Lecture Notes in Computer Science 4137

Commenced Publication in 1973
Founding and Former Series Editors:
Gerhard Goos, Juris Hartmanis, and Jan van Leeuwen

Christel Baier   Holger Hermanns (Eds.)

CONCUR 2006 – Concurrency Theory

17th International Conference, CONCUR 2006
Bonn, Germany, August 27-30, 2006
Proceedings

Springer

Volume Editors

Christel Baier
Institute for Informatics I
University of Bonn
Römerstraße 164
53117 Bonn, Germany
E-mail: baier@cs.uni-bonn.de

Holger Hermanns
Dependable Systems and Software
Department of Computer Science
Saarland University
Campus, E1 3
66123 Saarbrücken, Germany
E-mail: hermanns@cs.uni-sb.de

Library of Congress Control Number: 2006930603

CR Subject Classification (1998): F.3, F.1, D.3, D.1, C.2

LNCS Sublibrary: SL 1 – Theoretical Computer Science and General Issues

ISSN 0302-9743
ISBN-10 3-540-37376-4 Springer Berlin Heidelberg New York
ISBN-13 978-3-540-37376-6 Springer Berlin Heidelberg New York

Springer is a part of Springer Science+Business Media

springer.com

Typesetting: Camera-ready by author, data conversion by Scientific Publishing Services, Chennai, India
Printed on acid-free paper SPIN: 11817949 06/3142 5 4 3 2 1 0

Preface

This volume contains the proceedings of the 17th International Conference on Concurrency Theory (CONCUR) held in Bonn, Germany, August 27–30, 2006.

The purpose of the CONCUR conference series is to bring together researchers, developers and students in order to advance the theory of concurrency and promote its applications. Interest in this topic is continuously growing, as a consequence of the importance and ubiquity of concurrent systems and their applications and the scientific relevance of their foundations. The scope of CONCUR covers all areas of semantics, logics, and verification techniques for concurrent systems. Topics include basic models and logics of concurrent and distributed computation (such as process algebras, Petri nets, domain theoretic or game theoretic models, modal and temporal logics), specialized models or classes of systems (such as circuits, synchronous systems, real-time and hybrid systems, stochastic systems, databases, mobile and migrating systems, parametric protocols, security protocols), related verification techniques and tools (such as state-space exploration, model-checking, synthesis, abstraction, automated deduction, testing), and related programming models (such as distributed, constraint- or object-oriented, graph rewriting, as well as associated type systems, static analyses, abstract machines, and environments).

This volume starts with five invited papers covering the invited lectures and tutorials of the conference. The remaining 29 papers were selected by the Programme Committee out of 101 submissions after a very intensive reviewing and discussion phase. We would like to thank the members of the Programme Committee and the external reviewers for their excellent and hard work.

The conference programme contained three invited lectures and two invited tutorials. The invited talks were given by Edward A. Lee (University of California at Berkeley, USA), Jan Willem Klop, (Free University of Amsterdam, The Netherlands) and Orna Kupferman (Hebrew University, Israel), and the invited tutorials by Uwe Nestmann (Technical University of Berlin, Germany) and Roberto Segala (University of Verona, Italy).

Eleven workshops are affiliated to CONCUR 2006:

- Formal Methods for Industrial Critical Systems (FMICS) organized by Lubos Brim and Martin Leucker
- Verification of Infinite-State Systems (INFINITY) organized by Ahmed Bouajjani
- Expressiveness in Concurrency (EXPRESS) organized by Roberto Amadio and Iain Phillips
- Structural Operational Semantics (SOS) organized by Rob van Glabbeek and Peter D. Mosses
- Geometric and Topological Methods in Concurrency (GETCO) organized by Eric Goubault

– German Verification Day (GVD), organized by Werner Damm and Wolfgang Paul
– Foundations of Coordination Languages and Software Architectures (FOCLASA) organized by Carlos Canal and Mirko Viroli
– Parallel and Distributed Model Checking (PDMC) organized by Boudewijn Haverkort and Jaco van de Pol
– Security Issues in Coordination Models, Languages, and Systems (SecCo) organized by Dieter Gollmann and Peter Ryan
– Control and Observation of Real-Time Open Systems (CORTOS) organized by Franck Cassez
– Graph Transformation for Verification and Concurrency (GT-VC) organized by Arend Rensink

We would like to thank the CONCUR Steering Committee, the workshop organizers, the authors, and all Organizing Committee members for their contributions to the success of the conference. Finally, we gratefully acknowledge the generous support received from the Deutsche Forschungsgemeinschaft (DFG) and from the European Research Consortium for Informatics and Mathematics (ERCIM).

June 2006 Christel Baier and Holger Hermanns

Organization

Steering Committee

Roberto Amadio	University of Paris 7, France
Jos Baeten	Eindhoven University of Technology, The Netherlands
Eike Best	University of Oldenburg, Germany
Kim Larsen	Aalborg University, Denmark
Ugo Montanari	University of Pisa, Italy
Scott Smolka	SUNY, Stony Brook, USA

Programme Committee

Parosh Abdulla	Uppsala University, Sweden
Luca Aceto	Reykjavík University, Iceland
Luca De Alfaro	University of California, Santa Cruz, USA
Roberto Amadio	University of Paris 7, France
Jos Baeten	Eindhoven University of Technology, The Netherlands
Christel Baier	University of Bonn, Germany
Patricia Bouyer	École Normale Supérieure de Cachan, France
Franck van Breugel	York University, Canada
Kousha Etessami	University of Edinburgh, UK
Wan Fokkink	Free University of Amsterdam, The Netherlands
Philippa Gardner	Imperial College London, UK
Rob van Glabbeek	National ICT Australia, Sydney, Australia
Holger Hermanns	Saarland University, Germany
Barbara Koenig	University of Duisburg-Essen, Germany
Antonín Kučera	Masaryk University in Brno, Czech Republic
Kim Larsen	Aalborg University, Denmark
Gerald Luettgen	University of York, UK
Nancy Lynch	Massachusetts Institute of Technology, USA
Massimo Merro	University of Verona, Italy
Ugo Montanari	University of Pisa, Italy
Anca Muscholl	University of Paris 7, France
Catuscia Palamidessi	INRIA Futurs Saclay, France
Wojciech Penczek	ICS PAS and Podlasie Academy, Poland
Corrado Priami	University of Trento, Italy
Jean-Francois Raskin	Université Libre de Bruxelles, Belgium
Jan Rutten	Centre for Mathematics and Computer Science (CWI), The Netherlands
P.S. Thiagarajan	National University of Singapore, Singapore

Organizing Committee

Tobias Blechmann
Frank Ciesinski
Marcus Größer (Workshop Chair)
Martina Janssen
Joachim Klein
Sascha Klüppelholz
Jörn Ossowski
Reza Pulungan
Christa Schäfer

Referees

Samy Abbes
Rajeev Alur
Farhad Arbab
Pedro D'Argenio
Eugene Asarin
Michael Backes
Eric Badouel
Massimo Bartoletti
Twan Basten
Marek Bednarczyk
Emmanuel Beffara
Laurent Van Begin
Gerd Behrmann
Nick Benton
Nathalie Bertrand
Inge Bethke
Andreas Blass
Peter Bodorik
Michele Boreale
Johannes Borgström
Ahmed Bouajjani
Mario Bravetti
Tomáš Brázdil
Roberto Bruni
Nadia Busi
Diletta R. Cacciagrano
Nestor Catano
Didier Caucal
Matteo Cavaliere
Samarjit Chakraborty
Fabrice Chevalier
Yannick Chevalier
Federica Ciocchetta
D. Clarke
Hubert Comon-Lundh
Giovanni Conforti
D. Costa
Mads Dam
Philippe Darondeau
Giorgio Delzanno
Yuxin Deng
Rocco De Nicola
Laurent Doyen
Dominic Duggan
Claudio Eccher
Dirk Fahland
Harald Fecher
Cédric Fournet
Sibylle Froeschle
Pierre Ganty
Paul Gastin
Gilles Geeraerts
Blaise Genest
Hugo Gimbert
Jens Chr. Godskesen
Georges Gonthier
Andy Gordon
Jan Friso Groote
Dan Grossman
Maria L. Guerriero
Dilian Gurov
Cristian Haack
Bjœrn Haagensen
Jonathan Hayman
Keijo Heljanko
Claudio Hermida
Thomas Hildebrandt
Jane Hillston
Florian Horn
Hans Hüttel
Samuel Hym
Anna Ingolfsdottir
Florent Jacquemard
Radha Jagadeesan
Michael Jenkin
E. Johnsen
Bengt Jonsson
Marcin Jurdzinski
S. Kemper
Astrid Kiehn
Jetty Kleijn
Josva Kleist
Barbara Klunder
Beata Konikowska
Maciej Koutny
Steve Kremer
Jean Krivine
Morten Kühnrich
K. Narayan Kumar
Clemens Kupke

Table of Contents

Invited Contributions

Invited Tutorials

Model Checking

Process Calculi

Minimization and Equivalence Checking

Types

Semantics

Probability

Modeling Timed Concurrent Systems

Xiaojun Liu[1], Eleftherios Matsikoudis[2], and Edward A. Lee[2]

[1] Sun Microsystems, Inc.
xiaojun.liu@sun.com
[2] University of California, Berkeley
{ematsi, eal}@eecs.berkeley.edu

Abstract. Timed concurrent systems are widely used in concurrent and distributed real-time software, modeling of hybrid systems, design of hardware systems (using hardware description languages), discrete-event simulation, and modeling of communication networks. They consist of concurrent components that communicate using timed signals, that is, sets of (semantically) time-stamped events. The denotational semantics of such systems is traditionally formulated in a metric space, wherein causal components are modeled as contracting functions. We show that this formulation excessively restricts the models of time that can be used. In particular, it cannot handle super-dense time, commonly used in hardware description languages and hybrid systems modeling, finite time lines, and time with no origin. Moreover, if we admit continuous-time and mixed signals (essential for hybrid systems modeling) or certain Zeno signals, then causality is no longer equivalent to its formalization in terms of contracting functions. In this paper, we offer an alternative semantic framework using a generalized ultrametric that overcomes these limitations.

1 Introduction

This paper focuses on timed concurrent systems modeling. Timed concurrent systems are collections of concurrent components that communicate by use of timed signals. We will define this formally, but intuitively timed signals are functions of a globally defined time. They consist of either continuously evolving values or discrete events or some combination of the two. Semantically, time is a globally shared concept, and causality is intrinsically bound to chronological ordering.

Timed concurrent systems have a wide range of application. They are used in concurrent and distributed real-time software, modeling of hybrid systems, design of hardware systems (using hardware description languages), discrete-event simulation, and modeling of communication networks.

The importance of precise mathematical models for such systems cannot be overemphasized. In short, they establish canonical denotational definitions of timed programming languages, thereby providing the means for reasoning about the correctness of individual implementations, as well as allowing hidden commonalities of seemingly different timed systems to emerge.

C. Baier and H. Hermanns (Eds.): CONCUR 2006, LNCS 4137, pp. 1–15, 2006.

Unfortunately, timed systems are not amenable to standard order-theoretic denotational semantic approaches as they may realize non-monotonic functions over the sequences of observable actions [25]. Yet interesting results have been obtained by imposing a fixed lower bound on the reaction time of the involved components, effectively precluding Zeno behavior, where an infinite number of actions takes place over a finite interval of time. This has permitted the successful employment of traditional metric-space theory in the construction of well-defined mathematical models for these constrained classes of timed concurrent systems [23,25,11,2,4,6].

In this paper, we expose a number of limitations in the traditional metric-space approach that hinder generalization to broader classes of timed concurrent systems. We then proceed to develop the fundamentals of a semantic framework for timed concurrent systems that is more broadly applicable. The underlying assumption is that a timed concurrent system can be modeled as a single system function, and that the behavior of the system corresponds to a fixed point of that function. In practice, to obtain this function, we have to be concerned about composition. That is, given the functions for the interconnected components, we need to be able to compose them to obtain the system function. The techniques given in this paper facilitate such composition.

This paper begins with a brief review of metric spaces, a definition of timed signals, and a review of a metric-space semantics for timed concurrent systems. During this review, we point out several limitations in this traditional approach. We then develop an alternative based on generalized ultrametric spaces, and discuss how it overcomes these limitations.

2 Mathematical Preliminaries

A *metric space* (X, d) is a set X with a *metric distance function* $d\colon X \times X \to \mathbb{R}_0$ such that for all $x, y, z \in X$,

1. $d(x, y) = 0$ if and only if $x = y$,
2. $d(x, y) = d(y, x)$, and
3. $d(x, z) \leq d(x, y) + d(y, z)$.

If the metric distance function d also satisfies

4. $d(x, z) \leq \max(d(x, y), d(y, z))$

for all $x, y, z \in X$, then (X, d) is an *ultrametric space* and d an *ultrametric distance function.*

The value $d(x, y)$ quantifies how closely x approximates y. An element $x \in X$ is the *limit* of a sequence $\{x_k\}_{k\in\mathbb{N}}$, where $\mathbb{N}$ is the set of all natural numbers $\{0, 1, 2, \cdots\}$, iff for all $\epsilon > 0$, there exists $n \in \mathbb{N}$ such that for all $k \geq n$, $d(x_k, x) < \epsilon$. The sequence is then said to *converge* to x, denoted by $x_k \to x$. A sequence $\{x_k\}_{k\in\mathbb{N}}$ is *Cauchy* iff for all $\epsilon > 0$, there exists $n \in \mathbb{N}$ such that for all $k, l \geq n$, $d(x_k, x_l) < \epsilon$. A metric space (X, d) is *complete* iff every Cauchy sequence converges to some $x \in X$.

If $B_\delta(x)$ is the set $\{y \in X \mid d(y,x) < \delta\}$, then the collection of such sets $\{B_\delta(x) \mid x \in X,\ \delta \in \mathbb{R}_+\}$ is a basis of a *topology* on X. This topology is called the *metric topology* induced by d.

Let (X,d) and (X',d') be metric spaces. A function $f\colon X \to X'$ is *continuous* iff $x_k \to x$ implies $f(x_k) \to f(x)$. It is *contracting* iff for all $x, y \in X$,

$$d'(f(x), f(y)) \le d(x,y).$$

It is *strictly contracting* iff for all $x, y \in X$,

$$x \neq y \implies d'(f(x), f(y)) < d(x,y).$$

It is a *δ-contraction* iff there exists $\delta \in (0,1)$ such that for all $x, y \in X$,

$$d'(f(x), f(y)) \le \delta\, d(x,y).$$

From the theory of metric spaces, the key result used in programming language semantics is the Banach fixed-point theorem [7].

Theorem 1 (Banach). *Let (X,d) be a complete metric space. If the function $f\colon (X,d) \to (X,d)$ is a δ-contraction, then f has a unique fixed point in X, denoted by $\operatorname{fix} f$, and for all $x \in X$, $f^k(x) \to \operatorname{fix} f$.*

3 Timed Signals

In this paper, we are interested in concurrent components that communicate via *timed signals*. We model these using the tagged-signal model [12], where the communication between two components is represented by a set of events. Formally, let $\mathcal{T}$ be a non-empty set of *tags*, and $\mathcal{V}$ a non-empty set of *values*. An *event* is a pair (t, v) in $\mathcal{T} \times \mathcal{V}$. A *signal* is a set of events that typically represents the sum total of the communication between two components along some communication path. For the systems we are interested in, these sets are very likely infinite. Most applications of the tagged-signal model impose structure on the tag set $\mathcal{T}$ and study the consequences of that structure. For example, $\mathcal{T}$ might represent causality properties, time, or activation orders.

3.1 Models of Time

In general, in the tagged signal model, $\mathcal{T}$ is a partially ordered set. In this paper, $\mathcal{T}$ represents time. Our framework admits several models of time, but in all cases, $\mathcal{T}$ will be totally ordered.

Perhaps the most natural choice for $\mathcal{T}$ is the set of non-negative real numbers $\mathbb{R}_0$, reflecting a Newtonian physical view of time. The fact that we include only the non-negative reals implies that our timed concurrent networks have a starting point.

A more interesting model of time is the *super dense time* (SDT) model [19], where $\mathcal{T} = \mathbb{R}_0 \times \mathbb{N}$ equipped with the lexicographic order, that is, for all $(r_1, n_1), (r_2, n_2) \in \mathbb{R}_0 \times \mathbb{N}$,

$$(r_1, n_1) \leq (r_2, n_2) \iff r_1 < r_2 \text{ or } (r_1 = r_2 \ \& \ n_1 \leq n_2).$$

This is a total order. SDT can be similarly defined as $\mathcal{T} = I \times \mathbb{N}$, with I being any interval of real numbers. SDT has been used in studying the semantics of hybrid systems [10,14,18]. Its subset $\mathbb{N} \times \mathbb{N}$ is used as the model of time in the hardware description languages Verilog and VHDL. SDT is in a sense strictly richer than $\mathbb{R}_0$ as a model of time, in that there is no order-embedding from $\mathbb{R}_0 \times \mathbb{N}$ into $\mathbb{R}_0$, as may be easily verified.

3.2 Signals

A signal in the tagged-signal model is a set of events, or equivalently, a relation with domain some subset of $\mathcal{T}$ and range some subset of $\mathcal{V}$. In this paper, we constrain such relations to be single-valued, and thus commit to the following definition.

Definition 1 (Signal). *A set s is a signal if and only if $s \in (\mathcal{T} \rightharpoonup \mathcal{V})$.*[1]

We denote the set of all signals with tag set $\mathcal{T}$ and value set $\mathcal{V}$ by $\mathcal{S}(\mathcal{T}, \mathcal{V})$, that is, $\mathcal{S}(\mathcal{T}, \mathcal{V}) = (\mathcal{T} \rightharpoonup \mathcal{V})$. We adopt common practice in modern set theory and identify a function with its graph. The events of a signal s then are precisely the members of s. And the domain of the signal $\operatorname{dom} s$ is the set of all tags where events of the signal s are present. The signal with no events is simply the empty set $\emptyset$.

For notational convenience, we will write $s_1(t) \simeq s_2(t)$ iff the signals s_1 and s_2 are either both defined, or both undefined at tag t, and if defined $s_1(t) = s_2(t)$.

The following examples in $\mathcal{S}(\mathbb{R}_0, \mathbb{R})$ are sketched in Fig. 1:

$$\begin{aligned} const_1 &\stackrel{\text{def}}{=} \{(t, 1) \mid t \in \mathbb{R}_0\}, \\ clock_1 &\stackrel{\text{def}}{=} \{(k, 1) \mid k \in \mathbb{N}\}, \text{ and} \\ zeno &\stackrel{\text{def}}{=} \{(1 - 1/2^k, 1) \mid k \in \mathbb{N}\}. \end{aligned}$$

The *zeno* example is particularly interesting. It is really the timed systems version of Zeno's paradox [1], where an infinite number of events may take place before some finite instance of time. Although not physically realizable, such signals may easily crop up in simulation and modeling environments where time is represented as an actual program variable. In Section 4 we discuss some of the related subtleties that in the past have compelled researchers to invariably impose certain conditions on their systems that effectively preclude Zeno behavior [23,25,11].

---

[1] We denote the set of all functions f with $\operatorname{dom} f \subseteq A$ and $\operatorname{ran} f \subseteq B$ by $(A \rightharpoonup B)$.

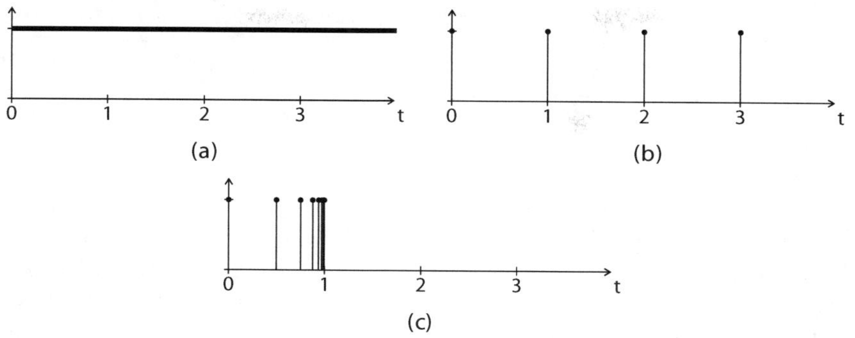

Fig. 1. Examples of timed signals: (a) $const_1$, (b) $clock_1$, (c) *zeno*

4 The Cantor Metric and Its Limitations

The Cantor metric is a distance function that may be defined on streams or sequences [5]. The same metric is called the Baire-distance in [6]. The focus here is on the Cantor metric for timed signals, a typical choice in the metric-space approach to the denotational semantics of timed concurrent systems [11,15,23].

Under the assumption that $\mathcal{T} = \mathbb{R}_0$, the Cantor metric for timed signals is a function $d_{\text{cantor}} \colon \mathcal{S}(\mathcal{T}, \mathcal{V}) \times \mathcal{S}(\mathcal{T}, \mathcal{V}) \to \mathbb{R}_0$ such that for all $s_1, s_2 \in \mathcal{S}(\mathcal{T}, \mathcal{V})$,

$$d_{\text{cantor}}(s_1, s_2) \stackrel{\text{def}}{=} 2^{-\sup \left\{ t \in \mathcal{T} \,\middle|\, (\forall \tau \leq t)(s_1(\tau) \simeq s_2(\tau)) \right\}}. \tag{1}$$

It is understood that since $\mathcal{T} = \mathbb{R}_0$, $2^{-\sup \emptyset} = 1$, and $2^{-\sup \mathbb{R}_0} = 0$. That is, two signals that differ at their start have distance one, and two signals that are everywhere identical have distance zero. It is easy to show that $(\mathcal{S}(\mathbb{R}_0, \mathcal{V}), d_{\text{cantor}})$ is a complete (ultra)metric space [16].

In the remainder of this section we discuss a number of limitations in the use of the Cantor metric in a semantic framework for timed concurrent systems, thus demonstrating our motivation for turning to the theory of generalized ultrametric spaces. This is not to say that the Cantor metric is the only metric applicable to timed signals. For example, any Hausdorff distance function, such as the Skorohod J2 metric in [8], may be used to endow the set of timed signals with the structure of a metric space. In the special case of discrete-event signals, even the Baire-distance on sequences, or other ad-hoc distance functions, as in [24], may be viable alternatives. However, all these alternatives seem to more or less suffer from the same limitations. And for timed concurrent systems modeling, the Cantor metric seems, at least to the authors, as the most prominent metric candidate, rendering causal components contracting functions on timed signals, and yielding a convergence process that closely resembles the actual operation of timed systems.

4.1 Convergence in the Cantor Metric Space

A sequence $\{s_k\}_{k\in\mathbb{N}}$ of signals is said to converge to a signal s if for any $\epsilon > 0$, there is an $n \in \mathbb{N}$ such that for all $k > n$,

$$d_{\text{cantor}}(s_k, s) < \epsilon.$$

Such convergence gives us a theory of approximation that enables assigning semantics to timed systems with infinite executions. If partial executions yield signals s_k, and these signals converge to some signal s, then in an operational semantics, s is the semantics of the signal. Of course, we would expect that this s be the same as the signal delivered by our denotational semantics. The main obstacle to achieving this in timed concurrent systems is the potential for Zeno conditions.

Consider, for example, finite approximations s_k to the signal *zeno* $\in \mathcal{S}(\mathbb{R}_0, \mathbb{R})$. Let $\{s_k\}_{k\in\mathbb{N}}$ be the sequence of signals where s_k is the defined by

$$s_k = \{(1 - 1/2^n, 1) \mid n \in \{0, \cdots, k\}\}. \tag{2}$$

That is, s_k is the prefix of *zeno* that contains the first k events. Intuitively, the sequence $\{s_k\}_{k\in\mathbb{N}}$ converges to *zeno*, but it does not converge in the Cantor metric. It is easy to see that for all k,

$$d_{\text{cantor}}(s_k, zeno) > 1/2.$$

It is also easy to see that for any k and k' such that $k \neq k'$,

$$d_{\text{cantor}}(s_k, s_{k'}) > 1/2.$$

So this sequence is not Cauchy. Although we have no mathematical contradiction, the Cantor metric has failed to provide us with a framework where we can consider the sequence of signals $\{s_k\}_{k\in\mathbb{N}}$ to be a sequence of finite approximations to the signal *zeno*.

On a related note, systems that give rise to Zeno signals cannot be modeled as δ-contractions in the Cantor metric space [25]. It is thus impossible to utilize the Banach fixed-point theorem for reasoning about the behavior of such systems. The generalized ultrametric space that we construct in Section 5 allows us to use a variant of the Banach fixed-point theorem that is less restrictive in terms of how contractive the system functions are.

4.2 Causal Components Versus Contracting Functions

Causality is the relationship between causes and effects. If a component in a timed concurrent system models a physical or computational process, the time of an effect cannot be earlier than the time of the corresponding cause. It is common to relate this intuitive notion of causality with contracting functions in the Cantor metric space [23,11]. However, this does not quite work with arbitrary timed signals.

Consider a deterministic component that accepts as input a timed signal and produces as output a timed signal. We can model such a component as a function $F\colon \mathcal{S}(\mathcal{T},\mathcal{V}) \to \mathcal{S}(\mathcal{T},\mathcal{V})$. If $\mathcal{T} = \mathbb{R}_0$, then the domain and range of this function are complete metric spaces under the Cantor metric. If F is contracting, then from the definition of the Cantor metric, we can see that if two possible inputs are identical up to some time, then the corresponding outputs are identical up to that same time. This motivates some authors to model causal components as contracting input-output functions.

Consider the following example. Let $u_1, u_2 \in \mathcal{S}(\mathbb{R}_0, \mathbb{R})$ be such that for all $t \in \mathbb{R}_0$,

$$u_1(t) = 0,$$

$$u_2(t) = \begin{cases} 0 & \text{if } t \in [0,1], \\ 1 & \text{if } t > 1. \end{cases}$$

Suppose a component with one input and one output is modeled by the function $F\colon \mathcal{S}(\mathbb{R}_0,\mathbb{R}) \to \mathcal{S}(\mathbb{R}_0,\mathbb{R})$, where for any input $s \in \mathcal{S}(\mathbb{R}_0,\mathbb{R})$ and any $t \in \mathbb{R}_0$,

$$F(s)(t) = \begin{cases} \lim_{r \to t^+} s(r) & \text{if the \textit{right limit} exists,} \\ 0 & \text{otherwise.} \end{cases} \tag{3}$$

The function F is contracting. However, $F(u_1) = u_1$, and

$$F(u_2)(t) = \begin{cases} 0 & \text{if } t \in [0,1), \\ 1 & \text{if } t \geq 1. \end{cases}$$

The input signals u_1 and u_2 are equal over $[0,1]$, whereas the output signals $F(u_1)$ and $F(u_2)$ are equal only over $[0,1)$. Consequently, the component is not causal.

The fact that contracting functions in the Cantor metric space are not necessarily causal is certainly disturbing. We can avoid this discrepancy by restricting our attention to a certain class of signals and components. The following definition comes from [11].

Definition 2 (DE Signals). *A timed signal $s \in \mathcal{S}(\mathcal{T},\mathcal{V})$ is a discrete-event (DE) signal if and only if there exists an order-embedding from* dom s *into* $\mathbb{N}$.

It is not hard to show that when equipped with the Cantor metric, the set of all DE signals yields a complete ultrametric space [16]. If we consider only DE signals and components that operate only on DE input signals yielding DE signals as outputs, then our informal notion of causality actually coincides with its classic formalization in terms of contracting functions, as the reader is invited to verify.

In Section 5 we define a generalized ultrametric that enables us to accurately formalize our informal notion of causality in terms of contracting functions in the respective generalized ultrametric space, and thus have a unified framework of causal systems that arbitrarily combine discrete (e.g. software) components with continuous (e.g. physical) processes.

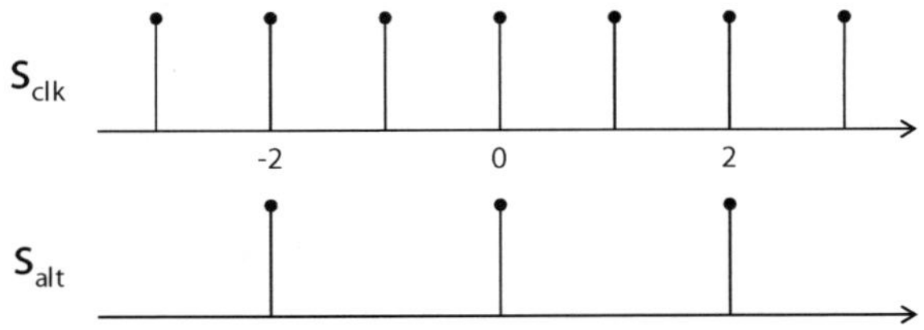

Fig. 2. Timed signals with tag set $\mathbb{R}$

4.3 Tag-Set Choices

When using the Cantor metric, the choice of tag set has a profound impact. We would like to be able to use any totally ordered set to model time but we cannot do this with the Cantor metric.

For example, we would like to be able to use super dense time as our model of time, an indispensable choice when studying hybrid systems. However, the fact that there is no order-embedding from $\mathbb{R}_0 \times \mathbb{N}$ into $\mathbb{R}_0$ makes this impossible.

Similarly, it is tempting to restrict the tag set to the interval $[0,1)$ so as to have the signal *zeno* extend over the whole time line. By the definition of Cantor metric in (1), for all signals $s_1, s_2 \in \mathcal{S}([0,1), \mathcal{V})$,

$$s_1 \neq s_2 \implies d_{\text{cantor}}(s_1, s_2) > \frac{1}{2}.$$

Hence, the metric topology induced by d_{cantor} on $\mathcal{S}([0,1), \mathcal{V})$ is the *discrete topology*. In other words, the Cantor metric does not provide any useful structure on $\mathcal{S}([0,1), \mathcal{V})$.

Another interesting case is to take $\mathbb{R}$ as the tag set. The Cantor distance between two signals in $\mathcal{S}(\mathbb{R}, \mathcal{V})$ may be infinity. For example, let

$$s_{\text{clk}} \stackrel{\text{def}}{=} \{(k,1) \mid k \in \mathbb{Z}\},$$
$$s_{\text{alt}} \stackrel{\text{def}}{=} \{(2k,1) \mid k \in \mathbb{Z}\},$$

where $\mathbb{Z}$ is the set of all integers. These signals, illustrated in Fig. 2, have an empty common prefix, and hence

$$\{t \in \mathbb{R} \mid (\forall \tau \leq t)(s_1(\tau) \simeq s_2(\tau))\} = \emptyset.$$

With $\mathbb{R}$ as the tag set, it is understood that $2^{-\sup \emptyset} = \infty$, so the Cantor distance between these signals is infinite.

$(\mathcal{S}(\mathbb{R}, \mathcal{V}), d_{\text{cantor}})$ is not a metric space[2], because a metric space is defined as a function into $\mathbb{R}_0$. We have a function onto $\mathbb{R}_0 \cup \{\infty\}$. Consequently, we cannot immediately use the Banach fixed point theorem, and in fact we can show that it does not hold in this space.

[2] It is erroneously assumed to be one in [20].

Consider a component $Delay_d$ that shifts every event in its input signal by $d \in \mathbb{R}_0$ into the future. That is, $Delay_d \colon \mathcal{S}(\mathbb{R},\mathcal{V}) \to \mathcal{S}(\mathbb{R},\mathcal{V})$ such that for any $s \in \mathcal{S}(\mathbb{R},\mathcal{V})$ and any $t \in \mathbb{R}$,

$$Delay_d(s)(t) \overset{\text{def}}{\simeq} \begin{cases} s(t-d) & \text{if } t-d \in \operatorname{dom} s, \\ \text{undefined} & \text{otherwise.} \end{cases} \tag{4}$$

It is easy to show that the function $Delay_d$ is a δ-contraction for any $d > 0$. In $\mathcal{S}(\mathbb{R},\mathcal{V})$, this function has more than one fixed point. In particular, note that with $d = 1$, both $\emptyset$ and s_{clk} are fixed points. Although the Banach fixed point theorem assures us that a δ-contraction has only one fixed point, there is no contradiction because $\mathcal{S}(\mathbb{R},\mathcal{V})$ is not a metric space.

$(\mathcal{S}(\mathbb{R},\mathcal{V}), d_{\text{cantor}})$ is an *extended metric space* [3]. This extended metric space can be divided into a set of complete metric spaces. Let relation R on $\mathcal{S}(\mathbb{R},\mathcal{V})$ be defined by

$$(s_1, s_2) \in R \iff d_{\text{cantor}}(s_1, s_2) < \infty.$$

An equivalent definition of relation R is that s_1 and s_2 have a non-empty common prefix—going back in time, s_1 and s_2 are eventually the same.

It is straightforward to show that R is an *equivalence relation*. For any signal $s \in \mathcal{S}(\mathbb{R},\mathcal{V})$, let

$$E_s \overset{\text{def}}{=} \left\{ s' \in \mathcal{S}(\mathbb{R},\mathcal{V}) \;\middle|\; d_{\text{cantor}}(s', s) < \infty \right\}$$

be the equivalence class containing s. (E_s, d_{cantor}) is a complete (ultra)metric space. The extended metric space $(\mathcal{S}(\mathbb{R},\mathcal{V}), d_{\text{cantor}})$ thus contains an infinite number of complete (ultra)metric spaces.

Consider $Delay_1$ as a function of the form $Delay_1 \colon E_{s_{\text{clk}}} \to E_{s_{\text{clk}}}$. This is legitimate, because given any $s \in E_{s_{\text{clk}}}$, $Delay_1(s) \in E_{s_{\text{clk}}}$. This function has a unique fixed point in $E_{s_{\text{clk}}}$, namely s_{clk}.

Consider $Delay_1$ as a function of the form $Delay_1 \colon E_\emptyset \to E_\emptyset$. This is legitimate, because given any $s \in E_\emptyset$, $Delay_1(s) \in E_\emptyset$. This function has a unique fixed point in $E_\emptyset$, namely $\emptyset$.

Notice that it is not possible to consider $Delay_1$ as a function of the form $Delay_1 \colon E_{s_{\text{alt}}} \to E_{s_{\text{alt}}}$, because in fact $Delay_1(s_{\text{alt}}) \notin E_{s_{\text{alt}}}$.

To borrow an analogy from cosmology, the equivalence classes of R partition $\mathcal{S}(\mathbb{R},\mathcal{V})$ into parallel universes, and all signals in an equivalence class originate from the same "Big Bang." If a (contracting) component can take us from one universe to another, then putting it in a feedback loop can yield multiple parallel behaviors.

We next develop a framework, based on the theory of generalized ultrametric spaces, that is far more admissive with respect to the tag-set choices. The generalized ultrametric space that we construct renders $Delay_d$ not strictly contracting.

5 Generalized Ultrametrics and Their Application

We have seen that the traditional approach to metric space semantics has a number of limitations for timed concurrent systems. Several restrictions have to be applied in order for it to be useful. It effectively rules out models of time that are used in practice (such as super dense time) or are interesting in theory (such as $\mathbb{R}$, which has no least time, or bounded intervals of $\mathbb{R}$). Moreover, even when time is modeled using $\mathbb{R}_0$, Zeno conditions can render the Banach fixed-point theorem irrelevant. Finally, the equivalence between our informal understanding of causality and its formalization in terms of contracting functions breaks down when continuous-time and mixed signals (essential for hybrid systems modeling) or certain Zeno signals are allowed.

In this section we resort to the theory of generalized ultrametric spaces and define a generalize ultrametric distance function on timed signals that eliminates the abovementioned problems.

5.1 Generalized Ultrametric Spaces

While the codomain of a metric distance function is required to be the set of all non-negative real numbers $\mathbb{R}_0$, the codomain of a generalized ultrametric distance function [21] may be chosen as any partially ordered set with a minimum element.

Definition 3 (Generalized Ultrametric Space). *Let X be a set, Γ a partially ordered set with a minimum element 0_Γ. Then (X, d, Γ) is a generalized ultrametric space iff $d\colon X \times X \to \Gamma$ is a function such that for all $x, y, z \in X$ and $\gamma \in \Gamma$,*

1. *$d(x, y) = 0_\Gamma$ if and only if $x = y$,*
2. *$d(x, y) = d(y, x)$, and*
3. *if $d(x, y) \leq \gamma$ and $d(y, z) \leq \gamma$, then $d(x, z) \leq \gamma$.*

A function $d\colon X \times X \to \Gamma$ that adheres to the above definition is called a *generalized ultrametric distance function.*

If (X, d, Γ) is a generalized ultrametric space, then for any $\gamma \in \Gamma \setminus \{0_\Gamma\}$ and $a \in X$, the set

$$B_\gamma(a) = \{x \in X \mid d(x, a) \leq_\Gamma \gamma\}$$

is called the *ball* with *center* a and *radius* γ. It is easy to verify that for all $x, y \in X$ and $\alpha, \beta \in \Gamma$, if $0_\Gamma < \alpha \leq \beta$ and $x \in B_\beta(y)$, then $B_\alpha(x) \subseteq B_\beta(y)$; every point in a ball is also its center.

The usual notion of completeness for metric spaces extends naturally to the case of generalized ultrametric spaces. However, it is the stronger notion of spherical completeness that most interesting results in the theory of generalized ultrametric spaces rely on.

Definition 4 (Spherical Completeness). *A generalized ultrametric space is spherically complete iff every chain of balls (ordered by inclusion) has a non-empty intersection.*

Let (X, d, Γ) and (X', d', Γ) be generalized ultrametric spaces. A function $f: X \to X'$ is *contracting* iff for all $x, y \in X$,

$$d'(f(x), f(y)) \leq d(x, y).$$

It is *strictly contracting* iff for all $x, y \in X$,

$$x \neq y \implies d'(f(x), f(y)) < d(x, y).$$

The above definitions are evidently identical to those introduced in the case of metric spaces. The notion of δ-contraction, however, has no immediate counterpart in the context of generalized ultrametric spaces. There is nevertheless an analogue, in some sense, to the Banach fixed-point theorem, namely the Priess-Crampe & Ribenboim fixed-point theorem. There are several variants of this theorem [21,22]. The following is from section 5.2 of [21].

Theorem 2 (Priess-Crampe & Ribenboim). *Let (X, d, Γ) is a spherically complete generalized ultrametric space. If the function $f: X \to X$ is strictly contracting, then f has a unique fixed point.*

We note that the proof of this theorem relies on the Axiom of Choice and is thus inherently non-constructive.

5.2 Generalized Ultrametrics on Timed Signals

Let s_1 and s_2 be signals in $\mathcal{S}(\mathbb{R}_0, \mathcal{V})$. The Cantor metric in essence maps the set $\{t \in \mathbb{R}_0 \mid (\forall \tau \leq t)(s(\tau) \simeq s_2(\tau))\}$, namely the largest down set[3] of $\mathbb{R}_0$ on which the signals s_1 and s_2 coincide, to an element of $\mathbb{R}_0$ such that for all $s'_1, s'_2 \in \mathcal{S}(\mathbb{R}_0, \mathcal{V})$,

$$\begin{array}{c} \{t \in \mathbb{R}_0 \mid (\forall \tau \leq t)(s_1(\tau) \simeq s_2(\tau))\} \;\supseteq\; \{t \in \mathbb{R}_0 \mid (\forall \tau \leq t)(s'_1(\tau) \simeq s'_2(\tau))\} \\ \Longrightarrow \\ d_{\text{cantor}}(s_1, s_2) \;\leq\; d_{\text{cantor}}(s'_1, s'_2). \end{array}$$

The inverse implication is not generally true, which is the reason that a contracting process is not necessarily causal.

Let $\mathcal{D}(\mathbb{R}_0)$ denote the set of all down sets of $\mathbb{R}_0$. We can define a totally ordered set $(\mathcal{D}(\mathbb{R}_0), \supseteq)$ whose order relation is reverse set containment $\supseteq$. It is easy to show that there is no order-embedding from $(\mathcal{D}(\mathbb{R}_0), \supseteq)$ into $\mathbb{R}_0$. Hence, it is impossible to define a metric d on $\mathcal{S}(\mathbb{R}_0, \mathcal{V})$ such that for all $s_1, s_2, s'_1, s'_2 \in \mathcal{S}(\mathbb{R}_0, \mathcal{V})$,

$$\begin{array}{c} \{t \in \mathbb{R}_0 \mid (\forall \tau \leq t)(s_1(\tau) \simeq s_2(\tau))\} \;\supseteq\; \{t \in \mathbb{R}_0 \mid (\forall \tau \leq t)(s'_1(\tau) \simeq s'_2(\tau))\} \\ \Longleftrightarrow \\ d_{\text{cantor}}(s_1, s_2) \;\leq\; d_{\text{cantor}}(s'_1, s'_2). \end{array}$$

[3] A subset D of a partially ordered set $(P, \leqslant)$ is a *down set* of P iff for all $p, p' \in P$, if $p' \in D$ and $p \leqslant p'$, then $p \in D$.

However, we can easily define a generalized ultrametric that satisfies this equivalence.

For any tag set $\mathcal{T}$, let the set of generalized ultrametric distances, $\Gamma_{\mathcal{T}}$, be the partially ordered set

$$\Gamma_{\mathcal{T}} \stackrel{\text{def}}{=} (\mathcal{D}(\mathcal{T}), \supseteq).$$

If we use the notation $\leq_{\Gamma}$ for the order relation of $\Gamma_{\mathcal{T}}$, then for any two down sets $D, D' \in \mathcal{D}(\mathcal{T})$, $D \leq_{\Gamma_{\mathcal{T}}} D'$ if and only if $D \supseteq D'$. That is, the order is reverse set containment. $\mathcal{T}$ is the minimum element of $\Gamma_{\mathcal{T}}$. That is, for all $D \in \mathcal{D}(\mathcal{T})$, $\mathcal{T} \leq_{\Gamma_{\mathcal{T}}} D$ because $\mathcal{T} \supseteq D$. Similarly, the maximum element is $\emptyset$, the empty set. It is easy to show that for any tag set $\mathcal{T}$, the partially ordered set $(\mathcal{D}(\mathcal{T}), \supseteq)$ is a complete lattice.

For any tag set $\mathcal{T}$ and any value set $\mathcal{V}$, we define the function $d_{\text{ds}}\colon \mathcal{S}(\mathcal{T}, \mathcal{V}) \times \mathcal{S}(\mathcal{T}, \mathcal{V}) \to \Gamma_{\mathcal{T}}$ such that for all $s_1, s_2 \in \mathcal{S}(\mathcal{T}, \mathcal{V})$,

$$d_{\text{ds}}(s_1, s_2) \stackrel{\text{def}}{=} \{t \in \mathcal{T} \mid (\forall \tau \leq t)(s_1(\tau) \simeq s_2(\tau))\}.$$

The following lemma establishes that d_{ds} is in fact a generalized ultrametric on timed signals [17].

Lemma 1 (Generalized Ultrametric on Timed Signals). *For any tag set $\mathcal{T}$ and any value set $\mathcal{V}$, d_{ds} is a generalized ultrametric distance function on $\mathcal{S}(\mathcal{T}, \mathcal{V})$.*

Stated differently, Lemma 1 shows that for any tag set $\mathcal{T}$ and any value set $\mathcal{V}$, $(\mathcal{S}(\mathcal{T}, \mathcal{V}), d_{\text{ds}}, \Gamma_{\mathcal{T}})$ is a generalized ultrametric space. In particular, we are no longer restricted to $\mathcal{T} = \mathbb{R}_0$. We can choose any totally ordered set to model time, including super dense time, time lines with no origin, and bounded intervals.

We remark here that if we choose $\mathcal{T}$ to be the interval of reals $[0, 1)$, then the sequence $\{s_k\}_{k \in \mathbb{N}}$ as specified in (2) actually converges to *zeno* in the respective generalized ultrametric space, whereas it failed to converge in the Cantor metric space.

On a similar note, observe that while the function $Delay_d \in \mathcal{S}(\mathbb{R}_0, \mathcal{V})$ as defined in (4) is a δ-contraction with respect to the Cantor metric, it is not strictly contracting in the respective generalized ultrametric space (consider any two $s_1, s_2 \in \mathcal{S}(\mathbb{R}, \mathcal{V})$ such that for all $t \in \mathbb{R}$, $s_1(t) \not\simeq s_2(t)$). Hence, and in accordance with intuition, we cannot apply the Priess-Crampe & Ribenboim fixed-point theorem to establish the existence of a unique fixed point for the function $Delay_d$.

Finally, notice that the function F defined in (3) is not contracting in the respective generalized ultrametric space. It can therefore no longer serve as a counterexample to the equivalence between the informal notion of causality and its formalization in terms of contracting functions. In fact, it is no longer possible to find such a counterexample. Contracting functions with respect to generalized ultrametrics on timed signals accurately capture the chronological precedence relationship between causes and effects. The following formal definition of causality is essentially equivalent to the respective definitions in [13] and [20].

Definition 5 (Causal Function). *A function* $f\colon \mathcal{S}(\mathcal{T},\mathcal{V}) \to \mathcal{S}(\mathcal{T},\mathcal{V})$ *is causal iff it is contracting in the generalized ultrametric space* $(\mathcal{S}(\mathcal{T},\mathcal{V}), d_{ds}, \Gamma_{\mathcal{T}})$.

Causal functions represent system components that are non-anticipative, in the sense that the output does not anticipate future events of the input. But non-anticipative components may still react instantaneously to input stimuli. The concept of strict causality is thus introduced in order to further assert, when appropriate, the impossibility of instantaneous reaction.

Definition 6 (Strictly Causal Function). *A function* $f\colon \mathcal{S}(\mathcal{T},\mathcal{V}) \to \mathcal{S}(\mathcal{T},\mathcal{V})$ *is strictly causal iff it is strictly contracting in the generalized ultrametric space* $(\mathcal{S}(\mathcal{T},\mathcal{V}), d_{ds}, \Gamma_{\mathcal{T}})$.

Again, the above formal definition of strict causality is equivalent to the respective definition in [20]. We remark here that δ-contractions in the Cantor metric space are strictly contracting functions in the respective generalized ultrametric space. The converse does not hold in general.

The next lemma ensures the applicability of the Priess-Crampe & Ribenboim fixed-point theorem in the context of timed concurrent systems [17].

Lemma 2. *For any tag set* $\mathcal{T}$ *and any value set* $\mathcal{V}$*, the generalized ultrametric space* $(\mathcal{S}(\mathcal{T},\mathcal{V}), d_{ds}, \Gamma_{\mathcal{T}})$ *is spherically complete.*

As a simple demonstration, we can immediately apply the Priess-Crampe & Ribenboim fixed-point theorem to establish the following result, first obtained by Naundorf in [20].

Theorem 3. *For any tag set* $\mathcal{T}$ *and any value set* $\mathcal{V}$*, if* $f\colon \mathcal{S}(\mathcal{T},\mathcal{V}) \to \mathcal{S}(\mathcal{T},\mathcal{V})$ *is a strictly causal function, then* f *has a unique fixed point in* $\mathcal{S}(\mathcal{T},\mathcal{V})$.

We remark that the above results can be specialized to certain classes of timed signals, including discrete-event signals [16].

The relative advantage of the approach taken here over that in [20] relates to the general formulation of the problem. The development of a semantic framework based on generalized ultrametric spaces makes it possible to apply off-the-shelf results from the theory of generalized ultrametric spaces, and share relevant findings with seemingly irrelevant research communities such as the programming logic community [9].

We conclude with the observation that the proof of Theorem 3 here (a trivial application of the Priess-Crampe & Ribenboim fixed-point theorem), as well as in [20], is non-constructive. At the moment, we can only guarantee the existence of a unique fixed point for strictly causal functions. This certainly limits our ability to reason about the behavior of strictly causal systems, a rather broad and interesting class of timed systems. It may nevertheless prove possible to construct a denotational semantics that accurately reflects the actual execution of such systems. In any case, a constructive proof of Theorem 3 is of both practical and theoretical interest, and is the subject of future work.

6 Conclusions

Timed concurrent systems are aggregations of components that communicate by use of timed signals. Such systems have been traditionally modeled in a semantic framework that leverages the theory of metric spaces, representing causal components as contracting functions. This approach has a number of limitations. In particular, it rules out models of time that are used in practice (such as super dense time) or are interesting in theory (such as finite time lines and time lines with no origin). Moreover, even when more conventional models of time are used, Zeno conditions can render key results from the theory of metric spaces (such as the Banach fixed-point theorem) irrelevant. Finally, the equivalence between the informal notion of causality and its formalization in terms of contracting functions breaks down when continuous-time and mixed signals or certain Zeno signals are allowed.

With these considerations in mind, we have introduced an alternative semantic framework for timed concurrent systems that relies on the theory of generalized ultrametric spaces. We defined an appropriate generalized ultrametric on timed signals that eliminates the aforementioned limitations, yielding a spherically complete generalized ultrametric space under any model of time. We also presented an elegant and formal definition of causality that is exactly equivalent to its informal counterpart. The resultant mathematical structure allows us to apply off-the-self results from the theory of generalized ultrametric spaces to reason about the behavior of timed concurrent systems. And as evidence for this thesis, we applied the Priess-Crampe & Ribenboim fixed-point theorem to trivially establish the fact that strictly causal functions have unique fixed points.

Acknowledgements

Thanks to Adam Cataldo for many helpful suggestions. This paper describes work that is part of the Ptolemy project, which is supported by the National Science Foundation (NSF award number CCR-00225610), and Chess (the Center for Hybrid and Embedded Software Systems), which receives support from NSF, the State of California Micro Program, and the following companies: Agilent, DGIST, General Motors, Hewlett Packard, Infineon, Microsoft, and Toyota.

References

1. M. Abadi and L. Lamport. An old-fashioned recipe for real time. *ACM Trans. Program. Lang. Syst.*, 16(5):1543–1571, 1994.
2. A. Arnold and M. Nivat. Metric interpretations of infinite trees and semantics of non deterministic recursive programs. *Fundamenta Informaticae*, 11(2):181–205, 1980.
3. N. Aronszajn and P. Panitchpakdi. Extension of uniformly continuous transformations and hyperconvex metric spaces. *Pacific Journal of Mathematics*, 6(3):405–439, 1956.

4. C. Baier and M. E. Majster-Cederbaum. Denotational semantics in the cpo and metric approach. *Theoretical Computer Science*, 135(2):171–220, 1994.
5. C. S. Calude, S. Marcus, and L. Staiger. A topological characterization of random sequences. *Information Processing Letters*, 88(5):245–250, 2003.
6. J. W. de Bakker and E. P. de Vink. Denotational models for programming languages: Applications of Banach's fixed point theorem. *Topology and its Applications*, 85:35–52, 1998.
7. A. Granas and J. Dugundji. *Fixed Point Theory*. Springer-Verlag, 2003.
8. V. Gupta, R. Jagadeesan, and P. Panangaden. Approximate reasoning for real-time probabilistic processes. In *Proceedings of the First International Conference on the Quantitative Evaluation of Systems (QEST'04)*, pages 304–313, Sep. 2004.
9. P. Hitzler and A. K. Seda. Generalized metrics and uniquely determined logic programs. *Theoretical Computer Science*, 305(1-3):187–219, 2003.
10. A. Kapur. *Interval and Point-Based Approaches to Hybrid Systems Verification*. Ph.d., Stanford University, 1997. Uses super dense time (super-dense, superdense).
11. E. A. Lee. Modeling concurrent real-time processes using discrete events. *Annals of Software Engineering*, 7:25–45, 1999.
12. E. A. Lee and A. Sangiovanni-Vincentelli. A framework for comparing models of computation. *IEEE Transactions on CAD*, 17(12), 1998.
13. E. A. Lee and P. Varaiya. *Structure and Interpretation of Signals and Systems*. Addison Wesley, 2003.
14. E. A. Lee and H. Zheng. Operational semantics of hybrid systems. In M. Morari and L. Thiele, editors, *Hybrid Systems: Computation and Control (HSCC)*, volume LNCS 3414, pages pp. 25–53, Zurich, Switzerland, 2005. Springer-Verlag.
15. J. Liu and E. A. Lee. On the causality of mixed-signal and hybrid models. In *6th International Workshop on Hybrid Systems: Computation and Control (HSCC '03)*, Prague, Czech Republic, 2003.
16. X. Liu. Semantic foundation of the tagged signal model. Phd thesis, EECS Department, University of California, December 20 2005.
17. X. Liu, E. Matsikoudis, and E. A. Lee. Modeling timed concurrent systems using generalized ultrametrics. Technical Report UCB/EECS-2006-45, EECS Department, University of California, Berkeley, May 1 2006.
18. O. Maler, Z. Manna, and A. Pnueli. From timed to hybrid systems. In *Real-Time: Theory and Practice, REX Workshop*, pages 447–484. Springer-Verlag, 1992.
19. Z. Manna and A. Pnueli. Verifying hybrid systems. *Hybrid Systems*, pages 4–35, 1992.
20. H. Naundorf. Strictly causal functions have a unique fixed point. *Theoretical Computer Science*, 238(1-2):483–488, 2000.
21. S. Priess-Crampe and P. Ribenboim. Logic programming and ultrametric spaces. *Rendiconti di Matematica, Serie VII*, 19:155–176, 1999.
22. S. Priess-Crampe and P. Ribenboim. Fixed point and attractor theorems for ultrametric spaces. *Forum Mathematicum*, 12:53–64, 2000.
23. G. M. Reed and A. W. Roscoe. Metric spaces as models for real-time concurrency. In *3rd Workshop on Mathematical Foundations of Programming Language Semantics*, pages 331–343, London, UK, 1988.
24. F. van Breugel. Comparative semantics for a real-time programming language with integration. In *TAPSOFT '91*, pages 397–411, New York, NY, USA, 1991. Springer-Verlag New York, Inc.
25. R. K. Yates. Networks of real-time processes. In E. Best, editor, *Proc. of the 4th Int. Conf. on Concurrency Theory (CONCUR)*, volume LNCS 715. Springer-Verlag, 1993.

Some Remarks on Definability of Process Graphs

Clemens Grabmayer[1,*], Jan Willem Klop[2], and Bas Luttik[3]

[1] Department of Computer Science, Vrije Universiteit Amsterdam,
De Boelelaan 1081a, 1081 HV Amsterdam, The Netherlands
clemens@cs.vu.nl
http://cs.vu.nl/~clemens

[2] Vrije Universiteit and CWI Amsterdam, and Radboud Universiteit Nijmegen
Postal address: Department of Computer Science, Vrije Universiteit Amsterdam,
De Boelelaan 1081a, 1081 HV Amsterdam, The Netherlands
jwk@cs.vu.nl
http://www.cs.vu.nl/~jwk

[3] Technische Universiteit Eindhoven, and CWI Amsterdam
Postal address: Department of Mathematics and Computer Science, TU/e,
P.O. Box 513, 5600 MB Eindhoven, The Netherlands
s.p.luttik@tue.nl
http://www.win.tue.nl/~luttik

Abstract. We propose the notions of "density" and "connectivity" of infinite process graphs and investigate them in the context of the well-known process algebras BPA and BPP. For a process graph G, the density function in a state s maps a natural number n to the number of states of G with distance less or equal to n from s. The connectivity of a process graph G in a state s is a measure for how many different ways "of going from s to infinity" exist in G.

For BPA-graphs we discuss some tentative findings about the notions density and connectivity, and indicate how they can be used to establish some non-definability results, stating that certain process graphs are not BPA-graphs, and stronger, not even BPA-definable. For BPP-graphs, which are associated with processes from the class of Basic Parallel Processes (BPP), we prove that their densities are at most polynomial. And we use this fact for showing that the paradigmatic process Queue is not expressible in BPP.

1 Introduction

An important topic in process theory is the issue of expressiveness or definability. There is a family of results, especially in the context of ACP [5,3], to the effect that a particular process can or cannot be defined by a finite recursive specification using a certain set of process operations.

A typical example is the process Stack. It can be defined by a finite recursive specification over BPA (for the axioms of BPA see Table 1), but not by a

* Supported by the Netherlands Organisation for Scientific Research NWO in project *GeoProc*("Geometry of Processes", Nr. 612.000.313).

C. Baier and H. Hermanns (Eds.): CONCUR 2006, LNCS 4137, pp. 16–36, 2006.

Table 1. BPA (Basic Process Algebra), left, and PA (Process Algebra), on the right

$$
\begin{aligned}
x + y &= y + x\\
x + (y + z) &= (x + y) + z\\
x + x &= x\\
(x + y) \cdot z &= x \cdot z + y \cdot z\\
(x \cdot y) \cdot z &= x \cdot (y \cdot z)
\end{aligned}
$$

$$
\begin{aligned}
x + y &= y + x\\
x + (y + z) &= (x + y) + z\\
x + x &= x\\
(x + y) \cdot z &= x \cdot z + y \cdot z\\
(x \cdot y) \cdot z &= x \cdot (y \cdot z)\\
x \parallel y &= x \mathbin{\lfloor\!\lfloor} y + y \mathbin{\lfloor\!\lfloor} x\\
\mathrm{a} \mathbin{\lfloor\!\lfloor} x &= \mathrm{a} \cdot x\\
\mathrm{a} \cdot x \mathbin{\lfloor\!\lfloor} y &= \mathrm{a} \cdot (x \parallel y)\\
(x + y) \mathbin{\lfloor\!\lfloor} z &= x \mathbin{\lfloor\!\lfloor} z + y \mathbin{\lfloor\!\lfloor} z
\end{aligned}
$$

Table 2. Stack, an infinite linear and a finite non-linear BPA-specification

$$
\begin{aligned}
&\mathrm{S}_\lambda = 0{\cdot}\mathrm{S}_0 + 1{\cdot}\mathrm{S}_1\\
&\mathrm{S}_{\mathrm{d}\sigma} = 0{\cdot}\mathrm{S}_{0\mathrm{d}\sigma} + 1{\cdot}\mathrm{S}_{1\mathrm{d}\sigma} + \underline{\mathrm{d}}{\cdot}\mathrm{S}_\sigma\\
&\quad (\text{for } d = 0 \text{ or } d = 1, \text{ and any string } \sigma)
\end{aligned}
$$

$$
\begin{aligned}
\mathrm{S} &= \mathrm{T}{\cdot}\mathrm{S}\\
\mathrm{T} &= 0{\cdot}\mathrm{T}_0 + 1{\cdot}\mathrm{T}_1\\
\mathrm{T}_0 &= \underline{0} + \mathrm{T}{\cdot}\mathrm{T}_0\\
\mathrm{T}_1 &= \underline{1} + \mathrm{T}{\cdot}\mathrm{T}_1
\end{aligned}
$$

finite recursive specification over BCCSP (which has action prefixing instead of sequential composition). See the infinite linear and the finite non-linear specification of Stack in Table 2. Moreover, it has been shown in [6] that a recursive BPA specification defining Stack has more than one equation; Stack cannot be defined by a single equation over BPA. Another example, well-known in the ACP literature, is that the process Bag cannot be defined by a finite recursive BPA specification, while it can be defined using a parallel operator as is present in the process algebra BPP [12] and in the axiom system PA[4] (see Table 1). The process Queue cannot be defined by a finite recursive specification in PA [7]; neither can it be defined in ACP with handshaking communicating [1]. Further well-known results are that communication adds, in the presence of global renaming operations, to the strength of PA (again [1]), and that abstraction via the τ-action and corresponding τ-laws further increase the expressive strength.

An appealing way of representing processes is by means of labeled transition graphs. In this paper, we propose to deal with expressiveness questions by considering geometric aspects of the labeled transition graphs associated with a class of recursive specifications. For instance, it is not hard to show that the labeled transition graphs associated with finite recursive BCCSP specifications have finitely many non-bisimilar vertices (modulo bisimulation). From this it follows that the process Stack is not definable by means of a finite recursive BCCSP specification, for the labeled transition graph of Stack depicted in Figure 1 has infinitely many non-bisimilar vertices.

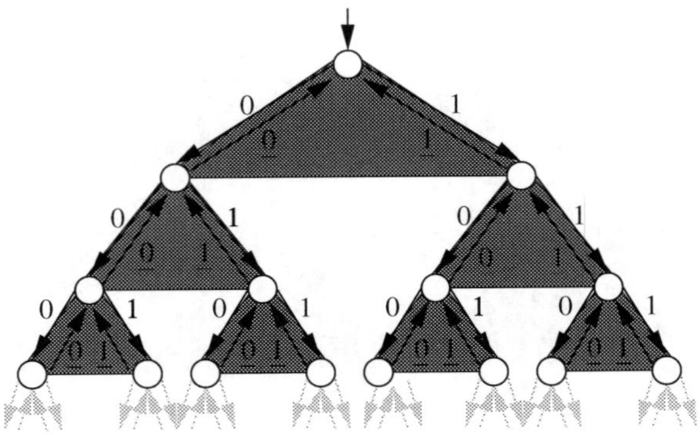

Fig. 1. The labeled transition graph STACK representing the process Stack

The main contribution of the present paper is the definition of two key concepts of the graph structure of processes, namely the density and the connectivity. For a process graph G, the density function maps a state s and a natural number n to the number of states of G with distance less or equal to n from s. The connectivity of a process graph G in a state s is a measure for how many different ways "of going from s to infinity" exist in G. Thus both density and connectivity are initially locally defined notions. It turns out that under certain conditions on a process graph both measures have also a global meaning.

The issue of properties of process graphs was also taken up by other researchers. In particular Caucal [10], Caucal and Montfort [9], and Burkart et al. [8] obtained sophisticated results from the mere appearance of the graphs. Although our primary motivation is the definability issue, one can imagine that progress in understanding the "geometry of processes" may have other benefits as well. Recently, there are major advances in visualising large state spaces of a plethora of processes (see work of Groote and van Ham reported in [15]). The process graphs of such large state spaces exhibit many interesting geometric phenomena that are at this moment largely unexplored. A better insight into the geometric structure of such processes is very likely to increase our awareness and intuition for such processes, with its obvious significance for verification applications.

We consider this study as a step towards a geometry of processes. It is to be expected that much more key notions will emerge. But already the present two parameters of graphs, density and connectivity, enable us to give "high-level" proofs of some non-definability theorems that before were obtained by intricate ad hoc proofs. Actually, the present note is not a first step towards a geometry of processes. Apart from the work already mentioned ([7,9,8]), one may also view the seminal paper [18] of Muller and Schupp to point in the direction of a geometrical study of processes, and likewise, there is a rich tradition of work on graphs, pattern graphs, graph grammars, and so on. There are also historical roots in the topological notion of Freudenthal, "ends" of topological spaces, followed up by the notion of context-free graph of Muller and Schupp.

2 Preliminaries on Labeled Transition Graphs

In this paper, we take the stance that a process is mathematically modeled as a rooted labeled transition graph. We fix the set A of *actions* that will be used as labels of edges in our graphs.

Definition 2.1. A *labeled transition graph* is a pair $(S, \rightarrow)$ consisting of a set S of *vertices* (or: *states*), and a *transition relation* $\rightarrow \subseteq S \times A \times S$. A *rooted* labeled transition graph is a triple $T = (S, \rightarrow, r)$ with $(S, \rightarrow)$ a labeled transition graph and $r \in S$ a distinguished state r called the *root* of T.

A labeled transition graph can be thought of as an edge-labeled directed graph with $\rightarrow$ as the set of labeled directed edges. It can also be thought of as an edge-labeled undirected graph if the direction of the edges, implied by the ordering of the triples in $\rightarrow$, is simply ignored. We shall rely on both views in the remainder of this paper. We proceed to define several general notions for labeled transition graphs. First we discuss the notions that depend on the direction of the edges, and then we discuss the notions that do not take the direction of the edges into account. Throughout, we fix a rooted labeled transition graph $T = (S, \rightarrow, r)$ (but most of our notions actually do not depend on the declaration of a distinguished root).

2.1 Labeled Transition Graphs as Directed Graphs

We write $s \xrightarrow{a} s'$ for $\langle s, a, s' \rangle \in \rightarrow$, and $s \rightarrow s'$ if there exists $a \in A$ such that $s \xrightarrow{a} s'$.

A *directed path* from a state s to a state s' in T is a sequence of states $s_0, \ldots, s_n$ such that $s = s_0 \rightarrow \cdots \rightarrow s_n = s'$. If there exists a path from s to s', then we also say that s' is *reachable* from s. It is convenient to take the number of transitions associated with a path as the length of the path (so the length of the path $s_0, \ldots, s_n$ is n, and not $n + 1$).

A state s is *normed* if there is a directed path from s to a state s' without outgoing transitions; the length of the shortest such path is called the *norm* of s. A labeled transition graph is *normed* if all its states are normed.

A state $s \in S$ is called a *coroot* of T if it has no outgoing transitions and there is a path to s from every other state in S. Note that if T has a coroot, then it is clearly unique, and, moreover, T is normed.

Let $T_i = (S_i, \rightarrow_i, r_i)$ $(i = 1, 2)$ be rooted labeled transition graphs. A binary relation $\mathcal{R} \subseteq S_1 \times S_2$ is a *bisimulation* between T_1 and T_2 if $s_1 \mathrel{\mathcal{R}} s_2$ implies for all $a \in A$:

(i) if $s_1 \xrightarrow{a} s_1'$, then there exists $s_2' \in S_2$ such that $s_2 \xrightarrow{a} s_2'$ and $s_1' \mathrel{\mathcal{R}} s_2'$;
(ii) if $s_2 \xrightarrow{a} s_2'$, then there exists $s_1' \in S_2$ such that $s_1 \xrightarrow{a} s_1'$ and $s_1' \mathrel{\mathcal{R}} s_2'$.

We write $s_1 \leftrightarroweq s_2$ if there exists a bisimulation $\mathcal{R}$ such that $s_1 \mathrel{\mathcal{R}} s_2$. Furthermore, we write $T_1 \leftrightarroweq T_2$ if there exists a bisimulation relation $\mathcal{R}$ such that $r_1 \mathrel{\mathcal{R}} r_2$.

A *self-bisimulation* on T is a bisimulation between T and itself. The rooted labeled transition graph T is *canonical* if every state is reachable from the root and the diagonal on S (i.e., the binary relation $\{\langle s, s\rangle \mid s \in S\}$) is the only self-bisimulation on T.

An *isomorphism* between T_1 and T_2 is a transition-preserving bijection between the subsets of states of T_1 and T_2 that are reachable from their respective roots. If there exists an isomorphism between T_1 and T_2, then we say that they are *isomorphic* (notation: $T_1 \simeq T_2$).

2.2 Labeled Transition Graphs as Undirected Graphs

We write $s \longleftrightarrow s'$ if $s \rightarrow s'$ or $s' \rightarrow s$. An *undirected path* between states s and s' is a sequence of states $s_0, \ldots, s_n$ such that $s = s_0 \longleftrightarrow \cdots \longleftrightarrow s_n = s'$. Two states s and s' are *connected* if there exists an undirected path between s and s'; a labeled transition graph is *connected* if any two states are connected.

The *distance* $d(s, s')$ of states s and s' is the length of the shortest undirected path between s and s' if s and s' are connected, and ∞ otherwise. Clearly, distance is commutative, i.e., $d(s, s') = d(s', s)$. The degree $deg(s)$ of a state s is the cardinality of the set of directed edges that have s as their source or as their target, that is, we let $deg(s) = \left|\{\, \langle s, a, s'\rangle, \langle s', a, s\rangle \mid s \xrightarrow{a} s' \text{ or } s' \xrightarrow{a} s\}\right|$. If every state in T has a finite degree, then we say that T is *locally finite*. For all states s in a locally finite labeled transition graph the set $\{s' \mid d(s, s') \leq n\}$ of states at a distance less or equal some $n \geq 0$ is finite.

A labeled transition graph $T' = (S', \rightarrow')$ is a *subgraph* of T (notation: $T' \subseteq T$) if $S' \subseteq S$ and $\rightarrow' \subseteq \rightarrow$. A *connected component* of T is a maximal connected subgraph of T, i.e., it is a connected subgraph T' of T and, for all T'' such that $T' \subseteq T'' \subseteq T$, either $T'' = T'$ or T'' is not connected.

2.3 Density and Connectivity

We introduce the notions of density and connectivity to classify labeled transition graphs according to their geometrical structure. The density of a labeled transition graph T in a state s is a function that describes the dependency on n of the number of states inside a sphere with radius n around s. The connectivity of a labeled graph T in a state s is the limit, as n tends to infinity, of the number of infinite connected parts into which T splits outside of a sphere around s with radius n.

Let $n \in \mathbb{N}$ and s a state of T. By $In(s, n, T)$ and $Out(s, n, T)$ we mean the subgraphs of T that result by removing all states with distance greater than n from s, and respectively, with distance less than n from s, i.e. we let

$$In(s, n, T) = (S_{\text{in}}(s, n), \rightarrow_{\text{in}}) , \qquad Out(s, n, T) = (S_{\text{out}}(s, n), \rightarrow_{\text{out}}) ,$$

with

$$S_{\text{in}}(s, n) = \{s' \in S \mid d(s, s') \leq n\} , \quad S_{\text{out}} = \{s' \in S \mid d(s, s') \geq n\} ,$$

$$\rightarrow_{\text{in}} = \{\langle s_1, a, s_2\rangle \in \rightarrow \mid a \in A \;\&\; s_1, s_2 \in S_{\text{in}}(s, n)\} ,$$

$$\rightarrow_{\text{out}} = \{\langle s_1, a, s_2\rangle \in \rightarrow \mid a \in A \;\&\; s_1, s_2 \in S_{\text{out}}(s, n)\} .$$

Definition 2.2. Suppose that T is a locally finite labeled transition graph. The *(undirected) density* in a state s of T is the function $\boldsymbol{d}_s : \mathbb{N} \to \mathbb{N}$ defined by

$$\boldsymbol{d}_s(n) = |S_{\text{in}}(s,n)| \ ,$$

which maps every natural number n to the number of states of the subgraph $In(s,n,T)$ of T. The *directed density* in a state s of T is the function $\boldsymbol{d}_s^{\rightarrow} : \mathbb{N} \to \mathbb{N}$ defined by

$$\boldsymbol{d}_s^{\rightarrow}(n) = \left\{ s' \mid \text{there is a path of length} \leq n \text{ from } s \text{ to } s' \right\} .$$

The *density* $\boldsymbol{d}_T$ (*directed density* $\boldsymbol{d}_T^{\rightarrow}$) of T is the density (the directed density) in the root of T. (Usually, T will be clear from the context, and then we shall drop the subscript T and simply write $\boldsymbol{d}$ and $\boldsymbol{d}^{\rightarrow}$ to denote the density, and respectively, the directed density of T.)

From this definition it is obvious that, for a locally finite and connected graph T, and for all states of s of T, the directed-density function $\boldsymbol{d}_s^{\rightarrow}$ of T in s is bounded by the density function $\boldsymbol{d}_s$ of T in s.

We shall generally be interested in bounds on the growth of the density function $\boldsymbol{d}$ locally in a vertex, or globally for all vertices. Let $f : \mathbb{N} \to \mathbb{R}$ a monotone increasing function, and s a state of T. We say that f is an *upper bound on the density of T in s* if and only if

$$(\exists\, n_0 \in \mathbb{N})\, (\forall n \in \mathbb{N}) \left[n \geq n_0 \quad \Rightarrow \quad \boldsymbol{d}_s(n) \leq f(n) \right] . \tag{1}$$

holds, that is iff $\boldsymbol{d}_s$ is almost everywhere bounded by f. We call f a *uniform upper bound* on the density of T if and only if, for all $s \in S$, f is an upper bound on the density of T in s. Analogously, upper bounds are defined for directed-density functions.

A function $f : \mathbb{N} \to \mathbb{R}$ is called *constant*, *linear*, *polynomial*, or *exponential* if $f \in \Theta(1)$, $f \in \Theta(n)$, $f \in \Theta(n^c)$ for some $c \geq 1$, or $f \in \Theta(c^n)$ for some $c > 1$, respectively. We agree to say that *the density of T is linear* (*polynomial*, or *exponential*) if and only if, for all $s \in S$, there exists a linear (and respectively, polynomial, or exponential) upper bound, but not a constant (and respectively, linear, or polynomial) upper bound on the density of T in s. We say that *the density of T is constant* iff, for all $s \in S$, there is a constant upper bound on the density of T in s. This agreement, which also applies for the density of T in a state s and for the directed density of T, is intended to allow succinct formulations of some of our statements. However, it has the consequence that some density functions are categorised imprecisely: graphs with super-linear, non-polynomial density functions like $n \log n$ are said to have polynomial density, and graphs with super-polynomial, but not-exponential functions like $n^{\log n}$ are agreed to have exponential density.

Without proof we now give a proposition, which relates the global property of a locally finite and connected labeled transition graph T to have linear, constant, polynomial, or exponential (undirected) density to the local property of T in a state s to have linear, constant, polynomial, or exponential (undirected) density in s, respectively.

Proposition 2.3. *Let T be a locally finite and connected labeled transition graph, and let s be a state of T. Then the density of T is linear (constant, polynomial, or exponential) if and only if the density of T in s is linear (or respectively, constant, polynomial, or exponential).*

Proposition 2.3 makes it possible to determine the "degree of growth" of the density in an arbitrary state of a locally finite and connected labeled transition graph by only considering the density in the root. For example, by a glance at the process graph STACK for the process Stack in Figure 1, one can recognise that STACK has exponential density in all of its states.

Now we are going to introduce the "connectivity" of a labeled transition graph T in a state s as the limit, as n goes to infinity, of the number of infinite connected components of $Out(s, n, T)$, the subgraph of T consisting of all states with distance greater or equal to n from s, and of all edges of T linking such states. This definition coincides with the definition of the "number of ends" of a locally finite, rooted graph that is used by Muller and Schupp in [17]. It seems to have played a motivating role for the concept of "context-free" graphs that has been introduced by the mentioned authors later in [18]. The "theory of ends", from which the definition of the "number of ends" stems, originated with Freudenthal's dissertation, on which [14] is based.

It is convenient to have notation for the set of all those connected components of a labeled transition graph that have infinitely many states; we define

$$icc(T) = \{T' \mid T' \text{ is an infinite connected component of } T\} .$$

(We say that a labeled transition graph is *infinite* if it has infinitely many states.) For the definition below of our connectivity measure it is important to note the following fact: For all locally finite and connected labeled transition graphs T and states s of T, the function $g : \mathbb{N} \to \mathbb{N},\ n \mapsto |icc(Out(s, n, T))|$ is well-defined and non-decreasing. This implies that the function g possesses a limit in $\mathbb{N} \cup \{\infty\}$, which we call the "connectivity of T in s."

Definition 2.4. Let T be a connected and locally finite rooted labeled transition graph and s a state of T. We define the *connectivity* $\boldsymbol{c}_s$ *of* T *in* s by

$$\boldsymbol{c}_s = \lim_{n\to\infty} |icc(Out(s, n, T))| \ \in \mathbb{N} \cup \{\infty\} .$$

By the *connectivity* $\boldsymbol{c}_T$ *of* T we mean the connectivity of T in its root.

Without proof we state the following proposition, which expresses the fact that, in locally finite and connected graphs, connectivity is a global concept that does not need to be relativised to individual states of a labeled transition graph. For such labeled transition graphs T, the connectivity of T is equal to the connectivity in every state of T.

Proposition 2.5. *Let T be a locally finite and connected labeled graph. Then, for all states s_1 and s_2 of T, $\boldsymbol{c}_{s_1} = \boldsymbol{c}_{s_2}$ holds, that is, the connectivity $\boldsymbol{c}_{s_1}$ of T in s_1 coincides with the connectivity $\boldsymbol{c}_{s_2}$ of T in s_2 (and hence also with the connectivity $\boldsymbol{c}_T$ of T, the connectivity of T in its root).*

Finally, it is important to note that both of the concepts "density function" and "connectivity" of labeled transition graphs are invariant under isomorphism, but not under bisimilarity.

3 BPA-Graphs and BPP-Graphs

BPA-graphs and BPP-graphs are the labeled transition graphs of processes definable in the process algebras BPA (Basic Process Algebra, [4]) and BPP (Basic Parallel Processes, [13]). Starting with work by Caucal and Montfort (see [9] and [11]) there have emerged a number of formal characterisations of the transition graphs of processes in well-known process algebras as the transition graphs described by certain labeled rewrite systems. These characterisations provide alternative definitions, which are widely used since, of process graphs belonging to process algebras like BPA and BPP. A particularly elegant framework is that of process rewrite systems due to Mayr in [16].

To limit technicalities in the two cases of classes of process graphs studied here, BPA-graphs and BPP-graphs, we base the definitions on the somewhat simpler framework of "labeled rewrite systems" (following the exposition in [8]).

Definition 3.1. An *alphabetic labeled (string) rewrite system* is a triple $\mathcal{R} = (V, \Sigma, R)$ where V is an *alphabet* (or set of *nonterminals*), and $R \subseteq V \times \Sigma \times V^*$ is a finite set of *rewrite rules*. We will generally denote a rewrite system $\mathcal{R} = (V, \Sigma, R)$ simply by R if V and Σ are clear from the context; rules $\langle u, a, v \rangle$ will generally be denoted as transitions $u \xrightarrow{a} v$.

Let (V, Σ, R) be a labeled rewrite system. Then the *prefix rewriting relation* $\mapsto$ of R is defined by

$$\mapsto \;=\; \{\langle uw, a, vw \rangle \mid \langle u, a, v \rangle \in R,\; w \in V^*\} .$$

We extend $\mapsto$ to a "more-step prefix rewriting relation" $\mapsto^* \subseteq V^* \times \Sigma^* \times V^*$ by defining, for all $v, v' \in V^*$, a more-step transition $v \mapsto^* v'$ to be possible if and only if $v \mapsto u_1 \mapsto u_2 \mapsto \ldots \mapsto u_{n-1} \mapsto v'$ holds for some $u_1, \ldots, u_{n-1} \in V^*$. By the labeled transition graph *generated by* $\mapsto$ *from* u we mean the rooted labeled transition graph

$$\mathcal{T}(\mapsto, u) \;=\; (\{v \in V^* \mid u \mapsto^* v\}, \mapsto, u) .$$

For an example, we consider the alphabetic rewrite system (V, Σ, R) with $V = \{A, B, C\}$, $\Sigma = \{a, b\}$, and set of rules

$$R = \{A \xrightarrow{a} \lambda,\; A \xrightarrow{b} AB,\; B \xrightarrow{a} \lambda,\; B \xrightarrow{b} BC,\; C \xrightarrow{a} \lambda\} . \tag{2}$$

The transition graph $\mathcal{T}(\mapsto, u)$, which we call TEMPLE, is illustrated in Figure 2. Alternatively, this graph is defined by the recursive specification

$$\langle \mathrm{A} \mid \mathrm{A} = \mathrm{a} + \mathrm{b\,AB},\; \mathrm{B} = \mathrm{a} + \mathrm{b\,BC},\; \mathrm{C} = \mathrm{a} \rangle \tag{3}$$

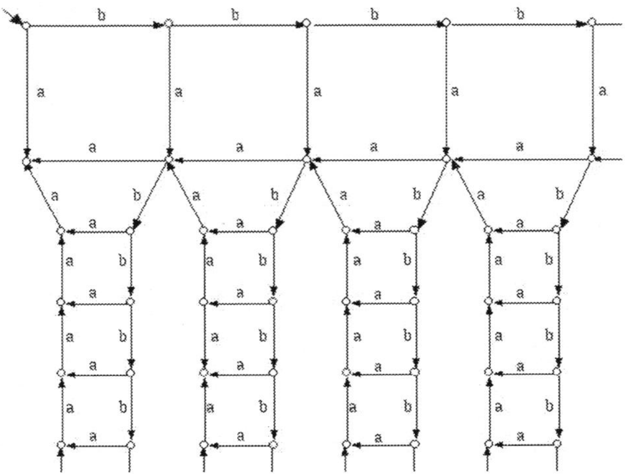

Fig. 2. The labeled transition graph TEMPLE

in the process algebra BPA, where the set of recursion equations is in "restricted Greibach normal form". The relationship indicated for this example between guarded recursive specifications in BPA and alphabetic rewrite systems justifies the following definition, by which the transition graph TEMPLE can be seen to be a "BPA-graph".

Definition 3.2. A rooted labeled transition graph $(T, \to, r)$ is called a BPA-*graph* iff there exists an alphabetic rewrite system (V, Σ, R) and $u \in V$ such that $(T, \to, r)$ is isomorphic to $\mathcal{T}(\mapsto, u)$.

For introducing transition graphs associated with recursive specifications in the process algebra BPP (of "Basic Parallel Processes"), we need some notation on multisets. Let V be a set. We denote by

$$\mathcal{M}(V) = \{\tilde{u} \mid \tilde{u} : V \to \mathbb{N},\ \tilde{u}(v) > 0 \text{ for finitely many } v \in V\}$$

the set of finite multisets over V. By $\oplus$ and $\ominus$ we denote the operations multiset union and multiset difference on the set $\mathcal{M}(V)$. For all $\tilde{u} \in \mathcal{M}(V)$, we let $|\tilde{u}| = \sum_{X \in V} \tilde{u}(X)$ the number of elements of the multiset $\tilde{u}$. Furthermore we designate by $\mathrm{ms}(w)$, for all $w \in V^*$, the multiset in $\mathcal{M}(V)$ that maps every $v \in V$ to the number of occurrences of v in w.

Let (V, Σ, R) be an alphabetic rewrite system. By the *multiset rewriting relation of* R we mean the rewriting relation $\rightsquigarrow \subseteq \mathcal{M}(V) \times \Sigma \times \mathcal{M}(V)$ that is defined, for all $\tilde{u}, \tilde{v} \in \mathcal{M}(\Sigma)$, by

$$\tilde{u} \rightsquigarrow \tilde{v} \iff (\exists \langle X, a, w\rangle \in R)\left[\,\tilde{u}(X) > 0 \ \&\ \tilde{v} = (\tilde{u} \ominus \mathrm{ms}(X)) \oplus \mathrm{ms}(w)\right]. \quad (4)$$

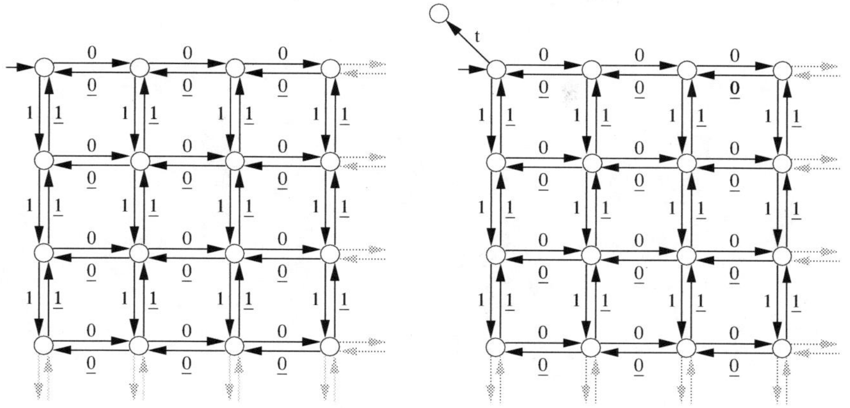

Fig. 3. The canonical process graphs of the process BAG (on the left-hand side), and of a terminating variant BAG_t of BAG (on the right-hand side)

Similar as the prefix-rewriting relation $\mapsto$ of R we extend $\rightsquigarrow$, to the "more-step multiset rewriting relation" $(\rightsquigarrow)^*$ of R. By the labeled transition graph *generated by from* $\tilde{u}$, where $\tilde{u} \in \mathcal{M}(V)$, we mean the rooted labeled transition graph

$$\mathcal{T}(\rightsquigarrow, \tilde{u}) = (\{\tilde{v} \in \mathcal{M}(V) \mid \tilde{u} \rightsquigarrow^* \tilde{v}\}, \rightsquigarrow, \tilde{u}) .$$

As an example, let (V, Σ, R) be the alphabetic rewrite system with $V = \{X, Y\}$, $\Sigma = \{0, \underline{0}, 1, \underline{1}\}$ and

$$R = \{X \xrightarrow{0} XY,\ X \xrightarrow{1} XZ,\ Y \xrightarrow{\underline{0}} \lambda,\ Z \xrightarrow{\underline{1}} \lambda\} .$$

The transition graph $\mathcal{T}(\rightsquigarrow, \mathrm{ms}(X))$ is the transition graph BAG on the left in Figure 3. This graph can also be specified by the recursive specification $\langle \mathrm{X} \mid \mathrm{X} = 0\,(\mathrm{X} \parallel \mathrm{Y}) + 1\,(\mathrm{X} \parallel \mathrm{Z}),\ \mathrm{Y} = \underline{0},\ \mathrm{Z} = \underline{1} \rangle$ in the process theory BPP, where $\parallel$ denotes the operator "merge" for parallel composition. Associativity and commutativity of $\parallel$ are the reason why BPP-specifications can be adequately formalised by multiset rewrite relations based on alphabetic rewrite relations. The relationship indicated here between guarded recursive specifications in BPP and alphabetic rewrite systems justifies the following definition, by which the process graph BAG can be recognised to be a "BPP-graph".

Definition 3.3. A rooted labeled transition graph $(T, \rightarrow, r)$ is called a *BPP-graph* if and only if there exists an alphabetic rewrite system (V, Σ, R) and some $u \in V$ such that $(T, \rightarrow, r)$ is isomorphic to $\mathcal{T}(\rightsquigarrow, \mathrm{ms}(u))$.

4 Density and Connectivity of BPA-Graphs

In this section we will discuss the notions of density and connectivity as they are found in BPA-graphs. We start with an experimental approach, by considering a number of examples.

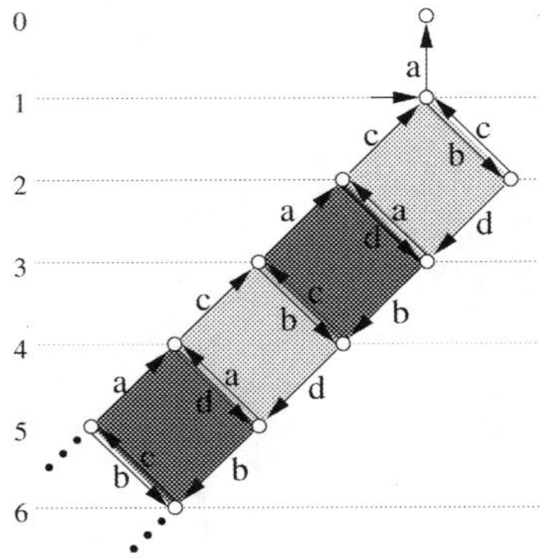

Fig. 4. The labeled transition graph RAILS

4.1 Examples

Example 4.1. The first example is the BPA-graph STACK in Figure 1 we encountered in Section 1. Its specification, both the easy to understand infinite one and the somewhat more sophisticated finite specification, have been given in Table 2 in the Introduction. It is straightforward to draw the infinite process graph corresponding to it. From the illustration in Figure 1 it is easy to read off the salient properties of the Stack graph:

- it is canonical (two different nodes are not bisimilar, i.e., they are the roots of subgraphs that are not bisimilar, or in our definition above, there is no non-trivial self-bisimulation of the whole graph);
- it is not normed, since all maximal traces are infinite (in other words, there is no coroot);
- the graph is not a tree since there are cycles, but it has a striking tree-like appearance which moreover is in some sense periodical, to be explained more precisely below;
- the density is exponential;
- the connectivity is infinite: cutting off a prefix of depth n, there arise 2^{n+1} icc's, so the limit for growing n is infinite.

Example 4.2. The BPA-graph in Figure 4, which we call RAILS, belongs to the guarded recursive BPA-specification $\langle \mathrm{X} \mid \mathrm{X} = \mathrm{a} + \mathrm{b}\,\mathrm{YX},\ \mathrm{Y} = \mathrm{c} + \mathrm{d}\,\mathrm{XY} \rangle$. Equivalently, it is given by the alphabetic rewrite system with set of rules $\{X \xrightarrow{a} \lambda,\ X \xrightarrow{b} YX,\ Y \xrightarrow{c} \lambda,\ Y \xrightarrow{d} XY\}$. The graph RAILS has the following properties:

- it is not canonical; nodes on the same level (i.e. distance to the coroot that is the highest node displayed) are bisimilar. So the graph can be compressed to its unique canonical form by identifying the nodes in a horizontal direction;
- the graph is normed;
- the density is linear;
- the connectivity is 1.

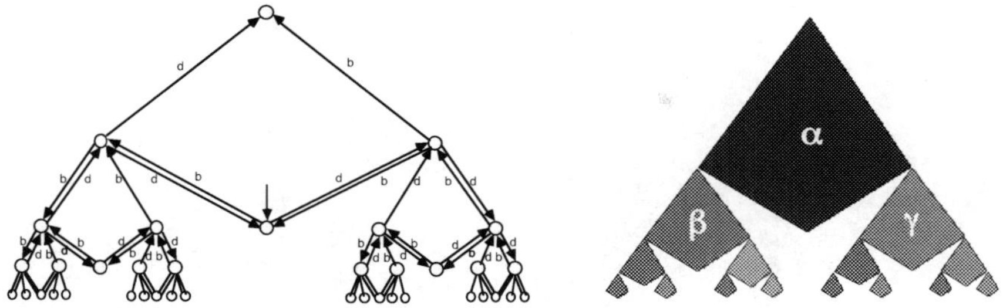

Fig. 5. The labeled transition graph KITES

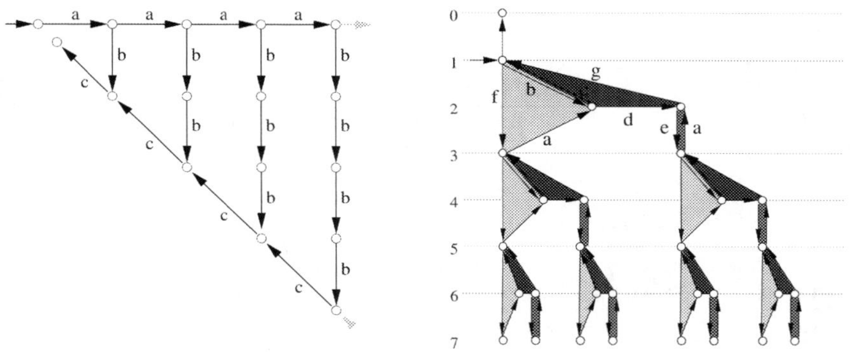

Fig. 6. The labeled transition graphsTRIANGLE and BUTTERFLIES

Example 4.3. KITES, in Figure 5. This is a canonical and normed BPA-graph, with exponential density and infinite connectivity. It corresponds to the recursive BPA-specification $\langle X \mid X = bY + dZ,\ Y = d + dX + bYY,\ Z = b + bX + dZZ \rangle$; its finite traces form the context-free language consisting of words containing as many b's as d's. Again it has a periodical tree-like decomposition.

Example 4.4. BUTTERFLIES, in Figure 6.

This BPA-graph has the recursive BPA-specification $\langle X \mid X = a + bY + fXY,\ Y = cX + dZ,\ Z = gX + eXZ \rangle$. The characteristics are as for KITES.

So far, our sequence of experiments revealed BPA-graphs that have either linear or exponential density. How about the graph BAG, or BAG_t in Figure 3? According to our discussion in the Introduction, BAG is not a BPA-graph. Clearly, it has polynomial (quadratic) density. Its connectivity is 1. It is not normed, but it is canonical. Here one could jump to the guess that all BPA-graphs have density linear or exponential—and not polynomial. However, Didier Caucal pointed out to us that, surprisingly, there are BPA-graphs with polynomial density. His beautiful example is displayed in Figure 2, as the graph called TEMPLE. It corresponds to the rewrite system with rules (2) and to the recursive

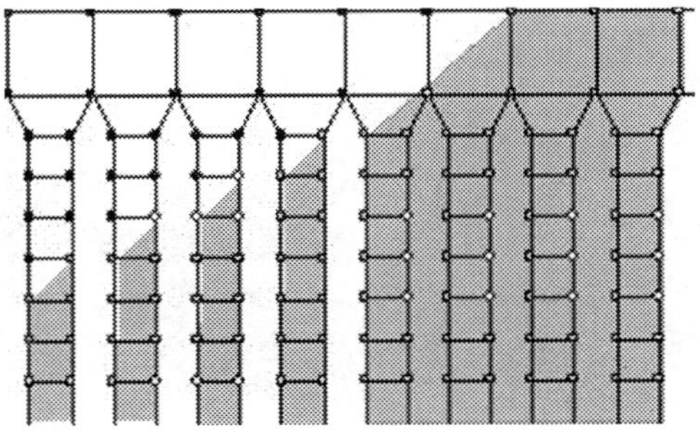

Fig. 7. Determining the connectivity of the graph TEMPLE

specification (3). It is a normed, canonical graph with quadratic density and infinite connectivity. That the connectivity is infinite, is clear from Figure 7, where the shadowy part, obtained by removing the prefix of depth 6, consists of 5 icc's; it is easy to see that the number of icc's grows to infinity with the prefix depth of nodes that are removed.

4.2 Periodic Decomposition

In the present note, we will not dwell on this phenomenon extensively, but refer instead to [2]. All BPA-graphs displayed above, including the quadratically dense TEMPLE, display a tree-like periodical decomposition, which was first observed and proved in [2]. That is, there are finitely many graph fragments that are strung together in a regular way.

So, for RAILS the graph fragment structure is described by the recursion term $\langle\alpha|\alpha = c(\alpha)\rangle$, where c stands for "connected to"; for STACK we have $\langle\alpha|\alpha = c(\alpha,\alpha)\rangle$; for TEMPLE we have $\langle\alpha|\alpha = c(\beta,\alpha),\, \beta = c(\beta)\rangle$; and for KITES, $\langle\alpha|\alpha = c(\beta,\gamma),\, \beta = c(\beta,\gamma),\, \gamma = c(\beta,\gamma)\rangle$. Alternatively, one may write these recursion terms as μ-terms, obtaining $\mu\alpha.c(\alpha)$, etc.

We continue by mentioning another important feature of BPA-graphs, this time with the restriction to normed graphs.

Theorem 4.5 (Caucal). *The class of normed* BPA*-graphs (or equivalently, the class of* BPA*-graphs with a coroot) is closed with respect to minimisation under bisimulation.*

It is a noteworthy fact that the restriction of normedness in this theorem is crucial: the class of all BPA-graphs is not closed under minimisation (for an example of an—unnormed—BPA-graph with a canonical graph that is not a BPA-graph, see Figure 3 in [8]).

4.3 Relating Density and Connectivity

We now state in Table 3 the relationship between the density and connectivity for BPA-graphs. Here we do not give the full proofs, but merely mention that they are obtained from an analysis of the structural μ-terms that describe tree-like

Table 3. Connectivity-density value pairs $\langle \boldsymbol{c}, \boldsymbol{d} \rangle$ that are possible for BPA-graphs

c versus d	constant	linear	polynomial	exponential
0	✓	—	—	—
finite, nonzero	—	✓	—	—
∞	—	—	✓	✓

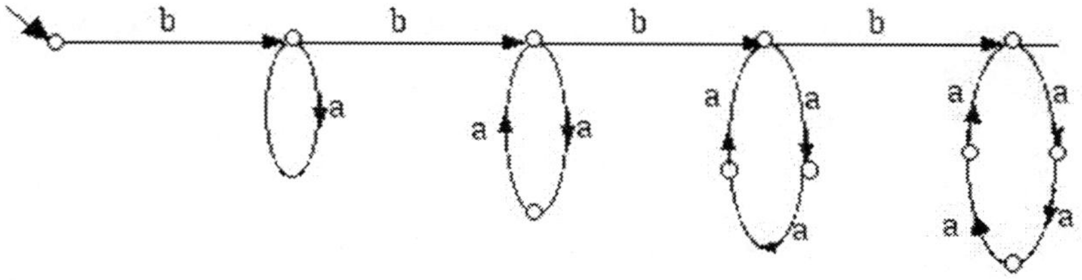

Fig. 8. The labeled transition graph RINGS

periodic decompositions obtained as described in [2]. As a caveat, we mention that the statements concerning Table 3 are still of tentative nature.

We now give an application. Figure 6 contains the graph TRIANGLE. Is it a BPA-graph? It corresponds to the context-sensitive language $\{a^n b^n c^n \mid n \in \mathbb{N}\}$, which is not context-free; so our suspicion is that it is not a BPA-graph. Indeed this is the case: it is normed, canonical, with quadratic density. However, its connectivity is 1, and according to the table above, it should be infinite. Hence TRIANGLE is not a BPA-graph. Similar for BAG_t.

Now the fact that TRIANGLE and BAG_t are not BPA-graphs, does not yet mean that they are not BPA-definable. It could be that for TRIANGLE there is a BPA-specification E, with process graph $g(E)$, such that the canonical form $\text{can}(g(E)) \leftrightarrows$ TRIANGLE. Since TRIANGLE is canonical, we even have $\text{can}(g(E)) \simeq$ TRIANGLE (recall that $\simeq$ stands for graph isomorphism). Now TRIANGLE is normed, hence $\text{can}(g(E))$ is normed. So $g(E)$ is normed (since $\text{can}(g(E)) \leftrightarrows g(E)$, and normedness is preserved by bisimilarity). So, we can apply Theorem 4.5 on the normed BPA-graph $g(E)$, and conclude that $\text{can}(g(E))$ is again a BPA-graph; say $\text{can}(g(E)) \simeq g(E')$ for some BPA-specification E'. Now we have that the BPA-graph $g(E') \simeq$ TRIANGLE hence $g(E')$ has the same connectivity and density as TRIANGLE, namely $\boldsymbol{c} = 1$ and $\boldsymbol{d}$ is quadratic. But this is impossible.

Now let us consider BAG and RINGS, in Figure 8. Both have quadratic density and connectivity 1. They are therefore not BPA-graphs. But are they not BPA-definable? Invoking Caucal's theorem (Theorem 4.5) does not work here, since both graphs are not normed. Here a more powerful theory is needed, and this is found in the notion of "context-free graph" of Muller and Schupp, in conjunction with more recent work of Caucal in [11] and [8].

Suppose that BAG is BPA-definable. Then there exists a recursive specification E in BPA such that BAG is bisimilar with a tree-like periodic graph $g(E)$ as defined by Baeten, Bergstra, and Klop in [2]. Then $g(E)$ is a BPA-graph (in the sense of Definition 3.2).[1]

In [8] Burkart, Caucal, and Steffen have shown that, for *every* BPA-graph T, the canonical graph of T is a "pattern graph", which means that it can be generated from a finite (hyper)graph by a reduction sequence of length ω according to a deterministic (hypergraph) grammar.[2] Since BAG is itself a canonical graph and since therefore BAG is the canonical graph of the BPA-graph $g(E)$, it follows that BAG is a pattern graph.

A theorem due to Caucal in [11] states that all (rooted) pattern graphs of finite degree are "context-free" according to the definition of Muller and Schupp in [18].[3] It follows that BAG is context-free. However, it is not difficult to verify that BAG is actually *not* a context-free graph according to the definition in [18].

In this way we have arrived at a contradiction with our assumption that BAG is definable in BPA. For RINGS the same reasoning applies.

We conclude this section by mentioning a useful fact due to Muller and Schupp in [18] that characterises the class of transition graphs corresponding to recursively defined specifications in the process algebra PDP (containing "Pushdown Processes") as the class of "context-free graphs".

Proposition 4.6. *Every* BPA*-graph is context-free.*

5 Density of BPP-Graphs

In this section we investigate the possible densities of BPP-graphs. We prove that BPP-graphs have at most polynomial density, and apply this result to show that the paradigmatic process Queue, which is definable in the process algebra ACP, cannot be defined in BPP.

For the proof of the mentioned result concerning the density of BPP-graphs the following technical lemma will be essential. This lemma contains a bound on the number of finite multisets with k members over a set with m elements.

Lemma 5.1. Let V be a finite set with $m \in \mathbb{N} \setminus \{0\}$ elements. Then, for all $k \in \mathbb{N}$, the number of multisets over V with k elements is equal to $\binom{m+k-1}{k}$.

---

1 In earlier papers of Caucal (e.g. in [9] and [11]) BPA-graphs were known under the name "alphabetic graphs".

2 "Pattern graphs" according to this definition used by Caucal and Montfort in [9] are called "regular graphs" in the later paper [8] by Burkart, Caucal, and Steffen. Because the use of the attribute "regular" for process graphs could lead to wrong associations, we avoid this terminology from (hyper)graph rewriting here.

3 Note that the class of "context-free" graphs in Muller and Schupp's definition does not coincide with the graphs associated with "context-free" processes (the class of BPA-graphs), but that it forms a strictly richer class of graphs corresponding to the class of transition graphs of push-down automata.

Furthermore it holds:

$$\Big(k \longmapsto \big|\{\tilde{v} \mid \tilde{v} \in \mathcal{M}(V),\, |\tilde{v}| = k\}\big|\Big) \in O(k^{m-1})\,, \tag{5}$$

$$\Big(k \longmapsto \big|\{\tilde{v} \mid \tilde{v} \in \mathcal{M}(V),\, |\tilde{v}| \le k\}\big|\Big) \in O(k^{m})\,. \tag{6}$$

Proof. Let $V = \{X_1, \ldots, X_m\}$ be a finite set with $m \in \mathbb{N}\backslash\{0\}$ elements. Then, for all $k \in \mathbb{N}$, the number of finite multisets over V with k elements can be computed as follows:

$$\begin{aligned}\big|\{\tilde{v} \mid \tilde{v} \in \mathcal{M}(V),\, |\tilde{v}| = k\}\big| &= \big|\{(x_1, \ldots, x_m) \mid 0 \le x_i \le k\,, \textstyle\sum_{i=1}^{k} x_i = k\}\big| \\ &= \big|\{(x_1, \ldots, x_{k+m-1}) \mid x_i \in \{0,1\},\, \textstyle\sum_{i=1}^{m+k-1} x_i = k\}\big| \\ &= \tbinom{m+k-1}{k}\,. \end{aligned} \tag{7}$$

For all $k \in \mathbb{N}$ with $k \ge m$ it holds:

$$\begin{aligned}\binom{m+k-1}{k} &= \frac{(m+k-1).(m+k-2)\,\ldots\,(m+1).m}{1.2\,\ldots\,(k-1).k} \\ &= \frac{(m+k-1)\,\ldots\,(k+1)}{1\,\ldots\,(m-1)} \le \frac{(2k)^{m-1}}{(m-1)!}\,.\end{aligned}$$

This implies $\big(k \mapsto \binom{m+k-1}{k}\big) \in O(k^{m-1})$, which in view of (7) demonstrates (5). Furthermore with $C_1 = \sum_{i=0}^{m-1} \binom{m+i-1}{i}$ and $C_2 = \frac{2^{m-1}}{(m-1)!}$ it follows:

$$\begin{aligned}\sum_{i=0}^{k} \tbinom{m+i-1}{i} &= \sum_{i=0}^{m-1} \tbinom{m+i-1}{i} + \sum_{i=m}^{k} \tbinom{m+i-1}{i} \\ &\le C_1 + C_2.\sum_{i=0}^{k} i^{m-1} \le C_1 + C_2.(k+1).k^{m-1} \\ &= C_1 + C_2.(k^m + k)\end{aligned}$$

which because of $(k \mapsto k^m + k) \in O(k^m)$ and (7) now demonstrates (6). □

Now we are able to state and prove our result concerning the density of BPP-graphs.

Theorem 5.2. *For every* BPP*-graph there exists a polynomial uniform upper bound on its density.*

Proof. Let $T = (S, \rightarrow, r)$ be a BPP-graph. That is, there exists an alphabetic rewrite system (V, Σ, R) with $V = \{X_1, \ldots, X_m\}$ such that T is isomorphic to the rooted labeled transition graph $\mathcal{T}(\rightsquigarrow, \mathrm{ms}(X_1))$, where $\rightsquigarrow$ is the multiset rewrite relation of R. Since the density of a labeled transition graph is invariant under isomorphism, we may assume, without loss of generality, that T actually *is* the rooted labeled transition graph $\mathcal{T}(\rightsquigarrow, \mathrm{ms}(X_1))$.

Now we let $\tilde{u}$, with $\tilde{u} \in \mathcal{M}(V)$, be an arbitrary state of T and investigate the density of T in $\tilde{u}$.

We let $N = \max\{1, (\max_{\langle X,a,v\rangle \in R} \lg(v)) - 1\}$. In particular, N is greater or equal to the maximal length of the right-hand side of a rule in R minus one. Therefore the definition of N implies, in view of the definition of $\rightsquigarrow$:

$$\tilde{v}_1 \rightsquigarrow \tilde{v}_2 \implies |\tilde{v}_2| \leq |\tilde{v}_1| + N \qquad \text{(for all } \tilde{v}_1, \tilde{v}_2 \in \mathcal{M}(V)) , \tag{8}$$

$$\tilde{v}_1 \rightsquigarrow \tilde{v}_2 \implies |\tilde{v}_1| \leq |\tilde{v}_2| + 1 \leq |\tilde{v}_2| + N \qquad \text{(for all } \tilde{v}_1, \tilde{v}_2 \in \mathcal{M}(V)) . \tag{9}$$

Now let, for all $n \in \mathbb{N}$, $=^{\leq n}_{(R)}$ be defined by

$$=^{\leq n}_{(R)} = \bigcup_{i=0}^{n} (\rightsquigarrow \cup (\rightsquigarrow)^{-1})^{i}$$

as the restriction of the convertibility relation $=_{(R)} = (\rightsquigarrow \cup (\rightsquigarrow)^{-1})^{*}$ of $\rightsquigarrow$ to conversions of length less or equal to n. Using (8) and (9) it can be proved by induction on n that, for all $n \in \mathbb{N}$,

$$\tilde{v}_1 =^{\leq n}_{(R)} \tilde{v}_2 \implies |\tilde{v}_2| \leq |\tilde{v}_1| + n.N \qquad \text{(for all } \tilde{v}_1, \tilde{v}_2 \in \mathcal{M}(V)) \tag{10}$$

holds. Since $\tilde{v}_1 =^{\leq n}_{(R)} \tilde{v}_2$ holds if and only if $d(\tilde{v}_1, \tilde{v}_2) \leq n$ is the case, (10) entails

$$d(\tilde{v}_1, \tilde{v}_2) \leq n \implies |\tilde{v}_2| \leq |\tilde{v}_1| + n.N \qquad \text{(for all } \tilde{v}_1, \tilde{v}_2 \in \mathcal{M}(V)) ,$$

for all $n \in \mathbb{N}$. Now this implies that, for all $n \in \mathbb{N}$, a superset of the set $S_{\text{in}}(\tilde{\boldsymbol{u}}, n)$ of states of the subgraph $In(\tilde{\boldsymbol{u}}, n, T)$ of T can be found as follows:

$$S_{\text{in}}(\tilde{u}, n) = \{\tilde{v} \in \mathcal{M}(V) \mid d(\tilde{u}, \tilde{v}) \leq n\} \subseteq \{\tilde{v} \in \mathcal{M}(V) \mid |\tilde{v}| \leq |\tilde{u}| + n.N\} .$$

By applying Lemma 5.1 now a bound on the density of T in $\tilde{\boldsymbol{u}}$ can be established as follows:

$$\boldsymbol{d}_{\tilde{u}} = (n \mapsto |S_{\text{in}}(\tilde{u}, n)|) \in O((|\tilde{u}| + n.N)^{m}) \subseteq O(n^{m}) .$$

Hence there is a polynomial upper bound on the density of T in $\tilde{\boldsymbol{u}}$; moreover, for such an upper bound a polynomial of the order of the number of variables in the alphabetic rewrite system underlying T can be chosen.

Since in this argument $\tilde{\boldsymbol{u}}$ has been an arbitrary state of T, we have established that there is a polynomial which is a uniform upper bound on the density of T. □

Now we turn to the paradigmatic process Queue in the first-in-first-out version with unbounded capacity. An infinite specification of Queue in BPA is given in Table 4. The canonical process graph of QUEUE is sketched, for the case $D = \{0, 1\}$ in Figure 9. Compared with the easier graphs of the paradigmatic processes Stack and Bag, the structure of this canonical graph is more complex. By using Proposition 2.5 it is easy to see from Figure 9 that $c_{\mathsf{QUEUE}} = 1$. Hence the connectivity of QUEUE is the same as that of BAG, but different from that of STACK. On the other hand, we will prove below that the density of QUEUE is greater than that of BAG.

Table 4. Queue, infinite BPA-specification

$$\mathrm{Q} = \mathrm{Q}_\lambda = \textstyle\sum_{d \in D} \mathrm{r}_1(\mathrm{d}) \cdot \mathrm{Q}_\mathrm{d}$$
$$\mathrm{Q}_{\sigma\mathrm{d}} = \mathrm{s}_2(\mathrm{d}) \cdot \mathrm{Q}_\sigma + \textstyle\sum_{e \in D} \mathrm{r}_1(\mathrm{e}) \cdot \mathrm{Q}_{\mathrm{e}\sigma\mathrm{d}}$$
(for $d \in D$, and $\sigma \in D^*$)

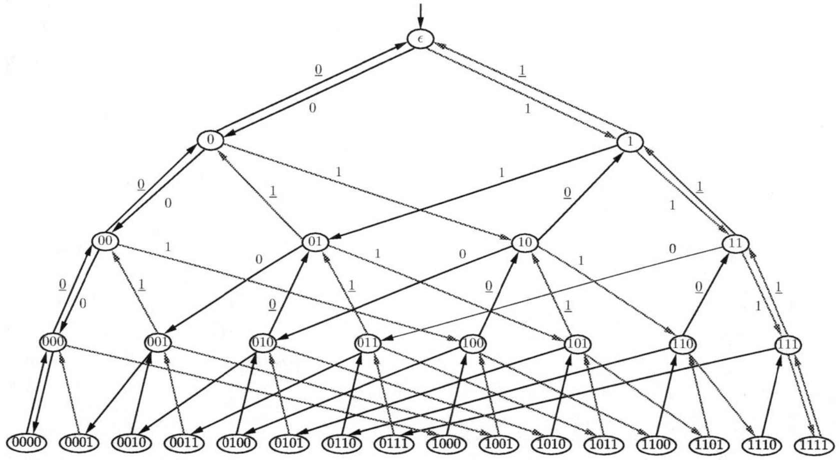

Fig. 9. The canonical process graph QUEUE of Queue

Table 5. Queue, finite ACP-specification with renaming

$$\mathrm{Q} = \textstyle\sum_{d \in D} \mathrm{r}_1(\mathrm{d})(\rho_{\mathrm{c}_3 \to \mathrm{s}_2} \circ \partial_H)(\rho_{\mathrm{s}_2 \to \mathrm{s}_3}(\mathrm{Q}) \parallel \mathrm{s}_2(\mathrm{d}) \cdot \mathrm{Z})$$
$$\mathrm{Z} = \textstyle\sum_{d \in D} \mathrm{r}_3(\mathrm{d}) \cdot \mathrm{Z}$$

It is clearly desirable to obtain a finite specification of this process. It was proved by Bergstra and Tiuryn in [7] that neither the process algebra BPA is sufficient for that, nor in fact is its extension PA. Building on this result, Baeten and Bergstra in [1] proved the even stronger statement that Queue cannot be defined in ACP *with handshaking communication* under the weak additional assumption that the pushing and popping actions are not the result of communications. However, in [1] also a finite recursive specification of Queue is given in ACP *with global renaming operators.* This beautiful specification (see Table 5) is originally due to Hoare who used a "chaining"-operation.

Proposition 5.3. *Let D be a finite set with $|D| > 1$. Then the canonical process graph* QUEUE(D) *of* Queue(D) *has exponential density.*

Proof. From the infinite BPA-specification for Queue in Table 4 it is easy to verify that, for all $\sigma_1, \sigma_2 \in D$ with $\sigma_1 \neq \sigma_2$, the subprocesses Q_{σ_1} and Q_{σ_2} of Q in Table 4 cannot be bisimilar: the sequence of popping moves for the processes Q_{σ_1} and Q_{σ_2} must be different. Hence the canonical process graph QUEUE for Queue can be drawn in tree space; for the example of $D = \{0,1\}$, QUEUE(D) is hinted in Figure 9.

We first consider the case $|D| = 2$. Then it is easy to verify that the function $(n \mapsto 2^{n+1} - 3)$ is an asymptotic lower bound on the density of QUEUE (for each vertex v by a sequences of length n of transitions in downwards-direction there are 2^n vertices reachable), and the function $\left(n \mapsto \frac{4}{3}(4^n - 1)\right)$ is an upper bound on the density of QUEUE (as an easy consequence of the summation formula for a geometric series in view of the fact that in QUEUE there are at most four vertices reachable from an arbitrary vertex by a single transition).

In the general case, where $k = |D|$, it is easy to verify that $\left(n \mapsto \frac{k(k^n-1)}{k-1} - 1\right)$ is an asymptotic lower bound on the density of QUEUE, and that $\left(n \mapsto \frac{2k((2k)^n-1)}{2k-1}\right)$ is an upper bound on the density of QUEUE. □

The following theorem states two conditions, canonicity and the existence of an exponential "lower bound" on the directed density, under which a labeled transition graph is not a BPP-graph. In the proof it is shown that these conditions enable to deduce a contradiction with Theorem 5.2, the statement that BPP-graphs have at most exponential density.

Theorem 5.4. *Let T be a rooted process graph that is canonical. Furthermore, there exists an exponential function that is not an upper bound on the directed density of T. Then T is not definable in* BPP.

Proof. Let $T = (S, \to, r)$ be a rooted process graph that is canonical and for which there exists an exponential function that is not an upper bound on the directed density of T.

Suppose that T is definable in BPP. Then there exists an alphabetic rewrite system $\mathcal{R} = (V, \Sigma, R)$ with $V = \{X_1, \ldots, X_m\}$ such that for the rooted transition graph $T' = (S', \to', r') = \mathcal{T}(\rightsquigarrow, \mathrm{ms}(X_1))$ it holds:

$$T' \leftrightarrows T\,. \tag{11}$$

By Theorem 5.2 the density of T' is at most polynomial, and hence there exists a polynomial upper bound p on the density of T' in the state $r' = \mathrm{ms}(X_1)$; hence $\boldsymbol{d}_{r'}(n) \leq p(n)$ holds for all but finitely many $n \in \mathbb{N}$. By assumption on T there exists an exponential function $f : \mathbb{N} \to \mathbb{R}$ that is not an upper bound on the directed density of T, which means that there are infinitely many $n \in \mathbb{N}$ such that $f(n) < \boldsymbol{d}_r^{\rightarrow}(n)$ holds. As a consequence of the fact that $p(n) < f(n)$ holds for all but finitely many n, $\boldsymbol{d}_{r'}(n) < \boldsymbol{d}_r^{\rightarrow}(n)$ must hold for infinitely many n. Due to this we can choose $n_0 \in \mathbb{N}$ with the property that

$$|(S')_{\mathrm{in}}(r', n_0)| = \boldsymbol{d}_{r'}(n_0) \;<\; \boldsymbol{d}_r^{\rightarrow}(n_0) = |S_{\mathrm{in}}^{\rightarrow}(r, n_0)| \tag{12}$$

holds, where

$$S_{\mathrm{in}}^{\rightarrow}(r, n_0) = \left\{ s \in S \mid \text{there is a path of length} \leq n_0 \text{ from } r \text{ to } s \right\}.$$

Now it follows from (11) by repeated applications of the back-condition for a bisimulation between T' and T linking r' and r that each state in T with distance less or equal to n_0 from r must be bisimilar to a state in T' with distance less or equal to n_0 from r'. Due to (12), the difference in cardinality between $(S')_{\text{in}}(r', n_0)$ and $S^{\rightarrow}_{\text{in}}(r, n_0)$, it follows that there must exist different states s_1 and s_2 in $S^{\rightarrow}_{\text{in}}(r, n_0)$, and hence of T, and a state s' in $(S')_{\text{in}}(r', n_0)$, and hence of T', such that s' (in T') is bisimilar both to s_1 and s_2 (in T). But this entails that actually s_1 and s_2 are two different bisimilar states of T, which is a contradiction with the assumption that T is a canonical graph.

Therefore the assumption that T is definable in BPP cannot be sustained. □

By using this theorem, we are finally able to show that, for sets D with more than one element, the paradigmatic process Queue(D) is not definable in BPP.

Corollary 5.5. *For all finite sets D with $|D| > 1$,* Queue(D) *is not definable in* BPP.

Proof. We assume that D is a finite set with more than one element and that Queue(D) is definable in BPP. This means that there exists a guarded recursive specification E in BPP with Queue(D) as a solution. From the specification E a BPP-graph T can be extracted which has the property that it is bisimilar to the canonical process graph QUEUE(D) of Queue(D), showing that the graph QUEUE(D) is definable in BPP. However, Theorem 5.4 implies, in view of Proposition 5.3, that QUEUE(D) is actually not definable in BPP. We have obtained a contradiction. □

We conclude with a question concerning the possible values of connectivity and the relationship between connectivity and density for BPP-graphs.

Question 5.6. What can be said about the connectivity of BPP*-graphs? Is there a useful concept of "regular decomposition" for* BPP*-graphs? Is there perhaps, similar as for* BPA*-graphs, a correspondence statement that relates density and connectivity also for* BPP*-graphs?*

Acknowledgement. We are very grateful to Didier Caucal for the graph TEMPLE with its specification, and for pointing out its consequences. We thank Henk Barendregt for discussions about this paper and posing the definability questions for the graphs RINGS and TRIANGLE.

References

1. J. C. M. Baeten and J. A. Bergstra. Global renaming operators in concrete process algebra. *Information and Computation*, pages 205–245, 1988.
2. J. C. M. Baeten, J. A. Bergstra, and J. W. Klop. Decidability of bisimulation equivalence for process generating context-free languages. *Journal of the ACM*, 40(3):653–682, 1993.
3. J. C. M. Baeten and W. P. Weijland. *Process Algebra.* Number 18 in Cambridge Tracts in Theoretical Computer Science. Cambridge University Press, 1990.

4. J. A. Bergstra and J. W. Klop. The algebra of recursively defined processes and the algebra of regular processes. In J. Paredaens, editor, *Proceedings of ICALP'84*, volume 172 of *LNCS*, pages 82–95. Springer, 1984.
5. J. A. Bergstra and J. W. Klop. Process algebra for synchronous communication. *Information and Control*, 60(1–3):109–137, January/February/March 1984.
6. J. A. Bergstra and J. W. Klop. Process algebra: specification and verification in bisimulation semantics. In M. Hazewinkel, J. K. Lenstra, and L. G. L. T. Meertens, editors, *CWI Monograph 4, Proceedings of the CWI Symposium Mathematics and Computer Science II*, pages 61–94, Amsterdam, 1986. North-Holland.
7. J. A. Bergstra and J. Tiuryn. Process algebra semantics for queues. *Fundamenta Informaticae*, X:213–224, 1987.
8. O. Burkart, D. Caucal, and B. Steffen. Bisimulation collapse and the process taxonomy. In *Proceedings of CONCUR'96*, 1996.
9. D. Caucal and R. Montfort. On the transition graphs of automata and grammars. In *Proceedings of WG 90*, volume 484 of *LNCS*, pages 61–86. Springer, 1990.
10. D. Caucal. Graphes canoniques de graphes algébriques. *Theoret. Inform. and Appl.*, 24(4):339–352, 1990.
11. D. Caucal. On the regular structure of prefix rewriting. *Theoretical Computer Science*, 1992.
12. S. Christensen. *Decidability and Decompostion in Process Algebras.* PhD thesis, University of Edinburgh, 1993.
13. Søren Christensen, Yoram Hirshfeld, and Faron Moller. Bisimulation equivalence is decidable for basic parallel processes. In *CONCUR*, pages 143–157, 1993.
14. H. Freudenthal. Über die Enden topologischer Räume und Gruppen. *Mathematische Zeitschrift*, 33:692–713, 1931.
15. J. F. Groote and F. J. J. van Ham. Interactive visualization of large state spaces. *International Journal on Software Tools for Technology Transfer*, 2005.
16. R. Mayr. Process rewrite systems. *Information and Computation*, 156(1):264–286, 2000.
17. D. E. Muller and P. E. Schupp. Groups, the theory of ends, and context-free languages. *Journal of Computer and System Sciences*, 26:295–310, 1983.
18. D. E. Muller and P. E. Schupp. The theory of ends, pushdown automata, and second-order logic. *Theoretical Computer Science*, 37:51–75, 1985.

Sanity Checks in Formal Verification*

Orna Kupferman**

Hebrew University, School of Engineering and Computer Science,
Jerusalem 91904, Israel
orna@cs.huji.ac.il
http://www.cs.huji.ac.il/~orna

Abstract. One of the advantages of temporal-logic model-checking tools is their ability to accompany a negative answer to the correctness query by a counterexample to the satisfaction of the specification in the system. On the other hand, when the answer to the correctness query is positive, most model-checking tools provide no additional information. In the last few years there has been growing awareness to the importance of suspecting the system or the specification of containing an error also in the case model checking succeeds. The main justification of such suspects are possible errors in the modeling of the system or of the specification. The goal of sanity checks is to detect such errors by further automatic reasoning. Two leading sanity checks are *vacuity* and *coverage*. In vacuity, the goal is to detect cases where the system satisfies the specification in some unintended trivial way. In coverage, the goal is to increase the exhaustiveness of the specification by detecting components of the system that do not play a role in verification process. For both checks, the challenge is to define vacuity and coverage formally, develop algorithms for detecting vacuous satisfaction and low coverage, and suggest methods for returning to the user helpful information. We survey existing work on vacuity and coverage and argue that, in many aspects, the two checks are essentially the same: both are based on repeating the verification process on some mutant input. In vacuity, mutations are in the specifications, whereas in coverage, mutations are in the system. This observation enables us to adopt work done in the context of vacuity to coverage, and vise versa.

1 Introduction

In temporal-logic *model checking*, we verify the correctness of a finite-state system with respect to a desired behavior by checking whether a labeled state-transition graph that models the system satisfies a temporal logic formula that specifies this behavior [CGL93]). Beyond being fully-automatic, an additional attraction of model-checking tools is their ability to accompany a negative answer to the correctness query by a counterexample to the satisfaction of the specification in the system. Thus, together with a negative answer, the model checker returns some erroneous execution of the system. These counterexamples are very important and they can be essential in detecting

* The paper is based on joint work with Hana Chockler, Moshe Y. Vardi, and Robert Kurshan, appearing in [CKV01, CKKV01, CKV03, Cho03].

** Supported in part by BSF grant 9800096, and by a grant from Minerva.

C. Baier and H. Hermanns (Eds.): CONCUR 2006, LNCS 4137, pp. 37–51, 2006.

subtle errors in complex designs [CGMZ95]. On the other hand, when the answer to the correctness query is positive, most model-checking tools provide no additional information. Since a positive answer means that the system is correct with respect to the specification, this at first seems like a reasonable policy. In the last few years, however, there has been growing awareness to the importance of suspecting the system and the specification of containing an error also in the case model checking succeeds. The main justification of such suspects are possible errors in the modeling of the system or of the behavior.

Early work on "suspecting a positive answer" concerns the fact that temporal logic formulas can suffer from antecedent failure [BB94]. For example, verifying a system with respect to the specification $\varphi = AG(req \rightarrow AF grant)$ ("every request is eventually followed by a grant"), one should distinguish between satisfaction of φ in systems in which requests are never sent, and satisfaction in which φ's precondition is sometimes satisfied. Evidently, the first type of satisfaction suggests some unexpected properties of the system, namely the absence of behaviors in which the precondition was expected to be satisfied.

In [BBER01], Beer et al. suggested a first formal treatment of vacuity. As described there, vacuity is a serious problem: "our experience has shown that typically 20% of specifications pass vacuously during the first formal-verification runs of a new hardware design, and that vacuous passes always point to a real problem in either the design or its specification or environment" [BBER01]. The definition of vacuity according to [BBER01] is based on the notion of subformulas that do not affect the satisfaction of the specification. Consider a model M satisfying a specification φ. A subformula ψ of φ *does not affect* (the satisfaction of) φ in M if M also satisfies all formulas obtained by modifying ψ. In the example above, the subformula $grant$ does not affect φ in a model with no requests. Now, M satisfies φ vacuously if φ has a subformula that does not affect φ in M. A general method for vacuity definition and detection was presented in [KV03], and the problem was further studied in [AFF$^+$03, CG04a, BFG$^+$05]. It is shown in these papers that for temporal logics such as LTL and CTL*, where an occurrence of the subformula ψ can be replaced by a universally quantified proposition, vacuity detection can be reduced to model checking specifications in the logic obtained by adding universally quantified atomic propositions. This leaves vacuity detection for LTL in PSPACE [AFF$^+$03], but makes vacuity detection for CTL and CTL* EXPTIME and 2EXPTIME complete — as hard as their satisfiability [CG04a]. Moreover, adding to the specification formalism a regular layer, such as the ability to use regular expressions in the formula as in Sugar [BBE$^+$01] and ForSpec [AFF$^+$02], also adds a need to replace some subformulas ψ by a university quantified interval, which makes vacuity detection more complex than model checking.

When the system is proven to be correct, and vacuity has been checked too, there is still a question of how complete the specification is, and whether it really covers all the behaviors of the system. It is not clear how to check completeness of the specification. Indeed, specifications are written manually, and their completeness depends entirely on the competence of the person who writes them. The motivation for a completeness check is clear: an erroneous behavior of the design can escape the verification efforts if this behavior is not captured by the specification. In fact, it is likely that a behavior not captured by the specification also escapes the attention of the designer, who is often the one to provide the specification.

The challenge of making the verification process as exhaustive as possible is even more crucial in *simulation-based* verification. Each input vector for the system induces a different execution of it, and a system is correct if it behaves as required for all possible input vectors. Checking all the executions of a system is an infeasible task. Simulation-based verification is traditionally used in order to check the system with respect to some input vectors [BF00]. The vectors are chosen so that the verification would be as exhaustive as possible, and it is crucial to measure the exhaustiveness of the input sequences that are checked. Indeed, there has been an extensive research in the simulation-based verification community on *coverage metrics*, which provide such a measure [TK01]. Coverage metrics are used in order to monitor progress of the verification process, estimate whether more input sequences are needed, and direct simulation towards unexplored areas of the system. Coverage metrics today play an important role in the system validation effort [Ver03]. For a survey on the variety of metrics that are used in simulation-based verification, see [ZHM97, Dil98, Pel01, TK01]

Measuring the exhaustiveness of a specification in formal verification ("are more properties need to be checked?") has a similar flavor as measuring the exhaustiveness of the input sequences in simulation-based verification ("are more sequences need to be checked?"). Nevertheless, while for simulation-based verification it is clear that coverage corresponds to activation during the execution on the input sequence, it is less clear what coverage should correspond to in formal verification, as in model checking all reachable parts of the system are visited. Early work on coverage metrics in formal verification [HKHZ99, KGG99] suggested two directions. Both directions reason about a state-transition graph that models the system. The metric in [HKHZ99], later followed by [CKV01, CKKV01, CK02], is based on *mutations* applied to the graph. Essentially, a state s in the graph is covered by the specification if modifying the value of a variable in the state renders the specification untrue. The metric in [KGG99] is based on a comparison between the graph and a reduced tableau for the specification.

In [CKV03], we adapted the work done on coverage in simulation-based verification to the formal-verification setting in order to obtain new coverage metrics. Interestingly, the adoption of metrics from simulation-based verification has brought vacuity to the front of the stage again, and this time, in the context of coverage. To see why, consider for example code-based coverage, where we check, for example, whether both branches of an *if* statement have been executed during the simulation. A straightforward adoption would check the satisfaction of the specification in a mutant system, one for each branch, in which the branch is disabled. Such a mutant system, however, has less behaviors than the original system, and would clearly satisfy all universal specifications (i.e., specifications that apply to *all* behaviors, as in linear temporal logic) that are satisfied by the original system. In general, the problem we are facing is the need to assess the role a behavior has played in the satisfaction of a universal specification – one that is clearly satisfied in the system obtained by removing this behavior. The way we suggested to do so is to check whether the specification is vacuously satisfied in a mutant system in which this behavior is disabled: a vacuous satisfaction of the specification in such a system (we assume that the specification is not vacuously satisfied in the original system) indicates that the specification does refer to this behavior; on the other hand, a non-vacuous satisfaction of the specification in the mutant system indicates that the specification does not refer to the missing behavior. Accordingly, coverage metrics adopted from the simulation-based word check both the satisfaction and the vacuous satisfaction of the specification in mutant systems.

The definition of vacuity coverage in [CKV03] has related vacuity and coverage. In this paper we strengthen the link between the two sanity checks further and argue that, from the algorithmic point of view, the problems are essentially identical. In both problems, we check whether all the components of the input to the model-checking problem have played a role in the model-checking process. In the case of vacuity, the components we check are subformulas of the specification. In the case of coverage, the components are elements of the system. This suggests that the solutions to the vacuity and coverage problems may be based on the same algorithm. We show that, indeed, ideas developed for coverage can be adopted for vacuity, and vice versa.

2 Vacuity and Coverage

In this section we describe the basic definitions of vacuity and coverage. We consider specifications in either linear or branching temporal logics. For a formula φ, a subformula ψ of φ, and a formula ξ, we use $\varphi[\psi \leftarrow \xi]$ to denote the formula obtained from φ by replacing all the occurrences of ψ in φ by ξ.

We define the semantics of temporal-logic formulas with respect to a *Kripke structure* $K = \langle AP, W, R, w_{in}, L\rangle$, where AP is a set of atomic propositions, W is a set of states, $R \subseteq W \times W$ is a total transition relation, $w_{in} \in W$ is an initial state, and $L : W \rightarrow 2^{AP}$ maps each state to the set of atomic propositions that hold in this state. A Kripke structure K can be unwound into an infinite computation tree in a straightforward way. Formally, the tree that is obtained by unwinding K is denoted by $\mathcal{K}$ and is the 2^{AP}-labeled W-tree $\langle T^K, V^K\rangle$, in which a node $x \cdot w$, for $x \in W^*$ and $w \in W$, is associated with state w. Formally, $\varepsilon \in T^K$ is associated with w_{in} and $V^K(\varepsilon) = L(w_{in})$. Now, for all w with $R(w_{in}, w)$, we have that $w \in T^K$, and for all $x \cdot w \in T^K$ and $v \in W$ with $R(w, v)$, we have $x \cdot w \cdot v \in T^K$ and $V^K(x \cdot w) = L(w)$. That is, V^K maps a node that was reached by taking the direction w to $L(w)$.

The definition of vacuity involves formulas with an atomic proposition that is universally quantified. Consider an atomic proposition x. A Kripke structure K satisfies a temporal logic formula $\forall x \varphi(x)$ iff φ is satisfied in all computation trees $\langle T, V\rangle$ that differ from $\langle T^K, V^K\rangle$ only in the label of the atomic proposition x. Note that different occurrences of the same state in K may have different x labels.

Let us start with the basic definition of vacuous satisfaction. Intuitively, a Kripke structure K satisfies a formula φ vacuously if K satisfies φ yet it does so in a non-interesting way, which is likely to point on some trouble with either K or φ. For example, a system in which requests are never sent satisfies $AG(req \rightarrow AF\,grant)$ vacuously. In order to formalize this intuition, it is suggested in [BBER01] to formalize first the notion of a subformula of φ affecting its truth value in K. We use the following definition for the latter:

Definition 1. [AFF$^+$03] *A subformula* ψ *of* φ does not affect the truth value of φ in K *(*ψ *does not affect* φ *in* K*, for short) if* K *satisfies* $\forall x \varphi[\psi \leftarrow x]$ *iff* K *satisfies* φ.

The definition in [AFF$^+$03] is semantic. Earlier definitions, and in particular the one in [BBER01], were syntactic, in the sense they consider a replacement of ψ by other subformulas. Thus, according to [BBER01], ψ does not affect φ in K if K satisfies $\varphi[\psi \leftarrow \xi]$ for all formulas ξ. A good reason to switch to the semantic-based definition is the fact that [BBER01]'s definition is not effective, as it requires evaluation of $\varphi[\psi \leftarrow \xi]$ for all formulas ξ. To deal with this difficulty, [BBER01] considers only a small class, called w-ACTL, of branching temporal logic formulas. Once we have defined when a subformula of φ affects its truth value in K, the definition of vacuity is as expected[1]:

Definition 2. *A system* K *satisfies a formula* φ vacuously *iff* $K \models \varphi$ *and there is some subformula* ψ *of* φ *such that* ψ *does not affect* φ *in* K.

In [KV03], we showed that when all the occurrences of a subformula ψ in φ are of a *pure polarity* (that is, they are either all under an even number of negations (positive polarity), or all are under an odd number of negations (negative polarity)), the syntactic and semantic definitions coincide, and checking whether ψ affects φ in K is easy. Formally, for a formula φ and a subformula ψ of φ, let $\varphi[\psi \leftarrow \bot]$ denote the formula obtained from φ by replacing ψ by **false**, in case ψ is positive in φ, and replacing ψ by **true**, in case ψ is negative in φ. Now, by [KV03], ψ does not affect φ iff K satisfies the formula obtained from φ by the single extreme modification of ψ. Formally, we have the following.

Theorem 1. [KV03] *For every formula* φ*, a subformula* ψ *of a pure polarity of* φ*, and a system* K *that satisfies* φ*, we have that* ψ *does not affect* φ *in* K *iff* K *satisfies* $\varphi[\psi \leftarrow \bot]$.

By Definition 2, vacuity detection can be reduced to checking whether K satisfied $\forall x \varphi[\psi \leftarrow x]$ for all subformulas ψ of φ. Also, by Theorem 1, when ψ is of a pure polarity [2], the latter can be done by checking whether K satisfies $\varphi[\psi \leftarrow \bot]$. In particular, when φ is *polar* (that is, all its subformulas are of a pure polarity), vacuity detection can be reduced to a sequence of model-checking executions, each for a single subformula (this is a naive algorithm for this task, and we later mention some heuristics). When, however, some subformula ψ is of a mixed polarity, the check is harder and requires model checking of formulas with quantified atomic propositions. For the case of CTL and CTL*, the problem of vacuity detection is then as hard as the satisfiability problem, namely it is EXPTIME and 2EXPTIME complete, respectively [CG04a]. For LTL, it can still be reduced to LTL model checking and stay PSPACE-complete, but is more complicated than simple model checking [AFF$^+$03].

---

[1] In [CG04b], the authors study an alternative definition of vacuity in which the *mutual vacuity* of some subformulas is taken into a consideration.

[2] Note that one can talk about a subformula ψ affecting φ in K or about an *occurrence* of ψ affecting φ in K. Since a single occurrence is of a pure polarity, Theorem 1 always applies in this setting.

Remark 2. The semantic approach turned out to be appropriate also when the specification formalism has a regular layer [BFG+05]. There, the subformula ψ may be a regular event, and the universal quantification that is needed is over intervals. Consider for example the formula $\varphi = G\,((req \cdot (\neg ack)^* \cdot ack)\ triggers\ X\,grant)$, which says that a grant is given exactly one cycle after the cycle in which a request is acknowledged. Note that if ack does not affect the satisfaction of φ in K, we can learn that acknowledgments are actually ignored: grants are given, and stay on forever, immediately after a request. Such a behavior is not referred to in the specification, but is detected by regular vacuity. Thus, while LTL vacuity involved only *monadic* quantification (over the set of points in which x may hold), regular vacuity also involves *dyadic* quantification (over intervals – sets of pairs of points, in which *int* may hold). This transition, from monadic to dyadic quantification, is technically very challenging, yet, as was shown in [BFG+05], the automata-theoretic approach to LTL [VW94] can be extended to handle regular vacuity, but the problem is much harder than LTL vacuity (it is in EXPSPACE and is EXPTIME-hard).

As with usual vacuity, when a subformula ψ has a pure polarity, checking whether it affects the truth value of φ can be reduced to checking whether K satisfies $\varphi[\psi \leftarrow \bot]$, with $\bot$ being $\mathbf{true}^*$ in case ψ is of a negative polarity and is **false** in case ψ is of a positive polarity. Thus, in the context of regular vacuity, pure polarity is even more crucial. □

We now turn to the basic definition of coverage in model checking. The idea, due to [HKHZ99], is to define coverage by examining the effect of modifications in the system on the satisfaction of the specification. Given a system modeled by a Kripke structure K, a formula φ that is satisfied in K, and a signal (atomic proposition) q, let us denote by $\tilde{K}_{w,q}$ the Kripke structure obtained from K by flipping the value of q in w. Thus, $\tilde{K}_{w,q} = \langle AP, W, R, W_{in}, \tilde{L}_{w,q}\rangle$, where $\tilde{L}_{w,q}(v) = L(v)$ for all $v \neq w$, and $\tilde{L}_{w,q}(w) = L(w) \setminus \{q\}$ if $q \in L(w)$ and $\tilde{L}_{w,q}(w) = L(w) \cup \{q\}$ if $q \notin L(w)$.

Definition 3. [HKHZ99] *A state w of a Kripke structure K is q-*covered by *φ, for a formula φ and an atomic proposition q, if K satisfies φ but $\tilde{K}_{w,q}$ does not satisfy φ.*

Thus, w is q-covered by φ if the Kripke structure obtained from K by flipping the value of q in w no longer satisfies φ. Indeed, this indicates that the value of q in w is crucial for the satisfaction of φ in K. Definition 3 is very basic not only since it considers only mutations of a very limited nature, but also, as pointed out in [CKV01], it ignores the fact that often, replacing the value of an atomic proposition also causes a change in the transitions of K, which are typically defined by means of the values of the atomic propositions in the target and source of each transition. As shown, however, in [CKV01], the latter weakness is technical and it is possible to extend coverage algorithms that consider mutations that do not change the transitions to mutations that do change them.

3 Adopting Ideas from Vacuity to Coverage

In this section we show how ideas that have been suggested in the context of coverage are actually an adoption of ideas in vacuity. We also point to ideas in vacuity that have not yet been adopted in coverage.

3.1 Single vs. Multiple Occurrences

We start with the definition of coverage. Recall that the basic definition of coverage considered a very simple mutation: flip the value of one atomic proposition in one state. Recall that the Kripke structure models a system, and that the execution of the system corresponds to unwinding the Kripke structure into an infinite computation tree. A state w of K may correspond to several nodes in the computation tree. The basic definition of coverage flips the value of q in w in all these occurrences. In a similar way, in the definition of vacuity, we have distinguished between a single occurrence of a subformula ψ of φ and all its occurrence. In the first case, we have replaced only this occurrence by a universally quantified proposition (in fact, in this case it is sufficient to replace the single occurrence by $\perp$), and in the second, we have replaced all the occurrences. Each approach may return a different answer to the vacuity query.

This suggest that the definition of coverage should also be refined to reflect the fact that the flipping of q in w can be performed in different ways. Such a refinement was suggested in [CKKV01], which made a distinction between "flipping always", "flipping once", and "flipping sometimes", which are formalized in the definitions of *structure coverage*, *node coverage*, and *tree coverage* below. We first need some notations.

For a domain Y, a function $V : Y \to 2^{AP}$, an observable signal $q \in AP$, and a set $X \subseteq Y$, the *dual function* $\tilde{V}_{X,q} : Y \to 2^{AP}$ is such that $\tilde{V}_{X,q}(x) = V(x)$ for all $x \notin X$, $\tilde{V}_{X,q}(x) = V(x) \setminus \{q\}$ if $x \in X$ and $q \in V(x)$, and $\tilde{V}_{X,q}(x) = V(x) \cup \{q\}$ if $x \in X$ and $q \notin V(x)$. When $X = \{x\}$ is a singleton, we write $\tilde{V}_{x,q}$. Recall that $\tilde{K}_{w,q} = \langle AP, W, R, W_{in}, \tilde{L}_{w,q} \rangle$. For $X \subseteq T^K$ we denote by $\tilde{\mathcal{K}}_{X,q}$ the tree that is obtained by flipping the value of q in all the nodes in X. Thus, $\tilde{\mathcal{K}}_{X,q} = \langle T^K, \tilde{V}^K_{X,q} \rangle$. When $X = \{x\}$ is a singleton, we write $\tilde{\mathcal{K}}_{x,q}$.

Definition 4. *Consider a Kripke structure K, a formula φ satisfied in K, and an observable signal $q \in AP$.*

- *A state w of K is* structure q-covered *by φ iff the structure $\tilde{K}_{w,q}$ does not satisfy φ.*
- *A state w of K is* node q-covered *by φ iff there is a w-node x in T^K such that $\tilde{\mathcal{K}}_{x,q}$ does not satisfy φ.*
- *A state w of K is* tree q-covered *by φ iff there is a set X of w-nodes in T^K such that $\tilde{\mathcal{K}}_{X,q}$ does not satisfy φ.*

Note that, structure coverage coincides with Definition 3. Also note that a state is structure q-covered iff $\tilde{\mathcal{K}}_{X,q}$ does not satisfy φ for the set X of all w-nodes in $\mathcal{K}$. In other words, a state w is structure q-covered if flipping the value of q in all the instances of w in $\mathcal{K}$ falsifies φ, it is node q-covered if a single flip of the value of q falsifies φ, and it is tree q-covered if some flips of the value of q falsifies φ.

3.2 A Semantic Approach to Coverage

Recall that earlier definitions of vacuity were syntactic and considered replacements of a subformula ψ by another formula [BBER01]. Later, in [AFF+03], researchers have moved to the semantic approach, where ψ is replaced by a universally quantified atomic proposition. We would like to use the idea of a universally quantified atomic proposition also in the context of coverage. Thus, we seek a definition according to which w is not covered by φ if $\forall x K[w \leftarrow x] \models \varphi$. In general, it is not clear what x is and what does $K[w \leftarrow x]$ stands for. There are, however, settings in which an appropriate definition for x exists. In particular, in symbolic methods, the state space is encoded by propositional variables [BCM$^+$92, BCC$^+$99], and universal quantification is naturally defined. The induced definition of coverage captures exactly our intuition of w not playing a role in the verification process. Indeed, if, for example, we have reduced bounded model checking to the non-satisfiability of a propositional formula θ and a vector $\boldsymbol{x}$ of variables encodes the value of the system's variables in state w in time t, then satisfiability of $\forall \boldsymbol{x} \theta$ indicates that the values of the variables in $\boldsymbol{x}$ did play a role in the model-checking procedure. Note that, as with usual coverage, there is a need to distinguish between structure, tree, and node coverage.

3.3 Returning an Interesting Witness to the User

A witness for the satisfaction of a specification in a system is a sub-system, usually a computation, that satisfies the specification. A witness is interesting if it satisfies the specification non-vacuously [BBER01, KV03]. For example, a computation in which both req and $\neg grant$ hold is an interesting witness for the satisfaction of $AG(req \rightarrow AF grant)$. An interesting witness gives the user a confirmation that his specification models correctly the desired behavior, and enables the user to study some nontrivial executions of the system.

An interesting witness in the context of coverage is a subformula that causes a component to be covered. It is easy to extend existing coverage algorithms to return, for each component of the system, the parts of the specification with respect to which it is covered. More informative, however, and closer to the way interesting witnesses are used in vacuity, is to return to the user information on how the component is covered. Thus, for every component c of the system, the user should be able to get witnesses to the coverage of c by means of an erroneous computations in which c is mutated. From an algorithmic point of view, this involves solving exactly the same problem as the problem of generating interesting witnesses in vacuity, namely the problem of generating counter examples [CGMZ95, KV03]. In the context of coverage, however, we return to the user a family of counterexamples – one for each sub-specification that is no longer satisfied in the system with c mutated.

4 Adopting Ideas from Coverage to Vacuity

The adoption we suggested in Section 4 considers the challenges of defining vacuity and coverage and of returning helpful information to the user. In the context of coverage, much effort has been put in order to develop efficient algorithms for computing coverage. As we shall detail below, this has to do with the fact that a naive algorithm for coverage increases the complexity of model checking by a factor that depends on the size of the system, whereas one for vacuity detection increases the complexity only by a factor that depends on the specification. While the specification is typically much smaller than the system, it is still desirable to get rid of this factor.

A naive algorithm for the detection of components of the system that are not covered by the specification proceeds by model checking mutations of the system. For example, in order to find the set of states not q-covered by φ in a Kripke structure K with n states, the naive algorithm executes the model-checking procedure n times, where in each execution $\tilde{K}_{w,q}$ is checked for a different state w. Likewise, a naive algorithm for vacuity detection proceeds by checking mutations of the specification, each obtained by replacing a single subformula by a universally quantified proposition (in case the subformula is of a mixed polarity) or by $\mathtt{true}$ or $\mathbf{false}$ (in case it is of a pure polarity).

In [CKV01, CKKV01], we presented two alternatives to the naive algorithm for coverage. The first is symbolic, and the second makes use of overlaps among different mutations of the same Kripke structures. In this section we briefly describe the two algorithms and show how exactly the same ideas can be used in order to detect vacuous satisfaction of polar formulas.

4.1 A Symbolic Approach

We start with the symbolic coverage detection algorithm for LTL specifications. The algorithm is described in [CKKV01]. For simplicity, we start with node coverage, and then explain how tree and structure coverage can be checked with the same idea. The algorithm extends the LTL automata-based model-checking algorithm. There, we translate an LTL specification φ to a nondeterministic Büchi automaton $\mathcal{A}_{\neg\varphi}$ that accepts all words that do not satisfy φ [VW94]. Model checking of K with respect to φ can then be reduced to checking the emptiness of the product $K \times \mathcal{A}_{\neg\varphi}$. Let $K = \langle AP, W, R, w_{in}, L\rangle$ be a Kripke structure that satisfies φ, and let $\mathcal{A}_{\neg\varphi}=\langle 2^{AP}, S, \delta, S_0, \alpha\rangle$ be the nondeterministic Büchi automaton for $\neg\varphi$. The product of K with $\mathcal{A}_{\neg\varphi}$ is the fair Kripke structure $K \times \mathcal{A}_{\neg\varphi} = \langle AP, W \times S, M, \{w_{in}\} \times S_0, L', W \times \alpha\rangle$, where $M(\langle w, s\rangle, \langle w', s'\rangle)$ iff $R(w, w')$ and $s' \in \delta(s, L(w))$, and $L'(\langle w, s\rangle) = L(w)$. Note that an infinite path π in $K \times \mathcal{A}_{\neg\varphi}$ is fair iff the projection of π on S satisfies the acceptance condition of $\mathcal{A}_{\neg\varphi}$. Since K satisfies φ, we know that no initialized path of K is accepted by $\mathcal{A}_{\neg\varphi}$. Hence, $L(K \times \mathcal{A}_{\neg\varphi})$ is empty.

Let $P \subseteq W \times S$ be the set of pairs $\langle w, s\rangle$ such that $\mathcal{A}_{\neg\varphi}$ can reach the state s as it reads the state w. That is, there exists a sequence $\langle w_0, s_0\rangle, \ldots, \langle w_k, s_k\rangle$ such that $w_0 = w_{in}$, $s_0 \in S_0$, $w_k = w$, $s_k = s$, and for all $i \geq 0$ we have $R(w_i, w_{i+1})$ and $s_{i+1} \in \delta(s_i, L(w_i))$. Note that $\langle w, s\rangle \in P$ iff $\langle w, s\rangle$ is reachable in $K \times \mathcal{A}_{\neg\varphi}$. For an observable signal $q \in AP$ and $w \in W$, we define the set $P_{w,q} \subseteq W \times S$ as the set of pairs $\langle w', s'\rangle$ such that w' is a successor of w and $\mathcal{A}_{\neg\varphi}$ can reach the state s' as it reads the state w' in a run in which the last occurrence of w has q flipped. Formally, if we denote by $\tilde{L}_q : W \to 2^{AP}$ the labeling function with q flipped (that is, $\tilde{L}_q(w) = L(w) \cup \{q\}$ if $q \notin L(w)$, and $\tilde{L}_q(w) = L(w) \setminus \{q\}$ if $q \in L(w)$), then

$$P_{w,q} = \{\langle w', s'\rangle : \text{ there is } s \in S \text{ such that } \langle w, s\rangle \in P, R(w, w'), \text{ and } s' \in \delta(s, \tilde{L}_q(w))\}.$$

Recall that a state w is node q-covered in K iff there exists a a w-node x in T^K such that $\tilde{K}_{x,q}$ does not satisfy φ. We can characterize node q-covered states also as follows

Theorem 3. *Consider a Kripke structure K, an LTL formula φ, and an observable signal q. A state w is node q-covered in K by φ iff there is a successor w' of w and a state s' such that $\langle w', s'\rangle \in P_{w,q}$ and there is a fair $\langle w', s'\rangle$-path in $K \times \mathcal{A}_{\neg\varphi}$.*

Theorem 3 reduces the problem of checking whether a state w is node q-covered to computing the relation $P_{w,q}$ and checking for the existence of a fair path from a state in the product $K \times \mathcal{A}_{\neg\varphi}$. Model-checking tools compute the relation P and compute the set of states from which we have fair paths. Therefore, Theorem 3 suggests an easy implementation for the problem of computing the set of node-covered states. We describe a possible implementation in the tool COSPAN, which is the engine of FormalCheck [HHK96, Kur98]. We also show that the implementation can be easily modified to handle structure and tree coverage.

In COSPAN, the system is modeled by a set of modules, and the desired behavior is specified by an additional module $\mathcal{A}$. The language $\mathcal{L}(\mathcal{A})$ is exactly the set of wrong behaviors, thus the module $\mathcal{A}$ stands for the automaton $\mathcal{A}_{\neg\varphi}$ in cases the specification is given an LTL formula φ. In order to compute the set of node q-covered states, the system has to nondeterministically choose a step in the synchronous composition of the modules, in which the value of q is flipped in all modules that refer to q. Note that this is the same as to choose a step in which the module $\mathcal{A}$ behaves as if it reads the dual value of q. This can be done by introducing two new Boolean variables *flip* and *flag*, local to $\mathcal{A}$. The variable *flip* is nondeterministically assigned **true** or **false** in each step. The variable *flag* is initialized to **true** and is set to **false** one step after *flip* becomes **true**. Instead of reading q, the module $\mathcal{A}$ reads $q \oplus (\mathit{flip} \wedge \mathit{flag})$. Thus, when both *flip* and *flag* hold, which happens exactly once, the value of q is flipped ($\oplus$ stands for exclusive or). So, the synchronous composition of the modules is not empty iff the state that was visited when *flip* becomes **true** for the first time is node q-covered.

With a small change in the implementation we can also check tree coverage. Since in tree coverage we can flip the value of q several times, the variable *flag* is no longer needed. Instead, we need $\log |W|$ variables $x_1, \ldots, x_{\log |W|}$ for encoding the state w that is now being checked for tree q-coverage. The state w is not known in advance and the variables $x_1, \ldots, x_{\log |W|}$ are initialized to some special value $\perp$. The variable *flip* is nondeterministically assigned **true** or **false** in each step. When *flip* is changed to **true** for the first time, the variables $x_1, \ldots, x_{\log |W|}$ are set to encode the current state w. Instead of reading q, the module $\mathcal{A}$ reads $q \oplus (\mathit{flip} \wedge \mathit{at\_w})$, where $\mathit{at\_w}$ holds iff the encoding of the current state coincides with $x_1, \ldots, x_{\log |W|}$. Thus, when both *flip* and $\mathit{at\_w}$ hold, which may happen several times, yet only when the current state is w, the value of q is flipped. So, the synchronous composition of the modules is not empty iff the state that was visited when *flip* becomes **true** for the first time is tree q-covered. Finally, by nondeterministically choosing the values of $x_1, \ldots, x_{\log |W|}$ at the first step of the run and fixing *flip* to **true**, we can also check structure coverage.

Note that our algorithm is independent of the fairness condition being Büchi, and it can handle any fairness condition for which the model-checking procedure supports the check for fair paths. Also, it is easy to see that the same algorithm can handle systems with multiple initial states. Finally, it is also easy to adjust the algorithm to definitions of coverage in which several mutations are checked mutually.

Remark 4. The above algorithm handles specifications in LTL. A different symbolic algorithm for coverage computation is described for CTL in [CKV01]. The algorithm addresses the fact that even if model checking of each of the mutant Kripke structures is checked symbolically, there may be many mutations to check. If we have, for example, a mutant structure for each state, then there are $|W|$ mutant structures to check, and we would like to refer also to these structures symbolically. Consider a Kripke structure $K = \langle AP, W, R, w_0, L\rangle$ and an atomic proposition $q \in AP$. For a CTL formula φ, we define

$$P(\varphi) = \{\langle w, v\rangle : \tilde{K}_{v,q}, w \models \varphi\}.$$

Thus, $P(\varphi) \subseteq W \times W$ contains exactly all pairs $\langle w, v\rangle$ such that w satisfies φ in the structure where we dualize the value of q in v. The q-covered set in K for φ can be derived easily from $P(\varphi)$ as it is the set $\{w : \langle w_0, w\rangle \notin P(\varphi)\}$.

The symbolic algorithm in [CKV01] computes the OBDDs $P(\psi)$ for all subformulas ψ. The algorithm works bottom-up, and is based on the symbolic CTL model-checking algorithm. The symbolic algorithm for CTL model-checking uses a linear number of OBDD variables. The algorithm in [CKV01] above doubles the number of OBDD variables, as it works with sets of pairs of states instead of sets of states. By the nature of the algorithm, it performs model-checking for all $\tilde{K}_{w,q}$ globally, and thus the OBDDs it computes contain information about the satisfaction of the specification in all the states of all the dual Kripke structures, and not only in their initial states. □

We now turn to describe how the same idea can be used in order to symbolically detect vacuity of polar formulas. The algorithm we describe can be viewed as a special case of the symbolic algorithm in [CKV03] for the detection of vacuity coverage. Recall that checking whether a system satisfies a specification vacuously involves model checking of a mutant specification. We can use the idea in [CKKV01] in order to check symbolically for vacuous satisfaction by adding a new variable x that encodes the subformula ψ that is being replaced with $\perp$. The subformula ψ belongs to the set $cl(\varphi)$ of subformulas of φ. The variable x is an integer in the range $0, \ldots, |cl(\varphi)|$, thus it can be encoded with $O(\log|\varphi|)$ Boolean variables. The value 0 of x stands for "no replacement", thus it checks the satisfaction of φ in the system. The value of (the variables that encode) x is chosen nondeterministically at initialization and is kept unchanged. For example, if $\varphi = y_1 \vee y_2$, and 1 encodes y_1 and 2 encodes y_2, then the value 1 of x corresponds to the replacement of y_1 with **false** (which is the $\perp$ value for y_1 in φ) resulting in the formula $(y_1 \vee y_2)[y_1 \leftarrow \textbf{false}] = y_2$. In the automaton $\mathcal{A}_{\neg\varphi}$, each state variable corresponds to a subformula (cf. [BCM+92]), thus the nondeterministic choice of the subformula leads to a mutant automaton $\mathcal{A}_{\neg\varphi[\psi\leftarrow\perp]}$. The state space of the augmented product now consists of triples $\langle x, u, s\rangle$, where x encodes the subformula replaced with $\perp$, and u and s are the components of the product automaton. The successors of $\langle x, u, s\rangle$ are the triples $\langle x, u', s'\rangle$ such that $\langle u', s'\rangle$ is a possible successor of $\langle u, s\rangle$ in a product between the system with the automaton $\mathcal{A}_{\neg\varphi[\psi\leftarrow\perp]}$, where ψ is the subformula encoded by x. The subformulas that affect the value of φ in the systems are these encoded by a value x for which there are initial states u_0 and s_0 of the system and the automaton, respectively, such that there is a fair path from $\langle x, u_0, s_0\rangle$. Let P be the set of triples from which a fair path exists in the augmented product (as above, P can be found symbolically), and let P' be the intersection of P with the initial states of the system and the automaton, projected on the first element. Note that $x \in P'$ iff the subformula associated with x affects the value of φ in the system. Thus, ψ is satisfied vacuously in the system if $\neg P'(0)$ and $P' \neq \{1, \ldots, cl(\psi)\}$.

4.2 Improving Average Complexity

Consider a Kripke structure $K = \langle AP, W, R, w_0, L\rangle$, a formula φ, and an atomic proposition q. Recall that the naive CTL coverage algorithm, which performs model checking for all dual Kripke structures, has running time of $O(|K| \cdot |\varphi| \cdot |W|)$. While for some dual Kripke structures model-checking may require less than $O(|K| \cdot |\varphi|)$, the naive algorithm always performs $|W|$ iterations of model checking; thus, its average complexity cannot be substantially better than its worst-case complexity. This unfortunate situation arises even when model checking of two dual Kripke structures is practically the same, and even when some of the states of K obviously do not affect the satisfaction of φ in K. In [CKV01] we presented an algorithm that makes use of such overlaps and redundancies. The expectant running time of our algorithm is $O(|K| \cdot |\varphi| \cdot \log |W|)$. Formally, we have the following:

Theorem 5. *The set q-cover(K, φ) can be computed in average*[3] *running time of* $O(|K| \cdot |\varphi| \cdot \log |W|)$.

Our algorithm is based on the fact that for each w, the dual Kripke structure $\tilde{K}_{w,q}$ differs from K only slightly. Therefore, there should be a large amount of work that we can share when we model check all the dual structures. In order to explain the algorithm, we introduce the notion of *incomplete model checking*. Informally, incomplete model checking of K is model checking of K with its labeling function L partially defined. The solution to the incomplete model checking problem can rely only on the truth values of the atomic propositions in states for which the corresponding L is defined. Obviously, in the general case we are not guaranteed to solve the model-checking problem without knowing the values of all atoms in all states. We can, however, perform some work in this direction, which is not needed to be performed again when missing parts of L are revealed.

Consider a partition of W into two equal sets, W_1 and W_2. Our algorithm essentially works as follows. For all the dual Kripke structures $\tilde{K}_{w,q}$ such that $w \in W_1$, the states in W_2 maintain their original labeling. Therefore, we start by performing incomplete model checking of φ in K with L that does not rely on the values of q in states in W_1. We end up in one of the following two situations. It may be that the values of q in states in W_2 (and the values of all the other atomic propositions in all the states) are sufficient to imply the satisfaction of φ in K. Then, we can infer that all the states in W_1 are not q-covered. It may also be that the values of q in states in W_2 are not sufficient to imply the satisfaction of φ in K. Then, we continue and partition the set W_1 into two equal sets, W_{11} and W_{12}, and perform incomplete model checking that does not rely on the values of q in states in W_{11}. The important observation is that incomplete model checking is now performed in a Kripke structure to which we have already applied incomplete model checking in the previous iteration. Thus, we only have to propagate information that involves the values of q in W_{12}. Thus, as we go deeper in the recursion described above, we perform less work. The depth of the recursion is bounded by $\log |W|$. As analyzed in [CKV01], the work in depth i amounts in average to model checking of φ in a Kripke structure of size $\frac{|K|}{2^i}$. Hence the $O(|K| \cdot |\varphi| \cdot \log |W|)$ complexity.

[3] Average is taken with respect to all possible inputs to the algorithm as well as all random choices made by the algorithm.

In case of vacuity for polar formulas, the naive algorithm performs model checking for each subformula, and thus has running time $O(|K| \cdot |\varphi|^2)$. The quadratic dependency in φ is less crucial than the quadratic dependency in $|W|$ in the case of coverage, but it is still a problem, and efforts to come up with better algorithms are described in [PS02, Nam04]. In order to improve the average complexity, we can encode all the mutations to the formula (each mutation corresponds to a subformula that is replaced by $\perp$) with a vector $\boldsymbol{x}$ of variables. We then proceed with incomplete model checking where in each iteration more variables get values. As with coverage, in each iteration we handle smaller structures, and the overall complexity is, in average, $O(|K| \cdot |\varphi| \log |\varphi|)$[Cho03].

5 Discussion

Sanity checks are applied to the system after model checking has successfully terminated. In addition to vacuity and coverage, other checks that have recently been advocated are *query checking* [Cha00] and *certification* [Nam01]. In query checking, some subformulas in the specification are replaced by the symbol "?" and the query-checking algorithm returns strongest possible replacements to "?" with which the specification is satisfied. In certification, the positive answer of the model-checking procedure is accompanied by a proof that the specification indeed holds. The idea is that it is much easier to check a given certificate than to find one.

The different checks have a lot in common, both conceptually and from the algorithmic point of view. Still, each approach has its own algorithms and tools. We believe that an effort should be made in order to accommodate sanity checks in one algorithmic framework. A good candidate is the theory of multi-valued logic (in fact, this has already been done for query checking in [BG01]). The idea is that typical sanity checks repeat the model-checking procedure with respect to "mutant inputs" — inputs that are slightly different from the original model-checking input. By associating different sets of mutations with different values, we can hopefully reduce the question of finding the set of mutants for which model checking no longer succeeds to the problem of multi-valued model checking [BG04]. In addition, as suggested in [Nam04] for the case of vacuity, it may be possible to carry the sanity checks with respect to the model-checking certificate, rather than with respect to the system and the specification.

References

[AFF+02] R. Armoni, L. Fix, A. Flaisher, R. Gerth, B. Ginsburg, T. Kanza, A. Landver, S. Mador-Haim, E. Singerman, A. Tiemeyer, M.Y. Vardi, and Y. Zbar. The ForSpec temporal logic: A new temporal property-specification logic. In *Proc. 8th International Conference on Tools and Algorithms for the Construction and Analysis of Systems*, volume 2280 of *Lecture Notes in Computer Science*, pages 296–211, Grenoble, France, April 2002. Springer-Verlag.

[AFF+03] R. Armon, L. Fix, A. Flaisher, O. Grumberg, N. Piterman, A. Tiemeyer, and M.Y. Vardi. Enhanced vacuity detection for linear temporal logic. In *Computer Aided Verification, Proc. 15th International Conference*. Springer-Verlag, 2003.

[BB94] D. Beatty and R. Bryant. Formally verifying a microprocessor using a simulation methodology. In *Proc. 31st Design Automation Conference*, pages 596–602. IEEE Computer Society, 1994.

[BBE+01] I. Beer, S. Ben-David, C. Eisner, D. Fisman, A. Gringauze, and Y. Rodeh. The temporal logic Sugar. In *Proc. 13th International Conference on Computer Aided Verification*, volume 2102 of *Lecture Notes in Computer Science*, pages 363–367, Paris, France, July 2001. Springer-Verlag.

[BBER01] I. Beer, S. Ben-David, C. Eisner, and Y. Rodeh. Efficient detection of vacuity in ACTL formulas. *Formal Methods in System Design*, 18(2):141–162, 2001.

[BCC+99] A. Biere, A. Cimatti, E.M. Clarke, M. Fujita, and Y. Zhu. Symbolic model checking using SAT procedures instead of BDDs. In *Proc. 36th Design Automation Conference*, pages 317–320. IEEE Computer Society, 1999.

[BCM+92] J.R. Burch, E.M. Clarke, K.L. McMillan, D.L. Dill, and L.J. Hwang. Symbolic model checking: 10^{20} states and beyond. *Information and Computation*, 98(2):142–170, June 1992.

[BF00] L. Bening and H. Foster. *Principles of verifiable RTL design – a functional coding style supporting verification processes*. Kluwer Academic Publishers, 2000.

[BFG+05] D. Bustan, A. Flaisher, O. Grumberg, O. Kupferman, and M.Y. Vardi. Regular vacuity. In *Proc. 13th Advanced Research Working Conference on Correct Hardware Design and Verification Methods*, volume 3725 of *Lecture Notes in Computer Science*, pages 191–206. Springer-Verlag, 2005.

[BG01] Glenn Bruns and Patrice Godefroid. Temporal logic query checking. In *Proceedings of the 16th Annual IEEE Symposium on Logic in Computer Science (LICS-01)*, pages 409–420, Los Alamitos, CA, June 16–19 2001. IEEE Computer Society.

[BG04] Bruns and Godefroid. Model checking with multi-valued logics. In *ICALP: Annual International Colloquium on Automata, Languages and Programming*, 2004.

[CG04a] M. Chechik and A. Gurfinkel. Extending extended vacuity. In *5th International Conference on Formal Methods in Computer-Aided Design*, volume 3312 of *Lecture Notes in Computer Science*, pages 306–321. Springer-Verlag, 2004.

[CG04b] M. Chechik and A. Gurfinkel. How vacuous is vacuous? In *10th International Conference on Tools and algorithms for the construction and analysis of systems*, volume 2988 of *Lecture Notes in Computer Science*, pages 451–466. Springer-Verlag, 2004.

[CGL93] E.M. Clarke, O. Grumberg, and D. Long. Verification tools for finite-state concurrent systems. In J.W. de Bakker, W.-P. de Roever, and G. Rozenberg, editors, *Decade of Concurrency – Reflections and Perspectives (Proceedings of REX School)*, volume 803 of *Lecture Notes in Computer Science*, pages 124–175. Springer-Verlag, 1993.

[CGMZ95] E.M. Clarke, O. Grumberg, K.L. McMillan, and X. Zhao. Efficient generation of counterexamples and witnesses in symbolic model checking. In *Proc. 32nd Design Automation Conference*, pages 427–432. IEEE Computer Society, 1995.

[Cha00] W. Chan. Temporal-logic queries. In *Computer Aided Verification, Proc. 12th International Conference*, volume 1855 of *Lecture Notes in Computer Science*, pages 450–463. Springer-Verlag, 2000.

[Cho03] H. Chockler. *Coverage metrics for model checking*. PhD thesis, Hebrew University, Jerusalem, Israel, 2003.

[CK02] H. Chockler and O. Kupferman. Coverage of implementations by simulating specifications. In R.A. Baeza-Yates, U. Montanari, and N. Santoro, editors, *Proceedings of 2nd IFIP International Conference on Theoretical Computer Science*, volume 223 of *IFIP Conference Proceedings*, pages 409–421, Montreal, Canada, August 2002. Kluwer Academic Publishers.

[CKKV01] H. Chockler, O. Kupferman, R.P. Kurshan, and M.Y. Vardi. A practical approach to coverage in model checking. In *Proc. 13th International Conference on Computer Aided Verification*, volume 2102 of *Lecture Notes in Computer Science*, pages 66–78. Springer-Verlag, 2001.

[CKV01] H. Chockler, O. Kupferman, and M.Y. Vardi. Coverage metrics for temporal logic model checking. In *7th International Conference on Tools and algorithms for the construction and analysis of systems*, number 2031 in Lecture Notes in Computer Science, pages 528–542. Springer-Verlag, 2001.

[CKV03] H. Chockler, O. Kupferman, and M.Y. Vardi. Coverage metrics for formal verification. In *12th Advanced Research Working Conference on Correct Hardware Design and Verification Methods*, volume 2860 of *Lecture Notes in Computer Science*, pages 111–125. Springer-Verlag, 2003.

[Dil98] D.L. Dill. What's between simulation and formal verification? In *Proc. 35st Design Automation Conference*, pages 328–329. IEEE Computer Society, 1998.

[HHK96] R.H. Hardin, Z. Har'el, and R.P. Kurshan. COSPAN. In *Computer Aided Verification, Proc. 8th International Conference*, volume 1102 of *Lecture Notes in Computer Science*, pages 423–427. Springer-Verlag, 1996.

[HKHZ99] Y. Hoskote, T. Kam, P.-H Ho, and X. Zhao. Coverage estimation for symbolic model checking. In *Proc. 36th Design automation conference*, pages 300–305, 1999.

[KGG99] S. Katz, D. Geist, and O. Grumberg. "Have I written enough properties ?" a method of comparison between specification and implementation. In *10th Advanced Research Working Conference on Correct Hardware Design and Verification Methods*, volume 1703 of *Lecture Notes in Computer Science*, pages 280–297. Springer-Verlag, 1999.

[Kur98] R.P. Kurshan. *FormalCheck User's Manual*. Cadence Design, Inc., 1998.

[KV03] O. Kupferman and M.Y. Vardi. Vacuity detection in temporal model checking. *Journal on Software Tools For Technology Transfer*, 4(2):224–233, February 2003.

[Nam01] K.S. Namjoshi. Certifying model checkers. In *13th Conference on Computer Aided Verification*, volume 2102 of *Lecture Notes in Computer Science*, pages 2–13. Springer-Verlag, 2001.

[Nam04] K.S. Namjoshi. An efficiently checkable, proof-based formulation of vacuity in model checking. In *16th Conference on Computer Aided Verification*, volume 2404 of *Lecture Notes in Computer Science*, pages 57–69. Springer-Verlag, 2004.

[Pel01] D. Peled. *Software Reliability Methods*. Springer-Verlag, 2001.

[PS02] M. Purandare and F. Somenzi. Vacuum cleaning CTL formulae. In *Proc. 14th Conference on Computer Aided Verification*, Lecture Notes in Computer Science, pages 485–499. Springer-Verlag, July 2002.

[TK01] S. Tasiran and K. Keutzer. Coverage metrics for functional validation of hardware designs. *IEEE Design and Test of Computers*, 18(4):36–45, 2001.

[Ver03] Verisity. Surecove's code coverage technology. http://www.verisity.com/ products/surecov.html, 2003.

[VW94] M.Y. Vardi and P. Wolper. Reasoning about infinite computations. *Information and Computation*, 115(1):1–37, November 1994.

[ZHM97] H. Zhu, P.V. Hall, and J.R. May. Software unit test coverage and adequacy. *ACM Computing Surveys*, 29(4):366–427, 1997.

Welcome to the Jungle: A Subjective Guide to Mobile Process Calculi

Uwe Nestmann

Technical University of Berlin, Germany

Abstract. Almost 30 years ago, the research on process calculi gained a lot of momentum with the invention of ACP, CCS and CSP. Later on, but also already 20 years ago, researchers started to consider so-called mobile variants of process calculi, in which communication channels were themselves treated as the exchanged data. The original Pi Calculus arose out of a reformulation and extension of CCS. In turn, it boosted the invention and study of a whole zoo of further process calculi.

In this tutorial, we provide a bird's-eye view on the jungle of results, techniques and subtleties about mobile process calculi. Next to a rough overview on the zoo of calculi, this includes the coverage of both semantic and pragmatic aspects, ranging from notions of equivalence and expressiveness to challenging application domains.

Disclaimer

This document does *not* intend to constitute yet another, possibly updated bibliographic article about mobile process calculi. There have been several already. To my knowledge, Kohei Honda did the first one in 1998, published online. Silvano Dal-Zilio did another one in 2001 [Dal01], integrating references to "truly mobile" calculi reminiscent of Mobile Ambients. Finally, during the years 1994–2003, Björn Victor and I actively co-maintained an online bibliography and web pages on the topic of Calculi for Mobile Processes [NV98]. When we stopped updating the bib-files, the corresponding LaTeX'ed version of the complete bibliography was 29 pages long, of course not even being complete at that time.

This document neither intends to constitute a typical technical tutorial-like introduction to mobile process calculi. There have been several already. The usual suspects that I would recommend are the ones listed on the mobility web pages, carefully written by Milner et. al. [MPW92, Mil99], Parrow [Par01], Pierce [Pie97], Sangiorgi [San01], Sewell [Sew00], etc.

This document, as well as the actual tutorial talk at CONCUR, rather tries to respond to typical critical questions that I often come across when having to defend mobile process calculi. The questions matter, especially when posed by "non-believers" who are very knowledgeable concerning *immobile* process calculi (like ACP, CCS and CSP) and who challenge that mobile process calculi would be truly foundational, canonical, elegant, or even useful at all. Especially when compared to the previous immobile calculi. The idea for such a document dates

C. Baier and H. Hermanns (Eds.): CONCUR 2006, LNCS 4137, pp. 52–63, 2006.

back to July 2003 when I proposed to the `moca` mailing list to develop a *Mobility FAQ*. Unfortunately, this idea had not taken off since, so here I go again.

To my colleagues in the Pi Calculus community, I apologize for possibly having missed to cite some of their own work, but there are simply too many interesting papers to include all that I probably should have. I also apologize for possibly trivializing too much on certain aspects within this informal guide.

The following questions (each listed as a separate section) represent just a starting point. Many more deserve to be posed and hopefully will be (cf. §10).

1 What's the Relation Between Ambient and Pi Calculi?

A welcome source of confusion. It is triggered by both families of calculi being equipped with the label "mobile", but interpreted on a quite different concept of "locations", i.e., places within a distributed system. The mobility difference is of course also manifest in the two quite different underlying basic computational paradigms. An obvious commonality is the role and treatment of names and the use of a restriction operator to dynamically create fresh names and to statically delimit and govern their scope during future computations. Both families of calculi are therefore nowadays also called *nominal* (cf. [Gor02]).

In Pi Calculi [MPW92], the location of a process can be understood as determined by its surrounding network configuration: the (current) set of active communication channels (a processes' communication interface), together with the set of partners reachable through these channels. Then, the location of a process changes whenever its surrounding network configuration changes. The role of name passing is precisely to implement such dynamic reconfigurations by means of explicit communication. This has been very clearly explained, e.g., by Milner [Mil99, §8]. The real expressive power of the Pi Calculus stems from the fact that also local (read: bound) names can be shipped in a controlled fashion.

In contrast, in Ambient Calculi [CG00], the location of a process is modeled explicitly by means of a syntactic entity. Locations usually appear as nested hierarchies. Processes themselves *are* locations. Computation occurs by having locations move around the hierarchy, thus by changing it. Depending on the set of Ambient primitives, location boundaries can also be dissolved dynamically.

In synthesis, there are also extensions of Pi Calculi with explicit concepts of location and movement, like the Distributed Pi Calculus or the Nomadic Pi Calculus. On the other hand, for convenience, also the Ambient Calculus and its descendants provide explicit communication concepts, although often bound to be used locally within a single ambient. To compare the expressive power of Pi and Ambient Calculi, mutual encodings have been studied in great detail.

With respect to this section, I also recommend Silvano Dal-Zilio's commented bibliography [Dal01]. In it, he structures the discourse by dividing mobile calculi into *labile* process systems (relating to chemistry) and *motile* (relating to biology) process systems. The former corresponds more to the first-order movement of names, the latter more to the higher-order movement of processes.

In this document, I will deliberately focus much more on Pi calculi.

2 The Pi Calculus Is Too Complicated!

There are actually many different reasons why people conceive the Pi Calculus as being complicated. In fact, sometimes it really is. But it does not have to be.

The Syntax Is Unreadable. Many different syntactic variants of the Pi Calculus have appeared over the years. However, for understanding how to send a value v over a channel a it should not matter that much whether you write it as $\overline{a}v$ or $\overline{a}\langle v\rangle$ or $a \leftarrow v$ or $a!v$. I do agree that the "bar" notation is not necessarily ideal, but it originates from CCS, and one can also get used to it. The arrow notation was introduced in Honda's ν-calculus, which is asynchronous (see below) and makes it resemble an assignment. The "bang" notation is closely related to ASCII syntax, which is useful when the goal is to discuss programming idioms, but you might confuse it with the replication bang (see below).

A quick word about names ... and (channel) constants ... and variables. In CCS with label passing [EN86], all of these entities were modeled as distinct syntactic concepts. In the original Pi Calculus [MPW92], they were unified into the single concept of names. Both approaches have their advantages and disadvantages. If you have just names, then many definitions get much more light-weight. If you have the distinction, then you get easier control when you have to distinguish names according to the positions in which they may occur. The differences are subtle, but most of the time just a matter of taste, philosophy or readability.

To Be Foundational, There Are Far Too Many Primitives. When compared to the Lambda Calculus, there are definitely more primitives. But, the domain of concurrent computation is also more complicated. On the other hand, one of the smallest and in my opinion very readable Pi Calculus with well enough expressivity is the Asynchronous Pi Calculus, my personal favorite, with or without the *matching* construct $[x = y]P$. Its syntax is generated from this grammar:

$$P \ ::= \ \underbrace{\mathbf{0}}_{nil} \ \mid \ \underbrace{P|P}_{parallel} \ \mid \ \underbrace{\overline{a}\langle v\rangle}_{message} \ \mid \ \underbrace{a(x).P}_{reception} \ \mid \ \underbrace{!\,a(x).P}_{replication} \ \mid \ \underbrace{(\boldsymbol{\nu} x)\,P}_{restriction}$$

It can also get smaller, but this is rather a debate covered by the study of (mutual) encodings between the various calculi. See Section 6, but also [Yos02] for a study of minimality based on combinators appealing to the Lambda Calculus.

The Labeled Semantics Has Too Many Side-Conditions. I got two answers. Labels characterize the interactions with the observing environment. Under dynamic reconfigurations, the scope of binding structures may span across the interface between an observed process system and its concurrently observing process. As a consequence, a labeled semantics must carefully keep track of which names may occur in free or bound position. This justifies the side-conditions.

Now, please have a look at §4, and then come back here. In the spirit of the various incarnations of the Pi Calculus, the labeled semantics is only used for the purpose of providing an underlying deductively defined transition relation on which to define labeled bisimilarities—as proof techniques. For understanding the execution of processes, reduction semantics plainly suffices.

There Are Far Too Many Kinds of Bisimulation. Yes and no. The problem that is usually referred to, when complaining about the many bisimilarities in Pi Calculi, is the different versions called *ground*, *early*, *late*, *open*, ...

First, consider that also for immobile process calculi, a frightening number of process equivalences have been defined, studied and compared [Gla93]. There, the usually accepted defense seems to be that the choice of process equivalence depends on the application under study: the strongest equivalence that is satisfied by a pair of processes tells you a lot about their intuition and semantics. For the many bisimilarities of Pi Calculi, such an argumentation does not quite play well, because the notions are too close to each other. The question of which bisimulation scheme implies the more natural equations leads to debatably subjective answers on whether they matter in practice [SW01].

Now, ultimately, we are interested in process *congruences*. I simply take this point of view for granted, so I will not further argue for it. In process calculi with explicit passing of data, congruences also need to consider closure properties w.r.t. input prefix, i.e., the appearance of processes as continuations of input clauses, where input variables are to be substituted by the received data.[1] All of the above-mentioned notions are just variants of bisimulation that differ in the treatment of substitution of names (variables) by other names (data). Unfortunately, the moment on *when* to apply substitutions, gives rise to strictly different bisimilarities. Which one is the good one? There are at least three answers.

If you want a bisimilarity that constitutes a congruence by itself, then choose the *open* variant. It is also the one, for which more verification tools exist (cf. §7).

If you are of the opinion that the Pi Calculus is no good, because all these bisimilarities differ, then you should be happy to see that there are Pi Calculi in which the bisimilarities actually coincide ... and are congruences themselves. This is one of the many reasons for which I (very subjectively) very much "like" the Asynchronous Pi Calculus (cf. §2 and §4). There is also the Private Pi Calculus (formerly called "Pi Calculus with internal mobility") [SW01]. Both of these are strict subcalculi of the "standard" Pi Calculus that nevertheless retain sufficient expressive power (cf. §6) for most if not all practical purposes.

Last but not least, please (unless you have already had) have a look at §4, and then come back here. Assume you agree that barbed congruence or reduction congruence is what your bisimulation-based congruence[2] shall coincide with. Then, depending on the calculus at hand, chances are very good that the bisimulation scheme to go for (i.e., to base your congruence on) is the *early* one.

[1] Note that some problems already arise in the context of Value Passing CCS [Ing94], so it is not only a problem of name passing calculi.

[2] Usually, we take the largest congruence contained in a given bisimilarity by requiring its closure under substitution. The result is called *full bisimilarity* in [SW01].

3 Why Are There So Many Different Calculi?

Counter-question: why are there so many different programming languages?

Surely, there are several different driving forces that triggered this abundance of Pi Calculi. We may classify them according to several quests, namely for:

Minimality. Which primitives are needed to retain sufficient expressive power? Usually, particular (combinations of) primitives are best studied in isolation, each time giving rise to a new variation of the calculus. Typical primitives of interest are the basic communication paradigms, which can be synchronous [MPW92], asynchronous [Bou92], include selection labels as in TyCO [Vas94], and the inclusion of matching and mismatching primitives (there would be too many papers to cite, here).

Applicability. For every application (domain), one usually has the choice between the use of the bare base calculus, or some syntactically sugared version. Then, it is often a matter of efficiency of available implementations or the precision and comprehension of feedback from formal analysis that triggers the decision to come up with yet another extension of the calculus. Suitable data types are a popular candidate to conveniently extend existing calculi (see also the Applied Pi Calculus [AF01]). Sometimes, however, completely new dimensions are explicitly added to some base calculus, driven by the application. Explicit notions of space [RH98, WS00, Uny01], time [Ber04], stochastics [Pri95], probabilities [HP00], ..., each give rise to new calculi.

Implementability. The interpretation of Pi Calculus as a computational formalism implies that it shall be implemented in order to execute its programs on computers, not just on paper. This quest contributed to the wide-spread use of (extended) sub-calculi often based on asynchronous communication like the ν-calculus [HT92], Lπ [MS04], and the Join Calculus [FG96]: synchronous communication, especially combined with general form of summation, is too hard to implement efficiently in a distributed setting [Pal03].

4 What Are These "Barbs"?

At the time of CCS, providing an operational semantics to a process calculus meant to write out deduction rules for a labeled transition relation, where the intuition is that labels characterize what a process is able to do. One distinguishes internal (invisible) from external (visible) steps. Visible steps model the interactions with an observer—a process that represents the actions of the observing environment. Technically, the labels were just copied from the occurrence of syntactic actions in process terms, with one exception: internal steps (labeled by τ) can also be triggered by the concurrent execution of two complementary (syntactic) actions, occurring at two different syntactic positions within the process. Back then, the world was mostly simple and elegant. ACP was a bit more flexible by allowing more varied new actions to be produced by means of combinations of concurrent actions. With the Pi Calculus, labeled semantics got more complicated since actions had to consider more structure: directed channels (subjects), data (objects) and even dynamically adaptable binding information. A labeled semantics to keep track of such aspects looks, at first, rather complicated to the outsider. Even worse, there seem to be several different but equally meaningful possibilities to characterize oberver actions through labels.

Let us take a step back. Initially, labeled transition semantics tried to prepare for (at least) three things at a time: (1) to define an execution semantics, which also considered actions at the interface to observers; (2) to define a sensible notion of observational congruence, and (3) to provide a tractable (co-inductive) proof technique for this notion. It is here that the Pi Calculus is too rich a setting in that it allows for many reasonable choices of how to define things (cf. §2). Now, the "barbed approach" [MS92] provides a simple and reasonably uniform solution, based on the separation of the above-mentioned three definitional tasks.

1. One defines a simple unlabeled transition semantics, called *reduction semantics* that only considers the execution of internal steps, which are independent of the observing environment. To this aim, and to cope with the syntactic distribution of the complementary parts of redexes, reduction is considered modulo structural rearrangement congruence (typically monoid laws for composition and summation, among others), according to

$$\frac{P \equiv Q \qquad Q \longrightarrow Q' \qquad Q' \equiv P'}{P \longrightarrow P'}$$

   The main reduction rule for the Asynchronous Pi Calculus above then is:

$$\overline{a}\langle v\rangle \mid a(x).P \longrightarrow \{{}^{v}\!/\!_{x}\}P$$

   In Pi Calculus, the treatment of fresh names is also conveniently pushed into the notion of structural congruence, essentially by the law

$$(\boldsymbol{\nu}x)\,(\ P \mid Q\ ) \equiv ((\boldsymbol{\nu}x)P) \mid Q \qquad \text{if } x \text{ does not occur freely in } Q$$

   that allows to extend or syntactically shrink the scope of bound names. Thus, to model the so-called *scope extrusion*, one just first structurally extends the scope—reading the above law from right to left—and then applies the simple standard reduction rule within the scope. As a result, the reduction semantics for the Pi Calculus looks actually almost as simple as the one for CCS.[3]
2. Based on a reduction semantics, one defines a bisimulation-like notion of observational congruence on top. Since reductions do not contain information about the observing environment, the congruence is defined by explicit quantification over sets of *contexts*, i.e., processes with a single hole. Formally, a symmetric relation $\mathcal{B}$ is a *barbed bisimulation*, if whenever $P\ \mathcal{B}\ Q$, then
   - $P \longrightarrow P'$ implies that there is $Q \Rightarrow Q'$ with $P'\ \mathcal{B}\ Q'$, and
   - P "has barb O" iff Q "has barb O".

[3] Exercise: to get a feeling for structural congruence, it is instructive to try to find a minimal set of structural rearrangement laws ($\equiv$) that suffice to define CCS reduction in 1-1 correspondence to the labeled τ-transitions of the respective CCS-terms.

The first item essentially requires the notion to be a *reduction bisimulation.*

In the second item, *barb* O is usually instantiated by some *observation predicate*, often written as $\Downarrow$ (or $\Downarrow_a$), telling that one can reach a state where some (or a particular kind of action involving the name a) action is enabled.

As usual, two processes P and Q are called *barbed bisimilar*, written $P \approx_{\mathrm{B}} Q$, if there is a barbed bisimulation $\mathcal{B}$ that contains (P, Q). Barbed bisimulation as such is not very interesting, because it does not consider interactions with an observing environment. Thus, we add this information explicitly. Two processes are *barbed congruent*, written $P \cong_{\mathrm{B}} Q$, if, for all contexts $C[\cdot]$, $C[P] \approx_{\mathrm{B}} C[Q]$. Thus, barbed congruence is a *contextual* notion. To prove two processes congruent, in addition to the otherwise simple obligations of the definition, one has to consider an infinite number of contexts.

But, since quantification is done over an explicit set of contexts, we now also have a convenient definitional scheme at hand to define coarser congruences by cutting down the number of contexts considered. The biggest beneficiaries are the following two: (1) notions of *typed barbed congruence* (cf. [PS96]), where the class of contexts to consider is characterized by only those that yield well-typed terms when plugging some process into the hole; (2) notions of *congruence up to translated contexts* in the study of encodings (cf. §6).

3. One is then looking for a labeled transition semantics and a suitable labeled notion of bisimulation congruence that—as a proof technique—approximates the previously defined uniform notion of barbed congruence. In other words, barbed congruence should guide the quest for finding the "right notion of labeled congruence". Ideally, of course, one finds a labeled version that is not only sound, but also complete w.r.t. the barbed notion.

Note that the above story is actually independent of the Pi Calculus. However, it was the Pi Calculus in whose rich context one felt the need to establish some more uniform way to capture observational equivalences. Later on, it has also been followed by many other calculi, e.g., Ambient Calculi and Spi Calculus.

Accompanying the discussion of barbed congruence, one should also mention the arguably more canonical definition of so-called *reduction congruence* [HY95]: the main difference is that no notion of observation predicate (i.e., barb) needs to be justified. Instead, the general notion of *process insensitivity* is used to govern the definition of process congruence on top of reduction-closed equality (roughly corresponding to reduction bisimulation). In most calculi, reduction congruence is finer than barbed congruence. Roughly, reduction congruence corresponds to the requirement of quantification over contexts after every step in the bisimulation game. Fournet and Gonthier [FG04] have proved, for the Asynchronous Pi Calculus with matching, that barbed congruence and reduction congruence coincide, also with labeled asynchronous bisimulation (cf. §2).

5 Are There Any Applications? More Precisely: Beyond What You Can Do with CCS ...

In the early years, there was the convincing analysis of (simple versions of) the GSM handover protocol, being reused in many papers, with more or less complicated scenarios. The situation reminds a bit of the numerous studies on the Alternating Bit Protocol within immobile process calculi and other concurrency formalisms during the 1980's. This is not necessarily bad, because it allows researchers to quickly get to the point and it allows referees to quickly understand the added value of the technique contributed by some submitted paper.

It is probably true that, for a too long time, the GSM handover has been the only truly mobile application example. Instead, those parts of the mobile process calculus community that were interested in "applications" went on studying the representations and implementations of high-level programming concepts by means of encoding them into a basic mobile process calculus (cf. §6). Examples include typed imperative, functional, object-oriented and even constraint-oriented programming, the latter two also in concurrent versions, whose semantics tends to be complex and difficult to get right. Although the modeling or encodings of high-level programming paradigms, as well as of typed data structures bears a number of similarities with assembler languages, the contributions can be stated as being surprisingly successful: the precision, depth and comprehensibility of results that could be achieved by translating concepts into Pi Calculi is astonishing, particularly in the functional and object-oriented domain. Also the Actor model—one of the sources of inspiration for the Pi Calculus—could be understood by representing it as a particular typed Pi Calculus [AT04].

Nevertheless, more and more truly mobile applications have been entering the landscape. The motivation to model Internet phenomena led to various distributed Pi Calculi, as well as versions that natively integrate XML datatypes, and also the Ambient Calculus. The Spi Calculus [AG99] has been used with success to model security protocols. Stochastic Pi Calculi have been used to model phenomena in Systems Biology [PRSS01]. This domain also inspired the development of tailor-made nominal calculi [DL04]. Finally, the domain of Business Process Modeling provides applications, where the standard original Pi Calculus has proved to be a useful modeling tool [PW05].

In most if not all of these applications, the expressive power and careful treatment of fresh name generation—a distinctive feature when compared to immobile process calculi—is the key to concise and successful modeling.

6 What's the Point of Studying Encodings?

Very many encodings that use Pi Calculi as target languages have been studied. So many that I do not include any explicit references in this part. The use of encodings is actually a quite standard technique. If you want to compare the *expressive power* of two calculi, then it is convenient to study mutual encodings between them.[4] If you want to represent *high-level programming concepts* (cf. §5) within some basic calculus, then you do this by means of an encoding function. Such encodings actually represent formal abstract implementations.

Encodings can be analyzed in many respects. Typically, a "good" encoding preserves and reflects as many semantic properties as possible, e.g., notions of equivalence, the decidability of properties, or just the existence of matching transitions according to the operational semantics. Although many criteria for the quality of encodings have been proposed, there is still not yet an agreed-upon "theory of encodings" that tells how all of those criteria relate. Ongoing debates include the following questions: (1) How compositional does an encoding have to be? Is it acceptable to translate $[\![P|Q]\!]$ as $C[[\![P]\!]|[\![Q]\!]]$, where C could be some powerful arbiter, or should we insist on C being the empty context? (2) Is it acceptable to require the intended behavior of encoded terms w.r.t. encoded contexts only, or should we insist on good behavior w.r.t. all contexts available in the target language? (3) Is it acceptable that an encoding introduces divergence?

7 What About Tools?

Actually, there are quite a few available (see an incomplete list at [Nes]). Some of them are compilers that allow one to efficiently run mobile programs written within some high-level programming language based on one the Pi Calculi, and this even in truly distributed settings. Others are analysis tools that allow one to simulate Pi Calculus executions, even for the Stochastic Pi Calculus. Further tools automate equivalence-checking, various forms of reachability analysis, some of them specialized for security protocols written in variants of the Spi Calculus. A member of the `moca` mailing list summarized the situation in 2003 as follows: "Process-calculists are not so interested in coding and coders don't read our papers, so cross fertilization has been somewhat lacking". I think it is fair to say that the situation has changed at least a bit, but we could still profit from more "efficient" analysis tools for mobile process calculi.

8 After 20 Years, What Are the Main Contributions?

This is a difficult question.

It is certainly the case that the fundamental role and pragmatic expressive power of fresh-name generation has proved to be useful for many practical programming and modeling problems (cf. §5).

The proliferation and extensive study of so many variations of the original Pi Calculus has helped to build up a large set of semantic techniques and results. It also helped to identify typical pitfalls and traps such that the development of further (domain-specific) variations is nowadays a much easier task. It has in fact become so easy to design new calculi (with notions of execution and observational

[4] Apparently, the question of expressive power is particularly appealing in the context of concurrency. The respective high quality 1-day workshop EXPRESS, which at its peak attracted 30 submissions, is now already running its 13th incarnation.

congruence, according to the scheme of § 4) that there is the running gag that we can "make up new calculi while having breakfast, several of them".

I think it is also fair to state that we have not yet discovered the process calculus that constitutes *the* foundation of mobile/global/distributed computation. Some sweet spots have been identified, e.g., where the many bisimulations collapse. Maybe, it could be stated as a contribution that there is reason to believe that there simply is no single one, e.g., with a fixed single concept of communication. Yet, if there is a single one, then it is likely a nominal calculus.

I also count as a main contribution the extensive study of name-based type systems in the context of mobile process calculi. Although they sometimes appear to be complicated, they are rich and flexible. The community even managed to convince an EU-official in the context of the GC-initiative of the importance of type systems for many concepts of distributed computation.

In this document, I have not at all covered the study of unifying models that are designed to capture the different notions of sequential, concurrent and distributed computation, e.g., Bi-Graphs. Their evolutionary development can certainly be counted as a main contribution, supported by mobile process calculi.

9 I Want to Use the Pi Calculus. Should I Take One off the Shelf, or Should I Assemble My Own Little Calculus?

There are some obviously good reasons for choosing a calculus off-the-shelf. (1) You want to use one of the tools that have been written to analyze Pi Calculus terms. (2) You do not yourself have to work out the theoretical results that you might need for your application. (3) You need to be able to state that you are using some "standard" calculus in order to convince your application community. (4) You only need to read one or two papers on Pi Calculus yourself.

Yet, there are also very good reasons for using your own home-brewed calculus. (1) The typical argument for the use of domain-specific languages applies: to model your application, existing calculi might not offer the right set of primitives, be it at the proper level of abstraction, or be it a completely independent modeling dimension that has not yet been considered appropriately. (2) You have a Pi Calculus guru next door who knows about the traps and pitfalls, who might help you work out the theory, or might even do it for you. (3) You might get another paper published by carefully motivating the design of your domain-specific process calculus. (4) You may help the process calculus community by inspiring the development of new techniques and theories.

10 Will There Be Further Work?

Concerning the Pi Calculi themselves, I am convinced that active research will continue for many more years, but I know of no roadmap that the community has agreed to pursue, possibly apart from the UK Grand Challenge on Sciences for Global Ubiquitous Computing. A list of open problems could be a good start.

Ideally, this document triggers many more questions that the "Pi Calculus community" should respond to. I will happily collect any such information—questions *and* responses—and provide an online resource, e.g., in the form of a Wiki, such that the guide will become less subjective as it appears herein.

Acknowledgments. Jos Baeten and Holger Hermanns for discussing related issues at the social event of CONCUR 2001. The members of the `moca` mailing list, in particular Martin Berger, for some discussion in July/August 2003.

References

[AF01] M. Abadi and C. Fournet. Mobile Values, New Names, and Secure Communication. In *Proceedings of POPL '01*, pages 104–115. ACM, Jan. 2001.

[AG99] M. Abadi and A. D. Gordon. A Calculus for Cryptographic Protocols: The Spi Calculus. *Information and Computation*, 148(1):1–70, 1999.

[AT04] G. Agha and P. Thati. An Algebraic Theory of Actors and Its Application to a Simple Object-Based Language. In *Essays in Memory of Ole-Johan Dahl*, volume 2635 of *LNCS*, pages 26–57. Springer, 2004.

[Ber04] M. Berger. Basic Theory of Reduction Congruence for Two Timed Asynchronous π-Calculi. In P. Gardner and N. Yoshida, eds, *Proceedings of CONCUR 2004*, volume 3170 of *LNCS*, pages 115–130. Springer, Aug. 2004.

[Bou92] G. Boudol. Asynchrony and the π-calculus (Note). Rapport de Recherche 1702, INRIA Sophia-Antipolis, May 1992.

[CG00] L. Cardelli and A. D. Gordon. Mobile Ambients. *Theoretical Computer Science*, 240(1):177–213, 2000.

[Dal01] S. Dal-Zilio. Mobile Processes: a Commented Bibliograhy. In *Proceedings of MOVEP'2K — 4th Summer school on Modelling and Verification of Parallel Processes)*, volume 2067 of *LNCS*, pages 206–222. Springer, 2001.

[DL04] V. Danos and C. Laneve. Formal Molecular Biology. *Theoretical Computer Science*, 325(1):69–110, 2004.

[EN86] U. Engberg and M. Nielsen. A Calculus of Communicating Systems with Label-passing. Technical Report DAIMI PB-208, Computer Science Department, University of Aarhus, Denmark, 1986.

[FG96] C. Fournet and G. Gonthier. The Reflexive Chemical Abstract Machine and the Join-Calculus. In *Proceedings of POPL '96*, pages 372–385. ACM, 1996.

[FG04] C. Fournet and G. Gonthier. A Hierarchy of Equivalences for Asynchronous Calculi. *Journal of Logic and Algebraic Programming*, 63(1):131–173, 2004.

[Gla93] R. Glabbeek. The Linear Time – Branching Time Spectrum II: The semantics of sequential systems with silent moves (Extended Abstract). In *Proceedings of CONCUR '93*, volume 715 of *LNCS*, pages 66–81. Springer, 1993.

[Gor02] A. D. Gordon. Notes on nominal calculi for security and mobility. In R. Focardi and R. Gorrieri, eds, *Foundations of Security Analysis and Design*, volume 2171 of *LNCS*, pages 262–330. Springer, 2002.

[HP00] O. M. Herescu and C. Palamidessi. Probabilistic Asynchronous π-Calculus. In J. Tiuryn, ed, *Proceedings of FoSSaCS 2000*, volume 1784 of *LNCS*, pages 146–160. Springer, 2000.

[HT92] K. Honda and M. Tokoro. On Asynchronous Communication Semantics. In M. Tokoro, O. Nierstrasz and P. Wegner, eds, *Object-Based Concurrent Computing 1991*, volume 612 of *LNCS*, pages 21–51. Springer, 1992.

[HY95] K. Honda and N. Yoshida. On Reduction-Based Process Semantics. *Theoretical Computer Science*, 152(2):437–486, 1995. An extract appeared in *Proceedings of FSTTCS '93*, LNCS 761.

[Ing94] A. Ingólfsdóttir. *Semantic Models for Communicating Processes with Value-Passing*. PhD thesis, University of Sussex, 1994.

[Mil99] R. Milner. *Communicating and Mobile Systems: the π-Calculus*. Cambridge University Press, May 1999.

[MPW92] R. Milner, J. Parrow and D. Walker. A Calculus of Mobile Processes, Part I/II. *Information and Computation*, 100:1–77, Sept. 1992.

[MS92] R. Milner and D. Sangiorgi. Barbed Bisimulation. In W. Kuich, ed, *Proceedings of ICALP '92*, volume 623 of *LNCS*, pages 685–695. Springer, 1992.

[MS04] M. Merro and D. Sangiorgi. On Asynchrony in Name-Passing Calculi. *Mathematical Structures in Computer Science*, 14(5):715–767, 2004.

[Nes] U. Nestmann. Calculi for Mobile Processes. http://move.to/mobility.

[NV98] U. Nestmann and B. Victor. Calculi for Mobile Processes: Bibliography and Web Pages. *EATCS Bulletin*, 64:139–144, Feb. 1998.

[Pal03] C. Palamidessi. Comparing the Expressive Power of the Synchronous and the Asynchronous π-calculus. *Mathematical Structures in Computer Science*, 13(5):685–719, 2003.

[Par01] J. Parrow. An Introduction to the pi-Calculus. In *Handbook of Process Algebra*, pages 479–543. Elsevier Science, 2001.

[Pie97] B. C. Pierce. Foundational Calculi for Programming Languages. In *Handbook of Computer Science and Engineering*, pages 2190–2207. CRC Press, 1997.

[Pri95] C. Priami. Stochastic π-Calculus. *The Computer Journal*, 38(6):578–589, 1995. Proceedings of PAPM '95.

[PRSS01] C. Priami, A. Regev, E. Y. Shapiro and W. Silverman. Application of a Stochastic Name-Passing Calculus to Representation and Simulation of Molecular Processes. *Information Processing Letters*, 80(1):25–31, 2001.

[PS96] B. C. Pierce and D. Sangiorgi. Typing and Subtyping for Mobile Processes. *Mathematical Structures in Computer Science*, 6(5):409–454, 1996. An extract appeared in *Proceedings of LICS '93*: 376–385.

[PW05] F. Puhlmann and M. Weske. Using the π-Calculus for Formalizing Workflow Patterns. In *Proceedings of BPM 2005*, volume 3649 of *LNCS*, pages 153–168. Springer, 2005.

[RH98] J. Riely and M. Hennessy. A Typed Language for Distributed Mobile Processes. In *Proceedings of POPL '98*. ACM, 1998.

[San01] D. Sangiorgi. Asynchronous process calculi: the first-order and higher-order paradigms (Tutorial). *Theoretical Computer Science*, 253(2):311–350, 2001.

[Sew00] P. Sewell. Applied Pi — A Brief Tutorial. Technical Report 498, Computer Laboratory, University of Cambridge, 2000.

[SW01] D. Sangiorgi and D. Walker. *The π-calculus: a Theory of Mobile Processes*. Cambridge University Press, 2001.

[Uny01] A. Unyapoth. *Nomadic Pi Calculi: Expressing and Verifying Infrastructure for Mobile Computation*. PhD thesis, University of Cambridge, June 2001.

[Vas94] V. T. Vasconcelos. Typed Concurrent Objects. In *Proceedings of ECOOP '94*, volume 821 of *LNCS*, pages 100–117. Springer, 1994.

[WS00] P. Wojciechowski and P. Sewell. Nomadic Pict: Language and Infrastructure Design for Mobile Agents. *IEEE Concurrency*, 8(2):42–52, 2000.

[Yos02] N. Yoshida. Minimality and separation results on asynchronous mobile processes — Representability theorems by concurrent combinators. *Theoretical Computer Science*, 274(1–2):231–276, 2002.

Probability and Nondeterminism in Operational Models of Concurrency

Roberto Segala*

Dipartimento di Informatica, Università di Verona, Italy

Abstract. We give a brief overview of operational models for concurrent systems that exhibit probabilistic behavior, focussing on the interplay between probability and nondeterminism. Our survey is carried out from the perspective of probabilistic automata, a model originally developed for the analysis of randomized distributed algorithms.

1 Introduction

The study of randomization in concurrency theory started almost two decades ago, leading to the proposal of several formalisms. In this paper we focus on operational nondeterministic models with discrete probabilities, and we analyze them from the perspective of Probabilistic Automata.

After giving the formal definition of probabilistic automata, we describe other existing proposals as extensions or restrictions of probabilistic automata, thus surveying the existing literature from a uniform point of view. We then turn to the definition of simulation and bisimulation relations. These relations are studied extensively for their mathematical simplicity; yet, several existing definitions appear incomparable. We show how to view the existing definitions based on the definitional style of probabilistic automata. We give several references along the way, including references to other relevant topics that we do not cover explicitly.

2 Preliminaries on Measure Theory

We start with some preliminary notions from measure theory. Although we define all the necessary concepts, some familiarity is useful. We refer the reader to any textbook on measure theory in case the use of some concepts is hard to grasp.

A *σ-field* over a set Ω is a subset $\mathcal{F}$ of 2^{Ω} that includes the empty set and is closed under complement and countable union. We call the pair $(\Omega, \mathcal{F})$ a *measurable space*. A special σ-field is the set 2^{Ω}, which we call the *discrete σ-field* over Ω. Given a subset $\mathcal{C}$ of 2^{Ω}, we denote by $\sigma(\mathcal{C})$ the smallest σ-field that includes $\mathcal{C}$, and we call it the σ-field *generated* by $\mathcal{C}$.

A *measure* over a measurable space $(\Omega, \mathcal{F})$ is a function $\mu : \mathcal{F} \rightarrow \mathcal{R}^{\geq 0}$ such that $\mu(\emptyset) = 0$ and, for each countable family $\{X_i\}_I$ of pairwise disjoint elements of $\mathcal{F}$, $\mu(\cup_I X_i) = \sum_I \mu(X_i)$. If $\mu(\Omega) \leq 1$, then we say that μ is a *sub-probability*

* Supported by MIUR project AIDA and INRIA project ProNoBiS.

C. Baier and H. Hermanns (Eds.): CONCUR 2006, LNCS 4137, pp. 64–78, 2006.

measure, and if $\mu(\Omega) = 1$, then we say that μ is a *probability measure.* If $\mathcal{F}$ is the discrete σ-field over Ω, then we say that μ is a *discrete* measure over Ω. In such case, for each set $X \subseteq \Omega$, $\mu(X) = \sum_{x \in X} \mu(\{x\})$. We drop brackets from singletons whenever this does not cause any confusion. We denote by $\mathsf{Disc}(\Omega)$ the set of discrete probability measures over Ω and by $\mathsf{SubDisc}(\Omega)$ the set of discrete sub-probability measures over Ω. We say that a set $X \subseteq \Omega$ is a *support* of a measure μ if $\mu(\Omega - X) = 0$. If μ is a discrete measure, then there is a minimum support of μ consisting of those elements $x \in \Omega$ such that $\mu(x) > 0$.

A function $f : \Omega_1 \to \Omega_2$ is said to be a *measurable function* from $(\Omega_1, \mathcal{F}_1)$ to $(\Omega_2, \mathcal{F}_2)$ if the inverse image under f of any element of $\mathcal{F}_2$ is an element of $\mathcal{F}_1$. In this case, given a measure μ on $(\Omega_1, \mathcal{F}_1)$ it is possible to define a measure on $(\Omega_2, \mathcal{F}_2)$ via f, called the *image measure* of μ under f and denoted by $f(\mu)$, as follows: for each $X \in \mathcal{F}_2$, $f(\mu)(X) = \mu(f^{-1}(X))$. In other words, the measure of X in $\mathcal{F}_2$ is the measure in $\mathcal{F}_1$ of those elements whose f-image is in X. The measurability of f ensures that $f(\mu)$ is indeed a well defined measure.

3 Probabilistic Automata

In this section we define probabilistic automata and we relate them to several other existing models.

3.1 Probabilistic Automata

The main idea behind probabilistic automata is that the target of a transition is not just a single state, but rather is determined by a probability measure. Thus, if a transition describes the act of flipping a fair coin, then the target state corresponds to head with probability 1/2 and tail with probability 1/2. However, in contraposition to ordinary Markov processes, for each state there may be several possible transitions.

A *probabilistic automaton* (PA) is a tuple $(Q, \bar{q}, A, D)$, where Q is a countable set of *states*, $\bar{q} \in Q$ is a *start* state, A is a countable set of *actions*, and $D \subseteq Q \times A \times \mathsf{Disc}(Q)$ is a *transition relation.* The set of actions A is further partitioned into two sets E, H of *external* and *internal* (hidden) actions, respectively.

The only difference with respect to ordinary automata is in the third element of the transition relation D, which is not a single state but rather a discrete probability measures over states. Indeed, an ordinary automaton can be seen as a special case of a probabilistic automaton where all transitions lead to *Dirac* measures, i.e., measures that assign probability 1 to a single state.

In the sequel we use $\mathcal{A}$ to denote a probabilistic automaton and we refer to the elements of $\mathcal{A}$ by $Q, \bar{q}, A, D$, propagating indices and primes as well. Thus, e.g., H_i' is the set of internal actions of a PA $\mathcal{A}_i'$.

Remark 1. The definition of probabilistic automaton given here includes a single start state; however, nothing prevents us from defining PAs with multiple start states or where start states are replaced by start probability measures. Such extensions do not provide much additional insight; however, they impose simple

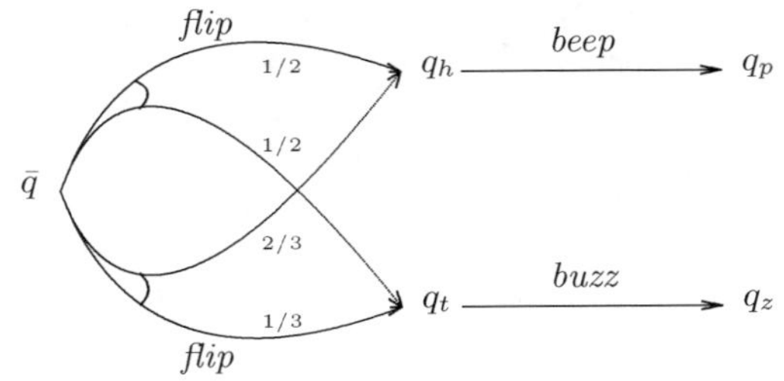

Fig. 1. A probabilistic automaton that flips a coin

cosmetic adjustments in several definitions that we prefer to avoid in favor of clarity. Similar reasons motivated the restrictions on the cardinality of Q and A.

Example 1. Figure 1 gives a graphical representation of a PA that performs an action flip and then beeps if the result of the coin flip is head and buzzes otherwise. The PA is nondeterministic since the coin to be flipped can be either fair or unfair, leading to head with probability 2/3 in the unfair case.

An *execution fragment* of a PA $\mathcal{A}$ is a sequence of alternating states and actions, $\alpha = q_0 a_1 q_1 \cdots$, starting with a state and, if the sequence is finite, ending with a state, such that, for each non final index i, there exists a transition $(q_i, a_{i+1}, \mu_{i+1})$ in D with $\mu_{i+1}(q_{i+1}) > 0$. We denote by $\mathsf{fstate}(\alpha)$ the first state q_0 of α, and, if the sequence is finite, we denote by $\mathsf{lstate}(\alpha)$ the last state of α. An *execution* of a PA $\mathcal{A}$ is an execution fragment of $\mathcal{A}$ whose first state if $\bar{q}$. We denote by $\mathsf{Frags}^*(\mathcal{A})$ the set of finite execution fragments of a PA $\mathcal{A}$.

An execution fragment is the result of resolving nondeterminism and fixing the outcomes of the probabilistic experiments. However, resolving nondeterministic choices only leads to more complex structures that should be studied.

Example 2. Consider the coin flipper of Example 1 and suppose we want to compute the probability that it beeps. We should note first that such probability depends on the coin that is flipped. Indeed, the coin flipper beeps with probability 1/2 if the fair coin is flipped, and with probability 2/3 if the unfair coin is flipped. Therefore, in order to answer our question, we should first fix the coin to be flipped, and then study probabilities on the structure that we get.

We can think of resolving nondeterminism by unfolding the transition relation of a PA and then choosing only one transition at each point. From the formal point of view it is more convenient to define a function, which we call *scheduler*, that chooses transitions based on the past history (i.e., the current position in the unfolding of the transition relation).

A *scheduler* for a PA $\mathcal{A}$ is a function $\sigma : \mathsf{Frags}^*(\mathcal{A}) \rightarrow \mathsf{SubDisc}(D)$ such that, for each finite execution fragment α and each transition tr with $\sigma(\alpha)(tr) > 0$, the source state of tr is $\mathsf{lstate}(\alpha)$. A scheduler σ is *deterministic* if, for each finite execution fragment α, either $\sigma(\alpha)$ assigns probability 1 to a single transition or

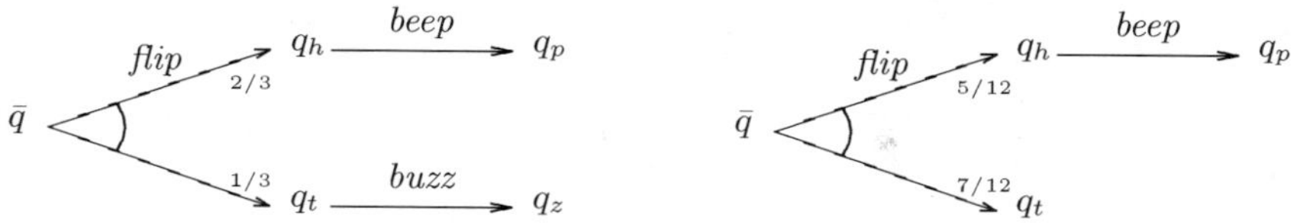

Fig. 2. Probabilistic executions

assigns probability 0 to all transitions. A scheduler σ is *memoryless* if it depends only on the last state of its argument, i.e., for each pair α_1, α_2 of finite execution fragments, if $\mathsf{lstate}(\alpha_1) = \mathsf{lstate}(\alpha_2)$, then $\sigma(\alpha_1) = \sigma(\alpha_2)$.

Informally, $\sigma(\alpha)$ describes the rule for choosing a transition after α has occurred. The rule itself may be randomized. Since $\sigma(\alpha)$ is a sub-probability measure, it is possible that with some non-zero probability no transition is chosen, which corresponds to terminating the computation (what in the purely nondeterministic case is called a finite execution fragment). Deterministic schedulers are not allowed to use randomization in their choices, while memoryless schedulers are not allowed to look at the past history in their choices. Deterministic and memoryless schedulers are easier to analyze compared to general schedulers, and several properties (e.g., reachability) can be studied by referring to deterministic memoryless schedulers only.

Remark 2. Terminology may be confusing at this point. In the original definition of PAs [35] a scheduler is called *adversary* since it is seen as a hostile entity that degrades performance as much as possible. In the field of Markov Decision Processes [15], a scheduler is called *policy* since it is seen as an entity that optimizes some cost function. In practice the three terms may be used interchangeably.

Example 3. Figure 2 gives two examples of probabilistic executions of the coin flipper of Example 1. In the left case the unfair coin is flipped, while in the right case each coin is flipped with probability 1/2 and the *buzz* transition is never scheduled. In general, considering that a scheduler may also terminate executions, we can say that the coin flipper beeps with probability at most 2/3. Furthermore, if we assume that transitions are scheduled whenever possible, then we can say that the coin flipper beeps with a probability between 1/2 and 2/3.

We now describe formally how to associate a probability measure to execution fragments once nondeterminism is resolved. Interestingly, we do not need to build explicitly the structures depicted in Figure 2. First we need to define the set of measurable events (when we talk about probabilities an element of the σ-field is called an event); then we associate probabilities to events. As basic measurable events we consider the set of *cones* of finite execution fragments, where the cone of a finite execution fragment α consists of all possible extensions of α and denotes the occurrence of α possibly followed by some other behavior. Formally, the cone of α, denoted by C_α, is the set $\{\alpha' \in \mathsf{Frags}(\mathcal{A}) \mid \alpha \leq \alpha'\}$, where $\leq$ is the standard prefix preorder on sequences. Informally, referring to Figure 2, the probability of a cone C_α is the product of the probabilities of all the edges of the path α. Formally, we give a recursive definition. Fixed a scheduler σ and a state s, we define a measure $\epsilon_{\sigma,s}$ on cones as follows.

$$\epsilon_{\sigma,s}(C_\alpha) = \begin{cases} 0 & \text{if } \alpha = q \text{ for some state } q \neq s, \\ 1 & \text{if } \alpha = s, \\ \epsilon_{\sigma,s}(C_{\alpha'}) \sum_{tr \in D(a)} \sigma(\alpha)(tr)\mu_{tr}(q) & \text{if } \alpha = \alpha' a q, \end{cases}$$

where $D(a)$ denotes the set of transitions of D with label a. Standard measure theoretical arguments ensure that $\epsilon_{\sigma,s}$ extends uniquely to the σ-field generated by cones. We call the measure $\epsilon_{\sigma,s}$ a *probabilistic execution fragment* of $\mathcal{A}$ and we say that it is generated by σ from s. If s is the start state of $\mathcal{A}$, then we say that $\epsilon_{\sigma,s}$ is a *probabilistic execution.*

The cone-based definition of σ-field is quite general, and indeed typical properties of interest are measurable. The occurrence of an action a (of a state s) is a union of cones, and thus measurable since there are countably many cones. Similarly, we retain measurability if we require n occurrences of an action or state. Also infinitely many occurrences of an action are measurable, since they can be expressed as the countable intersection, over all naturals n, of n occurrences. It is also known that any ω-regular language is measurable [39] and that the properties expressed by existing probabilistic temporal logics are measurable.

We conclude this section with the definition of a parallel composition operator. In our definition we synchronize two probabilistic automata on their common actions; however, many other synchronization styles are possible.

Two probabilistic automata $\mathcal{A}_1, \mathcal{A}_2$ are *compatible* if $H_1 \cap A_2 = A_1 \cap H_2 = \emptyset$. The composition of two compatible probabilistic automata $\mathcal{A}_1, \mathcal{A}_2$, denoted by $\mathcal{A}_1 \| \mathcal{A}_2$, is a probabilistic automaton $\mathcal{A}$ where $Q = Q_1 \times Q_2$, $\bar{q} = (\bar{q}_1, \bar{q}_2)$, $E = E_1 \cup E_2$, $H = H_1 \cup H_2$, and D is defined as follows: $((q_1, q_2), a, \mu_1 \times \mu_2) \in D$ iff, for each $i \in \{1, 2\}$, either $a \in A_i$ and $(q_i, a, \mu_i) \in D_i$, or $a \notin A_i$ and $\mu_i = \delta(q_i)$, where $\delta(q_i)$ denotes the probability measure that assigns probability 1 to q_i and $\mu_1 \times \mu_2((q'_1, q'_2))$ is defined to be $\mu_1(q'_1)\mu_2(q'_2)$.

3.2 Reactive, Generative, and Stratified Models

In [19] probabilistic models are classified into reactive, generative, and stratified. The paper was first written in 1990 in the context of concurrency theory, where the trend was to replace nondeterministic choices with probabilistic choices. The main driving idea was that the presence of probabilities does not hide the underlying nondeterminism, but rather gives more information.

A *reactive* system is a labeled transition system whose arcs are equipped with probabilities. Furthermore, for each state q and each action a, either there is no transition labeled by a from q, or the probabilities of all transition labeled by a from q add to 1. In other words, a reactive system does not provide any information about the way an action is chosen, but provides information about the way a transition is chosen once the action is fixed. The information about the underlying nondeterminism for an action a can be retrieved via an appropriate projection operation that removes all probabilities from the arcs.

A *generative* system is similar to a reactive system; however, this time the requirement is that for each state q either there is no transition from q, or the probabilities of all transition from q add to 1. In other words a generative system adds information about the way actions are chosen. The information about the actions available (i.e., the underlying reactive system) can be retrieved by an appropriate projection operation that renormalizes the probabilities of the transitions labeled by the same action.

A *stratified* system adds more information to a generative system in the sense that a measure over visible transitions is obtained via several non-visible transitions that reveal some hierarchy. This model has not received much attention in the literature and therefore we refer the interested reader to [19].

The view of [19] is that stratified is more general than generative and that generative is more general than stratified with the justification that the projection operators preserve bisimilarity. Our definition of probabilistic automata departs considerably from such view. Indeed, there is no way to encode the nondeterminism of the probabilistic automaton of Example 1 within a reactive or generative system. In contraposition to the underlying idea of [19], probabilistic automata keep explicitly both nondeterministic and probabilistic choices.

Observe that a reactive system can be seen also as a *deterministic* PA, i.e., a PA that from each state enables at most one transition for each action. However, this implies abandoning the idea of [19] that the underlying nondeterminism can be retrieved by removing probabilities.

3.3 Markov Decision Processes

Another well known model of probabilistic and nondeterministic systems is Markov Decision Processes (MDPs) [15], which in practice correspond to deterministic probabilistic automata. MDPs were studied originally within operational research: a process evolves probabilistically according to measures that depend only on the current states (Markovian property); however, from each state there are several possible actions available, each one leading to different evolutions. The objective is to choose actions from each state (choose a policy) so that some cost function is optimized. States may be associated with rewards that are used to compute the cost function. MDPs are deterministic in the sense that from each state each action identifies a unique evolution.

Another related model which is worth mentioning here are the probabilistic automata of Rabin [34]. Again, these correspond to deterministic probabilistic automata. They were studied originally in the context of language theory to show that finite-state probabilistic automata accept a class of languages which is strictly larger than regular languages.

3.4 Alternating Models

In [39] Vardi studies model checking algorithms for Markov processes in the presence of nondeterminism. For the purpose he distinguishes *probabilistic* states,

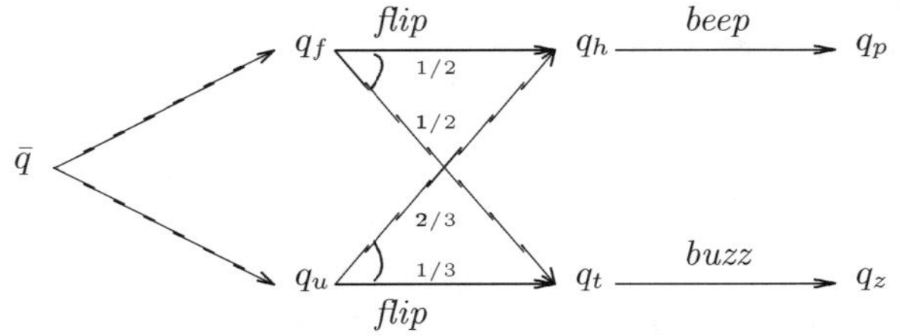

Fig. 3. An alternating representation of the coin flipper of Figure 1

where the next state is determined by a probability measure, from *nondeterministic* states, where several ordinary transitions may occur. The same idea is followed in [22] for the definition of Labeled Concurrent Markov Chains. The objective of [22] was to give a semantics to a probabilistic process algebra, where probability measures are expressed by appropriate expressions. Thus, a distinction between nondeterministic and probabilistic states follows naturally.

The models of [39,22] are currently referred to as *alternating* models, in contraposition to probabilistic automata which are *non-alternating*. The model of [22] is further called *strictly* alternating since it imposes a strict alternation between nondeterministic and probabilistic states, whereas the model of [39] permits transitions between nondeterministic states.

Since an ordinary transition is a special case of a probabilistic transition, the alternating models can be seen as special cases of probabilistic automata, where restrictions are imposed on the transition relations. This idea is formalized in [37] via appropriate embedding functions. The interesting aspect of viewing the alternating models as special cases of probabilistic automata is that several concepts that in the literature are defined on the models in very different styles turn out to be equivalent [37]. This is reassuring since it means that we can grasp the whole theory by understanding fewer concepts.

Example 4. Figure 3 represents the coin flipper of Figure 1 as an alternating probabilistic automaton. The main difference is that the transitions labeled by *flip* are split into two transitions, one from a nondeterministic state to a probabilistic state, and one from the probabilistic state to a probability measure over nondeterministic states. There is indeed a folklore idea, formalized in [37], on how to transform a non-alternating model into an alternating model by splitting transitions and vice-versa how to transform an alternating model into a non-alternating model by collapsing transitions. Observe also that the coin flipper of Figure 3 is a PA as well if we add dummy internal labels to the unlabeled arcs. This is the main idea behind the embedding functions of [37].

3.5 Generative Probabilistic Automata

The original definition of probabilistic automaton [35] was based on a more general notion of transition where not only the target state is determined by a probability measure, but also the action to be performed. In addition, it is also possible for a transition to deadlock with some probability. Although several concepts can be adapted to this general definition of probabilistic automaton, the main problem is that we are not aware yet of any meaningful definitions of composition that are conservative extensions of existing definitions in non probabilistic models. It is shown in [35] that several natural attempts break associativity of composition. A successful attempt is reported in [12] with the introduction of the *bundle* model. In this model a transition leads to a probability measure over sets of ordinary transitions and thus parallel composition can be defined easily. However, it is arguable whether this is really a conservative extension of ordinary automata or a faithful representation of generative systems. For example, in [5] it is argued that the bundle model is more expressive than generative probabilistic automata according to a classification that we describe in Section 5; however, we may also see a bundle system just as a special case of a probabilistic automaton in a similar way as we see the alternating models as special cases of probabilistic automata via embedding. This point of view is not investigated yet.

For the above reasons, as we do in this paper, it is now typical to use the term probabilistic automaton to refer to what in [35] is called a simple probabilistic automaton. Following the classification of [19] we could call the probabilistic automata of [35] probabilistic automata with *generative transitions* or generative probabilistic automata and the probabilistic automata of this paper, i.e., the simple probabilistic automata of [35], probabilistic automata with *reactive transitions* or reactive probabilistic automata.

3.6 Probabilistic I/O Automata

Following the style of [27], where the external actions of ordinary automata are partitioned into input and output actions, it is possible to introduce the input/output distinction on probabilistic automata as well. The advantage of this approach is that we can recover all the techniques used within I/O automata, including the task mechanisms used to describe fairness properties and the ability to use language inclusion to preserve fairness properties as well.

A probabilistic I/O automaton (PIOA) [10] is a probabilistic automaton whose external actions are partitioned into *input* and *output* actions such that for each state q and each input action a there is at least one transition labeled by a enabled from q (*input enabling* property). Output and internal actions are called *locally controlled* actions. Two PIOAs can be composed only if their locally controlled actions are disjoint. As a consequence, the external environment can never block any locally controlled action of a PIOA (the other automata may have the same action only as an input, which is always enabled), or, in other words, every PIOA is in full control of its locally controlled actions. We can say alternatively that each action is under the control of at most one component.

Another advantage of the input/output distinction is that it is possible to consider PIOAs with generative locally controlled transitions, and yet define a meaningful composition operator [40,35]. Indeed, the transitions of a composition can be obtained either by synchronizing input transitions, or by synchronizing a locally controlled transition of one component with appropriate input transitions of the other component.

The definition of PIOA of [40] does not include nondeterminism: each state enables exactly one reactive transition for each input action and possibly one generative transition with locally controlled actions. The nondeterminism that arises in a composition is resolved by assigning weights to each component and using relative weights as probabilities to solve conflicts determined by locally controlled transitions. It was observed later that this amounts to assuming that the locally controlled transitions of a component PIOA are performed with time delays governed by an exponential distribution whose delay parameter is the weight of the component. Thus, the PIOAs of [40] are special instances of the pure probabilistic models described later in Section 3.8.

3.7 Unlabeled Models

Probabilistic automata include labels; however, especially in the context of model checking, it is typical to consider unlabeled models and add structure to the states to define properties. For example, we could easily define probabilistic Kripke structures by removing labels from the transition relation of a PA and adding a labeling function that associates propositional symbols with states.

If we consider composition with synchronization between components, then synchronization occurs typically via shared variables. However, problems similar to those encountered with generative probabilistic automata arise if we do not impose any control structure on the values of the shared variables (e.g., the values of some variables are under the control of a single component). A successful attempt to solve the synchronization problem in unlabeled models appears in [13], where a probabilistic extension of reactive modules [1] is studied.

Example 5. Consider two unlabeled probabilistic automata $\mathcal{A}_1, \mathcal{A}_2$ whose states include a variable X. Suppose that $\mathcal{A}_1$ from its initial state flips a fair coin to set X either to 0 or 1, while $\mathcal{A}_2$ from its initial state flips a fair coin to set X either to 0 or 2. What transition should appear from the initial state of $\mathcal{A}_1 \| \mathcal{A}_2$? We have at least two choices: either we deadlock whenever the two automata set X in an incompatible way, and thus X is set to 0 with probability $1/4$ and the system deadlocks with probability $3/4$, or we consider only compatible choices and renormalize probabilities, and thus X is set to 0 with probability 1.

3.8 Pure Probabilistic Models

If we remove all nondeterminism and keep only probabilistic choices, then in the unlabeled case we obtain Markov processes, while in the labeled generative case we obtain Markov processes with actions. These models are used mainly for performance evaluation and are studied in the context of *stochastic process algebras* [20,24,6]. The underlying idea is that actions describe resources that are available with exponentially distributed delays, which means that there is a close correspondence between the delay parameter of the actions and their probability to occur. Each model manages actions in a slightly different way, but overall actions are partitioned into two sets. Actions from the first set occur according to some probability measures and describe the resources available, while actions from the second set are passive, and simply synchronize with actions from the first set. Passive actions describe the consumers of the resources. Thus some input/output distinction is present. Composition amounts to adding resources and users. If a resource cannot be used, then probabilities are renormalized.

A complete description of stochastic process algebras goes beyond the scope of this paper. Here we observe that composition of stochastic process algebras is not a conservative extensions of composition of ordinary automata and is not comparable with composition of probabilistic automata. A good understanding of the relationship between these models is still open.

We mention also the interesting approach to performance evaluation of Interactive Markov Chains [23]. In this case actions are immediate and time is described by explicit transitions with exponential delays. The advantage of this approach is that it is possible to keep nondeterminism in the model.

3.9 Models with Time

There is a vast literature on timed extension of probabilistic models. We have described before some ways to associate delays with actions and we refer the interested reader to a survey that appears in [7]. In the context of probabilistic automata one possibility to deal with time is by adding explicit time-passage transitions to the model and keep the underlying theory unchanged. This is done already in the work of Hansson and Jonsson [22] by discretizing time and representing the passage of a quantum of time via a "tick" action. Segala [35] considers a dense time domain and adds to probabilistic automata time-passage transitions labeled by the amount of time elapsed. However, in order to reuse the theory of probabilistic automata, schedulers can only be discrete.

A treatment of real-time with non-discrete measures poses non-trivial measurability problems that go beyond the scope of this paper. We refer the reader to [30,18] for an understanding of the problem on deterministic models and to [9] for an understanding of the problem in the presence of nondeterminism.

4 Simulations and Bisimulations

Simulation and bisimulation relations are attractive for their mathematical simplicity. They have been studied extensively in the context of probabilistic systems, including reactive systems [26], alternating models [21,32,2], and non alternating models [36,4]. The existing definitions are very different in style; however, as shown in [37], all the proposals end up being equivalent once we see the alternating models as special instances of probabilistic automata.

4.1 Lifting Relations

We start by lifting a relation on a set X to a relation on probability measures over X. This is useful since the target of a transition in a PA is a probability measure.

Let R be a relation on a set X. The *lifting* of R, denoted by $\mathcal{L}(R)$, is a relation on $\mathsf{Disc}(X)$ such that, $\mu_1\ \mathcal{L}(R)\ \mu_2$ iff for each upper closed set $C \subset X$, $\mu_1(C) \leq \mu_2(C)$, where the upper closure of a set C is the set $\{x \in X \mid \exists_{c \in C}, c\ R\ x\}$. This definition of lifting was first proposed in [16] in the context of non-discrete systems and is equivalent to an earlier proposal of [25,36] for discrete systems stating that $\mu_1\ \mathcal{L}(R)\ \mu_1'$ iff there exists a *weighting function* $w : Q \times Q \to [0,1]$ such that (1) $w(x_1, x_2) > 0$ implies $x_1\ R\ x_2$, (2) $\sum_{x_1} w(x_1, x_2) = \mu_2(x_2)$, and (3) $\sum_{x_2} w(x_1, x_2) = \mu_1(x_1)$. Informally, w redistributes probabilities between μ_1 and μ_2 respecting R. An important observation is that if R is an equivalence relation, then $\mu_1\ \mathcal{L}(R)\ \mu_2$ iff, for each equivalence class C of R, $\mu_1(C) = \mu_2(C)$.

4.2 Strong Simulations and Bisimulations

A *strong simulation* on a PA $\mathcal{A}$ is a relation R on Q such that, for each pair of states $(q_1, q_2) \in R$ and each transition (q_1, a, μ_1) of $\mathcal{A}$ there exists a transition (q_2, a, μ_2) of $\mathcal{A}$ such that $\mu_1\ \mathcal{L}(R)\ \mu_2$. If R is an equivalence relation, then we say that R is a *strong bisimulation.*

Sometimes it is more convenient to talk about simulation and bisimulation relations between two PAs $\mathcal{A}_1$ and $\mathcal{A}_2$. These definitions can be recovered from the definition above by considering the disjoint union of the states $Q_1 \uplus Q_2$, the union of the transition relations D_1, D_2, and requiring start states to be related.

If we apply the definition above to deterministic PAs, then we obtain the definition of bisimulation of [26], and similarly we obtain the definition of bisimulation of [21] if we consider strictly alternating PAs. There is also a definition of bisimulation for alternating PAs proposed in [32]. This definition, however, coincides with our definition above only if we transform an alternating automaton into a PA according to the construction of Example 4. Indeed, the definition of [32] was given by viewing alternation just as a formal artifact to describe PAs.

4.3 Strong Probabilistic Simulations and Bisimulations

Consider the two PAs of Figure 4. The two PAs are not bisimilar since the middle transition of $\mathcal{A}_2$ cannot be simulated by $\mathcal{A}_1$. On the other hand, the middle transition of $\mathcal{A}_2$ is just a convex combination of the other two transitions. If we are just interest in bounds to the probabilities of satisfying a property

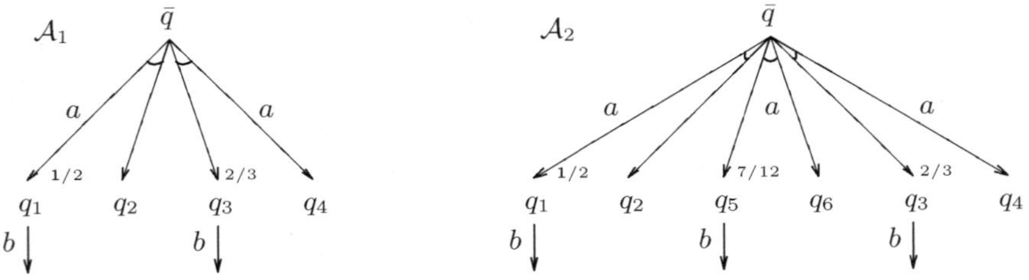

Fig. 4. Two PAs that are not strongly bisimilar

(say performing action *beep*), there should be no reason to distinguish $\mathcal{A}_1$ from $\mathcal{A}_2$. In [36] it is shown that $\mathcal{A}_1$ and $\mathcal{A}_2$ satisfy the same formulas of PCTL, a probabilistic temporal logic which indeed observes only bounds on probabilities, and thus it is argued that $\mathcal{A}_1$ and $\mathcal{A}_2$ should not be distinguished. This lead to the formulation of a *probabilistic* version of simulation and bisimulation relations, where transitions can be simulated by convex combinations of other transitions.

Let $\mathcal{A}$ be a probabilistic automaton, and let $\{(q, a, \mu_i)\}_I$ be a countable family of transitions of $\mathcal{A}$. Let $\{p_i\}_I$ be a family of probabilities such that $\sum_{i \in I} p_i = 1$. Then the triplet $(q, a, \sum_{i \in I} p_i \mu_i)$ is called a *combined transition* of $\mathcal{A}$.

A *strong probabilistic simulation* on a PA $\mathcal{A}$ is a relation R on Q such that, for each pair of states $(q_1, q_2) \in R$ and each transition (q_1, a, μ_1) of $\mathcal{A}$ there exists a combined transition (q_2, a, μ_2) of $\mathcal{A}$ such that $\mu_1 \; \mathcal{L}(R) \; \mu_2$. If R is an equivalence relation, then we say that R is a *strong probabilistic bisimulation.*

It turns out that in the alternating models strong bisimulation and strong probabilistic bisimulation coincide [37]. Thus, the distinction between the two kinds of bisimulation is relevant only for PAs.

Example 6. Observe that the ability to simulate a transition by convex combinations of transitions is lost in the alternating model, which is why strong and strong probabilistic bisimulation coincide. Indeed, if we transform the probabilistic automata of Figure 4 by splitting transitions, then they would not be bisimilar any more since the intermediate probabilistic state reached by the middle transition of $\mathcal{A}_2$ cannot be related to any state of the transformation of $\mathcal{A}_1$.

4.4 Weak Probabilistic Simulations and Bisimulations

The next step is to abstract from internal computation and extend weak simulations and bisimulations to PAs. The only interesting aspect is how to define a weak transition in the probabilistic case. On ordinary automata a weak transition is represented by a finite execution fragment whose trace consists of at most one external action. Here the trace of an execution fragment α, denoted by $\mathsf{trace}(\alpha)$, is the subsequence of external actions that occur in α. In the probabilistic case a weak transition is represented by a probabilistic execution fragment.

Let $\mathcal{A}$ be a probabilistic automaton, and let $\epsilon_{\sigma,q}$ be a probabilistic execution fragment of $\mathcal{A}$ generated by σ from state q. If $\epsilon_{\sigma,q}(\mathsf{Frags}^*(\mathcal{A})) = 1$ and there exists an action a such that $\mathsf{trace}(\epsilon_{\sigma,q}) = \mathsf{trace}(a)$, then we say that $(q, a, \mathsf{lstate}(\epsilon_{\sigma,q}))$ is a weak combined transition of $\mathcal{A}$. Here we have used implicitly the fact that functions trace and lstate are measurable.

A *weak probabilistic simulation* on a PA $\mathcal{A}$ is a relation R on Q such that, for each pair of states $(q_1, q_2) \in R$ and each transition (q_1, a, μ_1) of $\mathcal{A}$ there exists a weak combined transition (q_2, a, μ_2) of $\mathcal{A}$ such that $\mu_1 \; \mathcal{L}(R) \; \mu_2$. If R is an equivalence relation, then we say that R is a *weak probabilistic bisimulation.*

Since we have imposed no restrictions on the schedulers that generate weak transitions, we have defined directly the probabilistic versions of the weak relations. Indeed, it turns out that the non-probabilistic versions of the weak relations are not transitive [14]. A definition of weak bisimulation is proposed also for the alternating model [33] using deterministic schedulers. The definition uses conditional probability measures and is given in a very different style compared to this paper; however, our definition of weak probabilistic bisimulation restricted to the alternating model coincides with the definition of [32].

4.5 Other Kinds of Bisimulations

Bisimulation relations are studied extensively also in pure probabilistic models. The definitional style is very similar to ours and we refer the reader to [3] for an extensive comparative study. In particular in the absence of nondeterminism several relations coincide. There are also several variations of simulation and bisimulation relations in the literature, often proposed with specific applications in mind. Here we cite two important proposals.

In [36] there is a proposal for a probabilistic version of *branching bisimulation*, which is shown to preserve a weak version of PCTL. This definition is given in the same style of the previous subsections, except that some restrictions are imposed on the intermediate states of a weak transition, exactly as in the definition of branching bisimulation. A definition of branching bisimulation is also proposed in [2] for the alternating model. Once again, the definition of [36] coincides with the definition of [2] once restricted to the alternating model.

In [4] there is a proposal for a probabilistic version of *normed bisimulation* which has the advantage of being decidable efficiently. Indeed, strong bisimulations are decidable in polynomial time [8], while weak bisimulations are decidable in exponential time on probabilistic automata [8]. Interestingly, though, weak bisimulations are decidable in polynomial time in the alternating model [32] since the alternating structure ensures that two states are bisimilar iff for each action and each equivalence class the maximum probabilities of reaching the given class with the given action coincide. See [8] for more details.

5 Concluding Remarks

In this paper we have given an overview of the main operational models for probabilistic and nondeterministic systems. In doing so we have been forced to leave out other important approaches that the reader may want to investigate further. Within the field of domain theory and denotational semantics, several models have been proposed that combine probability and nondeterminism. The interested reader may start from [38,11] for more details. There has been also extensive research on probabilistic extensions of guarded command languages and their applications. The interested reader is referred to [28].

Our overview is given by taking probabilistic automata as reference model and viewing the others as special cases or generalizations. There are also other ways to classify models. In particular [5] proposes a hierarchy where a model is more expressive than another one if it is possible to transform objects of the least expressive model into objects of the other model so that bisimilarity is preserved and reflected. The transformations should preserve states; thus, for example, the transformations of [37] are not acceptable since they add or remove probabilistic states. Indeed, the alternating and non-alternating models are incomparable according to [5].

We have omitted here any reference to process algebras, axiomatizations and logical characterizations for probabilistic models. For process algebras the reader may look at [31] and references therein, while for logical characterizations the reader may look at [26,17]. The work in [17] is carried out in the context of alternating non-discrete systems and improves the results of [26].

References

1. R. Alur and T. Henzinger. Reactive modules. *Formal Methods in System Design* 15(1):7–48, 1999.
2. S. Andova, T. Willemse. Branching bisimulation for probabilistic systems: characteristics and decidability. *Theoretical Computer Science*, 356(3):325–355, 2006.
3. C. Baier, H. Hermanns, J-P.Katoen, and V. Wolf. Comparative branching-time semantics for markov chains. In *Proceedings of CONCUR 2003*, LNCS 2761, 2003.
4. C. Baier and M. Stoelinga. Norm functions for bisimulations with delays. In *Proceedings of FOSSACS*, LNCS 1784, pages 407–418, 2000.
5. F. Bartels, A. Sokolova, and E. de Vink. A hierarchy of probabilistic system types. *Theoretical Computer Science*, 327(1-2):3–22, 2004.
6. M. Bernardo and R. Gorrieri. Extended markovian process algebra. In [29].
7. M. Bravetti and P.R. D'Argenio. Tutte le algebre insieme: concepts, discussions and relations of stochastic process algebras with general distributions. In *Validation of Stochastic Systems*, LNCS 2925, pages 44–88, 2004.
8. S. Cattani and R. Segala. Decision algorithms for probabilistic bisimulation. In *Proceedings of CONCUR*, LNCS 2421, pages 371–385, 2002.
9. S. Cattani, R. Segala, M. Kwiatkowska, and G. Norman. Stochastic transition systems for continuous state spaces and non-determinism. In *Proceedings of FOSSACS*, LNCS 3441, pages 125–139, 2005.
10. L. Cheung, N. Lynch, R. Segala, and F. Vaandrager. Switched probabilistic I/O automata. In *Proceedings of ICTAC*, LNCS 3407, pages 494–510, 2004.
11. V. Daniele and G. Winskel. Distributing probability over non-determinism. *Mathematical Structures in Computer Science*, 16:87–113, 2006.
12. P. D'Argenio, H. Hermanns, and J.P. Katoen. On generative parallel composition. In *Proceedings of PROBMIV'98*, ENTCS 22, 1999.
13. L. de Alfaro, T.A. Henzinger, and R. Jhala. Compositional methods for probabilistic systems. In *Proceedings of CONCUR*, LNCS 2154, 2001.
14. Y. Deng. *Axiomatisations and types for probabilistic and mobile processes.* PhD thesis, Ecole de Mines, 2005.
15. C. Derman. *Finite State Markovian Decision Processes.* Academic Press, 1970.
16. J. Desharnais. *Labelled Markov Processes.* PhD thesis, McGill University, 1999.
17. J. Desharnais, A. Edalat, and P. Panangaden. A logical characterization of bisimulation for labelled Markov processes. In *Proceedings of LICS*, 1998.
18. J. Desharnais, A. Edalat, and P. Panangaden. Bisimulation for labelled Markov processes. *Information and Computation*, 179(2):163–193, 2002.
19. R. van Glabbeek, S. Smolka, B. Steffen. Reactive, generative, and stratified models of probabilistic processes. *Information and Computation*, 121(1):59–80, 1996.

20. N. Götz, U. Herzog, and M. Rettelbach. Multiprocessor and distributed system design: the integration of functional specification and performance analysis using stochastic process algebras. In *Performance Evaluation of Computer and Communication Systems. Joint Tutorial Papers of Performance '93 and Sigmetrics '93*, LNCS 729, pages 121–146, 1993.
21. H. Hansson. *Time and Probability in Formal Design of Distributed Systems*, volume 1 of *Real-Time Safety Critical Systems*. Elsevier, 1994.
22. H. Hansson and B. Jonsson. A calculus for communicating systems with time and probabilities. In *Proceedings of RTSS*, 1990.
23. H. Hermanns. *Interactive Markov Chains: The Quest for Quantified Quality*, LNCS 2428, 2002.
24. J. Hillston. *A Compositional Approach to Performance Modeling*. PhD thesis, Department of Computer Science, University of Edimburgh (UK), 1994.
25. B. Jonsson and K.G. Larsen. Specification and refinement of probabilistic processes. In *Proceedings of LICS*, pages 266–277, July 1991.
26. N.A. Lynch and E.W. Stark. A proof of the Kahn principle for Input/Output automata. *Information and Computation*, 82(1):81–92, 1989.
27. N.A. Lynch and M.R. Tuttle. Hierarchical correctness proofs for distributed algorithms. In *Proceedings of PoDC*, pages 137–151, 1987.
28. A. McIver and C. Morgan. *Abstraction, refinement, and proof for probabilistic systems*. Springer-Verlag, 2005.
29. U. Montanari and V. Sassone, editors. *Proceedings of CONCUR*, LNCS 1119, 1996.
30. P. Panangaden. Measure and probability for concurrency theorists. *Theoretical Computer Science*, 253(2):287–309, 2001.
31. A. Parma and R. Segala. Axiomatization of trace semantics for stochastic nondeterministic processes. In *Proceedings of QEST*, pages 294–303, 2004.
32. A. Philippou, I. Lee, and O. Sokolsky. Weak bisimulation for probabilistic systems. In *Proceedings of CONCUR 2000*, LNCS 1877, pages 334–349, 2000.
33. A. Pogosyants, R. Segala, and N. Lynch. Verification of the randomized consensus algorithm of Aspnes and Herlihy: a case study. *Distrib. Comp.* 13:155–186, 2000.
34. M.O. Rabin. Probabilistic automata. *Information and Control*, 6:230–245, 1963.
35. R. Segala. *Modeling and Verification of Randomized Distributed Real-Time Systems*. PhD thesis, MIT, 1995.
36. R. Segala and N.A. Lynch. Probabilistic simulations for probabilistic processes. *Nordic Journal of Computing*, 2(2):250–273, 1995.
37. R. Segala and A. Turrini. Comparative analysis of bisimulation relations on alternating and non-alternating probabilistic models. In *Proceedings of QEST*, 2005.
38. R. Tix, K. Keimel, and G. Plotkin. Semantic domains for combining probability and non-determinism. ENTCS 129:1–104, 2005.
39. M.Y. Vardi. Automatic verification of probabilistic concurrent finite-state programs. In *Proceedings of FoCS*, pages 327–338, 1985.
40. S.H. Wu, S. Smolka, and E.W. Stark. Composition and behaviors of probabilistic I/O automata. *Theoretical Computer Science*, 176(1-2):1–38, 1999.

A Livelock Freedom Analysis for Infinite State Asynchronous Reactive Systems

Stefan Leue, Alin Ştefănescu, and Wei Wei

Department of Computer and Information Science
University of Konstanz
D-78457 Konstanz, Germany
{Stefan.Leue, Alin.Stefanescu, Wei.Wei}@uni-konstanz.de

Abstract. We describe an incomplete but sound and efficient livelock freedom test for infinite state asynchronous reactive systems. The method abstracts a system into a set of simple control flow cycles labeled with their message passing effects. From these cycles, it constructs a homogeneous integer programming problem (IP) encoding a necessary condition for the existence of livelock runs. Livelock freedom is assured by the infeasibility of the generated homogeneous IP, which can be checked in polynomial time. In the case that livelock freedom cannot be proved, the method proposes a counterexample given as a set of cycles. We apply an automated cycle dependency analysis to counterexamples to check their spuriousness and to refine the abstraction. We illustrate the application of the method to Promela models using our prototype implementation named *aLive*.

1 Introduction

The main characteristic of a concurrent reactive system [17] is that of maintaining an ongoing activity of exchanging and processing information. One salient property that any reactive system must satisfy is deadlock freedom, i.e., the execution of the system is non-blocking. However, a system may be free of deadlock and yet it does no progress in executing its tasks. Such a situation is referred to as livelock. Freedom from livelock is highly desirable as it is important to ensure that the execution of a system is not only continuous but also meaningful.

Explicit state model checking techniques are mostly used to verify livelock freedom for finite state systems [4,11,9]. However, these techniques suffer from the state explosion problem especially when applied to asynchronous concurrent systems. Such systems usually possess a large global state space due to the combinatorial interleaving of the executions of local processes. On the contrary, integer programming (IP) based verification techniques do not rely on the enumeration of global states and thus avoid the state explosion problem. However, the existing IP based techniques focus on the analysis of synchronous systems.

In this paper we propose an incomplete analysis method for livelock freedom of asynchronous reactive systems, relying on the observation that control flow cycles play a central rôle in the setting of reactive systems with a "forever run" behavior. We consider asynchronous message-passing as the underlying communication paradigm of the systems that we analyze. The livelock freedom test is

C. Baier and H. Hermanns (Eds.): CONCUR 2006, LNCS 4137, pp. 79–94, 2006.

reduced to the solving of a homogeneous integer programming problem, which can be done in polynomial time. In case the incomplete analysis method that we propose cannot establish livelock freedom we use a heuristic abstraction refinement method to improve the accuracy of our analysis. Since the size of the communication channels is not relevant to the analysis, we can assume they are infinite, meaning that our method can verify infinite state systems that cannot be addressed via an explicit state space exploration.

The paper is structured as follows. Section 2 introduces the running example described in Promela. Section 3 properly defines the livelock freedom problem, while Section 4 presents the core idea of checking livelock freedom using integer programming solving. Section 5 gives the refinement procedure. We conclude with experimental results, related work, conclusions and future work.

2 Promela

We briefly introduce the *Promela* modeling language for concurrent systems and present the running example of this paper.

Promela is the input language of the *SPIN* explicit state model checker [11]. It has been successfully used for the modeling and analysis of many concurrent systems [12,4]. The Promela language supports asynchronous communication as well as synchronous rendez-vous communication and synchronization via shared variables. In the scope of this paper, we concentrate on asynchronous communication and exclude the use of any other types of communication that Promela offers.

```
mtype = {req, ack, rel};

chan c_s[2] = [1] of {mtype};
chan s_c[2] = [1] of {mtype};

proctype client(int index) {
  do
  :: c_s[index]!req;
     s_c[index]?ack ->
        // do some computation here
       c_s[index]!rel;

  od;
}
```

```
proctype server() {
  do
  :: c_s[0]?req -> s_c[0]!ack; c_s[0]?rel;
  :: c_s[1]?req -> s_c[1]!ack; c_s[1]?rel;
  od
}

init {
  run server();
  atomic {
    run client(0); run client(1);
  }
}
```

Fig. 1. The running example in Promela

Figure 1 shows a simple Promela model that will be used throughout the paper as a running example. The model consists of two instances of the *client* process type and one instance of the *server* process type. Each client *client[i]* exchanges messages with the server over two exclusive communication buffers *c_s[i]* and *s_c[i]*. The types of exchanged messages are defined as elements of the special enumeration type *mtype*. Each client performs a loop: it first sends a resource request (`req`) to the server; after it receives an acknowledgment (`ack`) from the server, it performs some local computation and then sends back a resource release notification (`rel`). The server can accept only one request at a time, and it chooses nondeterministically a request to handle.

The choice of the Promela language in the context of this paper is motivated by reasons of convenience. Promela possesses the salient features of most asynchronous concurrent system models, and a large number of models are publicly available. However, Promela was designed to be used for finite state verification and hence possesses some language features to ensure this property, such as limiting data to finite domains and requiring message buffers to have finite capacity. However, our livelock freedom analysis is applicable to both finite and infinite state systems which is why we simply ignore the respective Promela constructs. To facilitate our analysis we also assume that it is known at compile time how many Promela processes of which type will be instantiated at run time. In Section 4.3 we show that the soundness of our analysis does not rely on specifics of the Promela language, which is why we put forward that its application to other modeling and programming languages for asynchronous concurrent systems can easily be accomplished.

3 Livelock Freedom

Livelock has been defined variously in different contexts [10]. For concurrent systems, livelock often means "individual starvation": a process is prevented from performing some particular actions [17]. These actions are normally intended to make progress, deliver outputs, or respond to the environment and other peer processes. We call such an action a *progress action*. In the running example, a progress action of a client is to do the local computation after it receives an acknowledgment. In this paper we follow this meaning of livelock and give its definition in the setting of reactive systems.

We define that a *livelock* for a reactive system is an infinite run in which only non-progress actions are executed after a certain point of the run, i.e., all the progress actions are repeated only a finite number of times. If a reactive system has no livelock runs, then it is *livelock free*.

Both livelock and deadlock result in a lack of progress in the system. They are sometimes not distinguishable from a practical point of view. However, these two concepts are used to refer to two different sources of non-progress. Furthermore, from a formal point of view, they belong to two different types of properties: deadlock freedom is a safety property while livelock freedom is a liveness property. As a consequence, the techniques used to check these two properties are radically different. That is why we make a clear distinction of deadlock and livelock in our definition: a finite run, in particular a deadlocked run, is not a livelock run. In our analysis, we focus on checking the absence of livelock and ignore the existence of deadlocks: if a system is proved to be livelock free using our method, it may still have deadlocks.

The SPIN model checker distinguishes in a similar fashion between deadlock and livelock [11]. In Promela models, "progress" labels are attached to progress actions. SPIN then checks livelock freedom by checking the absence of non-progress global cycles by a nested depth first search in the global state space. However, such a state enumeration approach suffers from the state explosion problem and can only deal with finite state systems.

In this paper we will cover infinite state systems with unbounded communication buffers. A standard modeling framework for such systems are *communicating finite state machines* (CFSM) [22,1], which also serves as one intermediate abstraction level in our method. However, we can prove that the livelock freedom is undecidable for CFSM, using a simple reduction from the following problem proved to be undecidable in [1]:

Executability of a message reception in a CFSM system:

Instance: A CFSM M and a local state s of M having an outgoing edge labeled by the receive action '$?a$'

Question: Does there exist a run of M such that the message reception '$?a$' is executed in state s?

The reduction is as follows. Given M, s, and $?a$ as above, we construct another CFSM M' such that M' enters in a livelock after the reception '$?a$'. More precisely, M' is obtained from M by replacing the outgoing edge from s labeled by $?a$, with another edge also labeled by $?a$ but going to a new local state s_L that has a self-loop labeled by $!a_L$. Moreover, we add to M' a new state machine with a single state s'_L with a self-loop labeled by $?a_L$. In M' we set all actions except $!a_L$ and $?a_L$ as progress actions.

It is now easy to see that the reception $?a$ is executed in state s of M if and only if M' has a livelock run: For the direct implication, let r be a finite run of M in which $?a$ in state s is executed only once as the last step. Then, we can simulate the same run r in M' and reach the local state s_L. At this point we obtain a livelock by infinitely executing alternations of $!a_L$ and $?a_L$ which are the only non-progress actions of M'. For the reverse implication, if M' contains a livelock, this necessarily involves the sending of a_L messages, but it is possible only if state s_L is reached, which implies that the reception $?a$ is executable in s in M'. From the construction of M' upon M, we can find a run in M such that $?a$ is executed in s. □

4 Livelock Freedom Analysis

We propose an incomplete but sound method to prove livelock freedom for asynchronous reactive systems based on integer programming solving. The incompleteness follows from the undecidability of livelock freedom as proved above.

We outline the method as follows. Given a reactive system and a set of progress actions, we first carry out a series of abstractions that transforms the system into a set of independent control flow cycles labeled with their message passing effects. A cycle is a *progress cycle* if it contains one of the progress actions, and we identify the set of all the local progress cycles in the system. We give a *necessary condition* which ensures the existence of a livelock run, i.e., an infinite run in which all the progress cycles are repeated only a finite number of times. We translate this condition into a homogeneous *integer programming problem* (IP). If the resulting IP problem has no solution then the necessary condition cannot hold, which implies livelock freedom. On the other hand, if the resulting IP has solutions then the system may or may not be livelock free, which corresponds to the incomplete side of our test.

4.1 Abstraction

In asynchronous reactive systems, concurrent processes coordinate their actions by exchanging messages. Thus, the message passing behavior is a major factor to decide how cycles in the control flow are executed. This observation underlies the conservative abstraction approach sketched below for our livelock freedom analysis. The same abstraction steps were also used in our previous work on buffer boundedness analysis, which are detailed in [14,13]. In particular [13] deals with specifics of abstracting Promela models.

Code Abstraction. Given the program code of a reactive system we first abstract from variables, operations on data, the testing of conditions, etc., and retain only the finite control structure and the message passing behaviour of all processes. The resulting system is a CFSM system.

Message Orders. In the next step, we abstract from the order of messages in all communication buffers. We use an integer vector to represent how many messages of a certain type are currently stored in each buffer. In the running example, an integer vector $< 1, 0, 3, 2, 4, 6 >$ denotes that there is 1 *req* message in the buffer *c_s[0]*, no *ack* message in *s_c[0]*, 3 *rel* messages in *c_s[0]*, 2 *req* messages in *c_s[1]*, 4 *ack* messages in *s_c[1]*, and 6 *rel* messages in *c_s[1]*. We also use an integer vector, called an *effect vector*, to denote the message passing effect of a transition. A positive component in an effect vector corresponds to message sending, and a negative component corresponds to message consumption.

Activation Conditions and Dependencies of Control Flow Cycles. In this step, we assume that (1) any control flow cycle can be reached from the initial configuration of the system and that (2) the executions of these cycles are totally independent from one another. We detect all the local control flow cycles in each process of the system. We consider only simple cycles, i.e., cycles that cannot be decomposed into smaller cycles. For each cycle, we compute the sum of the effect vectors of all the transitions along the cycle. The resulting system is a set of independent control flow cycles with their effect vectors. In the running example, there are 4 cycles: one from the process *client[0]*, one from *client[1]*, and two from *server* given as the two nondeterministic choices within the `do` loop. Their effect vectors are respectively $< -1, 1, -1, 0, 0, 0 >$, $< 0, 0, 0, -1, 1, -1 >$, $< 1, -1, 1, 0, 0, 0 >$, and $< 0, 0, 0, 1, -1, 1 >$.

4.2 Determining Livelock Freedom

A reactive system is livelock free if at least one progress cycle can be repeated infinitely often in any infinite run. Let $C_1, \ldots, C_n$ be the set of control flow cycles that we collect from the system, and $C_{j_1}, \ldots, C_{j_m}$ ($j_1, \ldots, j_m \in \{1, \ldots, n\}$) be the set of progress cycles. We use c_i to denote the effect vector of a cycle C_i. We use the following IP problem to characterize a necessary condition for the existence of a livelock run, i.e., an infinite run in which any progress cycle can be repeated only a finite number of times.

$$x_1 c_1 + \ldots + x_n c_n \geq \bar{0} \quad (1) \qquad x_{j_1} + \ldots + x_{j_m} = 0 \quad (3)$$

$$x_1 + \ldots + x_n > 0 \quad (2) \qquad x_i \geq 0 \quad \text{for all } i \quad (4)$$

In the above inequalities, we assign an integer variable x_i to each cycle C_i to denote the number of times that it is repeated in a finite segment of a run. These variables may have only non-negative values as imposed by the inequalities 4. A particular assignment to all x_i's represents a *linear combination of cycle executions*. The inequality 1 states that the *overall* effect of a linear combination of cycle executions does not consume any messages. Thus, an infinite exclusive repetition of such a linear combination is possible since it does not run out of any type of messages. The inequality 2 excludes a trivial combination in which no cycle is executed at all. The inequalities 1 and 2 give a necessary condition for the existence of infinite runs. The inequality 3 then excludes any progress cycle C_{j_i} from a linear combination. Consequently, this condition excludes any progress cycle from being repeated infinitely often in any infinite run. The arguments in Section 4.3 ensure that the IP problem defined by the inequalities 1–4 gives indeed a necessary condition for the existence of livelock runs.

If the IP problem has no solutions, then the necessary condition cannot hold. In such a case, at least one progress cycle C_{j_i} has to be repeated infinitely often in any infinite run. This proves livelock freedom for the system. On the other hand, if the IP problem has solutions, then we do not know whether the system is livelock free since the IP problem gives a necessary but not sufficient livelock existence condition.

In the running example, let the only progress action be the local computation of one client, say *client[0]*. We use x_1 to correspond to the cycle in *client[0]*, x_2 to the cycle in *client[1]*, and x_3 and x_4 to the two cycles given as the two non-determinstic choices within the `do` loop in *server*. The resulting livelock freedom determination IP problem is given as below.

$$-x_1 + x_3 \geq 0 \quad (5) \qquad x_2 - x_4 \geq 0 \quad (9)$$

$$x_1 - x_3 \geq 0 \quad (6) \qquad -x_2 + x_4 \geq 0 \quad (10)$$

$$-x_1 + x_3 \geq 0 \quad (7) \qquad x_1 + x_2 + x_3 + x_4 > 0 \quad (11)$$

$$-x_2 + x_4 \geq 0 \quad (8) \qquad x_1 = 0 \quad (12)$$

$$x_1, x_2, x_3, x_4 \geq 0 \quad (13)$$

The inequalities 5–10 restrict the aggregate effect vector of a linear combination to be positive[1]. The inequality 11 excludes an all-zero combination. The inequality 12 excludes the only progress cycle in *client[0]*. There is one solution

[1] A vector is positive if all its components are non-negative.

satisfying these inequalities: $x_2 = x_4 = 1$ while assigning 0 to all other variables. As a consequence we cannot prove livelock freedom for the running example. However, we can construct a *counterexample* from the above obtained solution as a collection of cycles whose variable receives a nonzero value in the solution. A manual check of the counterexample reveals a real livelock scenario in which the server decides to accept only requests from *client[1]*. Note that due to the overapproximating abstractions that we use, a counterexample corresponds not always to a valid execution of the system. In such a case, the counterexample is called *spurious*. An automated method to determine spurious counterexamples will be discussed in depth in Section 5.

To eliminate the source of livelock that we uncovered above, we modify the model by removing the nondeterministic behavior of the server. We fix an order in which the server alternatively handles requests from the two clients as follows:

```
proctype server() {
  do
  :: c_s[0]?req -> s_c[0]!ack; c_s[0]?rel;
     c_s[1]?req -> s_c[1]!ack; c_s[1]?rel;
  od
}
```

The resulting IP problem for the revised model, given below, has no solutions, which implies livelock freedom.

$$-x_1 + x_3 \geq 0 \quad (14)$$
$$x_1 - x_3 \geq 0 \quad (15)$$
$$-x_1 + x_3 \geq 0 \quad (16)$$
$$-x_2 + x_3 \geq 0 \quad (17)$$
$$x_2 - x_3 \geq 0 \quad (18)$$
$$-x_2 + x_3 \geq 0 \quad (19)$$
$$x_1 + x_2 + x_3 > 0 \quad (20)$$
$$x_1 = 0 \quad (21)$$
$$x_1, x_2, x_3 \geq 0 \quad (22)$$

Complexity of the Livelock Freedom Test. Given a reactive system, the size of the constructed IP problem is linear in the number of message types and in the number of simple local control flow cycles. The number of simple cycles may be exponential in the size of the control flow graph. However, in practice the control flow graph extracted from the Promela code of a process is sparse, and we observed that the number of simple cycles is usually polynomial.

Furthermore, the IP problem that our method constructs is homogeneous, i.e., the right hand side of each inequality in the problem is 0. This homogeneous IP problem can be solved in polynomial time as follows. We solve the linear programming version of the IP problem to obtain a rational solution. This can be done in polynomial time [19]. If we obtain a rational solution, we can easily construct an integer solution by multiplying each component in the rational solution by the least common denominator of all the components.

4.3 Soundness Proof

The soundness proof of our method relies on the following preliminary lemma and proposition. In the following we denote by $[i..j]$ the set $\{i, \ldots, j\}$ (for $i \leq j$) and by $\bar{x}$ the n-dimensional integer vector $(x_1, \ldots, x_n) \in \mathbb{Z}^n$. For two n-dimensional vectors, we have $\bar{x} \leq \bar{y}$ iff $x_i \leq y_i$, for all $i \in [1..n]$. Moreover, $\bar{x} < \bar{y}$ iff $\bar{x} \leq \bar{y}$ and there exists $i \in [1..n]$ with $x_i < y_i$.

Lemma 1. *Let $\{\bar{c}_0, \ldots, \bar{c}_n\}$ be $n+1$ vectors of dimension m (with $n, m \geq 1$), i.e., $\bar{c}_i := (c_{i1}, \ldots, c_{im})$ for all $i \in [0..n]$. Then, if the following system of linear inequations has no integer solutions*

$$x_1\bar{c}_1 + \ldots + x_n\bar{c}_n \geq \bar{0} \tag{23}$$

$$x_1 + \ldots + x_n > 0 \tag{24}$$

$$x_i \geq 0 \quad \textit{for all } i \tag{25}$$

then, there exists an upper bound B such that for all integer solutions of

$$\bar{c}_0 + x_1\bar{c}_1 + \ldots + x_n\bar{c}_n \geq \bar{0} \tag{26}$$

$$x_1 + \ldots + x_n > 0 \tag{27}$$

$$x_i \geq 0 \quad \textit{for all } i \tag{28}$$

and any $k \in [1..m]$,

$$c_{0k} + x_1c_{1k} + \ldots + x_nc_{nk} \leq B.$$

Proof. Defining for each $k \in [1..m]$ a function $f_k : \mathbb{Z}^n \rightarrow \mathbb{Z}$ as $f_k(x_1, \ldots, x_n) := x_1c_{1k} + \ldots + x_nc_{nk}$, we will prove that f_k is bounded for any $k \in [1..m]$ on the domain of integer solutions of (26)–(28).

By contradiction, assume that there exists a $k \in [1..m]$ such that f_k is unbounded. This implies that there exists an infinite sequence $\{\bar{x}^i\}_{i\geq 1}$ of integer solutions of (26)–(28) such that $\lim_{i\rightarrow\infty} f_k(\bar{x}^i) = +\infty$ (the limit cannot be $-\infty$ because of (26)).

We first show that without loss of generality, we can assume that the sequence $\{\bar{x}^i\}_{i\geq 1}$ has the property that

$$\text{for any } i < j : \quad \bar{x}^i < \bar{x}^j \text{ and } f_k(\bar{x}^i) < f_k(\bar{x}^j) \tag{29}$$

This can be proved using standard mathematical analysis techniques as follows. Since $\lim_{i\rightarrow\infty} f_k(\bar{x}^i) = +\infty$, we can select an infinite subsequence $\{\bar{y}^i\}_{i\geq 1}$ of $\{\bar{x}^i\}_{i\geq 1}$ such that $\{f_k(\bar{y}^i)\}_{i\geq 1}$ is strictly increasing. Moreover, we can select $\{\bar{y}^i\}_{i\geq 1}$ to be also strictly increasing. This is possible because $\{\bar{y}^i\}_{i\geq 1}$ is on one hand bounded from below by $\bar{0}$ following (28), while on the other hand is an infinite sequence taking f_k to $+\infty$. In the following, we replace $\{\bar{x}^i\}_{i\geq 1}$ by $\{\bar{y}^i\}_{i\geq 1}$ (for the sake of consistency with the notation in (29)).

Next, we observe the behavior of the increasing sequence $\{\bar{x}^i\}_{i\geq 1}$ on the other functions $f_{k'}$, for $k' \neq k$. We have the following two possibilities for each $k' \in [1..m] \setminus \{k\}$:

- $\{f_{k'}(\bar{x}^i)\}_{i\geq 1}$ is bounded: In this case, since $\{f_{k'}(\bar{x}^i)\}_{i\geq 1}$ is also infinite, there exists an infinite increasing subsequence $\{\bar{y}^i\}_{i\geq 1}$ of $\{\bar{x}^i\}_{i\geq 1}$ such that $f_{k'}(\bar{y}^i) = f_{k'}(\bar{y}^j)$, for any $i, j \geq 1$.

– $\{f_{k'}(\bar{x}^i)\}_{i\geq 1}$ is unbounded: Because of (26), $\{f_{k'}(\bar{x}^i)\}_{i\geq 1}$ is bounded from below (by $-c_{0k}$), so necessarily there exists an infinite increasing subsequence $\{\bar{y}^i\}_{i\geq 1}$ of $\{\bar{x}^i\}_{i\geq 1}$ such that $f_{k'}(\bar{y}^i) < f_{k'}(\bar{y}^j)$, for any $i < j$ (similar to (29)).

From (29) and the above case analysis applied stepwise for each k', it is easy to see that there exists an infinite strictly increasing sequence $\{\bar{y}^i\}_{i\geq 1}$ (whose elements are solutions of (26)–(28)) such that $f_k(\bar{y}^i) \leq f_k(\bar{y}^j)$, for any $k \in [1..m]$, and $i < j$.

Finally, let us fix two indices $i < j$ (from $[1..m]$). Then, for all $k \in [1..m]$ we have $f_k(\bar{y}^i) \leq f_k(\bar{y}^j)$, which implies $f_k(\bar{y}^j) - f_k(\bar{y}^i) \geq 0$. But since all the functions f_k are linear, we have that $f_k(\bar{y}^j - \bar{y}^i) \geq 0$ (*). Moreover, since $\{\bar{y}^i\}_{i\geq 1}$ is strictly increasing, $\bar{y}^j - \bar{y}^i > \bar{0}$ (**). Slightly rewriting (*) and (**), we obtain that $\bar{y}^j - \bar{y}^i$ is a solution to the system of inequations (23)–(25), which is a contradiction with the hypothesis of the lemma. □

Proposition 1. *Let S be a CFSM system and C a subset of control flow cycles in S. Suppose that there exists no positive linear combination of effect vectors of cycles in C. Then, for any infinite execution in which only cycles in C are executed, the number of messages in all the communication buffers is always bounded.*

Proof. Given a CFSM and a subset of control flow cycles $C = \{C_1, \ldots, C_n\}$, we consider $\bar{c}_i$ as the effect vector of cycle C_i for each $i \in [1..n]$. Moreover, let $\bar{c}_0$ be an upper bound for all the effect vectors of the all acyclic paths of the CFSM.

First, since there exists *no positive* linear combination of effect vectors of cycles in C (from the hypothesis of Proposition 1), the hypothesis of Lemma 1 is satisfied, which implies that there is a global upper bound for $\bar{c}_0+x_1\bar{c}_1+\ldots+x_n\bar{c}_n$ for any fixed $\bar{c}_0$ and $\bar{x} := (x_1, \ldots, x_n)$. This means that there is an upper bound B on all the message buffers for all executions consisting of an acyclic path followed by a *linear combination* of simple cycles.

Secondly, suppose now by contradiction that there exists a run of the CFSM that strictly exceeds the bound B in one of the buffers and let us denote by r a finite run that increases the number of messages in one of the buffers to $B + 1$. Since r is necessarily composed of an acyclic path and a finite number of simple cycles (seen as a linear combination of cycles), the effect of r on the message buffers is bounded by B (according to the above application of Lemma 1), but this contradicts the previous assumption on r being able to fill $B + 1$ messages on one of the buffers. □

Theorem 1 (Soundness). *If we prove livelock freedom for a reactive system using the method described in Subsection 4.2, then the system is indeed livelock free.*

Proof. Consider a reactive system for which we use our method to prove livelock freedom. The first abstraction step constructs a CFSM from the original system in a conservative way in that it preserves the existence of livelock runs. Thus, if the CFSM is livelock free, then the original system is also livelock free.

Assume that the reactive system is proved to be livelock free. Then, in the corresponding CFSM there exists no positive linear combination of effect vectors of non-progress cycles (as there is no solution to the corresponding IP problem described by the inequalities 1–4). By Proposition 1, taking C to be the set of all non-progress cycles, we obtain that the number of messages in each communication buffer is bounded if only non-progress cycles are executed.

We prove that the CFSM is livelock free, which implies livelock freedom for the original system. We assume *by contradiction* that the CFSM has a livelock run r. In r all the progress cycles are repeated only a finite number of times. Then, there exists a particular point of time t in r after which only non-progress cycles are executed. As discussed above, following Proposition 1, the number of messages in each communication buffer must always be bounded after t in r. Note that any state machine in the CFSM has only finitely many local states. Thus, there will be only finitely many reachable configurations of the CFSM after t in r. Furthermore, since r is an infinite run, there must be two distinct points of time t' and t'' after t at which the CFSM reaches one same configuration. The finite segment of execution between t' and t'' can be represented as a linear combination of executions of non-progress cycles. The aggregate effect vector of this segment is however an all-zero vector. This contradicts the previous claim that no linear combination of effect vectors of non-progress cycles is positive. □

Note that the above proof does not use any assumption about buffer lengths. Consequently, if a system with unbounded buffers is proved to be livelock free, then the same system with bounded buffers of predefined lengths is also livelock free.

5 Counterexample-Based Refinements

The abstractions described in the previous section reduce the accuracy of the analysis, and our method may propose spurious counterexamples. We observed that the introducing of spurious counterexamples is often caused by the abstraction from those conditional statements that determine the repeatability of control flow cycles. As we will show later, such conditionals enforce dependencies among cycles that have been lost during the abstractions. In [15] we have proposed a counterexample-based refinement technique based on re-discovering local dependencies among the cycles of a same process. This technique can be adopted to the livelock freedom analysis in this paper and will be illustrated on a simple example. We will also present an improvement to the determination of cycle dependencies in [15] that is more efficient and precise in practice. We mention that all the techniques used in the refinement procedure are conservative with respect to livelock freedom.

Cycle Dependency Analysis. The details of the cycle dependency analysis can be found in [15]. Here we only illustrate the basic idea of the technique on a simple example. Figure 2 shows the control flow graph of a process in a reactive system. It contains four cycles C_1, C_2, C_3 and C_4. Suppose that none of them is a progress cycle and that the integer variable x is local. C_1 is enabled when

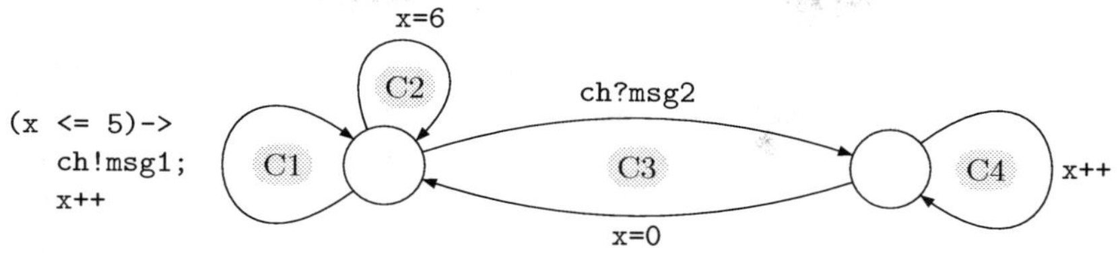

Fig. 2. Running example of Section 5

the value of x is no larger than 5. When executed, it sends a message `msg1` and increments the value of x by 1. C_1 leads to a spurious counterexample because the condition $x \leq 5$ is omitted during the abstraction, i.e., in the abstraction it is assumed that C_1 can be executed forever without interruption. To exclude this spurious counterexample, we perform the following cycle dependency analysis.

- We first determine that C_1 can be repeated without interruption at most 5 times before the condition $x \leq 5$ turns false. However, the determination of the maximal number of times that a cycle iterates relies on a termination decision which is undecidable. We recently proposed an incomplete automated termination proving technique [16] that can be easily extended to estimate cycle iteration counts, complementing the approach described in [15].
- We determine two sets of cycles that C_1 depends on. One set consists of all C_1's *neighbors*, i.e., cycles that share some common states with C_1. In our example the neighbors are C_2 and C_3. Another set of cycles that we determine consists of all the so-called *supplementary cycles* that, intuitively speaking, exert a positive effect to enable the execution of C_1 again, i.e., to render the condition $x \leq 5$ to become true. As can be easily seen, C_1 has only one such supplementary cycle which is C_3. However, in general it is hard to determine the exact set of supplementary cycles for a given cycle. Later in this section we will propose a so-called "next door" strategy that can be used to determine supplementary cycles more efficiently and precisely in practice.
- The following cycle dependencies can be determined from the above analysis: every 5 times that C_1 is repeated, (1) one of its neighbors has to be executed at least once; and (2) one of its supplementary cycles has to be executed at least once.

Refinement. We can easily express the two above determined dependencies using two linear inequalities. Let c_i be the variable corresponding to C_i in the respective livelock freedom determination IP problem. The inequality $c_1 \leq 5(c_2 + c_3)$ describes the first dependency regarding neighbors, and the inequality $c_1 \leq 5c_3$ describes the second one regarding supplementary cycles. These two inequalities are then added to the livelock freedom determination IP problem, which refines the abstraction by imposing the discovered cycle dependencies and thus ruling out the spurious counterexample consisting of only C_1.

In [15] we also consider other sources of cycle dependencies than those imposed by conditional statements in cycles. We leave out the discussion here due to limited space.

Next Door Strategy. In [15] two alternative methods were proposed to determine supplementary cycles. These methods are either relatively coarse or costly, and we give an improvement using what we call the “next door” strategy.

Note that, in the example in Figure 2, the incrementation of x in C_4 does not influence the satisfaction of the condition in C_1. This is because x is re-assigned with a constant by C_3, a neighbor of C_1, on the way back to C_1 from C_4. Thus, C_4 is not a supplementary cycle of C_1. In fact we can see that C_1 is *isolated* by all its neighbors in that, upon re-entering C_1, x is always reset to some constant by one of its neighbors. In such a case, the satisfaction of the condition in C_1 is totally decided by its neighbors, and thus no cycle other than a neighbor is supplementary to C_1.

Given a cycle whose supplementary cycles are to be determined, the next door strategy will first check whether the given cycle is isolated by all its neighbors. When this is the case, we can safely restrict the search for supplementary cycles to the set of its neighbors.

6 Case Studies

We implemented the livelock freedom proving method in a prototype system named *aLive*, and carried out a few case studies with realistic Promela models on a Pentium IV 1.60GHz machine with 1GB memory. We also compared the performance of aLive and the SPIN model checker on each model.

GARP. The *Group Address Registration Protocol* (*GARP*) is a network protocol allowing users to dynamically register to and detach themselves from a multicast group. A progress action is either for a user to join or leave a multicast group, or for the system to remove all the users from a group. The Promela implementation of GARP [18] consists of 7 concurrent processes with 131 local states, 212 local transitions, and 10 communication buffers. SPIN proved livelock freedom for the model within 56 seconds and visited 5×10^6 global states during the check. aLive used only 8 seconds to return the same result after 7 abstraction refinement steps. We contend that this seven fold speedup compared to SPIN is possible because aLive does not need to visit all reachable global states and thus avoids the combinatorial state space explosion caused by concurrency that the verification algorithm of SPIN is subject to. During the verification aLive identified 29 message types, collected 86 local control flow cycles, and generated altogether 21 IP problems. During the analysis 7 counterexamples were suggested and aLive automatically determined all of these to be spurious. One of these spurious counterexamples suggests the following scenario: While no other process moves on, one process keeps executing a cycle in which it sends a *join* message to inform a service process of some user’s decision to join a multicast group. However, after the message is sent, the user is included in the group, and the process cannot send another *join* message. This cycle can be repeated only if another cycle of the same process has been executed in which the process receives a message through which the user announces that he is leaving the group. aLive successfully detected this dependency between these two cycles and refined the abstraction accordingly.

GSM Handover. We also checked livelock freedom for a model of the *Handover* procedure in the GSM protocol. The model is included as an example in the latest SPIN 4.26 distribution. In this case a progress action is to hand over the control of communication from one base region to another one. We carefully revised the original model to remove the use of sending data objects corresponding to communication buffers from one process to another, which is a Promela language feature that we currently cannot handle. However, the revision does not change the behavior of the original model. The revised model consists of 6 processes with 49 local states, 62 local transitions, and 7 communication buffers. For the revised model, SPIN immediately reported an error trail with a length of 36 steps. aLive also found one counterexample in the first checking iteration and returned `unknown` after it failed to determine spuriousness for the counterexample. The counterexample consists of 6 control flow cycles and indicates the situation in which a base station is continuously forwarding messages between a mobile user and the system without handing over the control to another base region. Guided by this counterexample, we replayed the indicated scenario by a manual simulation of the *original* model within exactly 36 steps. Thus, the counterexample that aLive found is a real counterexample.

CORBA GIOP. Our analysis of the CORBA GIOP [12] protocol revealed a limitation of the current aLive approach that is rooted in the unavailability of suitable static analysis methods for global cycle dependencies in the abstraction refinement loop. aLive found 8 counterexamples during the analysis and determined spuriousness for all but the last one. The failure on the last counterexample results exactly from the existence of a global cycle dependency that we cannot currently handle. A manual inspection easily proves the spuriousness of this counterexample. On the contrary, SPIN proved livelock freedom for the GIOP model very efficiently.

Analysis of Parametric and Infinite State Models. Note that aLive actually proves livelock freedom for a class of Promela models that can be parameterized with *arbitrary* finite communication buffer capacities. SPIN, on the other hand, verifies only a given model with a fixed finite buffer length setting. As a consequence, if the buffer lengths specified in a Promela model are increased, SPIN may run out of memory due to an exponential growth of the size of the global state space and hence be unable to prove livelock freedom. On the contrary, aLive is insensitive to the size of the buffers bounds. Even more, if we assume that the (syntactically inadmissible) omission of buffer bounds in Promela channel declarations is interpreted as buffers with unbounded capacity, then our aLive analysis extends to the class of infinite state Promela models.

7 Related Work

Integer programming based techniques were previously used in the verification of concurrent systems [2,5,3,6,20]. INCA [2] relies on IP to provide an incomplete but sound method of verifying safety and liveness properties. However, INCA currently handles only synchronous rendezvous-like communication, although the theoretical framework is extensible to asynchronous communication. Furthermore, the analysis in INCA is restricted to control flow structures whereas our method also takes data into account. Also, the refinements of the control flow constraints proposed in [20] for INCA are different than the ones proposed in this paper. The work described in [5] uses a notion of T-invariants described in constraint programming (a more powerful framework than IP) to give an NP-complete semi-decision test ("yes" or "unknown") for LTL liveness properties on 1-safe Petri nets.

Livelock analysis was also studied in the context of process algebras. Tools explicitly verifying livelock freedom in the synchronous communication model of CSP are [7,21]. Note that our analysis focusses on the asynchronous communication model and is therefore fundamentally different.

In explicit state model checking, the verification of livelock freedom reduces to the detection of non-progress cycles using nested [11] or even simple [9] depth first state space traversals. In fact, any CTL or LTL model-checker is able to address livelock freedom checking [4], since livelock freedom can be expressed in both CTL and LTL temporal logics. SPIN [11] checks livelock-freedom of Promela models (attaching 'progress' labels to actions of interest and searching for non-progress cycles). Verisoft [8] addresses also the livelock freedom issue, but with a very restricted definition of livelock that is only applicable to finite executions.

8 Conclusion

In this paper we have presented an incomplete analysis method for the detection of livelock freedom for asynchronous infinite-state reactive systems. The method is based on a property conserving abstraction that reduces these systems to a system of numerical effect vectors. The livelock problem is then encoded into an integer programming problem over these effect vectors. The solvability of this IP problem answers the question, whether the program is livelock free, or whether livelock freedom cannot be proven. In the latter case the analysis returns a counterexample. We have devised automated heuristics to determine spuriousness of a given counterexample and to refine the abstraction, when applicable. We have evaluated the analysis using a number of real-life Promela models that we subjected to our prototype analysis tool aLive. The analysis together with the automated refinement in aLive have produced meaningful results. In one instance our automated counterexample refinement failed, which points at necessary improvements in the underlying static analysis. We have also compared our analysis with finite-state verification, in particular the SPIN model checker, and found that aLive performs very favorably. As we have argued, the soundness of our analyis does not hinge upon finiteness of the underlying model.

Further research aims at investigating how to encode other types of liveness properties, such as response properties, using effect vector analysis. Furthermore, we plan to use the counterexamples (linear combination of cycles) produced by our analysis to guide SPIN in its search for non-progress cycles (livelocks) using, for instance, as heuristic metric function the distance to a cycle in the counterexample. We also plan to improve our static analysis and extend it to global cycle dependencies so that impediments to automated abstraction refinement such as those occurring in GIOP will be eliminated.

Acknowledgments. This work was supported by the DFG-funded research project IMCOS (Grant No. LE 1342/1-/2). We thank George Avrunin, Javier Esparza and Keijo Heljanko for their pointers to relevant literature.

References

1. D. Brand and P. Zafiropulo. On communicating finite-state machines. *Journal of the ACM*, 30(2):323–342, 1983.
2. J.C. Corbett and G.S. Avrunin. Using integer programming to verify general safety and liveness properties. *Formal Methods in System Design*, 6(1):97–123, 1995.
3. S. Dellacherie, S. Devulder, and J.-L. Lambert. Software verification based on linear programming. In *Proc. of FM'99*, volume 1709 of *LNCS*, pages 1147–1165. Springer, 1999.
4. Y. Dong, X. Du, G.J. Holzmann, and S.A. Smolka. Fighting livelock in the GNU i-Protocol: a case study in explicit-state model checking. *Int. Journal on Software Tools for Technology Transfer (STTT)*, 4(4):505–528, 2003.
5. J. Esparza and S. Melzer. Model checking LTL using constraint programming. In *Proc. of ICATPN'97*, volume 1248 of *LNCS*, pages 1–20. Springer, 1997.
6. J. Esparza and S. Melzer. Verification of safety properties using integer programming: Beyond the state equation. *Formal Methods in System Design*, 16(2):159–189, 2000.
7. FDR2 tool. Formal Systems (Europe) Ltd. http://www.fsel.com.
8. P. Godefroid. Software model checking: The VeriSoft approach. *Formal Methods in System Design*, 26(2):77–101, 2005.
9. H. Hansen, W. Penczek, and A. Valmari. Stuttering-insensitive automata for on-the-fly detection of livelock properties. *ENTCS*, 66(2), 2002.
10. A. Ho, S. Smith, and S. Hand. On deadlock, livelock, and forward progress. Technical Report UCAM-CL-TR-633, Cambridge University, Computer Laboratory, 2005. 8 pp. http://www.cl.cam.ac.uk/TechReports/UCAM-CL-TR-633.pdf.
11. G.J. Holzmann. *The SPIN model checker: Primer and reference manual.* Addison Wesley, 2004.
12. M. Kamel and S. Leue. Formalization and validation of the general Inter-ORB protocol (GIOP) using PROMELA and SPIN. *Int. Journal on Software Tools for Technology Transfer (STTT)*, 2(4):394–409, 2000.
13. S. Leue, R. Mayr, and W. Wei. A scalable incomplete test for message buffer overflow in Promela models. In *Proc. of SPIN'04*, volume 2989 of *LNCS*, pages 216–233. Springer, 2004.
14. S. Leue, R. Mayr, and W. Wei. A scalable incomplete test for the boundedness of UML RT models. In *Proc. of TACAS'04*, volume 2988 of *LNCS*, pages 327–341. Springer, 2004.
15. S. Leue and W. Wei. Counterexample-based refinement for a boundedness test for CFSM languages. In *Proc. of SPIN'05*, volume 3639 of *LNCS*, pages 58–74. Springer, 2005.

16. S. Leue and W. Wei. A region graph based approach to termination proofs. In *Proc. of TACAS'06*, volume 3920 of *Lecture Notes in Computer Science*, pages 318–333. Springer, 2006.
17. Z. Manna and A. Pnueli. *The Temporal Logic of Reactive and Concurrent Systems – Specification.* Springer Verlag, 1992.
18. T. Nakatani. Verification of group address registration protocol using PROMELA and SPIN. In *Proc. of SPIN'97*, 1997. Available at http://spinroot.com/spin/Workshops/ws97/nakatani.pdf.
19. C. H. Papadimitriou and K. Steiglitz. *Combinatorial optimization: algorithms and complexity.* Prentice Hall, 1982.
20. S.F. Siegel and G.S. Avrunin. Improving the precision of INCA by eliminating solutions with spurious cycles. *IEEE Trans. Software Eng.*, 28(2):115–128, 2002.
21. SLAP tool (version 0.1): A static livelock analyzer for CSP processes. Webpage: http://web.comlab.ox.ac.uk/oucl/work/joel.ouaknine/software/slap.html.
22. G. von Bochmann. Finite state description of communication protocols. *Computer Networks*, 2:361–372, 1978.

Proving Liveness by Backwards Reachability*

Parosh Aziz Abdulla, Bengt Jonsson, Ahmed Rezine, and Mayank Saksena

Dept. of Information Technology, P.O. Box 337, S-751 05 Uppsala, Sweden
{parosh, bengt, rahmed, mayanks}@it.uu.se

Abstract. We present a new method for proving liveness and termination properties for fair concurrent programs, which does not rely on finding a ranking function or on computing the transitive closure of the transition relation. The set of states from which termination or some liveness property is guaranteed is computed by a backwards reachability analysis. A central technique for handling concurrency is a check for certain commutativity properties. The method is not complete. However, it can be seen as a complement to other methods for proving termination, in that it transforms a termination problem into a simpler one with a larger set of terminated states. We show the usefulness of our method by applying it to existing programs from the literature. We have also implemented it in the framework of Regular Model Checking, and used it to automatically verify non-starvation for parameterized algorithms.

1 Introduction

The last decade has witnessed impressive progress in the ability of tools to verify properties of hardware and software systems (e.g., [9,16,24]). The success has to a large extent concerned safety properties, e.g., absence of run-time errors, deadlocks, race conditions, etc. Progress in verification of liveness properties has been less prominent. A major reason is that they are harder to verify than safety properties. For finite-state systems and some parameterized systems, safety properties can be verified by computing (some approximation of) the set of reachable states. Verifying liveness properties, requires at least a repeated search through the state space in enumerative model checkers [24]. In symbolic model checkers, a natural but more expensive technique is to compute the transitive closure of the transition relation. Multiple fairness requirements can make the situation even more complicated. For general infinite-state systems, the difference between safety and liveness properties is even larger. For some classes of systems, such as lossy channel systems, checking safety properties is decidable [5], whereas checking liveness properties is undecidable [4].

The general approach for proving liveness involves finding auxiliary assertions associated with well-founded ranking functions and helpful directions (e.g., [26]). Finding such ranking functions is not easy, and automation requires techniques adapted to specific data domains. Techniques have been developed for programs with integers or reals [12,13,14,18,19], functional programs, [25], and parameterized systems [22,23].

The main technique of software model checking, using finite-state abstractions [16] has been difficult to apply when proving liveness properties, since abstractions may introduce spurious loops [33] that do not preserve liveness. Podelski and Rybalchenko

* This work was supported in part by the Swedish Research Council (http://www.vr.se/).

C. Baier and H. Hermanns (Eds.): CONCUR 2006, LNCS 4137, pp. 95–109, 2006.

therefore extended the framework of predicate abstraction to that of *transition predicate abstraction* [32], which involves constructing an abstraction of the transition relation and its transitive closure. However, the transitive closure is harder to compute or approximate than the set of reachable states.

Here, we present a new method for proving liveness using simple reachability analysis, which uses neither computation of transitive closure nor explicit construction of ranking functions. The method assumes that the liveness property has been transformed to the property of termination for a system; which is standard for many classes of liveness properties, including the so-called progress properties (of form $\Box(P \implies \Diamond Q)$). Termination is then checked by backwards reachability analysis, which computes the set of states that are backwards reachable from the set of terminated states under a particular transition relation, which we call a *convergence relation*. Computing the set of backwards reachable states is conceptually easier than finding ranking functions or computing the transitive closure. Thus, liveness properties can be established for a class of systems, provided that there is a powerful way to compute sets of backwards reachable states. For many classes of parameterized and infinite-state systems, the set of backwards reachable states is computable (e.g., [5,2]). For other classes of infinite-state systems, powerful acceleration techniques have been developed that compute or under-approximate the set of reachable states (e.g., [35,3]). It should be possible to develop equally powerful techniques for backwards reachability analysis, and apply them to proving liveness properties.

For a simple deterministic (non-concurrent) program, the set of states in which termination is guaranteed can be calculated as the set of states that are backwards reachable from some terminated state. We generalize this observation to develop techniques for using backwards reachability analysis to prove termination for general concurrent programs with arbitrary (weak) fairness (aka justice) requirements; backwards reachability analysis should be the only non-trivial computation on the verified program. A central new technique for handling concurrency is the use of commutativity properties between different actions of the program.

Our technique is in general not complete. It computes an under-approximation of the set of states from which termination is guaranteed. If this under-approximation does not include the states for which one intends to prove termination, there are several ways to increase the power of the method. One way is to repeat the backwards reachability analysis, letting the computed under-approximation play the role of terminated states. One then exploits the fact that our convergence relation increases when the set of terminated states increases: a repeated reachability analysis will therefore improve the under-approximation. Another way is to apply other techniques (e.g. based on ranks or transitive closure computation) to prove termination for the remaining states of interest. Here, we present such a complementary technique, developed particularly for parameterized systems.

To show the usefulness of our method, we apply it to several examples. The first is a program also considered by Podelski and Rybalchenko [32]; our method also handles the other programs in [32]. The second example is the well-known *alternating bit* protocol. This is an example of a lossy channel system, for which liveness properties are undecidable [4]. Our example shows that backwards reachability analysis (which is guaranteed to terminate [5]) can prove liveness properties for some of these systems, although in general they are undecidable. Finally, we have implemented our technique in the framework of regular model checking [7]. We prove starvation-freedom for several parameterized mutual exclusion protocols; some of which we have previously not been able to prove starvation-freedom for using transitive closure computation [6].

Related Work. For infinite-state systems, fair termination is typically proven by finding auxiliary assertions associated with well-founded ranking functions and helpful directions (e.g., [26,27]). Automated construction of such ranking functions is a challenging task, which requires techniques adapted to specific data domains. Recently, significant progress has been achieved for programs that operate on numerical domains, integers or reals [12,13,14,18,19,21]. Rather few papers present efficient techniques to prove termination for programs that operate on arbitrary data domains. For families of parameterized systems, where each system instance is finite-state, liveness can in principle be proven from the transitive closure, but computation of transitive closure is typically expensive [30]. Another approach is to develop heuristics to automate the search for rank functions [22,23] and procedures to check the conditions in a general proof rule [27] automatically. A third approach has been to find specialized abstractions, e.g., into integers, which work in certain cases [31].

Podelski and Rybalchenko extend the framework of predicate abstraction to that of *transition predicate abstraction* [32,33,29,20], which can be applied on arbitrary programs. The transitive closure of the transition relation is harder to compute or approximate than the set of reachable states. Extensions of predicate abstraction techniques for synthesizing ranking functions have also been developed by Balaban, Pnueli, and Zuck [8].

Our use of commutativity between actions is inspired by the use of commutativity in partial-order techniques to optimize state-space exploration [17] in finite-state model checking.

Organization of the Paper. Section 2 contains basic definitions, Section 3 an informal overview of our method, and Section 4 the formal presentation of the method. In Section 5, we verify an example also considered by Podelski and Rybalchenko [32], and the alternating bit protocol. In Section 6, we give experimental results on non-starvation for parameterized mutual exclusion algorithms, and describe our complementary termination rule, particularly developed for parameterized systems. Section 7 contains conclusions.

2 Preliminaries

Programs. We consider fair concurrent programs modeled as transition systems. A program may contain a set of actions with (weak) fairness requirements (aka justice), as in, e.g., UNITY [15].

Formally, a *program* $\mathcal{P}$ is a triple $\langle S, \longrightarrow, \mathcal{A} \rangle$, where

- S is a set of *states*,
- $\longrightarrow \subseteq S \times S$ is a *transition relation* on S. We require that the identity relation is included in $\longrightarrow$.

- $\mathcal{A}$ is a finite or countable set of *fair actions*, each of which is a subset of $\longrightarrow$, and required to be deterministic.

An *action* is any subset of the transition relation. We write $s \longrightarrow s'$ for $(s, s') \in \longrightarrow$. For an action α, we use $s \xrightarrow{\alpha} s'$ to denote $(s, s') \in \alpha$. An action α is *enabled* in a state s if there is some state s' such that $s \xrightarrow{\alpha} s'$. The set of states in which the action α is enabled is denoted $En(\alpha)$. If T is a set of states, then $\alpha \wedge T$ denotes the set of pairs (s, s') of states such that $s \xrightarrow{\alpha} s'$ and $s \in T$. For a set $\mathcal{B}$ of actions, let $\mathcal{B} \wedge T$ denote $\{\alpha \wedge T \mid \alpha \in \mathcal{B}\}$. A *computation* of $\mathcal{P}$ from a state $s \in S$ is an infinite sequence of states $s_0\ s_1\ s_2\ \ldots$ such that (i) $s = s_0$; (ii) $s_i \longrightarrow s_{i+1}$ for each $i \geq 0$; and (iii) for each fair action $\alpha \in \mathcal{A}$, there are infinitely many $i \geq 0$ where either $s_i \xrightarrow{\alpha} s_{i+1}$ or $s_i \notin En(\alpha)$.

For a set T of states and action α, let $Pre(\alpha, T)$ be the set of states s such that $s \xrightarrow{\alpha} t$ for some $t \in T$. For a set of actions $\mathcal{B}$, let $Pre^*(\mathcal{B}, T)$ be the union of T and the set of states s such that $s \xrightarrow{\alpha_1} \cdots \xrightarrow{\alpha_n} t$ for some $t \in T$ and $\alpha_1, \ldots, \alpha_n \in \mathcal{B}$.

Termination. Let $\mathcal{P}$ be a program $\langle S, \longrightarrow, \mathcal{A}\rangle$ and $F \subseteq S$ be a set of *terminated* states. We assume F to be *stable*, i.e., that $s \in F$ and $s \longrightarrow s'$ implies $s' \in F$. Define $\Diamond F$ as the set of states s such that any computation of $\mathcal{P}$ from s contains a state in F. In other words, $\Diamond F$ is the set of states from which termination is guaranteed, in the sense that each computation from s will eventually reach F. In this paper we present methods for computing (an under-approximation of) $\Diamond F$.

We can also consider many classes of liveness properties, e.g., progress properties (of form $\Box(P \implies \Diamond Q)$), by first transforming them to termination properties. There exist standard techniques for such reductions. For example, a program satisfies $\Box(P \implies \Diamond Q)$ if $\Diamond Q$ includes states that can be reached from an initial state in a sequence of transitions that visit P, but have not yet visited Q.

Remarks. The restriction that each fair action be deterministic can often be circumvented by representing a nondeterministic action as a union of several deterministic ones. Our definition of program does not mention initial states. When initial states are given, a typical use of our techniques will be to first compute the set of reachable states (or an over-approximation), and let them be the states of the program as defined above.

3 Overview of the Proof Method

In this section, we give an overview of our method for computing a (good) under-approximation of the set $\Diamond F$, where F is a set of states of a program $\mathcal{P} = \langle S, \longrightarrow, \mathcal{A}\rangle$. The inspiration for our method is the simple observation that when $\mathcal{P}$ is a deterministic program with only one fair action α, then $\Diamond F$ is the set $Pre^*(\alpha, F)$. Our goal is therefore a technique for proving termination and liveness properties, where the only non-trivial computation is a predecessor calculation, i.e., computing $Pre^*(\mathcal{B}, T)$ for some set of states T and actions $\mathcal{B}$.

Our method works by computing a so-called *convergence relation*, here denoted $\hookrightarrow_F$, on the states of $\mathcal{P}$; this is a relation with the property that if $s \hookrightarrow_F t$ and $t \in \Diamond F$

then also $s \in \Diamond F$. From this property it follows that $Pre^*(\hookrightarrow_F, F) \subseteq \Diamond F$ for any convergence relation $\hookrightarrow_F$. The construction of $\hookrightarrow_F$ depends in general on F. Since $\hookrightarrow_F$ will be employed in a predecessor calculation, it is natural to allow the use of predecessor calculations also in the construction of $\hookrightarrow_F$ itself, but to avoid computations of transitive closures or other more powerful techniques.

Our main technique for constructing $\hookrightarrow_F$ uses a commutativity argument to infer that it satisfies the required properties. To explain its intuition, consider the following simple program, which consists of two deterministic processes executing in parallel.

$$\begin{array}{llll} \alpha_1 : & x := x - 1 & \text{if} & x > 0 \\ \alpha_2 : & y := y - 1 & \text{if} & y > 0 \end{array}$$

Variables x and y assume values in the natural numbers. For $i = 1, 2$, process i repeatedly performs action α_i. Both α_1 and α_2 are fair actions. The transition relation is the union of both actions plus the identity relation. The set F of terminated states is the single state with $x = y = 0$.

In this example, our method computes $\hookrightarrow_F$ as $\alpha_1 \cup \alpha_2$. Our method implicitly ascertains that $\hookrightarrow_F$ is a convergence relation using a commutativity argument. To understand why α_1 is in $\hookrightarrow_F$, assume that $s \xrightarrow{\alpha_1} t$ and $t \in \Diamond F$. Consider any computation from s. If it goes first to t we are done. Otherwise, it first consists of a sequence of executions of action α_2. During this sequence, α_1 remains enabled, and so must eventually (by fairness) be executed, leading to some state t'. Now observe that since α_1 and α_2 commute, t' is reachable from t. Since $t \in \Diamond F$ we infer, using the fact that $\Diamond F$ is a stable set, that $t' \in \Diamond F$ and hence that $s \in \Diamond F$. We conclude that termination is guaranteed for all states in $Pre^*(\hookrightarrow_F, F)$, which here is the set of all states.

The above method can prove termination for many programs with a regular structure. It is in general incomplete. For programs where the above method computes a too small under-approximation of $\Diamond F$, we offer the following two ways to proceed.

The backwards reachability computation can be repeated several times. If one computation produces an under-approximation G of $\Diamond F$, the next application of our method will compute $\Diamond G$ using a convergence relation $\hookrightarrow_G$ that is larger than in the first computation, since it depends on G instead of F. Let us illustrate this by changing the above program by changing the guard of α_1 into $0 < x \leq y \vee y = 0$. This destroys commutativity between α_1 and α_2 in case $y = x$. However, a first backwards reachability computation will produce the set G consisting of states with $0 \leq x \leq 1$ or with $0 \leq y < x$ as an under-approximation to $\Diamond F$. A second backwards reachability computation thereafter reveals that all states are in $\Diamond G$, hence also in $\Diamond F$.

In many cases, the under-approximation of $\Diamond F$ computed by our method is sufficiently large that other techniques (e.g., standard techniques based on ranks or transitive closure computation) become computationally feasible. For the class of parameterized systems, we have developed a powerful method, whose only nontrivial computation is predecessor calculation, which can be used after applying the commutativity-based method.

4 Proving Termination as Backward Reachability

In this section, we formalize the methods for calculating (an under-approximation of) the set $\Diamond F$ by backwards reachability analysis, presented in the previous section. We first present the general approach, and then our main technique.

Assume a program $\langle S, \longrightarrow, \mathcal{A} \rangle$. Let F be a stable set of terminated states. Define a *convergence relation* on S for F to be a relation $\hookrightarrow_F$ on S such that whenever $s \hookrightarrow_F t$ and $t \in \Diamond F$ then also $s \in \Diamond F$. The point of convergence relations is that if $\hookrightarrow_F$ is a convergence relation for F, then $Pre^*(\hookrightarrow_F, F) \subseteq \Diamond F$, i.e., we can use predecessor calculation to prove that termination is guaranteed from a set of states. Larger convergence relations allow to prove termination for larger sets of states. Furthermore, even if we cannot precisely calculate $Pre^*(\hookrightarrow_F, F)$, any under-approximation of this set is also in $\Diamond F$.

To apply these ideas, we need techniques to compute sufficiently powerful convergence relations. Any number of convergence relations can be combined into one, since the union of two convergence relations is again a convergence relation. Now we present our main technique, which is based on a commutativity argument.

Definition 1. *Let α be a deterministic fair action, and let F be a set of states. Define the* left moving states for (α, F), *denoted $Left(\alpha, F)$, as the set of states s satisfying*

- *whenever there are states s', t' with $t' \notin F$ such that $s \longrightarrow s' \xrightarrow{\alpha} t'$, then there is a state t with $s \xrightarrow{\alpha} t \longrightarrow t'$.*

Intuitively, α can "move left" of $\longrightarrow$, and still reach the same state. The definition is illustrated in Figure 1.

$$\begin{array}{lccc} & \exists\, t & \longrightarrow & t' \notin F \\ \forall\, s', t' & \uparrow{\scriptstyle \alpha} & & \uparrow{\scriptstyle \alpha} \\ & s & \longrightarrow & s' \end{array}$$

Fig. 1. $s \in Left(\alpha, F)$. Action α commutes left at state s.

Definition 2. *Define the* α-helpful states, *denoted $Helpful(\alpha, F)$, as the largest set T of states such that $T \subseteq ((En(\alpha) \cap Left(\alpha, F)) \cup F)$, and*

- *whenever $s \in Helpful(\alpha, F)$ and $s \longrightarrow s'$ then either $s \xrightarrow{\alpha} s'$, or $s' \in F$, or $s' \in Helpful(\alpha, F)$.*

Intuitively, a state is α-helpful if the properties that α is enabled and left moving remain true when any sequence of transitions not in α are taken, unless F is reached. The above concepts can be used to define a convergence relation as follows.

Theorem 1. *Let α be a fair action of $\langle S, \longrightarrow, \mathcal{A} \rangle$ and F be a stable set of states. Then the relation $\overset{\alpha}{\hookrightarrow}_F$, defined by*

$$\overset{\alpha}{\hookrightarrow}_F \;\equiv\; \alpha \wedge Helpful(\alpha, F)$$

is a convergence relation for F.

Proof. Assume that $s \overset{\alpha}{\hookrightarrow}_F t$ and $t \in \Diamond F$. Consider any computation $s_0\ s_1\ s_2\ \ldots$ from $s = s_0$. We must show that it contains a state in F.

- If there is a k with $s_k \in F$ we are done.
- Otherwise, if there is a k with $s_k \overset{\alpha}{\longrightarrow} s_{k+1}$, let k be the least such index. By induction, using the definition of $\mathit{Helpful}(\alpha, F)$, we infer that $s_i \in \mathit{Helpful}(\alpha, F)$, hence $s_i \in En(\alpha)$ and $s_i \in \mathit{Left}(\alpha, F)$ for $i = 0, \ldots, k$. Let t_i be the unique state with $s_i \overset{\alpha}{\longrightarrow} t_i$, in particular $s_{k+1} = t_k$. By induction we infer, using the definition of $\mathit{Left}(\alpha, F)$, that t_i is reachable from t for all i with $0 \leq i \leq k$. In particular, $s_{k+1} = t_k$ is reachable from t. From $t \in \Diamond F$ we infer $s_{k+1} \in \Diamond F$ and hence the computation must contain a state in F. An illustration of this argument is provided in Figure 2.
- Otherwise, we infer by induction over k, using $s \in \mathit{Helpful}(\alpha, F)$, that α is enabled in all states of the computation. By fairness, α will eventually be executed, and we are back to the previous case. □

$$\begin{array}{ccccccccc}
t & \longrightarrow & t_1 & \longrightarrow & t_2 & \longrightarrow & \cdots & \longrightarrow & t_k \\
\uparrow{\scriptstyle\alpha} & & \uparrow{\scriptstyle\alpha} & & \uparrow{\scriptstyle\alpha} & & & & \uparrow{\scriptstyle\alpha} \\
s & \overset{\neg\alpha}{\longrightarrow} & s_1 & \overset{\neg\alpha}{\longrightarrow} & s_2 & \overset{\neg\alpha}{\longrightarrow} & \cdots & \overset{\neg\alpha}{\longrightarrow} & s_k
\end{array}$$

Fig. 2. $(s, t) \in \overset{\alpha}{\hookrightarrow}_F$. The α-successor of any successor of s, is either a successor of t, or in F.

Corollary 1. $\mathit{Pre}^*(\{\overset{\alpha}{\hookrightarrow}_F | \alpha \in \mathcal{A}\}\ ,\ F) \subseteq \Diamond F$

In order to show how termination can be proven by backwards reachability analysis, we must finally explain how to compute $\mathit{Helpful}(\alpha, F)$, or an under-approximation of it, by backwards reachability analysis. We first observe that:

$$\mathit{Left}(\alpha, F) = \neg \mathit{Pre}((\longrightarrow \circ\, \alpha) - (\alpha \circ \longrightarrow), \neg F)$$

Proposition 1. *The set $\mathit{Helpful}(\alpha, F)$ is the complement of the set*

$$\mathit{Pre}^*((\mathcal{A} - \alpha) \wedge \neg F\ ,\ (\neg \mathit{Left}(\alpha, F) \cup \neg En(\alpha))\ \cap\ \neg F)$$

Proof. According to Definition 2, a state s is not in $\mathit{Helpful}(\alpha, F)$ if and only if there is a sequence of transitions from s, none of which is in α or visits a state in F, which leads to a state neither in F nor in $En(\alpha)\ \cap\ \mathit{Left}(\alpha, F)$; exactly what the proposition formalizes. □

5 Examples

In this section we illustrate our method, by applying it to two examples from the literature.

5.1 Any-Down

The example *Any-Down* is used by Podelski and Rybalchenko [32] to illustrate their method of transition invariants. In fact, our method can handle, in two iterations or less, all the examples given in [32]. For readability, we reformulate the program into the action-based syntax of the example in Section 3, as follows.

$$\begin{array}{lll} \alpha_1 : y := y + 1 & \text{if} & x = 1 \\ \alpha_2 : x := 0 & \text{if} & \mathit{true} \\ \alpha_3 : y := y - 1 & \text{if} & x = 0 \wedge y > 0 \end{array}$$

The program variable y assumes values in the natural numbers, and the variable x assumes values in $\{0, 1\}$. Both α_2 and α_3 are fair actions. The transition relation is the union of all three actions plus the identity relation. The set F of terminated states is the single state with $x = y = 0$. It is well-known that a standard termination proof for this program will require a ranking function whose range is larger than the natural numbers. This suggests that we need at least two iterations of our method to compute the set $\Diamond F$. We describe each iteration below.

In the first iteration we compute $\mathit{Helpful}(\alpha_i, F)$ for $i = 2, 3$ (we omit α_1, since it is not a fair action). These computations are summarized in the below table.

	$\mathit{En}(\alpha_i)$	$\mathit{Left}(\alpha_i, F)$	$\mathit{Helpful}(\alpha_i, F)$
α_2	true	$x = 0$	$x = 0$
α_3	$x = 0 \wedge y > 0$	$x = 0 \vee y = 0 \vee y = 1$	$x = 0$

We explain the entries of the table for α_2. The corresponding entries for α_3 can be explained in a similar manner. The set $\mathit{Left}(\alpha_2, F)$ includes all states s where $x = 0$. This is since either (i) $y = 0$ in which case $s \in F$; or (ii) $y > 0$, which means that α_1 is not enabled, and α_2 commutes with α_3. On the other hand, $\mathit{Left}(\alpha_2, F)$ does not include any state s with $x = 1$, as follows. We have $s \xrightarrow{\alpha_1} \xrightarrow{\alpha_2} t$, for some t with $y > 0$. Obviously, $t \notin F$ and furthermore it is not the case that $s \xrightarrow{\alpha_2} \xrightarrow{\alpha_1} t$ since α_2 disables α_1. This means we have violated the condition for being a left mover.

The set $\mathit{Helpful}(\alpha_2, F)$ includes all states where $x = 0$; such a state s belongs to $\mathit{Left}(\alpha_2, F)$. The action α_2 is enabled from s. Furthermore, the action α_1 is disabled, while the execution of α_3 from s again leads to a state satisfying $\mathit{Helpful}(\alpha_2, F)$.

By Corollary 1, the following set is in $\Diamond F$:

$$G \equiv \mathit{Pre}^*((\alpha_2 \wedge \mathit{Helpful}(\alpha_2, F)) \cup (\alpha_3 \wedge \mathit{Helpful}(\alpha_3, F)), F) \quad \equiv \quad x = 0$$

In the second iteration we compute $\mathit{Helpful}(\alpha_i, G)$ for $i = 2, 3$ in the same way. The interesting difference is that $\mathit{Left}(\alpha_2, G)$, which is true, is larger than $\mathit{Left}(\alpha_2, F)$, since any execution of α_2 leads to G. Hence also $\mathit{Helpful}(\alpha_2, G)$, which is true, is larger than $\mathit{Helpful}(\alpha_2, F)$.

	$\mathit{En}(\alpha_i)$	$\mathit{Left}(\alpha_i, G)$	$\mathit{Helpful}(\alpha_i, G)$
α_2	true	true	true
α_3	$x = 0 \wedge y > 0$	true	$x = 0$

By Corollary 1, the following set is in $\Diamond G$, hence in $\Diamond F$:

$$Pre^*((\alpha_2 \wedge true) \cup (\alpha_3 \wedge Helpful(\alpha_3, F)), G) \quad \equiv \quad true$$

5.2 Alternating Bit Protocol

As a second example, we consider a protocol that consists of finite-state processes that communicate over unbounded and lossy FIFO channels. As shown in our earlier work, it is decidable whether a protocol satisfies a safety property [5], but undecidable whether a protocol satisfies a liveness property [4]. Using our technique, we can prove liveness properties for some of these protocols.

In the *Alternating Bit Protocol*, a sender and a receiver communicate via two unbounded and lossy FIFO channels. One channel, c_M, is used to transmit messages from the sender to the receiver, and another, c_A, to transmit acknowledgments from the receiver to the sender. The behavior of the sender and the receiver are depicted in Figure 3. The sender sends alternately the messages m_0 and m_1, while the receiver sends back acknowledgment a_i after receiving the message m_i. A state of the system is of form $s_i r_j(w_1, w_2)$ where s_i is a sender state (s_0 or s_1), r_j is a receiver state (r_0 or r_1), and w_1, w_2 are the contents of channels c_M, respectively c_A. The initial state is $s_0 r_0(\langle\rangle, \langle\rangle)$ with both channels empty. Here, a channel is modeled as a perfect FIFO buffer. Message loss is modeled as a nondeterministic choice between a send and a *skip* action. All actions, except *skip*, are fair. This corresponds to the assumption that if a message is continuously retransmitted, then eventually one of the messages is not lost.

In this example, we let the states S be those reachable from the initial state. This set can be computed, using e.g. the acceleration techniques based on *Queue-content Decision Diagram (QDD)* developed in [10], as the union of the four sets $s_0 r_0(m_0^* m_1^*, a_1^*)$, $s_0 r_1(m_0^*, a_0^* a_1^*)$, $s_1 r_0(m_1^*, a_1^* a_0^*)$, and $s_1 r_1(m_1^* m_0^*, a_0^*)$ where we use regular sets to denote the possible contents of each channel.

We use the method defined in Section 4 to prove the following four progress properties of the protocol.

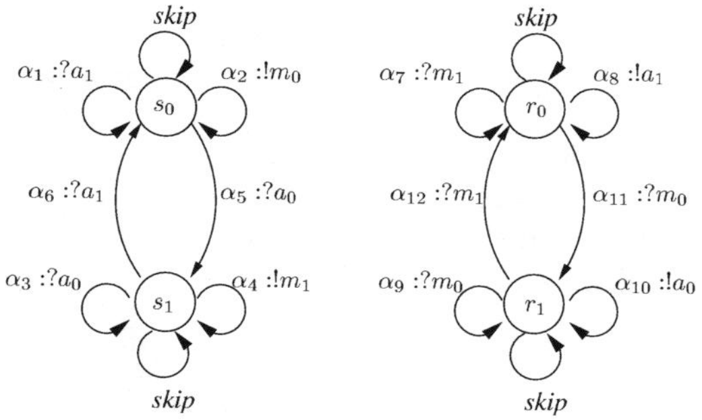

Fig. 3. The Alternating Bit Protocol

$$\begin{array}{ll} 1: & s_0r_0(m_0^*m_1^*, a_1^*) \subseteq \Diamond s_0r_1(m_0^*, a_0^*a_1^*) \\ 2: & s_0r_1(m_0^*, a_0^*a_1^*) \subseteq \Diamond s_1r_1(m_1^*m_0^*, a_0^*) \\ 3: & s_1r_1(m_1^*m_0^*, a_0^*) \subseteq \Diamond s_1r_0(m_1^*, a_1^*a_0^*) \\ 4: & s_1r_0(m_1^*, a_1^*a_0^*) \subseteq \Diamond s_0r_0(m_0^*m_1^*, a_1^*) \end{array}$$

These properties imply that the sender and the receiver indefinitely alternate sending m_0, a_0, m_1, and a_1. Here, we show how the first condition is proven; the other ones are analogous. Letting $F = s_0r_1(m_0^*, a_0^*a_1^*)$, we calculate a set of states included in $\Diamond F$.

To ensure the stability of F, we first modify each action α to $\alpha := \alpha \wedge \neg F$. Then we again use QDDs to compute the helpful set of states for every fair action in the protocol, according to Proposition 1. The results for actions α_2, α_7 and α_{11} are summarized in the following table.

	$En(\alpha_i) \cap Left(\alpha_i, F)$	$Helpful(\alpha_i, F)$
α_2	$s_0r_0(m_0^*m_1^*, a_1^*)$	$s_0r_0(m_0^*m_1^*, a_1^*) \cup s_0r_1(m_0^*, a_0^*a_1^*)$
α_7	$s_0r_0(m_0^*m_1^+, a_1^*) \cup s_1r_0(m_1^+, a_1^*a_0^*)$	$s_0r_0(m_0^*m_1^+, a_1^*) \cup s_1r_0(m_1^+, a_1^*a_0^*)$ $\cup\, s_0r_1(m_0^*, a_0^*a_1^*)$
α_{11}	$s_0r_0(m_0^+, a_1^*)$	$s_0r_0(m_0^+, a_1^*) \cup s_0r_1(m_0^*, a_0^*a_1^*)$

$Helpful(\alpha_7, F) = s_0r_0(m_0^*m_1^+, a_1^*) \cup s_1r_0(m_1^+, a_1^*a_0^*) \cup s_0r_1(m_0^*, a_0^*a_1^*)$ because for every state s in $Helpful(\alpha_7, F)$, it is the case that either (i) s is in F; or (ii) s is in $s_0r_0(m_0^*m_1^+, a_1^*) \cup s_1r_0(m_1^+, a_1^*a_0^*)$. In the second case we have that (i) α_7 is enabled from s and commutes with any other enabled action; and (ii) the execution of any other action from s leads again to $s_0r_0(m_0^*m_1^+, a_1^*) \cup s_1r_0(m_1^+, a_1^*a_0^*)$. The other sets can be explained in a similar way.

By Corollary 1, the set $G = Pre^*(\{\overset{\alpha_i}{\hookrightarrow}_F | i = 1, \ldots, 12\},\ F)$ is in $\Diamond F$. Observe that $s_0r_0(m_0^*m_1^*, a_1^*) = Pre^*(\{\alpha_i \wedge Helpful(\alpha_i, F) | i = 2, 7, 11\}, F)$ is a subset of G. We therefore conclude that $s_0r_0(m_0^*m_1^*, a_1^*) \subseteq \Diamond F$.

6 Parameterized Systems

In this section we consider verification of liveness properties for parameterized systems: these are systems with an arbitrary number of similar processes operating in parallel. A challenge is that they are not finite-state, since the number of processes is unbounded. We describe an implementation of our method in the framework of Regular Model Checking [7]. For several examples, the proof rule of Section 4 computes a strict under-approximation of the set $\Diamond F$; therefore we also present a complementary rule which can prove termination for those examples.

Example: Szymanski's Algorithm As an example of a parameterized system, we describe the mutual exclusion algorithm by Szymanski [34]. In the algorithm, an arbitrary number of processes compete for a critical section. The processes are numbered, say from 1 to N. The *local state* of each process consists of a control state ranging over the integers from 1 to 7 and of two Boolean flags, w and s. A pseudo-code description of the behavior of process number i is shown in Figure 4.

1: **await** $\forall j : j \neq i : \neg s[j]$

2: $w[i], s[i] := \mathit{true}, \mathit{true}$

3: **if** $\exists j : j \neq i : (pc[j] \neq 1) \wedge \neg w[j]$
  then $s[i] := \mathit{false}$; goto 4
  else $w[i] := \mathit{false}$; goto 5

4: **await** $\exists j : j \neq i : s[j] \wedge \neg w[j]$
  then $w[i], s[i] := \mathit{false}, \mathit{true}$

5: **await** $\forall j : j \neq i : \neg w[j]$

6: **await** $\forall j : j < i : \neg s[j]$

7: $s[i] := \mathit{false}$; goto 1

Fig. 4. Szymanski

For instance, according to the code on line 6, if the control state of a process i is 6, and if the value of s is *false* for all processes $j < i$, then the control state of i may be changed to 7. Line 7 represents the critical section. Each numbered line is modeled as an action: $\alpha_j(i)$ is the statement beginning at line j in the pseudo-code for process i. All actions are fair, except $\alpha_1(i)$; this action represents process i entering the competition for the critical section, and therefore its execution should not be enforced.

Starvation freedom can be formulated as follows: whenever any process is at line 2 it will eventually reach line 7. Define F_k to be all states in which process k is at line 7. To prove starvation freedom for process k we must show that all reachable states where process k is at line 2 are in $\Diamond F_k$.

6.1 A Complementary Termination Rule

In this section, we present a proof rule for termination, which is particularly suitable for the class of parameterized systems considered in this section. It will be used to complement the method of Corollary 1. The rule assumes that we select a finite number of fair actions of the program, and establishes that a state s is in $\Diamond F$ if computations from s satisfy

- whenever one of these actions is enabled, it remains enabled until it is executed,
- each of the actions can be executed at most once before F is reached, and
- when all these actions are disabled, the computation has reached F.

This rule is particularly useful for parameterized systems, since termination is often achieved by letting a selected subset of the processes execute a fixed sequence of actions (i.e., statements). Let us define the involved properties formally. Assume a program $\langle S, \longrightarrow, \mathcal{A} \rangle$. Let F be a set of terminated states.

- $\mathit{Persist}(\alpha, F)$ is the set of states s such that in any computation from s, whenever α is enabled, it remains enabled unless it is executed or F is reached.
- $\mathit{Twice}(\alpha, F)$ is the set of states, from which there exists a computation where α is executed twice (or more) without visiting F.
- Let $\mathcal{B}$ be a finite set of actions. $\mathit{After}(\mathcal{B}, F)$ is the set of states s such that in any computation from s, whenever all actions in $\mathcal{B}$ are disabled at a state s', then $s' \in F$.

The above sets are computable using backwards reachability analysis, in a manner analogous to the way $\mathit{Helpful}(\alpha, F)$ is computed in Proposition 1. Note that the set $\mathcal{B}$ used in $\mathit{After}(\mathcal{B}, F)$ is typically a parameterized set of actions, containing a set of actions of form $\alpha_j(i)$ for a finite set j, and an arbitrary i with $1 \leq i \leq N$. Thus the set $\mathcal{B}$ is unboundedly large, but still finite. Care must be taken to handle the parameters correctly when performing the predecessor calculations. Now we state the termination rule.

Theorem 2. *Let $\mathcal{B}$ be a set of fair actions of $\langle S, \longrightarrow, \mathcal{A}\rangle$, and let F be a set of states in S. Then*

$$\left[\mathit{After}(\mathcal{B}, F) \cap \bigcap_{\alpha \in \mathcal{B}} (\neg \mathit{Twice}(\alpha, F) \cap \mathit{Persist}(\alpha, F))\right] \subseteq \Diamond F$$

Proof. Let s be a state in the set defined by the left-hand side. Consider a computation from s. Assume that it contains no state in F. Then, since $s \in \mathit{After}(\mathcal{B}, F)$ it also contains no state in which all actions in $\mathcal{B}$ are disabled. This means that at any state in the computation, some action α is enabled. Since $s \in \mathit{Persist}(\alpha, F)$ the action α will remain enabled until it is executed, and thereafter (since $s \in \neg \mathit{Twice}(\alpha, F)$) never be executed again. This implies that after a finite number of computation steps, all actions in $\mathcal{B}$ have been executed. This contradicts the previous conclusion that thereafter some action in $\mathcal{B}$ is enabled, and will eventually be executed.

6.2 Implementation

We have implemented a verification method based on Corollary 1 and Theorem 2 in the framework of Regular Model Checking [7], and applied it to a number of well-known parameterized mutual exclusion protocols.

Verification Procedure. For each protocol, we have modeled F_k as the set of states where process k is in the critical section. We have thereafter computed an under-approximation G_k of $\Diamond F_k$ using the method of Section 4, and thereafter applied the complementary rule described in Section 6.1 to compute $\Diamond G_k$. To ensure that predecessors are reachable states, we computed the set of (forwards) reachable states, and restricted the actions to it.

In our experiments we manually chose what rules to apply and when, to test their expressive power. However, the approach may be fully automated by e.g. applying the rules alternatingly. As a termination condition one could use that the complementary rule does not increase the set $\Diamond F$, no matter which action it is applied to.

As an example, we describe how our verification of starvation freedom for Szymanski's algorithm works. Three successive applications of Corollary 1 establish starvation freedom for almost all the system states where process k is waiting. However, Corollary 1 cannot prove starvation freedom for system states where there are processes at both line 1 and line 2. The reason for this is that the actions of line 2 may disable the actions on line 1, thereby destroying commutativity. By using also one application of Theorem 2, starvation freedom is proven for all the system states where process k is waiting, as desired.

Results. The verification results of our implementation are presented in Table 1. We have computed the sets of states from which starvation freedom for process k is guaranteed, as a set which depends on k. In all cases, the computed *live states* contain all the terminating states. For example, the live states of Szymański's algorithm are: "whenever process k is at line 2". The column "Time" contains time measured from our implementation. The experiments were run on a PC with a 2.4 GHz processor and 1 GB of RAM. For the first three protocols, we need apply only Corollary 1. For the last three last protocols, we need also Theorem 2. Dijkstra's algorithm takes significantly longer time to verify because it contains an action where a global variable is set. Computing the effect of arbitrarily many executions of such an action is relatively expensive in our current implementation [7].

Table 1. Experimental results

Model	Token Pass	Token Ring	Bakery	Szymanski	Burns	Dijkstra
Time	9 s	14 s	36 s	7 min 15 s	7 min 30 s	55 min 11 s

Comparison with Related Work. Several works have considered verification of individual starvation freedom for parameterized mutual exclusion protocols. In papers [31,11] the Szymanski protocol and the Bakery protocol are verified in 95.87 seconds and 9 seconds respectively, using manually supplied abstractions. The works [22,23] verify the Bakery protocol using automatically generated ranking functions, but do not report running times. We have previously verified the Bakery protocol in 44.2 seconds using repeated reachability [28], on the same system. To our knowledge, starvation freedom for the algorithms of Burns and Dijkstra has not been successfully automatically verified before.

Techniques exist for quicker accelerations, which should significantly improve the performance ([1,30]). There is a need for quick automatic accelerations, which also cover global variables and compositions of actions.

7 Conclusions

We have presented a method for proving liveness and termination properties of fair concurrent programs using backwards reachability analysis. The method uses neither computation of transitive closure nor explicit construction of ranking functions and helpful directions, and relies instead on showing certain commutativity properties between different actions of the program. The advantage of our method is that reachability analysis can typically be expected to be simpler to perform than computation of transitive closures or ranking functions. We expect that it should be possible to use and develop powerful techniques for backwards reachability analysis for many classes of parameterized and infinite-state programs. The technique is in general incomplete, but its power can be increased by performing repeated applications and by applying complementary techniques afterwards. The examples in the paper indicate that the method should be applicable to several classes of infinite-state systems. In particular, we have shown that our technique is able to prove starvation-freedom for several parameterized mutual exclusion protocols, for which automated techniques have previously been too expensive.

References

1. P. A. Abdulla, A. Bouajjani, B. Jonsson, and M. Nilsson. Handling global conditions in parameterized system verification. In *Proc.* 11th *Int. Conf. on Computer Aided Verification*, volume 1633 of *Lecture Notes in Computer Science*, pages 134–145, 1999.
2. P. A. Abdulla, K. Čerāns, B. Jonsson, and T. Yih-Kuen. Algorithmic analysis of programs with well quasi-ordered domains. *Information and Computation*, 160:109–127, 2000.
3. P. A. Abdulla, A. Collomb-Annichini, A. Bouajjani, and B. Jonsson. Using forward reachability analysis for verification of lossy channel systems. *Formal Methods in System Design*, 25(1):39–65, 2004.
4. P. A. Abdulla and B. Jonsson. Undecidable verification problems for programs with unreliable channels. *Information and Computation*, 130(1):71–90, 1996.
5. P. A. Abdulla and B. Jonsson. Verifying programs with unreliable channels. *Information and Computation*, 127(2):91–101, 1996.
6. P. A. Abdulla, B. Jonsson, M. Nilsson, J. d'Orso, and M. Saksena. Regular model checking for LTL(MSO). In *Proc.* 16th *Int. Conf. on Computer Aided Verification*, volume 3114 of *Lecture Notes in Computer Science*, 2004.
7. P. A. Abdulla, B. Jonsson, M. Nilsson, and M. Saksena. A survey of regular model checking. In *Proc. CONCUR 2004,* 14th *Int. Conf. on Concurrency Theory*, volume 3170 of *LNCS*, pages 35–48, 2004.
8. I. Balaban, A. Pnueli, and L. D. Zuck. Shape analysis by predicate abstraction. In R. Cousot, editor, *VMCAI*, volume 3385 of *Lecture Notes in Computer Science*, pages 164–180. Springer Verlag, 2005.
9. T. Ball, R. Majumdar, T. Millstein, and S. K. Rajamani. Automatic predicate abstraction of C programs. In *PLDI 2001*, pages 203–213, 2001.
10. B. Boigelot and P. Godefroid. Symbolic verification of communication protocols with infinite state spaces using QDDs. In Alur and Henzinger, editors, *Proc.* 8th *Int. Conf. on Computer Aided Verification*, volume 1102 of *Lecture Notes in Computer Science*, pages 1–12. Springer Verlag, 1996.
11. A. Bouajjani, P. Habermehl, and T. Vojnar. Abstract regular model checking. In *Proc.* 16th *Int. Conf. on Computer Aided Verification*, volume 3114 of *Lecture Notes in Computer Science*, 2004.
12. A. Bradley, Z. Manna, and H. Sipma. Linear ranking with reachability. In M. Abadi and L. de Alfaro, editors, *Proc. CONCUR 2005,* 15th *Int. Conf. on Concurrency Theory*, volume 3653 of *Lecture Notes in Computer Science*, pages 491–504, 2005.
13. A. Bradley, Z. Manna, and H. Sipma. Termination analysis of integer linear loops. In K. Etessami and S. Rajamani, editors, *Proc.* 17th *Int. Conf. on Computer Aided Verification*, volume 3576 of *Lecture Notes in Computer Science*, pages 488–502, 2005.
14. A. Bradley, Z. Manna, and H. Sipma. Termination of polynomial programs. In R. Cousot, editor, *Proc. VMCAI 2005, Verification, Model Checking, and Abstract Interpretation, 6th International Conference, Paris, January 17-19*, volume 3385 of *Lecture Notes in Computer Science*, pages 113–129. Springer Verlag, 2005.
15. K. Chandy and J. Misra. *Parallel Program Design: A Foundation.* Addison-Wesley, 1988.
16. E. M. Clarke, O. Grumberg, S. Jha, Y. Lu, and H. Veith. Counterexample-guided abstraction refinement for symbolic model checking. *J. ACM*, 50(5):752–794, 2003.
17. E. M. Clarke, O. Grumberg, M. Minea, and D. Peled. State space reduction using partial order techniques. *Software Tools for Technology Transfer*, 2:279–287, 1999.
18. M. Colon and H. Sipma. Synthesis of linear ranking functions. In T. Margaria and W. Yi, editors, *Proc. TACAS '01,* 7th *Int. Conf. on Tools and Algorithms for the Construction and Analysis of Systems*, volume 2031 of *Lecture Notes in Computer Science*, pages 67–81. Springer Verlag, 2001.

19. M. Colon and H. Sipma. Practical methods for proving program termination. In Brinskma and Larsen, editors, *Proc. 14th Int. Conf. on Computer Aided Verification*, volume 2404 of *Lecture Notes in Computer Science*, pages 442–454. Springer Verlag, 2002.
20. B. Cook, A. Podelski, and A. Rybalchenko. Abstraction refinement for termination. In C. Hankin and I. Siveroni, editors, *Proc. 12th Int. Symp. on Static Analysis*, volume 3672 of *LNCS*, pages 87–101. Springer Verlag, 2005.
21. P. Cousot. Proving program invariance and termination by parametric abstraction, lagrangian relaxation and semidefinite programming. In R. Cousot, editor, *VMCAI*, volume 3385 of *Lecture Notes in Computer Science*, pages 1–24. Springer Verlag, 2005.
22. Y. Fang, N. Piterman, A. Pnueli, and L. Zuck. Liveness with incomprehensible ranking. In K. Jensen and A. Podelski, editors, *Proc. TACAS '04, 10th Int. Conf. on Tools and Algorithms for the Construction and Analysis of Systems*, volume 2988 of *Lecture Notes in Computer Science*, pages 482–496. Springer Verlag, 2004.
23. Y. Fang, N. Piterman, A. Pnueli, and L. Zuck. Liveness with invisible ranking. In B. Steffen and G. Leiv, editors, *Proc. VMCAI 2004, Verification, Model Checking, and Abstract Interpretation, 5th International Conference, Venice, January 11-13*, volume 2937 of *Lecture Notes in Computer Science*, pages 223–238. Springer Verlag, 2004.
24. G. Holzmann. The model checker SPIN. *IEEE Trans. on Software Engineering*, SE-23(5):279–295, May 1997.
25. C. S. Lee, N. D. Jones, and A. M. Ben-Amram. The size-change principle for program termination. In *Proc. 28th ACM Symp. on Principles of Programming Languages*, pages 81–92, 2001.
26. Z. Manna and A. Pnueli. Adequate proof principles for invariance and liveness properties of concurrent programs. *Science of Computer Programming*, 4(4):257–289, 1984.
27. Z. Manna and A. Pnueli. Tools and rules for the practicing verifier. In R. Rashid, editor, *CMU Computer Science: A 25th Anniversary Commemorative*, pages 125–159. ACM Press and Addison-Wesley, 1991.
28. M. Nilsson. *Regular Model Checking*. PhD thesis, Uppsala University, 2005.
29. A. Pnueli, A. Podelski, and A. Rybalchenko. Separating fairness and well-foundedness for the analysis of fair discrete systems. In N. Halbwachs and L. Zuck, editors, *Proc. TACAS '05, 11th Int. Conf. on Tools and Algorithms for the Construction and Analysis of Systems*, volume 3440 of *LNCS*, pages 124–139. Springer Verlag, 2005.
30. A. Pnueli and E. Shahar. Liveness and acceleration in parameterized verification. In *Proc. 12th Int. Conf. on Computer Aided Verification*, volume 1855 of *Lecture Notes in Computer Science*, pages 328–343. Springer Verlag, 2000.
31. A. Pnueli, J. Xu, and L. Zuck. Liveness with (0,1,infinity)-counter abstraction. In *Proc. 14th Int. Conf. on Computer Aided Verification*, volume 2404 of *Lecture Notes in Computer Science*, 2002.
32. A. Podelski and A. Rybalchenko. Transition invariants. In *Proc. LICS' 04 20th IEEE Int. Symp. on Logic in Computer Science*, pages 32–41, 2004.
33. A. Podelski and A. Rybalchenko. Transition predicate abstraction and fair termination. In *Proc. 32th ACM Symp. on Principles of Programming Languages*, pages 132–144, 2005.
34. B. K. Szymanski. Mutual exclusion revisited. In *Proc. Fifth Jerusalem Conference on Information Technology*, pages 110–117, Los Alamitos, CA, 1990. IEEE Computer Society Press.
35. P. Wolper and B. Boigelot. Verifying systems with infinite but regular state spaces. In *Proc. 10th Int. Conf. on Computer Aided Verification*, volume 1427 of *Lecture Notes in Computer Science*, pages 88–97, Vancouver, July 1998. Springer Verlag.

Model Checking Quantified Computation Tree Logic

Arend Rensink

Department of Computer Science, University of Twente
P.O. Box 217, 7500 AE, The Netherlands
rensink@cs.utwente.nl

Abstract. Propositional temporal logic is not suitable for expressing properties on the evolution of dynamically allocated entities over time. In particular, it is not possible to trace such entities through computation steps, since this requires the ability to freely mix quantification and temporal operators.

In this paper we study *Quantified Computation Tree Logic* (QCTL), which extends the well-known propositional computation tree logic, PCTL, with first and (monadic) second order quantification. The semantics of QCTL is expressed on *algebra automata*, which are automata enriched with abstract algebras at each state, and with reallocations at each transition that express an injective renaming of the algebra elements from one state to the next. The reallocations enable minimization of the automata modulo bisimilarity, essentially through symmetry reduction. Our main result is to show that each combination of a QCTL formula and a finite algebra automaton can be transformed to an equivalent PCTL formula over an ordinary Kripke structure, while maintaining the symmetry reduction. The transformation is structure-preserving on the formulae. This gives rise to a method to lift any model checking technique for PCTL to QCTL.

1 Introduction

Ever since its conception in the 80's, model checking has been based on modal extensions of propositional logic. That is to say, the properties that can be formulated and checked have as their smallest building blocks a finite set of atomic propositions, each of which is satisfied by a subset of the states of the model (Kripke structure, transition system, automaton) being checked. This means that, for the purpose of model checking, the information in each of the states is abstracted to the subset of propositions satisfied there.

Since the propositions themselves can be defined in any manner whatsoever (as long as only finitely many of them are considered at the same time) this setup can be used also in settings where the states have rich associated domains — for instance, the state snapshots of a software system. A good example of this principle arises in software models with a fixed set of variables over a finite set of values, such as can be written in, for instance, Spin's input language Promela [15]: there the states are essentially valuations of those variables, and typical propositions are (in)equations over the variables. As a more sophisticated example, one can define propositions that are actually closed first-order formulae interpreted over the states; this allows the expression of existential and universal properties even in a setting where the size of the state domains (such as the number of variables or entities) is not fixed. As an example, one may think of a

C. Baier and H. Hermanns (Eds.): CONCUR 2006, LNCS 4137, pp. 110–125, 2006.

property like "the buffer can always eventually become empty" interpreted in a model where values are added to and removed from cells of a buffer of variable (bounded) size; here the proposition "the buffer is empty" actually corresponds to the first-order property "no cell in the buffer contains a value".

(Note that a property such as this one is independent of the size of the buffer; this is why quantification is essential to be able to formulate it. When the model is fixed, so that the maximum size of the state domains is known, any closed first-order state formula can be *expanded* to an equivalent quantifier-free one by flattening the quantifiers to a finite disjunction or conjunction ranging over all existing values.)

This setup can also be explained in terms of a two-layered logic: at the bottom we have a language to express those properties of individual states that are considered interesting for verification purposes; on top of that we define a modal logic, in which the properties of the lower level are treated as propositions. There are, however, system-level properties that are relevant to the correctness of a system and yet cannot be expressed in this two-layered setup. Typically, these are properties where the *behaviour of individual entities over time* is at issue. An example that will be used throughout this paper is "values are removed from the buffer in the same order they are inserted" (or "the buffer has FIFO-behaviour"). Here it is important not only that a buffer cell contains *some* object, but also that *the same* object was (or was not) contained by some buffer cell in the next or previous state. In order to express this, we need to track the identity of the object over multiple states, which can only be done through quantification *outside* the modal operators; hence, the two-layer hierarchy no longer suffices.

From this observation, it follows that there is interest in logics in which quantification and modalities can be freely mixed — a point we have argued before in [11, 10, 19], and has been made independently by Yahav et al. in [21]. In contrast to the latter, we pursue a model checking approach. In our work cited above this was limited to multisets resp. singly-linked lists, which however were unbounded in size; in the current paper we study arbitrary algebraic structures (like [21]), albeit (in our case) for finite state, or in other words, bounded models only. As modal logic we take Quantified Computation Tree Logic (QCTL), which adds first and (monadic) second order quantification to Propositional Computation Tree Logic (PCTL, see [6]). The contribution of this paper is to show that:

1. Using second order quantification, QCTL formulae can not only be used to track entities over time, but also to express (de)allocation schedules, such as the fact that entities are deleted in their order of creation.
2. Any combination of a property in QCTL together with a finite model to be checked (in which the size of the state domains is variable) can be transformed to a combination of an expanded, quantifier-free formula and an expanded model, such that the model checking question has the same answer in both combinations.
3. This can be made to work on models that are minimized up to bisimilarity (using reallocations between states) without losing the reduction due to that minimization.

Regarding the latter point: for our models (which we call *algebra automata* since the state domains are algebras of some fixed signature) we use an idea from history-dependent automata (Montanari and Pistore [16, 17]): each transition carries a *reallocation* function from the entities in its source to thoses in its target state. This allows states with symmetrical domains to be merged, and thus can help to keep models small: [17] shows that history-dependent automata can be minimized with respect to bisimilarity. Depending on the amount of symmetry in the system, minimization can result in a logarithmically smaller model in terms of the number of states and transitions, while keeping the algebra sizes constant — at the price of the reallocations themselves.

In the terminology of quantified modal logic (see, e.g., Fitting [12, 13], Basin et al. [2]), our models have variable domains and non-rigid designators, and our transformation has a strong analogy to *Skolemization* — the introduction of a new constant (non-rigidly designating) for every quantified logical variable. The idea is essentially that of *case splitting* for existential quantifiers, modified to take (de)allocation and reallocations into account and to retain the state space reduction due to minimization.

The transformation theorem of this paper implies that existing tools and techniques for PCTL model checking (see, e.g., [7]) can be used directly for QCTL, once the property and model are both given. The complexity of the transformation of the automaton depends on the maximal nesting depth of quantifiers in the formula, d, and the maximum size of the algebras in the individual states, a: the transformation results in a worst-case blow-up exponential in d and a, or just linear in a if the formula contains first-order quantification only. On the formula the transformation results in blow-up linear in the number of temporal operators and quantifiers. Note that this complexity is no better than was to be expected by a simple combinatorial argument based on the boundedness of the model, but is still interesting in the light of the aforementioned potential for symmetry reduction.

Sect. 2 defines and discusses the logic, Sect. 3 defines its semantics and Sect. 4 defines the transformation and proves the main result. Sect. 5 discusses some improvements, including the addition of (Büchi) fairness. We draw conclusions and discuss related work in Sect. 6. For space reasons, most proofs had to be omitted; however, see http://www.cs.utwente.nl/~rensink/papers/concur2006-full.pdf.

2 The Logic

The structures that we will model and reason about in this paper are built on a set of *names* Name. The same names are used for functions and predicates in the model and for logical variables. Names will be interpreted by strict partial functions $\mathsf{Ent}_\bot^\alpha \rightharpoonup \mathsf{Ent}_\bot^\tau$ for some set of entities Ent (where $\bot \notin \mathsf{Ent}$ stands for undefinedness and $\mathsf{Ent}_\bot = \mathsf{Ent} \cup \{\bot\}$), with $\alpha \in \mathsf{Nat}$ (the *arity*) and $\tau \in \{0, 1\}$ (the *type*). In fact for the sake of conciseness we assume that every name $n \in \mathsf{Name}$ has a fixed arity αn and type τn, which are respected by the interpretation. We use $\mathsf{Name}^{i,j}$ with $i \in \mathsf{Nat}$ and $j = 0, 1$ for the subset of names with arity i and type j. The entities, which from the point of the formalism are uninterpreted, can in practice be made to stand for arbitrary data and reference values; for instance, in software models they can stand for stack frames or heap objects.

The intuition is that if $\tau n = 0$ then n denotes a partial function to a singleton set (since $\mathsf{Ent}^0 = \{\varepsilon\}$ consists of the empty sequence only), which in turn corresponds to the characteristic function for a predicate with arity αn (or a monadic second-order variable if used in the logic); the predicate is taken to hold in a given state if and only its value is defined. If, moreover, $\alpha n = 0$ then n corresponds to a proposition. On the other hand, if $\tau n = 1$ then n is a (partially defined) operator with arity αn; If, moreover, $\alpha n = 0$ then n corresponds to an ordinary constant (in the model) or first-order variable (in the logic).

As meta-variables over Name, we typically use p to range over predicates (including propositions), f for functions, and c for constants; for the general case we use x, y.

We now introduce the logic studied in this paper, QCTL. The syntax is given by the following grammar, which defines *terms* (meta-variables t, u) and *formulae* (meta-variables ϕ, ψ):

$$t ::= f(\boldsymbol{u})$$

$$\phi ::= t \mid t \equiv u \mid \exists x\, \phi \mid \phi \wedge \psi \mid \neg\phi \mid \mathsf{EX}\,\phi \mid \mathsf{E}(\phi\, \mathsf{U}\, \psi) \mid \mathsf{A}(\phi\, \mathsf{U}\, \psi)$$

In our examples, we assume that negation binds strongest, and quantification as well as EX bind weakest.

- A term $t = f(\boldsymbol{u})$ stands for the application of $f \in \mathsf{Name}$ to a vector of sub-terms $\boldsymbol{u}$, with $|\boldsymbol{u}| = \alpha f$. If $\alpha f = 0$ then $\boldsymbol{u} = \varepsilon$, in which case we usually omit the brackets and write only f.
  The notion of type can be extended from names to terms in a natural way, by specifying $\tau t = \tau f$ if $t = f(\boldsymbol{u})$; t is *well-typed* if for all $u_i \in \boldsymbol{u}$, $\tau u_i = 1$ and u_i is again well-typed. Since functions are generally partial, terms may evaluate to $\perp$.
- A formula $\phi = t$ expresses that (the interpretation of) t is defined; i.e., t does *not* evaluate to $\perp$. (Note that, due to the fact that our interpretations can be partial, we are not in classical logic.) In particular, if $\tau t = 0$ (meaning that $t = p(\boldsymbol{u})$ for some predicate p) then this is the usual interpretation of predicates. On the other hand, $\neg t$ with $\tau t = 1$ denotes that the entity denoted by t no longer exists — presumably because it has been deallocatied in a transition leading up to the current state.
- $\phi = t{\equiv}u$ expresses equality of the interpretations of t and u, where it is assumed that $\tau t = \tau u = 1$. Equality will be interpreted strictly, meaning that $t = u$ will be false if either t or u (or both) evaluate to $\perp$. Non-strict equality is expressed by $(t \vee u) \Rightarrow t \equiv u$.
- $\phi = \exists x\, \psi$ is existential quantification over x in ψ; it will be deemed valid if an appropriate (defined) value can be found for x such that ψ then holds. We limit this to first-order and monadic second-order quantification ($x \in \mathsf{Name}^{0,1}$ or $x \in \mathsf{Name}^{1,0}$, respectively).
  In the interpretation of the logic, to be defined below, a sub-formula x in the context of a quantified formula $\exists x\, \psi$ (i.e., the usage of a logical first-order variable as a formula) stands for the fact that the entity denoted by x is still "alive", i.e., has not been de-allocated. For second-order variables p, the sub-formula $p(x)$ in the context of $\exists p\, \psi$ denotes that x is among the (surviving) entities in the set p.

The other clauses correspond to the usual connectives from computation tree logic. Briefly:

- $\mathsf{EX}\,\phi$ expresses that ϕ holds in some state directly reachable from the current state;
- $\mathsf{E}(\phi\, \mathsf{U}\, \psi)$ expresses that there is a run of the system starting in the current state, in which ψ holds at some point, and ϕ holds at all earlier points;
- $\mathsf{A}(\phi\, \mathsf{U}\, \psi)$ expresses that for all runs of the system starting in the current state, ψ holds at some point, and ϕ holds in all earlier points.

We will also freely use the derived formulae $\forall x\, \phi$, $\phi \vee \psi$, $\mathsf{AX}\, \phi$ (the dual of $\mathsf{EX}\, \phi$), $\mathsf{AF}\, \phi$ and $\mathsf{EF}\, \phi$ (defined as $\mathsf{A}(\mathsf{tt}\ \mathsf{U}\ \phi)$ and $\mathsf{E}(\mathsf{tt}\ \mathsf{U}\ \phi)$, respectively) and their duals $\mathsf{EG}\, \phi$ and $\mathsf{AF}\, \phi$. We also define the *free names* of a formula ϕ, denoted $fn(\phi)$, as usual; we use $fn^{i,j}(\phi)$ $(= fn(\phi) \cap \mathsf{Name}^{i,j})$ to denote the subset of names with arity i and type j.

An important special class of formulae are the *propositional* ones. These are formulae for which the first- and second-order features of the logic are essentially unused: the only names are propositions (i.e., with $\alpha = \tau = 0$) and no quantification is used.

Definition 1 (propositional formulae). *A formula ϕ is called* propositional *if it is quantifier-free and $fn(\phi) \subseteq \mathsf{Name}^{0,0}$.*

Example 1. Assume $List, Cell, Data, S \in \mathsf{Name}^{1,0}$, $x, y \in \mathsf{Name}^{0,1}$, $next, val \in \mathsf{Name}^{1,1}$ and $connect \in \mathsf{Name}^{2,0}$. The following are example properties of QCTL:

1. $\mathsf{AG}\forall x\, (Cell(x) \Leftrightarrow Data(val(x)))$, expressing a type invariant, viz. that in all reachable states, val is defined only for, and for all, $Cell$-type entities, and always yields a $Data$-type entity.
2. $\forall x\, (Data(x) \Rightarrow \mathsf{AF}\, \neg x)$, expressing that all currently existing $Data$-type entities are eventually de-allocated.
3. $\forall S\, \mathsf{EF}\, \exists x\, (Data(x) \wedge \neg S(x))$, expressing that in all system behaviours, some new $Data$-type entity is eventually allocated. (Note that S is a second-order variable; $\neg S(x)$ expresses that x is not in the set S, meaning that the entity denoted by x did not exist in the state where S was bound.)
4. $\mathsf{AG}\, \forall x, y(List(x) \wedge Cell(y) \wedge connect(x, y) \Rightarrow (\mathsf{AG}\, y) \vee \mathsf{A}(connect(x, y)\, \mathsf{U}\, \neg y))$, expressing that cells can become disconnected from a $List$-type entity only when they are de-allocated.
5. $\mathsf{AG}\, \forall S\, (\forall x\, Data(x) \Leftrightarrow S(x)) \Rightarrow \mathsf{AG}\, \forall x,y\, S(x) \wedge Data(y) \Rightarrow S(y) \vee \mathsf{A}(y\, \mathsf{U}\, \neg x)$, expressing that $Data$-type entities are allocated and de-allocated in first-in-first-out order. To understand this, note that the sub-formula $\forall x\, Data(x) \Leftrightarrow S(x)$ specifies that the logical second-order variable S is equivalent (in the state where S is bound) to the predicate $Data$. Furthermore, $\mathsf{A}(y\, \mathsf{U}\, \neg x)$ expresses that y lives at least as long as x. Thus, $\forall x,y\, S(x) \wedge Data(y) \Rightarrow S(y) \vee \mathsf{A}(y\, \mathsf{U}\, \neg x)$ expresses that, for all $Data$-type entities x and y, if x existed in the (past) state where S was bound but y did not — meaning that y was created after x — then y will survive x.

We introduce some further syntactic sugar. In the following let $x \in \mathsf{Name}^{0,1}$, $S \in \mathsf{Name}^{1,0}$ and $T \in \mathsf{Name}^{1,\tau}$ for some τ, and let t be a term with $\tau t = 1$.

- $\exists x{:}T\, \phi$ stands for $\exists x\, T(x) \wedge \phi$;
- $\forall x{:}T\, \phi$ stands for $\forall x\, T(x) \Rightarrow \phi$;
- $\ulcorner x{\equiv}t\, \phi$ stands for $\exists x\, x{\equiv}t \wedge \phi$.
- $\ulcorner S{\equiv}T\, \phi$ stands for $\exists S\, (\forall x\, S(x) \Leftrightarrow T(x)) \wedge \phi$.
- $\ulcorner S\, \phi$ stands for $\exists S\, (\forall x\, S(x)) \wedge \phi$.

Thus, in $\exists x{:}T\, \phi$, the first-order variable x is bound to some entity of "type" T (i.e., on which T is defined), whereas in $\ulcorner x{\equiv}t\, \phi$ it is bound precisely to the current value of the term t (which has to be defined). Likewise, in $\ulcorner S{\equiv}T\, \phi$, the second-order variable S is bound to the set of all values of type T; finally, $\ulcorner S\,\phi$ binds S to the set of *all* currently existing values. The last three properties can be read as "let ... equal ... in ϕ."

Using this syntactic sugar, for instance, the property in Ex. 1.5 above becomes

$$\mathsf{AG}\,\ulcorner S{\equiv}Data\;\mathsf{AG}\,\forall x{:}S,\,y{:}Data(S(y) \vee \mathsf{A}(y\;\mathsf{U}\;\neg x)) \tag{1}$$

Valuations. To interpret the logic we need to express what the names stand for; in other words, we need the concept of a *valuation*. Valuations are defined in terms of *entities*: if $E \subseteq \mathsf{Ent}$ is some set of entities and $N \subseteq \mathsf{Name}$ a set of names, then a valuation of N over E is a function $V\colon N \to E^* \rightharpoonup E^{0,1}$ such that for all $x \in N$, $V(x)\colon E^{\alpha x} \rightharpoonup E^{\tau x}$; in words, V assigns to every name a partial function of the appropriate arity and type. The set of valuations of N over E is denoted $\mathsf{Val}[N, E]$. Valuations are strictly extended to terms, in the natural way:

$$V(f(\boldsymbol{u})) = \begin{cases} V(f)(V(u_1)\cdots V(u_{\alpha f})) & \text{if } V(u_i) \neq \bot \text{ for all } 1 \leq i \leq \alpha f \\ \bot & \text{otherwise.} \end{cases}$$

We call N the *domain* of V, denoted $dom(V)$. Note that we may actually have $V(x) = \bot$ for $x \in N^{0,1}$; in this case, the variable x is in the domain of V despite the fact that V assigns "undefined" to it.

Another way to understand the concept of a valuation $V \in \mathsf{Val}[N, E]$ is that it defines a partial N-*algebra* over the domain E (N being the signature of the algebra).

If $V \in \mathsf{Val}[N, E]$ and $W \in \mathsf{Val}[M, E]$, then $V\{W\}$ equals W wherever it is defined, and V otherwise. Furthermore, $V|_{-x}$ denotes V minus the value for x. Formally:

$$V\{W\} : y \mapsto \begin{cases} W(y) & \text{if } y \in dom(W) \\ V(y) & \text{otherwise.} \end{cases} \qquad V|_{-x} : y \mapsto V(y) \text{ if } x \neq y.$$

It follows that $dom(V\{W\}) = N \cup M$ and $dom(V|_{-x}) = N \setminus \{x\}$.

3 Algebra Automata

To express the semantics of QCTL we define an automata model that includes a fixed set of *model names*, as well as a separate domain of values at each state, with a corresponding valuation of the model names. In fact, the domain and valuation together constitute an *algebra* for the model names (considered as a signature). Furthermore, we use an idea from *History-Dependent Automata* proposed by Montanari and Pistore [17], namely to allow *reallocations* of values between states.

Definition 2. *Let* Ent *be a set of entities. An algebra automaton* $\mathcal{A}$ *over* Ent *is a tuple* $\langle N, S, D, A, \rightarrow, I\rangle$ *where*

- $N \subseteq \mathsf{Name}$ *is a finite set of names;*
- S *is a set of states;*
- $D\colon S \to \mathbf{2}^{\mathsf{Ent}}$ *associates with every* $s \in S$ *a domain* $D(s)$ *of values "existing" in* s*;*
- $A\colon S \to \mathsf{Val}[N, \mathsf{Ent}]$ *associates with every* $s \in S$ *an algebra* $A(s) \in \mathsf{Val}[N, D(s)]$*;*

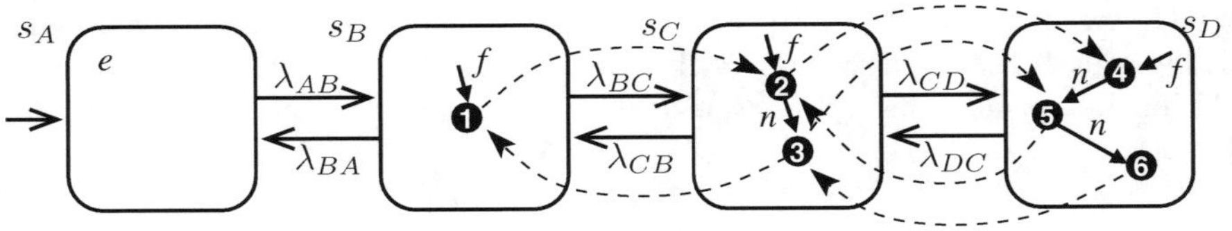

Fig. 1. First-in-first-out list

- $\rightarrow \subseteq S \times (\mathsf{Ent} \rightharpoonup \mathsf{Ent}) \times S$ *is an indexed binary relation between states, where the indices are partial injective functions that map the domain of the source state to the domain of the target state; thus,* $s \rightarrow_\lambda s'$ *implies* $\lambda\colon D(s) \rightharpoonup D(s')$. *Every state has at least one outgoing transition;*
- $I \subseteq S$ *is a set of initial states.*

$\mathcal{A}$ *is called finite if* S *is finite and* $D(s)$ *is finite for all* $s \in S$.

The index λ in a transition $s \rightarrow_\lambda s'$ stands for a *reallocation* (or renaming) of entities. That is, an entity $e \in D(s)$ that does not have an image in λ is *deallocated* (dies) during the transition; otherwise, the entity remains in existence but is known in s' as $\lambda(e)$. Entities $e' \in D(s')$ that are not in the range of λ are *allocated* (created, born). Note that λ is *not* required to preserve the algebraic structure of the state: indeed the structure may change, e.g., references or values may be reassigned, as in the transitions λ_{BC} and λ_{DC} in the following example.

Example 2. Let $e \in \mathsf{Name}^{0,0}, f \in \mathsf{Name}^{0,1}$ and $n \in \mathsf{Name}^{1,1}$ stand for *empty*, the *first* and *next* elements in a list; then **??** shows an algebra automaton with $N = \{e, f, n\}$ which models the behaviour of a list (of maximum length 3) of which the elements are allocated and deallocated in a first-in-first-out manner. The rounded rectangles are states, containing valuations $V \in \mathsf{Val}[N, \mathsf{Nat}]$ (so the numbered nodes represent the entities): proposition e holds in the state where it is inscribed, whereas the constant $V(f)$ and the partial function $V(n)$ are given as arrows. The reallocations λ are shown as dashed arrows, implicitly associated with the transitions in the corresponding direction.

From [17] we recall the important property that history-dependent automata can be minimized with respect to bisimilarity, defined appropriately to abstract from the entities while maintaining the algebraic structure up to isomorphism. That is, a bisimulation between algebra automata $\mathcal{A}_1$ and $\mathcal{A}_2$ is a family of symmetric relations $\{R_f \subseteq S_1 \times S_2\}_{f:\mathsf{Ent}\rightarrow\mathsf{Ent}}$, such that $(s_1, s_2) \in R_f$ implies

- f is an isomorphism from $A_1(s_1)$ to $A_2(s_2)$;
- $s_1 \rightarrow_\lambda s_1'$ implies $s_2 \rightarrow_\mu s_2'$ for some s_2' such that $(s_1', s_2') \in R_g$ with $g \circ \lambda = \mu \circ f$;
- $s_2 \rightarrow_\mu s_2'$ implies $s_1 \rightarrow_\lambda s_1'$ for some s_1' such that $(s_1', s_2') \in R_g$ with $g \circ \lambda = \mu \circ f$.

We call $\mathcal{A}_1$ and $\mathcal{A}_2$ bisimilar, denoted $\mathcal{A}_1 \sim \mathcal{A}_2$, if there exists such a bisimulation $\{R_f\}_f$, such that R_{id} is a total relation between I_1 and I_2.

Essentially, minimization w.r.t. $\sim$ comes down to *symmetry reduction*: all states with isomorphic algebras can be folded together, maintaining the connection with the entities in neighbouring states through the reallocations. In the automaton of Fig. 1, which is already minimized, this can be seen from the fact that the reallocations λ_{CD} and λ_{DC} between are not inverse to one another. Unfolding this example automaton so that all reallocations become (partial) identities results in a quadratic blowup (in the number of states). In the worst case the blowup is exponential in the size of the algebra — or in other words, minimization w.r.t. $\sim$ can result in a logarithmically smaller automaton.

The well-known model of Kripke structures appears as an important special case, where all the names are propositions (i.e., in $\mathsf{Name}^{0,0}$) and there are no entities. We call such automata *propositional.*

Definition 3 (propositional automata). *An algebra automaton is called* propositional *if $N \subseteq \mathsf{Name}^{0,0}$ and $D(s) = \emptyset$ for all $s \in S$.*

A key fact used in this paper (see Th. 2 below) is that for the special case of propositional automata and propositional formulae, efficient solutions to the model checking problem are well known from the literature (cf. [7]).

3.1 Semantics of QCTL

We now express the semantics of QCTL in terms of algebra automata. For this purpose we first need the notion of a *run* of such an automaton. Note that we have applied a common trick by enforcing every state to have at least one outgoing transition; this makes the presentation technically easier.

Definition 4 (paths runs). *Let $\mathcal{A}$ be an algebra automaton. A* path *through $\mathcal{A}$ is a finite or infinite alternating sequence $\sigma = s_0\,\lambda_1\,s_1\,\lambda_2\,s_2\cdots$, ending on a state if the sequence is finite, such that for all λ_i in the sequence, $s_{i-1} \rightarrow_{\lambda_i} s_i$ is a transition in $\mathcal{A}$. The path is called a* run *if it is infinite.*

The set of runs of $\mathcal{A}$ is denoted $\mathit{runs}(\mathcal{A})$. If $\sigma = s_0\,\lambda_1\,s_1\,\lambda_2\,\cdots$ is a run then

- For all $i \geq 0$, $\sigma|_i^s$ denotes the state at position i in the run, i.e., s_i;
- For all $i > 0$, $\sigma|_i^\lambda$ denotes the reallocation at position i in the run, i.e., λ_i;
- For all $i \geq 0$, $\sigma|_{\leq i}^\lambda$ denotes the reallocation *up to* position i in the run, i.e., $\lambda_i \circ \lambda_{i-1} \circ \cdots \circ \lambda_1$. This is interpreted to yield $id_{D(s_0)}$ if $i = 0$.

The semantics of QCTL is expressed by a relation $\mathcal{A}, s, V \models \phi$ where ϕ is a QCTL-formula, $\mathcal{A}$ is an algebra automaton, $s \in S$ is a state of $\mathcal{A}$ and $V \in \mathsf{Val}[M, D(s)]$ is a valuation, with $\mathit{fn}(\phi) \supseteq M \cup N_{\mathcal{A}}$. We write $\mathcal{A}, V \models \phi$ if $\mathcal{A}, s, V \models \phi$ for all $s \in I$. Moreover, we may omit V if $\mathit{dom}(V) = \emptyset$, and $\mathcal{A}$ if it is clear from the context. The modelling relation is defined by induction on the structure of ϕ, as follows:

$$
\begin{array}{lll}
\mathcal{A}, s, V \models t & :\Leftrightarrow & A(s)\{V\}(t) \neq \bot \\
\mathcal{A}, s, V \models t \equiv u & :\Leftrightarrow & A(s)\{V\}(t) = A(s)\{V\}(u) \;\; (\neq \bot) \\
\mathcal{A}, s, V \models \exists x\, \phi & :\Leftrightarrow & \mathcal{A}, s, V\{W\} \models \phi \text{ for some } W \in \mathsf{Val}[\{x\}, D(s)] \\
\mathcal{A}, s, V \models \mathsf{EX}\, \phi & :\Leftrightarrow & \mathcal{A}, s', \lambda \circ V \models \phi \text{ for some } s \rightarrow_\lambda s' \\
\mathcal{A}, s, V \models \mathsf{E}(\phi \,\mathsf{U}\, \psi) & :\Leftrightarrow & \text{there is a } \sigma \in \mathit{runs}(\mathcal{A}) \text{ with } \sigma|_0^s = s \text{ such that} \\
 & & \mathcal{A}, \sigma|_i^s, \sigma|_{\leq i}^\lambda \circ V \models \psi \text{ for some } i \geq 0 \text{ and} \\
 & & \mathcal{A}, \sigma|_j^s, \sigma|_{\leq j}^\lambda \circ V \models \phi \text{ for all } 0 \leq j < i; \\
\mathcal{A}, s, V \models \mathsf{A}(\phi \,\mathsf{U}\, \psi) & :\Leftrightarrow & \text{for all } \sigma \in \mathit{runs}(\mathcal{A}) \text{ with } \sigma|_0^s = s\text{:} \\
 & & \mathcal{A}, \sigma|_i^s, \sigma|_{\leq i}^\lambda \circ V \models \psi \text{ for some } i \geq 0 \text{ and} \\
 & & \mathcal{A}, \sigma|_j^s, \sigma|_{\leq j}^\lambda \circ V \models \phi \text{ for all } 0 \leq j < i.
\end{array}
$$

The following property (the proof of which is straightforward and omitted here) is important in the light of the discussion above regarding minimization up to bisimilarity:

Theorem 1. *If $\mathcal{A} \sim \mathcal{B}$, then $\mathcal{A}, V \models \phi$ iff $\mathcal{B}, V \models \phi$ for all* QCTL*-formulae ϕ.*

We can now formulate the "key fact" about model checking propositional formulae, referred to above:

Theorem 2 (See [7]). *Given a finite algebra automaton $\mathcal{A}$ and a propositional formula ϕ, $\mathcal{A} \models \phi$ can be decided in time linear in the size of ϕ and the size of $\mathcal{A}$.*

Example 3. Without proof, we assert that the automaton of Fig. 1 satisfies the formulae

$$\mathsf{AG}\, \forall x\; n(x) \Rightarrow \ulcorner y{\equiv}n(x)\, \mathsf{A}(y{\equiv}n(x)\; \mathsf{U} \neg x) \tag{2}$$

$$\mathsf{AG}\, \ulcorner S\; \mathsf{AF}\, \exists x\, \neg S(x) \tag{3}$$

$$\mathsf{AG}\, \forall x\; \mathsf{AF} \neg x \tag{4}$$

$$\mathsf{AG}\, \ulcorner S\; \mathsf{AG}\, \forall x{:}S\, \forall y\; S(y) \vee \mathsf{A}(y\; \mathsf{U} \neg x) \tag{5}$$

$$\mathsf{AG}\, \mathsf{EF}\; e\ . \tag{6}$$

Property (2) expresses that the n-pointers in the automaton are *immutable* in the sense that whenever the term $n(x)$ is defined for a given entity x, it will go on designating the same value until x itself is deallocated. Property (4) is a simplified form of Ex. 1.2 expressing that every entity is always eventually deallocated. Likewise, (3) is a simplified form of Ex. 1.3 expressing that a fresh entity is always eventually allocated. Property (5) is a simplified version of (1) expressing that entities are created and destroyed in a first-in-first-out schedule.

Finally, (6) expresses that the state where the list is empty always remains reachable. This is in fact a propositional formula and so can be model checked with existing methods (see Th. 2). Note that algebra automata include no fairness criterion, and so it is not true that the empty list is always eventually reached (i.e., the property $\mathsf{AG}\,\mathsf{AF}\; e$ is not satisfied). See, however, Sect. 5 where we discuss the extension of the model with just such a fairness criterion.

The following theorem states an intuitively straightforward property, heavily used in practice, namely that quantifier-free formulae can be treated as if they were propositional, by defining propositions for all basic formulae t and $t \equiv u$ and abstracting the models accordingly.

Theorem 3. *Let $\mathcal{A}$ be an algebra automaton and let ϕ be a formula with $fn(\phi) \subseteq N$. If ϕ is quantifier-free, then there is a propositional formula ϕ' and a propositional automaton $\mathcal{A}'$, with $size(\phi') = size(\phi)$, $S_{\mathcal{A}'} = S_{\mathcal{A}}$ and $\rightarrow_{\mathcal{A}'} = \{(s, \emptyset, s') \mid s \rightarrow_\lambda s'\}$, such that $\mathcal{A} \models \phi$ if and only if $\mathcal{A}' \models \phi'$.*

Proof. We sketch the proof. The idea is to introduce a propositional name $n_\beta \in \mathsf{Name}^{0,0}$ for every *base sub-formula* ψ in ϕ, where a base formula is of the form $\psi = t$ or $\psi = t{\equiv}u$. ϕ' equals ϕ with all base formulae ψ replaced by the corresponding names

n_ψ; $\mathcal{A}'$ is constructed from $\mathcal{A}$ by re-using the states, setting $D'(s) = \emptyset$ for all $s \in S$, re-using the transitions while stripping away the reallocations λ, and defining

$$A'(s)\colon n_\psi \mapsto \begin{cases} \varepsilon & \text{if } \psi = t \text{ and } A(s)(t) \neq \bot \\ \varepsilon & \text{if } \psi = t{\equiv}u \text{ and } A(s)(t) = A(s)(u) \neq \bot \\ \bot & \text{otherwise.} \end{cases}$$

The proof obligation is implied by the following property, which can be proved by induction on the structure of ϕ: For all $s \in S$, $\mathcal{A}, s \models \phi$ if and only if $\mathcal{A}', s \models \phi'$. □

4 Skolemization

The essential idea in model checking a QCTL formula ϕ over a given algebra automaton $\mathcal{A}$ is to turn the bound logical variables in ϕ into new (non-rigidly designating) model constants — a principle known as *Skolemization* — and to simulate the binding of a logical variable during the evaluation of the formula by a *random assignment* to the corresponding model constant. We can then equivalently model check a transformed formula ϕ^-, where all quantifications are changed into next-step modalities, over the extended automaton. Since ϕ^- is quantifier-free, due to Th. 3 we can apply existing theory to solve the transformed model checking problem.

In fact it is not enough to add the variables to the model and simulate their assignment: in addition we have to be able to distinguish between the transitions of the original automaton and the new "assignment transitions". This will be done by using *assignment flags*, which are proposition names $\alpha_x \in \mathsf{Name}^{0,0}$ for all variables x to be Skolemized, as well as one distinguished flag $\bar{\alpha}$, which stands for *no assignment* and behaves as the negated disjunction of the α_x. In the remainder we assume that the assignment flags are globally given and distinct from all other names in the automaton and the formula to be checked. Furthermore, for a given set of variables X we use $\alpha_X = \{\alpha_x \mid x \in X\} \cup \{\bar{\alpha}\}$ to denote the set of all assignment flags. We also use β, γ to range over α_X.

Definition 5. *Let $\mathcal{A}$ be an algebra automaton, and $X \subseteq \mathsf{Name}$. The X-Skolemization of $\mathcal{A}$, denoted $\mathcal{A}^{+X}$, is given by $\langle N', S', \rightarrow', D', A', I' \rangle$ with*

$$\begin{aligned}
N' &= N \cup X \cup \alpha_X \\
S' &= \{(s, W, \bar{\alpha}) \mid W \in \mathsf{Val}[X, D(s)]\} \cup \\
&\quad\ \{(s, W, \alpha_x) \mid W \in \mathsf{Val}[X, D(s)], x \in X, W(x) \neq \bot\} \\
\rightarrow' &= \{((s, W, \bar{\alpha}), \lambda, (s', \lambda \circ W, \bar{\alpha})) \mid s \rightarrow_\lambda s'\} \cup \\
&\quad\ \{((s, W, \bar{\alpha}), id_{D(s)}, (s, W', \alpha_x)) \mid (s, W, \bar{\alpha}) \in S', W'|_{-x} = W|_{-x}\} \cup \\
&\quad\ \{((s, W, \alpha_x), id_{D(s)}, (s, W, \bar{\alpha})) \mid (s, W, \bar{\alpha}) \in S'\} \\
D' &= \{((s, W, \beta), D(s)) \mid (s, W, \beta) \in S'\} \\
A' &= \{((s, W, \beta), A(s)\{W\}\{\varepsilon/\beta\}) \mid (s, W, \beta) \in S'\} \\
I' &= \{(s, W, \bar{\alpha}) \mid s \in I, dom(W) = \emptyset\}\ .
\end{aligned}$$

The principle of the construction is to allow, in every state, to "guess" a random value and assign it to one of the new variables in the set X. Each state of the extended automaton is a triple consisting of the corresponding state of the original automaton, a combined assignment W, and an assignment flag β indicating which (if any) of the Skolemized variables has been assigned a new value since the previous state. That is, either $\beta = \bar{\alpha}$ if the valuation was unchanged, or $\beta = \alpha_x$ for some $x \in X$ if a new value for x was guessed in the transitions leading up to the state. There are three types of transitions: those reflected from the original automaton, those reflecting random assignment steps, and those leading back from an assignment state to a "normal" state. In the first type, $\beta = \bar{\alpha}$ in source and target state and the guessed valuation W is kept constant (modulo the reallocation); in the second type, the state is unchanged, $\beta = \alpha_x$ (for some $x \in X$) in the target state and W may change (only) at x; in the third type, $\beta = \alpha_x$ in the source state, and the state and guessed valuation are kept constant.

The corresponding transformation of the formulae is defined as follows:

$$\begin{aligned}
t^- &= t \\
(t \equiv u)^- &= t \equiv u \\
(\neg\phi)^- &= \neg\phi^- \\
(\phi \vee \psi)^- &= \phi^- \vee \psi^- \\
(\exists x\, \phi)^- &= \mathsf{EX}(\alpha_x \wedge \mathsf{EX}\, \phi^-) \\
(\mathsf{EX}\, \phi)^- &= \mathsf{EX}(\bar{\alpha} \wedge \phi^-) \\
\mathsf{E}(\phi\, \mathsf{U}\, \psi)^- &= \mathsf{E}((\bar{\alpha} \wedge \phi^-)\, \mathsf{U}\, (\bar{\alpha} \wedge \psi^-)) \\
\mathsf{A}(\phi\, \mathsf{U}\, \psi)^- &= \mathsf{A}(\phi^-\, \mathsf{U}\, (\bar{\alpha} \Rightarrow \psi^-))
\end{aligned}$$

The intuition is that quantification is operationalised by a transition of the extended automaton, which guesses a value for the quantified variable — followed by another transition that returns to a "regular" state. The quantification operator itself is likewise turned into a pair of next-step operators. In order to distinguish "regular" from "assignment" next-steps, we test for the absence or presence of an assignment flag.

The following is the main theorem of this paper:

Theorem 4. *Let ϕ be an arbitrary formula; let X denote the set of names bound in ϕ. For any algebra automaton $\mathcal{A}$ with $fn(\phi) \subseteq N$, the following equivalence holds:*

$$\mathcal{A} \models \phi \qquad \textit{if and only if} \qquad \mathcal{A}^{+X} \models \phi^- \ .$$

Proof. The theorem follows from the following, stronger property, which holds for all $s \in S$ and $V \in \mathsf{Val}[Y, D(s)]$:

$$\mathcal{A}, s, V \models \phi \quad \text{if and only if} \quad \mathcal{A}^{+X}, (s, V, \bar{\alpha}) \models \phi^- \ .$$

This is proved by induction on the structure of ϕ. □

Example 4. Let ϕ denote property (4), and $\mathcal{A}$ the algebra automaton of Ex. 2, simplified to a list of maximum length 2. Fig. 2 shows $\mathcal{A}^{+\{x\}}$: the dotted arrows are the assignment transitions, and the λ's are indicated by pairs of entities, from the source resp. the target state. The skolemized formula is

$$\phi^- \quad = \quad \mathsf{AG}(\mathsf{AX}(\alpha_x \Rightarrow \mathsf{EX}\,\mathsf{AF}(\bar{\alpha} \Rightarrow \neg x)))$$

Clearly, checking ϕ^- over $\mathcal{A}^{+\{x\}}$ is a case of PCTL model checking. The states where $\bar{\alpha} \Rightarrow \neg x$ holds are shaded in the figure.

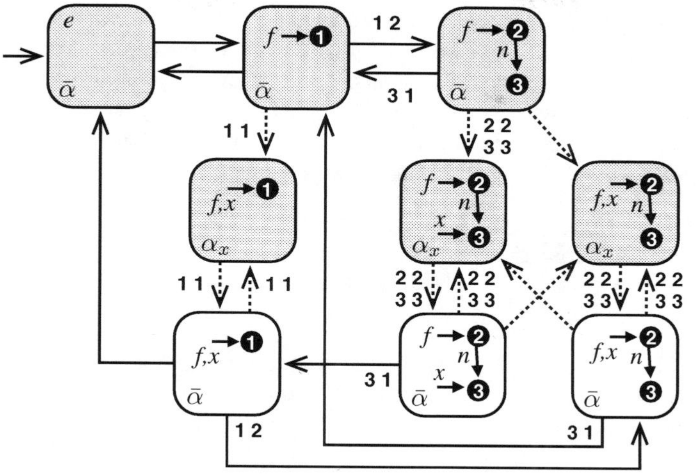

Fig. 2. Skolemization of part of the automaton of Fig. 1 w.r.t. $x \in \mathsf{Name}^{0,1}$

The size of $\mathcal{A}^{+X}$ can be computed as follows: for modelling the possible choices of a first-order variable we need $|D(s)|$ new states for each $s \in S_\mathcal{A}$; for a second-order variable this is $2^{|D(s)|}$. The number of "original" transitions between the new states grows with the same factor, and the number of "assignment" transitions is triple the number of new states. Thus Skolemizing a single variable blows up the automaton linearly (for first-order) resp. exponentially (for second-order) in the maximum domain size. This is repeated for every variable bound in ϕ, making the blow-up exponential in the number of variables. (Note that the domais themselves are not affected.)

Theorem 5 (complexity). *Let $\mathcal{A}$ be an algebra automaton with maximum algebra size a; let $X \subseteq \mathsf{Name}^{0,1} \cup \mathsf{Name}^{1,0}$ and let $d_1 = |X^{0,1}|$ and $d_2 = |X^{1,0}|$. If $\mathcal{B} = \mathcal{A}^{+X}$, then $|S_\mathcal{B}| \leq s \cdot |S_\mathcal{A}|$ and $|{\rightarrow_\mathcal{B}}| \leq s \cdot |{\rightarrow_\mathcal{A}}|$ with $s = O((d_1 + d_2) \cdot a^{d_1} \cdot 2^{a \cdot d_2})$.*

Skolemization of the formula also increases its size, but by a constant factor only.

Theorems 2, 3, 4 and 5 together give rise to the following worst-case time complexity:

Corollary 1. *A* QCTL *formula can be model checked over a finite algebra automaton in time linear in the number of states and transitions, exponential in the size of the formula and exponential in the maximum size of the state domains.*

5 Improvements

As defined above, skolemization only takes a set of (typed) names as input. By taking more information about the formula to be checked into account, the definition can be improved in several ways, resulting in a smaller automaton.

Collectively Bound Names. In Def. 5 the skolemized automaton receives assignment transitions everywhere. Yet they are used only to mimic quantification in the formula, say ϕ, that we want to model check. Through an analysis of ϕ, we can omit many of the assignment transitions or their target states that can clearly never be taken or reached, and thus achieve an appreciable reduction of the skolemized automaton.

A simple observation which can already cause a large reduction is that we only need to assign to sets of variables that occur *together* in some sub-formula. Define the *collectively bound names* $\mathcal{N}(\phi) \subseteq \mathbf{2}^{\mathsf{Name}}$ for arbitrary $\phi \in \mathsf{QCTL}$ as follows:

- $\mathcal{N}(\phi) = \{\emptyset\}$ whenever ϕ is quantifier-free;
- $\mathcal{N}(\neg\phi) = \mathcal{N}(\mathsf{EX}\,\phi) = \mathcal{N}(\phi)$;
- $\mathcal{N}(\phi \vee \psi) = \mathcal{N}(\mathsf{E}(\phi\,\mathsf{U}\,\psi)) = \mathcal{N}(\mathsf{A}(\phi\,\mathsf{U}\,\psi)) = \mathcal{N}(\phi) \cup \mathcal{N}(\psi)$;
- $\mathcal{N}(\exists x\,\phi) = \{Y \cup \{x\} \mid Y \in \mathcal{N}(\phi)\}$.

In model checking ϕ^-, all the states of $\mathcal{A}^{+X}$ that are actually encountered are of the form (s, V, β) with $\{x \in X \mid V(x) \neq \bot\} \subseteq M$ for some $M \in \mathcal{N}(\phi)$. It follows that we may omit all states that are *not* of this form, and still obtain the same answer to the model checking question for ϕ^-. This obviously affects the size of the resulting automaton, since the space over which the valuations V range is now possibly much smaller. In terms of Th. 5, the factor s is now of the order

$$\sum_{M \in \mathcal{N}(\phi), d_1 = |M^{0,1}|, d_2 = |M^{1,0}|} (d_1 + d_2) \cdot a^{d_1} \cdot 2^{a \cdot d_2} \quad .$$

Quantification Order. If we take the above analysis of the formula one step further, it becomes clear that assignment transitions need only ever be taken in the order in which we encounter quantifiers in ϕ, when traversing the syntax tree of ϕ top-down. For instance, in (2) this order is x followed by y, whereas in (5) it is S–x–y. This means that we may cut out transitions that attempt to assign the variables in any different order. Since we may also cut out non-reachable parts of the automaton, this may cause a further reduction.

For instance, in Fig. 2 the transitions leading from the bottom $\bar{\alpha}$-states back to the α_x-states would be removed by this optimization (without, however, a reduction in the number of states).

Assignment. A further optimization, causing a generally unpredictable but potentially large improvement, is to define a special treatment of the binders introduced as syntactic sugar in Sect. 2: $\exists x{:}T\,\phi$ and its dual, but especially $\ulcorner x{\equiv}t\,\phi$, $\ulcorner S{\equiv}T\,\phi$ and $\ulcorner S\,\phi$. Namely, in these cases the possible values assigned to the logical variables are *not* arbitrary values but satisfy some very strict constraints; in fact, in the latter three cases they are bound *precisely* to uniquely defined values.

In terms of Def. 5, if x is bound by such a special syntactic form then the assignment states for x, i.e., the states (s, V, α_x) in $\mathcal{A}^{+X}$, should all satisfy the corresponding constraint on V; i.e., $V(T)(V(x)) \neq \bot$ for $\exists x{:}T\,\phi$, $V(x) = V(t)$ for $\ulcorner x{\equiv}t\,\phi$, etc. Thus, the number of resulting assignment states (for a given s) is no longer $|D(s)|$ or $2^{|D(s)|}$, but much smaller and some cases just 1! Unfortunately, we cannot conclude from this that the whole skolemized automaton will always be that much smaller. This kind of constrained assignment may ruin the symmetry that has originally allowed states to be collapsed (while keeping track of entities through reallocations), and hence may partially or wholly undo the symmetry reduction discussed in Sect. 3.

Non-temporal Quantification In Th. 3 we have recalled how quantifier-free formulae may be reduced to PCTL. As recounted in the introduction, the same principle still works for quantified formulae, as long as all sub-formulae $\exists x\, \psi$ have the property that ψ is without temporal operators. We may take advantage of this by defining yet another optimization, in which all temporal-operator-free sub-formulae are reduced to propositional names, assigned the appropriate value by an extended valuation for the states.

As an example, regard property (3) (Page 118). The sub-formula $\psi = \exists x\, \neg S(x)$ is free of temporal operators and hence a candidate for this optimization. The resulting skolemized property becomes

$$\mathsf{AG}(\bar{\alpha} \Rightarrow \mathsf{EX}(\alpha_S \wedge \mathsf{EX}\,\mathsf{AF}(\bar{\alpha} \Rightarrow n_\psi)))$$

and the skolemized automaton needs to contain assignments to S only.

Fairness. Skolemization can still be applied if the algebra automata are extended with a fairness condition. This involves constructing a corresponding fairness condition for the skolemized automata, where the correspondence should be such that there is the same relation between the fair runs of $\mathcal{A}$ and those of $\mathcal{A}^{+X}$ as there is between the runs as originally defined in Def. 4. We show the necessary construction without proof.

Assume an algebra automaton $\mathcal{A}$ in addition has a component $\mathcal{F} \subseteq \mathbf{2}^S$, and that $runs(\mathcal{A})$ is restricted to those sequences σ such that $\{i \mid \sigma|_i^s \in F\} = \infty$ for all $F \in \mathcal{F}$. Then $\mathcal{A}^{+X}$ should receive a corresponding component $\mathcal{F}'$ defined by

$$\mathcal{F}' = \{\, \{(s, V, \beta) \in S \mid s \in F\} \;\mid F \in \mathcal{F}\} \;.$$

In words, $\mathcal{F}'$ consists of those sets that project onto the fair sets of $\mathcal{F}$. Note that there are, in fact, many fair runs in $\mathcal{A}^{+X}$ that do not project to fair runs of $\mathcal{A}$, because they just cycle around through the assignment states; however, the stripped formulae themselves prevent these "spurious" runs from making a difference to their validity, just as in the case without fairness.

With this adaptation, the proof of Th. 4 goes through just as before. Since, according to [7], model checking PCTL is linear in the size of $\mathcal{F}$, and this size is not affected by the skolemization defined above, Corollary 1 can also be extended with a dependency on the fairness criterion that is linear in the size of $\mathcal{F}$.

6 Conclusions

We have presented an effective technique for checking QCTL, which combines monadic second-order quantification with the temporal operators of CTL, on finite models with arbitrary (bounded) algebraic structure on the states and reallocations on the transitions. The reallocations allow models to be minimized up to bisimilarity (appropriately defined), resulting in a best-case logarithmic reduction in the size of the automata.

It is interesting to note that the technique used in our proof extends to other temporal logics in a limited way only. In order for the encoding of $\exists x\, \phi$ as $\mathsf{EX}(\alpha_x \wedge \mathsf{EX}\, \phi')$ to be valid, it seems crucial that ϕ is a state formula: if it is interpreted in the context of a path then this context is lost in the encoding. This means that the technique is useless for LTL, whereas it can still be used in the fragment of PCTL* where quantification is just allowed on state formulae (of the form $\mathsf{E}\,\phi$ or, dually, $\mathsf{A}\,\phi$).

On the other hand, it should be possible to extend Skolemization to a setting where the temporal modalities are defined through fixpoints, as in the μ-calculus [9]. Here the fact that we can repeatedly assign to the same variable may turn out to be crucial.

The proof theory of quantified modal logic has been studied in depth in the context of philosophical logic. An overview can be found in [14]; some more references were given in the introduction. Results on automated theorem proving (which is a much harder problem than the one studied here, since it is not restricted to finite models) are presented in Castellini and Smaill [4, 5]. Some decidability results on words over infinite alphabets can be found in [18, 3]. Finally, in [1] Baldan et al. present a translation of a quantified temporal logic to a Petri net logic, and so obtain an automatic way to approximate its verification.

As we pointed out in the introduction, a source of more closely related work is Yahav et al. [21]. Their Evolution Temporal Logic, which is a quantified extension of Linear Temporal Logic, is motivated by the same considerations as QCTL, namely to express properties that track entities over time. Through abstraction they can conservatively verify unbounded models, though they do not include reallocations.

As far as we are aware, however, the model checking question was not studied before, at least not for models with arbitrary algebraic structure on the states and quantified temporal logic. For models with unbounded domains (and consequently an infinite number of states, in a suitable finite representation) but very limited structure, some results on model checking were presented in [11, 10]. The first of these shows decidability of model checking for *unstructured* domains, i.e., just sets of entities; the second gives a safe approximation in the case where the domains are singly-linked lists. Finally, model checking for bounded domains and propositional temporal logic has been addressed in many software model checking tools; for instance, Bandera (e.g., [8]).

As future work, we plan to implement the algorithm presented here in the GROOVE tool for graph transformation-based verification [20], thereby realizing one important step of the programme, set out in [19], for model checking graph grammars.

References

[1] P. Baldan, A. Corradini, B. König, and A. LLuch Lafuente. A temporal graph logic for abstractions of graph rewrite systems. Draft, 2005.

[2] D. A. Basin, S. Matthews, and L. Vigano. Labelled modal logics: Quantifiers. *Journal of Logic, Language and Information*, 7(3):237–263, 1998.

[3] M. Bojanczyk, C. David, A. Muscholl, T. Schwentick, and L. Segoufin. Two-variable logic on words with data. Research Report 2005-004, LIAFA — Laboratoire d'Informatique Algorithmique: Fondements et Applications, 2005.

[4] C. Castellini and A. Smaill. A modular, tactic-based approach for first-order temporal theorem proving. In *International Conference on Temporal Logic (ICTL)*, 2000.

[5] C. Castellini and A. Smaill. Proof planning for first-order temporal logic. In Nieuwenhuis, ed., *20th International Conference on Automated Deduction (CADE)*, vol. 3632 of *LNCS*, pp. 235–249. Springer, 2005.

[6] E. M. Clarke and E. A. Emerson. Design and synthesis of synchronization skeletons using branching time temporal logic. In *Proceedings of the IBM Workshop on Logics of Programs*, vol. 131 of *LNCS*, pp. 52–71. Springer, 1982.
[7] E. M. Clarke, E. A. Emerson, and A. P. Sistla. Automatic verification of finite state concurrent systems using temporal logic specifications: A practical approach. In *Symposium on Principles of Programming Languages (POPL)*, pp. 117–126. ACM Press, 1983.
[8] J. C. Corbett, M. B. Dwyer, J. Hatcliff, and Robby. Expressing checkable properties of dynamic systems: the bandera specification language. *International Journal on Software Tools for Technology*, 4(1):34–56, 2002.
[9] M. Dam. CTL$\star$ and ECTL$\star$ as fragments of the modal μ-calculus. *Theoretical Comput. Sci.*, 126(1):77–96, 1994.
[10] D. Distefano, J.-P. Katoen, and A. Rensink. Who is pointing when to whom? on the automated verification of linked list structures. In K. Lodaya and M. Mahajan, eds., *Foundations of Software Technology and Theoretical Computer Science (FSTTCS)*, vol. 3328 of *LNCS*, pp. 250–262. Springer-Verlag, 2004.
[11] D. Distefano, A. Rensink, and J.-P. Katoen. Model checking birth and death. In Baeza-Yates, Montanari, and Santoro, eds., *Foundations of Information Technology in the Era of Network and Mobile Computing*, vol. 223 of *IFIP Conference Proceedings*, pp. 435–447. Kluwer Academic Publishers, 2002.
[12] M. Fitting. Bertrand Russell, Herbrand's theorem, and the assignment statement. In Calmet and Plaza, eds., *Artificial Intelligence and Symbolic Computation (AISC)*, vol. 1476 of *LNAI*, 1998.
[13] M. Fitting. On quantified modal logic. *Fundamenta Informaticae*, 39(1):5–121, 1999.
[14] J. W. Garson. Quantification in modal logic. In Guenthner and Gabbay, eds., *Handbook of Philosophical Logic, Vol. 3*, pp. 267–323. Kluwer, 2 edition, 2001.
[15] G. J. Holtzmann. *The Spin Model Checker: Primer and Reference Manual.* Addison-Wesley, 2003.
[16] U. Montanari and M. Pistore. History-dependent automata. Technical Report TR-11-98, Department of Computer Science, University of Pisa, 1998.
[17] U. Montanari and M. Pistore. History-dependent automata: An introduction. In Bernardo and Bogliolo, eds., *Formal Methods for Mobile Computing, 5th International School on Formal Methods for the Design of Computer, Communication, and Software Systems (SFM)*, vol. 3465 of *LNCS*, pp. 1–28. Springer, 2005.
[18] F. Neven, T. Schwentick, and V. Vianu. Towards regular languages over infinite alphabets. In Sgall, Pultr, and Kolman, eds., *Mathematical Foundations of Computer Science (MFCS)*, vol. 2136 of *LNCS*, pp. 560–572. Springer, 2001.
[19] A. Rensink. Towards model checking graph grammars. In Leuschel, Gruner, and Presti, eds., *Workshop on Automated Verification of Critical Systems (AVoCS)*, Technical Report DSSE–TR–2003–2, pp. 150–160. University of Southampton, 2003.
[20] A. Rensink. The GROOVE simulator: A tool for state space generation. In Pfalz, Nagl, and Böhlen, eds., *Applications of Graph Transformations with Industrial Relevance (AGTIVE)*, vol. 3062 of *LNCS*, pp. 479–485. Springer-Verlag, 2004.
[21] E. Yahav, T. Reps, M. Sagiv, and R. Wilhelm. Verifying temporal heap properties specified via evolution logic. In Degano, ed., *Programming Languages and Systems: 12th European Symposium on Programming (ESOP)*, vol. 2618 of *LNCS*, pp. 204–222. Springer, 2003.

Liveness, Fairness and Impossible Futures

Rob van Glabbeek[1,2] and Marc Voorhoeve[3]

[1] National ICT Australia, Sydney
[2] School of Computer Science and Engineering, The University of New South Wales
[3] Dept. of Mathematics and Computer Science, Eindhoven University of Technology

Abstract. Impossible futures equivalence is the semantic equivalence on labelled transition systems that identifies systems iff they have the same "AGEF" properties: temporal logic properties saying that reaching a desired outcome is not doomed to fail. We show that this equivalence, with an added root condition, is the coarsest congruence containing weak bisimilarity with explicit divergence that respects deadlock/livelock traces (or fair testing, or any liveness property under a global fairness assumption) and assigns unique solutions to recursive equations.

1 Introduction

This paper deals with a class of system requirements, and related notions of process equivalence, that we introduce by the following tale.

Pete's mobile phone allows a number to be redialed as long as connection attempts are unsuccessful. The phone's manual charts this functionality (Fig. 1, left hand side; *ok* and *nok* are internal actions that cannot be observed or interacted with). After having lost several valuable business opportunities, Pete finds out that his redial module contains a bug. During the redial process, data can become corrupted so that all connection attempts fail from then on. Pete contacts his vendor for damages, who denies responsibility, since all code has been certified by a company named TEI (Testing Equivalences Inc). Upon contacting TEI, their spokesman says: "We indeed have discovered the feature you complain about. Our technical people have even charted the functionality implemented (Fig. 1, right hand side, dashed arc omitted). However you have nothing to complain about, because we have verified that the two systems are equivalent with respect to ready simulation. This is our finest equivalence, highly recommended by concurrency specialists [4]." Our hero is considering his next step.

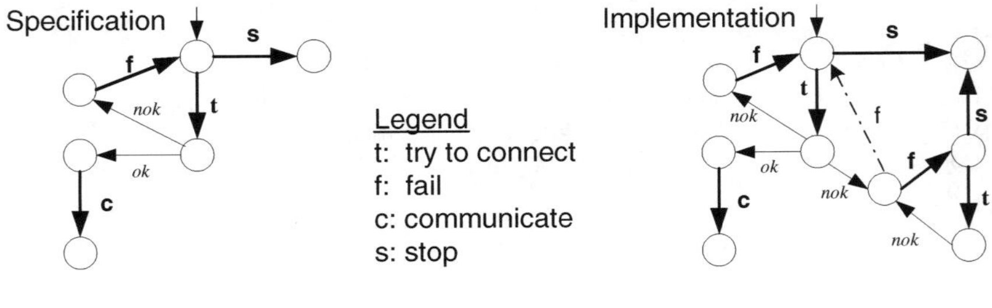

Fig. 1. Charts of Pete's mobile phone

C. Baier and H. Hermanns (Eds.): CONCUR 2006, LNCS 4137, pp. 126–141, 2006.

The specification in his manual led Pete to believe that his phone satisfies the requirement: every redial attempt *may* succeed. Of course, the attempts may fail, but attempts that are *doomed* to fail are not acceptable. In CTL [7], when taking observable histories of states as atomic propositions, Pete's requirement may be formulated as, for all $k \in \mathbb{N}$, $\mathbf{AG}((tf)^k$ has occurred $\Rightarrow \mathbf{EF} (tf)^k tc$ has occurred). We call such requirements *AGEF properties*. Pete's requirement is not preserved by testing equivalences such as ready simulation [4] or failures equivalence [6].

AGAF properties are (conditional) liveness requirements, stating that (depending on past activity) some condition will eventually hold. In Pete's case, such a requirement would be: if I keep hitting the redial button, I will eventually be connected. The implementation in Fig. 1 does not satisfy this AGAF property, but it is open to debate whether the specification satisfies it. In order to deduce that requirement, a *fairness* assumption is needed [9], e.g.: in a recurring state, a specific option cannot be avoided infinitely often. This assumption allows to distinguish the processes in Fig. 1, even without testing the AGEF property. We show that under a sufficiently strong fairness assumption any AGAF property can be reformulated as a conjunction of AGEF properties. Since the validity of AGEF properties does not depend on fairness, it appears preferable to directly verify the AGEF requirements rather than assume fairness and verify the AGAF requirement. *Fair testing equivalence* [5] preserves the subset of *testable* AGEF properties, including the reformulated AGAF properties. Absence of initial deadlock and livelock is an example of a testable AGEF property. However, many reasonable requirements such as Pete's not-doomed-to-fail requirement are in fact non-testable AGEF properties. If there is e.g. a possibility that the corrupted data in Pete's phone can become uncorrupted by redialling frantically, as indicated by the dashed arc in Fig. 1, the erroneous implementation is fair testing equivalent to the specification. However, Pete will still be far from satisfied.

In this paper we study the impossible futures (IF) equivalence of [13,14] that preserves all AGEF properties. We prove that any process equivalence that is a congruence w.r.t. the operators of calculi like CCS and CSP either preserves all AGEF properties, all testable properties only, or no proper AGEF property at all. Moreover, any equivalence that preserves just the testable AGEF properties and is coarser than weak bisimilarity with explicit divergence ($\underline{\leftrightarrow}^{\Delta}_{rw}$) does not respect the *recursive specification principle* (RSP), stating that solutions of guarded recursive equations are unique. This proof principle is of great importance in equational system verification [2]. So, among the semantic equivalences coarser than $\underline{\leftrightarrow}^{\Delta}_{rw}$,[1] IF is the coarsest congruence allowing both the preservation of any chosen proper AGEF property and equational system verification.

2   Labelled Transition Systems

Let Σ^* denote the set of finite sequences over a given set Σ. Write ε for the empty sequence, $\sigma\rho$ for the concatenation of sequences σ and ρ, and a for the

---

[1] We were unable to extend our results to equivalences incomparable with both $\underline{\leftrightarrow}^{\Delta}_{rw}$ and IF, preserving some AGEF property. However, no such equivalences are known.

sequence consisting of the single element $a \in \Sigma$. Write $\sigma \leq \rho$ if σ is a prefix of ρ, i.e. $\exists \nu \in \Sigma^* \cdot \sigma\nu = \rho$, and write $\sigma < \rho$ if $\sigma \leq \rho$ and $\sigma \neq \rho$.

We presuppose a countable action alphabet A, not containing the "silent" action τ and set $A_\tau = A \cup \{\tau\}$. We assume that our set A consists of complementary pairs; each $a \in A$ has a complement $\bar{a}$ such that $\bar{\bar{a}} = a$.

Definition 1. A *labelled transition system* (LTS) is a pair $(\mathbb{P}, \rightarrow)$, where $\mathbb{P}$ is a set (of *processes* or *states*) and $\rightarrow \subseteq \mathbb{P} \times A_\tau \times \mathbb{P}$ is a set of *transitions.*

Assuming a fixed transition system $(\mathbb{P}, \rightarrow)$, we write $p \xrightarrow{a} p'$ for $(p, a, p') \in \rightarrow$. $p \xrightarrow{a} p'$ means that process p can evolve into p', while performing the action a.

Definition 2. The ternary relation $\Longrightarrow \subseteq \mathbb{P} \times A^* \times \mathbb{P}$ is the least relation satisfying $p \overset{\varepsilon}{\Longrightarrow} p$, $\dfrac{p \xrightarrow{\tau} p'}{p \overset{\varepsilon}{\Longrightarrow} p'}$, $\dfrac{p \xrightarrow{a} p',\ a \neq \tau}{p \overset{a}{\Longrightarrow} p'}$, and $\dfrac{p \overset{\sigma}{\Longrightarrow} p' \overset{\rho}{\Longrightarrow} p''}{p \overset{\sigma\rho}{\Longrightarrow} p''}$.

We write $p \overset{\sigma}{\Longrightarrow}$ for $\exists p' \cdot p \overset{\sigma}{\Longrightarrow} p'$ and $p \overset{*}{\Longrightarrow} p'$ for $\exists \sigma \cdot p \overset{\sigma}{\Longrightarrow} p'$.

Let $\mathcal{T}(p) = \{\sigma \in A^* \mid p \overset{\sigma}{\Longrightarrow}\}$ be the set of *traces* of p, and $\mathcal{A}(p) = \{a \in A \mid a$ or $\bar{a}$ occurs in a trace of $p\}$ the *alphabet* of p.

In this paper we present particular processes that are instrumental in proving our results (cf. Figs. 2, 3). Therefore our results apply only to transition systems in which those processes exist. To ensure this, we assume that $(\mathbb{P}, \rightarrow)$

1. is closed under *action prefixing*, meaning that for any $p \in \mathbb{P}$ and $a \in A_\tau$ there is a process ap such that $ap \xrightarrow{c} q$ iff $a = c$ and $q = p$, and
2. is closed under *countable summation*, meaning that for every countable set of processes $P \subseteq \mathbb{P}$ there is a process $\sum P$ such that for all $a \in A$ we have $\sum P \xrightarrow{a} q$ iff there exists $p \in P$ such that $p \xrightarrow{a} q$.

Alternatively we may assume that $(\mathbb{P}, \rightarrow)$ contains finite-state processes only, and is closed under action prefixing and finite summation (cf. Remark 1 in Sect. 4). We also postulate the Fresh Atom Principle [11], allowing fresh actions in proofs.

When writing expressions with action prefixing and summation, we let 0 stand for $\sum \emptyset$ and $p + q$ for $\sum\{p, q\}$, and prefixing binds stronger than sum. We write a for $a0$ and, when $\sigma = a_1 \ldots a_n$, write σp for $a_1 \ldots a_n p$ and $\bar{\sigma}$ for $\bar{a}_1 \ldots \bar{a}_n$.

3 Coarsest Congruence Relations on Processes

Semantic equivalences on processes are used to assess whether an implementation has the same functionality as its specification, viz. Fig. 1. The equivalence of two processes should guarantee that if one has a certain desirable property, then so has the other. In the context of an LTS $(\mathbb{P}, \rightarrow)$, properties can be modelled as unary predicates $\varphi \subseteq \mathbb{P}$. A semantic equivalence relation $\sim \subseteq \mathbb{P} \times \mathbb{P}$ *respects* or *preserves* a property φ if $p \sim q \Rightarrow (\varphi(p) \Leftrightarrow \varphi(q))$. Thus, a semantic equivalence should respect all relevant properties of the systems on which it is applied. Naturally, what is relevant depends to a large extent on the intended application, and consequently many semantic equivalences have been proposed in the literature [10]. This paper focusses on system requirements that we call AGEF and AGAF properties; they will be defined in Section 4.

A transition system $(\mathbb{P}, \rightarrow)$ is often equipped with process algebraic operators $f : \mathbb{P}^n \rightarrow \mathbb{P}$. Throughout this paper, we shall assume that $(\mathbb{P}, \rightarrow)$ is equipped with the *parallel composition* $(\_|\_)$ and *restriction* $\_\backslash H$ for $H \subseteq A$ of CCS [12].

Definition 3. The CCS *parallel composition operator* is a binary operator $(\_|\_)$ defined on $\mathbb{P}$ in such a way that, for all $p, q, r \in \mathbb{P}$ and for all $a \in A_\tau$, $p\,|\,q \stackrel{a}{\longrightarrow} r$ iff

1. there exists $p' \in \mathbb{P}$ such that $p \stackrel{a}{\longrightarrow} p'$ and $r = p'\,|\,q$; or
2. there exists $q' \in \mathbb{P}$ such that $q \stackrel{a}{\longrightarrow} q'$ and $r = p\,|\,q'$; or
3. $a = \tau$ and $\exists p', q' \in \mathbb{P}$ and $b \in A$ such that $p \stackrel{b}{\longrightarrow} p'$, $q \stackrel{\bar{b}}{\longrightarrow} q'$ and $r = p'\,|\,q'$.

A *restriction operator* is a unary operator $\_\backslash H$ defined on $\mathbb{P}$ in such a way that, for all $p, q \in \mathbb{P}$ and for all $a \in A_\tau$, $p\backslash H \stackrel{a}{\longrightarrow} q$ iff $a, \bar{a} \notin H$ and there exists $p' \in \mathbb{P}$ such that $p \stackrel{a}{\longrightarrow} p'$ and $q = p'\backslash H$.

Component-based design often results in processes of the form $(p_0\,|\,\cdots\,|\,p_n)\backslash H$ when formalised in CCS. If the component p_i is replaced by an equivalent component q_i, we want to be able to conclude that the resulting composition is equivalent to the original. Due to the state explosion phenomenon, it is often infeasible to check this explicitly. Therefore, a second requirement on semantic equivalence relations is that they are congruences for all relevant composition operators; this in order to allow compositional verification.

Definition 4. A semantic equivalence relation $\sim\, \subseteq \mathbb{P} \times \mathbb{P}$ is a *congruence* for an operator $f : \mathbb{P}^n \rightarrow \mathbb{P}$, or f is *compositional* for $\sim$, if $p_i \sim q_i$ for $i = 1, ..., n$ implies that $f(p_1, ..., p_n) \sim f(q_1, ..., q_n)$.

Often, one requires compositionality of all operators of CCS and CSP; the minimum requirement typically involves just the operators $|$ and $\backslash H$ of CCS, or alternatively the *parallel composition* and *concealment* operators of CSP.

Let $\sim, \approx\, \subseteq \mathbb{P} \times \mathbb{P}$ be equivalence relations. Then $\sim$ is called *finer* than $\approx$ and $\approx$ *coarser* than $\sim$ if $\sim\, \subseteq\, \approx$. (Note that we use these concepts in a non-strict sense.) As explained above, we seek semantic equivalences that (1) preserve important properties of the processes on which they will be applied, (2) are congruences for the operators that are used to compose processes, and (3) possibly satisfy some other requirements, such as RSP (see the introduction). When the requirements are completely clear and not subject to change, amongst multiple equivalences that meet all requirements, the coarsest of them, if it exists, constitutes the ultimate criterion for system verification, as it enables more implementations to be shown correct with respect to a given specification. The main goal of this paper is to characterise such coarsest equivalences.

4 AGEF and AGAF Properties

Definition 5. The set $\mathcal{I}(p)$ of *impossible futures* of a process p is the set of pairs $(\sigma, G) \in A^* \times \mathcal{P}(A^*)$ satisfying

$$\exists p' \cdot p \stackrel{\sigma}{\Longrightarrow} p' \wedge G \cap \mathcal{T}(p') = \emptyset.$$

Processes p, q are *IF-equivalent*, notation $p \sim_{\mathcal{I}} q$, iff $\mathcal{I}(p) = \mathcal{I}(q)$.

Note that $(tf, \{tc\}) \in \mathcal{I}(q) \setminus \mathcal{I}(p)$, where p, q are respectively the left- and right-hand processes of Fig. 1. (The transitions *ok* and *nok* are labelled τ.) So p and q are not IF-equivalent. The statement $(\sigma, G) \notin \mathcal{I}(p)$ expresses the property

$$\forall p' \cdot p \stackrel{\sigma}{\Longrightarrow} p' \Rightarrow \exists \rho \in G \cdot p' \stackrel{\rho}{\Longrightarrow}.$$

Pete's redialling requirement consists of the conjunction of these properties for $\sigma = (tf)^k$ and $G = \{tc\}$. We call them *AGEF properties.*

Definition 6. For $\sigma \in A^*$ and $G \subseteq A^*$, let $\text{AGEF}(\sigma, G)$ be the property (subset) of processes with $p \in \text{AGEF}(\sigma, G)$ iff $\forall p' \cdot p \stackrel{\sigma}{\Longrightarrow} p' \Rightarrow \exists \rho \in G \cdot p' \stackrel{\rho}{\Longrightarrow}$.

Now a process p satisfies $\text{AGEF}(\sigma, G)$ iff $(\sigma, G) \notin \mathcal{I}(p)$. Thus, an equivalence on processes respects all AGEF properties if and only if it is finer than $\sim_{\mathcal{I}}$. Note that $\text{AGEF}(\sigma, G \cup G') = \text{AGEF}(\sigma, G)$ if every $\rho \in G'$ has a prefix $\rho' \in G$. We therefore assume w.l.o.g. that the sets G have the *prefix property*: $\forall \rho, \nu \in G \cdot \rho \not< \nu$.

The name AGEF is derived from a way to express such properties in *Computation Tree Logic* (CTL) [7]. CTL is a formalism to specify temporal properties of systems that are modelled as states in *Kripke structures.* The latter are transition systems in which states rather than transitions are labelled. Amongst others, CTL features the formulas, interpreted on a state s,

AFφ	meaning that every path from s eventually passes a state satisfying φ
EFφ	meaning that some path from s eventually passes a state satisfying φ
AGφ	meaning that on every path from s all states satisfy φ
EGφ	meaning that on some path from s all states satisfy φ
ℓ	meaning that state s has label ℓ.

Here φ is again a CTL formula. CTL formulas can also be combined with propositional connectives. In order to interpret CTL formulas on a process p in an LTS $\mathbb{L}$, we convert the part of $\mathbb{L}$ that is reachable from p into a Kripke structure by unwinding it into a tree, and labelling each state with the trace of the unique path leading to it. This leads to a Kripke structure $\mathbb{L}_p$ whose states are the finite paths π in $\mathbb{L}$ starting from p, labelled with the sequence of visible actions labelling π, and there is a transition $\pi \to \pi'$ iff the path π' can be obtained from π by adding one transition. We say that p satisfies a CTL formula φ iff the root of the tree-shaped Kripke structure $\mathbb{L}_p$ satisfies φ.[2] Now the property $\text{AGEF}(\sigma, G)$ is expressed in CTL as $\mathbf{AG}(\sigma \Rightarrow \mathbf{EF} \bigvee_{\rho \in G} \sigma\rho)$.

[2] Other translations from LTSs to Kripke structures have appeared in the literature [8], leading to different interpretations of CTL on LTSs.

We also consider *conditional liveness* requirements or *AGAF properties*, stating that *something good* will eventually happen when a specific past has been observed. The property $\text{AGAF}(\sigma, G)$ with $G \neq \emptyset$ states that every run with visible content σ *will* be completed to a run with visible content $\sigma\rho$ for $\rho \in G$, *provided no visible action occurs that disables the potential of achieving G*. In contrast, the property $\text{AGEF}(\sigma, G)$ says that any run with visible content σ *can* be completed to such a run. A liveness property of the form $\text{AGAF}(\varepsilon, G)$ states that something good will happen unconditionally. Pete's liveness requirement "if I keep hitting the redial button, I will eventually be connected" is $\text{AGAF}(\varepsilon, P)$ with $P = \{(tf)^k tc \mid k \in \mathbb{N}\}$.

We now formulate the fairness principle $\mathcal{F}$: during a system run, a specific set of states that remains reachable throughout cannot be avoided forever. This amounts to strong fairness [9] for finite-state processes. We say that a path satisfies $\mathcal{F}(\psi)$, with ψ a set of states, if it is not a infinite path with ψ reachable throughout and avoiding ψ forever. The requirement $\text{AGAF}(\sigma, G)$ under the assumption $\mathcal{F}$ is written $\text{AGAF}_{\mathcal{F}}(\sigma, G)$. The specification of Pete's phone satisfies $\text{AGAF}_{\mathcal{F}}(\varepsilon, P)$ but not $\text{AGAF}(\varepsilon, P)$. The implementation satisfies neither.

In order to conveniently express AGAF properties in temporal logic, we add a modality $\mathbf{A}^{\chi}\mathbf{F}$ to CTL. Here χ is a property on paths, and $\mathbf{A}^{\chi}\mathbf{F}\varphi$ holds in state s, if every (possibly infinite) path from s that is maximal (cannot be extended) amongst the paths satisfying χ, passes through a state satisfying φ. $\text{AGAF}(\sigma, G)$ with $\sigma \in A^*$ and $\emptyset \neq G \subseteq A^*$ can be expressed as $\mathbf{AG}(\sigma \Rightarrow \mathbf{A}^{[G]}\mathbf{F}\psi)$, and $\text{AGAF}_{\mathcal{F}}(\sigma, G)$ as $\mathbf{AG}(\sigma \Rightarrow \mathbf{A}^{\mathcal{F}(\psi)\wedge[G]}\mathbf{F}\psi)$, where $\psi = \bigvee_{\rho\in G}\sigma\rho$ and $[G]$ is the property of a path that all labels $\sigma\nu$ of its states satisfy $\exists\rho\in G \cdot \nu \leq \rho$.

Pete's liveness requirement cannot be expressed as a property of the form $\mathbf{AG}(\sigma \Rightarrow \mathbf{A}^{\mathcal{F}(\psi)}\mathbf{F}\psi)$ with $\psi = \bigvee_{\rho\in G}\sigma\rho$. When taking $\sigma = \varepsilon$ and $G = P$ this property says "eventual connection is guaranteed", which is easily refuted by hitting the *stop* button; taking $G = P \cup \{(tf)^k s \mid k \in \mathbb{N}\}$ yields a requirement that is satisfied by the buggy implementation.

We will show that any $\text{AGAF}_{\mathcal{F}}$ property can be formulated as a conjunction of AGEF properties. We write $\text{AGEF}\,C$ with $C \subseteq A^* \times \mathcal{P}(A^*)$ for the conjunction $\bigwedge_{(\sigma,G)\in C}\text{AGEF}(\sigma, G)$, and similarly for $\text{AGAF}\,C$ and $\text{AGAF}_{\mathcal{F}}\,C$.

Let $\sigma \in A^*$ and $\emptyset \neq G \subseteq A^*$. Then $\uparrow(\sigma, G) := \{(\sigma\rho, \rho^{-1}G) \mid \rho \in {\downarrow}G\}$, where ${\downarrow}G := \{\nu \in A^* \mid \exists\rho \cdot \nu\rho \in G\} \setminus \{\rho\nu \mid \rho \in G\}$ (the set of proper prefixes of G) and $\sigma^{-1}G := \{\rho \mid \sigma\rho \in G\}$. For instance, $\uparrow(a, \{b, cd\}) = \{(a, \{b, cd\}), (ac, \{d\})\}$.

Lemma 1. *Let $\sigma \in A^*$ and $\emptyset \neq G \subseteq A^*$. Then*

$$\text{AGAF}(\sigma, G) \subseteq \text{AGAF}_{\mathcal{F}}(\sigma, G) \subseteq \text{AGEF}(\sigma, G),$$
$$\text{AGAF}(\sigma, G) = \text{AGAF}{\uparrow}(\sigma, G) \textit{ and } \text{AGAF}_{\mathcal{F}}(\sigma, G) = \text{AGAF}_{\mathcal{F}}{\uparrow}(\sigma, G).$$

Proof. The inclusions are trivial; something that will happen must surely be possible. The equalities state e.g. that $\text{AGAF}(\sigma, G)$ implies $\text{AGAF}(\sigma\rho, \rho^{-1}G)$ for any $\rho \in {\downarrow}G$: a promise remains valid as long as it hasn't been delivered. □

Theorem 1. *The property $\text{AGAF}_{\mathcal{F}}(\sigma, G)$ is equal to $\text{AGEF}{\uparrow}(\sigma, G)$.*

Proof. By Lemma 1, we find $\text{AGAF}_{\mathcal{F}}(\sigma, G) = \text{AGAF}_{\mathcal{F}}\!\uparrow\!(\sigma, G) \subseteq \text{AGEF}\!\uparrow\!(\sigma, G)$. Let $\psi = \bigvee_{\rho \in G} \sigma\rho$. If $p \in \text{AGEF}\!\uparrow\!(\sigma, G)$ then from every p' with $p \overset{\sigma\rho}{\Longrightarrow} p'$ and $\rho \in \downarrow\! G$, a ψ-state is reachable. Any run from p that starts with σ, avoids states labelled $\sigma\nu$ with $\nexists \rho \in G \cdot \nu \leq \rho$, and satisfies $\mathcal{F}(\psi)$, will eventually reach ψ. □

By Theorem 1, Pete's liveness requirement $\text{AGAF}_{\mathcal{F}}(\varepsilon, P)$ (assuming fairness) is implied by $\text{AGEF}\!\uparrow\!(\varepsilon, P) = \text{AGEF}\{((tf)^n, P), ((tf)^n t, \{c\} \cup fP) \mid n \in \mathbb{N}\}$.

The property $\text{AGAF}(\sigma, G)$ can be expressed in CTL as $\text{AGEF}\!\uparrow\!(\sigma, G) \wedge \mathbf{AG}(\sigma \Rightarrow \mathbf{AF} \bigvee_{\rho \notin \downarrow G} \sigma\rho)$. We therefore do not need the modality $\mathbf{A}^{\chi}\mathbf{F}$ for stating AGAF properties with or without $\mathcal{F}$.

In [5] it is defined when a process p *should pass* a test. A *test* is given by a test process t, whose alphabet may contain an extra action ✓ that cannot occur in the alphabet of the process p. The test consists of running p and t in parallel using the CSP parallel composition operator $\|_A$ that forces all actions of p and t to synchronise, except for the action ✓. The occurrence of ✓ denotes a successful outcome of the test. We give an alternative formulation using the CCS operators: The process p *should pass* the test, notation p **shd** t, if $(p \,|\, t) \backslash (A \setminus \{✓\})$ satisfies $\text{AGEF}(\varepsilon, \{✓\})$. Processes p, q are *fair testing equivalent* [5], notation $p =_{\textbf{shd}} q$, iff p **shd** $t \Leftrightarrow q$ **shd** t for all tests t.

Definition 7. A property φ on transition systems is *(should-) testable* if there exists a test t such that for all processes p one has p **shd** t iff p satisfies φ.

A property is called *trivial* if it either always holds or always fails. As p **shd** ✓ for any p and p **shd** 0 for no p, all trivial properties are testable. The trivial AGEF properties are $\text{AGEF}(\sigma, G)$ with $\varepsilon \in G$, and $\text{AGEF}(\varepsilon, \emptyset)$.

Proposition 1. *A nontrivial AGEF property AGEF(σ, G) is testable iff for each sequence $b\rho$ in G also its prefix b is in G.*

Proof. "If": We assume $\varepsilon \notin G$ and G has the prefix property $(\forall \rho, \nu \in G \cdot \rho \not< \nu)$. So G consists of singleton traces only. Let $\sigma = a_1 \ldots a_m$. We define the processes T_i $(0 \leq i \leq m)$ by $T_i = \bar{a}_{i+1} T_{i+1} + ✓$ for $0 \leq i < m$ and $T_m = \sum\{\bar{b}✓ \mid b \in G\}$. Fig. 2 displays the processes T_i $(0 \leq i \leq m)$ for finite $G = \{b_1, \ldots, b_n\}$.

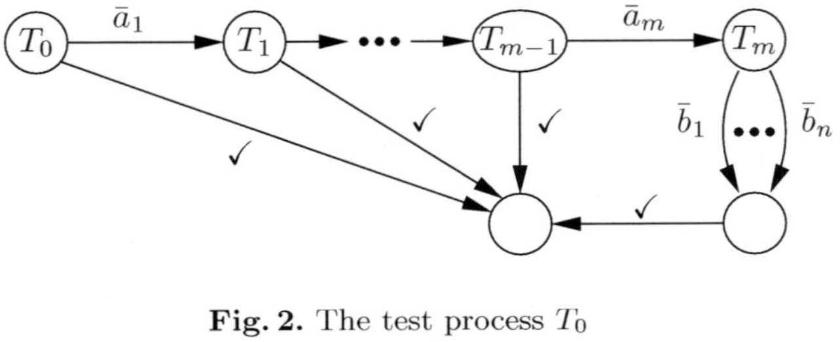

Fig. 2. The test process T_0

Now p satisfies $\text{AGEF}(\sigma, G)$ iff p **shd** T_0. Namely, if $(\sigma, G) \in \mathcal{I}(p)$, i.e. p does not satisfy $\text{AGEF}(\sigma, G)$, then there exists p' with $p \overset{\sigma}{\Longrightarrow} p'$ such that $\forall \rho \in G \cdot p' \overset{\rho}{\not\Longrightarrow}$, so $p \mid T_0 \stackrel{\varepsilon}{\Longrightarrow} p' \mid T_m \stackrel{\checkmark}{\not\Longrightarrow}$. Conversely, if $(\sigma, G) \notin \mathcal{I}(p)$, then for any (strict or not) prefix ν of σ and any p' with $p \stackrel{\nu}{\Longrightarrow} p'$ the $\checkmark$ can be done.

"Only if": Suppose G contains a sequence $b\rho$ but not b. Set $p := \sigma(b\rho + b)$ and $q := \sigma b\rho + \sigma b$ if $\sigma \neq \varepsilon$ and $p := \tau(b\rho + b)$ and $q := \tau b\rho + \tau b$ otherwise. Then p, q are fair testing equivalent [5], whereas $(\sigma, G) \in \mathcal{I}(q) \setminus \mathcal{I}(p)$. So $AGEF(\sigma, G)$ is not testable. □

Theorem 2. *All properties of the form* AGEF↑(σ, G) *are testable.*

Proof. Use the same test as above, but with T_m replaced by the deterministic process T_G with $\mathcal{T}(T_G) = \{\rho \in A^* \mid \exists \nu \cdot \rho\nu \in G\} \cup \{\rho\checkmark \mid \rho \in G\}$. □

Remark 1. When working in the context of a finite-state LTS, we only consider AGEF and AGAF properties with finite sets G. This way the test processes used above will be finite. That the correspondence between AGEF properties and $\sim_{\mathcal{I}}$ is unaffected by this change follows by

Lemma 2. *If* $(\sigma, G) \in \mathcal{I}(q) \setminus \mathcal{I}(q)$ *and* q *is a finite-state process, then there is a finite* G' *with* $(\sigma, G') \in \mathcal{I}(q) \setminus \mathcal{I}(q)$.

Proof. The set $R = \{r \mid q \stackrel{\sigma}{\Longrightarrow} r\}$ is finite and for each $r \in R$ we can choose a $\rho_r \in G$ such that $r \stackrel{\rho_r}{\Longrightarrow}$. Hence, $(\sigma, \{\rho_r \mid r \in R\}) \in \mathcal{I}(p) \setminus \mathcal{I}(q)$. □

A *safety property* says that *something bad will not happen.* Formalising "bad" as a predicate $B \subseteq A^*$ on the visible content of system runs, a safety property has the form $B \cap \mathcal{T}(x) = \emptyset$, and can be written as $\bigwedge_{\sigma \in B}$AGEF$(\sigma, \emptyset)$. Considering that the class of testable properties is closed under conjunction (for p **shd** $\tau t + \tau t'$ iff p **shd** t and p **shd** t'), Prop. 1 implies that safety properties are testable. A property AGEF(σ, G) or AGEF↑(σ, G) is called *proper* if it is neither trivial, nor a safety property, i.e. if $\varepsilon \notin G \neq \emptyset$.

5 Four Levels of Respect for AGEF Properties

In this section we show that only four types of congruences exist: those that respect all AGEF properties, those that respect all testable AGEF properties but no others, those that respect all safety properties but no other non-trivial AGEF properties, and those that do not respect a single non-trivial AGEF property. Examples in each of the four classes are weak bisimilarity [12], fair testing equivalence [5], trace equivalence—defined as $p =_{\mathcal{T}} q$ iff $\mathcal{T}(q) = \mathcal{T}(q)$—and failures equivalence [6] (where the absence of traces occurring past a divergence is not recorded), respectively. In this section "congruence" means congruence for the CCS parallel composition and restriction operators; we could also have used the CSP parallel composition and concealment operators. The results in this section are not needed further on, although we will reuse the proof of Lemma 3.

We say that a congruence $\sim$ is *non-IF* if there exist processes p, q with $p \sim q$ such that $\mathcal{I}(p) \neq \mathcal{I}(q)$. For a non-IF congruence there exists an AGEF property that it does not preserve; we shall now prove that in fact it does not preserve any non-testable AGEF property.

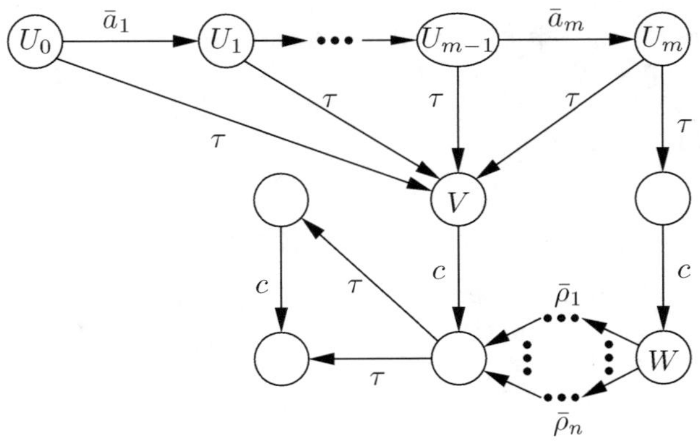

Fig. 3. The process U_0

Lemma 3. *If $\sim$ is a non-IF congruence, then for all $c \in A$ there exist processes p_c, q_c with $\mathcal{A}(p_c) = \mathcal{A}(q_c) = \{c\}$, such that $p_c \sim q_c$ and $(\varepsilon, \{cc\}) \in \mathcal{I}(p_c) \setminus \mathcal{I}(q_c)$.*

Proof. The congruence $\sim$ is non-IF, so there exist processes p, q and σ, G such that $p \sim q$ and $(\sigma, G) \in \mathcal{I}(p) \backslash \mathcal{I}(q)$. Note that $\varepsilon \notin G$: if $\varepsilon \in G$ then $(\sigma, G) \notin \mathcal{I}(p)$.

Let $\sigma = a_1 \dots a_m$ and define $H := \mathcal{A}(p) \cup \mathcal{A}(q)$. We first establish the lemma for all actions $c \notin H$, and then consider the case $c \in H$. Let U_i $(0 \leq i \leq m)$, V and W be defined by $U_i = \tau V + \bar{a}_{i+1} U_{i+1}$ for $0 \leq i < m$, $U_m = \tau V + \tau c W$, $V = c(\tau c + \tau)$ and $W = \sum_{\rho \in G} \bar{\rho}(\tau c + \tau)$ (Fig. 3 displays the processes U_i $(0 \leq i \leq m)$, V and W for the case that $G = \{\rho_1, \dots, \rho_n\}$). As we assume our alphabet A, and hence $G \subseteq A^*$, to be countable, the sum W is countable too. If q is a finite-state process, by Lemma 2 we may even assume it to be finite. Let $p_c = (U_0 \,|\, p) \backslash H$ and $q_c = (U_0 \,|\, q) \backslash H$. By construction, $\mathcal{A}(p_c) = \mathcal{A}(q_c) = \{c\}$. Since $p \sim q$ and $\sim$ is a congruence for $|$ and $\backslash H$, we have $(U_0 \,|\, p) \backslash H \sim (U_0 \,|\, q) \backslash H$. There exists a p' with $p \stackrel{\sigma}{\Longrightarrow} p'$ and $p' \not\stackrel{\rho}{\Longrightarrow}$ for all $\rho \in G$. Therefore, we have $(U_0 | p) \backslash H \stackrel{\varepsilon}{\Longrightarrow} (cW | p') \backslash H$ and $(cW | p') \backslash H \not\stackrel{\varepsilon c}{\Longrightarrow}$. Hence, $(\varepsilon, \{cc\}) \in \mathcal{I}((U_0 \,|\, p) \backslash H)$. However, as $\forall q' \cdot (q \stackrel{\sigma}{\Longrightarrow} q') \Rightarrow (\exists \rho \in G \cdot q' \stackrel{\rho}{\Longrightarrow})$, we have $(\varepsilon, \{cc\}) \notin \mathcal{I}((U_0 \,|\, q) \backslash H)$. This proves our lemma for all actions $c \notin H$.

To obtain the required results for $c \in H$, first choose $d \notin H$ (appealing to the Fresh Atom Principle [11] if $A \setminus H$ is empty). By the above, there exist p_d and q_d with $\mathcal{A}(p_d) = \mathcal{A}(q_d) = \{d\}$ such that $p_d \sim q_d$ and $(\varepsilon, \{dd\}) \in \mathcal{I}(p_d) \setminus \mathcal{I}(q_d)$. Now, since $c \in A \setminus \{d\}$, the required p_c and q_c are obtained by running the same arguments again, taking $p := p_d$, $q := q_d$, $\sigma := \varepsilon$, $G := \{dd\}$ and $H := \{d\}$. □

From this lemma we deduce that no non-testable AGEF property is preserved by a non-IF congruence.

Theorem 3. *Let $\sim$ be a non-IF congruence. Then for any non-testable property* AGEF(σ, G) *there are processes p, q such that $p \sim q$ and $(\sigma, G) \in \mathcal{I}(p) \setminus \mathcal{I}(q)$.*

Proof. Let (σ, G) be a non-testable AGEF property. Pick $b\rho \in G$ such that $\varepsilon, b \notin G$. Let c be an action that does not occur in $\sigma b\rho$. By Lemma 3 there are processes p and q with $\mathcal{A}(p) = \mathcal{A}(q) = \{c\}$, $p \sim q$ and $(\varepsilon, \{cc\}) \in \mathcal{I}(p) \setminus \mathcal{I}(q)$. As $\sim$ is a congruence for $|$ and $\backslash H$, we have $(p \,|\, \sigma b\bar{c}\bar{c}\rho)\backslash\{c\} \sim (q \,|\, \sigma b\bar{c}\bar{c}\rho)\backslash\{c\}$.

Whenever $(q \,|\, \sigma b\bar{c}\bar{c}\rho)\backslash\{c\} \stackrel{\sigma}{\Longrightarrow} r$, the process r must be of the form $(q' \,|\, b\bar{c}\bar{c}\rho)\backslash\{c\}$ with $q \stackrel{\varepsilon}{\Longrightarrow} q'$. Since $(\varepsilon, \{cc\}) \notin \mathcal{I}(q)$, we have $q' \stackrel{cc}{\Longrightarrow}$ and hence $(q' \,|\, b\bar{c}\bar{c}\rho)\backslash\{c\} \stackrel{b\rho}{\Longrightarrow}$. Thus $(\sigma, G) \notin \mathcal{I}((q \,|\, \sigma b\bar{c}\bar{c}\rho)\backslash\{c\})$.

Since $(\varepsilon, \{cc\}) \in \mathcal{I}(p)$, we have $p \stackrel{\varepsilon}{\Longrightarrow} p'$ for a process p' with $p' \stackrel{cc}{\not\Longrightarrow}$. Hence $(p \,|\, \sigma b\bar{c}\bar{c}\rho)\backslash\{c\} \stackrel{\sigma}{\Longrightarrow} (p' \,|\, b\bar{c}\bar{c}\rho)\backslash\{c\}$, and $(p' \,|\, b\bar{c}\bar{c}\rho)\backslash\{c\} \stackrel{\nu}{\Longrightarrow}$ only if $\nu = \varepsilon$ or $\nu = b$. It follows that $(\sigma, G) \in \mathcal{I}((p \,|\, \sigma b\bar{c}\bar{c}\rho)\backslash\{c\})$. □

Next, we prove that a congruence $\sim$ either preserves all testable properties (AGEF or otherwise) or does not preserve any proper AGEF property, nor any proper liveness property under the global fairness assumption $\mathcal{F}$.

Lemma 4. *If $\sim$ is a congruence that does not respect all testable properties, then for all $c \in A$ there exist processes p_c, q_c with $\mathcal{A}(p_c) = \mathcal{A}(q_c) = \{c\}$, such that $p_c \sim q_c$ and $(\varepsilon, \{c\}) \in \mathcal{I}(p_c) \setminus \mathcal{I}(q_c)$.*

Proof. Let φ be a testable property that is not preserved by $\sim$. As φ is testable, there is a test process t such that $\forall p \in \mathbb{P}$ one has p **shd** t iff p satisfies φ. As φ is not preserved by $\sim$, there are processes p, q such that $p \sim q$ and $\varphi(q)$ but not $\varphi(p)$. Hence q **shd** t but p ~~**shd**~~ t. Let $p_{\checkmark} = (p \,|\, t)\backslash(A \backslash \{\checkmark\})$ and $q_{\checkmark} = (q \,|\, t)\backslash(A \backslash \{\checkmark\})$. Then q satisfies AGEF$(\varepsilon, \{\checkmark\})$ but p does not, so $(\varepsilon, \{\checkmark\}) \in \mathcal{I}(p_{\checkmark}) \setminus \mathcal{I}(q_{\checkmark})$. $\mathcal{A}(p_{\checkmark}) = \mathcal{A}(q_{\checkmark}) = \{\checkmark\}$. As $\sim$ is a congruence for $|$ and $\backslash H$, we have $p_{\checkmark} \sim q_{\checkmark}$. The result for actions $c \neq \checkmark$ is obtained in a manner similar to the one used in the proof of Lemma 3. □

Theorem 4. *Let $\sim$ be a congruence that does not respect all testable properties. Then for any proper* AGEF *property* AGEF(σ, G) *there are processes p and q such that $p \sim q$ and $p \notin$* AGEF$(\sigma, G) \supseteq$ AGEF$\uparrow(\sigma, G) \ni q$.

Proof. Let (σ, G) be given, satisfying $\varepsilon \notin G \neq \emptyset$, and take $\rho \in G$. Let c be an action that does not occur in the sequence $\sigma\rho$. By Lemma 4 there are processes p and q with $\mathcal{A}(p) = \mathcal{A}(q) = \{c\}$, $p \sim q$ and $(\varepsilon, \{c\}) \in \mathcal{I}(p) \setminus \mathcal{I}(q)$. Since $\sim$ is a congruence for $|$ and $\backslash H$, we have $(p \,|\, \sigma\bar{c}\rho)\backslash\{c\} \sim (q \,|\, \sigma\bar{c}\rho)\backslash\{c\}$. As in the proof of Theorem 3, we find that $(\sigma, G) \in \mathcal{I}((p \,|\, \sigma\bar{c}\rho)\backslash\{c\}) \setminus \mathcal{I}((q \,|\, \sigma\bar{c}\rho)\backslash\{c\})$ and moreover $p \notin$ AGEF$(\sigma, G) \supseteq$ AGEF$\uparrow(\sigma, G) \ni q$. □

Finally we show that a congruence that fails to respect a safety property does not respect any nontrivial AGEF property.

Lemma 5. *If $\sim$ is a congruence that does not respect all safety properties, then for all $c \in A$ there exist processes p_c, q_c with $\mathcal{A}(p_c) = \mathcal{A}(q_c) = \{c\}$, such that $p_c \sim q_c$ and $c \in \mathcal{T}(p_c) \setminus \mathcal{T}(q_c)$.*

Proof. The congruence $\sim$ violates a safety property $\bigwedge_{\sigma \in G}$AGEF$(\sigma, \emptyset)$, so there must be an $\sigma \in G$ and processes p and q with $p \sim q$ and $(\sigma, \emptyset) \in \mathcal{I}(p) \setminus \mathcal{I}(q)$, i.e.

$\sigma \in \mathcal{T}(p) \setminus \mathcal{T}(q)$. Note that $\sigma \neq \varepsilon$: if $\sigma = \varepsilon$ then $(\sigma, \emptyset) \in \mathcal{I}(q)$. By placing p and q in a context $(\_ \,|\, \bar{\sigma}c)\backslash H$ with $c \notin H := \mathcal{A}(p) \cup \mathcal{A}(q)$ we obtain processes p_c, q_c as required. The result for $c \in H$ is obtained just as in the proof of Lemma 3. □

Theorem 5. *Let $\sim$ be a congruence that does not respect all safety properties. Then for any nontrivial property* AGEF(σ, G) *there are processes p and q with $p \sim q$ and $(\sigma, G) \in \mathcal{I}(p) \setminus \mathcal{I}(q)$, i.e. $q \in$* AGEF(σ, G) *and $p \notin$* AGEF(σ, G).

Proof. The case $\sigma = \varepsilon$ follows from Theorem 4, as safety properties are testable and nontrivial properties AGEF(ε, G) are proper. So assume $\sigma \neq \varepsilon$. Let c be an action that does not occur in σ. By Lemma 5 there are processes p, q with $p \sim q$, $\mathcal{A}(p) = \mathcal{A}(q) = \{c\}$ and $c \in \mathcal{T}(p)\setminus\mathcal{T}(q)$. Since $\sim$ is a congruence for $|$ and $\backslash H$, we have $(p \,|\, \bar{c}\sigma)\backslash\{c\} \sim (q \,|\, \bar{c}\sigma)\backslash\{c\}$. Now $(\sigma, G) \in \mathcal{I}((p \,|\, \bar{c}\sigma)\backslash\{c\}) \setminus \mathcal{I}((q \,|\, \bar{c}\sigma)\backslash\{c\})$. □

6 The Recursive Specification Principle

The *Recursive Specification Principle* (RSP) [3] says that systems of guarded recursive equations have unique solutions. Our aim is to characterise $\sim_\mathcal{I}$ as the coarsest congruence that respects a proper AGEF property and satisfies RSP. To this end, we only need a simplification of RSP, called RSP*, saying that equations of the form $X = \sigma X + p$ with $\sigma \in (A_\tau)^* \setminus \{\tau\}^*$ have unique solutions. We denote the unique solution of such an equation as $\sigma^* p$. Alternatively, we could introduce $\sigma^*\_$ as an operator on processes, with $\sigma^* p \xrightarrow{a} p'$ iff $p \xrightarrow{a} p'$ or ($\sigma = a\rho$ and $p' = \rho(\sigma^* p)$).

Definition 8. An equivalence relation $\sim$ satisfies RSP* if for all $\sigma \in (A_\tau)^* \setminus \{\tau\}^*$ and processes p, q

$$p \sim \sigma p + q \quad \Rightarrow \quad p \sim \sigma^* q\ .$$

Fair testing congruence [5] does not satisfy RSP*, since $t = a^*0 + a^*ab$ is fair testing congruent to $at + ab$ but not to a^*ab.

7 Impossible Futures Congruence

Just like weak bisimulation equivalence [12] and most other weak equivalences, impossible futures equivalence $\sim_\mathcal{I}$ (defined in Sect. 4) fails to be a congruence for the CCS choice operator $+$. We apply the usual fix to this problem: the addition of a root condition. Just like for failures or fair testing equivalence, a one-bit root condition is sufficient: we merely need to distinguish processes that can do an initial τ-step from those that can not.

Definition 9. Processes p, q are *IF-congruent* (notation $p =_\mathcal{I} q$) iff $p \sim_\mathcal{I} q \wedge (p \xrightarrow{\tau}) \Leftrightarrow (q \xrightarrow{\tau})$.

Theorem 12 in [5] (Theorem 4.8 in the journal preprint) shows that $=_\mathcal{I}$ is finer than fair testing equivalence, which is itself finer than trace equivalence. In [14], it is shown that $=_\mathcal{I}$ is coarser than weak bisimulation congruence. Since $a + \tau b$ and $\tau(a+b)+\tau b$ are IF congruent but not weakly bisimilar, $=_\mathcal{I}$ is strictly coarser. We now show that $=_\mathcal{I}$ is a congruence and satisfies RSP*.

Proposition 2. $=_{\mathcal{I}}$ *is a congruence satisfying* RSP (*and hence* RSP*).

Proof. The argument in [14] can be adapted and extended to yield the required result. For example, RSP follows from a standard deductive argument [3] based on the auxiliary finite projection operator and the induction principle AIP. □

Below, we show that $=_{\mathcal{I}}$ is the coarsest of all equivalences that (1) respect a proper AGEF property, (2) are congruences for the CCS parallel composition, restriction, choice and prefixing, (3) satisfy RSP*, and (4) are coarser than an equivalence $\leftrightarrows_{\max}$. We show that in (1) it does not matter which AGEF property we take, so it could for instance be the property AGEF(ε, A), saying that the system can always do a first visible action, i.e. has no initial livelock or deadlock. Instead of (1) we may also require that the equivalence respects a proper property AGAF$_{\mathcal{F}}(\sigma, G)$ = AGEF$\uparrow(\sigma, G)$, i.e. a conditional liveness property assuming global fairness. We do not know whether our result is valid without (4), but we use it in our proofs. Below, we establish our result with *rooted weak bisimilarity* in the rôle of $\leftrightarrows_{\max}$. In CCS, weak bisimilarity is the equivalence of choice for e.g. comparing specifications and implementations. This equivalence is not a congruence for all CCS operators, but it becomes so after extending it with a root condition, yielding *rooted weak bisimilarity* (*observational congruence*) [12].

Definition 10. A relation $R \subseteq \mathbb{P} \times \mathbb{P}$ is called a *weak bisimulation* if it satisfies for all processes p, q with $p\ R\ q$ and for all $\sigma \in A^*$:
– for all p' with $p \stackrel{\sigma}{\Longrightarrow} p'$ there exists q' such that $q \stackrel{\sigma}{\Longrightarrow} q'$ and $p'\ R\ q'$,
– for all q' with $q \stackrel{\sigma}{\Longrightarrow} q'$ there exists p' such that $p \stackrel{\sigma}{\Longrightarrow} p'$ and $p'\ R\ q'$.
Processes p, q are called *weakly bisimilar* (notation $p \leftrightarrows_w q$) if there exists a weak bisimulation R such that $p\ R\ q$. They are called *rooted weakly bisimilar* (notation $p \leftrightarrows_{rw} q$) if they satisfy the additional *root conditions*:
– for all p' with $p \stackrel{\tau}{\longrightarrow} p'$ there exists q' such that $q \stackrel{\varepsilon}{\Longrightarrow}\stackrel{\tau}{\longrightarrow} q'$ and $p'\ R\ q'$,
– for all q' with $q \stackrel{\tau}{\longrightarrow} q'$ there exists p' such that $p \stackrel{\varepsilon}{\Longrightarrow}\stackrel{\tau}{\longrightarrow} p'$ and $p'\ R\ q'$.

Write $\tau_a(p)$ for $(p\,|\,\bar{a}^*0)\backslash\{a\}$. The operator τ_a renames action a into τ (and disables $\bar{a}$). By construction of rooted weak bisimulations, one can deduce the following equivalences for $a \in A_\tau$, $\sigma \in \{a, \tau\}^* \setminus \{\tau\}^*$ and processes p:

$$\text{T1}: \quad a\tau p \leftrightarrows_{rw} ap \qquad\qquad \text{KFAR}: \quad \tau_a(\sigma^* p) \leftrightarrows_{rw} \tau\tau_a(p).$$

KFAR [3] identifies divergent processes (capable of an infinite sequence of τ steps) and non-divergent ones. We prove a lemma for later use.

Lemma 6. Let p, q, r be processes with $p \stackrel{\varepsilon}{\Longrightarrow}\stackrel{\tau}{\longrightarrow} r \leftrightarrows_w q$. Then $p \leftrightarrows_{rw} p + \tau q$.

Proof. Let R be $\leftrightarrows_w$ augmented with the pair $(p, p + \tau q)$. This is a weak bisimulation satisfying the root conditions. □

A process equivalence $\sim$ is called a *w-congruence* iff it is a congruence w.r.t. the CCS parallel composition, restriction, choice and prefixing, and is coarser than $\leftrightarrows_{rw}$. We proceed to characterise IF congruence as the coarsest w-congruence

Table 1. The relation R

simple term	merge term	condition
$\tau c(\tau c+\tau)$	$(U_0 \mid q)\backslash H$	*true*
$c(\tau c+\tau)$	$(U_k \mid q')\backslash H$	$0 \leq k \leq m \wedge q \stackrel{a_1\ldots a_k}{\Longrightarrow} q'$
$c(\tau c+\tau)$	$(V \mid q')\backslash H$	$q \stackrel{*}{\Longrightarrow} q'$
$\tau c+\tau$	$(\tau c+\tau \mid q')\backslash H$	$q \stackrel{*}{\Longrightarrow} q'$
c	$(c \mid q')\backslash H$	$q \stackrel{*}{\Longrightarrow} q'$
0	$(0 \mid q')\backslash H$	$q \stackrel{*}{\Longrightarrow} q'$
$c(\tau c+\tau)$	$(cW \mid q')\backslash H$	$q \stackrel{\sigma}{\Longrightarrow} q'$
$\tau c+\tau$	$(W \mid q')\backslash H$	$q \stackrel{\sigma}{\Longrightarrow} q'$
$\tau c+\tau$	$(\bar{\vartheta}(\tau c+\tau) \mid q')\backslash H$	$\exists \nu \neq \varepsilon \cdot \nu\vartheta \in G \wedge q \stackrel{\sigma}{\Longrightarrow}\stackrel{\nu}{\Longrightarrow} q' \stackrel{\vartheta}{\Longrightarrow}$
0	$(\bar{\vartheta}(\tau c+\tau) \mid q')\backslash H$	$\exists \nu \neq \varepsilon \cdot \nu\vartheta \in G \wedge q \stackrel{\sigma}{\Longrightarrow}\stackrel{\nu}{\Longrightarrow} q' \stackrel{\vartheta}{\not\Longrightarrow}$

that satisfies RSP* and preserves some arbitrary proper AGEF property. Recall that a congruence $\sim$ is called *non-IF* iff there exist processes p, q with $p \sim q$ such that $\mathcal{I}(p) \neq \mathcal{I}(q)$. We start with some lemmas.

Lemma 7. *If $\sim$ is a non-IF w-congruence, then for any $c \in A$*

$$\tau c(\tau c+\tau) \sim \tau c(\tau c+\tau)+\tau c$$

Proof. Start with the proof of Lemma 3, up to $(U_0 \mid p)\backslash H \sim (U_0 \mid q)\backslash H$. Next we define the relation R in Table 1. This relation is a weak bisimulation, which can be verified by checking all steps. The crucial argument is that for each q' satisfying $q \stackrel{\sigma}{\Longrightarrow} q'$ there exists a $\rho \in G$ such that $q' \stackrel{\rho}{\Longrightarrow}$. The relation satisfies the root conditions, so

$$\tau c(\tau c+\tau) \leftrightarroweq_{rw} (U_0 \mid q)\backslash H.$$

As $(\sigma, G) \in \mathcal{I}(p)$, there must be a process p' such that $p \stackrel{\sigma}{\Longrightarrow} p'$ and $\forall \rho \in G \cdot p' \stackrel{\rho}{\not\Longrightarrow}$. It is trivial to construct a weak bisimulation showing that $(cW \mid p')\backslash H \leftrightarroweq_w c$ and hence $(U_0 \mid p)\backslash H \stackrel{\varepsilon}{\Longrightarrow}\stackrel{\tau}{\longrightarrow} (cW \mid p')\backslash H \leftrightarroweq_w c$. Using Lemma 6, this implies that $(U_0 \mid p)\backslash H \leftrightarroweq_{rw} (U_0 \mid p)\backslash H + \tau c$. Therefore, as $\sim$ is a congruence, we have $\tau c(\tau c+\tau) \leftrightarroweq_{rw} (U_0 \mid q)\backslash H \sim (U_0 \mid p)\backslash H \leftrightarroweq_{rw} (U_0 \mid p)\backslash H + \tau c \sim (U_0 \mid q)\backslash H + \tau c$ $\leftrightarroweq_{rw} \tau c(\tau c+\tau)+\tau c$. Since $\sim$ is transitive and coarser than $\leftrightarroweq_{rw}$ we obtain the desired result for $c \in A\backslash H$. For $c \in H$, we proceed as in the proof of Lemma 3. □

Lemma 8. *If $\sim$ is a non-IF w-congruence, then for all processes P, Q and $a \in A$,*

$$\tau a(\tau P+Q) \sim \tau a(\tau P+Q)+\tau a P. \tag{1}$$

Proof. Pick $c \notin \mathcal{A}(P) \cup \mathcal{A}(Q) \cup \{a\}$ and place the processes equated by Lemma 7 in the context $(\_ \mid \tau a\bar{c}(\tau P+\bar{c}(\tau P+Q)))\backslash\{c\})$. □

We now use RSP* to show equivalence of processes with and without deadlock.

Lemma 9. *Let $\sim$ be a non-IF w-congruence satisfying RSP*. Then for any process Q we have $\tau(\tau Q+\tau) \sim \tau Q$.*

Proof. Choose Q and $a \notin \mathcal{A}(Q)$. Set $P = a^*0$ and $R = (\tau a)^*(\tau Q + \tau.P)$, so

$$(2)\ P \sim aP \qquad\qquad (3)\ R \sim \tau P + \tau Q + \tau a R.$$

Since $\tau a R = \tau a(\tau P + \tau Q + \tau a R)$, (1) yields $\tau a R \sim \tau a R + \tau a P$. Hence,

$$\tau a R + \tau Q \sim \tau a R + \tau a P + \tau Q \overset{2}{\sim} \tau a R + \tau P + \tau Q \overset{3}{\sim} R.$$

Since $R \sim \tau a R + \tau Q$, RSP* yields $R \sim (\tau a)^* \tau Q$. So, since $\sim$ is a congruence,

$$\tau.(\tau Q + \tau\tau 0) \leftrightarroweq_{rw} \tau_a((\tau a)^*(\tau Q + \tau(a^*0))) \sim \tau_a((\tau a)^*\tau Q) \leftrightarroweq_{rw} \tau\tau Q$$

applying KFAR and $\tau_a(Q) = Q$. Using T1, we obtain $\tau(\tau Q + \tau) \sim \tau Q$. □

Fair testing [5] is a non-IF w-congruence that preserves all testable AGEF properties. However, non-IF w-congruences satisfying RSP do not preserve *any* proper AGEF property, nor any nontrivial property $\text{AGAF}_{\mathcal{F}}(\sigma, G) = \text{AGEF}{\uparrow}(\sigma, G)$.

Theorem 6. *Let $\sim$ be a non-IF w-congruence satisfying RSP*. Then for any proper* AGEF *property* $\text{AGEF}(\sigma, G)$ *there are processes p and q such that $p \sim q$ and $p \notin \text{AGEF}(\sigma, G) \supseteq \text{AGEF}{\uparrow}(\sigma, G) \ni q$.*

Proof. Let (σ, G) be proper, i.e. $\varepsilon \notin G \neq \emptyset$, and pick $\rho \in G$. Set $Q = \rho$. By Lemma 9, the fact that $\sim$ is a congruence for the prefix operator, and by identity T1, we have $p = \sigma(\tau Q + \tau) \sim \sigma Q = q$. Clearly, $(\sigma, G) \in \mathcal{I}(p) \setminus \mathcal{I}(q)$ and $p \notin \text{AGEF}(\sigma, G) \supseteq \text{AGEF}{\uparrow}(\sigma, G) \ni q$. □

This theorem also gives a partial answer to van Glabbeek's first problem in [1]: what is the coarsest congruence $\sim$ satisfying RSP and respecting deadlock/livelock traces?

Definition 11. A sequence $\sigma \in A^*$ is a *deadlock/livelock trace* of a process p if $\exists p' \cdot p \overset{\sigma}{\Longrightarrow} p' \wedge \mathcal{T}(p') = \{\varepsilon\}$. A process equivalence $\sim$ *respects deadlock/livelock traces* iff $p \sim q$ implies that p and q have the same deadlock/livelock traces.

Note that σ is a deadlock/livelock trace of p iff $(\sigma, A) \in \mathcal{I}(p)$. This is the negation of a proper AGEF property, so from Theorem 6 we deduce that $=_{\mathcal{I}}$ is the coarsest w-congruence satisfying RSP and respecting deadlock/livelock traces. The answer is partial, since there exist congruences that respect deadlock/livelock traces but are not coarser than $\leftrightarroweq_{rw}$, such as branching bisimilarity [10]. So the existence of (non-w) congruences respecting deadlock/livelock traces and satisfying RSP that are incomparable with $=_{\mathcal{I}}$ is conceivable.

The results in this section can be generalised to a divergence sensitive setting. Divergence of a process is the possibility to perform an infinite sequence of τ steps. By only allowing to relate divergent processes to divergent processes, one defines *weak bisimulation congruence with explicit divergence* (notation $\leftrightarroweq^{\Delta}_{rw}$) [10]. We now relax the requirement in Theorem 6 that $\sim$ must be a *w*-congruence. Instead of requiring $\sim$ to be coarser than $\leftrightarroweq_{rw}$ we merely require it to be coarser than $\leftrightarroweq^{\Delta}_{rw}$, i.e. we use $\leftrightarroweq^{\Delta}_{rw}$ for $\leftrightarroweq_{\max}$. The proof, which is omitted due to lack of space, requires a slight extension of RSP*, still implied by RSP.

Theorem 7. *$=_{\mathcal{I}}$ is the coarsest congruence coarser than $\leftrightarrow^{\Delta}_{rw}$, satisfying* RSP *and respecting deadlock/livelock traces.*

This is a useful addition, because many equivalences in the linear time – branching time spectrum of [10], such as the CSP failures equivalence [6], fail to be coarser than $\leftrightarrow_{rw}$, although virtually all are coarser than $\leftrightarrow^{\Delta}_{rw}$. Moreover, the few equivalences from [10] that are not coarser than $\leftrightarrow^{\Delta}_{rw}$ are certainly finer than $\sim_{\mathcal{I}}$ or do not respect deadlock/livelock traces; thus no known equivalence is ruled out by the restriction "coarser than $\leftrightarrow^{\Delta}_{rw}$".

8 Conclusion

We have discussed the connection between AGAF properties, expressing (conditional) lifeness requirements, AGEF properties, expressing not-doomed-to-fail requirements, and impossible futures congruence, which we have characterised, under a mild side-condition, as the coarsest congruence that allows verification of testable AGEF properties—or AGAF properties under a global fairness assumption—and assigns unique solutions to guarded recursive equations. Thus, where such properties are deemed important, equational system verification [2] requires a semantic equivalence at least as fine as impossible futures congruence.

The fact that we have used the operators of CCS bears no relevance. We could have used any process calculus that allows action prefix, choice, communication merge, restriction and abstraction, such as CSP, ACP, LOTOS and many others.

Acknowledgement. We are grateful for the support and advice of our colleague Bas Luttik.

References

1. L. Aceto (moderator) (2003): *Some open problems in Process Algebra.* `http://www.cs.auc.dk/~luca/BICI/open-problems.html`
2. J.C.M. Baeten, editor (1990): *Applications of Process Algebra.* Cambridge Tracts in Theoretical Computer Science 17. Cambridge University Press.
3. J.C.M. Baeten, J.A. Bergstra & J.W. Klop (1987): *On the consistency of Koomen's fair abstraction rule. Theoretical Computer Science* 51(1/2), pp. 129–176.
4. B. Bloom, S. Istrael & A. Meyer (1995): *Bisimulation Can't Be Traced. Journal of the ACM* 42(1), pp. 232–268.
5. E. Brinksma, A. Rensink & W. Vogler (1995): *Fair Testing.* In *Proceedings CONCUR '95* (I. Lee & S.A. Smolka, eds.), LNCS 962, Springer, pp. 311–327. Journal preprint: `http://eprints.eemcs.utwente.nl/1623/01/submitted.pdf`
6. S.D. Brookes, C.A.R. Hoare & A.W. Roscoe (1984): *A theory of communicating sequential processes. Journal of the ACM* 31(3), pp. 560–599.
7. E.M. Clarke & E.A. Emerson (1981): *Design and synthesis of synchronization skeletons using branching-time temporal logic.* In Proceedings workshop on *Logic of Programs* (D. Kozen, ed.), LNCS 131, Springer, pp. 52–71.
8. R. De Nicola & F.W. Vaandrager (1995): *Three logics for branching bisimulation. Journal of the ACM* 42(2), pp. 458–487.

9. N. Francez (1986): *Fairness.* Springer.
10. R.J. van Glabbeek (1993): *The Linear Time – Branching Time Spectrum II: The semantics of sequential systems with silent moves (extended abstract).* In *Proceedings CONCUR '93* (E. Best, ed.), LNCS 715, Springer, pp. 66–81.
11. R.J. van Glabbeek (2005): *A Characterisation of Weak Bisimulation Congruence.* In *Processes, Terms and Cycles: Steps on the Road to Infinity:* Essays Dedicated to J.W. Klop on the Occasion of His 60th Birthday (A. Middeldorp, V. van Oostrom, F. van Raamsdonk & R. de Vrijer, eds.), LNCS 3838, Springer, pp. 26-39.
12. R. Milner (1990): *Communication and Concurrency,* Prentice-Hall International, Englewood Cliffs, 1989. An earlier version appeared as *A Calculus of Communicating Systems,* LNCS 92, Springer-Verlag, 1980.
13. W. Vogler (1992): *Modular Construction and Partial Order Semantics of Petri nets.* LNCS 625, Springer.
14. M. Voorhoeve & S. Mauw (2001): *Impossible Futures and Determinism. Information Processing Letters* 80(1), Elsevier, pp. 51–58.

Checking a Mutex Algorithm in a Process Algebra with Fairness

Flavio Corradini[1], Maria Rita Di Berardini[1], and Walter Vogler[2]

[1] Dipartimento di Matematica e Informatica, Università di Camerino
{flavio.corradini, mariarita.diberardini}@unicam.it
[2] Institut für Informatik, Universität Augsburg
vogler@informatik.uni-augsburg.de

Abstract. In earlier work, we have shown that two variants of weak fairness can be expressed comparatively easily in the timed process algebra PAFAS. To demonstrate the usefulness of these results, we complement work by Walker [11] and study the liveness property of Dekker's mutual exclusion algorithm within our process algebraic setting. We also present some results that allow to reduce the state space of the PAFAS process representing Dekker's algorithm, and give some insight into the representation of fair behaviour in PAFAS.

1 Introduction

This paper was inspired by the work of Walker [11] who aimed at automatically verifying six mutual exclusion algorithms – including Dekker's. Walker translated the algorithms into the process algebra CCS [9] and then verified with the Concurrency Workbench [1] that all of them satisfy the *safety property* that the two competing processes are never in their critical sections at the same time.

The *liveness property* that a requesting process will always eventually enter the critical section is more difficult to verify, since one has to assume some fairness, which is not so easy to do in a process algebraic setting; with respect to the verification of liveness, Walker was less successful.

Costa and Stirling [6,7] have studied some notions of fairness in a process algebra. While their formalisation captures the intuition of fairness faithfully, it is technically involved and leads to processes with infinite state spaces – at least for processes that have an infinite computation. In [2,3], we have defined fair runs in the spirit of Costa and Stirling and characterised them in the timed process algebra PAFAS [5] as those runs that take infinitely long; here, processes that are finite state in a standard process algebra without time still have a finite transition system in the setting where fairness can be studied. The present paper complements the work by Walker, taking the liveness of Dekker's algorithm as a case study to demonstrate how our approach to fairness can be used.

Attempting the verification of the liveness property, Walker used the following version in [11] – which could be expressed as a modal mu-calculus formula and checked with the Concurrency Workbench:

C. Baier and H. Hermanns (Eds.): CONCUR 2006, LNCS 4137, pp. 142–157, 2006.

Whenever at some point in a run the process P_i *requests the execution of its critical section, then in any continuation of that run from that point in which between them the processes execute an infinite number of critical sections,* P_i *performs its critical section at least once.*

The fairness (or progress) assumed here is that infinitely often a critical section is entered. This assumption allows a run where one process enters its critical section repeatedly, while the other requests the execution of its critical section, but then – for no good reason at all – refuses to take the necessary steps to actually enter it. Thus, it is maybe not so surprising that four of the six mutual exclusion algorithms – including Dekker's – fail to satisfy this property. Walker then discusses how fairness could be assumed to enable a proof of liveness, but the ideas discussed could not be expressed for use of the Concurrency Workbench.

Here, we will model Dekker's algorithm in the CCS-typė process algebra PAFAS and study whether all fair runs satisfy the liveness property. Actually, we consider two versions of PAFAS. The first one is suitable for (weak) *fairness of actions*, i.e. in a fair run each enabled action must be performed or disabled eventually; if this action is a synchronisation, then the action is already disabled if one partner of this synchronisation offers a different instance of the action. As a consequence, repeated accesses to a variable can block another access, and for this reason some fair runs of Dekker's algorithm violate liveness; this is not so different from Walker's result, but we can point to a realistic reason for the failure, namely the blocking of a variable. We provide two fair runs, one in which one process repeatedly enters its critical section while the other is stuck, and one where both processes are stuck.

It is equally realistic to assume that access to a variable cannot be blocked indefinitely. In the second version of PAFAS, we deal with (weak) *fairness of components*, i.e. in a fair run each enabled component must be performed or disabled eventually. Thus, if a process wants to read a binary variable, it will offer two read-actions (one for each value); if none of these is performed, then in every future state one or the other will be enabled, i.e. the process will be enabled indefinitely; fairness now implies that the process actually will read the variable eventually. Assuming fairness of components, we will show that Dekker's algorithm indeed satisfies the liveness property. In this proof, we have to take into account all possible derivatives reachable from *Dekker* along fair computations. In particular, we will consider those states where one process has just performed a request to enter a critical section, and show that from those states the respective process does eventually enter the critical section.

Modelling fairness involves a certain blow-up of the state space, so for a proof by hand the number of states we had to deal with was rather large. Consequently, to manage the proof, we had to rely on structural properties of the processes, which may be of interest independently of the main aims of this paper. Previously, we have characterised fair runs as those action sequences that arise from timed computations with infinitely many unit time steps by deleting these time steps. Our first result states that we can restrict attention to a particular subclass of such timed computations and still cover all fair runs. A considerable reduction of states comes from switching some components to "permanently lazy", i.e. to require fairness only for the other components. In our case study, the "permanently lazy components" correspond to the variables; so this is a very realistic change, since it seems natural that only the processes are active, while a variable never forces to be read or to be written. In general, switching some components to permanently lazy gives an overapproximation for the fair runs, and it is clearly sufficient to prove a desired property for this possibly larger set of runs. Finally, we take advantage of symmetries in the *Dekker* algorithm. The two processes that compete for the execution of their critical section, indeed, have a symmetric structure so that their derivatives follow a symmetric pattern. Thus, we check liveness of a generic fair-reachable derivative to deduce the same property of the symmetric one; see [4] for many details omitted here. These observations have allowed a proof by hand. We believe, however, that they are not specific to this work but really add some general knowledge to the theory of PAFAS useful to be embedded within an automatic tool for the verification based on fairness.

2 Fairness and PAFAS

We now recall PAFAS, its timed behaviour and the fairness notions we consider, namely fairness of actions and components. Instead of using the very involved direct formalisations of fairness in the spirit of [6,7], we define the two types of fair traces on the basis of our characterisations with everlasting timed execution sequences in the two respective versions of PAFAS.

2.1 Fairness of Actions and PAFAS

We use the following notation: $\mathbb{A}$ is an infinite set of basic actions. An additional action τ is used to represent internal activity, which is unobservable for other components. We define $\mathbb{A}_\tau = \mathbb{A} \cup \{\tau\}$. Elements of $\mathbb{A}$ are denoted by $a, b, c, \ldots$ and those of $\mathbb{A}_\tau$ are denoted by $\alpha, \beta, \ldots$ Actions in $\mathbb{A}_\tau$ can let time 1 pass before their execution, i.e. 1 is their maximal delay. After that time, they become *urgent* actions written $\underline{a}$ or $\underline{\tau}$; these have maximal delay 0. The set of urgent actions is denoted by $\underline{\mathbb{A}}_\tau = \{\underline{a} \mid a \in \mathbb{A}\} \cup \{\underline{\tau}\}$ and is ranged over by $\underline{\alpha}, \underline{\beta}, \ldots$. Elements of $\mathbb{A}_\tau \cup \underline{\mathbb{A}}_\tau$ are ranged over by μ. $\mathcal{X}$ is the set of process variables, used for recursive definitions. Elements of $\mathcal{X}$ are denoted by $x, y, z, \ldots$ $\Phi : \mathbb{A}_\tau \to \mathbb{A}_\tau$ is a *general relabelling function* if the set $\{\alpha \in \mathbb{A}_\tau \mid \emptyset \neq \Phi^{-1}(\alpha) \neq \{\alpha\}\}$ is finite and $\Phi(\tau) = \tau$. Such a function can also be used to define *hiding*: P/A, where the actions in A are made internal, is the same as $P[\Phi_A]$, where the relabelling function Φ_A is defined by $\Phi_A(\alpha) = \tau$ if $\alpha \in A$ and $\Phi_A(\alpha) = \alpha$ if $\alpha \notin A$.

Definition 1. (*timed process terms*) The set $\tilde{\mathbb{P}}_1$ of *initial (timed) process terms* is generated by the following grammar

$$P ::= \mathsf{nil} \;\big|\; x \;\big|\; \alpha.P \;\big|\; P + P \;\big|\; P \|_A P \;\big|\; P[\Phi] \;\big|\; \mathsf{rec}\, x.P$$

where nil is a constant, $x \in \mathcal{X}$, $\alpha \in \mathbb{A}_\tau$, Φ is a general relabelling function and $A \subseteq \mathbb{A}$ possibly infinite. We assume that recursion is guarded (see below).

The set $\tilde{\mathbb{P}}$ of (general) *(timed) process terms* is generated by the following grammar:

$$Q ::= P \mid \underline{\alpha}.P \mid Q + Q \mid Q \parallel_A Q \mid Q[\Phi] \mid \mathsf{rec}\, x.Q$$

where $P \in \tilde{\mathbb{P}}_1$, $x \in \mathcal{X}$, $\alpha \in \mathbb{A}_\tau$, Φ is a general relabelling function and $A \subseteq \mathbb{A}$ possibly infinite. We assume that the recursion is *guarded*, i.e. for $\mathsf{rec}x.Q$ variable x only appears in Q within the scope of a prefix $\mu.()$ with $\mu \in \mathbb{A}_\tau \cup \underline{\mathbb{A}}_\tau$. A term Q is *guarded* if each occurrence of a variable is guarded in this sense. A timed process term Q is closed, if every variable x in Q is bound by the corresponding $\mathsf{rec}x$-operator; such Q in $\tilde{\mathbb{P}}$ and $\tilde{\mathbb{P}}_1$ are simply called *processes* and *initial processes* resp., and their sets are denoted by $\mathbb{P}$ and $\mathbb{P}_1$ resp.[1]

Initial processes are just standard processes of a standard process algebra. General processes are defined here such that they include all processes reachable from the initial ones according to the operational semantics to be defined below.

We can now define the set of activated actions in a process term. Given a process term Q, $\mathcal{A}(Q, A)$ will denote the set of the *activated* (or enabled) actions of Q when the environment prevents the actions in A.

Definition 2. (*activated basic actions*) Let $Q \in \tilde{\mathbb{P}}$ and $A \subseteq \mathbb{A}$. The set $\mathcal{A}(Q, A)$ is defined by induction on Q.

Nil, Var: $\mathcal{A}(\mathsf{nil}, A) = \mathcal{A}(x, A) = \emptyset$

Pref: $\mathcal{A}(\alpha.P, A) = \mathcal{A}(\underline{\alpha}.P, A) = \begin{cases} \{\alpha\} & \text{if } \alpha \notin A \\ \emptyset & \text{otherwise} \end{cases}$

Sum: $\mathcal{A}(Q_1 + Q_2, A) = \mathcal{A}(Q_1, A) \cup \mathcal{A}(Q_2, A)$

Par: $\mathcal{A}(Q_1 \parallel_B Q_2, A) = \mathcal{A}(Q_1, A \cup A') \cup \mathcal{A}(Q_2, A \cup A'')$
where $A' = (\mathcal{A}(Q_1) \backslash \mathcal{A}(Q_2)) \cap B$ and $A'' = (\mathcal{A}(Q_2) \backslash \mathcal{A}(Q_1)) \cap B$

Rel: $\mathcal{A}(Q[\Phi], A) = \Phi(\mathcal{A}(Q, \Phi^{-1}(A)))$

Rec: $\mathcal{A}(\mathsf{rec}\, x.Q, A) = \mathcal{A}(Q, A)$

The *activated actions* of Q are defined as $\mathcal{A}(Q, \emptyset)$ which we abbreviate to $\mathcal{A}(Q)$.

Definition 3. (*urgent activated action*) Let $Q \in \tilde{\mathbb{P}}$ and $A \subseteq \mathbb{A}$. The set $\mathcal{U}(Q, A)$ is defined as in Definition 2 when $\mathcal{A}(\_)$ is replaced by $\mathcal{U}(\_)$ and the Pref-rule is replaced by the following one:

Pref: $\mathcal{U}(\alpha.P, A) = \emptyset$ $\qquad$ $\mathcal{U}(\underline{\alpha}.P, A) = \begin{cases} \{\alpha\} & \text{if } \alpha \notin A \\ \emptyset & \text{otherwise} \end{cases}$

The *urgent activated actions* of Q are defined as $\mathcal{U}(Q) = \mathcal{U}(Q, \emptyset)$

The operational semantics exploits two functions on process terms: $\mathsf{clean}(\_)$ and $\mathsf{unmark}(\_)$. Function $\mathsf{clean}(\_)$ removes *all inactive urgencies* in a process term

[1] In [5], we prove that $\mathbb{P}_1$ processes do not have time-stops; i.e. every finite process run can be extended such that time grows unboundedly. This result was proven for a different operational semantics than that defined in this paper but a similar proof applies also in the current setting.

$Q \in \tilde{\mathbb{P}}$. When a process evolves and a synchronized action is no longer urgent or enabled in some synchronization partner, then it should also lose its urgency in the others; the corresponding change of markings is performed by clean, where again set A in $\mathsf{clean}(Q, A)$ denotes the set of actions that are not enabled or urgent due to restrictions of the environment. Function $\mathsf{unmark}(\_)$ simply removes all urgencies (inactive or not) in a process term $Q \in \tilde{\mathbb{P}}$. We provide the formal definition of the former function. The second one is as expected.

Definition 4. (*cleaning inactive urgencies*) Given a process term $Q \in \tilde{\mathbb{P}}$ we define $\mathsf{clean}(Q)$ as $\mathsf{clean}(Q, \emptyset)$ where, for a set $A \subseteq \mathbb{A}$, $\mathsf{clean}(Q, A)$ is defined as:

Nil, Var: $\mathsf{clean}(\mathsf{nil}, A) = \mathsf{nil}, \qquad \mathsf{clean}(x, A) = x$

Pref: $\mathsf{clean}(\alpha.P, A) = \alpha.P \qquad \mathsf{clean}(\underline{\alpha}.P, A) = \begin{cases} \alpha.P & \text{if } \alpha \in A \\ \underline{\alpha}.P & \text{otherwise} \end{cases}$

Sum: $\mathsf{clean}(Q_1 + Q_2, A) = \mathsf{clean}(Q_1, A) + \mathsf{clean}(Q_2, A)$

Par: $\mathsf{clean}(Q_1 \parallel_B Q_2, A) = \mathsf{clean}(Q_1, A \cup A') \parallel_B \mathsf{clean}(Q_2, A \cup A'')$
where $A' = (\mathcal{U}(Q_1) \backslash \mathcal{U}(Q_2)) \cap B$ and $A'' = (\mathcal{U}(Q_2) \backslash \mathcal{U}(Q_1)) \cap B$

Rel $\mathsf{clean}(Q[\Phi], A) = \mathsf{clean}(Q, \Phi^{-1}(A))[\Phi]$

Rec: $\mathsf{clean}(\mathsf{rec}\, x.Q, A) = \mathsf{rec}\, x.\ \mathsf{clean}(Q, A)$

The Functional Behaviour of PAFAS Process. The transitional semantics describing the functional behaviour of PAFAS processes indicates which basic actions they can perform.

Definition 5. (*Functional operational semantics*) The following SOS-rules define the action transition relations $\xrightarrow{\alpha} \subseteq (\tilde{\mathbb{P}} \times \tilde{\mathbb{P}})$ for $\alpha \in \mathbb{A}_\tau$. As usual, we write $Q \xrightarrow{\alpha} Q'$ if $(Q, Q') \in \xrightarrow{\alpha}$ and $Q \xrightarrow{\alpha}$ if there exists a $Q' \in \tilde{\mathbb{P}}$ such that $(Q, Q') \in \xrightarrow{\alpha}$, and similar conventions will apply later on.

$$\textsc{Pref}_{a1}\frac{}{\alpha.P \xrightarrow{\alpha} P} \qquad \textsc{Pref}_{a2}\frac{}{\underline{\alpha}.P \xrightarrow{\alpha} P} \qquad \textsc{Sum}_a\frac{Q_1 \xrightarrow{\alpha} Q'}{Q_1 + Q_2 \xrightarrow{\alpha} Q'}$$

$$\textsc{Par}_{a1}\frac{\alpha \notin A,\ Q_1 \xrightarrow{\alpha} Q_1'}{Q_1 \|_A Q_2 \xrightarrow{\alpha} \mathsf{clean}(Q_1' \|_A Q_2)} \qquad \textsc{Par}_{a2}\frac{\alpha \in A,\ Q_1 \xrightarrow{\alpha} Q_1',\ Q_2 \xrightarrow{\alpha} Q_2'}{Q_1 \|_A Q_2 \xrightarrow{\alpha} \mathsf{clean}(Q_1' \|_A Q_2')}$$

$$\textsc{Rel}_a\frac{Q \xrightarrow{\alpha} Q'}{Q[\Phi] \xrightarrow{\Phi(\alpha)} Q'[\Phi]} \qquad \textsc{Rec}_a\frac{Q\{\mathsf{rec}\, x.\mathsf{unmark}(Q)/x\} \xrightarrow{\alpha} Q'}{\mathsf{rec}\, x.Q \xrightarrow{\alpha} Q'}$$

Additionally, there are symmetric rules for $\textsc{Par}_{a1}$ and $\textsc{Sum}_a$ for actions of Q_2. For an *initial* process P_0, we say that a finite or infinite sequence $\alpha_0\alpha_1 \ldots$ of actions from $\mathbb{A}_\tau$ is a *trace* of P_0, if there is a sequence $P_0 \xrightarrow{\alpha_0} P_1 \xrightarrow{\alpha_1} \ldots$ of action transitions, possibly ending with a process P_n.

The Temporal Behaviour of PAFAS Process. Now, we consider transitions corresponding to the passage of one unit of time. The function urgent marks all *enabled* actions of a process as urgent when a time step is performed. Before the next time step, all such actions must occur or get disabled.

Definition 6. (*time step, timed execution sequences*) For $P \in \tilde{\mathbb{P}}_1$, we write $P \xrightarrow{1} Q$ when $Q = \mathsf{urgent}(P)$, where $\mathsf{urgent}(P)$ abbreviates $\mathsf{urgent}(P, \emptyset)$ and $\mathsf{urgent}(P, A)$ is defined as:

Nil, Var:	$\mathsf{urgent}(\mathsf{nil}, A) = \mathsf{nil}, \quad \mathsf{urgent}(x, A) = x$
Pref:	$\mathsf{urgent}(\alpha.P, A) = \begin{cases} \underline{\alpha}.P & \text{if } \alpha \notin A \\ \alpha.P & \text{otherwise} \end{cases}$
Sum:	$\mathsf{urgent}(P_1 + P_2, A) = \mathsf{urgent}(P_1, A) + \mathsf{urgent}(P_2, A)$
Par:	$\mathsf{urgent}(P_1 \parallel_B P_2, A) = \mathsf{urgent}(P_1, A \cup A') \parallel_B \mathsf{urgent}(P_2, A \cup A'')$ where $A' = (\mathcal{A}(P_1) \backslash \mathcal{A}(P_2)) \cap B$ and $A'' = (\mathcal{A}(P_2) \backslash \mathcal{A}(P_1)) \cap B$
Rel:	$\mathsf{urgent}(P[\Phi, A) = \mathsf{urgent}(P, \Phi^{-1}(A))[\Phi]$
Rec:	$\mathsf{urgent}(\mathsf{rec}\, x.P, A) = \mathsf{rec}\, x.\, \mathsf{urgent}(P, A)$

For an initial process P_0, we say that a sequence of transitions $\gamma = P_0 \xrightarrow{1} Q_0 \xrightarrow{\lambda_1} \ldots$ with $\lambda_i \in \mathbb{A}_\tau \cup \{1\}$ is a *timed execution sequence* if it is an infinite sequence of action transitions and time steps (starting with a time step)[2]. A timed execution sequence is *everlasting* in the sense of having infinitely many time steps if and only if it is *non-Zeno*; a Zeno run would have infinitely many actions in a finite amount of time.

Fairness of Actions and Timing. We can now define the (weakly) fair traces in terms of non-Zeno execution sequences.

Definition 7. (*fair traces*) Let $P_0 \in \mathbb{P}_1$ and $\alpha_0, \alpha_1, \alpha_2, \ldots \in \mathbb{A}_\tau$. A trace of P_0 is *fair (w.r.t. fairness of actions)* if it can be obtained as the sequence of actions in a non-Zeno timed execution sequence. In detail:

1. A finite trace $\alpha_0\alpha_1 \ldots \alpha_n$ is fair if and only if there exists a timed execution sequence $P_{i_0} \xrightarrow{1} Q_{i_0} \xrightarrow{v_0} P_{i_1} \xrightarrow{1} Q_{i_1} \xrightarrow{v_1} P_{i_2} \ldots P_{i_{m-1}} \xrightarrow{1} Q_{i_{m-1}} \xrightarrow{v_{m-1}} P_{i_m} \xrightarrow{1} Q_{i_m} \xrightarrow{1} Q_{i_m} \ldots$, where $P_{i_0} = P_0$ and $v_0\, v_1 \ldots v_{m-1} = \alpha_0\, \alpha_1 \ldots \alpha_n$;
2. an infinite trace $\alpha_0\alpha_1\alpha_2 \ldots$ is fair if and only if there exists a timed execution sequence $P_{i_0} \xrightarrow{1} Q_{i_0} \xrightarrow{v_0} P_{i_1} \xrightarrow{1} Q_{i_1} \xrightarrow{v_1} P_{i_2} \cdots P_{i_m} \xrightarrow{1} Q_{i_m} \xrightarrow{v_m} P_{i_{m+1}} \cdots$, where $P_{i_0} = P_0$ and $v_0\, v_1 \ldots v_m \ldots = \alpha_0\, \alpha_1 \ldots \alpha_i \ldots$.

This is a characterisation for fair traces obtained in [2] on the basis of a more intuitive, but very complex definition of fair traces in the spirit of [6,7].

2.2 Fairness of Components and PAFAS^{c}

In this section, we concentrate on weak *fairness of components*. We have found a suitable variation of PAFAS and its semantics which allows us to characterize Costa and Stirling's fairness of components again in terms of a simple filtering

[2] Note that a maximal sequence of such transitions/steps is never finite, since for $\gamma = Q_0 \xrightarrow{\lambda_0} Q_1 \xrightarrow{\lambda_1} \ldots \xrightarrow{\lambda_{n-1}} Q_n$, we have $Q_n \xrightarrow{\alpha}$ or $Q_n \xrightarrow{1}$ (see Proposition 3.13 in [2]).

of system executions. Conceptually, we proceed analogously to Section 2.1, but a number of technical changes are needed. Since we associate time bounds to components in the present section, we may also mark - besides prefixes - the other dynamic operator $+$ as urgent: a process $P+Q$ becomes $P \underline{+} Q$ after a time step. This variant of PAFAS is called PAFAS^{C} henceforth.

Definition 8. (*timed process terms*) Let $\tilde{\mathbb{P}}_1$ be the set of *initial timed process terms* as given in Definition 1. The set $\tilde{\mathbb{P}}_c$ of (component-oriented) *timed process terms* is generated by the grammar:

$$Q ::= P \mid \underline{\alpha}.P \mid P \underline{+} P \mid Q \|_A Q \mid Q[\Phi] \mid \mathsf{rec}\, x.Q$$

where $P \in \tilde{\mathbb{P}}_1$, $x \in \mathcal{X}$, $\alpha \in \mathbb{A}_\tau$, Φ is a general relabelling function, and $A \subseteq \mathbb{A}$ possibly infinite. Again, we assume that recursion is always guarded. The set of closed timed process terms in $\tilde{\mathbb{P}}_c$, simply called *processes* is denoted by $\mathbb{P}_c$.

Function $\mathcal{A}(\_)$ on process terms, returns the *activated* (or enabled) actions of a process term.

Definition 9. (*activated basic actions*) Let $Q \in \tilde{\mathbb{P}}_c$ and $A \subseteq \mathbb{A}$. The set $\mathcal{A}(Q, A)$ can be defined as in Definition 2 when rule Sum is replaced as follows:

$$\text{Sum:} \quad \mathcal{A}(P_1 + P_2, A) = \mathcal{A}(P_1 \underline{+} P_2, A) = \mathcal{A}(P_1, A) \cup \mathcal{A}(P_2, A)$$

The Operational Behaviour of PAFAS^{C} Processes. A new definition of function $\mathsf{clean}(\_)$ is needed

Definition 10. (*cleaning inactive urgencies*) For a process $Q \in \mathbb{P}_c$, define $\mathsf{clean}(Q)$ as $\mathsf{clean}(Q, \emptyset)$, $A \subseteq \mathbb{A}$, $\mathsf{clean}(Q, A)$ is defined as in Definition 4 where rules Sum and Par are replaced by:

$$\text{Sum: } \mathsf{clean}(P_1 + P_2, A) = P_1 + P_2$$
$$\mathsf{clean}(P_1 \underline{+} P_2, A) = \begin{cases} P_1 + P_2 & \text{if } \mathcal{A}(P_1) \cup \mathcal{A}(P_2) \subseteq A \\ P_1 \underline{+} P_2 & \text{otherwise} \end{cases}$$
$$\text{Par: } \mathsf{clean}(Q_1 \|_B Q_2, A) = \mathsf{clean}(Q_1, A \cup A') \|_B \mathsf{clean}(Q_2, A \cup A'')$$
$$\text{where } \quad A' = (\mathcal{A}(Q_1) \backslash \mathcal{A}(Q_2)) \cap B \text{ and } A'' = (\mathcal{A}(Q_2) \backslash \mathcal{A}(Q_1)) \cap B$$

Definition 11. (*Functional operational semantics*) The functional operational semantics for $\tilde{\mathbb{P}}_c$-terms is as in Definition 5 where $\rightarrow$ is replaced by $\longmapsto$ and rule Sum$_a$ (and symmetrically its symmetric rules) are replaced by:

$$\textsc{Sum}_{a1}\frac{P_1 \overset{\alpha}{\longmapsto} P_1'}{P_1 + P_2 \overset{\alpha}{\longmapsto} P_1'} \qquad \textsc{Sum}_{a2}\frac{P_1 \overset{\alpha}{\longmapsto} P_1'}{P_1 \underline{+} P_2 \overset{\alpha}{\longmapsto} P_1'}$$

and function clean is the one in Definition 10. Consequently, traces out of an initial process P_0 consider $\longmapsto$ (instead of $\rightarrow$).

The Temporal Behaviour of PAFAS^c Process. As in Section 2.1, we define *timed execution sequences* to be infinite sequences of action transitions and time steps starting at some initial process P_0 (again a maximal sequence of such transitions/steps starting is never finite) and the property *non-Zeno*, where:

Definition 12. (*time step, timed execution sequence*) For $P \in \tilde{\mathbb{P}}_1$, we write $P \xmapsto{1} Q$ when $Q = \mathsf{urgent}(P)$, where $\mathsf{urgent}(P)$ abbreviates $\mathsf{urgent}(P, \emptyset)$ and $\mathsf{urgent}(P, A)$ is defined as in Definition 6 but rule Sum is replaced as follows:

$$\text{Sum: } \mathsf{urgent}(P_1 + P_2, A) = \begin{cases} P_1 \underline{+} P_2 & \text{if } (\mathcal{A}(P_1) \cup \mathcal{A}(P_2)) \backslash A \neq \emptyset \\ P_1 + P_2 & \text{otherwise} \end{cases}$$

Fairness of Components and Timing. As in Section 2.1, we can now define (weak) *fairness w.r.t. components* in terms of non-Zeno timed execution sequences. In fact, *fair traces* (w.r.t. fairness of components) can be defined just as in Definition 7 by replacing each action transition $\xrightarrow{\alpha}$ and time step $\xrightarrow{1}$ with its counterpart in the component-oriented timed operational semantics, i.e. $\xmapsto{\alpha}$ and $\xmapsto{1}$. To keep things short, we do not report here the formal definition.

3 Dekker's Algorithm and Its Liveness Property

In this section we briefly describe Dekker's mutex algorithm. There are two processes P_1 and P_2, two boolean-valued variables b_1 and b_2, whose initial values are *false*, and a variable k, which may take the values 1 and 2 and whose initial value is arbitrary. The ith process (with $i = 1, 2$) can be described as follows, where j is the index of the other process:

```
while true do
begin
    ⟨noncritical section⟩;
    b_i = true;
    while b_j do if k = j then begin
           b_i := false;   while k = j do skip;   b_i := true;
    end;
    ⟨critical section⟩;
    k := j;   b_i := false;
end;
```

Informally, the b variables are "request" variables and k is a "turn" variable: b_i is *true* if P_i is requesting entry to its critical section and k is i if it is P_i's turn to enter its critical section. Only P_i writes b_i, but both processes read it.

3.1 Translating the Algorithm into PAFAS Processes

In our translation of the algorithm into PAFAS, we use essentially the same coding as given by Walker in [11]. Each program variable is represented as a family of processes. For instance, the process $\mathsf{B}_1(\mathit{false})$ denotes the variable b_1 with value *false*. The *sort* of the process $\mathsf{B}_1(\mathit{false})$ is the set $\{b_1 rf, b_1 rt, b_1 wf, b_1 wt\}$ where $b_1 rf$ and $b_1 rt$ represent the actions of reading the values *false* and *true* from b_1, $b_1 wf$ and $b_1 wt$ represent, respectively, the writing of the values *false* and *true* into b_1. Let $\mathbb{B} = \{\mathit{false}, \mathit{true}\}$ and $\mathbb{K} = \{1, 2\}$.

Definition 13. (*program variables*) Let $i \in \{1, 2\}$. We define the processes representing program variables as follows:

$$\begin{array}{l} \mathsf{B}_i(\mathit{false}) = b_i rf.\mathsf{B}_i(\mathit{false}) + (b_i wf.\mathsf{B}_i(\mathit{false}) + b_i wt.\mathsf{B}_i(\mathit{true})) \\ \mathsf{B}_i(\mathit{true}) = b_i rt.\mathsf{B}_i(\mathit{true}) + (b_i wf.\mathsf{B}_i(\mathit{false}) + b_i wt.\mathsf{B}_i(\mathit{true})) \\ \mathsf{K}(i) = kri.\mathsf{K}(i) + (kw1.\mathsf{K}(1) + kw2.\mathsf{K}(2)) \end{array}$$

Let $B = \{b_i rf, b_i rt, b_i wf, b_i wt \mid i \in \{1, 2\}\} \cup \{kr1, kr2, kw1, kw2\}$ be the union of the sorts of all variables and Φ_B the relabelling function such that $\Phi_B(\alpha) = \tau$ if $\alpha \in B$ and $\Phi_B(\alpha) = \alpha$ if $\alpha \notin B$. Given $b_1, b_2 \in \mathbb{B}$, $k \in \mathbb{K}$ and using $\|$ as a shorthand for $\|_\emptyset$, we define $\mathsf{PV}(b_1, b_2, k) = (\mathsf{B}_1(b_1) \parallel \mathsf{B}_2(b_2)) \parallel \mathsf{K}(k)$.

Definition 14. (*the algorithm*) The processes $\mathtt{P}_1$ and $\mathtt{P}_2$ are represented by the following PAFAS processes; the actions $\mathtt{req}_i$ and cs_i have been added to indicate the request to enter and the execution of the critical section by the process $\mathtt{P}_i$.

$$\begin{array}{ll} P_1 = \mathtt{req}_1.b_1 wt.P_{11} + \tau.P_1 & P_2 = \mathtt{req}_2.b_2 wt.P_{21} + \tau.P_2 \\ P_{11} = b_2 rf.P_{14} + b_2 rt.P_{12} & P_{21} = b_1 rf.P_{24} + b_1 rt.P_{22} \\ P_{12} = kr1.P_{11} + kr2.b_1 wf.P_{13} & P_{22} = kr2.P_{21} + kr1.b_2 wf.P_{23} \\ P_{13} = kr1.b_1 wt.P_{11} + kr2.P_{13} & P_{23} = kr2.b_2 wt.P_{21} + kr1.P_{23} \\ P_{14} = \mathsf{cs}_1.kw2.b_1 wf.P_1 & P_{24} = \mathsf{cs}_2.kw1.b_2 wf.P_2 \end{array}$$

Now we define the algorithm as $\mathit{Dekker} = ((P_1 \parallel P_2) \parallel_B \mathsf{PV}(\mathit{false}, \mathit{false}, 1))[\Phi_B]$. The sort of *Dekker* is the set $\mathbb{A}_d = \{\mathtt{req}_i, \mathsf{cs}_i \mid i = 1, 2\}$.

3.2 Liveness Property of Dekker's Algorithm

As discussed in the introduction, a mutex algorithm satisfies its liveness property if whenever at any point in any computation a process $\mathtt{P}_i$ requests the execution of its critical section, then, in any continuation of that computation, there is a point at which $\mathtt{P}_i$ will perform its critical section. We can expect this property to hold only under some fairness assumption; so for the formal property we want to check, we replace 'computation' by 'fair trace' (in one of our two interpretations). In other words, a mutex algorithm satisfies its *liveness property* if any occurrence of $\mathtt{req}_i$ in a fair trace is eventually followed by cs_i, $i = 1, 2$. Due to our definition of fair trace, this amounts to checking that each non-Zeno timed execution sequence is live according to the following definition.

Definition 15. (*live execution sequences*) Let $P_0 \in \mathbb{P}_1$, $\lambda_0, \lambda_1, \ldots \in (\mathbb{A}_d \cup \{\tau\} \cup \{1\})$. A *timed execution sequence* γ from P_0 with $\gamma = P_0 \xrightarrow{1} Q_0 \xrightarrow{\lambda_0} Q_1 \xrightarrow{\lambda_1} \ldots$ ($\gamma = P_0 \overset{1}{\longmapsto} Q_0 \overset{\lambda_0}{\longmapsto} Q_1 \overset{\lambda_1}{\longmapsto} \ldots$) is *not live* if there exists $j \in \mathbb{N}_0$ such that $\lambda_j = \mathtt{req}_i$ and cs_i is not performed in the execution sequence $Q_{j+1} \xrightarrow{\lambda_{j+1}} Q_{j+2} \xrightarrow{\lambda_{j+2}} \ldots$ ($Q_{j+1} \overset{\lambda_{j+1}}{\longmapsto} Q_{j+2} \overset{\lambda_{j+2}}{\longmapsto} \ldots$ respectively). Otherwise, we say that γ is live.

4 Fairness of Actions and Liveness

This section shows that fairness of actions is not sufficiently strong to ensure the liveness property. We present two fair traces with respect to fairness of actions, which violate the liveness property, i.e. two non-Zeno timed execution sequences in PAFAS (cf. Section 2.1) which are not live. We now describe how program variables and the processes P_1 and P_2 evolve by letting one time unit pass.

Definition 16. (*urgent program variables*) According to Definitions 13 and 6, *urgent program variables* can be defined as follows:

$$\begin{array}{l}\underline{\mathsf{B}_i}(\mathit{false}) = \underline{b_i rf}.\mathsf{B}_i(\mathit{false}) + (\underline{b_i wf}.\mathsf{B}_i(\mathit{false}) + \underline{b_i wt}.\mathsf{B}_i(\mathit{true}))\\ \underline{\mathsf{B}_i}(\mathit{true}) = \underline{b_i rt}.\mathsf{B}_i(\mathit{true}) + (\underline{b_i wf}.\mathsf{B}_i(\mathit{false}) + \underline{b_i wt}.\mathsf{B}_i(\mathit{true}))\\ \underline{\mathsf{K}}(i) = \underline{kri}.\mathsf{K}(i) + (\underline{kw1}.\mathsf{K}(1) + \underline{kw2}.\mathsf{K}(2))\end{array}$$

Let us denote with $\underline{\mathbb{B}} = \{\underline{false}, \underline{true}\}$ and with $\underline{\mathbb{K}} = \{\underline{1}, \underline{2}\}$. Then, given $b'_1, b'_2 \in \mathbb{B} \cup \underline{\mathbb{B}}$ and $k' \in \mathbb{K} \cup \underline{\mathbb{K}}$, we define $\mathsf{PV}(b'_1, b'_2, k') = ((B_1 \parallel B_2) \parallel K)$, where:

$$B_i = \begin{cases} \mathsf{B}_i(b) & \text{if } b'_i = b \in \mathbb{B}\\ \underline{\mathsf{B}_i}(b) & \text{if } b'_i = \underline{b} \in \underline{\mathbb{B}}\end{cases} \qquad K = \begin{cases} \mathsf{K}(k) & \text{if } k' = k \in \mathbb{K}\\ \underline{\mathsf{K}}(k) & \text{if } k' = \underline{k} \in \underline{\mathbb{K}}\end{cases}$$

As an example, we have that $\mathsf{PV}(\underline{true}, \mathit{false}, \underline{2}) = (\underline{\mathsf{B}_1}(\mathit{true}) \parallel \mathsf{B}_2(\mathit{false})) \parallel \underline{\mathsf{K}}(2)$.

The urgent versions of processes P_1 and P_2, denoted by $\underline{P_1}$ and $\underline{P_2}$ resp., are as in Definition 14 where initial actions are urgent. We use $\underline{P_{ij}}$ ($i = 1, 2$ and $j = 1, 2, 3, 4$) to denote the urgent versions of their derivatives (ex. $\underline{P_{12}} = \underline{kr1}.P_{11} + \underline{kr2}.b_1 wf.P_{13}$). As a consequence of the above definitions (and by the action-oriented operational semantics) we have that *Dekker* can let one time unit pass evolving into $\underline{\mathit{Dekker}} = ((\underline{P_1} \parallel \underline{P_2}) \parallel_B \mathsf{PV}(\mathit{false}, \mathit{false}, 1))[\Phi_B]$. Our first example shows how an infinite τ-loop can result in the starvation of both processes.

Example 1. Let us consider the following timed computation from *Dekker*:

$$\begin{array}{rl} \mathit{Dekker} \xrightarrow{1} \underline{\mathit{Dekker}} = & ((\underline{P_1} \parallel \underline{P_2}) \parallel_B \mathsf{PV}(\mathit{false}, \mathit{false}, 1))[\Phi_B] \quad \xrightarrow{\mathtt{req}_1} \xrightarrow{\mathtt{req}_2} \xrightarrow{\tau^4}\\ P_0 = & ((P_{11} \parallel b_2 wf.P_{23}) \parallel_B \mathsf{PV}(\mathit{true}, \mathit{true}, 1))[\Phi_B] \xrightarrow{1}\\ Q_0 = & ((\underline{P_{11}} \parallel \underline{b_2 wf}.P_{23}) \parallel_B \mathsf{PV}(\mathit{true}, \underline{\mathit{true}}, 1))[\Phi_B] \xrightarrow{\tau^2}\\ P_0 = & ((P_{11} \parallel b_2 wf.P_{23}) \parallel_B \mathsf{PV}(\mathit{true}, \mathit{true}, 1))[\Phi_B]\end{array}$$

Repeating the last three transitions, we get a non-Zeno timed execution sequence that is not live, i.e. *Dekker* can perform a fair trace $\mathit{Dekker} \xrightarrow{\mathtt{req}_1\, \mathtt{req}_2\, \tau^4} P_0 \xrightarrow{\tau^2} P_0 \xrightarrow{\tau^2} P_0 \ldots$ that violates liveness since no process will ever enter its critical section. Intuitively speaking, once in P_0, repeated reading of variables b_2 and k blocks indefinitely P_2 which will never set its request variable b_2 to false. On the other hand, P_1 cannot enter its critical section and, hence, cannot proceed until the value of b_2 is true. Thus, both processes are stuck. The next example shows a different kind of computation which also causes a violation of liveness; along such a computation, one process is stuck while the other repeatedly executes its critical section. Consider the following computation:

$$\begin{array}{l} Dekker \xrightarrow{1} \underline{Dekker} = ((\underline{P}_1 \parallel \underline{P}_2) \parallel_B \mathsf{PV}(\mathit{false}, \mathit{false}, 1))[\Phi_B] \xrightarrow{\texttt{req}_1\ \texttt{req}_2\ \tau^2\ \texttt{cs}_1\ \tau} \\ \qquad P_0 = ((b_1 \mathit{wf}.P_1 \parallel b_2 \mathit{wt}.P_{21}) \parallel_B \mathsf{PV}(\mathit{true}, \mathit{false}, 2))[\Phi_B] \xrightarrow{1} \\ \qquad ((\underline{b_1 \mathit{wf}}.P_1 \parallel \underline{b_2 \mathit{wt}}.P_{21}) \parallel_B \mathsf{PV}(\underline{\mathit{true}}, \underline{\mathit{false}}, 2))[\Phi_B] \xrightarrow{\tau\ \texttt{req}_1\ \tau^2\ \texttt{cs}_1\ \tau} \\ \qquad P_0 = ((b_1 \mathit{wf}.P_1 \parallel b_2 \mathit{wt}.P_{21}) \parallel_B \mathsf{PV}(\mathit{true}, \mathit{false}, 2))[\Phi_B] \end{array}$$

Again, the trace performed in $Dekker \xrightarrow{\texttt{req}_1\ \texttt{req}_2\ \tau^2\ \texttt{cs}_1\ \tau} P_0 \xrightarrow{\tau\ \texttt{req}_1\ \tau^2\ \texttt{cs}_1\ \tau} P_0 \ldots$ is fair but violates liveness since P_2 never enters its critical section. Here, P_1 repeatedly executes its critical section, again preventing P_2 to set its request variable b_2 to *true*. As a consequence, P_2 cannot enter its critical section even if the value of turn variable k is two.

5 Fairness of Components and Liveness

This section proves that any fair trace of *Dekker* according to fairness of components satisfies the liveness property. We present three ideas to reduce the number of states we have to deal with.

5.1 Permanently Lazy Components

The state space of a process in PAFAS^{c} is considerably larger than in an untimed process algebra because process components switch from lazy to urgent. We can achieve a considerable reduction, if we prevent this by declaring some components as permanently lazy. As an application, we regard the three program variables as one component of *Dekker*; declaring it as permanently lazy results in a process denoted by *Dekker*[PV]. A non-Zeno timed execution sequence of the original process can be simulated by one of the new process. Thus, instead of proving that all non-Zeno timed execution sequences of *Dekker* are live, it is sufficient to prove that all non-Zeno timed execution sequences of *Dekker*[PV] are live. We have also a good intuitive reason to request it to be true. Since fairness is required for all components, a program variable can, intuitively speaking, enforce to be read or written - provided there is always some component that could do so. But our intuition for variables is that they are passive, that we really only want fairness towards P_1 and P_2. Assuming this kind of fairness is indeed enough. We now extend PAFAS^{c} with a new operator, which can only be applied to a top-level component.

Definition 17. (*permanently lazy processes*) Given $P \in \tilde{\mathbb{P}}_1$, we define the *permanently lazy version* of P, written $[P]$, to be the process with the same syntactical structure of P (and, hence, the same functional behaviour) but which permanently ignores the passage of time. The timed operational semantics of $[P]$ can be defined by the following rules:

$$\textsc{Act}_L \frac{P \overset{\alpha}{\longmapsto} P'}{[P] \overset{\alpha}{\longmapsto} [P']} \qquad \textsc{Time}_L \frac{}{[P] \overset{1}{\longmapsto} [P]}$$

The set $\tilde{\mathbb{P}}_{\ell 1}$ of initial processes with one permanently lazy top-level component is generated by:

$$S ::= P \parallel_A [P] \mid S[\Phi]$$

where $P \in \tilde{\mathbb{P}}_1$, $A \subseteq \mathbb{A}$ (possibly infinite) and Φ is a general relabelling function. Similarly, the set $\tilde{\mathbb{P}}_\ell$ of *(general) processes with one permanently lazy top-level component* is generated by the following grammar:

$$R ::= Q \parallel_A [P] \mid R[\Phi]$$

where $Q \in \tilde{\mathbb{P}}_c$, $P \in \tilde{\mathbb{P}}_1$, $A \subseteq \mathbb{A}$ (possibly infinite) and Φ is a general relabelling function.

We define the operational semantics for processes with one permanently lazy top-level component.

Definition 18. (*Functional operational semantics*) The following SOS-rules define the transition relations $\overset{\alpha}{\longmapsto} \subseteq (\tilde{\mathbb{P}}_\ell \times \tilde{\mathbb{P}}_\ell)$ for $\alpha \in \mathbb{A}_\tau$, the *action transitions*.

$$\textsc{LPar}_{a1} \frac{\alpha \notin A,\ Q \overset{\alpha}{\longmapsto} Q'}{Q \parallel_A [P] \overset{\alpha}{\longmapsto} \mathsf{clean}(Q' \parallel_A [P])} \qquad \textsc{LPar}_{a2} \frac{\alpha \notin A, P \longmapsto_\alpha P'}{Q \parallel_A [P] \overset{\alpha}{\longmapsto} \mathsf{clean}(Q \parallel_A [P'])}$$

$$\textsc{LSynch}_a \frac{\alpha \in A,\ Q \overset{\alpha}{\longmapsto} Q',\ P \longmapsto_\alpha P'}{Q \parallel_A [P] \longmapsto_\alpha \mathsf{clean}(Q' \parallel_A [P'])} \qquad \textsc{LRel}_a \frac{R \overset{\alpha}{\longmapsto} R'}{R[\Phi] \longmapsto_{\Phi(\alpha)} R'[\Phi]}$$

where $\mathsf{clean}(Q \parallel_A [P]) = \mathsf{clean}(Q, A') \parallel_A [P]$ and $A' = (\mathcal{A}(Q) \backslash \mathcal{A}(P)) \cap A$.

Definition 19. (*time step*) For $S \in \tilde{\mathbb{P}}_{\ell 1}$, we write that $S \overset{1}{\longmapsto} R$ when $R = \mathsf{urgent}(S)$ where function $\mathsf{urgent}(S)$ is defined as follows:

Par: $\mathsf{urgent}(P_1 \parallel_B [P_2]) = \mathsf{urgent}(P_1, A') \parallel_B [P_2]$ where $A' = (\mathcal{A}(P_1) \backslash \mathcal{A}(P_2)) \cap A$
Rel: $\mathsf{urgent}(S[\Phi]) = \mathsf{urgent}(S)[\Phi]$

Definition 20. Let $Q \in \tilde{\mathbb{P}}$ and $R \in \tilde{\mathbb{P}}_\ell$. We write that $Q \preceq R$ if either $Q = Q_1 \parallel_A Q_2$ and $R = Q_1 \parallel_A [\mathsf{unmark}(Q_2)]$ or $Q = Q_1[\Phi]$ and $R = R_1[\Phi]$ with $Q_1 \preceq R_1$.

Proposition 1. Let $P \in \tilde{\mathbb{P}}_1$, $S \in \tilde{\mathbb{P}}_{\ell 1}$ with $P \preceq S$ and $v \in (\mathbb{A}_\tau)^*$. Then $P \overset{1}{\longmapsto} Q \overset{v}{\longmapsto} P' \in \tilde{\mathbb{P}}_1$ implies $S \overset{1}{\longmapsto} R \overset{v}{\longmapsto} S'$ with $P' \preceq S'$ (S simulates each non-Zeno timed execution sequence of P).

This proposition states that all non-Zeno timed execution sequences of *Dekker* can be simulated by non-Zeno timed execution sequences of *Dekker*[PV].

5.2 F-Steps

We can group the transitions of a non-Zeno timed execution sequence into infinitely many steps of the form $S \overset{1}{\longmapsto} R \overset{v}{\longmapsto} S'$, where $v \in (\mathbb{A}_\tau)^*$ and S' is the next process to perform a time step. Such a step is minimal in a sense, if S' is the first process in the transition sequence $R \overset{v}{\longmapsto} S'$ that could perform a time step, i.e. the first initial process. We call such minimal steps f-steps and the processes reachable by them fair-reachable. We will show in this subsection that we only have to consider timed execution sequences built from infinitely such f-steps.

Definition 21. (*f-executions*) A transition sequence $S \overset{1}{\longmapsto} R \overset{v}{\longmapsto} S'$ with $S, S' \in \mathbb{P}_{\ell 1}$ and $v \in (\mathbb{A}_\tau)^*$ is an *f-step* if S' is the only initial process in the transition sequence $R \overset{v}{\longmapsto} S'$ (allowing $R = S'$ if v is the empty sequence). An *f-execution* from $S_0 \in \mathbb{P}_{\ell 1}$ is any infinite sequence of f-steps of the form: $\gamma = S_0 \overset{1}{\longmapsto} R_0 \overset{v_0}{\longmapsto} S_1 \overset{1}{\longmapsto} R_1 \overset{v_1}{\longmapsto} S_2 \ldots$ We call the processes $S_1, S_2, \ldots$ *fair-reachable* from S_0.

F-executions are special non-Zeno timed execution sequences. To show that checking them for liveness suffices, we need the following proposition.

Proposition 2. For each non-Zeno timed execution sequence from $S_0 \in \mathbb{P}_{\ell 1}$, $\gamma = S_0 \overset{1}{\longmapsto} R_0 \overset{v_0}{\longmapsto} S_1 \overset{1}{\longmapsto} R_1 \overset{v_1}{\longmapsto} S_2 \ldots$ there exists a corresponding f-execution $\gamma' = S'_0 \overset{1}{\longmapsto} R'_0 \overset{v'_0}{\longmapsto} S'_1 \overset{1}{\longmapsto} R'_1 \overset{v'_1}{\longmapsto} S'_2 \ldots$, where $S'_0 = S_0$, $v_0 v_1 \ldots = v'_0 v'_1 \ldots$ and each step $S'_i \overset{1}{\longmapsto} R'_i \overset{v'_i}{\longmapsto} S'_{i+1}$ is minimal.

5.3 Symmetry of Fair-Reachable Processes

Half of the processes which are fair-reachable from *Dekker*[PV] are denoted by $D_1, \ldots, D_{47}$; see Table 1 and [4] for a full list of the processes. We also consider all possible symmetries and use S_y to denote the process which is symmetric to D_y with respect to the local state of P_1 and P_2 and the value of the variables b_1, b_2 and k. For each $y \in [1, 47]$, $S_y = \mathcal{S}(D_y)$ where function $\mathcal{S}(\_)$ on processes is given below. Moreover, $\mathcal{S}(S_y) = D_y$ for any y.

Table 1. Fair-Reachable Processes

$D_1 = ((b_1 wt.P_{11} \parallel b_2 wt.P_{21}) \parallel_B [\mathsf{PV}(\mathit{false}, \mathit{false}, 1)])[\Phi_B]$
$\vdots$
$D_{23} = ((b_1 wf.P_1 \parallel P_{21}) \parallel_B [\mathsf{PV}(\mathit{true}, \mathit{true}, 2)])[\Phi_B]$
$\vdots$
$D_{47} = (P_{13} \parallel b_2 wt.P_{21}) \parallel_B [\mathsf{PV}(\mathit{false}, \mathit{false}, 2)])[\Phi_B]$

Definition 22. (*symmetric processes*) Let $P_1, P_{11}, \ldots P_{14}, P_2, P_{21}, \ldots P_{24}$ be processes as given in Definition 14. Let moreover $x \in [1, 4]$ and $\{i, j\} = \{1, 2\}$. Then:

$$\mathcal{S}(P_i) = P_j \qquad \mathcal{S}(P_{ix}) = P_{jx}$$
$$\mathcal{S}(b_i wt.P_{i1}) = b_j wt.P_{j1} \qquad \mathcal{S}(b_i wf.P_{i3}) = b_j wf.P_{j3}$$
$$\mathcal{S}(kwj.b_i wf.P_i) = kwi.b_j wf.P_j \qquad \mathcal{S}(b_i wf.P_i) = b_j wf.P_j$$

Now, let $b_1, b_2 \in \mathbb{B}$, $k \in \mathbb{K}$ and $S = ((S_1 \parallel S_2) \parallel_B [\mathsf{PV}(b_1, b_2, k)])[\Phi]$ be action-reachable from *Dekker*[PV]. We can define the symmetric process of S as follows:

$$\mathcal{S}(S) = ((\mathcal{S}(S_2) \parallel \mathcal{S}(S_1)) \parallel_B [\mathsf{PV}(b_2, b_1, (k \mod 2) + 1)])[\Phi_B]$$

We say that two processes S and S' action-reachable from *Dekker*[PV] are symmetric, written $S \approx S'$, if either $S' = \mathcal{S}(S)$ or $S = \mathcal{S}(S')$.

Definition 23. *(symmetric sequences of actions)* Given $v \in (\mathbb{A}_d \cup \{\tau\})^*$, the string $\mathcal{S}(v)$ is defined, by induction on the length of v, as follows: $\mathcal{S}(\varepsilon) = \varepsilon$, $\mathcal{S}(\tau\, v') = \tau\, \mathcal{S}(v')$, $\mathcal{S}(\mathtt{req}_i\, v') = \mathtt{req}_j\, v'$ and $\mathcal{S}(\mathsf{cs}_i\, v') = \mathsf{cs}_j\, v'$ where $i, j \in \{1, 2\}$

Proposition 3 states that symmetric processes have symmetric behaviours: they perform symmetric f-steps and evolve into processes which are still symmetric.

Proposition 3. Let $S \approx S'$ and $v \in (\mathbb{A}_d \cup \{\tau\})^*$. Then: $S' \overset{1}{\longmapsto} R' \overset{v}{\longmapsto} S'_0 \in \tilde{\mathbb{P}}_{\ell 1}$ implies $S \overset{1}{\longmapsto} R \overset{\mathcal{S}(v)}{\longmapsto} S_0 \in \tilde{\mathbb{P}}_{\ell 1}$ with $S_0 \approx S'_0$, and one is an f-step if and only if the other one is.

Let $D_0 = \mathit{Dekker}[\mathsf{PV}]$, $\mathtt{D} = \{D_0, \ldots D_{47}\}$ and $\mathtt{S} = \{S_0, \ldots S_{47}\}$. The following proposition shows that all processes fair-reachable from *Dekker*[PV] are in $\mathtt{D} \cup \mathtt{S}$.

Proposition 4. Let $S \in \mathtt{D} \cup \mathtt{S}$ and $v \in (\mathbb{A}_d \cup \{\tau\})^*$. $S \overset{1}{\longmapsto} R \overset{v}{\longmapsto} S' \in \tilde{\mathbb{P}}_{\ell 1}$ implies $S' \in \mathtt{D} \cup \mathtt{S}$.

5.4 Progressing Processes

We distinguish terms in $\mathtt{D} \cup \mathtt{S}$ depending on how many processes are waiting to perform their critical section, i.e. depending on how many actions cs_i are still pending. The action cs_i is *pending*, for a given $S \in \mathtt{D} \cup \mathtt{S}$, if there exist sequences of basic actions $v, w \in (\mathbb{A}_d \cup \{\tau\})^*$ such that $\mathit{Dekker}[\mathsf{PV}] \overset{v\, \mathtt{req}_i\, w}{\longmapsto} S$ and $\mathsf{cs}_i \notin w$. Trivially, each process may have at most two pending actions and hence $\mathtt{D} \cup \mathtt{S} = \mathtt{R}_1 \cup \mathtt{R}_2 \cup \mathtt{R}_{1,2}$, where $\mathtt{R}_1$ ($\mathtt{R}_2$) is the set of fair-reachable states with only cs_1 (cs_2, resp.) pending and $\mathtt{R}_{1,2}$ is the set of fair-reachable states with both cs_1 and cs_2 pending.

We may check if a given fair-reachable process S belongs to $\mathtt{R}_1$, $\mathtt{R}_2$ or $\mathtt{R}_{1,2}$ by considering its syntactical structure and, in particular, the local states of $\mathtt{P}_1$ and $\mathtt{P}_2$ in S. In detail, we distinguish the following subsets of fair-reachable processes: $\mathtt{D}_1 = \mathtt{D} \cap \mathtt{R}_1 = \{D_2, D_5, D_9, D_{14}, D_{22}, D_{32}\}$, $\mathtt{D}_2 = \mathtt{D} \cap \mathtt{R}_2 = \{D_3, D_7, D_{11}, D_{12}, D_{16}, D_{21}, D_{23}, D_{29}, D_{30}, D_{31}, D_{33}, \ldots, D_{36}, D_{40}\}$ and $\mathtt{D}_{1,2} = \mathtt{D} \cap \mathtt{R}_{1,2} = \{D_1, D_4, D_6, D_8, D_{10}, D_{18}, D_{19}, D_{20}, D_{24}, .., D_{28}, D_{37}, D_{38}, D_{39}, D_{41}, D_{42}, \ldots, D_{47}\}$. Processes D_0, D_{13}, D_{15} and D_{17} have no pending sections. Since $S \in \mathtt{R}_1$, $S \in \mathtt{R}_2$ and $S \in \mathtt{R}_{1,2}$ imply $\mathcal{S}(S) \in \mathtt{R}_2$, $\mathcal{S}(S) \in \mathtt{R}_1$ and $\mathcal{S}(S) \in \mathtt{R}_{1,2}$, respectively, we also have: $\mathtt{S}_1 = \mathtt{S} \cap \mathtt{R}_1 = \mathcal{S}(\mathtt{D}_2)$, $\mathtt{S}_2 = \mathtt{S} \cap \mathtt{R}_2 = \mathcal{S}(\mathtt{D}_1)$ and $\mathtt{S}_{1,2} = \mathtt{S} \cap \mathtt{R}_{1,2} = \mathcal{S}(\mathtt{D}_{1,2})$. Finally, S_0, S_{13}, S_{15} and S_{17} have no pending actions.

Definition 24. (*progressing processes*) We say that a string $v = \alpha_1 \dots \alpha_n \in (\mathbb{A}_d \cup \{\tau\})^*$ contains the action cs_i ($i \in \{1,2\}$), writen $\mathsf{cs}_i \in v$, if $\alpha_j = \mathsf{cs}_i$ for some $j \in [1,n]$. Trivially, $\mathsf{cs}_1, \mathsf{cs}_2 \in v$ if both $\mathsf{cs}_1 \in v$ and $\mathsf{cs}_2 \in v$.

A given $S \in \mathtt{D} \cup \mathtt{S}$ implies the execution of the action cs_i, denoted by $S \rhd \mathsf{cs}_i$, if each f-execution from S contains the action cs_i; $S \rhd \mathsf{cs}_1, \mathsf{cs}_2$ if both $S \rhd \mathsf{cs}_1$ and $S \rhd \mathsf{cs}_2$. Finally, we say that $S \in \mathtt{R}_1$ (symmetrically for $S \in \mathtt{R}_2$ and $S \in \mathtt{R}_{1,2}$) is *making progress (progressing)* if $S \rhd \mathsf{cs}_1$ ($S \rhd \mathsf{cs}_2$, $S \rhd \mathsf{cs}_1, \mathsf{cs}_2$, respectively).

Proposition 5. Let $S, S' \in \mathtt{D} \cup \mathtt{S}$ with $S \approx S'$. Then: (*i*) $S \rhd \mathsf{cs}_i$ implies $S' \rhd \mathsf{cs}_j$ with $\{i,j\} \in \{1,2\}$; (*ii*) if S is making progress then also S' is making progress.

Now, we prove that all processes in $\mathtt{D}$ and hence, by Proposition 5-(*ii*), all processes in $\mathtt{D} \cup \mathtt{S}$ are progressing. We need the following statement.

Proposition 6. A given $D_y \rhd \mathsf{cs}_i$ if for any f-step from D_y of the form $D_y \overset{1}{\longmapsto} R \overset{v}{\longmapsto} S \in \tilde{\mathbb{P}}_{\ell 1}$ we have either $\mathsf{cs}_i \in v$ or $S \rhd \mathsf{cs}_i$.

Iterative application of Proposition 6 allows us to state which processes can perform specific actions.

Lemma 1. All processes in $\mathtt{D} \cup \mathtt{S}$ are making progress.

Proposition 7. Each f-execution from *Dekker*[PV] is live.

As an immediate consequence of the relationships between fair traces of *Dekker* and f-executions of *Dekker*[PV], we have the main result of this section:

Theorem 1. Each fair trace of *Dekker* satisfies the liveness property.

References

1. R. Cleaveland, J. Parrow, and B. Steffen. The concurrency workbench: a semantics-based tool for the verification of concurrent systems. In *Proceedings of ACM Transaction on Programming Languages and Systems*, **15**, 1993.
2. F. Corradini, M.R. Di Berardini, and W. Vogler. Fairness of Actions in System Computations. To appear in *Acta Informatica* Extended abstract: Relating Fairness and Timing in Process Algebras. Proc. of *Concur'03*, Lect. Notes Comp. Sci. 2761, pp. 446-460, 2003.
3. F. Corradini, M.R. Di Berardini, and W. Vogler. Fairness of Components in System Computations. *Theoretical Computer Science* **356**, pp. 291-324, 2006.
4. F. Corradini, M.R. Di Berardini, and W. Vogler. Checking a Mutex Algorithm in a Process Algebra with Fairness. Full Version, Avalilable on line at http://www.cs.unicam.it/docenti/flavio.corradini
5. F. Corradini, W. Vogler, and L. Jenner. Comparing the Worst-Case Efficiency of Asynchronous Systems with PAFAS. *Acta Informatica* **38**, pp. 735-792, 2002.
6. G. Costa, C. Stirling. A Fair Calculus of Communicating Systems. *Acta Informatica* **21**, pp. 417-441, 1984.
7. G. Costa, C. Stirling. Weak and Strong Fairness in CCS. *Information and Computation* **73**, pp. 207-244, 1987.

8. C.A.R. Hoare. *Communicating Sequential Processes.* Prentice Hall, 1985.
9. R. Milner. *Communication and Concurrency.* International series in computer science, Prentice Hall International, 1989.
10. J.L. Peterson, A. Silberschatz . *Operating Systems Concepts.* Addison Wiley, 1985.
11. D.J. Walker. Automated Analysis of Mutual Exclusion algorithms using CCS. *Formal Aspects of Computing* **1**, pp. 273-292, 1989.

A Complete Axiomatic Semantics for the CSP Stable-Failures Model

Yoshinao Isobe[1] and Markus Roggenbach[2,*]

[1] National Institute of Advanced Industrial Science and Technology, Japan
y-isobe@aist.go.jp
[2] University of Wales Swansea, United Kingdom
M.Roggenbach@Swan.ac.uk

Abstract. Traditionally, the various semantics of the process algebra CSP are formulated in denotational style. For many CSP models, e.g., the traces model, equivalent semantics have been given in operational style. A CSP semantics in axiomatic style, however, has been considered problematic in the literature.

In this paper we present a sound and complete axiomatic semantics for CSP with unbounded nondeterminism over an alphabet of arbitrary size.

This result is connected in various ways with our tool CSP-Prover: (1) the CSP dialect under discussion is the input language of CSP-Prover; (2) all theorems presented have been verified with CSP-Prover; (3) CSP-Prover implements the given axiom system.

1 Introduction

Among the various frameworks for the description and modelling of reactive systems, process algebra plays a prominent role. Here, the process algebra CSP [2,8] has successfully been applied in various areas, ranging from train control systems over software for the international space station to the verification of security protocols.

Traditionally, CSP semantics such as the traces model, the failures-divergences model, or the stable-failures model, are formulated in denotational style, c.f. [8]. However, the success of the model checker FDR [6], which clearly is the standard proof tool for CSP, relies on the formulation of operational semantics equivalent to the given denotational ones.

A similar success story with theorem proving for CSP, see, e.g., [1,4,5,9,10] for various approaches, will require an axiomatic (or algebraic) formulation of the CSP models. A *complete* axiomatic semantics for CSP, however, is considered problematic in the literature. There are issues concerning normalisation. The best known results apply for finitely nondeterministic CSP over a finite alphabet of communications only [8]. Consequently, all the implementations listed above are based on a denotational semantics. While this is satisfactory from a theoretical point of view (every true proposition over the denotational semantics

* This cooperation was supported by the EPSRC Project EP/D037212/1.

C. Baier and H. Hermanns (Eds.): CONCUR 2006, LNCS 4137, pp. 158–172, 2006.

can be proven within the theorem prover — up to the incompleteness of the underlying logic[1]), the actual proof-practise relies on an known to be *incomplete* set of algebraic laws and proof rules derived from the denotational semantics implemented.

In this paper we present a sound and complete axiomatic semantics for CSP with unbounded nondeterminism over an alphabet of arbitrary size. Here, we consider full CSP, where the generic internal choice operator has been replaced by a restricted one (this is necessary in order to obtain a *set* of processes rather than a *class*), and where recursion is replaced by infinite nondeterminism over depth-finite processes. We show in Theorem 1 that this language is expressive with respect to the stable-failures domain.

The considered CSP dialect is the input language of our tool CSP-Prover [3,4,5]. CSP-Prover is an interactive theorem prover which supports refinement proofs over various denotational semantics of the process algebra CSP. In the context of this paper, we use CSP-Prover to verify that our axiom system is sound (in this process we found some of the CSP laws established in the literature to be incorrect — see Section 3) as well as to show that the two transformations involved in the completeness proof are semantics preserving.

The paper is organised as follows: First, we introduce our CSP dialect and show that it is expressive. In Section 3 we present a sound axiom system $\mathcal{A}_\mathcal{F}$ for stable-failures equivalence. The proof that the axiom system $\mathcal{A}_\mathcal{F}$ is complete involves two steps: (1) sequentialisation, see Section 4, and (2) normalisation of sequential processes, see Section 5. Finally, we briefly discuss how to verify the theorems given in this paper with CSP-Prover.

2 The CSP-Dialect

This section summarises syntax and semantics of the input language of CSP-Prover. Especially, we show that it is expressive and that it can deal with infinitely many mutual recursive processes.

2.1 Syntax

Fig. 1 shows the syntax of CSP implemented in CSP-Prover: given an alphabet of communications Σ and the data type of natural numbers Nat, we form a set $Sel(\Sigma)$ of *selectors* to be explained below. $Proc_\Sigma$ denotes the set of the processes whose alphabet is Σ.

The set $Sel(\Sigma)$ of *selectors* used in the replicated internal choice is defined as the disjoint sum of the powerset over Σ and the set of the natural numbers:

$$Sel(\Sigma) = \{(set)\,A \mid A \subseteq \Sigma\} \uplus \{(nat)\,n \mid n \in Nat\}$$

Note that replicated internal choice takes a *subset* of $Sel(\Sigma)$ as its parameter.

[1] The traditional formulation of the denotational CSP semantics involves higher-order concepts such as chain-completeness or metric-completeness.

$P ::=$	$Skip$	%% successful terminating process
$\mid$	$Stop$	%% deadlock process
$\mid$	Div	%% divergence
$\mid$	$a \to P$	%% action prefix
$\mid$	$?\, x : A \to P(x)$	%% prefix choice
$\mid$	$P \,\Box\, P$	%% external choice
$\mid$	$P \sqcap P$	%% internal choice
$\mid$	$!!\, s : S \bullet P(s)$	%% replicated internal choice
$\mid$	$\mathit{if}\ b\ \mathit{then}\ P\ \mathit{else}\ P$	%% conditional
$\mid$	$P\, [\![X]\!]\, P$	%% generalized parallel
$\mid$	$P \setminus X$	%% hiding
$\mid$	$P[[r]]$	%% relational renaming
$\mid$	$P \,\mathbin{;}\, P$	%% sequential composition
$\mid$	$P \downarrow n$	%% depth restriction

where $A, X \subseteq \Sigma$, $S \subseteq Sel(\Sigma)$, b is a condition, $r \in \mathbb{P}(\Sigma \times \Sigma)$, and $n \in Nat$.

Fig. 1. Syntax of basic CSP processes in CSP-Prover

One difference from conventional CSP is that we replace the generic internal choice $\sqcap \mathcal{P}$ by a replicated internal choice $!!\, s : S \bullet P(s)$, i.e., instead of having internal choice over an arbitrary class of processes $\mathcal{P} \subseteq Proc_\Sigma$, internal choice is restricted to run over an indexed set of processes $P(s) : Sel(\Sigma) \Rightarrow Proc_\Sigma$ only, where the index set S is a subset of $Sel(\Sigma)$. The other difference is that we introduce restriction $\downarrow$ as a basic operator. Restriction plays an important role in full-normalisation. In the stable-failures model, restriction cannot be defined in terms of the other basic operators, see [8].

The following shortcuts have proven to be useful:

$$\begin{aligned} !set\ A : \mathcal{A} \bullet P(A) &= !!\, s : \{(set)\, A \mid A \in \mathcal{A}\} \bullet P((set)^{-1}(s)) \\ !nat\ n : N \bullet P(n) &= !!\, s : \{(nat)\, n \mid n \in N\} \bullet P((nat)^{-1}(s)) \\ !\ x : A \bullet P(x) &= !set\ X : \{\{x\} \mid x \in A\} \bullet P(contents(X)) \end{aligned}$$

where $\mathcal{A} \subseteq \mathbb{P}(\Sigma)$, $N \subseteq Nat$, $A \subseteq \Sigma$, and $contents(\{x\}) = x$. Moreover, if the range of the selector is the universe, the universe is often omitted, for example we write $!nat\ n \bullet P(n)$ instead of $!nat\ n : Nat \bullet P(n)$.

2.2 Semantics

In this paper, we concentrate on the denotational stable-failures model $\mathcal{F}$ of CSP. Its domain $\mathcal{F}_\Sigma$ is given as the set of all pairs (T, F) that satisfy certain healthiness conditions, where $T \subseteq \Sigma^{*\checkmark}$ and $F \subseteq \Sigma^{*\checkmark} \times \mathbb{P}(\Sigma^{\checkmark})$[2], see [8] for the details. The semantics of a process P is denoted by $[\![P]\!]_\mathcal{F}$, where the map $[\![\cdot]\!]_\mathcal{F} : Proc_\Sigma \to \mathcal{F}_\Sigma$ is expressed in terms of two functions: $[\![P]\!]_\mathcal{F} = (traces(P), failures(P))$. Our definitions of *traces* and *failures* are identical to those given in [8]. However, we

[2] $\Sigma^{\checkmark} := \Sigma \cup \{\checkmark\}$, $\Sigma^{*\checkmark} := \Sigma^* \cup \{t \frown \langle \checkmark \rangle \mid t \in \Sigma^*\}$.

need to add semantical clauses for our two new operators, namely replicated internal choice[3] and depth restriction:

$$\begin{aligned} traces(!!\ s : S \bullet P(s)) &= \bigcup\{traces(P(s)) \mid s \in S\} \cup \{\langle\rangle\} \\ failures(!!\ s : S \bullet P(s)) &= \bigcup\{failures(P(s)) \mid s \in S\} \\ traces(P \downarrow n) &= traces(P) \downarrow n \\ failures(P \downarrow n) &= failures(P) \downarrow n \end{aligned}$$

where the restriction functions over traces and failures are given as follows:

$$\begin{aligned} T \downarrow n &= \{t \in T \mid length(t) \leq n\} \\ F \downarrow n &= \{(t, X) \in F \mid length(t) < n \vee (\exists t'.\ t = t' \frown \langle\checkmark\rangle, length(t) = n)\} \end{aligned}$$

Note that on the domain, which general internal choice and replicated internal choice share, they have the same semantics, see the semantical clauses for general internal choice in the stable-failures model as defined in [8] (note $\mathcal{P} \neq \emptyset$):

$$\begin{aligned} traces(\sqcap \mathcal{P}) &= \bigcup\{traces(P) \mid P \in \mathcal{P}\} \\ failures(\sqcap \mathcal{P}) &= \bigcup\{failures(P) \mid P \in \mathcal{P}\} \end{aligned}$$

Process equivalence $=_\mathcal{F}$ and process refinement $\sqsubseteq_\mathcal{F}$ over the stable failures model are then defined as usual:

$$\begin{aligned} P =_\mathcal{F} Q &\Leftrightarrow traces(P) = traces(Q) \wedge failures(P) = failures(Q), \\ P \sqsubseteq_\mathcal{F} Q &\Leftrightarrow traces(P) \supseteq traces(Q) \wedge failures(P) \supseteq failures(Q). \end{aligned}$$

2.3 Expressiveness

At first glance, the above defined input language of CSP-Prover seems to be weaker than full CSP as the generic internal choice operator $\sqcap \mathcal{P}$ is missing. However, we can show our language to be expressive.

First, we define a function $Proc_{\mathcal{T}(n)}$ on sets of traces and a function $Proc_{\mathcal{F}(n)}$ on the domain $\mathcal{F}_\Sigma$, inductively on n as follows:

$$\begin{aligned} Proc_{\mathcal{T}(0)}(T) &= Div \\ Proc_{\mathcal{T}(n+1)}(T) &= ((!\,x : head(T) \bullet (x \rightarrow Proc_{\mathcal{T}(n)}(tail(T, x)))) \,\Box\, Div) \\ &\quad \sqcap (if\ (\langle\checkmark\rangle \in T)\ then\ Skip\ else\ Div) \\ Proc_{\mathcal{F}(0)}(T, F) &= \ !set\ A : accept(T, F) \bullet (?\,x : A \rightarrow Div) \\ Proc_{\mathcal{F}(n+1)}(T, F) &= (!\,x : head(F) \bullet (x \rightarrow Proc_{\mathcal{F}(n)}(tail(T, x), tail(F, x)))) \,\Box\, Div \end{aligned}$$

where *head*, *tail*, and *accept* are defined as

$$\begin{aligned} head(T) &= \{x \in \Sigma \mid \exists\, t. \langle x\rangle \frown t \in T\} \\ head(F) &= \{x \in \Sigma \mid \exists\, t\ X. (\langle x\rangle \frown t, X) \in F\} \\ tail(T, x) &= \{t \mid \langle x\rangle \frown t \in T\} \\ tail(F, x) &= \{(t, X) \mid (\langle x\rangle \frown t, X) \in F\} \\ accept(T, F) &= \{(\Sigma - Y) \mid (\langle\rangle, Y) \in F \wedge \checkmark \in Y \wedge (\forall x \notin Y. \langle x\rangle \in T)\}. \end{aligned}$$

[3] To make the implementation easier we allow the empty set $\emptyset$ as a set S of selectors. Consequently we need to add $\{\langle\rangle\}$ to the set of traces. However, this makes sense only in models with a refinement top.

Intuitively, $A \in accept(T, F)$ is the set of communications which are not refused by F and can be performed by T. Next, define a function $Proc_{\mathcal{F}}$ as follows:

$$Proc_{\mathcal{F}}(T, F) = (!nat\ n \bullet Proc_{\mathcal{T}(n)}(T)) \ \sqcap \ (!nat\ n \bullet Proc_{\mathcal{F}(n)}(T, F))$$

With these functions defined, we show that $[\![\cdot]\!]_{\mathcal{F}}$ is surjective on $\mathcal{F}_{\Sigma}$:

Theorem 1. *For all $(T, F) \in \mathcal{F}_{\Sigma}$, $[\![Proc_{\mathcal{F}}(T, F)]\!]_{\mathcal{F}} = (T, F)$.*

Proof sketch. We prove by induction on n : if $t \in traces(Proc_{\mathcal{T}(n)}(T))$ or $t \in traces(Proc_{\mathcal{F}(n)}(T, F))$ for some n, then $t \in T$. Then we show by induction on the length of t : if $t \in T$ then $t \in traces(Proc_{\mathcal{T}(length(t))}(T))$. Hence, $traces(Proc_{\mathcal{F}}(T, F)) = T$. Equality for *failures* follows by a similar argument. □

2.4 Recursive Processes

Infinite processes can be effectively expressed by fixed points. For example, a buffer *Buffer*, which iteratively receives a real number r from the channel *in* and sends it to a channel *out* together with an increasing natural number *id*, can be defined by using a solution f of the following system of equations[4]:

$$\begin{aligned} f\,(Empty\,(id)) &=_{\mathcal{F}} \ in\,?\,r \rightarrow (f\,(Full\,(r, id))) \\ f\,(Full\,(r, id)) &=_{\mathcal{F}} \ out\,(r, id) \rightarrow (f\,(Empty\,(id + 1))) \end{aligned}$$

where *Empty* and *Full* are *names*, and f is a function whose domain is

$$Dom(f) = \{Empty\,(id) \mid id \in Nat\} \cup \{Full\,(r, id) \mid r \in Real, id \in Nat\}$$

and whose range is the set of all processes. Any solution f is a fixed point $(Fix\ fun)$ of the function $fun : (Dom(f) \Rightarrow Proc_{\Sigma}) \Rightarrow (Dom(f) \Rightarrow Proc_{\Sigma})$ given as:

$$\begin{aligned} fun(f)(Empty\,(id)) &:= in\,?\,r \rightarrow (f\,(Full\,(r, id))) \\ fun(f)(Full\ (r, id)) &:= out\,(r, id) \rightarrow (f\,(Empty\,(id + 1))) \end{aligned}$$

Therefore, the process *Buffer*, which initially has no data and whose initial *id* is zero, is given as $(Fix\ fun)(Empty\,(0))$.

CSP offers two standard approaches to deal with fixed-points: complete partial orders (cpo) with Tarski's fixed point theorem or complete metric spaces (cms) with Banach's fixed point theorem. The limits $(Fix\ fun)$ and $(Fix!\ fun)$ of the converging sequences in Tarski's and Banach's fixed point theorems can be defined in our CSP-dialect as follows:

$$\begin{aligned} (Fix\ fun)(x) &:= \ !nat\ n \bullet ((fun^{(n)}(\lambda\,y.\,Div))(x)) \\ (Fix!\ fun)(x) &:= \ !nat\ n \bullet (((fun^{(n)}(\lambda\,y.\,Any))(x)) \downarrow n) \end{aligned}$$

where *Div* plays the role of the bottom element in the cpo approach and *Any* stands for any process, which corresponds to the arbitrary initial point of Banach's theorem. Then, as expected, the following properties hold:

[4] $in\,?\,r \rightarrow P(r)$ is a syntactic sugar for $?\,x : \{in(r) \mid r \in Real\} \rightarrow P(in^{-1}(x))$.

1. Let $fun \in ProcFun_\Sigma$. Then $(Fix\, fun)(x) =_\mathcal{F} (fun\,(Fix\, fun))(x)$ for all x; furthermore, for any f with $(\forall x. f(x) =_\mathcal{F} fun(f)(x))$ holds $f(x) \sqsubseteq_\mathcal{F} (Fix\, fun)(x)$. Thus, $(Fix\, fun)$ is the greatest fixed point on $\sqsubseteq_\mathcal{F}$, in other words, it is the least fixed point in the semantic domain.
2. Let $fun \in ProcFun_\Sigma$ be guarded and without hiding operator. Then we have $(Fix!\ fun)(x) =_\mathcal{F} (fun\,(Fix!\ fun))(x)$ for all x; furthermore, for every f, if $(\forall\, x.\ f(x) =_\mathcal{F} fun(f)(x))$ then $f(x) =_\mathcal{F} (Fix!\ fun)(x)$. Thus, $(Fix!\ fun)$ is the unique fixed point on $=_\mathcal{F}$.

Here, $ProcFun_\Sigma$ is the set of functions fun such that for all x, $(\lambda f.\ fun(f)(x))$ is a *process-function.* Each process-function $P(f)$ is a process that may contain a process-function variable f, see, e.g., the above example *Buffer*.

Thus, both ways of CSP of dealing with systems of recursive equations, the cpo approach using Tarski's fixed point theorem as well as the cms approach using Banach's fixed point theorem, are expressible in the input language of CSP-Prover.

3 Axiom System

In this section, we present a sound axiom system $\mathcal{A}_\mathcal{F}$ for the CSP stable-failures model. The completeness of $\mathcal{A}_\mathcal{F}$ is shown later in the Sections 4 and 5.

We write $\mathcal{A}_\mathcal{F} \vdash P = Q$ if the equality of two processes P and Q can be proven by equational and inductive reasoning from the axiom system $\mathcal{A}_\mathcal{F}$. Fig. 2 summarizes changes from the axiom system for finite processes given in [8]. The superscript $*$ denotes modified laws, the superscript $+$ denotes added laws.

Our axiom system $\mathcal{A}_\mathcal{F}$ replaces the usual unwinding laws for recursive processes such as $(\mu\, X.\, P(X)) = P(\mu\, X.\, P(X))$ by new axioms (Tarski-fix) and (Banach-fix). While the unwinding laws have proven to be handy for verifying practical systems with CSP-Prover, at the same time they cause problems with normalization: see the discussion on infinite unwinding of divergent processes such as $(\mu\, X.\, X)$ in [8], p. 273. Our laws (Tarski-fix) and (Banach-fix), however, transforms recursive processes to unbounded nondeterministic processes. Such processes can then be analyzed via induction on n. We give an example of how to normalise a divergent process at the end of Section 5.

Secondly, we found that the well-known laws ($\|[X]\|$-$\rhd$-split) and ($\|[X]\|$-$\rhd$-input) (P.288–289 in [8]) are not correct:

$$\begin{aligned}&(P \rhd P')\, \|[\, X\,]\|\, (Q \rhd Q')\\ &= (P\, \|[\, X\,]\|\, Q) \rhd ((P'\, \|[\, X\,]\|\, (Q \rhd Q')) \sqcap ((P \rhd P')\, \|[\, X\,]\|\, Q')), \qquad (\|[X]\|\text{-}\rhd\text{-split})\end{aligned}$$

$$\begin{aligned}&(P \rhd P')\, \|[\, X\,]\|\, (?x : A \to Q(x))\\ &= (?x : (A - X) \to ((P \rhd P')\, \|[\, X\,]\|\, Q(x)))\\ &\quad \Box\, ((P\, \|[\, X\,]\|\, (?x : A \to Q(x))) \rhd (P'\, \|[\, X\,]\|\, (?x : A \to Q(x)))). \quad (\|[X]\|\text{-}\rhd\text{-input})\end{aligned}$$

For example, instantiate the processes in ($\|[X]\|$-$\rhd$-split) as follows: $P = a \to Stop$, $P' = Stop$, $Q = Stop$, $Q' = b \to Stop$, and $X = \emptyset$, where $a \neq b$. In this case, the semantics of the left hand side of ($\|[X]\|$-$\rhd$-split) does not contain the failure $(\langle a\rangle, b)$

$$(\mathit{Fix}\ \mathit{fun})(x) = !\mathit{nat}\ n \bullet ((\mathit{fun}^{(n)}(\lambda\, y.\, \mathit{Div}))(x)) \qquad \text{(Tarski-fix)}^{+}$$
$$(\mathit{Fix!}\ \mathit{fun})(x) = !\mathit{nat}\ n \bullet (((\mathit{fun}^{(n)}(\lambda\, y.\, P))(x)) \downarrow n) \qquad \text{(Banach-fix)}^{+}$$

$$\begin{array}{l}
\text{if } P = (?x : A \to P'(x)) \triangleright P'' \text{ and } Q = (?x : B \to Q'(x)) \triangleright Q'' \text{ then} \\
\quad P \,[\![X]\!]\, Q \\
\quad = (?x : ((X \cap A \cap B) \cup (A - X) \cup (B - X)) \to \\
\qquad\quad \mathit{if}\ (x \in X)\ \mathit{then}\ (P'(x) \,[\![X]\!]\, Q'(x)) \\
\qquad\quad \mathit{else\ if}\ (x \in A \cap B)\ \mathit{then}\ ((P'(x) \,[\![X]\!]\, Q) \sqcap (P \,[\![X]\!]\, Q'(x))) \\
\qquad\qquad\quad \mathit{else\ if}\ (x \in A)\ \mathit{then}\ (P'(x) \,[\![X]\!]\, Q)\ \mathit{else}\ (P \,[\![X]\!]\, Q'(x))) \\
\qquad \triangleright ((P'' \,[\![X]\!]\, Q) \sqcap (P \,[\![X]\!]\, Q''))
\end{array} \qquad ([\![X]\!]\text{-}\triangleright\text{-split})^{*}$$

$$\begin{array}{l}
\text{if } P = (?x : A \to P'(x)) \triangleright P'' \text{ and } Q = ?x : B \to Q'(x) \text{ then} \\
\quad P \,[\![X]\!]\, Q \\
\quad = (?x : ((X \cap A \cap B) \cup (A - X) \cup (B - X)) \to \\
\qquad\quad \mathit{if}\ (x \in X)\ \mathit{then}\ (P'(x) \,[\![X]\!]\, Q'(x)) \\
\qquad\quad \mathit{else\ if}\ (x \in A \cap B)\ \mathit{then}\ ((P'(x) \,[\![X]\!]\, Q) \sqcap (P \,[\![X]\!]\, Q'(x))) \\
\qquad\qquad\quad \mathit{else\ if}\ (x \in A)\ \mathit{then}\ (P'(x) \,[\![X]\!]\, Q)\ \mathit{else}\ (P \,[\![X]\!]\, Q'(x))) \\
\qquad \triangleright (P'' \,[\![X]\!]\, Q)
\end{array} \qquad ([\![X]\!]\text{-}\triangleright\text{-input})^{*}$$

$$!!\, s : \emptyset \bullet P(s) = \mathit{Div} \qquad \text{(!!-emptyset)}^{+}$$
$$\text{if } S \neq \emptyset \text{ and } (\forall s \in S.\ P(s) = Q) \text{ then } !!\, s : S \bullet P(s) = Q \qquad \text{(!!-const)}^{*}$$
$$!!\, s : (S_1 \cup S_2) \bullet P(s) = (!!\, s : S_1 \bullet P(s)) \sqcap (!!\, s : S_2 \bullet P(s)) \qquad (\text{!!-union-}\sqcap)^{*}$$
$$\begin{array}{l}
!!\, s : S \bullet (?\, x : A(s) \to P(s, x)) \\
\quad = !\mathit{set}\ X : \{A(s) \mid s \in S\} \bullet \\
\qquad\quad (?\, x : X \to (!!\, s : \{s \in S \mid x \in A(s)\} \bullet P(s, x)))
\end{array} \qquad \text{(!!-input-!set)}^{+}$$
$$\begin{array}{l}
\text{if } \forall s \in S.\ Q(s) \in \{\mathit{Skip}, \mathit{Div}\} \text{ then} \\
\quad !!\, s : S \bullet (P(s) \,\Box\, Q(s)) = (!!\, s : S \bullet P(s)) \,\Box\, (!!\, s : S \bullet Q(s))
\end{array} \qquad (\text{!!-}\Box\text{-Dist})^{+}$$
$$\begin{array}{l}
\text{if } Q \in \{\mathit{Skip}, \mathit{Div}\} \text{ then} \\
\quad (!\mathit{set}\ X : \mathcal{X} \bullet (?\, x : X \to P(x))) \,\Box\, Q = (?\, x : \bigcup \mathcal{X} \to P(x)) \,\Box\, Q
\end{array} \qquad \text{(!!-input-Dist)}^{+}$$

$$P \downarrow 0 = \mathit{Div} \qquad (\downarrow\text{-zero})^{+}$$
$$(P \downarrow n) \downarrow m = P \downarrow \min(n, m) \qquad (\downarrow\text{-min})^{+}$$
$$P = !\mathit{nat}\ n \bullet (P \downarrow n) \qquad (!\text{nat-}\downarrow)^{+}$$
$$(!!\, s : S \bullet P(s)) \downarrow n = !!\, s : S \bullet (P(s) \downarrow n) \qquad (\downarrow\text{-Dist})^{+}$$
$$(P_1 \sqcap P_2) \downarrow n = (P_1 \downarrow n) \sqcap (P_2 \downarrow n) \qquad (\downarrow\text{-dist})^{+}$$
$$(P_1 \,\Box\, P_2) \downarrow n = (P_1 \downarrow n) \,\Box\, (P_2 \downarrow n) \qquad (\downarrow\text{-}\Box\text{-dist})^{+}$$
$$\mathit{Skip} \downarrow (n + 1) = \mathit{Skip} \qquad (\text{skip-}\downarrow)^{+}$$
$$\mathit{Div} \downarrow n = \mathit{Div} \qquad (\text{div-}\downarrow)^{+}$$
$$(?\, x : A \to P(x)) \downarrow (n + 1) = ?\, x : A \to (P(x) \downarrow n) \qquad (\downarrow\text{-step})^{+}$$

$$?\, x : A \to P(x) = ((?\, x : A \to P(x)) \,\Box\, \mathit{Div}) \sqcap (?\, x : A \to \mathit{Div}) \qquad \text{(?-div)}^{+}$$
$$\begin{array}{l}
!!\, s : S \bullet (!\mathit{set}\ X : \mathcal{X}(s) \bullet (?\, x : X \to \mathit{Div})) \\
\quad = !\mathit{set}\ X : \bigcup\{\mathcal{X}(s) \mid s \in S\} \bullet (?\, x : X \to \mathit{Div})
\end{array} \qquad \text{(!!-!set-div)}^{+}$$
$$\begin{array}{l}
\text{if } \mathcal{X} \subseteq \mathcal{Y} \text{ and } (\forall\, Y \in \mathcal{Y}.\ \exists\, X \in \mathcal{X}.\ X \subseteq Y \subseteq A) \text{ then} \\
\quad ((?\, x : A \to P(x)) \,\Box\, Q) \sqcap (!\mathit{set}\ X : \mathcal{X} \bullet (?\, x : X \to \mathit{Div})) \\
\quad = ((?\, x : A \to P(x)) \,\Box\, Q) \sqcap (!\mathit{set}\ X : \mathcal{Y} \bullet (?\, x : X \to \mathit{Div}))
\end{array} \qquad (\text{?-!set-}\subseteq)^{+}$$

Fig. 2. The axiom system $\mathcal{A}_{\mathcal{F}}$ (differences from [8])

because $(Stop \rhd (b \rightarrow Stop))$ can perform b even after P has performed a. On the other hand, the semantics of the right hand side of ($\|[X]\|$-$\rhd$-split) contains the failure $(\langle a \rangle, b)$ because it has a subexpression $((a \rightarrow Stop) \|[\emptyset]\| Stop)$. Therefore, the law ($\|[X]\|$-$\rhd$-split) does not hold. Similarly, there is a counter example (e.g. $P = Stop$, $P' = b \rightarrow Stop$, $A = \{a\}$, $Q(a) = Stop$, and $X = \emptyset$) for the law ($\|[X]\|$-$\rhd$-input). Hence, we modified the laws ($\|[X]\|$-$\rhd$-split) and ($\|[X]\|$-$\rhd$-input) as shown in Fig. 2. The modified laws are less generic than the original ones, but they are expressive enough to gain completeness.

Thirdly, we added laws (!!-$\cdots$) for replicated internal choice $!!\, s : S \bullet P(s)$, as shown in Fig. 2, by modifying the laws for the (generic) internal choice $\sqcap$. The laws (!!-input-!set), (!!-$\Box$-Dist), and (!!-input-Dist) are used for replacing replicated internal choice by (external) prefix choice, considering the effects of *Skip* or *Div*. These laws were added instead of the following law for the binary internal choice (P.289 in [8]): $(P \Box Skip) \sqcap (Q \Box Skip) = (P \Box Q \Box Skip)$.

Furthermore, we added the laws ($\downarrow$-$\cdots$) for the restriction operator as shown in Fig. 2. The most important law is (!nat-$\downarrow$) which is used for finitising the depth of infinite processes.

Finally, we added the laws (?-div), (!!-!set-div), and (?-!set-$\subseteq$) for normalising sequential processes. The law (?-!set-$\subseteq$) is used to satisfy the condition (N_3) of full normal forms, stated in Definition 2 in Section 5.

The presented axiom system $\mathcal{A}_{\mathcal{F}}$ is sound:

Theorem 2. *Let $P, Q \in Proc_\Sigma$. Then $\mathcal{A}_{\mathcal{F}} \vdash P = Q$ implies $P =_{\mathcal{F}} Q$.*

4 Full Sequentialisation

In this section, we define a method to fully sequentialise a process. The purpose of this transformation is to remove hiding. Hiding operators can cause a problem when normalising processes with the help of depth restriction operators: $P \downarrow n =_{\mathcal{F}} Q \downarrow n$ does not necessarily imply $(P \setminus X) \downarrow n =_{\mathcal{F}} (Q \setminus X) \downarrow n$ due to hidden communications.

First, we define the set $SeqProc_\Sigma$ of processes in *full sequential forms*. Processes in full sequential form are built using the various CSP choice operators and the basic processes *Skip*, *Stop* and *Div* only. More formally:

Definition 1. *The set $SeqProc_\Sigma$ is defined as the smallest set satisfying*

1. $(?\, x : A \rightarrow P(x)) \Box Q \in SeqProc_\Sigma$,
   if $P(x) \in SeqProc_\Sigma$ for all $x \in A$ and $Q \in \{Skip, Div, Stop\}$.
2. $!!\, s : S \bullet P(s) \in SeqProc_\Sigma$,
   if $P(s) \in SeqProc_\Sigma$ for all $s \in S$, where $S \neq \emptyset$.

If $P \in SeqProc_\Sigma$, we say that P is in full sequential form.

As the set A in the first condition is allowed to be the empty set, we have for example $(?\, x : \emptyset \rightarrow Div) \Box Skip \in SeqProc_\Sigma$.

Next, we define for each CSP operator op a sequentialising function f_{op}. Applying f_{op} to a CSP process P which has op as its out-most operator, the function will transform this process into a semantically equivalent CSP process $f_{op}(P)$ in

$$
\begin{aligned}
(Pr)_{seq} &= (?\,x:\emptyset \to Div) \,\Box\, Pr \qquad (Pr \in \{Skip, Div, Stop\})\\
a \to_{seq} P_1 &= (?\,x:\{a\} \to P_1) \,\Box\, Stop\\
?\,x:A \to_{seq} P(x) &= (?\,x:A \to P(x)) \,\Box\, Stop\\
!!\,s:S \bullet_{seq} P'(s) &= \begin{cases} (Div)_{seq} & ;\ S=\emptyset\\ !!\,s:S \bullet P'(s) & ;\ \text{otherwise}\end{cases}\\
P_1 \sqcap_{seq} P_2 &= !nat\ n:\{0,1\} \bullet (\text{if } (n=0) \text{ then } P_1 \text{ else } P_2)\\[1em]
P_1 \,\Box_{seq}\, Pr &= !!\,s:S_1 \bullet (R_1'(s) \,\Box_{seq}\, Pr) \qquad (Pr \in \{P_2, R_2\})\\
R_1 \,\Box_{seq}\, P_2 &= !!\,s:S_2 \bullet (R_1 \,\Box_{seq}\, R_2'(s))\\
R_1 \,\Box_{seq}\, R_2 &= (?\,x:(A_1 \cup A_2) \to\\
&\qquad \text{if } (x \in A_1 \cap A_2) \text{ then } P_1'(x) \sqcap_{seq} P_2'(x)\\
&\qquad \text{else if } (x \in A_1) \text{ then } P_1'(x) \text{ else } P_2'(x))\\
&\qquad \Box \text{ if } (Q_1 = Skip \lor Q_2 = Skip) \text{ then } Skip\\
&\qquad\quad \text{else if } (Q_1 = Div \lor Q_2 = Div) \text{ then } Div \text{ else } Stop\\
Pr_1 \rhd_{seq} Pr_2 &= (Pr_1 \sqcap_{seq} (Stop)_{seq}) \,\Box_{seq}\, Pr_2 \qquad (Pr_i \in \{P_i, R_i\})\\[1em]
P_1 \,[\![X]\!]_{seq}\, Pr &= !!\,s:S_1 \bullet (R_1'(s) \,[\![X]\!]_{seq}\, Pr) \qquad (Pr \in \{P_2, R_2, Skip, Div\})\\
R_1 \,[\![X]\!]_{seq}\, P_2 &= !!\,s:S_2 \bullet (R_1 \,[\![X]\!]_{seq}\, R_2'(s))\\
R_1 \,[\![X]\!]_{seq}\, Skip &= ((?\,x:(A_1 - X) \to (P_1'(x) \,[\![X]\!]_{seq}\, Skip)) \,\Box\, Q_1)\\
R_1 \,[\![X]\!]_{seq}\, Div &= ((?\,x:(A_1 - X) \to (P_1'(x) \,[\![X]\!]_{seq}\, Div)) \,\Box\, Div)\\
R_1 \,[\![X]\!]_{seq}\, R_2 &= \text{if } (Q_1 = Stop \land Q_2 = Stop) \text{ then } R_1 \,[\![X]\!]^{step}_{seq}\, R_2\\
&\quad \text{else } (R_1 \,[\![X]\!]^{step}_{seq}\, R_2)\\
&\qquad \rhd_{seq} (\text{if } (Q_1 = Stop) \text{ then } (R_1 \,[\![X]\!]_{seq}\, Q_2)\\
&\qquad\qquad \text{else if } (Q_2 = Stop) \text{ then } (R_2 \,[\![X]\!]_{seq}\, Q_1)\\
&\qquad\qquad \text{else } (R_1 \,[\![X]\!]_{seq}\, Q_2) \sqcap_{seq} (R_2 \,[\![X]\!]_{seq}\, Q_1))\\
R_1 \,[\![X]\!]^{step}_{seq}\, R_2 &= ?\,x:((X \cap A_1 \cap A_2) \cup (A_1 - X) \cup (A_2 - X)) \to\\
&\quad (\text{if } (x \in X) \text{ then } (P_1'(x) \,[\![X]\!]_{seq}\, P_2'(x))\\
&\quad\ \text{else if } (x \in A_1 \cap A_2)\\
&\qquad \text{then } ((P_1'(x) \,[\![X]\!]_{seq}\, R_2) \sqcap_{seq} (R_1 \,[\![X]\!]_{seq}\, P_2'(x)))\\
&\qquad \text{else if } (x \in A_1)\\
&\qquad\quad \text{then } (P_1'(x) \,[\![X]\!]_{seq}\, R_2) \text{ else } (R_1 \,[\![X]\!]_{seq}\, P_2'(x)))\\
&\quad \Box\, Stop\\
P_1 \setminus_{seq} X &= !!\,s:S_1 \bullet (R_1'(s) \setminus_{seq} X)\\
R_1 \setminus_{seq} X &= \text{if } (Q_1 = Stop) \text{ then}\\
&\quad \text{if } (A_1 \cap X = \emptyset)\\
&\quad \text{then } ((?\,x:A_1 \to (P_1'(x) \setminus_{seq} X)) \,\Box\, Q_1)\\
&\quad \text{else } ((?\,x:(A_1 - X) \to (P_1'(x) \setminus_{seq} X)) \,\Box\, Q_1)\\
&\qquad \rhd_{seq} (!\,x:(A_1 \cap X) \bullet_{seq} (P_1'(x) \setminus_{seq} X))\\
&\quad \text{else } (((?\,x:(A_1 - X) \to (P_1'(x) \setminus_{seq} X)) \,\Box\, Q_1)\\
&\qquad \sqcap_{seq} (!\,x:(A_1 \cap X) \bullet_{seq} (P_1'(x) \setminus_{seq} X)))
\end{aligned}
$$

In this figure, it is assumed that
$P(x) \in SeqProc_\Sigma$ for all $x \in A$,
$P'(s) \in SeqProc_\Sigma$ for all $s \in S$,
$P_i = !!\,s:S_i \bullet R_i'(s) \in SeqProc_\Sigma$ for each $i \in \{1,2\}$, and
$R_i = (?\,x:A_i \to P_i'(x)) \,\Box\, Q_i \in SeqProc_\Sigma$ for each $i \in \{1,2\}$.

Fig. 3. Sequentialising functions (part)

full sequential form, provided its subprocesses are already in full sequential form. Here, we actually prove a stronger proposition, namely $\mathcal{A}_{\mathcal{F}} \vdash P = f_{op}(P)$. For example, we have $\mathcal{A}_{\mathcal{F}} \vdash P \,[\![\, X \,]\!]\, Q = f_{par}(P \,[\![\, X \,]\!]\, Q)$, which according to Theorem 2 implies $P \,[\![\, X \,]\!]\, Q =_{\mathcal{F}} f_{par}(P \,[\![\, X \,]\!]\, Q)$, and $f_{par}(P \,[\![\, X \,]\!]\, Q) \in \mathit{SeqProc}_{\Sigma}$ for $P, Q \in \mathit{SeqProc}_{\Sigma}$. For convenience, we use infix notation to write the functions f_{op}, for example we write $P \,[\![\, X \,]\!]_{seq}\, Q$ instead of $f_{par}(P \,[\![\, X \,]\!]\, Q)$. Note the inductive structure of the sequentialising functions presented in Fig. 3.

Finally, we define an overall sequentialisation function $\mathit{Seq} : \mathit{Proc}_{\Sigma} \Rightarrow \mathit{SeqProc}_{\Sigma}$ inductively on the syntactic structure of processes:

$$\begin{aligned}
\mathit{Seq}(P) &= (P)_{seq} && (P \in \{\mathit{Skip}, \mathit{Div}, \mathit{Stop}\})\\
\mathit{Seq}(a \to P) &= a \to_{\mathrm{seq}} \mathit{Seq}(P)\\
\mathit{Seq}(?x : A \to P(x)) &= ?x : A \to_{\mathrm{seq}} \mathit{Seq}(P(x))\\
\mathit{Seq}(P \oplus Q) &= \mathit{Seq}(P) \oplus_{\mathrm{seq}} \mathit{Seq}(Q) && (\oplus \in \{\Box, \sqcap, [\![X]\!], \fatsemi\})\\
\mathit{Seq}(!!\, s : S \bullet P(s)) &= !!\, s : S \bullet_{\mathrm{seq}} \mathit{Seq}(P(s)) \quad \cdots
\end{aligned}$$

For this function *Seq*, Theorem 3 holds:

Theorem 3. *$\mathit{Seq}(P) \in \mathit{SeqProc}_{\Sigma}$ and $\mathcal{A}_{\mathcal{F}} \vdash P = \mathit{Seq}(P)$ for all $P \in \mathit{Proc}_{\Sigma}$.*

Proof sketch. First we show that each sequentialising function f_{op} indeed sequentialises processes, e.g., if $P, Q \in \mathit{SeqProc}_{\Sigma}$ then $\mathcal{A}_{\mathcal{F}} \vdash P \,[\![\, X \,]\!]\, Q = P \,[\![\, X \,]\!]_{seq}\, Q$ and $P \,[\![\, X \,]\!]_{seq}\, Q \in \mathit{SeqProc}_{\Sigma}$, by induction on the structures of full sequential forms P and Q. Equality can often be derived by using the *distributive-laws* and *step-laws* taking into account the special role of *Skip* and *Div*. From this, the result on $\mathit{Seq}(P)$ follows easily. □

5 Full Normalisation

Semantically equivalent processes $P =_{\mathcal{F}} Q$ in full sequential form can still be different syntactically: Let $A \neq B$ and $R(x, y) = (x \to_{seq} y \to_{seq} (\mathit{Skip})_{seq})$. Then $!\, x : A \bullet_{seq} (!\, y : B \bullet_{seq} R(x, y)) \neq !\, x : B \bullet_{seq} (!\, y : A \bullet_{seq} R(y, x))$, are both in full sequential form, although the two processes have the same semantics; semantically it does not matter in which order the selector sets are defined. Therefore, the next step is to study normalisation.

First, we define a new full normal form, which differs slightly from the full normal form for finite processes presented in [8]:

Definition 2. *A process $P \in \mathit{Proc}_{\Sigma}$ is said to be in full normal form if and only if P has the form $((?x : A \to P(x)) \,\Box\, Q) \sqcap (!\mathit{set}\ X : \mathcal{X} \bullet (?x : X \to \mathit{Div}))$ and the following four conditions $(N_1), \ldots, (N_4)$ are satisfied: (N_1) for all x, if $x \in A$ then $P(x)$ is already in full normal form else $P(x)$ is Div*[5]*, (N_2) $\bigcup \mathcal{X} \subseteq A$, (N_3) $\forall X. ((\exists X_0 \in \mathcal{X}. X_0 \subseteq X \subseteq A) \Rightarrow X \in \mathcal{X})$, and (N_4) $Q \in \{\mathit{Skip}, \mathit{Div}\}$.*

The set of full normal forms is denoted by $\mathit{NormProc}_{\Sigma}$.

[5] $?x : A \to P(x) =_{\mathcal{F}} ?x : A \to Q(x)$ implies $P(x) =_{\mathcal{F}} Q(x)$ for all $x \in A$. However, for $x \in \Sigma \backslash A$ we do not necessarily have $P(x) =_{\mathcal{F}} Q(x)$. Since $P(x)$ and $Q(x)$ are total functions over Σ, for values outside of A we need to fix them to some constant as, e.g., *Div* in order to obtain uniqueness.

Our definition 2 differs from [8] only in condition (N_3). [8] requires all elements of $\mathcal{X}$ to be incomparable. In fact, if $\mathcal{X}$ is *finite*, we can replace our set $\mathcal{X}$ in the full normal form by the incomparable set $\{\bigcap\{X_0 \in \mathcal{X} \mid X_0 \subseteq X\} \mid X \in \mathcal{X}\}$ without changing the semantics of the process. However, if $\mathcal{X}$ is *infinite*, the semantics may change: $\bigcap\{X_0 \in \mathcal{X} \mid X_0 \subseteq X\}$ is not always contained in $\mathcal{X}$. Therefore, we require (N_3) instead of incomparability.

Next we prove that for processes in $NormProc_\Sigma$ syntactic and semantic equality are the same:

Theorem 4. *For all $P, Q \in NormProc_\Sigma$, $P =_\mathcal{F} Q$ if and only if $P = Q$.*

Proof. Almost identical to the proof presented in [8]. □

While for every *finitely* nondeterministic process P with a finite alphabet, there is a process P' in full normal form such that $P =_\mathcal{F} P'$, this does not hold for *infinitely* nondeterministic processes with an arbitrary alphabet as follows.

Theorem 5. *There exist $P \in Proc_\Sigma$ with $P \neq_\mathcal{F} P'$ for all $P' \in NormProc_\Sigma$.*

Proof. Consider the process $Loop_a := (Fix\ fun_a)(A)$ with $fun_a(f)(A) := a \rightarrow f(A)$, thus, $Loop_a$ satisfies the equation $Loop_a =_\mathcal{F} a \rightarrow Loop_a$. Note that $(Fix\ fun_a)$ is expressed by infinite nondeterminism over Nat. Assume there exists some $P' \in NormProc_\Sigma$ with $Loop_a =_\mathcal{F} P'$. Define

$$\begin{aligned} P'' := {} & ((?\,x : \{a\} \rightarrow (\text{if } (x = a) \text{ then } P' \text{ else } Div)) \,\Box\, Div) \\ & \sqcap (!set\ X : \{\{a\}\} \bullet (?\,x : X \rightarrow Div)) \end{aligned}$$

Consequently $P' \neq P''$. On the other hand, we can prove that $P'' \in NormProc_\Sigma$ and $P' =_\mathcal{F} P''$ — contradiction to Theorem 4. □

To deal with this weakness, we define an *extended* full normal form.

Definition 3. *A process P is in extended full normal form iff P is of the form $!nat\ n \bullet P'(n)$, where the processes $P'(n)$ are in full normal form and $P'(n) =_\mathcal{F} P \downarrow n$ for all $n \in Nat$. We denote the set of extended full normal forms by $XNormProc_\Sigma$.*

The extended full normal form consists of an infinite nondeterministic choice between a family of fully normalised processes $P(n)$, where the depth of the processes $P(n)$ is restricted to n by the restriction operator $\downarrow$.

First we give an example of extended full normal form of an infinite process.

Example 1. For $n \in Nat$ define the process $Inc(n)$ as $(Fix\ fun_{inc})(n)$ with $fun_{inc}(f)(n) := !nat\ m : GT(n) \bullet m \rightarrow f(m)$ and $GT(n) = \{m \mid n < m\}$. $Inc(n)$ produces a sequence of natural numbers $> n$ where the increment is nondeterministically chosen. Let $Ninc(n)$ be the process $!nat\ i \bullet Ninc(i, n)$ with

$$\begin{aligned} Ninc(0, n) &:= (Div)_{norm} \\ Ninc(i+1, n) &:= ((?\,m : GT(n) \rightarrow (\text{if } (n < m) \text{ then } Ninc(i, m) \text{ else } Div)) \,\Box\, Div) \\ &\quad\ \sqcap (!set\ N : \{N \mid N \neq \emptyset, N \subseteq GT(n)\} \bullet (?\,m : N \rightarrow Div)) \end{aligned}$$

$$
\begin{aligned}
&!!s : S \bullet^{(0)}_{norm} P(s) = (Div)_{norm} \\
&!!s : S \bullet^{(n+1)}_{norm} P(s) = ((?x : A' \rightarrow \\
&\qquad\qquad \text{if } (x \in A') \text{ then } (!!s : \{s \in S \mid x \in A(s)\} \bullet^{(n)}_{norm} P'(s,x)) \\
&\qquad\qquad \text{else } Div) \\
&\qquad\qquad \Box \text{ if } (\exists\, s \in S. Q(s) = Skip) \text{ then } Skip \text{ else } Div) \\
&\qquad\qquad \sqcap\ !set\ X : (complete(A', \mathcal{X}')) \bullet (?x : X \rightarrow Div) \\
&\text{where} \\
&\qquad (Div)_{norm} = ((?x : \emptyset \rightarrow Div) \Box Div) \sqcap (!set\ X : \emptyset \bullet (?x : X \rightarrow Div)), \\
&\qquad complete(A', \mathcal{X}') = \{X \mid \exists\, X_0 \in \mathcal{X}'.\ X_0 \subseteq X \subseteq A'\}, \\
&\qquad \forall\, s \in S.\ P(s) = ((?x : A(s) \rightarrow P'(s,x)) \Box Q(s)) \sqcap \\
&\qquad\qquad (!set\ X : \mathcal{X}(s) \bullet (?x : X \rightarrow Div)) \in NormProc_\Sigma, \\
&\qquad A' = \bigcup\{A(s) \mid s \in S\}, \text{ and } \mathcal{X}' = \bigcup\{\mathcal{X}(s) \mid s \in S\}.
\end{aligned}
$$

Fig. 4. Normalising function for replicated internal choice

Here, $(Div)_{norm}$ is the full normal form of Div as defined in Fig. 4. $Ninc(n) =_\mathcal{F} Inc(n)$ and $Ninc(n) \in XNormProc_{Nat}$.

Next we prove that for processes in $XNormProc_\Sigma$ syntactic and semantic equality are the same:

Theorem 6. *For all $P, Q \in XNormProc_\Sigma$, $P =_\mathcal{F} Q$ if and only if $P = Q$.*

Proof. Let $P, Q \in XNormProc_\Sigma$ and $P =_\mathcal{F} Q$. Thus, for some P' and Q', $P = !nat\ n \bullet P'(n)$ and $Q = !nat\ n \bullet Q'(n)$. Further, for all n, $P'(n) =_\mathcal{F} P \downarrow n =_\mathcal{F} Q \downarrow n =_\mathcal{F} Q'(n)$. Thus, $P'(n) = Q'(n)$ by Theorem 4. Hence, $P = Q$. □

Then we define a function that transforms processes of the form $!!\,s : S \bullet P(s)$ into full normal form, see Fig. 4. Note that the function $!!\,s : S \bullet^{(n)}_{norm} P(s)$ is defined inductively on n (and not on the process structure). The reason for this is that structural induction on processes is not possible over a family of processes $P(s)$. The following lemma shows that our transformation up to depth n indeed yields a process in full normal form and is semantics preserving:

Lemma 1. *If $P(s) \in NormProc_\Sigma$ for all $s \in S$, then for any n, $!!\,s : S \bullet^{(n)}_{norm} P(s) \in NormProc_\Sigma$, and $\mathcal{A}_\mathcal{F} \vdash (!!\,s : S \bullet P(s)) \downarrow n = !!\,s : S \bullet^{(n)}_{norm} P(s)$.*

Proof sketch. By induction on n. The transformation by $\mathcal{A}_\mathcal{F}$ is established in three steps: (1) for the first subexpression $((?x : A(s) \rightarrow P(s,x)) \Box Q(s))$ of $P(s)$, the nondeterminism over S can be rewritten to (external) prefix choice by (!!-input-!set), (!!-□-Dist), and (!!-input-Dist). (2) for the second subexpression $(!set\ X : \mathcal{X}(s) \bullet (?\,x : X \rightarrow Div))$ of $P(s)$, the two nondeterminism by S and $\mathcal{X}(s)$ can be rewritten to one nondeterminism by (!!-!set-div). (3) Finally, (?-!set-⊆) is applied for replacing $\mathcal{X}'$ by $complete(A', \mathcal{X}')$. □

Finally, for each $n \in Nat$ we define a function $Norm_{(n)}(P)$ inductively on the structure of P, see Fig. 5. The following lemma shows that the function $Norm_{(n)}$

$$
\begin{array}{l}
Norm_{(0)}(Pr) = (Div)_{norm} \qquad\qquad\qquad\qquad (Pr \in SeqProc_{\Sigma}) \\
Norm_{(n+1)}(P) = \,!!\, s : S \bullet^{(n+1)}_{norm} Norm_{(n+1)}(R'(s)) \\
Norm_{(n+1)}(R) = (?\, x : A \to (\text{if } x : A \text{ then } Norm_{(n)}(P'(x)) \text{ else } Div) \\
\qquad\qquad\qquad\qquad \Box\, (\text{if } (Q = Skip) \text{ then } Skip \text{ else } Div)) \\
\qquad\qquad\qquad\quad \sqcap\, (!set\ X : (\text{if } Q = Stop \text{ then } \{A\} \text{ else } \emptyset) \bullet (?\, x : X \to Div)) \\
\text{where } P = \,!!\, s : S \bullet R'(s) \in SeqProc_{\Sigma}, \\
\qquad\quad R = ((?x : A \to P'(x)) \,\Box\, Q) \in SeqProc_{\Sigma},
\end{array}
$$

Fig. 5. Normalising function

transforms a process in full sequential forms whose depth is restricted to n into full normal form.

Lemma 2. *Let $P \in SeqProc_{\Sigma}$. Then for any n, $Norm_{(n)}(P) \in NormProc_{\Sigma}$ and $\mathcal{A}_{\mathcal{F}} \vdash P \downarrow n = Norm_{(n)}(P)$.*

Proof sketch. By induction on the structure of the full sequential form P. If P has the form $!!\, s : S \bullet R'(s)$, it can be normalised by Lemma 1. Otherwise, P is of the form $(?\, x : A \to P'(x)) \,\Box\, Q$. If $Q \neq Stop$ then it can be transformed to a full normal form by ($\sqcap$-unit) and (!!-emptyset), otherwise by (?-div). □

With the function *XNorm* defined as

$$XNorm(P) = \,!nat\ n \bullet (Norm_{(n)}(Seq(P))),$$

we finally obtain the expected theorem:

Theorem 7. *Let $P \in Proc_{\Sigma}$. Then, $XNorm(P) \in XNormProc_{\Sigma}$ and $\mathcal{A}_{\mathcal{F}} \vdash P = XNorm(P)$.*

Proof sketch. By the law (!nat-↓), Theorem 3, and Lemma 2, $\mathcal{A}_{\mathcal{F}} \vdash P = \,!nat\ n \bullet (P \downarrow n) = \,!nat\ n \bullet (Seq(P) \downarrow n) = \,!nat\ n \bullet (Norm_{(n)}(Seq(P))) = XNorm(P)$, and for all n, $Norm_{(n)}(Seq(P)) =_{\mathcal{F}} XNorm(P) \downarrow n$. □

From this follows as a corollary that the axiom system $\mathcal{A}_{\mathcal{F}}$ is sound and complete for stable-failures equivalence.

Corollary 1. *Let $P, Q \in Proc_{\Sigma}$. Then, $\mathcal{A}_{\mathcal{F}} \vdash P = Q$ if and only if $P =_{\mathcal{F}} Q$.*

Proof. By Theorems 2, 6, and 7 □

At the end of this section, we give an example to show how to normalise divergent infinite processes by the axiom system $\mathcal{A}_{\mathcal{F}}$.

Example 2. We normalise the divergent infinite process $(Fix\ count)(0)$ by $\mathcal{A}_{\mathcal{F}}$, where the function $count :: (Nat \Rightarrow Proc_{Nat}) \Rightarrow (Nat \Rightarrow Proc_{Nat})$ is defined as:

$$count\,(f)\,(n) \;:=\; (n \to f(n+1)) \setminus \{n\}$$

The process $(Fix\ count)(0)$ increases the natural number n from the initial value 0 – which is hidden to the outside world. For $(Fix\ count)(0)$, we can for example prove the equality: $(Fix\ count)(0) =_{\mathcal{F}} (0 \to (1 \to (Fix\ count)(2)) \setminus \{1\}) \setminus \{0\}$. To do so, first expand the fixed point by the law (Tarski-fix),

$$\mathcal{A}_{\mathcal{F}} \vdash (Fix\ count)(0) = !nat\ n \bullet ((count^{(n)}(\lambda\, y.\, Div))(0))$$

Next, we show by induction on n that $\mathcal{A}_{\mathcal{F}} \vdash count^{(n)}(\lambda\, y.\, Div)(m) = Div$ for all n, m. The base case ($n = 0$) is trivial because $\mathcal{A}_{\mathcal{F}} \vdash count^{(0)}(\lambda\, y.\, Div)(m) = (\lambda\, y.\, Div)(m) = Div$. The induction case $(n + 1)$ is proven as follows:

$$\begin{array}{lll}
\mathcal{A}_{\mathcal{F}} \vdash & count^{(n+1)}(\lambda\, y.\, Div)(m) & \\
& = count(count^{(n)}(\lambda\, y.\, Div))(m) & \\
& = (m \to (count^{(n)}(\lambda\, y.\, Div))(m+1)) \setminus \{m\} & \\
& = (m \to Div) \setminus \{m\} & \text{by induction} \\
& = (?\, x : \emptyset \to (Div \setminus \{m\})) \rhd (!\, x : \{m\} \bullet (Div \setminus \{m\})) & \text{by (hide-step)} \\
& = Stop \rhd (!\, x : \{m\} \bullet (Div \setminus \{m\})) & \text{by (stop-step)} \\
& = !\, x : \{m\} \bullet Div & \text{by (unit-laws)} \\
& = Div & \text{by (!!-const)}
\end{array}$$

Finally, since $\mathcal{A}_{\mathcal{F}} \vdash Div = (Div)_{norm} \in NormProc_{\Sigma}$, we have

$$\mathcal{A}_{\mathcal{F}} \vdash (Fix\ count)(0) = !nat\ n \bullet (Div)_{norm} \in XNormProc_{\Sigma},$$

where $(Div)_{norm}$ given in Fig. 4 and $!nat\ n \bullet (Div)_{norm}$ are the full normal form and the extended full normal form of Div, respectively. □

6 Verification by CSP-Prover

The tool CSP-Prover [3,4] provides a deep encoding of CSP in the generic theorem prover Isabelle [7]. CSP-Prover contains fundamental theorems such as fixed point theorems on complete metric spaces and complete partial order, the definitions of CSP syntax and semantics, and many CSP-laws and semi-automatic proof tactics for verification of refinement relation. Therefore, CSP-Prover can be used for

1. Verification of infinite state systems. For example, we applied CSP-Prover to verify a part of the specification of the EP2 system, which is a new industrial standard of electronic payment systems, see [4].
2. Establishing new theorems on CSP. For example, CSP-Prover assisted us in proving the theorems given in this paper.

All proofs (including the examples) given in this paper have been verified by CSP-Prover. However, CSP-Prover also implements the axiom system $\mathcal{A}_{\mathcal{F}}$, besides the verification of this paper. Therefore, it is possible to prove the stable-failures equivalence over processes by syntactical rewriting with CSP-Prover.

In Isabelle, theorems, together with definitions and proof-scripts needed for their proof, can be stored in *theory-files*. Currently, CSP-Prover consists of three packages of theory-files: `CSP`, `CSP_T`, and `CSP_F`. The package `CSP` is the reusable part independent of specific CSP models. For example, it contains fixed point theorems on cms and cpo, and the definition of CSP syntax. The packages `CSP_T` and `CSP_F` are instantiated parts for the traces model and the stable failures model.

The packages have a hierarchical organisation as: `CSP_F` on `CSP_T` on `CSP` on Isabelle/HOL-Complex. The total number of lines of theory-files in `CSP`, `CSP_T`, and `CSP_F` are about 12,000 lines, 11,000 lines, and 18,000 lines, respectively.

The theorems for sequentialisation and normalisation given in this paper are stored in a new package `FNF_F` implemented on `CSP_F`. The total line number of theory-files in `FNF_F` is about 6,000 lines. All the packages can be downloaded from the web-site [3] of CSP-Prover.

7 Conclusion

We have shown that the CSP-dialect under discussion has the same expressive power as full CSP. We also presented a sound and complete axiom system $\mathcal{A}_{\mathcal{F}}$ of stable-failures equivalence for processes with unbounded nondeterminism over an arbitrary (possibly infinite) alphabet. The theorems presented in this paper have been verified by CSP-Prover.

Our results are of practical relevance for theorem proving for CSP in general: besides having a complete axiom system available, it is also possible to base proof rules and tactics on the extended full normal form. On the theoretical side, the here presented axioms, transformations, and normal forms provide new insight into the semantics of the process algebra CSP.

Acknowledgement. The authors are grateful to Erwin R. Catesbeiana Jr for pointing out the incompleteness problem in the first place and for good advice on how to avoid inconsistencies in the axiom system.

References

1. B. Dutertre and S. Schneider. Using a PVS embedding of CSP to verify authentication protocols. In E. L. Gunter and A. P. Felty, editors, *TPHOL 1997*, LNCS 1275, pages 121–136. Springer, 1997.
2. C. A. R. Hoare. *Communicating Sequential Processes*. Prentice Hall, 1985.
3. Y. Isobe and M. Roggenbach. Webpage on CSP-Prover. `http://staff.aist.go.jp/y-isobe/CSP-Prover/CSP-Prover.html`.
4. Y. Isobe and M. Roggenbach. A generic theorem prover of CSP refinement. In N. Halbwachs and L. D. Zuck, editors, *TACAS 2005*, LNCS 3440, pages 108–123. Springer, 2005.
5. Y. Isobe, M. Roggenbach, and S. Gruner. Extending CSP-Prover by deadlock-analysis: Towards the verification of systolic arrays. In *FOSE 2005*, Japanese Lecture Notes Series 31, pages 257–266. Kindai-kagaku-sha, 2005.
6. F. S. E. Limited. Failures-divergence refinement: FDR2. `http://www.fsel.com/`.
7. L. C. Paulson. *A Generic Theorem Prover*. LNCS 828. Springer, 1994.
8. A. W. Roscoe. *The Theory and Practice of Concurrency*. Prentice Hall, 1998. Or No.68 in `http://web.comlab.ox.ac.uk/oucl/work/bill.roscoe/pubs.html`.
9. S. Schneider. Verifying authentication protocol implementations. In B. Jacobs and A. Rensink, editors, *FMOODS 2002*, volume 209 of *IFIP Conference Proceedings*, pages 5–24. Kluwer, 2002.
10. H. Tej and B. Wolff. A corrected failure-divergence model for CSP in Isabelle/HOL. In J. Fitzgerald, C. Jones, and P. Lucas, editors, *FME'97*, LNCS 1313, pages 318–337. Springer, 1997.

Transition Systems of Elementary Net Systems with Localities

Maciej Koutny and Marta Pietkiewicz-Koutny

School of Computing Science, University of Newcastle
Newcastle upon Tyne, NE1 7RU, United Kingdom
{maciej.koutny, marta.koutny}@newcastle.ac.uk

Abstract. In this paper, we investigate transition systems of a class of Petri nets suitable for the modelling and behavioural analysis of globally asynchronous locally synchronous systems. The considered model of Elementary Net Systems with Localities (ENL-systems) is basically that of Elementary Net Systems (EN-systems) equipped with an explicit notion of locality. Each locality identifies a distinct set of events which may only be executed synchronously, i.e., in a maximally concurrent manner. For this reason, the overall behaviour of an ENL-system cannot be represented by an interleaved transition system, with arcs being labelled by single events, but rather by a suitable notion of a step transition system, with arcs being labelled by sets of events executed concurrently.

We completely characterise transition systems which can be generated by Elementary Net Systems with Localities under their intended concurrency semantics. In developing a suitable characterisation, we follow the standard approach in which key relationships between a Petri net and its transition system are established via the regions of the latter defined as specific sets of states of the transition system. We argue that this definition is insufficient for the class of transition systems of ENL-systems, and then augment the standard notion of a region with some additional information, leading to the notion of a region with explicit input and output events (or io-region).

We define, and show consistency of, two behaviour preserving translations between ENL-systems and their transition systems. As a result, we provide a solution to the synthesis problem of Elementary Net Systems with Localities, which consists in constructing an ENL-system for a given transition system in such a way that the transition system of the former is isomorphic to the latter.

Keywords: Theory of concurrency, Petri nets, elementary net systems, localities, analysis and synthesis, step sequence semantics, structure and behaviour of nets, theory of regions, transition systems.

1 Introduction

Several real-life computational systems exhibit dynamic behaviour which could best be described as following the 'globally asynchronous locally (maximally) synchronous' paradigm. Prominent examples of such systems can be found in

C. Baier and H. Hermanns (Eds.): CONCUR 2006, LNCS 4137, pp. 173–187, 2006.

hardware design, where a VLSI chip may contain multiple clocks responsible for synchronising different subsets of gates [6], and in biologically motivated computing, where a membrane system models a cell with compartments, inside which reactions are carried out in co-ordinated pulses [13]. In these cases, the activities in different localities can proceed independently, subject to communication and/or synchronisation constraints. To express such systems in a formal manner, [9] introduced *Place/Transition-nets with localities* (PTL-nets), which are basically PT-nets equipped with the notion a locality. Each locality identifies a distinct set of transitions which may only be executed synchronously, i.e., in a maximally concurrent manner. The aim of [9] was then to look at the way in which the standard concurrency techniques of Petri nets could be used to provide a similar treatment for the new model. In this paper, we adapt the model of [9] to the case of Elementary Net Systems (EN-systems), which are a fundamental class of safe Petri nets, and set ourselves the task of finding a characterisation of all transition systems generated by such nets.

ENL-Systems

To explain the basic concepts relating to ENL-systems, we consider the net shown in figure 1(a), which models a concurrent system consisting of one producer (the left triangle-like subnet), and one consumer process (the right square-like subnet). The two subsystems are connected by a buffer-like condition b_0 which holds items produced by the producer using the event p2, and consumed by the consumer using the event c1. The net would be a standard EN-system if we ignored the integer labels, 1 and 2, shown in the middle of the events. These labels represent *localities* to which the various events belong. We can then observe that events p1 and p2 belong to the same locality, while the remaining events to a different one.

In general, the way events are assigned to different localities will have a strong impact on the step sequences generated by an ENL-system, as it is required that within each locality events are executed in a maximally concurrent way. For the net in figure 1(a), this does not have any apparent effect since the subnets corresponding to the two localities are strictly sequential. This changes radically for the slightly modified example shown in figure 1(b), which models a system consisting of one producer and two co-located consumers (indicated by the two tokens in the right subnet).

For example, though under the standard EN-systems' semantics this net generates the step sequence $\{\mathtt{p2}\}\{\mathtt{c1}\}$, the execution model of ENL-systems will reject it for the following reason: After executing the initial step $\{\mathtt{p2}\}$, the net can execute the step $\{\mathtt{c1}, \mathtt{c4}\}$ consisting of two co-located events, and so executing c1 alone violates the maximal concurrency execution rule within locality 2. A possible way of executing a valid step could then be to add the 'missing' event c4, resulting in the legal step sequence $\{\mathtt{p2}\}\{\mathtt{c1}, \mathtt{c4}\}$. Another legal step sequence, according to the intended semantics, could be $\{\mathtt{p2}\}\{\mathtt{c1}, \mathtt{c4}, \mathtt{p1}\}$. Note that in the latter case the second step $\{\mathtt{c1}, \mathtt{c4}, \mathtt{p1}\}$ is maximally concurrent in a global sense, as it cannot be extended any further.

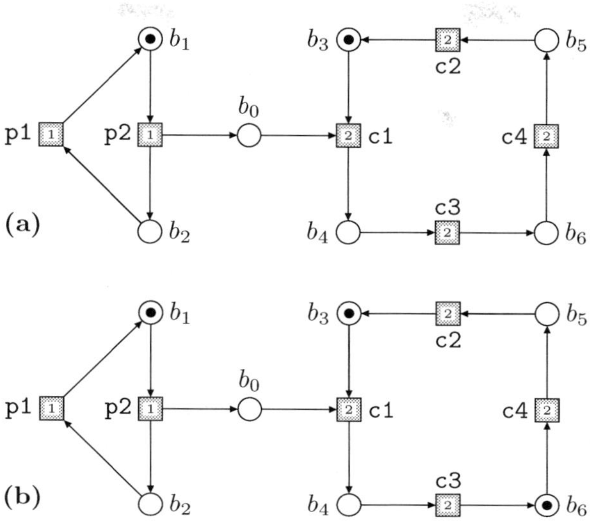

Fig. 1. ENL-system for the one-producer/one-consumer scenario **(a)**; and for the one-producer/two-consumers scenario **(b)**

If all the events of an ENL-system belong to the same locality (and so no extra labelling is really needed), then the notion of an ENL-system reduces to that of an Elementary Net System with Maximal Concurrency. In a nutshell, such a system is an EN-system executed under the maximal concurrency rule, i.e., in such a way that an executed step cannot be extended any further without violating the basic constraint embodied in the structure of the net.

ENL-Systems and the Synthesis Problem

Let us consider the EN-system together with its interleaving transition system shown in figure 2(a,b), and the ENL-system together with its step transition system shown in figure 2(c,d). Suppose that we are to solve the synthesis problem for the ENL-systems in the case of the example shown in figure 2. It can be formulated as a task of finding a method which, given a transition system, constructs a net in such a way that its behaviour (expressed as a transition system) is isomorphic to the given transition system.

This problem was solved for the class of EN-systems in [7], using the notion of a region which links nodes of transition systems (global states) with conditions in the corresponding nets (local states). The solution was later extended to the pure bounded PT-nets [4], general Petri nets [11], safe nets [16] and EN-systems with inhibitor arcs [5,10,14], by adopting the definition of a region or using some extended notion of a generalised region [3].

The way the standard region construction works can be explained in the following way. Let us try to retrieve the original EN-system from the interleaving transition system in figure 2(b). A region of a transition system is meant to

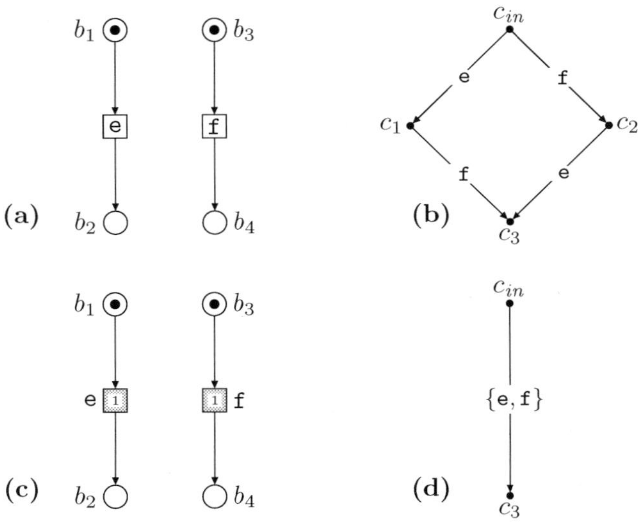

Fig. 2. An EN-system **(a)**; its interleaving transition system **(b)**; an ENL-system **(c)**; and step transition system **(d)**. Note that $c_{in} = \{b_1, b_3\}$, $c_1 = \{b_2, b_3\}$, $c_2 = \{b_1, b_4\}$ and $c_3 = \{b_2, b_4\}$.

encompass precisely those states where a given condition of the EN-system holds. So, for example, the region corresponding to the condition b_1 is the set comprising of two states, $r_1 = \{c_{in}, c_2\}$. Its defining characteristics is that is has the same 'crossing relationship' with both events `e` and `f`. Indeed, both `e`-arcs leave r_1, and both `f`-arcs do not cross r_1's boundary. There are three further regions with similar 'stable' crossing characteristics: $r_2 = \{c_1, c_3\}$ (`e`-arcs enter it and `f`-arcs do not cross the boundary), $r_3 = \{c_{in}, c_1\}$ (`f`-arcs leave it and `e`-arcs do not cross the boundary) and $r_4 = \{c_2, c_3\}$ (`f`-arcs enter it and `e`-arcs do not cross the boundary).[1] The synthesis procedure then derives an EN-system in the following way: for each region r_i a fresh condition b'_i is constructed and its input and output events are determined by the crossing relationships mentioned above, e.g., for r_1 `e` is an output event, and `f` is not joined to it by any arc. In this particular case, the resulting EN-system is actually isomorphic to the original one, though in the general case this cannot be guaranteed. But what can be guaranteed is that the transition systems of the two EN-systems are isomorphic.

One might attempt to apply the same procedure also in the case of the step transition system in figure 2(d), under the assumption that `e` and `f` are co-located events. However, this is not going to get us back to a desired ENL-system since there are at most 2 non-trivial regions there, $r_1 = \{c_{in}\}$ and $r_2 = \{c_3\}$, and so the construction can at best generate 2 conditions. However, we need at least 4 conditions in the resulting ENL-system, to be able to support a pair of concurrent

[1] Note that there are two more 'trivial' regions, $r = \{c_{in}, c_1, c_2, c_3\}$ and $r' = \varnothing$, which are ignored by the synthesis procedure.

events which were executed at the initial state. In other words, we have too few standard regions to construct enough conditions if the target is an appropriate ENL-system.

About This Paper

An intuitive reason why the standard construction failed to work for the step transition system in figure 2(d) was that the set-of-states notion of region is not rich enough for the purposes of synthesising ENL-systems.

The modification to the original notion we will propose is based on the explicit *input and output events* of a set of states, which is consistent with the underlying idea of static crossing relationship between events and regions. More precisely, we will work with *io-regions*, each such region being a triple: $\mathfrak{r} = (in, r, out)$, where r is a set of states, in is a set of events which are responsible for entering r, and out is a set of events which are responsible for leaving r. Intuitively, we will require that in each step leaving (or entering) r there is a unique event belonging to out (resp. to in) responsible for it, and, conversely, executing an event from out or from in always results in crossing of the boundary of r in an appropriate way. In the case of the example transition system, we will identify four io-regions: $\mathfrak{r}_1 = (\varnothing, \{c_{in}\}, \{\mathtt{e}\})$ $\mathfrak{r}_2 = (\{\mathtt{e}\}, \{c_3\}, \varnothing\})$, $\mathfrak{r}_3 = (\varnothing, \{c_{in}\}, \{\mathtt{f}\})$ and $\mathfrak{r}_4 = (\{\mathtt{f}\}, \{c_3\}, \varnothing)$. Now we have enough regions to re-constitute the conditions of the original ENL-system, namely each $\mathfrak{r}_i$ corresponds to b_i. The rest of the construction is basically the same as in the standard approach.

The paper is organised as follows. In the next section, we introduce step transition systems and their io-regions. After that we define ENL-transition systems. In section 3, we introduce formally ENL-systems and show that their transition systems are ENL-transition systems. We also demonstrate how to construct a corresponding ENL-system for a given ENL-transition system. In the concluding section, we compare our approach with other works, and outline how the modified notion of region could be used to solve the synthesis problem for other semantics of EN-systems.

2 Step Transition Systems and io-regions

In this section, we set the scene by introducing general step transition systems, which after further restrictions will be used to provide a behavioural model for ENL-systems, and the key notion of an io-region of a step transition system.

Let $\mathcal{E}$ be a non-empty set of *events* fixed throughout this paper. We also assume that there is a *locality mapping*, $\mathfrak{L} : \mathcal{E} \to \mathbb{N}$, associating to each event $e \in \mathcal{E}$ its locality $\mathfrak{L}(e)$; implicitly, each non-empty inverse image $\mathfrak{L}^{-1}(n)$ determines a set of co-located events.

A *step transition system* [1,8] is a triple $\mathfrak{ts} \stackrel{\mathrm{df}}{=} (S, T, s_{in})$ where:

TS1 S is a non-empty finite set of *states*.
TS2 $T \subseteq S \times (2^{\mathcal{E}} \setminus \{\varnothing\}) \times S$ is a finite set of *transitions*.
TS3 $s_{in} \in S$ is the *initial state*.

Throughout the rest of this section, the step transition system $\mathfrak{ts}$ will be fixed. We will denote by $\mathcal{E}_{\mathfrak{ts}}$ the set of all the events appearing in steps labelling the transitions of $\mathfrak{ts}$, i.e.,

$$\mathcal{E}_{\mathfrak{ts}} \stackrel{\mathrm{df}}{=} \bigcup_{(s,u,s')\in T} u .$$

We will use $s \xrightarrow{u} s'$ whenever $(s,u,s') \in T$, and respectively call s the *source* and s' the *target* of this transition. We will also say that the step u is *enabled* at s, and denote this by $s \xrightarrow{u}$. Moreover, we will denote $s \longrightarrow s'$ if $s \xrightarrow{u} s'$, for some u.

We now introduce a central notion whose aim is to link the nodes of a transition system (global states) with the conditions in the corresponding net (local states).

Definition 1. *A region with explicit input and output events (or* io-region*) is a triple* $\mathfrak{r} \stackrel{\mathrm{df}}{=} (in, r, out) \in 2^{\mathcal{E}_{\mathfrak{ts}}} \times 2^S \times 2^{\mathcal{E}_{\mathfrak{ts}}}$ *such that the following four conditions are satisfied, for every transition* $s \xrightarrow{u} s'$ *of the step transition system* $\mathfrak{ts}$*:*

1. *If* $s \in r$ *and* $s' \notin r$ *then* $|u \cap in| = 0$ *and* $|u \cap out| = 1$.
2. *If* $s \notin r$ *and* $s' \in r$ *then* $|u \cap in| = 1$ *and* $|u \cap out| = 0$.
3. *If* $u \cap out \neq \varnothing$ *then* $s \in r$ *and* $s' \notin r$.
4. *If* $u \cap in \neq \varnothing$ *then* $s \notin r$ *and* $s' \in r$.

We denote $\|\mathfrak{r}\| \stackrel{\mathrm{df}}{=} r$, ${}^\bullet\mathfrak{r} \stackrel{\mathrm{df}}{=} in$ *and* $\mathfrak{r}^\bullet \stackrel{\mathrm{df}}{=} out$.

An io-region $\mathfrak{r}$ is *trivial* if $\|\mathfrak{r}\| = \varnothing$ or $\|\mathfrak{r}\| = S$; otherwise it is *non-trivial.*

Proposition 1. *There are exactly two trivial io-regions:* $(\varnothing, \varnothing, \varnothing)$ *and* $(\varnothing, S, \varnothing)$.

Proof. From definition 1(3,4) and TS2, if $\mathfrak{r}$ is trivial then it must be the case that ${}^\bullet\mathfrak{r} = \mathfrak{r}^\bullet = \varnothing$. □

Proposition 2. $\mathfrak{r} = (in, r, out)$ *is an io-region if and only if* $\overline{\mathfrak{r}} \stackrel{\mathrm{df}}{=} (out, S \setminus r, in)$ *is an io-region.*

Proof. Follows directly from definition 1. □

In general, an io-region $\mathfrak{r}$ cannot be identified only by its set of states $\|\mathfrak{r}\|$; in other words, ${}^\bullet\mathfrak{r}$ and $\mathfrak{r}^\bullet$ may not be recoverable from $\|\mathfrak{r}\|$. However, if the transition system is *thin*, i.e., for every event $e \in \mathcal{E}_{\mathfrak{ts}}$ there is a transition $s \xrightarrow{\{e\}} s'$ of $\mathfrak{ts}$, then different io-regions are based on different sets of states.[2]

Proposition 3. *If* $\mathfrak{ts}$ *is thin and* $\mathfrak{r} \neq \mathfrak{r}'$ *are io-regions, then* $\|\mathfrak{r}\| \neq \|\mathfrak{r}'\|$.

[2] As we have already seen being thin is not, in general, a property of step transition systems generated by ENL-systems. However, transition systems generated by, e.g., EN-systems or EN-systems with inhibitor arcs, are thin and then the standard definition of a region as a set of states is sufficient.

Proof. Suppose that $\|\mathfrak{r}\| = \|\mathfrak{r}'\|$. Since $\mathfrak{r} \neq \mathfrak{r}'$, we have that ${}^\bullet\mathfrak{r} \neq {}^\bullet\mathfrak{r}'$ or $\mathfrak{r}^\bullet \neq \mathfrak{r}'^\bullet$. Assume, without loss of generality, that ${}^\bullet\mathfrak{r} \neq {}^\bullet\mathfrak{r}'$. Then, again without loss of generality, we have that ${}^\bullet\mathfrak{r} \neq \varnothing$.

Let us take any $e \in {}^\bullet\mathfrak{r}$. Since $\mathfrak{ts}$ is thin, there is a transition $s \xrightarrow{\{e\}} s'$ of $\mathfrak{ts}$. By definition 1(4), we have $s \notin \|\mathfrak{r}\|$ and $s' \in \|\mathfrak{r}\|$. Hence, by $\|\mathfrak{r}\| = \|\mathfrak{r}'\|$, we also have that $s \notin \|\mathfrak{r}'\|$ and $s' \in \|\mathfrak{r}'\|$. Thus, by $s \xrightarrow{\{e\}} s'$ and definition 1(2), $e \in {}^\bullet\mathfrak{r}'$. As a result, ${}^\bullet\mathfrak{r} \subseteq {}^\bullet\mathfrak{r}'$. By proceeding in a similar way, we may then show that ${}^\bullet\mathfrak{r} = {}^\bullet\mathfrak{r}'$ and $\mathfrak{r}^\bullet = \mathfrak{r}'^\bullet$. This, together with $\|\mathfrak{r}\| = \|\mathfrak{r}'\|$, produces a contradiction with $\mathfrak{r} \neq \mathfrak{r}'$. □

The set of all *non-trivial* io-regions will be denoted by $\mathfrak{R}_{\mathfrak{ts}}$ and, for every state $s \in S$, we will denote by $\mathfrak{R}_s$ the set of non-trivial io-regions containing s,

$$\mathfrak{R}_s \stackrel{\mathrm{df}}{=} \{\mathfrak{r} \in \mathfrak{R}_{\mathfrak{ts}} \mid s \in \|\mathfrak{r}\|\} .$$

The sets of *pre-io-regions*, $^\circ e$, and *post-io-regions*, e°, of an event $e \in \mathcal{E}_{\mathfrak{ts}}$ are then defined as:

$$^\circ e \stackrel{\mathrm{df}}{=} \{\mathfrak{r} \in \mathfrak{R}_{\mathfrak{ts}} \mid e \in \mathfrak{r}^\bullet\} \quad \text{and} \quad e^\circ \stackrel{\mathrm{df}}{=} \{\mathfrak{r} \in \mathfrak{R}_{\mathfrak{ts}} \mid e \in {}^\bullet\mathfrak{r}\} .$$

Moreover, the sets of pre-io-regions and post-io-regions of a set of events $u \subseteq \mathcal{E}_{\mathfrak{ts}}$ are respectively given by:

$$^\circ u \stackrel{\mathrm{df}}{=} \bigcup_{e \in u} {}^\circ e \quad \text{and} \quad u^\circ \stackrel{\mathrm{df}}{=} \bigcup_{e \in u} e^\circ .$$

Proposition 4. *If $s \xrightarrow{u} s'$ is a transition of $\mathfrak{ts}$, then*

1. *$\mathfrak{r} \in {}^\circ u$ implies $s \in \|\mathfrak{r}\|$ and $s' \notin \|\mathfrak{r}\|$.*
2. *$\mathfrak{r} \in u^\circ$ implies $s \notin \|\mathfrak{r}\|$ and $s' \in \|\mathfrak{r}\|$.*

Proof. Follows directly from the definitions of $^\circ u$ and u°, as well as definition 1(3,4). □

The sets of pre- and post-io-regions of a step involved in a transition of $\mathfrak{ts}$ are, in fact, disjoint unions of sets of respectively pre- and post-io-regions of events it comprises.

Proposition 5. *If u is a step appearing in one of the transitions of $\mathfrak{ts}$, then*

$$^\circ u = \biguplus_{e \in u} {}^\circ e \quad \text{and} \quad u^\circ = \biguplus_{e \in u} e^\circ .$$

Proof. Let $s \xrightarrow{u} s'$ and $e, f \in u$ be such that $e \neq f$. Suppose that $\mathfrak{r} \in {}^\circ e \cap {}^\circ f$ which means that $e, f \in \mathfrak{r}^\bullet$. This means, by definition 1(3), that $s \in \|\mathfrak{r}\|$ and $s' \notin \|\mathfrak{r}\|$. Thus, by definition 1(1), $|u \cap \mathfrak{r}^\bullet| = 1$, a contradiction with $e, f \in u \cap \mathfrak{r}^\bullet$. Hence the first part of the result holds. The second one can be shown in a similar way. □

Proposition 6. *If u is a step appearing in one of the transitions of $\mathfrak{ts}$, then $^\circ u \cap u^\circ = \varnothing$.*

Proof. Suppose that $s \xrightarrow{u} s'$ and $\mathfrak{r} \in {}^\circ u \cap u^\circ$. Then, by proposition 4, $s \notin \|\mathfrak{r}\|$ and $s \in \|\mathfrak{r}\|$. We thus obtained a contradiction. □

Proposition 7. *If $s \xrightarrow{u} s'$ then $\mathfrak{R}_s \setminus \mathfrak{R}_{s'} = {}^\circ u$ and $\mathfrak{R}_{s'} \setminus \mathfrak{R}_s = u^\circ$.*

Proof. We show that $\mathfrak{R}_s \setminus \mathfrak{R}_{s'} = {}^\circ u$, as the second part can be shown in a similar way. By proposition 4, $^\circ u \subseteq \mathfrak{R}_s$ and $^\circ u \cap \mathfrak{R}_{s'} = \varnothing$. Hence $^\circ u \subseteq \mathfrak{R}_s \setminus \mathfrak{R}_{s'}$. Suppose that $\mathfrak{r} \in \mathfrak{R}_s \setminus \mathfrak{R}_{s'}$, which implies that $s \in \|\mathfrak{r}\|$ and $s' \notin \|\mathfrak{r}\|$. Hence, by definition 1(1) and $s \xrightarrow{u} s'$, $u \cap \mathfrak{r}^\bullet \neq \varnothing$. Hence $\mathfrak{r} \in {}^\circ u$ and so $\mathfrak{R}_s \setminus \mathfrak{R}_{s'} \subseteq {}^\circ u$. Consequently, $\mathfrak{R}_s \setminus \mathfrak{R}_{s'} = {}^\circ u$. □

To characterise fully transition systems generated by ENL-systems, we will need the notion of a potential step. The set of all *potential steps* $\mathbb{U}_{\mathfrak{ts}}$ of $\mathfrak{ts}$ is defined as follows:

$$\mathbb{U}_{\mathfrak{ts}} \stackrel{\mathrm{df}}{=} \{u \subseteq \mathcal{E}_{\mathfrak{ts}} \mid u \neq \varnothing \wedge \forall e, f \in u : (e \neq f \Rightarrow ({}^\circ e \cup e^\circ) \cap ({}^\circ f \cup f^\circ) = \varnothing)\} .$$

Proposition 8. *If $s \xrightarrow{u} s'$ then $u \in \mathbb{U}_{\mathfrak{ts}}$.*

Proof. Follows from TS2 and propositions 5 and 6. □

2.1 ENL-Transition Systems

A step transition system $\mathfrak{ts} = (S, T, s_{in})$ is an *ENL-transition system* if it satisfies the following axioms:

- **A1** For every $s \in S \setminus \{s_{in}\}$, there are $(s_0, u_0, s_1), \ldots, (s_{n-1}, u_{n-1}, s_n) \in T$ such that $s_0 = s_{in}$ and $s_n = s$.
- **A2** For every event $e \in \mathcal{E}_{\mathfrak{ts}}$, both $^\circ e$ and e° are non-empty.
- **A3** For all states $s, s' \in S$, if $\mathfrak{R}_s = \mathfrak{R}_{s'}$ then $s = s'$.
- **A4** Let $s \in S$ and $u \in \mathbb{U}_{\mathfrak{ts}}$ be such that $^\circ u \subseteq \mathfrak{R}_s$ and $u^\circ \cap \mathfrak{R}_s = \varnothing$, and there is no $u \uplus \{e\} \in \mathbb{U}_{\mathfrak{ts}}$ satisfying $\mathfrak{L}(e) \in \mathfrak{L}(u)$ and $^\circ e \subseteq \mathfrak{R}_s$ and $e^\circ \cap \mathfrak{R}_s = \varnothing$. Then $s \xrightarrow{u}$.
- **A5** If $s \xrightarrow{u}$ then there is no $u \uplus \{e\} \in \mathbb{U}_{\mathfrak{ts}}$ satisfying $\mathfrak{L}(e) \in \mathfrak{L}(u)$ and $^\circ e \subseteq \mathfrak{R}_s$ and $e^\circ \cap \mathfrak{R}_s = \varnothing$.

The (A1) axiom implies that all the states in $\mathfrak{ts}$ are reachable from the initial state. (A2) will ensure that every event in a synthesised ENL-system will have at least one input condition and at least one output condition. (A3) was used for other transition systems as well, and is usually called the *state separation property* [3,12], and it guarantees that $\mathfrak{ts}$ is deterministic. (A4) is a variation of the *forward closure property* [12] or the *event/state separation property* [3]. (A5) ensures that every step in a transition system is indeed a maximal step w.r.t. localities of the events it comprises.

Proposition 9. *If $s \xrightarrow{u} s'$ and $s \xrightarrow{u} s''$ then $s' = s''$.*

Proof. Follows from proposition 7 and (A3). □

3 ENL-Systems

A *net* is a tuple $\mathfrak{net} \stackrel{\mathrm{df}}{=} (B, E, F)$ such that B and $E \subseteq \mathcal{E}$ are finite disjoint sets, and $F \subseteq (B \times E) \cup (E \times B)$. The meaning and graphical representation of B (conditions), E (events) and F (flow relation) is the same as in the standard net theory. Moreover, in diagrams, boxes representing events with localities are shaded with the actual locality being shown in the middle (see figure 1). We denote, for every $x \in B \cup E$,

$$^\bullet x \stackrel{\mathrm{df}}{=} \{y \mid (y, x) \in F\} \quad \text{and} \quad x^\bullet \stackrel{\mathrm{df}}{=} \{y \mid (x, y) \in F\} ,$$

and we call them the *pre-elements* and *post-elements*, respectively. The dot-notation extends in the usual way to sets:

$$^\bullet X \stackrel{\mathrm{df}}{=} \bigcup_{x \in X} {^\bullet x} \text{ and } X^\bullet \stackrel{\mathrm{df}}{=} \bigcup_{x \in X} x^\bullet .$$

It is assumed that for every $e \in E$, the sets $^\bullet e$ and $e^\bullet$ are non-empty and disjoint.

An *elementary net system with localities* (ENL-system) is a tuple

$$\mathfrak{enl} \stackrel{\mathrm{df}}{=} (B, E, F, c_{in})$$

such that $\mathfrak{net}_{\mathfrak{enl}} \stackrel{\mathrm{df}}{=} (B, E, F)$ is the (underlying) net and $c_{in} \subseteq B$ is the *initial case* (in general, any subset of B is a *case*). We will assume that $\mathfrak{enl}$ is fixed until the end of this section.

The concurrency semantics of ENL-systems will be based on steps of simultaneously executed events. We first define the set of *valid steps* of the ENL-system:

$$\mathbb{U}_{\mathfrak{enl}} \stackrel{\mathrm{df}}{=} \{u \subseteq E \mid u \neq \varnothing \ \wedge \ \forall e, f \in u : \ (e \neq f \Rightarrow (^\bullet e \cup e^\bullet) \cap (^\bullet f \cup f^\bullet) = \varnothing)\} .$$

A step $u \in \mathbb{U}_{\mathfrak{enl}}$ is *enabled* at a case $c \subseteq B$ if $^\bullet u \subseteq c$ and $u^\bullet \cap c = \varnothing$, and there is no step $u \uplus \{e\} \in \mathbb{U}_{\mathfrak{enl}}$ satisfying $\mathfrak{L}(e) \in \mathfrak{L}(u)$ and $^\bullet e \subseteq c$ and $e^\bullet \cap c = \varnothing$.

The transition relation of $\mathfrak{net}_{\mathfrak{enl}}$, denoted by $\rightarrow_{\mathfrak{net}_{\mathfrak{enl}}}$, is then given as the set of all triples

$$(c, u, c') \in 2^B \times \mathbb{U}_{\mathfrak{enl}} \times 2^B$$

such that u is enabled at c and $c' = (c \setminus {^\bullet u}) \cup u^\bullet$.

The *state space* of $\mathfrak{enl}$, denoted by $C_{\mathfrak{enl}}$, is the least subset of 2^B containing c_{in} such that if $c \in C_{\mathfrak{enl}}$ and $(c, u, c') \in \rightarrow_{\mathfrak{net}_{\mathfrak{enl}}}$ then $c' \in C_{\mathfrak{enl}}$. The *transition relation* of $\mathfrak{enl}$, denoted by $\rightarrow_{\mathfrak{enl}}$, is then defined as $\rightarrow_{\mathfrak{net}_{\mathfrak{enl}}}$ restricted to $C_{\mathfrak{enl}} \times \mathbb{U}_{\mathfrak{enl}} \times C_{\mathfrak{enl}}$. We will use $c \xrightarrow{u}_{\mathfrak{enl}} c'$ to denote that $(c, u, c') \in \rightarrow_{\mathfrak{enl}}$. Also, $c \xrightarrow{u}_{\mathfrak{enl}}$ if $(c, u, c') \in \rightarrow_{\mathfrak{enl}}$, for some c'.

Proposition 10. *If $c \xrightarrow{u}_{\mathfrak{enl}} c'$ then $c \setminus c' = {^\bullet u}$ and $c' \setminus c = u^\bullet$.*

Proof. From $c \xrightarrow{u}_{\mathfrak{enl}} c'$ we have that u is enabled at c (which implies $^\bullet u \subseteq c$ and $u^\bullet \cap c = \varnothing$) and $c' = (c \setminus {^\bullet u}) \cup u^\bullet$. One can easily check that these imply $c \setminus c' = {^\bullet u}$ and $c' \setminus c = u^\bullet$. □

3.1 Transition Systems Generated by ENL-Systems

The construction of a step transition system for a given ENL-system is straightforward.

Let $\mathfrak{enl} = (B, E, F, c_{in})$ be an ENL-system. Then

$$\mathfrak{ts}_{\mathfrak{enl}} \stackrel{\text{df}}{=} (C_{\mathfrak{enl}}, \rightarrow_{\mathfrak{enl}}, c_{in})$$

is the *transition system generated* by $\mathfrak{enl}$.

Theorem 1. *$\mathfrak{ts}_{\mathfrak{enl}}$ is an ENL-transition system.*

Proof. Clearly, $\mathfrak{ts}_{\mathfrak{enl}}$ is a step transition system. We need to prove that it satisfies the five axioms defining ENL-transition systems. Before doing this, we will show that, for every $b \in B$,

$$\mathfrak{r}_b \stackrel{\text{df}}{=} ({}^\bullet b, \{c \in C_{\mathfrak{enl}} \mid b \in c\}, b^\bullet)$$

is a (possibly trivial) io-region of $\mathfrak{ts}_{\mathfrak{enl}}$. Moreover, if $\varnothing \neq \|\mathfrak{r}_b\| \neq C_{\mathfrak{enl}}$ then $\mathfrak{r}_b$ is non-trivial.

To show that definition 1 holds for $\mathfrak{r}_b$, we assume that $c \stackrel{u}{\longrightarrow}_{\mathfrak{enl}} c'$ in $\mathfrak{ts}_{\mathfrak{enl}}$, and proceed as follows:

Proof of definition 1(1) for $\mathfrak{r}_b$. We need to show that $c \in \|\mathfrak{r}_b\|$ and $c' \notin \|\mathfrak{r}_b\|$ implies $|u \cap {}^\bullet b| = 0$ and $|u \cap b^\bullet| = 1$.

From $c \in \|\mathfrak{r}_b\|$ ($c' \notin \|\mathfrak{r}_b\|$) it follows that $b \in c$ (resp. $b \notin c'$). Hence $b \in c \setminus c'$. From proposition 10 we have $c \setminus c' = {}^\bullet u$ and $c' \setminus c = u^\bullet$. Hence $b \in {}^\bullet u$ and, as a consequence, there exists $e \in u$ such that $b \in {}^\bullet e$, and so $e \in b^\bullet$. We therefore have $e \in u \cap b^\bullet$. Hence $u \cap b^\bullet \neq \varnothing$. Suppose that there is $f \neq e$ such that $f \in u \cap b^\bullet$. Then we have $f \in u$ and $b \in {}^\bullet f$ which implies $b \in {}^\bullet f \cap {}^\bullet e$. We obtained a contradiction with $e, f \in u \in \mathbb{U}_{\mathfrak{enl}}$. Hence $|u \cap b^\bullet| = 1$.

From $b \notin c'$ and $c' \setminus c = u^\bullet$, we have $b \notin u^\bullet$. Let $e \in u$ ($u \neq \varnothing$ by definition). Then $b \notin e^\bullet$, and therefore $e \notin {}^\bullet b$. Hence $|u \cap {}^\bullet b| = 0$.

Proof of definition 1(2) for $\mathfrak{r}_b$. Can be proved similarly as definition 1(1).

Proof of definition 1(3) for $\mathfrak{r}_b$. We need to show that $u \cap b^\bullet \neq \varnothing$ implies $c \in \|\mathfrak{r}_b\|$ and $c' \notin \|\mathfrak{r}_b\|$.

From proposition 10, we have $c \setminus c' = {}^\bullet u$ and $c' \setminus c = u^\bullet$. From $u \cap b^\bullet \neq \varnothing$, we have that there is $e \in u$ such that $e \in b^\bullet$, and so $b \in {}^\bullet e$. Consequently, $b \in {}^\bullet u = c \setminus c'$, and so $b \in c$ and $b \notin c'$. We therefore obtained that $c \in \|\mathfrak{r}_b\|$ and $c' \notin \|\mathfrak{r}_b\|$.

Proof of definition 1(4) for $\mathfrak{r}_b$. Can be proved similarly as definition 1(3).

Clearly, if $\varnothing \neq \|\mathfrak{r}_b\| \neq C_{\mathfrak{enl}}$ then $\mathfrak{r}_b$ is a non-trivial io-region.

We may now proceed with the proof proper.

Proof of (A1). Follows directly from the definition of $C_{\mathfrak{enl}}$.

Proof of (A2). We observe that if $e \in \mathcal{E}_{\mathfrak{ts}_{\mathfrak{enl}}}$ then $\{\mathfrak{r}_b \mid b \in {}^{\bullet}e\} \subseteq {}^{\circ}e$ and $\{\mathfrak{r}_b \mid b \in e^{\bullet}\} \subseteq e^{\circ}$ (follows from the definitions of ${}^{\circ}e$, e° and $\mathfrak{r}_b$). This and ${}^{\bullet}e \neq \varnothing \neq e^{\bullet}$ yields ${}^{\circ}e \neq \varnothing \neq e^{\circ}$.

Proof of (A3). Suppose that $c \neq c'$ are two cases in $C_{\mathfrak{enl}}$. Without loss of generality, we may assume that there is $b \in c \setminus c'$. Hence $c \in \|\mathfrak{r}_b\|$ and $c' \notin \|\mathfrak{r}_b\|$. Thus, by the fact that $\mathfrak{r}_b$ is not trivial ($\varnothing \neq \|\mathfrak{r}_b\| \neq C_{\mathfrak{enl}}$) and $\mathfrak{r}_b \in \mathfrak{R}_c \setminus \mathfrak{R}_{c'}$, (A3) holds.

Proof of (A4). Suppose that $c \in C_{\mathfrak{enl}}$ and $u \in \mathbb{U}_{\mathfrak{ts}_{\mathfrak{enl}}}$ are such that ${}^{\circ}u \subseteq \mathfrak{R}_c$ and $u^{\circ} \cap \mathfrak{R}_c = \varnothing$ and there is no $u \uplus \{e\} \in \mathbb{U}_{\mathfrak{ts}_{\mathfrak{enl}}}$ satisfying: $\mathfrak{L}(e) \in \mathfrak{L}(u)$ and ${}^{\circ}e \subseteq \mathfrak{R}_c$ and $e^{\circ} \cap \mathfrak{R}_c = \varnothing$. We need to show that $c \xrightarrow{u}_{\mathfrak{enl}}$.

First we show ${}^{\bullet}u \subseteq c$. Let $e \in u$. Consider $b \in {}^{\bullet}e$. We have already shown that this implies $\mathfrak{r}_b \in {}^{\circ}e$. From ${}^{\circ}u \subseteq \mathfrak{R}_c$, we have that $\mathfrak{r}_b \in \mathfrak{R}_c$, and so $c \in \|\mathfrak{r}_b\|$. Consequently, $b \in c$. Hence, for all $e \in u$ we have ${}^{\bullet}e \subseteq c$, and so ${}^{\bullet}u \subseteq c$.

Now we show that ${}^{\bullet}u \cap c = \varnothing$. Let $e \in u$. Consider $b \in e^{\bullet}$. We have already shown that this implies $\mathfrak{r}_b \in e^{\circ}$. From $u^{\circ} \cap \mathfrak{R}_c = \varnothing$, we have that $\mathfrak{r}_b \notin \mathfrak{R}_c$, and so $c \notin \|\mathfrak{r}_b\|$. Consequently, $b \notin c$. Hence, for all $e \in u$ we have $e^{\bullet} \cap c = \varnothing$, and so $u^{\bullet} \cap c = \varnothing$. Now we need to prove that there is no step $u \uplus \{e\} \in \mathbb{U}_{\mathfrak{enl}}$ satisfying: $\mathfrak{L}(e) \in \mathfrak{L}(u)$ and ${}^{\bullet}e \subseteq c$ and $e^{\bullet} \cap c = \varnothing$.

Suppose that this is not the case. Let $u \uplus \{e_1\} \in \mathbb{U}_{\mathfrak{enl}}$ be a step satisfying these conditions. Now we have two cases.

Case 1: There is no $u \uplus \{e_1\} \uplus \{f\} \in \mathbb{U}_{\mathfrak{enl}}$ such that $\mathfrak{L}(f) \in \mathfrak{L}(u \uplus \{e_1\})$ and ${}^{\bullet}f \subseteq c$ and $f^{\bullet} \cap c = \varnothing$. This implies $c \xrightarrow{u \uplus \{e_1\}}_{\mathfrak{enl}}$. By proposition 8, we have that $u \uplus \{e_1\} \in \mathbb{U}_{\mathfrak{ts}_{\mathfrak{enl}}}$. Moreover, $\mathfrak{L}(e_1) \in \mathfrak{L}(u)$ and, by proposition 7, we have ${}^{\circ}(u \uplus \{e_1\}) \subseteq \mathfrak{R}_c$ and $(u \uplus \{e_1\})^{\circ} \cap \mathfrak{R}_c = \varnothing$. We therefore obtained a contradiction with our assumptions.

Case 2: We can find $u \uplus \{e_1\} \uplus \{e_2\} \in \mathbb{U}_{\mathfrak{enl}}$ such that $\mathfrak{L}(e_2) \in \mathfrak{L}(u \uplus \{e_1\})$ and ${}^{\bullet}e_2 \subseteq c$ and $e_2^{\bullet} \cap c = \varnothing$. Then we consider Cases 1 and 2 again, taking $u \uplus \{e_1\} \uplus \{e_2\}$ instead of $u \uplus \{e_1\}$. Since the number of events in E is finite, we will eventually end up in Case 1. This means that, eventually, we will obtain a contradiction.

Proof of (A5). We need to show that, if $c \xrightarrow{u}_{\mathfrak{enl}}$ then there is no $u \uplus \{e\} \in \mathbb{U}_{\mathfrak{ts}_{\mathfrak{enl}}}$ satisfying $\mathfrak{L}(e) \in \mathfrak{L}(u)$ and ${}^{\circ}e \subseteq \mathfrak{R}_c$ and $e^{\circ} \cap \mathfrak{R}_c = \varnothing$.

Suppose that there *is* $u \uplus \{e\} \in \mathbb{U}_{\mathfrak{ts}_{\mathfrak{enl}}}$ satisfying $\mathfrak{L}(e) \in \mathfrak{L}(u)$ and ${}^{\circ}e \subseteq \mathfrak{R}_c$ and $e^{\circ} \cap \mathfrak{R}_c = \varnothing$ (†).

We have already shown that for $e \in \mathcal{E}_{\mathfrak{ts}_{\mathfrak{enl}}}$, $b \in {}^{\bullet}e$ implies $\mathfrak{r}_b \in {}^{\circ}e$, and $b \in e^{\bullet}$ implies $\mathfrak{r}_b \in e^{\circ}$. From this and $u \uplus \{e\} \in \mathbb{U}_{\mathfrak{ts}_{\mathfrak{enl}}}$ we have $u \uplus \{e\} \in \mathbb{U}_{\mathfrak{enl}}$.

We will show that ${}^{\bullet}e \subseteq c$. We have $b \in {}^{\bullet}e$ implies $\mathfrak{r}_b \in {}^{\circ}e$. But ${}^{\circ}e \subseteq \mathfrak{R}_c$, so $\mathfrak{r}_b \in \mathfrak{R}_c$. This means $c \in \|\mathfrak{r}_b\|$, and consequently, $b \in c$. Hence ${}^{\bullet}e \subseteq c$

We will show that $e^{\bullet} \cap c = \varnothing$. We have $b \in e^{\bullet}$ implies $\mathfrak{r}_b \in e^{\circ}$. But $e^{\circ} \cap \mathfrak{R}_c = \varnothing$, so $\mathfrak{r}_b \notin \mathfrak{R}_c$. This means $c \notin \|\mathfrak{r}_b\|$, and consequently, $b \notin c$. Hence $e^{\bullet} \cap c = \varnothing$.

As a result, assuming (†) leads to a contradiction with $c \xrightarrow{u}_{\mathfrak{enl}}$. □

3.2 ENL-Systems Generated by ENL-Transition Systems

The reverse translation, from ENL-transition systems to ENL-systems, is based on the pre- and post-io-regions of events appearing in a transition system.

Let $\mathfrak{ts} = (S, T, s_{in})$ be an ENL-transition system. The net system *associated* with $\mathfrak{ts}$ is defined as

$$\mathfrak{enl}_{\mathfrak{ts}} \stackrel{\mathrm{df}}{=} (\mathfrak{R}_{\mathfrak{ts}}, \mathcal{E}_{\mathfrak{ts}}, F_{\mathfrak{ts}}, \mathfrak{R}_{s_{in}})$$

where $F_{\mathfrak{ts}}$ is defined thus:

$$F_{\mathfrak{ts}} \stackrel{\mathrm{df}}{=} \{(\mathfrak{r}, e) \in \mathfrak{R}_{\mathfrak{ts}} \times \mathcal{E}_{\mathfrak{ts}} \mid \mathfrak{r} \in {}^{\circ}e\} \cup \{(e, \mathfrak{r}) \in \mathcal{E}_{\mathfrak{ts}} \times \mathfrak{R}_{\mathfrak{ts}} \mid \mathfrak{r} \in e^{\circ}\} . \quad (1)$$

Proposition 11. *For every $e \in \mathcal{E}_{\mathfrak{ts}}$, ${}^{\circ}e = {}^{\bullet}e$ and $e^{\circ} = e^{\bullet}$.*

Proof. Follows directly from the definition of $\mathfrak{enl}_{\mathfrak{ts}}$. □

Note that the above construction produces a net which is saturated with conditions.

Theorem 2. *$\mathfrak{enl}_{\mathfrak{ts}}$ is an ENL-system.*

Proof. The only thing we need to observe is that, for every event e of $\mathcal{E}_{\mathfrak{ts}}$, it is the case that: ${}^{\bullet}e \neq \varnothing \neq e^{\bullet}$, which follows from (A2) and proposition 11; and ${}^{\bullet}e \cap e^{\bullet} = \varnothing$, which follows from propositions 6 and 11. □

We will now show that the ENL-system associated with an ENL-transition system $\mathfrak{ts}$ generates a transition system which is isomorphic to $\mathfrak{ts}$.

Proposition 12. *Let $\mathfrak{ts} = (S, T, s_{in})$ be an ENL-transition system and*

$$\mathfrak{enl} = \mathfrak{enl}_{\mathfrak{ts}} = (\mathfrak{R}_{\mathfrak{ts}}, \mathcal{E}_{\mathfrak{ts}}, F_{\mathfrak{ts}}, \mathfrak{R}_{s_{in}}) = (B, E, F, c_{in})$$

be the ENL-system associated with it.

1. $C_{\mathfrak{enl}} = \{\mathfrak{R}_s \mid s \in S\}$.
2. $\rightarrow_{\mathfrak{enl}} = \{(\mathfrak{R}_s, u, \mathfrak{R}_{s'}) \mid (s, u, s') \in T\}$.

Proof. Note that from the definition of $C_{\mathfrak{enl}}$, every $c \in C_{\mathfrak{enl}}$ is a case reachable from c_{in} in $\mathfrak{enl}$; and that from axiom (A1), every $s \in S$ is a state reachable from s_{in} in $\mathfrak{ts}$.

We first show that if $c \xrightarrow{u}_{\mathfrak{enl}} c'$ and $c = \mathfrak{R}_s$, for some $s \in S$, then there is $s' \in S$ such that $s \xrightarrow{u} s'$ and $c' = \mathfrak{R}_{s'}$. By $c \xrightarrow{u}_{\mathfrak{enl}} c'$, $u \in \mathbb{U}_{\mathfrak{enl}}$ is a step such that ${}^{\bullet}u \subseteq c$ and $u^{\bullet} \cap c = \varnothing$, and there is no step $u \uplus \{e\} \in \mathbb{U}_{\mathfrak{enl}}$ satisfying $\mathfrak{L}(e) \in \mathfrak{L}(u)$ and ${}^{\bullet}e \subseteq c$ and $e^{\bullet} \cap c = \varnothing$. Moreover, $c' = (c \setminus {}^{\bullet}u) \cup u^{\bullet}$.
Hence, by proposition 11 and (A4), $u \in \mathbb{U}_{\mathfrak{ts}}$ and $s \xrightarrow{u} s'$, for some $s' \in S$. Then, by proposition 7, $\mathfrak{R}_{s'} = (\mathfrak{R}_s \setminus {}^{\circ}u) \cup u^{\circ}$. At the same time, we have $c' = (c \setminus {}^{\bullet}u) \cup u^{\bullet}$.
Hence, by proposition 11 and $c = \mathfrak{R}_s$, we have that $c' = \mathfrak{R}_{s'}$.
As a result, we have shown (note that $c_{in} = \mathfrak{R}_{s_{in}} \in \{\mathfrak{R}_s \mid s \in S\}$) that

$$\begin{aligned} C_{\mathfrak{enl}} &\subseteq \{\mathfrak{R}_s \mid s \in S\} \\ \rightarrow_{\mathfrak{enl}} &\subseteq \{(\mathfrak{R}_s, u, \mathfrak{R}_{s'}) \mid (s, u, s') \in T\} . \end{aligned}$$

We now prove the reverse inclusions. By definition, $\mathfrak{R}_{s_{in}} \in C_{\mathfrak{enl}}$. It is enough to show that if $s \xrightarrow{u} s'$ and $\mathfrak{R}_s \in C_{\mathfrak{enl}}$, then $\mathfrak{R}_{s'} \in C_{\mathfrak{enl}}$ and $\mathfrak{R}_s \xrightarrow{u}_{\mathfrak{enl}} \mathfrak{R}_{s'}$. By (A5) and propositions 7, 8 and 11, u is a valid step in $\mathfrak{enl}$ which is enabled at the case $\mathfrak{R}_s$. So, there is a case c' such that $\mathfrak{R}_s \xrightarrow{u}_{\mathfrak{enl}} c'$ and $c' = (\mathfrak{R}_s \setminus {}^\bullet u) \cup u^\bullet$. From propositions 7 and 11 we have that $c' = \mathfrak{R}_{s'}$. Hence we obtain that $\mathfrak{R}_s \xrightarrow{u}_{\mathfrak{enl}} \mathfrak{R}_{s'}$ and so also $\mathfrak{R}_{s'} \in C_{\mathfrak{enl}}$. □

Theorem 3. *Let* $\mathfrak{ts} = (S, T, s_{in})$ *be an ENL-transition system and* $\mathfrak{enl} = \mathfrak{enl}_{\mathfrak{ts}}$ *be the ENL-system associated with it. Then* $\mathfrak{ts}_{\mathfrak{enl}}$ *is isomorphic to* $\mathfrak{ts}$.

Proof. Let $\psi : S \to C_{\mathfrak{enl}}$ be a mapping given by $\psi(s) = \mathfrak{R}_s$, for all $s \in S$ (note that, by proposition 12(1), ψ is well-defined). We will show that ψ is an isomorphism for $\mathfrak{ts}$ and $\mathfrak{ts}_{\mathfrak{enl}}$.

Note that $\psi(s_{in}) = \mathfrak{R}_{s_{in}}$. By proposition 12(1), ψ is onto. Moreover, by (A3), it is injective. Hence ψ is a bijection. We then observe that, by proposition 12(2), we have $(s, u, s') \in T$ if and only if $(\psi(s), u, \psi(s')) \in \longrightarrow_{\mathfrak{enl}}$. Hence ψ is an isomorphism for $\mathfrak{ts}$ and $\mathfrak{ts}_{\mathfrak{enl}}$. □

4 Concluding Remarks

In this paper, we have completely characterised transition systems which can be generated by the elementary net systems with localities. In doing so, we followed the standard approach in which key relationships between a Petri net and its transition system are established via the notion of a region. The standard definition of regions is insufficient for the class of transition systems of ENL-systems, and we augmented it with some additional information, leading to the notion of an io-region.

In this paper, we have completely characterised transition systems which can be generated by the elementary net systems with localities. In doing so, we followed the standard approach in which key relationships between a Petri net and its transition system are established via the notion of a region. The standard definition of regions is insufficient for the class of transition systems of ENL-systems, and we augmented it with some additional information, leading to the notion of an io-region.

We defined, and showed consistency of, two behaviour preserving translations between ENL-systems and their transition systems. As a result, we provided a solution to the synthesis problem of ENL-systems, which consists in constructing an ENL-system for a given transition system in such a way that the transition system of the former is isomorphic to the latter.

The previous work which appears to be closest to what has been proposed in this paper is due to Badouel and Darondeau [3]. It discusses the notion of a step transition system (generalising that introduced by Mukund [11]), which provides much more general a framework than the basic Elementary Net Systems; in particular, by dropping the assumption that a transition system should exhibit the so-called *intermediate state property*:

$$s \xrightarrow{\alpha+\beta} s' \;\Rightarrow\; \exists s'' : s \xrightarrow{\alpha} s'' \xrightarrow{\beta} s' \,.$$

This clearly is a characteristic shared by the class of the ENL-transition systems. But the step transition systems of [3] still exhibit what one might call a *weak intermediate state property* (or *subset property*):

$$s \xrightarrow{\alpha+\beta} s' \;\Rightarrow\; \exists s'' : s \xrightarrow{\alpha} s'' \,.$$

However, this is a key property which is *not satisfied* by the ENL-transition systems. We feel that it is an important question to find out whether or to what extent the theory of Badouel and Darondeau [3] could be adopted to work for the ENL-transition systems and their extensions.

Future Work. We expect that the notion of an io-region may be used to characterise transition systems of other extensions of EN-systems, as well as non-safe Petri nets (after suitable adaptations, of course). We now briefly outline some initial thoughts, which all boil down to suitable modifications of the last two axioms, (A4) and (A5).

Let us consider EN-systems with maximal concurrency semantics. In this case we do not consider localities, but only assume that all enabled steps are chosen according to the maximal concurrency paradigm.

A4a Let $s \in S$ and $u \in \mathbb{U}_{\mathfrak{ts}}$ be such that $^\circ u \subseteq \mathfrak{R}_s$ and $u^\circ \cap \mathfrak{R}_s = \varnothing$, and there is no $u \uplus \{e\} \in \mathbb{U}_{\mathfrak{ts}}$ satisfying $^\circ e \subseteq \mathfrak{R}_s$ and $e^\circ \cap \mathfrak{R}_s = \varnothing$. Then $s \xrightarrow{u}$.

A5a If $s \xrightarrow{u}$ then there is no $u \uplus \{e\} \in \mathbb{U}_{\mathfrak{ts}}$ satisfying $^\circ e \subseteq \mathfrak{R}_s$ and $e^\circ \cap \mathfrak{R}_s = \varnothing$.

As a second example, we consider EN-systems with what might be thought of as 'constrained parallelism'. Again, in this case we do not consider localities, but rather assume that no enabled step can comprise less than m events and more than $n \in \mathbb{N} \cup \{\infty\}$ events, where $0 < m < n \leq \infty$. (When $m = 0$, this roughly corresponds to assuming that the system is run on n processors.)

A4b Let $s \in S$ and $u \in \mathbb{U}_{\mathfrak{ts}}$ be such that $^\circ u \subseteq \mathfrak{R}_s$ and $u^\circ \cap \mathfrak{R}_s = \varnothing$ and $m \leq |u| \leq n$. Then $s \xrightarrow{u}$.

A5b If $s \xrightarrow{u}$ then $m \leq |u| \leq n$.

As a third example, we consider EN-systems where there are two kinds of events, $\mathcal{E}_s$ and $\mathcal{E}_h$, modelling respectively software and hardware actions. It is also assumed that the occurrence of each software event $e \in \mathcal{E}_s$ is supported by one of the hardware events of a pre-defined set $supp_e \subseteq \mathcal{E}_h$.

A4c Let $s \in S$ and $u \in \mathbb{U}_{\mathfrak{ts}}$ be such that $^\circ u \subseteq \mathfrak{R}_s$ and $u^\circ \cap \mathfrak{R}_s = \varnothing$ and, for every $e \in u \cap \mathcal{E}_s$, it is the case that $u \cap supp_e \neq \varnothing$. Then $s \xrightarrow{u}$.

A5c If $s \xrightarrow{u}$ then, for every $e \in u \cap \mathcal{E}_s$, it is the case that $u \cap supp_e \neq \varnothing$.

Finally, without going into technical details, we feel that if the enabling relation for a class of EN-systems' extensions can be expressed by a formula which refers to pre-sets and post-set of steps, possibly using quantifiers without referring to specific conditions, then one can derive a suitable modification of the axioms (A4) and (A5) by suitably replacing references to pre- and post-sets by the corresponding references to pre- and post-io-regions.

Acknowledgment. We would like to thank the referees for their comments and suggestions. This research was supported by the EPSRC project CASINO.

References

1. Arnold, A.: Finite Transition Systems. Prentice Hall International (1994)
2. Badouel, E., Bernardinello, L., Darondeau, Ph.: The Synthesis Problem for Elementary Net Systems is NP-complete. Theoretical Computer Science **186** (1997) 107–134
3. Badouel, E., Darondeau, Ph.: Theory of Regions. In: Reisig, W., Rozenberg, G. (eds.): Lectures on Petri Nets I: Basic Models, Advances in Petri Nets. Lecture Notes in Computer Science, Vol. 1491. Springer-Verlag, Berlin Heidelberg New York (1998) 529–586
4. Bernardinello, L., De Michelis, G., Petruni, K., Vigna, S.: On the Synchronic Structure of Transition Systems. In: Desel, J. (ed.): Structures in Concurrency Theory. Berlin 1995, Workshops in Computing. Springer-Verlag, Berlin Heidelberg New York (1995) 69–84
5. Busi, N., Pinna, G.M.: Synthesis of Nets with Inhibitor Arcs. In: Mazurkiewicz, A., Winkowski, J. (eds.): CONCUR 1997. Lecture Notes in Computer Science, Vol. 1243. Springer-Verlag, Berlin Heidelberg New York (1997) 151–165
6. Dasgupta, S., Potop-Butucaru, D., Caillaud, B., Yakovlev, A.: Moving from Weakly Endochronous Systems to Delay-Insensitive Circuits. Electronic Notes in Theoretical Computer Science **146** (2006) 81–103
7. Ehrenfeucht, A., Rozenberg, G.: Partial 2-structures; Part I: Basic Notions and the Representation Problem, and Part II: State Spaces of Concurrent Systems. Acta Informatica **27** (1990) 315–368
8. Keller, R.M.: Formal Verification of Parallel Programs. CACM **19** (1976) 371–389
9. Kleijn, H.C.M., Koutny, M., Rozenberg, G.: Towards a Petri Net Semantics for Membrane Systems. In: Freund, R., Paun, G., Rozenberg, G., Salomaa, A. (eds.): WMC 2005. Lecture Notes in Computer Science, Vol. 3850. Springer-Verlag, Berlin Heidelberg New York (2006) 292–309
10. Montanari, U., Rossi, F.: Contextual Nets. Acta Informatica **32** (1995) 545–596
11. Mukund, M.: Petri Nets and Step Transition Systems. International Journal of Foundations of Computer Science **3** (1992) 443–478
12. Nielsen, M., Rozenberg, G., Thiagarajan, P.S.: Elementary Transition Systems. Theoretical Computer Science **96** (1992) 3–33
13. Păun, G.: Membrane Computing, An Introduction. Springer-Verlag, Berlin Heidelberg New York (2002)
14. Pietkiewicz-Koutny, M.: The Synthesis Problem for Elementary Net Systems with Inhibitor Arcs. Fundamenta Informaticae **40** (1999) 251–283
15. Pietkiewicz-Koutny, M.: Synthesising Elementary Net Systems with Inhibitor Arcs from Step Transition Systems. Fundamenta Informaticae **50** (2002) 175–203
16. Winskel, G., Nielsen, M.: Models for Concurrency. In: Abramsky, S., Gabbay D.M., Maibaum, T.S.E. (eds.): Handbook of Logic in Computer Science **4** (1995) 1–148

Operational Determinism and Fast Algorithms

Henri Hansen and Antti Valmari

Tampere University of Technology, Institute of Software Systems
PO Box 553, FI-33101 Tampere, Finland
{henri.hansen, antti.valmari}@tut.fi

Abstract. The main contribution of this work is a fast algorithm for checking whether a labelled transition system (LTS) is *operationally deterministic*. Operational determinism is a condition on the LTS designed to capture the notion of "deterministic behaviour" without ruling out invisible actions and divergence, and without strictly devoting oneself to any single process-algebraic semantics. Indeed, we show that in the case of operationally deterministic LTSs, all divergence-sensitive equivalences between divergence-sensitive branching bisimilarity and trace + divergence trace equivalence collapse to the same equivalence. The running time of the algorithm is linear except a term that, roughly speaking, grows as slowly as Ackermann's function grows quickly. If the original LTS is operationally deterministic, the algorithm produces as a by-product a structurally deterministic LTS that is divergence-sensitive branching bisimilar to the original one. This LTS can be minimised like a deterministic finite automaton. The overall approach is so cheap that it makes almost always sense to first try it and revert to a semantics-specific reduction or minimisation algorithm only if the LTS proves operationally nondeterministic.

1 Introduction

In the theory of finite automata, "deterministic" means that there are no invisible transitions, and for each state and symbol, there is at most one transition from that state labelled with that symbol. The definition implies that if a sequence of visible symbols leads to any state at all, it leads to a unique state. We will call this and similar notions *structural* determinism.

Structural determinism is usually too restrictive in the context of concurrent systems. Therefore, notions of determinism have been suggested that are based on observable aspects of the behaviour of the system. In CSP, "deterministic" means that there are no divergences, and it is not possible to both execute and refuse the same action after the same trace [8, Section 3.3]. A similar definition that ignores divergences instead of ruling them out was presented in [12]. In our terminology, these are examples of *operational* determinism.

The implications of operational determinism resemble those of *determinacy*, which requires that after different executions of the same trace, the system behaves in an equivalent manner. When divergences are ignored, determinacy is

C. Baier and H. Hermanns (Eds.): CONCUR 2006, LNCS 4137, pp. 188–202, 2006.

known to be largely independent of the equivalence and it collapses a significant part of the linear time–branching time spectrum [5].

An algorithm for checking whether a system is operationally deterministic is useful in security analysis, for instance [7,9,13]. Furthermore, as we will show in this paper, if a labelled transition system (LTS) happens to be operationally deterministic, then it can be minimised very cheaply.

The contribution of this paper is twofold. First, to promote generality, we introduce a notion of operational determinism that neither forbids nor ignores divergences, and prove that it collapses the divergence-sensitive part of the linear time–branching time spectrum. Second, we present an efficient algorithm for deciding whether an LTS is operationally deterministic. In the positive case, the algorithm can be used to return a structurally deterministic LTS that is divergence-sensitively branching bisimilar with the original one. The algorithm is applicable, with minimal adjustments, to divergence-banning and divergence-ignoring determinism.

Section 2 presents the background definitions. Our notions of structural and operational determinism are introduced and investigated in Section 3. In Section 4 we present our algorithm for deciding the operational determinism of LTSs. The correctness and efficiency of the algorithm are proven. Section 5 adds to the algorithm a back-end that produces a minimal equivalent LTS, if the input LTS is operationally deterministic.

2 Background

Definition 1. *A* labelled transition system *or an* LTS *is a 4-tuple* $(S, \Sigma, \Delta, \hat{S})$, *where*

- S *is a set of* states.
- Σ *is a set called the* alphabet. *It satisfies* $\tau \notin \Sigma$.
- $\Delta \subseteq S \times (\Sigma \cup \{\tau\}) \times S$ *is the* transition relation.
- $\hat{S} \subseteq S$ *is the set of* initial states. *We assume* $\hat{S} \neq \emptyset$.

Our definition differs from the established definition in that we allow for multiple initial states. This is not an important detail. We have found the need for it when modelling systems with uninitialised variables. The results in this paper can be applied to the standard LTSs simply by using singleton sets of initial states.

Let $a \in \Sigma$, $u \in \Sigma \cup \{\tau\}$, and $\alpha = a_1 a_2 \cdots a_n \in \Sigma^*$. We define the following:

- $s -u\rightarrow s'$, meaning $(s, u, s') \in \Delta$.
- $s -u\rightarrow$ means $\exists s' : s -u\rightarrow s'$.
- $s =\varepsilon\Rightarrow s'$, when for some n, $\exists s_0, s_1, \ldots, s_n : s = s_0 -\tau\rightarrow s_1 -\tau\rightarrow \cdots -\tau\rightarrow s_n = s'$.
- $s =a\Rightarrow s'$, when $\exists s_1, s_2 : s =\varepsilon\Rightarrow s_1 -a\rightarrow s_2 =\varepsilon\Rightarrow s'$.
- $s =\alpha\Rightarrow s'$ means $\exists s_0, \ldots, s_n : s = s_0 =a_1\Rightarrow \cdots =a_n\Rightarrow s_n = s'$.
- $s =\alpha\Rightarrow$ means $\exists s' : s =\alpha\Rightarrow s'$.
- $s -\tau^\omega\rightarrow$ means that there is an infinite sequence $s_1 s_2 \cdots$ of states such that $s = s_1 -\tau\rightarrow s_2 -\tau\rightarrow \cdots$.

Definition 2. *The* reachable part *of an LTS* $(S, \Sigma, \Delta, \hat{S})$ *is the LTS* $(S', \Sigma, \Delta', \hat{S})$, *where*

- $S' = \{ s \in S \mid \exists \sigma \in \Sigma^* : \exists \hat{s} \in \hat{S} : \hat{s} =\sigma\Rightarrow s \}$, *and*
- $\Delta' = \Delta \cap (S' \times (\Sigma \cup \{\tau\}) \times S')$.

Definition 3. *Let* $L_1 = (S_1, \Sigma_1, \Delta_1, \hat{S}_1)$ *and* $L_2 = (S_2, \Sigma_2, \Delta_2, \hat{S}_2)$. *The* parallel composition *of* L_1 *and* L_2, *denoted by* $L_1 \,||\, L_2$ *is the reachable part of the LTS* $(S, \Sigma, \Delta, \hat{S})$, *where:*

- $S = S_1 \times S_2$,
- $\Sigma = \Sigma_1 \cup \Sigma_2$,
- $\Delta = \{ ((s_1, s_2), u, (s_1', s_2')) \mid u \in \Sigma_1 \cap \Sigma_2 \wedge (s_1, u, s_1') \in \Delta_1 \wedge (s_2, u, s_2') \in \Delta_2$
  $\vee\; u \in (\Sigma_1 - \Sigma_2) \cup \{\tau\} \wedge (s_1, u, s_1') \in \Delta_1 \wedge s_2 = s_2'$
  $\vee\; u \in (\Sigma_2 - \Sigma_1) \cup \{\tau\} \wedge (s_2, u, s_2') \in \Delta_2 \wedge s_1 = s_1' \}$, *and*
- $\hat{S} = \hat{S}_1 \times \hat{S}_2$.

Definition 4. *Let* $L = (S, \Sigma, \Delta, \hat{S})$ *be an LTS. We define the following:*

- $\Sigma(L) = \Sigma$.
- $\{ \sigma \in \Sigma^* \mid \exists \hat{s} \in \hat{S} : \hat{s} =\sigma\Rightarrow \}$ *is the set of* traces *of* L, *denoted by* $\mathsf{Tr}(L)$.
- $\{ \sigma \in \Sigma^* \mid \exists \hat{s} \in \hat{S} : \exists s \in S : \hat{s} =\sigma\Rightarrow s -\tau^\omega\rightarrow \}$ *is the set of* divergence traces *of* L, *denoted by* $\mathsf{Divtr}(L)$.
- $\{ (\sigma, A) \in \Sigma^* \times 2^\Sigma \mid \exists \hat{s} \in \hat{S} : \exists s \in S : \hat{s} =\sigma\Rightarrow s \wedge \forall u \in A \cup \{\tau\} : \neg(s -u\rightarrow) \}$ *is the set of* stable failures *of* L, *which we denote by* $\mathsf{Sfail}(L)$.

We will need three different notions of bisimilarity. Branching bisimilarity [11] is defined in the usual way (except for multiple initial states). D-bisimilarity is a divergence-sensitive variant of weak bisimilarity presented in [4]. Δ-branching bisimilarity adds divergence-sensitivity to branching bisimilarity the same way as in [10,11]. It is motivated after the definition.

Definition 5. *Let* $L_1 = (S_1, \Sigma, \Delta_1, \hat{S}_1)$ *and* $L_2 = (S_2, \Sigma, \Delta_2, \hat{S}_2)$ *be LTSs, and* "$\rightleftharpoons$" $\subseteq S_1 \times S_2$.

- *We say that* $\rightleftharpoons$ *is a* branching bisimulation *if and only if the following hold:*
  1. *Whenever* $r \rightleftharpoons s$, $u \in \Sigma \cup \{\tau\}$, $r' \in S_1$, *and* $r -u\rightarrow r'$, *then*
     $(\dagger_1)$ $u = \tau \wedge r' \rightleftharpoons s$ *or* $\exists s', s'' : s =\varepsilon\Rightarrow s' -u\rightarrow s'' \wedge r \rightleftharpoons s' \wedge r' \rightleftharpoons s''$.
  2. *Whenever* $r \rightleftharpoons s$, $u \in \Sigma \cup \{\tau\}$, $s' \in S_2$, *and* $s -u\rightarrow s'$, *then*
     $(\ddagger_1)$ $u = \tau \wedge r \rightleftharpoons s'$ *or* $\exists r', r'' : r =\varepsilon\Rightarrow r' -u\rightarrow r'' \wedge r' \rightleftharpoons s \wedge r'' \rightleftharpoons s'$.

  L_1 *and* L_2 *are* branching bisimilar, *denoted* $L_1 \cong_{\mathsf{SB}} L_2$ *if and only if there is a branching bisimulation* "$\rightleftharpoons$" *such that* $\forall \hat{s}_1 \in \hat{S}_1 : \exists \hat{s}_2 \in \hat{S}_2 : \hat{s}_1 \rightleftharpoons \hat{s}_2$ *and* $\forall \hat{s}_2 \in \hat{S}_2 : \exists \hat{s}_1 \in \hat{S}_1 : \hat{s}_1 \rightleftharpoons \hat{s}_2$.
- D-bisimulation *and* D-bisimilarity $\cong_{\mathsf{DB}}$ *are defined similarly, with* $(\dagger_1)$ *and* $(\ddagger_1)$ *replaced by*
  $(\dagger_2)$ $\exists s' : r' \rightleftharpoons s' \wedge (u = \tau \wedge s =\varepsilon\Rightarrow s' \vee u \neq \tau \wedge s =u\Rightarrow s')$ *and*
  $(\ddagger_2)$ $\exists r' : r' \rightleftharpoons s' \wedge (u = \tau \wedge r =\varepsilon\Rightarrow r' \vee u \neq \tau \wedge r =u\Rightarrow r')$,
  and additionally requiring $r -\tau^\omega\rightarrow \;\Leftrightarrow\; s -\tau^\omega\rightarrow$ *whenever* $r \rightleftharpoons s$.

– *Δ-branching bisimulation and Δ-branching bisimilarity $\cong_{\mathsf{BB}^\Delta}$ are obtained by adding the following requirement to the definition of branching bisimilarity:*
  - *whenever $r_0 -\tau\rightarrow r_1 -\tau\rightarrow \ldots$ and $\forall i : r_i \rightleftharpoons s_0$, there are $s_1, s_2, \ldots$ such that $s_0 -\tau\rightarrow s_1 -\tau\rightarrow \ldots$ and $\forall i : \forall j : r_i \rightleftharpoons s_j$, and*
  - *whenever $s_0 -\tau\rightarrow s_1 -\tau\rightarrow \ldots$ and $\forall i : r_0 \rightleftharpoons s_i$, there are $r_1, r_2, \ldots$ such that $r_0 -\tau\rightarrow r_1 -\tau\rightarrow \ldots$ and $\forall i : \forall j : r_i \rightleftharpoons s_j$.*

Δ-branching bisimilarity can be found in [10]. An equivalent notion is defined in [11], where it was called *branching bisimulation with explicit divergence*. Another, not equivalent definition, with a subtle difference in the handling of deadlocks, was presented in [3]. Yet another definition with a different meaning was given in [4]. The condition on divergences that defines Δ-branching bisimilarity may seem complicated, but in all our proofs we show that the following stronger condition holds: whenever $r_0 -\tau\rightarrow r_1 -\tau\rightarrow \ldots$ and $r_0 \rightleftharpoons s_0$, there are s_1, s_2, $\ldots$ such that $s_0 -\tau\rightarrow s_1 -\tau\rightarrow \ldots$ and $\forall i : \forall j : r_i \rightleftharpoons s_j$, and symmetrically for $s_0 -\tau\rightarrow^\omega$.

3 Structural and Operational Determinism

By "structural" determinism we refer to the property that each trace always leads to the *same* (not just equivalently behaving) state. The classical notion of (structural) determinism forbids invisible actions altogether. To make our theory useful also in the presence of divergences, we generalise a bit by allowing local τ-loops in our notion of structural determinism.

Definition 6. *An LTS $(S, \Sigma, \Delta, \hat{S})$ is* structurally deterministic *if and only if*

1. *$|\hat{S}| = 1$,*
2. *$\forall s, s' : (s -\tau\rightarrow s' \Rightarrow s = s')$, and*
3. *$\forall s, s_1, s_2, a : (s -a\rightarrow s_1 \wedge s -a\rightarrow s_2 \Rightarrow s_1 = s_2)$.*

To relax the rather strong structural requirements imposed by structural determinism, we define operational determinism so that only the observable behaviour the system can exhibit is fully determined by the trace observed so far.

Definition 7. *We say that an LTS L is* operationally deterministic *if and only if for any two states s_1 and s_2 such that there are initial states $\hat{s}_1$ and $\hat{s}_2$ and a trace σ such that $\hat{s}_1 =\sigma\Rightarrow s_1$ and $\hat{s}_2 =\sigma\Rightarrow s_2$, the following hold:*

1. *$\forall a \in \Sigma(L) : (s_1 =a\Rightarrow \;\Rightarrow s_2 =a\Rightarrow)$, and*
2. *$s_1 -\tau^\omega\rightarrow \;\Rightarrow s_2 -\tau^\omega\rightarrow$.*

In other words, if σa is a trace of L, then after executing σ, it is always possible to continue with a. Also, if σ is a divergence trace, then *all* executions of σ lead to a divergence. Operational determinism, like determinism in CSP [8, Section 3.3]: $(\mathsf{Divtr}(L) = \emptyset \wedge \forall \sigma, a : \sigma a \in \mathsf{Tr}(L) \Rightarrow (\sigma, \{a\}) \notin \mathsf{Sfail}(L))$, is preserved under action prefixing, alphabet-based parallel composition and one-to-one renaming. The proof for parallel composition is given towards the end of this section.

In [5] it is proven that *determinacy*, which is actually our operational determinism with divergences ignored, has the following characteristic: If we restrict ourselves to determinate systems, all equivalences in the branching time–linear time spectrum that are between trace equivalence and weak bisimulation are the same equivalence. A stronger result is actually true; the divergence-ignoring part of the spectrum collapses all the way to branching bisimulation. This is noted in [12].

We will prove soon (Theorem 3) that a similar collapse takes place when divergences are taken into account, if our notion of operational determinism is used, branching bisimilarity is replaced by Δ-branching bisimilarity, and trace equivalence is amplified by divergence traces. However, before attacking this more complicated result, we observe that an LTS is CSP-deterministic if and only if it is operationally deterministic and has no divergences.

Theorem 1. *If* L *is operationally deterministic, then* $\mathsf{Sfail}(L) =$
$$\{ (\sigma, A) \mid \sigma \in \mathsf{Tr}(L) - \mathsf{Divtr}(L) \wedge A \subseteq \Sigma(L) \wedge \forall a \in A : \sigma a \notin \mathsf{Tr}(L) \}.$$

Proof. If $(\sigma, A) \in \mathsf{Sfail}(L)$, then there are $\hat{s} \in \hat{S}$ and s such that $\hat{s} =\sigma\Rightarrow s$ and $\neg(s -\tau\rightarrow)$. Definition 7(2) implies that $\sigma \notin \mathsf{Divtr}(L)$. Furthermore, if $a \in A$, then $\neg(s -a\rightarrow)$, from which Definition 7(1) yields $\sigma a \notin \mathsf{Tr}(L)$. If (σ, A) belongs to the set on the right hand side, then, by executing σ and then taking as many τ-transitions as possible, a state s is reached such that $\forall u \in A \cup \{\tau\} : \neg(s - u \rightarrow)$. Taking τ-transitions terminates because $\sigma \notin \mathsf{Divtr}(L)$. So $(\sigma, A) \in \mathsf{Sfail}(L)$. □

The converse of this result does not hold. More generally, the following LTSs demonstrate that our operational determinism cannot be characterised in terms of $\Sigma(L)$, $\mathsf{Tr}(L)$, $\mathsf{Divtr}(L)$, and $\mathsf{Sfail}(L)$: 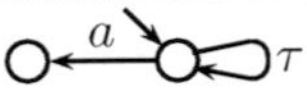 and 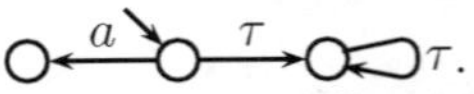. One of them is deterministic and the other is not, but they do not differ in terms of the given sets.

Most of the rest of this paper is based on an auxiliary notion of D-relation.

Definition 8. *Let* $(S, \Sigma, \Delta, \hat{S})$ *be an LTS. Let* $a \in \Sigma$ *below. We say that "*$\sim$*"* $\subseteq S \times S$ *is a* D-relation, *if and only if it is an equivalence with the following properties:*

D1 $\forall s_1, s_2, a : (s_1 \sim s_2 \wedge s_1 =a\Rightarrow \ \Rightarrow s_2 =a\Rightarrow)$
D2 $\forall s_1, s_2 : (s_1 \sim s_2 \wedge s_1 -\tau^\omega\rightarrow \ \Rightarrow s_2 -\tau^\omega\rightarrow)$
D3 $\forall s_1, s_2, s_1', s_2', a : (s_1 \sim s_2 \wedge s_1 -a\rightarrow s_1' \wedge s_2 -a\rightarrow s_2' \Rightarrow s_1' \sim s_2')$
D4 $\forall s_1, s_2 : (s_1 -\tau\rightarrow s_2 \Rightarrow s_1 \sim s_2)$
D5 $\forall \hat{s}_1, \hat{s}_2 : (\hat{s}_1 \in \hat{S} \wedge \hat{s}_2 \in \hat{S} \Rightarrow \hat{s}_1 \sim \hat{s}_2)$

Lemma 1. *An LTS is operationally deterministic if and only if its reachable part has a D-relation.*

Proof. First, suppose there is an equivalence $\sim$ on the reachable states of L that has the properties D1 to D5. Let s_1 and s_2 be states, $\sigma \in \Sigma^*$ and $\hat{s}_1 \in \hat{S}$,

$\hat{s}_2 \in \hat{S}$ such that $\hat{s}_1 = \sigma \Rightarrow s_1 \wedge \hat{s}_2 = \sigma \Rightarrow s_2$. By property D5 we write $\hat{s}_1 \sim \hat{s}_2$. By straightforward induction, relying on D3 and D4 and the fact that $\sim$ is an equivalence, also $s_1 \sim s_2$. Together with D1 and D2, this implies that L must be operationally deterministic.

Conversely, suppose that L is operationally deterministic. We define the relation "$\triangleq$" $\subseteq S \times S$ by $s_1 \triangleq s_2 \Leftrightarrow \exists \hat{s}_1, \hat{s}_2 \in \hat{S} : \exists \sigma \in \Sigma^* : \hat{s}_1 = \sigma \Rightarrow s_1 \wedge \hat{s}_2 = \sigma \Rightarrow s_2$. Furthermore, we define the relation $\doteqdot$ as the transitive closure of $\triangleq$. We are going to show that $\doteqdot$ is a D-relation over the reachable part of L. It is clearly symmetric, transitive and reflexive over the states of the reachable part, that is, it is an equivalence. Since L is operationally deterministic, $\triangleq$ must satisfy D1 and D2, and by transitivity, so must $\doteqdot$.

To see that $\doteqdot$ satisfies D3, suppose that $s_1 \doteqdot s_2$ and that $s_1 - a \rightarrow s_1' \wedge s_2 - a \rightarrow s_2'$. We observe that $s_1 \doteqdot s_2 \Leftrightarrow \exists z_0, z_1, \ldots, z_n : z_0 = s_1 \wedge z_n = s_2 \wedge \forall i; 1 \leq i \leq n : z_{i-1} \triangleq z_i$. By D1, the states $z_1, \ldots, z_{n-1}$ all have $z_i = a \Rightarrow z_i'$ for some z_i'. Furthermore, by the definition of $\triangleq$ we have $s_1' \triangleq z_1'$, $z_{i-1}' \triangleq z_i'$, and $z_{n-1}' \triangleq s_2'$. Thus, by transitivity, $s_1' \doteqdot s_2'$, which proves D3.

D4 is obvious from the definition of $\triangleq$, and D5 follows by choosing $\sigma = \varepsilon$ as the trace in the definition of $\triangleq$. □

D-relations make it possible to show that for each operationally deterministic LTS, there is a structurally deterministic Δ-branching bisimilar LTS.

Definition 9. *Let $(S, \Sigma, \Delta, \hat{S})$ be the reachable part of an operationally deterministic LTS, and $\sim$ a D-relation on it. Its* quotient LTS *is $(S', \Sigma, \Delta', \hat{S}')$, where*

- *If $s \in S$, then $[[s]] = \{ s' \in S \mid s \sim s' \}$.*
- $S' = \{ [[s]] \mid s \in S \}$,
- $\Delta' = \{ ([[s]], a, [[s']]) \mid (s, a, s') \in \Delta \wedge a \in \Sigma \} \cup$
  $\{ ([[s]], \tau, [[s]]) \mid s \in S \wedge s - \tau^\omega \rightarrow \}$, *and*
- $\hat{S}' = \{ [[\hat{s}]] \mid \hat{s} \in \hat{S} \}$.

Because there may be many D-relations, the quotient LTS is not necessarily unique.

Theorem 2. *A quotient LTS is structurally deterministic, and Δ-branching bisimilar to the original LTS.*

Proof. D5 implies item 1 of Definition 6. Item 2 follows immediately from the definition of Δ', and D3 yields item 3.

We now prove that the relation "$\rightleftharpoons$" $\subseteq S \times S'$ defined by $r \rightleftharpoons s \Leftrightarrow s = [[r]]$ is a Δ-branching bisimulation. Let $r \rightleftharpoons s$. If $r - \tau \rightarrow r'$ then $[[r']] = [[r]]$ by D4, so $r' \rightleftharpoons s$. If $s - \tau \rightarrow s'$ then $s' = s$, so $r \rightleftharpoons s'$. If $r - a \rightarrow r'$ where $a \neq \tau$, then $s = [[r]] - a \rightarrow [[r']]$, so s qualifies as the s' and $[[r']]$ qualifies as the s'' in $\dagger_1$. Let $s - a \rightarrow s'$ where $a \neq \tau$. By the construction, there are some x and $x' \in S$ such that $x - a \rightarrow x'$, $s = [[x]]$ and $s' = [[x']]$. Because $s = [[r]]$, we get $x \sim r$. D1 implies that there are r' and r'' such that $r = \varepsilon \Rightarrow r' - a \rightarrow r''$. D4 implies that $r \sim r'$, so $[[r']] = [[r]] = s$ and $r' \rightleftharpoons s$. Because $x \sim r \sim r'$, D3 gives $x' \sim r''$. So $[[r'']] = [[x']] = s'$ and $r'' \rightleftharpoons s'$, and $\ddagger_1$ holds.

By the construction of $\hat{S}'$, "$\rightleftharpoons$" obviously satisfies the condition on initial states in Definition 5.

If $r_0 -\tau\rightarrow r_1 -\tau\rightarrow \ldots$ and $r_0 \rightleftharpoons s_0$, then $s_0 = [[r_0]] = [[r_1]] = \ldots$ by D4. Furthermore, the definition of Δ' yields $s_0 -\tau\rightarrow s_0$. So we may choose $s_0 = s_1 = s_2 = \ldots$ to get $s_0 -\tau\rightarrow s_1 -\tau\rightarrow \ldots$ and $\forall i : \forall j : r_i \rightleftharpoons s_j$. Let $s_0 -\tau\rightarrow s_1 -\tau\rightarrow \ldots$ and $r_0 \rightleftharpoons s_0$. By the construction, $s_0 = s_1 = s_2 = \ldots$, and there is $x \in [[r_0]]$ such that $x -\tau^\omega\rightarrow$. By D2, also $r_0 -\tau^\omega\rightarrow$, that is, there are $r_1, r_2, \ldots$ such that $r_0 -\tau\rightarrow r_1 -\tau\rightarrow \ldots$. D4 gives $[[r_0]] = [[r_1]] = [[r_2]] = \ldots$, so $\forall i : \forall j : r_i \rightleftharpoons s_j$. □

Theorem 3. *Let L_1 and L_2 be operationally deterministic LTSs with $\Sigma(L_1) = \Sigma(L_2)$, $\mathsf{Tr}(L_1) = \mathsf{Tr}(L_2)$, and $\mathsf{Divtr}(L_1) = \mathsf{Divtr}(L_2)$. Then $L_1 \cong_{\mathsf{BB}^\Delta} L_2$.*

Proof. Let "$\sim$" $\subseteq S_1 \times S_2$ such that $s_1 \sim s_2 \Leftrightarrow \exists \hat{s}_1 \in \hat{S}_1 : \exists \hat{s}_2 \in \hat{S}_2 : \exists \sigma \in \Sigma^* : \hat{s}_1 =\sigma\Rightarrow s_1 \wedge \hat{s}_2 =\sigma\Rightarrow s_2$. We show that "$\sim$" is a Δ-branching bisimulation.

By definition, it is clear that $\forall \hat{s}_1 \in \hat{S}_1 : \forall \hat{s}_2 \in \hat{S}_2 : \hat{s}_1 \sim \hat{s}_2$, by considering $\varepsilon = \sigma$ as the common trace in the definition of "$\sim$".

Let $s_1 \sim s_2$ and σ be the common trace, starting from initial states $\hat{s}_1$ and $\hat{s}_2$, respectively.

1. Let $s_1 -\tau\rightarrow s_1'$. Since $\hat{s}_1 =\sigma\Rightarrow s_1$ implies $\hat{s}_1 =\sigma\Rightarrow s_1'$, we have $s_1' \sim s_2$.
2. Let $s_1 -a\rightarrow s_1'$. Then $\hat{s}_1 =\sigma\Rightarrow s_1$ implies $\hat{s}_1 =\sigma a\Rightarrow s_1'$. By trace equivalence, $\hat{s}_2 =\sigma a\Rightarrow$ and by operational determinism $s_2 =\varepsilon\Rightarrow s_2'' -a\rightarrow s_2'$, for some s_2', s_2''. By definition of "$\sim$", $s_1 \sim s_2''$ and $s_1' \sim s_2'$.
3. Let $s_1 -\tau\rightarrow s_1^{(1)} -\tau\rightarrow \cdots$. Because $\mathsf{Divtr}(L_1) = \mathsf{Divtr}(L_2)$, $\hat{s}_2' =\sigma\Rightarrow s_2' -\tau^\omega\rightarrow$ for some $\hat{s}_2', s_2'$. By operational determinism then $s_2 -\tau\rightarrow s_2^{(1)} -\tau\rightarrow \cdots$. Since $\hat{s}_1 =\sigma\Rightarrow s_1^{(i)}$ and $\hat{s}_2 =\sigma\Rightarrow s_2^{(i)}$ for all i, we have $\forall i : \forall j : s_1^{(j)} \sim s_2^{(i)}$.

($\ddagger_1$) and the symmetric case for divergence are proven analogously. □

Theorem 4. *Let L be a structurally deterministic LTS and let L' be D-bisimilar to L. Then L' is operationally deterministic.*

Proof. Let $L' = (S', \Sigma, \Delta', \hat{S}')$ such that $L' \cong_{\mathsf{DB}} L$. Let $\hat{s}$ be the unique initial state of L, and let $\rightleftharpoons$ be a D-bisimulation such that $\forall \hat{s}' \in \hat{S}' : \hat{s}' \rightleftharpoons \hat{s}$.

Let $\sigma \in \Sigma^*$, $\hat{s}_1', \hat{s}_2' \in \hat{S}'$ and $r_1, r_2 \in S'$ such that $\hat{s}_1' =\sigma\Rightarrow r_1 \wedge \hat{s}_2' =\sigma\Rightarrow r_2$. By letting L simulate according to $\dagger_2$ the executions of σ that lead to r_1 and r_2, such s_1 and s_2 are found that $r_1 \rightleftharpoons s_1$ and $r_2 \rightleftharpoons s_2$. However, $s_1 = s_2$ because L is structurally deterministic. If $r_1 =a\Rightarrow$, then by $\dagger_2$ $s_1 =a\Rightarrow$, and by $\ddagger_2$ $r_2 =a\Rightarrow$. By the last requirement of D-bisimulation, $r_1 -\tau^\omega\rightarrow \Leftrightarrow s_1 -\tau^\omega\rightarrow \Leftrightarrow r_2 -\tau^\omega\rightarrow$. Therefore, L' is operationally deterministic. □

Corollary 1. *Let $L_1 \cong_{\mathsf{DB}} L_2$. Then L_1 is operationally deterministic if and only if L_2 is operationally deterministic.*

Proof. If L_1 is operationally deterministic, then let L_1' be its quotient LTS. A Δ-branching bisimulation is also a D-bisimulation, so $L_1 \cong_{\mathsf{DB}} L_1'$. So $L_2 \cong_{\mathsf{DB}} L_1'$, from which Theorem 4 gives that L_2 is operationally deterministic. □

Lemma 2. *Let* $L_1 = (S_1, \Sigma_1, \Delta_1, \hat{S}_1)$ *and* $L_2 = (S_2, \Sigma_2, \Delta_2, \hat{S}_2)$ *be structurally deterministic LTSs. Then* $L_1 \,||\, L_2$ *is structurally deterministic.*

Proof. Let $(S, \Sigma, \Delta, \hat{S}) = L_1||L_2$. Firstly, note that $|\hat{S}| = |\hat{S}_1| \cdot |\hat{S}_2| = 1$. Secondly, let $(s, u, s') \in \Delta$ and $(s, u, s'') \in \Delta$, where $s = (s_1, s_2)$, $s' = (s'_1, s'_2)$, and $s'' = (s''_1, s''_2)$. If $u = \tau$, then, by structural determinism and the definition of $||$ we must have $s_1 = s'_1 = s''_1$ and $s_2 = s'_2 = s''_2$, and hence $s = s' = s''$. Suppose then that $u \neq \tau$. If $u \in \Sigma_1$ we have $(s_1, u, s'_1) \in \Delta_1$ and $(s_1, u, s''_1) \in \Delta_1$, so $s'_1 = s''_1$ by structural determinism. Otherwise, $s'_1 = s_1$ and $s''_1 = s_1$. So, in both cases $s'_1 = s''_1$. Similarly $s'_2 = s''_2$. Therefore, $s' = s''$. □

Theorem 5. *Let* L_1 *and* L_2 *be operationally deterministic LTSs. Then* $L_1 \,||\, L_2$ *is operationally deterministic.*

Proof. Let L'_1 and L'_2 be quotient LTSs of L_1 and L_2. By Theorem 2 and Lemma 2, $L'_1 \,||\, L'_2$ is structurally deterministic. Because D-bisimilarity is implied by Δ-branching bisimilarity and is a congruence with respect to $||$ [4], $L_1 \,||\, L_2 \cong_{\mathsf{DB}} L'_1 \,||\, L'_2$. Therefore, Theorem 4 gives the claim. □

4 Fast Checking of Operational Determinism

In this section we introduce a simple yet efficient algorithm for checking whether an LTS $(S, \Sigma, \Delta, \hat{S})$ is operationally deterministic. Throughout this section we use a convention that $s_1, s_2, \ldots \in S$ and $a \in \Sigma$. Some concepts and notation need to be defined, along with a brief discussion on implementation details.

We use a disjoint set structure presented in data structure textbooks [2, Chapter 21]. It is a simple way of maintaining a collection of disjoint sets featuring the operations of creating a singleton set, taking a union of two sets, and testing whether two elements belong to the same set.

Each element is stored in a record that also has a pointer field. In each set, one member, the *representative*, has a pointer to itself, while others have a pointer to another element in the same set so that following the chain of pointers eventually leads to the representative. Whether or not two elements belong to the same set is tested by finding their representatives and checking whether they are the same. Union is computed by re-directing the pointer of one representative to point to the other.

Two heuristics are used to speed up processing. First, each time a chain of pointers is followed, all pointers along the chain are re-directed to point directly to the representative. Second, a *rank*, an upper approximation of the length of the longest chain, is maintained in each set. When taking the union of two sets with different ranks, the representative of the set with the greater rank is chosen as the representative of the union. The rank is initially zero, and incremented when computing the union of two sets of equal rank.

If a total of m operations are performed, of which n are singleton-set creations, the total time consumption is $O(m\alpha(n))$, where α is a very slowly growing function, practically a constant [2].

We denote by $\textsc{Rep}(s)$ the representative of s. The definition of representative implies that $\textsc{Rep}(\textsc{Rep}(s)) = \textsc{Rep}(s)$. $\textsc{Union}(s_1, s_2)$ takes the sets which s_1 and s_2 are members of and transforms them into a single set. Instead of using the operation that creates a singleton set, we use $\textsc{InitRep}(s_1, s_2)$ that makes the pointer of s_1 point to s_2. We will use it in such a way that the result is equivalent to first making each s a singleton set and then calling the union operation less than $|S|$ times, choosing the representative in a certain way whenever the two ranks are equivalent. Therefore, the n in the total time consumption formula will be the number of states in the LTS.

The algorithm is shown in Figure 2. The LTS must be preprocessed in what we shall call stage 0. All strongly connected components consisting of τ-transitions are collapsed into single states. As a result of the operation τ-COLLAPSE, an LTS $(S, \Sigma, \Delta, \hat{S})$ is replaced by $(S', \Sigma, \Delta', \hat{S}')$, where

- $S' = \{ [[s]] \mid s \in S \}$, where $[[s]] = \{ s' \mid s =\varepsilon\Rightarrow s' \wedge s' =\varepsilon\Rightarrow s \}$,
- $\Delta' = \{ ([[s]], u, [[s']]) \mid u \in \Sigma \cup \{\tau\} \wedge (s, u, s') \in \Delta \}$, and
- $\hat{S}' = \{ [[\hat{s}]] \mid \hat{s} \in \hat{S} \}$.

After such an operation, we can talk about the set S_b of *bottom states*. A bottom state is a state s for which $\forall s' : (s -\tau\rightarrow s' \Rightarrow s = s')$. For each state s, there is at least one bottom state s_b such that $s =\varepsilon\Rightarrow s_b$.

For each bottom state s_b and a non-τ action a we choose a representative transition and denote by $s_b.tr[a]$ the destination state of this transition, and let $s_b.tr[a] = \textsc{Nil}$ if no such transition exists for a. Also, for any state s, bottom or otherwise, $s.div$ is used to indicate whether or not a local τ-loop is present in the state. As a consequence, $s -\tau^\omega\rightarrow$ if and only if $\exists s' : s =\varepsilon\Rightarrow s' \wedge s'.div$. One can think of "$s.div$" as a notational convention or it may be implemented, e.g., as a bit. In the latter case, local τ-loops may be removed. When we later write $s -\tau^\omega\rightarrow$ we actually mean that $\exists s' : s =\varepsilon\Rightarrow s' \wedge s'.div$.

After stage 1, each state has a representative and that representative is a bottom state. Due to the implementation of the union operation sketched earlier, this will remain true until the algorithm terminates. Each bottom state is now its own representative, but this will change later.

For the next stage we need a subroutine to check whether two states can be joined. This subroutine is shown in Figure 1. We use a set *Pending*, initially empty, to store pairs of states that need to be checked later on. $\textsc{Exit}(\textsc{Nondet})$ means that the algorithm has found that the LTS is not operationally deterministic, and terminates.

We now proceed to analyse what takes place in stages 2 and 3.

Lemma 3. *If the LTS has a D-relation* $\sim$, *then* $\textsc{Exit}(\textsc{Nondet})$ *is not called and the following invariant holds throughout the execution of stages 2 and 3: if* s_1 *and* s_2 *are states and* $\textsc{Rep}(s_1) = \textsc{Rep}(s_2) \vee (s_1, s_2) \in \textit{Pending}$, *then* $s_1 \sim s_2$.

Proof. Recall that for each s, $\textsc{Rep}(\textsc{Rep}(s)) = \textsc{Rep}(s)$, so the invariant will also imply $\textsc{Rep}(s) \sim s$.

The invariant holds initially, since *Pending* is empty, $\forall s : s =\varepsilon\Rightarrow \textsc{Rep}(s)$, and $\sim$ satisfies D4 and is an equivalence.

global variable $Pending \subseteq S^2 := \emptyset$

Check(s_1, s_2)

1     $s_1 := $ Rep(s_1); $s_2 := $ Rep(s_2)
2   **if** $s_1 = s_2$ **then return**
3   **if** $s_1.div \neq s_2.div$ **then** Exit(Nondet)
4   **for** $a \in \Sigma$ **do**
5   **if** $(s_1.tr[a] = $ Nil$)$ exclusive-or $(s_2.tr[a] = $ Nil$)$ **then** Exit(Nondet)
6   **if** $s_1.tr[a] \neq $ Nil **then** add $(s_1.tr[a], s_2.tr[a])$ to $Pending$
7   **endfor**
8   Union(s_1, s_2)

Fig. 1. State checking subroutine

stage0
9   remove unreachable states and transitions
10   τ-collapse
Stage1
11   **for** each state s **do**
12   find a bottom state s_b such that $s =\varepsilon\Rightarrow s_b$ and call InitRep(s, s_b)
13   **endfor**
Stage2
14   **for** each bottom state s_b **do**
15   **for** each transition (s_b, a, s') **do** Check$(s_b.tr[a], s')$ **endfor**
16   **endfor**
17   **for** each non-bottom state s **do**
18   **if** $s.div \wedge \neg$Rep$(s).div$ **then** Exit(Nondet)
19   **endfor**
20   **for** $a \in \Sigma$ **do**
21   **for** each $(s, a, s') \in \Delta$ such that s is a non-bottom state **do**
22   **if** Rep$(s).tr[a] = $ Nil **then** Exit(Nondet)
23   Check$($Rep$(s).tr[a], s')$
24   **endfor**
25   **endfor**
26   **for** each invisible transition (s, τ, s') **do** Check(s, s') **endfor**
27   choose $\hat{s} \in \hat{S}$
28   **for** each $\hat{s}' \in \hat{S} - \{\hat{s}\}$ **do** Check$(\hat{s}, \hat{s}')$ **endfor**
Stage3
29   **while** $Pending \neq \emptyset$ **do**
30   take any (s_1, s_2) from $Pending$
31   Check(s_1, s_2)
32   **endwhile**
33   Exit(Deterministic)

Fig. 2. Fast determinism checking

The invariant is at risk only when Rep is changed or pairs are added to *Pending*. These only happen inside Check, so we must examine each call of Check.

First we prove that if $s_1 \sim s_2$ when $\text{CHECK}(s_1, s_2)$ is called, the invariant is preserved.

We have $\text{REP}(s_1) \sim s_1 \wedge \text{REP}(s_2) \sim s_2$, which implies $\text{REP}(s_1) \sim \text{REP}(s_2)$. To avoid confusion, let z_1 and z_2 denote the variables s_1 and s_2 in the code of CHECK. $z_1 = \text{REP}(s_1) \sim z_2 = \text{REP}(s_2)$ holds after line 1. Line 3 will not cause termination, because of D2 and the fact that $z -\tau^\omega\rightarrow \Leftrightarrow z.div$ for bottom states. Similarly D1 guarantees that line 5 will not cause termination. By property D3, when the pair $(z_1.tr[a], z_2.tr[a])$ goes to *Pending* on line 6, we do have $z_1.tr[a] \sim z_2.tr[a]$. The UNION in the end cannot violate the invariant, since if it makes $\text{REP}(s_1') = \text{REP}(s_2')$ hold for some s_1' and s_2', then before the call of CHECK, $\text{REP}(s_1') = \text{REP}(s_1)$ and $\text{REP}(s_2') = \text{REP}(s_2)$ (or $\text{REP}(s_2') = \text{REP}(s_1)$ and $\text{REP}(s_1') = \text{REP}(s_2)$) held, so $s_1' \sim \text{REP}(s_1) = z_1 \sim z_2 = \text{REP}(s_2) \sim s_2'$.

We must now show that $s_1 \sim s_2$ holds every time $\text{CHECK}(s_1, s_2)$ is called.

On line 15, $\text{CHECK}(s_1, s_2)$ is called when $\exists a : \exists s_b \in S_b : s_b -a\rightarrow s_1 \wedge s_b -a\rightarrow s_2$. Because a D-relation is reflexive and D3 holds, we must have $s_1 \sim s_2$.

On line 23, $s \sim \text{REP}(s)$. We have $s -a\rightarrow s'$ and $\text{REP}(s) -a\rightarrow \text{REP}(s).tr[a]$, so, because of D3, $\text{REP}(s).tr[a] \sim s'$.

For line 26, $s \sim s'$ is guaranteed by D4. D5 takes care of line 28.

As for line 31, the invariant itself guarantees that $s_1 \sim s_2$.

Line 18 will not cause termination because of D2 and the fact that a bottom state may diverge only by having $s.div$. Similarly, the safety of line 22 is guaranteed by D1. □

Corollary 2. *If the algorithm executes* EXIT(NONDET) *then L is nondeterministic.*

Proof. Lemma 3 implies that then L has no D-relation, from which Lemma 1 gives the claim. □

To see that false positives are not produced, we need the following:

Definition 10. *Let the relation "$\frown$" $\subseteq S \times S$ be defined as follows: $s_1 \frown s_2$ if and only if $\text{REP}(s_1) = \text{REP}(s_2)$, $(s_1, s_2) \in$ Pending, or $(s_2, s_1) \in$ Pending. We denote by $\asymp$ the transitive closure of $\frown$.*

Lemma 4. *The following hold during stages 2 and 3:*

1. *The truth value of "$\text{REP}(s) -a\rightarrow$" never changes.*
2. *The truth value of "$\text{REP}(s).div$" never changes.*
3. *If $\text{REP}(s_1) = \text{REP}(s_2)$ becomes true, it holds until the algorithm terminates.*
4. *If $\text{REP}(s).tr[a] \asymp s'$ becomes true and* EXIT(NONDET) *is not executed, it holds (except inside the loop of stage 3) until the algorithm terminates.*

Proof. Claims 1 and 2 are checked before UNION is called in line 8 in CHECK. Claim 3 is obvious from the operation of the disjoint set structure. Claim 4 holds because when the REP changes, the pair consisting of the old and the new $\text{REP}(s).tr[a]$ is put into *Pending*, and $\asymp$ is transitive. □

Lemma 5. *If the algorithm does not execute* EXIT(NONDET)*, the following hold after stages 2 and 3:*

E1 $\forall s_1, s_2, a : (\text{REP}(s_1) = \text{REP}(s_2) \wedge s_1 =a\Rightarrow \Rightarrow s_2 =a\Rightarrow)$
E2 $\forall s_1, s_2 : (\text{REP}(s_1) = \text{REP}(s_2) \wedge s_1 -\tau^\omega\rightarrow \Rightarrow s_2 -\tau^\omega\rightarrow)$
E3 $\forall s_1, s_2, s_1', s_2', a : (\text{REP}(s_1) = \text{REP}(s_2) \wedge s_1 -a\rightarrow s_1' \wedge s_2 -a\rightarrow s_2' \Rightarrow s_1' \asymp s_2')$
E4 $\forall s_1, s_2 : (s_1 -\tau\rightarrow s_2 \Rightarrow \text{REP}(s_1) = \text{REP}(s_2))$
E5 $\forall \hat{s}_1, \hat{s}_2 : (\hat{s}_1 \in \hat{S} \wedge \hat{s}_2 \in \hat{S} \Rightarrow \text{REP}(\hat{s}_1) = \text{REP}(\hat{s}_2))$

Proof. E4: Since all τ-transitions are covered in line 26 this is obvious.

E5: Again, obvious due to line 28.

E1: Let $\text{REP}(s_1) = \text{REP}(s_2) \wedge s_1 =a\Rightarrow$ at the end of stage 2 or 3. By definition, we have $\exists s_1' : s_1 =\varepsilon\Rightarrow s_1' -a\rightarrow$. Because of E4 we must have $\text{REP}(s_1') = \text{REP}(s_1) = \text{REP}(s_2)$ in the end of stage 2 or 3. If $s_1' \in S_b$, then $s_1' = \text{REP}(s_1')$ and thus $\text{REP}(s_1') -a\rightarrow$ held in the beginning of stage 2. Otherwise $\text{REP}(s_1') -a\rightarrow$ held when line 22 was executed for s_1' and a, because EXIT(NONDET) was not executed. By Lemma 4(1), $\text{REP}(s_1') -a\rightarrow$ and thus $\text{REP}(s_2) -a\rightarrow$ hold at the end of stage 2 or 3. Again, using Lemma 4(1), $\text{REP}(s_2) -a\rightarrow$ held at the beginning of stage 2 or 3. Then also $s_2 =\varepsilon\Rightarrow \text{REP}(s_2)$ held. This completes our proof of E1.

E2: The reasoning is analogous to E1. Clearly $s_1 -\tau^\omega\rightarrow \Leftrightarrow \exists s_1' : s_1 =\varepsilon\Rightarrow s_1' \wedge s_1'.div$. If s_1' is not a bottom state, then $\text{REP}(s_1').div$ holds in line 18. If s_1' is a bottom state, then $\text{REP}(s_1').div$ held initially. In both cases Lemma 4(2) gives that $\text{REP}(s_1').div$ holds at the end of stage 2 or 3. E4 makes sure that then also $\text{REP}(s_1') = \text{REP}(s_1)$. So $\text{REP}(s_2).div$ holds at the end of stage 2 or 3. Thus, $\text{REP}(s_2).div$ held also at the beginning of stage 2, which proves that $s_2 -\tau^\omega\rightarrow$.

E3: Let $\text{REP}(s_1) = \text{REP}(s_2) \wedge s_1 -a\rightarrow s_1' \wedge s_2 -a\rightarrow s_2'$ hold at the end of stage 2 or 3. If s_1 is not a bottom state, $\text{REP}(s_1).tr[a] \asymp s_1'$ held immediately after line 23. Due to Lemma 4(4), $\text{REP}(s_1).tr[a] \asymp s_1'$ also holds at the end of stage 2 or 3. Proving the same when s_1 is a bottom state is more complicated. $s_1.tr[a] \asymp s_1'$ held immediately after line 15. By Lemma 4(3), it holds at the end of stage 2 or 3. On the other hand, $\text{REP}(s_1) = s_1$ and thus $\text{REP}(s_1).tr[a] \asymp s_1.tr[a]$ held at the beginning of stage 2. Lemma 4(4) carries this fact to the end of stage 2 or 3. Together these yield $\text{REP}(s_1).tr[a] \asymp s_1'$. Similar reasoning applies to s_2 and s_2'. Since we assumed that $\text{REP}(s_1) = \text{REP}(s_2)$ holds at the end of stage 2 or 3, we have $s_1' \asymp \text{REP}(s_1).tr[a] = \text{REP}(s_2).tr[a] \asymp s_2'$. □

Now, after the completion of stage 3, $Pending = \emptyset$. Therefore, $s_1' \asymp s_2' \Leftrightarrow \text{REP}(s_1') = \text{REP}(s_2')$, and E3 becomes:

E3′ $\forall s_1, s_2, s_1', s_2', a :$
$(\text{REP}(s_1) = \text{REP}(s_2) \wedge s_1 -a\rightarrow s_1' \wedge s_2 -a\rightarrow s_2' \Rightarrow \text{REP}(s_1') = \text{REP}(s_2'))$

The relation $s_1 \sim s_2 \Leftrightarrow \text{REP}(s_1) = \text{REP}(s_2)$ is now clearly a D-relation. Lemma 1 gives the following.

Theorem 6. *If the algorithm executes* EXIT(DETERMINISTIC) *then L is operationally deterministic.*

Theorem 7. *The running time of the algorithm is $O(|S| + (|\Delta| + |\hat{S}|)\alpha(|S|))$.*

Proof. Stages 0 and 1 can be implemented in linear ($O(|S| + |\Delta|)$) time with well-known graph search and strong component algorithms. During stages 2 and 3, CHECK is critical in assessing the cost.

In the worst case, CHECK executes lines 4–7, which at a first glance amount to $O(|\Sigma|)$. However, the loop need not do more than $|\{ a \mid s_1.tr[a] \neq \text{NIL} \wedge s_2.tr[a] \neq \text{NIL} \}|$ iterations, if the non-τ output transitions of each state s are represented as a list of lists, where each higher level list record contains an a and $tr[a]$ where $tr[a] \neq \text{NIL}$, plus a link to a lower level list containing the remaining s' for which $(s, a, s') \in \Delta$. The higher level list is sorted according to a. Note that if at some point $s_1.tr[a] \neq \text{NIL} \wedge s_2.tr[a] = \text{NIL}$, the algorithm terminates immediately.

These lines are executed only if $\text{REP}(s_1) \neq \text{REP}(s_2)$ and, if they are, $\text{REP}(s_1) = \text{REP}(s_2)$ after the call. Therefore, the worst case can happen at most $O(|S|)$ times. This also makes sure that of the transitions corresponding to $s_1.tr[a]$ and $s_2.tr[a]$, one will never re-appear on lines 5 and 6. So, at most $|\Delta|$ iterations of the loop in CHECK are executed in total and thus $|\Delta|$ additions are applied to *Pending*, each of which is constant time.

When the loop is not executed, the execution time of CHECK is almost constant. Finding the REP for a state requires amortized time $\alpha(|S|)$, where α is an extremely slowly growing function. For more details and analysis of the disjoint set data structure, see [2].

At most $|\Delta| + |\hat{S}|$ calls of CHECK take place during stage 2. The number of calls of CHECK during stage 3 is at most the number of additions to *Pending*, that is, $|\Delta|$. As a consequence, the algorithm as a whole is $O(|S| + (|\Delta| + |\hat{S}|)\alpha(|S|))$. □

5 Deterministic LTS Minimisation

Quotient LTSs were introduced in Definition 9. Because the relation $\text{REP}(s_1) = \text{REP}(s_2)$ is a D-relation on line 33 of Figure 2, a quotient LTS can be constructed with it.

We can speed up the computation by using the representative states as the states of the result. Because representative states are bottom states, they cannot have τ-transitions to other states. Therefore, if $s -\tau^\omega\rightarrow$, then $\text{REP}(s).div$; and if $s -a\rightarrow s'$, then there is s'' such that $\text{REP}(s) -a\rightarrow s''$ and $\text{REP}(s') = \text{REP}(s'')$. Thus a quotient LTS can be constructed as follows.

- $S' = \{ \text{REP}(s) \mid s \in S \}$
- $\Delta' = \{ (s, a, s') \mid s \in S' \wedge a \neq \tau \wedge \exists s_1 \in S : (s, a, s_1) \in \Delta \wedge s' = \text{REP}(s_1) \}$
  $\cup \{ (s, \tau, s) \mid s \in S' \wedge s.div \}$
- $\hat{S}' = \{ \text{REP}(\hat{s}) \mid \hat{s} \in \hat{S} \}$

Structurally deterministic LTSs can be minimised with the block splitting construction of deterministic finite automata. To use the construction, for each $a \in \Sigma$, the transition relation $-a\rightarrow$ must be made total by adding one common "non-trace" state and directing all missing transitions to it. As a consequence, all $\sigma \in \Sigma^*$ that are not traces lead to the non-trace state. To save memory, this state and its incoming transitions should not be actually implemented. However, block splittings must be computed as if the state were there. To guarantee that divergence traces are preserved in the minimisation, the initial partitioning of states consists of three blocks: diverging (in this case that is, $s -\tau\rightarrow s$) states, non-diverging states, and the above-mentioned non-trace state.

The result is the smallest structurally deterministic LTS that has the same traces and divergence traces as the original LTS. By Theorem 3, it is Δ-branching bisimilar, and consequently equivalent according to many other notions, to the input LTS. Because this application of block splitting is simpler than in typical LTS minimisation algorithms (no τ-transitions between different states, no multiple transitions with the same label from the same state), it can be implemented at least as efficiently.

The deterministic LTS minimisation algorithm thus starts by running the algorithm in Figure 2. If the result is NONDET, then the algorithm gives up and some other approach must be used. Otherwise, a quotient LTS is constructed and minimised as was described above.

6 Conclusions

We defined the concept of operational determinism and studied its consequences and showed how operational determinism of LTSs can be detected. In light of the results we have given, operational determinism captures the notion of "deterministic behaviour" in a natural way. Operational determinism is preserved under all branching time equivalences that are at least as strong as divergence-sensitive weak bisimulation. In addition, the parallel composition of two operationally deterministic LTSs is operationally deterministic.

We have proven that the distinction between branching time and linear time disappears when restricting to operationally deterministic processes, so that all the equivalences between trace + divergence trace equivalence and Δ-branching bisimulation equivalence are the same.

The handling of τ-transitions affects significantly the complexity of known branching bisimulation [6,1] and weak bisimulation minimisation algorithms. Therefore, we suggest first testing if the LTS is operationally deterministic. If it is, it is minimised by computing the quotient LTS and then applying the minimisation algorithm for deterministic finite automata. If it is not, the ordinary algorithm for branching bisimulation, etc., is applied. The testing is cheap and does not affect the overall complexity. For operationally deterministic LTSs, the significant cost of handling τ-structures during the latter stage is avoided.

Our algorithm is also suitable for detecting the kind of determinism where divergence is not allowed: nondeterminism may be declared as soon as a divergence is found. It is also applicable when using divergence-blind semantics, by simply ignoring the divergence information.

References

1. S. Blom and S. Orzan. Distributed branching bisimulation reduction of state spaces. In *PDMC 2003, Parallel and Distributed Model Checking (Satellite workshop of CAV'03*, volume 89(1) of *ENTCS*, pages 99–113. Elsevier, 2003.
2. T. Cormen, C. Leiserson, R. Rivest, and C. Stein. *Introduction to Algorithms.* MIT Press, second edition, 2001.
3. R. De Nicola and F. Vaandrager. Three logics for branching bisimulation. *Journal of the ACM*, 42(2):458–487, 1995.
4. J. Eloranta. *Minimal Transition Systems with Respect to Divergence Preserving Behavioural Equivalences.* PhD thesis, University of Helsinki, 1994.
5. J. Engelfriet. Determinacy $\longrightarrow$ (observation equivalence $=$ trace equivalence). *Theoretical Computer Science*, 36(1):21–25, 1985.
6. J. F. Groote and F. Vaandrager. An efficient algorithm for branching bisimulation and stuttering equivalence. In Mike Paterson, editor, *ICALP90,* $17^t h$ *International Colloquim on Automata Languages and Programming*, volume 443 of *LNCS*, pages 626–638. Springer, 1990.
7. A. W. Roscoe. CSP and determinism in security modelling. In *Proceedings of IEEE Symposium on Security and Privacy*, pages 114–127. IEEE, 1995.
8. A. W. Roscoe. *The Theory and Practice of Concurrency.* Prentice-Hall, 1998. 565 p.
9. P. Y. A. Ryan and S. A. Schneider. Process algebra and non-interference. In *Proceedings of Computer Security Foundations Workshop*, pages 214–227. IEEE, 1999.
10. R. J. Van Glabbeek. The linear time – branching time spectrum II; the semantics of sequential systems with silent moves. In E. Best, editor, *Proceedings of* CONCUR'93, 4th *International Conference on Concurrency Theory, Hildesheim, Germany, August 1993*, number 715 in LNCS, pages 66–81. Springer, 1993.
11. R. J. Van Glabbeek and W. P. Weijland. Branching time and abstraction in bisimulation semantics. *Journal of the ACM*, 43(3):555–600, 1996.
12. M. Voorhoeve and S. Mauw. Impossible futures and determinism. *Information Processing Letters*, 80(1):51–58, 2001.
13. S. Zdancewic and A. Myers. Observational determinism for concurrent program security. In *Proceedings of the 16th IEEE Computer Security Foundations Workshop*, pages 29–43. IEEE, 2003.

Minimization, Learning, and Conformance Testing of Boolean Programs

Viraj Kumar*, P. Madhusudan, and Mahesh Viswanathan**

University of Illinois at Urbana-Champaign, Urbana, IL, USA
{kumar, madhu, vmahesh}@cs.uiuc.edu

Abstract. Boolean programs with recursion are convenient abstractions of sequential imperative programs, and can be represented as recursive state machines (RSMs) or pushdown automata. Motivated by the special structure of RSMs, we define a notion of modular visibly pushdown automata (modular VPA) and show that for the class of languages accepted by such automata, unique minimal modular VPA exist. This yields an efficient *approximate* minimization theorem that minimizes RSMs to within a factor of k of the minimal RSM, where k is the maximum number of parameters in any module. Using the congruence defined for minimization, we show an active learning algorithm (with a minimally adequate teacher) for context free languages in terms of modular VPAs. We also present an algorithm that constructs complete test suites for Boolean program specifications. Finally, we apply our results on learning and test generation to perform model checking of black-box Boolean programs.

1 Introduction

The abstraction-based approach to model-checking is based on building finite models, say using predicates over variables, and subjecting the finite models to systematic state-space exploration [10]. Recursion of control in programs leads to models with recursion, which can be captured using pushdown automata. The model of recursive state machines (RSMs) [1] is an alternate model, which is equivalent in power but whose notation is closer to programs.

The class of visibly pushdown languages is a subclass of context-free languages, defined as those languages that can be accepted by pushdown automata whose action on the stack is determined by the letter the automaton reads. Given that a model of a program is naturally visibly pushdown (since we can make calls and returns to modules visible), visibly pushdown languages are a tighter model for Boolean programs. The class of visibly pushdown languages enjoys closure and decidability properties, making several problems like model-checking pushdown program models against visibly pushdown specifications decidable [3,5].

In this paper we reap more benefits from the visibly pushdown modeling of programs, by showing that pushdown program models can be *minimized*, can be

* Supported by DARPA/AFOSR MURI award F49620-02-1-0325.
** Supported by NSF CCF 04-29639 and NSF CCF 04-48178.

C. Baier and H. Hermanns (Eds.): CONCUR 2006, LNCS 4137, pp. 203–217, 2006.

learnt and *tested for conformance*, and subject to *black-box checking*, paralleling results for finite-state models. We now outline these results.

In a recent paper [4], we showed that visibly pushdown languages have a *congruence* based characterization. However, this congruence does not yield minimal visibly pushdown automata, and in fact, unique minimal visibly pushdown automata do not exist in general. The main reason why the minimization result fails is that when implementing functions in the automata model there are two choices available. One option is to have function modules that "compute" the value for multiple (or all the) parameters, and then let the caller decide which result to pick when the function returns. The second option is for the function to only "compute" the answer to the specific parameter with which it was called.

In [4], we showed a minimization result for a special class of models. We looked at visibly pushdown machines with a modular structure (similar to recursive state machines) which have the additional property that modules, when called, compute the answers to all parameters and let the caller decide the right answer on return. This results in *modular*, *single-entry* (i.e., the state the machine enters on function calls is the same, no matter what the parameter is) machines. We showed that for any visibly pushdown language there is a unique minimal modular single-entry machine.

The restriction to single-entry machines is awkward. First they do not correspond to program models, as programs typically do not compute answers to all parameters on function calls. Second, combining the computation for multiple parameters can result in requiring a lot more memory, which in the context of automata corresponds to larger number of states.

The first contribution of this paper is a minimization result of a variant of modular VPAs that has multiple entry points in each module, corresponding to the multiple parameters. This variant is inspired by the recursive state machine model in two ways: (a) the parameters passed to modules are explicit and visible, and (b) we demand that when a module is called, the state *but not the parameter* is pushed onto the stack. Requiring that the parameter not be pushed onto the stack is crucial in achieving a unique minimization result; since the program does not "remember" the parameter it called the module with, it cannot choose the result for a parameter from a combined result. Thus, we get minimal program models that are more faithful to the semantics of programming languages. Technically, if we allow automata models that are not complete (i.e., certain transitions being disabled from certain states) then it is possible to encode the parameter in the calling state. Thus our minimization result only applies to complete models. However, we also show that any incomplete recursive state machine model for a program can be translated into a *canonical*, complete, recursive state machine model which is at most k times larger than the incomplete model, where k is the maximum number of parameters in any module. This results in an approximate minimization procedure for incomplete RSMs that transforms a deterministic RSM in polynomial time into one whose size is at most k times the size of the minimal deterministic RSM.

Next, we look at the problem of learning modular VPA models for context free languages. The learning model that we consider is one where the learning algorithm is allowed to interact with a knowledgeable teacher who answers two types of queries: *membership* queries, where the learner can ask whether a string belongs to the target language, and *equivalence* queries, where the learner can ask whether a hypothesis machine does indeed recognize exactly the target language. Learning algorithms identifying machine models for formal languages in such a learning framework have recently been extensively used in formal verification in a variety of contexts (see [8,2,12,7,21,14,25] for some examples). However, all these applications use algorithms that learn finite state models based on the algorithm originally proposed by Angluin [9]. The reason for this is because known learning algorithms apply only to very limited push-down models: Chomsky Normal Form grammars with known non-terminals [9] (which corresponds to knowing all the states of a pushdown model and discovering only the transitions), and deterministic one-counter machines [11].

Our main result in the context of the learning problem is that we can learn the smallest complete, deterministic, modular VPA for a language in time which is polynomial in the length of the longest counter-example provided by the teacher, and the size of the smallest machine model. The algorithm is based on the congruence based characterization of the minimum machine that we present in this paper[1].

We would like to contrast this learning algorithm with the implicit one suggested by the results of [5,22]. The results in [5] show that associated with every visibly pushdown language is the tree language of *stack trees* which is regular. Using Sakakibara's algorithm [22] one could learn the deterministic bottom-up tree automaton accepting the language of stack trees, and convert that to obtain a visibly pushdown automaton for the language using the results of [5]. There are two downsides to using this approach. First, the resulting VPA is non-deterministic, and one would need to pay the exponential cost in obtaining a deterministic machine. Second, even the non-deterministic VPA obtained thus has an awkward structure, as it may not be modular, or have one entry for each parameter, that we expect of program models.

The number of membership and equivalence queries made by our learning algorithm has the same dependence on the size of the minimal machine and length of the longest counter-example as Angluin's algorithm for learning finite state machines. However, in the case of regular languages, it is possible for a *cooperative teacher* to present counter-examples that are linear in the size of the smallest deterministic finite automaton accepting the language. For modular VPAs this is not the case; one can construct examples where the shortest counter-example is exponential in the size of the smallest modular VPA recognizing the language. However, we observe that the counter-examples (even if long) are

[1] The learning, conformance testing, and black-box checking algorithms in this paper can also be adapted to the congruence presented in [4] to construct single-entry VPA models. We present results using the congruence presented in this paper as we believe that multiple entry modular VPAs are a more natural and succinct model.

highly structured, and can be succinctly represented using an equation system. Our learning algorithm can be shown to have the same running time even when the teacher presents such succinct counter-examples, thus yielding a polynomial learning algorithm for such cooperative teachers.

We can also PAC learn modular-VPAs with membership queries. The PAC learning with membership queries model [24,9] is a weaker learning framework, where the equivalence queries are replaced by an oracle that samples strings (based on any fixed probability distribution) and labels them as either belonging to the language or not; the learning algorithm is required to identify the concept "approximately" in polynomial time, using the sampling oracle, with "high probability". We can show that one can PAC learn modular VPAs provided one has an oracle that samples strings represented succinctly using the equational representation. Because of lack of space we do not outline the PAC learning algorithm, but the extension to this framework is standard based on our results on learning with a knowledgeable teacher.

Next, we study the problem of *conformance testing* modular VPAs. In this framework, one is given a black-box implementation, whose internal transition structure is assumed to be unknown. The specification is another machine, but one whose transition structure is fully known. The objective in conformance testing is to construct a sequence of test inputs (based on the specification) such that if the implementation does not "conform" to the specification, then the implementation gives a different output than the specification on the test. Typically the notion of "conformance" is taken to be language equivalence, though weaker notions such as ioco have also been explored [23]. Since Moore's seminal work [20], there have been many algorithms to generate such test sequences; major results are summarized in [16,13,19,18] [2]. These algorithms construct complete suites (i.e., guaranteed to catch all buggy implementations) when both the specification and the implementation are known to be finite state machines. Further, these algorithms also assume that an a priori bound on the number of states of the implementation is known. We extend these results on conformance testing to the case when the specification and implementation are modeled as complete modular VPAs. The size of our test suite and the running time to construct the test suite depend on the number of states in the unknown black-box implementation, and the construction of the test suite relies on our characterization of the minimal modular VPA recognizing a language.

Finally, we show how we can apply our results to verify third-party programs. *Black Box Checking* [21] is a framework to model check unknown systems, by first learning the model of the system and then model checking the constructed model. This framework has been applied to construct finite state models, using Angluin's learning algorithm and conformance testing algorithms for finite models. Our extension to learning and testing boolean programs, allows one to extend this framework to verify recursive systems.

---

[2] The references here only talk about algorithms to construct complete test suites, which is the focus of this paper. There is also extensive work on constructing incomplete test suites that catch all bugs in the limit.

An alternative formulation of visibly pushdown automata is *nested word automata* [6], which are *finite* automata (without stack) on words endowed with a nesting relation (corresponding to the nesting relation defined between calls and their matching returns). A nested word automaton can decide the state at a return based on the previous state and the state before its matching call. This model already has the implicit restriction that at a call the module and parameter cannot be "pushed", and hence conforms to the restriction we introduce in this paper. Consequently, all results in this paper also hold for appropriately defined *modular* nested word automata.

The paper is organized as follows. We first introduce the model of modular VPAs and RSMs, along with useful definitions and notation. In Section 3 we present our results on the existence of unique, minimal, complete modular VPAs, and show how these results can be used to construct approximately minimal RSM models. After this we focus our attention exclusively on complete machines. Our learning algorithm is presented in Section 4, while our conformance testing results are presented in Section 5. Finally, we conclude in Section 6 by showing how these results can be combined to perform black-box checking.

2 Preliminaries

In this section, we define modular VPAs, and introduce notation that we will use in the rest of the paper.

We model Boolean programs as modular VPAs by modeling each module as a finite-state machine that also allows calls to and returns from other modules: modules representing different procedures are modeled separately, the usage of stack is implicit in that when a call to a module occurs, the local state of the module is pushed into the stack automatically, but neither the name of the called module nor the parameter passed is stored in the stack.

Let us fix M, a finite set of *modules*, with $m_0 \in M$ as the *initial module.* For each $m \in M$, let us fix a nonempty finite set of *parameters* P_m, with $P_{m_0} = \{p_0\}$.

A *call* c is a pair (m, p) where $m \in M \setminus \{m_0\}$ and $p \in P_m$, and denotes the action calling the module m with parameter p (we won't allow the initial module to be called except at the beginning, and hence (m_0, p_0) will not be a call). Let Σ_{call} denote the set of all calls. Let us also fix a finite set of internal actions Σ_{int}, and let $\Sigma_{\text{ret}} = \{r\}$ be the alphabet of returns, containing the unique symbol r. Let $\widehat{\Sigma} = (\Sigma_{\text{call}}, \Sigma_{\text{int}}, \Sigma_{\text{ret}})$ and let $\Sigma = \Sigma_{\text{call}} \cup \Sigma_{\text{int}} \cup \Sigma_{\text{ret}}$.

Definition 1 (Modular VPAs). *A modular VPA over* $\langle M, \{P_m\}_{m \in M}, m_0, \widehat{\Sigma}\rangle$ *is a tuple* $(\{Q_m, \{q_m^p\}_{p \in P_m}, \delta_m\}_{m \in M}, F)$ *where for each* $m \in M$

- Q_m *is a finite set of states. We assume that for* $m \neq m'$, $Q_m \cap Q_{m'} = \emptyset$. *Let* $Q = \bigcup_{m \in M} Q_m$ *denote the set of all states.*
- *For each parameter* $p \in P_m$, q_m^p *is a state associated with* p; *we will call this the* entry *associated with the call* (m, p).
  (Note that we do not insist that q_m^p *be different from* $q_m^{p'}$, *when* $p \neq p'$.*)*
- $F \subseteq Q_0$ *is the set of final states.*

– $\delta_m = \langle \delta^m_{\text{call}}, \delta^m_{\text{int}}, \delta^m_{\text{ret}} \rangle$ *is a triple of transition relations, one for calls, one for internals and one for returns, where*
  - $\delta^m_{\text{call}} \subseteq \{(q, (n,p), q^p_n) \mid q \in Q_m, (n,p) \in \Sigma_{\text{call}}\}$;
  - $\delta^m_{\text{int}} \subseteq \{(q, a, q') \mid q, q' \in Q_m, a \in \Sigma_{\text{int}}\}$;
  - $\delta^m_{\text{ret}} \subseteq \{(q, q', q'') \mid q', q'' \in Q_m, q \in Q\}$;

Notation: We write $q \xrightarrow{(n,p)} q^p_n$ to mean $(q, (n,p), q^p_n) \in \delta^m_{\text{call}}$, $q \xrightarrow{a} q'$ to mean $(q, a, q') \in \delta^m_{\text{int}}$, and $q \xrightarrow{q'} q''$ to mean $(q, q', q'') \in \delta^m_{\text{ret}}$.

Semantics: A *stack* is a finite sequence over Q; let the set of all stacks be $St = Q^*$. A *configuration* is any pair (q, σ) where $q \in Q$, and $\sigma \in St$. Let *Conf* denote the set of all configurations, along with the special configuration c_0.

The configuration graph of a modular VPA is (V, E) where $V = \mathit{Conf}$ and E is the smallest set of Σ-labeled edges that satisfies:

(Initial edge) $c_0 \xrightarrow{(m_0,p_0)} (q^{p_0}_{m_0}, \epsilon) \in E$.

(Internal edges) If $(q, \sigma) \in V$ $(q \in Q_m)$ and $(q, a, q') \in \delta^m_{\text{int}}$, then $(q, \sigma) \xrightarrow{a} (q', \sigma) \in E$.

(Call edges) If $(q, \sigma) \in V$ and $q \xrightarrow{(m,p)} q^p_m$, then $(q, \sigma) \xrightarrow{(m,p)} (q^p_m, \sigma q) \in E$.

(Return edges) If $(q, \sigma q') \in V$ $(q' \in Q_m)$, and $(q, q', q'') \in \delta^m_{\text{ret}}$, then $(q, \sigma q') \xrightarrow{r} (q'', \sigma) \in E$.
(Note that q'' and q' belong to the same module m.)

A *run* of A on a word u is a path in the configuration graph on u. Let $\rho : \mathit{Conf} \times \Sigma^* \to 2^{\mathit{Conf}}$ be the function where $\rho(\mathit{conf}, u)$ is the set of configurations reached at the end of all runs from *conf* on u in the configuration graph. An *accepting run* of A on u is a run from the initial configuration c_0 that ends in a configuration whose state is in the final set F. A word u is *accepted* by A if there is an accepting run of A on u, i.e. if $\rho(c_0, u) \cap (F \times St) \neq \emptyset$. The *language* of A, $L(A)$, is defined as the set of words $u \in \Sigma^*$ accepted by A.

Let *WM* be the set of well-matched words over $\widehat{\Sigma}$, i.e, the set of all words generated by the grammar: $S \to cSrS$ (for each $c \in \Sigma_{\text{call}}$), $S \to aS$ (for each $a \in \Sigma_{\text{int}}$), and $S \to \epsilon$. We will denote by $w, w', w_i, \ldots$ words in *WM*. Note that a modular VPA accepts only words that are in $\{(m_0, p_0)\}.\mathit{WM}$ (since the final states are in module m_0, and the initial symbol (m_0, p_0) is not considered a call).

A word u *reaches* state q in A if $(q, \sigma) \in \rho(c_0, u)$ for some $\sigma \in St$. Note that if q belongs to module m, then $u = u_1(m,p)w$ for some $p \in P_m$ and $w \in \mathit{WM}$. We say that $(m,p)w$ is an *access string* for state q in A.

A (complete) modular VPA is said to be *deterministic* if its transition relation is deterministic, i.e. for each $m \in M$:

– $\forall q \in Q_m, a \in \Sigma_{\text{int}}$, there is at most one q' such that $(q, a, q') \in \delta^m_{\text{int}}$; and
– $\forall q \in Q, q' \in Q_m$, there is exactly one q'' such that $(q, q', q'') \in \delta^m_{\text{ret}}$.

Note that transitions on calls are always deterministic since the target state is always the unique entry state associated with the call.

A modular VPA is said to be *complete* if a transition of every label is enabled from every state, i.e. for each $m \in M$,

- for each $q \in Q_m$ and $(n,p) \in \Sigma_{\text{call}}$, $(q,(n,p),q_n^p) \in \delta_{\text{call}}^m$;
- for each $q \in Q_m$ and $a \in \Sigma_{\text{int}}$, $\exists q'$ such that $(q,a,q') \in \delta_{\text{int}}^m$; and
- for each $q \in Q$ and $q' \in Q_m$, $\exists q''$ such that $(q,q',q'') \in \delta_{\text{ret}}^m$.

A *recursive state machine* (RSM) is a modular VPA with no final states set and where every word that has a run on it can be completed to a well-matched word. More precisely, the language defined by an RSM R is the set of words u such that there is a path in the configuration graph from the initial configuration, and we require that for every $u \in L(R)$, there is some word $w \in (\{(m_0,p_0)\}.WM) \cap L(R)$, such that u is a prefix of w.

Let MR be the set of all words with "matched-returns", i.e. where every return has a matching call, i.e. $MR = \{u \in \Sigma^* \mid \exists v \in \Sigma^*, uv \in WM\}$. It is easy to see then that the language of an RSM consists of words in $(m_0,p_0).MR$.

The *size* of a modular VPA (or RSM) is the number of states in it; when we refer to minimization, we mean minimizing the number of states.

The definition of modular VPAs above has been chosen carefully with final states only in the initial module, and disallowing calls to the initial module. Note that if we did allow final states in non-initial modules, then complete VPAs are less powerful than incomplete ones. For example, if $u(m,p)$ is accepted by a complete VPA, then $u'(m,p)$ is also accepted by it. An incomplete VPA can disallow the call after u' and hence reject $u'(m,p)$. However, incomplete VPAs are too ill behaved in the sense that we can encode parameters into the state being pushed at a call in an incomplete VPA, leading minimization results to fail. The focus on complete VPAs is a subtle and tricky restriction that allows our minimization result to go through.

Section 4 and Section 5 will consider only complete modular VPAs, and show the learning and conformance testing results for them. In the latter half of Section 3, we show how to handle (incomplete) RSMs by using the results for complete machines.

3 Minimization of VPAs and RSMs

Minimization of Complete Modular VPAs: In this section, we will show that for any *complete* modular VPA A, there exists a unique minimal (with respect to number of states) deterministic modular VPA that accepts the same language as A does. As a corollary, it will follow that deterministic complete modular VPAs are as powerful as non-deterministic complete ones.

Lemma 1. *For any complete modular VPA A, there exists a unique minimal complete modular VPA A' such that $L(A') = L(A)$. Further, given a complete deterministic modular VPA A, the unique minimal deterministic modular VPA equivalent to it can be constructed in polynomial time.*

Proof. (sketch)
Let $A = (\{Q_m, \{q_m^p\}_{p \in P_m}, \delta_m\}_{m \in M}, F)$ and let $L(A) = L$. For every $m \in M$, we define an equivalence relation $\sim_m$ on $P_m \times WM$ which depends on L (and not on A) as: $(p_1, w_1) \sim_m (p_2, w_2)$ **iff** $\forall u, v \in \Sigma^*$

$$u(m, p_1)w_1 v \in L \text{ iff } u(m, p_2)w_2 vinL$$

Note that $\sim_m$ is a congruence in the sense that if $(p_1, w_1) \sim_m (p_2, w_2)$, then for any well-matched word w, $(p_1, w_1 w) \sim_m (p_2, w_2 w)$.

Let $[(p, w)]_m$ denote the equivalence class of (p, w) with respect to $\sim_m$. It can be shown that $\sim_m$ has at most $2^{|Q_m|}$ equivalence classes. These equivalence classes correspond to states of the unique minimal complete deterministic modular VPA. The details of the construction and complexity, and the proof of minimality can be found in [17]. □

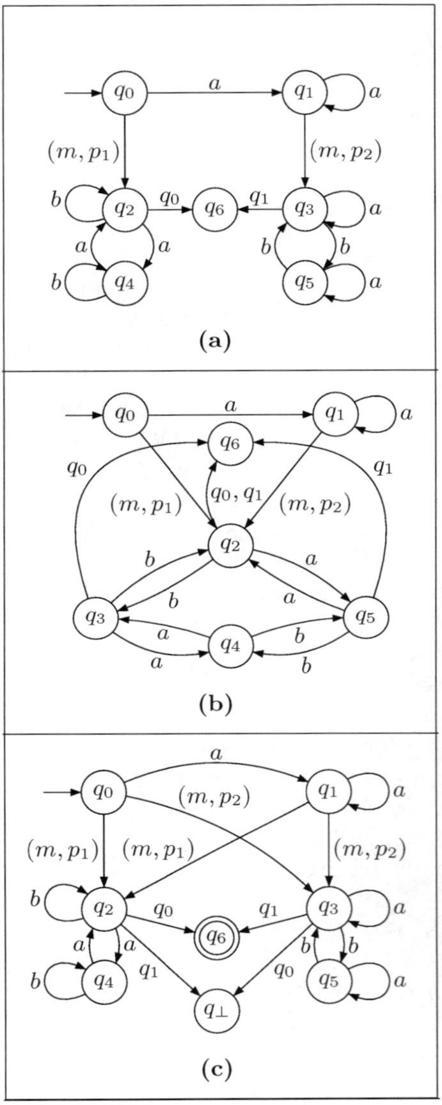

Fig. 1. (a) and (b): Two non-isomorphic minimum-state RSMs; (c) completing the RSM

Let A be a complete modular VPA. For distinct states q_1, q_2 in module m of A with access strings $(m, p_1)w_1$ and $(m, p_2)w_2$ respectively, a pair of strings (u, v) is a *distinguishing test* for $\{q_1, q_2\}$ if exactly one of $u(m, p_1)w_1 v$ and $u(m, p_2)w_2 v$ is in $L(A)$. By the above theorem, for a *minimal* complete modular VPA A, there is a set D of distinguishing tests such that for every module m and distinct states q_1, q_2 in module m of A, there is a distinguishing test $(u, v) \in D$ for $\{q_1, q_2\}$. We call such a set D a *complete* set of distinguishing tests.

Minimization of Recursive State Machines: Figure 1 shows two non-isomorphic (incomplete) RSMs that use minimal number of states and accept the same language. The call with parameter p_1 checks if there are an even number of a's (from the call to the return) while the parameter p_2 checks if there are an even number of b's. The first machine processes the parameters separately, while the second machine processes both parameters and lets the caller choose the appropriate result. However, if we restrict to complete machines, then we can complete the first machine by enabling all calls from q_0 and q_1, to get a modular VPA that accepts the language $L' = \{w \in WM \mid \forall v \preceq w, v \in L\}$ [3], where L is the language accepted by the RSM (see Fig. 1(c); all edges are not drawn). However, the second automaton cannot be transformed this way: if we enable the call (m, p_2) from q_0, then upon returning from a call, we would not know whether the module was called with p_1 or p_2, and hence cannot accept the right language.

Our strategy for minimizing RSMs is to translate an RSM into a complete modular VPA, minimize it, and translate it back to an RSM. This results in an RSM whose size is at most a factor k of the minimal size possible, where k is bound by the maximum number of parameters in any module of the RSM.

Lemma 2. *Let $R = (\{Q_m, \{q_m^p\}_{p \in P_m}, \delta_m\}_{m \in M})$ be an RSM and let k be the maximum number of parameters for any module. Then there exists a complete modular VPA A such that $L(A) = \{w \in WM \mid \forall v \preceq w, v \in L(R)\}$. Further, the size of A is at most k times R, and A is deterministic if R is deterministic.*

Lemma 3. *Let R be an RSM, and let $\hat{A}$ be the complete minimal deterministic automaton such that $L(\hat{A}) = \{w \in WM \mid \forall v \preceq w, v \in L(R)\}$. Then there exists a deterministic RSM R' with at most the number of states in $\hat{A}$, such that $L(R') = L(R)$.*

Using the lemmas above and Lemma 1, we can show:

Theorem 1. *Given a deterministic RSM R, we can compute in polynomial time an RSM $\hat{R}$ that accepts the same language, such that if R' is any RSM accepting $L(R)$, then $\hat{R}$ has at most k times the number of states R' has.*

Proof. Given R, we complete it (using Lemma 2), minimize it (using Lemma 1), and using Lemma 3, build an incomplete RSM $\hat{R}$ (all this takes polynomial time). If R' is another RSM accepting the same language as R does, then its completion results in the same language as the completion of R, and is at most k times size of R'. Since $\hat{R}$ was obtained using incompletion of a minimal machine (and the incompletion process only removes states), the result follows.

4 Learning Complete Modular VPAs

We will now consider the problem of exactly learning a target context free language L (over $\langle M, \{P_m\}_{m \in M}, m_0, \hat{\Sigma}\rangle$) by constructing a complete, modular VPA for L from examples of strings in L and those not in L. In our learning model, we will assume that the learning algorithm is interacting with a knowledgeable teacher (often called a *minimally adequate teacher*) who assists the learner in identifying L. We can think of the teacher as an oracle answering two types of queries.

---

[3] $\preceq$ denotes the prefix relation on words.

Membership Query The learning algorithm may select any string x and ask whether x is a member of L.

Equivalence Query In such a query, the algorithm submits a hypothesis RSM $\widehat{A}$. If $L = L(\widehat{A})$ then the teacher informs the learning algorithm that it has correctly identified the target language. Otherwise, in response to the query, the learner receives a *counter-example* word $(m_0, p_0)x$ where x is a well-matched string and $(m_0, p_0)x \in (L \setminus L(\widehat{A})) \cup (L(\widehat{A}) \setminus L)$. No assumptions are made about how the counter-example is chosen. In particular the counter-example x maybe picked adversarially.

Our goal is to design an algorithm that identifies L in time which is polynomial in the size of the smallest modular VPA recognizing L and the length of the longest counter-example presented to it. The algorithm that we present is very similar to the learning algorithm for regular languages due to Angluin [9]. However our presentation is closer in spirit to the algorithm due to Kearns and Vazirani [15].

4.1 Overview of Algorithm

Let A be the smallest, complete, deterministic, modular VPA that recognizes the target language L and let $size(A)$ be the number of states of A. Recall from Lemma 1, that the states of A correspond to the equivalence classes of $\sim_m$. The main idea behind the learning algorithm will be to progressively identify the equivalence classes of $\sim_m$; the construction of the VPA A from $\sim_m$ will be the same as that outlined in Lemma 1 (see [17]).

The learning algorithm will proceed in phases. During the execution, the algorithm will maintain equivalence relations (not necessarily congruences) $\equiv_m$ on $P_m \times WM$ such that if $(p_1, w_1) \sim_m (p_2, w_2)$ then $(p_1, w_1) \equiv_m (p_2, w_2)$. In other words, $\sim_m$ will always be a refinement of $\equiv_m$. The algorithm will also ensure that if it knows $(m_0, p_0)w_1 \in L$ and $(m_0, p_0)w_2 \notin L$, then $(p_0, w_1) \not\equiv_{m_0} (p_0, w_2)$. Further the equivalence $\equiv_m$ itself will be maintained implicitly using a data structure called a *classification forest*, such that deciding if $(p_1, w_1) \equiv_m (p_2, w_2)$ is efficient; this is formally stated next. A classification forest is very similar to a classification tree, introduced by Vazirani and Kearns. Readers unfamiliar with the Vazirani-Kearns data structure are referred to [17].

Proposition 1. *Given (p_1, w_1) and (p_2, w_2), $(p_1, w_1) \equiv_m (p_2, w_2)$ can be decided using $O(size(A))$ membership queries.*

In addition to maintaining the equivalence relation $\equiv_m$, the algorithm will maintain a representative (p, w) for each equivalence class $[(p, w)]_m$ of $\equiv_m$. In what follows we will denote the representative of $[(p, w)]_m$ by $\text{rep}([(p, w)]_m)$. In particular, the algorithm will ensure that (p_0, ϵ) is always among the representatives. In each phase of the algorithm, these representatives will be used to construct a hypothesis machine $\widehat{A}$. A module m will have one state corresponding to each representative $\text{rep}([(p, w)]_m)$. The transitions are naturally determined by the relation $\equiv_m$ as follows. On a call symbol (m, p), every state has a transition to the state $\text{rep}([(p, \epsilon)]_m)$. On an internal symbol a, a state $(p, w) = \text{rep}([(p, w)]_m)$

has a transition to the state rep($[(p, wa)]_m$). Finally on a return with $(p_1, w_1) =$ rep($[(p_1, w_1)]_{m_1}$) on top of the stack, the state $(p_2, w_2) =$ rep($[(p_2, w_2)]_{m_2}$) has a transition to the state rep($[(p_1, w_1(m_2, p_2)w_2r)]_{m_1}$). Observe that since $\equiv_m$ is not necessarily a congruence, the machine $\widehat{A}$ depends on the representatives chosen. Finally, by using special data structures, this machine can be constructed efficiently from $\equiv_m$ and the representatives (details are in [17]).

In each phase, the algorithm will construct the hypothesis machine $\widehat{A}$ based on the current $\equiv_m$ and representatives. It will then ask an equivalence query with the machine $\widehat{A}$. If the query has a positive answer, the learning algorithm will stop and one can show that in this case $\equiv_m = \sim_m$ and that $\widehat{A}$ is exactly the machine A. On the other hand the equivalence oracle may present a counter example string w. The algorithm will process this counter example to refine $\equiv_m$ to discover a new equivalence class of $\sim_m$. The details of how the counter-example is processed is similar to Angluin's algorithm and is skipped in the interests of space; the interested reader is referred to [17].

The overall algorithm is thus as follows. The algorithm starts with a hypothesis machine, where each module has exactly one state; thus $(p_1, w_1) \equiv_m (p_2, w_2)$ for any p_1, p_2, w_1, w_2. In each phase the algorithm asks an equivalence query with the current hypothesis, and uses the answer to refine the equivalence $\equiv_m$ by identifying one more equivalence class of $\sim_m$. This process repeats until the algorithm has identified all the equivalence classes of $\sim_m$. This algorithm can be implemented efficiently and this is the main theorem of this section.

Theorem 2. *Let L be a language accepted by a complete, deterministic VPA and let A be the smallest modular VPA accepting L. The learning algorithm identifies A by making at most $size(A)$ calls to the equivalence oracle, and $O(size(A)(size(A) + n))$ calls to the membership oracle, where n is the length of the longest counter-example returned by the equivalence oracle.*

4.2 Cooperative Teacher

The running time of the learning algorithm presented in the previous section has the same dependence on the size of the minimal machine and the length of counter-examples, as the learning algorithm for regular languages. However, there is one important difference. For regular languages, a *cooperative* teacher can always find a counter-example of length at most $size(A)$ in response to an equivalence query, yielding a polynomial running time in the presence of cooperative teachers. This is, however not the case for VPAs as the shortest counter-example in response to an equivalence query maybe as long as $2^{size(A)}$. Thus, even if the counter-examples are guaranteed to be the shortest possible, the learning algorithm for VPAs will not run in polynomial time.

There is, however, one form of cooperative teacher who can assist in learning the target VPA fast. Observe that even though the shortest counter-example maybe exponentially long, it is typically highly structured and has a very small, succinct representation. Consider an equation system $\{x_i = t_i\}_{i \geq 1}^{k}$, where x_i is a variable and t_i is a well-matched string over $\Sigma \cup \{x_1, \ldots x_{i-1}\}$. The variable x_k

in such an equation system represents a string over *WM* that can be obtained by progressively solving for x_i for increasing values of i, by replacing solutions for $x_1, \ldots x_{i-1}$. It can be shown that there is an equation system of size at most *size*(A) that represents a counter-example to any equivalence query. Further, given a counter-example represented by an equation system (instead of explicitly), we can process the counter example using linearly many (in the size of the equation system) membership queries to discover a new state in the hypothesis machine. The details are a straightforward extension of the ideas already presented, and are skipped in the interests of space.

5 Conformance Testing

We now describe the setting for conformance testing. We are given a *specification machine* $\mathcal{S}$ and a "black-box" *implementation machine* $\mathcal{I}$ that are both deterministic complete modular VPAs over $\langle M, \{P_m\}_{m\in M}, \Sigma_{\text{int}}, \Sigma_{\text{ret}}\rangle$. The task is to test whether or not $\mathcal{I}$ is equivalent to $\mathcal{S}$, i.e. $L(\mathcal{I}) = L(\mathcal{S})$. In order to achieve this, we make the following assumptions:

1. $\mathcal{S}$ is minimized and has n states;
2. $\mathcal{I}$ is equivalent to a deterministic complete modular VPA that has at most N states;
3. $\mathcal{I}$ does not change during the testing experiment.

Note that assumption 1 can be made with no loss of generality, since the specification $\mathcal{S}$ is known, and hence we can assume it is minimized. Assumption 2 is necessary in order to guarantee that every state of the implementation is explored. The need for assumption 3 is obvious.

A *sample* over Σ is a pair (T^+, T^-), where T^+, T^- are finite subsets of Σ^*. A modular VPA A is *consistent* with sample (T^+, T^-) if $T^+ \subseteq L(A)$ and $T^- \subseteq \overline{L(A)}$.

Definition 2. *A* conformance test *for* $(\mathcal{S}, \mathcal{I})$ *is a sample* (T^+, T^-) *over* Σ *such that* $\mathcal{S}$ *is consistent with* (T^+, T^-) *and, for any* $\mathcal{I}$ *satisfying the above assumptions,* $\mathcal{I}$ *is consistent with* (T^+, T^-) *if and only if* $L(\mathcal{I}) = L(\mathcal{S})$.

Let $Q_\mathcal{S}$ (the states of $\mathcal{S}$) be $\{q_1, q_2, \ldots, q_n\}$, with access strings $(m_1, p_1)w_1$, $(m_2, p_2)w_2$, …, $(m_n, p_n)w_n$ respectively, and let the set of final states of $\mathcal{S}$ be $F_\mathcal{S}$. Assume without loss of generality that the access string for every entry state q_m^p of $\mathcal{S}$ is (m, p), and that $q_1 = q_{m_0}^{p_0}$. Let $Q_\mathcal{I}$ (the set of states of $\mathcal{I}$) be $\{\hat{q}_1, \hat{q}_2, \ldots, \hat{q}_N\}$, let $\hat{q}_1 = \hat{q}_{m_0}^{p_0}$, and let the set of final states of $\mathcal{I}$ be $F_\mathcal{I}$.

Since $\mathcal{S}$ is minimized and has n states, for $\mathcal{I}$ to be equivalent to $\mathcal{S}$ it is necessary for $\mathcal{I}$ to have at least n distinct states. Using the fact that $\mathcal{S}$, being minimized, has a complete set of distinguishing tests, we construct a sample (T_0^+, T_0^-) such that any modular VPA consistent with it has at least n states. Let D be a complete set of distinguishing tests for $\mathcal{S}$. Hence, for every distinct pair of states q_i, q_j in module m, there is a distinguishing test $(u_{ij}, v_{ij}) \in D$ for $\{q_i, q_j\}$. For every $i = 1, \ldots, n$, let $D_i = \bigcup_j \{(u_{ij}, v_{ij})\}$. Define $T_0 = \bigcup_{i=1}^n \{u(m_i, p_i)w_i v \mid (u, v) \in D_i\}$. Let $T_0^+ = T_0 \cap L(\mathcal{S})$ and $T_0^- = T_0 \setminus L(\mathcal{S})$. The following lemma is easy to prove.

Lemma 4. *If $\mathcal{I}$ is consistent with (T_0^+, T_0^-), then*

1. *for every $i \neq j$, $(m_i, p_i)w_i$ and $(m_j, p_j)w_j$ are access strings for* distinct *states of $\mathcal{I}$ (hence $N \geq n$)*
2. *there are access strings $\{x_i\}_{i=1}^N$ for all states of $\mathcal{I}$, where $x_i = (m_i, p_i)w_i$ for $i = 1, \ldots, n$ and for $i > n$, x_i is of one of the following forms: $x_i = ya$, where $a \in \Sigma_{\text{int}}$; or $x_i = yzr$, where $y, z \in \{x_1, x_2, \ldots, x_{i-1}\}$ and $z \neq x_1$.*

Note that every access string x_i of $\mathcal{I}$ is of the form $(m,p)w$ for some $m \in M, p \in P_m, w \in WM$. Assume without loss of generality that for each i, x_i is an access string for $\hat{q}_i$. If $\mathcal{I}$ is equivalent to $\mathcal{S}$, it is necessary that for each i, x_i is an access string of a final state of $\mathcal{I}$ if and only if x_i is an access string of a final state in $\mathcal{S}$. We define a sample (T_1^+, T_1^-) such that $\mathcal{I}$ is consistent with this sample if this condition holds.

Define $h : Q_{\mathcal{I}} \to Q_{\mathcal{S}}$ as follows: $h(\hat{q}_i) = q_j$ iff x_i is an access string for q_j in $\mathcal{S}$. Define $T_1 = \{x_i \mid i = 1, \ldots, N\}$. Let $T_1^+ = T_1 \cap L(\mathcal{S})$ and $T_1^- = T_1 \setminus L(\mathcal{S})$. We immediately have the following lemma:

Lemma 5. *If $\mathcal{I}$ is consistent with (T_1^+, T_1^-), then for every $1 \leq i \leq n$, $\hat{q}_i \in F_{\mathcal{I}}$ iff $h(\hat{q}_i) \in F_{\mathcal{S}}$.*

Our goal is to design a sample (T^+, T^-) such that if $\mathcal{I}$ is consistent with it, then $L(\mathcal{I}) = L(\mathcal{S})$. In view of Lemma 5, it is enough to construct a sample such that if $\mathcal{I}$ is consistent with it, then for every $u \in MR$, $h(\hat{q}_i) \xrightarrow{u}_{\mathcal{S}} h(\hat{q}_j)$ whenever $\hat{q}_i \xrightarrow{u}_{\mathcal{I}} \hat{q}_j$. Define

$$T_2 = \bigcup_{i=1}^n \{ux_iav \mid a \in \Sigma_{\text{int}}, (u,v) \in D_j \text{ where } h(\hat{q}_i) \xrightarrow{a}_{\mathcal{S}} q_j\}$$
$$T_3 = \bigcup_{i,j=1}^n \{ux_jx_irv \mid (u,v) \in D_k \text{ where } h(\hat{q}_i) \xrightarrow{h(\hat{q}_j)}_{\mathcal{S}} q_k\}$$

It is not hard to see that if $\mathcal{I}$ is consistent with $(T_2 \cap L(\mathcal{S}), T_2 \setminus L(\mathcal{S}))$, then for every $a \in \Sigma_{\text{int}}$, $h(\hat{q}_i) \xrightarrow{a}_{\mathcal{S}} h(\hat{q}_j)$ whenever $\hat{q}_i \xrightarrow{a}_{\mathcal{I}} \hat{q}_j$. Similarly, it can be show that if $\mathcal{I}$ is consistent with $(T_3 \cap L(\mathcal{S}), T_3 \setminus L(\mathcal{S}))$, then $h(\hat{q}_i) \xrightarrow{h(\hat{q}_j)}_{\mathcal{S}} h(\hat{q}_k)$ whenever $\hat{q}_i \xrightarrow{\hat{q}_j}_{\mathcal{I}} \hat{q}_k$. Finally, since we had assumed that the access string for each entry state q_m^p of $\mathcal{S}$ was (m,p) and $x_j = (m,p)$ for some $1 \leq j \leq n$, it follows that $h(\hat{q}_m^p) = q_m^p$. Hence, $h(\hat{q}_i) \xrightarrow{(m,p)}_{\mathcal{S}} h(\hat{q}_m^p)$ whenever $\hat{q}_i \xrightarrow{(m,p)}_{\mathcal{I}} \hat{q}_m^p$. The following theorem now follows.

Theorem 3. *Let $T = T_0 \cup T_1 \cup T_2 \cup T_3$. If $\mathcal{I}$ is consistent with $(T \cap L(\mathcal{S}), T \setminus L(\mathcal{S}))$, then $L(\mathcal{I}) = L(\mathcal{S})$.*

Proof. By the above observations, for any string $u \in MR$, it follows by induction on the length of u that $h(\hat{q}_i) \xrightarrow{u}_{\mathcal{S}} h(\hat{q}_j)$ whenever $\hat{q}_i \xrightarrow{u}_{\mathcal{I}} \hat{q}_j$. Now Lemma 5 implies that $L(\mathcal{I}) = L(\mathcal{S})$. □

By the above Theorem, a conformance test (T^+, T^-) for $(\mathcal{S}, \mathcal{I})$ can be constructed given a complete set of distinguishing tests D for $\mathcal{S}$, and a set of access strings for all states of $\mathcal{I}$. We show how these requirements can be met.

Constructing a complete set of distinguishing tests

Lemma 6. *If $\mathcal{S}$ is a minimized deterministic complete modular VPA, a complete set of distinguishing tests D can be constructed effectively.*

The proof of the above lemma is presented in the full version [17]. Let $\Omega = \Sigma \cup \{x_i\}_{i=1}^{n}$. The following lemma is a simple corollary to Lemma 6.

Lemma 7. *A complete set of distinguishing tests D for $\mathcal{S}$ can be represented as $\binom{n}{2}$ strings in Ω^*, each of length $O(n^2)$, where n is the number of states of $\mathcal{S}$.*

Constructing access strings

Let Ω be as defined above, and let $\Omega' = \Omega \cup \{x_{n+1}, \ldots, x_N\}$. By Lemma 4, if $\mathcal{I}$ is consistent with (T_0^+, T_0^-), there is a system of $N-n$ equations, each representable by $O(1)$ symbols in Ω', describing the set of access strings for all states in $\mathcal{I}$. There are at most $\left(N|\Sigma| + N^2\right)^{N-n}$ such systems of equations, at least one of which describes a correct set of access strings for $\mathcal{I}$. Assuming $|\Sigma|$ is a constant, a set of access strings for $\mathcal{I}$ can be represented in $O(n \log n + N^{2(N-n)} \log N)$ space.

6 Black Box Checking

Our learning algorithm, along with our algorithm to generate conformance tests, can be used in a powerful way to model check black-box programs whose structure is unknown. Black-box checking was introduced in [21], and in this framework one assumes that while the structure of the system is unknown, it can be simulated to see if it exhibits certain behaviors. The main idea is to use a machine learning algorithm to construct a model of the program and then use the constructed machine model for verification. Our learning algorithm requires a teacher to answer both membership and equivalence queries. So in order to use our learning algorithm to construct a model of the program, we will need to find a way to answer these queries. Membership queries correspond to whether a certain sequence of steps is executed by the system; thus they can be answered by simulating the system. Equivalence queries are handled by constructing a conformance test. We assume that an *a priori* upper bound on the size of the model of the program is known. When the learning algorithm builds a hypothesis machine, we construct a conformance test using the hypothesis as the specification and the program as the implementation. If the program behaves the same way as the constructed hypothesis, then we have constructed a faithful model of the program. On the other hand, if the program differs from the hypothesis, then the conformance test gives us the counter-example needed for the learning algorithm to refine its hypothesis. Thus, using the learning and testing algorithms presented here, we can perform black-box checking of recursive programs.

References

1. R. Alur, M. Benedikt, K. Etessami, P. Godefroid, T. W. Reps, and M. Yannakakis. Analysis of recursive state machines. *TOPLAS*, 27(4):786–818, 2005.
2. R. Alur, P. Cerný, P. Madhusudan, and W. Nam. Synthesis of interface specifications for Java classes. In *POPL*, pages 98–109. ACM Press, 2005.
3. R. Alur, K. Etessami, and P. Madhusudan. A temporal logic of nested calls and returns. In *TACAS*, LNCS 2988, pages 467–481. Springer, 2004.
4. R. Alur, V. Kumar, P. Madhusudan, and M. Viswanathan. Congruences for visibly pushdown languages. In *ICALP*, LNCS 3580, pages 1102–1114. Springer, 2005.
5. R. Alur and P. Madhusudan. Visibly pushdown languages. In *STOC*, pages 202–211. ACM Press, 2004.
6. R. Alur and P. Madhusudan. Adding nesting structure to words. In *DLT*, LNCS 4036, pages 1–13, 2006.
7. R. Alur, P. Madhusudan, and W. Nam. Symbolic compositional verification by learning assumptions. In *CAV*, LNCS 3576, pages 548–562. Springer, 2005.
8. G. Ammons, R. Bodik, and J. R. Larus. Mining specifications. *SIGPLAN Not.*, 37(1):4–16, 2002.
9. D. Angluin. Learning regular sets from queries and counterexamples. *Information and Computation*, 75:87–106, 1987.
10. T. Ball and S. Rajamani. Bebop: A symbolic model checker for boolean programs. In *SPIN*, LNCS 1885, pages 113–130. Springer, 2000.
11. P. Berman and R. Roos. Learning one–counter languages in polynomial time. In *FOCS*, pages 61–67. IEEE, 1987.
12. J. M. Cobleigh, D. Giannakopoulou, and C. S. Pasareanu. Learning assumptions for compositional verification. In *TACAS*, LNCS 2619, pages 331–346, 2003.
13. A. Friedman and P. Menon. *Fault Detection in Digital Circuits*. PrenticeHall, Inc., Englewood Cliffs, New Jersey, 1971.
14. A. Groce, D. Peled, and M. Yannakakis. Adaptive model checking. In *TACAS*, LNCS 2280, pages 357–370. Springer-Verlag, 2002.
15. M. Kearns and U. Vazirani. *An introduction to computational learning theory*. MIT Press, 1994.
16. Z. Kohavi. *Switching and Finite Automata Theory*. McGraw-Hill, New York, 1978.
17. V. Kumar, P. Madhusudan, and M. Viswanathan. Minimization, learning, and conformance testing of Boolean programs. Technical Report UIUCDCS-R-2006-2736, University of Illinois at Urbana-Champaign, June 2006.
18. D. Lee and M. Yannakakis. Principles and methods of testing finite state machines - A survey. In *Proceedings of the IEEE*, volume 84, pages 1090–1126, 1996.
19. R. Linn and M. Üyar. *Conformance testing methodologies and architectures for OSI protocols*. IEEE Computer Society Press, 1995.
20. E. F. Moore. Gedanken-experiments on sequential machines. In *Automata Studies*, pages 129–153, Princeton University Press, Princeton, NJ, 1956.
21. D. Peled, M. Y. Vardi, and M. Yannakakis. Black box checking. *J. Autom. Lang. Comb.*, 7(2):225–246, 2001.
22. Y. Sakakibara. Efficient learning of context-free grammars from positive structural examples. *Inf. Comput.*, 97(1):23–60, 1992.
23. J. Tretmans. A formal approach to conformance testing. In *Protocol Test Systems*, volume C-19 of *IFIP Trans.*, pages 257–276. North-Holland, 1994.
24. L. Valiant. A theory of the learnable. *Comm. of the ACM*, 27(11):1134–1142, 1984.
25. A. Vardhan, K. Sen, M. Viswanathan, and G. Agha. Actively learning to verify safety for FIFO automata. In *FSTTCS*, LNCS 3328, pages 494–505, 2004.

A Capability Calculus for Concurrency and Determinism*

Tachio Terauchi[1] and Alex Aiken[2]

[1] EECS Department, University of California, Berkeley
[2] Computer Science Department, Stanford University

Abstract. We present a capability calculus for checking partial confluence of channel-communicating concurrent processes. Our approach automatically detects more programs to be partially confluent than previous approaches and is able to handle a mix of different kinds of communication channels, including shared reference cells.

1 Introduction

Deterministic programs are easier to debug and verify than non-deterministic programs, both for testing (or simulation) and for formal methods. However, sometimes programs are written as communicating concurrent processes, for speed or for ease of programming, and therefore are possibly non-deterministic. In this paper, we present a system that can automatically detect more programs to be deterministic than previous methods [7,10,8,9,5]. Our system is able to handle programs communicating via a mix of different kinds of channels: rendezvous, output buffered, input buffered, and shared reference cells. Section 3.2 shows a few examples that can be checked by our system: producer consumer, token ring, and barrier synchronization. The companion technical report contains the omitted proofs [12].

We cast our system as a *capability calculus* [4]. The capability calculus was originally proposed as a framework for reasoning about resources in sequential computation, but has recently been extended to reason about determinism in concurrent programs [3,11]. However, these systems can only reason about synchronization at join points, and therefore cannot verify determinism of channel-communicating processes. This paper extends the capability calculus to reason about synchronization due to channel communications. A key insight comes from our previous work [11] which showed that confluence can be ensured in a principled way from ordering dependencies between the side effects; dependencies are enforced by finding a flow assignment (which can be interpreted as *fractional capabilities* [3]) in the dependence graph.

2 Preliminaries

We focus on the simple concurrent language shown in Figure 1. A program, p, is a parallel composition of finitely many processes. A process, s, is a sequential

* This research was supported in part by NSF Grant No. CCR-0326577.

C. Baier and H. Hermanns (Eds.): CONCUR 2006, LNCS 4137, pp. 218–232, 2006.

$p ::= s_1 \| s_2 \| \ldots \| s_n$	*(program)*	$s ::= s_1; s_2$	*(sequence)*
$e ::= c$	*(channel)*	$\mid$ `if` e `then` s_1 `else` s_2	*(branch)*
$\mid x$	*(local variable)*	$\mid$ `while` e `do` s	*(loop)*
$\mid n$	*(integer constant)*	$\mid$ `skip`	*(skip)*
$\mid e_1\ op\ e_2$	*(integer operation)*	$\mid x$ `:=` e	*(assignment)*
		$\mid\ !(e_1, e_2)$	*(write channel)*
		$\mid\ ?(e, x)$	*(read channel)*

Fig. 1. The syntax of the small concurrent language

statement consisting of the usual imperative features as well as channel communication operations. Here, $!(e_1, e_2)$ means writing the value of e_2 to the channel e_1, and $?(e, x)$ means storing the value read from the channel e to the variable x. The variables are process-local, and so the only means of communication are channel reads and writes. We use meta-variables x, y, z, etc. for variables and c, d, etc. for channels.

The language cannot dynamically create channels or spawn new processes, but these restrictions are imposed only to keep the main presentation to the novel features of the system. Section 3.3 shows that techniques similar to previous work in the capability calculus can be used to handle dynamic channels and processes.

2.1 Channel Kinds

The literature on concurrency includes several forms of channels with distinct semantics. We introduce these channel kinds and show how they affect determinism.

If c and d are *rendezvous* channels, then the following program is deterministic[1] because $(x, y) = (1, 2)$ when the process terminates:

$$!(c, 1); !(d, 2) \mid\mid\ !(d, 3); ?(c, x) \mid\mid ?(d, y); ?(d, y)$$

The same program is non-deterministic if c is *output buffered* because $!(c, 1)$ does not need to wait for the reader $?(c, x)$, and therefore (x, y) could be $(1, 2)$ or $(1, 3)$.

While all the processes share one output buffer per channel, each process has its own input buffer per channel. Therefore, $!(c, 1); !(c, 2) \mid\mid ?(c, x) \mid\mid ?(c, y)$ is deterministic if c is input buffered but not if c is output buffered or rendezvous. Input buffered channels are the basis of Kahn process networks [7].

We also consider a buffered channel whose buffer is overwritten by every write but never modified by a read. Such a channel is equivalent to a reference cell. If c is a reference cell, $!(c, 1); !(c, 2) \mid\mid ?(c, x)$ is not deterministic because $!(c, 2)$ may or may-not overwrite 1 in the buffer before $?(c, x)$ reads the buffer. The program is deterministic if c is any other channel kind. On the other hand, $!(c, 1); !(c, 2); !(d, 3); ?(c, x) \mid\mid ?(d, x); ?(c, y)$ is deterministic if c is a reference

[1] Here, we use the term informally. Determinism is formally defined in Section 2.2.

cell and d is rendezvous because both reads of c happen after $!(c, 2)$ overwrites the buffer. But the program is not deterministic if c is output buffered.

2.2 Operational Semantics

The operational semantics of the language is defined as a series of reductions from states to states. A state is represented by the triple (B, S, p) where B is a buffer, S is a store, and p is a program such that each concurrent process in p is indexed by a process number, i.e., $p ::= 1.s_1||2.s_2|| \ldots ||n.s_n$. Indexes are used to connect a process to its input buffer and its store.

A store is a mapping from process indexes to histories of assignments where a *history* is a sequence of pairs (x, e), meaning e was assigned to x. We use meta-variables h, h', etc. for histories. Let :: be append. A lookup in a history is defined as: $(h :: (x, e))(x) = e$ and $(h :: (y, e))(x) = h(x)$ if $y \neq x$. We use history instead of memory for the purpose of defining determinism.

Expressions are evaluated entirely locally. The semantics of expressions are defined as: $(h, c) \Downarrow c$, $(h, x) \Downarrow h(x)$, $(h, n) \Downarrow n$, and $(h, e_1 \ op\ e_2) \Downarrow e_1' \ op\ e_2'$ if $(h, e_1) \Downarrow e_1'$ and $(h, e_2) \Downarrow e_2'$.

Figure 2 shows the reduction rules. Programs are equivalent up to re-ordering of parallel processes, e.g., $p_1||p_2 = p_2||p_1$. If p is an empty program (i.e., p

$$\frac{(S(i), e) \Downarrow n \qquad n \neq 0}{(B, S, i.(\texttt{if}\ e\ \texttt{then}\ s_1\ \texttt{else}\ s_2); s||p) \rightarrow (B, S, i.s_1; s||p)}\ \textbf{IF1}$$

$$\frac{(S(i), e) \Downarrow 0}{(B, S, i.(\texttt{if}\ e\ \texttt{then}\ s_1\ \texttt{else}\ s_2); s||p) \rightarrow (B, S, i.s_2; s||p)}\ \textbf{IF2}$$

$$\frac{(S(i), e) \Downarrow n \qquad n \neq 0}{(B, S, i.(\texttt{while}\ e\ \texttt{do}\ s_1); s||p) \rightarrow (B, S, i.s_1; (\texttt{while}\ e\ \texttt{do}\ s_1); s||p)}\ \textbf{WHILE1}$$

$$\frac{(S(i), e) \Downarrow 0}{(B, S, i.(\texttt{while}\ e\ \texttt{do}\ s_1); s||p) \rightarrow (B, S, i.s||p)}\ \textbf{WHILE2}$$

$$\frac{(S(i), e) \Downarrow e' \qquad S' = S[i \mapsto S(i) :: (x, e')]}{(B, S, i.x := e; s||p) \rightarrow (B, S', i.s||p)}\ \textbf{ASSIGN}$$

$$\frac{\begin{array}{ccc}(S(i), e_1) \Downarrow c & (S(i), e_2) \Downarrow e_2' & (S(j), e_3) \Downarrow c \\ \neg \mathit{buffered}(c) & & S' = S[j \mapsto S(j) :: (x, e_2')]\end{array}}{(B, S, i.!(e_1, e_2); s_1||j.?(e_3, x); s_2||p) \rightarrow (B, S', i.s_1||j.s_2||p)}\ \textbf{UNBUF}$$

$$\frac{(S(i), e_1) \Downarrow c \qquad (S(i), e_2) \Downarrow e_2' \qquad \mathit{buffered}(c) \qquad B' = B.\mathit{write}(c, e_2')}{(B, S, i.!(e_1, e_2); s||p) \rightarrow (B', S, i.s||p)}\ \textbf{BUF1}$$

$$\frac{\begin{array}{cc}(S(i), e) \Downarrow c & \mathit{buffered}(c) \\ (B', e') = B.\mathit{read}(c, i) & S' = S[i \mapsto S(i) :: (x, e')]\end{array}}{(B, S, i.?(e, x); s||p) \rightarrow (B', S', i.s||p)}\ \textbf{BUF2}$$

Fig. 2. The operational semantics of the small concurrent language

contains 0 processes), then $p' || p = p'$. Also, we let $s = s;\texttt{skip} = \texttt{skip};s$. Note that the rules only reduce the left-most processes, and so we rely on process re-ordering to reduce other processes. The rules **IF1**, **IF2**, **WHILE1**, and **WHILE2** do not involve channel communication and are self-explanatory. **ASSIGN** is also a process-local reduction because variables are local. Here, $S[i \mapsto h]$ means $\{j \mapsto S(j) \mid j \neq i \wedge j \in dom(S)\} \cup \{i \mapsto h\}$. We use the same notation for other mappings.

UNBUF handles communication over rendezvous channels. The predicate $\neg buffered(c)$ says c is unbuffered (and therefore rendezvous). Note that the written value e_2' is immediately transmitted to the reader. **BUF1** and **BUF2** handle communication over buffered channels, which include output buffered channels, input buffered channels, and reference cells. The predicate $buffered(c)$ says that c is a buffered channel. We write $B.write(c, e_2')$ for the buffer B after e_2' is written to the channel c, and $B.read(c, i)$ for the pair (B', e') where e' is the value process i read from channel c and B' is the buffer after the read.

Formally, a buffer B is a mapping from channels to buffer contents. If c is a rendezvous channel, then $B(c) = nil$ indicating that c is not buffered. If c is output buffered, then $B(c) = q$ where q is a FIFO queue of values. If c is input buffered, then $B(c) = \langle q_1, q_2, \dots, q_n \rangle$, i.e., a sequence of FIFO queues where each q_i represents the buffer content for process i. If c is a reference cell, then $B(c) = e$ for some value e. Let $enq(q, e)$ be q after e is enqueued. Let $deq(q)$ be the pair (q', e) where q' is q after e is dequeued. Buffer writes and reads are defined as shown in Figure 3. Note that $B.read(c, i)$ and $B.write(c, e)$ are undefined if c is rendezvous.

We write $P \rightarrow^* Q$ for 0 or more reduction steps from P to Q. We define partial confluence and determinism.

Definition 1. *Let Y be a set of channels. We say that P is partially confluent with respect to Y if for any $P \rightarrow^* P_1$ communicating only over channels in Y, and for any $P \rightarrow^* P_2$, there exists a state Q such that $P_2 \rightarrow^* Q$ communicating only over channels in Y and $P_1 \rightarrow^* Q$.*

$$B.write(c, e) = \begin{cases} B[c \mapsto enq(B(c), e)] & \text{if } c \text{ is output buffered} \\ B[c \mapsto \langle enq(q_1, e), \dots, enq(q_n, e)\rangle] \\ \quad \text{where } B(c) = \langle q_1, \dots, q_n \rangle & \text{if } c \text{ is input buffered} \\ B[c \mapsto e] & \text{if } c \text{ is a reference cell} \end{cases}$$

$$B.read(c, i) = \begin{cases} (B[c \mapsto q'], e) \\ \quad \text{where } B(c) = q \text{ and } (q', e) = deq(q) & \text{if } c \text{ is output buffered} \\ (B[c \mapsto \langle q_1, \dots, q_i', \dots, q_n \rangle], e) \\ \quad \text{where } B(c) = \langle q_1, \dots, q_i, \dots, q_n \rangle & \text{if } c \text{ is input buffered} \\ \qquad (q_i', e) = deq(q_i) \\ (B, B(c)) & \text{if } c \text{ is a reference cell} \end{cases}$$

Fig. 3. Buffer operations

Definition 2. *Let Y be a set of channels. We say that P is deterministic with respect to Y if for each process index i, there exists a (possibly infinite) sequence h_i such that for any $P \to^* (B, S, p)$ that communicates only over channels in Y, $S(i)$ is a prefix of h_i.*

Determinism implies that for any single process, interaction with the rest of the program is deterministic. Determinism and partial confluence are related in the following way.

Lemma 1. *If P is partially confluent with respect to Y then P is deterministic with respect to Y.*

Note that the definitions are sufficient for programs interacting with the environment because an environment can be modeled as a process using integer operators with unknown (but deterministic) semantics.

3 Calculus of Capabilities

We now present a capability calculus for ensuring partial confluence. While capability calculi are typically presented as a type system in the literature, we take a different approach and present the capability calculus as a dynamic system. We then construct a type system to statically reason about the dynamic capability calculus. This approach allows us to distinguish approximations due to the type abstraction from approximations inherent in the capability concept. (We have taken a similar approach in previous work [11].)

We informally describe the general idea. To simplify matters, we begin this initial discussion with rendezvous channels and total confluence. Given a program, the goal is to ensure that for each channel c, at most one process can write c and at most one process can read c at any point in time. To this end, we introduce capabilities $r(c)$ and $w(c)$ such that a process needs $r(c)$ to read from c and $w(c)$ to write to c. Capabilities are distributed to the processes at the start of the program and are not allowed be duplicated.

Recall the following confluent program from Section 2:

$$1.!(c, 1); !(d, 2) \,||\, 2.!(d, 3); ?(c, x) \,||\, 3.?(d, y); ?(d, y)$$

Note that for both c and d, at most one process can read and at most one process can write at any point in time. However, because both process 1 and process 2 write to d, they must somehow share $w(d)$. A novel feature of our capability calculus is the ability to pass capabilities between processes. The idea is to let capabilities be passed when the two processes synchronize, i.e., when the processes communicate over a channel. In our example, we let process 2 have $w(d)$ at the start of the program. Then, when process 1 and process 2 communicate over c, we pass $w(d)$ from process 2 to process 1 so that process 1 can write to d.

An important observation is that capability passing works in this example because $!(d, 3)$ is guaranteed to occur before the communication on c due to c

being rendezvous. If c is buffered (recall that the program is not confluent in this case), then $!(c,1)$ may occur before $!(d,3)$. Therefore, process 1 cannot obtain $w(d)$ from process 2 when c is written because process 2 may still need $w(d)$ to write on d. In general, for a buffered channel, while the read is guaranteed to occur after the write, there is no ordering dependency in the other direction, i.e., from the read to the write. Therefore, capabilities can be passed from the writer to the reader but not vice versa, whereas capabilities can be passed in both directions when communicating over a rendezvous channel.

Special care is needed for reference cells. If c is a reference cell, the program $1.!(c,1);\ !(c,2)||2.?(c,x)$ is not deterministic although process 1 is the only writer and process 2 is the only reader. We use *fractional capabilities* [3,11] such that a read capability is a fraction of the write capability. Capabilities can be split into multiple fractions, which allows concurrent reads on the same reference cell, but must be re-assembled to form the write capability. Fractional capabilities can be passed between processes in the same way as other capabilities. Recall the following confluent program from Section 2 where c is a reference cell and d is rendezvous:

$$1.!(c,1);\ !(c,2);\ !(d,3);\ ?(c,x)\ ||\ 2.?(d,x);\ ?(c,y)$$

Process 1 must start with the capability to write c. Because both processes read from c after communicating over d, we split the capability for c such that one half of the capability stays in process 1 and the other half is passed to process 2 via d. As a result, both processes obtain the capability to read from c. We have shown previously that fractional capabilities can be derived in a principled way from ordering dependencies [11].

We now formally present our capability calculus. Let

$$\begin{aligned}\textbf{Capabilities} = &\ \{w(c), r(c) \mid c \text{ is rendezvous or output buffered}\}\\ &\cup \{w(c) \mid c \text{ is input buffered}\} \cup \{w(c) \mid c \text{ is a reference cell}\}\end{aligned}$$

A *capability set* C is a function from **Capabilities** to rational numbers in the range $[0,1]$. If c is rendezvous, output buffered, or input buffered, $C(w(c)) = 1$ (resp. $C(r(c)) = 1$) means that the capability to write (resp. read) c is in C. Read capabilities are not needed for input buffered channels because each process has its own buffer. For reference cells, $C(w(c)) = 1$ means that the capability to write is in C, whereas $C(w(c)) > 0$ means that the capability to read is in C. To summarize, we define the following predicates:

$$hasWcap(C,c) \Leftrightarrow C(w(c)) = 1$$

$$hasRcap(C,c) \Leftrightarrow \begin{cases} C(r(c)) = 1 & \text{if } c \text{ is rendezvous or output buffered} \\ true & \text{if } c \text{ is input buffered} \\ C(w(c)) > 0 & \text{if } c \text{ is reference cell} \end{cases}$$

To denote capability merging and splitting, we define:

$$C_1 + C_2 = \{cap \mapsto C_1(cap) + C_2(cap) \mid cap \in \textbf{Capabilities}\}$$

We define $C_1 - C_2 = C_3$ if $C_1 = C_3 + C_2$. (We avoid negative capabilities.)

$$\frac{(S(i), e) \Downarrow n \qquad n \neq 0}{(X, B, S, i.C.(\texttt{if } e \texttt{ then } s_1 \texttt{ else } s_2); s||p) \rightarrow (X, B, S, i.C.s_1; s||p)} \ \textbf{IF1}'$$

$$\frac{(S(i), e) \Downarrow 0}{(X, B, S, i.C.(\texttt{if } e \texttt{ then } s_1 \texttt{ else } s_2); s||p) \rightarrow (X, B, S, i.C.s_2; s||p)} \ \textbf{IF2}'$$

$$\frac{(S(i), e) \Downarrow n \qquad n \neq 0}{\begin{array}{l}(X, B, S, i.C.(\texttt{while } e \texttt{ do } s_1); s||p) \\ \qquad \rightarrow (X, B, S, i.C.s_1; (\texttt{while } e \texttt{ do } s_1); s||p)\end{array}} \ \textbf{WHILE1}'$$

$$\frac{(S(i), e) \Downarrow 0}{(X, B, S, i.C.(\texttt{while } e \texttt{ do } s_1); s||p) \rightarrow (X, B, S, i.C.s||p)} \ \textbf{WHILE2}'$$

$$\frac{(S(i), e) \Downarrow e' \qquad S' = S[i \mapsto S(i) :: (x, e')]}{(X, B, S, i.C.x \texttt{ := } e; s||p) \rightarrow (X, B, S', i.C.s||p)} \ \textbf{ASSIGN}'$$

Fig. 4. The capability calculus: sequential reductions

$$\frac{\begin{array}{ccc}(S(i), e_1) \Downarrow c & (S(i), e_2) \Downarrow e_2' & (S(j), e_3) \Downarrow c \\ \neg buffered(c) & & S' = S[j \mapsto S(j) :: (x, e_2')] \\ \multicolumn{3}{c}{\ell = (confch(c) \Rightarrow (hasWcap(C_i, c) \wedge hasRcap(C_j, c)))}\end{array}}{\begin{array}{l}(X, B, S, i.C_i.!(e_1, e_2); s_1||j.C_j?(e_3, x); s_2||p) \\ \quad \xrightarrow{\ell} (X, B, S', i.(C_i - C + C').s_1||j.(C_j + C - C').s_2||p)\end{array}} \ \textbf{UNBUF}'$$

$$\frac{\begin{array}{ccc}(S(i), e_1) \Downarrow c & (S(i), e_2) \Downarrow e_2' & buffered(c) \\ B' = B.write(c, e_2') & \multicolumn{2}{c}{\ell = (confch(c) \Rightarrow hasWcap(C, c))}\end{array}}{(X, B, S, i.C.!(e_1, e_2); s||p) \xrightarrow{\ell} (X[c \mapsto X(c) + C'], B', S, i.(C - C').s||p)} \ \textbf{BUF1}'$$

$$\frac{\begin{array}{ccc}(S(i), e) \Downarrow c & buffered(c) & (B', e') = B.read(c, i) \\ S' = S[i \mapsto S(i) :: (x, e')] & \multicolumn{2}{c}{\ell = (confch(c) \Rightarrow \neg hasRcap(C, c))}\end{array}}{(X, B, S, i.C.?(e, x); s||p) \xrightarrow{\ell} (X[c \mapsto X(c) - C'], B', S', i.(C + C').s||p)} \ \textbf{BUF2}'$$

Fig. 5. The capability calculus: communication reductions

Figure 4 and Figure 5 show the reduction rules of the capability calculus. The reduction rules (technically, labeled transition rules) are similar to those of operational semantics with the following differences.

Each concurrent process is prefixed by a capability set C representing the current capabilities held by the process. The rules in Figure 4 do not utilize capabilities (i.e., capabilities are only passed sequentially) and are self-explanatory. Figure 5 shows how capabilities are utilized at communication points. **UNBUF′** sends capabilities C from the writer process to the reader process and sends capabilities C' from the reader process to the writer process. **UNBUF′** checks whether the right capabilities are present by $hasWcap(C_i, c) \wedge hasRcap(C_j, c)$. The label ℓ records whether the check succeeds. Because we are interested in partial confluence with respect to some set Y of channels, we only check the capabilities if $c \in Y$. To this end, the predicate *confch*() parameterizes the system so that *confch*(c) iff $c \in Y$.

BUF1′ and **BUF2′** handle buffered communication. Recall that the writer can pass capabilities to the reader. **BUF1′** takes capabilities C' from the writer process and stores them in X. **BUF2′** takes capabilities C' from X and gives them to the reader process. The mapping X from channels to capability sets maintains the capabilities stored in each channel.

We now formally state when our capability calculus guarantees partial confluence. Let $erase((X, B, S, 1.C_1.s_1 || \ldots || n.C_n.s_n)) = (B, S, 1.s_1 || \ldots || n.s_n)$, i.e., *erase*() erases all capability information from the state. We use meta-variables P, Q, R, etc. for states in the operational semantics and underlined meta-variables $\underline{P}$, $\underline{Q}$, $\underline{R}$, etc. for states in the capability calculus.

A *well-formed state* is a state in the capability calculus that does not carry duplicated capabilities. More formally,

Definition 3. *Let* $\underline{P} = (X, B, S, 1.C_1.s_1 || \ldots || n.C_n.s_n)$*. Let* $C = \sum_{i=1}^{n} C_i + \sum_{c \in dom(X)} X(c)$*. We say* $\underline{P}$ *is well-formed if for all* $cap \in dom(C)$, $C(cap) = 1$.

We define *capability-respecting states.* Informally, $\underline{P}$ is capability respecting with respect to a set of channels Y if for any sequence of reductions from *erase*($\underline{P}$), there exists a strategy to pass capabilities between the processes such that every communication over the channels in Y occurs under the appropriate capabilities. More formally,

Definition 4. *Let* Y *be a set of channels and let* $confch(c) \Leftrightarrow c \in Y$*. Let* M *be a set of states in the capability calculus.* M *is said to be capability-respecting with respect to* Y *if for any* $\underline{P} \in M$*,*

- $\underline{P}$ *is well-formed, and*
- *for any state* Q *such that* $erase(\underline{P}) \rightarrow Q$*, there exists* $\underline{Q} \in M$ *such that,* $erase(\underline{Q}) = Q$, $\underline{P} \xrightarrow{\ell} \underline{Q}$*, and if* ℓ *is not empty then* $\ell = true$*.*

We now state the main claim of this section.

Theorem 1. *Let* P *be a state. Suppose there exists* M *such that* M *is capability-respecting with respect to* Y *and there exists* $\underline{P} \in M$ *such that* $erase(\underline{P}) = P$*. Then* P *is partially confluent with respect to* Y*.*

3.1 Static Checking of Capabilities

Theorem 1 tells us that to ensure that P is partially confluent, it is sufficient to find a capability-respecting set containing some $\underline{P}$ such that $erase(\underline{P}) = P$. [2] Ideally, we would like to use the largest capability-respecting set, but such a set is not recursive (because it is reducible from the halting problem). Instead, we use a type system to compute a safe approximation of the set.

[2] It is not a necessary condition, however. For example, $!(c,1)||!(c,1)||?(c,x)||?(c,x)$ is confluent but does not satisfy the condition.

We define four kinds of channel types, one for each channel kind.

$$\begin{array}{lll} \tau ::= & ch(\rho, \tau, \Psi_1, \Psi_2) & (\textit{rendezvous}) \\ \mid & ch(\rho, \tau, \Psi) & (\textit{output buffered}) \\ \mid & ch(\rho, \tau, \langle \Psi_1, \ldots, \Psi_n \rangle) & (\textit{input buffered}) \\ \mid & ch(\rho, \tau) & (\textit{reference cell}) \\ \mid & int & (\textit{integers}) \end{array}$$

Meta-variables ρ, ρ', etc. are *channel handles.* Let **Handles** be the set of channel handles. Let **StaticCapabilities** $= \{w(\rho), r(\rho) \mid \rho \in$ **Handles**$\}$. Meta-variables Ψ, Ψ', etc. are mappings from **StaticCapabilities** to $[0, 1]$. We call such a mapping a *static capability set.* The rendezvous channel type can be read as follows: the channel communicates values of type τ, any writer of the channel sends capabilities Ψ_1, and any reader of the channel sends capabilities Ψ_2. For an output buffered channel, because readers cannot send capabilities, only one static capability set, Ψ, is present in its type. For an input buffered channel, the sequence $\langle \Psi_1, \ldots, \Psi_n \rangle$ lists capabilities such that each process i gets Ψ_i from a read. Because a value stored in a reference cell may be read arbitrarily many times, our type system cannot statically reason about processes passing capabilities through reference cells, and so a reference cell type does not carry any static capability set.

Additions and subtractions of static capabilities are analogous to those of (actual) capabilities:

$$\begin{array}{l} \Psi_1 + \Psi_2 = \{cap \mapsto \Psi_1(cap) + \Psi_2(cap) \mid cap \in \textbf{StaticCapabilities}\} \\ \Psi_1 - \Psi_2 = \Psi_3 \quad \text{if } \Psi_1 = \Psi_3 + \Psi_2 \end{array}$$

We say $\Psi_1 \geq \Psi_2$ if there exists Ψ_3 such that $\Psi_1 = \Psi_2 + \Psi_3$.

For channel type τ, $hdl(\tau)$ is the handle of the channel, and $valtype(\tau)$ is the type of the communicated value. That is, $hdl(ch(\rho, \ldots)) = \rho$ and $valtype(ch(\rho, \tau, \ldots)) = \tau$. Also, $writeSend(\tau)$ (resp. $readSend(\tau)$) is the set of capabilities sent by a writer (resp. reader) of the channel. More formally,

$$\begin{array}{l} writeSend(ch(\rho, \tau, \Psi_1, \Psi_2)) = \Psi_1 \\ writeSend(ch(\rho, \tau, \Psi)) = \Psi \\ writeSend(ch(\rho, \tau, \langle \Psi_1, \ldots, \Psi_n \rangle)) = \sum_{i=1}^{n} \Psi_i \\ writeSend(ch(\rho, \tau)) = \mathit{0} \\ readSend(\tau) = \begin{cases} \Psi_2 & \text{if } \tau = ch(\rho, \tau', \Psi_1, \Psi_2) \\ \mathit{0} & \text{otherwise} \end{cases} \end{array}$$

($\mathit{0}$ is the constant zero function $\lambda x.0$.) Similarly, $writeRecv(\tau)$ (resp. $readRecv(\tau, i)$) is the set of capabilities received by the writer (resp. the reader process i):

$$\begin{array}{l} writeRecv(\tau) = readSend(\tau) \\ readRecv(\tau, i) = \begin{cases} \Psi_i & \text{if } \tau = ch(\rho, \tau, \langle \Psi_1, \ldots, \Psi_n \rangle) \\ writeSend(\tau) & \text{otherwise} \end{cases} \end{array}$$

$$\frac{\Gamma, i, \Psi \vdash s_1 : \Psi_1 \quad \Gamma, i, \Psi_1 \vdash s_2 : \Psi_2}{\Gamma, i, \Psi \vdash s_1; s_2 : \Psi_2} \ \textbf{SEQ}$$

$$\frac{\Gamma \vdash e : int \quad \Gamma, i, \Psi \vdash s_1 : \Psi_1 \quad \Gamma, i, \Psi \vdash s_2 : \Psi_2 \quad \Psi_1 \geq \Psi_3 \quad \Psi_2 \geq \Psi_3}{\Gamma, i, \Psi \vdash \texttt{if } e \texttt{ then } s_1 \texttt{ else } s_2 : \Psi_3} \ \textbf{IF}$$

$$\frac{\Gamma \vdash e : int \quad \Gamma, i, \Psi_1 \vdash s : \Psi_2 \quad \Psi_2 \geq \Psi_1 \quad \Psi \geq \Psi_1}{\Gamma, i, \Psi \vdash \texttt{while } e \texttt{ do } s : \Psi_2} \ \textbf{WHILE}$$

$$\frac{}{\Gamma, i, \Psi \vdash \texttt{skip} : \Psi} \ \textbf{SKIP} \qquad \frac{\Gamma \vdash e : \Gamma(x)}{\Gamma, i, \Psi \vdash x \texttt{ := } e : \Psi} \ \textbf{ASSIGN}$$

$$\frac{\Gamma \vdash e_1 : \tau \quad \Gamma \vdash e_2 : valtype(\tau) \quad confch(\tau, \Gamma) \Rightarrow hasWcap(\Psi, \tau)}{\Gamma, i, \Psi \vdash \texttt{!}(e_1, e_2) : \Psi - writeSend(\tau) + writeRecv(\tau)} \ \textbf{WRITE}$$

$$\frac{\Gamma \vdash e : \tau \quad \Gamma(x) = valtype(\tau) \quad confch(\tau, \Gamma) \Rightarrow hasRcap(\Psi, \tau)}{\Gamma, i, \Psi \vdash \texttt{?}(e, x) : \Psi - readSend(\tau) + readRecv(\tau, i)} \ \textbf{READ}$$

Fig. 6. Type checking rules

Note that the writer of the input buffered channel $ch(\rho, \tau, \langle \Psi_1, \ldots, \Psi_n \rangle)$ must be able to send the sum of all capabilities to be received by each process (i.e., $\sum_{i=1}^{n} \Psi_i$), whereas the reader receives only its own share (i.e., Ψ_i).

For channel type τ, $hasWcap(\Psi, \tau)$ and $hasRcap(\Psi, \tau)$ are the static analog of $hasWcap(C, c)$ and $hasRcap(C, c)$. More formally,

$$hasWcap(\Psi, \tau) \Leftrightarrow \Psi(w(hdl(\tau))) = 1$$

$$hasRcap(\Psi, \tau) \Leftrightarrow \begin{cases} \Psi(r(hdl(\tau))) = 1 & \text{if } \tau \text{ is rendezvous or output buffered} \\ true & \text{if } \tau \text{ is input buffered} \\ \Psi(w(hdl(\tau))) > 0 & \text{if } \tau \text{ is reference cell} \end{cases}$$

A *type environment* Γ is a mapping from channels and variables to types such that for each channel c and d,

- the channel type kind of $\Gamma(c)$ coincides with the channel kind of c, and
- if $c \neq d$ then $hdl(\Gamma(c)) \neq hdl(\Gamma(d))$, i.e., each handle ρ uniquely identifies a channel. (Section 3.3 discusses a way to relax this restriction.)

We sometimes write $\Gamma[c]$ to mean $hdl(\Gamma(c))$.

Expressions are type-checked as follows:

$$\frac{}{\Gamma \vdash c : \Gamma(c)} \qquad \frac{}{\Gamma \vdash x : \Gamma(x)} \qquad \frac{}{\Gamma \vdash n : int} \qquad \frac{\Gamma \vdash e_1 : int \quad \Gamma \vdash e_2 : int}{\Gamma \vdash e_1 \ op \ e_2 : int}$$

Figure 6 shows the type checking rules for statements. The judgments are of the form $\Gamma, i, \Psi \vdash s : \Psi'$ where i is the index of the process where s appears in, Ψ the capabilities before s, and Ψ' the capabilities after s. **SEQ**, **IF**, **WHILE**, **SKIP**, and **ASSIGN** are self-explanatory. **WRITE** handles channel writes and

READ handles channel reads. Here, $\mathit{confch}(\tau, \Gamma)$ is defined as:

$$\mathit{confch}(\tau, \Gamma) \Leftrightarrow \exists c.\Gamma[c] = \mathit{hdl}(\tau) \wedge \mathit{confch}(c)$$

We write $\Gamma \vdash B(c)$ if the buffer $B(c)$ is well-typed, i.e., $\Gamma \vdash e : \mathit{valtype}(\Gamma(c))$ for each value e stored in the buffer $B(c)$. We write $\Gamma \vdash h$ if the history h is well-typed, i.e, $\Gamma \vdash h(x) : \Gamma(x)$ for each $x \in \mathit{dom}(h)$. We write $\Gamma \vdash C : \Psi$ if Ψ represents C, i.e., for each $w(c) \in \mathit{dom}(C)$, $\Psi(w(\Gamma[c])) = C(w(c))$ and for each $r(c) \in \mathit{dom}(C)$, $\Psi(r(\Gamma[c])) = C(r(c))$.

Let $\underline{P} = (B, X, S, 1.C_1.s_1 || \ldots || n.C_n.s_n)$. An *environment* for $\underline{P}$ consists of a type environment Γ for typing the channels, a type environment Γ_i for typing each process i, the starting static capability Ψ_i for each process i, and the mapping W from handles to static capabilities that represents X. We say $\underline{P}$ is well-typed under the environment $(\Gamma, \Gamma_1, \ldots, \Gamma_n, \Psi_1, \ldots, \Psi_n, W)$, written $(\Gamma, \Gamma_1, \ldots, \Gamma_n, \Psi_1, \ldots, \Psi_n, W) \vdash \underline{P}$, if

- For each c, $\Gamma \vdash B(c)$.
- For each i, $\Gamma_i \supseteq \Gamma$, $\Gamma_i \vdash S(i)$, $\Gamma \vdash C_i : \Psi_i$, and $\Gamma_i, i, \Psi_i \vdash s_i : \Psi_i'$ for some Ψ_i'.
- For each c, $\Gamma \vdash X(c) : W(\Gamma[c])$, i.e., W is a static representation of X.
- Let $\Psi_{total} = \sum_{i=1}^{n} \Psi_i + \sum_{\rho \in \mathit{dom}(W)} W(\rho)$. Then for each $\mathit{cap} \in \mathit{dom}(\Psi_{total})$, $\Psi_{total}(\mathit{cap}) = 1$, i.e., there are no duplicated capabilities.
- For all output buffered channels c, $W(\Gamma[c]) = |B(c)| \times \mathit{writeSend}(\Gamma(c))$. For all input buffered channels c, $W(\Gamma[c]) = \sum_{i=1}^{n} |B(c).i| \times \mathit{readRecv}(\Gamma(c), i)$.

In the last condition, $|B(c)|$ denotes the length of the queue $B(c)$, and $|B(c).i|$ denotes the length of the queue for process i (for input buffered channels). The condition ensures that there are enough capabilities in X for buffered reads. We now state the main claim of this section.

Theorem 2. *Let Y be a set of channels and let $\mathit{confch}(c) \Leftrightarrow c \in Y$. Let $M = \{\underline{P} \mid \exists \mathit{Env}.\mathit{Env} \vdash \underline{P}\}$. Then M is capability-respecting with respect to Y.*

Theorem 2 together with Theorem 1 implies that to check if P is confluent, it suffices to find a well-typed $\underline{P}$ such that $P = \mathit{erase}(\underline{P})$. More formally,

Corollary 1. *Let Y be a set of channels and let $\mathit{confch}(c) \Leftrightarrow c \in Y$. P is partially-confluent and deterministic with respect to Y if there exists $\underline{P}$ and Env such that $P = \mathit{erase}(\underline{P})$ and $\mathit{Env} \vdash \underline{P}$.*

The problem of finding $\underline{P}$ and Env such that $P = \mathit{erase}(\underline{P})$ and $\mathit{Env} \vdash \underline{P}$ can be formulated as linear inequality constraints satisfaction problem. The details are similar to the type inference algorithm from our previous work [11]. The constraints can be generated in time polynomial in the size of P, which can then be solved efficiently by a linear programming algorithm.

3.2 Examples

Producer Consumer. Let c be an output buffered channel. The program 1.`while` 1 `do` !$(c, 1)$ || 2.`while` 1 `do` ?(c, x) is a simple but common communication pattern of sender and receiver processes being fixed for each channel;

no capabilities need to be passed between processes. The type system can prove confluence by assigning the starting capabilities $\mathit{0}[w(\rho) \mapsto 1]$ to process 1 and $\mathit{0}[r(\rho) \mapsto 1]$ to process 2 where $c : \mathit{ch}(\rho, \mathit{int}, \mathit{0})$.

Token Ring. Let c_1, c_2, c_3 be rendezvous and d be output buffered. The program below models a token ring where processes 1, 2, and 3 take turns writing to d:

$$\begin{array}{l} 1.\texttt{while}\ 1\ \texttt{do}\ (?(c_3, x);\ !(d, 1);\ !(c_1, 0)) \\ \|\ 2.\texttt{while}\ 1\ \texttt{do}\ (?(c_1, x);\ !(d, 2);\ !(c_2, 0)) \\ \|\ 3.!(c_3, 0); \texttt{while}\ 1\ \texttt{do}\ (?(c_2, x);\ !(d, 3);\ !(c_3, 0)) \\ \|\ 4.\texttt{while}\ 1\ \texttt{do}\ ?(d, y) \end{array}$$

Recall that variables x and y are process local. The type system can prove confluence by assigning the channel d the type $\mathit{ch}(\rho_d, \mathit{int}, \mathit{0})$ and each c_i the type $\mathit{ch}(\rho_{c_i}, \mathit{int}, \mathit{0}[w(\rho_d) \mapsto 1], \mathit{0})$, which says that a write to c_i sends $w(d)$ to the reader. The starting capabilities are $\mathit{0}[r(\rho_{c_3}) \mapsto 1, w(\rho_{c_1}) \mapsto 1]$ for process 1, $\mathit{0}[r(\rho_{c_1}) \mapsto 1, w(\rho_{c_2}) \mapsto 1]$ for process 2, $\mathit{0}[r(\rho_{c_2}) \mapsto 1, w(\rho_{c_3}) \mapsto 1, w(\rho_d) \mapsto 1]$ for process 3, and $\mathit{0}[r(\rho_d) \mapsto 1]$ for process 4.

Barrier Synchronization. Let c_1, c_2, c_3 be reference cells. Let d_1, d_2, d_3, d'_1, d'_2, d'_3 be input buffered channels. Consider the following program:

$$\begin{array}{l} 1.\texttt{while}\ 1\ \texttt{do}\ (!(c_1, e_1);\ !(d_1, 0); \mathbf{BR}; ?(c_1, y); ?(c_2, z); ?(c_3, w);\ !(d'_1, 0); \mathbf{BR}') \\ \|\ 2.\texttt{while}\ 1\ \texttt{do}\ (!(c_2, e_2);\ !(d_2, 0); \mathbf{BR}; ?(c_1, y); ?(c_2, z); ?(c_3, w);\ !(d'_2, 0); \mathbf{BR}') \\ \|\ 3.\texttt{while}\ 1\ \texttt{do}\ (!(c_3, e_3);\ !(d_3, 0); \mathbf{BR}; ?(c_1, y); ?(c_2, z); ?(c_3, w);\ !(d'_3, 0); \mathbf{BR}') \end{array}$$

Here, $\mathbf{BR} = ?(d_1, x); ?(d_2, x); ?(d_3, x)$ and $\mathbf{BR}' = ?(d'_1, x); ?(d'_2, x); ?(d'_3, x)$. The program is an example of barrier-style synchronization. Process 1 writes to c_1, process 2 writes to c_2, process 3 writes to c_3, and then the three processes synchronize via a barrier so that none of the processes can proceed until all are done with their writes. Note that $!(d_i, 0); \mathbf{BR}$ models the barrier for each process i. After the barrier synchronization, each process reads from all three reference cells before synchronizing themselves via another barrier, this time modeled by $!(d'_i, 0); \mathbf{BR}'$, before the next iteration of the loop.

The type system can prove confluence by assigning the following types (assume e_1, e_2, and e_3 are of type *int*): $c_1 : \mathit{ch}(\rho_{c1}, \mathit{int})$, $c_2 : \mathit{ch}(\rho_{c2}, \mathit{int})$, $c_3 : \mathit{ch}(\rho_{c3}, \mathit{int})$, and for each $i \in \{1, 2, 3\}$,

$$\begin{array}{l} d_i : \mathit{ch}(\rho_{d_i}, \mathit{int}, \langle \mathit{0}[w(\rho_{c_i}) \mapsto \frac{1}{3}], \mathit{0}[w(\rho_{c_i}) \mapsto \frac{1}{3}], \mathit{0}[w(\rho_{c_i}) \mapsto \frac{1}{3}] \rangle) \\ d'_i : \mathit{ch}(\rho_{d'_i}, \mathit{int}, \langle \mathit{0}[w(\rho_{c_1}) \mapsto \frac{1}{3}], \mathit{0}[w(\rho_{c_2}) \mapsto \frac{1}{3}], \mathit{0}[w(\rho_{c_3}) \mapsto \frac{1}{3}] \rangle) \end{array}$$

The initial static capability set for each process i is $\mathit{0}[w(\rho_{c_i}) \mapsto 1, w(\rho_{d_i}) \mapsto 1, w(\rho_{d'_i}) \mapsto 1]$. Note that fractional capabilities are passed at barrier synchronization points to enable reads and writes on c_1, c_2, and c_3.

Type inference fails if the program is changed so that d_1, d_2, d_3 are also used for the second barrier (in place of d'_1, d'_2, d'_3) because while the first write to d_i must send the capability to read c_i, the second write to d_i must send to each process j the capability to access c_j, and there is no single type for d_i to express this behavior. This demonstrates the *flow-insensitivity* limitation of our type system, i.e., a channel must send and receive the same capabilities every time it is used.

However, if synchronization points are syntactically identifiable (as in this example) then the program is easily modified so that flow-insensitivity becomes sufficient by using distinct channels at each syntactic synchronization point.[3] In our example, the first barrier in each process matches the other, and the second barrier in each process matches the other. Synchronizations that are not syntactically identifiable are often considered as a sign of potential bugs [1]. Note that reference cells c_1 and c_2 are not used for synchronization and therefore need no syntactic restriction.

3.3 Extensions

We discuss extensions to our system.

Regions. Aliasing becomes an issue when channels are used as values, e.g., like in a π calculus program. For example, our type system does not allow two different channels c and d to be passed to the same channel because two different channels cannot be given the same handle. One way to resolve aliasing is to use *regions* so that each ρ represents a set of channels. Then, we may give both c and d the same type $ch(\rho, \ldots)$ at the cost of sharing $w(\rho)$ (and $r(\rho)$) for all the channels in the region ρ.

Existential Abstraction and Linear Types. Another way to resolve aliasing is to existentially abstract capabilities as in $\exists\rho.\tau \otimes \Psi$. Any type containing a capability set must be handled linearly[4] to prevent the duplication of capabilities. The capabilities are recovered by opening the existential package. Existential abstraction can encode linearly typed channels [10,8] (for rendezvous channels) as: $\exists\rho.ch(\rho, \tau, 0, 0) \otimes 0[w(\rho) \mapsto 1, r(\rho) \mapsto 1]$. Note that the type encapsulates both a channel and the capability to access the channel. This encoding allows transitions to and from linearly typed channels to the capabilities world, e.g., it is possible to use once a linearly-typed channel multiple times. An analogous approach has been applied to express updatable recursive data structures in the capability calculus [13].

Dynamically Created Channels. Dynamically created channels can be handled in much the same way heap allocated objects are handled in the capability calculus [4] (we only show the rule for the case where c is rendezvous):

$$\frac{\rho \text{ is not free in the conclusion} \quad \Gamma \cup \{c \mapsto ch(\rho, \tau, \Psi_1, \Psi_2)\}, i, \Psi + 0[w(\rho) \mapsto 1][r(\rho) \mapsto 1] \vdash s : \Psi'}{\Gamma, i, \Psi \vdash \nu c.s : \Psi'}$$

[3] This can be done without changing the implementation. See *named barriers* in [1].

[4] Actually, a more relaxed sub-structural type system is preferred for handling fractional capabilities [11].

Existential abstraction allows dynamically created channels to leave their lexical scope. An alternative approach is to place the newly created channel in an existing region. In this case, we can remove the hypothesis "ρ is not free in the conclusion", but we also must remove the capabilities $\mathit{0}[w(\rho) \mapsto 1][r(\rho) \mapsto 1]$.

Dynamically Spawned Processes. Dynamic spawning of processes can be typed as follows:

$$\frac{\Gamma, i, \Psi_2 \vdash s : \Psi'}{\Gamma, i, \Psi_1 + \Psi_2 \vdash \mathtt{spawn}(s) : \Psi_1}$$

(For simplicity, we assume that the local store of the parent process is copied for the spawned process. Details for handling input buffered channels are omitted.) Note that the spawned process may take capabilities from the parent process.

4 Related Work

We discuss previous approaches to inferring partial confluence. Kahn process networks [7] restrict communication to input buffered channels with a unique sender process to guarantee determinism. Edwards et al. [5] restricts communication to rendezvous channels with a unique sender process and a unique receiver process to model deterministic behavior of embedded systems. These models are the easy cases for our system where capabilities are not passed between processes.

Linear type systems can infer partial confluence by checking that each channel is used at most once [10,8].[5] Section 3.3 discusses how to express linearly typed channels in our system. König presents a type system that can be parameterized to check partial confluence in the π-calculus [9]. Her system corresponds to the restricted case of our system where each (rendezvous) channel is given a type of the form $\mathit{ch}(\rho, \tau, \mathit{0}[w(\rho) \mapsto 1], \mathit{0}[r(\rho) \mapsto 1])$, i.e., each channel sends its own write capability at writes and sends its own read capability at reads. Therefore, for example, while her system can check the confluence of $\mathtt{!}(c, 1); \mathtt{?}(c, x) || \mathtt{?}(c, x); \mathtt{!}(c, 2)$, it cannot check the confluence of $\mathtt{!}(c, 1); \mathtt{!}(c, 2) || \mathtt{?}(c, x); \mathtt{?}(c, x)$.

A more exhaustive approach for checking partial confluence has been proposed in which the confluence for every state of the program is individually checked by following the transitions from that state [6,2]. These methods are designed specifically to drive state space reduction, and hence have somewhat a different aim from our work. They have been shown effective for programs with a small number of states.

This work was motivated by our previous work on inferring confluence in functional languages with side effects [11] (see also [3]). These systems can only reason about synchronization at join points, and therefore cannot infer confluence of channel-communicating processes.

---

[5] [8] uses asynchronous π calculus, and so is not entirely comparable with our work.

5 Conclusions

We have presented a system for inferring partial confluence of concurrent programs communicating via a mix of different kinds of communication channels. We casted our system as a capability calculus where fractional capabilities can be passed at channel communications, and presented a type system for statically inferring partial confluence by finding an appropriate capability passing strategy in the calculus.

References

1. A. Aiken and D. Gay. Barrier inference. In *Proceedings of the 25th Annual ACM SIGPLAN-SIGACT Symposium on Principles of Programming Languages*, pages 342–354, San Diego, California, Jan. 1998.
2. S. Blom and J. van de Pol. State space reduction by proving confluence. In *Proceedings of the 14th International Conference on Computer Aided Verification*, pages 596–609, Copenhagen, Denmark, July 2002.
3. J. Boyland. Checking interference with fractional permissions. In R. Cousot, editor, *Static Analysis, Tenth International Symposium*, volume 2694 of *Lecture Notes in Computer Science*, pages 55–72, San Diego, CA, June 2003. Springer-Verlag.
4. K. Crary, D. Walker, and G. Morrisett. Typed memory management in a calculus of capabilities. In *Proceedings of the 26th Annual ACM SIGPLAN-SIGACT Symposium on Principles of Programming Languages*, pages 262–275, San Antonio, Texas, Jan. 1999.
5. S. A. Edwards and O. Tardieu. Shim: a deterministic model for heterogeneous embedded systems. In *Proceedings of the 5th ACM International Conference On Embedded Software*, pages 264–272, Jersey City, NJ, Sept. 2005.
6. J. F. Groote and J. van de Pol. State space reduction using partial tau-confluence. In *Proceedings of 25th International Symposium on the Mathematical Foundations of Computer Science 2000*, pages 383–393, Bratislava, Slovakia, Aug. 2000.
7. G. Kahn. The semantics of a simple language for parallel programming. In *Information processing*, pages 471–475, Stockholm, Sweden, Aug 1974.
8. N. Kobayashi, B. C. Pierce, and D. N. Turner. Linearity and the pi-calculus. *ACM Transactions on Programming Languages and Systems*, 21(5):914–947, Sept. 1999.
9. B. König. Analysing input/output-capabilities of mobile processes with a generic type system. In *Proceedings of the 27th International Colloquium on Automata, Languages and Programming*, pages 403–414, Geneva, Switzerland, July 2000.
10. U. Nestmann and M. Steffen. Typing confluence. In *Proceedings of FMICS '97*, pages 77–101, 1997.
11. T. Terauchi and A. Aiken. Witnessing side-effects. In *Proceedings of the 10th ACM SIGPLAN International Conference on Functional Programming*, pages 105–115, Tallinn, Estonia, Sept. 2005. ACM.
12. T. Terauchi and A. Aiken. A capability calculus for concurrency and determinism. Technical Report UCB/EECS-2006-84, University of California, Berkeley, 2006.
13. D. Walker and G. Morrisett. Alias types for recursive data structures. In *International Workshop on Types in Compilation*, Montreal, Canada, Sept. 2000.

A New Type System for Deadlock-Free Processes

Naoki Kobayashi

Graduate School of Information Sciences, Tohoku University

Abstract. We extend a previous type system for the π-calculus that guarantees deadlock-freedom. The previous type systems for deadlock-freedom either lacked a reasonable type inference algorithm or were not strong enough to ensure deadlock-freedom of processes using recursion. Although the extension is fairly simple, the new type system admits type inference and is much more expressive than the previous type systems that admit type inference. In fact, we show that the simply-typed λ-calculus with recursion can be encoded into the deadlock-free fragment of our typed π-calculus. To enable analysis of realistic programs, we also present an extension of the type system to handle recursive data structures like lists. Both extensions have already been incorporated into the recent release of `TyPiCal`, a type-based analyzer for the π-calculus.

1 Introduction

Various type systems for the π-calculus have been proposed, some of which can guarantee that processes are deadlock-free in the sense that certain communications will eventually succeed unless the process diverges [3, 5–7, 10, 15]. (Some of them guarantee even a stronger property.) Earlier type systems for deadlock-freedom [5, 6, 14, 15] required explicit type annotations, so that they were not suitable for automatic analysis of deadlock-freedom. Kobayashi et al. [7, 10] later modified the type systems so that the resulting type systems have a type inference algorithm, and deadlock-freedom of processes can be automatically analyzed through type inference.

Based on the type system of [7], Kobayashi has implemented the first version of `TyPiCal` (ver. 1.0), a type-based analyzer for the π-calculus. Figure 1 shows a sample input and output of the deadlock analysis of `TyPiCal`. The first line in the input program runs two servers, one of which waits for a request on channel `server1` and sends 1 back to the reply channel `r`, and the other of which waits for a request on channel `server2` and may or may not send a reply, depending on the value of `b`. (Here, ?, !, and | represent an input action, an output action, and parallel composition respectively. `O` represents an inaction.) The second line runs a client process, which creates a fresh communication channel `r1` for receiving a reply, sends a request on `server1`, and waits for a reply. The client process on the third line behaves similarly, except that it sends a request on `server2`. Given that program, `TyPiCal`'s deadlock analyzer automatically finds input and

C. Baier and H. Hermanns (Eds.): CONCUR 2006, LNCS 4137, pp. 233–247, 2006.

output operations that are guaranteed to succeed if they are ever executed and if the whole process does not diverge, and mark them with `??` and `!!`. The output shown in the figure indicates that the first client can eventually receive a reply (note that `r1?x` has been replaced by `r1??x`), while the second client may not be able to receive a reply (`r2?x` remains the same).

Input program:
```
  *(server1?r.r!1) | *(server2?r.if b then r!1 else O)  /* Servers */
| new r1 in server1!r1.r1?x  /* A client for the first server */
| new r2 in server2!r2.r2?x  /* A client for the second server */
```

Output:
```
  *(server1?r.r!!1) | *(server2?r.if b then r!!1 else O)
| new r1 in server1!!r1.r1??x | new r2 in server2!!r2.r2?x
```

Fig. 1. A sample input and output of the deadlock analysis of `TyPiCal`

To enable type inference, however, we have traded the strength of the type system [7, 10]. In particular, the previous type systems for deadlock-freedom equipped with type inference algorithms cannot well handle recursive processes. For example, consider the following function server, which computes the factorial:

```
*fact?(n,r).if n=0 then r!1
            else new r1 in (fact!(n-1,r1) | r1?x.r!(x*n))
```

The server is deadlock-free in the sense that given a request, it will eventually returns a result unless the process diverges (actually, the process does not diverge, but the termination analysis is out of scope of this paper), but the previous type systems fail to conclude that. Even the simply-typed λ-calculus (without recursion) could not be encoded into the deadlock-free fragment of the previous type systems [7, 10]. On the other hand, an earlier type system of Kobayashi [5] could handle the above recursive process, but it was so complicated that a type inference algorithm could not be developed.

In this paper, we introduce a simple extension of the type system for deadlock-freedom [7, 10], which allows us to handle recursive processes like above, while keeping the existence of a type inference algorithm. Unlike the previous type systems which deal with pure polyadic π-calculus, we also extend the target language with data structures like pairs and lists. We have already incorporated those extensions into the recent version of `TyPiCal`.

The rest of this paper is structured as follows. Section 2 introduces our target language (with only pairs as data structures). Section 3 introduces our new type system for deadlock-freedom, and shows its soundness. To demonstrate the strength of our type system, Section 4 shows that the simply-typed λ-calculus with recursion can be encoded into the deadlock-free fragment of our typed calculus. Section 5 informally explains how to deal with list data structures. Missing definitions and proofs are found in the full version of this paper [8].

2 Target Language

This section introduces the target language of our deadlock analysis, which is a subset of π-calculus [12] extended with booleans, pairs, and conditionals.

2.1 Syntax

Definition 2.1. *The set of processes, ranged over by P, is defined by:*

$$\begin{aligned} P &::= \mathbf{0} \mid x!^t v.\, P \mid x?^t y.\, P \\ &\quad \mid (P \,|\, Q) \mid *P \mid (\nu x)\, P \mid \textbf{if } v \textbf{ then } P \textbf{ else } Q \mid \textbf{let } x = e \textbf{ in } P \\ e &::= \mathit{true} \mid \mathit{false} \mid x \mid \langle e_1, e_2 \rangle \mid \mathit{proj}_1(e) \mid \mathit{proj}_2(e) \\ v &::= \mathit{true} \mid \mathit{false} \mid x \mid \langle v_1, v_2 \rangle \end{aligned}$$

Here, x and y range over a countably infinite set **Var** *of variables. t ranges over* $\mathbf{Nat} \cup \{\infty\}$.

Notation 2.1. *The prefix $x?y$ binds variables y and (νx) binds x. As usual, we identify processes up to α-conversions (renaming of bound variables), and assume that α-conversions are implicitly applied so that bound variables are always different from each other and from free variables. We write $[x \mapsto v]P$ for the process obtained by replacing all the free occurrences of x in P with v. We often omit $\mathbf{0}$ and write $x!v$ and $x?y$ for $x!v.\,\mathbf{0}$ and $x?y.\,\mathbf{0}$ respectively.*

We assume that prefixes ($x!v$, $x?y$, (νx), and $*$) bind tighter than the parallel composition operator $|$, so that $x!y.\,P \,|\, Q$ means $(x!y.\,P) \,|\, Q$, not $x!y.\,(P \,|\, Q)$. We often write $x?(y,z).\,P$ for $x?p.$ **let** *$y = \mathit{proj}_1(p)$* **in let** *$z = \mathit{proj}_2(p)$* **in** *P (where we assume p does not appear in P).*

Process $\mathbf{0}$ does nothing. Process $x!^t v.\, P$ sends v on x, and then (after v is received by some process) the process behaves like P. The label t indicates whether the output operation is deadlock-free: If $t \neq \infty$, then the output is deadlock-free, i.e., if it is ever executed, v will eventually be received by some process or the whole process diverges. The exact value of t can be ignored at this moment; it will only be used in the type system. We call t a *capability annotation*. Note that programmers actually need not supply capability annotations; They are automatically inferred through type inference. We often omit t when it is unimportant. Process $x?^t y.\, P$ waits to receive a value v on x and then behaves like $[y \mapsto v]P$. The label t indicates whether the input operation is deadlock-free: If $t \neq \infty$, then the input is deadlock-free, i.e., if it is ever executed, the process will eventually be able to receive a message on x or the whole process diverges. $P \,|\, Q$ represents concurrent execution of P and Q. $*P$ represents infinitely many copies of the process P running in parallel, and $(\nu x)\, P$ denotes a process that creates a fresh communication channel x and then behaves like P. **if** v **then** P **else** Q behaves like P if v is *true*, and behaves like Q if v is *false*. **let** $x = e$ **in** P evaluates e to some value v, binds x to it, and then behaves like P.

As usual, we define the operational semantics using a structural relation $P \preceq Q$, and a reduction relation $P \longrightarrow Q$. The former relation means that

P can be restructured to Q by using the commutativity and associativity laws on $|$, etc. The latter relation means that P is reduced to Q by one communication on a channel. The formal definition of the relations are given in the full paper [8]. We write $\longrightarrow^*$ for the reflexive and transitive closure of $\longrightarrow$.

3 Type System

3.1 Overview

We first review the idea of previous type systems for deadlock-freedom [7, 10], identify the weakness of them, and then explain how to get rid of the weakness.

Ideas of Previous Type Systems for Deadlock-Freedom. The main idea of previous type systems for deadlock-freedom was to extend channel types with the following information:

- Channel-wise usage information, which describes how often and in which order each channel is used for input and output.
- Capability and obligation of each input/output action, which captures certain inter-channel dependency information.

We express channel-wise usage information by using a small, CCS-like process calculus, which has two primitive actions ? and !. For example, usage of x in the process $x?y \,|\, x!1 \,|\, x!2$ is expressed by $? \,|\, ! \,|\, !$, which means that x is used once for input and twice for output possibly in parallel. The usage of x in $x?y.\,x!y$ is expressed by ?.!, which means that x is first used for input, and then used for output. The usage conveys some information about whether each action succeeds or not. For example, x having usage $? \,|\, ! \,|\, !$ indicates that at least one of the two outputs fails to succeed. Similarly, x having usage ?.! (in the whole process) indicates that neither an input action nor an output action succeeds, since the input and output do not occur in parallel.

Channel-wise usage information alone is not sufficient for the analysis of deadlock. For example, it cannot distinguish between a deadlocked process $x?z.\,y!z \,|\, y?z.\,x!1$ and a non-deadlocked process $x?z.\,y!z \,|\, x!1.\,y?z.$. To control the dependency between communications on different channels, we have introduced the notion of *capabilities* and *obligations* [6, 7]. Let us explain why $x?z.\,y!z \,|\, y?z.\,x!1$ deadlocks in terms of *capabilities* (to successfully receive or send a message) and *obligations* (to wait for or to send a message). In order for the left sub-process $x?z.\,y!z$ to succeed in receiving a message on x, some process has to fulfill an *obligation* to send a message on x. The right sub-process, however, tries to exercise a *capability* to receive a message on y before fulfilling the obligation. In order for the right sub-process to be able to exercise a capability, the left process must fulfill an obligation to send a message on y, but the left process tries to exercise a capability to receive a message on x before fulfilling the obligation. Thus, the capability/obligation dependency is circular, so that no communication can succeed. To avoid such circular dependency, each action (? or !) in the channel-wise usage is associated with the *levels* of obligations and capabilities, which range over $\{0, 1, 2, \ldots\} \cup \{\infty\}$. The capability and obligation levels impose the following rules on the behavior of a process and its environment.

A. An obligation of level $n(\neq \infty)$ must be fulfilled by using only capabilities of level less than n. For example, suppose that x has usage $?^0_0$ and y has usage $!^1_1$, where the subscript of an action describes its capability level and the superscript describes its obligation level. Then, $x?z.\,y!z$ and $x?z \,|\, y!1$ are valid, but $y!1.\,x?z$ is invalid: the last process tries to exercise a capability of level 1 before fulfilling the obligation of lower level.

B. For an action of capability level $n(\neq \infty)$, there must exist a co-action of obligation level less than or equal to n (so as to guarantee that the capability can be eventually exercised).

Therefore, the obligation level describes a requirement for the process being concerned, while the capability level describes an assumption about the environment of the process being concerned. The two rules above ensure that there is no cyclic dependency between capabilities and obligations of finite levels; thus, deadlock-freedom is ensured for any action of a finite capability level.

Let us come back to the deadlocked process $x?z.\,y!z \,|\, y?z.\,x!1$. Suppose that the usages of x and y are $?^{o_{x1}}_{c_{x1}} \,|\, !^{o_{x2}}_{c_{x2}}$ and $?^{o_{y1}}_{c_{y1}} \,|\, !^{o_{y2}}_{c_{y2}}$, where c_{x1} and c_{y1} are finite. Rule **A** above implies that $c_{x1} < o_{y2}$ and $c_{y1} < o_{x2}$, while rule B implies that $o_{x2} \leq c_{x1}$, $o_{x1} \leq c_{x2}$, $o_{y2} \leq c_{y1}$, and $o_{y1} \leq c_{y2}$. So, we get $c_{x1} < o_{y2} \leq c_{y1} < o_{x2} \leq c_{x1}$, a contradiction.

Weakness of Previous Type Systems. The main weakness of the previous type systems based on the idea above was that they cannot handle recursive processes well. Consider the following function server computing the factorial:

$$*\mathit{fact}?(n, r).\,\textbf{if}\ n = 0\ \textbf{then}\ r!1\ \textbf{else}\ (\nu r')\,(\mathit{fact}!(n-1, r') \,|\, r'?m.\,r!(m \times n))$$

The second argument r of *fact* is assigned a type of the form $\textbf{chan}(\mathit{int}, !^{t_o}_{t_c})$, which says that the channel is used for sending an integer, and the levels of the obligation and capability to do so are t_o and t_c respectively. Since r' is sent on *fact*, it is also assigned the type $\textbf{chan}(\mathit{int}, !^{t_o}_{t_c})$. Then, because of rule **B**, however, the capability level of the input action on r' in $r'?m.\ \cdots$ must be greater than t_o. So, the sub-process $r'?m.\,r!(m \times n)$ violates rule **A** (if t_o is not ∞). The same problem arises even in handling a process simulating a term of the simply-typed λ-calculus (without recursion). One way to overcome the problem above is to use dependent types, so that the obligation level of the second argument r can depend on the value of the first argument n [6]. The resulting type system would, however, require heavy type annotations.

The Idea of the Extension. To get rid of the weakness mentioned above, we weaken rule **A** as follows:

A′. An obligation of level n on a channel x must be fulfilled by using only capabilities of level less than or *equal to* n, and if the capability level is n, the capability must be on a channel which has been created more recently than x.

For example, in the factorial server above, the level of an obligation to return a value on r and that of a capability to receive a value on r' are the same, but since r' has been created more recently, $r'?m.\, r!(m \times n)$ conforms to rule **A′**. Rule **A′** is sufficient to prevent deadlock by avoiding circular dependency between different channels. Since information about which channels has been created more recently is dynamic, a static analysis is required to estimate the information. In this paper, we use a simple syntactic analysis, which concludes that, in the process $(\nu x)\, P$, x has been created more recently than any other free channel of P. Fortunately, that turns out to be sufficient for handling recursive processes like the factorial server and processes simulating λ-terms.

In the formal operational semantics, a channel x being created more recently than another channel y corresponds to the condition that the prefix (νx) is inside the scope of the prefix (νy). Note that our operational semantics disallows the usual structural rule $(\nu x)\,(\nu y)\, P \equiv (\nu y)\,(\nu x)\, P$. The condition in **A′** could be the other way around; we could require that the capability must be on a channel which has been created *less* recently than x. We, however, found the condition above more useful than this alternative requirement. That is because one of the common channel creation patterns is $(\nu x)\,(P \,|\, x?y.\, Q)$, where P performs some sub-computation and sends the result on x.

3.2 Usages

This subsection introduces the syntax and semantics of usages more formally. They are almost identical to those of the previous type system [7].

Definition 3.1 (usages). *The set* $\mathcal{U}$ *of* usages, *ranged over by* U, *is given by:*

$$U ::= \mathbf{0} \mid \alpha^{t_1}_{t_2}.U \mid (U_1 \,|\, U_2) \mid *U \mid \uparrow^t U \mid U_1 \,\&\, U_2 \mid \rho \mid \mu\rho.U$$
$$\alpha ::= ? \mid !$$

Here, t *ranges over* $\mathbf{Nat} \cup \{\infty\}$ *(where* $\mathbf{Nat}$ *is the set of natural numbers).*

We often omit $\mathbf{0}$ and write $\alpha^{t_1}_{t_2}$ for $\alpha^{t_1}_{t_2}.\mathbf{0}$. We extend the usual binary relation $\leq$ on $\mathbf{Nat}$ to that on $\mathbf{Nat} \cup \{\infty\}$ by $\forall t \in \mathbf{Nat} \cup \{\infty\}.t \leq \infty$. We also extend $+$ by $\infty + t = t + \infty = \infty$. We write $\mathbf{min}(x_1, \ldots, x_n)$ for the least element of $\{x_1, \ldots, x_n\}$ (∞ if $n = 0$) with respect to $\leq$ and write $\mathbf{max}(x_1, \ldots, x_n)$ for the greatest element of $\{x_1, \ldots, x_n\}$ (0 if $n = 0$). We assume that $\mu\rho$ binds ρ. We write $[\rho \mapsto U_1]U_2$ for the usage obtained by replacing the free occurrences of ρ in U_2 with U_1. We write $FV(U)$ for the set of free usage variables. A usage is *closed* if $FV(U) = \emptyset$.

Intuitive meaning of usages is summarized in Table 1. If t_o is finite, a channel of usage $\alpha^{t_o}_{t_c}.U$ must be used for the action α, while if t_o is ∞, the action need

Table 1. Meaning of Usage Expressions

Usages	Interpretation
$\mathbf{0}$	Cannot be used at all
$?^{t_o}_{t_c}.U$	Used once for input, and then used according to U
$!^{t_o}_{t_c}.U$	Used once for output, and then used according to U
$U_1 \mid U_2$	Used according to U_1 and U_2, possibly in parallel
$*U$	Used according to U by infinitely many processes
$\uparrow^t U$	The same as U, except that input and output obligation levels are lifted to t.
$U_1 \,\&\, U_2$	Used according to either U_1 or U_2
ρ	Usage variable (used in combination with recursive usages below)
$\mu\rho.U$	Recursively used according to $[\rho \mapsto \mu\rho.U]U$.

not be performed. When t_c is finite, the action will eventually succeed if it is ever executed and the whole process does not diverge. If t_c is ∞, there is no such guarantee. Note that a channel of usage $\alpha^{t_o}_{t_c}.U$ must be used according to U only if it has been used for the action α and the action succeeds. For example, a channel of usage $?^{\infty}_{0}.!^{0}_{\infty}$ can be used for input (but need not be used), and if it has been used for input and the input has succeeded, it *must* be used for output. That is similar to the usage of a lock: a lock may be acquired (but need not be acquired), and after the lock has been acquired, the lock must be released. In fact, a lock can be expressed as a channel of such usage: see Example 1. Usage $\uparrow^t U$ lifts the obligation levels occurring in U (except for those guarded by ? or !) so that the input obligations and output obligations become greater than or equal to t. For example, $\uparrow^1(?^0_0.!^0_{\infty})$ is the same as $?^1_0.!^0_{\infty}$.

We give a higher precedence to prefixes ($\alpha^{t_o}_{t_c}$ and $*$) than to $\mid$. We write $\overline{\alpha}$ for the co-action of α ($\overline{?} =!$ and $\overline{!} =?$).

Example 1. Linear channels [9] are given a usage of the form $?^{n_1}_{n_2} \mid !^{n_3}_{n_4}$. Affine channels, which can be used *at most once*, are given a usage $?^{\infty}_{\infty} \mid !^{\infty}_{\infty}$. A reference cell can be implemented as a channel holding the current value as a message. Then, the read operation is expressed as $x?y.\,(x!y \mid \cdots)$, while the write operation is expressed as $x?y.\,(x!v \mid \cdots)$. The usage of a reference cell is thus represented as $!^0_{\infty} \mid *?^{\infty}_0.!^0_{\infty}$. Similarly, a binary semaphore can be expressed as a channel holding at most one message. The semaphore can be acquired by receiving the message, and released by sending the message back to the channel. Thus, the usage of a semaphore is represented as $!^0_{\infty} \mid *?^{\infty}_n.!^n_{\infty}$. Here, the level n controls which locks should be acquired first when multiple locks need to be acquired.

Next, we define capability/obligation levels of a usage.

Definition 3.2 (capabilities). *$cap_?(U)$ and $cap_!(U)$ are defined by:*

$$\begin{array}{ll} cap_\alpha(\mathbf{0}) = cap_\alpha(\overline{\alpha}^{t_o}_{t_c}.U) = cap_\alpha(\rho) = \infty & cap_\alpha(\alpha^{t_o}_{t_c}.U) = t_c \\ cap_\alpha(*U) = cap_\alpha(\uparrow^t U) = cap_\alpha(\mu\rho.U) = cap_\alpha(U) & \\ cap_\alpha(U_1 \mid U_2) = cap_\alpha(U_1 \,\&\, U_2) = \mathbf{min}(cap_\alpha(U_1), cap_\alpha(U_2)) & \end{array}$$

Definition 3.3 (obligations). *$ob_?(U)$ and $ob_!(U)$ are defined by:*

$$ob_\alpha(\mathbf{0}) = ob_\alpha(\overline{\alpha}^{t_o}_{t_c}.U) = \infty \qquad ob_\alpha(\rho) = 0$$
$$ob_\alpha(\alpha^{t_o}_{t_c}.U) = t_o \qquad ob_\alpha(U_1 \,|\, U_2) = \mathbf{min}(ob_\alpha(U_1), ob_\alpha(U_2))$$
$$ob_\alpha(\uparrow^t U) = \mathbf{max}(t, ob_\alpha(U)) \qquad ob_\alpha(U_1 \,\&\, U_2) = \mathbf{max}(ob_\alpha(U_1), ob_\alpha(U_2))$$
$$ob_\alpha(*U) = ob_\alpha(\mu\rho.U) = ob_\alpha(U)$$

We write $ob(U)$ for $\mathbf{max}(ob_?(U), ob_!(U))$.

We next introduce the usage reduction relation $U \longrightarrow U'$. Intuitively, $U \longrightarrow U'$ means that if a channel of usage U has been used for a communication, then it should be used according to U' afterwards. For example, $!^0_\infty \,|\, ?^\infty_0.!^0_\infty \longrightarrow !^0_\infty$ holds. The formal definition of the relation is given in the full paper [8].

Relations and Operations on Usages. As described in rule **B** in Subsection 3.1, if some action has a capability of level n, the obligation level of its co-action should be at most n. The relation $rel(U)$ defined below ensures that condition.

Definition 3.4 (reliability). *We write $con_\alpha(U)$ when $ob_{\overline{\alpha}}(U) \leq cap_\alpha(U)$. A usage U is* reliable, *written $rel(U)$, if $con_?(U')$ and $con_!(U')$ hold for any U' such that $U \longrightarrow^* U'$.*

The subusage relation $U_1 \leq U_2$ defined below means that U_1 expresses more liberal usage of channels than U_2, so that a channel of usage U_1 may be used as that of usage U_2. The first and second conditions require that the subusage relation is closed under contexts and reduction. The third and fourth conditions allow capabilities to be weakened and obligations to be strengthened.

Definition 3.5 (subusage). *The* subusage relation $\leq$ *on closed usages is the largest binary relation on usages such that the following conditions hold whenever $U_1 \leq U_2$.*

1. *$[\rho \mapsto U_1]U \leq [\rho \mapsto U_2]U$ for any usage U such that $FV(U) = \{\rho\}$.*
2. *If $U_2 \longrightarrow U_2'$, then there exists U_1' such that $U_1 \longrightarrow U_1'$ and $U_1' \leq U_2'$.*
3. *For each $\alpha \in \{?, !\}$, $cap_\alpha(U_1) \leq cap_\alpha(U_2)$ holds.*
4. *For each $\alpha \in \{?, !\}$, if $con_{\overline{\alpha}}(U_1)$, then $ob_\alpha(U_1) \geq ob_\alpha(U_2)$.*

3.3 Types

Definition 3.6 (types). *The set of* types *is given by:*

$$\tau \ (types) ::= \mathbf{bool} \mid \tau_1 \times \tau_2 \mid \mathbf{chan}(\tau, U)$$

Type **bool** is the type of booleans. The type $\tau_1 \times \tau_2$ describes pairs consisting of a value of type τ_1 and a value of type τ_2. The type $\mathbf{chan}(\tau, U)$ describes channels that should be used according to U for transmitting values of type τ.

We extend relations and operations on usages to those on types.

Definition 3.7 (subtyping). *A subtyping relation $\leq$ is the least reflexive relation closed under the following rule:*

$$\frac{U \leq U'}{\mathbf{chan}(\tau, U) \leq \mathbf{chan}(\tau, U')} \qquad \frac{\tau_1 \leq \tau_1' \quad \tau_2 \leq \tau_2'}{\tau_1 \times \tau_2 \leq \tau_1' \times \tau_2'}$$

Definition 3.8. *The* obligation level *of type τ, written $ob(\tau)$, is defined by: $ob(\mathbf{bool}) = \infty$, $ob(\tau_1 \times \tau_2) = \mathbf{min}(ob(\tau_1), ob(\tau_2))$, and $ob(\mathbf{chan}(\tau, U)) = ob(U)$.*

Definition 3.9. *Unary operations $*$ and $\uparrow^t$ on types is defined by: $*\mathbf{bool} = \uparrow^t\mathbf{bool} = \mathbf{bool}$, $*(\tau_1 \times \tau_2) = (*\tau_1) \times (*\tau_2)$, $\uparrow^t(\tau_1 \times \tau_2) = (\uparrow^t\tau_1) \times (\uparrow^t\tau_2)$, $*(\mathbf{chan}(\tau, U)) = \mathbf{chan}(\tau, *U)$, and $\uparrow^t(\mathbf{chan}(\tau, U)) = \mathbf{chan}(\tau, \uparrow^t U)$,*

Definition 3.10. *A (partial) binary operation $|$ on types is defined by: $\mathbf{bool} \,|\, \mathbf{bool} = \mathbf{bool}$, $(\tau_{11} \times \tau_{12}) \,|\, (\tau_{21} \times \tau_{22}) = (\tau_{11} \,|\, \tau_{21}) \times (\tau_{12} \,|\, \tau_{22})$, and $(\mathbf{chan}(\tau, U_1)) \,|\, (\mathbf{chan}(\tau, U_2)) = \mathbf{chan}(\tau, (U_1 \,|\, U_2))$. $\tau_1 \,|\, \tau_2$ is undefined if it does not match any of the above rules.*

3.4 Type Environment

A type environment is a mapping from a finite set of variables to types. We use metavariables Γ and Δ for type environments. We write $\emptyset$ for the type environment whose domain is empty. When $x \notin dom(\Gamma)$, we write $\Gamma, x : \tau$ for the type environment Γ' such that $dom(\Gamma') = dom(\Gamma) \cup \{x\}$, $\Gamma'(x) = \tau$, and $\Gamma'(y) = \Gamma(y)$ for all $y \in dom(\Gamma)$.

The operations and relations on types are pointwise extended to those on type environments below.

Definition 3.11. *A binary relation $\leq$ on type environments is defined by: $\Gamma_1 \leq \Gamma_2$ if and only if (i) $dom(\Gamma_1) \supseteq dom(\Gamma_2)$, (ii) $\Gamma_1(x) \leq \Gamma_2(x)$ for each $x \in dom(\Gamma_2)$, and (iii) $ob(\Gamma_1(x)) = \infty$ for each $x \in dom(\Gamma_1) \backslash dom(\Gamma_2)$.*

Definition 3.12. *The operations $|$ and $*$ on type environments are defined by:*

$$(\Gamma_1 \,|\, \Gamma_2)(x) = \begin{cases} \Gamma_1(x) \,|\, \Gamma_2(x) & \text{if } x \in dom(\Gamma_1) \cap dom(\Gamma_2) \\ \Gamma_1(x) & \text{if } x \in dom(\Gamma_1) \backslash dom(\Gamma_2) \\ \Gamma_2(x) & \text{if } x \in dom(\Gamma_2) \backslash dom(\Gamma_1) \end{cases}$$
$$(*\Gamma)(x) = *(\Gamma(x))$$

3.5 Typing Rules

We have two kinds of judgments: $\Gamma \vdash e : \tau$ for expressions, and $\Gamma \vdash_{\prec} P$ for processes. The latter means that P uses free variables as specified by Γ. $\prec$ is a partial order that statically estimates the order between the times when channels are created. $x \prec y$ means that x must have been created more recently than y. Because of rule $\mathbf{A}'$, $x : \mathbf{chan}(\mathbf{bool}, ?^0_1), y : \mathbf{chan}(\mathbf{bool}, !^1_\infty) \vdash_{\{(x,y)\}} x?z.\, y!z$ and $x : \mathbf{chan}(\mathbf{bool}, ?^0_0), y : \mathbf{chan}(\mathbf{bool}, !^1_\infty) \vdash_\emptyset x?z.\, y!z$ are valid judgments, while $x : \mathbf{chan}(\mathbf{bool}, ?^0_1), y : \mathbf{chan}(\mathbf{bool}, !^1_\infty) \vdash_\emptyset x?z.\, y!z$ is invalid.

For expressions

$$\frac{}{x:\tau \vdash x:\tau}\ (\text{Tv-Var}) \qquad \frac{\Gamma \vdash e : \tau_1 \times \tau_2 \quad i \in \{1,2\} \quad ob(\tau_{3-i}) = \infty}{\Gamma \vdash proj_i(e) : \tau_i}\ (\text{Tv-Proj})$$

$$\frac{b \in \{true, false\}}{\emptyset \vdash b : \mathbf{bool}}\ (\text{Tv-Bool})$$

$$\frac{\Gamma_1 \vdash e_1 : \tau_1 \quad \Gamma_2 \vdash e_2 : \tau_2}{\Gamma_1 \mid \Gamma_2 \vdash \langle e_1, e_2\rangle : \tau_1 \times \tau_2}\ (\text{Tv-Pair}) \qquad \frac{\Gamma \vdash e : \tau \quad \Gamma' \leq \Gamma}{\Gamma' \vdash e : \tau}\ (\text{Tv-Weak})$$

For Processes

$$\frac{\Gamma, x : \mathbf{chan}(\tau, U) \vdash_{\prec \cup \{(x,y) \mid y \in FV(P)\setminus\{x\}\}} P \quad rel(U)}{\Gamma \vdash_{\prec} (\nu x)\, P}\ (\text{T-New})$$

$$\frac{}{\emptyset \vdash_{\prec} \mathbf{0}}\ (\text{T-Zero}) \qquad \frac{\Gamma' \vdash_{\prec} P \quad \Gamma \leq \Gamma'}{\Gamma \vdash_{\prec} P}\ (\text{T-Weak})$$

$$\frac{\Gamma_1 \vdash_{\prec} P_1 \quad \Gamma_2 \vdash_{\prec} P_2}{\Gamma_1 \mid \Gamma_2 \vdash_{\prec} P_1 \mid P_2}\ (\text{T-Par}) \qquad \frac{\Gamma \vdash_{\prec} P}{*\Gamma \vdash_{\prec} *P}\ (\text{T-Rep})$$

$$\frac{\Gamma_1 \vdash_{\prec} P \quad \Gamma_2 \vdash v : \tau}{x : \mathbf{chan}(\tau, !^0_{t_c});_{\prec} (\Gamma_1 \mid \Gamma_2) \vdash_{\prec} x!^{t_c} v.\, P}\ (\text{T-Out}) \qquad \frac{\Gamma, y : \tau \vdash_{\prec} P}{x : \mathbf{chan}(\tau, ?^0_{t_c});_{\prec} \Gamma \vdash_{\prec} x?^{t_c} y.\, P}\ (\text{T-In})$$

$$\frac{\Gamma_1 \vdash e : \tau \quad \Gamma_2, x : \tau \vdash_{\prec} P}{\Gamma_1 \mid \Gamma_2 \vdash_{\prec} \mathbf{let}\ x = e\ \mathbf{in}\ P}\ (\text{T-Let}) \qquad \frac{\Gamma_1 \vdash v : \mathbf{bool} \quad \Gamma_2 \vdash_{\prec} P \quad \Gamma_2 \vdash_{\prec} Q}{\Gamma_1 \mid \Gamma_2 \vdash_{\prec} \mathbf{if}\ v\ \mathbf{then}\ P\ \mathbf{else}\ Q}\ (\text{T-If})$$

Fig. 2. Typing Rules

We assume that α-conversion is implicitly applied so that the variables in Γ and $\prec$ are always different from the bound variables in P. The typing rules for deriving valid type judgments are given in Figure 2.

We explain some key rules. In T-New, $\prec$ is extended with the assumption that x has been created more recently than any other free channels in P.

In T-Out and T-In, we use the operation $x : \mathbf{chan}(\tau, \alpha^{t_o}_{t_c});_{\prec} \Gamma$ on type environments. It represents the type environment Δ defined by:

$$\begin{aligned}
dom(\Delta) &= \{x\} \cup dom(\Gamma) \\
\Delta(x) &= \begin{cases} \mathbf{chan}(\tau, \alpha^{t_o}_{t_c}.U) & \text{if } \Gamma(x) = \mathbf{chan}(\tau, U) \\ \mathbf{chan}(\tau, \alpha^{t_o}_{t_c}) & \text{if } x \notin dom(\Gamma) \end{cases} \\
\Delta(y) &= \begin{cases} \uparrow^{t_c} \Gamma(y) & \text{if } y \neq x \wedge x \prec y \\ \uparrow^{t_c+1} \Gamma(y) & \text{if } y \neq x \wedge x \not\prec y \end{cases}
\end{aligned}$$

For example, $x\colon \mathbf{chan}(\tau, ?^0_2);_{\{(x,y)\}}(x\colon \mathbf{chan}(\tau, !^0_0), y\colon \mathbf{chan}(\tau_1, !^0_0), z\colon \mathbf{chan}(\tau_2, !^0_0))$ is $x:\mathbf{chan}(\tau, ?^0_2.!^0_0), y:\mathbf{chan}(\tau_1, !^2_0), z:\mathbf{chan}(\tau_2, !^3_0))$.

Intuitively, the environment $x:\mathbf{chan}(\tau, \alpha^{t_o}_{t_c});_{\prec}\Gamma$ means that x may be first used for the action α, and then communications can be performed according to Γ. Since the capability of level t_c is exercised before fulfilling obligations in Γ, the level of each obligation in Γ are lifted either to t_c or t_c+1, depending on $\prec$.

In rule T-In, the premise means that P performs communications according to Γ. Since $x?^{t_c}y.\,P$ tries to exercise a capability of level t_c to receive a value on x, the process is well-typed under $x:\mathbf{chan}(\tau, ?^0_{t_c});_{\prec}\Gamma$.

Example 2. Let us consider the following process P:

$$*f?r.\,(\mathbf{if}\ b\ \mathbf{then}\ r!\mathit{true}\ \mathbf{else}\ (\nu r')\,(f!r' \mid r'?x.\,r!x)).$$

It is typed as follows.

$$\dfrac{\dfrac{\dfrac{\Gamma \vdash_\emptyset r!\mathit{true} \qquad \Gamma \vdash_\emptyset (\nu r')\cdots}{\Gamma \vdash_\emptyset \mathbf{if}\ b\ \mathbf{then}\ r!\mathit{true}\ \mathbf{else}\ \cdots}}{f:\mathbf{chan}(\mathbf{chan}(\mathbf{bool}, !^1_\infty), ?^0_\infty.!^\infty_0), b:\mathbf{bool} \vdash_\emptyset f?r.\cdots}}{f:\mathbf{chan}(\mathbf{chan}(\mathbf{bool}, !^1_\infty), *?^0_\infty.!^\infty_0), b:\mathbf{bool} \vdash_\emptyset P}$$

Here, Γ is $f:\mathbf{chan}(\mathbf{chan}(\mathbf{bool}, !^1_\infty), !^\infty_0), b:\mathbf{bool}, r:\mathbf{chan}(\mathbf{bool}, !^1_\infty)$, and $\Gamma \vdash_\emptyset (\nu r')\cdots$ is derived by:

$$\dfrac{\dfrac{\Gamma_1 \vdash_{\{(r',r)\}} f!r' \qquad r:\mathbf{chan}(\mathbf{bool}, !^1_\infty), r':\mathbf{chan}(\mathbf{bool}, ?^0_1) \vdash_{\{(r',r)\}} r'?x.\,r!x}{\Gamma, r':\mathbf{chan}(\mathbf{bool}, !^1_\infty \mid ?^0_1) \vdash_{\{(r',r)\}} f!r' \mid r'?x.\,r!x}}{\Gamma \vdash_\emptyset (\nu r')\cdots}$$

Here, $\Gamma_1 = f:\mathbf{chan}(\mathbf{chan}(\mathbf{bool}, !^1_\infty), !^\infty_0), r':\mathbf{chan}(\mathbf{bool}, !^1_\infty)$. Note that if $r' \prec r$ did not hold, we could only obtain $r:\mathbf{chan}(\mathbf{bool}, !^2_\infty)$, $r':\mathbf{chan}(\mathbf{bool}, ?^0_1) \vdash_\emptyset r'?x.\,r!x$, so that $f:\mathbf{chan}(\mathbf{chan}(\mathbf{bool}, !^1_\infty), *?^0_\infty.!^\infty_0)$, $b:\mathbf{bool} \vdash_\emptyset P$ were not derivable.

3.6 Type Soundness

The following theorems imply that if a process is well-typed in our type system, an input or output process that is annotated with a finite capability level is deadlock-free, in the sense that if the process is ready (i.e., it appears at the top-level, without being guarded by any other input or output prefix), the whole process can be reduced further.

We write $\Gamma \longrightarrow \Gamma'$ when $\Gamma = \Gamma_1, x:\mathbf{chan}(\tau, U)$ and $\Gamma' = \Gamma_1, x:\mathbf{chan}(\tau, U')$ with $U \longrightarrow U'$ for some Γ_1, x, τ, U, and U'.

Theorem 1 (type preservation). *If $\Gamma \vdash_\prec P$ and $P \longrightarrow Q$, then $\Gamma' \vdash_\prec Q$ for some Γ' such that $\Gamma' = \Gamma$ or $\Gamma \longrightarrow \Gamma'$.*

Theorem 2. *If* $\emptyset \vdash_{\prec} P$ *and either* $P \preceq (\nu\widetilde{x})\,(x!^n v.\,Q_1 \mid Q_2)$ *or* $P \preceq (\nu\widetilde{x})\,(x?^n y.\,Q_1 \mid Q_2)$ *with* $n \in \mathbf{Nat}$*, then* $P \longrightarrow R$ *for some* R*.*

Corollary 1. *Suppose* $\emptyset \vdash_{\prec} P$*. If* $P \longrightarrow^* Q$*, and either* $Q \preceq (\nu\widetilde{x})\,(x!^n v.\,Q_1 \mid Q_2)$ *or* $Q \preceq (\nu\widetilde{x})\,(x?^n y.\,Q_1 \mid Q_2)$ *with* $n \in \mathbf{Nat}$*, then* $Q \longrightarrow R$ *for some* R*.*

3.7 Type Inference

Given a closed process P (without any capability annotations on input and output processes), there is a complete algorithm to decide whether there exists P' such that $\emptyset \vdash_{\emptyset} P'$ holds and P and P' coincide except for capability annotations. Moreover, such an algorithm tries to infer the least capability for each input/output process. Since the algorithm is almost the same as that of the previous type system [7], we do not re-describe the algorithm here; The algorithm first extract constraints on types, reduce them step by step to obtain constraints of the form $rel(U)$, and then solve $rel(U)$ by reduction to Petri net reachability problems [7]. The only extra work compared with the previous one is to expand the relation $\prec$ when the algorithm encounters the ν-prefix. We have already implemented the algorithm in `TyPiCal` [4].

4 Encoding of λ-Calculus

To demonstrate the power of the new type system, we show that the call-by-value simply-typed λ-calculus with recursion can be encoded into the deadlock-free fragment. Concurrent objects can also be encoded as in our previous paper [5].

Definition 4.1. *The sets of types and terms of* $\lambda^{\rightarrow,\mathit{fix}}$ *are given by the following syntax:*

$$\begin{array}{ll} \theta \ (\mathit{types}) & ::= \mathbf{bool} \mid \theta_1 \rightarrow \theta_2 \\ M \ (\mathit{terms}) & ::= x \mid \boldsymbol{\mathit{fix}}(f, x, M) \mid M_1 M_2 \end{array}$$

Here, $\mathbf{fix}(f, x, M)$ represents a recursive function f defined by $f(x) \stackrel{\triangle}{=} M$. If f does not appear in M, it is the same as the usual λ-abstraction $\lambda x.M$.

Typing rules are given as follows.

$$\frac{}{\mathcal{T}, x : \theta \vdash x : \theta} \qquad \text{(TL-VAR)}$$

$$\frac{\mathcal{T}, f : \theta_1 \rightarrow \theta_2, x : \theta_1 \vdash M : \theta_2}{\mathcal{T} \vdash \mathbf{fix}(f, x, M) : \theta_1 \rightarrow \theta_2} \qquad \text{(TL-FIX)}$$

$$\frac{\mathcal{T} \vdash M_1 : \theta_1 \rightarrow \theta_2 \qquad \mathcal{T} \vdash M_2 : \theta_1}{\mathcal{T} \vdash M_1 M_2 : \theta_2} \qquad \text{(TL-APP)}$$

We encode terms, types, and type environments into our typed π-calculus as follows, in a standard manner [5, 11, 13].

$$\begin{aligned}
[\![x]\!]^r &= r!x \\
[\![\mathbf{fix}(f,x,M)]\!]^r &= (\nu y)\,(r!y \mid *y?(x,r').\, [\![M]\!]^{r'}\,) \\
[\![M_1 M_2]\!]^r &= (\nu r_1)\,(\nu r_2)\,([\![M_1\,]\!]^{r_1} \mid [\![\,M_2\,]\!]^{r_2} \mid r_1?f.\, r_2?x.\, f!(x,r))
\end{aligned}$$

$$\begin{aligned}
[\![\mathbf{bool}]\!] &= \mathbf{bool} \\
[\![\theta_1 \to \theta_2]\!] &= \mathbf{chan}([\![\theta_1\,]\!] \times \mathbf{chan}([\![\theta_2]\!], !^1_\infty), *!^\infty_0) \\
[\![x_1:\theta_1,\ldots,x_n:\theta_n]\!] &= x_1 :\, [\![\,\theta_1]\!],\ldots,x_n :\, [\![\,\theta_n]\!]
\end{aligned}$$

Intuitively, a term M is encoded into $[\![M]\!]^r$ which evaluates M and sends the result on channel r. The usage $*!^\infty_0$ in the encoding of function types means that a function can be invoked an arbitrary number of times, and the usage $!^1_\infty$ means that the function will eventually returns a result (or diverge).

It is easy to check that the typing is preserved by encoding.

Lemma 1. *If $\mathcal{T} \vdash M:\theta$, then $[\![\mathcal{T}]\!], r:\mathbf{chan}([\![\theta]\!], !^1_\infty) \vdash_\emptyset [\![M]\!]^r$.*

The following is an immediate corollary of the above lemma, which means that a process that simulates functional computation does not get deadlocked before returning a result.

Corollary 2. *If $\emptyset \vdash M:\theta$ and $[\![M]\!]^r \longrightarrow^* P$, then $P \longrightarrow Q$ for some Q or $P \preceq (\nu\widetilde{x})\,(r!v.\,Q_1 \mid Q_2)$ for some v, Q_1, Q_2.*

Proof. Suppose $\emptyset \vdash M:\theta$ and $[\![M]\!]^r \longrightarrow^* P$. By Lemma 1, $r:\mathbf{chan}([\![\theta]\!], !^1_\infty) \vdash_\emptyset [\![M]\!]^r$. By Theorem 1, we have $r:\mathbf{chan}([\![\theta]\!], !^1_\infty) \vdash_\emptyset P$. Let $R = (\nu r)\,(P \mid r?^1x.\,\mathbf{0})$. Then, $\emptyset \vdash_\emptyset R$. By Theorem 2, we have $R \longrightarrow R'$, which implies either $P \longrightarrow Q$ or $P \preceq (\nu\widetilde{x})\,(r!v.\,Q_1 \mid Q_2)$.

5 Extension for Recursive Data Structures

The language discussed so far is the π-calculus extended with pairs. We briefly discuss a subtle point that arises when dealing with recursive data structures, using the list data structure as an example.

Let us consider the following process, which waits to receive a list l of channels, and sends *true* to all the channels in the list.

$$\begin{aligned}
&*broadcast?l.\,\mathbf{if}\ null(l)\ \mathbf{then}\ \mathbf{0}\ \mathbf{else} \\
&\qquad\qquad (\mathbf{let}\ x = \mathbf{hd}(l)\ \mathbf{in}\ (x!true \mid broadcast!\mathbf{tl}(l)))
\end{aligned}$$

Here, $\mathbf{hd}(l)$ is the first element of the list l, and $\mathbf{tl}(l)$ is the rest.

A naive way to handle lists is to introduce list types of the form $\mathbf{list}(\tau)$, which describes lists whose elements are of type τ, and the following typing rules:

$$\frac{\Gamma \vdash e : \mathbf{list}(\tau)}{\Gamma \vdash \mathbf{hd}(e) : \tau} \qquad\qquad \frac{\Gamma \vdash e : \mathbf{list}(\tau)}{\Gamma \vdash \mathbf{tl}(e) : \mathbf{list}(\tau)}$$

However, we have to add the condition that $ob(\tau) = \infty$ in both rules (just like we had to impose the condition $ob(\tau_{3-i}) = \infty$ in the rule for projections), since

$\mathbf{hd}(e)$ throws away the elements other than the head, and $\mathbf{tl}(e)$ throws away the head. Thus, we can only assign $\mathbf{list}(\mathbf{chan}(\mathbf{bool}, !^{\infty}_{t}))$ to l in the above example, failing to infer that the server eventually sends messages to all the elements in the list.

To overcome the problem above, we represent list types as $\mathbf{list}(\tau_1, \tau_2)$, where τ_1 is the type of the first element, and τ_2 is the type of the rest of the elements, and use the following types:

$$\frac{\Gamma \vdash e : \mathbf{list}(\tau_1, \tau_2) \qquad ob(\tau_2) = \infty}{\Gamma \vdash \mathbf{hd}(e) : \tau_1} \qquad \frac{\Gamma \vdash e : \mathbf{list}(\tau_1, \tau_2) \qquad ob(\tau_1) = \infty}{\Gamma \vdash \mathbf{tl}(e) : \mathbf{list}(\tau_2, \tau_2)}$$

With these rules, we can assign $\mathbf{list}(\mathbf{chan}(\mathbf{bool}, !^{1}_{\infty}), \mathbf{chan}(\mathbf{bool}, !^{1}_{\infty}))$ to l in the example above, so that we can infer that the server eventually sends messages to all the elements in the list.

The replacement of $\mathbf{list}(\tau)$ with $\mathbf{list}(\tau_1, \tau_2)$ corresponds to the unfolding of the recursive type $\mu\alpha.(1 + (\tau \times \alpha))$ to $1 + \tau \times \mu\alpha.(1 + (\tau \times \alpha))$. As in the case of lists above, unfolding of recursive types in general seems to be useful to make our type system for deadlock-freedom more robust.

6 Related Work

As already mentioned in Section 1, earlier type systems that can guarantee deadlock-freedom [5, 14, 15] required explicit type annotations, having no reasonable type inference algorithm. We have later modified the type systems to make type inference tractable [7, 10], with the sacrifice of some expressive power. The type system proposed in this paper can be considered a reunion of the earlier type systems [5, 14] and recent ones [7, 10].

Some type systems [6, 7] can guarantee a stronger property that certain communications will eventually succeed no matter whether the process diverges. There are also type systems that guarantee the termination of processes [1, 16]. Unfortunately, the idea proposed in the present paper does not work for guaranteeing those stronger properties.

There are some studies of abstract interpretation for the π-calculus [2]. To the best of our knowledge, deadlock-freedom analysis has not been studied in that context. Our type-based analysis relies on a syntactic analysis of the order in which channels are created. Abstract interpretation [2] might be useful for obtaining more precise information about the order of channel creation.

7 Conclusion

We have proposed a new type system for deadlock-freedom of π-calculus processes. The new type system admits type inference, while it is strictly more expressive than the previous type systems that admit type inference. We have also extended the type system to handle data structures like pairs and lists.

References

1. Y. Deng and D. Sangiorgi. Ensuring termination by typability. In *Proceedings of IFIP TCS 2004*, pages 619–632, 2004.
2. J. Feret. Abstract interpretation of mobile systems. *Journal of Logic and Algebraic Programming*, 63(1), 2005.
3. K. Honda and N. Yoshida. A uniform type structure for secure information flow. In *Proceedings of ACM SIGPLAN/SIGACT Symposium on Principles of Programming Languages*, pages 81–92, 2002.
4. N. Kobayashi. TyPiCal: A type-based static analyzer for the pi-calculus. Tool available at `http://www.kb.ecei.tohoku.ac.jp/~koba/typical/`.
5. N. Kobayashi. A partially deadlock-free typed process calculus. *ACM Transactions on Programming Languages and Systems*, 20(2):436–482, 1998.
6. N. Kobayashi. A type system for lock-free processes. *Information and Computation*, 177:122–159, 2002.
7. N. Kobayashi. Type-based information flow analysis for the pi-calculus. *Acta Informatica*, 42(4-5):291–347, 2005.
8. N. Kobayashi. A new type system for deadlock-free processes, 2006. Full version. Available from `http://www.kb.ecei.tohoku.ac.jp/~koba/`.
9. N. Kobayashi, B. C. Pierce, and D. N. Turner. Linearity and the pi-calculus. *ACM Transactions on Programming Languages and Systems*, 21(5):914–947, 1999.
10. N. Kobayashi, S. Saito, and E. Sumii. An implicitly-typed deadlock-free process calculus. Technical Report TR00-01, Dept. Info. Sci., Univ. of Tokyo, January 2000. A summary has appeared in Proceedings of CONCUR 2000, Springer LNCS1877, pp.489-503, 2000.
11. R. Milner. Function as processes. In *Automata, Language and Programming*, volume 443 of *Lecture Notes in Computer Science*, pages 167–180. Springer-Verlag, 1990.
12. R. Milner. The polyadic π-calculus: a tutorial. In F. L. Bauer, W. Brauer, and H. Schwichtenberg, editors, *Logic and Algebra of Specification*. Springer-Verlag, 1993.
13. B. Pierce and D. Sangiorgi. Typing and subtyping for mobile processes. In *Proceedings of IEEE Symposium on Logic in Computer Science*, pages 376–385, 1993.
14. E. Sumii and N. Kobayashi. A generalized deadlock-free process calculus. In *Proc. of Workshop on High-Level Concurrent Language (HLCL'98)*, volume 16(3) of *ENTCS*, pages 55–77, 1998.
15. N. Yoshida. Graph types for monadic mobile processes. In *FST/TCS'16*, volume 1180 of *Lecture Notes in Computer Science*, pages 371–387. Springer-Verlag, 1996.
16. N. Yoshida, M. Berger, and K. Honda. Strong normalisation in the pi-calculus. *Information and Computation*, 191(2):145–202, 2004.

Sortings for Reactive Systems*

Lars Birkedal, Søren Debois, and Thomas Hildebrandt

IT University of Copenhagen
{birkedal, debois, hilde}@itu.dk

Abstract. We investigate *sorting* or *typing* for Leifer and Milner's reactive systems. We focus on transferring congruence properties for bisimulations from unsorted to sorted systems. Technically, we give a general definition of sorting; we adapt Jensen's work on the transfer of congruence properties to this general definition; we construct a *predicate sorting*, which for any decomposible predicate P filters out agents not satisfying P; we prove that the predicate sorting preserves congruence properties and that it suitably retains dynamics; and finally, we show how the predicate sortings can be used to achieve *context-aware reaction*.

1 Introduction

The last decade has seen a series of definitions of reactive systems for which it is possible to derive labeled transition systems with an associated bisimulation relation that is guaranteed to be a congruence relation [1,2,3,4,5,6,7,8]. Sewell proposed to use suitable contexts of the reactive system as labels in the derived labeled transition system [1]. Leifer and Milner refined this approach by suggesting that it suffices to consider minimal contexts, with minimality captured by the notion of *relative pushout* (RPO) in the category corresponding to the reactive system [2]. Milner and Jensen suggested further refinements in their work on bigraphical reactive systems, technically by representing the reactive systems as quotients of precategories, which in turn possess the requisite relative pushouts [3,4,5]. An alternative approach using 2-categories was suggested by Sassone and Sobocinski [6,7], and subsequently transferred to double categories by Bruni, Gadducci, Montanari and Sobocinski in [8].

One aim of these abstract definitions of reactive systems is to unify and generalize existing calculi for concurrency and mobility, by providing a uniform behavioral theory: the congruential bisimulation relation associated with the derived labeled transition system. For bigraphical reactive systems, this aim has been evaluated with encouraging results: existing behavioral theories have been recovered for CCS [5], π-calculus [9], and mobile ambients [9]; and bigraphical semantics has contributed to that of Petri-nets [10] and Homer [11].

Bigraphical reactive systems aim also to model aspects of ubiquitous systems directly. An evaluation of this aim was initiated in [12].

* This work was funded in part by the Danish Research Agency (grant no.: 2059-03-0031) and the IT University of Copenhagen (the LaCoMoCo project).

C. Baier and H. Hermanns (Eds.): CONCUR 2006, LNCS 4137, pp. 248–262, 2006.

A *sorting* for a reactive system is analogous to a typing discipline for terms: Each sort gives an abstract view of its morphisms, in the same way that each type gives an abstract view of its terms. Various notions of sorting have turned out to be useful for both the meta-modeling aim and for the ubiquitous system aim.

1. In representations of existing calculi in bigraphical reactive systems, sortings remove "junk" morphisms — morphisms not representing anything. These are removed to get a tight correspondence between the bisimulation derived in bigraphs and the intended bisimulation [10,5,9,11].
2. For the modeling of context-aware systems, sortings help restricting reaction rules to apply only in certain contexts, to get "context-aware reaction rules" [13,12].

The sortings used in *loc.cit.* are all defined by first adding sorts to each object in the category of bigraphs, second stipulating a well-sortedness condition using this extra information, and finally declaring that we will only consider well-sorted morphisms. (Notice again the analogy to typing disciplines.) For representation applications (Item 1 above), sorts and conditions are chosen to make well-sorted all but the junk morphisms. For modeling applications (Item 2 above), sorts are used simply to distinguish sets of contexts; by choosing an appropriate sort for a reaction, we restrict it to specific contexts.

However, we cannot tinker arbitrarily with our underlying category; we must preserve relative pushouts in order to keep bisimulation a congruence. In each example cited above, this preservation property is shown by hand. Moreover, sorting is itself defined explicitly in each case: both Jensen [9] and Milner [5] define sorting for bigraphical place graphs; and Leifer and Milner define bigraphical link graph sorting in [10].

In this paper we investigate sortings for reactive systems and make the following contributions.

1. We give a general definition of sorting, encompassing all the different notions seen in the above examples (Definition 4).
2. We lift Jensen's safety theorem to this general setting (Theorem 12). Jensen's safety theorem gives a sufficient condition under which RPOs may be transferred between sorted and unsorted worlds, but only in the setting of bigraphical place-graph sorting [9].
3. We present a general construction of sorting, the *predicate sorting* (Definition 15). For any predicate P which is preserved under under de-composition, this sorting filters out morphisms not satisfying P.
4. We prove that predicate sortings transfer RPOs (Theorem 20). Thus, if the bisimulation of an unsorted system is a congruence, then so is the bisimulation of the corresponding predicate-sorted system.
5. We prove a *correspondence theorem* (Theorem 25) for predicate sortings: A predicate sorted system suitably preserves the dynamics of its unsorted counterpart.

6. We show that predicate sortings can be used to model some context-aware reaction systems, notably those where some reaction rules should apply only in contexts which do not contain a given sub-context (Theorem 30).

Our setting is reactive systems over categories rather than precategories (the home of bigraphs) or 2-categories. We believe the extension of our work to either setting to be straightforward, but have yet to justify that belief.

This paper is an abridged version of the technical report [14]; refer to that report for omitted proofs.

Overview. In Section 2, we recall Leifer and Milner's reactive systems; in Section 3, we give our general definition of sorting and lift Jensen's transfer theorem; in Section 4, we define predicate sortings; in Section 5, we prove that predicate sortings transfers RPOs; in Section 6, we prove the correspondence theorem; in Section 7, we demonstrate that predicate sortings can be used to define context-aware reaction rules; and in Section 8, we conclude.

Notation and Terminology. We will need a tiny bit of standard terminology from the study of (op-)fibrations (see, e.g., [15]). Let $p : \mathbb{E} \to \mathbb{B}$ be a functor. A morphism of $\mathbb{B}$ has a *lift at* E iff it is the p-image of a morphism $f : E \to X$. A morphism f is *above* $p(f)$. A morphism ϕ is *vertical* if it is above an identity. The verticals above a particular identity id_B forms a category, the *fibre* over B. A morphism f is *opcartesian* iff whenever h, f is a span and h is above $g \circ p(f)$, then there exists a unique $\bar{g}$ s.t. $p(\bar{g}) = g$ and $h = \bar{g} \circ f$. (Two morphisms f, g form a *span* if they share domain, a *cospan* if they share codomain.)

2 Reactive Systems

We give a brief introduction to Leifer and Milner's reactive systems [2]. First, terminology and a little intuition. Let $\mathbb{B}$ be a category, and let ϵ be a distinguished object of $\mathbb{B}$. We shall think of morphisms with domain ϵ as *agents* and all other morphisms as *contexts*. Notice that the composition $C \circ a$ of a context $C : X \to Y$ with an agent $a : \epsilon \to X$ yields an agent $C \circ a : \epsilon \to Y$. A *reaction rule* (l, r) is a span of agents, i.e., both $l : \epsilon \to X$ and $r : \epsilon \to X$ for some X. Intuitively, l and r are the left- and right-hand sides of rewrite rule. A set $\mathcal{R}$ of reaction rules gives rise to a *reaction relation*, $\longmapsto$, by closing reaction rules under contexts:

$$a \longmapsto b \quad \text{iff} \quad \exists C \in \mathbb{B}, \exists (l, r) \in \mathcal{R}.\ a = C \circ l, b = C \circ r. \tag{1}$$

Altogether, these components constitute a reactive system.

Definition 1 (Reactive systems). *A reactive system over a category $\mathbb{B}$ comprises a distinguished object ϵ and a set $\mathcal{R}$ of reaction rules; the reaction rules gives rise to a reaction relation by (1) above.*

Thus far, we have merely restated well-known concepts in the language of category theory. The contribution of Leifer and Milner is their method for deriving labeled transitions from *any* reactive system: Provided the underlying category has sufficient structure, the bisimulation on these labeled transitions is guaranteed to be a congruence. To give the labeled transitions, we will need the concept of relative pushouts (RPOs).

Definition 2 (Relative pushout). *Consider the following diagram.*

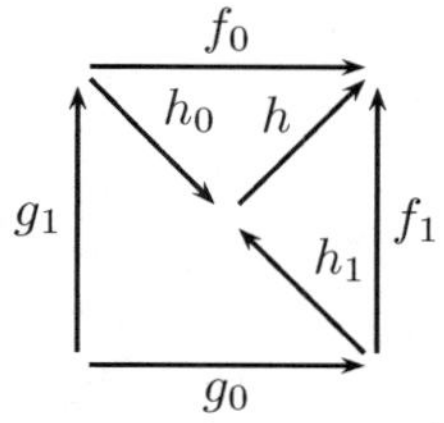

Suppose the outer square commutes. The triple (h_0, h_1, h) *is an RPO for* g_0, g_1 *to* f_0, f_1 *iff the entire diagram commutes and* (h_0, h_1, h) *is universal, that is, if* (h'_0, h'_1, h') *has* $h'_0 \circ g_0 = h'_1 \circ g_1$ *and* $f_i = h' \circ h'_i$*, then there exists a unique* k *s.t.* $h = h' \circ k$ *and* $h_i = k \circ h'_i$*. If* (f_0, f_1, id) *is an RPO for* g_0, g_1 *to* f_0, f_1*, we say that* (f_0, f_1) *is an* idem pushout *(IPO) for* g_0, g_1*.*

(For category-theory buffs: The RPO for g_i to f_i is a pushout of appropriate g_i in the slice-category over the codomain of the f_i.)

Intuitively, if (h_i, h) is an RPO for g_i to f_i, then h is the common part of the contexts f_i. The universality condition says that h is as big as possible: If h' is an alternative common part, then it must factor h, and there are thus commonalities in the f_i captured by h but not by h'. With this intuition, if f_i is an IPO for g_i, the f_i are minimal contexts making up for the differences between the g_i.

Leifer and Milner proceed to construct their labeled transition systems by taking as labels such minimal contexts enabling reaction.

Definition 3. *For a reactive system* $(\mathcal{R}, \epsilon)$ *over* $\mathbb{B}$*, we define the* standard transition relation $\longrightarrow$ *by taking* $a \xrightarrow{L} b$ *iff there exists a context* C *and a reaction rule* $(l, r) \in \mathcal{R}$ *s.t. the following diagram commutes, and the square is an IPO.*

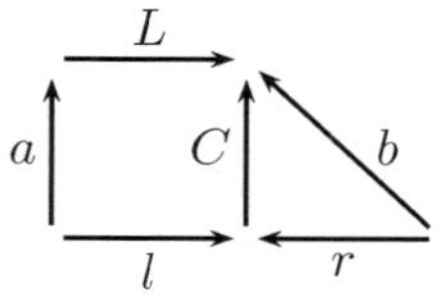

As mentioned, if $\mathbb{B}$ has all RPOs, then the bisimulation induced by the standard transitions is a congruence [2].

3 Sortings

The process of adding sort information, then removing morphisms based on that information is really the construction of a category $\mathbb{E}$, based on some existing category $\mathbb{B}$. There is obviously a forgetful functor $p : \mathbb{E} \to \mathbb{B}$ which is surjective on objects; both Jensen [9] and Milner/Leifer [10] note so. Clearly, this functor characterizes the sorting — Milner and Leifer states: "We shall often confuse [a sorting] with its functor" [10, p.44]. Hence, we suggest taking the existence of such a functor as the *definition* of a sorting.

Definition 4 (Sorting). *A* sorting *of a category* $\mathbb{B}$ *is a functor into* $\mathbb{B}$ *that is faithful and surjective on objects.*

It is perhaps helpful to think of a sorting functor p as a refinement of homsets: A homset $\mathbb{B}(B, B')$ is refined into the homsets $\mathbb{E}(E, E')$, where each E and E' are p-preimages of B and B'. Because p is surjective on objects, every homset of $\mathbb{B}$ is so refined; because p is faithful, each such refined homset simply consists of a subset of the morphisms of the original homset.

We are interested in sortings that allow us to infer the existence of RPOs in $\mathbb{E}$ from the existence of RPOs in $\mathbb{B}$. Jensen gives a sufficient condition, *safety*, for making such inferences. However, Jensen formulates safety in the setting of bigraphical place-graph sortings, so we would like to lift Jensen's definition of safety and his RPO-transfer theorem [9, Theorem 4.32] to our general definition of sorting. Remarkably, *virtually nothing needs to be done*: Jensen's definition, theorems and proofs are all formulated exclusively in terms of the (induced) forgetful functor p, so we may transfer his work verbatim to our more general setting. Thus, Definition 5 and Theorems 6, 8, and 12 are essentially due to Jensen, although our formulations are much more general than his[1]. Jensen's proofs of Theorems 6, 8, and 12 can be found either in Jensen's forthcoming thesis [9] or (restated more verbosely) in [14].

Definition 5 (Transfer of RPOs). *A functor* $p : \mathbb{E} \to \mathbb{B}$ *transfers RPOs iff whenever the* p*-image of an* $\mathbb{E}$*-square* s *has an RPO, then that RPO has a* p*-preimage that is an RPO for* s.

This definition is sufficient to infer the existence of RPOs in $\mathbb{E}$ from the existence of RPO in $\mathbb{B}$:

Theorem 6. *If* $\mathbb{B}$ *has RPOs and* $p : \mathbb{E} \to \mathbb{B}$ *transfers RPOs, then* $\mathbb{E}$ *has RPOs and* p *preserves RPOs.*

In order to characterize RPOs in $\mathbb{E}$, we have concocted the following generalization of "opcartesian". The notion is inspired by Jensen's notion of minimally sorted sets of morphisms; it is a vehicle for transferring factorization of contexts from $\mathbb{B}$ to $\mathbb{E}$.

Definition 7 (Jointly opcartesian). *Let* $p : \mathbb{E} \to \mathbb{B}$ *be a functor. A cospan* f, g *in* $\mathbb{E}$ *is said to be* jointly opcartesian *iff whenever* f', g' *is a cospan,* f, f' *is a*

1 In the words of Poincaré [16, p. 34]: "When language has been well-chosen, one is astonished to find that all demonstrations made for a known object apply immediately to many new objects: nothing requires to be changed, not even the terms, since the names have become the same."

span, and g, g' is a span (see the diagram below, left side) with $p(f') = k \circ p(f)$ and $p(g') = k \circ p(g)$ (see the diagram below, right side), then there exists a unique lift $\bar{k}$ of k s.t. $f' = \bar{k} \circ f$ and $g' = \bar{k} \circ f'$.

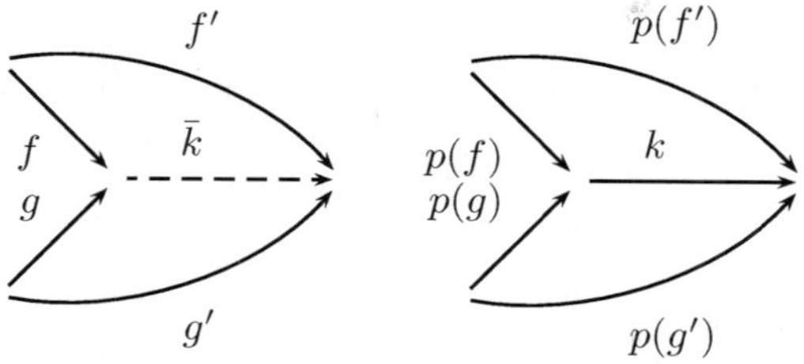

Theorem 8. *If $\mathbb{B}$ has RPOs and $p : \mathbb{E} \to \mathbb{B}$ transfers RPOs, then the diagram below is an RPO in $\mathbb{E}$ iff its p-image is an RPO and h_0, h_1 are jointly opcartesian.*

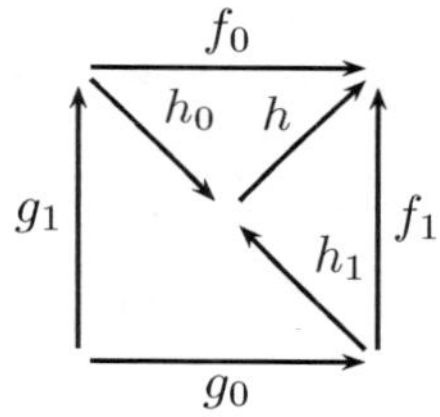

Intuitively, an RPO is the best way to factor a square; h_0, h_1 jointly opcartesian ensures that this best factorization can be lifted from $\mathbb{B}$ to $\mathbb{E}$.

Now that we have a characterization of IPOs for sortings that transfer RPOs sortings, we look for a way to establish that a sorting actually does transfer RPOs. The following generalization of the notion of opfibration will do.

Definition 9 (Weak opfibration). *A functor $p : \mathbb{E} \to \mathbb{B}$ is a* weak opfibration *iff whenever a morphism f of $\mathbb{B}$ has a lift at E, it has an opcartesian lift at E.*

This definition relaxes the requirement of an opfibration (see, e.g., [15]), where each morphism of $\mathbb{B}$ must have an opcartesian lift at each preimage of its domain. However, it does retain the key property that every morphism can be written as the composition of a vertical and an opcartesian.

Proposition 10. *Suppose $p : \mathbb{E} \to \mathbb{B}$ is a sorting. Then p is a weak opfibration iff every morphism f of $\mathbb{E}$ can be written $f = \phi \circ f'$ where ϕ is a vertical and f' is opcartesian.*

Proof. "$\Longrightarrow$". For any $f : E \to E' \in \mathbb{E}$, $p(f)$ must have an opcartesian lift at E, say $\bar{f}$. But $p(\bar{f}) = p(f)$ factors $p(f) \circ \mathrm{id}$, so for some vertical ϕ, $f = \phi \circ \bar{f}$. "$\Longleftarrow$". Any lift $f : E \to E'$ of $p(f)$ can be written $f = \phi \circ \bar{f}$, ϕ vertical and $\bar{f}$ opcartesian, whence $\bar{f}$ is the requisite opcartesian lift. □

Definition 11 (Reflects prefixes, Vertical pushouts). *A functor $p : \mathbb{E} \to \mathbb{B}$* reflects prefixes *iff whenever f is above $g \circ h$ then h has a lift at the domain of f; p has* vertical pushouts *iff the fibres have pushouts and such pushouts are also pushouts in $\mathbb{E}$.*

Theorem 12. *Let $p : \mathbb{E} \to \mathbb{B}$ be a sorting. If p is a weak opfibration, reflects prefixes, and has vertical pushouts, then p transfers RPOs. If $\mathbb{B}$ also has RPOs, then $\mathbb{E}$ has RPOs and p preserves RPOs.*

We note that sortings can be composed by composing their functors, and we can form conjunctions of sortings by taking their pullbacks. Composition preserves RPO-transfer, and pullbacks preserve both RPO-transfer and the preconditions for Theorem 12; refer to [14] for proofs and details.

4 Predicate Sortings

The example sortings referenced in the introduction are all intended to ban morphisms from the underlying category $\mathbb{B}$. The adding of sort information is but a means to this end; in each case, the authors construct a category $\mathbb{E}$ which resembles $\mathbb{B}$, except that morphisms not satisfying some predicate P are no longer present. We have identified a common feature of these sortings: When read as predicates on morphisms of $\mathbb{B}$, they all define *de*-composible predicates.

Definition 13. *A predicate P on the morphisms of a category $\mathbb{B}$ is* decomposible *iff $P(f \circ g)$ implies $P(f)$ and $P(g)$.*

This commonality may appear remarkable, but it is not, really, once we realize that the decomposible predicates are precisely those that disallow morphisms that are factored by morphisms in some given set.

Proposition 14. *A predicate P on the morphisms of a category $\mathbb{B}$ is decomposible iff there exists a set Φ of $\mathbb{B}$-morphisms s.t. $P(f)$ iff for any g, ψ, h, $f = g \circ \psi \circ h$ implies $\psi \notin \Phi$.*

Proof. Suppose P decomposible; take $\Phi = \{\phi \mid \neg P(\phi)\}$. If $P(f)$ and $f = g \circ \psi \circ h$, then $P(\psi)$, so $\psi \notin \Phi$. If $f = g \circ \psi \circ h$ implies $\psi \notin \Phi$, then $f = \mathrm{id} \circ f \circ \mathrm{id}$, so $f \notin \Phi$, thus $P(f)$. Define instead for some Φ, $P(f)$ iff $f = g \circ \psi \circ h$ implies $\psi \notin \Phi$. If $P(f \circ g)$ and, say, $f = h \circ \phi \circ i$, then $f \circ g = h \circ \phi \circ (i \circ g)$, so $\phi \notin \Phi$. □

In an encoding $[\![-]\!]$ of a calculus as a reactive system, it is natural to take Φ to be the complement of the image of the encoding $[\![-]\!]$. However, the resulting predicate is different from just defining "$P(f)$ iff f is in the image of $[\![-]\!]$"; the former definition always allows decompositions of morphisms in the image of $[\![-]\!]$ where as the latter does so only if $[\![-]\!]$ is closed under decomposition in the first place. Because the encodings listed in the introduction all use sortings that are manifestations of decomposible predicates, it appears that so far, images of encodings either turn out to closed under decomposition, or can be closed under decomposition without adversely affecting the resulting bisimulation.

Proposition 14 gives a connection to BiLog [17,18], a spatial logic for bigraphs. Given a BiLog formula ψ which characterizes a set Ψ of unwanted morphisms, the BiLog formula $(\neg\psi)^{\forall\circ}$ characterizes the morphisms f s.t. $f = x \circ \phi \circ y$

implies $\phi \notin \Psi$. By Proposition 14, the set of morphisms satisfying $(\neg\psi)^{\forall\circ}$ is decomposible, and thus gives rise to a *predicate sorting* as defined below.

We proceed to construct, for any decomposible predicate P on a category $\mathbb{B}$, a corresponding sorting $p : \mathbb{E} \to \mathbb{B}$. The problem we face when constructing any sorting is that we would like to retain as many morphisms of $\mathbb{B}$ as possible, while guaranteeing that we never inadvertently violate P by composition. Suppose for instance that we have morphisms $f : A \to B$ and $g : B \to C$, and that we have both $P(f)$ and $P(g)$, but *not* $P(g \circ f)$. We must either disallow f and allow g, or allow f and disallow g. In the predicate sorting, we retain both options: As preimage of an object B, we take all pairs (X, Y) of sets of morphisms into and out of B such that every morphism in X can safely be composed with every morphism in Y.

Definition 15 (Predicate sorting). *Let $\mathbb{B}$ be a category, and let P be a decomposible predicate on the morphisms of $\mathbb{B}$; we define the* predicate sorting *$p : \mathbb{E} \to \mathbb{B}$ for P. The category $\mathbb{E}$ has pairs (X, Y) as objects, where, for some object B of $\mathbb{B}$, X is a set of $\mathbb{B}$ morphisms with codomain B and Y is a set of $\mathbb{B}$-morphisms with domain B, subject to the following conditions.*

$$\mathrm{id}_B \in X, Y \qquad (\text{ID})$$

$$f \in X \cup Y \implies P(f) \qquad (\text{SOUND})$$

$$f \in X, g \in Y \implies P(g \circ f) \qquad (\text{COMP})$$

$$g \circ f \in X \implies g \in X \qquad (\text{SUFFIX})$$

$$g \circ f \in Y \implies f \in Y \qquad (\text{PREFIX})$$

There is a morphism $f : (X, Y) \to (U, V)$ whenever the following holds.

$$f \in Y, f \in U \qquad (\text{VALID})$$

$$x \in X \implies f \circ x \in U \qquad (\text{PRESERVE})$$

$$v \in V \implies v \circ f \in Y \qquad (\text{REFLECT})$$

We put this definition in words. For an object (X, Y), we require that X, Y contain the identity (ID); that morphisms in X, Y satisfy P (SOUND); that morphisms in X, Y are composible (COMP); that X is suffix-closed (SUFFIX); and that Y is prefix-closed (PREFIX). The first three requirements picks out all possible combinations of morphisms satisfying P. The latter two requirements ensures the existence of opcartesians and that the sorting reflects prefixes, respectively; we will need these properties to transfer RPOs. Notice that decomposibility of P is integral only to these latter two requirements.

For a morphism f, we require that it is contained in the sets at its domain and codomain (VALID); that it preserves validity of its domain (PRESERVE); and that it reflects validity at its codomain (REFLECT). The latter two requirements ensure that we do not accidentally violate P by successive compositions. (Technically, we could do without (VALID), which follows from (PRESERVE), (REFLECT) and (ID); we feel that the definition is clearer as it stands.)

5 Transfer Theorem for Predicate Sortings

In this section, we prove that a predicate sorting $p : \mathbb{E} \to \mathbb{B}$ transfers RPOs. First, we establish that each fibre is a lattice (Proposition 16); second, we characterize the opcartesians (Definition 17 and Proposition 18); third, we use this characterization to show that p is a weak opfibration (Proposition 19); and fourth, we show that p transfers RPOs (Theorem 20). First, each fibre is a lattice.

Proposition 16. *If $\phi : (X,Y) \to (U,V)$ is vertical, then $X \subseteq U$ and $Y \supseteq V$. Ordered pointwise under $\subseteq$ and $\supseteq$, each fibre is a lattice with joins $(X,Y) \sqcup (U,V) = (X \cup U, Y \cap V)$ and meets $(X,Y) \sqcap (U,V) = (X \cap U, Y \cup V)$.*

We characterize the opcartesians. For a morphism $f : A \to B$ and a preimage (X,Y) of A, we use (PRESERVE) and (REFLECT) to *define* a preimage of B.

Definition 17. *Let $f : A \to B$ be a morphism of $\mathbb{B}$, and let $X \subseteq \{g \mid \mathrm{cod}(g) = A\}$ and $Y \subseteq \{h \mid \mathrm{dom}(h) = A\}$. We define operators $\bullet$ and $\circ$ by $f \circ X = \{f \circ x \mid x \in X\}$ and $Y \bullet f = \{g \mid g \circ f \in Y\}$. For any set Z of morphisms, we define the* suffix *and* prefix closures $Z^{\mathbf{s}} = \{h \mid \exists g.\ h \circ g \in Z\}$ *and* $Z^{\mathbf{P}} = \{g \mid \exists h.\ h \circ g \in Z\}$.

Proposition 18. *A morphism $f : (X,Y) \to (U,V)$ is opcartesian if and only if $U = (f \circ X)^{\mathbf{s}}$ and $V = (Y \bullet f)^{\mathbf{P}}$.*

Proposition 19. *A predicate sorting $p : \mathbb{E} \to \mathbb{B}$ is a weak opfibration.*

It is straightforward to establish that p reflects prefixes and has vertical pushouts; see [14]. Thus, by Theorem 12, we have the desired transfer theorem.

Theorem 20. *If $\mathbb{B}$ has RPOs, then a predicate sorting $p : \mathbb{E} \to \mathbb{B}$ transfers RPOs.*

6 Correspondence Theorem for Predicate Sortings

Taking the view that sortings exist to get rid of junk morphisms, when is a sorting good enough? Not just any sorting will do. For instance, for any category $\mathbb{B}$ and predicate P, we can construct a category $\mathbb{E}$ that has, for each f with $P(f)$, unique objects f_X, f_Y and a morphism $f : f_X \to f_Y$. This category gives a sorting $p : \mathbb{E} \to \mathbb{B}$ that transfers RPOs and has as image precisely the morphisms f with $P(f)$, but surely, this sorting is untenable: It supports no non-trivial compositions, reactions, or transitions. We believe that a sorting will prove usable if our chosen reactive system in $\mathbb{B}$ and restricted to morphisms satisfying P can be recovered in $\mathbb{E}$, and similarly for transitions. We establish that our predicate sortings maintain this correspondence between reactions and transitions in Theorem 25 below. First, we must make our notion of correspondence precise. For a predicate sorting $p : \mathbb{E} \to \mathbb{B}$, we let $\mathbb{E}$ *inherit* reactions from $\mathbb{B}$. Inheritance will in turn require a lift of the distinguished object ϵ, the domain of agents.

Lemma 21. *Write $\bar{\epsilon}$ for the pair $((\mathrm{id}_\epsilon)^{\mathrm{s}}, \{f : \epsilon \to X \mid P(f)\})$. Then $\bar{\epsilon}$ is an object above ϵ, and any morphism $f : \epsilon \to X$ with $P(f)$ has a lift at $\bar{\epsilon}$.*

Definition 22 (p-inherited reactive system). *Let $p : \mathbb{E} \to \mathbb{B}$ be a sorting, and let $\mathcal{R}$ be a ground reactive system on $\mathbb{B}$. The* p-inherited reactive system *has distinguished object $\bar{\epsilon}$ and reaction rules $\bar{\mathcal{R}}$ defined by*

$$\bar{\mathcal{R}} = \{(f, g) \mid f, g : \bar{\epsilon} \to X \textit{ for some } X, \textit{ and } (p(f), p(g)) \in \mathcal{R}\}.$$

Conversely, reactions and transitions in $\mathbb{E}$ can be translated to $\mathbb{B}$.

Definition 23 (p-induced reactions and transitions). *Let $p : \mathbb{E} \to \mathbb{B}$ be a sorting, and let $\longmapsto$ be a reaction relation on $\mathbb{E}$. We define the* p-induced reaction relation $[\![\longmapsto]\!]$ *in $\mathbb{B}$ by taking for any f, g,*

$$p(f) \, [\![\longmapsto]\!] \, p(g) \quad \textit{iff} \quad f \longmapsto g.$$

Let $\longrightarrow$ be the corresponding transition relation. We define the p-induced transition relation $[\![\longrightarrow]\!]$ *in $\mathbb{B}$ by taking for any f, g, h,*

$$p(f) \, [\![\xrightarrow{p(h)}]\!] \, p(g) \quad \textit{iff} \quad f \xrightarrow{h} g.$$

Having moved reactions up, and reactions and transitions back down, we compare the result to restricting the original $\mathbb{B}$ reactions to P.

Definition 24 (P-restricted reactions and transitions). *Let $\longmapsto$ be a reaction relation. We define the* P-restricted reaction relation $\lfloor\longmapsto\rfloor$ *(in the obvious way) by*

$$f \lfloor\longmapsto\rfloor g \quad \textit{iff} \quad f \longmapsto g \textit{ and } P(f), P(g).$$

Let $\longrightarrow$ be the corresponding transition relation. We define the P-restricted transition relation $\lfloor\longrightarrow\rfloor$ *by*

$$f \lfloor\xrightarrow{h}\rfloor g \quad \textit{iff} \quad f \xrightarrow{h} g \textit{ and } P(f), P(g), P(h), P(h \circ f).$$

Theorem 25 (Correspondence). *Let $\mathbb{B}$ be a category with RPOs, let P be a decomposible predicate, let $p : \mathbb{E} \to \mathbb{B}$ be the predicate sorting for P, let $\mathcal{R}$ be a reactive system on $\mathbb{B}$, and let $\bar{\mathcal{R}}$ be the p-inherited reactive system on $\mathbb{E}$. Then*

1. *the p-induced and P-restricted reaction relations coincide, and*
2. *the p-induced and P-restricted transition relations coincide.*

To prove the correspondence theorem, we will need better understanding of the jointly opcartesians: Using Theorem 8, the jointly opcartesian pairs help us find IPOs.

Definition 26 (Nearly jointly opcartesian). *For $p : \mathbb{E} \to \mathbb{B}$, a cospan f, g is* nearly jointly opcartesian *iff there exists a jointly opcartesian pair f', g' and a vertical ϕ s.t. $f = \phi \circ f'$ and $g = \phi \circ g'$.*

Using that each fibre is a lattice, we find that all cospans are nearly jointly opcartesian.

Proposition 27. *In a predicate sorting $p : \mathbb{E} \to \mathbb{B}$, f, g are jointly opcartesian iff $f = \phi \circ \bar{f}$ and $g = \psi \circ \bar{g}$ where $\bar{f}, \bar{g}$ are opcartesians and ϕ, ψ are the unique verticals given by* $\mathrm{cod}(\bar{f}) \sqcup \mathrm{cod}(\bar{g})$.

Proposition 28. *In a predicate sorting $p : \mathbb{E} \to \mathbb{B}$, every cospan f, g is nearly jointly opcartesian.*

Proof. By Proposition 10, we may write $f = \rho \circ \bar{f}$ and $g = \tau \circ \bar{g}$ where $\bar{f}, \bar{g}$ are opcartesian and ρ, τ are verticals. Take ϕ, ψ to be the unique verticals given by $\bar{f} \sqcup \bar{g}$. By Proposition 27, $\phi \circ \bar{f}$ and $\psi \circ \bar{g}$ are jointly opcartesians, hence there exists a vertical α with $f = \alpha \circ \phi \circ \bar{f}$ and $g = \alpha \circ \psi \circ \bar{g}$. □

Proposition 29. *Let $p : \mathbb{E} \to \mathbb{B}$ be a predicate sorting, and consider a cospan*

$$p(X, Y) \xrightarrow{\ f\ } B \xleftarrow{\ g\ } p(U, V)$$

If f and g have lifts at $p(X, Y)$ and $p(U, V)$, respectively, then they have jointly opcartesian lifts there.

Proof. We have opcartesian lifts $\bar{f}$ of f and $\bar{g}$ of g, and because f, g is a cospan, we may form $\bar{f} \sqcup \bar{g}$; Proposition 27 now gives a jointly opcartesian lift. □

In light of Theorem 8, the above proposition gives us a very tight grip on the relation between IPOs in $\mathbb{B}$ and $\mathbb{E}$. We now use that grip to prove the correspondence theorem.

Proof (of Theorem 25). Part 1. Suppose first that a $[\![\longmapsto]\!]$ b. Then for some f, g with $a = p(f)$ and $b = p(g)$, $f \longmapsto g$. Thus $f = D \circ e$ and $g = D \circ e'$ with $(e, e') \in \bar{\mathcal{R}}$, so $a = p(D) \circ p(e)$ and $b = p(D) \circ p(e')$, with $(p(e), p(e')) \in \mathcal{R}$, so $a \longmapsto b$; clearly $P(a)$ and $P(b)$, hence a $\lfloor\longmapsto\rfloor$ b.

Suppose instead that f $\lfloor\longmapsto\rfloor$ g. There exists C, r and s with $(r, s) \in \mathcal{R}$ s.t. $f = C \circ r$ and $g = C \circ s$. By Lemma 21 we can find lifts of r, s at $\bar{\epsilon}$, so by Proposition 29, we have a jointly opcartesian lift $\bar{r}, \bar{s}$ of r, s at ϵ. Again by Lemma 21, we can lift $\overline{C \circ r}$ and $\overline{C \circ s}$ at ϵ; so by $\bar{r}, \bar{s}$ jointly opcartesian, there is a lift $\bar{C}$ of C at $\mathrm{cod}(\bar{r}) = \mathrm{cod}(\bar{s})$. Clearly $(\bar{r}, \bar{s}) \in \bar{R}$, so we have $\bar{C} \circ \bar{r} \longmapsto \bar{C} \circ \bar{s}$, and in turn $f = C \circ r$ $[\![\longmapsto]\!]$ $C \circ s = g$.

Part 2. Suppose a $\lfloor\xrightarrow{L}\rfloor$ b. Thus there exists $(r, s) \in \mathcal{R}$ and a context C s.t. the following diagram commutes and the square is an IPO.

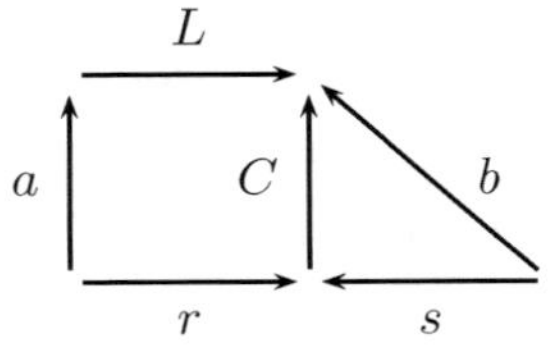

We find $P(C \circ r)$ because $P(L \circ a)$, and $P(C \circ s)$ because $P(b)$. By Lemma 21 and Proposition 19, we have opcartesian lifts $\bar{a}$, $\overline{L \circ a}$, $\bar{r}$, $\bar{s}$, $\overline{C \circ r}$ and $\overline{C \circ s}$ at $\bar{\epsilon}$. Because $\bar{a}$ is opcartesian, we find may a lift of $\bar{L}$ at the codomain of $\bar{a}$; we may assume this lift opcartesian. By Proposition 29, we may assume $\bar{r}, \bar{s}$ jointly opcartesian and $\overline{C \circ r}, \overline{C \circ s}$ cospan, so there exists a lift $\bar{C}$ of C at $\mathrm{cod}(\bar{r}) = \mathrm{cod}(\bar{s})$. Again by Proposition 29, we may assume $\bar{L}, \bar{C}$ jointly opcartesian. Altogether, we have erected the following diagram.

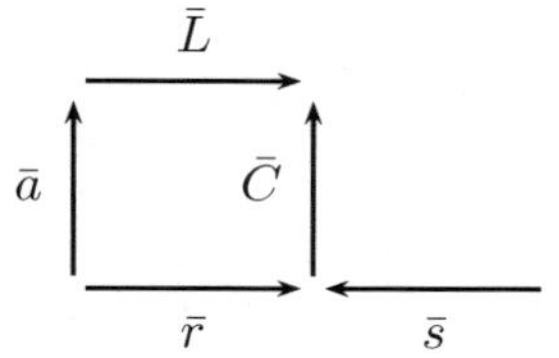

By Theorem 8, we have constructed an IPO, and clearly $(p(\bar{r}), p(\bar{s})) \in \mathcal{R}$, so we have a transition $\bar{a} \xrightarrow{\bar{L}} \bar{C} \circ \bar{s}$. Because $C \circ s = b$, we have obtained the desired transition $a \;[\![\xrightarrow{L}]\!]\; b$.

Suppose instead $a \;[\![\xrightarrow{L}]\!]\; b$. For some f, g, h, we have $a = p(f), b = p(g), L = p(h)$ and $f \xrightarrow{h} g$, so there exists $(r, s) \in \bar{\mathcal{R}}$ and a C s.t. the following diagram commutes, and the square is an IPO.

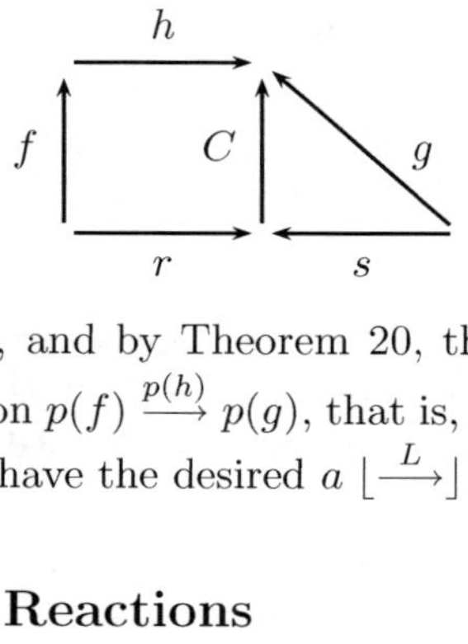

Clearly, $(p(r), p(s)) \in \mathcal{R})$, and by Theorem 20, the image of the square is an IPO, so there is a transition $p(f) \xrightarrow{p(h)} p(g)$, that is, $a \xrightarrow{L} b$. Clearly, $P(a)$, $P(L)$, $P(b)$ and $P(L \circ a)$, so we have the desired $a \lfloor\xrightarrow{L}\rfloor\; b$. □

7 Context-Aware Reactions

Ubiquitous computing is inextricably linked to context-aware computing: computations that are aware of and depend on the present context of the computing agent. Here are two examples. (1) An electronic tour guide device, carried around by visitors at a museum, should provide information about the physically closest exhibit. (2) Doors in a shop which open automatically unless an RFID-tag of an item not registered as sold is too close. Notice the dual requirements in these examples: The first stipulates a positive requirement (the presence of an exhibit), whereas the second stipulates a negative requirement (the absence of an unsold item). Thus, for modeling such applications, it is very convenient if we can specify reaction rules that apply in some but not all contexts. However, as observed in [19], work on process calculi tends to supply at most a rudimentary distinction between active and passive contexts, a distinction insufficient for the above examples.

We can use sorting to better control reaction: We simply specify our reactive system directly in the sorted category $\mathbb{E}$. By choosing the right codomain for a reaction rule (l, r) we specify in what contexts it applies. In particular, we may use sorting to capture absence of something in the context. In some categories — in particular bigraphs — we model contexts as morphisms and the presence of something as factorization. Thus, we say that $a : A' \to B'$ is present in the context $c : A \to B$ iff $c = x \circ a \circ y$ for some x, y. Under this notion of presence, the predicate sorting can be used to capture *absence* to the extent of the following theorem.

Theorem 30. *Let $p : \mathbb{E} \to \mathbb{B}$ be the predicate sorting, let $f : \epsilon \to B$ be a morphism of $\mathbb{B}$, and let T be any set of morphisms with domain B. Then f has a lift $\bar{f}$ at $\bar{\epsilon}$ s.t. each $g : B \to X$ has a lift at $\mathrm{cod}(\bar{f})$ precisely when $g \in T$ iff T is prefix closed and respects P.*

Put another way: If we want the left-hand side of a reaction rule (l, r) to apply precisely in a set T of contexts, we can do so within any predicate sorting, provided T is prefix-closed and respects the predicate P. Notice that we may take P to be everywhere true, should we so desire.

What does the restriction to prefix-closed sets T mean? Reconsidering the examples with presence and absence, we see that absence is prefix-closed whereas presence is not. Clearly, if a does not occur in a context c, then it also does not occur in any sub-context of c; in particular, it does not occur in any prefix of c. On the other hand, we may very well have a context c that contains some a, but a prefix of c which does not.

In the case of bigraphs or, more generally, wide reactive systems [4,5], the monoidal structure enables us to express presence without the use of sortings: If we insist that (l, r) applies only when a is present in the context, we simply give the rule as $(a \otimes l, a \otimes r)$. Thus, in sorted wide reactive systems, we can model both presence and absence.

8 Conclusion

Building on earlier work on more specific sortings, ours is the first investigation of general sortings, or type systems, for reactive systems. However, type systems have been investigated for related frameworks, notably for hypergraph rewriting systems in [20], and for process algebras in [21]. Our work is alone in addressing the impact of sorting on labeled transition systems, bisimulations, and congruence properties.

König's typings for hypergraph rewriting systems [20] resembles our sortings in that the aim of typing is explicitly stated to be identifying hypergraphs satisfying a given predicate; that decomposition preserves well-typedness; that composition does not necessarily preserve well-typedness; and that there is a notion of minimal type, roughly comparable to our use of opcartesian lifts. The method differs from ours — the setting of hypergraphs not withstanding — in that the typing relation is required to satisfy subject reduction, whereas we simply disregard type-altering reductions (cf. the P-restriction of reaction, Definition 24).

Honda's work on typed process algebras [21] is reminiscent of ours in that it focuses explicitly on controlling which morphisms are composible and which are not. However, Honda's notion of process is quite specific to process calculi compared to our more general setting of reactive systems over categories.

For future work, we see as the most urgent the reconciliation of present work with precategories, bridging the gap to bigraphs. Observing that our notion of sorting applies immediately to abstract bigraph, we are hopeful that we can transfer our results across the quotient functors to precategories.

Other directions include further investigating compositionality of sortings. In Section 3, we demonstrated how to compose sortings sequentially and how to form their conjunction; it is natural to wonder about other connectives, particularly negation. Another direction is investigating the use of sortings for encoding typed calculi in reactive systems. Yet another is that for bigraphs, it would be interesting if there were stronger connections between BiLog [17,18] and sorted bigraphs than those noted in Section 4. For instance, BiLog formulas might form the basis of a syntactic formulation of sorting, which could in turn be useful for implementations of reactive systems. Finally, it would be interesting to know if the predicate sorting is in some sense universal.

Acknowledgments. We gratefully acknowledge good suggestions from the anonymous referees and vibrant discussions with Rasmus Lerchedahl Petersen and Mikkel Bundgaard.

References

1. Sewell, P.: From rewrite rules to bisimulation congruences. Theoretical Computer Science **274**(1–2) (2002) 183–230
2. Leifer, J.J., Milner, R.: Deriving bisimulation congruences for reactive systems. In: CONCUR '00: Proceedings of the 11th International Conference on Concurrency Theory, Springer-Verlag (2000) 243–258
3. Jensen, O.H., Milner, R.: Bigraphs and transitions. In: POPL '03: Proceedings of the 30th ACM SIGPLAN-SIGACT symposium on Principles of programming languages, ACM Press (2003) 38–49
4. Jensen, O.H., Milner, R.: Bigraphs and mobile processes (revised). Technical Report UCAM-CL-TR-580, University of Cambridge Computer Laboratory (2004)
5. Milner, R.: Pure bigraphs: Structure and dynamics. Information and Computation **204**(1) (2006) 60–122
6. Sassone, V., Sobocinski, P.: Deriving bisimulation congruences: 2-categories vs. precategories. In: FOSSACS '03: Proceedings of Foundations of Software Science and Computation Structures. Volume 2620 of Lecture Notes in Computer Science., Springer-Verlag (2003) 409–424
7. Sassone, V., Sobocinski, P.: Reactive systems over cospans. In: LICS '05: Proceedings of the twentieth annual IEEE symposium on Logic in computer science, IEEE Computer Society Press (2005) 311–320

8. Bruni, R., Gadducci, F., Montanari, U., Sobociński, P.: Deriving weak bisimulation congruences from reduction systems. In: CONCUR '05: Proceedings of the 16th international conference on Concurrency theory. Volume 3653 of Lecture Notes in Computer Science., Springer-Verlag (2005) 293–307
9. Jensen, O.H.: Mobile Processes in Bigraphs. PhD thesis, University of Aalborg (2006) Forthcoming.
10. Milner, R., Leifer, J.J.: Transition systems, link graphs and Petri nets. Technical report, University of Cambridge, Computer Laboratory (2004)
11. Bundgaard, M., Hildebrandt, T.: Bigraphical semantics of higher-order mobile embedded resources with local names. In: GT-VC '05: Proceedings of the Graph Transformation for Verification and Concurrency workshop. Volume 154 of Electronic Notes in Theoretical Computer Science., Elsevier (2006) 7–29
12. Birkedal, L., Debois, S., Elsborg, E., Hildebrandt, T., Niss, H.: Bigraphical Models of Context-aware Systems. Technical Report 74, IT University of Copenhagen (2005) ISBN: 87-7949-110-3.
13. Birkedal, L., Debois, S., Elsborg, E., Hildebrandt, T., Niss, H.: Bigraphical Models of Context-aware Systems. In: FOSSACS '06: Proceedings of 9th International Conference on Foundations of Software Science and Computation Structures. Volume 3921 of Lecture Notes in Computer Science., Springer-Verlag (2006)
14. Birkedal, L., Debois, S., Hildebrandt, T.: Sortings for reactive systems. Technical Report 84, IT University of Copenhagen (2006) ISBN 87-7949-124-3.
15. Jacobs, B.: Categorical logic and type theory. Volume 141 of Studies in logic and the foundation of mathematics. Elsevier (1999)
16. Poincaré, H.: Science and Method. Dover Publications (1914) Translation by Francis Maitland.
17. Conforti, G., Macedonio, D., Sassone, V.: Spatial logics for bigraphs. In: ICALP '05: Proceedings of the 32nd international colloquium on Automata, languages and programming. Volume 3580 of Lecture Notes in Computer Science., Springer-Verlag (2005) 766–778
18. Conforti, G., Macedonio, D., Sassone, V.: Spatial logics for bigraphs. Computer Science Report 02, University of Sussex (2005)
19. Braione, P., Picco, G.P.: On calculi for context-aware coordination. In: COORDINATION '04: Proceedings of the 7th International Conference on Coordination Models and Languages. Volume 2949 of Lecture Notes in Computer Science., Springer (2004) 38–54
20. König, B.: A general framework for types in graph rewriting. In: FST TCS '00: Proceedings of the 20th Conference on Foundations of software technology and Theoretical computer science. Volume 1974 of Lecture Notes in Computer Science., Springer-Verlag (2000) 373–384
21. Honda, K.: Composing processes. In: POPL '96: Proceedings of the 23rd ACM SIGPLAN-SIGACT symposium on Principles of programming languages. (1996) 344–357

Dynamic Access Control in a Concurrent Object Calculus

Avik Chaudhuri

Computer Science Department
University of California, Santa Cruz
avik@cs.ucsc.edu

Abstract. We develop a variant of Gordon and Hankin's concurrent object calculus with support for flexible access control on methods. We investigate safe administration and access of shared resources in the resulting language. Specifically, we show a static type system that guarantees safe manipulation of objects with respect to dynamic specifications, where such specifications are enforced via access changes on the underlying methods at runtime. By labeling types with secrecy groups, we show that well-typed systems preserve their secrets amidst dynamic access control and untrusted environments.

1 Introduction

Systems that share resources almost always exercise some control on access to those resources. The access control typically relies on a set of rules that decide which access requests to accept; furthermore, those rules may be subject to change to reflect changing requirements on resource access at runtime. While access control mechanisms are often easy to deploy—they are both common and various—they are surprisingly difficult to marshal towards achieving higher safety goals. For instance, users who have access to a file with sensitive content can often share the content, intentionally or by mistake, with those who do not have access; even if the privileged users are careful, a change in the access rules can allow other users to read that content, or write over it.

A convenient view of access control results from its characterization in terms of - capabilities: a resource may be accessed if and only if a corresponding capability is shown for its access. For one, this view provides an immediate low-level abstraction of access control "by definition"; two, the view is independent of higher level specifications on resource usage (say, in terms of types, or identities of principals). The separation facilitates higher level proofs, since it suffices to guarantee that the flow of a capability that protects a resource respects the corresponding high-level intention on resource usage. We develop methods to provide such guarantees in this paper. The methods in turn rely on a sound low-level implementation of access control in terms of capabilities. Fortunately, to that end, a capability for a resource can be identified with a pointer to that resource. Exporting a direct link to a resource, however, poses problems for dynamic access control, as discussed by Redell in his dissertation (1974). Redell suggests a simple alternative that uses indirection: export indirect pointers to a local, direct reference to the resource, and overwrite this local pointer to modify access to that resource [30]. We revisit that idea in this paper.

C. Baier and H. Hermanns (Eds.): CONCUR 2006, LNCS 4137, pp. 263–278, 2006.

We study safe dynamic access control in a concurrent object language. Resources are often built over other resources; dependencies between resources may entail dependencies on their access assumptions for end-to-end safety. For example, suppose two users read the same file to obtain what they believe is a shared secret key that they then use to encrypt secret messages between themselves; it does not help if a third user can write a Trojan key on that file and then decrypt the "secret" messages. A natural way to capture such dependencies is to group the related resources into objects. (In the example above, the object would be the file in question, and the resources would be a "key" field and "read" and "write" methods that manipulate that field.)

We develop a variant of Gordon and Hankin's concurrent object calculus $\mathbf{conc}\varsigma$ [14] for our study. In $\mathbf{conc}\varsigma$, as in most previous object calculi (*e.g.*, [2,4,32]), a method is accessed by providing the name of the parent object and a label that identifies the method. For example, for a timer object t in the calculus, with two methods, tick and set, knowing the name t is sufficient to call (or even redefine) both methods (t.tick, t.set). We may, however, want to restrict access to set to the owner of t, while allowing other users to access tick; such requirements are not directly supported by $\mathbf{conc}\varsigma$. In languages like Java, there is limited support for method-level access control via access modifiers—however, such modifiers can only sometimes be changed in a very restricted way, and moreover they implement a policy design that is fixed by the language.

Our calculus provides *veils* for implementing flexible access control of methods. Veils are similar to Redell's indirect access pointers. More specifically, a veil is an alias (or "handle") for the label that identifies a particular method inside an object definition. A method is invoked by sending a message on its veil; method access is modified by re-exporting a different veil for its label. A method call crucially does not require the name of the parent object. An object name, on the other hand, is required for access modification and redefinition of methods—thus object names are similar to Redell's local references (or "capabilities"). In the sequel, informally, a *capability* is a reference to an object, and veils are indirect references to its methods. A capability is meant to be shared between the owner and other administrators of an object, and veils are meant to be made available to the users of its methods. Dependencies between object methods often require their redefinitions and access modifications to be simultaneous—therefore the calculus replaces $\mathbf{conc}\varsigma$'s method update with a more general "administration" primitive. Veils allow a relatively straightforward encoding of the mutex primitives of $\mathbf{conc}\varsigma_{\mathrm{m}}$ (an extension of $\mathbf{conc}\varsigma$ that facilitates encodings of locks, communication channels, *etc.*), so we do not include those primitives in the syntax.

We show a type system for the resulting language that guarantees safe manipulation of objects with respect to dynamically changing specifications. Informally, we allow object methods to change their exported "type views" at runtime: in other words, resource administrators can not only control resource usage at runtime, but also dynamically specify why they do so (*i.e.*, their higher level intentions). This flexibility is desirable since persistent resources (*e.g.*, file systems, memory) are typically used in several different contexts over time. For example, files are often required to pass through intervals of restricted access; memory locations are dynamically allocated/deallocated to map different data structures over several program executions. By a combination of access control (as provided by the language) and static discipline (provided by the type system) we can show that the intentions of the users and administrators of those resources are respected through and between such phases of flux. In particular, by labeling types with secrecy groups, we show that well-typedness guarantees secrecy under dynamic access control, even in the presence of possibly untyped, active environments.

Outline of the Paper. In the next section we present a concurrent object calculus with veils for dynamic access control (the "veil calculus", for brevity). We accompany the formal syntax and semantics of our language with commentary on the conceptual and technical differences with Gordon and Hankin's original calculus. In Section 3, we present a type system for the language, show examples of well-typed programs, and state our main theorem, *viz.* typing guarantees secrecy under dynamically changing type views and even under untyped environments. We discuss related work in Section 4 and conclude by summarizing our contributions.

2 The Untyped Veil Calculus

In this section we present a variant of the calculus **conc**ς [14]. The novel aspects of the language lie in the separation of roles for method definition and invocation; this separation is induced by a fresh treatment of method names via veils.

The syntax is very similar to that of **conc**ς; as such, it retains most of the simplicity, compactness, and expressivity of the original. Although we make minimal changes to the original calculus (specifically, in the manner of method call and update), the changes have a clear effect on the suitability of the resulting language as a core calculus for studying security properties of concurrent objects. As argued in Section 1, the original calculus cannot separate the ability to call a method (*i.e.*, use a resource) from the ability to redefine it (*i.e.*, do administration on it); moreover, it cannot distinguish between method-access abilities within the same object. Persistent resources characteristically require support for such distinctions for security. The new language improves upon **conc**ς in this respect, since veils can enforce those distinctions quite naturally.

$u, v, w ::=$	results
$\quad x$	variable
$\quad m, n, p, q, \theta$	name (capability, veil)
$d ::=$	denotations
$\quad \widetilde{\theta}[\widetilde{\ell} \Mapsto \varsigma(x)\widetilde{(y)b}]$	object
$a, b ::=$	expressions
$\quad u$	result
$\quad p \mapsto d$	denomination
$\quad (\nu n)\, a$	restriction
$\quad a \upharpoonright b$	fork
$\quad \text{let } x = a \text{ in } b$	evaluation
$\quad \ell(u)$	internal method call
$\quad \ell \Lleftarrow (y)b$	internal method update
$\quad \breve{v}\langle u\rangle$	external method call
$\quad u \hookleftarrow d$	external update ("administration")

Names in the veil calculus fall into two conceptual categories (that we do not distinguish syntactically): object names, which we call capabilities, and method alias names, which we call veils. An object is defined by a map from labels to expressions, and a map from labels to veils. The former map defines the methods of the object. The method bodies abstract on a "self" variable that gets bound to the name of the object at runtime. Unlike **conc**ς, they also abstract on an "argument" variable—while parameter passing can be encoded even otherwise, having explicit argument abstraction allows better typings. The map from labels to veils defines the external aliases for the methods of the object. As usual, these (finite) maps are written as associated sequences for convenience. We use the notation $\widetilde{\varphi}$ to abbreviate a sequence $\varphi_1, \ldots \varphi_k$, where k is given by $|\widetilde{\varphi}|$. Thus in the object $\widetilde{\theta}[\widetilde{\ell} \Mapsto \varsigma(x)\widetilde{(y)b}]$, the variable x abstracts "self"; for each label $\ell_i \in \widetilde{\ell}$, the name θ_i is a veil for the method identified by that label; the method's body b_i takes the parameter y_i. The maps are sometimes made explicit by writing the object as $\Theta[\varsigma(x)\Delta]$, where $\Theta(\ell_i) = \theta_i$ and $\Delta(\ell_i)(y_i) = b_i$ for each $\ell_i \in \widetilde{\ell}$.

There are separate "internal" and "external" primitives in the syntax for method call and update. The internal primitives $\ell(u)$ and $\ell \Lleftarrow (y)b$ noticeably do not carry any object reference (*cf.* the forms $p.\ell$ and $p.\ell \Lleftarrow b$ in **conc**ς [14]). Labels by themselves have no meaning outside objects; hence the use of internal primitives is limited to within objects. The external primitives, on the other hand, can be used in any context. An external method call $\widetilde{v}\,\langle u\rangle$ is a message on a veil. Crucially, an object reference is not required for invoking a method (*cf.* [14]). Object references are required for administration. Administration is done via external update $u \hookleftarrow d$, which is a generalization of **conc**ς's method update: it modifies an object by re-exporting veil bindings and augmenting/overriding several method definitions.

The rest of the syntax is the same as that of **conc**ς. Informally, the syntactical forms have the following meanings. (The formal semantics is shown later in the section.)

- u is a result (a variable or name) that is returned by an expression.
- $p \mapsto d$ attaches the capability p to an object d.
- $(\nu n)\ a$ creates a new name n that is bound in the expression a, and executes a.
- $a \upharpoonright b$ is the (non-commutative) parallel composition of the expressions a and b; it returns any result returned by b, while executing a for side-effect. This form, introduced in [14], is largely responsible for the compactness of the syntax, since it provides an uniform way to write expressions that return results, and "processes" that exhibit behaviours. (Of course, expressions that return results can also have side-effects.)
- let $x = a$ in b binds the result of the expression a to the variable x and then executes the expression b; here x is bound in b.
- $\ell(u)$ means a local method call inside an object; see external call.
- $\ell \Lleftarrow (y)b$ means a local method update inside an object; see external update.
- $\widetilde{v}\,\langle u\rangle$ means an external call on the veil v, with argument u; in the presence of a denomination $p \mapsto d$ where d exports v for a defined method, the corresponding method expression is exported by substituting veiled calls for internal calls, self updates for internal updates, p for the abstracted self variable, and u for the formal parameter. The details of method export are given below.

– $u \mapsfrom d$ means an external update on the capability u; in the presence of a denomination $u \mapsto d'$, the veils exported by d replace those exported by d', and the methods defined by d augment or override those defined by d'; the capability u is returned.

Example 1. Assume that integers can be encoded in the language, and there is a method handle $\theta_{\texttt{pre}}$ for decrementing a positive integer. Consider the following code. A server creates a new timer object, exports the tick and set methods of the timer on veils $\theta_{\texttt{tick}}$ and $\theta_{\texttt{set}}$, and sets the value of the timer to an integer N by invoking $\theta_{\texttt{set}}$. A client repeatedly ticks the timer by invoking $\theta_{\texttt{tick}}$. At some point, the server creates a new veil $\theta_{\texttt{ntick}}$, and re-exports the tick method of the timer object on this veil. Consequently, since the client does not know this new veil, it can no longer tick the timer. (We elide unnecessary self-bindings $\varsigma(x)$, formal parameters (y), and unit arguments in the code.)

$$
\begin{array}{rlr}
\text{System} \stackrel{\text{def}}{=} & (\nu p, \theta_{\texttt{val}}, \theta_{\texttt{set}}, \theta_{\texttt{tick}})\ (\text{Server} \Rsh \text{Client}) & \\
\text{Server} \stackrel{\text{def}}{=} & p \mapsto \theta_{\texttt{val}}\theta_{\texttt{set}}\theta_{\texttt{tick}}[\,\texttt{val} \Mapsto \texttt{val}, & \text{\# timer on capability } p \text{, with} \\
 & \qquad \texttt{set}(y) \Mapsto \text{let } \_ = \texttt{val} \Mapsfrom y \text{ in } y, & \text{\# \texttt{set} exported on veil } \theta_{\texttt{set}} \\
 & \qquad \texttt{tick} \Mapsto \text{let } z = \texttt{val} \text{ in} & \text{\# \texttt{tick} exported on veil } \theta_{\texttt{tick}} \\
 & \qquad\qquad \text{let } z' = \grave{\theta}_{\texttt{pre}}\langle z \rangle \text{ in } \texttt{set}(z')\,] \Rsh & \\
 & \grave{\theta}_{\texttt{set}}\langle N \rangle \Rsh \ldots \Rsh & \text{\# timer gets activated...} \\
 & (\nu\theta_{\texttt{ntick}})\ p \mapsfrom \theta_{\texttt{val}}\theta_{\texttt{set}}\theta_{\texttt{ntick}}[\,\texttt{val} \Mapsto \texttt{val}\,] & \text{\# timer gets deactivated} \\
\text{Client} \stackrel{\text{def}}{=} & (\grave{\theta}_{\texttt{tick}} \Rsh \ldots \Rsh \grave{\theta}_{\texttt{tick}}) & \text{\# timer ticks}
\end{array}
$$

We show a chemical semantics for the language, much as in [14]. Following the presentation in [13], we employ a grammar of evaluation contexts to tighten the rules.

$\mathcal{E}$ ::=	evaluation contexts
$\bullet$	hole
let $x = \mathcal{E}$ in b	evaluation
$\mathcal{E} \Rsh b$	fork side
$a \Rsh \mathcal{E}$	fork main
$(\nu n)\ \mathcal{E}$	restriction

Informally, an evaluation context is an expression container with exactly one hole. By plugging an expression a into the hole of an evaluation context $\mathcal{E}$, we obtain the expression $\mathcal{E}[\![a]\!]$. (In general, plugging may not be capture-free with respect to names or variables.) We define structural congruence of expressions as usual.

Structural congruence $a \equiv b$ # fn (*resp.* bn) collects free (*resp.* bound) names

(STRUCT RES)
$$\frac{n \notin \mathsf{fn}(\mathcal{E}) \cup \mathsf{bn}(\mathcal{E})}{(\nu n)\ \mathcal{E}[\![a]\!] \equiv \mathcal{E}[\![(\nu n)\ a]\!]}$$

(STRUCT PAR)
$$\frac{\mathsf{fn}(a) \cap \mathsf{bn}(\mathcal{E}) = \varnothing}{a \Rsh \mathcal{E}[\![b]\!] \equiv \mathcal{E}[\![a \Rsh b]\!]}$$

(STRUCT EQV)
$\equiv$ is an equivalence

Next, we define reduction of expressions. Not surprisingly, perhaps, there are no reduction rules for internal call and update: we restrict the sites of action to the external primitives. The reductions for external call and update, (Red Call) and (Red Upd), have some important differences from the corresponding reductions in $\mathbf{conc}\varsigma$. First, when a method body is exported on call reduction, the free labels in the body are "frozen" via substitutions of veiled calls for internal calls, and self updates for internal updates. The export translation $\lightning^{\Theta}_{x}$ is shown below. Second, while object update is a straightforward generalization of method update, such an update also re-exports veil bindings for the methods of the object. In general, the update can block or unblock method calls that are invoked on past or present veils: thus it serves as an access control mechanism in the language. Update is therefore synonymous with *administration* in this paper.

In the following, we use the notation Δ', Δ to mean the map obtained by augmenting the map Δ with Δ', while overriding bindings for the common labels.

Export $a \lightning^{\Theta}_{x}$ **and structural reduction** $a \longrightarrow b$

$$\frac{\Theta(\ell) = v}{\ell(u) \lightning^{\Theta}_{x} \stackrel{\text{def}}{=} \grave{v}\langle u \rangle} \qquad (\ell \Lleftarrow (y)b) \lightning^{\Theta}_{x} \stackrel{\text{def}}{=} x \mapsfrom \Theta[\ell \Mapsto \varsigma(x)(y)b \lightning^{\Theta}_{x}]$$

$$(a \Rsh b) \lightning^{\Theta}_{x} \stackrel{\text{def}}{=} a \lightning^{\Theta}_{x} \Rsh b \lightning^{\Theta}_{x} \qquad (\text{let } z = a \text{ in } b) \lightning^{\Theta}_{x} \stackrel{\text{def}}{=} \text{let } z = a \lightning^{\Theta}_{x} \text{ in } b \lightning^{\Theta}_{x}$$

$$((\nu n)\ a) \lightning^{\Theta}_{x} \stackrel{\text{def}}{=} (\nu n)\ a \lightning^{\Theta}_{x} \qquad \frac{a = u,\ p \mapsto d,\ \grave{v}\langle u \rangle, \text{ or } u \mapsfrom d}{a \lightning^{\Theta}_{x} \stackrel{\text{def}}{=} a}$$

(RED CALL)

$$\frac{d = \Theta[\varsigma(x)\Delta] \quad \Theta(\ell_j) = \theta \qquad \Delta(\ell_j)(y) = b}{(p \mapsto d) \Rsh \grave{\theta}\langle m \rangle \longrightarrow (p \mapsto d) \Rsh b \lightning^{\Theta}_{x}\{p/x, m/y\}}$$

(RED UPD)

$$\frac{d = \_[\varsigma(x)\Delta] \qquad d' = \Theta'[\varsigma(x)\Delta'] \quad d'' = \Theta'[\varsigma(x)\Delta', \Delta]}{(p \mapsto d) \Rsh p \mapsfrom d' \longrightarrow (p \mapsto d'') \Rsh p}$$

(RED EVAL)

$$\text{let } x = n \text{ in } b \longrightarrow b\{n/x\}$$

(RED CONTEXT)

$$\frac{a \longrightarrow b}{\mathcal{E}[\![a]\!] \longrightarrow \mathcal{E}[\![b]\!]}$$

(RED STRUCT)

$$\frac{a \equiv a' \qquad a' \longrightarrow b' \qquad b' \equiv b}{a \longrightarrow b}$$

Freezing labels (by a veil map) in the export translation makes intuitive sense: it assigns a definite meaning to a method expression outside the syntactical scope of its parent object. Freezing labels also facilitates the enforcement of static object invariants (Section 3) amidst runtime administration; indeed labels in isolation cannot provide any runtime access guarantees.

Notice that an update returns the object reference (as in [14]): therefore, say, if an internal update is the rightmost branch of a method definition, a call to the method might return a reference to its parent object. This result is potentially dangerous—a user of the method can obtain administrative abilities on the object. We however do not complicate the semantics to prevent such "errors", partly because they are easy to catch statically. The update in question can of course be localized by a "let" if necessary.

To illustrate the semantics, next we show some sample reductions for parts of the code of Example 1. Here, let $\Theta(\texttt{tick}) = \theta_{\texttt{tick}}$, $\Theta'(\texttt{tick}) = \theta_{\texttt{ntick}}$, $\Delta(\texttt{val}) = \texttt{val}$, $\Delta'(\texttt{val}) = N$, $\Delta''(\texttt{val}) = N - 1$, and let the remaining bindings be as given by the initial denomination of p in the code.

$$\begin{aligned} p \mapsto \Theta[\varsigma(x)\Delta] \Rsh \grave{\theta}_{\texttt{set}}\langle N \rangle &\longrightarrow p \mapsto \Theta[\varsigma(x)\Delta] \Rsh \\ &\qquad \text{let } \_ = p \mapsfrom \Theta[\texttt{val} \Mapsto N] \text{ in } N \\ &\longrightarrow p \mapsto \Theta[\varsigma(x)\Delta'] \Rsh N \qquad \# \text{ activate} \end{aligned}$$

$$p \mapsto \Theta[\varsigma(x)\Delta'] \Lsh \grave{\theta}_{\texttt{tick}} \longrightarrow p \mapsto \Theta[\varsigma(x)\Delta'] \Lsh$$
$$\text{let } z = \grave{\theta}_{\texttt{val}} \text{ in let } z' = \grave{\theta}_{\texttt{pre}}\langle z\rangle \text{ in } \grave{\theta}_{\texttt{set}}\langle z'\rangle$$
$$\longrightarrow^{\star} p \mapsto \Theta[\varsigma(x)\Delta''] \Lsh N - 1 \qquad \#\ \text{tick}$$

$$p \mapsto \Theta[\varsigma(x)\Delta''] \Lsh p \leftarrow\!\dashv \Theta'[\texttt{val} \Mapsto \texttt{val}] \longrightarrow p \mapsto \Theta'[\varsigma(x)\Delta] \Lsh p \qquad \#\ \text{deactivate}$$

3 Flux-Robust Typing

In this section we show a type discipline for systems with concurrent objects that export dynamic "type views". More specifically, we allow methods to change types at runtime: the type of a method corresponds dynamically to the type of the veil it exports. For example, suppose the owner of a file wants to change the type of the content from "public" to "secret". Clearly, the veil for the content field must be changed: while the previous veil could have been public, the new veil has to be secret. If the file additionally has read and write methods that depend on the content field, their types change accordingly: therefore the veils for these methods need to be changed as well.

Changing veils is however not enough for end-to-end secrecy. (This inadequacy is typical of access control mechanisms, as mentioned in Section 1.) A user who can now read the file on its new veil will regard the content as secret (even if it is not). Suppose that the user reads the (previously public) content θ on the new veil, and exports θ as a handle to read a secret key k that he has written to another file: it now becomes possible to publicly read k by invoking θ. Indeed, it is almost always possible to exploit such "type interpretation" errors to leak secrets. (For instance, interpreting secret content as public can be equally bad.) To prevent such errors, the content field must be overridden to reflect its new type. By the same argument, then, it appears that the read and write methods need to be overridden as well—we can however do better. Typically read and write have types that are parametric with respect to the type of the content: informally, whenever the content type is X, the read and write methods have types $(\mathbf{1})X$ and $(X)\mathbf{1}$ (where $\mathbf{1}$ is the unit type). Therefore, those methods reflect their new types as soon as the content field is overridden.

We summarize these insights in the following general principles that govern the type system below. First, an object update is consistent only if the types of the new veils match up with the types of the method definitions. Second, type consistency forces some methods to be overridden; methods whose types are parametric with respect to the types of the overridden methods however need not be overridden themselves. This form of polymorphism is typically exhibited by higher-order (generic) functions, compositionally defined procedures, or (in the degenerate case) methods that have static types, *i.e.*, whose types do not change. We prefer to call these methods "natural" to avoid nomenclatural confusion with any particular brand of polymorphism.

3.1 A Type System for Secrecy Despite Flux

The primary goal of the type discipline is *flux robustness*, *i.e.*, type safety despite dynamic changes to type assumptions for methods. Access control is used in an integral way to enforce safety. In the type system, methods are qualified as "flat" or "natural".

Flat methods must be overridden whenever veils change. Natural methods may be overridden; if they are, they must remain polymorphically typed, as indicated above.

To specify and verify secrecy, we introduce a system of principals. More specifically, we use indices to identify "owners" of code, and let the type declaration for a name specify the group of indices within which that name is intended to be confined. We then use type safety to verify that each such intention is preserved at runtime.

Secrecy groups as presented are close to those developed in [10]; the basic concepts appear earlier in, *e.g.*, the pi calculus with group creation [9] and the confined lambda calculus [23]. Let ∞ be a countable universe of indices—this is the largest group, also called "public", since a name that belongs to this group may be shared by all principals. Other groups (trusted) are proper subsets of ∞, or group variables (ranged over by $\mathcal{X}$).

$\rho ::=$	qualifiers
$\flat$	flat method
$\natural$	natural method
$\mathcal{H}, \mathcal{I} ::=$	groups
∞	countable universe of indices (public)
$\mathcal{G}$	trusted
$\mathcal{G} ::=$	trusted groups
$\mathcal{X}$	group variable
$\{\ldots\}$	proper subset of ∞
$S, T, U ::=$	types
X	type variable
$\mathsf{Obj}^{\mathcal{G}}[\widetilde{\ell : (S)T^{\rho}}]$	capability type scheme
$\mathsf{Veil}^{\mathcal{G}}(u.\ell : (S)T)$	veil type
$(\exists x)T$	dependent union type
Null	null type
Un	untrusted type

Typed processes declare types for new names (with $(\nu n : T)\ a$, instead of $(\nu n)\ a$ in Section 2). Informally, the type sorts have the following meanings:

- X ranges over type variables. Group and type variables appear in capability signatures (see below).
- A capability signature $\mathsf{Obj}^{\mathcal{G}}[\widetilde{\ell : (S)T^{\rho}}]$ is a type scheme that assigns types $(S_i)T_i$ and qualifiers ρ_i to the methods $\ell_i \in \widetilde{\ell}$ of a denoted object. The group $\mathcal{G}$ corresponds to the set of administrators for that object. The scheme binds group and type variables that are shared by the types of the methods in the signature. We interpret a type scheme as an universally quantified type over its bound variables, while leaving the bound variables implicit (*à la* polymorphic types in ML [26]).
- A veil type $\mathsf{Veil}^{\mathcal{G}}(u.\ell : (S)T)$ is dependent on a capability u, and instantiates the type scheme for a method ℓ in the signature of that capability. The veil expects an argument of type S and returns a result of type T. The group $\mathcal{G}$ corresponds to the set of users—the "access-control list"—for the method referenced by the veil. We use dependence in the veil type to prevent the same veil from being exported by different objects. (A similar "no-confusion" property is required, for instance, of datatype constructors [11].)

- Dependent union types $(\exists x)T$ allow capability dependencies to be passed without explicit communication of the capabilities themselves. The type system thus supports the separation of roles of veils and capabilities (as intended) despite enforcing necessary dependencies between them.
- The type Null is given to an expression whose result, if any, is ignored.
- Finally, the type Un is given to any expression whose result, if any, is untrusted.

For example, the signature of a file capability might look like:

$$\mathsf{Obj}^{\{\mathrm{Owner}\}}[\mathtt{content} : (\mathbf{1})X^{\flat}, \mathtt{read} : (\mathbf{1})X^{\natural}, \mathtt{write} : (X)\mathbf{1}^{\natural}]$$

where $\mathbf{1} \stackrel{\text{def}}{=} \mathsf{Obj}[\,]$. If, say, the content is of type T, a veil for `write` may have the type:

$$(\exists z)\mathsf{Veil}^{\{\mathrm{Writer,Owner}\}}(z.\mathtt{write} : (T)\mathbf{1})$$

As another example, an authenticated encryption object may be given the signature:

$$\mathsf{Obj}^{\{\mathrm{KeyManager}\}}[\mathtt{key} : X^{\flat}, \mathtt{authencrypt} : (Y)(\exists z)\mathsf{Veil}^{\mathcal{X}}(z.\mathtt{decrypt} : (X)Y)^{\natural}]$$

where the group $\mathcal{X}$ of the decryption handle returned by encryption can be controlled by KeyManager. Let, *e.g.*, $R \stackrel{\text{def}}{=} \{\text{Reader, KeyManager}\}$, $W \stackrel{\text{def}}{=} \{\text{Writer, KeyManager}\}$, $RW \stackrel{\text{def}}{=} R \cup W$, key type $T_X \stackrel{\text{def}}{=} \mathsf{Obj}^R[\,]$, and content type $T_Y \stackrel{\text{def}}{=} \mathsf{Obj}^{RW}[\,]$. Then `authencrypt` may be exported on a veil with type

$$(\exists z')\mathsf{Veil}^{W}(z'.\mathtt{authencrypt} : (T_Y)(\exists z)\mathsf{Veil}^{RW}(z.\mathsf{decrypt} : (T_X)T_Y))$$

The relationship between types and groups is made explicit by a *reach* function, defined below. Informally, the reach of a type is the group within which the inhabitants of that type may be shared (but not without). For example, Un has reach ∞. Group and type variables do not constrain the reach of the type they appear in. Otherwise, the topmost group that appears in a type is taken to be the reach of that type.

Type reach $\|T\|$ with group variables $\mathcal{X}$ equated to ∞

$$\|X\| = \infty \qquad \|(\exists x)T\| = \|T\| \qquad \|\mathsf{Un}\| = \infty \qquad \|\mathsf{Obj}^{\mathcal{G}}[\_ : \_]\| = \mathcal{G} \qquad \|\mathsf{Veil}^{\mathcal{G}}(\_ : \_)\| = \mathcal{G}$$

Let σ range over substitutions of group and type variables, that is, $\sigma : (\mathcal{X} \to \mathcal{H}) + (X \to T)$. We define substitution below; it is mostly standard, except for the substitution of ∞ for a group variable that annotates a type, which "rounds off" that type as untrusted. We say that σ is a *proper* substitution for U if $U\sigma$ is defined.

Group and type substitution $\mathcal{G}\sigma$, $U\sigma$

$$\mathcal{X}\sigma = \sigma(\mathcal{X}) \qquad \{\ldots\}\sigma = \{\ldots\} \qquad X\sigma = \sigma(X) \qquad ((\exists x)T)\sigma = (\exists x)T\sigma \qquad \mathsf{Un}\,\sigma = \mathsf{Un}$$

$$\frac{\mathcal{G}\sigma \neq \infty}{\mathsf{Obj}^{\mathcal{G}}[\widetilde{\ell : (S)T^{\rho}}]\sigma = \mathsf{Obj}^{\mathcal{G}\sigma}[\widetilde{\ell : (S\sigma)T\sigma^{\rho}}]} \qquad \frac{\mathcal{G}\sigma = \infty \quad \widetilde{S}\sigma = \mathsf{Un} \quad \widetilde{T}\sigma = \mathsf{Un}}{\mathsf{Obj}^{\mathcal{G}}[\widetilde{\ell : (S)T^{\rho}}]\sigma = \mathsf{Un}}$$

$$\frac{\mathcal{G}\sigma \neq \infty}{\mathsf{Veil}^{\mathcal{G}}(u.\ell : (S)T)\sigma = \mathsf{Veil}^{\mathcal{G}\sigma}(u.\ell : (S\sigma)T\sigma)} \qquad \frac{\mathcal{G}\sigma = \infty \quad S\sigma = \mathsf{Un} \quad T\sigma = \mathsf{Un}}{\mathsf{Veil}^{\mathcal{G}}(u.\ell : (S)T)\sigma = \mathsf{Un}}$$

Next, we show typing rules. Let Γ be a sequence of type assumptions $u : T$. The rules judge well-formed assumptions $\Gamma \vdash \diamond$, good types $\Gamma \vdash T$, good subtyping $\Gamma \vdash T <: U$, and well-typed expressions $\Gamma \vdash_{\mathcal{I}} a : T$. In the rules for $\Gamma \vdash T <: U$, we implicitly include the condition $\Gamma \vdash T$ in the antecedent. In the rules for $\Gamma \vdash T$ and $\Gamma \vdash_{\mathcal{I}} a : T$, whenever there are no $\vdash$ judgments in the antecedent, we implicitly include the condition $\Gamma \vdash \diamond$.

In the judgment $\Gamma \vdash_{\mathcal{I}} a : T$, the group $\mathcal{I}$ under $\vdash$ indicates the "trust level" under which the program is to be typed: any result in the program must have a type whose reach intersects $\mathcal{I}$. Informally, principals with indices in $\mathcal{I}$ are allowed to collude—their programs may contain results that have types whose reaches include at least one of the indices in $\mathcal{I}$, but may not contain any result whose type is "out of reach" (*i.e.*, whose reach does not include any index in $\mathcal{I}$). For instance, $\vdash_\infty$ is the most liberal typing relation. In fact $\vdash$ is monotone: $\mathcal{H} \subseteq \mathcal{I}$ implies $\vdash_{\mathcal{H}} \subseteq \vdash_{\mathcal{I}}$.

Let $\mathsf{Veil}^{\mathcal{G}}(u.\ell : (S)T) \in \mathsf{veiltype}(u.\ell : (S)T)$ for all trusted groups $\mathcal{G}$, and $\mathsf{Un} \in \mathsf{veiltype}(u.\ell : (\mathsf{Un})\mathsf{Un})$. Finally, let σ_∞ range over special substitutions that map group variables to ∞ and type variables to Un, that is, $\sigma_\infty : (\mathcal{X} \to \infty) + (X \to \mathsf{Un})$.

Typing rules $\Gamma \vdash \diamond$, $\Gamma \vdash T$, $\Gamma \vdash T <: U$, $\Gamma \vdash_{\mathcal{I}} a : T$

(HYP NONE)
$$\varnothing \vdash \diamond$$

(HYP NEXT)
$$\frac{\Gamma \vdash T \qquad u \notin \mathsf{dom}(\Gamma)}{\Gamma, u : T \vdash \diamond}$$

(TYP VAR)
$$\Gamma \vdash X$$

(TYP EXST)
$$\frac{\Gamma, x : X \vdash T}{\Gamma \vdash (\exists x)T}$$

(TYP OBJ)
$$\frac{\widetilde{\ell} \text{ distinct} \qquad \forall \{\ell_i \in \widetilde{\ell}\}.\ \Gamma \vdash S_i, T_i}{\Gamma \vdash \mathsf{Obj}^{\mathcal{G}}[\widetilde{\ell} : \widetilde{(S)T^{\rho}}]}$$

(TYP VEIL)
$$\frac{u \in \mathsf{dom}(\Gamma) \qquad \Gamma \vdash S, T}{\Gamma \vdash \mathsf{Veil}^{\mathcal{G}}(u.\ell : (S)T)}$$

(TYP UN)
$$\Gamma \vdash \mathsf{Un}$$

(SUB REFL)
$$\Gamma \vdash T <: T$$

(SUB TRAN)
$$\frac{\Gamma \vdash T <: S \qquad \Gamma \vdash S <: U}{\Gamma \vdash T <: U}$$

(EXP SUB)
$$\frac{\Gamma \vdash_{\mathcal{I}} a : T \qquad \Gamma \vdash T <: U}{\Gamma \vdash_{\mathcal{I}} a : U}$$

(DEP GRNT)
$$\frac{x \notin \mathsf{dom}(\Gamma)}{\Gamma \vdash T\{u/x\} <: (\exists x)T}$$

(DEP ASSM)
$$\frac{x \text{ not free in } U \qquad X \text{ fresh} \qquad \Gamma, x : X, u : T \vdash_{\mathcal{I}} a : U}{\Gamma, u : (\exists x)T \vdash_{\mathcal{I}} a : U}$$

(SUB OBJ)
$$\frac{\widetilde{\ell} : \widetilde{(S)T^{\rho}} \subseteq \widetilde{\ell'} : \widetilde{(S')T'^{\rho'}}}{\Gamma \vdash \mathsf{Obj}^{\mathcal{G}}[\widetilde{\ell'} : \widetilde{(S')T'^{\rho'}}] <: \mathsf{Obj}^{\mathcal{G}}[\widetilde{\ell} : \widetilde{(S)T^{\rho}}]}$$

(NULL EXP)
$$\Gamma \vdash T <: \mathsf{Null}$$

(EXP RES)
$$\frac{\mathcal{I} \cap \|T\| \neq \varnothing \qquad \Gamma(u) = T}{\Gamma \vdash_{\mathcal{I}} u : T}$$

(EXP NEW)
$$\frac{\Gamma, n : T \vdash_{\mathcal{I}} a : U}{\Gamma \vdash_{\mathcal{I}} (\nu n : T)\, a : U}$$

(EXP FORK)
$$\frac{\Gamma \vdash_{\mathcal{I}} a : T \qquad \Gamma \vdash_{\mathcal{I}} b : U}{\Gamma \vdash_{\mathcal{I}} a \upharpoonright b : U}$$

(EXP EVAL)
$$\frac{\Gamma \vdash_{\mathcal{I}} a : T \qquad \Gamma, x : T \vdash_{\mathcal{I}} b : U}{\Gamma \vdash_{\mathcal{I}} \mathsf{let}\ x = a\ \mathsf{in}\ b : U}$$

(EXP CALL)
$$\frac{\Gamma \vdash_{\mathcal{I}} v : \mathsf{Veil}^{\mathcal{G}}(w.\ell : (S)T) \qquad \Gamma \vdash_{\mathcal{I}} u : S \qquad \mathcal{I} \cap \|T\| \neq \varnothing}{\Gamma \vdash_{\mathcal{I}} \tilde{v}\langle u \rangle : T}$$

(EXP CALL UN)
$$\frac{\Gamma \vdash_{\mathcal{I}} v : \mathsf{Un} \qquad \Gamma \vdash_{\mathcal{I}} u : \mathsf{Un}}{\Gamma \vdash_{\mathcal{I}} \tilde{v}\langle u \rangle : \mathsf{Un}}$$

(NULL DEN)

$$\frac{\begin{array}{c} \Gamma \vdash_{\mathcal{I}} p : \mathsf{Obj}^{\mathcal{G}}[\widetilde{\ell} : \widetilde{(S)T^{\rho}}] \qquad \mathsf{dom}(\Theta) \cup \mathsf{dom}(\Delta) \subseteq \widetilde{\ell} \qquad \widetilde{(S)T}\sigma = \widetilde{(S')T'} \\ \forall\{\ell_i \in \mathsf{dom}(\Theta)\}.\ \Gamma \vdash_{\mathcal{I}} \Theta(\ell_i) : U'_i \in \mathsf{veiltype}(p.\ell_i : (S'_i)T'_i) \\ \forall\{\ell_i \in \mathsf{dom}(\Delta)\}.\ \Gamma, y_i : S'_i \vdash_{\mathcal{I}} \Delta(\ell_i)(y_i) \lightning^{\Theta}_{x} \{p/x\}\sigma : T'_i \\ \forall\{\ell_i \in \mathsf{dom}(\Delta) \mid \rho_i = \natural\}.\ \forall\sigma_{\infty}. \\ \Gamma, \widetilde{z} : \widetilde{U} \in \mathsf{veiltype}(p.\widetilde{\ell} : \widetilde{(S)T}\sigma_{\infty}), y_i : S_i\sigma_{\infty} \vdash_{\mathcal{I}} \Delta(\ell_i)(y_i) \lightning^{\widetilde{z}/\widetilde{\ell}}_{x} \{p/x\}\sigma_{\infty} : T_i\sigma_{\infty} \end{array}}{\Gamma \vdash_{\mathcal{I}} p \mapsto \Theta[\varsigma(x)\Delta] : \mathsf{Null}}$$

(DEN UN)

$$\frac{\begin{array}{c} \Gamma \vdash_{\mathcal{I}} p : \mathsf{Un} \qquad \forall\{\ell_i \in \mathsf{dom}(\Theta)\}.\ \Gamma \vdash_{\mathcal{I}} \Theta(\ell_i) : \mathsf{Un} \\ \forall\{\ell_i \in \mathsf{dom}(\Delta)\}.\ \Gamma, y_i : \mathsf{Un} \vdash_{\mathcal{I}} \Delta(\ell_i)(y_i) \lightning^{\Theta}_{x} \{p/x\} : \mathsf{Un} \end{array}}{\Gamma \vdash_{\mathcal{I}} p \mapsto \Theta[\varsigma(x)\Delta] : \mathsf{Un}}$$

(EXP UPD)

$$\frac{\begin{array}{c} \Gamma \vdash_{\mathcal{I}} u : \mathsf{Obj}^{\mathcal{G}}[\widetilde{\ell} : \widetilde{(S)T^{\rho}}] \qquad \mathsf{dom}(\Theta) \cup \mathsf{dom}(\Delta) \subseteq \widetilde{\ell} \qquad \{\ell_i \mid \rho_i = \flat\} \subseteq \mathsf{dom}(\Delta) \\ \widetilde{(S)T}\sigma = \widetilde{(S')T'} \qquad \forall\{\ell_i \in \mathsf{dom}(\Theta)\}.\ \Gamma \vdash_{\mathcal{I}} \Theta(\ell_i) : U'_i \in \mathsf{veiltype}(u.\ell_i : (S'_i)T'_i) \\ \forall\{\ell_i \in \mathsf{dom}(\Delta)\}.\ \Gamma, y_i : S'_i \vdash_{\mathcal{I}} \Delta(\ell_i)(y_i) \lightning^{\Theta}_{x} \{u/x\}\sigma : T'_i \\ \forall\{\ell_i \in \mathsf{dom}(\Delta) \mid \rho_i = \natural\}.\ \forall\sigma_{\infty}. \\ \Gamma, \widetilde{z} : \widetilde{U} \in \mathsf{veiltype}(u.\widetilde{\ell} : \widetilde{(S)T}\sigma_{\infty}), y_i : S_i\sigma_{\infty} \vdash_{\mathcal{I}} \Delta(\ell_i)(y_i) \lightning^{\widetilde{z}/\widetilde{\ell}}_{x} \{u/x\}\sigma_{\infty} : T_i\sigma_{\infty} \end{array}}{\Gamma \vdash_{\mathcal{I}} u \leftarrow\!\!\dashv \Theta[\varsigma(x)\Delta] : \mathsf{Obj}^{\mathcal{G}}[\widetilde{\ell} : \widetilde{(S)T^{\rho}}]}$$

(EXP UPD UN)

$$\frac{\begin{array}{c} \Gamma \vdash_{\mathcal{I}} u : \mathsf{Un} \qquad \forall\{\ell_i \in \mathsf{dom}(\Theta)\}.\ \Gamma \vdash_{\mathcal{I}} \Theta(\ell_i) : \mathsf{Un} \\ \forall\{\ell_i \in \mathsf{dom}(\Delta)\}.\ \Gamma, y_i : \mathsf{Un} \vdash_{\mathcal{I}} \Delta(\ell_i)(y_i) \lightning^{\Theta}_{x} \{u/x\} : \mathsf{Un} \end{array}}{\Gamma \vdash_{\mathcal{I}} u \leftarrow\!\!\dashv \Theta[\varsigma(x)\Delta] : \mathsf{Un}}$$

Notice that Null is not a "good" type—we have Null as a type only because it allows us to give compact rules for well-typed expressions. (Dep Assm) and (Dep Grnt) are standard assume/guarantee rules for propagating dependencies. (Den Un), (Exp Call Un), and (Exp Upd Un) can type arbitrary "untrusted" expressions whose names and type declarations are all public.

(Exp Call) checks that veil invocation is type-safe, *i.e.*, the type of the result matches that suggested by the veil type. (Exp Res) and (Exp Call) check if the typing group intersects the reach of an expected result type. These checks do not constrain irrelevant type assumptions, even if those types are out of reach of the typing group.

(Null Den) and (Exp Upd) are largely similar. There, σ ranges over proper substitutions for group and type variables that are bound by the capability signature. Additionally, σ_{∞} ranges over all proper *partial* substitutions that map some of those variables to ∞ and Un. Both rules check if the capability signature is properly instantiated (via σ) by the types of the new veil bindings and the new method bodies. Crucially, every application of (Null Den) and (Exp Upd) can present a different instantiation for the type scheme of the same capability. This allows "dynamic specification" of type assumptions for the methods of an object. For those methods that are qualified natural, (Null Den) and (Exp Upd) also check if the method bodies can be typed polymorphically to match their type schema, with fresh veil bindings and partially instantiated types (via σ_{∞}). The checks are necessary because we do not require natural methods to be overridden on each update of the object, yet want them to be robust to any changes in type assumptions within the object. (Indeed, (Exp Upd) requires only those methods that are qualified flat to be overridden on update.) There are only finitely many σ_∞ to consider (since there are only finitely many bound group and type variables in the signature). Group variables suffice to account for instantiations with trusted groups; the substitutions σ_∞ account for those instantiations that may map some group variables to ∞, thereby collapsing some types to Un and changing type structure. (Similar subtleties appear in a secrecy type system for asymmetric communication [1] while exploiting polymorphism across trusted types and Un.)

Example 2. Assume that name matching can be encoded in the language. Recall the example with authenticated encryption objects. Assume that p has the shown signature, $\theta_{\texttt{enc}}$ has the shown veil type, k has type T_X, and $\theta_{\texttt{key}}$ has type $(\exists z')\mathsf{Veil}^R(z'.\texttt{key} : T_X)$. Then the following denomination is well-typed under $\vdash_{\{\text{KeyManager}\}}$. A proper σ_∞ that must be considered when typechecking authencrypt maps $\mathcal{X}$ to ∞, and X and Y to Un; another such is the empty substitution that does not instantiate any variable.

$$
\begin{aligned}
&p \mapsto \theta_{\texttt{key}}\theta_{\texttt{enc}}[\,\texttt{key} \Mapsto k, \texttt{authencrypt}(y) \Mapsto \\
&\quad (\nu q : \mathsf{Obj}^{\mathcal{X}}[\texttt{decrypt} : (X)Y^{\natural}])\ (\nu \theta_{\texttt{dec}} : \mathsf{Veil}^{\mathcal{X}}(q.\texttt{decrypt} : (X)Y)) \\
&\qquad \text{let } x' = \texttt{key} \text{ in } q \mapsto \theta_{\texttt{dec}}[\,\texttt{decrypt}(x) \Mapsto \text{if } x \text{ is } x' \text{ then } y\,] \Rsh \theta_{\texttt{dec}}\,]
\end{aligned}
$$

Next, say we can type Reader's code a_r under $\vdash_{\{\text{Reader}\}}$ and Writer's code a_w under $\vdash_{\{\text{Writer}\}}$. Informally, a_r can obtain the key k by invoking $\theta_{\texttt{key}}$; a_w can encrypt a term of type T_Y by invoking $\theta_{\texttt{enc}}$, and share the resulting decryption handle $\theta_{\texttt{dec}}$ with a_r; and a_r can retrieve the encrypted term by invoking $\theta_{\texttt{dec}}$ with argument k. However, a_r can never encrypt a term with $\theta_{\texttt{enc}}$, and a_w can never decrypt a term encrypted with $\theta_{\texttt{enc}}$.

Example 3. Suppose that Bonnie and Clyde wish to start a session sometime in the future, with a session secret generated by Clyde. Moreover, they wish to use a file p owned by Bonnie to establish that secret when they are ready. We show a safe, well-typed protocol in which the file is used in at least three different ways over time. Bonnie initializes the file content to a new name $\theta_{\texttt{nw}}$, binding its access to a name $\theta_{\texttt{c}}$ known to Clyde; the content $\theta_{\texttt{nw}}$ is a future write handle to the file. Additionally, she programs the file to transition into a publicly usable phase as soon as that content is read off (since she has other tasks for the file). Since Clyde knows $\theta_{\texttt{c}}$, he can read the file to obtain $\theta_{\texttt{nw}}$. Later, Bonnie brings the file back into restricted usage, with $\theta_{\texttt{nw}}$ as its new write handle. She then listens for the secret she expects from Clyde. Accordingly Clyde creates a new secret and writes it to the file by invoking (the earlier obtained) $\theta_{\texttt{nw}}$. Both Bonnie and Clyde now share the new secret, and can safely start their session.

Let $B \overset{\text{def}}{=} \{\text{Bonnie}\}$, $C \overset{\text{def}}{=} \{\text{Clyde}\}$, $BC \overset{\text{def}}{=} B \cup C$, $\mathbf{1} \overset{\text{def}}{=} \mathsf{Un}$, $\mathsf{Sec}^{BC} \overset{\text{def}}{=} \mathsf{Obj}^{BC}[\,]$, and $a; b \overset{\text{def}}{=} \text{let } x = a \text{ in } b$ for fresh x. Assume $p : \mathsf{Obj}^B[\texttt{content} : (\mathbf{1})X^{\flat}, \texttt{write} : (X)\mathbf{1}^{\natural}]$, $\theta_{\texttt{c}} : \mathsf{Veil}^{BC}(p.\texttt{content} : (\mathbf{1})(\exists z)\mathsf{Veil}^{BC}(z.\texttt{write} : (\mathsf{Sec}^{BC})\mathbf{1}))$, $\theta_{\texttt{uc}} : \mathsf{Un}$, and $\theta_{\texttt{uw}} : \mathsf{Un}$. Then we can type Bonnie's code b under $\vdash_B$ and Clyde's code c under $\vdash_C$.

$$
\begin{aligned}
b \;=\; & (\nu\theta_{\mathtt{nw}} : \mathsf{Veil}^{BC}(p.\mathtt{write} : (\mathsf{Sec}^{BC})\mathbf{1}))\\
& (\nu\theta_{\mathtt{w}} : \mathsf{Veil}^{B}(p.\mathtt{write} : ((\exists z)\mathsf{Veil}^{BC}(z.\mathtt{write} : (\mathsf{Sec}^{BC})\mathbf{1}))\mathbf{1}))\\
& \quad p \mapsto \theta_{\mathtt{c}}\theta_{\mathtt{w}}[\,\mathtt{content} \Mapsto \varsigma(x)\; x \leftarrow\!\dashv \theta_{\mathtt{uc}}\theta_{\mathtt{uw}}[\,\mathtt{content} \Mapsto \mathtt{content}\,]; \theta_{\mathtt{nw}},\\
& \qquad\qquad \mathtt{write}(y) \Mapsto \mathtt{content} \Leftarrow\!\dashv y;\ ] \ \vec{\upharpoonright}\\
& \quad \ldots\\
& \quad (\nu\theta_{\mathtt{nc}} : \mathsf{Veil}^{B}(p.\mathtt{content} : (\mathbf{1})\mathsf{Sec}^{BC}))\\
& \qquad p \leftarrow\!\dashv \theta_{\mathtt{nc}}\theta_{\mathtt{nw}}[\,\mathtt{content} \Mapsto \mathtt{content}\,];\\
& \qquad \text{let } x = \overset{\frown}{\theta}_{\mathtt{nc}} \text{ in } \ldots\\
c \;=\; & \text{let } x = \overset{\frown}{\theta}_{\mathtt{c}} \text{ in } (\nu k : \mathsf{Sec}^{BC})\ \overset{\frown}{x}\langle k\rangle; \ldots
\end{aligned}
$$

3.2 Properties of Well-Typed Code

The main result for the type system of Section 3 is that well-typed code never leaks secrets beyond declared boundaries, even under arbitrary untrusted environments. The result relies on a standard but non-trivial preservation property: well-typed expressions preserve their types on execution. This property justifies our typing approach.

Proposition 1 (Preservation). *Let $\Gamma \vdash_{\mathcal{I}} a : T$. If $a \longrightarrow b$, then $\Gamma \vdash_{\mathcal{I}} b : T$.*

Additionally, the type system has two important properties. First, the type given to an expression is not beyond reach, *i.e.*, at least one index in the typing group falls within the reach of the expression type. (Additionally, reaches are preserved by subtyping.)

Proposition 2 (Reach soundness). *Let $\Gamma \vdash_{\mathcal{I}} a : T \neq \mathsf{Null}$. Then $\|T\| \cap \mathcal{I} \neq \varnothing$.*

Second, the type system can accommodate arbitrary expressions, as long as they do not contain trusted names. This property is important, since we cannot assume that attackers attempting to learn secrets would politely follow our typing discipline.

Proposition 3 (Typability). *Let a be any expression without free labels or variables. Suppose all declared types in a are* Un, *and $\Gamma(n) = \mathsf{Un}$ for all free names n in a. Then $\Gamma \vdash_{\mathcal{I}} a : \mathsf{Un}$ for all $\mathcal{I}$.*

Finally, we present the main result. Let a be trusted code typed under group $\mathcal{I}$, and b be (perhaps partially) untrusted code typed under the complement group $\infty - \mathcal{I}$. In general, b may be any adversarial code written jointly by an arbitrary attacker in collusion with trusted principals outside $\mathcal{I}$; the trusted part of b may even share trusted names with a. Then if the principals in $\mathcal{I}$ eventually declare an exclusive secret n, this secret can never be learnt by executing b in composition with a.

Theorem 1 (Secrecy). *Let $\Gamma \vdash_{\mathcal{I}} a : S$ and $\Gamma \vdash_{\infty-\mathcal{I}} b : T$. If $a \vec{\upharpoonright} b \longrightarrow^{\star} (\nu\widetilde{m} : \widetilde{U'})\,(\nu n : U)\,c$ such that $\|U\| \subseteq \mathcal{I}$, then $c \not\longrightarrow^{\star} n$.*

The proof is based on a simple argument: if n can be learnt, then T must be the same as U—but the reach of T must contain at least one index in $\infty - \mathcal{I}$, *i.e.*, outside $\mathcal{I}$ (contradiction). A weaker version of the theorem that deals with top-level secrets also holds: for all names m such that $\|\Gamma(m)\| \subseteq \mathcal{I}$, it must be the case that $a \vec{\upharpoonright} b \not\longrightarrow^{\star} m$.

4 Conclusion

Static analyses have been quite helpful in guaranteeing high-level safety properties of distributed systems: indeed, a significant body of work focuses specifically on safe resource usage [13,5,22,24,25,6,7,8,29]. Some analyses use access levels, as declared via static type annotations, to guarantee the absence of access violations at runtime [21,28,7,29]. In our previous work [10], we go further by studying the interplay of static secrecy specifications with dynamically acquired permissions, and verify that access checks help respect the specifications at runtime. A similar approach is reflected in hybrid typechecking [12], a type system for secure information flow in a Java-like language [3], and a type system that supports dynamic revocation [19].

An alternative, and perhaps more natural stance is to allow specifications to be inherently dynamic to reflect changing assumptions during execution. Dynamic specifications are often desirable when reasoning about resources in the long run. When additional runtime guarantees can be exploited, dynamic specifications typically also allow finer analyses than static specifications. Along those lines, one body of work studies the enforcement of policies specified as security automata [31,18]. Yet another studies systems with declassification, *i.e.*, conservative relaxation of secrecy assumptions at runtime [27]. There is also some recent work on compromised secrets [15,17] in the context of network protocols. In comparison, our analyses apply more generally to changing assumptions at runtime. Perhaps closest to our work are analyses developed for dynamic access control in languages with locality and migration [20,16]. Similar ideas also appear in a type system for noninterference that allows the use of dynamic security labels [33].

Our contributions in this paper are two-fold. We develop low-level access control features in an existing object language to make it suitable as a core calculus for studying security properties of concurrent, stateful resources. We then show a typing approach for verifying high-level intentions on resource manipulation in the resulting language. The type system allows dynamic access control specifications, and crucially relies on corresponding low-level guarantees provided by the language runtime to verify those specifications. This combination helps in developing precise security analyses for shared resources that are used under changing assumptions over time.

Acknowledgments. Martín Abadi suggested $\mathbf{conc}\varsigma$ as a possible starting point for the calculus. In addition, he and Cormac Flanagan helped with comments on an earlier draft. This work was partly supported by the National Science Foundation under Grants CCR-0208800 and CCF-0524078, and by Livermore National Laboratory, Los Alamos National Laboratory, and Sandia National Laboratory under Contract B554869.

References

1. M. Abadi and B. Blanchet. Secrecy types for asymmetric communication. *Theoretical Computer Science*, 298(3):387–415, 2003.
2. M. Abadi and L. Cardelli. An imperative object calculus. In *TAPSOFT'95: Theory and Practice of Software Development*, pages 471–485. Springer, 1995.

3. A. Banerjee and D. Naumann. Using access control for secure information flow in a Java-like language. In *CSFW'03: Computer Security Foundations Workshop*, pages 155–169. IEEE, 2003.
4. P. D. Blasio and K. Fisher. A calculus for concurrent objects. In *CONCUR'96: Concurrency Theory*, pages 655–670. Springer, 1996.
5. P. D. Blasio, K. Fisher, and C. Talcott. A control-flow analysis for a calculus of concurrent objects. *IEEE Transactions on Software Engineering*, 26(7):617–634, 2000.
6. C. Braghin, D. Gorla, and V. Sassone. A distributed calculus for role-based access control. In *CSFW'04: Computer Security Foundations Workshop*, pages 48–60. IEEE, 2004.
7. M. Bugliesi, G. Castagna, and S. Crafa. Access control for mobile agents: The calculus of boxed ambients. *ACM Transactions on Programming Languages and Systems*, 26(1):57–124, 2004.
8. M. Bugliesi, D. Colazzo, and S. Crafa. Type based discretionary access control. In *CONCUR'04: Concurrency Theory*, pages 225–239. Springer, 2004.
9. L. Cardelli, G. Ghelli, and A. D. Gordon. Secrecy and group creation. *Information and Computation*, 196(2):127–155, 2005.
10. A. Chaudhuri and M. Abadi. Secrecy by typing and file-access control. In *CSFW'06: Computer Security Foundations Workshop*. To appear. IEEE, 2006.
11. T. Coquand. Pattern matching with dependent types. In *Workshop on Types for Proofs and Programs*. Electronic proceedings, 1992.
12. C. Flanagan. Hybrid type checking. In *POPL '06: Principles of programming languages*, pages 245–256. ACM, 2006.
13. C. Flanagan and M. Abadi. Object types against races. In *CONCUR '99: Concurrency Theory*, pages 288–303. Springer, 1999.
14. A. D. Gordon and P. D. Hankin. A concurrent object calculus: Reduction and typing. In *HLCL'98: High-Level Concurrent Languages*, pages 248–264. Elsevier, 1998.
15. A. D. Gordon and A. Jeffrey. Secrecy despite compromise: Types, cryptography, and the pi-calculus. In *CONCUR'05: Concurrency Theory*, pages 186–201. Springer, 2005.
16. D. Gorla and R. Pugliese. Resource access and mobility control with dynamic privileges acquisition. In *ICALP'03: International Colloquium on Automata, Languages, and Programming*, pages 119–132. Springer, 2003.
17. C. Haack and A. Jeffrey. Timed spi-calculus with types for secrecy and authenticity. In *CONCUR'05: Concurrency Theory*, pages 202–216. Springer, 2005.
18. K. W. Hamlen, G. Morrisett, and F. B. Schneider. Certified in-lined reference monitoring on .NET. In *PLAS'06: Programming Languages and Analysis for Security*. To appear. ACM, 2006.
19. C. Hawblitzel and T. von Eicken. Type system support for dynamic revocation. In *Workshop on Compiler Support for System Software*. Electronic proceedings, 1999.
20. M. Hennessy, M. Merro, and J. Rathke. Towards a behavioural theory of access and mobility control in distributed systems. In *FOSSACS'03: Foundations of Software Science and Computational Structures*, pages 282–298. Springer, 2003.
21. M. Hennessy and J. Riely. Resource access control in systems of mobile agents. In *HLCL '98: High-Level Concurrent Languages*, pages 174–188. Elsevier, 1998.
22. M. Hennessy and J. Riely. Information flow vs. resource access in the asynchronous pi-calculus. *ACM Transactions on Programming Languages and Systems*, 24(5):566–591, 2002.
23. Z. D. Kirli. Confined mobile functions. In *CSFW'01: Computer Security Foundations Workshop*, pages 283–294. IEEE, 2001.
24. J. Kleist and D. Sangiorgi. Imperative objects as mobile processes. *Science of Computer Programming*, 44(3):293–342, 2002.
25. G. Miklau and D. Suciu. Controlling access to published data using cryptography. In *VLDB'03: Very Large Data Bases*, pages 898–909. Springer, 2003.

26. R. Milner, M. Tofte, R. Harper, and D. MacQueen. *The Definition of Standard ML (Revised)*. The MIT Press, 1997.
27. A. Myers, A. Sabelfeld, and S. Zdancewic. Enforcing robust declassification. In *CSFW'04: Computer Security Foundations Workshop*, pages 172–186. IEEE, 2004.
28. R. D. Nicola, G. Ferrari, R. Pugliese, and B. Venneri. Types for access control. *Theoretical Computer Science*, 240(1):215–254, 2000.
29. F. Pottier, C. Skalka, and S. Smith. A systematic approach to static access control. *ACM Transactions on Programming Languages and Systems*, 27(2):344–382, 2005.
30. D. D. Redell. Naming and protection in extendible operating systems. Technical Report 140, Project MAC, MIT, 1974.
31. F. B. Schneider. Enforceable security policies. *ACM Transactions on Information and System Security*, 3(1):30–50, 2000.
32. V. T. Vasconcelos. Typed concurrent objects. In *ECOOP'94: European Conference on Object-Oriented Programming*, pages 100–117. Springer, 1994.
33. L. Zheng and A. Myers. Dynamic security labels and noninterference. In *FAST'04: Formal Aspects in Security and Trust*, pages 27–40. Springer, 2004.

Concurrent Rewriting for Graphs with Equivalences*

Paolo Baldan[1], Fabio Gadducci[2], and Ugo Montanari[2]

[1] Dipartimento di Scienze dell'Informazione, Università Ca' Foscari di Venezia
[2] Dipartimento di Informatica, Università of Pisa

Abstract. Several applications of graph rewriting systems (notably, some encodings of calculi with name passing) require rules which, besides deleting and generating graph items, are able to coalesce some parts of the graph. This latter feature forbids the development of a satisfactory concurrent semantics for rewrites (intended as a partial order description of the steps in a computation). This paper proposes the use of *graphs with equivalences*, i.e., (typed hyper-) graphs equipped with an equivalence over nodes, for the analysis of distributed systems. The formalism is amenable to the tools of the double-pushout approach to rewriting, including the theoretical results associated to its concurrent features. The formalism is tested against the encoding of a simple calculus with name mobility, namely the *solo calculus*.

Keywords: Concurrent graph rewriting, DPO approach, graphical encoding of nominal calculi, graph process semantics.

1 Introduction

Recent years have seen an increasing use of graphical formalisms for the modeling of concurrent and distributed systems. Graph-like structures naturally provide a formal yet flexible view of system states, while the rewriting rules suitably model local state transformations. Among the different formalisms proposed in the literature, the so-called *double pushout* (DPO) approach offers a large variety of theoretical and practical tools for the visual specification of a system (as witnessed by [6] and the many areas where it found applications), abstracting away from the often unnecessary details of the state representation. As an example, DPO rewriting techniques for simulating reductions in nominal calculi [17,4], as presented in [9,10], views a (possibly recursive) process as a graph, thus modeling reductions by rewrites. The use of graphs allows for getting rid of the problems concerning the implementation of reduction over the structural congruence, such as e.g. α-conversion of (bound) names, since equivalent processes turn out to be mapped into isomorphic graphs.

However, the widespread diffusion of the formalism raises unresolved issues concerning the analysis of its concurrency aspects. Consider again the graphical

* Research partially supported the EC RTN 2-2001-00346 SEGRAVIS, the EU IST-2004-16004 SENSORIA and the MIUR Project ART.

C. Baier and H. Hermanns (Eds.): CONCUR 2006, LNCS 4137, pp. 279–294, 2006.

encodings for nominal calculi we mentioned above: a concurrent semantics for the graph rewriting formalism would provide a concurrent semantics for process reduction, but unfortunately these encodings fall outside the canon of DPO concurrent semantics. More specifically, the matching morphisms (those morphisms identifying the occurrence of the left-hand side of a rule into the graph to be rewritten) are forced to be injective. More importantly, the right-hand side of the rules resulting from the encoding are specified by non-injective morphisms (operationally, they force some node coalescing in the graph to be rewritten).

Such features are general enough to deserve to be properly addressed. Recall that concurrency in the DPO approach was originally defined by using the *shift equivalence* [6], which equates those derivations that could be related via the repeated application of an interchange operator swapping consecutive rewriting steps that are *sequentially independent* (roughly, such that they act on disjoint parts of the graph). *Graph processes*, as proposed in [5], generalise the notion of non-sequential process from the Petri net mold, representing concurrency and causal dependency in a synthetic manner as a partial ordering on the rewrites occurring in a derivation. Shift equivalent derivations correspond to isomorphic processes. Additionally, each total order on rule instances, compatible with the partial order of the graph process, uniquely characterises a derivation which is shift equivalent to the original one [1] (*complete concurrency* property). The above theory has been developed for rules with injective right-hand morphisms. When considering coalescing rules, as argued in [14,11], a connection between graph processes and shift-equivalent derivations may still be drawn, but no partial order can be distilled anymore from a graph process.

In order to allow the use of coalescing rules, while retaining a satisfactory theory of concurrency, we advocate the use of rewriting over a novel family of structures, *graphs with equivalences*, which are ordinary (hyper-)graphs equipped with an equivalence relation over their nodes. The underlying intuition is simple: the coalescing of nodes is replaced by the handling of equivalence classes over nodes. Avoiding the fusion of these graph items (and thus preserving the identities of the nodes involved in a computation) allows for recovering the theoretical results associated to the concurrent features of the DPO approach: the paradigm of graph processes for representing shift-equivalent derivations can be lifted to the new formalism, and the complete concurrency property once more holds.

For the sake of presentation, the formalism is tested against the encoding of (a fragment of the) *solo calculus* [16], one of the dialects of those nominal calculi whose distinctive feature is name fusion [12,18]. The choice of such a simple calculus is functional to the main focus of the paper, but it is noteworthy that the formalism is expressive enough to properly recast the graphical encodings of nominal calculi proposed in e.g. [9,10]. With respect to those encodings, where the presence of node coalescing rules forbade the development of a suitable concurrent presentation of reductions, the use of equivalences on nodes allows the extraction of a meaningful notion of causal order from a process.

The paper has the following structure. In Section 2 we introduce the formalism of graphs with equivalences, which is proved to be amenable to the DPO approach to rewriting. In Section 3 we develop a concurrency theory for rewriting of graphs with equivalences. Section 4 presents an encoding of the solo calculus into graphs with equivalences, showing how it allows for an analysis of its concurrency properties. Finally, Section 5 concludes the paper, discussing open issues and directions of future research.

2 Rewriting Graphs with Equivalences

In this section we introduce the category of graphs with equivalences, which are graphs endowed with an equivalence over the set of nodes. Rewriting systems over such structures are proposed as a technically convenient replacement of rewriting over ordinary graphs where rules may coalesce nodes.

2.1 The Category of Graphs with Equivalences

A *(hyper-)graph* G is a tuple $\langle V_G, E_G, c_G \rangle$ for V_G the set of nodes, E_G the set of edges and $c_G : E_G \to V_G^*$ the connection function. An (hyper-)graph morphism $f : G \to H$ is a pair $f = \langle f_V : V_G \to V_H, f_E : E_G \to E_H \rangle$ satisfying $c_H(f_E(e)) = f_V^*(c_G(e))$ for any $e \in E_G$. The corresponding category is denoted by **Graph**.

Definition 1 (graphs with equivalences). *A* graph with equivalences (e-graph) *is a pair* $\mathbb{G} = \langle G, \sim_G \rangle$ *where* G *is a graph and* $\sim_G \subseteq V_G \times V_G$ *is an equivalence over the set of nodes. Given two e-graphs* $\mathbb{G}$ *and* $\mathbb{H}$*, a morphism* $f : \mathbb{G} \to \mathbb{H}$ *is a graph morphism* $f : G \to H$ *such that for all* $n, n' \in V_G$*, if* $n \sim_G n'$ *then* $f(n) \sim_H f(n')$*. The category of e-graphs and their morphisms is denoted by* **EGraph**.

An e-graph $\mathbb{G}$ is intended to provide an alternative representation for the graph $G/_{\sim_G}$ obtained by quotienting G with respect to $\sim_G$. Formally, we can define a quotient functor $\mathcal{Q} :$ **EGraph** $\to$ **Graph** defined on objects as $\mathcal{Q}(\mathbb{G}) = G/_{\sim_G} = \langle V/_{\sim_G}, E, c' \rangle$ where $c'([e]_{\sim_G}) = [v_1]_{\sim_G} \ldots [v_n]_{\sim_G}$ if $c(e) = v_1 \ldots v_n$. Given $f : \mathbb{G} \to \mathbb{H}$ we have $\mathcal{Q}(f)$ defined by $\mathcal{Q}(f)([v]_{\sim_G}) = [f(v)]_{\sim_G}$.

In order to define rewriting over e-graphs some considerations are in order.

Observe that monos in **EGraph** are morphisms $f : \mathbb{G} \to \mathbb{H}$ such that $f : G \to H$ is a mono in **Graph**. This is easily proved observing that **Graph** is equivalent to the full subcategory of **EGraph** where objects are e-graphs with all non-equivalent nodes (i.e., e-graphs $\mathbb{G}$ where $\sim_G$ is the identity). *Regular* monos are monos $f : \mathbb{G} \to \mathbb{H}$ which reflect as well as preserve the equivalences of nodes, i.e., such that for all $n, n' \in V_G$ if $f(n) \sim_H f(n')$ then $n \sim_G n'$. Note that regular monos over e-graphs induce monos over the corresponding quotient graphs, i.e., if $f : \mathbb{G} \to \mathbb{H}$ is regular mono then $\mathcal{Q}(f) : \mathcal{Q}(\mathbb{G}) \to \mathcal{Q}(\mathbb{H})$ is injective.

The category **EGraph** has all pushouts, which are computed by taking the pushout in **Graph**, endowed with the equivalence arising as the "union" of the equivalences of the components.

2.2 Rewriting e-Graphs

We next define rewriting systems over e-graphs according to the algebraic double-pushout (DPO) approach to rewriting, as presented in [6,7]. For technical reasons it is convenient to work with *typed e-graphs*, which are e-graphs labelled over a structure that is itself an e-graph (see e.g. [5] for the idea of graph typing).

Given an e-graph $\mathbb{T}$, the category of e-graphs typed over $\mathbb{T}$ is the slice category **EGraph** $\downarrow \mathbb{T}$, later denoted $\mathbb{T}$-**EGraph**. Explicitly, the objects of the category are the e-graph morphisms $f : \mathbb{G} \to \mathbb{T}$ with target $\mathbb{T}$, and arrows are e-graph morphisms making the obvious diagram commutes. Given a $\mathbb{T}$-typed e-graph $\mathbb{G}$, we write $|\mathbb{G}|$ for the underlying e-graph and $t_{\mathbb{G}}$ for the typing arrow $t_{\mathbb{G}} : |\mathbb{G}| \to \mathbb{T}$.

Rewriting systems over typed e-graphs will be used as a replacement of rewriting systems over ordinary graphs where rules can coalesce nodes. Intuitively, the coalescing of nodes in rewriting systems over graphs becomes the generation of an equivalence between such nodes in the setting of e-graphs.

Definition 2 (e-graph production). *A* $\mathbb{T}$*-typed* e-graph production *is a span* $\mathbb{L} \stackrel{l}{\leftarrow} \mathbb{K} \stackrel{r}{\rightarrow} \mathbb{R}$ *in* $\mathbb{T}$-**EGraph** *such that* l *and* r *are mono. It is called left-linear if* l *is regular mono. A* typed e-graph transformation system *(*e-GTS*) is a tuple* $\langle \mathbb{T}, P, \pi \rangle$ *where* $\mathbb{T}$ *is a fixed graph,* P *is a set of production names, and* π *is a function mapping each name to a* $\mathbb{T}$*-typed production. An* e-GTS *is called* left-linear *if all its productions are left-linear.*

Observe that, given a left-linear production p, in the graph production $\mathcal{Q}(\mathbb{L}) \stackrel{\mathcal{Q}(l)}{\longleftarrow} \mathcal{Q}(\mathbb{K}) \stackrel{\mathcal{Q}(r)}{\longrightarrow} \mathcal{Q}(\mathbb{R})$ the left morphism is mono, while the right morphism may coalesce some nodes.

Definition 3 (derivation). *Given a* $\mathbb{T}$*-typed production* $p : \mathbb{L} \stackrel{l}{\longleftarrow} \mathbb{K} \stackrel{r}{\longrightarrow} \mathbb{R}$, *a match of* p *in a* $\mathbb{T}$*-typed e-graph* $\mathbb{G}$ *is a morphism* $m_L : \mathbb{L} \to \mathbb{G}$. *A* direct derivation *from* $\mathbb{G}$ *to* $\mathbb{H}$ *via production* p *at a match* m *is a diagram as depicted in Fig. 1, where (1) and (2) are pushout squares in* $\mathbb{T}$-**EGraph**. *It is called* strict *if the match is regular mono. We write* $\mathbb{G} \stackrel{p/m}{\Longrightarrow} \mathbb{H}$, *where* $m = \langle m_L, m_K, m_R \rangle$, *or simply* $\mathbb{G} \Longrightarrow \mathbb{H}$.

Roughly, concerning the graphical part, the application of a production p first removes all the items of G matched by $L - l(K)$, leading to the context graph D. Then the items of $R - r(K)$ are added to D, thus obtaining H.

Concerning the equivalence part, the fact that l is a regular mono intuitively means that equivalences among nodes are never deleted, that is, two nodes which

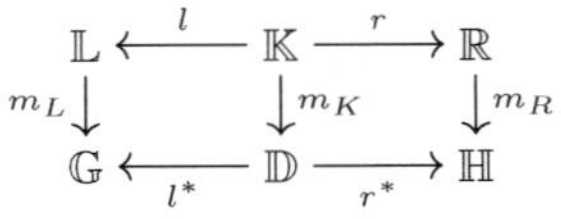

Fig. 1. A direct derivation

are equivalent in the e-graph $\mathbb{L}$ will still be equivalent in the e-graph $\mathbb{R}$. Hence, the equivalence in $\mathbb{D}$ is just the restriction of the equivalence in $\mathbb{G}$. Instead, whenever r is not a regular mono, as an effect of taking the second pushout, some nodes which were not equivalent in $\mathbb{D}$ might become equivalent in $\mathbb{H}$. On the formal side, the regular mono requirement for l ensures that the pushout complement, when it exists, is unique.

In several applications, e.g., in the encoding of nominal calculi, it is necessary to consider injective matches only. When dealing with e-graphs, this property corresponds to the requirement of having regular mono matches. The rest of the paper will focus on strict derivations and left-linear e-GTS, hence both qualifications "strict" and "left-linear" will be omitted.

A drawback of the approach is given by the fact that a single node in the standard approach can be represented by an equivalence class of possibly unbounded size. Therefore, in order to model node deletion, also an unbounded number of rules deleting equivalence classes of arbitrary size must be inserted into a transformation system. However, notice that for modelling purposes, it is often not restrictive to consider only rules which never delete nodes: indeed, this is what happens on most graphical encodings of process calculi. Node deletion is then simulated by leaving a node isolated, thus assuming an implicit mechanism for performing garbage collection.

3 Concurrency in E-Graph Rewriting

In this section we show that the notion of sequential independence, characterising independent steps in a computation, may be extended to the setting of e-graphs. More importantly, also the notion of process may be generalised, thus providing a partial order description of concurrency in computations: a generalization that fails when considering standard graphs with coalescing rules.

3.1 Sequential Independence and Shift-Equivalence

The notion of sequential independence is aimed at characterising direct derivations which do not interfere with each other and thus which could be potentially applied in any order (and concurrently). The definition below, a stronger version of the standard one, is inspired to the notion proposed in [14] for DPO rewriting with injective matches.

Definition 4 (sequential independence). *Let* $\mathbb{G} \stackrel{p_1/m_1}{\Longrightarrow} \mathbb{H} \stackrel{p_2/m_2}{\Longrightarrow} \mathbb{M}$ *be a derivation as in Fig. 2. Then, its components are* sequentially independent *if there exists an* independence pair *among them, i.e., two e-graph morphisms* $i_1 : \mathbb{R}_1 \to \mathbb{D}_2$ *and* $i_2 : \mathbb{L}_2 \to \mathbb{D}_1$ *such that* $l_2^* \circ i_1 = m_{L_2}$, $r_1^* \circ i_2 = m_{R_1}$ *and* $r_2^* \circ i_1$ *is regular mono.*

Requiring $r_2^* \circ i_1$ to be regular mono is motivated by the interplay between the equivalences the application of a rule may produce and the request for the matches to be regular mono. Roughly, the second direct derivation must not

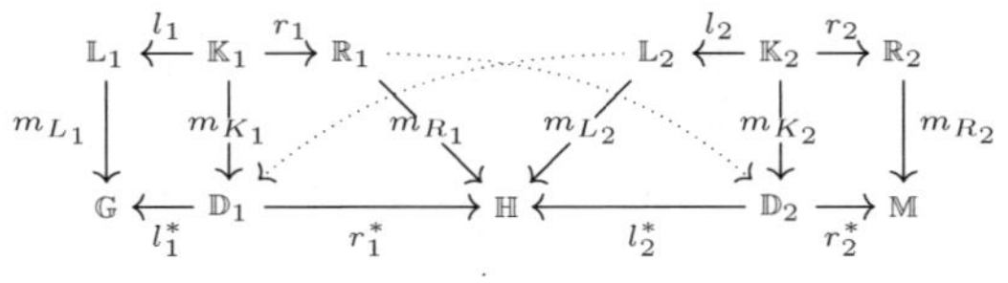

Fig. 2. (Strong) sequential independence for derivation $\rho = \mathbb{G} \overset{p_1/m_1}{\Longrightarrow} \mathbb{H} \overset{p_2/m_2}{\Longrightarrow} \mathbb{M}$

equate items which are read by the first one: otherwise, the application of the two productions could not be swapped, keeping the matches regular mono.

Proposition 5 (interchange operator). *Let $\rho = \mathbb{G} \overset{p_1/m_1}{\Longrightarrow} \mathbb{H} \overset{p_2/m_2}{\Longrightarrow} \mathbb{M}$ be a derivation, and let its components be sequentially independent via an independence pair ξ. Then, a derivation $IC_\pi(\rho) = \mathbb{G} \overset{p_2/m_2^*}{\Longrightarrow} \mathbb{H}^* \overset{p_1/m_1^*}{\Longrightarrow} \mathbb{M}$ can be uniquely chosen, such that its components are sequentially independent via a canonical independence pair ξ^*.*

The interchange operator can be used to formalise a notion of shift-equivalence [6], identifying (as for the analogous, better-known *permutation equivalence* of λ-calculus) those derivations which differ only for the scheduling of independent steps. This equivalence abstracts also from the concrete identity of items involved in a derivation, i.e., it considers derivations up-to isomorphism (defined component-wise, in the obvious way).

Definition 6 (shift-equivalence). *Two derivations ρ and ρ' are* shift-equivalent, *written $\rho \equiv_s \rho'$, if repeatedly applying the interchange operator to ρ we can obtain a derivation isomorphic to ρ'.*

The shift-equivalence class $[\rho]_s$ of a derivation ρ can be considered as a representation of a concurrent derivation which abstracts from the order of non-interfering rewriting steps.

3.2 Processes for e-Graphs

A more concrete, yet equivalent notion of abstract derivation for an e-GTS is obtained by generalising the so-called *graph process semantics* [1]. As for the similar notion on Petri nets [13], a *graph process* is aimed at describing a derivation abstracting away from the ordering of causally unrelated steps, and thus it offers at the same time a concrete representative for a class of shift-equivalent derivations. We will see that, differently from what happens in the case of graph transformation systems with coalescing rules, the notion of process for e-graphs provides a faithful partial order representation of concurrency in a derivation.

Definition 7 (e-graph process). *Let $\mathcal{G}$ be an* e-GTS *and $\rho = \mathbb{G}_0 \overset{p_1/m_1}{\Longrightarrow} \dots \overset{p_n/m_n}{\Longrightarrow} \mathbb{G}_n$ a derivation (upper part of Fig. 3). The* e-graph process *associated to ρ is a tuple $\phi = \langle \mathcal{O}_\phi, \phi_T, \phi_P, \mathbb{I}, \mathbb{F} \rangle$, where $\mathcal{O}_\phi = \langle \mathbb{T}_\phi, P_\phi, \pi_\phi \rangle$ is an* e-GTS *and $\phi_T : \mathbb{T}_\phi \to \mathbb{T}$ is an e-graph morphism and $\phi_P : P_\phi \to P$ is a function, defined as*

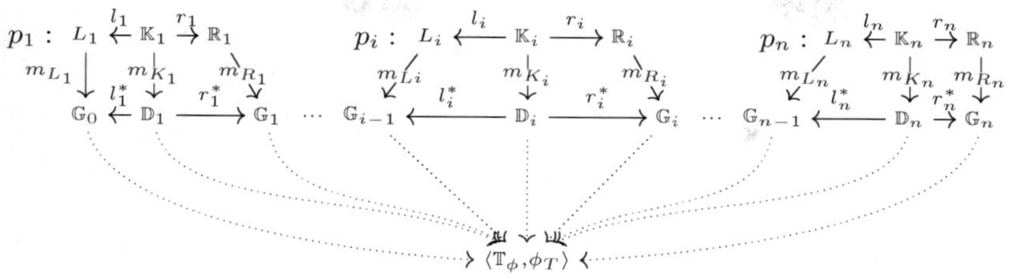

Fig. 3. Colimit construction for derivation $\rho = \mathbb{G}_0 \stackrel{p_1/m_1}{\Longrightarrow} \ldots \stackrel{p_n/m_n}{\Longrightarrow} \mathbb{G}_n$

- $\langle \mathbb{T}_\phi, \phi_T \rangle$ *is a colimit object (in* $\mathbb{T}$-**Graph***) of the diagram representing derivation* ρ*, as depicted in Fig. 3;*
- $P_\phi = \{\langle p_j, j\rangle \mid j \in \{1, \ldots, n\}\}$*. For all* j*,* $\pi_\phi(\langle p_j, j\rangle)$ *is essentially the production* p_j*, but retyped over* $\mathbb{T}_\phi$ *by the morphisms uniquely induced by the colimit (see Fig. 3). Moreover,* $\phi_P(\langle p_j, j\rangle) = p_j$*;*
- $\mathbb{I}$ *and* $\mathbb{F}$ *are the graphs* $\mathbb{G}_0$ *and* $\mathbb{G}_n$*, typed over* $\mathbb{T}_\phi$ *by the morphisms induced by the colimit. They are called* source *and* target *of the process and denoted* $src(\Pi(\rho))$ *and* $trg(\Pi(\rho))$*.*

The process associated to a derivation ρ*, as defined above, is denoted by* $\Pi(\rho)$*.*

The colimit construction applied to a derivation ρ essentially constructs the type graph as a copy of the source graph plus the items created during the derivation. Productions are instances of production applications. Additionally, the colimit operation "collects" the generated equivalences: the equivalence on the e-graph arising as type graph of $\Pi(\rho)$ is the "union" of the equivalences of the graphs occurring in ρ.

It can now be shown that two derivations are shift equivalent iff the corresponding processes are isomorphic, and thus processes properly capture the notion of concurrency as expressed by shift-equivalence.

Proposition 8 (Shift equivalence vs processes). *Let* ρ *and* ρ' *be derivations. Then* $\rho \equiv_s \rho'$ *if and only if the processes* $\Pi(\rho)$ *and* $\Pi(\rho')$ *are isomorphic.*

The result above is standard in graph rewriting theory for rules where both morphisms are monos. It was generalized to strict derivations and rules coalescing nodes in [11, Thms 1–2]. However, in that setting it was impossible to provide a technique for extracting from a process any information about the dependencies between the single direct derivations occurring in it (see [11, Section 4.2]).

3.3 Full Concurrency for e-Graph Processes

In order to extract from a process ϕ sound information about the dependencies between events, as for rewriting over ordinary graphs, we define the pre-set, post-set and context of a production, which roughly identify the items which are deleted, produced and preserved by a production.

Definition 9 (pre-set, post-set, context). *Let $\phi = \langle \mathcal{O}_\phi, \phi_T, \phi_P, \mathbb{I}, \mathbb{F} \rangle$ be a process, where $\mathcal{O}_\phi = \langle \mathbb{T}_\phi, P_\phi, \pi_\phi \rangle$. For any $p \in P_\phi$ we define*

$$^\bullet p = t_{\mathbb{L}_p}(|\mathbb{L}_p| - l_p(|\mathbb{K}_p|)) \qquad p^\bullet = t_{\mathbb{R}_p}(|\mathbb{R}_p| - r_p(|\mathbb{K}_p|)) \qquad \underline{p} = t_{\mathbb{K}_p}(|\mathbb{K}_p|)$$

considered as sets of nodes and edges, and we say that p consumes, produces *and* preserves *items in $^\bullet p$, $p^\bullet$ and $\underline{p}$, respectively.*

The mutual relationships between the pre-sets, post-sets and contexts of productions naturally lead to a precedence relation between the productions in a process (generalising to e-graphs the asymmetric conflict relation [3]).

Definition 10 (precedence relation). *Let ϕ be a process as in Def. 9. The* precedence relation *is the binary relation $\nearrow_\phi$ over the set P_ϕ of productions, defined by $p \nearrow_\phi p'$ if (1) $p^\bullet \cap (^\bullet p' \cup \underline{p'}) \neq \emptyset$ and $p \neq p'$ or (2) $\underline{p} \cup \cap ^\bullet p' \neq \emptyset$.*

Observe that when p' uses something produced by p necessarily p' follows p (point 1). Similarly, when p' consumes an item read by p, the only possible order of execution is p followed by p' (point 2).

However, $\nearrow_\phi$ alone does not suffice to faithfully mirror the relationship between productions since additional dependencies arise whenever productions "read" equivalences among nodes and generate new ones. Hence, we now characterise the equalities between nodes needed and generated by any production.

Definition 11 (read and produced equivalences). *Let ϕ be a process as in Def. 9. For any $p \in P_\phi$ we define*

$$req(p) = t_{\mathbb{L}_p}(\sim_{L_p}) \qquad \text{and} \qquad grel(p) = t_{\mathbb{R}_p}(\sim_{R_p} - t_{\mathbb{K}_p}(\sim_{K_p}))$$

and call them the (symmetric) relations read and produced by p. Given a set of productions $X \subseteq P_\phi$ we write $geq(X)$ for the set $(\bigcup_{p \in X} grel(p) \cup \sim_{src(\phi)})^*$.

Note that since all matches are regular monos, the application of a production never generates an already existing equivalence. This implies that any equivalence between nodes has a uniquely determined history, whose events are thus causes for productions which read that equivalence.

Proposition 12 (generating relation). *Let ϕ be a process as in Def. 9. Then for any production $p \in P_\phi$ there exists a least subset of productions $eq(p) \subseteq P_\phi$ such that $req(p) \subseteq geq(eq(p))$.*

Now, all events in $eq(p)$ must precede p in the computation, as expressed by the relation defined below.

Definition 13 (e-precedence relation). *Let ϕ be a process as in Def. 9. The* e-precedence relation *is the binary relation $\nearrow^e_\phi$ over the set P_ϕ of productions, defined by*

$$\nearrow_\phi \cup (\bigcup_{p \in P_\phi} eq(p) \times \{p\})$$

Then it can be shown that relation $\nearrow^{e}_{\phi}$ faithfully captures the dependencies between events in a process, i.e., we can prove the following result.

Proposition 14 (full concurrency). *Let ϕ be a process. Then the productions of ϕ, applied to in any order compatible with $\nearrow^{e}_{\phi}$, rewrite $src(\phi)$ into $trg(\phi)$ and all such derivations are shift equivalent.*

This "permutation" result does not hold for graph rewriting rules that may coalesce nodes, hence the notion of process fails to work when dealing with standard graphs. The reason for this failure is due to the fact that node identity is lost after a fusion, while node equivalences allow for a natural way of taking into account these additional dependencies.

4 Encoding a Simple Process Calculus

In this section we put the e-graph formalism at work, showing that it allows for encoding a simple (the simplest available, in fact) process calculus, namely, the monadic *solo calculus* [16], one of the dialects of those nominal calculi whose distinctive feature is name fusion [12,18]. We will see that the tools introduced in the previous section, like shift-equivalence and process semantics, allow for providing a characterisation of concurrent reductions in the solo calculus.

4.1 The Monadic Fragment of the Solo Calculus

We next shortly introduce the monadic variant of the *solo calculus*, its structural equivalence and the associated reduction semantics.

Definition 15 (processes). *Let $\mathcal{N}$ be a set of* names, *ranged over by $x, y, w, \ldots$. The set of* processes *Proc is generated by the syntax*

$$P ::= 0,\ \sigma,\ (\nu x)P,\ P_1 \mid P_2 \qquad \textit{for } \sigma \in \{x(y), \overline{x}y\}$$

The operators $x(y)$ and $\overline{x}y$ are denoted as *input* and *output*, respectively, even if their symmetric behaviour makes the distinction (typical instead of other calculi) immaterial; collectively, each instance of them is called a *solo*, to emphasise its lack of connections, except for some possible name sharing, with the other operators. Finally, the first argument of the two operators, indicated by x, is usually called the *channel* where the communication of information takes place.

We assume the standard definitions for the set of free names of a process P, denoted by $fn(P)$. Similarly for α-convertibility, with respect to the *restriction* operators $(\nu y)P$: the name y is bound in P, and it can be freely α-converted. Using these definitions, the behaviour of a process P is described as a relation obtained by closing a set of basic rules under a suitable congruence.

Definition 16 (reduction semantics). *The* reduction relation *for processes is the relation $R_\sigma \subseteq Proc \times Proc$, closed under the structural congruence $\equiv$ induced by the equations in Fig. 4, generated by the following inference rules*

$$(r_1)\ \frac{y \neq w}{(\nu w)(x(y) \mid \overline{x}w \mid P) \rightarrow P\{^y/_w\}} \qquad (r_2)\ \frac{y \neq w}{(\nu y)(x(y) \mid \overline{x}w \mid P) \rightarrow P\{^w/_y\}}$$

$$(r_3)\ \frac{}{x(y) \mid \overline{x}y \rightarrow 0} \qquad (r_4)\ \frac{P \rightarrow Q}{(\nu x)P \rightarrow (\nu x)Q} \qquad (r_5)\ \frac{P \rightarrow Q}{P \mid R \rightarrow Q \mid R}$$

where $P \rightarrow Q$ *means that* $\langle P, Q\rangle \in R_\sigma$.

The top rules characterise the communication between restricted processes. Consider the second: the process $\overline{x}w$ is ready to communicate the name w along the channel x; it then synchronises with the process $x(y)$, and the bound name y is thus substituted by w on *all the occurrences* inside the residual process P. Hence, the communication has a global effect on the process as a whole. Note that one of the names among $\{y, w\}$ *has to be bound*, so that, in principle, the rule does not to alter the number of free names floating around and the possible choice requires the presence of two different rules. The third rule expresses the fact that there is no reason to bind a name during a reduction, if no substitution has actually to occur. The latter two rules simply state the closure of the reduction relation with respect to the operators of restriction and parallel composition.

The axioms for structural congruence in Fig. 4 state that a process is a collection of solos floating around, and interacting by forcing some name fusion. The only difference with respect to the monadic fragment of the calculus proposed in [16] is the lack of a *match* operator $[x = y]$, avoided to simplify the presentation, and the explicit presentation of the three reduction rules, which in [16] are summarised as a unique rule equipped with constraints on the substitution induced by the name fusion.

4.2 The Graphical Encoding of Solos

This section informally presents an encoding of solos based on e-graphs. It resembles the encoding using standard graphs presented in [11, Section 5], basically replacing node coalescing rules with rules generating node equivalences. Its formal definition is not presented for space limitation: it is easily obtained by adapting the proposals for mobile ambients and π-calculus in [9,10].

In order to help intuition, we begin with a description of a suitable normal form for structurally congruent processes. First notice that any process P is equivalent to a process of the shape $(\nu x_1)\ldots(\nu x_n)(\sigma_1 \mid \ldots \mid \sigma_m)$ where all x_i's are different, all σ_j's are solos, and the set $X = \{x_1 \ldots x_n\}$ contains only names occurring in $S = \sigma_1 \mid \ldots \mid \sigma_m$, that is, $X \subseteq \mathtt{fn}(S)$. Thus we can denote a process in normal form as $(\nu X)\mathcal{P}$, for $\mathcal{P}$ a set of solos, since the order of the restriction operators and of the solos is immaterial.

$$P \mid Q = Q \mid P \qquad P \mid 0 = P \qquad P \mid (Q \mid R) = (P \mid Q) \mid R$$

$$(\nu x)(\nu y)P = (\nu y)(\nu x)P \qquad (\nu x)0 = 0 \qquad (\nu x)(P \mid Q) = P \mid (\nu x)Q \ \text{ for } x \notin fn(P)$$

Fig. 4. The set of structural axioms

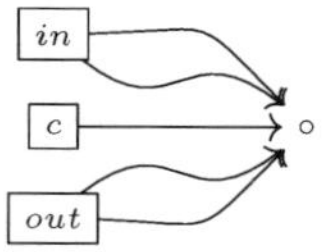

Fig. 5. The type graph T_σ

Definition 17 (disjoint normal form). *Let P be a solo process and let $(\nu X)\mathcal{P}$ be its normal form. We call* disjoint normal form *of P an expression of the kind $(\nu X)\mathcal{D}\xi$, where $\mathcal{D}$ is a set of solos with disjoint names such that $X \cap fn(\mathcal{D}) = \emptyset$ and $\xi : fn(\mathcal{D}) \to fn(\mathcal{P})$ is a surjective name substitution satisfying $\mathcal{D}\xi = \mathcal{P}$.*

After renaming the solos, the substitution ξ picks a canonical representative for each equivalence class of names. For example, the process $P_e = (\nu w)(x(y) \mid \overline{x}w \mid w(z) \mid \overline{y}z)$ can be described by the disjoint normal form $(\nu w)\mathcal{D}_e\xi_e$ where $\mathcal{D}_e = \{x_2(y_2), \overline{x}_1 w_2, w_1(z_2), \overline{y}_1 z_1\}$ and ξ_e is the obvious substitution.

The above characterisation naturally suggests a representation using typed e-graphs. The type e-graph $\mathbb{T}_\sigma$, represented in Fig. 5, has one node and three different edges, corresponding to the operators of the calculus. The equivalence on nodes is the identity, i.e., $\mathbb{T}_\sigma$ is essentially a standard graph. The typing will be represented by labelling graph edges with *in*, *out* and *c*.

Let P be a process, and $(\nu X)\mathcal{D}\xi$ its disjoint normal form. Then the typed e-graph $\mathbb{G}_P$ associated to P has as many edges and nodes as operators and names, respectively, occurring in $\mathcal{D}$. The effect of the substitution ξ is represented by using the equivalence $\sim_{G_P}$ between nodes: given two nodes x and y we have $x \sim_{G_P} y$ iff $\xi(x) = \xi(y)$ or $\xi(x) = y$. So, consider again the process $P_e = (\nu w)(x(y) \mid \overline{x}w \mid w(z) \mid \overline{y}z)$ and its disjoint normal form. Its encoding is represented in Fig. 6(a), where nodes, for the sake of clarity, are equipped with the name they represent. Equivalence classes are represented by a dotted rectangle, encompassing those nodes belonging to the class. In the example there are four equivalence classes: $\{y_1, y_2\}$, $\{x_1, x_2\}$, $\{z_1, z_2\}$ and $\{w, w_1, w_2\}$. Some intuition may be gained by looking at the graph $\mathcal{Q}(\mathbb{G}_{P_e})$ depicted in Fig. 6(b), obtained by collapsing equivalent nodes (this was indeed the encoding proposed for process P_e in [11, Fig. 11]).

4.3 Encoding Reductions

We now introduce the e-GTS $\mathcal{G}_\sigma$ in $\mathbb{T}_\sigma$-**EGraph**, showing how it simulates the reduction semantics for solo processes. It it basically contains just three productions (i.e., one for each axiom of the reduction system), plus some "instances" of them. The first production p_1^σ is depicted in Fig. 7: the e-graph on the left-hand side (center, right-hand side) is $\mathbb{L}_1^\sigma$ ($\mathbb{K}_1^\sigma$ and $\mathbb{R}_1^\sigma$, respectively). The action of the rule is described by the names of the nodes: as an example, the nodes identified by y and w_i's, distinct in $\mathbb{L}_1^\sigma$, are made equivalent in $\mathbb{R}_1^\sigma$. The node identifiers are of course arbitrary: they are used just to characterise the span of morphisms.

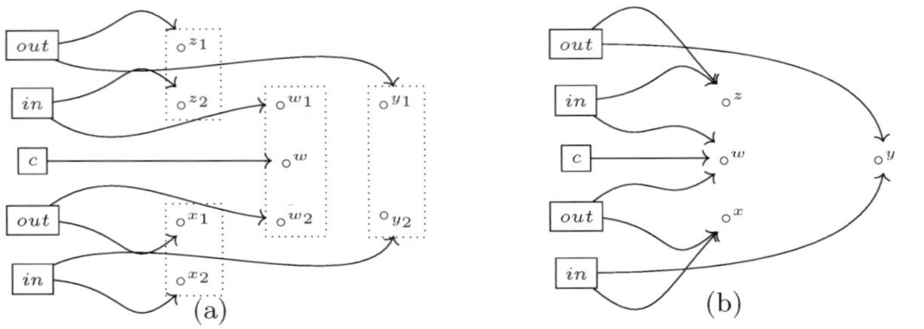

Fig. 6. (a) The e-graph $\mathbb{G}_{P_e}$ encoding a process P_e and (b) the quotient graph $\mathcal{Q}(\mathbb{G}_{P_e})$

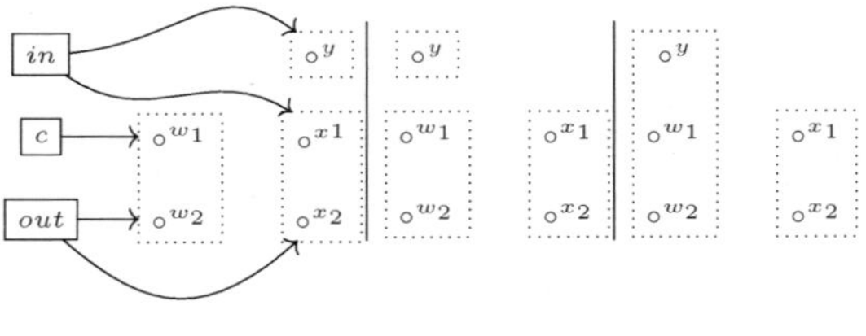

Fig. 7. The first production of $\mathcal{G}_\sigma$

The rule mimics (a disjoint variant of) the first axiom of the reduction semantics, as given in Def. 16. Constraining the matches to be regular monos ensures that the production is not applied to a graph where nodes y and w_i's are equivalent. Nevertheless, this turns out to be too restrictive, since a reduction step can be performed if name x coincides with either y or w. Hence, two additional productions are needed: they are variations of p_1^σ, where nodes x_i's are equivalent either to the node y or to the nodes w_i's. We leave these productions unnamed, since they play a minor role in the paper.

A similar situation occurs when the name y on the input operator, instead of the name w on the output operator, is bound: it suffices a production p_2^σ (together with two instances) mirroring p_1^σ. Most important, a production p_3^σ is needed, where nodes y and w_i's are already coalesced and the restriction operator is not required, as depicted in Fig. 8. Additionally, an instance where the two names coincide, and the corresponding nodes are thus equivalent, has to be included.

Observe that, during the reductions, isolated nodes may arise in correspondence of unused names. Hence, in the encoding a process P actually corresponds to a class of e-graphs, including $\mathbb{G}_P$, as defined in the previous section, and all the e-graphs which differ from $\mathbb{G}_P$ for the presence of additional isolated nodes.

4.4 Concurrency Via Fusion

Consider the process $(\nu w)(x(y) \mid \overline{x}w \mid w(z) \mid \overline{y}z)$, and its graphical depiction $\mathbb{G}_{P_e}$ in Fig. 6(a). A possible derivation consists of the two steps below, applying rules r_1 and r_3, respectively.

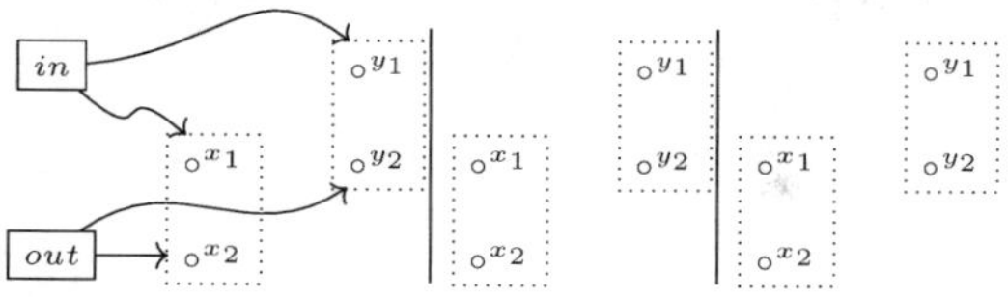

Fig. 8. The third production of $\mathcal{G}_\sigma$

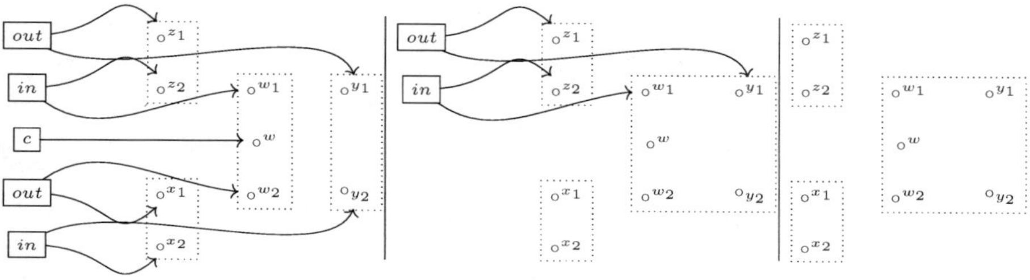

Fig. 9. The derived graphs of a derivation first applying p_1^σ and then p_3^σ

$$(\nu w)(x(y) \mid \overline{x}w \mid w(z) \mid \overline{y}z) \quad \to \quad (w(z) \mid \overline{y}z)\{^y/_w\} = y(z) \mid \overline{y}z \quad \to \quad 0$$

Being the context rules immaterial, we end up by applying to the graph in the left-hand side of Fig. 9 first the rule p_1^σ, and then the rule p_3^σ. The derivation (the derived graphs) is shown in Fig. 9, and the associated process is in Fig. 10.

It can be easily seen that the two steps are *not* sequentially independent. This is indeed recorded in the process $\Pi(\rho)$, as depicted in Fig. 10. The production p_1^σ consumes three edges, reads three equivalence classes (namely, those for nodes $\{w, w_2\}$, x_i's and y_i's), and generates the symmetric relation containing $\{\langle w, y_j\rangle, \langle w_i, y_j\rangle \mid i, j = 1, 2\}$. For the sake of readability, productions have dotted arrows only to (the smallest) equivalence relations including $\sim_{src(\rho)}$ that they read or generate. Now, p_3^σ reads the class $\{w_1, y_1\}$, so that $req(p_3^\sigma)$ is contained in $geq(\{p_1^\sigma\})$: thus, differently from what happens considering just the relation $\nearrow$, here $p_1^\sigma \nearrow^e p_3^\sigma$, i.e., the dependency between (the applications of) the production p_1^σ and the production p_3^σ is properly recorded.

Let us now consider the process $(\nu w)(x(y) \mid \overline{x}w \mid w(z) \mid \overline{w}z)$, which differs from the process above just for the name occurring in the right-most solo (namely, $\overline{w}z$ instead of $\overline{y}z$). The same sequence of rule applications as for the derivation depicted in Fig. 9 can now be replicated, and the result (the derived graphs) is presented in Fig. 11. The process $\Pi(\rho')$ is depicted in Fig. 12: with respect to the process in Fig. 10, production p_3^σ now reads the equivalence class containing $\{w_0, w_1\}$, instead of the class containing the w, w_i's and y generated by p_1^σ: thus, $req(p_3^\sigma)$ is contained in $\sim_{src(\rho')}$, and no casual dependency holds between the production occurrences. Hence the components of the derivation

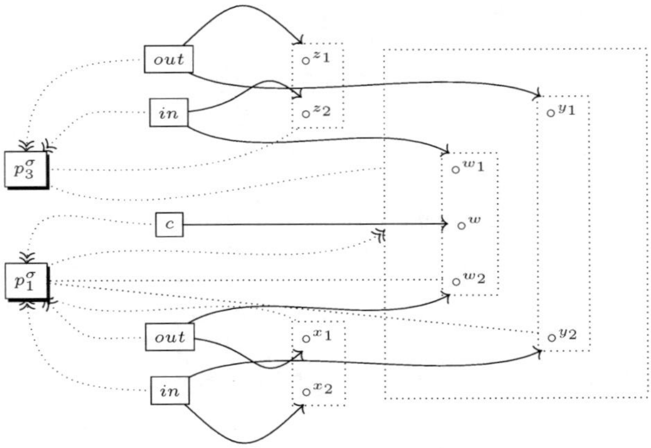

Fig. 10. The process of the derivation in Fig. 9

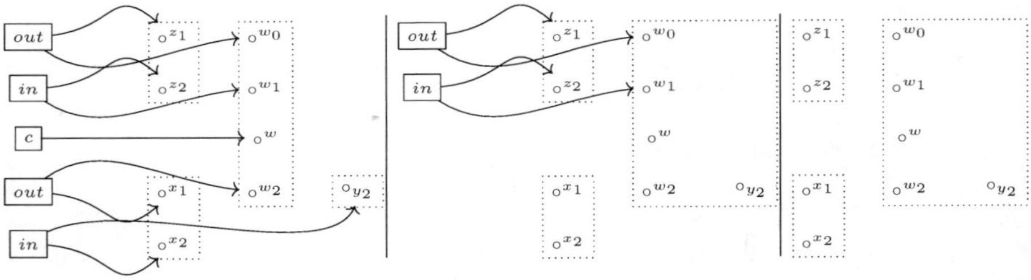

Fig. 11. The derived graphs of another derivation first applying p_1^σ and then p_3^σ

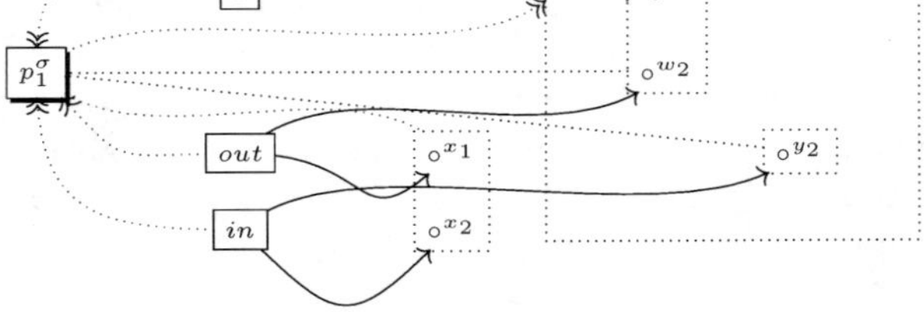

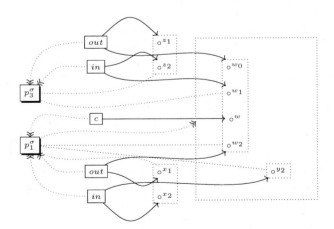

Fig. 12. The process of the derivation in Fig. 11

are sequentially independent, since the coalescing of nodes w, w_i's and y is not needed for the second direct derivation.

5 Conclusions and Further Works

The paper introduces a novel formalism for the analysis of distributed systems, *graphs with equivalences*: typed (hyper-)graphs equipped with an equivalence relation over their nodes. The formalism is amenable to the usual tools of the DPO approach to graph transformation: in particular, the theoretical results associated to the concurrent features of the approach (the paradigm of graph processes for representing shift-equivalent derivations) can be lifted to the new formalism.

We are planning two related strands of research. On the one side, we would like to properly establish the connection between the category of graphs and of graph with equivalences, making precise the correspondence briefly hinted at in Section 2. On the other side, we need to further develop the theory surrounding the graph process construction, drawing a link with respect to a suitable notion of event structure, amenable to model non-determinism in derivations. The latter characterisation would provide a further sanity check, providing a concurrent semantics for nominal calculi, to be compared with already existing proposals.

As a final remark, observe that e-graphs resemble the so-called *structures*, as defined in [8]. Indeed, along the same lines of [15, Section 6] that the category **EGraph** can be proved *quasi-adhesive*, thus inheriting part of the rich theory developed for such formalism. That very same paper develops a general theory of DPO rewriting for (quasi-)adhesive categories and a theory of processes is proposed in [2]. Unfortunately, this could not be helpful for our purposes, since the use of rules where right-hand side morphisms are not regular monos makes a relevant part of such theory not applicable.

References

1. P. Baldan, A. Corradini, H. Ehrig, M. Löwe, U. Montanari, and F. Rossi. Concurrent semantics of algebraic graph transformation. In H. Ehrig, H.-J. Kreowski, U. Montanari, and G. Rozenberg, editors, *Handbook of Graph Grammars and Computing by Graph Transformation*, volume 3, pages 107–187. World Scientific, 1999.
2. P. Baldan, A. Corradini, T. Heindel, B. König, and P. Sobociński. Processes for adhesive rewriting systems. In L. Aceto and A. Ingólfsdóttir, editors, *Foundations of Software Science and Computation Structures*, volume 3921 of *Lect. Notes Comp. Sc.*, pages 202–216. Springer, 2006.
3. P. Baldan, A. Corradini, and U. Montanari. Unfolding and event structure semantics for graph grammars. In W. Thomas, editor, *Foundations of Software Science and Computation Structures*, volume 1578 of *Lect. Notes Comp. Sc.*, pages 73–89. Springer, 1999.
4. L. Cardelli and A. Gordon. Mobile ambients. *Th. Comp. Sc.*, 240:177–213, 2000.
5. A. Corradini, U. Montanari, and F. Rossi. Graph processes. *Fundamenta Informaticae*, 26:241–265, 1996.

6. A. Corradini, U. Montanari, F. Rossi, H. Ehrig, R. Heckel, and M. Löwe. Algebraic approaches to graph transformation I: Basic concepts and double pushout approach. In G. Rozenberg, editor, *Handbook of Graph Grammars and Computing by Graph Transformation*, volume 1, pages 163–245. World Scientific, 1997.
7. F. Drewes, A. Habel, and H.-J. Kreowski. Hyperedge replacement graph grammars. In G. Rozenberg, editor, *Handbook of Graph Grammars and Computing by Graph Transformation*, volume 1, pages 95–162. World Scientific, 1997.
8. H. Ehrig, A. Habel, H.-J. Kreowski, and F. Parisi-Presicce. Parallelism and concurrency in high-level replacement systems. *Math. Str. Comp. Sc.*, 1:361–404, 1991.
9. F. Gadducci. Term graph rewriting and the π-calculus. In A. Ohori, editor, *Programming Languages and Semantics*, volume 2895 of *Lect. Notes Comp. Sc.*, pages 37–54. Springer, 2003.
10. F. Gadducci and U. Montanari. A concurrent graph semantics for mobile ambients. In S. Brookes and M. Mislove, editors, *Mathematical Foundations of Programming Semantics*, volume 45 of *El. Notes Th. Comp. Sc.* Elsevier Science, 2001.
11. F. Gadducci and U. Montanari. Graph processes with fusions: concurrency by colimits, again. In H.-J. Kreowski, U. Montanari, F. Orejas, G. Rozenberg, and G. Taentzer, editors, *Formal Methods (Ehrig Festschrift)*, volume 3393 of *Lect. Notes Comp. Sc.*, pages 84–100. Springer, 2005.
12. P. Gardner and L. Wischik. Explicit fusion. In M. Nielsen and B. Rovan, editors, *Mathematical Foundations of Computer Science*, volume 1893 of *Lect. Notes Comp. Sc.*, pages 373–382. Springer, 2000.
13. U. Golz and W. Reisig. The non-sequential behaviour of Petri nets. *Information and Control*, 57:125–147, 1983.
14. A. Habel, J. Müller, and D. Plump. Double-pushout graph transformation revisited. *Math. Str. Comp. Sc.*, 11:637–688, 2001.
15. S. Lack and P. Sobociński. Adhesive and quasiadhesive categories. *Informatique Théorique et Applications/Theor. Informatics and Applications*, 39:511–545, 2005.
16. C. Laneve and B. Victor. Solos in concert. *Math. Str. Comp. Sc.*, 13:675–683.
17. R. Milner, J. Parrow, and D. Walker. A calculus of mobile processes. Part I and II. *Information and Computation*, 100:1–77, 1992.
18. J. Parrow and B. Victor. The fusion calculus: Expressiveness and simmetry in mobile processes. In V. Pratt, editor, *Logic in Computer Science*, pages 176–185. IEEE Computer Society Press, 1998.

Event Structure Semantics for Nominal Calculi*

Roberto Bruni[1], Hernán Melgratti[2], and Ugo Montanari[1]

[1] Dipartimento di Informatica, Università di Pisa, Italia
[2] IMT Lucca Institute for Advance Studies, Italia
bruni@di.unipi.it, hernan.melgratti@imtlucca.it, ugo@di.unipi.it

Abstract. Event structures have been used for giving true concurrent semantics to languages and models of concurrency such as CCS, Petri nets and graph grammars. Although certain nominal calculi have been modeled with graph grammars, and hence their event structure semantics could be obtained as instances of the general case, the main limitation is that in the case of graph grammars the construction is more complex than strictly necessary for dealing with usual nominal calculi and, speaking in categorical terms, it is not as elegant as in the case of Petri nets. The main contribution of this work is the definition of a particular class of graph grammars, called *persistent*, that are expressive enough to model name passing calculi while simplifying the denotational domain construction, which can be expressed as an adjunction. Finally, we apply our technique to derive event structure semantics for pi-calculus and join-calculus processes.

1 Introduction

The paper by Varacca and Yoshida [23] advocates the definition of true concurrent semantics for π-calculus, renewing the interest in the use of event structures in connection with process calculi, a long-standing thread initiated by Winskel's semantics of Milner's CCS [24]. Their main contribution is an original typing system on the event structure for controlling the behavior of linear processes. Actually, they also suggest that their formalization is the first event structure semantics for the π-calculus, which (as also discussed in their concluding section) is true just in part.

We argue that the techniques were already available for deriving an event structure semantics (but not the results in [23]), even if the pieces were not put together yet. To explain this, we have to go back to the joint work of the third author with Pistore [19] on the encoding of π-calculus in Graph Transformation Systems (GTS), under the so-called Double Pushout approach (DPO) [9,10]. While Petri nets can account for CCS-like languages, it seems that nominal calculi fit better in the GTS approach, where name creation, dynamic network topology, and causality due to name passing can be more easily accounted for. However, some of the latest results about concurrent semantics for GTS were not available at that time, and the existing techniques were not as much sophisticated as available today, so that no explicit definition of the associated event structure semantics was given. More recently, [1] made some substantial advancements on the true concurrent semantics of DPO, by explaining in

* Research supported by the EU FET-GC2 IST-2004-16004 Integrated Project SENSORIA.

C. Baier and H. Hermanns (Eds.): CONCUR 2006, LNCS 4137, pp. 295–309, 2006.

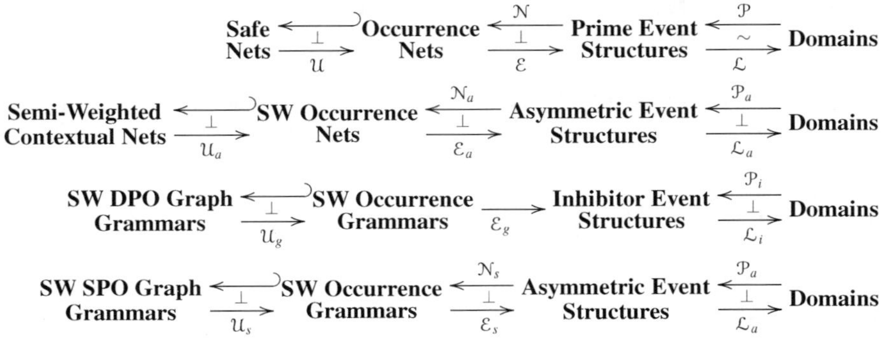

Fig. 1. A recollection of event structure semantics

terms of the so-called *inhibitor event structures* the semantics of a large class of GTS. This result was achieved as part of a larger research programme aimed at extending the chain of coreflections defined for Petri nets [20,24,18] first to contextual nets [3] (using *asymmetric event structures*) and then to graph grammars (exploiting some analogy between these two models). The price to pay was the introduction of much more sophisticated event structures. For DPO grammars the adjunction between unfolding and event structures breaks down to a functorial construction in just one direction. A recent result [4] has shown that the missing link can be re-established when considering the Single Pushout (SPO) approach [17,12]. This is summarized in Figure 1. The category of prime algebraic domains is equivalent to the category of prime event structures (PES), thus all constructions can ultimately lead to PES. It is worth noting that, under a mild assumption on graph grammars, namely *node preservation*, the elegant SPO constructions can be transferred also to the DPO approach. To some extent, the above informal discussion paves the way to the definition of an event structure semantics of π-calculus, (almost) obtained by applying the PES construction available for GTS to the encoding in [19].

We observe that the event structure semantics in this case are unnecessarily complicated (by the need of dealing with features pertaining to graph grammars but not needed in the encoding). Hence, we devise a simpler class of grammars, large enough to allow the encoding, but restricted as much as needed to obtain a PES via a chain of coreflections. Incidentally, the class we take is node preserving, and thus we can carry the construction under both the DPO and the SPO approach, still getting the same result. Our contribution aims to promote GTS as a suitable modeling framework for nominal calculi. The technique is demonstrated by addressing the case studies of π-calculus and join-calculus. We remark that this is the first event structure semantics for the latter, whose synchronization pattern challenges the reuse of other techniques in the literature.

Structure of the Paper. Section 2 summarizes the basics of typed graph grammars under the DPO (§ 2.1) and SPO (§ 2.2) approaches, and their event structure semantics (§ 2.3). Section 3 defines the class of persistent grammars. Sections 4 and 5 illustrate, respectively, how to associate PES to π-calculus processes and join calculus processes. Related works and final remarks are in Section 6.

2 Typed Graph Grammars and True Concurrency

Given a partial function $f : A \rightarrowtail B$ its *domain* is $dom(f) = \{a \in A \mid f(a) \text{ is defined}\}$. For $f, g : A \rightarrowtail B$ partial functions, we write $f \subseteq g$ when $dom(f) \subseteq dom(g)$ and $f(x) = g(x)$ for all $x \in dom(f)$. When $dom(f) = A$ we say that f is *total* and write $f : A \to B$.

A *(directed, unlabeled) graph* is a tuple $G = \langle N_G, E_G, s_G, t_G \rangle$, where N_G is a set of *nodes* (or *vertices*), E_G is a set of *edges* (or *arcs*), and $s_G, t_G : E_G \to N_G$ are the *source* and *target* functions. We shall omit subscripts when obvious from the context.

A *partial graph morphism* $f : G \rightarrowtail G'$ is a couple $f = \langle f_N : N \rightarrowtail N', f_E : E \rightarrowtail E' \rangle$ such that: $s' \circ f_E \subseteq f_N \circ s$ and $t' \circ f_E \subseteq f_N \circ t$. It is *total* if both components are total. The inclusions ensure that *any* subgraph of a graph G can be the domain of a partial morphism $f : G \rightarrowtail H$. Instead, the stronger constraint $s' \circ f_E = f_N \circ s$ and $t' \circ f_E = f_N \circ t$ would require f to be defined over an edge if it is defined on its source or target nodes.

In *typed graph grammars* [9], graphs are typed over a structure that is itself a graph, i.e., the typing is a graph homomorphism. In this setting, category theory serves as a tool to characterize constructions in a succinct, elegant way, favoring flexibility and generality. Since category theory is mainly a *theory of morphisms*, structure / behavior preserving mappings play a key role. Given a *graph of types* T, a T*-typed graph* is a pair $\langle |G|, \tau_G \rangle$, where $|G|$ is the *underlying* graph and $\tau_G : |G| \to T$ is a total morphism.

In GTS the graph $|G|$ defines the (dynamically evolving) configuration of the system and its elements (nodes and edges) model resources, while τ_G defines the (static) *typing* of the resources. For example, when encoding Petri nets in GTS the places of the net form the (discrete) graph of types, while tokens form the configuration of the system.

A *partial (resp. total) morphism* between T-typed graphs $f : G_1 \rightarrowtail G_2$ is a partial (resp. total) graph morphism $f : |G_1| \rightarrowtail |G_2|$ consistent with the typing, i.e., such that $\tau_{G_1} \supseteq \tau_{G_2} \circ f$. We denote by T-**PGraph** the category of T-typed graphs and partial morphisms and by T-**Graph** its subcategory of total morphisms. Focusing on total morphisms, the DPO approach is based T-**Graph**, whereas the SPO approach exploits T-**PGraph**. Since in this paper we work only with typed notions, we will usually omit the qualification "typed", and we will not indicate explicitly the typing morphisms.

In GTS the key notion to *glue* graphs together is that of a categorical pushout. Roughly, a pushout pastes two graphs together by injecting them in a larger graph that is (isomorphic to) their disjoint union modulo the collapsing of some common part. We recall that a *span* is a pair (b, c) of morphisms $b : A \to B$ and $c : A \to C$. A *pushout* of the span (b, c) is then an object D together with two (co-final) morphisms $f : B \to D$ and $g : C \to D$ such that: (i) $f \circ b = g \circ c$ and (ii) for any other choice of $f' : B \to D'$ and $g' : C \to D'$ s.t. $f' \circ b = g' \circ c$ there is a unique $d : D \to D'$ s.t. $f' = d \circ f$ and $g' = d \circ g$. If the pushout is defined, then c and g is called the *pushout complement* of $\langle b, f \rangle$.

2.1 DPO Direct Derivations

A *(T-typed) DPO production* $p : (L \stackrel{l}{\leftarrow} K \stackrel{r}{\rightarrow} R)$ is a span of injective typed graph morphisms $l : K \to L$ and $r : K \to R$. The T-typed graphs L, K, and R are called the *left-hand side*, the *interface*, and the *right-hand side* of the production, respectively. The production is called *consuming* if the morphism $l : K \to L$ is not surjective.

(a) A DPO direct derivation.

(b) An SPO direct derivation.

Fig. 2. Graph grammar derivations

Definition 2.1 (DPO graph grammar). *A* (T-typed) DPO graph grammar $\mathcal{G}$ *is a tuple* $\langle T, G_{in}, P\rangle$, *where* G_{in} *is the* initial (T-typed) graph *and* P *is a set of DPO* productions.

Given a graph G, a production $p : (L \stackrel{l}{\leftarrow} K \stackrel{r}{\rightarrow} R)$, and a *match* (i.e., a total graph morphism) $g : L \rightarrow G$, a *direct derivation* δ *from* G *to* H *using* p *(based on* g*)* exists, written $\delta : G \Rightarrow_p H$, if and only if the diagram in Figure 2(a) can be constructed, where both squares are pushouts in T-**Graph**: (1) the rewriting step removes from the graph G the items $g(L - l(K))$ (images of the left-hand side but not of the interface), yielding the graph D (with k, b as a pushout complement of $\langle g, l\rangle$); (2) then, fresh copies of the items in the right-hand side R that are not in the image of the interface, namely $R - r(K)$, are added to D yielding H (as a pushout of (k, r)). The interface K specifies both what is preserved and how fresh items must be glued to the existing part.

The existence of the pushout complement of $\langle g, l\rangle$ is subject to the satisfaction of the following *gluing conditions* [10]:

- *identification condition:* $\forall x, y \in L$ if $x \neq y$ and $g(x) = g(y)$ then $x, y \in l(K)$ (note however that the match can be non-injective on preserved items: the same resource can be used with multiplicity greater than one if preserved by the derivation);
- *dangling condition:* no arc in $G - g(L)$ is attached to a node in $g(L - l(K))$ (otherwise the derivation would leave such arc dangling after the removal of the node).

The identification condition is satisfied by the so-called *valid matches*: a match is not valid if it requires an item to be consumed twice, or to be both deleted and preserved.

2.2 SPO Direct Derivations

A *(T-typed) SPO production* is an injective partial graph morphism $q : L \rightarrowtail R$. It is called *consuming* if the morphism is not total. Without loss of generality, we will assume that q is just the partial inclusion $L \cap R \subseteq R$. The typed graphs L and R are called the *left-hand side* and the *right-hand side* of the production, respectively.

Definition 2.2 (SPO graph grammar). *A* (T-typed) SPO graph grammar $\mathcal{G}$ *is a tuple* $\langle T, G_{in}, Q\rangle$, *where* G_{in} *is the* initial (T-typed) graph *and* Q *is a set of* productions.

Given a graph G and a *match* $g : L \rightarrow G$, there is a *direct derivation* δ *from* G *to* H *using* q *(based on* g*)*, written $\delta : G \Rightarrow_q H$, if the diagram in Figure 2(b) forms a pushout square in T-**PGraph**. Roughly, the rewriting step removes from the graph G the image of the items of the left-hand side that are not in the domain of q, namely $g(L-R)$, and it adds the items of the right-hand side that are not in the image of q, namely $R-L$. The items in the image of $dom(q) = L \cap R$ are preserved by the rewriting step.

The key difference w.r.t. the DPO approach is that in SPO there is no *dangling condition* preventing a rule to be applied. In fact, as T-**PGraph** is the base category, when a node is deleted by the application of a rule, then all the edges having such node as source or target are deleted by the rewriting step, as a kind of *side-effect*.

On the contrary, the *identification condition* and the notion of *valid match* are still required to hold for the correct application of a production.

In the special case of *node preserving* grammars, the effect of SPO and DPO is very close. An SPO grammar is node preserving if each production $q : L \rightarrowtail R$ defines a total map on nodes. Similarly, a DPO grammar is node preserving if in each production $p : (L \stackrel{l}{\leftarrow} K \stackrel{r}{\rightarrow} R)$ the functions l and r are surjective on nodes. Then there is an isomorphism between SPO and DPO node preserving grammars that maps each production $q : L \rightarrowtail R$ to $D(q) : (L \stackrel{l}{\leftarrow} dom(q) \stackrel{r}{\rightarrow} R)$, with l and r the obvious inclusions.

2.3 Unfolding Constructions and Event Structure Semantics

A DPO/SPO *derivation* $\rho = \{G_{i-1} \Rightarrow_{q_{i-1}} G_i\}_{i \in \{1,\dots,n\}}$ in $\mathcal{G}$ is a sequence of direct derivations, with $G_0 = G_{in}$. A derivation is *valid* if it involves only valid matches.

We will consider only *consuming* graph grammars and *valid* derivations. The restriction to consuming grammars is essential to obtain a meaningful semantics combining concurrency and nondeterminism. In fact, the presence of non-consuming productions, which can be applied without deleting any item, would lead to an unbounded number of concurrent events with the same causal history. This would not fit with the approach to concurrency (see, e.g., [16,24]) where events in computations are identified with their causal history (formally, the unfolding construction would not work properly). This corresponds, in the theory of Petri nets, to the common requirement that transitions must have non-empty preconditions. The requirement about valid derivations is needed to have a computational interpretation that is resource-conscious, i.e., where a resource can be consumed only once.

To equip graph grammars with event structure semantics, by analogy with Petri nets, the idea is to first unfold all graph grammar derivations into the same "space of computations", collecting all items that can ever be produced and relating them to the applicable direct derivations. Then, we can project such unfolding so to keep just the events and the causality $\prec$, concurrency **co** and conflict # relationship between them.

In the case of Petri nets, the unfolding can be represented as a special kind of acyclic net, called occurrence net, whose places model all the tokens that can ever be produced and whose transitions model all the possible firings (events). For example, two events requesting the same token are in conflict, while an event is causally dependent on those events that generated the tokens it fetches and two events can be concurrently executed if they are neither causally dependent nor in conflict. The event structure is then obtained by keeping the events and forgetting the tokens. The appropriateness of the construction is supported by categorical arguments: (1) the maps from Petri nets to their unfoldings and from unfoldings to event structures are functors, i.e. they preserve net morphisms; (2) it is possible to go backward, in the sense of deriving a standard occurrence net from each event structure, and a standard net from each occurrence net (actually itself); (3) the backward maps are again functors; (4) forward and backward maps form a particularly nice kind of adjunctions, called co-reflections, which are the categorical means to relate different domains in the best possible way (formally, the unit of the adjunction is a natural isomorphism establishing an equivalence between a full subcategory of the domain of computational models and the denotational domain).

The case of DPO grammars is complicated by the fact that derivations can introduce subtle dependencies between events. Here the "tokens" are both the nodes and the arcs of the graph, hence it is possible: (1) to access the same resource concurrently, in read-only modality so to speak; (2) to have *asymmetric conflicts* between a direct derivation that attempts to read a resource and one that wants to fetch it; (3) to have events that by attempting to remove a node are inhibited by the presence of edges connected to that node. The consequences are that: (1) it is still possible to unfold DPO grammars in special acyclic DPO occurrence grammars accounting for all the above features; (2) a more complicated notion of event structure is needed, called *inhibitor event structures*; (3) the constructions are still functorial, but there is no fully satisfactory way back from inhibitor event structures to occurrence graph grammars.

The case of SPO is still more sophisticated than Petri nets, but more satisfactory than DPO. In fact: (1) it is possible to unfold SPO graph grammars in special acyclic SPO occurrence grammars; (2) a more sophisticated notion of event structure is needed, called *asymmetric event structures*, which can account for multiple concurrent readings and asymmetric conflicts; (3) all the constructions are coreflections.

Notably, for the special case of node preserving grammars the DPO construction can be carried on in close analogy with SPO, yielding the same asymmetric event structures. We do not have enough space here to formalize the above discussion, but details are not needed to follow the rest of this paper. Interested readers can check [4] for technicalities.

An important point to mention is that all the above constructions work only for a special kind of grammars, called *semi-weighted* and inspired by a similar requirements on Petri nets. Roughly, semi-weighted grammars enforce disambiguation in the semantics by preventing the generation of "equivalent" resources carrying the same history. We recall that a typed graph G is called *injective* if the typing morphism τ_G is injective.

Definition 2.3 (Semi-Weighted Grammar). *A graph grammar* $\mathcal{G} = \langle T, G_{in}, P\rangle$ *is* semi-weighted *if* G_{in} *is injective and the target of every production* $p \in P$ *is injective.*

3 Persistent Graph Grammars

In this section we revisit the general theory developed for SPO and DPO approaches when considering a special kind of graph grammars, called *persistent*. Sections 4 and 5 show that such restriction is a reasonable enough compromise between the applicability of the approach to nominal calculi and the categorical adequacy of the semantics.

A type graph T is *persistent* if its edges are partitioned in two subsets: E_T^+ of persistent edges and E_T^- of removable edges. Given a persistent T, and a T-typed graph G, we denote by E_G^+ and E_G^- the set of edges mapped respectively to persistent edges and to removable edges of T. In the following assume a persistent type graph T is given.

Definition 3.1 (Persistent Productions). *A DPO production* $p : (L \xleftarrow{l} K \xrightarrow{r} R)$ *is* persistent *if all of the following hold:*

- node persistence: $N_L = l(N_K)$ *(i.e., all nodes in L are images of nodes in K);*
- removal of removable arcs: $E_K^- = \emptyset$ *(i.e., no removable arc is in K);*
- preservation of persistent arcs: $E_L^+ = l(E_K^+)$ *(i.e., all persistent arcs in L are images of persistent arcs in K).*

Similarly, an SPO production $q : L \rightarrowtail R$ *is* persistent *if:*

- node persistence: $N_L \subseteq N_R$ *(i.e., all nodes in L are also in R);*
- removal of removable arcs: $E_L^- \cap E_R = \emptyset$ *(i.e., no removable arc in L is preserved);*
- preservation of persistent arcs: $E_L^+ \subseteq E_R^+$ *(i.e., all persistent arcs in L are in R).*

Definition 3.2 (Persistent graph grammar). *A* (T-typed, DPO/SPO) graph grammar $\mathcal{G}$ *is* persistent *if all its productions are consuming, semi-weighted and persistent.*

We have already analyzed and discussed the requirements about the grammar being consuming and semi-weighted. A first motivation for the persistence requirement is the fact that it characterizes a whole class of grammars for which there is no need of checking the dangling arc condition when applying any direct derivation.

Lemma 3.1. *Given any (T-typed) graph G, any persistent DPO production* $p : (L \xleftarrow{l} K \xrightarrow{r} R)$*, and any valid match* $g : L \rightarrow G$*, the dangling arc condition is trivially satisfied.*

Lemma 3.2. *Given any (T-typed) graph G, any persistent SPO production* $q : L \rightarrowtail R$*, and any valid match* $g : L \rightarrow G$*, no side-effect is produced on G.*

The proofs of the above lemmas exploit just node persistence. A remarkable consequence of the above properties is that in the unfolding construction we can completely disregard the precedences between productions induced by the dangling arc condition.

A second motivation is that there is no resource that can be both read and consumed during a derivation: nodes and persistent arcs can be just produced once and then read; removable arcs can be produced (once) and removed (once) but never read. A remarkable consequence of this property is that the event structure associated to the unfolding does not impose inhibitor conditions between events.

Theorem 3.1. *The construction of the prime event structure associated to a persistent graph grammar is expressed by the chain of coreflections in Figure 3.*

The isomorphism between node preserving SPO grammars and node preserving DPO grammars (see end of § 2.2) makes the result independent from the approach, in the sense that the PES $\mathcal{E}_p(\mathcal{U}_p(\mathcal{G}))$ associated to a persistent SPO grammar $\mathcal{G}$ is isomorphic to the one associated with the corresponding persistent DPO grammar $D(\mathcal{G})$.

The proof of the main result (for SPO) is carried on along the lines of [4], but it is omitted because of space limitation. We are confident that the case studies in Sections 4 and 5 can be understood without looking at the details of our constructions. Proofs will be included in the full version of this work. We just remark that the unfolding functor ($\mathcal{U}_p$) and the event structure ($\mathcal{E}_p$) are just the restrictions to the domain of persistent

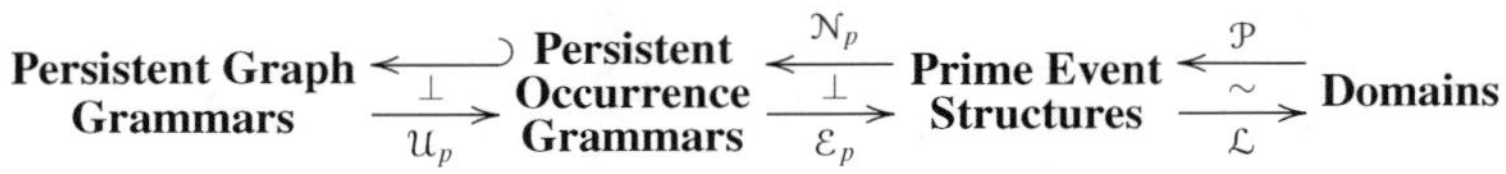

Fig. 3. True concurrent semantics of persistent graph grammars

$$P ::= 0 \mid \overline{x}\langle y\rangle \mid x(y).P \mid !x(y).P \mid (\nu x)P \mid P|P$$

(a) Syntax

$$P \mid 0 \equiv P \qquad P \mid Q \equiv P \mid Q \qquad (P \mid Q) \mid R \equiv P \mid (Q \mid R)$$
$$P \equiv Q \;\; if \; P \equiv_\alpha Q \qquad (\nu x)(\nu y)P \equiv (\nu y)(\nu x)P \qquad (\nu x)P \mid Q \equiv (\nu x)(P|Q) \;\; if \; x \notin fn(Q)$$

(b) Structural equivalence

$$(\text{SYNC}) \quad \overline{x}\langle y\rangle \mid x(z).P \to P\{^y/_z\} \qquad (!\text{SYNC}) \quad \overline{x}\langle y\rangle \mid !x(z).P \to P\{^y/_z\} \mid !x(z).P$$
$$(\text{PAR}) \quad P \to P' \Rightarrow P|Q \to P'|Q \qquad (\text{RES}) \quad P \to P' \Rightarrow (\nu x)P \to (\nu x)P'$$

(c) Reduction Semantics

Fig. 4. Syntax and reduction Semantics of the asynchronous *pi*-calculus

graph grammars of the functors already designed for (node preserving) graph grammars ($\mathcal{U}_s$ and $\mathcal{E}_s$). Moreover, asymmetric conflicts are due to ordinary mutual exclusion arguments (and causality) and thus the event structure associated to the unfolding is morally a PES (in disguise). Hence, the only adjunct that must be redefined is the one associating a (persistent) occurrence graph grammar to a PES, as otherwise the adjoint functor $\mathcal{N}_s$ would generate a node preserving, but non persistent occurrence graph grammar.

4 Event Structure Semantics for the π-Calculus

In this section we show the encoding of asynchronous π processes as persistent graph grammars and the construction of their event structure.

Given an infinite set of names $\mathcal{N}$ ranged over by $a, b, x, y, z, \ldots$, the *asynchronous π processes* over $\mathcal{N}$ are defined by the grammar in Figure 4(a). The reduction semantics is the least relation satisfying the rules in Figure 4(c) (modulo the structural congruence rules in Figure 4(b)). Free and bound names (written $fn(P)$ and $bn(P)$) are defined as usual. A process P is a *sequential agent* if it is either $\overline{x}\langle y\rangle$, $x(y).P$ or $!x(y).P'$.

For simplicity, we represent π processes as *hypergraphs* instead of graphs, like in [19]. A hyperarc can be connected to several nodes. Hence, any hyperarc has an ordered set of attachment points, which is represented by a sequence. As usual, $|s|$ stands for the length of the sequence s, and $s[i]$ for $0 < i \leq |s|$ refers to the ith element of s.

Definition 4.1 (Hypergraph). *A* (hyper)graph *is a triple $H = (N_H, E_H, \phi_H)$, where N_H is the set of nodes, E_H is the set of edges, and $\phi_H : E_H \to N_H^*$ describes the connections of the graph. We call $|\phi_H(e)|$ the* rank *of e and assume that $|\phi_H(e)| > 0$ for any e.*

Note that every hypergraph H can be straightforwardly encoded as a graph G, whose nodes are the nodes and arcs of H, and whose arcs connect the nodes corresponding to edges with the original nodes of H. Formally, $G = (N_H \cup E_H, E, s, t)$, where $E = \bigcup_{e \in E_H} \{e_1, \ldots, e_{|e|}\}$, $s(e_i) = e$ and $t(e_i) = \phi_H(e)[i]$ for all $e_i \in E$.

A process P corresponds to a hypergraph $H = (N_H, E_H, \phi_H)$, where nodes stand for the names used by P, and hyperarcs denote sequential agents of P. Given $e \in E_H$ denoting a sequential agent S, the definition of ϕ_H attaches e to the nodes corresponding to the free names $fn(S)$ of S. In particular, $|\phi(e)|$ is equal to the number of occurrences of free variables in S, and $\phi(e)[i] = n_x$ if n_x is the node associated to the variable x and the ith occurrence of a free name in S corresponds to x (we assume free names in S to be ordered in some fixed form, e.g., from left to right).

For simplicity, and w.l.o.g., we will consider a canonical form for processes in which all bound variables are different from each other. The canonical form of P is $can(P) = P'$ where $\{[P]\}_1 = P', n$ and $\{[\_]\}_n : P \to P \times \mathbb{N}$ is defined s.t. $\{[P]\}_n = P', n'$ iff P' is obtained by renaming (from the left to the right) all bound variables of P with consecutive natural numbers in the range $[n, n'-1]$. Moreover, we assume $fn(P) \cap \mathbb{N} = \emptyset$.

$$
\begin{array}{rll}
\{[0]\}_n = & 0, n & \\
\{[\overline{x}\langle y\rangle]\}_n = & \overline{x}\langle y\rangle, n & \\
\{[x(y).P]\}_n = & x(n).P', n' & where \{[P\{^n/_y\}]\}_{n+1} = P', n' \\
\{[(\nu x)P]\}_n = & (\nu n)P', n' & where \{[P\{^n/_x\}]\}_{n+1} = P', n' \\
\{[P_1 | P_2]\}_n = & P_1' \mid P_2', n' & where \{[P_1]\}_n = P_1', n'' \; and \; \{[P_2]\}_{n''} = P_2', n' \\
\{[!P]\}_n = & !P', n' & where \{[P]\}_n = P', n'
\end{array}
$$

We associate a type $\lfloor S \rfloor$ to any sequential agent S, defined as follows:

$$
\begin{array}{rll}
\lfloor \overline{x}\langle y\rangle \rfloor = & \overline{x}\langle \bullet \rangle & \\
\lfloor x(n).P \rfloor = & x(n).(P\{^\bullet/_{x_1}, \ldots, ^\bullet/_{x_n}\}) & where \; \{x_1, \ldots, x_n\} = fn(P) \backslash \{n\} \\
\lfloor !x(n).P \rfloor = & !x(n).(P\{^\bullet/_{x_1}, \ldots, ^\bullet/_{x_n}\}) & where \; \{x_1, \ldots, x_n\} = fn(P) \backslash \{n\}
\end{array}
$$

The special mark $\bullet$ denotes an occurrence of a free variable. We say $n+1$ the rank of $\lfloor S \rfloor$ with n the number of occurrences of $\bullet$ in $\lfloor S \rfloor$.

Example 4.1. Consider the following process $P = x(z).(\overline{z}\langle y\rangle \mid \overline{z}\langle y\rangle) \mid \overline{x}\langle y\rangle \mid \overline{x}\langle x\rangle$. Then $can(P) = x(1).(\overline{1}\langle y\rangle \mid \overline{1}\langle y\rangle) \mid \overline{x}\langle y\rangle \mid \overline{x}\langle x\rangle$. Moreover, the types of all sequential agents in P are $x(1).(\overline{1}\langle \bullet\rangle \mid \overline{1}\langle \bullet\rangle)$ and $\overline{x}\langle \bullet\rangle$.

Differently from the encoding of [19], sequential agents differing on their first free name have different types. For instance, here $P_1 = \overline{x}\langle z\rangle$, $P_2 = \overline{x}\langle x\rangle$ and $P_3 = \overline{z}\langle z\rangle$ are typed $\lfloor P_1 \rfloor = \lfloor P_2 \rfloor = \overline{x}\langle \bullet\rangle \neq \lfloor P_3 \rfloor = \overline{z}\langle \bullet\rangle$ (contrastingly to the original proposal that assigns the same type $\overline{\bullet}\langle \bullet\rangle$ to all of them). Our definition generates more productions, but it produces semi-weighted grammars in many more cases, as explained below.

Given a set A of agent types, the *type graph* associated with A is $T_A = \langle \{x\}, A, \phi_{T_A} \rangle$ s.t. for all t, $\phi_{T_A}(t) = s$, and $s[i] = x$ for $0 < i \leq |s| = rank(t)$. The set of T_A-typed hypergraphs we consider is the least set built using the following constants and operations.

- 0 is the empty graph $(\emptyset, \emptyset, \emptyset)$.
- x denotes the discrete graph $(\{x\}, \emptyset, \emptyset)$ containing the node x.
- $H_1 \oplus H_2 = (N_{H_1} \cup N_{H_2}, E_{H_1} + E_{H_2}, \phi)$ is the composition of H_1 and H_2 , where $+$ stands for the disjoint union of sets and ϕ is defined as follows

$$
\phi(e) = \phi_{H_1}(e) \quad if \; e \in E_{H_1}(e) \qquad\qquad \phi(e) = \phi_{H_2}(e) \quad if \; e \in E_{H_2}(e)
$$

- $H_1\{^y/x\}$ is the graph obtained by renaming the node x of H_1 by y, i.e., $H_1\{^y/x\} = ((N_{H_1} \setminus \{x\}) \cup \{y\}, E_{H_1}, \phi_H)$, where $\phi_H(e) = \phi_{H_1}(e)\{^y/_x\}$ for all $e \in E_{H_1}$.
- S s.t $\lfloor S \rfloor \in A$ is the graph whose nodes are the free names of S and its unique arc has type $\lfloor S \rfloor$, i.e., $H = (fn(S), \{\lfloor S \rfloor\}, \{\lfloor S \rfloor \mapsto s\})$, where $|s|$ is equal to the rank of $\lfloor S \rfloor$ and $s[i] = x$ if the ith occurrence of a free name in S is x.

In all cases, the typing morphisms map nodes to x and arcs to their type.

Remark 4.1. The graphs $H_1 = \overline{x}\langle y \rangle$ and $H_2 = \overline{k}\langle y \rangle\{^x/_k\}$ are different since they contain the same nodes $\{x, y\}$, but H_1 has a unique arc with type $\overline{x}\langle \bullet \rangle$, while the arc of H_2 has type $\overline{k}\langle \bullet \rangle$. Differently, $H_3 = \overline{x}\langle y \rangle$ and $H_4 = \overline{x}\langle k \rangle\{^x/_k\}$ are identical. In this case, we will use the first notation as an abbreviation for the second one.

The next definition provides the mapping from π processes to (hyper)graphs.

Definition 4.2. *Given a canonical π process P, its corresponding agent hypergraph is $H_P = unw(P)$, where unw is inductively defined as follows:*

$$unw(0) = 0 \qquad unw(\overline{x}\langle y \rangle) = \overline{x}\langle y \rangle \qquad unw(x(y).P) = x(y).P$$
$$unw(!x(y).P) = !x(y).P \quad unw((\nu x)P) = unw(P) \quad unw(P_1|P_2) = unw(P_1) \oplus unw(P_2)$$

Example 4.2. The agent hypergraph corresponding to the process P in Example 4.1 is $H_P = x(1).(\overline{1}\langle y \rangle \mid \overline{1}\langle y \rangle) \oplus \overline{x}\langle y \rangle \oplus \overline{x}\langle x \rangle$.

Then, the graph grammar corresponding to a particular process is defined as follows. We use $I \underset{C}{\rightarrow} O$ to denote rule patterns that can be instantiated by providing agent types.

Any instance is a production $q : L \overset{l}{\leftarrow} K \overset{r}{\rightarrow} R$ with $K = C \oplus n(I)$, $L = I$ and $R = O \oplus K$, with $n(I)$ being the nodes of I, and where the morphisms are the obvious inclusions.

Definition 4.3 (π process as a graph grammar). *The graph grammar corresponding to a π process P is $\mathcal{G}_P = \langle T, G_{in}, Q \rangle$, where T contains the types of all possible subagents of P, $G_{in} = H_P = unw(P)$ and productions $q \in Q$ are obtained by instantiating the two patterns below (where $\overline{k_1}\langle \bullet \rangle$,$k_2(y).P$ and $k_2(y).P$ are types of T and z is a fresh name) with the types of the subagents of P.*

$$\text{GRAPH-SYNC}: \quad \overline{k_1}\langle z \rangle\{^x/_{k_1}\} \oplus k_2(y).P\{^x/_{k_2}\} \longrightarrow unw(P)\{^x/_{k_2}\}\{^z/_y\}$$
$$\text{GRAPH-!SYNC}: \quad \overline{k_1}\langle z \rangle\{^x/_{k_1}\} \xrightarrow[!k_2(y).P\{^x/_{k_2}\}]{} unw(P)\{^x/_{k_2}\}\{^z/_y\}$$

The rewriting rules do not specify the actual name over which the communication takes place, but just that the output and the input action take place over the same node.

Example 4.3. Consider P defined in Example 4.1. The corresponding graph grammar $\mathcal{G}_P = \langle T, G_{in}, Q \rangle$ is defined as follows:

- T contains a unique node, and its arcs correspond to the different types of all the sequential agents occurring in P, i.e., $E_T = \{\overline{1}\langle \bullet \rangle, \overline{x}\langle \bullet \rangle, x(1).(\overline{1}\langle \bullet \rangle \mid \overline{1}\langle \bullet \rangle)\}$.
- $G_{in} = H_P = x(1).(\overline{1}\langle y \rangle \mid \overline{1}\langle y \rangle) \oplus \overline{x}\langle y \rangle \oplus \overline{x}\langle x \rangle$;

- $Q = \{p_1, p_2\}$, where:

$$p_1 : \overline{x}\langle z\rangle \oplus x(1).(\overline{1}\langle y\rangle \mid \overline{1}\langle y\rangle) \xleftarrow{l_1} x \oplus y \oplus z \xrightarrow{r_1} \overline{1}\langle y\rangle\{^z/_1\} \oplus \overline{1}\langle y\rangle\{^z/_1\} \oplus x$$

$$p_2 : \overline{1}\langle z\rangle\{^x/_1\} \oplus x(1).(\overline{1}\langle y\rangle \mid \overline{1}\langle y\rangle) \xleftarrow{l_2} x \oplus y \oplus z \xrightarrow{r_2} \overline{1}\langle y\rangle\{^z/_1\} \oplus \overline{1}\langle y\rangle\{^z/_1\} \oplus x$$

with l_1, l_2, r_1 and r_2 being inclusion morphisms.

By applying rule p_1, we can derive $G_{in} \Rightarrow_{p_1} \overline{1}\langle y\rangle\{^y/_1\} \oplus \overline{1}\langle y\rangle\{^y/_1\} \oplus \overline{x}\langle x\rangle$.

The evolution of any process P is described by a finite rewriting system (since the set of sequential agents contained in P is finite). Moreover, graph productions are persistent since all nodes are persistent and removable arcs do not appear in contexts. Nevertheless, the grammar may not be semi-weighted. In fact, the initial graph G_{in} in Example 4.3 is not injective (it contains two arcs with the same type $\overline{x}\langle\bullet\rangle$). Similarly, the targets of both productions are not injective (they have two arcs with type $\overline{1}\langle\bullet\rangle$). In what follows, we restrict our analysis to semi-weighted processes, i.e., processes that produce semi-weighted grammars. Semi-weighted processes disambiguate the production of identical elements having the same history. Hence, P can be written as

$$P' = x(1).(\overline{1}\langle y\rangle \mid (\nu 2)(2(3).\overline{1}\langle y\rangle|\overline{2}\langle 2\rangle)) \mid \overline{x}\langle y\rangle \mid (\nu 4)(4(5).\overline{x}\langle y\rangle|\overline{4}\langle 4\rangle)$$

where the production of identical elements with the same history is avoided by introducing an internal reduction. Note that the initial graph

$$G'_{in} = x(1).(\overline{1}\langle y\rangle \mid (\nu 2)(2(3).\overline{1}\langle y\rangle|\overline{2}\langle 2\rangle)) \oplus \overline{x}\langle y\rangle \oplus 4(5).\overline{x}\langle y\rangle \oplus \overline{4}\langle 4\rangle$$

is injective (arcs of graphs $\overline{x}\langle y\rangle$ and $\overline{4}\langle 4\rangle$ have different types). Similarly, the target of associated transitions are injective, and hence, the associated grammar is semi-weighted.

Remark 4.2. PGGs do not imply a severe limitation for encoding the π-calculus since (i) node and arc persistency have no influence, (ii) consuming rules have no effect when following a reduction approach, (iii) although semi-weighted rules prevent us from encoding processes having tokens with identical causal history, it is possible to encode any process as a PGGs by disambiguating identical tokens (for instance, by introducing internal reductions).

Example 4.4 (Event Structure). Consider the following asynchronous π process corresponding to the encoding of the synchronous process $\overline{x}\langle y\rangle.\overline{c}\langle c\rangle.0|x(z).\overline{b}\langle z\rangle.0$.

$$P = (\nu k)(\overline{x}\langle k\rangle|k(a).(\overline{a}\langle y\rangle|\overline{c}\langle c\rangle)) \mid x(k).(\nu a)(\overline{k}\langle a\rangle|a(z).\overline{b}\langle z\rangle)$$

After obtaining the canonical form of P by renaming all bound names by natural numbers, the initial graph of the corresponding grammar is

$$G_{in} = \overline{x}\langle 1\rangle \oplus 1(2).(\overline{2}\langle y\rangle|\overline{c}\langle c\rangle) \oplus x(3).(\overline{3}\langle 4\rangle|4(5).\overline{b}\langle 5\rangle)$$

The set of productions is obtained by instantiating the pattern rule for GRAPH-SYNC with all possible agent types: $\overline{x}\langle\bullet\rangle$, $1(2).(\overline{2}\langle\bullet\rangle|\overline{\bullet}\langle\bullet\rangle)$, $\overline{2}\langle\bullet\rangle$, $\overline{c}\langle\bullet\rangle$, $x(3).(\overline{3}\langle\bullet\rangle|\bullet(5).\overline{\bullet}\langle 5\rangle)$, $\overline{3}\langle\bullet\rangle$, $4(5).\overline{\bullet}\langle 5\rangle$, $\overline{b}\langle\bullet\rangle\}$. For instance, one possible instantiation is:

$$p_1 : \overline{x}\langle y\rangle \oplus (1(2).(\overline{2}\langle v\rangle|\overline{w}\langle z\rangle))\{^x/_1\} \xleftarrow{l_1} x \oplus y \oplus v \oplus w \oplus z \xrightarrow{r_1} \overline{2}\langle v\rangle\{^y/_2\} \oplus \overline{w}\langle z\rangle \oplus x$$

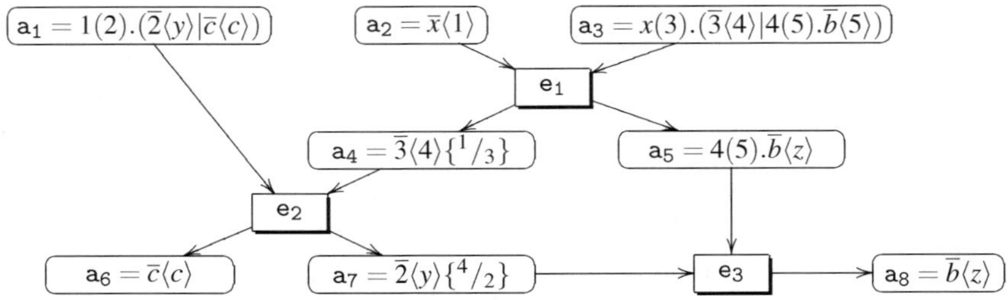

Fig. 5. Unfolding of the grammar corresponding to the π process P

The corresponding unfolding is in Figure 5. We use a net-like pictorial representation, where productions are shadow-shaped boxes connected to the consumed and produced resources by incoming and outcoming arrows respectively. For the sake of clarity, we omit the representation of graph nodes (i.e., names x and y) and edge attachments, since nodes are preserved by productions and they do not introduce additional dependencies to those shown in Figure 5. The minimal elements of the unfolding, i.e., a_1, a_2 and a_3, are the elements of G_{in}. Any event stands for the application of a production on a set of concurrent events. Note that a_6 and a_8 causally depend on $\mathsf{a}_1, \mathsf{a}_2$ and a_3. In particular, the output in a_6 causally depends on the input action in a_3, even though a_1 and a_3 share no names.

5 Event Structure Semantics for Join-Calculus

As done for the π calculus, we provide the event structure semantics of join processes through its mapping to persistent graph grammars. For simplicity, we focus on *core (recursive) join-calculus* [13], but our approach smoothly extends to full join.

The syntax of core Join is in Figure 6(a). The occurrences of x and u in $x\langle u\rangle$ are *free*, while x and y occur bound in $P = \textbf{def}\ x\langle u\rangle|y\langle v\rangle \rhd P_1\ \textbf{in}\ P_2$, and u and v occur bound in $x\langle u\rangle|y\langle v\rangle \rhd P_1$. Free and bound names of P are written respectively $fn(P)$ and $bn(P)$.

The semantics of the join calculus relies on the *reflexive chemical abstract machine* model [13]. In this model a solution is a multiset of active definitions and processes (separated by comma). New definitions may become active dynamically. Moves are distinguished between *structural* $\equiv$, which heat or cool processes, and reductions $\rightarrow$, which are the basic computational steps (disjoint reductions can be executed in parallel). The rewriting rules are shown in Figure 6(b).

As done for π processes, we only consider canonical processes. The canonical form of P is $can(P) = P'$ for $\{[P]\}_1 = P', n$ and

$$\begin{aligned}
\{[x\langle u\rangle]\}_n &= \overline{x}\langle u\rangle, n\\
\{[P_1|P_1]\}_n &= P_1' \mid P_2', n' \ \textit{where} \{[P_1]\}_n = P_1', n'' \ \textit{and}\ \{[P_2]\}_{n''} = P_2', n'\\
\{[\textbf{def}\ x\langle u\rangle|y\langle v\rangle \rhd P_1\ \textbf{in}\ P_2]\}_n &= \textbf{def}\ n\langle n+1\rangle|n+2\langle n+3\rangle \rhd P_1'\ \textbf{in}\ P_2', n'\\
&\quad \textit{where}\ \{[P_1\{{}^{n}/_{x}, {}^{n+1}/_{u}, {}^{n+2}/_{y}, {}^{n+3}/_{v}\}]\}_{n+4} = P_1', n''\\
&\quad \textit{and}\ \{[P_2\{{}^{n}/_{x}, {}^{n+2}/_{y}\}]\}_{n''} = P_2', n'
\end{aligned}$$

$$P = x\langle u\rangle \mid P|P \mid \textbf{def}\ x\langle u\rangle|y\langle v\rangle \triangleright P\ \textbf{in}\ P$$

(a) Syntax

$$P\,|\,Q \equiv P\,,\,Q$$
$$\textbf{def}\ x\langle u\rangle|y\langle v\rangle \triangleright P_1\ \textbf{in}\ P_2 \equiv (x\langle u\rangle|y\langle v\rangle \triangleright P_1)\sigma\,,\,P_2\sigma$$
$(\sigma$ *renames x and y with globally fresh names*$)$
$$x\langle u\rangle|y\langle v\rangle \triangleright P,\ x\langle z_1\rangle,\ y\langle z_2\rangle \rightarrow x\langle u\rangle|y\langle v\rangle \triangleright P,\ P\{^{z_1}/_x, {}^{z_2}/_y\}$$

(b) Semantics

Fig. 6. Core Join

By analogy with π, we consider subterms $x\langle u\rangle$ and $x\langle u\rangle|y\langle v\rangle \triangleright P$ as sequential agents. Then, the type $\lfloor S \rfloor$ of a sequential agent S is defined as follows:

$$\lfloor \overline{x}\langle y\rangle \rfloor = \overline{x}\langle\bullet\rangle$$
$$\lfloor x\langle u\rangle|y\langle v\rangle \triangleright P\rfloor = x\langle u\rangle|y\langle v\rangle \triangleright (P\{^{\bullet}/_{x_1},\ldots,{}^{\bullet}/_{x_n}\})\ \textit{where}\ \{x_1,\ldots,x_n\} = fn(P)\backslash\{u,v\}$$

The mapping of processes to graph grammar is defined below.

Definition 5.1. *Given a canonical join process P, its corresponding hypergraph is* $H_P = unw(P)$*, where unw is inductively defined as follows:*

$$unw(x\langle u\rangle) = x\langle u\rangle$$
$$unw(\textbf{def}\ x\langle u\rangle|y\langle v\rangle \triangleright P_1\ \textbf{in}\ P_2) = x\langle u\rangle|y\langle v\rangle \triangleright P_1 \oplus unw(P_2)$$
$$unw(P_1|P_2) = unw(P_1) \oplus unw(P_2)$$

Definition 5.2 (Join process as a graph grammar). *The graph grammar* $\mathcal{G}_P$ *corresponding to the join process P is* $\mathcal{G}_P = \langle T, G_{in}, Q\rangle$*, where T contains the types of all the subagents of P,* $G_{in} = H_P = unw(P)$ *and productions* $q \in Q$ *are obtained by instantiating the following pattern with the types in T.*

$$\overline{k_1}\langle u\rangle\{^x/_{k_1}\} \oplus \overline{k_2}\langle v\rangle\{^y/_{k_2}\} \xrightarrow[(k_3\langle u_1\rangle|k_4\langle v_1\rangle\triangleright P)\{^x/_{k_3},{}^y/_{k_4}\}]{} unw(P)\{^x/_{k_3},{}^y/_{k_4}\}\{^u/_{u_1},{}^v/_{v_1}\}$$

Example 5.1. Consider the canonical join process $P = \textbf{def}\ D\ \textbf{in}\ 1\langle 3\rangle \mid 3\langle 1\rangle$, with $D = 1\langle 2\rangle|3\langle 4\rangle \triangleright 4\langle 3\rangle|3\langle 1\rangle$. Then, the initial graph of the grammar is

$$G_{in} = H_P = D \oplus 1\langle 3\rangle \oplus 3\langle 1\rangle$$

and the types $\{1\langle 2\rangle|3\langle 4\rangle \triangleright 4\langle\bullet\rangle|\bullet\langle\bullet\rangle,\ 1\langle\bullet\rangle,\ 3\langle\bullet\rangle,\ 4\langle\bullet\rangle\}$. Hence, we have nine possible rules p_{k_1,k_2}, one for any possible combination of $k_1,k_2 \in 1,3,4$, defined as follows

$$D\{^x/_1,{}^y/_3\} \oplus \overline{k_1}\langle u\rangle\{^x/_{k_1}\} \oplus \overline{k_2}\langle v\rangle\{^y/_{k_2}\} \xleftarrow{l_1} D\{^x/_1,{}^y/_3\} \oplus u \oplus v$$
$$\xrightarrow{r_1} D\{^x/_1,{}^y/_3\} \oplus \overline{4}\langle y\rangle\{^v/_4\} \oplus \overline{3}\langle 1\rangle\{^x/_1,{}^y/_3\} \oplus u$$

Then, we have the following computation

$$G_{in} \Rightarrow_{p_{1,3}} D \oplus 4\langle 3\rangle\{^1/_4\} \oplus 3\langle 1\rangle \Rightarrow_{p_{4,3}} D \oplus 4\langle 3\rangle\{^1/_4\} \oplus 3\langle 1\rangle$$

The unfolding of $\mathcal{G}_P$ can be obtained as for π processes. In this case, the causal relation of the event structure is the total order $\mathsf{e}_1 \prec \mathsf{e}_2, \ldots$, while the $\# = \emptyset$ and $\mathbf{co} = \emptyset$.

6 Related Works and Concluding Remarks

We have introduced Persistent Graph Grammars (PGGs) as a convenient model for equipping nominal calculi with truly concurrent semantics. Our results collect, so to say, the best of two worlds: the event structure semantics is defined by a chain of coreflections as in [4] and the encoding of nominal calculi is rather direct as in [19]

We improve on [4] by restricting the format of productions so as to guarantee that there is no information loss when viewing the asymmetric event structure associated to the grammar as a PES. The restricted format considerably simplifies the construction w.r.t. fully general grammars. We improve on [19] by refining the type system so as to apply the unfolding construction to a much broader class of π-processes that comprises all those processes whose associated productions are semi-weighted. The generality of our technique is also supported by the original case study of join calculus.

Being a special case of semi-weighted grammars, PGGs enjoys the nice property of reconciling the SPO with the DPO approach. Note that two other event structure semantics proposed in the literature for DPO [8,22] coincide with the one obtained from the unfolding, which thus can be called *the* event structure semantics of GTS.

We exploit a "hierarchical" encoding of sequential processes, as opposed to the "flat" (DPO) encodings of [14,15], where finitely many productions encode all (finite) agents and where node fusion is requested in the right-hand side of some productions. The latter feature prevented the straightforward reuse of some techniques, although [5] develops a non-sequential semantics also in the presence of node fusion.

Due to space limitation we leave the comparison with previous non-interleaving semantics of the π-calculus [11,6] to the full version of this paper. The linearity constraint in [23] shares some similarities with the semi-weightedness criterion and it would be interesting to see if their type systems can be transferred to graph grammar productions.

Acknowledgement. We warmfully thank Paolo Baldan for his guidance and support during the writing of the paper. We also thank the referees for their careful revisions.

References

1. P. Baldan. *Modelling concurrent computations: from contextual Petri nets to graph grammars*. PhD thesis, University of Pisa, 2000.
2. P. Baldan, A. Corradini, and B. König. Verifying Finite-State Graph Grammars: An Unfolding-Based Approach. *Proc. CONCUR'04, LNCS* 3170, pp. 83–98. Springer, 2004.
3. P. Baldan, A. Corradini, and U. Montanari. Contextual Petri nets, asymmetric event structures and processes. *Inform. and Comput.*, 171(1):1–49, 2001.
4. P. Baldan, A. Corradini, U. Montanari, and L. Ribeiro. Concurrency and Nondeterminism in Graph Rewriting: From Graph Grammars to Asymmetric Event Structures and Backwards. *Technical Report CS-2005-2*, University Ca' Foscari of Venice, 2005.
5. P. Baldan, F. Gadducci, and U. Montanari. Concurrent Semantics for Graph Rewriting with Fusions. *Proc. CONCUR'06*. This volume.
6. M. Boreale and D. Sangiorgi. A fully abstract semantics for causality in the pi-calculus. *Acta Informatica*, 35(3):353–400, 1998.
7. A. Corradini, H. Ehrig, M. Löwe, U. Montanari, and J. Padberg. The category of typed graph grammars and its adjunctions with categories of derivations. *Proc. TAGT'94, LNCS* 1073, pp. 56–74. Springer, 1996.

8. A. Corradini, H. Ehrig, M. Löwe, U. Montanari, F. Rossi. An event structure semantics for graph grammars with parallel productions. *Proc. TAGT'94, LNCS* 1073, pp.240–256, 1996.
9. A. Corradini, U. Montanari, and F. Rossi. Graph processes. *Fund. Inf.*, 26:241–265, 1996.
10. A. Corradini, U. Montanari, F. Rossi, H. Ehrig, R. Heckel, and M. Löwe. Algebraic approaches to graph transformation I: Basic concepts and double pushout approach. In [21].
11. P. Degano and C. Priami. Non-interleaving semantics for mobile processes. *Theoret. Comput. Sci.*, 216(1-2):237–270, 1999.
12. H. Ehrig, R. Heckel, M. Korff, M. Löwe, L. Ribeiro, A. Wagner, A. Corradini. Algebraic approaches to graph transformation II: SPO approach and comparison with DPO. In [21].
13. C. Fournet and G. Gonthier. The reflexive chemical abstract machine and the Join calculus. In *Proc. POPL'96*, pp. 372–385. ACM Press, 1996.
14. F. Gadducci. Term Graph Rewriting for the phi-Calculus. In *Proc. APLAS'03, LNCS* 2895, pp. 37–54. Springer, 2003.
15. F. Gadducci and U. Montanari. A Concurrent Graph Semantics for Mobile Ambients. In *Proc. MFPS'01, ENTCS* 45. Elsevier, 2001.
16. U. Golz and W. Reisig. The non-sequential behaviour of Petri nets. *Information and Control*, 57:125–147, 1983.
17. M. Löwe. Algebraic approach to single-pushout graph transformation. *Theoret. Comput. Sci.*, 109:181–224, 1993.
18. J. Meseguer, U. Montanari, and V. Sassone. On the semantics of Place/Transition Petri nets. *Mathematical Structures in Computer Science*, 7:359–397, 1997.
19. U. Montanari and M. Pistore. Concurent semantics for the π-calculus. *ENTCS* 1. 1995.
20. M. Nielsen, G. Plotkin, and G. Winskel. Petri Nets, Event Structures and Domains, Part 1. *Theoret. Comput. Sci.*, 13:85–108, 1981.
21. Grzegorz Rozenberg, editor. *Handbook of Graph Grammars and Computing by Graph Transformation. Vol. 1: Foundations.* World Scientific, 1997.
22. G. Schied. On relating Rewriting Systems and Graph Grammars to Event Structures. *Proc. Graph Transformations in Computer Science, LNCS* 776, pp. 326–340. Springer, 1994.
23. D. Varacca and N. Yoshida. Typed event Structures and the π-calculus. In *Proc. MFPS'06.*
24. G. Winskel. Event Structures. *Advances in Petri Nets'86, LNCS* 255, pp. 325–392. 1987.

Encoding $\mathbb{C}$Duce in the $\mathbb{C}\pi$-Calculus*

Giuseppe Castagna[1], Mariangiola Dezani-Ciancaglini[2], and Daniele Varacca[3]

[1] École Normale Supérieure de Paris
[2] Universitá di Torino
[3] Imperial College London

Abstract. We present a type faithful encoding of $\mathbb{C}$Duce into the $\mathbb{C}\pi$-calculus. These calculi are two variants of, respectively, the λ-calculus and the π-calculus, characterised by rich typing and subtyping systems with union, negation, and intersection types.

The encoding is interesting because it sheds new light on the Milner-Turner encoding, on the relations between sequential and remote execution of functions/services, and on the validity of the equational laws for union and intersection types in π-calculus.

1 Introduction and Motivations

The language $\mathbb{C}$Duce [11,10] is a functional programming language for XML documents manipulation, with a very rich type system. Types and subtyping play a central role in $\mathbb{C}$Duce: for its design (patterns and pattern matching are built around types), for its execution (functions can be overloaded with run-time code selection), and for its implementation (pattern matching compilation and query computation use static type information to optimise execution). All these multifarious usages of types rely on a common foundational core: the *semantic subtyping* framework. An introduction to semantic subtyping can be found in [8], while [5] discusses several aspects and perspectives; technical details are given in [11,10]. In a nutshell, given a typed language with some (possibly recursive) type constructors (e.g., $\rightarrow$, $\times$, `list()`, ...), semantic subtyping is a technique to enrich the language with *type combinators*, i.e. set-theoretic union, intersection, and negation types. The behaviour of combinators is specified via the subtyping relation (rather than via the typing of the terms). The subtyping relation is "semantic" since instead of axiomatising it by a set of inference rules, one describes a set-theoretic interpretation of the types $[\![\ ]\!] : \mathbf{Types} \rightarrow \mathscr{P}(\mathscr{D})$ (where $\mathscr{P}$ denotes the powerset operator and $\mathscr{D}$ some domain) and then defines the subtyping relation as $s \leq t \stackrel{\text{def}}{\iff} [\![s]\!] \subseteq [\![t]\!]$. Such a set-theoretic interpretation must satisfy at least three design goals.

1. It must ensure that type *combinators* have a set-theoretic interpretation. This is done by imposing that union, intersection, and negation types are respectively interpreted as the set-theoretic union, intersection, and complement operations of $\mathscr{P}(\mathscr{D})$.
2. It must ensure that type *constructors* have a "natural" interpretation (at least, for what concerns subtyping), e.g., that product types are interpreted as set-theoretic products, function types as sets of maps from domain to co-domain, and so on.

* Work partially supported by FP6-2004-510996 Coordination Action TYPES, Cofin'04 project McTafi, Tralala ACI project, EPSRC grant GR/T04724/01 "Program Analysis and the Typed Pi-Calculus", and by an ENS visiting professorship grant for Mariangiola Dezani.

C. Baier and H. Hermanns (Eds.): CONCUR 2006, LNCS 4137, pp. 310–326, 2006.

3. It must allow for an interpretation of types as sets of values. This means that if we take as $\mathscr{D}$ the set of values of the language and as interpretation the function that maps a type to the set of all values of that type, then this new interpretation must induce the very same subtyping relation as the one used to type values.

Finding a domain $\mathscr{D}$ and an interpretation function $[\![-]\!]$ that satisfy the last two points is far from being trivial: a set-theoretic interpretation of functional and recursive types or the circularity between the typing of values and definition of subtyping are difficult constraints. As described in [8] and outlined later on, semantic subtyping provides a technique to do so.

In [6] the $\mathbb{C}\pi$-calculus is devised. $\mathbb{C}\pi$ is a type system for the π-calculus which exploits the same principles as $\mathbb{C}$Duce to enrich Pierce and Sangiorgi's types [16] with (set-theoretic) unions, intersections, and negations. In the cited paper, a higher-order extension of the $\mathbb{C}\pi$-calculus with functional values is discussed. However the question arises whether the extension is necessary or whether it is possible to encode functions as processes. It is well known that several such encodings are possible from the λ-calculus into the π-calculus [15,17,18]. In the Join-calculus language [9], the functional part is simply syntactic sugar for its coding in the concurrent part.

Contributions. In this paper we describe an encoding of $\mathbb{C}$Duce into the $\mathbb{C}\pi$-calculus. The encoding turned out not to be so straightforward as one may expect. The difficulty arises in finding an encoding of the types that respects the subtyping relation. The Milner-Turner translation of arrow types [17] respects the subtyping relation in the context of the simply typed λ-calculus, but it breaks down in the presence of intersection types.

Strictly speaking the technical contribution of this paper is twofold: first it introduces the local $\mathbb{C}\pi$-calculus, a variant of the $\mathbb{C}\pi$-calculus that admits unrestricted recursion on types, a feature not allowed in the version of the calculus presented in [6]; secondly it defines an encoding of $\mathbb{C}$Duce (hence, of intersection, union, and negation types) into local $\mathbb{C}\pi$ that preserves the typing and subtyping relations as well as the reduction semantics.

But beyond these technicalities, or actually hidden right in the technical details, there lies the main interest of this work. As we detail in Sections 4 and 5, the translation sheds new light on the Milner-Turner encoding as it shows the respective roles of argument and return channel that are used to simulate functions in a concurrent world. In particular, it shows that in the presence of type-case constructions, the latter must be scrambled by introducing some noise at the type level so that the receiver cannot gain information by testing the type of the return channel. The translation is a further confirmation of the validity of the equational laws for union and intersection types in the π-calculus, since a different axiomatisation proposed in the literature is incompatible with the Milner-Turner technique. This is not the only contribution to the type theory of the π-calculus, since the encoding also outlines the different roles played by the two contra-variant constructors of $\mathbb{C}\pi$, namely input channel and negation, and shows how they interplay when considering them from a logical point of view. Finally, at term level the translation formalises the nice correspondence between functional pattern matching and π-calculus guarded sums on a same input channel.

Structure. In Section 2 we present the local variant of the $\mathbb{C}\pi$-calculus. In Section 3 we present the functional core of $\mathbb{C}$Duce. Section 4 is devoted to explaining the main difficulties we encountered when encoding $\mathbb{C}$Duce types into $\mathbb{C}\pi$ types. Section 5 contains the formalisation of the encoding of the language, while Section 6 presents the correctness results. In Section 7 we conclude by giving some insight on more general aspects of this work and trying to convey the intuition of why we believe that the main contribution lies well beyond the technical result we present. For lack of space some definitions and all proofs are omitted; the interested reader can find them in [7].

2 The $\mathbb{C}\pi$-Calculus

The $\mathbb{C}\pi$-calculus is a variant of the asynchronous π-calculus with pattern matching in input and rich typing and subtyping systems [6]. We introduce here a further simplification of the calculus, following ideas of the Join calculus [9] and of the local π-calculus [14]. The key idea is that if a process is communicated a channel, then it cannot use that channel in input. Only global channels already known to the process or newly generated channels can be used in input. This policy is enforced syntactically, even before processes are typed. In the typing system, this implies that input channel types are no longer necessary. The consequent subtyping relation is much easier to decide and, unlike the system for full $\mathbb{C}\pi$-calculus, can be also extended to recursive types.

2.1 Types and Subtyping

A type is coinductively defined by applying *type constructors*, namely base type constructors (e.g. integers, strings, etc...), the channel or product type constructors, or by applying a *boolean combinator*, i.e., union, intersection, and negation. More formally, types are regular trees generated by the following grammar

$$
\begin{array}{llll}
\mathbb{C}\pi\ \textit{Types} & t ::= & \mathbf{b} \mid ch^{-}(t) \mid t\times t & \text{constructors} \\
 & & \mid\ \mathbf{0} \mid \mathbf{1} \mid \neg t \mid t\vee t \mid t\wedge t & \text{combinators}
\end{array}
$$

and that are contractive, that is for which on every infinite branch of the tree there are infinitely many occurrences of constructors. Combinators are self-explaining, with $\mathbf{0}$ being the empty type and $\mathbf{1}$ the type of all values. We use $\mathbf{b}$ to range over base types. The channel type constructor $ch^{-}(t)$ denotes the type of channels that can be used to *output* values of type t. The set of all types (sometimes referred to as "type algebra") will be denoted by $\mathscr{T}$. Contractivity ensures, as usual, the absence of meaningless recursively defined types such as $t = \neg t$. The subtyping relation is defined semantically. This means that we first give a set-theoretical interpretation of types $[\![-]\!] : \mathscr{T} \to \mathscr{P}(\mathscr{D})$, for some domain $\mathscr{D}$, and then define subtyping as inclusion of the interpretations: $s \leq t \stackrel{\text{def}}{\iff} [\![s]\!] \subseteq [\![t]\!]$. It is out of the scope of this work to precisely define $\mathscr{D}$ or the interpretation $[\![-]\!]$ (see [6] for details). All we need for this work is to precisely define the subtyping relation these definitions entail. This is *completely* characterised by the subtyping relation on the basic types and by the following property:

$$[\![s]\!] \subseteq [\![t]\!] \iff \mathbb{E}(s) \subseteq \mathbb{E}(t) \tag{1}$$

where $\mathbb{E}(-)$ is defined as follows

Definition 2.1 (Extensional interpretation). *The* extensional interpretation *of the types is the function* $\mathbb{E}(-) : \mathscr{T} \to \mathscr{P}(\mathscr{D} + \mathscr{D}\times\mathscr{D} + \mathscr{P}(\mathscr{D}))$*, defined as follows:*

a. $\mathbb{E}(\mathbf{1}) = \mathscr{D} + \mathscr{D}\times\mathscr{D} + \mathscr{P}(\mathscr{D})$, $\mathbb{E}(\mathbf{0}) = \varnothing$, $\mathbb{E}(\mathbf{b}) = [\![\mathbf{b}]\!]$;

b. $\mathbb{E}(t_1 \vee t_2) = \mathbb{E}(t_1) \cup \mathbb{E}(t_2)$, $\mathbb{E}(t_1 \wedge t_2) = \mathbb{E}(t_1) \cap \mathbb{E}(t_2)$, $\mathbb{E}(\neg t) = \mathbb{E}(\mathbf{1}) \setminus \mathbb{E}(t)$;

c. $\mathbb{E}(t_1 \times t_2) = [\![t_1]\!] \times [\![t_2]\!]$;

d. $\mathbb{E}(ch^{-}(t)) = \{[\![s]\!] \mid [\![s]\!] \supseteq [\![t]\!]\}$.

The intuition underlying property (1) is that, *for what concerns subtyping*, we can consider that $[\![t]\!]$, i.e. the semantics of t, is precisely $\mathbb{E}(t)$. Thus in Definition 2.1, (b.) states that the type combinators are interpreted as the corresponding set operations and (c.) that the product type is interpreted as set-theoretic product. Point (d.) gives us the semantics of channels. Intuitively, if a type denotes the set of all values with that type, then the type $ch^{-}(t)$ denotes the set of all channels in which one can safely put objects of type t. Therefore it will denote all channels that can contain objects of type s, for any $s \geq t$. Let us write c^t for a channel named c and transporting objects of type t. We have $[\![ch^{-}(t)]\!] = \{c^s \mid s \geq t\}$. The derived subtyping relation is insensitive to the actual number of channels of a given type or to their names. We can therefore assume that for every equivalence class of types, there is only one such channel, which may as well be identified with $[\![t]\!]$, so that the intended semantics of channel types would be

$$[\![ch^{-}(t)]\!] = \Big\{[\![s]\!] \mid s \geq t\Big\} \tag{2}$$

which by definition of subtyping gives point (d.) of the previous definition. The subtyping relation of the local $\mathbb{C}\pi$-calculus is decidable and the decision algorithm is much simpler than the one for the full $\mathbb{C}\pi$-calculus presented in [6].

In order to stress that property (1) and Definition 2.1 completely define the subtyping relation, let us show as an example how to deduce the contra-variance of the output type channel constructor: $ch^{-}(s) \leq ch^{-}(t) \Leftrightarrow [\![ch^{-}(s)]\!] \subseteq [\![ch^{-}(t)]\!] \Leftrightarrow \mathbb{E}(ch^{-}(s)) \subseteq \mathbb{E}(ch^{-}(t)) \Leftrightarrow \{[\![u]\!] \mid [\![u]\!] \supseteq [\![s]\!]\} \subseteq \{[\![u]\!] \mid [\![u]\!] \supseteq [\![t]\!]\} \Leftrightarrow [\![t]\!] \subseteq [\![s]\!] \Leftrightarrow t \leq s$.

Similarly we can derive interesting equations and inequations between types. For instance, $ch^{-}(t) \leq ch^{-}(\mathbf{0})$ is a special case of the contra-variance we just derived. It states that every channel c can be safely used in a process that does not write on c. If we define $s = t \overset{\text{def}}{\Longleftrightarrow} [\![s]\!] = [\![t]\!]$, then we have

$$ch^{-}(t_1) \wedge ch^{-}(t_2) = ch^{-}(t_1 \vee t_2) \tag{3}$$

which states that if on a channel we can write values of type t_1 and values of type t_2, then we can also write values of type $t_1 \vee t_2$, and vice versa. Union of channel types behaves differently since the inequation below is strict (see [6] for a discussion on this)

$$ch^{-}(t_1) \vee ch^{-}(t_2) \lneq ch^{-}(t_1 \wedge t_2)\ .$$

2.2 Patterns

Both $\mathbb{C}\pi$ and $\mathbb{C}$Duce feature powerful pattern matching. Patterns perform type-cases, decompose values by capturing subcomponents in variables, and can be recursive.

Definition 2.2. *Given a type algebra $\mathscr{T}$, and a set of variables $\mathbb{V}$, a* pattern *p on $(\mathbb{V},\mathscr{T})$ is a regular tree generated by the following grammar*

$$p ::= x \mid t \mid p \wedge p \mid p|p \mid (p,p)$$

such that (i) on every infinite branch of p there are infinitely many occurrences of the pair pattern, (ii) for every subterm $p_1 \wedge p_2$ of p we have $Var(p_1) \cap Var(p_2) = \varnothing$, and (iii) for every subterm $p_1|p_2$ of p we have $Var(p_1) = Var(p_2)$ (where $x \in \mathbb{V}$, $t \in \mathscr{T}$, and $Var(p)$ is the set of variables occurring in p).

The semantics of patterns is given in terms of a matching operation that returns either a substitution for the variables of the pattern or a failure denoted by Ω. Matching can be defined independently from the language, via the domain $\mathscr{D}$ of a model of types. We use d/p to denote the matching of the element d against the pattern p. Intuitively, x is the pattern that always succeeds and captures the matched element in x (i.e., d/x returns the substitution $\{x \mapsto d\}$); t succeeds if the element is in the interpretation of t, in which case it returns the empty substitution; the intersection succeeds only if both patterns succeed and it returns the union of the substitutions; the alternation follows a first-match policy by applying the pattern on the right only if the one on the left failed; the pair decomposes the element and applies the patterns to the respective sub-components. See [6] for the formal definition. It can be shown that the set of all elements for which a pattern p does not fail is the denotation of a type. We denote this type by $(\!| p |\!)$, that is by definition $[\![(\!| p |\!)]\!] = \{d \mid d/p \neq \Omega\}$. Matching can be extended to types as stated by the following theorem:

Theorem 2.3 (A.5 in [11]). *There is an algorithm mapping every pair (t,p), where p is a pattern and t a type such that $t \leq (\!| p |\!)$, to a type environment $(t/p) \in \mathscr{T}^{Var(p)}$ such that $[\![(t/p)(x)]\!] = \{(d/p)(x) \mid d \in [\![t]\!]\}$.*

2.3 The Language

The syntax of $\mathbb{C}\pi$ is similar to that of the asynchronous π-calculus [3,13], extended with call-by-value pattern matching (obtained by pattern-guarded sums of inputs on the same channel) and an extra condition which guarantees "locality" [14].

Processes $P ::=$	$\overline{\alpha}M$	output	*Channels* $\alpha ::=$	x	variables
$\mid$	$\Sigma_{i\in I} c^t(p_i).P_i$	patterned input	$\mid$	c^t	constant
$\mid$	$P \parallel P$	parallel			
$\mid$	$(\nu c^t)P$	restriction	*Messages* $M ::=$	n	constants
$\mid$	$!P$	replication	$\mid$	α	channel
			$\mid$	(M,M)	pair

where I is a possibly empty finite set of indexes, t ranges over the types defined in Section 2.1 and p_i are patterns as defined in Definition 2.2. As customary, empty sum corresponds to the inert process, denoted by $\mathsf{0}$. The *values* of the language are the closed messages $v ::= n \mid c^t \mid (v,v)$. We use $\mathscr{V}$ to denote the set of all values.

Observe that we force input to happen on channel constants. This ensures that channels sent by other processes cannot be used in input. Output instead can be performed on non-constant channels, too. Since pattern matching performs type-case, we must define the typing of messages before the reduction semantics, see Figure 1. We suppose

Messages

$$\frac{}{\Gamma \vdash n : \mathbf{b}_n}\ (\text{const}) \qquad \frac{s_i \not\leq t}{\Gamma \vdash c^t : \mathit{ch}^{-}(t) \wedge \neg \mathit{ch}^{-}(s_1) \wedge \ldots \wedge \neg \mathit{ch}^{-}(s_n)}\ (\text{chan})$$

$$\frac{}{\Gamma \vdash x : \Gamma(x)}\ (\text{var}) \qquad \frac{\Gamma \vdash M : s \leq t}{\Gamma \vdash M : t}\ (\text{subs}) \qquad \frac{\Gamma \vdash M_1 : t_1,\ \Gamma \vdash M_2 : t_2}{\Gamma \vdash (M_1, M_2) : t_1 \times t_2}\ (\text{pair})$$

Processes

$$\frac{\Gamma \vdash P}{\Gamma \vdash (\nu c^t)P}\ (\text{new}) \qquad \frac{\Gamma \vdash P}{\Gamma \vdash !P}\ (\text{repl}) \qquad \frac{\Gamma \vdash P_1 \quad \Gamma \vdash P_2}{\Gamma \vdash P_1 \| P_2}\ (\text{para})$$

$$\frac{t \leq \bigvee_{i\in I} \langle\!| p_i |\!\rangle \quad \Gamma, (t \wedge \langle\!| p_i |\!\rangle)/p_i \vdash P_i}{\Gamma \vdash \sum_{i\in I} c^t(p_i).P_i}\ (\text{input}) \qquad \frac{\Gamma \vdash M : t \quad \Gamma \vdash \alpha : \mathit{ch}^{-}(t)}{\Gamma \vdash \overline{\alpha} M}\ (\text{output})$$

Fig. 1. ℂπ typing rules

that every basic constant n is associated to an atomic basic type $\mathbf{b}_n$. The rules, and in particular rule (chan), are designed so that we can interpret a type as the set of all values of that type. The interpretation $[\![\ ]\!]_{\mathscr{V}} : \mathscr{T} \to \mathscr{P}(\mathscr{V})$ defined as

$$[\![t]\!]_{\mathscr{V}} = \{v \mid \varnothing \vdash v : t\} \tag{4}$$

satisfies property (1) and, furthermore, it generates the same subtyping relation as $\leq$.[1]

Then, the definition for pattern matching given in Section 2.2 applies for v being a value and we can use it to define the reduction semantics of ℂπ:

$$\overline{c^t} v \ \| \ \sum_{i\in I} c^t(p_i).P_i \quad \longrightarrow \quad P_j[v/p_j]$$

where $P[\mathbf{s}]$ denotes the application of substitution $\mathbf{s}$ to process P. The asynchronous output of a *value* on the channel c^t synchronises with a summand in a sum guarded by the same channel, only if the pattern of the summand matches the communicated value (the type system ensures the existence of such a pattern). If more than one pattern matches, then one of them is non-deterministically chosen and the corresponding process executed, but before its execution the pattern variables are replaced by the captured values. As usual, the notion of reduction must be completed with reductions in evaluation contexts and up to structural congruence, whose definitions are standard and can be found in [6]. We use $\longrightarrow^*$ to denote the reflexive and transitive closure of $\longrightarrow$.

The typing of processes is defined in the lower half of Figure 1. Notice that the rule for restrictions (new) does not rely on the type environment Γ, since channels are decorated by the type of their messages, and that in the rule (input) the condition $t \leq \bigvee_{i\in I} \langle\!| p_i |\!\rangle$ ensures that for every message that may arrive on the channel, there exists at least one pattern that matches it. The system satisfies subject reduction [6].

[1] Without the intersection of the negated channel types in (chan), we could not prove that, say, $c^{\mathtt{int}} : \neg \mathit{ch}^{-}(\mathtt{bool})$. More generally, the property $\vdash v : t \Leftrightarrow \not\vdash v : \neg t$ would not hold, and this is necessary to $[\![-]\!]_{\mathscr{V}}$ to satisfy (1): cf. Definition 2.1(b). For a broader discussion on such inference rules with negated types see Section 4.6 of [5].

3 The Functional Language $\mathbb{C}$Duce

$\mathbb{C}$Duce is a very efficient functional language for rapid design and development of applications that manipulate XML data [2]. In this work we concentrate on the foundational aspects of $\mathbb{C}$Duce [11] a detailed survey of which can be found in [8]. In that respect, $\mathbb{C}$Duce features the same syntactic types as $\mathbb{C}\pi$, with just a single exception, namely, the channel type constructor is replaced by the function type constructor:

$$\begin{array}{llll} \mathbb{C}\text{Duce } \textit{Types} & \tau ::= \mathbf{b} \mid \tau \to \tau \mid \tau \times \tau & & \text{constructors} \\ & \quad\mid \mathbf{0} \mid \mathbf{1} \mid \neg\tau \mid \tau \vee \tau \mid \tau \wedge \tau & & \text{combinators} \end{array}$$

where the same regularity and contractivity restrictions as in Section 2.1 apply. We use σ, τ to range over $\mathbb{C}$Duce types and to typographically distinguish them from $\mathbb{C}\pi$ ones, these latter still ranged over by s and t. Subtyping is characterised in the same way as for $\mathbb{C}\pi$, by defining an interpretation from the above types into a domain $\mathscr{D}$ (that we leave unspecified, see [11]) which satisfies property (1). Definition 2.1 is modified to account for the new type constructor for functions. We have $\mathbb{E}(-) : \mathscr{T} \to \mathscr{P}(\mathscr{D} + \mathscr{D} \times \mathscr{D} + \mathscr{P}(\mathscr{D} \times \mathscr{D}_\Omega))$ (where $\mathscr{D}_\Omega = \mathscr{D} + \{\Omega\}$, the disjoint union of the domain and of a distinguished error element Ω) while point (d.) of Definition 2.1 becomes:

d. $\mathbb{E}(\sigma \to \tau) = \mathscr{P}\left(\overline{[\![\sigma]\!] \times \overline{[\![\tau]\!]}^{\mathscr{D}_\Omega}}^{\mathscr{D} \times \mathscr{D}_\Omega}\right)$

where $\overline{X}^Y$ denotes the complement of X with respect to Y (i.e., $Y \setminus X$). In words, the extensional interpretation of $\sigma \to \tau$ is the set of graphs such that if the first element is in $[\![\sigma]\!]$, then the second element is in $[\![\tau]\!]$ (otherwise the second element can be anything, in particular the error Ω). Therefore, *for what concerns subtyping*, we can consider that arrow types are interpreted as follows:

$$[\![\sigma \to \tau]\!] = \{f \subseteq \mathscr{D} \times \mathscr{D}_\Omega \mid \forall (d_{\text{in}}, d_{\text{out}}) \in f.\ d_{\text{in}} \in [\![\sigma]\!] \Rightarrow d_{\text{out}} \in [\![\tau]\!]\}.$$

As we did for $\mathbb{C}\pi$, we can use this characterisation to deduce several type equality and containment relations.[2] For the goals of this work an utmostly interesting equation is

$$(\sigma \to \tau) \wedge (\sigma \to \tau') = \sigma \to \tau \wedge \tau' \tag{5}$$

whose validity can be easily checked by the reader, by applying the definition of $\mathbb{E}(-)$.

$\mathbb{C}$Duce is a λ-calculus with pairs, overloaded recursive functions, and pattern matching. This is reflected by the following syntax:

$$e ::= x \mid n \mid ee \mid (e,e) \mid \mu f^{\bigwedge_{i\in I}(\sigma_i \to \tau_i)}(x).e \mid \texttt{match}\ e\ \texttt{with}\ p \Rightarrow e \mid p \Rightarrow e$$

where patterns p are those defined in Definition 2.2 (but use $\mathbb{C}$Duce types). The type-case expression $(x = e \in \tau)\,?e_1 : e_2$ can be added as syntactic sugar for the matching expression $\texttt{match}\ e\ \texttt{with}\ x \wedge \tau \Rightarrow e_1 \mid x \wedge \neg\tau \Rightarrow e_2$.

---

[2] The error Ω is included in the codomain of the functions since without it every function would have type $\mathbf{1} \to \mathbf{1}$, therefore every application would be well-typed (with type $\mathbf{1}$). The error element Ω stands for the result of ill-typed applications. Thanks to it $\sigma \to \tau \leq \mathbf{1} \to \mathbf{1}$ does not hold in general, hence, it explicitly avoids the problem above.

$$\frac{}{\Delta;\Gamma\vdash n:\mathbf{b}_n}(const) \quad \frac{}{\Delta;\Gamma\vdash x:\Gamma(x)}(var) \quad \frac{}{\Delta;\Gamma\vdash f:\Delta(f)}(fvar) \quad \frac{\Delta;\Gamma\vdash e:\sigma\leq\tau}{\Delta;\Gamma\vdash e:\tau}(subs)$$

$$\frac{\Delta;\Gamma\vdash e_1:\tau_1 \quad \Delta;\Gamma\vdash e_2:\tau_2}{\Delta;\Gamma\vdash (e_1,e_2):\tau_1\times\tau_2}(pair) \qquad \frac{\Delta;\Gamma\vdash e_1:\sigma\to\tau \quad \Delta;\Gamma\vdash e_2:\sigma}{\Delta;\Gamma\vdash e_1e_2:\tau}(appl)$$

$$(\text{for } \sigma_1\equiv\sigma\wedge\langle p_1\rangle,\ \sigma_2\equiv\sigma\wedge\neg\langle p_1\rangle)$$
$$\frac{\Delta;\Gamma\vdash e:\sigma\leq\langle p_1\rangle\vee\langle p_2\rangle \quad \Delta;\Gamma,(\sigma_i/p_i)\vdash e_i:\tau_i}{\Delta;\Gamma\vdash \texttt{match}\ e\ \texttt{with}\ p_1\Rightarrow e_1\mid p_2\Rightarrow e_2:\bigvee_{\{i\mid\sigma_i\not\simeq\mathbf{0}\}}\tau_i}(match)$$

$$(\text{for } \tau\equiv\textstyle\bigwedge_{i\in I}(\sigma_i\to\tau_i)) \quad (\forall i\in I, h\in I, j\in J)$$
$$\frac{\sigma_h\wedge\sigma_i=\mathbf{0} \qquad \tau\not\leq\sigma'_j\to\tau'_j \qquad \Delta,f:\tau;\Gamma,x:\sigma_i\vdash e:\tau_i}{\Delta;\Gamma\vdash \mu f^{\tau}(x).e:\tau\wedge\bigwedge_{j\in J}\neg(\sigma'_j\to\tau'_j)}(abstr)$$

Fig. 2. ℂDuce typing rules

Function abstractions use a μ-abstracted name for recursion and specify at their index several arrow types, indicating that the function has all these types (i.e., their intersection). This is formally stated by the rule (*abstr*) in Figure 2 which for each $i\in I$ checks that the body e has type τ_i under the hypothesis that x has type σ_i. Note that the types of μ-abstracted variables are recorded in a distinct environment Δ. The distinction here is totally useless (we could have used a unique Γ) but it will be handy when we define the encoding (since μ-abstracted variables are translated into channel constants, then the encoding will be parametric only in Γ).

The only difficult rule is (*match*). It first deduces the type σ of the matched expression and checks whether patterns cover all its possible results (i.e., $\sigma\leq\langle p_1\rangle\vee\langle p_2\rangle$); then it separately checks the first branch under the hypothesis that p_1 is selected (i.e. e is in $\sigma\wedge\langle p_1\rangle$) and the second branch under the hypothesis that p_2 is selected (i.e., e in $\sigma\wedge\neg\langle p_1\rangle$); finally it discards the return types of the branches *that cannot be selected*, which is safely approximated by the fact that the corresponding σ_i is empty.[3]

The rules in Figure 2 are the same as those defined in [11] (to which the reader can refer for more details) with just a single exception: in rule (*abstr*) we require that the arrows specified at the index of the function have disjoint domains: $\forall i,h<i.\sigma_h\wedge\sigma_i=\mathbf{0}$. This restriction is necessary (but not sufficient) in order to avoid the problem of output-driven overloading explained in Section 4.2. However, it causes no loss of generality, since every ℂDuce function $\mu f^{\bigwedge_{i\in I}(\sigma_i\to\tau_i)}(x).e$ can be put into this form by iterating on its index the rewriting that replaces $(\sigma_h\wedge\sigma_k\to\tau_h\wedge\tau_k)\wedge(\sigma_k\wedge\neg\sigma_h\to\tau_k)\wedge(\sigma_h\wedge\neg\sigma_k\to$

[3] The reader may wonder why the system does not return a type error when one of the two branches cannot be selected. As a matter of fact this is a key feature for typing overloaded functions, where the body is repeatedly checked under different hypothesis for some of which the σ_i of some typecase may be empty. This simple function should clarify the point: $\mu f^{(\mathsf{Int}\to\mathsf{Int};\mathsf{Bool}\to\mathsf{Bool})}(x).(y=x\in\mathsf{Int})\,?(y+1):\mathsf{not}(y)$ when we type the body under the hypothesis $x:\mathsf{Int}$, then the second branch cannot be selected, while under $x:\mathsf{Bool}$ is the first one that cannot be selected. Without the selective union in the typing rule the best type we could have given to this function would have been $(\mathsf{Int}\vee\mathsf{Bool})\to(\mathsf{Int}\vee\mathsf{Bool})$.

$\tau_h)$ for every pair of arrows $\sigma_h \to \tau_h$, $\sigma_k \to \tau_k$ such that $\sigma_h \wedge \sigma_k \neq \mathbf{0}$. This rewriting is sound and it is easy to show that the two functions are operationally indistinguishable (e.g., by applicative bisimilarity).

As the intersection of negated channels in the rule (chan) ensures that values of $\mathbb{C}\pi$ yield a model that induces the same subtyping relation as the initial one, so does for $\mathbb{C}$Duce the intersection of negated arrows in the rule (*abstr*): the interpretation defined by (4) where values are closed terms generated by $v ::= n \mid \mu f^{\bigwedge_{i\in I}(\sigma_i \to \tau_i)}(x).e \mid (v,v)$ and types are $\mathbb{C}$Duce types, enjoys the same properties. Therefore, we can again use the pattern semantics of Section 2.2 to define the call-by-value operational semantics of $\mathbb{C}$Duce (we omit the straightforward context rules that can be found in [11]).

$$
\begin{array}{rcll}
v_1 v_2 & \longrightarrow & e[v_1/f; v_2/x] & \text{if } v_1 = \mu f^{\tau}(x).e \\
\texttt{match}\ v\ \texttt{with}\ p_1 \Rightarrow e_1 \mid p_2 \Rightarrow e_2 & \longrightarrow & e_1[v/p_1] & \text{if } v/p_1 \neq \Omega \\
\texttt{match}\ v\ \texttt{with}\ p_1 \Rightarrow e_1 \mid p_2 \Rightarrow e_2 & \longrightarrow & e_2[v/p_2] & \text{if } v/p_1 = \Omega, v/p_2 \neq \Omega
\end{array}
$$

The calculus satisfies the subject reduction property [2].

4 Roadmap to the Encoding

In this section we discuss the main difficulties encountered in the definition of an encoding of $\mathbb{C}$Duce into $\mathbb{C}\pi$. It lists some failed attempts which will clarify the reasons behind the successful attempt.

4.1 The Milner-Turner Encoding

Since our encoding involves languages with subtyping, the first approach we tried was to adapt the Milner-Turner (MT) encoding of the call-by-value typed λ-calculus with subtyping into the typed π-calculus with subtyping, as presented in [17]. The translation of arrow types presented there is:

$$
(\!|\sigma \to \tau|\!) \;=\; ch^{-}((\!|\sigma|\!) \times ch^{-}((\!|\tau|\!)))\ .
$$

The encoding of λ-terms, decorated by their minimum types, is:

$$
\begin{array}{ll}
(\!|x^{\tau}|\!)_c^{\Gamma,x:\tau} & = \overline{c}(x) \\
(\!|\lambda x^{\sigma}.e^{\tau}|\!)_c^{\Gamma} & = (\nu\, a^{(\!|\sigma|\!)\times ch^{-}((\!|\tau|\!))})(\overline{c}(a) \parallel\ !(a(x,b).(\!|e^{\tau}|\!)_b^{\Gamma,x:\sigma})) \\
(\!|e_1^{\sigma\to\tau} e_2^{\rho}|\!)_c^{\Gamma} & = (\nu\, a^{(\!|\sigma|\!)\times ch^{-}((\!|\tau|\!))})(\nu\, b^{(\!|\rho|\!)})((\!|e_1^{\sigma\to\tau}|\!)_a^{\Gamma} \parallel a(w).((\!|e_2^{\rho}|\!)_b^{\Gamma} \parallel b(h).\overline{w}(h,c)))
\end{array}
$$

The encoding of an expression e is parametrised by a type environment Γ such that $\Gamma \vdash e : \tau$ and by a channel $c^{(\!|\tau|\!)}$ on which the value of the expression is returned to the environment. A function is represented by a channel (the "name" of the function) which can be called by sending the input value and a channel on which the output value should be returned. These two parameters are used by a replicated process (the "body" of the function) which returns the output value upon termination. In the encoding of the application, the encoding of the function is called on the encoding of the argument, and the returned value is returned as the value of the whole expression. This encoding bears a strong resemblance with the continuation passing style transform. In this sense, the return channel of an expression could be seen as the address of the continuation.

Since we translate only well-typed terms, in the case of the application we must have $\rho \leq \sigma$. The encoding of the application (in particular, the $\overline{w}(h,c)$ subterm) is well-typed only if this implies $(\!|\rho|\!) \leq (\!|\sigma|\!)$. This holds true in the simply typed λ-calculus with subtyping, but fails as soon as we add intersection types. In that case, the translation of the types does not preserve the identity of types: in ℂDuce, we have seen that the identity (5) holds (i.e., $(\sigma \to \tau) \wedge (\sigma \to \tau') = \sigma \to \tau \wedge \tau'$), while the same does not hold on the encodings of the types at issue since, in general, it is not true that

$$ch^{-}(s \times ch^{-}(t)) \wedge ch^{-}(s \times ch^{-}(t')) \leq ch^{-}(s \times ch^{-}(t \wedge t'))\ .$$

Using this observation we can indeed show that the MT encoding maps a well-typed ℂDuce expression into an ill-typed ℂπ process.

4.2 Output-Driven Overloading

In order to give an operational intuition of why the MT encoding does not work, recall that intersections of arrow types are commonly assimilated to the types of overloaded functions. In ℂDuce, the identity $(\sigma \to \tau) \wedge (\sigma \to \tau') = \sigma \to \tau \wedge \tau'$ is justified because overloaded functions can perform a type-case only on the type of the input. Therefore, if on the same input a function returns values of type τ *and* values of type τ' it must return only values that have both types.

In ℂπ, however, a process that encodes a function receives in input also the return channel. In principle such process could perform a type-case on this extra piece of information and then execute different computations according to whether the expected result is of type τ or τ'. Such "output-driven" overloaded function can, on the same input, return a value of type τ and a *different* value of type τ' (and not in τ). This is a function that is in $(\!|(\sigma \to \tau) \wedge (\sigma \to \tau')|\!)$ and not in $(\!|\sigma \to \tau \wedge \tau'|\!)$, therefore we expect that $(\!|\sigma \to \tau \wedge \tau'|\!) \lneq (\!|(\sigma \to \tau) \wedge (\sigma \to \tau')|\!)$ which is indeed the case.

4.3 The Distributive Law

At a first analysis, it may seem that the problem is the subtyping relation of ℂπ. We may be tempted to change it by adding the following inequation:

$$ch^{-}(t_1 \wedge t_2)\ \leq\ ch^{-}(t_1) \vee ch^{-}(t_2)\ .$$

Since the converse inequality already holds (as seen in Section 2), we would obtain a "contravariant" distributive law of the channel constructor over the intersection. A similar distributive law is used by Hennessy and Riely in [12] to *define* the intersection type. As explained in [6], the above inequation is not justified in a calculus endowed with dynamic type-case. It is also not clear at first sight whether introducing the inequation is at all possible using a semantic approach. In any case, this new subtyping relation would not make the translation work either as it would introduce *too many* equations in the translation. For example, being $\texttt{int} \wedge \texttt{bool} = \mathbf{0}$, we would get

$$ch^{-}(\mathbf{0} \times ch^{-}(\texttt{int} \vee \texttt{bool}))\ \leq\ ch^{-}(\texttt{int} \times ch^{-}(\texttt{bool})) \vee ch^{-}(\texttt{bool} \times ch^{-}(\texttt{int})).$$

The type on the left is the encoding of $\mathbf{0} \to \texttt{int} \vee \texttt{bool}$ and the other type is the encoding of $(\texttt{int} \to \texttt{bool}) \vee (\texttt{bool} \to \texttt{int})$. This subtyping gives a problem already for the identity function, which has type $\mathbf{0} \to \texttt{int} \vee \texttt{bool}$ but not $(\texttt{int} \to \texttt{bool}) \vee (\texttt{bool} \to \texttt{int})$.

4.4 The Negation Translation

Intuitively, to find an encoding that respects type equality, we need that, when encoding the arrow type, the operator that encodes the output type distributes over the intersection, while the operator that encodes the input type should not distribute over the intersection. One possible encoding that satisfies this requirement is the following:

$$(\!|\sigma \to \tau|\!) \;=\; ch^{-}((\!|\sigma|\!) \times \neg(\!|\tau|\!)) \,.$$

Indeed the negation is a contravariant constructor that distributes over the intersection. However it was not clear to us what operational interpretation we could attach to this translation. Under this translation of the types, the MT translation of the λ-terms would not be well-typed.

This however was the sparkle that brought us to our solution: (i) We want to preserve the naturalness of the MT encoding, that is, to encode functions calls by RPCs that send along with the argument a channel on which the call must return the result; thus the type of the second argument of the call (i.e., the one that encodes the output type τ) must allow for messages of type $ch^{-}((\!|\tau|\!))$. (ii) We also want the type of this argument to distribute over intersections, in order to respect the subtyping relation; the use of negation, $\neg(\!|\tau|\!)$, seems to help in this direction. Finally, (iii) we want this second argument to be contravariant (since it is under a $ch^{-}(\,)$, it will then respect the covariance of the output type it is meant to encode); but the joint use of two contravariant constructors, $ch^{-}(\,)$ and $\neg$, would make it covariant, thus we may need to add a further negation to make it contravariant. All this yields, for the encoding of $\sigma \to \tau$, a second argument of type $\neg(ch^{-}(\neg(\!|\tau|\!)))$, which is *almost* what we are looking for. We say "almost" since it still does not satisfy (i) insofar as it is not a supertype of $ch^{-}((\!|\tau|\!))$; as we will explain in Section 5.2 one point is still missing from it: $ch^{-}(\mathbf{1})$ — to verify it, simply compute the difference $ch^{-}((\!|\tau|\!)) \setminus \neg ch^{-}(\neg(\!|\tau|\!))$. So we add it, obtaining for the second argument the following encoding $\neg ch^{-}(\neg(\!|\tau|\!)) \vee ch^{-}(\mathbf{1})$. This idea is carried out in details and generalised in the following section.

5 The Encoding

We propose a modification of the Milner-Turner encoding that respects type equality, and it is very close to the original translation.

5.1 The λ-Channel Constructor

The encoding of the types we propose is parametric with respect to a constructor of $\mathbb{C}\pi$ types that we call "λ-channel" type. This notion is designed to make the translation of types to respect the type equality (unlike the Milner-Turner and distributive approach), and to make the translation of terms to make sense (unlike the negation approach).

Definition 5.1. *A* λ-channel *(noted, $ch^{\lambda}(-)$) is a unary constructor of $\mathbb{C}\pi$ types s.t.:* (1.) $ch^{-}(t) \leq ch^{\lambda}(t)$; (2.) $ch^{\lambda}(s \wedge t) = ch^{\lambda}(s) \vee ch^{\lambda}(t)$; (3.) $s \leq t \iff ch^{\lambda}(t) \leq ch^{\lambda}(s)$.

Observe that the three conditions of the definition above correspond to the requirements $(i\text{-}iii)$ we outlined at the end of the previous section. Therefore, Condition (1) is necessary for a meaningful translation of terms, while Conditions (2) and (3) are necessary for respecting the identity of types. Using λ-channel types we can now define a mapping of ℂDuce types to ℂπ-calculus types that respects type equality.

Definition 5.2. *The interpretation function* $\{\{-\}\} : \mathscr{T}_{\mathbb{C}\text{Duce}} \to \mathscr{T}_{\mathbb{C}\pi}$ *is defined as follows*

$$\{\{\mathbf{b}\}\} = \mathbf{b} \qquad \{\{\mathbf{0}\}\} = \mathbf{0} \qquad \{\{\mathbf{1}\}\} = \mathbf{1} \qquad \{\{\neg\tau\}\} = \neg\{\{\tau\}\}$$
$$\{\{\sigma \vee \tau\}\} = \{\{\sigma\}\} \vee \{\{\tau\}\} \qquad \{\{\sigma \wedge \tau\}\} = \{\{\sigma\}\} \wedge \{\{\tau\}\}$$
$$\{\{\sigma \times \tau\}\} = \{\{\sigma\}\} \times \{\{\tau\}\} \qquad \{\{\sigma \to \tau\}\} = ch^{-}(\{\{\sigma\}\} \times ch^{\lambda}(\{\{\tau\}\})).$$

Theorem 5.3. *Let* σ *and* τ *be* ℂDuce *types. Then* $\sigma \leq \tau \iff \{\{\sigma\}\} \leq \{\{\tau\}\}$.

5.2 Incarnations of λ-Channels and Their Intuition

Possible choices for $ch^{\lambda}(t)$ are of the form $ch^{\lambda_0}(t) \wedge \varphi$ where $ch^{\lambda_0}(t) = \neg ch^{-}(\neg t) \vee ch^{-}(\mathbf{1})$ and φ is a constant type such that $ch^{-}(\mathbf{0}) \leq \varphi$.

As the Condition (1) in Definition 5.1 clearly states, the λ-channel $ch^{\lambda}(t)$ essentially is $ch^{-}(t)$ plus some extra stuff, some "garbage", that makes the other two conditions —hence type identity preservation— hold. The extra stuff that is added to $ch^{-}(t)$ is basically given by $ch^{\lambda_0}(t)$. To understand the precise role played by this garbage, it is interesting to consider the following properties:

a. $ch^{\lambda_0}(\mathbf{0}) = \mathbf{1}$
b. $ch^{\lambda_0}(\mathbf{1}) = \neg ch^{-}(\mathbf{0}) \vee ch^{-}(\mathbf{1})$
c. $[\![(ch^{\lambda_0}(t) \wedge \neg ch^{-}(t)) \wedge ch^{-}(\mathbf{0})]\!] = \{c^s \mid t \not\leq s \;\&\; \neg t \not\leq s\} \cup \{c^{\mathbf{1}}\}$.

The first two properties say that $ch^{\lambda_0}(-)$ adds as garbage *at most* (point (a.)) everything and *at least* (point (b.)) all non-channel types plus the channel which outputs everything. In order to exactly determine which channels $ch^{\lambda_0}(t)$ adds to to $ch^{-}(t)$ let us take out all $ch^{-}(t)$ and consider just the channels that remained: this is exactly what $(ch^{\lambda_0}(t) \wedge \neg ch^{-}(t)) \wedge ch^{-}(\mathbf{0})$ does. Point (c.) states that these are all channels that can send values both inside and outside t. That is, these are all the channels for which it is not possible to predict the result of a test that checks whether the messages they transport are of type t.

This last observation is the key to understand why the complicated definition of $ch^{\lambda_0}(-)$ is necessary. We have observed that the MT translation does not work because it allows a "output-driven" overloading whereby a function can have different behaviours for different expected types of the result. The more general channel type $ch^{\lambda_0}(-)$ allows (potentially, in the types) the caller to "confuse" such output-driven functions, by sending "garbage" reply channels. Although in practice, encodings don't do that, the possibility of a output-driven function is ruled out also at the level of the types. It is like the presence of the Police in Utopia: everybody behaves well in Utopia, and the Police never works. But the presence of the Police is the visible representation of the fact the everybody behaves well.

To put it otherwise, if we take a channel that has type $ch^{\lambda}(s) \vee ch^{\lambda}(t)$, it is impossible to deduce whether it is only of type $ch^{\lambda}(s)$ or only of type $ch^{\lambda}(t)$. Even if it can transport all messages of type, say, t, it could be because the channel was in the garbage generated by $ch^{\lambda}(s)$. So λ-channels introduce some latent noise that makes it impossible to determine which output type they encode.

Although the constructor is parametric on a type φ, non-channel types play no active role in the encoding. Therefore it is reasonable (and it makes the encoding more understandable) to minimise φ (that is, $\varphi = \mathit{ch}^{-}(\mathbf{0})$) so that $[\![\mathit{ch}^{\lambda}(t)]\!]$ only contains channels. In particular, this choice implies that $\mathit{ch}^{\lambda}(\mathbf{0}) = \mathit{ch}^{-}(\mathbf{0})$ (all channels), $\mathit{ch}^{\lambda}(\mathbf{1}) = \mathit{ch}^{-}(\mathbf{1})$ (just the channel which outputs everything). All the development, however, is independent from this choice.

5.3 Encoding of the Terms

We describe here the mapping of $\mathbb{C}$Duce terms to $\mathbb{C}\pi$-calculus terms. What we translate are in fact typing derivations. To simplify the notation, we write e^{τ} assuming that τ is the type of e in the last step of the derivation. We use a similar convention for the immediate sub-expressions of e which are in the premises of the last applied rule. The translation is parametrised by a "continuation channel" α of type $\mathit{ch}^{-}(\{\!\{\tau\}\!\})$. For readability we decorate the channels with their types only when we restrict them and in rule (*fvar*). We also adopt the $\mathbb{C}$Duce's convention to write $x{:}\tau$ for the pattern $x \wedge \tau$. The translation also requires a straightforward translation of the patterns (it just encodes the types occurring in them) whose details are omitted.

Definition 5.4. *The translation of the expression e^{τ} on a channel α is defined by cases on the last applied typing rule:*

$$(\mathit{const})\ \{\!\{n^{\mathbf{b}_n}\}\!\}^{\Gamma}_{\alpha} = \overline{\alpha}(n)$$

$$(\mathit{var})\ \{\!\{x^{\tau}\}\!\}^{\Gamma,x:\tau}_{\alpha} = \overline{\alpha}(x)$$

$$(\mathit{fvar})\ \{\!\{f^{\tau}\}\!\}^{\Gamma}_{\alpha} = \overline{\alpha}(f^{\bigvee_{i\in I}(\{\!\{\sigma_i\}\!\}\times \mathit{ch}^{\lambda}(\{\!\{\tau_i\}\!\}))}) \qquad (\text{where } \tau = \textstyle\bigwedge_{i\in I}(\sigma_i \to \tau_i))$$

$$(\mathit{pair})\ \{\!\{(e_1^{\sigma_1}, e_2^{\sigma_2})^{\tau}\}\!\}^{\Gamma}_{\alpha} = (\nu\, a^{\{\!\{\sigma_1\}\!\}})(\nu\, b^{\{\!\{\sigma_2\}\!\}})(\{\!\{e_1^{\sigma_1}\}\!\}^{\Gamma}_{a} \parallel a(w{:}\{\!\{\sigma_1\}\!\}).(\{\!\{e_2^{\sigma_2}\}\!\}^{\Gamma}_{b} \parallel b(h{:}\{\!\{\sigma_2\}\!\}).\overline{\alpha}(w,h))) \qquad (\text{where } \tau = \sigma_1 \times \sigma_2)$$

$$(\mathit{appl})\ \{\!\{(e_1^{\sigma\to\tau} e_2^{\sigma})^{\tau}\}\!\}^{\Gamma}_{\alpha} = (\nu\, a^{\{\!\{\sigma\to\tau\}\!\}})(\nu\, b^{\{\!\{\sigma\}\!\}})(\{\!\{e_1^{\sigma\to\tau}\}\!\}^{\Gamma}_{a} \parallel a(w{:}\{\!\{\sigma\to\tau\}\!\}).(\{\!\{e_2^{\sigma}\}\!\}^{\Gamma}_{b} \parallel b(h{:}\{\!\{\sigma\}\!\}).\overline{w}(h,\alpha)))$$

$$(\mathit{subs})\ \{\!\{(e^{\sigma})^{\tau}\}\!\}^{\Gamma}_{\alpha} = (\nu\, a^{\{\!\{\sigma\}\!\}})(\{\!\{e^{\sigma}\}\!\}^{\Gamma}_{a} \parallel a(w{:}\{\!\{\sigma\}\!\}).\overline{\alpha}(w)) \qquad (\text{where } \sigma \leq \tau)$$

$$\begin{aligned}(\mathit{match})\ & \{\!\{(\mathtt{match}\ e^{\sigma}\ \mathtt{with}\ p_1 \Rightarrow e_1^{\tau_1} \mid p_2 \Rightarrow e_2^{\tau_2})^{\tau}\}\!\}^{\Gamma}_{\alpha} = \\ & (\nu\, a^{\{\!\{\sigma\}\!\}})(\nu\, b^{(\{\!\{\sigma_1\}\!\}\times \mathit{ch}^{-}(\{\!\{\tau_1\}\!\}))\vee(\{\!\{\sigma_2\}\!\}\times \mathit{ch}^{-}(\{\!\{\tau_2\}\!\}))})((P_1 + P_2) \parallel Q) \\ \text{where } P_1 &= b(\{\!\{p_1\}\!\}, d{:}\mathit{ch}^{-}(\{\!\{\tau_1\}\!\})).\{\!\{e_1^{\tau_1}\}\!\}^{\Gamma,\sigma_1/p_1}_{d}, \\ P_2 &= b(\{\!\{p_2 \wedge \neg \llparenthesis p_1 \rrparenthesis\}\!\}, d{:}\mathit{ch}^{-}(\{\!\{\tau_2\}\!\})).\{\!\{e_2^{\tau_2}\}\!\}^{\Gamma,\sigma_2/p_2}_{d}, \\ Q &= \{\!\{e^{\sigma}\}\!\}^{\Gamma}_{a} \parallel a(h{:}\{\!\{\sigma\}\!\}).\overline{b}(h,\alpha) \\ \sigma_1 &= \sigma \wedge \llparenthesis p_1 \rrparenthesis,\ \ \sigma_2 = \sigma \wedge \neg \llparenthesis p_1 \rrparenthesis,\ \ \tau = \textstyle\bigvee_{\{i \mid \sigma_i \neq \mathbf{0}\}} \tau_i\end{aligned}$$

$$\begin{aligned}(\mathit{abstr})\ & \{\!\{(\mu f^{\bigwedge_{i\in I}(\sigma_i\to\tau_i)}(x).e)^{\tau}\}\!\}^{\Gamma}_{\alpha} = (\nu\, f^{\bigvee_{i\in I}(\{\!\{\sigma_i\}\!\}\times \mathit{ch}^{\lambda}(\{\!\{\tau_i\}\!\}))})(\overline{\alpha}(f) \parallel \mathsf{body}(f)) \\ \text{where } \mathsf{body}(f) &= !(\textstyle\sum_{i\in I} f(x{:}\{\!\{\sigma_i\}\!\}, b{:}\mathit{ch}^{-}(\{\!\{\tau_i\}\!\})).\{\!\{e^{\tau_i}\}\!\}^{\Gamma,x:\sigma_i}_{b} \\ &\quad + f(x{:}\textstyle\bigvee_{i\in I}\{\!\{\sigma_i\}\!\}, b{:}\bigvee_{i\in I}(\mathit{ch}^{\lambda}(\{\!\{\tau_i\}\!\}) \wedge \neg \mathit{ch}^{-}(\{\!\{\tau_i\}\!\})).0) \\ \tau &= \textstyle\bigwedge_{i\in I}(\sigma_i \to \tau_i) \wedge \bigwedge_{j\in J} \neg(\sigma'_j \to \tau'_j).\end{aligned}$$

In rule (*fvar*), we assume that every μ-abstracted variable f has a corresponding channel constant f^{t} for every suitable $\mathbb{C}\pi$ type t. This allows the encoding to be parametric only in the Γ environment, and not in the Δ one.

In a match the expressions e_1 and e_2 play the role of two functions to be chosen in alternative according to the type of the argument e. Therefore we encode the match with a patterned sum of the encodings of e_1 and e_2 in parallel with the encoding of e.

The translation of a functional term is very similar to the original MT translation. To deal with overloading, the body of the function features a patterned choice. This choice includes all different behaviours that the function can produce on different inputs, and the special sub-term $f(x{:}\bigvee_{i\in I}\{\{\sigma_i\}\}, b{:}\bigvee_{i\in I}(ch^{\lambda}(\{\{\tau_i\}\})\wedge\neg ch^{\neg}(\{\{\tau_i\}\})).0$, which we call the *functional garbage*. The role of this sub-term is to obtain well-typed terms. However we will see that, within the context of translation of ℂDuce terms, the functional garbage choice is never taken. Indeed, carrying on with our analogy, this functional garbage corresponds to the prison of Utopia: it is there to capture misbehaving terms, even if we all know that there isn't any.

6 Correctness of the Encoding

We start by stating that the translation produces well-typed terms.

Theorem 6.1. *If* $\Delta;\Gamma\vdash e:\tau$, *then* $\{\{\Gamma\}\}\vdash\{\{e^{\tau}\}\}^{\Gamma}_{c^{\{\{\tau\}\}}}$ *and* $\{\{\Gamma\}\}, x: ch^{\neg}(\{\{\tau\}\})\vdash\{\{e^{\tau}\}\}^{\Gamma}_{x}$, *where* $\{\{\Gamma\}\}=\{y:\{\{\sigma\}\}\mid y:\sigma\in\Gamma\}$.

In the following we convene that when we write $\{\{e\}\}^{\Gamma}_{c}$, then there are τ and Δ such that $\Delta;\Gamma\vdash e:\tau$ and $ch^{\neg}(\{\{\tau\}\})$ is the type of c.

A first observation is that all reductions out of the encoding of a ℂDuce expression are deterministic (since patterns in sums are mutually exclusive) and never use the functional garbage in the body of functions. A *functional redex* is a redex of the shape $\mathsf{body}(f)\parallel\overline{f}(v,c)$. A reduction is *safe* if it is deterministic and each functional redex is reduced by choosing an alternative in $\mathsf{body}(f)$ different from the functional garbage. We denote safe reductions by $\longrightarrow_s$: as usual $\longrightarrow_s^*$ is the reflexive and transitive closure of $\longrightarrow_s$.

Lemma 6.2. *All reductions starting from* $\{\{e\}\}^{\varnothing}_{c}$ *where e is an arbitrary* ℂDuce *expression are safe.*

In order to state the correctness of the encoding, it is crucial to understand how ℂDuce values are mapped to ℂπ processes. As it is clear from the encoding, a functional value is mapped into the output of a private channel name in parallel with the encoding of the function body. We can then say that the ℂπ value corresponding to a functional value is a channel name. The encoding of a pair of ℂDuce values reduces to a process which outputs the pair of the corresponding ℂπ values in parallel with the function bodies of all functions which occur in the two values.

To formalise the above we will assume that *all function names* in the current value are *distinct* and *fixed*, so that we cannot rename them. We define two mappings, one from ℂDuce values to ℂπ values and one from ℂDuce values to sets of channel names.

Definition 6.3

1. *The mapping* $\mathsf{cpv}(-)$ *is defined by induction on* $\mathbb{C}$Duce *values as follows:*
   - $\mathsf{cpv}(n) = n$;
   - $\mathsf{cpv}(\mu f^{\bigwedge_{i\in I}(\sigma_i \to \tau_i)}(x).e) = f^{\bigvee_{i\in I}(\{\{\sigma_i\}\} \times ch^{\lambda}(\{\{\tau_i\}\}))}$;
   - $\mathsf{cpv}((v_1, v_2)) = (\mathsf{cpv}(v_1), \mathsf{cpv}(v_2))$.
2. *The mapping* $\mathsf{func}(-)$ *is defined by induction on* $\mathbb{C}$Duce *values as follows:*
   - $\mathsf{func}(n) = \varnothing$;
   - $\mathsf{func}(\mu f^{\bigwedge_{i\in I}(\sigma_i \to \tau_i)}(x).e) = \{f^{\bigvee_{i\in I}(\{\{\sigma_i\}\} \times ch^{\lambda}(\{\{\tau_i\}\}))}\}$;
   - $\mathsf{func}((v_1, v_2)) = \mathsf{func}(v_1) \cup \mathsf{func}(v_2)$.

Let $\mathsf{body}(f)$ be defined as in the last clause of Definition 5.4, then the above mappings can express the normal forms of processes encoding values:

Lemma 6.4. $\{\{v\}\}_c^{\varnothing} \longrightarrow_s^* (\nu\, \mathsf{func}(v))(\overline{c}(\mathsf{cpv}(v)) \|_{f \in \mathsf{func}(v)} \mathsf{body}(f))$.

More generally, one would like to have that if e is a well-typed $\mathbb{C}$Duce expression and $e \longrightarrow^* v$, then $\{\{e\}\}_c^{\varnothing} \longrightarrow_s^* (\nu\, \mathsf{func}(v))(\overline{c}(\mathsf{cpv}(v)) \|_{f \in \mathsf{func}(v)} \mathsf{body}(f))$. Unfortunately, the corresponding result does not even hold for the MT encoding of λ-calculus into π-calculus [15], *a fortiori* nor does for our encoding.

Our encoding of $\mathbb{C}$Duce into $\mathbb{C}\pi$ being essentially an extension of the MT encoding has luckily no more problems than the original one, so we can show similar soundness results. To formulate these results we need to define for $\mathbb{C}\pi$ processes a standard notion of typed barbed congruence with respect to an environment Γ ($\Gamma \triangleright P \cong Q$), see [17]. The main theorem of this section states that if a $\mathbb{C}$Duce expression reduces to a value, then its encoding reduces to a process which is barbed congruent to the normal form of the encoding of that value, and vice versa if the evaluation of a $\mathbb{C}$Duce expression does not terminate, then the evaluation of its encoding does not terminate either.

Theorem 6.5 (Correctness). *If* $e \longrightarrow^* v$, *then* $\{\{e\}\}_c^{\varnothing} \longrightarrow_s^* P$ *for some* P *such that* $\varnothing \triangleright P \cong (\nu\, \mathsf{func}(v))(\overline{c}(\mathsf{cpv}(v)) \|_{f \in \mathsf{func}(v)} \mathsf{body}(f))$. *If* e *diverges, then so does* $\{\{e\}\}_c^{\varnothing}$.

From this, and from compositionality, it is easy to obtain soundness. Given two $\mathbb{C}$Duce terms $\Delta;\Gamma \vdash e : \tau$ and $\Delta;\Gamma \vdash e' : \tau$ we denote by $\Delta;\Gamma \triangleright e \approx e'$ the standard Morris-style observational congruence (as defined, for instance, in [17] pag. 478).

Corollary 6.6 (Soundness). *If* $\Delta;\Gamma \vdash e : \tau$ *and* $\Delta;\Gamma \vdash e' : \tau$ *and* $\{\{\Gamma\}\} \triangleright \{\{e\}\}_c^{\Gamma} \cong \{\{e'\}\}_c^{\Gamma}$, *then* $\Delta;\Gamma \triangleright e \approx e'$.

Notice that completeness fails for our encoding, for the same reason as it fails for the original MT encoding.

7 Conclusion

In this paper we presented a localised version of the $\mathbb{C}\pi$-calculus which allows for fully recursive types, on top of the already rich type structure of $\mathbb{C}\pi$. We then showed how this can be used to type-faithfully encode $\mathbb{C}$Duce.

If we merely stop at the technical result, then the interest of this work is quite limited: sure, it shows the correspondence between overloading and guarded choices; sure, this can be seen as the work that paves the way toward a concrete implementation of a concurrent programming language based on $\mathbb{C}$Duce, similarly to the way the JoCaml language was derived from OCaml and Join. But again this would look as some solid, technically impeccable, and extremely boring achievement.

However, we think that the added value of this work lies more in the lessons we learnt and the techniques we developed, than directly in its result.

Foremost, we learnt that the process that encodes a function has much more power than the function it encodes. This is because it has more elements to work on, both the argument and the return channel, and it is thus characterised by a wider spectrum of possible choices. This looks bluntly obvious, worthy of Monsieur De La Palice's troops, but note that this aspect was totally hidden in all previous encodings. Indeed this is emphasised only by the presence of linguistic branching constructs for which the type system must cover all alternatives. This is the case of pattern matching, where the pattern exhaustiveness requirement forces types to take into account all possible combinations.

This situation requires the introduction of some noise at the level of the types in order to compensate for the asymmetry between the caller of the function (the service client) and the executor of the function (the service server). This technique could be seen as a security policy that the client implements at type level to defend itself from possible misbehaviour of the server. The client performs a type obfuscation: in this way it reserves for itself the possibility to send rogue arguments and so it threatens the server against misbehaviour. We hope that these techniques of type obfuscation could be generalised to various security scenarios and we aim to explore them in the future.

As noted, the Milner-Turner encoding bears strong resemblance with the continuation passing style (CPS) techniques used in functional programming. All the above observations can be indeed carried over to such framework. Using these intuitions, we plan to study CPS transforms for $\mathbb{C}$Duce. This should have a very important practical impact: $\mathbb{C}$Duce (we mean, the implemented language) was recently extended to deal with Web-services and active Web pages, and we consider CPS as the key technique to implement stateless Web sessions on the top of them.

The other important aspect of this work is that it constitutes an independent, though indirect, confirmation that $\mathbb{C}\pi$ yields the right equational theory of union and intersection types for the π-calculus. Pierce and Sangiorgi's subtyping for the π-calculus, though very elegant, is structurally very poor: it essentially amounts to compare the levels of nesting of channel constructors with the same polarity. In order to obtain a much richer and expressive subtyping relation, one can resort to union and intersection types. However, the problem arises on which equational theory to use for these types. $\mathbb{C}\pi$ gives a precise and semantically grounded answer for it (and for negation types): its semantic justification for the equational theory, and its correspondence with set-theory constitute a first strong justification for it.

The equational theory of $\mathbb{C}\pi$ is partially justified in practice, since works such as the PiDuce project carried out at the University of Bologna [4] and the language XPi developed at the University of Marseille [1], feature restrictions of the $\mathbb{C}\pi$ type system that fit XML data manipulation. The present work is another, more theoretical, confirmation of the validity of the $\mathbb{C}\pi$ theory. If we admit that the Milner-Turner encoding is very natural, then we see how perfectly the laws of $\mathbb{C}\pi$ fit the MT encoding, stressing the asymmetry of the roles of client and server, and pushing the emergence of the type obfuscation technique. This is what we consider the most important achievement of this work.

References

1. L. Acciai and M. Boreale. XPi: A typed process calculus for XML messaging. In *FMOODS*, volume 3535 of *LNCS*, pages 47–66. Springer-Verlag, 2005.
2. V. Benzaken, G. Castagna, and A. Frisch. CDuce: an XML-friendly general purpose language. In *ICFP '03*, pages 51–63. ACM Press, 2003.
3. G. Boudol. Asynchrony and the π-calculus. Research Report 1702, INRIA, `http://www.inria.fr/rrrt/rr-1702.html`, 1992.
4. A. L. Brown, C. Laneve, and L. G. Meredith. PiDuce: A process calculus with native XML datatypes. In *EPEW/WS-FM*, volume 3670 of *LNCS*, pages 18–34. Springer-Verlag, 2005.
5. G. Castagna. Semantic subtyping: challenges, perspectives, and open problems. In *ICTCS 2005*, volume 3701 of *LNCS*, pages 1–20. Springer-Verlag, 2005.
6. G. Castagna, R. De Nicola, and D. Varacca. Semantic subtyping for the π-calculus. In *LICS '05*, pages 92–101. IEEE Computer Society Press, 2005.
7. G. Castagna, M. Dezani-Ciancaglini, and D. Varacca. Encoding $\mathbb{C}$Duce in the $\mathbb{C}\pi$-calculus. Extended version, `http://www.di.unito.it/~dezani/papers/cdv.pdf`, 2006.
8. G. Castagna and A. Frisch. A gentle introduction to semantic subtyping. In *PPDP '05, ACM Press* (full version) and *ICALP '05, LNCS* volume 3580, Springer-Verlag (summary), 2005. Joint ICALP-PPDP keynote talk.
9. C. Fournet, G. Gonthier, J.-J. Lévy, L. Maranget, and D. Rémy. A calculus of mobile agents. In *CONCUR '96*, volume 1119 of *LNCS*, pages 406–421. Springer-Verlag, 1996.
10. A. Frisch. *Théorie, conception et réalisation d'un langage de programmation fonctionnel adapté à XML*. PhD thesis, Université Paris 7, 2004.
11. A. Frisch, G. Castagna, and V. Benzaken. Semantic subtyping. In *LICS '02*, pages 137–146. IEEE Computer Society Press, 2002.
12. M. Hennessy and J. Riely. Resource access control in systems of mobile agents. *Information and Computation*, 173:82–120, 2002.
13. K. Honda and M. Tokoro. An object calculus for asynchronous communication. In *ECOOP 91*, volume 512 of *LNCS*, pages 133–147. Springer-Verlag, 1991.
14. M. Merro and D. Sangiorgi. On asynchrony in name-passing calculi. In *ICALP'98*, volume 1443 of *LNCS*, pages 856–867. Springer-Verlag, 1998.
15. R. Milner. Functions as processes. *Mathematical Structures in Computer Science*, 2(2):119–141, 1992.
16. B. Pierce and D. Sangiorgi. Typing and subtyping for mobile processes. *Mathematical Structures in Computer Science*, 6(5), 1996.
17. D. Sangiorgi and D. Walker. *The π-calculus*. Cambridge University Press, 2002.
18. N. Yoshida, M. Berger, and K. Honda. Strong Normalisation in the π-Calculus. *Information and Computation*, 191(2):145–202, 2004.

A Complete Axiomatisation of Branching Bisimulation for Probabilistic Systems with an Application in Protocol Verification

Suzana Andova[1,*], Jos C.M. Baeten[2], and Tim A.C. Willemse[3]

[1] Department of Telematics, Norwegian University of Science, Trondheim, Norway
[2] Department of Mathematics and Computer Science, Eindhoven University of Technology, P.O. Box 513, 5600 MB Eindhoven, The Netherlands
[3] Faculty of Science, Mathematics and Computing Science, University of Nijmegen, P.O. Box 9010, 6500 GL Nijmegen, The Netherlands
suzana@item.ntnu.no, josb@win.tue.nl, timw@cs.ru.nl

Abstract. We consider abstraction in probabilistic process algebra. The process algebra can be employed for specifying processes that exhibit both probabilistic and non-deterministic choices in their behaviour. We give a set of axioms that completely axiomatises the branching bisimulation for the strictly alternating probabilistic graph model. In addition, several recursive verification rules are identified, allowing us to remove redundant internal activity.

Using the axioms and the verification rules, we have successfully conducted a verification of the *Concurrent Alternating Bit Protocol*. This is a simple communication protocol, slightly more 'sophisticated' than the well-known Alternating Bit Protocol. As channels are lossy, sending continuous streams of data through the channels is a method to overcome this possible loss of data. This instigates a considerable level of parallelism (parallel activities) and as such requires more complex techniques for proving the protocol correct. Using our process algebra we show that after abstraction of internal activity, the protocol behaves as a buffer.

1 Introduction

Being able to specify the probabilistic behaviour of a system, enables a designer to analyse not only the functional aspects of his system, but also non-functional aspects of his system, such as performance. Examples of inherently probabilistic systems are data-link protocols, where decisions in the protocol can be based on a probabilistic process, and fluctuations in bandwidth and noise (which can be modelled using probabilities) affect the quality of underlying communications channels. Notice that a probabilistic choice is inherently different from a non-deterministic choice. The latter is still required in the specification of systems if, e.g. it is the environment that determines the choice, or to model interleaving [4,9].

The introduction of abstraction into a framework that already includes probabilities and non-determinism, however, remains challenging. Recently, an equivalence relation

* This work was carried out during the tenure of an ERCIM fellowships of the author visiting the Department of Telematics at Norwegian University of Science and Technology.

C. Baier and H. Hermanns (Eds.): CONCUR 2006, LNCS 4137, pp. 327–342, 2006.

called *branching bisimulation* is described in [2]. Although the relation is explained using alternative mathematical characterisations, its intricacies remain rather tricky, which is why we provide a *process algebraic* characterisation of the relation in this paper.

Process algebras provide the means for studying behaviours of processes by investigating the ways in which these can be constructed from basic operators and constants [8,15]. The interplay between the operators, constants and processes is typically described by axioms. Often, this axiomatic perspective is preferable over more operational perspectives, since the latter one may be highly dependent on the model and may involve some complex notions such as equivalences and basic composition methods. Branching bisimulation for probabilistic systems is a prime example of such a complex operational perspective, which requires in-depth knowledge of probability theory and complex notions such as schedulers.

Even though branching bisimulation has received much attention in the non-probabilistic setting, it remains little-studied in the probabilistic setting. Branching and weak bisimulation are compared in detail in [12], and advantages of branching bisimulation are pointed out. We focus our attention to branching bisimulation in the alternating model [13] and propose a complete axiomatisation for it, together with a set of sound verification rules. The completeness result is for closed (recursion free) expressions. The verification rules are sound with respect to the branching bisimulation and can be used to remove inert τ transitions and loops. A subset of the proposed rules already suffices to reduce the behaviour of complex protocols (such as the Concurrent Alternating Bit Protocol [14]) with respect to branching bisimulation.

The problem of abstraction in probabilistic process algebra has been addressed by several authors. Bandini and Segala [10] provide complete axiomatisations for recursion free processes for the weak bisimulation equivalences for the two models for probabilistic systems mainly in use, viz. the alternating and non-alternating model. Recently, in [11] an extension of the recursion free complete axiomatisation has been defined over guarded processes for the non-alternating model. However, the language we use is more expressive and (if a convex combination is not included) the verification rules we propose cover wider range of branching (weak) equivalent processes. Note here that branching bisimulation is a finer equivalence than weak bisimulation, therefore, our rules are sound with respect to the weak bisimulation as defined in [16].

This paper is structured as follows. Section 2 provides a brief overview of branching bisimulation for probabilistic systems. In Section 3 we introduce the process algebra pBPA_τ and discuss its axiomatisation. Section 4 describes several additional verification rules, and in Section 5 we employ our process algebra and the rules in a verification of the *Concurrent Alternating Bit Protocol* [14]. Section 6 ends with conclusions.

2 Preliminaries

We briefly introduce the semantic model and branching bisimulation. For an in-depth introduction, we refer to [2]. Probabilistic systems are modelled using *finite probabilistic graphs*, henceforth simply called *graphs*. Graphs consist of two types of nodes: *probabilistic nodes* and *non-deterministic nodes*, which are connected by two types of directed edges, viz. *probabilistic transitions* and *non-deterministic transitions*. The latter are labelled with *actions* from a set Act or with the *unobservable event*, τ ($\tau \notin$ Act). We assume the existence of a different special terminal node nil, which is not part of the set of nodes of any graph; nil is used to indicate successful termination.

Definition 1. *A* graph *is a 7-tuple* $\langle N, P, r, Act, \to, \rightsquigarrow, \mathsf{pr}\rangle$*, in which* N *is a non-empty finite set of* non-deterministic nodes*;* P *is a non-empty finite set of* probabilistic nodes. *We write* S *for* $P \cup N$*,* S_{nil} *for the set* $S \cup \{\mathsf{nil}\}$*, likewise* P_{nil}*. The node* $r \in P$ *is the* initial node*, also called* root*; Act is a finite set of* action labels*; we write* Act_τ *for* $Act \cup \{\tau\}$*. The relation* $\to \subseteq N \times Act_\tau \times P_{\mathsf{nil}}$ *is the* non-deterministic transition relation *and* $\rightsquigarrow \subseteq P \times N$ *is a* probabilistic transition relation*;* $\mathsf{pr}\colon \rightsquigarrow \to (0,1]$ *is a total function for which* $\sum_{n \in N} \mathsf{pr}(p,n) = 1$ *for all* $p \in P$.

For the remainder of this section, we assume a graph $\mathsf{x} = \langle N, P, r_{\mathsf{x}}, \mathrm{Act}, \to, \rightsquigarrow, \mathsf{pr}\rangle$. We let a, b, $c\ldots$ range over Act_τ, s, t, $n\ldots$ over S_{nil} and $\mathcal{M}$, $\mathcal{M}'$ over the subsets of S_{nil}. If $t \in S_{\mathsf{nil}}$, $[t]_{\mathcal{R}}$ denotes the equivalence class of t for some equivalence relation $\mathcal{R}$ defined on S_{nil}. The set of all graphs is denoted $\mathbf{G}$, and $\mathsf{x}, \mathsf{y}, \ldots$ range over $\mathbf{G}$. As usual, $n \xrightarrow{a} p$ abbreviates $(n, a, p) \in\to$ and $p \rightsquigarrow n$ abbreviates $(p, n) \in\rightsquigarrow$. If $t \in N$ such that t does not have any outgoing edge we write $t \not\to$. A *path* starting in a node $s_0 \in S_{\mathsf{nil}}$ is an alternating finite sequence $c \equiv s_0\ l_1 \ldots l_n\ s_n$, or an alternating infinite sequence $c \equiv s_0\ l_1\ s_1\ \ldots$ of nodes $s_i \in S_{\mathsf{nil}}$ and labels $l_i \in \mathrm{Act}_\tau \cup (0,1]$, satisfying:

1. for all nodes $s_j \in N$, we require $s_j \xrightarrow{l_{j+1}} s_{j+1}$, and
2. for all nodes $s_j \in P$, we require $s_j \rightsquigarrow s_{j+1}$ and $l_{j+1} = \mathsf{pr}(s_j, s_{j+1})$.

We write $\mathsf{first}(c) = s_0$, and, if c is a finite path, we write $\mathsf{last}(c)$ for the last node of c. The set of all nodes occurring in c is denoted $\mathsf{nodes}(c)$. By $\mathsf{trace}(c)$ we denote the sequence of *action labels* from the set Act_τ that occur in c. $\mathcal{P}(c)$ is the probability of a finite path c induced by function pr in the obvious way. The set of *all paths* starting in s_0 is denoted $\mathsf{Path}(s_0)$ and the set of finite paths starting in s_0 is denoted $\mathsf{Path}_f(s_0)$. A path c is a *maximal path* iff c is a finite path with $\mathsf{last}(c) = \mathsf{nil}$ or $\mathsf{last}(c) \not\to$, or c is an infinite path. The set of maximal paths starting in s_0 is denoted $\mathsf{Path}_m(s_0)$.

Definition 2. *A* scheduler *of paths starting in a node* s_0 *is a partial function* $\sigma\colon\mathsf{Path}_f(s_0) \mapsto (\to \cup \{\perp\})$ *satisfying:*

1. $\sigma(c)$ *is defined for all* $c \in \mathsf{Path}_f(s_0)$ *for which* $\mathsf{last}(c) \in N$*. Then* $\sigma(c) = \perp$ *or* $\sigma(c) = \mathsf{last}(c) \xrightarrow{a} t$ *for some* a *and* t.
2. *If* $\mathsf{last}(c) \in P_{\mathsf{nil}}$ *and* $\sigma(c)$ *is defined, then* $\sigma(c) = \perp$.
3. *For all* $c \in \mathsf{Path}_m(s_0) \cap \mathsf{Path}_f(s_0)$ *we have* $\sigma(c) = \perp$.

$\mathsf{Sched}(s_0)$ denotes the set of *all* schedulers of paths starting in node s_0. For $\sigma \in \mathsf{Sched}(s_0)$, we denote the set of scheduled paths starting in s_0 by $\mathsf{SPath}(s_0, \sigma)$. The probability $\mathcal{P}(\cdot)$ induces a probability space associated to $\sigma \in \mathsf{Sched}(s_0)$ on the set of σ-scheduled paths starting in s_0. Furthermore, let $\mathcal{B}_\sigma(s \xRightarrow{a}_{\mathcal{M}} \mathcal{M}')$ be the set of all σ-scheduled paths that, starting in s, traverse through a set of nodes $\mathcal{M}$ using τ actions only, and reach a node in $\mathcal{M}'$ by executing action a:

$$\mathcal{B}_\sigma(s \overset{a}{\Longrightarrow}_{\mathcal{M}} \mathcal{M}') = \{c \in \mathsf{SPath}(s,\sigma) \mid \sigma(c) = \bot \text{ and either } \\ c \equiv s \Longrightarrow_{\mathcal{M}} \cdot \overset{a}{\longrightarrow} s', s' \in \mathcal{M}', \text{ or} \\ c \equiv s \Longrightarrow_{\mathcal{M}} \cdot \rightsquigarrow s', s' \in \mathcal{M}', a = \tau, \text{ or} \\ c \equiv s, a = \tau, \mathcal{M} = \mathcal{M}'\},$$

where $c \equiv s \Longrightarrow_{\mathcal{M}} \cdot \overset{a}{\longrightarrow} s'$ denotes that $\exists c' : c \equiv c'as'$, $\mathsf{first}(c') = s$, $\mathsf{last}(c') \overset{a}{\longrightarrow} s'$, $\mathsf{trace}(c') = \tau^*$ and $\mathsf{nodes}(c') \subseteq \mathcal{M}$, and similar for $c \equiv s \Longrightarrow_{\mathcal{M}} \cdot \rightsquigarrow s'$

The probability over $\mathcal{B}_\sigma(s \overset{a}{\Longrightarrow}_{\mathcal{M}} \mathcal{M}')$ is given by $\mathcal{P}(\mathcal{B}_\sigma(s \overset{a}{\Longrightarrow}_{\mathcal{M}} \mathcal{M}'))$, and, since the set of probabilities is ordered, a maximal probability exists:

$$\mathcal{P}_{\max}(s \overset{a}{\Longrightarrow}_{\mathcal{M}} \mathcal{M}') \overset{\text{def}}{=} \max_{\sigma \in \mathsf{Sched}(s)} \mathcal{P}(\mathcal{B}_\sigma(s \overset{a}{\Longrightarrow}_{\mathcal{M}} \mathcal{M}'))$$

Note that even though the maximal probability is a unique number, there can be more than one scheduler inducing this maximal probability.

Definition 3. *Let* x *and* y *be two graphs, and denote the set of their nodes by* S. *A relation* $\mathcal{R}$ *on* S_{nil} *is a branching bisimulation relation iff the following three conditions are met for all nodes* $p, q \in S_{\mathsf{nil}}$ *satisfying* $p\mathcal{R}q$*:*

1. $\mathcal{P}_{max}(p \overset{a}{\Longrightarrow}_{[p]_{\mathcal{R}}} \mathcal{M}') = \mathcal{P}_{max}(q \overset{a}{\Longrightarrow}_{[q]_{\mathcal{R}}} \mathcal{M}')$ *for all* $a \in Act$ *and* $\mathcal{M}' \in S_{\mathsf{nil}/\mathcal{R}}$.
2. $\mathcal{P}_{max}(p \overset{\tau}{\Longrightarrow}_{[p]_{\mathcal{R}}} \mathcal{M}') = \mathcal{P}_{max}(q \overset{\tau}{\Longrightarrow}_{[q]_{\mathcal{R}}} \mathcal{M}')$ *for all* $\mathcal{M}' \in S_{\mathsf{nil}/\mathcal{R}} \setminus \{[p]_{\mathcal{R}}\}$.
3. $\mathcal{P}_{max}(p \overset{\tau}{\Longrightarrow}_{[p]_{\mathcal{R}}} \{\mathsf{nil}\}) = \mathcal{P}_{max}(q \overset{\tau}{\Longrightarrow}_{[q]_{\mathcal{R}}} \{\mathsf{nil}\})$.

A branching bisimulation relation $\mathcal{R}$ *is a* rooted *branching bisimulation relation iff the following two additional conditions are met:*

4. *For all* $\mathcal{M} \in S_{\mathsf{nil}/\mathcal{R}}$, *we require* $\sum_{n \in \mathcal{M}} \mathsf{pr}(r_{\mathsf{x}}, n) = \sum_{n \in \mathcal{M}} \mathsf{pr}(r_{\mathsf{y}}, n)$.
5. *If* $r_{\mathsf{x}} \rightsquigarrow n_{\mathsf{x}}$ *and* $n_{\mathsf{x}} \overset{a}{\longrightarrow} p_{\mathsf{x}}$, *then also* $r_{\mathsf{y}} \rightsquigarrow n_{\mathsf{y}}$ *and* $n_{\mathsf{y}} \overset{a}{\longrightarrow} p_{\mathsf{y}}$ *and* $n_{\mathsf{x}}\mathcal{R}n_{\mathsf{y}}$ *and* $p_{\mathsf{x}}\mathcal{R}p_{\mathsf{y}}$ *for some* n_{y} *and* p_{y}*; vice versa for* y.

x *and* y *are rooted branching bisimilar,* $\mathsf{x} \leftrightarrows_{rb} \mathsf{y}$, *iff there is a rooted branching bisimulation* $\mathcal{R}$ *such that* $r_{\mathsf{x}}\mathcal{R}r_{\mathsf{y}}$.

Note that the way $\mathcal{B}_\sigma(s \overset{a}{\Longrightarrow}_{\mathcal{M}} \mathcal{M}')$ is defined demonstrates the idea of branching bisimulation to preserve the branching structure in all intermediate states that are passed through, even if silent moves are involved [12]. The third condition in Definition 3 distinguishes successful (nil) from unsuccessful ($t \not\longrightarrow$) terminal nodes.

3 Probabilistic Process Algebra

The equivalence relation defined in the previous section is difficult to understand: it is rooted in probability theory and relies on notions such as schedulers. The alternative characterisations that are studied in [2] provide more insight into the properties of the equivalence relation, but these characterisations do not provide insights into the way the equivalence relation can be used in calculations. In other papers branching and weak bisimulations are defined by means of "weak" ($\overset{\tau^*}{\Longrightarrow}$) transitions (from a node to a distribution) e.g. [17,18], but again additional knowledge and good understanding of the model are required.

To overcome this problem, we define the probabilistic process algebra pBPA$_\tau$ which gives a complete axiomatisation (for closed processes) of branching bisimulation. In addition, we give several rules that capture branching bisimulation on *finite-state* graphs.

3.1 pBPA$_\tau$

pBPA$_\tau$ extends a subtheory of ACP, called BPA$_\tau$ [8] with the means to reason about probabilistic systems and abstraction. Probabilistic behaviours of processes are captured by means of a probabilistic choice operator. This binary operator models a choice between two processes, based on a probability distribution. The implications of adding this operator to the theory of BPA are studied in detail in [6,5].

Let Act again denote a set of (observable) atomic actions and τ the unobservable action ($\tau \notin$ Act). The syntax for pBPA$_\tau$ is given by the following grammar:

$$S ::= \delta \mid \tau \mid a \mid S \cdot S \mid S + S \mid S \boxplus_\pi S \mid \tau_I(S) \mid x$$

for $a \in$Act and $\pi \in (0,1)$, $I \subseteq$ Act and $x \in V$, where V is a set of recursion variables; p, q, r range over the set of all (process) expressions of pBPA$_\tau$. A *recursive specification* is a set of equations of the form $x = s_x(V)$, where x is a variable from V and s is a possibly open pBPA$_\tau$ expression containing variables from V. We consider guarded recursive specifications only (see e.g. [8] for definition). By means of guarded recursive specifications we are able to define infinite processes. pBPA$_\tau$ expressions that do not contain any variables are called *closed* expressions. Throughout this paper, we assume the following binding strengths: $\cdot > + > \tau_I > \boxplus$, i.e. $\cdot$ binds strongest.

Each pBPA$_\tau$ expression can be interpreted as a graph. We refrain from giving a formal interpretation of these expressions (it can be found in [3,5]), but, instead we give an informal explanation of the intended meaning of the constants and operators. Note that a closed expression determines a *finite* graph in which all paths are finite.

The constant δ represents unsuccessful termination with probability 1. An expression a performs, with probability 1, an observable activity that is modelled by action a and terminates successfully; the expression τ on the other hand, performs an *unobservable* activity with probability 1. Figure 1 depicts the graphs that are associated to the constants δ and τ, and the atomic actions a.

The binary operator $\cdot$ models sequential composition; the process $p \cdot q$ intuitively behaves as process p, and, upon successful termination, behaves as process q. This is

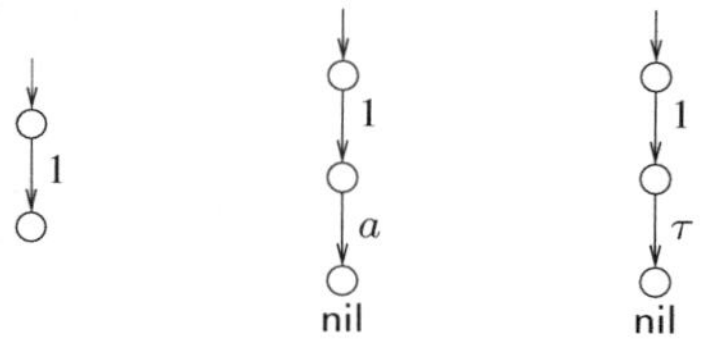

Fig. 1. Graph representation of δ, a ($a \in$ Act) and τ

also reflected in the graph p · q that belongs to the process $p \cdot q$: it is represented by the graph with the root of p as its root and for which all non-deterministic transitions $n \xrightarrow{a}$ nil in p are replaced by $n \xrightarrow{a} r_{\mathsf{q}}$, where r_{q} is the root node of q.

Alternative composition (commonly referred to as *non-deterministic choice*) is modelled by $+$; process $p + q$ behaves either as process p or process q, dependent on which process performs the first action. The graph interpretation of the alternative composition of two processes, process p, given by $(a \cdot p_0) \boxplus_{1/2} (b \cdot p_1)$ and process q, given by $(a \cdot q_0) \boxplus_{3/4} (c \cdot q_1)$ is illustrated in Fig. 2.

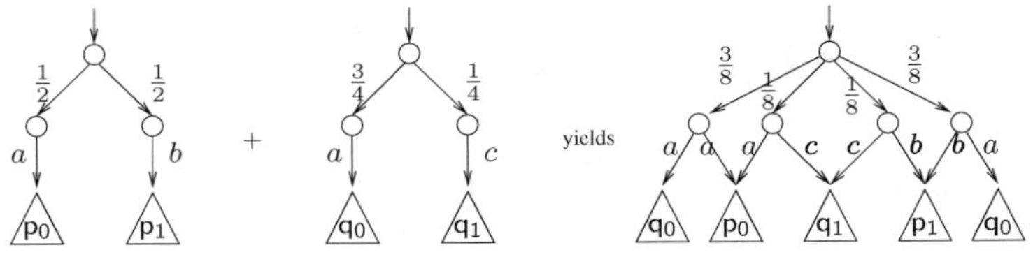

Fig. 2. Example for alternative composition of two graphs

The probabilistic extension lies in the addition of the binary operator $\boxplus_\pi$. A probabilistic process $p \boxplus_\pi q$ behaves as process p with probability π and as process q with probability $1 - \pi$. The choice between p and q in process $p \boxplus_\pi q$ is resolved differently from the non-deterministic choice: it is assumed that this type of choice is made *before* the first action occurs, but, the exact moment is not known. That is, there is an internal behaviour of the process which determines the outcome of the choice $p \boxplus_\pi q$ which takes place *before* p or q performs any action. The outcome of this choice cannot be influenced by the environment, it can only be observed. To illustrate, the graph interpretations of a probabilistic choice of $1/2$ between the processes p and q of Fig. 2 is depicted in Fig. 3.

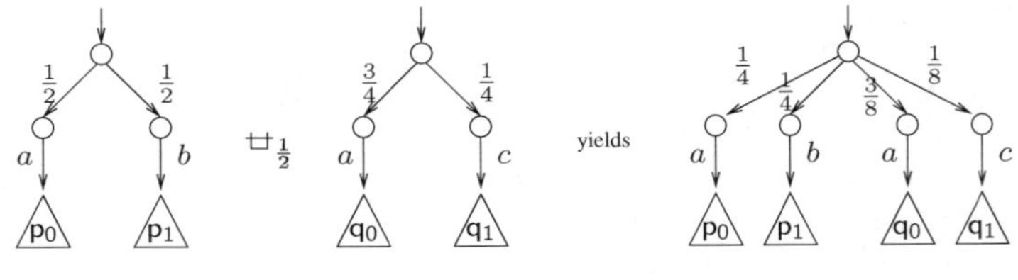

Fig. 3. Example for probabilistic choice of two graphs

The unary operator τ_I can be used to hide observable actions that are part of the set of actions I, i.e. any action $a \in I$, occurring in a process p, is mapped onto τ in the process $\tau_I(p)$. Given a graph p for the pBPA$_\tau$ process p, the graph for $\tau_I(p)$ is obtained by renaming all actions $a \in I$ that appear on the non-deterministic transitions into τ. The complete proof of the following theorem is given in [1].

Theorem 1. *Rooted branching bisimulation is a congruence for the operators in pBPA$_\tau$.*

3.2 Axiomatising Rooted Branching Bisimulation

An axiomatic perspective on the operators, their interplay, and the equivalences between pBPA$_\tau$ expressions are formalised by a set of axioms (see Table 1), which completely axiomatises rooted branching bisimulation as defined in Section 2.

Table 1. Axioms of pBPA$_\tau$. $a \in \text{Act} \cup \{\delta\}$, $I \subseteq \text{Act}$, $w, x, y, z \in V$

A1	$x + y$	$= y + x$	PrAC1	$x \boxplus_\pi y$	$= y \boxplus_{1-\pi} x$
A2	$(x + y) + z$	$= x + (y + z)$	PrAC2	$x \boxplus_\pi (y \boxplus_\rho z)$	$= (x \boxplus_{\frac{\pi}{\pi+\rho-\pi\rho}} y) \boxplus_{\pi+\rho-\pi\rho} z$
AA3	$a + a$	$= a$	PrAC3	$x \boxplus_\pi x$	$= x$
A4	$(x + y) \cdot z$	$= x \cdot z + y \cdot z$	PrAC4	$(x \boxplus_\pi y) \cdot z$	$= x \cdot z \boxplus_\pi y \cdot z$
A5	$x \cdot (y \cdot z)$	$= (x \cdot y) \cdot z$	PrAC5	$(x \boxplus_\pi y) + z$	$= (x + z) \boxplus_\pi (y + z)$
A6	$x + \delta$	$= x$			
A7	$\delta \cdot x$	$= \delta$			
TI0	$\tau_I(\tau)$	$= \tau$			
TI1	$\tau_I(a)$	$= a$		if $a \notin I$ or $a = \delta$	
TI1'	$\tau_I(a)$	$= \tau$		if $a \in I$	
TI2	$\tau_I(x + y)$	$= \tau_I(x) + \tau_I(y)$			
TI3	$\tau_I(x \cdot y)$	$= \tau_I(x) \cdot \tau_I(y)$			
TI4	$\tau_I(x \boxplus_\pi y)$	$= \tau_I(x) \boxplus_\pi \tau_I(y)$			
PrB1	$x \cdot \tau$	$= x$			
PrB2	$x \cdot ((y + \tau \cdot (y + z)) \boxplus_\pi w)$	$= x \cdot ((y + z) \boxplus_\pi w)$		if $y = y + y$ and $z = z + z$	
PrB3	$x \cdot (\tau \cdot z \boxplus_\pi z)$	$= x \cdot z$			

We briefly discuss the axioms of Table 1. The axioms A1 through A7 and PrAC1 through PrAC5 are the standard axioms for the *concrete* probabilistic process algebra pBPA (see [6]), which provide a complete axiomatisation of strong bisimulation. The axioms TI0 through TI4 are standard axioms for the hiding operator in ACP-like process algebras (e.g. [8,3,5]). Axioms PrB1 through PrB3 are the more interesting axioms, which we discuss in some more detail.

Unlike ordinary atomic actions, τ cannot be *observed* directly, but in some cases, its presence can be inferred. However, some unobservable actions in a process can be removed without affecting the (observable parts of the) behaviour of a process. Such redundant τ actions are also called *inert* τ actions. In BPA$_\tau$ there are two rules that allow us to remove redundant τ actions [8,12]:

B1 $x \cdot \tau \;=\; x$, and
B2 $x \cdot (\tau \cdot (y + z) + z) \;=\; x \cdot (y + z)$.

While axiom B1 remains valid in pBPA$_\tau$ (here renamed into axiom PrB1), it is not immediately clear whether axiom B2 should still hold in all cases. As a matter of fact, B2 does not hold in our setting, as illustrated by the processes $a \cdot (\tau \cdot ((b \boxplus_{1/3} c) + d) + d)$ and $a \cdot ((b \boxplus_{1/3} c) + d)$. The two processes do not have the same branching structure, therefore they are not equivalent. The informal explanation is as follows. After the successful execution of a, the first process reaches a state from which: 1) d can be executed immediately, 2) b can be executed by a positive probability after making an unobservable transition, 3) c can be executed by a positive probability after making an unobservable transition. On the other hand, after the successful termination of a, the second process cannot execute d immediately. First, a probabilistic choice has to be resolved. But by doing this, the process probabilistically chooses between b and c, but at the same time it excludes any possibilities of executing the other action.

The axioms PrB2 and PrB3 capture exactly the situations in which axiom B2 holds in the probabilistic setting. Remark that the conditions of the form $y = y+y$ hold for all probabilistic processes that have their probabilistic choice resolved, i.e. they are "ready" to perform an (non-deterministic) activity. In other words, y cannot choose probabilistically between processes that are not equivalent. This is expressed in Proposition 1. In the sequel we refer to these processes as *dynamic processes*.

Proposition 1. *Let* x *be a graph such that* $\mathsf{x} \leftrightarrow_{rb} \mathsf{x} + \mathsf{x}$. *There is a rooted branching bisimulation* $\mathcal{R}$ *such that* $r_{\mathsf{x}} \mathcal{R} r_{\mathsf{x}+\mathsf{x}}$ *and if* $r_{\mathsf{x}} \leadsto n$ *and* $r_{\mathsf{x}} \leadsto n'$, *then* $n \mathcal{R} n'$. r_{x} *and* $r_{\mathsf{x}+\mathsf{x}}$ *denote the roots of* x *and* $\mathsf{x} + \mathsf{x}$.

Having the meaning of this condition in mind, the reader may recognise B2 in PrB2, but applied on a sub-process which appears as a possible outcome of a probabilistic choice.

The axiom PrB3 can be derived from PrB2, but only for processes for which z is a dynamic process, $z = z + z$. Nevertheless, this axiom holds for all z, and this is why PrB3 is added. Both parts of the probabilistic choice lead to the same options.

Our main result is stated in the following two theorems. For detailed proofs see [1].

Theorem 2 (Soundness theorem). *The algebra pBPA*$_\tau$ *is sound with respect to the structure* $(\mathbf{G}/\leftrightarrow_{rb}, \delta, \cdot, +, \boxplus_\pi, \tau_I(p), Act_\tau)$.

Theorem 3 (Completeness theorem). *Let* p *and* q *be closed expressions and let* p *and* q *be their graph interpretations in* $\mathbf{G}$. *Then* $\mathsf{p} \leftrightarrow_{rb} \mathsf{q}$ *implies pBPA*$_\tau \vdash p = q$.

Proof. The proof follows the lines of the completeness proof for BPA$_\tau$ as given in [12]. Roughly speaking, it goes in several steps: 1. The notions of coloured probabilistic traces and coloured graphs that capture probabilities are introduced. 2. An equivalence relation on coloured graphs is defined for which we prove that it coincides with branching bisimulation (see also [2]). 3. We define a confluent and normalising system of rewriting rules for coloured graphs. Every rule removes an inert τ-transition or a node that is a copy of another node from the graph. We show that every coloured graph reduces to a unique normal form. 4. We show that every rewriting rule corresponds to an equation in the algebra.

4 Verification Rules

In a setting without probabilities, the correctness of an implementation (with respect to a specification) often hinges on fairness assumptions about the resolution of non-deterministic choices. Algebraically, such fairness assumptions are described through the use of *Koomen's fair abstraction rules* (KFARs) [7]. These rules capture the idea that in abstracting from a set of internal events (events that will become τ steps), eventually an observable event will be chosen. The eventuality arises as a result of an implicit fairness mechanism underlying a non-deterministic choice.

In the presence of probabilities, a fairness assumption for probabilistic choice is superfluous. By assigning a non-zero probability to every alternative in a probabilistic choice we can quantify the otherwise implicit fairness assumptions. Despite the fact that we do not need fairness assumptions to resolve a probabilistic choice, additional verification rules for probabilistic processes are still needed to reason about systems in which internal activity and probability distributions over observable events are involved.

For instance, consider process $x = a \boxplus_\pi \tau \cdot x$, where a is an observable activity. Using the axioms of pBPA$_\tau$, process x cannot be simplified further. Yet, when we examine the intuition behind this process, we find that with a probability of π, action a is executed immediately; if a is not executed immediately, there is a probability of $\pi(1-\pi)$ to be executed upon the second resolution of the choice. The pattern is obvious: action a is executed with probability $\sum_{0 \leq k < n} \pi(1-\pi)^k$ within n consecutive resolutions of the probabilistic choice. When n tends to infinity, the probability that a is executed tends to 1, so, in the limit, we find that process x should equal process a (see rule PVR$_1$).

Following a similar line of reasoning and using maximal probabilities with which observable actions are executed (as defined in Section 2), we identify the following verification rules.

$$\frac{x = y \boxplus_\pi i \cdot x \qquad i \in I}{\tau \cdot \tau_I(x) = \tau \cdot \tau_I(y)} \tag{PVR$_1$}$$

$$\frac{x = y + i \cdot x \qquad y = y + y \qquad i \in I}{\tau \cdot \tau_I(x) = \tau \cdot \tau_I(y)} \tag{PVR$_2$}$$

$$\frac{x = (z \boxplus_\pi y) + i \cdot x \qquad y = y + y \qquad i \in I}{\tau \cdot \tau_I(x) = \tau \cdot \tau_I(x') \text{ for } x' = z + y + i \cdot x'} \tag{PVR$_3$}$$

$$\frac{x = y_0 + i_0 \cdot x_1 \quad x_1 = y_1 + i_1 \cdot x_2 \quad \ldots \quad x_n = y_n + i_n \cdot x \quad i_k \in I,\ \exists i_j \neq \tau}{\tau \cdot \tau_I(x) = \tau \cdot \tau_I(x') \ \text{ for } x' = y_0 + y_1 \ldots y_n + i_0 \cdot x'} \tag{PKR$_n^b$}$$

$$\frac{x = z \boxplus_\pi (u + i \cdot x) \qquad z = z + u \qquad z = z + z \qquad i \in I}{\tau \cdot \tau_I(x) = \tau \cdot \tau_I(z)} \tag{PVR$_4$}$$

$$\frac{x = z + i \cdot y \qquad y = z \boxplus_\pi (u + j \cdot x) \qquad z = z + z \quad z = z + u \quad i, j \in I}{\tau \cdot \tau_I(x) = \tau \cdot \tau_I(y') \text{ for } y' = z \boxplus_\pi (u + i \cdot y')} \tag{PVR$_5$}$$

Rule PVR$_1$ has been already discussed. Rule PVR$_2$ is a variant of the KFAR rule for probabilistic setting. As such it is restricted on dynamic processes ($y = y + y$). Other probabilistic variants of the KFAR rules, the rules PKFAR$_n^b$, are given in [1].

In addition, we define rules PKR$_n^b$, $n \geq 1$, that also resemble the KFAR rules. Actually if all y_k are dynamic processes, by a proper combination of PKR$_n^b$ and PVR$_2$ we can derive PKFAR$_n^b$ for $n \geq 2$. But the PKR rules are applicable in more general cases since $y_k, k = 1, \ldots, n$ can be any pBPA$_\tau$ expressions. Let us consider the specification $x_1 = (a \boxplus_{1/2} b) + i \cdot x_2$ and $x_2 = (c \boxplus_{1/2} d) + j \cdot x_1$ for some internal actions i and j. For process x_1 (the same holds for x_2) the maximal probability to execute a, possibly preceded by finitely many internal activities, is equal to 1. Clearly, it is obtained by resolving all nondeterministic choices in favour of a and if a is not possible then in favour of τ. Thus we aim on relating x_1 after abstraction to a process in which a can be executed with maximal probability 1. Since we conclude the same for b, c and d, we obtain that x_1 shall be related to the process $a + b + c + d$.[1] The PKR rules do not imply this equality directly, but they can be used to reduce the specification to a form on which rule PVR_3 can be applied.

Rule PVR_3 expresses that in some cases a τ-loop makes the probability distribution irrelevant. Take $z = a \boxplus_{1/2} b$ and $y = c$. Note that $y = y + y$. According to this rule the presence of the τ-loop in $x = ((a \boxplus_{1/2} b) \boxplus_{1/3} c) + i \cdot x$ (after abstraction from i) makes the probability distribution over a, b and c irrelevant. Thus, it allows us to equate x to $x' = (a \boxplus_{1/2} b) + c + i \cdot x'$ in which the probabilistic choice between $(a \boxplus_{1/2} b)$ and c is replaced by a non-deterministic choice. By applying the rule once more and using some technical tricks (introducing new internal actions, renaming them, assuming that every guarded specification has a unique solution, etc.) we can obtain $\tau \cdot \tau_I(x) = \tau \cdot \tau_I(a + b + c + i \cdot x)$ for some set of internal actions $I, i \in I$. Finally, we can apply the PVR_2 rule and remove the remaining τ-loop and obtain $\tau \cdot \tau_I(x) = \tau \cdot (a + b + c)$ (again, slightly abusing notation).

Rules PVR_4 and PVR_5 have a condition of the form $z = z + u$. Informally, it states that every process which can be reached from z with a positive probability can mimic all activities of u. Hence, all activities of process u are also captured by process z.

Proposition 2. *Let* z *and* u *be graphs such that* $\mathsf{z} \underline{\leftrightarrow}_{rb} \mathsf{z} + \mathsf{u}$. *There is a rooted branching bisimulation* $\mathcal{R}$ *such that* $r_{\mathsf{z}} \mathcal{R} r_{\mathsf{z+u}}$ *and, for all* n, n', t' *such that* $r_{\mathsf{z}} \rightsquigarrow n$, $r_{\mathsf{u}} \rightsquigarrow n'$ *and* $n' \xrightarrow{a} t'$ *for* $a \in Act_\tau$, *there exists a transition* $n \xrightarrow{a} t$ *for some* $t \in S_{\mathsf{z}}$ *and* $t \mathcal{R} t'$. r_{z} *and* $r_{\mathsf{z+u}}$ *denote the root nodes of* z *and* $\mathsf{z} + \mathsf{u}$.

Next we focus on rule PVR_4 and give only a short example for PVR_5. Rule PVR_4 expresses a situation in which, due to a τ-loop, a summand u of probabilistic process x can be dropped without affecting the behaviour of the process x. The two conditions: $z = z + z$ expressing that z is a dynamic process (see Proposition 1), and $z = z + u$ stating that all activities of process u are captured by process z (see Proposition 2) guarantee that every node reachable from the root of the graph for x, x, can perform the *same* set of actions that z can perform, and continue with the equivalent behaviour to the one of z afterwards. These actions can be performed either directly in one step or after performing a τ-transition back to the root of x. For the latter case, the specification of x guarantees that the nodes that cannot perform an action immediately (as stated above) can make the τ step back to the root of x. Under these conditions, the root of x and all nodes reachable from it in one probabilistic transition, are equivalent. Therefore, they can all be lumped in a single node, the root of the graph of z as the rule states. This is not possible if z is not a dynamic process.

Note that this rule (and the processes involved) can be translated into the non-alternating model (as simple probabilistic automata [17] or as probabilistic automata [11]). Clearly, it is sound for weak bisimilulation equivalences as defined in [17,18,11]. However, so far there have not been algebraic laws proposed that characterises the property of weak bisimulation to relate these processes.

[1] Note that at this point and in several discussions later in this section we are not precise since we omit the τ prefix for the sake of simplicity.

Rule PVR5 has two conditions: z restricted to dynamic processes, and u must be a process (possibly not a dynamic process) that is mimicked by z (see Proposition 2). For simplicity take both z and u to be dynamic processes (in which case u is a sub-process of z) $z = a + b$ and $u = b$. Rule PVR5 states that process $x = (a + b) + i \cdot ((a + b) \boxplus_{1/2}(b + j \cdot x))$ is equal to $x' = (a + b) \boxplus_{1/2}(b + i \cdot x')$ after abstraction from i and j. Obviously, PVR_5 is an extension of PVR_4 to a specification with two equations. We believe that a generalisation of these rules to any finite specifications is feasible, but this may require more complex conditions.

Theorem 4 (Soundness of verification rules). *The verification rules PVR_1,...,PVR_5 and PKR^b_n, $n \geq 1$, are sound for the structure $(\mathbf{G}/\underline{\leftrightarrow}_{rb}, \delta, \cdot, +, \boxplus_\pi, \tau_I(p), Act_\tau)$.*

5 Application

The main intention of this section is to show that our probabilistic process algebra and the verification rules from Section 4 can be used for the verification of complex protocols which exhibit both probabilistic and non-deterministic behaviour. We do not aim at giving a complete description of the protocol. We refer the reader to [19] for more details. The specifications we provide use two other operators, viz. *parallel composition* and *encapsulation*. The parallel operator $\|$ models the interleavings and communications (synchronisations) of two processes. The unary encapsulation operator ∂_H is in a sense a special renaming operator, renaming all actions from the set H to δ. Using the elimination theorem for parallel composition, and encapsulation, all guarded recursive equations containing the parallel operator can be rewritten to equivalent guarded recursive equations using only the operators from the algebra pBPA_τ. For a detailed treatment on these operators in the probabilistic setting, we refer to [6,5].

The CABP is a more complex variant of the well-known *Alternating Bit Protocol* (ABP). Both protocols are used to reliably send and receive data via an unreliable channel, using a system of *acknowledgements*, also sent via unreliable channels. While the ABP resends messages that have not been received correctly only after receiving a *negative acknowledgement*, the CABP continuously (re)sends the same message until it receives a *positive acknowledgement*, confirming a correct delivery of the datum. Due to this phenomenon many activities are executed in parallel.

5.1 Specification of the CABP

The specification we use for the CABP is based on the description given in [19]. While in [19], the channels for transmitting data and acknowledgements are modelled using non-determinism, we shall use probabilities to model the behaviours of the channels. The CABP is described by six separate processes that need to communicate with one another. A sketch of the system is provided in Fig. 4. The numbers 1 through 8 represent the gates at which actions are communicated. Together, the six processes model the entire protocol. We represent the *sender* and *receiver* of data by process S and R, respectively. The sender and receiver of an acknowledgement are specified by processes AS and AR, respectively. In turn, the channel, carrying the data is represented by process K, and the channel carrying the acknowledgements is represented by process L. We

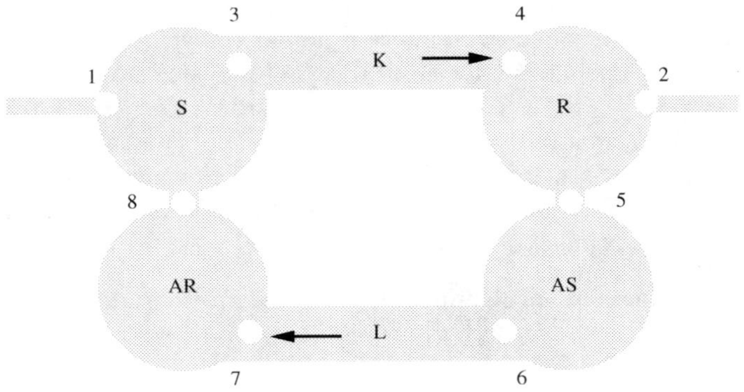

Fig. 4. Layout of the *Concurrent Alternating Bit Protocol*

Table 2. Specification of the sender, the receiver and the channel. The probabilities π and ρ model the probability that a message is sent correctly and the probability that a message is corrupted. With a probability of $1-\pi-\rho$ the message is lost in a channel.

Sender:

$$
\begin{aligned}
&S &&= \mathit{RM}(0)\\
&\mathit{RM}(b{\in}\mathit{Bit}) &&= \textstyle\sum_{d\in D} r_1(d)\cdot \mathit{SF}(d,b)\\
&\mathit{SF}((d,b){\in}D{\times}\mathit{Bit}) &&= s_3(d,b)\cdot \mathit{SF}(d,b) + r_8(ac)\cdot \mathit{RM}(1-b)
\end{aligned}
$$

Receiver:

$$
\begin{aligned}
&R &&= \mathit{RF}(0)\\
&\mathit{RF}(b{\in}\mathit{Bit}) &&= \textstyle\sum_{d\in D} r_4(d,b)\cdot \mathit{RS}(d,b)\\
& &&\quad + \textstyle\sum_{d\in D} r_4(d,1-b)\cdot \mathit{RF}(b) + r_4(\bot)\cdot \mathit{RF}(b)\\
&\mathit{RS}((d,b){\in}D{\times}\mathit{Bit}) &&= s_2(d)\cdot s_5(ac)\cdot \mathit{RF}(1-b)
\end{aligned}
$$

Channel:

$$
\begin{aligned}
&K &&= \textstyle\sum_{(d,b)\in D\times \mathit{Bit}} r_3(d,b)\cdot K_s(d,b)\\
&K_s((d,b){\in}D{\times}\mathit{Bit}) &&= (s_4(d,b) \boxplus_\pi s_4(\bot) \boxplus_\rho k)\cdot K
\end{aligned}
$$

group these processes in two logical modules, viz. a module M_1 responsible for transmitting and receiving data, containing processes S, K and R, and a module M_2 responsible for transmitting and receiving acknowledgements, containing processes AS, L and AR. The CABP is then described by the parallel composition of these two modules. Since the behaviour of both modules is quite similar, we here only investigate the behaviour of module M_1. The specifications for the sender, the receiver and the data channel are given in Table 2. The difference between our specification and the one appearing in [19] is mainly in the definition of the channel.

We briefly sketch the intuition behind the processes of module M_1. The set D denotes a finite set of data elements. The sender, modelled by process S uses action r_1 to receive a datum from its environment. This datum, augmented with a bit (for acknowledgement purposes), is then repeatedly sent using action s_3. Alternatively, an acknowledgement is received using action r_8. The receiver reads data from the communication channel K using action r_4. A corrupted datum is represented by $\perp$ (a mechanism for detecting faulty data is assumed). If a non-corrupted, expected datum is received (i.e. it carries the expected acknowledgement bit), it is sent to the environment via action s_2 and the acknowledgement sender is triggered via action s_5. Finally, the unreliable channel uses action r_3 for receiving a datum, action s_4 for sending a (possibly corrupted) datum and action k for losing a datum.

We distinguish between the external and the internal behaviour of module M_1. The communications between the actions of module M_1 are defined using a (commutative and associative) function γ, given by $\gamma(r_3(d,b), s_3(d,b)) = c_3(d,b)$ and $\gamma(r_4(d,b), s_4(d,b)) = c_4(d,b)$ and $\gamma(r_4(\perp), s_4(\perp)) = c_4(\perp)$ for all data $(d,b) \in D \times \mathit{Bit}$ (here, c_3 and c_4 are fresh actions). Process $\partial_H(S \| R \| K)$ then describes the internal behaviour of module M_1, where $H = \{s_3(d,b), r_3(d,b), s_4(d,b), r_4(d,b), s_4(\perp), r_4(\perp) \mid (d,b) \in D \times \mathit{Bit}\}$ contains all actions that need to be blocked to enforce communication. The external behaviour of module M_1 is the behaviour of module M_1 *after* abstracting from the actions from the set $I = \{c_3(d,b), c_4(d,b), c_4(\perp), k \mid (d,b) \in D \times \mathit{Bit}\}$. The external behaviour of module M_1 can thus be represented by $Y = \tau_I \circ \partial_H(S \| R \| K)$.

5.2 Verification of the CABP

Our aim is to rewrite the process, representing the external behaviour of module M_1 to a simpler process, for which it is easier to check that it behaves the way it is meant to behave. For lack of space, we will not go into the full detail, but pick out several interesting bits of the verification. For the full verification, we refer to [1]. Apart from using the rules we gave in Section 4 and the use of axiomatic reasoning, we employ a technique called *language matching*, which is explained and used in [19]. This is not essential for the verification but it reduces it significantly. Language matching builds on the idea that certain behaviours of one separate process when considered in isolation, cannot occur when the process is composed in parallel with some other process(es). Consider for example process $\partial_{\{a,c,d\}}(x \| y)$, where $x = a \cdot x + c \cdot z$ and $y = d \cdot y$, and the actions a and d are meant to communicate to action b. Clearly, c is a redundant summand because it gets encapsulated, and it is not involved in communications. The intuition, how to identify redundant summands, is that actions often occur in a fixed sequence. The language matching operator, denoted by $\triangle_Z$, where Z is a collection of traces, checks for a given process if the actions that occur are executed according to the order, specified by a trace in Z. If so, the remainder of the process is inspected. If not, then the remainder of the process is apparently not of any interest to the overall behaviour of the system, and hence, it is replaced by the special symbol $\Re$, which is not present in the alphabet Act.

Analysis of the CABP. We start with analysing the subprocess $\partial_{H'}(R \| K)$, where H' is the set $\{r_4(d,b), s_4(d,b), r_4(\perp), s_4(\perp) \mid (d,b) \in D \times \mathit{Bit}\}$. Removing parallelism using the elimination theorem we arrive at the description for this process, given in Table 3 for which actions k, $c_4(\perp)$ and $c_4(d,b)$ occur as internal actions.

The sender itself can always receive an acknowledgement of the correct reception of a message (action $r_8(ac)$), and thereby change the entire global state. However, in the overall behaviour of the CABP, the reception of an acknowledgement only happens

Table 3. Process $R\|K$ after encapsulation of the actions in set H'

$X_1(b{\in}Bit)$	$= \sum_{d\in D} r_3(d,b)\cdot X_3(b,d) + \sum_{d\in D} r_3(d,1-b)\cdot X_2(b,d)$
$X_2(b{\in}Bit, d{\in}D)$	$= (c_4(d,1-b) \boxplus_{\pi} c_4(\bot) \boxplus_{\rho} k)\cdot X_1(b)$
$X_3(b{\in}Bit, d{\in}D)$	$= c_4(d,b)\cdot X_4(b,d) \boxplus_{\pi} c_4(\bot)\cdot X_1(b) \boxplus_{\rho} k\cdot X_1(b)$
$X_4(b{\in}Bit, d{\in}D)$	$= \sum_{d'\in D} r_3(d',b)\cdot X_5(b,d,d')$
	$+ \sum_{d'\in D} r_3(d',1-b)\cdot X_6(b,d,d')$
	$+ s_2(d)\cdot X_9(b)$
$X_5(b{\in}Bit, d, d'{\in}D)$	$= s_2(d)\cdot X_7(b,d') + (\delta \boxplus_{\pi+\rho} k)\cdot X_4(b,d)$
$X_6(b{\in}Bit, d, d'{\in}D)$	$= s_2(d)\cdot X_8(b,d') + (\delta \boxplus_{\pi+\rho} k)\cdot X_4(b,d)$
$X_7(b{\in}Bit, d{\in}D)$	$= s_5(ac)\cdot X_2(1-b,d) + (\delta \boxplus_{\pi+\rho} k)\cdot X_9(b)$
$X_8(b{\in}Bit, d{\in}D)$	$= s_5(ac)\cdot X_3(1-b,d) + (\delta \boxplus_{\pi+\rho} k)\cdot X_9(b)$
$X_9(b{\in}Bit)$	$= \sum_{d\in D} r_3(d,b)\cdot X_7(b,d)$
	$+ \sum_{d\in D} r_3(d,1-b)\cdot X_8(b,d)$
	$+ s_5(ac)\cdot X_1(1-b)$

when an acknowledgement has been sent earlier. Thus, to filter out the reception of the ill-timed acknowledgements, we apply the language matching. In short, all alternatives in the specification for module M_1 that are in traces that do not match the language containing concatenations of traces $r_1(d)\ s_2(d)\ s_5(ac)\ r_8(ac)$ for arbitrary $d{\in}D$ should be marked with the symbol $\Re$. We define $Z = \{r_1(d)\ s_2(d)\ s_5(ac)\ r_8(ac) \mid d{\in}D\}^*$, and subsequently study process $\triangle_{Z'} \circ \partial_H(SF(d,b)\|X_4(b,d))$, where $Z' = \{z \mid d{\in}D, r_1(d)z{\in}Z\}$ contains all traces of Z from which the first action $r_1(d)$ has been removed. The complete specification for the process $Y(b) = \triangle_{Z'} \circ \partial_H(RM(b)\|RF(b)\|K)$ is given in [1]. We discuss one step of the verification. We derive

$$\triangle_{Z'} \circ \partial_H(SF(d,b)\|X_4(b,d))$$
$$= r_8(ac)\cdot\Re + s_2(d)\cdot U_1 + c_3(d,b)\cdot \triangle_{Z'} \circ \partial_H(SF(d,b)\|X_5(b,d,d))$$

Process U_1 is not of our interest at this point. Note that after action $r_8(ac)$, the remainder of the process has become unimportant, as the action $r_8(ac)$ is not a valid option at this point in the overall behaviour. We continue, and derive that

$$\triangle_{Z'} \circ \partial_H(SF(d,b)\|X_5(b,d,d))$$
$$= (r_8(ac)\cdot\Re + s_2(d)\cdot U_2)$$
$$\boxplus_{\pi+\rho}(r_8(ac)\cdot\Re + s_2(d)\cdot U_2 + k\cdot \triangle_{Z'} \circ \partial_H(SF(d,b)\|X_4(b,d))$$

Again, the exact process U_2 is not of our interest at this point (for details see [1]). It turns out that (by carrying the verification through to the end), we can prove that $\tau_I(U_1) = \tau_I(U_2)$, for I not containing the communications with the channel K. Hence, by hiding the communications that occur on gates 3 and 4, using verification rule PVR$_5$ and then PVR$_4$ (for $z = u = r_8(ac)\cdot\Re + s_2(d)\cdot\tau_I(U_2)$)), we derive

$$\tau\cdot\tau_{I_K} \circ \triangle_{Z'} \circ \partial_H(SF(d,b)\|X_4(b,d)) = \tau\cdot(r_8(ac)\cdot\Re + s_2(d)\cdot\tau_{I_K}(U_2))$$

where I_K contains all communications with the channel K. Repeatedly applying the rules and axioms in a fashion we just sketched (in total there are 10 steps), we can derive that $Y = \sum_{d\in D} r_1(d)\cdot(r_8(ac)\cdot\Re + s_2(d)\cdot(r_8(ac)\cdot\Re + s_5(ac)\cdot r_8(ac)\cdot Y))$. By carrying the verification to the end, we can derive that the whole CABP behaves as a reliable buffer, i.e.

$$\tau\cdot\tau_{I'} \circ \partial_{H''}(S\|K\|R\|AS\|L\|AR)$$
$$= \tau\cdot\sum_{d\in D} r_1(d)\cdot s_2(d)\cdot\tau_{I'} \circ \partial_{H''}(S\|K\|R\|AS\|L\|AR)$$

for I' containing all activities over communication gates $3, 4, 5, 6, 7$ and 8 (i.e. all activities in and between modules M_1 and M_2), and H'' containing all send and read activities that do not synchronise in the interleaving.

6 Summary

We presented a probabilistic process algebra pBPA$_\tau$ with capabilities for hiding internal activity of a process by renaming observable actions to an unobservable action. We furthermore presented a number of axioms that allow for the removal of inert unobservable actions, i.e. unobservable actions whose presence cannot be detected. This set of axioms forms a complete axiomatisation of branching bisimilarity for the strictly alternating model [2]. Analogously with rules such as Koomen's Fair Abstraction Rules (KFARs) [7], which are used in a setting without probabilities, we introduced a number of rules that proved useful in a setting with probabilities. With this method, without having to resort to probability theory or schedulers, we can do a complete algebraic verification of the Concurrent Alternating Bit Protocol [19] that contains non-removable non-deterministic choices. It turns out that the rules and the axioms we provided are indeed needed and sufficient to come to the desired result.

References

1. S. Andova, J.C.M. Baeten, T.A.C. Willemse, *Complete axiomatisation of probabilistic branching bisimulation*, preliminary version available via `http://www.cs.ru.nl/~timw/completeness.pdf`. To appear as CSR, 2006.
2. S. Andova, T.A.C. Willemse, *Branching bisimulation for probabilistic systems: characteristics and decidability*. Theor. Comp. Sci. Vol 356, No 3., J.C.M. Baeten, F. Corradini, (eds.), pg. 325-355, 2006. Also appeared as a CSR, University of Twente, TR-CTIT-05-08, 2005
3. S. Andova, J.C.M. Baeten *Abstraction in probabilistic process algebra*, Proc. TACAS 2001, T. Margaria, Wang Yi, eds., LNCS 2031 Springer Verlag, pp. 204-219, 2001.
4. S. Andova, J.C.M. Baeten *Alternative composition does not imply non-determinism*, Bulletin of the European Association for Theoretical Computer Science 76, pp. 125-127, 2002.
5. S. Andova, *Probabilistic process algebra*, Ph.D. thesis, Eindhoven University of Technology, 2002.
6. S. Andova, *Process algebra with probabilistic choice*, ARTS'99, J.-P. Katoen (ed.), LNCS 1601, Springer-Verlag, pp. 111-129, 1999.
7. J.C.M. Baeten, J.A. Bergstra, J.W. Klop, *On the consistency of Koomen's fair abstraction rule*, Theor. Comp. Sci. 51, pp.129-176, 1987.
8. J.C.M. Baeten, W.P. Weijland, *Process algebra*, Cambridge University Press, 1990.
9. C. Baier, *On algorithmic verification methods for probabilistic systems*, Habilitation thesis, University of Mannheim, 1998.
10. E. Bandini, R. Segala, *Axiomatizations for probabilistic bisimulation*, ICALP'01, F. Orejas, P.G. Spirakis, J. van Leeuwen, eds., LNCS 2076, Springer Verlag, pp. 370-381, 2001.
11. Y. Deng, C. Palamidessi *Axiomatizations for probabilistic finite-state behaviors*, Proc. FoSSaCS'05, LNCS 3441, pp. 110–124, 2005.
12. R. J. van Glabbeek, W. P. Weijland, *Branching time and abstraction in bisimulation semantics*, Journal of ACM, Vol. 43-3, pp.555-600, 1996.
13. H. Hansson, *Time and probability in formal design of distributed systems*, Ph.D. thesis, DoCS 91/27, University of Uppsala, 1991.

14. C.P.J. Koymans and J.C. Mulder, *A modular approach to protocol verification using process algebra*, In: Applications of Process Algebra, J.C.M. Baeten, ed., Cambridge Tracts in Theoretical Computer Science 17, Cambridge University Press, pp. 261-306, 1990.
15. R. Milner, *Communication and concurrency*, International Series in Computer Science, Prentice Hall, 1989.
16. A. Philippou, I. Lee, O. Sokolsky, *Weak bisimulation for probabilistic systems*, Proc. CONCUR'00, C. Palamidessi, ed., LNCS 1877, Springer Verlag, pp. 334-349, 2000.
17. R. Segala, N.A. Lynch, *Probabilistic simulations for probabilistic processes*, Nordic Journal of Computing, 2(2):250-273,1995.
18. M. Stoelinga, *Alea jacta est: Verification of probabilistic, real-time and parametric systems*, Ph.D. thesis, Katholieke Universiteit Nijmegen, The Netherlands, 2002.
19. J. van Wamel, *Process Algebra with Language Matching*, Theor. Comput. Sci. 177(2):425-458, 1997.

Probabilistic I/O Automata: Theories of Two Equivalences*

Eugene W. Stark[1], Rance Cleaveland[2], and Scott A. Smolka[1]

[1] Department of Computer Science, State University of New York at Stony Brook, Stony Brook, NY 11794 USA
{stark, sas}@cs.sunysb.edu
[2] Department of Computer Science, University of Maryland, College Park, Maryland 20742 USA
rance@cs.umd.edu

Abstract. Working in the context of a process-algebraic language for Probabilistic I/O Automata (PIOA), we study the notion of *PIOA behavior equivalence* by obtaining a complete axiomatization of its equational theory and comparing the results with a complete axiomatization of a more standard equivalence, *weighted bisimulation*. The axiomatization of behavior equivalence is achieved by adding to the language an operator for forming *convex combinations* of terms.

Keywords: stochastic process algebras; process equivalences; continuous-time Markov chains; equational theories; complete axiomatizations.

1 Introduction

In previous work [SCS03], we presented a process-algebraic language, motivated by the *probabilistic I/O automaton* model, that provides a compositional formalism for defining continuous-time Markov chains (CTMCs). The constructs in our language are similar to those in other "Markovian process algebra" languages that have been studied by a number of other researchers (see [HH02] for a survey), especially EMPA [BDG98]. In our language, we classify transitions as either *output* ("active") transitions or *input* ("passive") transitions. Output transitions, which can occur spontaneously, have associated positive *rates*. Rates are dimensional quantities with units of 1/time, which are regarded as the parameters of exponential probability distributions. When multiple output transitions are available for a process, the choice between them is made probabilistically by a "race policy" semantics: an exponentially distributed random future time

* This research was supported in part by the National Science Foundation under Grant CCR-9988155 and the Army Research Office under Grants DAAD190110003 and DAAD190110019. Any opinions, findings, and conclusions or recommendations expressed in this material are those of the author(s) and do not necessarily reflect the views of the National Science Foundation, the Army Research Office, or other sponsors.

C. Baier and H. Hermanns (Eds.): CONCUR 2006, LNCS 4137, pp. 343–357, 2006.

is chosen for the occurrence of each transition (using the associated rate as the parameter of the distribution) and the transition for which the earliest time is chosen "wins the race" and becomes the next transition to occur. Input transitions, which can occur for a process only in conjunction with a similarly labeled output transition performed by its environment, have associated positive *weights*, which are dimensionless. When multiple input transitions labeled by the same action are available, the choice between them is made probabilistically on the basis of their proportionate weights.

In this paper, we consider a fragment of our language having the following syntax, where *Act* is a set of *actions*, variables $a, b, c, \ldots$ are used to range over *Act*, and variables $t, u, v, \ldots$ are used to range over process terms:

$$\mathrm{nil}_I \mid \langle a?_w \rangle\, t \mid \langle b!_r \rangle\, t \mid t + t' \mid t\ {}_O\|_{O'}\ t'$$

The informal meaning of the constructs is as follows:

- nil_I denotes a process that passively accepts an input from the set $I \subseteq Act$, assigning such an input a weight of 1, and then continues to behave as nil_I.
- $\langle a?_w \rangle\, t$ denotes an *input-prefixed* process that can accept an input $a \in Act$ with positive *weight* w and then become the process t.
- $\langle b!_r \rangle\, t$ denotes an *output-prefixed* process that can spontaneously perform output action $b \in Act$ with positive *rate* r and then become the process denoted by t.
- $t + t'$ denotes a *choice* between alternatives offered by t and t'.
- $t\ {}_O\|_{O'}\ t'$ denotes the *parallel composition* of t and t'. Here O and O' are disjoint sets of output actions *controlled by* t and t', respectively.

Synchronization of actions, which occurs between the components of a parallel composition, is restricted to the input/input and input/output cases only. Output/output synchronization is not permitted. This seems to be the simplest version of action synchronization that has an intuitively meaningful stochastic interpretation. As our goal is to understand the relationship between input and output in the simplest possible setting, we do not complicate the language with immediate actions, priorities, or other extraneous constructs.

The standard notions of process equivalence in the context of stochastic process algebra are based on variants of *probabilistic bisimulation* [LS91], which is closely related to the concept of *lumpability* in the theory of Markov chains. A typical example of such an equivalence is *Markovian bisimulation* [Hil96], in which terms regarded as equivalent are required to have the same aggregate transition rate, and which is such that equivalent terms have identical total transition probabilities to each equivalence class of terms for each action. In this paper we use *weighted bisimulation*, which uses the same fundamental idea and covers the cases of weight-labeled and rate-labeled transitions.

Behavior equivalence is an alternative to weighted bisimulation equivalence that we have studied in earlier papers. This equivalence is strictly coarser than weighted bisimulation equivalence, but still substitutive with respect to the process algebraic operations listed above. The original motivation of behavior equivalence was as a testing equivalence, and in this context a full-abstractness result was established in [WSS97]. The original definitions were reformulated in subsequent papers as our understanding of behavior equivalence improved. In [Sta03] we were able to compare weighted bisimulation equivalence and behavior equivalence by viewing them both as certain "invariant" equivalences on formal *linear combinations* of process terms, rather than as equivalences on individual terms. We showed, roughly: (1) that weighted bisimulation equivalence can be characterized as the largest invariant equivalence on combinations of terms that is in a sense generated by equations between individual terms, (2) that behavior equivalence can be characterized as the largest invariant equivalence on combinations of terms that in a sense separates terms having distinct aggregate rates, and (3) that behavior equivalence is strictly coarser than weighted bisimulation equivalence, even when restricted to individual terms.

For example, the following intuitively reasonable equation between terms in our language holds for behavior equivalence but not for weighted bisimulation equivalence:

$$\langle b!_r\rangle\ (\langle c!_{\pi s}\rangle\ t + \langle d!_{(1-\pi)s}\rangle\ u) \quad = \quad \langle b!_{\pi r}\rangle\ \langle c!_s\rangle\ t + \langle b!_{(1-\pi)r}\rangle\ \langle d!_s\rangle\ u$$

where π can be any value in the interval $(0, 1)$. Intuitively, both sides above can perform the output b with the same aggregate rate r. After doing so, the term on the left-hand side evolves to the derivative term $\langle c!_{\pi s}\rangle\ t + \langle d!_{(1-\pi)s}\rangle\ u$, which can do output c with rate πs and output d with rate $(1-\pi)s$, for an aggregate rate of s. In contrast, there is no individual term that expresses the derivative of the right-hand side after output b has been performed. The best we can do is to think of this derivative as a *probability distribution* that assigns probability π to term $\langle c!_s\rangle\ t$ and probability $1-\pi$ to term $\langle d!_s\rangle\ t$. Intuitively, there is no observable difference between such a probability distribution and the individual term $\langle c!_{\pi s}\rangle\ t + \langle d!_{(1-\pi)s}\rangle\ u$, which explains why the original equation is a reasonable one to expect.

Consideration of the preceding example suggests that an axiomatization of behavior equivalence might be achieved if we augment the language with an explicit notation for expressing convex combinations of terms; for example: $\langle c!_s\rangle\ t\ {}_{\pi}{\oplus}_{1-\pi}\ \langle d!_s\rangle\ u$. We would then be able to express the equivalence between the derivatives of the left and right-hand sides of the equation above as follows:

$$\langle c!_{\pi s}\rangle\ t + \langle d!_{(1-\pi)s}\rangle\ u \quad = \quad \langle c!_s\rangle\ t\ {}_{\pi}{\oplus}_{1-\pi}\ \langle d!_s\rangle\ u.$$

In fact, for the $\|$-free fragment of the language, an axiomatization of behavior equivalence can be achieved in this way and the details are the subject of the present paper. A key point, which took us a long time to discover, is that we cannot permit the the formation of combinations $t\ {}_{\pi}{\oplus}_{1-\pi}\ u$ for arbitrary terms t and u. Rather, we must require as a condition of well-formedness that terms t and u have an *identical aggregate rate*, which then becomes the aggregate rate of the combined term. Failing to impose this requirement results in the possibility of having "terms" that do not have unique aggregate rates, which produces seemingly insurmountable complications in the semantics and axiomatization.

Another detail that required some care to work out properly concerns keeping track of the "types" of terms, by which we mean the sets of input and output actions in which a term is required to participate.

As a result of our investigation, we have further clarified our understanding of behavior equivalence and its relationship to weighted bisimulation equivalence. Perhaps the simplest way to summarize what we have learned is to compare the normal form used in the proofs of completeness for the axiomatization of weighted bisimulation equivalence with that used in the proof for behavior equivalence. Employing $\sum$-notation in a standard way and (for the moment) ignoring special cases that arise with empty summations, the following is a generic normal form for a term with respect to weighted bisimulation equivalence:

$$\sum_{i=1}^{m} \langle a_i?_{w_i} \rangle \, t_i + \sum_{j=1}^{n} \langle b_j!_{r_j} \rangle \, t_j$$

In the above, the t_i and t_j are recursively required to be normal forms. Moreover, it is required that for no distinct i and i' do we have both $a_i = a_{i'}$ and t_i equivalent to $t_{i'}$ and for no distinct j and j' do we have both $b_j = b_{j'}$ and t_j equivalent to $t_{j'}$. Thus, w_i is the aggregate weight of a_i-transitions to the equivalence class of t_i, and r_j is the aggregate rate of b_j-transitions to the equivalence class of t_j.

In contrast, a generic normal form for a term with respect to behavior equivalence is the following:

$$\sum_{a \in I} \sum_{s \in R_a} \langle a?_{w_{a,s}} \rangle \, t_{a,s} + \sum_{b \in O} \sum_{s \in R_b} \langle b!_{r_{b,s}} \rangle \, t_{b,s},$$

where each set R_a and R_b is nonempty and each term $t_{a,s}$ and $t_{b,s}$ is required recursively to be a normal form with aggregate rate s. The main point here is that, once input a has been chosen, there is a unique derivative term $t_{a,s}$ for each aggregate rate in the set R_a, and once output b has been chosen, there is a unique derivative term $t_{b,s}$ for each aggregate rate in the set R_b. Terms $t_{a,s}$ and $t_{a,s'}$ cannot be equivalent for distinct values of s because they have distinct aggregate rates. Similar considerations hold for $t_{b,s}$ and $t_{b,s'}$. A normal form for behavior equivalence is thus also a normal form for weighted bisimulation equivalence, but not conversely. So, the essential difference between weighted bisimulation equivalence and behavior equivalence is that the former will in general draw distinctions between terms based on the existence of multiple derivatives having the same aggregate rate, whereas the latter will not.

Note that, although the operator ${}_{\pi}\oplus_{1-\pi}$ does not appear in the normal form for behavior equivalence, achieving a reduction to normal form will in general require passing through terms in which explicit use is made of this operator.

The remainder of the paper is organized as follows: In Section 2, we summarize the basic definitions pertaining to our process-algebraic language and its semantics. In Section 3, we define the notion of weighted bisimulation equivalence for our language and present a sound and complete set of axioms for this equivalence. In Section 4, we define the notion of behavior equivalence, extend

$$\mathrm{nil}_I : I/I \Rightarrow \emptyset$$

$$\frac{t : J/J \Rightarrow O \quad a \in J}{\langle a?_w \rangle\, t : \{a\}/J \Rightarrow O} \qquad \frac{t : J/J \Rightarrow O \quad b \notin J}{\langle b!_r \rangle\, t : \emptyset/J \Rightarrow O \cup \{b\}}$$

$$\frac{t : I_t/J \Rightarrow O_t \quad u : I_u/J \Rightarrow O_u}{t + u : I_t \cup I_u/J \Rightarrow O_t \cup O_u}$$

$$\frac{t : I_t/I_t \Rightarrow O_t \quad u : I_u/I_u \Rightarrow O_u \quad I = (I_t \cup I_u) \setminus (O_t \cup O_u)}{t \;{}_{O_t}\|_{O_u}\; u : I/I \Rightarrow O_t \cup O_u}$$

$$\frac{t : I/J \Rightarrow O \quad O \subseteq O' \quad O' \cap J = \emptyset}{t : I/J \Rightarrow O'}$$

Fig. 1. Type-Inference Rules

the language with the convex combination operator ${}_\pi\oplus_{1-\pi}$ discussed above, present a sound and complete set of axioms for behavior equivalence in the extended language, and sketch the main ideas of the completeness proof. Although we include the parallel composition construct in the language defined in section 2, the results of Sections 3 and 4 concern only the $\|$-free fragment. We hope to extend our results to include parallel composition in a future paper.

Though we give here complete definitions for all important notions, space limitations force us to omit almost all proofs from this paper. The interested reader can find the omitted proofs in the full version [SCS06] available online.

2 Basic Definitions

2.1 Types

As detailed in our previous paper [SCS03], our PIOA language is equipped with a set of rules for inferring *typing judgements* of the form $t : I/J \Rightarrow O$, where I, J, and O are sets of actions. We write $\vdash t : \phi$ to assert that a typing judgement $t : \phi$ is inferable. A term t is *well-typed* if $\vdash t : \phi$ for some ϕ. Let $\mathrm{Proc}(I/J \Rightarrow O)$ denote the set of all terms t such that $\vdash t : I/J \Rightarrow O$.

Intuitively, a typing judgement $t : I/J \Rightarrow O$ asserts that I is a set of actions for which input transitions are guaranteed to be enabled at the first step of t, that J is a set of actions for which input transitions are guaranteed to be enabled at all steps of t after the first, and O is a set of actions that includes at least all the outputs that may be produced by t (but which may be larger). The primary purpose of the typing system is to identify those terms that are *input-enabled*, in order to rule out the formation of parallel compositions involving non-input-enabled terms. Non-input-enabled terms are required in the language to permit the building up of sets of alternatives using $+$. The reason why only input-enabled terms are permitted in parallel compositions is that we do not wish to allow stochastically unclear situations in which one component in a system is attempting to perform an output with a definite rate, but is inhibited from doing so by another component that will not accept that action as an input.

Figure 1 presents the type-inference rules applicable to the language fragment we consider here. We have included an additional "weakening" rule (the last rule), which was not present in our previous paper. The purpose of the weakening rule is to ensure that if $\vdash t : I/J \Rightarrow O$ then also $\vdash t : I/J \Rightarrow O'$ for all $O' \supseteq O$ such that $O' \cap J = \emptyset$; this is a useful property that did not hold of the typing system in our previous paper.

Proposition 1. *If* $\vdash t : I/J \Rightarrow O$ *for some* I, J, *and* O, *then*

1. $I \subseteq J$ *and* $J \cap O = \emptyset$.
2. *There exists* $\hat{O}$ *such that* $\vdash t : I/J \Rightarrow \hat{O}$, *and such that whenever* $\vdash t : I'/J' \Rightarrow O'$ *then* $I' = I$, $J' = J$, *and* $O' \supseteq \hat{O}$.

A technical issue with our PIOA language is that of "native" versus "non-native" actions. If $t \in \mathrm{Proc}(I/J \Rightarrow O)$, then actions $e \in J \cup O$ are called *native* to t and actions outside this set are called *non-native*. Intuitively, native actions are those in which t must participate and non-native actions are those that t ignores. This distinction is important because if t has no transition for a particular output action in which it must participate, then that action is inhibited from occurring, whereas if t ignores an action then it may occur freely. Note that whether an action is considered native or non-native depends on our having fixed a particular type $I/J \Rightarrow O$ inferable for t. All such types have the same input sets I and J, but the output sets O may differ. Thus, in the sequel it will be necessary for us to parameterize certain notions by the particular output set on which they depend.

2.2 Transition Semantics

In our previous paper, we gave structural operational semantics rules that defined the transitions that could be taken by terms in our language. Though our present purposes do not require a full presentation of the transition semantics given in our previous paper, we do need a notation for the aggregate *weight* or *rate* $\Delta_e^O(t,v)$ of e-labeled transitions from t to v.

Suppose $t \in \mathrm{Proc}(I/J \Rightarrow O)$. Define $\Delta_e^O(t,v)$ as follows: If $e \notin J \cup O$ (non-native case), then $\Delta_e^O(t,v) = 1$ if $v = t$, and $\Delta_e^O(t,v) = 0$ otherwise. If $e \in J \cup O$ (native case), then

1. $\Delta_e^O(\mathrm{nil}_I, v) = \begin{cases} 1, & \text{if } e \in I \text{ and } v = \mathrm{nil}_I. \\ 0, & \text{otherwise.} \end{cases}$

2. $\Delta_e^O(\langle a?_w \rangle\, t, v) = \begin{cases} w, & \text{if } e = a \text{ and } v = t \\ 0, & \text{otherwise.} \end{cases}$

3. $\Delta_e^O(\langle b!_r \rangle\, t, v) = \begin{cases} r, & \text{if } e = b \text{ and } v = t \\ 0, & \text{otherwise.} \end{cases}$

4. $\Delta_e^O(t + u, v) = \Delta_e^O(t,v) + \Delta_e^O(u,v)$.

5. $\Delta_e^O(t \;{}_{O_t}\!\|_{O_u}\; u, v) = \begin{cases} \Delta_e^{O \setminus O_u}(t,t') \cdot \Delta_e^{O \setminus O_t}(u,u'), & \text{if } v = t' \;{}_{O_t}\!\|_{O_u}\; u' \\ 0, & \text{otherwise.} \end{cases}$

In the sequel, if $\mathcal{C}$ is a set of terms, then $\Delta_e^O(t, \mathcal{C})$ will be an abbreviation for the sum $\sum_{v \in \mathcal{C}} \Delta_e^O(t, v)$, which is always finite.

It is important for us that inferable types are preserved under transitions. Formally, we have the following result, which was stated in our previous paper and remains true in the presence of the weakening rule.

Proposition 2. *Suppose* $t \in \mathrm{Proc}(I/J \Rightarrow O)$. *If* $\Delta_e^O(t, u) \neq 0$, *then* $u \in \mathrm{Proc}(J/J \Rightarrow O)$. *In particular,* $\mathrm{Proc}(J/J \Rightarrow O)$ *is closed under transitions and terms in* $\mathrm{Proc}(I/J \Rightarrow O)$ *reach* $\mathrm{Proc}(J/J \Rightarrow O)$ *after one transition.*

A term $t \in \mathrm{Proc}(J/J \Rightarrow O)$ is called *input-stochastic* if for all $e \in J$ we have $\sum_{v \in \mathrm{Proc}(J/J \Rightarrow O)} \Delta_e^O(t, v) = 1$.

3 Weighted Bisimulation

In this paper, we discuss weighted bisimulation equivalence primarily for the purposes of comparison with behavior equivalence. Modulo minor differences in the formal setup, the properties of this equivalence are standard, and have been established before by other authors (*e.g.* [HR94]). Consequently, in this section we simply give the basic definitions and state the results briefly without proof.

A *weighted bisimulation* on $\mathrm{Proc}(J/J \Rightarrow O)$ is an equivalence relation R on $\mathrm{Proc}(J/J \Rightarrow O)$ such that the following condition is satisfied:

- Whenever $t\, R\, t'$ then for all actions e and all equivalence classes $\mathcal{C}$ of R we have $\Delta_e^O(t, \mathcal{C}) = \Delta_e^O(t', \mathcal{C})$.

Terms t and t' in $\mathrm{Proc}(I/J \Rightarrow O)$ are defined to be *weighted bisimulation equivalent* if there exists a weighted bisimulation relation R on $\mathrm{Proc}(J/J \Rightarrow O)$ such that for all actions e and all equivalence classes $\mathcal{C}$ of R we have $\Delta_e^O(t, \mathcal{C}) = \Delta_e^O(t', \mathcal{C})$. In this case we write $t \underset{O}{\sim} t'$ (there is no need to mention the input sets I and J which are uniquely determined by t and t').

Without giving a formal statement (it is similar to the one given later for behavior equivalence), we comment at this point that a substitutivity result can be established for weighted bisimulation equivalence, which makes an equational axiomatization feasible.

3.1 Axioms

Axioms for weighted bisimulation equivalence are shown in Table 1. In axiom (nil-fold), we have used the summation notation $\sum_{a \in I} \langle a?_1 \rangle\ \mathrm{nil}_I$ in an obvious way. The soundness of axioms (choice-comm) and (choice-assoc) will permit us in the sequel to manipulate this summation notation in the conventional fashion without further comment.

Lemma 1. *The axioms shown in Table 1 are sound for weighted bisimulation equivalence.*

Table 1. Axioms for Weighted Bisimulation Equivalence

$$t + \mathrm{nil}_\emptyset = t \qquad \text{(choice-unit)}$$
$$t + u = u + t \qquad \text{(choice-comm)}$$
$$(t + u) + v = t + (u + v) \qquad \text{(choice-assoc)}$$

$$\langle a?_p\rangle\, t + \langle a?_q\rangle\, t = \langle a?_{p+q}\rangle\, t \qquad \text{(input-choice)}$$
$$\langle b!_r\rangle\, t + \langle b!_s\rangle\, t = \langle b!_{r+s}\rangle\, t \qquad \text{(output-choice)}$$

$$\text{If } I \neq \emptyset, \text{ then} \quad \sum_{a \in I} \langle a?_1\rangle\, \mathrm{nil}_I = \mathrm{nil}_I \qquad \text{(nil-fold)}$$

3.2 Completeness

We say that two terms are *identical up to permutation of sums* if they can be proved equivalent to each other using only axioms (choice-comm) and (choice-assoc).

Let the notions *input normal form*, *output normal form*, and *normal form* be defined mutually recursively as follows:

- An *input normal form* is a well-typed term u that is either nil_I for some $I \neq \emptyset$, or else has the form $\sum_{i=1}^{m} \langle a_i?_{p_i}\rangle\, t_i$, where we require that:
  1. Each t_i is a normal form.
  2. For no distinct i, i' do we have $a_i = a_{i'}$ and t_i identical to $t_{i'}$ up to permutation of sums.
  3. u is not an instance (up to permutation of sums) of the left-hand side of axiom (nil-fold).
- An *output normal form* is a well-typed term v that is either $\mathrm{nil}_\emptyset$ or else has the form $\sum_{j=1}^{n} \langle b_j!_{r_j}\rangle\, t_j$, where we require that:
  1. Each t_j is a normal form.
  2. For no distinct j, j' do we have $b_j = b_{j'}$ and t_j identical to $t_{j'}$ up to permutation of sums.

  An output normal form is called *nontrivial* if it is not $\mathrm{nil}_\emptyset$.
- A *normal form* is either an input normal form, an output normal form, or a sum $u + v$, where u is an input normal form and v is a nontrivial output normal form.

Lemma 2. *Any $\|$-free term t in* $\mathrm{Proc}(I/J \Rightarrow O)$ *can be proved equivalent to a normal form using the axioms in Table 1.*

Lemma 3. *If normal forms t and t' in* $\mathrm{Proc}(I/J \Rightarrow O)$ *are weighted bisimulation equivalent, then they are identical up to permutation of sums.*

Theorem 1. *The axioms in Table 1 are sound and complete for weighted bisimulation equivalence of $\|$-free terms.*

4 Behavior Equivalence

4.1 Behavior Maps

We now consider the theory of behavior equivalence. To define behavior equivalence, we need some auxiliary concepts. First is the notion of the *aggregate rate* $\mathrm{rt}(t)$ of a term $t \in \mathrm{Proc}(I/J \Rightarrow O)$. This is defined by: $\mathrm{rt}(t) = \sum_{e \in O} \sum_{t'} \Delta_e^O(t, t')$. The following can then be established by structural induction:

- If t has the form nil_I or $\langle a?_w \rangle\ u$, then $\mathrm{rt}(t) = 0$.
- If t has the form $\langle b!_r \rangle\ u$, then $\mathrm{rt}(t) = r$.
- If t has the form $u + v$, then $\mathrm{rt}(t) = \mathrm{rt}(u) + \mathrm{rt}(v)$.
- If t has the form $u\ {}_{O_u}\|_{O_v}\ v$, where u and v are input-stochastic (*cf.* Section 2.2), then $\mathrm{rt}(t) = \mathrm{rt}(u) + \mathrm{rt}(v)$.

Next, we define a *rated action* to be a pair $\langle e, r \rangle \in Act \times [0, \infty)$. A *rated trace* is a finite sequence of rated actions. We use ϵ to denote the empty rated trace.

An *observable* is a mapping from rated traces to real numbers. We use Obs to denote the set of all observables. The *derivative* of an observable Φ by a rated action $\langle e, r \rangle$ is the observable $\langle e, r \rangle^{-1} \Phi$ defined by

$$(\langle e, r \rangle^{-1} \Phi)(\alpha) = \Phi(\langle e, r \rangle\ \alpha)$$

for all all rated traces α.

To each term t in $\mathrm{Proc}(I/J \Rightarrow O)$ we associate a *behavior map* $\mathcal{B}_t^O : \mathrm{Obs} \rightarrow \mathrm{Obs}$ defined by induction on the length of a rated trace as follows:

1. $\mathcal{B}_t^O[\Phi](\epsilon) = \Phi(\epsilon)$.
2. $\mathcal{B}_t^O[\Phi](\langle e, r \rangle \alpha) = \sum_{u \in \mathrm{Proc}(J/J \Rightarrow O)} \Delta_e^O(t, u) \cdot \mathcal{B}_u^O[\langle e, r + \mathrm{rt}(t) \rangle^{-1} \Phi](\alpha)$

Terms t and t' in $\mathrm{Proc}(I/J \Rightarrow O)$ are defined to be *behavior equivalent*, and we write $t \underset{O}{\equiv} t'$, if $\mathcal{B}_t^O = \mathcal{B}_{t'}^O$.

The following result gives a syntax-directed characterization of $\mathcal{B}_t^O$ that is useful in proofs. Case (1) is concerned with non-native actions.

Lemma 4. *For all terms* $t \in \mathrm{Proc}(I/J \Rightarrow O)$, *all observables* Φ, *all rated traces* α *and rated actions* $\langle e, r \rangle$:

1. $\mathcal{B}_t^O[\Phi](\langle e, r \rangle \alpha) = \mathcal{B}_t^O[\langle e, r + \mathrm{rt}(t) \rangle^{-1} \Phi](\alpha), \qquad \text{if } e \notin J \cup O.$
2. $\mathcal{B}_{\mathrm{nil}_J}^O[\Phi](\langle e, r \rangle \alpha) = \begin{cases} \mathcal{B}_{\mathrm{nil}_J}^O[\langle e, r \rangle^{-1} \Phi](\alpha), & \text{if } e \in J, \\ 0, & \text{if } e \in O. \end{cases}$
3. $\mathcal{B}_{\langle a?_w \rangle\ t}^O[\Phi](\langle e, r \rangle \alpha) = \begin{cases} w \cdot \mathcal{B}_t^O[\langle a, r \rangle^{-1} \Phi](\alpha), & \text{if } e = a \\ 0, & \text{if } e \in (J \cup O) \setminus \{a\}. \end{cases}$

4. $\mathcal{B}^O_{\langle b!_s\rangle\, t}[\Phi](\langle e,r\rangle\alpha) = \begin{cases} s \cdot \mathcal{B}^O_t[\langle b, r+s\rangle^{-1}\Phi](\alpha), & \text{if } e = b \\ 0, & \text{if } e \in (J \cup O) \setminus \{b\}. \end{cases}$
5. $\mathcal{B}^O_{t+u}[\Phi](\langle e,r\rangle\alpha) = \mathcal{B}^O_t[\Phi](\langle e, r+\mathrm{rt}(u)\rangle\alpha) + \mathcal{B}^O_u[\Phi](\langle e, r+\mathrm{rt}(t)\rangle\alpha)$.
6. $\mathcal{B}^O_{t\ {}_{O_t}\|_{O_u}\ u} = \mathcal{B}^{O\setminus O_u}_t \circ \mathcal{B}^{O\setminus O_t}_u = \mathcal{B}^{O\setminus O_t}_u \circ \mathcal{B}^{O\setminus O_u}_t$, *assuming* t *and* u *are input-stochastic.*

Input-stochasticity is required in (6) in order to ensure that $\mathrm{rt}(t'\ {}_{O_t}\|_{O_u}\ u') = \mathrm{rt}(t') + \mathrm{rt}(u')$ for all derivatives t' of t and u' of u. Further discussion of behavior maps and their properties can be found in our previous papers [WSS97, Sta03, SCS03].

4.2 Combinations

As indicated in the introduction, in order to axiomatize behavior equivalence, we extend our language by adding a construct for forming (convex) *combinations* of terms. Specifically, we add an additional binary operator ${}_\pi\!\oplus_{1-\pi}$, where the parameter π is a real number in the open interval $(0, 1)$.

The following typing rule applies to this new operator:

$$\frac{t : I/J \Rightarrow O \quad u : I/J \Rightarrow O \quad \mathrm{rt}(t) = \mathrm{rt}(u)}{t\ {}_\pi\!\oplus_{1-\pi}\ u : I/J \Rightarrow O}$$

This rule requires that, for $t\ {}_\pi\!\oplus_{1-\pi}\ u$ to be well-typed, terms t and u must have the same aggregate rate as well as a common type. In this case we extend the notion of aggregate rate by defining $\mathrm{rt}(t\ {}_\pi\!\oplus_{1-\pi}\ u)$ to be the common value $\mathrm{rt}(t) = \mathrm{rt}(u)$.

We formally extend the transition semantics Δ^O_e given in Section 2.2 to encompass terms containing $t\ {}_\pi\!\oplus_{1-\pi}\ u$ by adding to the defining clauses given there the additional clause:

$$\Delta^O_e(t\ {}_\pi\!\oplus_{1-\pi}\ u,\ v) \quad = \quad \pi \cdot \Delta^O_e(t, v) + (1-\pi) \cdot \Delta^O_e(u, v).$$

Note that in making the extension we are implicitly re-interpreting the original clauses from Section 2.2 by allowing for the possibility of terms containing ${}_\pi\!\oplus_{1-\pi}$. For example, we now have

$$\Delta^O_a(\langle a?_w\rangle\ (t\ {}_\pi\!\oplus_{1-\pi}\ u),\ t\ {}_\pi\!\oplus_{1-\pi}\ u) \quad = \quad w.$$

We similarly re-interpret the definition of $\mathcal{B}^O_t$ given earlier in this section to allow for the possibility of terms containing ${}_\pi\!\oplus_{1-\pi}$. These particular definitions are intuitively motivated by our desire for $t\ {}_\pi\!\oplus_{1-\pi}\ u$ to represent a probabilistic choice between (or superposition of) t and u; as considered, for example, in [And99]. Formally, we obtain the following result:

Lemma 5. *For all terms* t, u *in* $\mathrm{Proc}(I/J \Rightarrow O)$ *such that* $\mathrm{rt}(t) = \mathrm{rt}(u)$, *for all observables* Φ *and all rated traces* α *we have:*

$$\mathcal{B}^O_{t\ {}_\pi\oplus_{1-\pi}\ u}[\Phi](\alpha) \quad = \quad \pi \cdot \mathcal{B}^O_t[\Phi](\alpha) + (1-\pi) \cdot \mathcal{B}^O_u[\Phi](\alpha).$$

Lemma 6. *Behavior equivalence is substitutive for input prefixing, output prefixing, choice, and combination of arbitrary terms, and also for parallel composition of input-stochastic terms. That is, each of the following assertions holds for terms t and t' in* $\mathrm{Proc}(I/J \Rightarrow O)$ *whenever all the terms mentioned are well-typed and the equivalences make sense:*

1. *If* $t \underset{O}{\equiv} t'$ *then* $\langle a?_w \rangle\, t \underset{O}{\equiv} \langle a?_w \rangle\, t'$.
2. *If* $t \underset{O}{\equiv} t'$ *then* $\langle b!_r \rangle\, t \underset{O}{\equiv} \langle b!_r \rangle\, t'$.
3. *If* $t \underset{O}{\equiv} t'$ *then* $t + u \underset{O}{\equiv} t' + u$ *and* $u + t \underset{O}{\equiv} u + t'$.
4. *If* $t \underset{O}{\equiv} t'$ *then* $t \;{}_{\pi}{\oplus}_{1-\pi}\; u \underset{O}{\equiv} t' \;{}_{\pi}{\oplus}_{1-\pi}\; u$ *and* $u \;{}_{\pi}{\oplus}_{1-\pi}\; t \underset{O}{\equiv} u \;{}_{\pi}{\oplus}_{1-\pi}\; t'$.
5. *If* $t \underset{O}{\equiv} t'$ *then* $t \;{}_{O}\|_{O_u}\; u \underset{O'}{\equiv} t' \;{}_{O}\|_{O_u}\; u$ *and* $u \;{}_{O_u}\|_{O}\; t \underset{O'}{\equiv} u \;{}_{O_u}\|_{O}\; t'$, *assuming* t, t', *and* u *are input-stochastic.*

4.3 Axioms

Axioms for behavior equivalence are shown in Table 2. Note that an equation is only regarded an axiom if all the terms involved are well-formed and the same type can be inferred for the left and right-hand sides. Particular care must be taken when using axioms (input-distr) and (output-distr), to see that these equations are never applied in such a way as to create combinations whose operands have different rates.

In contrast to the axioms for weighted bisimulation equivalence, the axioms for behavior equivalence expose some distinction between input and output. For example, comparison of axiom (input-comb) and (output-comb) reveals that in (output-comb) the two output actions are permitted to be distinct. This is not permitted in (input-comb), because in that case the right-hand side would never be well-typed. Also, the axiom (input-extract) exhibits a special property of input that is not shared by output. The content of axiom (interchange) is that the two types of sums commute freely with each other, subject only to the conditions on rates imposed by well-typedness.

Note that Table 2 includes all the axioms for weighted bisimulation equivalence, except for the axioms (input-choice) and (output-choice). However, it is not difficult to show that these axioms are derivable, so that all equations provable for weighted bisimulation equivalence are also provable for behavior equivalence.

Lemma 7. *The axioms in Table 2 are sound for behavior equivalence.*

Proof. We prove the case of (input-extract) to give the basic flavor of working with behavior maps. We must show that

$$\mathcal{B}^{O}_{\langle a?_{\pi p}\rangle\, t + (u \;{}_{\pi}{\oplus}_{1-\pi}\; v)}[\Phi](\alpha) \;=\; \mathcal{B}^{O}_{(\langle a?_p\rangle\, t + u) \;{}_{\pi}{\oplus}_{1-\pi}\; v}[\Phi](\alpha)$$

for all observables Φ and rated traces α. We proceed by induction on the length of the rated trace α. The basis case $\alpha = \epsilon$ is immediate, because by definition of behavior maps:

$$\mathcal{B}^{O}_{\langle a?_{\pi p}\rangle\, t + (u \;{}_{\pi}{\oplus}_{1-\pi}\; v)}[\Phi](\epsilon) \;=\; \Phi(\epsilon) \;=\; \mathcal{B}^{O}_{(\langle a?_p\rangle\, t + u) \;{}_{\pi}{\oplus}_{1-\pi}\; v}[\Phi](\epsilon).$$

Table 2. Axioms for Behavior Equivalence

$$t + \mathrm{nil}_\emptyset = t \qquad \text{(choice-unit)}$$
$$t + u = u + t \qquad \text{(choice-comm)}$$
$$(t + u) + v = t + (u + v) \qquad \text{(choice-assoc)}$$

$$\sum_{a \in I} \langle a?_1 \rangle\ \mathrm{nil}_I = \mathrm{nil}_I \qquad \text{(nil-fold)}$$

$$\langle a?_p \rangle\ t + \langle a?_q \rangle\ u = \langle a?_{p+q} \rangle\ t\ {}_{\frac{p}{p+q}}\!\oplus_{\frac{q}{p+q}} \langle a?_{p+q} \rangle\ u \qquad \text{(input-comb)}$$
$$\langle b!_r \rangle\ t + \langle c!_s \rangle\ u = \langle b!_{r+s} \rangle\ t\ {}_{\frac{r}{r+s}}\!\oplus_{\frac{s}{r+s}} \langle c!_{r+s} \rangle\ u \qquad \text{(output-comb)}$$

$$t = t\ {}_\pi\!\oplus_{1-\pi}\ t \qquad \text{(comb-idemp)}$$
$$t\ {}_\pi\!\oplus_{1-\pi}\ u = u\ {}_{1-\pi}\!\oplus_\pi\ t \qquad \text{(comb-comm)}$$
$$(t\ {}_\pi\!\oplus_{1-\pi}\ u)\ {}_\rho\!\oplus_{1-\rho}\ v = t\ {}_\sigma\!\oplus_{1-\sigma}\ (u\ {}_\tau\!\oplus_{1-\tau}\ v), \qquad \text{(comb-assoc)}$$
$$\text{whenever } \pi\rho = \sigma \text{ and } (1-\rho) = (1-\sigma)(1-\tau).$$

$$\langle a?_p \rangle\ t\ {}_\pi\!\oplus_{1-\pi} \langle a?_p \rangle\ u = \langle a?_p \rangle\ (t\ {}_\pi\!\oplus_{1-\pi}\ u) \qquad \text{(input-distr)}$$
$$\langle b!_r \rangle\ t\ {}_\pi\!\oplus_{1-\pi} \langle b!_r \rangle\ u = \langle b!_r \rangle\ (t\ {}_\pi\!\oplus_{1-\pi}\ u) \qquad \text{(output-distr)}$$

$$(t\ {}_\pi\!\oplus_{1-\pi}\ w) + (u\ {}_\pi\!\oplus_{1-\pi}\ v) = (t + u)\ {}_\pi\!\oplus_{1-\pi}\ (w + v) \qquad \text{(interchange)}$$
$$\langle a?_{\pi p} \rangle\ t + (u\ {}_\pi\!\oplus_{1-\pi}\ v) = (\langle a?_p \rangle\ t + u)\ {}_\pi\!\oplus_{1-\pi}\ v \qquad \text{(input-extract)}$$

Suppose now that $\alpha = \langle e, r \rangle \beta$. Let $s = \mathrm{rt}(\langle a?_{\pi p} \rangle\ t + (u\ {}_\pi\!\oplus_{1-\pi}\ v)) = \mathrm{rt}((\langle a?_p \rangle\ t + u)\ {}_\pi\!\oplus_{1-\pi}\ v)$. In case $e \notin J \cup O$ (*i.e.* e is non-native), then applying Lemma 4 (1) and the induction hypothesis we have

$$\begin{aligned}
\mathcal{B}^O_{\langle a?_{\pi p} \rangle\ t + (u\ {}_\pi\oplus_{1-\pi}\ v)}[\Phi](\langle e, r \rangle \beta) &= \mathcal{B}^O_{\langle a?_{\pi p} \rangle\ t + (u\ {}_\pi\oplus_{1-\pi}\ v)}[\langle e, r+s \rangle^{-1} \Phi](\beta) \\
&= \mathcal{B}^O_{(\langle a?_p \rangle\ t + u)\ {}_\pi\oplus_{1-\pi}\ v}[\langle e, r+s \rangle^{-1} \Phi](\beta) \\
&= \mathcal{B}^O_{(\langle a?_p \rangle\ t + u)\ {}_\pi\oplus_{1-\pi}\ v}[\Phi](\langle e, r \rangle \beta).
\end{aligned}$$

It remains for us to consider the case $e \in J \cup O$. We compute, using Lemma 4:

$$\begin{aligned}
&\mathcal{B}^O_{\langle a?_{\pi p} \rangle\ t + (u\ {}_\pi\oplus_{1-\pi}\ v)}[\Phi](\langle e, r \rangle \beta) \\
&= \mathcal{B}^O_{\langle a?_{\pi p} \rangle\ t}[\Phi](\langle e, r+s \rangle \beta) + \mathcal{B}^O_{u\ {}_\pi\oplus_{1-\pi}\ v}[\Phi](\langle e, r+0 \rangle \beta) \\
&= \pi \cdot \mathcal{B}^O_{\langle a?_p \rangle\ t}[\Phi](\langle e, r+s \rangle \beta) + \pi \cdot \mathcal{B}^O_u[\Phi](\langle e, r \rangle \beta) + (1-\pi) \cdot \mathcal{B}^O_v[\Phi](\langle e, r \rangle \beta) \\
&= \pi \cdot \mathcal{B}^O_{\langle a?_p \rangle\ t + u}[\Phi](\langle e, r \rangle \beta) + (1-\pi) \cdot \mathcal{B}^O_v[\Phi](\langle e, r \rangle \beta) \\
&= \mathcal{B}^O_{(\langle a?_p \rangle\ t + u)\ {}_\pi\oplus_{1-\pi}\ v}[\Phi](\langle e, r \rangle \beta).
\end{aligned}$$

Note that the first and third steps crucially depend on the fact that the input-prefixed terms $\langle a?_{\pi p} \rangle\ t$ and $\langle a?_p \rangle\ t$ have aggregate rate 0, and that $s = \mathrm{rt}(\langle a?_{\pi p}\rangle\, t + (u\ {}_{\pi}\!\oplus_{1-\pi}\, v)) = \mathrm{rt}(u\ {}_{\pi}\!\oplus_{1-\pi}\, v) = \mathrm{rt}(u) = \mathrm{rt}(v) = \mathrm{rt}((\langle a?_p\rangle\, t + u)\ {}_{\pi}\!\oplus_{1-\pi}\, v)$.

4.4 Normal Forms

Let the notions *input normal form*, *output normal form*, and *normal form* be defined mutually recursively as follows:

- An *input normal form* is a well-typed term u that is either nil_I for some $I \neq \emptyset$, or else has the form: $\sum_{a\in I}\sum_{s\in R_a}\langle a?_{p_{a,s}}\rangle\, t_{a,s}$, where we require that:
  1. $I \neq \emptyset$.
  2. Each $t_{a,s}$ is a normal form, with $\mathrm{rt}(t_{a,s}) = s$.
  3. For each $a \in I$ the set R_a is a nonempty finite subset of $(0, \infty)$.
  4. u is not an instance (up to permutation of sums) of the left-hand side of axiom (nil-fold).
- An *output normal form* is a well-typed term u that is either $\mathrm{nil}_\emptyset$ or else has the form: $\sum_{b\in O}\sum_{s\in R_b}\langle b!_{\sigma_{b,s}\cdot r}\rangle\, t_{b,s}$, where we require that:
  1. $O \neq \emptyset$.
  2. Each $t_{b,s}$ is a normal form, with $\mathrm{rt}(t_{b,s}) = s$.
  3. For each $b \in O$ the set R_b is a nonempty finite subset of $(0, \infty)$.
  4. Each $\sigma_{b,s}$ satisfies $0 < \sigma_{b,s} \leq 1$ and $\sum_{b\in O}\sum_{s\in R_b}\sigma_{b,s} = 1$.

  An output normal form is called *nontrivial* if it is not $\mathrm{nil}_\emptyset$.
- A *normal form* is either an input normal form, an output normal form, or a sum $u + v$, where u is an input normal form and v is a nontrivial output normal form.

Lemma 8. *Any $\|$-free term t in* $\mathrm{Proc}(I/J \Rightarrow O)$ *can be proved equivalent to a normal form using the axioms in Table 2.*

4.5 Completeness

Key to the completeness proof is Lemma 9 below, which shows how certain information about the structure of t can be extracted from its behavior. In case t is a normal form, this information is essentially the entire structure of t, except for the ordering of terms in sums. Suppose a type $I/J \Rightarrow O$ has been fixed and let $*$ be an arbitrarily chosen (non-native) action in $Act \setminus (J \cup O)$. Given $e \in Act$ and $r \geq 0$, let $\Xi_{e,r}$ be the observable defined as follows:

$$\Xi_{e,r}(\alpha) = \begin{cases} s, & \text{if } \alpha = \langle *, s\rangle, \\ 1, & \text{if } \alpha = \langle e, s\rangle\langle *, r\rangle, \\ 0, & \text{otherwise.} \end{cases}$$

We call such an observable a *probe*.

Lemma 9. *Suppose $t \in$ $\mathrm{Proc}(I/J \Rightarrow O)$. Then the probe $\Xi_{e,r}$ has the following properties:*

1. $\mathcal{B}_t^O[\Xi_{*,0}](\langle *, 0\rangle) = \mathrm{rt}(t)$.
2. *For $e \in J \cup O$,* $\mathcal{B}_t^O[\Xi_{e,r}](\langle e, 0\rangle\langle *, 0\rangle) = \sum_{\{u:\mathrm{rt}(u)=r\}} \Delta_e^O(t, u)$.

Lemma 10. *Suppose t and t' are normal forms in* $\mathrm{Proc}(I/J \Rightarrow O)$. *If* $\mathcal{B}_t^O = \mathcal{B}_{t'}^O$, *then t and t' are identical up to permutation of sums.*

Theorem 2. *The axioms in Table 2 are sound and complete for behavior equivalence of $\|$-free terms.*

5 Conclusion

By comparing complete axiomatizations (and especially the normal forms arising in the completeness proofs), we have improved our understanding of the relationship between two notions of equivalence for processes with Markovian behavior. In contrast to the axiomatization of weighted bisimulation equivalence, the axiomatization of behavior equivalence exhibits differences in the role of input actions and output actions.

If we restrict to the output-only fragment of the language, then a complete axiomatization of behavior equivalence is given by axioms (choice-unit), (choice-comm), (choice-assoc), (comb-idemp), (comb-comm), (comb-assoc), (output-comb), (output-distr), and (interchange). This axiomatization may be compared to the axiomatization given in [Ber05] for the "Markovian trace equivalence" notion originally defined in [BC00]. In fact, each of the axioms for Markovian trace equivalence is sound for behavior equivalence, so (applying Bernardo's completeness result) Markovian trace equivalent processes are also behavior equivalent.

Conversely, given a sequence of actions (*i.e.* a trace) $x \in Act^*$ and a time T in $[0, \infty)$, it is possible to define an observable $\Phi_{x,T}$ such that "the probability of performing an execution compatible with x in average time $\leq T$" is given by $\sum_\alpha \mathcal{B}_t^O[\Phi_{x,T}](\alpha)$, where α ranges over all rated traces that contain only actions in O. Thus, behavior equivalent output-only processes are also Markovian trace equivalent. So, one part of what we have achieved is to show that the introduction of the operator ${}_\pi\oplus_{1-\pi}$ permits a finite axiomatization of Markovian trace equivalence, as opposed to the infinite axiom scheme given in [Ber05].

We have not yet succeeded in extending our results to include parallel composition. For weighted bisimulation equivalence there is an evident "expansion theorem" that permits parallel composition to be eliminated in favor of choice. For behavior equivalence, one might attempt a similar expansion for the parallel composition of two normal forms. One difficulty in doing this arises from the fact that behavior equivalence fails to be substitutive for parallel composition unless we restrict to input-stochastic terms. Thus we cannot employ various useful manipulations that move individual input-prefixed terms into and out of the scope of a parallel operator, as these do not preserve input-stochasticity, in general. Another subtlety is the following: if $t \in \mathrm{Proc}(I/J \Rightarrow O)$ and $J' \cap (J \cup O) = \emptyset$, then there is no way to eliminate parallel composition from a term of the form $t\ {}_O\|_{O'}\ \mathrm{nil}_{J'}$. Such a term amounts to a kind of "input expansion" of t which, in the absence of a recursion operator, cannot be otherwise expressed. So in the absence of recursion (or alternatively, an explicit input expansion operator) there can be no expansion theorem that completely eliminates parallel composition. To attempt an axiomatization of recursion would first require an extension of the completeness results of the present paper to open terms. We leave these explorations as subjects for future research.

References

[And99] S. Andova. Process algebra with probabilistic choice. In *ARTS '99: Proceedings of the 5th International AMAST Workshop on Formal Methods for Real-Time and Probabilistic Systems*, pages 111–129, London, UK, 1999. Springer-Verlag.

[BC00] M. Bernardo and R. Cleaveland. A theory of testing for Markovian processes. In C. Palamidessi, editor, *CONCUR*, volume 1877 of *Lecture Notes in Computer Science*, pages 305–319, 2000.

[BDG98] M. Bernardo, L. Donatiello, and R. Gorrieri. A formal approach to the integration of performance aspects in the modeling and analysis of concurrent systems. *Information and Computation*, 144(2):83–154, 1998.

[Ber05] M. Bernardo. Markovian testing and trace equivalences exactly lump more than Markovian bisimilarity. In L. Aceto and A. D. Gordon, editors, *International Workshop on Algebraic Process Calculi: The First Twenty Five Years and Beyond (APC 25)*, Electronic Notes in Theoretical Computer Science. Springer-Verlag, 2005.

[HH02] J.-P. Katoen H. Hermanns, U. Herzog. Process algebra for performance evaluation. *Theoretical Computer Science*, 274:43–97, 2002.

[Hil96] J. Hillston. *A Compositional Approach to Performance Modelling.* Cambridge University Press, 1996.

[HR94] H. Hermanns and M. Rettelbach. Syntax, semantics, equivalences, and axioms for MTIPP, 1994.

[LS91] K. G. Larsen and A. Skou. Bisimulation through probabilistic testing. *Information and Computation*, 94(1):1–28, September 1991.

[SCS03] E. W. Stark, R. Cleaveland, and S. A. Smolka. A process-algebraic language for probabilistic I/O automata. In Roberto M. Amadio and Denis Lugiez, editors, *CONCUR 2003 - Concurrency Theory, 14th International Conference, Marseille, France, September 3-5, 2003, Proceedings*, volume 2761 of *Lecture Notes in Computer Science*, pages 189–203. Springer-Verlag, 2003.

[SCS06] E. W. Stark, R. Cleaveland, and S. A. Smolka. Probabilistic I/O automata: Theories of two equivalences. Full version available at `http://bsd7.cs.sunysb.edu/~stark/REPORTS/pioa-equivalences.pdf`, June 2006.

[Sta03] E. W. Stark. On behaviour equivalence for probabilistic I/O automata and its relationship to probabilistic bisimulation. *Journal of Automata, Languages and Combinatorics*, 8(2):361–395, 2003.

[WSS97] S.-H. Wu, S. A. Smolka, and E. W. Stark. Composition and behaviors of probabilistic I/O automata. *Theoretical Computer Science*, 176(1-2):1–38, 1997.

Reachability in Recursive Markov Decision Processes*

Tomáš Brázdil, Václav Brožek, Vojtěch Forejt, and Antonín Kučera

Faculty of Informatics, Masaryk University,
Botanická 68a, 60200 Brno,
Czech Republic
{brazdil, xbrozek, xforejt, kucera}@fi.muni.cz

Abstract. We consider a class of infinite-state Markov decision processes generated by stateless pushdown automata. This class corresponds to $1\frac{1}{2}$-player games over graphs generated by BPA systems or (equivalently) 1-exit recursive state machines. An *extended reachability objective* is specified by two sets S and T of *safe* and *terminal* stack configurations, where the membership to S and T depends just on the top-of-the-stack symbol. The question is whether there is a suitable strategy such that the probability of hitting a terminal configuration by a path leading only through safe configurations is equal to (or different from) a given $x \in \{0, 1\}$. We show that the qualitative extended reachability problem is decidable in polynomial time, and that the set of all configurations for which there is a winning strategy is effectively regular. More precisely, this set can be represented by a deterministic finite-state automaton with a fixed number of control states. This result is a generalization of a recent theorem by Etessami & Yannakakis which says that the qualitative termination for 1-exit RMDPs (which exactly correspond to our $1\frac{1}{2}$-player BPA games) is decidable in polynomial time. Interestingly, the properties of winning strategies for the extended reachability objectives are quite different from the ones for termination, and new observations are needed to obtain the result. As an application, we derive the **EXPTIME**-completeness of the model-checking problem for $1\frac{1}{2}$-player BPA games and qualitative PCTL formulae.

1 Introduction

$1\frac{1}{2}$-player games (or Markov decision processes) are a fundamental model in the area of system design and control optimization [11,8]. Formally, a $1\frac{1}{2}$-player game G is a directed graph where the vertices are split into two disjoint subsets $V_\Box$ and $V_\bigcirc$. For every $v \in V_\bigcirc$, there is a fixed probability distribution over the set of its outgoing transitions. A *play* is initiated by putting a token on some vertex. The token is then moved from vertex to vertex by one "real" player $\Box$ (controller) and one "virtual" player $\bigcirc$ (stochastic environment), who are responsible for

* Supported by the research center Institute for Theoretical Computer Science (ITI), project No. 1M0545.

C. Baier and H. Hermanns (Eds.): CONCUR 2006, LNCS 4137, pp. 358–374, 2006.

selecting outgoing transitions in the vertices of $V_\Box$ and $V_\bigcirc$, respectively. Player $\bigcirc$ does not make a real choice, but selects his next move randomly according to the fixed probability distribution over the outgoing transitions. A *strategy* specifies how player $\Box$ should play. In general, a strategy may or may not depend on the history of a play (we say that a strategy is *history-dependent (H)* or *memoryless (M)*), and the transitions may be chosen deterministically or randomly (*deterministic (D)* and *randomized (R)* strategies). In the case of randomized strategies, player $\Box$ chooses a probability distribution on the set of outgoing transitions. Note that deterministic strategies can be seen as restricted randomized strategies, where one of the outgoing transitions has probability 1. Each strategy σ determines a unique Markov chain $G(\sigma)$ where the states are finite paths in G, and $wu \to wuu'$ with probability x iff (u, u') is a transition in the game and x is the probability chosen by player $\Box$, or the fixed probability of the transition (u, u') when $u \in V_\bigcirc$. A *winning objective* for player $\Box$ is some property of Markov chains that is to be achieved. A *winning strategy* is a strategy that achieves the objective. In the context of "classical" MDP theory, winning objectives are typically related to long-time characteristics such as the expected total reward, the expected reward per transition, etc. [11,8]. In the context of formal verification, winning objectives are often specified as formulae of suitable temporal logics and their probabilistic variants such as PCTL or PCTL* [9]. For games with finitely many vertices, the corresponding decision algorithms have been designed [9,2,1] and also implemented in verifications tools such as PRISM (see, e.g., [10]). Recently, the scope of this study has been extended to a class of *infinite-state* games generated by *recursive state machines (RSM)* [6,7]. Intuitively, a RSM is a finite collection of finite-state automata which can call each other in a recursive fashion, maintaining the (unbounded) stack of activation records. RSM are semantically equivalent to *pushdown automata (PDA)*, and there are effective linear-time translations between the two models. A given RSM can be encoded in PDA syntax by storing the collection of finite-state automata in the control unit, and the recursive calls/returns are modeled by pushing/popping symbols onto/from the stack. An important subclass of RSM are *1-exit RSM*, where each finite-state automaton in the collection terminates in exactly one state. This means that no information can be returned back to the caller. In PDA terms, this means that whenever a given stack symbol X is popped from the stack, the same control state p_X is entered. Hence, the finite-state control unit can be encoded directly into the stack alphabet and simulated in top-of-the-stack symbol. Thus, 1-exit RSM can effectively be represented as *stateless* PDA, which are also denoted BPA in the context of concurrency theory.

Now we briefly summarize some of the results presented in [6,7]. To be able to give a clear comparison with our work, we reformulate these results in PDA/BPA terminology. A *termination objective* is specified by two control states p, q and one stack symbol X of a given PDA. The task of player $\Box$ is to maximize/minimize the probability of hitting $q\varepsilon$ from pX (each "head" rY in a given PDA is either probabilistic or non-deterministic; transitions from probabilistic heads are chosen randomly according to a fixed distribution, while the transitions from non-deterministic heads can be chosen by player □). In the case of BPA, there are no control states and the termination objective is specified simply by the stack symbol which is to be removed.

In [6,7], it has been shown that optimal minimizing/maximizing strategies in general $1\frac{1}{2}$-player PDA games with termination objectives do not always exist, and that the problem whether there is a strategy such that termination is achieved with probability 1 is undecidable. The situation is different for $1\frac{1}{2}$-player BPA games, where the optimal minimizing/maximizing strategies do exist, and can be constructed so that they depend only on top-of-the-stack symbol of a given configuration. Hence, the optimal strategies are stackless, memoryless, and deterministic (SMD). Furthermore, the corresponding minimal/maximal termination probabilities are expressible as the least solution of an effectively constructible system of non-linear recursive equations. Since the least solution of this system can effectively be expressed in first-order theory of the reals, this entails the decidability of the *quantitative* termination problem, i.e., the question whether the minimal/maximal achievable termination probability is bounded by a given constant. For the *qualitative* subcase (i.e., the problem whether the minimal/maximal achievable termination probability is equal to one), polynomial-time algorithms have been designed. On the other hand, in [6] it was noted that model-checking $1\frac{1}{2}$-player BPA games against *qualitative LTL objectives* is already undecidable.

Our contribution: In this paper we consider $1\frac{1}{2}$-player BPA games with *extended reachability objectives (EROs)*. An ERO is specified by two sets of *safe* and *terminal* stack symbols. A configuration is safe/terminal iff its top-of-the-stack symbol is safe/terminal. A run w satisfies a given ERO iff w visits a terminal configuration and all configurations preceding this visit are safe. The goal of player □ is to minimize/maximize the probability of all runs satisfying a given ERO. Note that termination objectives can easily be encoded as EROs (this may require a new bottom-of-the-stack symbol). However, the properties of EROs are surprisingly different from the ones of termination objectives (in contrast, methods for termination can easily be extended to EROs for fully probabilistic PDA [4]). We show that optimal maximizing strategies may not exist at all, and even if they do exist, they are not necessarily SMD. The optimal minimizing strategies are guaranteed to exist, but are not necessarily SMD. The method of expressing the minimal/maximal termination probability by a system of non-linear equations used in [6] cannot be easily extended to EROs, and the reasons seem to be fundamental.

At the core of our paper are results about *qualitative* EROs. We show that the sets of all configurations for which there exists a strategy such that the probability of all runs satisfying a given ERO is equal to zero (equal to one, larger than zero, less than one, resp.) are regular and the corresponding finite-state automata can be constructed in polynomial time. In our algorithms, we use the results about qualitative termination as "black boxes" and concentrate on problems that are specific to EROs. We note that the subcase "equal to one", and particularly the subcase "less than one", require non-trivial methods and observations.

As an application, we design an exponential-time model-checking algorithm for $1\frac{1}{2}$-player BPA games and the qualitative fragment of the logic PCTL. More precisely, our algorithm is polynomial in the size of a given BPA and exponential in the size of a given formula (hence, the algorithm becomes polynomial for each fixed formula). Since there is a matching **EXPTIME** lower bound [3], we yield the **EXPTIME**-completeness of the problem. As a consequence we also obtain the **EXPTIME**-completeness of the model-checking problem for fully probabilistic BPA and qualitative PCTL (fully probabilistic BPA correspond to a subclass of $1\frac{1}{2}$-player BPA games where all heads are probabilistic). This problem has been studied in [4,3], but the best known upper complexity bound was **EXPSPACE**. Finally, let us note that since model-checking $1\frac{1}{2}$-player BPA games against qualitative LTL properties is already undecidable [6], our result cannot be extended to the qualitative fragment of PCTL*.

2 Basic Definitions

In this paper, the set of all positive integers, non-negative integers, rational numbers, real numbers, and non-negative real numbers are denoted $\mathbb{N}$, $\mathbb{N}_0$, $\mathbb{Q}$, $\mathbb{R}$, and $\mathbb{R}^{\geq 0}$, respectively.

We start by recalling basic notions of probability theory. Let A be a finite or countably infinite set. A *probability distribution* on A is a function $f : A \to [0,1]$ such that $\sum_{a \in A} f(a) = 1$. A distribution f is *rational* if $f(a) \in \mathbb{Q}$ for every $a \in A$, *positive* if $f(a) > 0$ for every $a \in A$, and *Dirac* if $f(a) = 1$ for some $a \in A$. The set of all distributions on A is denoted $\mathcal{D}(A)$.

A *σ-field* over a set X is a set $\mathcal{F} \subseteq 2^X$ that includes X and is closed under complement and countable union. A *measurable space* is a pair $(X, \mathcal{F})$ where X is a set called *sample space* and $\mathcal{F}$ is a σ-field over X. A *probability measure* over a measurable space $(X, \mathcal{F})$ is a function $\mathcal{P} : \mathcal{F} \to \mathbb{R}^{\geq 0}$ such that, for each countable collection $\{X_i\}_{i \in I}$ of pairwise disjoint elements of $\mathcal{F}$, $\mathcal{P}(\bigcup_{i \in I} X_i) = \sum_{i \in I} \mathcal{P}(X_i)$, and moreover $\mathcal{P}(X) = 1$. A *probabilistic space* is a triple $(X, \mathcal{F}, \mathcal{P})$ where $(X, \mathcal{F})$ is a measurable space and $\mathcal{P}$ is a probability measure over $(X, \mathcal{F})$.

Markov Chains. A *Markov chain* is a triple $\mathcal{M} = (M, \to, Prob)$ where M is a finite or countably infinite set of *states*, $\to \subseteq M \times M$ is a *transition relation* such that for every $s \in M$ there is some transition $s \to t$, and *Prob* is a function which to each $s \in M$ assigns a positive probability distribution over the set of its outgoing transitions.

In the rest of this paper we also write $s \xrightarrow{x} t$ instead of $Prob(s \to t) = x$. A *path* in $\mathcal{M}$ is a finite or infinite sequence $w = s_0, s_1, \cdots$ of states such that $s_i \to s_{i+1}$ for every i. We also use $w(i)$ to denote the state s_i of w, and w_i to denote the path $s_i, s_{i+1}, \cdots$ (by writing $w(i) = s$ or w_i we implicitly impose the condition that the length of w is at least $i + 1$). A *run* is an infinite path. The sets of all finite paths and all runs of $\mathcal{M}$ are denoted $FPath(\mathcal{M})$ and $Run(\mathcal{M})$, respectively. Similarly, the sets of all finite paths and runs that start in a given $s \in M$ are denoted $FPath(\mathcal{M}, s)$ and $Run(\mathcal{M}, s)$, respectively.

Each $w \in FPath(\mathcal{M})$ determines a *basic cylinder* $Run(\mathcal{M}, w)$ which consists of all runs that start with w. To every $s \in M$ we associate the probabilistic space $(Run(\mathcal{M}, s), \mathcal{F}, \mathcal{P})$ where $\mathcal{F}$ is the σ-field generated by all basic cylinders $Run(\mathcal{M}, w)$ where w starts with s, and $\mathcal{P} : \mathcal{F} \rightarrow [0, 1]$ is the unique probability function such that $\mathcal{P}(Run(\mathcal{M}, w)) = \Pi_{i=0}^{m-1} x_i$ where $w = s_0, \cdots, s_m$ and $s_i \stackrel{x_i}{\rightarrow} s_{i+1}$ for every $0 \leq i < m$ (if $m = 0$, we put $\mathcal{P}(Run(\mathcal{M}, w)) = 1$).

For all $S, T \subseteq M$ and $s \in M$, we define the sets

- $Run(\mathcal{M}, s, S\,\mathcal{U}\,T) = \{w \in Run(\mathcal{M}, s) \mid \exists j \geq 0 : w(j) \in T \wedge \forall i < j : w(i) \in S\}$
- $Run(\mathcal{M}, s, \mathcal{F}T) = \{w \in Run(\mathcal{M}, s) \mid \exists j \geq 0 : w(j) \in T\}$
- $Run(\mathcal{M}, s, \neg\mathcal{F}T) = \{w \in Run(\mathcal{M}, s) \mid \forall j \geq 0 : w(j) \notin T\}$
- $Run(\mathcal{M}, s, \mathcal{X}\,S) = \{w \in Run(\mathcal{M}, s) \mid w(1) \in S\}$

Games, Strategies, and Objectives. A $1\frac{1}{2}$*-player game* (or *Markov decision process*) is a tuple $G = (V, E, (V_\Box, V_\bigcirc), Prob)$ where V is a finite or countably infinite set of *vertices*, $E \subseteq V \times V$ is a set of *transitions*, $(V_\Box, V_\bigcirc)$ is a partition of V, and $Prob$ is a *probability assignment* which to each $v \in V_\bigcirc$ assigns a positive probability distribution on the set of its outgoing transitions. For technical convenience, we assume that each vertex has at least one outgoing transition. We say that G is *finitely-branching* if for each $v \in V$ there are only finitely many $u \in V$ such that $(v, u) \in E$.

The game is played by a player $\Box$ who selects the moves in the $V_\Box$ vertices, and a "virtual" player $\bigcirc$ who selects the moves in the $V_\bigcirc$ vertices according to the corresponding probability distribution.

A *strategy* for player $\Box$ is a function σ which to each $wv \in V^*V_\Box$ assigns a probability distribution on the set of outgoing transitions of v. We say that a strategy σ is *memoryless (M)* if $\sigma(wv)$ depends just on the last vertex v, and *deterministic (D)* if $\sigma(wv)$ is a Dirac distribution for each $wv \in V^*V_\Box$. Strategies that are not necessarily memoryless are called *history-dependent (H)*, and strategies that are not necessarily deterministic are called *randomized (R)*. Hence, we can define the following four classes of strategies: MD, MR, HD, and HR, where MD $\subseteq$ HD $\subseteq$ HR and MD $\subseteq$ MR $\subseteq$ HR, but MR and HD are incomparable.

Remark 1. Each MD strategy σ determines a unique function $f_\sigma : V_\Box \rightarrow V$. Conversely, each function $f : V_\Box \rightarrow V$ such that $(v, f(v)) \in E$ for every $v \in V_\Box$ determines a unique MD strategy σ_f.

Each strategy σ for player $\Box$ determines a unique *play* of the game G, which is a Markov chain $G(\sigma)$ where V^+ is the set of states, and $wu \stackrel{x}{\rightarrow} wuu'$ iff $(u, u') \in E$ and one of the following conditions holds:

- $u \in V_\bigcirc$ and $Prob(u, u') = x$;
- $u \in V_\Box$ and $\sigma(wu)$ assigns x to (u, u').

For every $w \in Run(G(\sigma))$ and every $i \in \mathbb{N}_0$, we define $w[i]$ to be the last vertex of $w(i)$ (realize that $w(i)$ is a finite sequence of vertices of the game G).

The logic PCTL. The logic PCTL, the probabilistic extension of CTL, was introduced by Hansson & Jonsson in [9]. Let $Ap = \{p, q, \ldots\}$ be a countably infinite set of *atomic propositions*. The syntax of PCTL formulae is given by the following abstract syntax equation:

$$\Phi ::= p \mid \Phi_1 \wedge \Phi_2 \mid \neg \Phi \mid \mathcal{X}^{\bowtie \varrho} \Phi \mid \Phi_1 \mathcal{U}^{\bowtie \varrho} \Phi_2$$

Here $p \in Ap$, $\varrho \in [0,1]$, and $\bowtie \in \{\leq, <, \geq, >, =, \neq\}$.

Let $G = (V, E, (V_\Box, V_\bigcirc), Prob)$ be a $1\frac{1}{2}$-player game, and let $\nu : Ap \to 2^V$ be a *valuation*. The semantics of PCTL is defined below.

$$\begin{aligned}
[\![p]\!]^\nu &= \nu(p)\\
[\![\Phi_1 \wedge \Phi_2]\!]^\nu &= [\![\Phi_1]\!]^\nu \cap [\![\Phi_2]\!]^\nu\\
[\![\neg\Phi]\!]^\nu &= V \setminus [\![\Phi]\!]^\nu\\
[\![\mathcal{X}^{\bowtie\varrho}\Phi]\!]^\nu &= \{u \in V \mid \forall \sigma \in \mathrm{HR} : \mathcal{P}(Run(G(\sigma), u, \mathcal{X}\,[\![\Phi]\!]^\nu)) \bowtie \varrho\}\\
[\![\Phi_1 \mathcal{U}^{\bowtie\varrho}\Phi_2]\!]^\nu &= \{u \in V \mid \forall \sigma \in \mathrm{HR} : \mathcal{P}(Run(G(\sigma), u, [\![\Phi_1]\!]^\nu\, \mathcal{U}\, [\![\Phi_2]\!]^\nu)) \bowtie \varrho\}
\end{aligned}$$

The $\mathcal{F}^{\bowtie\varrho}$ and $\mathrm{G}^{\bowtie\varrho}$ operators are defined in the standard way: $\mathcal{F}^{\bowtie\varrho}\Phi$ stands for $\mathtt{tt}\,\mathcal{U}^{\bowtie\varrho}\Phi$, and $\mathrm{G}^{\bowtie\varrho}\Phi$ stands for $\mathtt{tt}\,\mathcal{U}^{\bar{\bowtie} 1-\varrho}\neg\Phi$, where $\bar{\bowtie}$ is $<$, $>$, $\leq$, $\geq$, $=$, or $\neq$, depending on whether $\bowtie$ is $>$, $<$, $\geq$, $\leq$, $=$, or $\neq$, respectively.

Various natural fragments of PCTL can be obtained by restricting the PCTL syntax to certain modal connectives and/or certain operator/number combinations. The *qualitative* fragment of PCTL is obtained by restricting the allowed operator/number combinations to '$\bowtie 0$' and '$\bowtie 1$'. Hence, $a\mathcal{U}^{<1}b \vee \mathcal{F}^{>0}c$ is a qualitative PCTL formula.

BPA Games. A $1\frac{1}{2}$-*player BPA game* is a tuple $\Delta = (\Gamma, \hookrightarrow, (\Gamma_\Box, \Gamma_\bigcirc), Prob)$ where Γ is a finite *stack alphabet*, $\hookrightarrow \subseteq \Gamma \times \Gamma^{\leq 2}$ is a set of *rules* (where $\Gamma^{\leq 2} = \{w \in \Gamma^* : |w| \leq 2\}$) such that for each $X \in \Gamma$ there is some $X \hookrightarrow \alpha$, $(\Gamma_\Box, \Gamma_\bigcirc)$ is a partition of Γ, and *Prob* is a *probability assignment* which to each $X \in \Gamma_\bigcirc$ assigns a rational positive probability distribution on the set of all rules of the form $X \hookrightarrow \alpha$.

Each $1\frac{1}{2}$-player BPA game $\Delta = (\Gamma, \hookrightarrow, (\Gamma_\Box, \Gamma_\bigcirc), Prob)$ determines a unique $1\frac{1}{2}$-player game $G_\Delta = (\Gamma^*, E_\Delta, (\Gamma_\Box\Gamma^*, \Gamma_\bigcirc\Gamma^* \cup \{\varepsilon\}), Prob_\Delta)$ where the transitions of E_Δ are determined as follows: $\varepsilon \to \varepsilon$, and $X\beta \to \alpha\beta$ iff $X \hookrightarrow \alpha$. The probability assignment $Prob_\Delta$ is the natural extension of *Prob*, i.e., $Prob_\Delta(X\beta \to \alpha\beta) = Prob(X \hookrightarrow \alpha)$, and $Prob_\Delta(\varepsilon \to \varepsilon) = 1$. Note that G_Δ is finitely branching.

Given a configuration $X\alpha \in \Gamma^*$, we put $head(X\alpha) = X$.

3 $1\frac{1}{2}$-Player BPA Games with Extended Reachability Objectives

In this section we present several results about $1\frac{1}{2}$-player BPA games with extended reachability objectives.

Definition 2. *Let $G = (V, E, (V_\Box, V_\bigcirc), Prob)$ be an (arbitrary) $1\frac{1}{2}$-player game. An* extended reachability objective (ERO) *is a pair (S,T), where $S,T \subseteq V$ are the subsets of* safe *and* terminal *vertices.*

Let (S,T) be an ERO. For every HR strategy σ and every $u \in V$ we define the σ-value *of u, denoted $Val^\sigma(u)$, as follows:*

$$Val^\sigma(u) = \mathcal{P}(Run(G(\sigma), u, S\mathcal{U}T))$$

Furthermore, we define the upper *and* lower *value of u, denoted $Val^+(u)$ and $Val^-(u)$, as the* sup *and* inf *of the set $\{Val^\sigma(u) \mid \sigma \in HR\}$, respectively.*

If the player $\Box$ wants to maximize (or minimize) the value of a certain vertex u, he uses a maximizing (or minimizing) strategy. An *optimal maximizing* (or *optimal minimizing*) strategy for a vertex u is a strategy σ such that $Val^\sigma(u)$ is equal to $Val^+(u)$ (or to $Val^-(u)$, resp.).

It has been shown in [2] that optimal maximizing/minimizing strategies always exist in $1\frac{1}{2}$-player games with *finitely* many vertices; moreover, there are efficiently constructible optimal maximizing/minimizing MD strategies. This does *not* hold for games with infinitely many vertices—one can easily give an example of a game with countably many vertices where an optimal minimizing strategy does not exist for a certain vertex u, and

$$1 = \inf_{\sigma \in \mathrm{MD}} \{\mathcal{P}(Run(G(\sigma), u, S\mathcal{U}T))\} > \inf_{\sigma \in \mathrm{HR}} \{\mathcal{P}(Run(G(\sigma), u, S\mathcal{U}T))\} = 0$$

We are primarily interested in finitely-branching games, where the situation is somewhat specific. The following proposition gives a full characterization:

Proposition 3. *Let $G = (V, E, (V_\Box, V_\bigcirc), Prob)$ be a finitely-branching $1\frac{1}{2}$-player game, $u \in V$, and (S,T) an ERO. Then*

(a) there is an optimal minimizing MD strategy for u;
(b) $\sup_{\sigma \in MD}\{\mathcal{P}(Run(G(\sigma), u, S\mathcal{U}T))\} = \sup_{\sigma \in HR}\{\mathcal{P}(Run(G(\sigma), u, S\mathcal{U}T))\}$
(c) if there is an optimal maximizing HR strategy for u, then there is also an optimal maximizing MD strategy for u.

Proposition 3 admits the non-existence of an optimal maximizing strategy for u. This can indeed happen, even for $1\frac{1}{2}$-player BPA games (see also [6]):

Example 4. Let $\Delta = (\{X, A, D\}, \hookrightarrow, (\{X\}, \{A, D\}), Prob)$ be a $1\frac{1}{2}$-player BPA game, where

$$X \hookrightarrow XA,\ X \hookrightarrow \varepsilon,\ A \overset{1/2}{\hookrightarrow} D,\ A \overset{1/2}{\hookrightarrow} \varepsilon,\ D \overset{1}{\hookrightarrow} D.$$

Let $S = \{X, A, D\}^*$ and $T = \{D\}\{A\}^*$. One can easily verify that $Val^+(X) = 1$. However, for every HR strategy σ we have that $Val^\sigma(X) < 1$.

In the rest of this section we restrict our attention to $1\frac{1}{2}$-player BPA games. Due to Proposition 3, from now on we can safely consider just MD strategies because they are equivalently powerful as HR strategies in the context of extended reachability objectives.

To simplify our notation, for the rest of this section we fix a $1\frac{1}{2}$-player BPA game $\Delta = (\Gamma, \hookrightarrow, (\Gamma_\Box, \Gamma_\bigcirc), Prob)$. Realize that all of the previously introduced game-theoretic notions (strategy, upper/lower value, etc.) apply to $G(\Delta)$, not directly to Δ. In particular, the vertices of $G(\Delta)$ are stack configurations of Γ^*, which means that MD strategies generally depend on the whole sequence of symbols which form a given vertex. An MD strategy σ is *stackless (SMD)* if it depends just on the top-of-the-stack symbol of a given vertex.

A *termination objective* is an ERO where $S = \Gamma^*$ and $T = \{\varepsilon\}$. In [6,7], it has been shown that $1\frac{1}{2}$-player BPA games with termination objectives have the following properties:

(a) There are optimal SMD minimizing and maximizing strategies.
(b) For each $X \in \Gamma$, the values $\mathit{Val}^+(X)$ and $\mathit{Val}^-(X)$ are expressible as the least solution of an effectively constructible system of non-linear equations. This allows to express the values $\mathit{Val}^+(X)$ and $\mathit{Val}^-(X)$ in $(\mathbb{R}, +, *, \leq)$, i.e., first-order arithmetic of the reals.
(c) The problems whether $\mathit{Val}^+(\alpha) = x$, where $x \in \{0,1\}$, and whether $\mathit{Val}^-(\alpha) = x$, where $x \in \{0,1\}$, are solvable in polynomial time.

In this paper we consider $1\frac{1}{2}$-player BPA games with more general EROs, where the sets S and T are *simple*:

Definition 5. *A set $M \subseteq \Gamma^*$ is* simple *iff there is a* characteristic set $C(M) \subseteq \Gamma$ *such that $M = \bigcup_{Y \in C(M)} \{Y\}\Gamma^*$. An ERO (S,T) is simple if S and T are simple.*

The properties (a)–(c) stated above do not hold for BPA games with simple EROs. In particular, note the following:

(A) An optimal minimizing SMD strategy may not exist (though there must be an optimal minimizing MD strategy by Proposition 3). An optimal maximizing strategy may not exist at all (see Example 4), and the existence of an optimal maximizing strategy does not imply the existence of an optimal maximizing SMD strategy.
(B) The system of non-linear recursive equations which was used in [6] for termination objectives cannot be immediately generalized to simple EROs. Intuitively, the reason is that the optimal minimizing/maximizing strategy in a configuration $X\alpha$ does not depend just on X but also on α, and a small modification of α may lead to a completely different optimal strategy. This is because one has to "balance" between the probability of termination and the probability of hitting a terminal configuration for each stack symbol, depending on what is achievable for the symbols stored below in the stack.
(C) For a given $\alpha \in \Gamma^*$, the problems whether $\mathit{Val}^-(\alpha) = 0$, whether $\mathit{Val}^+(\alpha) = 0$, and whether $\mathit{Val}^-(\alpha) = 1$ are solvable in polynomial time. The decidability of the problem whether $\mathit{Val}^+(\alpha) = 1$ is left open. Nevertheless, we show that the problem whether there is an optimal maximizing strategy σ such that $\mathit{Val}^\sigma(\alpha) = 1$ is decidable in polynomial time (remember that $\mathit{Val}^+(\alpha)$ can be 1 even if no optimal maximizing strategy exists).

The property (A) is demonstrated in the following example:

Example 6. Let $\Delta = (\{X, R\}, \hookrightarrow, (\{X, R\}, \emptyset), Prob)$ be a $1\frac{1}{2}$-player BPA game, where $X \hookrightarrow XR$, $X \hookrightarrow \varepsilon$, $R \hookrightarrow R$. Let us consider an ERO (S, T) where $C(S) = \{X\}$ and $C(T) = \{R\}$. Then $Val^{+}(X) = 1$ and there an optimal maximizing MD strategy, but there is no optimal maximizing SMD strategy.

Let $\Delta' = (\{X, Y, Z, H, R\}, \hookrightarrow, (\{X, Y, Z, R\}, \{H\}), Prob)$ be a $1\frac{1}{2}$-player BPA game, where

$$X \hookrightarrow YR,\ Y \hookrightarrow H,\ Y \hookrightarrow \varepsilon,\ R \hookrightarrow R,\ Z \hookrightarrow Z,\ H \overset{1/2}{\hookrightarrow} YZ,\ H \overset{1/2}{\hookrightarrow} R.$$

Let us consider an ERO (S, T) where $C(S) = \{X, Y, Z, H\}$ and $C(T) = \{R\}$. Then $Val^{-}(X) = 1/2$ and there an optimal minimizing MD strategy, but there is no optimal minimizing SMD strategy.

Now we present a sequence of results from which (C) follows as a simple consequence, and which allow to design the model-checking algorithm for $1\frac{1}{2}$-player games and qualitative PCTL formulae presented in Section 4.

For the rest of this section, let us fix a simple ERO (S, T). Let $\Delta' = (\Gamma, \leadsto, (\Gamma_\Box, \Gamma_\bigcirc), Prob')$ be a modification of the game Δ obtained by replacing all rules of the form $P \hookrightarrow \alpha$, where $P \in C(T) \cup (\Gamma \setminus C(S))$, with a single rule $P \leadsto P$ (the other rules are preserved). One can easily verify that for every strategy σ and every $\alpha \in \Gamma^*$ we have that $\mathcal{P}(G_\Delta(\sigma), \alpha, S\mathcal{U}T) = \mathcal{P}(G_{\Delta'}(\sigma), \alpha, \mathcal{F}T)$, and this fact is heavily used in the proofs of subsequent theorems where we freely "shift" between Δ and Δ'.

Theorem 7. *Let $[S\mathcal{U}^{>0}T]$ be the set of all $\alpha \in \Gamma^*$ for which there is a strategy σ such that $\mathcal{P}(G_\Delta(\sigma), \alpha, S\mathcal{U}T) > 0$. Then there are $\mathcal{A}, \mathcal{B} \subseteq \Gamma$ computable in polynomial time such that $[S\mathcal{U}^{>0}T] = \mathcal{A}^*\mathcal{B}\Gamma^*$.*

Proof. Let $\mathcal{A} = \{X \in \Gamma \mid X \leadsto^* \varepsilon\}$ and $\mathcal{B} = \{X \in \Gamma \mid X \leadsto^* R\beta$, where $R \in C(T)$ and $\beta \in \Gamma^*\}$. Now observe that $\alpha \in [S\mathcal{U}^{>0}T]$ iff $\alpha \leadsto^* R\beta$ for some $R \in C(T)$ and $\beta \in \Gamma^*$ iff $\alpha \in \mathcal{A}^*\mathcal{B}\Gamma^*$. The sets $\mathcal{A}, \mathcal{B}$ can be computed using standard algorithms for PDA reachability. □

Theorem 8. *Let $[S\mathcal{U}^{=0}T]$ be the set of all $\alpha \in \Gamma^*$ for which there is a strategy σ such that $\mathcal{P}(G_\Delta(\sigma), \alpha, S\mathcal{U}T) = 0$. Then there are $\mathcal{A}, \mathcal{B} \subseteq \Gamma$ computable in polynomial time such that $[S\mathcal{U}^{=0}T] = \mathcal{B}^* \cup (\mathcal{B}^*\mathcal{A}\Gamma^*)$.*

Proof. We define the sets $\mathcal{A}$ and $\mathcal{B}$ as follows:

- $X \in \mathcal{A}$ iff there is a strategy σ such that $\mathcal{P}(Run(G_{\Delta'}(\sigma), X, \mathcal{F}(T \cup \{\varepsilon\}))) = 0$
- $X \in \mathcal{B}$ iff there is a strategy σ such that $\mathcal{P}(Run(G_{\Delta'}(\sigma), X, \mathcal{F}T)) = 0$

It is easy to verify that $\mathcal{A}$ and $\mathcal{B}$ satisfy the property that $[S\mathcal{U}^{=0}T] = \mathcal{B}^* \cup \mathcal{B}^*\mathcal{A}\Gamma^*$.

We show that the sets $\mathcal{A}$ and $\mathcal{B}$ can be computed as the greatest fixpoint of a monotonic function $\Theta : 2^\Gamma \times 2^\Gamma \to 2^\Gamma \times 2^\Gamma$, where $\Theta(M, N) = (M', N')$ is defined as follows:

- $X \in M'$ iff $X \in M \setminus C(T)$ and the following conditions are satisfied:
  - If $X \in \Gamma_{\Box}$, then there is a rule of one of the following forms: $X \rightsquigarrow Y$ where $Y \in M$, or $X \rightsquigarrow YZ$ where either $Y \in M$, or $Y \in N$ and $Z \in M$.
  - If $X \in \Gamma_{\bigcirc}$, then all rules of the form $X \rightsquigarrow \alpha$ satisfy either $\alpha = Y$ where $Y \in M$, or $\alpha = YZ$ where either $Y \in M$, or $Y \in N$ and $Z \in M$.
- $X \in N'$ iff $X \in N \setminus C(T)$ and the following conditions are satisfied:
  - If $X \in \Gamma_{\Box}$, then there is a rule of one of the following forms: $X \rightsquigarrow \varepsilon$, or $X \rightsquigarrow Y$ where $Y \in N \cup M$, or $X \rightsquigarrow YZ$ where either $Y \in M$, or $Y, Z \in N \cup M$.
  - If $X \in \Gamma_{\bigcirc}$, then all rules of the form $X \rightsquigarrow \alpha$ satisfy either $\alpha = \varepsilon$, or $\alpha = Y$ where $Y \in N \cup M$, or $\alpha = YZ$ where either $Y \in M$, or $Y, Z \in N \cup M$.

It is easy to show that:

(1) $(\mathcal{A}, \mathcal{B})$ is a fixpoint of Θ.
(2) If (C, D) is a fixpoint of Θ, then $C \subseteq \mathcal{A}$ and $D \subseteq \mathcal{B}$.

Hence, the sets $\mathcal{A}$ and $\mathcal{B}$ can be computed in polynomial time by a simple iterative algorithm. □

Theorem 9. *Let $[S\mathcal{U}^{=1}T]$ be the set of all $\alpha \in \Gamma^*$ for which there is a strategy σ such that $\mathcal{P}(G_\Delta(\sigma), \alpha, S\mathcal{U}T) = 1$. Then there are $\mathcal{A}, \mathcal{B}, \mathcal{C} \subseteq \Gamma$ computable in polynomial time such that $[S\mathcal{U}^{=1}T] = (\mathcal{B} \cup \mathcal{C})^* \mathcal{A} \Gamma^*$.*

Proof. We define the sets $\mathcal{A}$, $\mathcal{B}$ and $\mathcal{C}$ as follows:

- $X \in \mathcal{A}$ iff there is a strategy σ such that $\mathcal{P}(Run(G_{\Delta'}(\sigma)), X, \mathcal{F}T) = 1$
- $X \in \mathcal{B}$ iff there is a strategy σ such that $\mathcal{P}(Run(G_{\Delta'}(\sigma)), X, \mathcal{F}(T \cup \{\varepsilon\})) = 1$ and $\mathcal{P}(Run(G_{\Delta'}(\sigma)), X, \mathcal{F}T) > 0$
- $X \in \mathcal{C}$ iff there is a strategy σ such that $\mathcal{P}(Run(G_{\Delta'}(\sigma)), X, \mathcal{F}\{\varepsilon\}) = 1$

Observe that $\mathcal{C}$ can be computed in polynomial time using the algorithm of [7]. Moreover, it is easy to show that $[S\mathcal{U}^{=1}T] = (\mathcal{B} \cup \mathcal{C})^* \mathcal{A} \Gamma^*$ and $[S\mathcal{U}^{=1}(T \cup \{\varepsilon\})] = (\mathcal{B} \cup \mathcal{C})^* \cup (\mathcal{B} \cup \mathcal{C})^* \mathcal{A} \Gamma^*$.

We prove that the sets $\mathcal{A}$ and $\mathcal{B}$ can be computed in polynomial time. The proof proceeds as follows: first we define a monotone function $\Theta : 2^\Gamma \times 2^\Gamma \to 2^\Gamma \times 2^\Gamma$ and show that $(\mathcal{A}, \mathcal{B})$ is the greatest fixpoint of Θ. Second, we show how to compute Θ (and hence also its greatest fixpoint) in polynomial time.

In order to define the function Θ we need to introduce some notation. Let $R, H \subseteq \Gamma$. For every MD strategy π, we define two predicates $Q_{R,H}$ and $Q'_{R,H}$ over $FPath(G_{\Delta'}(\pi), X)$ as follows: Given a path $u \in FPath(G_{\Delta'}(\pi), X)$ of length $n \geq 0$, the predicate $Q_{R,H}(u)$ (or $Q'_{R,H}(u)$) holds iff $u[n] \in T$ and for all $0 \leq i < n$ such that $u[i] \in \Gamma_{\bigcirc}\Gamma^*$ we have that *all* successors of $u(i)$ are of the form $(H \cup \mathcal{C})^* R \Gamma^*$ (or $(H \cup \mathcal{C})^* R \Gamma^* \cup (H \cup \mathcal{C})^*$, resp.). Now, we put $\Theta(R, H) = (R', H')$ where

$$R' = \{X \in R \cup C(T) \mid \exists \pi \exists u \in FPath(G_{\Delta'}(\pi), X), Q_{R \cup C(T), H \cup C(T)}(u) = \text{true}\}$$
$$H' = \{X \in H \cup C(T) \mid \exists \pi \exists u \in FPath(G_{\Delta'}(\pi), X), Q'_{R \cup C(T), H \cup C(T)}(u) = \text{true}\}$$

It follows directly from the definition that Θ is monotone. It remains to show that $(\mathcal{A}, \mathcal{B})$ is the greatest fixpoint of Θ. First, we prove that $(\mathcal{A}, \mathcal{B})$ is a fixpoint.

Let $\Theta(\mathcal{A}, \mathcal{B}) = (\mathcal{A}', \mathcal{B}')$. Since $\mathcal{A}' \subseteq \mathcal{A}$ and $\mathcal{B}' \subseteq \mathcal{B}$ by definition of Θ, it suffices to show the opposite inclusions. Let $X \in \mathcal{A}$ and let σ be a strategy which witnesses that $X \in \mathcal{A}$. Let us consider a path of minimal length in $G_{\Delta'}(\sigma)$ from X to a configuration of T. Since every configuration reachable from X along a path which does not visit T belongs to $[S\mathcal{U}^{=1}T] = (\mathcal{B} \cup \mathcal{C})^* \mathcal{A} \Gamma^*$, we can conclude $X \in \mathcal{A}'$. Similarly, we can show that $\mathcal{B} \subseteq \mathcal{B}'$ which implies that $\Theta(\mathcal{A}, \mathcal{B}) = (\mathcal{A}, \mathcal{B})$.

Now, suppose that (R, H) is a fixpoint of Θ. We prove that $R \subseteq \mathcal{A}$ and $H \subseteq \mathcal{B}$. For every $Y \in R$ (or $Y \in H$), let us fix a path u_Y which witnesses that $Y \in R$ (or $Y \in H$, resp.). It follows from the definition of Θ that if $Y \in R$ (or $Y \in H$) then all successors of all stochastic configurations that appear on u_Y are of the form $(H \cup \mathcal{C})^* R \Gamma^*$ (or $(H \cup \mathcal{C})^* R \Gamma^* \cup (H \cup \mathcal{C})^*$, resp.). Note that for every configuration of the form $(H \cup \mathcal{C})^* R \Gamma^*$ there is a strategy which forces almost all runs to reach a configuration of the form $R\Gamma^* \cup (H(H \cup \mathcal{C})^* R \Gamma^*)$. Let us consider a strategy π which from configurations of the form $\{X\}\Gamma^*$ where $X \in R$ (or configurations of the form $\{X\}(H \cup \mathcal{C})^* R \Gamma^*$ where $X \in H$) follows the path u_X and for all successors of stochastic configurations on u_X strives to reach configurations of the form $R\Gamma^* \cup (H(H \cup \mathcal{C})^* R \Gamma^*)$ with probability 1. Now, observe that almost every run of $Run(G_{\Delta'}(\pi), X)$, where $X \in R$, enters configurations with a head $Y \in R \cup H$ infinitely often, which implies that almost every run takes a path u_Y for some $Y \in R \cup H$. It follows that $\mathcal{P}(Run(G_{\Delta'}(\pi), X, \mathcal{F}T)) = 1$. Similarly, we prove that for $X \in H$ there is a strategy π such that $\mathcal{P}(Run(G_{\Delta'}(\pi), X, \mathcal{F}(T \cup \{\varepsilon\})) = 1$ and $\mathcal{P}(Run(G_{\Delta'}(\pi), X, \mathcal{F}T) > 0$.

So, we proved that $(\mathcal{A}, \mathcal{B})$ is the greatest fixpoint of Θ. Now we indicate how to compute $\Theta(R, H)$ in polynomial time.

We can consider Δ' as a non-probabilistic BPA (just ignoring the probabilities on transitions from the stochastic configurations). Observe that there is a path u with the properties stated in the definition of R' (or H') iff in the non-probabilistic BPA Δ' the set T is reachable via configurations with all successors in $(H \cup \mathcal{C})^* R \Gamma^*$ (or $(H \cup \mathcal{C})^* R \Gamma^* \cup (H \cup \mathcal{C})^*$, resp.). This variant of reachability problem is decidable in polynomial time for BPA processes using standard techniques. □

Theorem 10. *Let $[S\mathcal{U}^{<1}T]$ be the set of all $\alpha \in \Gamma^*$ for which there is a strategy σ such that $\mathcal{P}(G_\Delta(\sigma), \alpha, S\mathcal{U}T) < 1$. Then there are $\mathcal{A}, \mathcal{B} \subseteq \Gamma$ computable in polynomial time such that $[S\mathcal{U}^{<1}T] = \mathcal{A}^* \cup (\mathcal{A}^* \mathcal{B} \Gamma^*)$.*

Proof. Let us define the sets $\mathcal{A}$ and $\mathcal{B}$ as follows:

- $X \in \mathcal{A}$ iff there is a strategy σ such that $\mathcal{P}(Run(G_{\Delta'}(\sigma), X, \mathcal{F}\{\varepsilon\})) > 0$
- $X \in \mathcal{B}$ iff there is a strategy σ such that $\mathcal{P}(Run(G_{\Delta'}(\sigma), X, \neg\mathcal{F}(T \cup \{\varepsilon\}))) > 0$

It is easy to prove that $\mathcal{A}$ and $\mathcal{B}$ satisfy the desired property $[S\mathcal{U}^{<1}T] = \mathcal{A}^* \cup (\mathcal{A}^* \mathcal{B} \Gamma^*)$. It follows from Theorem 7 that the membership to $\mathcal{A}$ is decidable in polynomial time. For the rest of this proof we fix some $X \in \Gamma$ and examine the conditions under which $X \in \mathcal{B}$.

One sufficient condition for $X \in \mathcal{B}$ is the existence of some $Y \in \Gamma \setminus C(T)$ and two strategies σ, π where $\mathcal{P}(Run(G_{\Delta'}(\sigma), X, \mathcal{F}(\{Y\}\Gamma^*)) > 0$ and $\mathcal{P}(Run(G_{\Delta'}(\pi), Y, \mathcal{F}(T \cup \{\varepsilon\}))) = 0$. The strategies σ and π can be combined into a single strategy σ' which behaves like σ until a configuration with the head Y is reached, and then it behaves like π. Obviously, $\mathcal{P}(Run(G_{\Delta'}(\sigma'), X, \neg\mathcal{F}(T \cup \{\varepsilon\}))) > 0$. The existence of such Y, σ and π can be decided in polynomial time using Theorem 7 and Theorem 8. However, this condition is not necessary as the following example illustrates. Let us consider a $1\frac{1}{2}$-player BPA game with rules

$$A \overset{1/2}{\hookrightarrow} C,\ A \overset{1/2}{\hookrightarrow} B,\ B \overset{3/4}{\hookrightarrow} BB,\ B \overset{1/4}{\hookrightarrow} \varepsilon,\ C \overset{1}{\hookrightarrow} C.$$

Note that this example closely ressembles one-dimensional (asymmetric) random walk. It can be shown that using the only (empty) strategy the probability of reaching ε or (a configuration with a head) C from A is less than 1 but every Y reachable from A reaches ε or C with a non-zero probability.

Hence, let us assume that *there are no suitable* Y, σ and π such that $\mathcal{P}(Run(G_{\Delta'}(\sigma), X, \mathcal{F}(\{Y\}\Gamma^*)) > 0$ and $\mathcal{P}(Run(G_{\Delta'}(\pi), Y, \mathcal{F}(T \cup \{\varepsilon\}))) = 0$. For now, let us assume that $X \in \mathcal{B}$ and let us fix a strategy σ which witnesses that $X \in \mathcal{B}$.

Claim (1). There are $Y \in \Gamma \setminus C(T)$ where $\mathcal{P}(G_{\Delta'}(\sigma), X, \mathcal{F}(\{Y\}\Gamma^*)) > 0$, sets $A \subseteq \Gamma \setminus C(T)$ and $R \subseteq \rightsquigarrow$, a strategy σ', and a set of runs $V \subseteq Run(G_{\Delta'}(\sigma'), Y)$ such that

1. $\mathcal{P}(V) > 0$;
2. for all $w \in V$ and $i \geq 0$ we have that $head(w[i]) \in A$ (in particular, $Y \in A$) and $w(i) \rightarrow w(i+1)$ is induced by a transition rule of R;
3. for every $Z \in A$ there are infinitely many $i \geq 0$ such that $head(w[i]) = Z$ and for every rule $Z \rightsquigarrow \alpha \in R$ there are infinitely many $i \geq 0$ such that $w(i) \rightarrow w(i+1)$ is induced by $Z \rightsquigarrow \alpha$.

Proof (of Claim (1)). For all $A \subseteq \Gamma$ and $R \subseteq \rightsquigarrow$, we denote $L_{A,R}$ the set of all $w \in Run(G_{\Delta'}(\sigma), X, \neg\mathcal{F}(T \cup \{\varepsilon\}))$ such that exactly the heads of A and exactly the transitions induced by the rules of R occur infinitely often along w. Since there are only finitely many sets $L_{A,R}$, $Run(G_{\Delta'}(\sigma), X, \neg\mathcal{F}(T \cup \{\varepsilon\})) = \bigcup L_{A,R}$, and $\mathcal{P}(Run(G_{\Delta'}(\sigma), X, \neg\mathcal{F}(T \cup \{\varepsilon\}))) > 0$, we have that $\mathcal{P}(L_{A,R}) > 0$ for some A and R. Let us fix such sets A and R.

For every $v \in FPath(G_{\Delta'}(\sigma), X)$, we denote U_v the set of all runs w of $L_{A,R}$ such that v is a prefix of w, $w(|v|-1)$ is a *minimum* of w (i.e. for all $j \geq |v|$ we have that the length of $w[j]$ is not strictly less than the length of $w[|v|-1]$), and for all $i \geq |v|-1$ we have that $head(w[i]) \in A$ and $w(i) \rightarrow w(i+1)$ is induced by a rule of R. Clearly, $L_{A,R} = \bigcup_{v \in FPath(G_{\Delta'}(\sigma), X)} U_v$. It follows that $0 < \mathcal{P}(L_{A,R}) \leq \sum_{v \in FPath(G_{\Delta'}(\sigma), X)} \mathcal{P}(U_v)$ and thus there is $v \in FPath(G_{\Delta'}(\sigma), X)$ such that $\mathcal{P}(U_v) > 0$.

Let us assume that $v[|v|-1] = Y\alpha$ and let $w \in U_v$. Since $w(|v|-1)$ is a minimum of w, for all $i \geq 0$ we have that $w(i+|v|-1) = \beta_i\alpha$ where $\beta_i \neq \varepsilon$. We define $\Theta(w) = \beta_0, \beta_0\beta_1, \beta_0\beta_1\beta_2, \ldots$. Now, let us consider a strategy σ' which, along a run $\Theta(w)$ of $\Theta(U_v)$, behaves similarly as σ over w after the prefix v (ignoring the context α). It can be proved using standard arguments for Markov chains that $\mathcal{P}(U_v) = \mathcal{P}(Run(G_{\Delta'}(\sigma), v)) \cdot \mathcal{P}(\Theta(U_v))$, which implies that

$$\mathcal{P}(\Theta(U_v)) = \frac{\mathcal{P}(U_v)}{\mathcal{P}(Run(G_{\Delta'}(\sigma), v))} > 0$$

Now it is easy to verify that we can safely put $V = \Theta(U_v)$. ◇

For all $A' \subseteq \Gamma$ and $R' \subseteq \rightsquigarrow$, we put $\Delta'_{A',R'} = (A', R', (A' \cap \Gamma_\square, A' \cap \Gamma_\bigcirc), Prob)$.

Claim (2). $\Delta'_{A,R}$ is a $1\frac{1}{2}$-player BPA game, and there is a strategy π for $\Delta'_{A,R}$ such that $\mathcal{P}(Run(G_{\Delta'_{A,R}}(\pi), Y, \mathcal{F}\{\varepsilon\})) < 1$.

Proof (of Claim (2)). First we take a closer look at the rules in R. Let $Z \in \Gamma_\bigcirc \cap A$ and let $Z \rightsquigarrow D$. We claim that $(Z, D) \in R$ and $D \in A$. Indeed, all runs of V enter a configuration having Z as its head infinitely often which implies that almost all runs of V take the rule $Z \rightsquigarrow D$ infinitely often. Thus, if $(Z, D) \notin R$ or $D \notin A$, then $\mathcal{P}(V) = 0$. Similarly, we prove that if $Z \rightsquigarrow \varepsilon$ then $(Z, \varepsilon) \in R$.

Let us consider a rule $Z \rightsquigarrow DE$. By the same argument as above we conclude that $(Z, DE) \in R$ and $D \in A$. We show that $E \in A$. Suppose the converse, i.e., $E \notin A$. We claim that then for every $\xi > 0$ there is a strategy ζ such that $\mathcal{P}(Run(G_{\Delta'}(\zeta), D, \mathcal{F}(T \cup \{\varepsilon\}))) < \xi$, because otherwise $\mathcal{P}(V) = 0$. Indeed, if for every ζ we have $\mathcal{P}(Run(G_{\Delta'}(\zeta), D, \mathcal{F}(T \cup \{\varepsilon\}))) \geq \xi$ for a fixed $\xi > 0$, then almost all runs of V enter E infinitely often, because all runs of V enter a configuration with the head Z infinitely often and no run of V enters T. Now, we employ Proposition 3 (a) and conclude that there is a strategy ζ' such that $\mathcal{P}(Run(G_{\Delta'}(\zeta'), D, \mathcal{F}(T \cup \{\varepsilon\})) = 0$. However, D is reachable from X (using a suitable strategy) which contradicts our assumption. Hence, $E \in A$.

Now let us assume that $Z \in \Gamma_\square \cap A$. Observe that $(Z, \alpha) \in R$ for at least one rule $Z \rightsquigarrow \alpha$. Let us assume that $(Z, D) \in R$. We have that $Z \rightsquigarrow D$ is used infinitely often along every run of V and thus $D \in A$. Similarly, if $(Z, DE) \in R$ then $D \in A$ and using similar arguments as above (for $Z \in \Gamma_\bigcirc \cap A$) we can show that $E \in A$.

The above arguments imply that $\Delta'_{A,R}$ is a $1\frac{1}{2}$-player BPA game. Now, let us consider an arbitrary strategy π for $\Delta'_{A,R}$ which behaves similarly as σ' over runs of V. The existence of such a strategy is guaranteed by Claim (1). Using standard arguments for Markov chains, it can be proven that the probability of V remains the same (i.e., non-zero) in $G_{\Delta'_{A,R}}(\pi)$ as in $G_{\Delta'}(\sigma')$, which implies that $\mathcal{P}(G_{\Delta'_{A,R}}, Y, \mathcal{F}\{\varepsilon\}) < 1$. ◇

So far, we have proved that if $X \in \mathcal{B}$, then

- there are $Y \in \Gamma \setminus C(T)$, $A \subseteq \Gamma \setminus C(T)$ and $R \subseteq \rightsquigarrow$ such that $Y \in A$ and $\Delta'_{A,R}$ is a $1\frac{1}{2}$-player BPA game;
- there is a strategy σ satisfying $\mathcal{P}(Run(G_{\Delta'}(\sigma), Y, \mathcal{F}(\{Y\}\Gamma^*)) > 0$;
- there is a strategy π satisfying $\mathcal{P}(Run(G_{\Delta'_{A,R}}(\pi), Y, \mathcal{F}\{\varepsilon\})) < 1$.

Using the strategies σ and π, we can easily define a strategy ζ for Δ' which witnesses that $X \in \mathcal{B}$ (ζ behaves like σ until Y is reached and then behaves like π).

Now, it is easy to see that if $\Delta'_{A',R'}$ is a $1\frac{1}{2}$-player BPA game for some $A' \supseteq A$ and $R' \supseteq R$, then the strategy π can be extended to a strategy π' in $\Delta'_{A',R'}$ which satisfies $\mathcal{P}(Run(G_{\Delta'_{A',R'}}(\pi'), Y, \mathcal{F}\{\varepsilon\})) = \mathcal{P}(Run(G_{\Delta'_{A,R}}(\pi), Y, \mathcal{F}\{\varepsilon\})) < 1$. Furthermore, if for A', R' and A'', R'' we have that $\Delta'_{A',R'}$ and $\Delta'_{A'',R''}$ are $1\frac{1}{2}$-player BPA games, then $\Delta'_{A' \cup A'', R' \cup R''}$ is a $1\frac{1}{2}$-player BPA game.

Hence, in order to decide whether $X \in \mathcal{B}$, it suffices to compute the largest sets $A \subseteq \Gamma \smallsetminus C(T)$ and $R \subseteq \rightsquigarrow$ for which $\Delta'_{A,R}$ is a $1\frac{1}{2}$-player BPA game, and to decide whether there are $Y \in A$, σ, and π such that $\mathcal{P}(Run(G_{\Delta'}(\sigma), X, \mathcal{F}(\{Y\}\Gamma^*)) > 0$ and $\mathcal{P}(Run(G_{\Delta'_{A,R}}(\pi), Y, \mathcal{F}\{\varepsilon\})) < 1$. The problem whether there is π such that $\mathcal{P}(Run(G_{\Delta'_{A,R}}(\pi), Y, \mathcal{F}\{\varepsilon\})) < 1$ can be decided in polynomial time using the algorithm of [7]. The maximal sets A and R can be computed using a simple fixpoint algorithm. □

4 Model-Checking Qualitative PCTL for $1\frac{1}{2}$-Player BPA Games

In this section we show that the results about $1\frac{1}{2}$-player BPA games with extended reachability objectives (see Section 3) can be used to design an essentially optimal model-checking algorithm for the qualitative fragment of PCTL and $1\frac{1}{2}$-player BPA games. For technical convenience, we restrict ourselves to *simple* valuations, where $\nu(p)$ is a simple set for each $p \in Ap$ (see Definition 5).

Infinite sets of stack configurations will be represented by deterministic finite-state automata (DFA) which read the stack bottom-up. Formally, a DFA is a tuple $\mathcal{F} = (Q, \Sigma, \delta, \hat{q}, F)$ where Q is a finite set of *control states*, Σ is a finite *input alphabet*, $\delta : (Q \times \Sigma) \to Q$ is a total *transition function*, $\hat{q} \in Q$ is the *initial state*, and $F \subseteq Q$ is a subset of *final* states. The function δ is extended to the elements of $Q \times \Sigma^*$ in the natural way. A word $w \in \Sigma^*$ is *accepted* by $\mathcal{F}$ iff $\delta(q_0, w) \in F$.

Let Δ be a $1\frac{1}{2}$-player BPA game with the stack alphabet Γ, and let $\mathcal{F}$ be a DFA with the input alphabet Γ. We say that a stack configuration $\alpha \in \Gamma^*$ is *recognized* by $\mathcal{F}$ iff the *reverse* of α is accepted by $\mathcal{F}$. Note that stack configurations are traditionally written as words starting with the top-of-the-stack symbol, but for technical reasons we prefer to read them in the bottom-up (i.e., right to left) direction.

In the proof of our next theorem we use the standard technique of simulating DFA in the stack alphabet (see, e.g., [5]).

Theorem 11. *Let $\Delta = (\Gamma, \hookrightarrow, (\Gamma_\Box, \Gamma_\bigcirc), Prob)$ by a $1\frac{1}{2}$-player BPA game. Let ν be a simple valuation and Φ a qualitative PCTL formula. Then there is a DFA $\mathcal{F}_\Phi$ of size $|\Delta| \cdot 2^{\mathcal{O}(|\Phi|)}$ constructible in time which is polynomial in $|\Delta|$ and exponential in $|\Phi|$ such that for all $\alpha \in \Gamma^*$ we have that $\alpha \models^\nu \Phi$ iff α is recognized by $\mathcal{F}_\Phi$.*

Proof. We proceed by induction on the structure of Φ. The cases when $\Phi \equiv p$, $\Phi \equiv \Phi_1 \wedge \Phi_2$, and $\Phi \equiv \neg\Phi_1$ follow immediately.

Let $\Phi \equiv \mathcal{X}^{=1}\Phi_1$, and let $\mathcal{F}_1 = (Q_1, \Gamma, \delta_1, \hat{q}, F_1)$ be the DFA associated with Φ_1. The automaton $\mathcal{F}$ associated with Φ should then recognize exactly all $\alpha \in \Gamma^*$ such that for every transition $\alpha \to \beta$ we have that β is recognized by $\mathcal{F}_1$. Hence, we put $\mathcal{F} = (Q_1 \cup Q_1', \Gamma, \delta, \hat{r}, Q_1')$, where $Q_1' = \{q' \mid q \in Q_1\}$ and the transition function δ is constructed as follows: Let $q \in Q_1$, $A \in \Gamma$, and let $t = \delta_1(q, A)$. If for all rules $A \hookrightarrow \gamma$ we have that $\delta_1(q, \gamma^r) \in F_1$ (where γ^r denotes the reverse of γ), then $\delta(q, A) = \delta(q', A) = t'$. Otherwise, $\delta(q, A) = \delta(q', A) = t$. The initial state $\hat{r}$ of $\mathcal{F}$ is either $\hat{q}'$ or $\hat{q}$, depending on whether ε is recognized by $\mathcal{F}_1$ or not, respectively.

The cases when $\Phi \equiv \mathcal{X}^{<1}\Phi_1$, $\Phi \equiv \mathcal{X}^{=0}\Phi_1$, and $\Phi \equiv \mathcal{X}^{>0}\Phi_1$ are handled similarly.

Now, let us consider the case when $\Phi \equiv \Phi_1 \mathcal{U}^{=1}\Phi_2$. Note that $\alpha \models^\nu \Phi_1 \mathcal{U}^{=1}\Phi_2$ iff there is no MD strategy σ such that $\mathcal{P}(Run(G_\Delta(\sigma), \alpha, [\![\Phi_1]\!]\,\mathcal{U}\,[\![\Phi_2]\!])) < 1$. Let $\mathcal{F}_1 = (Q_1, \Gamma, \delta_1, \hat{q}, F_1)$ and $\mathcal{F}_2 = (Q_2, \Gamma, \delta_2, \hat{r}, F_2)$ be the DFA associated with Φ_1 and Φ_2. We construct another DFA $\mathcal{F}$ which accepts exactly those $\alpha \in \Gamma^*$ for which there *exists* an MD strategy σ such that $\mathcal{P}(Run(G_\Delta(\sigma), \alpha, [\![\Phi_1]\!]\,\mathcal{U}\,[\![\Phi_2]\!])) < 1$. The desired DFA is then obtained simply by complementing the automaton $\mathcal{F}$. First we construct a $1\frac{1}{2}$-player BPA game $\bar{\Delta}$ which is obtained from Δ by encoding the automata $\mathcal{F}_1, \mathcal{F}_2$ into the stack alphabet and simulating them "on-the-fly". Formally, $\bar{\Delta} = (\bar{\Gamma}, \rightsquigarrow, (\bar{\Gamma}_\Box, \bar{\Gamma}_\bigcirc), Pr)$ where $\bar{\Gamma} = (\Gamma \cup \{\varepsilon\}) \times Q_1 \times Q_2$, $\bar{\Gamma}_\Box = \Gamma_\Box \times Q_1 \times Q_2$, $\bar{\Gamma}_\bigcirc = (\Gamma_\bigcirc \cup \{\varepsilon\}) \times Q_1 \times Q_2$ and the transition relation $\rightsquigarrow$ together with Pr are defined as follows (A, q, and r range over Γ, Q_1, and Q_2, respectively):

- $(A, q, r) \overset{x}{\rightsquigarrow} \varepsilon$ iff $A \overset{x}{\rightsquigarrow} \varepsilon$;
- $(A, q, r) \overset{x}{\rightsquigarrow} (B, q, r)$ iff $A \overset{x}{\rightsquigarrow} B$
- $(A, q, r) \overset{x}{\rightsquigarrow} (B, q', r')(C, q, r)$ iff $A \overset{x}{\rightsquigarrow} BC$, $\delta_1(q, C) = q'$ and $\delta_2(r, C) = r'$;
- $(\varepsilon, q, r) \overset{1}{\rightsquigarrow} (\varepsilon, q, r)$.

For every configuration $\alpha \in \Gamma^*$ of the form $A_n \cdots A_1$ there is a unique configuration $[\alpha] \in \bar{\Gamma}^*$ of the form $(A_n, q_n, r_n) \cdots (A_1, q_1, r_1)(\varepsilon, \hat{q}, \hat{r})$ where $q_1 = \hat{q}$, $r_1 = \hat{r}$, and for all $0 \leq i < n$ we have that $\delta_1(q_i, A_i) = q_{i+1}$ and $\delta_2(r_i, A_i) = r_{i+1}$. Note that for every $\alpha \in \Gamma^*$, the subgraphs of G_Δ and $G_{\bar{\Delta}}$ which consist of all vertices reachable from α and $[\alpha]$ are isomorphic. Let $S, T \subseteq \bar{\Gamma}^*$ be the simple sets where

- $C(S) = \{(x, q, r) \mid x \in \Gamma \cup \{\varepsilon\}, \delta_1(q, x) \in F_1, r \in Q_2\}$
- $C(T) = \{(x, q, r) \mid x \in \Gamma \cup \{\varepsilon\}, q \in Q_1, \delta_2(r, x) \in F_2\}$.

Now it is easy to see that $\{\alpha \in \Gamma^* \mid \exists\sigma : \mathcal{P}(Run(G_\Delta(\sigma), \alpha, [\![\Phi_1]\!]\,\mathcal{U}\,[\![\Phi_2]\!])) < 1\}$ is equal to the set $K = \{\alpha \in \Gamma^* \mid \exists\sigma : \mathcal{P}(Run(G_{\bar{\Delta}}(\sigma), [\alpha], S\,\mathcal{U}\,T)) < 1\}$. By Theorem 10, there effectively exist the sets $\mathcal{A}, \mathcal{B} \subseteq \bar{\Gamma}$ such that $K = \{\alpha \in \Gamma^* \mid [\alpha] \in \mathcal{A}^* \cup (\mathcal{A}^*\mathcal{B}\bar{\Gamma}^*)\}$. Hence, the automaton $\mathcal{F}$ recognizing the set K can now be constructed as follows: we put $\mathcal{F} = (Q, \Gamma, \delta, \hat{t}, F)$ where

- $Q = Q_1 \times Q_2 \times \{0,1\}$.
- For all $A \in \Gamma$, $q \in Q_1$, $r \in Q_2$, and $i \in \{0,1\}$ we put $\delta((q,r,i),A) = (\delta_1(q,A),\delta_2(r,A),j)$, where
  - $j = 0$ iff either $i = 0$ and $(q,r,A) \in \mathcal{A} \cup \mathcal{B}$, or $i = 1$ and $(q,r,A) \in \mathcal{B}$;
  - $j = 1$ iff either $i = 0$ and $(q,r,A) \in \Gamma \setminus (\mathcal{A} \cup \mathcal{B})$, or $i = 1$ and $(q,r,A) \in \Gamma \setminus \mathcal{B}$.
- The initial state $\hat{t}$ is either $(\hat{q},\hat{r},0)$ or $(\hat{q},\hat{r},1)$, depending on whether $(\varepsilon,\hat{q},\hat{r}) \in \mathcal{A} \cup \mathcal{B}$ or not, respectively.
- $F = Q_1 \times Q_2 \times \{0\}$.

The cases when $\Phi \equiv \Phi_1 \mathcal{U}^{=0} \Phi_2$, $\Phi \equiv \Phi_1 \mathcal{U}^{>0} \Phi_2$, and $\Phi \equiv \Phi_1 \mathcal{U}^{<1} \Phi_2$ are handled similarly, using Theorem 7, 8, and 9, respectively.

The complexity of the whole algorithm is easy to evaluate (it suffices to consider the worst subcase $\Phi \equiv \Phi_1 \mathcal{U}^{\bowtie \varrho} \Phi_2$). □

Since the model-checking problem for qualitative PCTL and fully probabilistic BPA (i.e., the subclass of $1\frac{1}{2}$-player BPA games where $\Gamma_\Box = \emptyset$) is known to be **EXPTIME**-hard [3], we obtain the following:

Corollary 12. *The model-checking problem for qualitative PCTL and $1\frac{1}{2}$-player BPA games is* ***EXPTIME****-complete. For each fixed formula, the problem becomes solvable in polynomial time.*

Acknowledgement. We thank an anonymous reviewer for fixing a mistake in the proof of Theorem 9.

References

1. C. Baier and M. Kwiatkowska. Model checking for a probabilistic branching time logic with fairness. *Distributed Computing*, 11(3):125–155, 1998.
2. A. Bianco and L. de Alfaro. Model checking of probabalistic and nondeterministic systems. In *Proceedings of FST&TCS'95*, vol. 1026 of *LNCS*, pp. 499–513. Springer, 1995.
3. T. Brázdil, A. Kučera, and O. Stražovský. On the decidability of temporal properties of probabilistic pushdown automata. In *Proceedings of STACS'2005*, vol. 3404 of *LNCS*, pp. 145–157. Springer, 2005.
4. J. Esparza, A. Kučera, and R. Mayr. Model-checking probabilistic pushdown automata. In *Proceedings of LICS 2004*, pp. 12–21. IEEE, 2004.
5. J. Esparza, A. Kučera, and S. Schwoon. Model-checking LTL with regular valuations for pushdown systems. *I&C*, 186(2):355–376, 2003.
6. K. Etessami and M. Yannakakis. Recursive Markov decision processes and recursive stochastic games. In *Proceedings of ICALP 2005*, vol. 3580 of *LNCS*. Springer, 2005.
7. K. Etessami and M. Yannakakis. Efficient qualitative analysis of classes of recursive Markov decision processes and simple stochastic games. In *Proceedings of STACS'2006*, LNCS. Springer, 2006.

8. E. Feinberg and A. Shwartz, editors. *Handbook of Markov Decision Processes.* Kluwer, 2002.
9. H. Hansson and B. Jonsson. A logic for reasoning about time and reliability. *Formal Aspects of Computing*, 6:512–535, 1994.
10. A. Hinton, M. Kwiatkowska, G. Norman, and D. Parker. PRISM: a tool for automatic verification of probabilistic systems. In *Proceedings of TACAS 2006*, LNCS. Springer, 2006. To appear.
11. M.L. Puterman. *Markov Decision Processes.* Wiley, 1994.

Strategy Improvement for Stochastic Rabin and Streett Games*

Krishnendu Chatterjee[1] and Thomas A. Henzinger[1,2]

[1] UC Berkeley, USA
[2] EPFL, Switzerland
c_krish@eecs.berkeley.edu, tah@epfl.ch

Abstract. A stochastic graph game is played by two players on a game graph with probabilistic transitions. We consider stochastic graph games with ω-regular winning conditions specified as Rabin or Streett objectives. These games are NP-complete and coNP-complete, respectively. The *value* of the game for a player at a state s given an objective Φ is the maximal probability with which the player can guarantee the satisfaction of Φ from s. We present a strategy-improvement algorithm to compute values in stochastic Rabin games, where an improvement step involves solving Markov decision processes (MDPs) and nonstochastic Rabin games. The algorithm also computes values for stochastic Streett games but does not directly yield an optimal strategy for Streett objectives. We then show how to obtain an optimal strategy for Streett objectives by solving certain nonstochastic Streett games.

1 Introduction

Graph games. A stochastic graph game [6] is played on a directed graph with three kinds of states: player-1, player-2, and probabilistic states. At player-1 states, player 1 chooses a successor state; at player-2 states, player 2 chooses a successor state; at probabilistic states, a successor state is chosen according to a given probability distribution. The outcome of playing the game forever is an infinite path through the graph. If there are no probabilistic states, we refer to the game as a *2-player graph game*; otherwise, as a *2$^1\!/_2$-player graph game.* If there are only player 1 states and probabilistic states, we refer to the game as a Markov decision process (MDP).

Games with Rabin and Streett objectives. The theory of graph games with ω-regular winning conditions is the foundation for modeling and synthesizing reactive processes with fairness constraints [16,15,17]. In the case of 2$^1\!/_2$-player graph games, the two players represent a reactive system (or plant) and its environment (or controller), and the probabilistic states represent uncertainty. The fairness constraints of reactive processes lead to ω-regular objectives [13]. Strong-fairness

* This research was supported in part by the NSF grants CCR-0225610 and CCR-0234690, and by the SNSF under the Indo-Swiss Joint Research Programme.

C. Baier and H. Hermanns (Eds.): CONCUR 2006, LNCS 4137, pp. 375–389, 2006.

constraints correspond to Streett objectives; and Rabin objectives are their dual. Moreover, every ω-regular objective can be specified as a Rabin and a Streett objective. The quantitative solution problem for a $2^1\!/\!_2$-player game with a Rabin objective Φ asks for each state s, for the maximal probability with which player 1 can ensure the satisfaction of Φ if the game is started from s (this probability is called the *value* of the game at the state s). An *optimal strategy* for player 1 is a strategy that enables player 1 to win with that maximal probability. The existence of *pure memoryless* optimal strategies for $2^1\!/\!_2$-player games with Rabin objectives was established recently [3] (a pure memoryless strategy chooses for each player-1 state a unique successor state; it uses neither randomization nor the history of the game). The existence of pure memoryless optimal strategies implies that the quantitative solution problem for $2^1\!/\!_2$-player games with Rabin objectives can be decided in NP; and the problem is NP-hard even for 2-player games [10]. Hence $2^1\!/\!_2$-player games with Rabin objectives are NP-complete, and dually, coNP-complete for Streett objectives. The optimal strategies for the Streett player require memory, but finite-memory optimal strategies exist.

Algorithms. Emerson-Jutla [10] showed that 2-player Rabin and Streett games (*without* probabilistic states) are NP-complete and coNP-complete, respectively. Several algorithms are known to solve 2-player Rabin and Streett games: recursive algorithms on game graphs [10]; algorithms obtained by reduction to checking the emptiness of weak alternating automata [12]; and algorithms based on ranking functions [14]. These algorithms are much better than a brute-force enumeration of all possible pure memoryless strategies, especially for Rabin objectives with few Rabin pairs. For example the algorithm of [14] works in time $O(m \cdot n^{d+1} \cdot d!)$ for game graphs with n states and m edges, and Rabin objectives with d pairs. For $2^1\!/\!_2$-player games (*with* probabilistic states), Condon [6] proved containment in NP $\cap$ coNP and gave a strategy-improvement algorithm for the restricted case of *reachability* objectives. A strategy-improvement scheme iterates local optimizations of a pure memoryless strategy; this works if the iteration can be shown to converge to the global optimum [11]. For $2^1\!/\!_2$-player games with *parity* objectives (parity objectives are a complementation-closed subclass of Rabin and Streett objectives) containment in NP $\cap$ coNP was shown in [5] and a strategy-improvement algorithm was given in [4]. However, for $2^1\!/\!_2$-player games with general Rabin objectives, no algorithm has been known other than either a brute-force enumeration of the set of all possible pure memoryless strategies (choosing the best one as the optimal strategy), or a reduction of Rabin objectives to parity objectives. However, first reducing Rabin to parity objectives, and then applying the strategy-improvement algorithm for $2^1\!/\!_2$-player parity games, yields a worst-case complexity of double-exponential time.

Our results and techniques. We present a direct strategy-improvement algorithm for $2^1\!/\!_2$-player Rabin games. The improvement step involves solving MDPs with Streett objectives and solving 2-player Rabin games. Our algorithm combines techniques for 2-player Rabin games and for $2^1\!/\!_2$-player reachability games, employing a novel reduction from $2^1\!/\!_2$-player Rabin games (with quantitative winning criteria) to 2-player Rabin games (with qualitative winning criteria). A similar idea has been used to obtain a strategy-improvement algorithm for $2^1/_2$-player parity games [4]; however, our present algorithm is more subtle for the following reasons. First, for parity objectives pure memoryless optimal strategies exist for both players, and the analysis of the strategy-improvement algorithm for $2^1/_2$-player parity games can be restricted to pure memoryless strategies. However, the complement of a Rabin objective is a Streett objective: optimal strategies for Streett objectives require memory for $2^1/_2$-player games, and pure optimal strategies require memory even for MDPs. A key insight to our analysis is as follows: once a pure memoryless strategy for a player is fixed, we obtain an MDP, and in MDPs with Streett objectives, randomized (not necessarily pure) memoryless optimal strategies exist. Since pure memoryless optimal strategies exist for $2^1/_2$-player games with Rabin objectives, we consider only pure memoryless strategies for the player with the Rabin objective. Then the analysis of the counter-optimal strategies for the other player is restricted to randomized memoryless strategies. Second, the algorithm for $2^1/_2$-player parity games relies on the existence of a strategy-improvement algorithm for 2-player parity games. The present algorithm does not depend on any specific algorithm to solve 2-player Rabin games, but uses as a black-box any algorithm to solve 2-player Rabin games for the improvement step.

Our strategy-improvement algorithm requires exponentially many improvement steps in the worst case; the running time can be bounded by $O(2^{n \cdot \log n} \cdot (m \cdot d) \cdot (n \cdot d)^{d+2} \cdot (d+1)!)$ for game graphs with n states and m edges, and Rabin objectives with d pairs. We also present a randomized strategy-improvement algorithm with an expected subexponential number of iterations, using the techniques of [1] (note that since improvement steps need to solve 2-player Rabin games, the improvement steps may take exponential time). The expected running time of the randomized algorithm can be bounded by $O(2^{\sqrt{n \cdot \log n}} \cdot (m \cdot d) \cdot (n \cdot d)^{d+2} \cdot (d+1)!)$. By determinacy, the Rabin algorithms obtain the values for Streett objectives also, but they do not directly yield optimal strategies for stochastic Streett games, because optimal Streett strategies in general are not pure memoryless. We show that how, once the values are computed, we can construct optimal strategies for Streett objectives by solving certain 2-player games with Streett objectives.

2 Definitions

We consider several classes of turn-based games, namely, two-player turn-based probabilistic games ($2^1/_2$-player games), two-player turn-based deterministic games (2-player games), and Markov decision processes ($1^1/_2$-player games).

Game graphs. A *turn-based probabilistic game graph* (*$2^1/_2$-player game graph*) $G = ((S, E), (S_1, S_2, S_\bigcirc), \delta)$ consists of a directed graph (S, E), a partition $(S_1$, S_2, $S_\bigcirc)$ of the finite set S of states, and a probabilistic transition function δ: $S_\bigcirc \to \mathcal{D}(S)$, where $\mathcal{D}(S)$ denotes the set of probability distributions over the state space S. The states in S_1 are the *player*-1 states, where player 1 decides the successor state; the states in S_2 are the *player*-2 states, where player 2 decides the successor state; and the states in $S_\bigcirc$ are the *probabilistic* states, where the successor state is chosen according to the probabilistic transition function δ. We assume that for $s \in S_\bigcirc$ and $t \in S$, we have $(s,t) \in E$ if and only if $\delta(s)(t) > 0$, and we often write $\delta(s,t)$ for $\delta(s)(t)$. For technical convenience we assume that every state in the graph (S,E) has at least one outgoing edge. For a state $s \in S$, we write $E(s)$ to denote the set $\{t \in S \mid (s,t) \in E\}$ of possible successors.

A set $U \subseteq S$ of states is *δ-closed* if for every probabilistic state $u \in U \cap S_\bigcirc$, we have $E(u) \subseteq U$. The set U is *δ-live* if for every nonprobabilistic state $u \in U \cap (S_1 \cup S_2)$, we have $E(u) \cap U \neq \emptyset$. A δ-closed and δ-live subset U of S induces a *subgame graph* of G, indicated by $G \upharpoonright U$.

The *turn-based deterministic game graphs* (*2-player game graphs*) are the special case of the $2^1\!/_2$-player game graphs with $S_\bigcirc = \emptyset$. The *Markov decision processes* (*$1^1\!/_2$-player game graphs*) are the special case of the $2^1\!/_2$-player game graphs with $S_1 = \emptyset$ or $S_2 = \emptyset$. We refer to the MDPs with $S_2 = \emptyset$ as *player*-1 *MDPs*, and to the MDPs with $S_1 = \emptyset$ as *player*-2 *MDPs*.

Plays and strategies. An infinite path, or *play*, of the game graph G is an infinite sequence $\omega = \langle s_0, s_1, s_2, \ldots \rangle$ of states such that $(s_k, s_{k+1}) \in E$ for all $k \in \mathbb{N}$. We write Ω for the set of all plays, and for a state $s \in S$, we write $\Omega_s \subseteq \Omega$ for the set of plays that start from the state s.

A *strategy* for player 1 is a function $\sigma\colon S^* \cdot S_1 \to \mathcal{D}(S)$ that assigns a probability distribution to all finite sequences $\boldsymbol{w} \in S^* \cdot S_1$ of states ending in a player-1 state (the sequence represents a prefix of a play). Player 1 follows the strategy σ if in each player-1 state, given that the current history of the game is $\boldsymbol{w} \in S^* \cdot S_1$, she chooses the next state according to the probability distribution $\sigma(\boldsymbol{w})$. A strategy must prescribe only available moves, i.e., for all $\boldsymbol{w} \in S^*$, $s \in S_1$, and $t \in S$, if $\sigma(\boldsymbol{w} \cdot s)(t) > 0$, then $(s,t) \in E$. The strategies for player 2 are defined analogously. We denote by Σ and Π the sets of strategies for player 1 and player 2, respectively.

Once a starting state $s \in S$ and strategies $\sigma \in \Sigma$ and $\pi \in \Pi$ for the two players are fixed, the outcome of the game is a random walk $\omega_s^{\sigma,\pi}$ for which the probabilities of events are uniquely defined, where an *event* $\mathcal{A} \subseteq \Omega$ is a measurable set of plays. Given strategies σ for player 1 and π for player 2, a play $\omega = \langle s_0, s_1, s_2, \ldots \rangle$ is *feasible* if for every $k \in \mathbb{N}$ the following three conditions hold: (1) if $s_k \in S_\bigcirc$, then $(s_k, s_{k+1}) \in E$; (2) if $s_k \in S_1$, then $\sigma(s_0, s_1, \ldots, s_k)(s_{k+1}) > 0$; and (3) if $s_k \in S_2$, then $\pi(s_0, s_1, \ldots, s_k)(s_{k+1}) > 0$. Given two strategies $\sigma \in \Sigma$ and $\pi \in \Pi$, and a state $s \in S$, we denote by $\mathrm{Outcome}(s,\sigma,\pi) \subseteq \Omega_s$ the set of feasible plays that start from s given strategies σ and π. For a state $s \in S$ and an event $\mathcal{A} \subseteq \Omega$, we write $\mathrm{Pr}_s^{\sigma,\pi}(\mathcal{A})$ for the probability that a play belongs to $\mathcal{A}$ if the game starts from the state s and the players follow the strategies σ and π, respectively.

We classify strategies according to their use of randomization and memory. The strategies that do not use randomization are called pure. A player-1 strategy σ is *pure* if for all $\boldsymbol{w} \in S^*$ and $s \in S_1$, there is a state $t \in S$ such that $\sigma(\boldsymbol{w} \cdot s)(t) = 1$. We denote by $\Sigma^P \subseteq \Sigma$ the set of pure strategies for player 1. A strategy that is not necessarily pure is called *randomized.* Let $\mathtt{M}$ be a set called *memory.* A player-1 strategy can be described as a pair of functions: a *memory-update* function $\sigma_u\colon S \times \mathtt{M} \to \mathtt{M}$ and a *next-move* function $\sigma_m\colon S_1 \times \mathtt{M} \to \mathcal{D}(S)$. The strategy (σ_u, σ_m) is *finite-memory* if the memory $\mathtt{M}$ is finite. We denote by Σ^F the set of finite-memory strategies for player 1, and by Σ^{PF} the set of *pure finite-memory* strategies; that is, $\Sigma^{PF} = \Sigma^P \cap \Sigma^F$. The strategy (σ_u, σ_m) is *memoryless* if $|\mathtt{M}| = 1$. A memoryless player-1 strategy does not depend on the history of the play, but only on the current state, and hence can be represented as a function $\sigma\colon S_1 \to \mathcal{D}(S)$. A *pure memoryless strategy* is a pure strategy that is memoryless. A pure memoryless strategy for player 1 can be represented as a function $\sigma\colon S_1 \to S$. We denote by Σ^M the set of memoryless strategies for player 1, and by Σ^{PM} the set of pure memoryless strategies; that is, $\Sigma^{PM} = \Sigma^P \cap \Sigma^M$. Analogously we define the families Π^P, Π^M, and Π^{PM} of pure, memoryless, and pure memoryless strategies for player 2, respectively.

Given a memoryless strategy $\sigma \in \Sigma^M$, let G_σ be the game graph obtained from G under the constraint that player 1 follows the strategy σ. The corresponding definition G_π for a player-2 strategy $\pi \in \Pi^M$ is analogous, and we write $G_{\sigma,\pi}$ for the game graph obtained from G if both players follow the memoryless strategies σ and π, respectively. Observe that given a $2^1\!/_2$-player game graph G and a memoryless player-1 strategy σ, the result G_σ is a player-2 MDP. Similarly, for a player-1 MDP G and a memoryless player-1 strategy σ, the result G_σ is a Markov chain. Hence if G is a $2^1\!/_2$-player game graph and the two players follow memoryless strategies σ and π, the result $G_{\sigma,\pi}$ is a Markov chain. These observations will be useful in the analysis of $2^1\!/_2$-player games.

Objectives. We specify objectives for the players by providing the set of *winning plays* $\Phi \subseteq \Omega$ for each player. In this paper we consider *ω-regular objectives* [17] specified as Rabin and Streett objectives: a Rabin objective for player 1, and the complementary Streett objective for player 2. For a play $\omega = \langle s_0, s_1, s_2, \ldots \rangle$, let $\mathrm{Inf}(\omega)$ be the set $\{s \in S \mid s = s_k \text{ for infinitely many } k \geq 0\}$ of states that occur infinitely often in ω. We use colors to define objectives independent of game graphs. For a set C of colors, we write $[\![\cdot]\!]\colon C \to 2^S$ for a function that maps each color to a set of states. Inversely, given a set $U \subseteq S$ of states, we write $[U] = \{c \in C \mid [\![c]\!] \cap U \neq \emptyset\}$ for the set of colors that occur in U. Note that a state can have multiple colors.

A *Rabin objective* is specified as a set $P = \{(e_1, f_1), \ldots, (e_d, f_d)\}$ of pairs of colors $e_i, f_i \in C$. Intuitively, the Rabin condition P requires that for some $1 \leq i \leq d$, all states of color e_i be visited finitely often and some state of color f_i be visited infinitely often. Let $[\![P]\!] = \{(E_1, F_1), \ldots, (E_d, F_d)\}$ be the corresponding set of so-called *Rabin pairs*, where $E_i = [\![e_i]\!]$ and $F_i = [\![f_i]\!]$ for all $1 \leq i \leq d$. Formally, the set of winning plays is $\mathrm{Rabin}(P) = \{\omega \in \Omega \mid \exists\, 1 \leq i \leq d.\ (\mathrm{Inf}(\omega) \cap E_i = \emptyset \ \wedge\ \mathrm{Inf}(\omega) \cap F_i \neq \emptyset)\}$. Without loss of generality, we require that $\bigcup_{i \in \{1,2,\ldots,d\}} (E_i \cup F_i) = S$. The *parity* (or *Rabin-chain*) objectives are the special case of Rabin objectives such that $E_1 \subset F_1 \subset E_2 \subset F_2 \subset \cdots \subset E_d \subset F_d$.

A *Streett objective* is again specified as a set $P = \{(e_1, f_1), \ldots, (e_d, f_d)\}$ of pairs of colors. The Streett condition P requires that for each $1 \leq i \leq d$, if some state of color f_i is visited infinitely often, then some state of color e_i be visited infinitely often. Formally, the set of winning plays is Streett$(P) = \{\omega \in \Omega \mid \forall\, 1 \leq i \leq d.\ (\mathrm{Inf}(\omega) \cap E_i \neq \emptyset \ \vee\ \mathrm{Inf}(\omega) \cap F_i = \emptyset)\}$, for the set $[\![P]\!] = \{(E_1, F_1), \ldots, (E_d, F_d)\}$ of so-called *Streett pairs*. Note that the Rabin and Streett objectives are dual; i.e., the complement of a Rabin objective is a Streett objective, and vice versa. Moreover, every parity objective is both a Rabin objective and a Streett objective.

Sure winning, almost-sure winning, and optimality. Given a player-1 objective Φ, a strategy $\sigma \in \Sigma$ is *sure winning* for player 1 from a state $s \in S$ if for every strategy $\pi \in \Pi$ for player 2, we have Outcome$(s, \sigma, \pi) \subseteq \Phi$. The strategy σ is *almost-sure winning* for player 1 from the state s for the objective Φ if for every player-2 strategy π, we have $\Pr_s^{\sigma,\pi}(\Phi) = 1$. The sure and almost-sure winning strategies for player 2 are defined analogously. Given an objective Φ, the *sure winning set* $\langle\!\langle 1 \rangle\!\rangle_{sure}(\Phi)$ for player 1 is the set of states from which player 1 has a sure winning strategy. The *almost-sure winning set* $\langle\!\langle 1 \rangle\!\rangle_{almost}(\Phi)$ for player 1 is the set of states from which player 1 has an almost-sure winning strategy. The sure winning set $\langle\!\langle 2 \rangle\!\rangle_{sure}(\Omega \setminus \Phi)$ and the almost-sure winning set $\langle\!\langle 2 \rangle\!\rangle_{almost}(\Omega \setminus \Phi)$ for player 2 are defined analogously. It follows from the definitions that for all $2^1\!/\!_2$-player game graphs and all objectives Φ, we have $\langle\!\langle 1 \rangle\!\rangle_{sure}(\Phi) \subseteq \langle\!\langle 1 \rangle\!\rangle_{almost}(\Phi)$. A game is sure (resp. almost-sure) winning for player i, if player i wins surely (resp. almost-surely) from every state in the game. Computing sure and almost-sure winning sets and strategies is the *qualitative* analysis of $2^1\!/\!_2$-player games [9].

Given objectives $\Phi \subseteq \Omega$ for player 1 and $\Omega \setminus \Phi$ for player 2, we define the *value* functions $\langle\!\langle 1 \rangle\!\rangle_{val}$ and $\langle\!\langle 2 \rangle\!\rangle_{val}$ for the players 1 and 2, respectively, as the following functions from the state space S to the interval $[0, 1]$ of reals: for all states $s \in S$, let $\langle\!\langle 1 \rangle\!\rangle_{val}(\Phi)(s) = \sup_{\sigma \in \Sigma} \inf_{\pi \in \Pi} \Pr_s^{\sigma,\pi}(\Phi)$ and $\langle\!\langle 2 \rangle\!\rangle_{val}(\Omega \setminus \Phi)(s) = \sup_{\pi \in \Pi} \inf_{\sigma \in \Sigma} \Pr_s^{\sigma,\pi}(\Omega \setminus \Phi)$. In other words, the value $\langle\!\langle 1 \rangle\!\rangle_{val}(\Phi)(s)$ gives the maximal probability with which player 1 can achieve her objective Φ from state s, and analogously for player 2. The strategies that achieve the value are called optimal: a strategy σ for player 1 is *optimal* from the state s for the objective Φ if $\langle\!\langle 1 \rangle\!\rangle_{val}(\Phi)(s) = \inf_{\pi \in \Pi} \Pr_s^{\sigma,\pi}(\Phi)$. The optimal strategies for player 2 are defined analogously. Computing values and optimal strategies is the *quantitative* analysis of $2^1\!/\!_2$-player games.

Let $\mathcal{C} \in \{P, M, F, PM, PF\}$ and consider a family $\Sigma^{\mathcal{C}} \subseteq \Sigma$ of special strategies for player 1. The family $\Sigma^{\mathcal{C}}$ of strategies *suffices* with respect to a player-1 objective Φ on a class $\mathcal{G}$ of game graphs for *sure winning* if for every game graph $G \in \mathcal{G}$ and state $s \in \langle\!\langle 1 \rangle\!\rangle_{sure}(\Phi)$, there is a player-1 strategy $\sigma \in \Sigma^{\mathcal{C}}$ such that for every player-2 strategy $\pi \in \Pi$, we have Outcome$(s, \sigma, \pi) \subseteq \Phi$. Similarly, the family $\Sigma^{\mathcal{C}}$ *suffices* with respect to the objective Φ on the class $\mathcal{G}$ of game graphs for *almost-sure winning* if for every game graph $G \in \mathcal{G}$ and state $s \in \langle\!\langle 1 \rangle\!\rangle_{almost}(\Phi)$, there is a player-1 strategy $\sigma \in \Sigma^{\mathcal{C}}$ such that for every player-2 strategy $\pi \in \Pi$, we have $\Pr_s^{\sigma,\pi}(\Phi) = 1$; and for *optimality*, if for every game graph $G \in \mathcal{G}$ and state $s \in S$, there is a player-1 strategy $\sigma \in \Sigma^{\mathcal{C}}$ such that $\langle\!\langle 1 \rangle\!\rangle_{val}(\Phi)(s) = \inf_{\pi \in \Pi} \Pr_s^{\sigma,\pi}(\Phi)$.

For sure winning, the $1\frac{1}{2}$-player and $2\frac{1}{2}$-player games coincide with 2-player (deterministic) games where the random player (who chooses the successor at the probabilistic states) is interpreted as an adversary, i.e., as player 2. Theorem 1 and Theorem 2 state the classical determinacy results for 2-player and $2\frac{1}{2}$-player game graphs with Rabin and Streett objectives.

Theorem 1 (Qualitative determinacy). [10] *For all 2-player game graphs with state space S, and all Rabin objectives Φ and Streett objectives $\Omega \setminus \Phi$, we have $\langle\langle 1\rangle\rangle_{sure}(\Phi) = S \setminus \langle\langle 2\rangle\rangle_{sure}(\Omega \setminus \Phi)$. Moreover, on 2-player game graphs, the family of pure memoryless strategies suffices for sure winning with respect to Rabin objectives, and the family of pure finite-memory strategies suffices for sure winning with respect to Streett objectives.*

Theorem 2 (Quantitative determinacy). [3] *For all $2\frac{1}{2}$-player game graphs, all Rabin objectives Φ and Streett objectives $\Omega \setminus \Phi$, and all states s, we have $\langle\langle 1\rangle\rangle_{val}(\Phi)(s) + \langle\langle 2\rangle\rangle_{val}(\Omega \setminus \Phi)(s) = 1$. Moreover, on $2\frac{1}{2}$-player game graphs, the family of pure memoryless strategies suffices for optimality with respect to Rabin objectives, and the family of pure finite-memory strategies suffices for optimality with respect to Streett objectives.*

Since in $2\frac{1}{2}$-player games with Rabin objectives, the pure memoryless strategies suffice for optimality, in the sequel we consider only pure memoryless strategies for the player with the Rabin objective (i.e., player 1).

3 Strategy-Improvement Algorithm

We first recall a few key properties of $2\frac{1}{2}$-player games with Rabin objectives that were proved in [3]. We will use these properties to develop a strategy-improvement algorithm for $2\frac{1}{2}$-player games with Rabin objectives.

Key properties. We present a reduction of $2\frac{1}{2}$-player parity games to 2-player parity games capturing the ability of player 1 to win almost-surely.

Reduction. Given a $2\frac{1}{2}$-player game graph $G = ((S, E), (S_1, S_2, S_\bigcirc), \delta)$, a set $C = \{e_1, f_1, \ldots, e_d, f_d\}$ of colors, and a color map $[\cdot]\colon S \to 2^C \setminus \emptyset$, we construct a 2-player game graph $\overline{G} = ((\overline{S}, \overline{E}), (\overline{S}_1, \overline{S}_2), \overline{\delta})$ together with a color map $[\cdot]$: $\overline{S} \to 2^{\overline{C}} \setminus \emptyset$ for the extended color set $\overline{C} = C \cup \{e_{d+1}, f_{d+1}\}$. The construction is specified as follows. For every nonprobabilistic state $s \in S_1 \cup S_2$, there is a corresponding state $\overline{s} \in \overline{S}$ such that (1) $\overline{s} \in \overline{S}_1$ if and only if $s \in S_1$, and (2) $[\overline{s}] = [s]$, and (3) $(\overline{s}, \overline{t}) \in \overline{E}$ if and only if $(s,t) \in E$. Every probabilistic state $s \in S_\bigcirc$ is replaced by the following gadget. From state $\overline{s}$ with $[\overline{s}] = [s]$, the players play the following 3-step game in $\overline{G}$. First, in state $\overline{s}$ player 2 chooses a successor $(\widetilde{s}, 2k)$, for $k \in \{0, 1, \ldots, d\}$. For every state $(\widetilde{s}, 2k)$, we have $[(\widetilde{s}, 2k)] = [s]$. For $k \geq 1$, in state $(\widetilde{s}, 2k)$ player 1 chooses from two successors: state $(\widehat{s}, 2k-1)$ with $[(\widehat{s}, 2k-1)] = e_k$, or state $(\widehat{s}, 2k)$ with $[(\widehat{s}, 2k)] = f_k$. The state $(\widetilde{s}, 0)$ has only one successor, $(\widehat{s}, 0)$, with $[(\widehat{s}, 0)] = f_{d+1}$. Note that no state in $\overline{S}$ is labeled by the new color e_{d+1}, that is, $[\![e_{d+1}]\!] = \emptyset$. Finally, in each state $(\widehat{s}, j)$ the choice is between all states $\overline{t}$ such that $(s,t) \in E$, and it belongs to player 1 if k is odd, and to player 2 if k is even.

We consider 2½-player games played on the graph G with the Rabin objective Rabin(P) for player 1, where $P = \{(e_1, f_1), \ldots, (e_d, f_d)\}$. We denote by $\overline{G} = \mathrm{Tr}^1_{\mathrm{as}}(G)$ the 2-player game with the Rabin objective Rabin($\overline{P}$), where $\overline{P} = \{(e_1, f_1), \ldots, (e_{d+1}, f_{d+1})\}$, as defined by the reduction above. Also, given a (pure memoryless) strategy $\overline{\sigma}$ in the 2-player game $\overline{G}$, a strategy $\sigma = \mathrm{Tr}^1_{\mathrm{as}}(\overline{\sigma})$ in the 2½-player game G is defined as follows: for all $s \in S_1$, let $\sigma(s) = t$ if and only if $\overline{\sigma}(\overline{s}) = \overline{t}$. Similar definitions hold for player 2.

Lemma 1. [3] *Given a 2½-player game graph G with the Rabin objective Rabin(P) for player 1, let $\overline{U}_1$ and $\overline{U}_2$ be the sure winning sets for players 1 and 2, respectively, in the 2-player game graph $\overline{G} = \mathrm{Tr}^1_{\mathrm{as}}(G)$ with the modified Rabin objective Rabin($\overline{P}$). Define the sets U_1 and U_2 in the original 2½-player game graph G by $U_1 = \{s \in S \mid \overline{s} \in \overline{U}_1\}$ and $U_2 = \{s \in S \mid \overline{s} \in \overline{U}_2\}$. Then the following assertions hold: (1) $U_1 = \langle\langle 1 \rangle\rangle_{almost}(\mathit{Rabin}(P)) = S \setminus U_2$; and (2) if $\overline{\sigma}$ is a pure memoryless sure winning strategy for player 1 from $\overline{U}_1$ in $\overline{G}$, then $\sigma = \mathrm{Tr}^1_{\mathrm{as}}(\overline{\sigma})$ is a pure memoryless almost-sure winning strategy for player 1 from U_1 in G.*

A similar reduction preserves almost-sure winning for player 2 (i.e., the player with the Streett objective), and we refer to the reduction for player 2 as $\mathrm{Tr}^2_{\mathrm{as}}$. Also, there is a simple mapping of finite-memory sure winning strategies $\overline{\pi}$ in $\mathrm{Tr}^2_{\mathrm{as}}(G)$ to finite-memory almost-sure winning strategies $\pi = \mathrm{Tr}^2_{\mathrm{as}}(\overline{\pi})$ in G.

Boundary probabilistic states. Given a set U of states, let $\mathit{Bnd}(U) = \{s \in U \cap S_{\bigcirc} \mid \exists t \in E(s).\ t \notin U\}$ be the set of *boundary* probabilistic states, which have an edge out of U. Given a set U of states and a Rabin objective Rabin(P) for player 1, we define two transformations $\mathrm{Tr}_{\mathrm{win}_1}(U)$ and $\mathrm{Tr}_{\mathrm{win}_2}(U)$ of U as follows: every state s in $\mathit{Bnd}(U)$ is converted to an *absorbing* state (i.e., a state with only a self-loop), and (1) in $\mathrm{Tr}_{\mathrm{win}_1}(U)$ it is assigned the color f_1, and (2) in $\mathrm{Tr}_{\mathrm{win}_2}(U)$ it is assigned the color e_1; i.e., every state in $\mathit{Bnd}(U)$ is converted to a sure winning state for player 1 in $\mathrm{Tr}_{\mathrm{win}_1}(U)$ and every state in $\mathit{Bnd}(U)$ is converted to a sure winning state for player 2 in $\mathrm{Tr}_{\mathrm{win}_2}(U)$. Observe that if U is δ-live, then $\mathrm{Tr}_{\mathrm{win}_1}(G \upharpoonright U)$ and $\mathrm{Tr}_{\mathrm{win}_2}(G \upharpoonright U)$ are game graphs.

Value classes. Given a Rabin objective Φ, for every real $r \in [0,1]$ the *value class* with value r, denoted $\mathrm{VC}(r) = \{s \in S \mid \langle\langle 1 \rangle\rangle_{val}(\Phi)(s) = r\}$, is the set of states with value r for player 1. For every $r > 0$, the value class $\mathrm{VC}(r)$ is δ-live. The following lemma establishes a connection between value classes, the transformations $\mathrm{Tr}_{\mathrm{win}_1}$ and $\mathrm{Tr}_{\mathrm{win}_2}$, and almost-sure winning states.

Lemma 2. [3] *For all $r > 0$, the game $\mathrm{Tr}_{\mathrm{win}_1}(G \upharpoonright \mathrm{VC}(r))$ is almost-sure winning for player 1. For all $r < 1$, the game $\mathrm{Tr}_{\mathrm{win}_2}(G \upharpoonright \mathrm{VC}(r))$ is almost-sure winning for player 2.*

Lemma 3 (Optimal strategies). [3] *Consider a strategy σ for player 1 (resp. π for player 2) such that the strategy is an almost-sure winning strategy in the* *game* $\mathrm{Tr}_{\mathrm{win}_1}(G \upharpoonright \mathrm{VC}(r))$, *for all* $r > 0$ *(resp. in the game* $\mathrm{Tr}_{\mathrm{win}_2}(G \upharpoonright \mathrm{VC}(r))$, *for all* $r < 1$*). Then* σ *(resp.* π*) is an optimal strategy in* G.

It follows from Lemma 1 and Lemma 2, that for every value class $\mathrm{VC}(r)$, with $r > 0$, the game $\mathrm{Tr}^1_{\mathrm{as}}(\mathrm{Tr}_{\mathrm{win}_1}(G \upharpoonright \mathrm{VC}(r)))$ is sure winning for player 1.

Properties of almost-sure winning states. It follows from the results of [9] that for parity objectives, if the set of almost-sure winning states for a player is empty, then the other player wins almost-surely from all states in the game. Since games with Rabin and Streett objectives can be reduced to games with parity objectives [17], Lemma 4 follows. Lemma 5 is a result from [2].

Lemma 4. *Given a* $2^1\!/_2$*-player game graph* G *with state space* S*, and a Rabin objective* Φ*, if* $\langle\langle 1\rangle\rangle_{almost}(\Phi) = \emptyset$*, then* $\langle\langle 2\rangle\rangle_{almost}(\Omega \setminus \Phi) = S$.

Lemma 5. [2] *The family of randomized memoryless strategies suffices for optimality with respect to Streett objectives on MDPs.*

Strategy-improvement algorithm. We now present an algorithm to compute the values for $2^1\!/_2$-player games with a Rabin objective Φ for player 1. By quantitative determinacy (Theorem 2), the algorithm also computes the values for the Streett objective $\Omega \setminus \Phi$ for player 2. Recall that optimal pure memoryless strategies exist for Rabin objectives, and hence we consider only pure memoryless strategies for player 1.

Definitions. Given a player-1 strategy σ and a Rabin objective Φ, we denote the value of player 1 *given* the strategy σ as follows: $\langle\langle 1\rangle\rangle^{\sigma}_{val}(\Phi)(s) = \inf_{\pi \in \Pi} \mathrm{Pr}^{\sigma,\pi}_{s}(\Phi)$. We define the value classes *given* strategy σ by $\mathrm{VC}^{\sigma}(r) = \{s \in S \mid \langle\langle 1\rangle\rangle^{\sigma}_{val}(\Phi)(s) = r\}$, for all $r > 0$. We define an ordering relation $\prec$ on strategies as follows: given two strategies σ and σ', we have $\sigma \prec \sigma'$ if and only if (1) for all states $s \in S$, we have $\langle\langle 1\rangle\rangle^{\sigma}_{val}(\Phi)(s) \leq \langle\langle 1\rangle\rangle^{\sigma'}_{val}(\Phi)(s)$, and (2) for some state $s \in S$, we have $\langle\langle 1\rangle\rangle^{\sigma}_{val}(\Phi)(s) < \langle\langle 1\rangle\rangle^{\sigma'}_{val}(\Phi)(s)$.

Strategy-improvement step. Given a strategy σ for player 1, we describe a procedure `Improve` to "improve" the strategy for player 1. The procedure is described in Algorithm 1. An informal description of the procedure is as follows: given a strategy σ, the algorithm computes the values $\langle\langle 1\rangle\rangle^{\sigma}_{val}(\Phi)(s)$ for all states. Since σ is a pure memoryless strategy, $\langle\langle 1\rangle\rangle^{\sigma}_{val}(\Phi)(s)$ can be computed by solving the MDP G_{σ} with the Streett objective $\Omega \setminus \Phi$. If there is a state $s \in S_1$ such that the strategy can be "value improved," i.e., there is a state $t \in E(s)$ with $\langle\langle 1\rangle\rangle^{\sigma}_{val}(\Phi)(t) > \langle\langle 1\rangle\rangle^{\sigma}_{val}(\Phi)(s)$, then the strategy σ is modified by setting $\sigma(s)$ to t. This is achieved in Step 2.1 of `Improve`. Otherwise in every value class $\mathrm{VC}^{\sigma}(r)$, the strategy σ is "improved" for the game $\mathrm{Tr}^1_{\mathrm{as}}(\mathrm{Tr}_{\mathrm{win}_2}(G \upharpoonright \mathrm{VC}^{\sigma}(r)))$ by solving the 2-player game $\mathrm{Tr}^1_{\mathrm{as}}(\mathrm{Tr}_{\mathrm{win}_2}(G \upharpoonright \mathrm{VC}^{\sigma}(r)))$ by an algorithm to solve 2-player Rabin games.

The complexity of `Improve` will be discussed in Lemma 10. In the algorithm the strategy σ for player 1 is always a pure memoryless strategy (this is sufficient, because pure memoryless strategies suffice for optimality in $2^1\!/_2$-player games

Algorithm 1. `Improve`

Input: A 2½-player game graph G, a Rabin objective Φ for player 1, and a pure memoryless strategy σ for player 1.
Output: A pure memoryless strategy σ' for player 1 such that $\sigma' = \sigma$ or $\sigma \prec \sigma'$.
[Step 1] Compute $\langle\langle 1 \rangle\rangle_{val}^{\sigma}(\Phi)(s)$ for all states s.
[Step 2] Consider the set $I = \{s \in S_1 \mid \exists t \in E(s).\ \langle\langle 1 \rangle\rangle_{val}^{\sigma}(\Phi)(t) > \langle\langle 1 \rangle\rangle_{val}^{\sigma}(\Phi)(s)\}$.
  2.1 (Value improvement) **if** $I \neq \emptyset$ **then** choose σ' as follows:
    $\sigma'(s) = \sigma(s)$ for $s \in S_1 \setminus I$; and
    $\sigma'(s) = t$ for $s \in I$, where $t \in E(s)$ such that $\langle\langle 1 \rangle\rangle_{val}^{\sigma}(\Phi)(t) > \langle\langle 1 \rangle\rangle_{val}^{\sigma}(\Phi)(s)$.
  2.2 (Qualitative improvement) **else**
    for each value class $\mathrm{VC}^{\sigma}(r)$ with $r < 1$ **do**
      Let $\overline{G}_r$ be the 2-player game $\mathrm{Tr}_{\mathrm{as}}^{1}(\mathrm{Tr}_{\mathrm{win}_2}(G \upharpoonright \mathrm{VC}^{\sigma}(r)))$.
      Let $\overline{U}_r$ be the sure winning states for player 1 in $\overline{G}_r$;
        let U_r the corresponding set in G; and
        let $\overline{\sigma}_r$ be the sure winning strategy for player 1 in $\overline{U}_r$.
      Choose $\sigma'(s) = \mathrm{Tr}_{\mathrm{as}}^{1}(\overline{\sigma}_r \upharpoonright \overline{U}_r)(s)$ for all states in U_r; and
        $\sigma'(s) = \sigma(s)$ for all states in $\mathrm{VC}^{\sigma}(r) \setminus U_r$.
  return σ'.

with Rabin objectives (Theorem 2)). Moreover, given a pure memoryless strategy σ, the game G_σ is a player-2 MDP, and by Lemma 5, there is a randomized memoryless counter-optimal strategy for player 2. Hence, fixing a pure memoryless strategy for player 1, we only consider randomized memoryless strategies for player 2. We now define the notion of Rabin winning set, and then present Fact 1 and Fact 2, which are useful in the correctness proof of the algorithm.

Rabin winning set. Consider a Rabin objective $\mathrm{Rabin}(P)$ and let $[\![P]\!] = \{(E_1, F_1), (E_2, F_2), \ldots, (E_d, F_d)\}$ be the set of Rabin pairs. A set $C \subseteq S$ is *Rabin winning* if there exists $1 \leq i \leq d$ such that $C \cap E_i = \emptyset$ and $C \cap F_i \neq \emptyset$, i.e., for all plays ω if $\mathrm{Inf}(\omega) = C$, then $\omega \in \mathrm{Rabin}(P)$.

Fact 1. For all strategies σ for player 1, all $r \in [0,1]$, and all states $s \in \mathrm{VC}^{\sigma}(r) \cap S_2$, if $t \in E(s)$, then $\langle\langle 1 \rangle\rangle_{val}^{\sigma}(\Phi)(t) \geq r$, that is, $E(s) \subseteq \bigcup_{q \geq r} \mathrm{VC}^{\sigma}(q)$. ∎

Fact 2. For all strategies σ for player 1 and all memoryless strategies $\pi \in \Pi^M$ for player 2, if there is a closed recurrent class C in the Markov chain $G_{\sigma,\pi}$ with $C \subseteq \mathrm{VC}^{\sigma}(r)$ for some $r > 0$, then C is Rabin winning. ∎

Lemma 6. *Consider a strategy σ to be an input to Algorithm 1, and let σ' be the corresponding output, i.e., $\sigma' =$ `Improve`(G, σ). If the set I in Step 2 of Algorithm 1 is nonempty, then (1) $\langle\langle 1 \rangle\rangle_{val}^{\sigma'}(\Phi)(s) \geq \langle\langle 1 \rangle\rangle_{val}^{\sigma}(\Phi)(s)$ for all states $s \in S$; and (2) $\langle\langle 1 \rangle\rangle_{val}^{\sigma'}(\Phi)(s) > \langle\langle 1 \rangle\rangle_{val}^{\sigma}(\Phi)(s)$ for all states $s \in I$.*

Proof. Consider a switch of the strategy of player 1 from σ to σ', as constructed in Step 2.1 of Algorithm 1. Consider a strategy $\pi \in \Pi^M$ for player 2 and a closed recurrent class C in $G_{\sigma',\pi}$ such that $C \subseteq \bigcup_{r>0} \mathrm{VC}^{\sigma}(r)$. Let $z = \max\{r > 0 \mid C \cap \mathrm{VC}^{\sigma}(r) \neq \emptyset\}$, that is, $\mathrm{VC}^{\sigma}(z)$ is the greatest value class with a nonempty intersection with C. A state $s \in \mathrm{VC}^{\sigma}(z) \cap C$ satisfies the following conditions:

1. If $s \in S_2$, then for all $t \in E(s)$ if $\pi(s)(t) > 0$, then $t \in \mathrm{VC}^{\sigma}(z)$. This follows, because by Fact 1 we have $E(s) \subseteq \bigcup_{q \geq z} \mathrm{VC}^{\sigma}(q)$ and $C \cap \mathrm{VC}^{\sigma}(q) = \emptyset$ for $q > z$.
2. If $s \in S_1$, then $\sigma'(s) \in \mathrm{VC}^{\sigma}(z)$. This follows, because by construction $\sigma'(s) \in \bigcup_{q \geq z} \mathrm{VC}^{\sigma}(q)$ and $C \cap \mathrm{VC}^{\sigma}(q) = \emptyset$ for $q > z$. Also, since $s \in \mathrm{VC}^{\sigma}(z)$ and $\sigma'(s) \in \mathrm{VC}^{\sigma}(z)$, it follows that $\sigma'(s) = \sigma(s)$.
3. If $s \in S_{\bigcirc}$, then $E(s) \subseteq \mathrm{VC}^{\sigma}(z)$. This follows, because for $s \in S_{\bigcirc}$, if $E(s) \subsetneq \mathrm{VC}^{\sigma}(z)$, then $E(s) \cap \bigcup_{q>z} \mathrm{VC}^{\sigma}(q) \neq \emptyset$. Since C is closed, and $C \cap \mathrm{VC}^{\sigma}(q) = \emptyset$ for $q > z$, the claim follows.

It follows that $C \subseteq \mathrm{VC}^{\sigma}(z)$, and for all states $s \in C \cap S_1$, we have $\sigma'(s) = \sigma(s)$. Hence, by Fact 2, we conclude that C is Rabin winning.

It follows that if player 1 switches to the strategy σ', as constructed when Step 2.1 of Algorithm 1 is executed, then for all strategies $\pi \in \Pi^M$ for player 2 the following assertion holds: if there is a closed recurrent class $C \subseteq S \setminus \mathrm{VC}^{\sigma}(0)$ in the Markov chain $G_{\sigma',\pi}$, then C is Rabin winning for player 1. Hence given strategy σ', a counter-optimal strategy for player 2 maximizes the probability to reach $\mathrm{VC}^{\sigma}(0)$. The desired result follows from arguments similar to $2^1/_2$-player games with reachability objectives [7], with $\mathrm{VC}^{\sigma}(0)$ as the target for player 2, and the value improvement step (Step 2.1 of Algorithm 1). ∎

Lemma 7. *Consider a strategy σ to be an input to Algorithm 1, and let σ' be the corresponding output, that is, $\sigma' =$ `Improve`(G, σ), such that $\sigma' \neq \sigma$. If the set I in Step 2 of Algorithm 1 is empty, then (1) $\langle\langle 1 \rangle\rangle_{val}^{\sigma'}(\Phi)(s) \geq \langle\langle 1 \rangle\rangle_{val}^{\sigma}(\Phi)(s)$ for all states $s \in S$; and (2) $\langle\langle 1 \rangle\rangle_{val}^{\sigma'}(\Phi)(s) > \langle\langle 1 \rangle\rangle_{val}^{\sigma}(\Phi)(s)$ for some state $s \in S$.*

Proof. It follows from Fact 2 that for all strategies $\pi \in \Pi^M$ for player 2, if C is a closed recurrent class in $G_{\sigma,\pi}$ and $C \subseteq \mathrm{VC}^{\sigma}(r)$, for $r > 0$, then C is Rabin winning. Let σ' be the strategy constructed from σ in Step 2.2 of Algorithm 1. Let the set of states where σ is modified to obtain σ' be U_r. Then by construction, the strategy $\sigma' \upharpoonright U_r$ is an almost-sure winning strategy in U_r in the subgame $\mathrm{Tr}_{\mathrm{win}_2}(G \upharpoonright \mathrm{VC}^{\sigma}(r))$. This follows from Lemma 1, because $\sigma' \upharpoonright U_r = \mathrm{Tr}^1_{\mathrm{as}}(\overline{\sigma} \upharpoonright \overline{U}_r)$ and $\overline{\sigma} \upharpoonright \overline{U}_r$ is a sure winning strategy for player 1 in $\overline{U}_r$ in the subgame $\mathrm{Tr}^1_{\mathrm{as}}(\mathrm{Tr}_{\mathrm{win}_2}(G \upharpoonright \mathrm{VC}^{\sigma}(r)))$. It follows that if C is a closed recurrent class in $G_{\sigma',\pi}$ and $C \subseteq \mathrm{VC}^{\sigma}(r)$, for $r > 0$, then C is Rabin winning. Arguments similar to Lemma 6 show that the following assertion holds: for all strategies $\pi \in \Pi^M$ for player 2, if there is a closed recurrent class $C \subseteq (S \setminus \mathrm{VC}^{\sigma}(0))$ in the Markov chain $G_{\sigma',\pi}$, then C is Rabin winning. Since in strategy σ' player 1 chooses every edge in the same value class as σ, it can be shown that for all states $s \in S$, we have $\langle\langle 1 \rangle\rangle_{val}^{\sigma'}(\Phi)(s) \geq \langle\langle 1 \rangle\rangle_{val}^{\sigma}(\Phi)(s)$.

If $\sigma \neq \sigma'$, then the set U_r where the strategy σ is modified is nonempty. Since $\sigma' \upharpoonright U_r$ is an almost-sure winning strategy in U_r in $\mathrm{Tr}_{\mathrm{win}_2}(G \upharpoonright \mathrm{VC}^{\sigma}(r))$, it follows that given σ', any counter-optimal strategy $\pi \in \Pi^M$ of player 2 either moves to a higher value class, or player 1 wins almost-surely in U_r. In either case, for some state $s \in U_r$, we have $\langle\langle 1 \rangle\rangle_{val}^{\sigma'}(\Phi)(s) > \langle\langle 1 \rangle\rangle_{val}^{\sigma}(\Phi)(s)$. ∎

Lemma 8. *If* $\sigma \neq \texttt{Improve}(G, \sigma)$, *then* $\sigma \prec \texttt{Improve}(G, \sigma)$.

Lemma 9. *If* $\sigma = \texttt{Improve}(G, \sigma)$, *then σ is an optimal strategy for player 1.*

Lemma 8 follows from Lemma 6 and Lemma 7. The key argument to establish Lemma 9 is as follows: let σ be a strategy such that $\sigma = \texttt{Improve}(G, \sigma)$. It follows that the strategy σ cannot be "value-improved." Moreover, for all $r < 1$, the set of almost-sure winning states in $\mathrm{Tr}_{\mathrm{win}_2}(G \upharpoonright \mathrm{VC}^{\sigma}(r))$ for player 1 is empty. By Lemma 4 it follows that for all $r < 1$, all states in $\mathrm{Tr}_{\mathrm{win}_2}(G \upharpoonright \mathrm{VC}^{\sigma}(r))$ are almost-sure winning for player 2. Consider a strategy π for player 2 such that the strategy π is almost-sure winning in $\mathrm{Tr}_{\mathrm{win}_2}(G \upharpoonright \mathrm{VC}^{\sigma}(r))$ for all $r < 1$. Let $U_{<1} = S \setminus \mathrm{VC}^{\sigma}(1)$. For all strategies σ' of player 1 and all states $s \in U_{<1}$, we have $\mathrm{Pr}_s^{\sigma',\pi}(\Phi \mid \mathrm{Safe}(U_{<1})) = 0$, where $\mathrm{Safe}(U_{<1}) = \{\omega = \langle s_0, s_1, \ldots \rangle \mid \forall k \geq 0.\ s_k \in U_{<1}\}$ denotes the set of plays that only visit states in $U_{<1}$. Hence, given the strategy π, any counter-optimal strategy for player 1 maximizes the probability to reach $\mathrm{VC}^{\sigma}(1)$. Since the strategy σ cannot be "value improved," it follows from arguments similar to [7] for $2^1\!/\!_2$-player reachability games that for all player-1 strategies σ', all $r < 1$, and all states $s \in \mathrm{VC}^{\sigma}(r)$, we have $\mathrm{Pr}_s^{\sigma',\pi}(\Phi) \leq r$. Hence for all $r \in [0, 1]$ and all states $s \in \mathrm{VC}^{\sigma}(r)$, we have $\langle\langle 1 \rangle\rangle_{val}(\Phi)(s) \leq r$. For all $r \in [0, 1]$ and all states $s \in \mathrm{VC}^{\sigma}(r)$, we have $r = \langle\langle 1 \rangle\rangle_{val}^{\sigma}(\Phi)(s) \leq \langle\langle 1 \rangle\rangle_{val}(\Phi)(s)$. This establishes the optimality of σ.

Lemma 10. *The procedure* `Improve` *can be computed in time* $O(poly(n)) \cdot O(\texttt{TwoPlRabinGame}(n \cdot d, m \cdot d, d + 1))$, *where poly is a polynomial function.*

In Lemma 10 we denote by $O(\texttt{TwoPlRabinGame}(n \cdot d, m \cdot d, d + 1))$ the time complexity of an algorithm for solving 2-player Rabin games with $n \cdot d$ states, $m \cdot d$ edges, and $d + 1$ Rabin pairs. Recall the reduction $\mathrm{Tr}_{\mathrm{as}}^1$ blows up states in and outgoing edges from $S_{\bigcirc}$ by a factor of d, and adds a new Rabin pair. A call to `Improve` requires solving an MDP with Streett objectives quantitatively (Step 1 of `Improve`; this can be achieved in polynomial time), and computing Step 2.2 requires to solve at most n two-player Rabin games (since there can be at most n value classes). Lemma 10 follows. Also recall that by the results of [14] we have $O(\texttt{TwoPlRabinGame}(n \cdot d, m \cdot d, d + 1)) = O\big((m \cdot d) \cdot (n \cdot d)^{d+2} \cdot (d + 1)!\big)$.

A strategy-improvement algorithm using the `Improve` procedure is described in Algorithm 2. Observe that it follows from Lemma 8 that, if Algorithm 2 outputs a strategy σ^*, then $\sigma^* = \texttt{Improve}(G, \sigma^*)$. The correctness of the algorithm follows from Lemma 9 and yields Theorem 2. Given an optimal strategy σ for player 1, the values for both the players can be computed in polynomial time by computing the values of the MDP G_{σ} [3,8]. Since there are at most $\left(\frac{m}{n}\right)^n \leq 2^{n \cdot \log n}$ possible pure memoryless strategies, it follows that Algorithm 2 requires at most $2^{n \cdot \log n}$ iterations. This along with Lemma 10 gives us the following theorem.

Algorithm 2. StrategyImprovementAlgorithm

Input: A $2^1\!/_2$-player game graph G and a Rabin objective Φ for player 1.
Output: An optimal strategy σ^* for player 1.
1. Choose an arbitrary pure memoryless strategy σ for player 1.
2. **while** $\sigma \neq \texttt{Improve}(G, \sigma)$ **do** $\sigma = \texttt{Improve}(G, \sigma)$.
3. **return** $\sigma^* = \sigma$.

Theorem 3 (Correctness of Algorithm 2). *For every $2^1\!/_2$-player game graph G and Rabin objective Φ, the output σ^* of Algorithm 2 is an optimal strategy for player 1. The running time of Algorithm 2 is bounded by $2^{O(n \cdot \log n)} \cdot O((m \cdot d) \cdot (n \cdot d)^{d+2} \cdot (d+1)!)$ if G has n states and m edges, and Φ has d pairs.*

4 Randomized Algorithm

We now present a randomized algorithm for $2^1\!/_2$-player Rabin games, by combining an algorithm of Björklund et al. [1] and the procedure `Improve`.

Games and improving subgames. Given $l, m \in \mathbb{N}$, let $\mathcal{G}(l, m)$ be the class of $2^1\!/_2$-player game graphs with the set S_1 of player 1 states partitioned into two sets as follows: (1) $O_1 = \{s \in S_1 \mid |E(s)| = 1\}$, i.e., the set of states with outdegree 1; and (2) $O_2 = S_1 \setminus O_1$, with $O_2 \leq l$ and $\sum_{s \in O_2} |E(s)| \leq m$. There is no restriction for player 2. Given a game $G \in \mathcal{G}(l, m)$, a state $s \in O_2$, and an edge $e = (s, t)$, we define the subgame $\widetilde{G}_e$ of G by deleting all outgoing edges from s other than the edge e. Observe that $\widetilde{G}_e \in \mathcal{G}(l-1, m - |E(s)|)$, and hence also $\widetilde{G}_e \in \mathcal{G}(l, m)$. If σ is a strategy for player 1 in $G \in \mathcal{G}(l, m)$, then a subgame $\widetilde{G}$ of G is *σ-improving* if some player-1 strategy σ' in $\widetilde{G}$ satisfies $\sigma \prec \sigma'$.

Informal description of the randomized algorithm. We refer to the randomized algorithm as Algorithm 3. The algorithm takes a $2^1\!/_2$-player Rabin game and an initial strategy σ^0, and proceeds in two steps. Given the game graph G, consider the least l and m such that $G \in \mathcal{G}(l, m)$. In Step 1, the algorithm constructs r subgames $\widetilde{G}$ that are σ^0-improving, together with the corresponding improved player-1 strategies σ, that is, $\sigma^0 \prec \sigma$. This is achieved by the procedure `ImprovingSubgames`. The parameter r will be chosen to obtain a suitable complexity analysis. In Step 2, the algorithm selects uniformly at random one of the improving subgames $\widetilde{G}$ with corresponding strategy σ, and recursively computes an optimal strategy σ^* in $\widetilde{G}$ from σ as the initial strategy. If the strategy σ^* is optimal in the original game G, then the algorithm terminates and returns σ^*. Otherwise it improves σ^* by a call to `Improve`, and continues at Step 1 with the improved strategy $\texttt{Improve}(G, \sigma^*)$ as the initial strategy.

The procedure `ImprovingSubgames` constructs a sequence of game graphs $G^0, G^1, \ldots, G^{r-l}$ with $G^i \in \mathcal{G}(l, l+i)$ such that all $(l+i)$-subgames $\widetilde{G}^i_e$ of G^i are σ^0-improving. The subgame G^{i+1} is constructed from G^i as follows:

we compute an optimal strategy σ^i in G^i, and if σ^i is optimal in G, then we have discovered an optimal strategy; otherwise we construct G^{i+1} by adding an edge e of $\texttt{Improve}(G, \sigma^i)$ to G^i, that is, e is any edge required in the strategy $\texttt{Improve}(G, \sigma^i)$ that is not in the strategy σ^i. The formal description of the algorithm coincides with Algorithm 3 of [4], with the strategy-improvement step replaced by a call to the procedure Improve.

The correctness of the algorithm can be seen as follows. Observe that every time Step 1 is executed, the initial strategy is improved with respect to the ordering $\prec$ on strategies. Since the number of strategies is bounded, the termination of the algorithm is guaranteed. The termination conditions guarantee that the output of the algorithm is an optimal strategy. Lemma 11 bounds the expected number of iterations of Algorithm 3. The analysis is similar to the results of [1].

Lemma 11. *Algorithm 3 computes an optimal strategy. The expected number of iterations $T(\cdot,\cdot)$ of Algorithm 3 for a game $G \in \mathcal{G}(l, m)$ is bounded by the recurrence:* $T(l,m) \leq \sum_{i=l}^{r} T(l,i) + T(l-1, m-2) + \frac{1}{r} \cdot \sum_{i=1}^{r} T(l, m-i) + 1$.

For a game graph G with n states, we obtain a bound of n^2 for m. Using this fact and an analysis of Kalai for linear programming, Björklund et al. [1] showed that $m^{O\left(\sqrt{n/\log n}\right)} = 2^{O\left(\sqrt{n \cdot \log n}\right)}$ is a solution to the recurrence of Lemma 11, by choosing $r = \max\{n, \frac{m}{2}\}$. This analysis and Lemma 10 yield Theorem 4.

Theorem 4. *Given a $2^1\!/\!_2$-player game graph G with n states and m edges, and a Rabin objective Φ with d pairs, the value $\langle\langle 1 \rangle\rangle_{val}(\Phi)(s)$ can be computed for all states s of G in expected time* $2^{O(\sqrt{n \cdot \log n})} \cdot O((m \cdot d) \cdot (n \cdot d)^{d+2} \cdot (d+1)!)$.

5 Optimal-Strategy Construction for Streett Objectives

The algorithms, Algorithm 2 and the randomized algorithm, compute values for both player 1 and player 2 (i.e., both for Rabin and Streett objectives), but only construct an optimal strategy for player 1 (i.e., the player with the Rabin objective). Since pure memoryless optimal strategies exist for the Rabin player, it is much simpler to analyze and obtain the values and an optimal strategy for player 1. We now show that how, once these values have been computed, we can obtain an optimal strategy for the Streett player as well. We do this by computing sure winning strategies in 2-player games with Streett objectives.

Given a $2^1\!/\!_2$-player game G with Rabin objective Φ for player 1, and the complementary objective $\Omega \setminus \Phi$ for player 2, first we compute $\langle\langle 1 \rangle\rangle_{val}(\Phi)(s)$ for all states $s \in S$. An optimal strategy π^* for player 2 is constructed as follows: for a value class $\mathrm{VC}(r)$, for $r < 1$, obtain a sure winning strategy $\overline{\pi}_r$ for player 2 in $\mathrm{Tr}_{\mathrm{as}}^2(\mathrm{Tr}_{\mathrm{win}_2}(G \upharpoonright \mathrm{VC}(r)))$, and in $\mathrm{VC}(r)$ the strategy π^* follows the strategy $\mathrm{Tr}_{\mathrm{as}}^2(\overline{\pi}_r)$. By Lemma 3, it follows that π^* is an optimal strategy, and given all values, the construction of π^* requires n calls to a procedure for solving 2-player games with Streett objectives.

Theorem 5. *Let G be a $2^1\!/\!_2$-player game graph with n states and m edges, and let Φ and $\Omega \setminus \Phi$ be a Rabin and Streett objective, respectively, with d pairs. Given* *the values* $\langle\langle 1 \rangle\rangle_{val}(\Phi)(s) = 1 - \langle\langle 2 \rangle\rangle_{val}(\Phi)(s)$ *for all states* s *of* G*, an optimal strategy* π^* *for player 2 can be constructed in time* $n \cdot O(\texttt{TwoPlStreettGame}(n \cdot d, m \cdot d, d+1))$*, where* $\texttt{TwoPlStreettGame}(n \cdot d, m \cdot d, d+1)$ *is any algorithm for solving 2-player Streett games with* $n \cdot d$ *states,* $m \cdot d$ *edges, and* $d+1$ *Streett pairs.*

References

1. H. Bjorklund, S. Sandberg, and S. Vorobyov. A discrete subexponential algorithms for parity games. In *STACS*, LNCS 2607, pp. 663–674. Springer, 2003.
2. K. Chatterjee, L. de Alfaro, and T.A. Henzinger. Trading memory for randomness. In *QEST*, pp. 206–217. IEEE Computer Society, 2004.
3. K. Chatterjee, L. de Alfaro, and T.A. Henzinger. The complexity of stochastic Rabin and Streett games. In *ICALP*, LNCS 3580, pp. 878–890. Springer, 2005.
4. K. Chatterjee and T.A. Henzinger. Strategy improvement and randomized subexponential algorithms for stochastic parity games. In *STACS*, LNCS 3884, pp. 512–523. Springer, 2006.
5. K. Chatterjee, M. Jurdziński, and T. A. Henzinger. Simple stochastic parity games. In *CSL*, LNCS 2803, pp. 100–113. Springer, 2003.
6. A. Condon. The complexity of stochastic games. *Information and Computation*, 96:203–224, 1992.
7. A. Condon. On algorithms for simple stochastic games. In *Advances in Computational Complexity Theory*, volume 13 of *DIMACS Series in Discrete Mathematics and Theoretical Computer Science*, pp. 51–73. AMS, 1993.
8. L. de Alfaro. *Formal Verification of Probabilistic Systems*. PhD thesis, Stanford University, 1997.
9. L. de Alfaro and T.A. Henzinger. Concurrent ω-regular games. In *LICS*, pp. 141–154. IEEE Computer Society, 2000.
10. E.A. Emerson and C. Jutla. The complexity of tree automata and logics of programs. In *FOCS*, pp. 328–337. IEEE Computer Society, 1988.
11. A. Hoffman and R. Karp. On nonterminating stochastic games. *Management Science*, 12:359–370, 1966.
12. O. Kupferman and M.Y. Vardi. Weak alternating automata and tree-automata emptiness. In *STOC*, pp. 224–233. ACM, 1998.
13. Z. Manna and A. Pnueli. *The Temporal Logic of Reactive and Concurrent Systems: Specification*. Springer, 1992.
14. N. Piterman and A. Pnueli. Faster solutions of Rabin and Streett games. In *LICS*. IEEE Computer Society, 2006 (to appear).
15. A. Pnueli and R. Rosner. On the synthesis of a reactive module. In *POPL*, pp. 179–190. ACM, 1989.
16. P.J. Ramadge and W.M. Wonham. Supervisory control of a class of discrete-event processes. *SIAM J. Control and Optimization*, 25:206–230, 1987.
17. W. Thomas. Languages, automata, and logic. In *Beyond Words*, volume 3 of *Handbook of Formal Languages*, pp. 389–455. Springer, 1997.

Weak Bisimulation Up to Elaboration*

Damien Pous

ENS Lyon

Abstract. We study the use of the elaboration preorder (due to Arun-Kumar and Natarajan) in the framework of up-to techniques for weak bisimulation. We show that elaboration yields a correct technique that encompasses the commonly used up to expansion technique. We also define a theory of up-to techniques for elaboration that in particular validates an elaboration up to elaboration technique, while it is known that weak bisimulation up to weak bisimilarity is unsound. In this sense, the resulting setting improves over previous works in terms of modularity.

Our results are obtained using nontrivial proofs that exploit termination arguments. In particular, we need the termination of internal computations for the up-to techniques to be correct. We show how this condition can be relaxed to some extent in order to handle processes exhibiting infinite internal behaviour.

Introduction

Weak bisimilarity ($\approx$) is a commonly used behavioural equivalence for the analysis of concurrent systems. *Weak* here means distinguishing between visible actions of a system, that express interactions with its environment, and τ *transitions*, that are treated as internal moves, and hence unobservable. To prove a weak bisimilarity result, one usually exhibits a relation $\mathcal{R}$ between states of the systems being compared, and shows that $\mathcal{R}$ is a weak bisimulation relation (we shall often simply use 'bisimilarity' and 'bisimulation' in the sequel, and refer explicitly to the strong version of these relations when necessary).

The crux of a bisimulation proof is often the study of silent transitions, as this part of the proof expresses the fact that internal calculations do not introduce unexpected behaviours. Typically, this is where it is shown that an optimisation is valid, that an encoding is fully abstract, or that some invariant about a data structure is preserved. Because one has to take into account all possible silent transitions, this makes bisimulation relations grow a lot, although, intuitively, many of the τ transitions being examined are irrelevant from the point of view of the overall behaviour of the system.

Several *up-to techniques* have been proposed to alleviate the task of bisimulation proofs. The idea of up-to techniques is to manipulate functions from

* This work has been supported by the french initiatives "Action Concertée Nouvelles Interfaces des Mathématiques GEOCAL" and "ANR ARASSIA, projet ModyFiable".

C. Baier and H. Hermanns (Eds.): CONCUR 2006, LNCS 4137, pp. 390–405, 2006.

relations to relations, that compute a form of closure. These functions are used in the bisimulation game as shown on the diagram on the left below:

$$\begin{array}{ccc} P & \mathcal{R} & Q \\ {\scriptstyle\alpha}\downarrow & & \Downarrow{\scriptstyle\widehat{\alpha}} \\ P' & \mathcal{F}(\mathcal{R}) & Q' \end{array} \qquad \begin{array}{l} \mathcal{U} : \mathcal{R} \mapsto \mathcal{R} \cup \approx \\ \mathcal{W} : \mathcal{R} \mapsto \approx \mathcal{R} \approx \end{array} \qquad \begin{array}{l} \mathcal{X} : \mathcal{R} \mapsto \gtrsim \mathcal{R} \approx \\ \mathcal{E} : \mathcal{R} \mapsto \gtrapprox \mathcal{R} \approx \end{array}$$

When the symmetric candidate relation $\mathcal{R}$ contains a pair $\langle P, Q\rangle$, and P does a transition to P' along an action α, Q has to perform the same action, modulo some internal computation (τ transitions), to yield a process Q'. The point is that the resulting pair $\langle P', Q'\rangle$ has to belong to $\mathcal{F}(\mathcal{R})$ instead of $\mathcal{R}$ (bisimulation is obtained by taking the identity function for $\mathcal{F}$).

For example, if we take for $\mathcal{F}$ the function $\mathcal{U}$ above, we can use known facts about $\approx$ when examining the transitions of processes related by $\mathcal{R}$. More interestingly, function $\mathcal{W}$ allows one to apply known bisimilarity laws to transform P' and Q' in order to obtain a pair belonging to $\mathcal{R}$. Unfortunately, the technique given by $\mathcal{W}$ is unsound, as shown by the following standard counterexample (written in CCS): consider a process P which is not bisimilar to 0, and define $\mathcal{R} \triangleq \{\langle \tau.P, 0\rangle\}$. Since $\tau.P \approx P$, we can use $\mathcal{W}$ to repeatedly undo the silent transition $\tau.P \xrightarrow{\tau} P$, so that in the game of weak bisimulation up to weak bisimilarity, we never explore the actual behaviour of P.

$$\begin{array}{ccccccc} \tau.P & \mathcal{R} & 0 & & & & \\ {\scriptstyle\tau}\downarrow & & & & & & \\ P & \approx & \tau.P & \mathcal{R} & 0 & & \\ & & {\scriptstyle\tau}\downarrow & & & & \\ & & P & \approx & \tau.P & \mathcal{R} & 0 \\ & & & & {\scriptstyle\tau}\downarrow & & \\ & & & & & \ldots & \end{array}$$

To address this difficulty, [10] introduces *expansion* ($\gtrsim$), a behavioural preorder included in weak bisimilarity, that leads to the up-to technique given by function $\mathcal{X}$ defined above. Unlike $\mathcal{W}$, $\mathcal{X}$ yields a correct proof technique, because expansion expresses a kind of efficiency constraint: intuitively, if $P \gtrsim Q$, then Q is 'faster' than P, in the sense that P and Q exhibit the same behaviour, but Q has to require less silent transitions to do so (we define $\gtrsim$ formally below). Since $P \gtrsim \tau.P$ does not hold, $\mathcal{X}$ rules out the above counterexample.

However, as experience shows [5,7], there are cases where reasoning up to expansion does not suffice, because the silent moves one would like to factor out in a bisimulation proof are not contained in expansion. Typically, this occurs when the 'faster process' has to spend some time at certain points to do some internal bookkeeping, for instance to update a data structure. To go beyond expansion, we have proposed in [7] a general and, at least to some extent, modular theory of up-to techniques for weak bisimulation. [7] introduces a notion of *controlled relation*, which guarantees that a given relation can be used in place of expansion. Several sufficient conditions for a relation to be controlled are given, among which, most notably, a criterion based on a termination property that prevents the existence of what we call 'infinite ladders' like depicted on the diagram above (which shows an infinite $\xrightarrow{\tau}\approx$ ladder).

Nevertheless, the resulting setting lacks flexibility, essentially because the property of being a controlled relation is not stable by union. This prevents the incremental construction of bisimulation proofs, and thus represents a drawback in terms of modularity: in this setting, extending a proof requires an involved knowledge of the up-to techniques at work, in order to check that relations remain controlled along the extension (we discuss this at the end of Sect. 3).

In this paper, we focus on the *elaboration* preorder, which has been introduced in [2]. Elaboration, written $\gtrapprox$, is somehow the dual of expansion: informally, $P \gtrapprox Q$ means that P performs *at least as many silent transitions* as Q, while exhibiting the same behaviour. Elaboration strictly contains expansion, and is in some sense very close to $\approx$. The focus in [2] is on congruence properties of $\gtrapprox$ in the setting of CCS, and on the axiomatisation of this relation.

The first result we establish is that $\gtrapprox$ yields a correct up-to technique for bisimulation when the system is *terminating*, that is, when it does not exhibit infinite sequences of silent transitions. Rather remarkably, this result cannot be derived by a simple diagram chasing (as is the case for the up to expansion technique). The proof relies instead on the approach of [7], the termination hypothesis being used to derive the absence of infinite 'ladders'.

Our second contribution is to show that $\gtrapprox$ supports the development of a modular theory of up-to techniques, along the lines of the treatment of up-to techniques for strong bisimulation presented in [9]. This represents a significant step forward w.r.t. [7] in terms of modularity, notably because the *up to transitivity* proof technique, given by $\mathcal{T} : \mathcal{R} \mapsto \mathcal{R}^*$, is shown to be correct for elaboration (under the previous termination hypothesis). We devote particular attention to this important result: when applicable to reason about a coinductively defined relation $\simeq$, $\mathcal{T}$ provides the powerful techniques given by $\mathcal{R} \mapsto (\mathcal{R} \cup \simeq)^\star$, or the more restrictive (but more commonly used) $\mathcal{R} \mapsto \simeq \mathcal{R} \simeq$. As we show in the paper, an application of the resulting framework is the study of an *up to polyadic contexts* proof technique (a polyadic context is a context with possibly many holes in it). Establishing directly the correctness of this technique can be really tedious, while correctness of $\mathcal{T}$ allows one to derive a modular proof that boils down to correctness in the – simpler – monadic case.

Although it can be argued that the termination of silent transitions is realistic in many systems (typically, when silent moves are used to update the internal representation of a data structure), some programming techniques may be the source of deliberate infinite internal behaviours, such as busy waiting loops. In order to be able to handle some of these situations, we move to a setting where silent transitions are decomposed into two kinds of internal moves, respectively called the *progressive* and *non-progressive* silent transitions (as in [4]). Only progressive silent transitions are supposed to be terminating. We show that under this relaxed hypothesis, the previous results can be adapted, by validating an 'up to progressive elaboration' technique for bisimulation, and showing the correctness of progressive elaboration up to transitivity. While being similar to the proofs of the results above, establishing the properties for non-terminating systems involves rather intricate usages of well-founded induction. Beyond this technical aspect, we believe that the general proof pattern adopted in this paper exposes an interesting application of rewriting techniques to concurrency.

Outline of the paper. In Sect. 1, we introduce our notations and briefly recall the results of [7] that will be used in the sequel. In Sect. 2 we define the elaboration preorder, and establish correctness of the up to elaboration proof technique when silent transitions of the system are terminating. We develop in Sect. 3 a theory of up-to techniques for elaboration, and draw a comparison with existing techniques. We extend these results to non-terminating systems in Sect. 4, and give final remarks in Sect. 5.

1 Preliminaries

1.1 Labelled Transition Systems, Definitions

We consider labelled transition systems (LTS) $\langle \mathcal{P}, \mathcal{L}, \rightarrow \rangle$, with domain $\mathcal{P}$, *labels* or *actions* in $\mathcal{L}$ and transition relation $\rightarrow \subseteq \mathcal{P} \times \mathcal{L} \times \mathcal{P}$. The elements of $\mathcal{P}$ are called *processes* and are denoted by P, Q. Except in Sect. 4, $\mathcal{L}$ will always implicitly contain a distinguished *silent action*, noted τ. We let α, β (resp. a, b) range over actions, in $\mathcal{L}$ (resp. *visible actions*, in $\mathcal{L} \backslash \{\tau\}$). Some examples will be given using the syntax of CCS, which we suppose known to the reader.

We let $\mathcal{R}, \mathcal{S}, \mathcal{B}$ range over binary relations (simply called *relations* in the sequel) between processes. We denote respectively by $\mathcal{R}^+, \mathcal{R}^=, \mathcal{R}^\star$ the transitive, reflexive, transitive and reflexive closures of a relation $\mathcal{R}$. $P\mathcal{R}Q$ means $\langle P, Q \rangle \in \mathcal{R}$. The composition of two relations $\mathcal{R}$ and $\mathcal{S}$, written $\mathcal{RS}$, is defined by $\mathcal{RS} \triangleq \{\langle P, Q \rangle / P\mathcal{R}T \text{ and } T\mathcal{S}Q \text{ for some process } T\}$. We also define the inverse of a relation: $\mathcal{R}^{-1} \triangleq \{\langle P, Q \rangle / Q\mathcal{R}P\}$. $\mathcal{I}$ is the identity relation, defined by $\mathcal{I} \triangleq \{\langle P, P \rangle / P \in \mathcal{P}\}$. We say that $\mathcal{R}$ *contains* $\mathcal{S}$ (alternatively, that $\mathcal{S}$ is contained in $\mathcal{R}$), written $\mathcal{S} \subseteq \mathcal{R}$, if $P\mathcal{S}Q$ implies $P\mathcal{R}Q$. Given an action α, the set of transitions along α induces a relation denoted by $\xrightarrow{\alpha}$: $\xrightarrow{\alpha} \triangleq \{\langle P, Q \rangle / \langle P, \alpha, Q \rangle \in \rightarrow\}$. Its inverse is written using a reversed arrow: $\xleftarrow{a} = (\xrightarrow{a})^{-1}$, and similarly for other forms of arrows, defined below. Finally, we call *function* a mapping from relations to relations.

Definition 1.1 (Termination). *A relation $\mathcal{R}$* terminates *if there is no infinite sequence $(P_i)_{i \in \mathbb{N}}$ such that $\forall i, P_i \mathcal{R} P_{i+1}$.*

Such terminating relations are also called *Nœtherian* in the literature. They lead to the powerful technique of proof by *well-founded induction* on which we heavily rely in the sequel. We will also make use of *lexicographic inductions*, that is, inductions based on lexicographic orders. In our case, such orders will always consist of the product of a terminating relation $\mathcal{R}$ with the standard ordering of natural numbers: $\langle P, n \rangle \succ \langle Q, m \rangle$ iff $P\mathcal{R}Q$ or ($P = Q$ and $n > m$).

The definitions of behavioural equivalences and preorders will make use of the following *weak transition* relations.

Definition 1.2 (Weak transitions).

$$\xrightarrow{\widehat{\alpha}} \triangleq \begin{cases} \xrightarrow{\tau}^{=} & \text{if } \alpha = \tau \\ \xrightarrow{a} & \text{if } \alpha = a \in \mathcal{L}\backslash\{\tau\} \end{cases} \qquad \begin{array}{l} \stackrel{\alpha}{\Rightarrow} \triangleq \xrightarrow{\tau}^{\star}\xrightarrow{\alpha}\xrightarrow{\tau}^{\star} \\ \stackrel{\widehat{\alpha}}{\Rightarrow} \triangleq \xrightarrow{\tau}^{\star}\xrightarrow{\widehat{\alpha}}\xrightarrow{\tau}^{\star} \end{array}$$

We can remark the following properties: $\stackrel{\widehat{\tau}}{\Rightarrow} = \xrightarrow{\tau}^{\star}$, $\stackrel{\tau}{\Rightarrow} = \xrightarrow{\tau}^{+}$, $\stackrel{\widehat{a}}{\Rightarrow} = \stackrel{a}{\Rightarrow}$ (note in particular the difference between $\stackrel{\widehat{\tau}}{\Rightarrow}$ and $\stackrel{\tau}{\Rightarrow}$).

Definition 1.3 (Evolution of relations). *Let α be an action and $\mathcal{R}, \mathcal{S}$ two relations. We say that $\mathcal{R}$* α-evolves *to $\mathcal{S}$ if whenever $P\mathcal{R}Q$, $P \xrightarrow{\alpha} P'$ implies $Q \stackrel{\widehat{\alpha}}{\Rightarrow} Q'$ and $P'\mathcal{S}Q'$ for some Q'. Given two relations $\mathcal{R}$ and $\mathcal{S}$, we say that:*

- $\mathcal{R}$ evolves *to $\mathcal{S}$ if $\mathcal{R}$ α-evolves to $\mathcal{S}$ for all $\alpha \in \mathcal{L}$,*
- $\mathcal{R}$ evolves silently *to $\mathcal{S}$ if $\mathcal{R}$ τ-evolves to $\mathcal{S}$,*
- $\mathcal{R}$ evolves visibly *to $\mathcal{S}$ if $\mathcal{R}$ a-evolves to $\mathcal{S}$ for all $a \in \mathcal{L}\backslash\{\tau\}$.*

Definition 1.4 (Bisimulation, Bisimilarity). *Let $\mathcal{R}$ be a relation. $\mathcal{R}$ is a* bisimulation *if it is symmetric and evolves to itself.* Bisimilarity, *denoted by $\approx$, is defined as the union of all bisimulations.*

1.2 Existing Up-to Techniques for Bisimulation

The following lemma will be useful in the sequel. It states correctness of reasoning up to transitivity on visible actions.

Lemma 1.5. *Let $\mathcal{R}$ be a relation. If $\mathcal{R}$ evolves silently to itself, and visibly to $\mathcal{R}^\star$, then $\mathcal{R}^\star$ evolves to itself.*

Proof. By two successive inductions, we show that for any n, $\mathcal{R}^n$ evolves silently to itself, and $\mathcal{R}^n$ evolves visibly to $\mathcal{R}^\star$ ($\mathcal{R}^n$ is the composition of $\mathcal{R}$ with itself, n times). □

Some important up-to techniques for bisimulation are given by the two following results which are simple reformulations of [7, Theorems 2.6 and 3.6].

Theorem 1.6. *Let $\mathcal{R}$ be a symmetric relation. If $\mathcal{R}$ evolves silently to $\succcurlyeq \mathcal{R} \approx$ and visibly to $\mathcal{R}^\star$, then $\mathcal{R}$ is contained in bisimilarity.*

Theorem 1.7. *Let $\mathcal{B}$ be a relation contained in bisimilarity, evolving to $\mathcal{B}^\star$, and such that $\mathcal{B}^+\stackrel{\tau}{\Rightarrow}$ terminates. If $\mathcal{R}$ is a symmetric relation that evolves silently to $\mathcal{B}^\star\mathcal{R} \approx$ and visibly to $\mathcal{R}^\star$, then $\mathcal{R}$ is contained in bisimilarity.*

In both cases, visible and silent transitions are treated differently, and up to transitivity is allowed on visible actions only. The difference between these two results is in the up-to technique that is allowed after a silent action: in the first case, one uses the compression preorder, written $\succcurlyeq$ ($\succcurlyeq$ will be defined in Sect. 2.1). This result is essentially already present in [10,11], without the transitivity on visible actions. In the second case, the up-to technique is given by a relation $\mathcal{B}$, which has to satisfy a termination property. In [7], the actual requirement for $\mathcal{B}$ is to be a *controlled relation* [7, Definition 3.1], and it is shown that the conditions in the above theorem are sufficient for $\mathcal{B}$ to be controlled.

The compression, used in Theorem 1.6, is not as involved as the sufficient condition expressed by Theorem 1.7. On the other hand, as will be discussed in Sect. 3, the technique given by the former theorem is more amenable to the incremental development of proofs than the setting of the latter.

2 Elaboration

2.1 Definition and Basic Properties

We now define elaboration, that has been introduced in the setting of CCS in [2].

Definition 2.1 (Elaboration relation, Elaboration). *A relation $\mathcal{R}$ is an* elaboration relation *(in short, an* elaboration*) if whenever $P\mathcal{R}Q$:*

(i) if $P \xrightarrow{\alpha} P'$, then $Q \stackrel{\widehat{\alpha}}{\Rightarrow} Q'$ with $P'\mathcal{R}Q'$,
(ii) if $Q \xrightarrow{\alpha} Q'$, then $P \stackrel{\alpha}{\Rightarrow} P'$ with $P'\mathcal{R}Q'$.

Elaboration, *denoted by $\gtrapprox$, is the union of all elaboration relations.*

Note that [2] uses a reversed version of the symbol for elaboration – we adopted this choice to follow the convention in other papers about up-to techniques and behavioural preorders, notably [10].

The intuition behind elaboration is that if $P \gtrapprox Q$, then P is able to always be *at least as slow* as Q, as expressed by clause *(ii)*. In relation to this, we may remark that divergences blur the difference between elaboration and bisimilarity: if $P \approx Q$, then $P|!\tau \gtrapprox Q$. This observation suggests that elaboration is a coarse relation, rather close to $\approx$ (see also Prop. 2.3 below). Moreover, if we consider the bisimilarity defined by using clause *(ii)* on both sides, we obtain *progressing bisimulation* [6]. On CCS agents, the latter equivalence (which is contained in $\gtrapprox$) coincides with the greatest weak bisimulation that is a congruence.

To draw a comparison between $\gtrapprox$ and other behavioural preorders, we recall the definition of *expansion* [10,11] (called *efficiency preorder* in [1]). A slightly coarser definition of expansion appears in [3,7], here we call it *compression* in order to avoid confusions. The difference has consequences as far as up-to techniques are concerned, as will be explained in Sect. 3.

Definition 2.2 (Expansion, Compression).

Expansion, *denoted by $\gtrsim$, is the largest relation such that whenever $P \gtrsim Q$,*
- *if $P \xrightarrow{\alpha} P'$, then $Q \xrightarrow{\widehat{\alpha}} Q'$ with $P' \gtrsim Q'$,*
- *if $Q \xrightarrow{\alpha} Q'$, then $P \stackrel{\alpha}{\Rightarrow} P'$ with $P' \gtrsim Q'$.*

Compression, *denoted by $\succcurlyeq$, is the largest relation such that whenever $P \succcurlyeq Q$,*
- *if $P \xrightarrow{\alpha} P'$, then $Q \xrightarrow{\widehat{\alpha}} Q'$ with $P' \succcurlyeq Q'$,*
- *if $Q \xrightarrow{\alpha} Q'$, then $P \stackrel{\widehat{\alpha}}{\Rightarrow} P'$ with $P' \succcurlyeq Q'$.*

In contrast with $\succapprox$, $P \succsim Q$ intuitively captures the fact that Q is able to be always faster than P (and similarly for $P \succeq Q$).

Proposition 2.3. *In any LTS, we have* $\sim \subset \succsim \subset \succapprox \subset \approx$ *and* $\succsim \subset \succeq \subset \approx$. *Moreover, in CCS,* $a|\tau \overset{\not\succeq}{\succapprox} \tau.a$ *and* $a \overset{\succeq}{\not\succapprox} a|\tau$.

As shown by the examples above, elaboration and compression are not comparable in general. These examples can be used to make the same observation with *almost weak bisimulation* [10] or *relaxed expansion* [7] instead of compression.

2.2 Bisimulation Up to Elaboration

In order for elaboration to yield a correct up-to technique, we need a termination hypothesis, for which we introduce the following terminology.

Definition 2.4 (α-terminating LTS). *Let* $\mathbb{S} = \langle \mathcal{P}, \mathcal{L}, \to \rangle$ *be an LTS, and* $\alpha \in \mathcal{L}$ *a label of* $\mathbb{S}$. *We say that* $\mathbb{S}$ *is* α-terminating *if* $\stackrel{\alpha}{\Rightarrow}$ *terminates.*

Lemma 2.5. *Let* α *be an action and* $\mathcal{R}$ *a relation such that* $\mathcal{R} \stackrel{\alpha}{\Rightarrow} \subseteq \stackrel{\alpha}{\Rightarrow} \mathcal{R}$. *If* $\stackrel{\alpha}{\Rightarrow}$ *terminates, then so does* $\mathcal{R} \stackrel{\alpha}{\Rightarrow}$.

Proof. First we prove $\varphi : \forall n, \mathcal{R}^n \stackrel{\alpha}{\Rightarrow} \subseteq \stackrel{\alpha}{\Rightarrow} \mathcal{R}^n$. Then, suppose that $\mathcal{R} \stackrel{\alpha}{\Rightarrow}$ does not terminate: there exists an infinite sequence $(Q_i)_{i \geq 0}$ such that $Q_i \ \mathcal{R} \stackrel{\alpha}{\Rightarrow} Q_{i+1}$. Using φ, we can define by induction an infinite sequence $(P_i)_{i \geq 0}$ such that $P_i \stackrel{\alpha}{\Rightarrow} P_{i+1}$ and $P_i \mathcal{R}^i Q_i$. This sequence is contradictory with the termination of $\stackrel{\alpha}{\Rightarrow}$. □

Theorem 2.6 (Bisimilarity up to Elaboration). *In a* τ*-terminating LTS, any symmetric relation* $\mathcal{R}$ *that evolves silently to* $\succapprox \mathcal{R} \approx$ *and visibly to* $\mathcal{R}^\star$ *is contained in bisimilarity.*

Proof. We show easily $\succapprox \stackrel{\tau}{\Rightarrow} \subseteq \stackrel{\tau}{\Rightarrow} \succapprox$, so that $\succapprox \stackrel{\tau}{\Rightarrow}$ terminates by Lemma 2.5. Then we check that $\succapprox$ and $\mathcal{R}$ satisfy the hypotheses of Theorem 1.7. □

We make some comments about this result and its proof.

We have $\stackrel{\tau}{\Rightarrow} = \stackrel{\tau}{\to}^+$, so that the τ-termination is actually the termination of $\stackrel{\tau}{\to}$ (a property called *convergence* in [4]). Without this hypothesis, up to elaboration fails to be correct: in CCS, we have $!\tau|a \succapprox !\tau|\tau.a$, and hence the (symmetric) relation $\mathcal{R} = \{\langle !\tau|\tau.a, 0 \rangle; \langle 0, !\tau|\tau.a \rangle\}$ evolves to $\succapprox \mathcal{R}$, but $\mathcal{R} \not\subseteq \approx$. We show in Sect. 4 how to relax the τ-termination requirement in some cases.

Theorem 2.6 is an application of the results proved in [7] – summed up in Theorem 1.7 – that exploit the termination of *ladders* (that is, sequences of processes related by $\mathcal{B}^+ \stackrel{\tau}{\Rightarrow}$). Remarkably, we are able to require here a termination property that does no longer involve the relation of interest ($\succapprox$). This is achieved by using the right-to-left part of the elaboration game: as shown in the proof of Lemma 2.5, and depicted on the left diagram below, we use this part of the elaboration game in order to transform any infinite ladder into an infinite sequence of τ-transitions, that would contradict the τ-termination hypothesis.

By contrast, when considering $\approx$ instead of $\gtrapprox$, the same argument does not hold, as shown on the right diagram, which recasts the counterexample seen in the introduction: in a bisimulation game, the left hand side process is allowed not to move and hence an infinite ladder may yield a finite sequence of τ-moves.

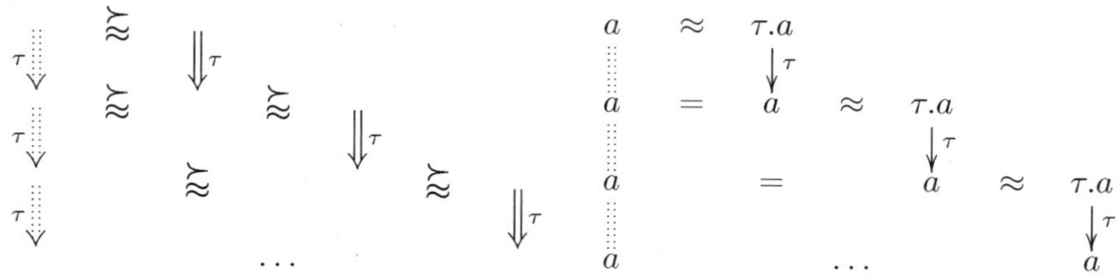

We can moreover remark that Lemma 2.5 actually entails that $\gtrapprox$ can be used in the general setting proposed in [7] (it is a *controlled relation* – cf. [7]). In particular, in systems where $\gtrapprox$ is a precongruence, up to elaboration can be combined with the 'up to context' technique, yielding a powerful tool for bisimulation proofs.

3 Up-to Techniques for Elaboration

We now present some techniques that can be used to establish elaboration results, which in turn can be used for bisimulation proofs, by Theorem 2.6. We develop a theory of up-to techniques for elaboration along the lines of the study of up-to techniques for strong bisimulation in [9].

Definition 3.1 (Progression). *Let $\mathcal{R}, \mathcal{S}$ be two relations. We say that $\mathcal{R}$ progresses to $\mathcal{S}$, denoted by $\mathcal{R} \rightsquigarrow \mathcal{S}$, if whenever $P\mathcal{R}Q$,*

- *if $P \xrightarrow{\alpha} P'$, then $Q \stackrel{\widehat{\alpha}}{\Rightarrow} Q'$ with $P'\mathcal{S}Q'$,*
- *if $Q \xrightarrow{\alpha} Q'$, then $P \stackrel{\alpha}{\Rightarrow} P'$ with $P'\mathcal{S}Q'$.*

This notion of progression is the counterpart of evolution (Definition 1.3) where an 'elaboration game' replaces the 'simulation game'. In particular, $\mathcal{R}$ is an elaboration iff $\mathcal{R}$ progresses to itself.

First we show that like strong bisimilarity, elaboration validates the powerful up to transitivity technique. As a corollary, elaboration up to elaboration is a correct technique: this means in particular that the elaboration preorder does not suffer from the irregularities of weak bisimilarity.

Theorem 3.2 (Elaboration up to transitivity). *In a τ-terminating LTS, if $\mathcal{R}$ is a relation that progresses to $\mathcal{R}^\star$, then $\mathcal{R}$ is contained in elaboration.*

Proof. We show that $\mathcal{R}^\star$ is an elaboration relation. For $\alpha \in \mathcal{L}$, let $\varphi_\alpha(P,n)$ denote the predicate: "for any Q' such that $P\mathcal{R}^n \stackrel{\alpha}{\Rightarrow} Q'$, $P \stackrel{\alpha}{\Rightarrow} \mathcal{R}^\star Q'$". We prove $\mathcal{R}^\star \stackrel{\tau}{\Rightarrow} \subseteq \stackrel{\tau}{\Rightarrow} \mathcal{R}^\star$ (1) by a lexicographic induction based on the termination of $\stackrel{\tau}{\Rightarrow}$, with the predicate φ_τ. The argument for the non-trivial case is sketched on the left diagram below:

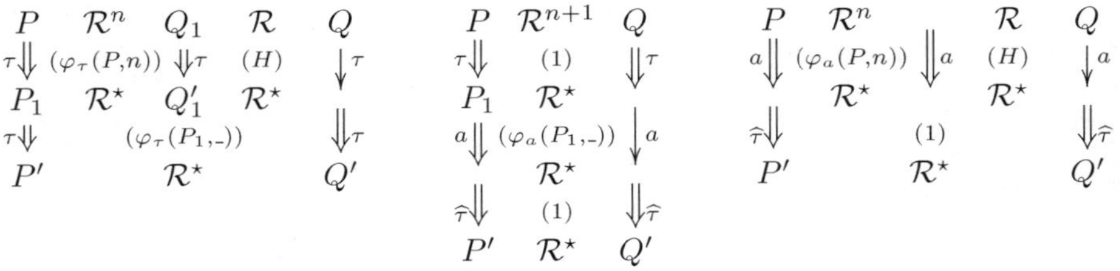

Then we prove $\mathcal{R}^\star \overset{a}{\Rightarrow} \subseteq \overset{a}{\Rightarrow} \mathcal{R}^\star$ (2) by a second lexicographic induction with the predicate φ_a. The two diagrams on the right above give the interesting cases. Finally, by applying Lemma 2.5 to $\mathcal{R}^\star$ and (1), we obtain the termination of $\mathcal{R}^\star \overset{\tau}{\Rightarrow}$, that leads to $\overset{\alpha}{\leftarrow} \mathcal{R}^\star \subseteq \mathcal{R}^\star \overset{\widehat{\alpha}}{\Leftarrow}$ using [7, Theorem 3.12]. □

We now introduce a class of functions corresponding to correct up-to techniques, that enjoys nice compositional properties.

Definition 3.3 (Safe function). *A function $\mathcal{F}$ is* safe *if for any relations $\mathcal{R}$ and $\mathcal{S}$,*
$$\text{if } \begin{cases} \mathcal{R} \subseteq \mathcal{S} \\ \mathcal{R} \rightsquigarrow \mathcal{S}^\star \end{cases} \quad \text{then } \begin{cases} \mathcal{F}(\mathcal{R}) \subseteq \mathcal{F}(\mathcal{S}) \\ \mathcal{F}(\mathcal{R}) \rightsquigarrow \mathcal{F}(\mathcal{S})^\star \end{cases}$$

This definition corresponds to [9, Definition 2.5]. The main difference is that we consider progressions to the reflexive transitive closures of relations. As shown in the following theorem, using Theorem 3.2, this makes it possible to use safe functions 'up to transitivity'.

Theorem 3.4 (Correctness of safe functions). *Let $\mathcal{F}$ be a safe function. In a τ-terminating LTS, if a relation $\mathcal{R}$ progresses to $\mathcal{F}(\mathcal{R})^\star$, then it is contained in elaboration.*

Proof. Let $\mathcal{R}_0 = \mathcal{R}$, $\mathcal{R}_{n+1} = \mathcal{R}_n \cup \mathcal{F}(\mathcal{R}_n)$, $\mathcal{R}_\omega = \bigcup_n \mathcal{R}_n$. We show by induction $\forall n,\ \mathcal{R}_n \rightsquigarrow \mathcal{R}_{n+1}^\star$. Hence $\mathcal{R}_\omega \rightsquigarrow \mathcal{R}_\omega^\star$, and finally $\mathcal{R}_\omega \subseteq \gtrsim$ using Theorem 3.2. □

The main point of safe functions is that they can be combined in a modular way: given two safe functions $\mathcal{F}$ and $\mathcal{G}$, their union $\mathcal{F} \cup \mathcal{G} : \mathcal{R} \mapsto \mathcal{F}(\mathcal{R}) \cup \mathcal{G}(\mathcal{R})$ and their functional composition $\mathcal{F} \circ \mathcal{G} : \mathcal{R} \mapsto \mathcal{F}(\mathcal{G}(\mathcal{R}))$ are safe. Hence, we can define correct up-to techniques incrementally (see for example the proof of Corollary 3.7). By contrast with [9], composing functions using the *chaining operator* $\mathcal{F}^\frown\mathcal{G} : \mathcal{R} \mapsto \mathcal{F}(\mathcal{R})\mathcal{G}(\mathcal{R})$ does not preserve safety, essentially for the same reasons as in the weak bisimilarity case [11] (in particular, τ-termination does not help). However, chaining can be 'emulated' since we are allowed to use safe functions up to transitivity: instead of $\mathcal{F}^\frown\mathcal{G}$, we can work with $(\mathcal{F} \cup \mathcal{G})^\star$, which we believe provides enough flexibility for actual elaboration proofs.

Elaboration up to context. We further enrich the set of up-to techniques for elaboration with an up to context technique. We call *context* a mapping from processes to processes (like in [7], we adopt an approach that allows us to abstract over the details of the underlying syntax). We denote by $C[P]$ the application of a context C to a process P. In the following technical definition, both $\xrightarrow{\epsilon}$ and $\xRightarrow{\epsilon}$ are synonyms for the identity relation $\mathcal{I}$ (we suppose $\epsilon \notin \mathcal{L}$).

Definition 3.5 (Faithfulness). *Let $\mathcal{C}$ be a family of contexts. We say that $\mathcal{C}$ is* faithful *if for all $C \in \mathcal{C}$, whenever $C[P] \xrightarrow{\alpha} R$, there are $C' \in \mathcal{C}$, $P' \in \mathcal{P}$ and $\delta \in \mathcal{L} \cup \{\epsilon\}$ such that $R = C'[P']$ and $P \xrightarrow{\delta} P'$, and for any Q, Q' such that $Q \xRightarrow{\delta} Q'$, $C[Q] \xRightarrow{\alpha} C'[Q']$.*

This is the direct adaptation to the weak case of the notion of faithfulness found in [9]. In CCS *non-degenerate* contexts [11] are faithful; in the π-calculus, *non-input guarded* contexts are faithful. The following proposition shows that these families of contexts yield correct up-to techniques for elaboration. The proof is very similar to the proof of the corresponding result in [11].

Proposition 3.6 (Safety of faithful families of contexts). *Let $\mathcal{C}$ be a faithful family of contexts; the following* closure up to $\mathcal{C}$ *function is safe:*

$$\widetilde{\mathcal{C}} : \mathcal{R} \mapsto \{\langle C[P], C[Q] \rangle \ / \ C \in \mathcal{C} \text{ and } P \mathcal{R} Q\} \ .$$

The following corollary sums up all previous results, yielding a powerful up-to technique for elaboration. It appears that the theory of up-to techniques for elaboration is as smooth as that for strong bisimilarity. Also notice that while we considered only *monadic* contexts in Prop. 3.6, Theorem 3.4 allows us to use $\widetilde{\mathcal{C}}$ transitively, thus validating the up to *polyadic* contexts technique.

Corollary 3.7 (Elaboration up to context and transitivity). *Let $\mathcal{C}$ be a faithful family of contexts and $\mathcal{R}$ a relation. If $\xrightarrow{\tau}$ terminates and $\mathcal{R}$ progresses to $(\widetilde{\mathcal{C}}(\mathcal{R}) \cup \gtrsim)^\star$, then $\mathcal{R}$ is contained in elaboration.*

Proof. The functions $\mathcal{R} \mapsto \gtrsim$ and $\widetilde{\mathcal{C}}$ are safe, hence so is $\mathcal{R} \mapsto \widetilde{\mathcal{C}}(\mathcal{R}) \cup \gtrsim$. □

Up to deterministic transitions. Let us finally mention a corollary of Theorem 3.2, that extends a technique which has been introduced in [3, Chap. 4] in the setting of barbed bisimilarity. Together with Theorem 2.6, this result gives the possibility, when $\xrightarrow{\tau}$ is terminating and deterministic, to normalise processes w.r.t. $\xrightarrow{\tau}$ along a bisimulation proof. Notice that [3] does not suppose τ-termination, but requires the stronger commutation hypothesis $\xleftarrow{\alpha}\xrightarrow{\tau} \subseteq \xrightarrow{\widehat{\tau}}\xleftarrow{\widehat{\alpha}}$.

Corollary 3.8. *If $\xrightarrow{\tau}$ terminates and for all $\alpha \in \mathcal{L}$, $\xleftarrow{\alpha}\xrightarrow{\tau} \subseteq \xRightarrow{\widehat{\tau}}\xLeftarrow{\widehat{\alpha}}$, then $\xrightarrow{\tau} \subseteq \gtrsim$.*

Proof. We remark that $\xrightarrow{\tau}\xrightarrow{\alpha} \subseteq \xRightarrow{\alpha} \subseteq \xRightarrow{\alpha}\xRightarrow{\widehat{\tau}}$, so that relation $\xrightarrow{\tau}$ satisfies the requirements of Theorem 3.2, and hence is an elaboration up to transitivity. □

On Modularity Properties of Up-to Techniques. Introducing the up to elaboration proof technique enriches the existing landscape of up-to techniques for bisimulation. We have seen that this behavioural preorder enjoys nice properties, allowing one to develop elaboration proofs in an incremental and modular fashion. We now study other up-to techniques from this point of view.

On the use of compression. As shown in [3,7], compression also yields a correct up-to technique. By Proposition 2.3 above, elaboration and compression are not comparable. The following example in CCS shows that they are neither compatible, in the sense that they cannot be used in the same bisimulation proof. Let $P = \tau.\tau.a$ and $Q = \tau.(\tau.\tau|a)$; we have $P \xrightarrow{\tau} \tau.a \succeq Q \xrightarrow{\tau} \tau.\tau|a \succapprox P$ so that the symmetric relation $\mathcal{R} = \{\langle P, 0\rangle; \langle Q, 0\rangle; \langle 0, P\rangle; \langle 0, Q\rangle\}$ evolves to $(\succeq \cup \succapprox)\mathcal{R}$, but obviously $\mathcal{R} \not\subseteq \approx$.

Another observation we can make about compression is that unlike elaboration, compression result cannot be proved up to transitivity, even when the LTS is τ-terminating. Indeed, the relation $\{\langle 0, \tau.a\rangle; \langle \tau.a, a\rangle; \langle 0, 0\rangle; \langle a, a\rangle\}$ over finite CCS processes is a 'compression up to transitivity', but it is clearly not contained in bisimilarity, and thus neither in compression.

Incrementality in the setting of [7]. Stability by union for up-to techniques provides a form of modularity, since it allows one to extend an existing proof by simply adding new behavioural laws. This property is immediate for coinductively defined relations such as $\succapprox$, $\succsim$ or $\succeq$. On the contrary, the setting of [7] lacks this facility: in order to extend a bisimulation proof up to $\mathcal{B}_1^*$ using a relation $\mathcal{B}_2$ ($\mathcal{B}_1$ and $\mathcal{B}_2$ are supposed to satisfy the hypotheses of Theorem 1.7), one needs to prove the termination of $(\mathcal{B}_1 \cup \mathcal{B}_2)^+ \overset{\tau}{\Rightarrow}$, which involves some knowledge about $\mathcal{B}_1$. To illustrate the difficulties, consider the following example in CCS:

$$\mathcal{B}_1 = \{(a + a, \tau.\tau.a), (\tau.\tau.a, \tau.a)\}$$
$$\mathcal{B}_2 = \{(a, a + a)\}$$

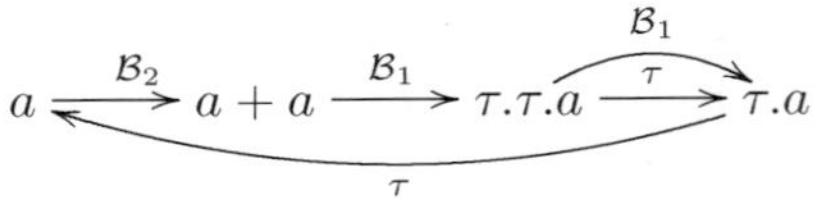

These relations satisfy the required property: for $i \in \{1, 2\}$, $\mathcal{B}_i$ evolves to $\mathcal{B}_i^*$ and $\mathcal{B}_i^+ \overset{\tau}{\Rightarrow}$ terminates. But $(\mathcal{B}_1 \cup \mathcal{B}_2)^+$ contains the pair $\langle a, \tau.a\rangle$, and hence $\mathcal{B}_1 \cup \mathcal{B}_2$ does not qualify to apply Theorem 1.7. We return to this question in Sect. 5.

4 The Case of Non-terminating Systems

We now show how the results from the two previous sections can be adapted to cases where the τ-termination assumption is not satisfied. Before moving to the formal definitions, we make a few remarks on the τ-termination requirement. It should be noticed that for the up to elaboration technique to be applicable, *the whole LTS* does not necessarily need to be τ-terminating. What we need is rather a transition closed subset of (pairs of) processes for which this condition holds. For instance, we might want to represent a system in CCS, a calculus where divergences are of course expressible, but the processes used for the modelling do not exhibit τ-divergences.

If, on the contrary, the system we would like to reason about does contain divergences, a first approach could be to 'tag' non-terminating silent moves and treat these as visible. However, such visible transitions must be mapped to some visible actions on the other side of the elaboration game, in order to play these in one-to-one correspondence. This of course might be too demanding in some cases, typically when divergences arise because implementing a given behaviour introduces some loops (that are not present in the original specification). In order to address such situations, we adopt an approach from [4], which consists in isolating a subset of the τ transitions that are terminating, while still treating all τ moves as silent.

In the following we consider a LTS where silent moves are split into two special actions: $\{\tau_>, \tau_=\} \subseteq \mathcal{L}$. Transitions $\xrightarrow{\tau_>}$ and $\xrightarrow{\tau_=}$ will respectively be called *progressive* and *non-progressive* silent transitions. *Silent transitions*, written $\xrightarrow{\tau}$, are *defined* by $\xrightarrow{\tau} \triangleq \xrightarrow{\tau_>} \cup \xrightarrow{\tau_=}$. Coherently, a, b will range over $\mathcal{L} \setminus \{\tau_>, \tau_=\}$. We recall our notations for weak transitions (Definition 1.2) below.

$$\stackrel{\widehat{\tau}}{\Rightarrow} = \xrightarrow{\tau}{}^{\star} \qquad \stackrel{\widehat{a}}{\Rightarrow} = \stackrel{a}{\Rightarrow} = \xrightarrow{\tau}{}^{\star} \xrightarrow{a} \xrightarrow{\tau}{}^{\star} \qquad \stackrel{\tau_>}{\Rightarrow} = \xrightarrow{\tau}{}^{\star} \xrightarrow{\tau_>} \xrightarrow{\tau}{}^{\star}$$

In this setting the notions of bisimulation and bisimilarity ignore the distinction between the two kinds of silent transitions (in particular, these relations do not coincide with what we would obtain by treating $\tau_=$ as visible actions). The definition of elaboration is adapted so as to control progressive transitions only:

Definition 4.1 ($\tau_>$-Elaboration). $\tau_>$-Elaboration, *denoted by* $\gtrsim^>$, *is the largest relation such that whenever* $P \gtrsim^> Q$,

(i) if $P \xrightarrow{\alpha} P'$ *then* $Q \stackrel{\widehat{\alpha}}{\Rightarrow} Q'$ *with* $P' \gtrsim^> Q'$, *for any* $\alpha \in \mathcal{L}$,
(ii) if $Q \xrightarrow{\alpha} Q'$ *then* $P \stackrel{\widehat{\alpha}}{\Rightarrow} P'$ *with* $P' \gtrsim^> Q'$, *for any* $\alpha \neq \tau_>$,
(iii) if $Q \xrightarrow{\tau_>} Q'$ *then* $P \stackrel{\tau_>}{\Rightarrow} P'$ *with* $P' \gtrsim^> Q'$.

$\tau_>$-expansion is the 'progressive elaboration' we alluded to in the introduction. Clause (i) corresponds to bisimulation, while when playing from right to left, we ensure that progressive silent transitions are 'preserved' (iii). We can easily check that $\gtrsim^>$ is a preorder, and that we have $\sim\, \subset\, \gtrsim^>\, \subset\, \approx$.

This adaptation leads to the following theorem, where the termination hypothesis concerns progressive silent transitions. As expected, up to transitivity is allowed on visible transitions (i), and up to $\tau_>$-elaboration is supported only on progressive silent transitions (ii). Clause (iii) for non-progressive transitions does not allow up-to reasoning on the left of $\mathcal{R}$. We show in [8] how to relax this condition by using an adapted version of expansion. We omit this development here for the sake of simplicity.

Theorem 4.2 (Bisimulation up to $\tau_>$-Elaboration). *Let* $\mathcal{R}$ *be a symmetric relation. If the following conditions hold whenever* $P\mathcal{R}Q$:

(i) if $P \xrightarrow{a} P'$ *then* $Q \stackrel{a}{\Rightarrow} Q'$ *with* $P'\mathcal{R}^{\star}Q'$,
(ii) if $P \xrightarrow{\tau_>} P'$ *then* $Q \stackrel{\widehat{\tau}}{\Rightarrow} Q'$ *with* $P' \gtrsim^> \mathcal{R} \approx Q'$, *and*
(iii) if $P \xrightarrow{\tau_=} P'$ *then* $Q \stackrel{\widehat{\tau}}{\Rightarrow} Q'$ *with* $P'\mathcal{R} \approx Q'$,

and the LTS is $\tau_>$*-terminating then* $\mathcal{R}$ *is contained in bisimilarity.*

Proof. We first prove the termination of $\gtrsim^> \stackrel{\tau_>}{\Rightarrow}$ using Lemma 2.5. Then we show that the symmetric relation $(\mathcal{R} \cup \approx)^{\star}$ is a bisimulation. Let $\mathcal{S} = \gtrsim^> \mathcal{R} \approx$; we remark that $(\mathcal{R} \cup \approx)^\star = \approx \mathcal{S}^\star$, so that it is sufficient to show that $\mathcal{S}^\star$ evolves to itself. This is established by proving successively the following inclusions:

$$(1)\ \xleftarrow{\tau_=}^\star \mathcal{R} \subseteq \mathcal{R} \approx \overset{\widehat{\tau}}{\Leftarrow} \qquad (2)\ \overset{\tau}{\Leftarrow} \mathcal{S} \subseteq \mathcal{S} \overset{\widehat{\tau}}{\Leftarrow} \qquad (3)\ \xleftarrow{a} \mathcal{S} \subseteq \mathcal{S}^\star \overset{a}{\Leftarrow}$$

We obtain (1) from *(iii)* and a simple induction over the sequence $\xrightarrow{\tau_=}^\star$. We prove (2) by well-founded induction using the termination of $\gtrsim_{\approx}^{>} \overset{\tau_>}{\Rightarrow}$ and the predicate $\varphi(P)$: "for any P', Q such that $P \overset{\widehat{\tau}}{\Rightarrow} P'$ and $P\mathcal{S}Q$, we have $P'\mathcal{S} \overset{\widehat{\tau}}{\Leftarrow} Q$". This leads to the diagrams below, where we reason by cases according to whether there is a progressive silent transition between P_0 and P_0' or not. In the former case, $P \gtrsim_{\approx}^{>} \overset{\tau}{\Rightarrow} P_1$ so that $\varphi(P_1)$ holds. Otherwise, we just use (1).

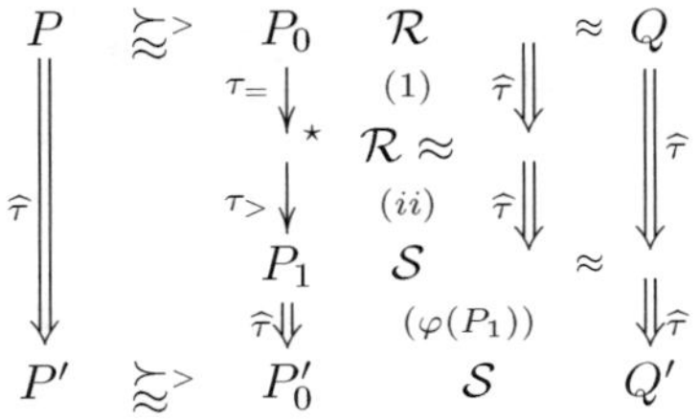

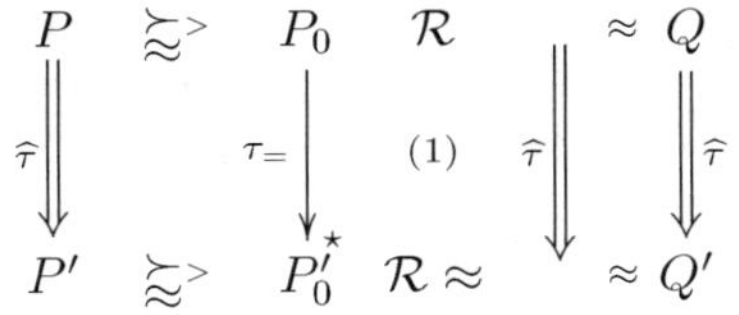

Then we prove (3) by well-founded induction using the termination of $\gtrsim_{\approx}^{>} \overset{\tau_>}{\Rightarrow}$ and the predicate $\psi(P)$: "for any P', Q such that $P \xrightarrow{a} P'$ and $P\mathcal{S}Q$, we have $P'\mathcal{S}^\star \overset{a}{\Leftarrow} Q$". As depicted in the following diagrams, if there is a progressive silent transition transition between P_0 and P_1, we use the induction hypothesis, otherwise, (1) is sufficient to close the diagram.

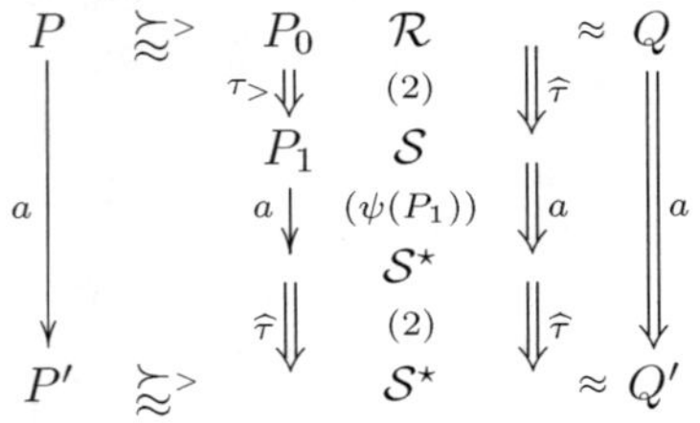

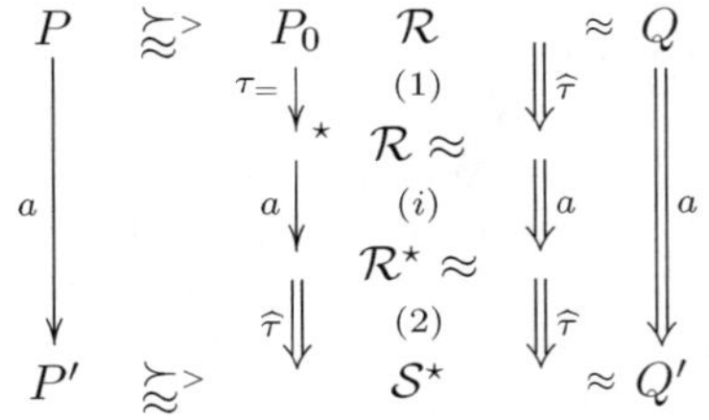

Finally, we apply Lemma 1.5 with (2) and (3) so that $\mathcal{S}^\star$ evolves to itself. □

We now show that $\tau_>$-elaboration validates the powerful up to transitivity proof technique on visible and progressive silent actions.

Theorem 4.3 ($\tau_>$-Elaboration up to Transitivity). *Let $\mathcal{R}$ be a relation. If the following conditions hold whenever $P\mathcal{R}Q$:*

(i) if $P \xrightarrow{\alpha} P'$ then $Q \overset{\widehat{\alpha}}{\Rightarrow} Q'$ with $P'\mathcal{R}^\star Q'$, for any $\alpha \neq \tau_=$,
(ii) if $P \xrightarrow{\tau_=} P'$ then $Q \overset{\widehat{\tau}}{\Rightarrow} Q'$ with $P'\mathcal{R}Q'$,
(iii) if $Q \xrightarrow{\alpha} Q'$ then $P \overset{\alpha}{\Rightarrow} P'$ with $P'\mathcal{R}^\star Q'$, for any $\alpha \neq \tau_=$, and
(iv) if $Q \xrightarrow{\tau_=} Q'$ then $P \overset{\widehat{\tau}}{\Rightarrow} P'$ with $P'\mathcal{R}Q'$,

and the LTS is $\tau_>$-terminating then $\mathcal{R}$ is contained in $\tau_>$-elaboration.

Proof. We show that $\mathcal{R}^\star$ is a $\tau_>$-elaboration relation by successively establishing the following properties.

$$\mathcal{R} \stackrel{\tau_=}{\rightarrow}^{\star} \subseteq \stackrel{\hat{\tau}}{\Rightarrow} \mathcal{R} \qquad (1)$$

$$\mathcal{R}^\star \stackrel{\tau_=}{\rightarrow}^{\star} \subseteq \stackrel{\hat{\tau}}{\Rightarrow} \mathcal{R}^\star \qquad (2)$$

$$\mathcal{R}^\star \stackrel{\tau_>}{\Rightarrow} \subseteq \stackrel{\tau_>}{\Rightarrow} \mathcal{R}^\star \qquad (3)$$

$$\mathcal{R}^\star \stackrel{a}{\Rightarrow} \subseteq \stackrel{a}{\Rightarrow} \mathcal{R}^\star \qquad (4)$$

$$\mathcal{R}^\star \stackrel{\tau_>}{\Rightarrow} \text{ terminates} \qquad (5)$$

$$\stackrel{\tau_=}{\leftarrow}^{\star} \mathcal{R} \subseteq \mathcal{R} \stackrel{\hat{\tau}}{\Leftarrow} \qquad (6)$$

$$\stackrel{\tau}{\Leftarrow} \mathcal{R}^\star \subseteq \mathcal{R}^\star \stackrel{\hat{\tau}}{\Leftarrow} \qquad (7)$$

$$\stackrel{a}{\Leftarrow} \mathcal{R}^\star \subseteq \mathcal{R}^\star \stackrel{\hat{a}}{\Leftarrow} \qquad (8)$$

A simple induction and (*iv*) yields (1), we prove (2) and (3) simultaneously by a lexicographic induction, using the termination of $\stackrel{\tau}{\Rightarrow}$ and $\varphi(P, n)$: "for any Q, Q' such that $P\mathcal{R}^n Q$, if $Q \stackrel{\tau_=}{\rightarrow}^{\star} Q'$ then $P \stackrel{\hat{\tau}}{\Rightarrow} \mathcal{R}^\star Q'$, and if $Q \stackrel{\tau_>}{\Rightarrow} Q'$ then $P \stackrel{\tau_>}{\Rightarrow} \mathcal{R}^\star Q'$". The non-trivial cases are respectively depicted on the two diagrams below.

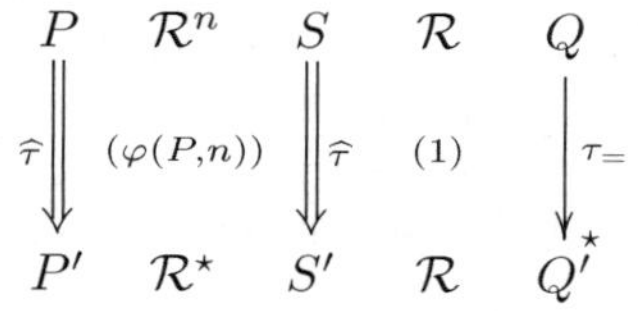

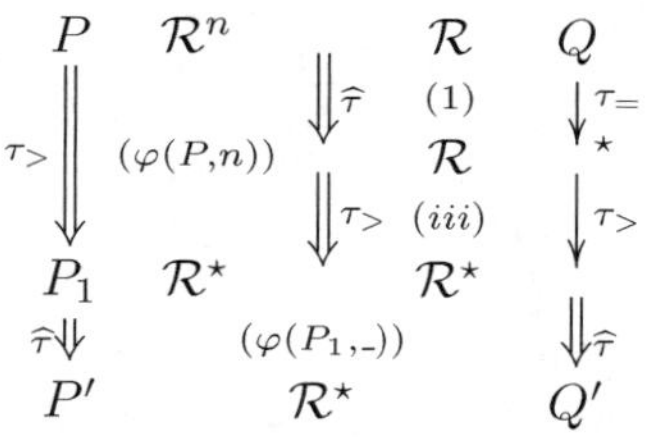

We prove (4) with another lexicographic induction, with the predicate $\psi(P, n)$: "for any Q' if $P\mathcal{R}^n \stackrel{a}{\Rightarrow} Q'$ then $P \stackrel{a}{\Rightarrow} \mathcal{R}^\star Q'$". Depending on the existence of a progressive silent transition before the visible action of the transition $Q \stackrel{a}{\Rightarrow} Q'$, we close the diagrams as depicted below.

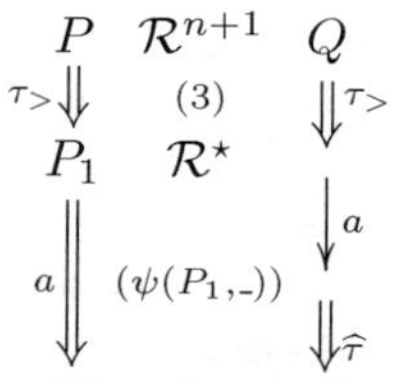

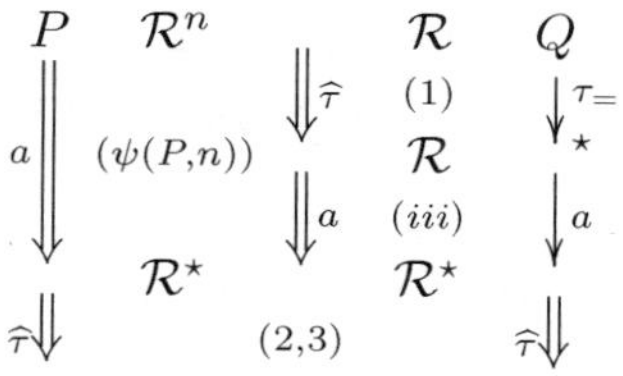

We obtain (5) by applying Lemma 2.5 to $\mathcal{R}^\star$ and (3). A simple induction and (*ii*) give (6). We show (7) with a lexicographic induction using the termination of $\mathcal{R}^\star \stackrel{\tau_>}{\Rightarrow}$ and the predicate $\Phi(P, n)$: "if $P\mathcal{R}^n Q$ and $P \stackrel{\alpha}{\Rightarrow} P'$ then $P'\mathcal{R}^\star \stackrel{\hat{\alpha}}{\Leftarrow} Q$".

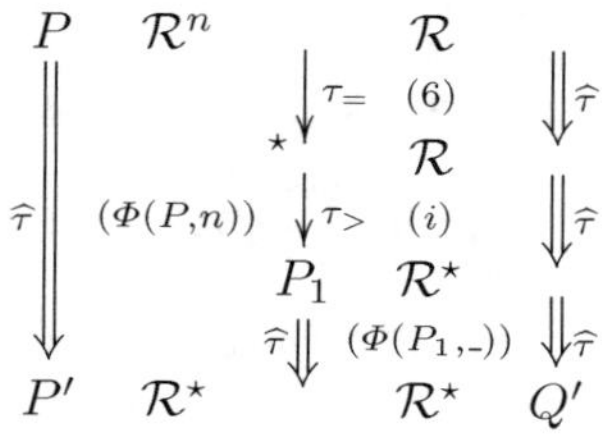

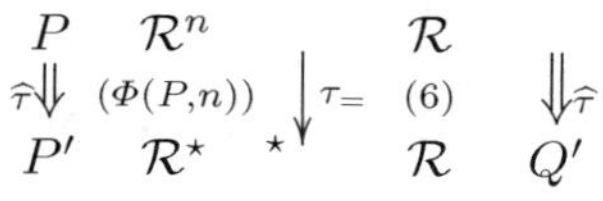

The proof of (8) follows the lines of (7). □

5 Concluding Remarks

We have proposed the new up to elaboration proof technique for bisimulation as an alternative to existing approaches. The proofs in this paper demonstrate how nontrivial termination arguments can be used to validate sophisticated proof techniques for bisimulation.

We have argued that up to elaboration offers advantages with respect to existing up-to techniques, in terms of expressiveness, flexibility or modularity. Our hope is that this technique can help addressing more complex weak bisimulation proofs. That it could be the case is suggested by the mathematical elegance of the framework we obtain, which opens the way for modular and incremental construction of proofs. This should nevertheless be confirmed by actual experiments in the study of systems involving manipulation of large bisimulation relations.

Several results in this paper suggest directions for future investigations. To enhance further our framework, it would be interesting to study how to integrate different kinds of methods in order to guarantee τ-termination, which is necessary for the results in Sect. 2. A possible approach would be to provide a measure together with the LTS, or to adopt syntactical criteria when the LTS is given by a calculus (a process algebra). Another interesting idea in this direction is given by type systems for termination. In Sect. 4, we proposed a way to handle the case of non terminating systems. We can however think of other approaches; in particular, we would like to study LTS where non-termination of $\xrightarrow{\tau}$ comes from cycles only, or where any state has a finite number of derivatives.

Finally, we would like to have a better understanding of the main problem of the setting of [7] (to which this paper proposes an alternative solution), namely the fact that controlled relations are not stable by union. An interesting direction would be to look for connections with the question of termination of the union of terminating rewrite systems, that has been widely studied in rewriting theory.

Acknowledgements. We are very thankful to Daniel Hirschkoff for his numerous comments and suggestions, and his great help during the redaction process. We would also like to thank an anonymous referee for pointing out an incorrect proof.

References

1. S. Arun-Kumar and M. Hennessy. An Efficiency Preorder for Processes. *Acta Informatica*, 29(9):737–760, 1992.
2. S. Arun-Kumar and V. Natarajan. Conformance: A Precongruence Close to Bisimilarity. In *Proc. Struct. in Concurrency Theory*, pages 55–68. Springer Verlag, 1995.
3. C. Fournet. *The Join-Calculus: a Calculus for Distributed Mobile Programming.* PhD thesis, Ecole Polytechnique, 1998.
4. J. Groote and M. Reniers. Algebraic Process Verification. In *Handbook of Process Algebra*, pages 1151–1208. Elsevier, 2001.
5. D. Hirschkoff, D. Pous, and D. Sangiorgi. A Correct Abstract Machine for Safe Ambients. In *Proc. COORD '05*, volume 3454 of *LNCS*. Springer Verlag, 2005.

6. U. Montanari and V. Sassone. Dynamic Congruence vs. Progressing Bisimulation for CCS. *Fundamenta Informaticae*, 16(1):171–199, 1992.
7. D. Pous. Up-to Techniques for Weak Bisimulation. In *Proc. 32th ICALP*, volume 3580 of *LNCS*, pages 730–741. Springer Verlag, 2005.
8. D. Pous. Weak Bisimulation up to Elaboration. Long version of this paper, with full proofs – available from `http://perso.ens-lyon.fr/damien.pous/upto`, 2006.
9. D. Sangiorgi. On the Bisimulation Proof Method. *Journal of Mathematical Structures in Computer Science*, 8:447–479, 1998.
10. D. Sangiorgi and R. Milner. The problem of "Weak Bisimulation up to". In *Proc. 3rd CONCUR*, volume 630 of *LNCS*, pages 32–46. Springer Verlag, 1992.
11. D. Sangiorgi and D. Walker. *The π-calculus: a Theory of Mobile Processes*. Cambridge University Press, 2001.

Generic Forward and Backward Simulations*

Ichiro Hasuo**

Institute for Computing and Information Sciences
Radboud University Nijmegen, The Netherlands
http://www.cs.ru.nl/~ichiro

Abstract. The technique of forward/backward simulations has been applied successfully in many distributed and concurrent applications. In this paper, however, we claim that the technique can actually have more genericity and mathematical clarity. We do so by identifying forward/backward simulations as lax/oplax morphisms of coalgebras. Starting from this observation, we present a systematic study of this generic notion of simulations. It is meant to be a generic version of the study by Lynch and Vaandrager, covering both non-deterministic and probabilistic systems. In particular we prove soundness and completeness results with respect to trace inclusion: the proof is by coinduction using the generic theory of traces developed by Jacobs, Sokolova and the author. By suitably instantiating our generic framework, one obtains the appropriate definition of forward/backward simulations for various kinds of systems, for which soundness and completeness come *for free*.

1 Introduction

The theory of forward/backward simulations for non-deterministic automata has been extensively studied, notably by Lynch and Vaandrager [12]. It has been applied successfully in many distributed and concurrent applications, described as transition systems. For example, in [9] trace-based anonymity properties for network protocols are proved by building backward simulations. The notions of forward/backward simulations are also extended to different kinds of state-based systems such as probabilistic ones [15].

In this paper we claim that this theory of forward/backward simulations can actually have more genericity and mathematical clarity. We do so by revealing a simple mathematical structure hidden behind various notions of simulations defined for different kinds of systems. The slogan is:

Forward/backward simulations are lax/oplax morphisms
of coalgebras in Kleisli categories.

* An extended version of this paper appears as [6].

** Part of this work was done during the author's stay at Research Center for Verification and Semantics, National Institute of Advanced Industrial Science and Technology (AIST), Japan. The author is grateful for the hospitality.

C. Baier and H. Hermanns (Eds.): CONCUR 2006, LNCS 4137, pp. 406–420, 2006.

Based on this observation, we aim at presenting a generic version of the systematic study [12]. The outcome is satisfactory. We employ the generic theory of traces in [5] and show:

– *Soundness.* Existence of a forward or backward simulation implies trace inclusion.
– *Completeness.* Trace inclusion implies existence of a certain kind of hybrid simulation, namely a backward-forward simulation.

The important point is that all these definitions and proofs are stated in abstract coalgebraic terms, hence come with ample genericity. In fact they are parametrized by:

– The type of branching. It can be either non-determinism (with a set of possible transitions) or probabilism (with a distribution over possible transitions).
– The type of transitions. For example, a context-free grammar can be considered as a state-based system—non-terminals as states—with non-deterministic branching. It has a different transition type from, say, LTS's: a CFG transits to a word over symbols and states, while an LTS transits to a pair of a symbol and a (next) state. Our result covers a wide variety of transition types.

Hence for each application from such a wide variety, one can obtain a definition of forward/backward simulations by instantiating our general framework with suitable parameters. Moreover one is assured that this definition is the *right* one: good properties such as soundness and completeness come for free. Therefore we expect abundant practical implication of this work.

Now let us take a completely different standpoint, namely that of a coalgebra-theorist. This work cultivates a new field of coalgebraic methods in computer science: coalgebras in a Kleisli category. The standard theory of coalgebras (e.g. [14]) is based in **Sets**, establishing the (successful) second row of the table. This paper, following the previous work [5], extends this table downwards.

base category	morphisms of coalgebras		coinduction gives
Sets	functional bisimulation		bisimilarity
Kleisli	lax $\cdots$ forward simulation oplax $\cdots$ backward simulation	[this paper]	trace semantics [5]

The paper is organized as follows. In Section 2 our basic (coalgebraic) setting is presented. State-based systems are formulated as coalgebras with explicit start states in Section 3. The key notion of generic forward/backward simulations is presented in Section 4. In Section 5 we recall the generic theory of coalgebraic traces from [5]. The materials of the previous two sections are combined in Section 6 to prove soundness and completeness. We conclude in Section 7.

2 Preliminaries

This section presents preliminaries from category theory and theory of coalgebras. They are put in an elementary and descriptive manner. For more details the reader is referred to [5].

In this paper we identify forward/backward simulations as lax/oplax morphisms of coalgebras in a Kleisli category $\mathcal{K}\ell(T)$ for a monad T on **Sets**. This observation is inspired by a series of work (stemming from [13]) on trace semantics for/via coalgebras: a Kleisli category is a suitable base category there. Our basic story is as follows.

We model a state-based system as a coalgebra $X \to TFX$ in **Sets**, with T a monad, F a functor and a distributive law $FT \Rightarrow TF$ implicit. The intuition is:

- a monad T describes the type of *branching* (non-determinism, probabilism, etc.) of the system;
- a functor F describes the *transition* type of the system, which determines the type of linear-time behavior (e.g. words over action symbols);
- a distributive law $FT \Rightarrow TF$ describes the way how T's effect of branching is distributed over the transition type represented by F.

It turns out that having $X \to TFX$ in **Sets** is equivalent to having a coalgebra $X \to \overline{F}X$ in the Kleisli category $\mathcal{K}\ell(T)$, where $\overline{F} : \mathcal{K}\ell(T) \to \mathcal{K}\ell(T)$ is a canonical lifting of $F : \mathbf{Sets} \to \mathbf{Sets}$ with $\overline{F}X = FX$. This lifting $\overline{F}$ is induced by the distributive law. To summarize:

- In modeling a system as a coalgebra $X \to TFX$, we separate the type of branching T from the transition type F.
- By moving from **Sets** to $\mathcal{K}\ell(T)$, this coalgebra becomes a coalgebra $X \to \overline{F}X$ for a functor $\overline{F}$—instead of a combination TF. Then we can start the usual coalgebraic business such as morphisms, final coalgebras and coinduction.

2.1 Monads for Types of Branching

A *monad* T on **Sets** is an endofunctor on **Sets** equipped with two kinds of functions: for each set X, the *unit* $X \stackrel{\eta_X}{\to} TX$ and the *multiplication* $TTX \stackrel{\mu_X}{\to} TX$. These functions must satisfy certain coherence conditions.

In coalgebraic settings, it is shown in [5] that monads with a certain order structure are suitable for modeling state-based systems with branching, especially for analyzing their trace semantics. We are interested in such monads in this paper. We have two examples:

- The *powerset monad* $\mathcal{P}$, modeling the *non-deterministic* branching.
- The *subdistribution monad* $\mathcal{D}$, modeling the *probabilistic* branching. For a set X, $\mathcal{D}X$ is given by: $\mathcal{D}X = \{\, \xi : X \to [0,1] \mid \sum_{x \in X} \xi(x) \le 1 \,\}$. Here ξ is called a *probability subdistribution* over X. It is "sub" because the sum of all probabilities is not necessarily equal to 1.

We take the subdistribution monad $\mathcal{D}$, instead of the distribution monad $\mathcal{D}_{=1}X = \{\xi \mid \sum_x \xi(x) = 1\}$, since the latter lacks a suitable order structure. This point is elaborated in Section 2.3.

2.2 Kleisli Categories for Monads

For each monad T on **Sets**, we construct the *Kleisli category* for T, denoted by $\mathcal{K}\ell(T)$, in the following way. The crucial part is that an arrow $X \to Y$ in $\mathcal{K}\ell(T)$ is actually a function $X \to TY$ in **Sets**.

- Objects in $\mathcal{K}\ell(T)$ are the same as in **Sets**: they are just sets.
- An arrow $X \to Y$ in $\mathcal{K}\ell(T)$ is a function $X \to TY$ in **Sets**.
- Composition of arrows is defined using multiplication $\mu_X : TTX \to TX$.
- The identity arrow $X \stackrel{\mathrm{id}}{\to} X$ in $\mathcal{K}\ell(T)$ is the unit $X \stackrel{\eta_X}{\to} TX$ in **Sets**.

This $\mathcal{K}\ell(T)$ will be our base category. Notice that when we write $X \to Y$ in $\mathcal{K}\ell(T)$, a branching nature of this arrow is implicit because it is a function $X \to TY$.

For the monads $\mathcal{P}$ and $\mathcal{D}$ of our interest, we shall describe more details of their Kleisli categories.

The category $\mathcal{K}\ell(\mathcal{P})$ is in fact isomorphic to the category **Rel** of sets and relations. That is, an arrow $X \to Y$ in $\mathcal{K}\ell(\mathcal{P})$ is a relation between X and Y via the standard "relation-into-function" trick: given a function $f : X \to \mathcal{P}Y$ in **Sets** we obtain a relation $R_f = \{(x, y) \mid y \in f(x)\}$. In particular, composition of arrows in $\mathcal{K}\ell(\mathcal{P})$ is given by the relational composition $S \circ R = \{(x, z) \mid \exists y.\, xRy \wedge ySz\}$ of the corresponding relations. The identity arrow id_X is the diagonal relation $\{(x, x) \mid x \in X\}$.

In $\mathcal{K}\ell(\mathcal{D})$ an arrow $X \to Y$ assigns to each $x \in X$ a probability subdistribution over Y. The identity arrow $X \stackrel{\mathrm{id}}{\to} X$ maps $x \in X$ to the so-called *Dirac distribution* for x. The composition of arrows $X \stackrel{f}{\to} Y \stackrel{g}{\to} Z$ in $\mathcal{K}\ell(\mathcal{D})$ is such that: for $x \in X$ and $z \in Z$, $(g \circ f)(x)(z) = \sum_{y \in Y} f(x)(y) \cdot g(y)(z)$.

2.3 Order-Enriched Structure of Kleisli Categories

The notion of branching—such as non-determinism and probabilism—come with natural notions of order. For non-determinism we have the inclusion order between sets of possible transitions. For probabilism a subdistribution ξ is bigger than ψ if, to each possible transition, ξ assigns bigger probability than ψ does.

These natural orders accompanying the notion of branching appear in our setting as a $\mathbf{DCpo}_\perp$-enriched structure of Kleisli categories. This order structure is fully exploited in the definition of forward/backward simulations: a system simulates another one if it has *more* behavior.

For $T = \mathcal{P}$ or $\mathcal{D}$, the Kleisli category $\mathcal{K}\ell(T)$ is $\mathbf{DCpo}_\perp$*-enriched*. This means:

- For any pair of sets X and Y, the set $\mathrm{Hom}_{\mathcal{K}\ell(T)}(X, Y)$ of the arrows from X to Y has a dcpo structure $\sqsubseteq$ with bottom. In particular we can take the supremum $\bigsqcup_{n<\omega} f_n$ of an increasing chain $f_0 \sqsubseteq f_1 \sqsubseteq \cdots$ of arrows, and there is the minimum arrow $\perp_{X,Y} : X \to Y$.
- Composition of arrows is continuous: $g \circ (\bigsqcup_n f_n) = \bigsqcup_n (g \circ f_n)$ and $(\bigsqcup_n f_n) \circ h = \bigsqcup_n (f_n \circ h)$. In particular composition is monotone.

Indeed, for $T = \mathcal{P}$ or $\mathcal{D}$, a set TY has a $\mathbf{DCpo}_\bot$ structure $\sqsubseteq_{TY}$. This extends to the order between arrows in $\mathcal{K}\ell(T)$ in a pointwise manner: for $f, g : X \rightrightarrows Y$, $f \sqsubseteq g$ if for each $x \in X$, $f(x) \sqsubseteq_{TY} g(x)$.

We need the minimum arrow $\bot_{X,Y} : X \to Y$ in $\mathcal{K}\ell(T)$ for the trace semantics results in Section 5. It is not available for the distribution monad $\mathcal{D}_{=1}$: that is why we use the subdistribution monad $\mathcal{D}$ instead.

2.4 Shapely Functors for Transition Types

We restrict a functor F—which models the transition type of a system—to be *shapely*. The reason to do so is: we know the results on coalgebraic trace semantics in Section 5 hold for shapely functors,[1] and also in most of the interesting examples we can take as F a shapely functor. The family of shapely functors is almost as broad as that of polynomial functors: it is defined inductively by the following BNF notation.

$$F, G, F_i ::= \mathrm{id} \mid \Sigma \mid F \times G \mid \textstyle\coprod_{i \in I} F_i \enspace ,$$

where Σ denotes the constant functor into an arbitrary set Σ, and I is an arbitrary index set. Here are some virtue of shapely functors which we will exploit.

- An initial F-algebra exists, obtained via the initial sequence of length ω.
- For $T = \mathcal{P}$ or $\mathcal{D}$, there is a canonical distributive law $FT \Rightarrow TF$. Equivalently, F has a canonical lifting $\overline{F}$ on $\mathcal{K}\ell(T)$. On objects $\overline{F}X = FX$, and on arrows $\overline{F}$'s action is what one might think of at first sight.

3 Coalgebraic Modeling of Systems

In this section we model a wide variety of branching state-based systems as what we call (T, F)-*systems*. A (T, F)-system is a $\overline{F}$-coalgebra in the Kleisli category $\mathcal{K}\ell(T)$ plus explicit start states. This definition of (T, F)-systems will be motivated by several illustrating examples.

Two parameters in the notion of (T, F)-systems are: T is a monad, being either $\mathcal{P}$ or $\mathcal{D}$, representing the branching type; F is a shapely functor describing the transition type. In the sequel we assume that T and F are such.

Definition 3.1 ((T, F)-systems). A (T, F)-*system* is a pair of arrows

$$1 \xrightarrow{\ s\ } X \xrightarrow{\ c\ } \overline{F}X \qquad \text{in the Kleisli category } \mathcal{K}\ell(T).$$

That is, a pair of functions $(s : 1 \to TX,\ c : X \to TFX)$ in **Sets**, recalling that $\overline{F}X = FX$. The arrow s is called the *start states map*, and the $\overline{F}$-coalgebra c is called the *dynamics*. The set X is called the *state space*. The only element of the singleton 1 appearing here[2] is denoted by $*$.

[1] This does not say that those results hold exclusively for shapely functors.

[2] In this paper we will have singletons with different computational meanings. Accordingly, their only elements will be denoted by different symbols.

In most literature on coalgebras the start state (or the set of start states) is left implicit. However in our setting we need to have them explicit. See [6, Appendix 1] for further discussion.

Example 3.2 (Non-deterministic automata). Let us take the powerset monad $\mathcal{P}$ for T, hence non-deterministic branching. For an endofunctor F we take $1 + \Sigma \times \_$, where $1 = \{\checkmark\}$ is a singleton and Σ is a non-empty set of symbols. A (T, F)-system then is a pair of functions in **Sets**,

$$\left(1 \xrightarrow{s} \mathcal{P}X, \quad X \xrightarrow{c} \mathcal{P}(1 + \Sigma \times X) \right) ,$$

which should be interpreted as follows. The subset $s(*)$ of X is the set of possible start states. For a state $x \in X$, the set $c(x)$ contains $\checkmark$ if x is an accepting state; it contains a tuple (a, x') if there is a (possible) transition $x \xrightarrow{a} x'$. In this way a (T, F)-system for these T and F is thought of as a non-deterministic automaton.

Example 3.3 (Probabilistic automata). Let us take $T = \mathcal{D}$ instead of $\mathcal{P}$ in the previous example. A (T, F)-system is a pair of functions in **Sets**:

$$\left(1 \xrightarrow{s} \mathcal{D}X, \quad X \xrightarrow{c} \mathcal{D}(1 + \Sigma \times X) \right) .$$

This is understood as follows. The subdistribution $s(*)$ over X represents the probability with which each state $x \in X$ is chosen as a starting state. An execution successfully terminates at x with the probability $c(x)(\checkmark)$; a transition $x \xrightarrow{a} x'$ is made with the probability $c(x)(a, x')$. Such a system is called a *generative probabilistic transition system* [17,16]: in this paper we shall call it simply a *probabilistic automaton*. Here is an example of a probabilistic automaton.

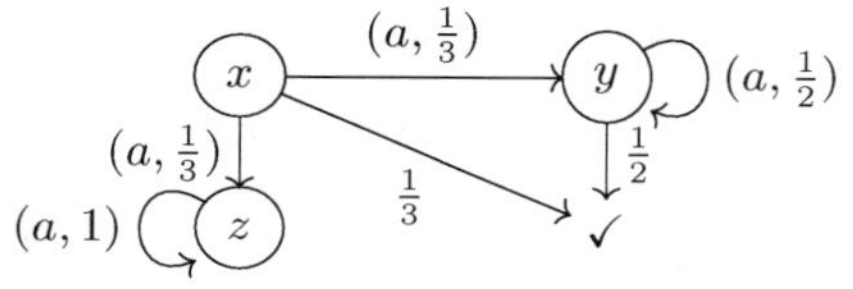

with start states: $\begin{bmatrix} x \mapsto 1/3 \\ y \mapsto 2/3 \end{bmatrix}$.

This is modeled as the following $(\mathcal{D}, 1 + \Sigma \times \_)$-system.

- The start state map $1 \xrightarrow{s} \mathcal{D}X$ is such that $s(*) = \begin{bmatrix} x \mapsto 1/3 \\ y \mapsto 2/3 \end{bmatrix}$, and
- the dynamics coalgebra $X \xrightarrow{c} \mathcal{D}(1 + \Sigma \times X)$ is such that $c(x) = [\ (a, y) \mapsto 1/3,\ (a, z) \mapsto 1/3,\ \checkmark \mapsto 1/3\ ]$, etc.

Remark 3.4 (Systems with both non-determ./probabilistic branching). Probabilistic I/O automata [18] are another kind of well-studied models for state-based systems. One of their features is that they are equipped with both non-deterministic and probabilistic branching. Unfortunately, we are yet to find a suitable monad to model this combined branching: that is why probabilistic I/O automata are currently out of the scope of our generic framework.

Context-free grammars (without finiteness assumptions) can be also modeled as (T, F)-systems with $T = \mathcal{P}$ and a suitable F (see [4]).

The notion of morphisms of coalgebras extends to (T, F)-systems in an obvious manner [6].

4   Forward/Backward Simulations, Coalgebraically

This section presents the key notions of this paper: generic forward, backward and backward-forward simulations. The intuition about order accompanying the notion of "branching"—now substantiated as the $\mathbf{DCpo}_\perp$-enriched structure of a Kleisli category—is fully exploited here.

In this section again $T = \mathcal{P}$ or $\mathcal{D}$, and F is a shapely functor.

Definition 4.1 (Forward simulation). Let $1 \xrightarrow{s} X \xrightarrow{c} FX$ and $1 \xrightarrow{t} Y \xrightarrow{d} FY$ be (T, F)-systems, presented in $\mathcal{K}\ell(T)$. A *forward simulation* from (t, d) to (s, c) is an arrow $f : X \to Y$ in $\mathcal{K}\ell(T)$ such that:

$$t \sqsubseteq f \circ s \quad \text{and} \quad d \circ f \sqsubseteq \overline{F}f \circ c \ ,$$

where $\sqsubseteq$ refers to the order available due to the $\mathbf{DCpo}_\perp$-enriched structure of the Kleisli category. Diagrammatically presented,

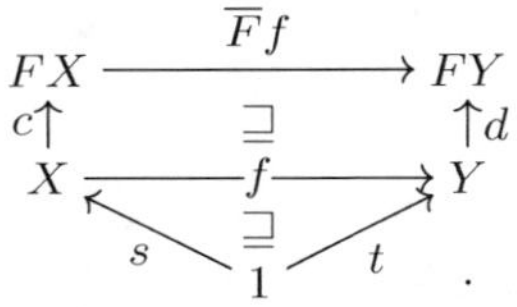

$$
\begin{array}{ccc}
FX & \xrightarrow{\ \overline{F}f\ } & FY \\
c\uparrow & \sqsupseteq & \uparrow d \\
X & \xrightarrow{\quad f \quad} & Y \\
& {}_s\!\!\searrow \ \ \overset{\sqsupseteq}{\underset{1}{\ }} \ \nearrow{}_t &
\end{array}
\tag{1}
$$

In other words, a forward simulation is a *lax morphism* from (s, c) to (t, d).

We write $(t, d) \sqsubseteq_{\mathbf{F}} (s, c)$ if there is a forward simulation from (t, d) to (s, c).

The use of lax morphisms in categorical accounts of simulation/refinement is found in [10]. In a coalgebraic setting, [2] uses lax morphisms to investigate order-enriched version of bisimulation. However, to the best of our knowledge, we are the first to notice the significance of lax morphisms in Kleisli categories.

The dual notion, with the order of arrows opposed, has also a significant computational meaning.

Definition 4.2 (Backward simulation). Let $1 \xrightarrow{s} X \xrightarrow{c} FX$ and $1 \xrightarrow{t} Y \xrightarrow{d} FY$ be (T, F)-systems, presented in $\mathcal{K}\ell(T)$. A *backward simulation* from (s, c) to (t, d) is an arrow $f : X \to Y$ in $\mathcal{K}\ell(T)$ such that: $f \circ s \sqsubseteq t$ and $\overline{F}f \circ c \sqsubseteq d \circ f$.

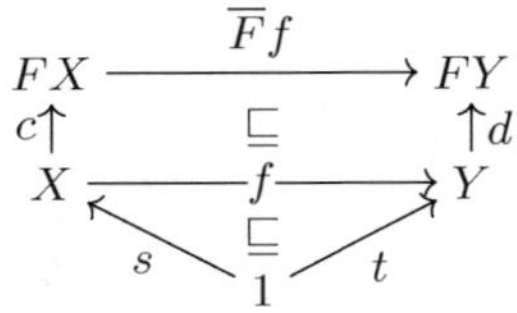

$$
\begin{array}{ccc}
FX & \xrightarrow{\ \overline{F}f\ } & FY \\
c\uparrow & \sqsubseteq & \uparrow d \\
X & \xrightarrow{\quad f \quad} & Y \\
& {}_s\!\!\searrow \ \ \overset{\sqsubseteq}{\underset{1}{\ }} \ \nearrow{}_t &
\end{array}
\tag{2}
$$

Hence a backward simulation is an *oplax morphism* of systems.

We write $(s, c) \sqsubseteq_{\mathbf{B}} (t, d)$ if there is a backward simulation from (s, c) to (t, d).

Remark 4.3. Note the direction of forward/backward simulations and lax/oplax morphisms. In general, the system which appears on the smaller sides of inequalities is simulated by the other one. For example, a lax morphism from (s,c) to (t,d) in Diagram (1) is a forward simulation *from* (t,d) *to* (s,c), through which (s,c) *forward-simulates* (t,d); hence $(t,d) \sqsubseteq_{\mathbf{F}} (s,c)$.

Let us be convinced of these abstract definitions by looking at examples.

Example 4.4 (Non-deterministic automata). In the setting of Example3.2, an arrow $X \to Y$ in $\mathcal{K}\ell(T)$ is a relation R from X to Y since $\mathcal{K}\ell(\mathcal{P}) \cong \mathbf{Rel}$. The previous definitions boil down as follows: R is a forward simulation from (t,d) to (s,c) if and only if it satisfies the following conditions.

$$\begin{array}{rcl} y \in \mathsf{start}_{(t,d)} & \Longrightarrow & \exists x \in \mathsf{start}_{(s,c)}.\quad xRy \ , \\ xRy \ \wedge \ y \to_d \checkmark & \Longrightarrow & x \to_c \checkmark \ , \\ xRy \ \wedge \ y \stackrel{a}{\to}_d y' & \Longrightarrow & \exists x' \in X. \quad (\, x \stackrel{a}{\to}_c x' \ \wedge \ x'Ry' \,) \ , \end{array}$$

where $\mathsf{start}_{(s,c)}$ denotes the set $s(*)$. These conditions are much like those in the standard literature [12]. Notice in particular that the third condition is of the following familiar form, working "forwards".

$$\begin{array}{ccc} x & & \\ R \,\vdots & & \\ y & \stackrel{a}{\longrightarrow} & y' \end{array} \quad \Longrightarrow \quad \begin{array}{ccc} x & \stackrel{a}{\longrightarrow} & \exists x' \\ R \,\vdots & & \vdots\, R \\ y & \stackrel{a}{\longrightarrow} & y' \end{array}$$

Similarly, a relation R from X to Y is a backward simulation from (s,c) to (t,d) if and only if:

$$\begin{array}{rcl} x \in \mathsf{start}_{(s,c)} \ \wedge \ xRy & \Longrightarrow & y \in \mathsf{start}_{(t,d)} \ , \\ x \to_c \checkmark & \Longrightarrow & \exists y \in Y. \quad (\, xRy \ \wedge \ y \to_d \checkmark \,) \ , \\ x \stackrel{a}{\to}_c x' \ \wedge \ x'Ry' & \Longrightarrow & \exists y \in Y. \quad (\, xRy \ \wedge \ y \stackrel{a}{\to}_d y' \,) \ . \end{array}$$

The third condition here works "backwards" in the following way.

$$\begin{array}{ccc} x & \stackrel{a}{\longrightarrow} & x' \\ & & \vdots\, R \\ & & y' \end{array} \quad \Longrightarrow \quad \begin{array}{ccc} x & \stackrel{a}{\longrightarrow} & x' \\ R \,\vdots & & \vdots\, R \\ \exists y & \stackrel{a}{\longrightarrow} & y' \end{array}$$

Example 4.5 (Probabilistic automata). In the setting of Example 3.3, the abstract Definition 4.1 is instantiated as follows: a function $f : X \to \mathcal{D}Y$ in **Sets** is a forward simulation from (t,d) to (s,c) if and only if:

$$\begin{array}{rcl} t(*)(y) & \leq & \sum_{x \in X} s(*)(x) \cdot f(x)(y) \ , \\ \sum_{y \in Y} f(x)(y) \cdot d(y)(\checkmark) & \leq & c(x)(\checkmark) \ , \\ \sum_{y \in Y} f(x)(y) \cdot d(y)(a,y') & \leq & \sum_{x' \in X} c(x)(a,x') \cdot f(x')(y') \ . \end{array} \tag{3}$$

It is also straightforward to instantiate Definition 4.2 of backward simulations.

One may wonder why we can call such f a forward simulation, although one can notice that a "forward" argument similar to the previous example is going on. The point is that, however, by the abstract theorems in the following sections we know that this definition (3) of forward simulations—derived from the coalgebraic definition—satisfies desirable properties such as soundness/completeness with respect to trace inclusion.

We define a simulation from one probabilistic system to another to be a function $X \to \mathcal{D}Y$. This is different from the approach in [7]: there a simulation is always a relation between state spaces X and Y.

By suitably instantiating the generic definitions, we also obtain appropriate notions of simulations for context-free grammars.

Forward and backward simulations will be shown to be sound with respect to trace inclusion. But they in general fail to be complete. Instead, a completeness result is proved for a certain combination of forward and backward simulations (*hybrid* simulations), as is done in [12].

Definition 4.6 (Backward-forward simulations). Let (s, c) and (t, d) be (T, F)-systems. A *backward-forward simulation* from (s, c) to (t, d) is a pair of

- a backward simulation f from (s, c) to an intermediate system (r, b), and
- a forward simulation g from the intermediate system (r, b) to (t, d).

Diagrammatically presented in $\mathcal{K}\ell(T)$ (note the direction of arrows),

$$\begin{array}{ccccc} FX & \xrightarrow{\overline{F}f} & FU & \xleftarrow{\overline{F}g} & FY \\ c\uparrow & \sqsubseteq & b\uparrow & \sqsubseteq & \uparrow d \\ X & \xrightarrow{f} & U & \xleftarrow{g} & Y \\ & {}^{s}\nwarrow \;\sqsubseteq & r\uparrow & \sqsubseteq\; \nearrow^{t} & \\ & & 1 & & \end{array} \qquad (4)$$

We write $(s, c) \sqsubseteq_{\mathbf{BF}} (t, d)$ if there is a backward-forward simulation from (s, c) to (t, d). Obviously,

$$(s, c) \sqsubseteq_{\mathbf{BF}} (t, d) \quad \Longleftrightarrow \quad \exists (r, b). \;\; \big(\, (s, c) \sqsubseteq_{\mathbf{B}} (r, b) \;\wedge\; (r, b) \sqsubseteq_{\mathbf{F}} (t, d) \, \big) \; .$$

Remark 4.7 (Forward-backward simulations). It is straightforward to define the notion of *forward-backward simulations* and the relation $\sqsubseteq_{\mathbf{FB}}$, as a suitable dual of Definition 4.6. This is done in [12] for a restricted class of non-deterministic systems. In the same paper $\sqsubseteq_{\mathbf{BF}}$ and $\sqsubseteq_{\mathbf{FB}}$ are shown to coincide.

However we have not yet found the coincidence of $\sqsubseteq_{\mathbf{BF}}$ and $\sqsubseteq_{\mathbf{FB}}$ in general: in the light of Theorem 6.2, it seems that $\sqsubseteq_{\mathbf{BF}}$ is the more fundamental notion. The coincidence for non-deterministic systems in [12] may be because $\mathcal{K}\ell(\mathcal{P})$ is self-dual, i.e. $\mathcal{K}\ell(\mathcal{P}) \cong \mathcal{K}\ell(\mathcal{P})^{\mathrm{op}}$. Details are yet to be elaborated.

5 Finite Trace Semantics Via Coinduction

In this paper we take (finite) traces as our semantics for systems. It is with respect to trace semantics that soundness and completeness of forward/backward simulations are shown. This section establishes the basics of trace semantics for systems by revisiting our previous work [5]. The main points are:

- a final coalgebra in the Kleisli category $\mathcal{K}\ell(T)$ is (interestingly) induced by an initial algebra in **Sets**;
- the principle of coinduction, when employed in $\mathcal{K}\ell(T)$, yields finite trace semantics for branching systems.

We also cite a fact from [2] about an order-theoretic property of a final coalgebra. Again in this section a monad T is $\mathcal{P}$ or $\mathcal{D}$ and F is a shapely functor.

The following result identifies a final coalgebra in the Kleisli categories.

Theorem 5.1 (Main theorem of [5]). *Let $\alpha\colon FA \xrightarrow{\cong} A$ be an initial F-algebra in* **Sets**.

1. *An initial $\overline{F}$-algebra in $\mathcal{K}\ell(T)$ is induced by α as $\eta_A \circ \alpha : FA \xrightarrow{\cong} A$ in $\mathcal{K}\ell(T)$.*
2. *In $\mathcal{K}\ell(T)$, an initial $\overline{F}$-algebra and a final $\overline{F}$-coalgebra coincide. The latter is given as follows. We shall denote this coalgebraic structure map by ζ.*

$$\zeta = (\eta_A \circ \alpha)^{-1} = \eta_{FA} \circ \alpha^{-1} : A \xrightarrow{\cong} FA \qquad \text{in } \mathcal{K}\ell(T) . \qquad \square$$

As a corollary we obtain the final coalgebra semantics for an $\overline{F}$-coalgebra. Recall that such a coalgebra is a dynamics of a (T, F)-system.

Corollary 5.2 (Trace semantics for coalgebras, [5]). *Given an $\overline{F}$-coalgebra $X \xrightarrow{c} FX$ in $\mathcal{K}\ell(T)$, there exists a unique morphism tr_c which makes the following diagram commute. Here $\alpha : FA \xrightarrow{\cong} A$ is an initial F-algebra in* **Sets**.

$$\begin{array}{ccc} FX & \xrightarrow{\overline{F}(\mathsf{tr}_c)} & FA \\ c\uparrow & & \cong\uparrow\zeta \text{ (final)} \\ X & \xrightarrow[\mathsf{tr}_c]{} & A \end{array} \qquad (5)$$

$\square$

The induced map $\mathsf{tr}_c : X \to A$ in $\mathcal{K}\ell(T)$, i.e. $\mathsf{tr}_c : X \to TA$ in **Sets**, in fact becomes what is usually called the finite trace map: it assigns to each state its "trace" in a suitable sense. The following examples show that the commutation of Diagram (5) actually amounts to standard and natural recursive definition of finite trace maps.

Example 5.3 (Non-deterministic automata). In the setting of Example3.2, an initial F-algebra in **Sets** is carried by finite lists, or words, over Σ.

$$1 + \Sigma \times \Sigma^* \xrightarrow[\cong]{[\mathsf{nil}, \mathsf{cons}]} \Sigma^*$$

Now Diagram (5) commutes if and only if the function $\mathsf{tr}_c : X \to \mathcal{P}(\Sigma^*)$ satisfies the following conditions. For each $a \in \Sigma$ and $\sigma \in \Sigma^*$.

$$\begin{array}{rcl} \langle\rangle \in \mathsf{tr}_c(x) & \iff & x \to \checkmark\ , \\ a \cdot \sigma \in \mathsf{tr}_c(x) & \iff & \exists x' \in X.\ \ \big(\, x \stackrel{a}{\to} x' \ \wedge\ \sigma \in \mathsf{tr}_c(x')\,\big)\ . \end{array}$$

This is the standard recursive (or corecursive, if you like) definition of the *accepted languages* of non-deterministic automata. The language $\mathsf{tr}_c(x) \subseteq \Sigma^*$ is the set of all the linear-time behavior of x which eventually terminates within a finite number of steps (hence the name *finite* trace).

Example 5.4 (Probabilistic automata). Let us look at the example of a probabilistic automaton in Example 3.3. What is the "trace" of the state x of this system? A natural answer, as suggested in [8], is the probability subdistribution over lists on Σ:

$$\langle\rangle \mapsto \frac{1}{3}, \quad a \mapsto \frac{1}{3}\cdot\frac{1}{2}, \quad aa \mapsto \frac{1}{3}\cdot\frac{1}{2}\cdot\frac{1}{2}, \quad \ldots, \quad a^n \mapsto \frac{1}{3}\cdot\left(\frac{1}{2}\right)^{n-1}\cdot\frac{1}{2}, \quad \ldots \tag{6}$$

This is explained as follows. For the state x to output the list aa, it has to take the path of transitions: $x \stackrel{a}{\to} y \stackrel{a}{\to} y \to \checkmark$. This path occurs with the probability $\frac{1}{3}\cdot\frac{1}{2}\cdot\frac{1}{2}$.

This notion of "probabilistic trace" is again obtained via coinduction in the Kleisli category. Let us instantiate Diagram (5) with T and F in Example 3.3. The commutativity of the diagram amounts to the following (co)recursive definition of a function $\mathsf{tr}_c : X \to \mathcal{D}(\Sigma^*)$:

$$\mathsf{tr}_c(x) = \begin{bmatrix} \langle\rangle & \mapsto & c(x)(\checkmark) \\ a\cdot\sigma & \mapsto & \sum_{y\in X} c(x)(a,y)\cdot \mathsf{tr}_c(y)(\sigma) \end{bmatrix} .$$

Here the probability $c(x)(a,y) \cdot \mathsf{tr}_c(y)(\sigma)$ is for the event that x makes an a-move to y and then y yields the list σ as its trace. Taking the sum over all the possible successors y of x, we get a natural recursive definition of the probability with which x yields $a \cdot \sigma$ as its trace.

As an additional remark we point out that the subdistribution (6) sums up only to $2/3$. The remaining $1/3$ is for the path $x \stackrel{a}{\to} z \stackrel{a}{\to} z \stackrel{a}{\to} \cdots$: the probability for a^ω, or *livelock*. This entry $a^\omega \mapsto 1/3$ is absent in $\mathsf{tr}_c(x)$ because $\mathsf{tr}_c : X \to \mathcal{D}(\Sigma^*)$ is the *finite* trace. This also demonstrates why we use the subdistribution monad $\mathcal{D}$ instead of the distribution monad $\mathcal{D}_{=1}$: although the system can be described using $\mathcal{D}_{=1}$, we do not get tr_c of the type $X \to \mathcal{D}_{=1}(\Sigma^*)$.

Example 5.5 (Context-free grammar, [4]). Take $T = \mathcal{P}$ and a suitable F for context-free grammars. Then the trace map tr_c assigns to each non-terminal x the set of finite-depth parse trees generated by the context-free grammar c starting from x.

From a different point of view, the previous examples are seen as proofs that standard recursive definitions uniquely determine trace maps, due to the finality result in Corollary 5.2.

The trace map tr_c, being a morphism of coalgebras, automatically becomes a lax morphism of coalgebras. It is in fact characterized as the biggest one.

Proposition 5.6 (Trace map as the biggest lax morphism) *In the situation of Diagram (5), the trace map* tr_c *is the biggest one among the lax coalgebra morphisms from* c *to the final* ζ.

Dually, the trace map tr_c *is the smallest one among the oplax coalgebra morphisms from* c *to the final* ζ.

Proof. Although the proposition follows from a general result [2, Proposition 6.7], in this specific setting of a Kleisli category we can give another proof. It does not depend on the local continuity of $\overline{F}$ but only on its local monotonicity. This alternative proof is found in [6, Appendix 2]. □

So far the trace map induced by coinduction gives the semantics for a single state of a coalgebra. This is extended to the semantics of a (T, F)-system—a coalgebra with explicit start states—in the obvious way.

Definition 5.7 (Finite trace semantics of (T, F)-systems). Given a (T, F)-system $1 \xrightarrow{s} X \xrightarrow{c} FX$ in $\mathcal{K}\ell(T)$, its *finite trace* (or just *trace*) $\mathrm{tr}_{(s,c)}$ is the following composite in $\mathcal{K}\ell(T)$.

$$\begin{array}{ccc} FX & \overset{\overline{F}(\mathrm{tr}_c)}{\dashrightarrow} & FA \\ c\uparrow & & \cong\uparrow\zeta \\ X & \overset{\mathrm{tr}_c}{\dashrightarrow} & A \\ s\uparrow & \nearrow_{\mathrm{tr}_{(s,c)}} & \\ 1 & & \end{array}$$

One can readily show that a morphism of systems preserves trace semantics.

6 Soundness and Completeness Theorems

In the last two sections we have built up the notions of (and some results on) forward/backward simulations and trace semantics, with a high level of genericity and abstraction. In this section we relate those materials—with the same genericity and abstraction—by proving soundness of $\sqsubseteq_{\mathbf{F}}, \sqsubseteq_{\mathbf{B}}, \sqsubseteq_{\mathbf{BF}}$ and completeness of $\sqsubseteq_{\mathbf{BF}}$ with respect to trace inclusion. This is the main technical result of this paper.

In the rest of this section we assume $1 \xrightarrow{s} X \xrightarrow{c} FX$ and $1 \xrightarrow{t} Y \xrightarrow{d} FY$ to be (T, F)-systems, where $T = \mathcal{P}$ or $\mathcal{D}$ and F is shapely.

Theorem 6.1 (Soundness of $\sqsubseteq_{\mathbf{F}}, \sqsubseteq_{\mathbf{B}}, \sqsubseteq_{\mathbf{BF}}$).

$$\begin{array}{llcl} \mathit{1.} & (s,c) \sqsubseteq_{\mathbf{F}} (t,d) & \Longrightarrow & \mathrm{tr}_{(s,c)} \sqsubseteq \mathrm{tr}_{(t,d)}\ , \\ \mathit{2.} & (s,c) \sqsubseteq_{\mathbf{B}} (t,d) & \Longrightarrow & \mathrm{tr}_{(s,c)} \sqsubseteq \mathrm{tr}_{(t,d)}\ , \\ \mathit{3.} & (s,c) \sqsubseteq_{\mathbf{BF}} (t,d) & \Longrightarrow & \mathrm{tr}_{(s,c)} \sqsubseteq \mathrm{tr}_{(t,d)}\ . \end{array}$$

Proof. 1. By definition of $\sqsubseteq_{\mathbf{F}}$ we have a forward simulation $f : Y \to X$. In particular we have in $\mathcal{K}\ell(T)$,

$$
\begin{array}{ccccc}
FY & \xrightarrow{\ \overline{F}f\ } & FX & \dashrightarrow^{\ \overline{F}(\mathsf{tr}_c)\ } & FA \\
{\scriptstyle d}\uparrow & \sqsupseteq & {\scriptstyle c}\uparrow & = & \cong\uparrow{\scriptstyle \zeta}\ (\text{final}) \\
Y & \xrightarrow{\ f\ } & X & \dashrightarrow_{\ \mathsf{tr}_c\ } & A
\end{array}
$$

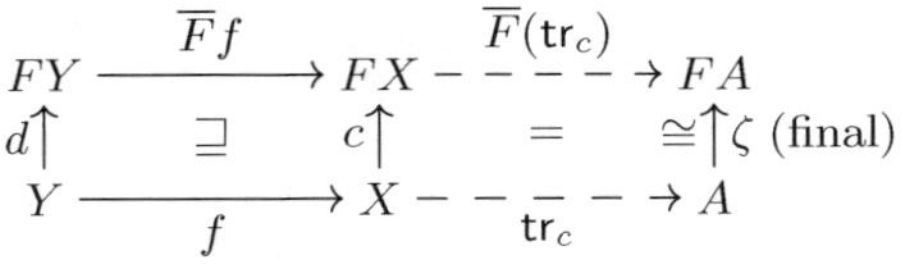

where the coinduction diagram appears on the right. This shows that the arrow $\mathsf{tr}_c \circ f$ is a lax coalgebra morphism from d to the final coalgebra. Since the trace map is the biggest lax coalgebra morphism (Proposition 5.6), we have $\mathsf{tr}_c \circ f \sqsubseteq \mathsf{tr}_d$. This inequality is combined with f's condition on start states.

$$
\mathsf{tr}_{(s,c)} \ = \ \mathsf{tr}_c \circ s \ \sqsubseteq \ \mathsf{tr}_c \circ f \circ t \ \sqsubseteq \ \mathsf{tr}_d \circ t \ = \ \mathsf{tr}_{(t,d)}
$$

This proves 1. Similar arguments prove 2.

3. The relation $\sqsubseteq_{\mathbf{BF}}$ is a relational composition $\sqsubseteq_{\mathbf{F}} \circ \sqsubseteq_{\mathbf{B}}$. We use 1. and 2. of the theorem and transitivity of the order $\sqsubseteq$ between arrows $1 \rightrightarrows A$. □

Completeness—the converse of the soundness result above—does not hold for $\sqsubseteq_{\mathbf{F}}, \sqsubseteq_{\mathbf{B}}$ but does hold for the weaker notion of $\sqsubseteq_{\mathbf{BF}}$. For a restricted class of non-deterministic systems the completeness result is shown in [11,12].

Theorem 6.2 (Completeness of $\sqsubseteq_{\mathbf{BF}}$).

$$
\mathsf{tr}_{(s,c)} \sqsubseteq \mathsf{tr}_{(t,d)} \quad \Longrightarrow \quad (s,c)\ \sqsubseteq_{\mathbf{BF}}\ (t,d) \ .
$$

Proof. From a (T,F)-system (s,c), we construct its "canonical system" as

$$
1 \xrightarrow{\ \mathsf{tr}_{(s,c)}\ } A \xrightarrow[\cong]{\ \zeta\ } FA \qquad \text{in } \mathcal{K}\ell(T) \ .
$$

That is, the dynamics is the final $\overline{F}$-coalgebra and the start states map is the trace of the system. It is obvious by definition that the map tr_c is a morphism of systems from (s,c) to this canonical system (the left side of Diagram (7) below). We apply the same construction to (t,d) yielding the right side of the diagram. Then the assumption $\mathsf{tr}_{(s,c)} \sqsubseteq \mathsf{tr}_{(t,d)}$ fits in the lower middle of the diagram.

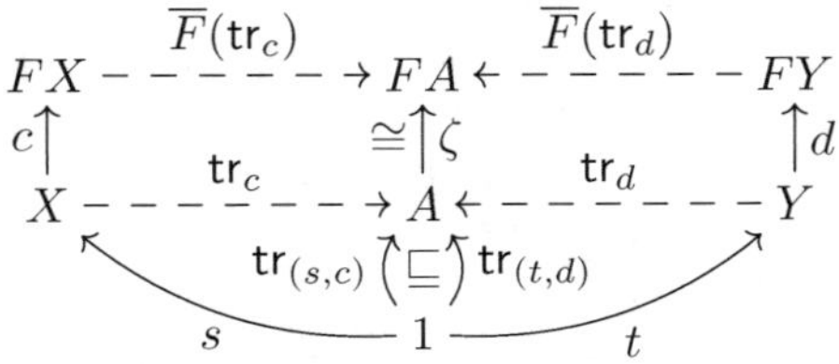

$$
\begin{array}{ccccc}
FX & \dashrightarrow^{\ \overline{F}(\mathsf{tr}_c)\ } & FA & \xleftarrow{\ \overline{F}(\mathsf{tr}_d)\ } & FY \\
{\scriptstyle c}\uparrow & & \cong\uparrow{\scriptstyle \zeta} & & \uparrow{\scriptstyle d} \\
X & \dashrightarrow_{\ \mathsf{tr}_c\ } & A & \xleftarrow{\ \mathsf{tr}_d\ } & Y \\
& {\scriptstyle s}\ \searrow\ \mathsf{tr}_{(s,c)} & \big(\sqsubseteq\big) & \mathsf{tr}_{(t,d)}\ \nearrow\ {\scriptstyle t} & \\
& & 1 & &
\end{array}
\tag{7}
$$

From this we have two diagrams of backward-forward simulations—like Diagram (4) in Definition 4.6—depending on our choice of the intermediate system.

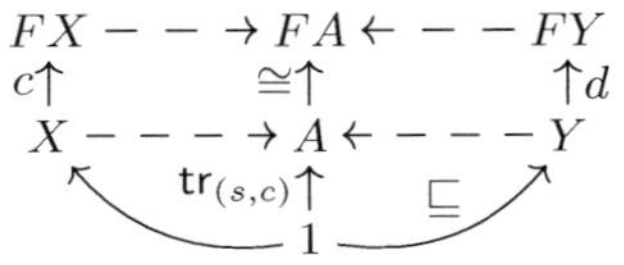

$$
\begin{array}{ccc}
FX \dashrightarrow FA \leftarrow\!-\!- FY & & FX \dashrightarrow FA \leftarrow\!-\!- FY \\
{\scriptstyle c}\uparrow \quad \cong\uparrow \quad \uparrow{\scriptstyle d} & & {\scriptstyle c}\uparrow \quad \cong\uparrow \quad \uparrow{\scriptstyle d} \\
X \dashrightarrow A \leftarrow\!-\!- Y & \text{or} & X \dashrightarrow A \leftarrow\!-\!- Y \\
\quad\searrow \mathsf{tr}_{(s,c)}\uparrow\quad\sqsubseteq\quad\nearrow & & \quad\searrow\quad\sqsubseteq\quad\uparrow\mathsf{tr}_{(t,d)}\nearrow \\
1 & & 1
\end{array}
$$

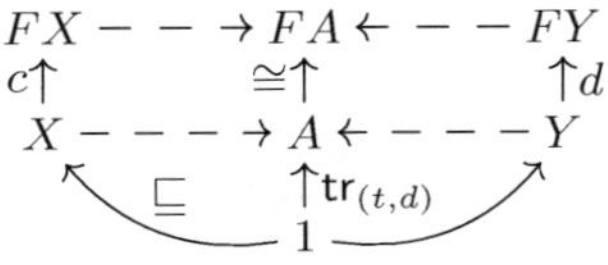

Either diagram shows $(s,c) \sqsubseteq_{\mathbf{BF}} (t,d)$. □

Using the completeness result we can prove that the simulation relation $\sqsubseteq_{\mathbf{BF}}$—now equivalent to trace inclusion—is actually transitive.

Proposition 6.3 *The simulation relations* $\sqsubseteq_{\mathbf{F}}, \sqsubseteq_{\mathbf{B}}$ *and* $\sqsubseteq_{\mathbf{BF}}$ *are preorders. That is, they are reflexive and transitive.*

Proof. Except for transitivity of $\sqsubseteq_{\mathbf{BF}}$, the proof is straightforward. See [6, Propositions 6.3, 6.4]. □

7 Conclusions and Future Work

We have developed a generic theory of branching state-based systems in terms of coalgebras in Kleisli categories. Notions such as forward/backward simulations and traces are defined and related via soundness and completeness results. Several illustrating examples suggest practical implications of this theory.

There are a number of issues on branching systems that remain to be elaborated in our generic framework. To name a few: composition of systems, compositionality of semantics, modal logic, preservation of logical formulas, infinite traces and internal actions.

As mentioned in Remark 3.4, systems with both non-deterministic and probabilistic branching do not fit in our general framework. There are many semantical questions (see e.g. [1]) about this combination of different branching: hopefully categorical approaches will contribute to clarify the picture.

More examples of types of systems to which our framework applies are to be found. For example, the author is interested in a probabilistic version of anonymous simulations [9] .

IOA Toolset [3] is a formal verification tool in which systems are described as I/O automata and analyzed using simulations. Now that its base theory is made generic, one might as well work on a generic version of the toolset itself.

Acknowledgments

Thanks are due to Chris Heunen, Bart Jacobs, Yoshinobu Kawabe, Koki Nishizawa, Ana Sokolova, Frits Vaandrager and Hiroshi Watanabe for helpful discussions.

References

1. L. Cheung. *Reconciling Nondeterministic and Probabilistic Choices.* PhD thesis, Radboud Univ. Nijmegen, 2006.
2. M. Fiore. A coinduction principle for recursive data types based on bisimulation. *Inf. & Comp.*, 127(2):186–198, 1996.
3. S. Garland, N. Lynch, and M. Vaziri. *IOA: a language for specifying, programming, and validating distributed systems.* MIT Laboratory for Computer Science, 1997.

4. I. Hasuo and B. Jacobs. Context-free languages via coalgebraic trace semantics. In *Algebra and Coalgebra in Computer Science (CALCO'05)*, volume 3629 of *Lect. Notes Comp. Sci.*, pages 213–231. Springer, Berlin, 2005.
5. I. Hasuo, B. Jacobs, and A. Sokolova. Generic trace theory. In *Coalgebraic Methods in Computer Science (CMCS 2006)*, Elect. Notes in Theor. Comp. Sci. Elsevier, Amsterdam, 2006.
6. I. Hasuo. Generic forward and backward simulations. Technical report, Research Center for Verification and Semantics, National Institute of Advanced Industrial Science and Technology (AIST), Japan, 2006. `http://www.cs.ru.nl/~ichiro/papers/`.
7. J. Hughes and B. Jacobs. Simulations in coalgebra. *Theor. Comp. Sci.*, 327(1-2):71–108, 2004.
8. C. Jou and S. Smolka. Equivalences, congruences and complete axiomatizations for probabilistic processes. In *CONCUR'90*, volume 458 of *Lect. Notes Comp. Sci.*, pages 367–383. Springer-Verlag, 1990.
9. Y. Kawabe, K. Mano, H. Sakurada, and Y. Tsukada. Backward simulations for anonymity. In *International Workshop on Issues in the Theory of Security (WITS '06)*, 2006.
10. Y. Kinoshita and J. Power. Data refinement and algebraic structure. *Acta Informatica*, 36:693–719, 2000.
11. N. Klarlund and F. Schneider. Verifying safety properties using infinite-state automata. Technical Report 89-1039, Department of Computer Science, Cornell University, Ithaca, New York, 1989.
12. N. Lynch and F. Vaandrager. Forward and backward simulations. I. Untimed systems. *Inf. & Comp.*, 121(2):214–233, 1995.
13. J. Power and D. Turi. A coalgebraic foundation for linear time semantics. In *Category Theory and Computer Science*, number 29 in Elect. Notes in Theor. Comp. Sci. Elsevier, Amsterdam, 1999.
14. J. Rutten. Universal coalgebra: a theory of systems. *Theor. Comp. Sci.*, 249:3–80, 2000.
15. R. Segala and N. Lynch. Probabilistic simulations for probabilistic processes. *Nordic Journ. Comput.*, 2(2):250–273, 1995.
16. A. Sokolova. *Coalgebraic Analysis of Probabilistic Systems.* PhD thesis, TU Eindhoven, 2005.
17. R. van Glabbeek, S. Smolka, and B. Steffen. Reactive, generative, and stratified models of probabilistic processes. *Inf. & Comp.*, 121:59–80, 1995.
18. S.H. Wu, S.A. Smolka, and E.W. Stark. Composition and behaviors of probabilistic I/O automata. *Theor. Comp. Sci.*, 176(1–2):1–38, 1997.

On Finite Alphabets and Infinite Bases III: Simulation*

Taolue Chen[1,2] and Wan Fokkink[1,3]

[1] CWI, Department of Software Engineering, PO Box 94079, 1090 GB Amsterdam, The Netherlands
chen@cwi.nl
[2] Nanjing University, State Key Laboratory of Novel Software Technology, Nanjing, Jiangsu, P.R. China, 210093
[3] Vrije Universiteit Amsterdam, Department of Theoretical Computer Science, De Boelelaan 1081a, 1081 HV Amsterdam, The Netherlands
wanf@cs.vu.nl

Abstract. This paper studies the (in)equational theory of simulation preorder and equivalence over the process algebra BCCSP. We prove that in the presence of a finite alphabet with at least two actions, the (in)equational theory of BCCSP modulo simulation preorder or equivalence does not have a finite basis. In contrast, in the presence of an alphabet that is infinite or a singleton, the equational theory for simulation equivalence does have a finite basis.

1 Introduction

Labeled transition systems constitute a fundamental model of concurrent computation which is widely used in light of its flexibility and applicability. They model processes by explicitly describing their states and their transitions from state to state, together with the actions that produce them. Several notions of behavioral equivalence have been proposed, with the aim to identify those states of labeled transition systems that afford the same observations. The lack of consensus on what constitutes an appropriate notion of observable behavior for reactive systems has led to a large number of proposals for behavioral equivalences for concurrent processes.

Van Glabbeek [9] presented the linear time - branching time spectrum of behavioral preorders and equivalences for finitely branching, concrete, sequential processes. In this paper we focus on the *simulation* semantics in this spectrum. A relation R between processes is a simulation if $s_0 \; R \; s_1$ and $s_0 \xrightarrow{a} s_0'$ implies $s_1 \xrightarrow{a} s_1'$ with $s_0' \; R \; s_1'$. It was introduced by Milner in his seminal work on CCS [21], and the first branching-time semantics to be used studied in the setting of process algebra (before the formulation of bisimulation by Park [27] appeared). The

* Partially supported by the Dutch Bsik project BRICKS (Basic Research in Informatics for Creating the Knowledge Society), 973 Program of China (No. 2002CB312002), NNSFC (No. 60233010, No. 60273034, No. 60403014).

C. Baier and H. Hermanns (Eds.): CONCUR 2006, LNCS 4137, pp. 421–434, 2006.

notion of simulation is well studied in the literatures, both from the theoretical and from the practical point of view, see e.g. [14,17].

Other semantics in the linear time - branching time spectrum are based on simulation notions or on decorated traces. Figure 1 depicts the linear time - branching time spectrum, where a directed edge from one equivalence to another means that the source of the edge is finer than the target.

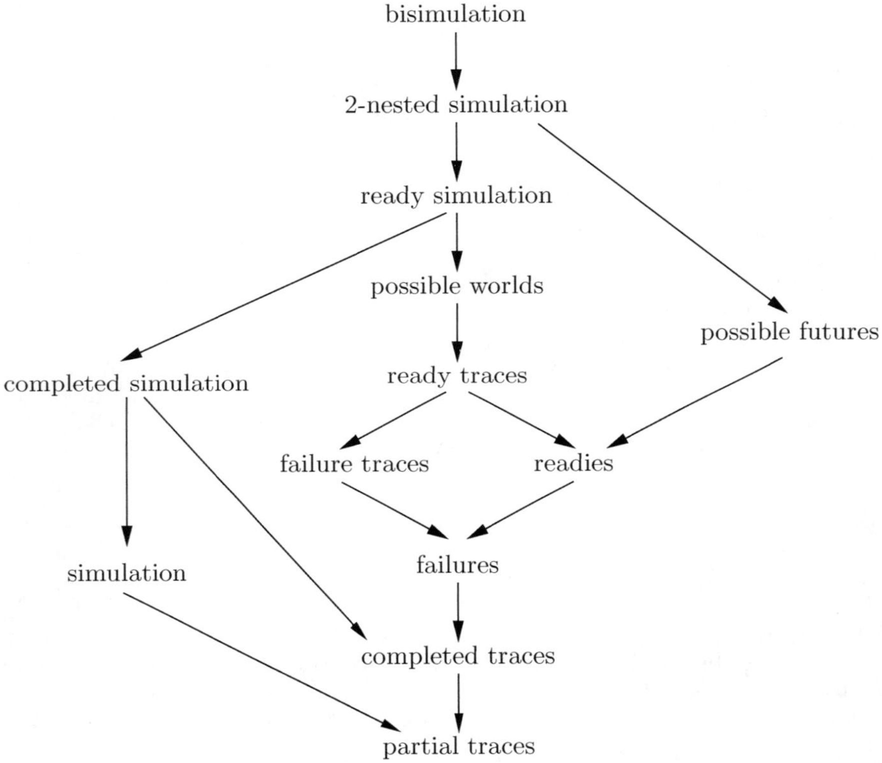

Fig. 1. The linear time - branching time spectrum

Van Glabbeek [9] studied the semantics in his spectrum in the setting of the process algebra BCCSP, which contains only the basic process algebraic operators from CCS and CSP, but is sufficiently powerful to express all finite synchronization trees. Van Glabbeek gave axiomatizations for the semantics in the spectrum, such that two closed BCCSP terms can be equated by the axioms if and only if they are equivalent.

Having defined a model of an axiomatization for a process algebra in terms of labeled transition systems, it is natural to study the connection between the equations that are valid in the chosen model, and those that are derivable from the axioms using the rules of equational logic. A key question here is whether there is a finite axiomatization that is ω-complete. That is, if all closed instances of an equation can be derived, does this imply that the equation itself can be derived from the axiomatization using the rules of equational logic? (We also refer to an ω-complete axiom system as a *basis* for the equational theory.) An ω-complete axiomatization of a behavioral congruence yields a purely syntactic characterization, independent of labeled transition systems and of the actual details of the definition of the behavioral congruence. This bridge between syntax and semantics plays an important role in both the practice and the theory of process algebras. From the point of view of practice, these proof systems can be used to perform system verifications in a purely syntactic way using general purpose theorem provers or proof checkers, and form the basis of purpose-built axiomatic verification tools like, e.g., PAM [15]. In particular, for theorem proving applications, it is convenient if an axiomatization is ω-complete, because it means that proofs by (structural) induction can be avoided in favor of purely equational reasoning; see [16]. In [12] it was argued that ω-completeness is desirable for the partial evaluation of programs.

The existence of a finite basis for an equational theory is a classic topic of study in universal algebra (see, e.g., [20]), dating back to Lyndon [18]. Murskiĭ [26] proved that "almost all" finite algebras (namely all quasi-primal ones) are finitely based, while in [25] he presented an example of a three-element algebra that has no finite basis. Henkin [13] showed that the algebra of naturals with addition and multiplication is finitely based, while Gurevič [11] showed that after adding exponentiation the algebra is no longer finitely based. McKenzie [19] settled Tarski's Finite Basis Problem in the negative, by showing that the general question whether a finite algebra is finitely based is undecidable.

Notable examples of ω-incomplete axiomatizations in the literature are the $\lambda K\beta\eta$-calculus (see [28]) and the equational theory of CCS [24]. Therefore laws such as commutativity of parallelism, which are valid in the initial model but which cannot be derived, are often added to the latter equational theory. For such extended equational theories, ω-completeness results were presented in the setting of CCS [23,3] and ACP [6].

A number of positive and negative results regarding finite ω-complete axiomatizations for BCCSP occur in the literature. For a comprehensive survey and discussion of open problems, the interested reader is referred to [2].

- *Infinite alphabets:*[1] Moller [23] proved that the ground-complete axiomatization for BCCSP modulo bisimulation equivalence is ω-complete. Groote [10] presented ω-completeness proofs for completed trace equivalence, for trace equivalence (in the presence of an alphabet A with $|A| > 1$), and for readiness and failures equivalence (if $|A| = \infty$). Van Glabbeek [9] noted (without proof) that Groote's technique of inverted substitutions can also be used to prove that the ground-complete axiomatizations for BCCSP modulo simulation, ready simulation and failure trace equivalence are ω-complete if $|A| = \infty$.

[1] In case of an infinite alphabet, occurrences of action names in axioms should be interpreted as variables, as otherwise most of the axiomatizations mentioned in this paragraph would be infinite.

Blom, Fokkink and Nain [4] proved that BCCSP modulo ready trace equivalence does not have a finite sound and ground-complete axiomatization if $|A| = \infty$. Aceto, Fokkink, van Glabbeek and Ingolfsdottir [1] proved such a negative result for 2-nested simulation and possible futures equivalence, independent of the cardinality of A.

– *Finite alphabets*: Fokkink and Nain [8] obtained an ω-complete axiomatization for BCCSP modulo failures equivalence if $|A| < \infty$, by adding one extra axiom that uses the cardinality of A. In [7] they proved that if $1 < |A| < \infty$, BCCSP modulo any semantics in between readiness and possible worlds equivalence does not have a finite basis. In [5], Chen, Fokkink and Nain proved that BCCSP modulo completed simulation equivalence does not have a finite basis if $|A| > 1$, and that BCCSP modulo ready simulation equivalence does not have a finite basis if $1 < |A| < \infty$.

If $|A| = 1$, then the semantics in the linear time - branching time spectrum from completed trace up to ready simulation equivalence all coincide with completed trace equivalence, while simulation equivalence coincides with trace equivalence. And there exists a finite basis for the equational theories of BCCSP modulo completed trace and trace equivalence if $|A| = 1$.

In this paper we consider BCCSP modulo simulation semantics. We prove that if $1 < |A| < \infty$, then no finite sound and ground-complete axiomatization for BCCSP modulo simulation preorder and equivalence is ω-complete. This solves an open question mentioned by van Glabbeek [9, p78] and Aceto et al. [2, p355]. To give some intuition for the infinite family of inequations on which our negative result for simulation preorder is based, we present one of these inequations, for $A = \{a, b\}$:

$$\begin{aligned} a(x + aa\mathbf{0} + ab\mathbf{0} + ba\mathbf{0} + bb\mathbf{0}) \preccurlyeq\ & a(x + aa\mathbf{0} + ab\mathbf{0} + ba\mathbf{0}) \\ & + a(x + aa\mathbf{0} + ab\mathbf{0} + bb\mathbf{0}) \\ & + a(x + aa\mathbf{0} + ba\mathbf{0} + bb\mathbf{0}) \\ & + a(x + ab\mathbf{0} + ba\mathbf{0} + bb\mathbf{0}) \\ & + a(a(a\mathbf{0} + b\mathbf{0}) + b(a\mathbf{0} + b\mathbf{0})) \end{aligned}$$

It is sound modulo simulation preorder. Namely, given a closed substitution ρ, $\rho(x) + aa\mathbf{0} + ab\mathbf{0} + ba\mathbf{0} + bb\mathbf{0}$ is simulated either by $a(a\mathbf{0} + b\mathbf{0}) + b(a\mathbf{0} + b\mathbf{0})$, if $\rho(x)$ cannot perform a trace of length two, or by for instance $\rho(x) + aa\mathbf{0} + ab\mathbf{0} + bb\mathbf{0}$, if $\rho(x)$ can perform the trace ba. The equation above can be generalized to a family of equations of any depth (see Section 3.1) that blocks the existence of a finite basis. Our proof of this fact is based on what in [2, Section 2.3] is called a proof-theoretic technique. Given a finite sound axiomatization E, we give a property of equations that:

– holds true for each instantiation of the axioms in E;
– is preserved by the rules of equational logic; and
– fails for one of the equations in the aforementioned infinite family.

So then this latter sound equation cannot be derived from E.

In contrast, using the technique of inverted substitutions from [10], we present a proof of the claim in [9] that if $|A| = \infty$, then the ground-complete axiomatization of BCCSP modulo simulation equivalence is ω-complete. As remarked above, if $|A| = 1$, then simulation equivalence coincides with trace equivalence, and in that case a finite basis also exists.

We note that only one open question regarding ω-complete axiomatizations for BCCSP modulo the semantics in the linear time - branching time spectrum remains. Namely, it is unknown whether BCCSP modulo failure trace equivalence has a finite basis if $1 < |A| < \infty$.

This paper is set up as follows. Section 2 presents basic definitions regarding simulation semantics, the process algebra BCCSP, and (in)equational logic. Section 3 contains the proofs of the negative results for simulation preorder and equivalence in case $1 < |A| < \infty$. Section 4 contains a short proof of the positive result for simulation equivalence in case $|A| = \infty$.

2 Preliminaries

Simulation semantics: A *labeled transition system* contains a set of states, with typical element s, and a set of transitions $s \xrightarrow{a} s'$, where a ranges over some set A of labels.

Definition 1 (Simulation). *Assume a labeled transition system. A* simulation *is a binary relation R on states such that $s_0 \; R \; s_1$ and $s_0 \xrightarrow{a} s_0'$ imply $s_1 \xrightarrow{a} s_1'$ with $s_0' \; R \; s_1'$.*

We write $s_0 \precsim s_1$ if $s_0 \; R \; s_1$ with R a simulation. Simulation equivalence, *i.e., $\precsim \cap \precsim^{-1}$, is denoted by $\simeq$. If $s_0 \simeq s_1$, we say that s_0 is* similar *to s_1.*

Syntax of BCCSP: BCCSP(A) is a basic process algebra for expressing finite process behavior. Its syntax consists of closed (process) terms p, q that are constructed from a constant $\mathbf{0}$, a binary operator $\_+\_$ called *alternative composition*, and unary *prefix* operators $a\_$, where a ranges over some nonempty set A of *actions* (with typical elements a, b). Open terms t, u, v, w can moreover contain variables from a countably infinite set V (with typical elements x, y, z). The sets of closed and open terms are denoted by T(BCCSP) and $\mathbb{T}$(BCCSP), respectively. We let $var(t)$ denote the set of variables occurring in term t.

A (closed) substitution maps variables in V to (closed) terms. For every term t and substitution σ, the term $\sigma(t)$ is obtained by replacing every occurrence of a variable x in t by $\sigma(x)$.

Transition rules: Intuitively, closed BCCSP(A)-terms represent finite process behaviors, where $\mathbf{0}$ does not exhibit any behavior, $p + q$ is the nondeterministic choice between the behaviors of p and q, and ap executes action a to transform into p. This intuition is captured, in the style of Plotkin, by the transition rules below, which give rise to A-labeled transitions between closed terms.

$$\frac{}{ax \xrightarrow{a} x} \qquad \frac{x \xrightarrow{a} x'}{x + y \xrightarrow{a} x'} \qquad \frac{y \xrightarrow{a} y'}{x + y \xrightarrow{a} y'}$$

Simulation preorder $\precsim$ constitutes a *precongruence* for closed BCCSP(A)-terms. That is, $p_1 \precsim q_1$ and $p_2 \precsim q_2$ implies $ap_1 \precsim aq_1$ for $a \in A$ and $p_1 + p_2 \precsim q_1 + q_2$. Likewise, simulation equivalence constitutes a *congruence* for closed BCCSP(A)-terms.

Equations and inequations: An *axiomatization* E is a collection of either inequations $t \preccurlyeq u$ or equations $t \approx u$. We write $E \vdash t \preccurlyeq u$ or $E \vdash t \approx u$ if this (in)equation can be derived from the (in)equations in E using the standard rules of (in)equational logic, where the rule for symmetry can be applied for equational derivations but not for inequational ones. An axiomatization E is *sound* modulo $\precsim$ (or $\simeq$) if for any open terms t, u, from $E \vdash t \preccurlyeq u$ (or $E \vdash t \approx u$) it follows that $\rho(t) \precsim \rho(u)$ (or $\rho(t) \simeq \rho(u)$) for all closed substitutions ρ. E is *ground-complete* modulo $\precsim$ (or $\simeq$) if $p \precsim q$ (or $p \simeq q$) implies $E \vdash p \preccurlyeq q$ (or $E \vdash p \approx q$), for all closed terms p and q. Finally, E is ω*-complete* if for any open terms t, u with $E \vdash \rho(t) \preccurlyeq \rho(u)$ (or $E \vdash \rho(t) \approx \rho(u)$) for all closed substitutions ρ, we have $E \vdash t \preccurlyeq u$ (or $E \vdash t \approx u$).

The core axioms A1-4 [22] for BCCSP(A) below are ω-complete, and sound and ground-complete modulo bisimulation equivalence, which is the finest semantics in the linear time - branching time spectrum (see Figure 1).

A1	$x + y \approx y + x$
A2	$(x + y) + z \approx x + (y + z)$
A3	$x + x \approx x$
A4	$x + \mathbf{0} \approx x$

In the remainder of this paper, process terms are considered modulo A1-4. A term x or at is a *summand* of each term $x + u$ or $at + u$, respectively. We use *summation* $\sum_{i\in\{i_1,\ldots,i_k\}} t_i$ (with $k \geq 0$) to denote $t_{i_1} + \cdots + t_{i_k}$, where the empty sum denotes $\mathbf{0}$. As binding convention, alternative composition and summation bind weaker than prefixing.

Open terms: For open terms t and u, we define $t \precsim u$ (or $t \simeq u$) if $\rho(t) \precsim \rho(u)$ (resp. $\rho(t) \simeq \rho(u)$) for all closed substitutions ρ.

Since we will be interested in ω-completeness, it is useful to extend the operational semantics to open terms, by assuming that variables do not exhibit any behavior.

Definition 2 (Traces). *A sequence* $a_1 \cdots a_m \in A^*$*, with* $m \geq 0$*, is a* trace *of a term* t_0 *if there exists a sequence of transitions* $t_0 \xrightarrow{a_1} t_1 \xrightarrow{a_2} \cdots \xrightarrow{a_m} t_m$*. We write* $t_0 \xrightarrow{a_1\cdots a_m} t_m$*.*

The depth *of a term* t*, denoted* $depth(t)$*, is the length of a longest trace of* t*.*

We prove some basic facts for relations $t \precsim u$.

Lemma 1

1. *Let* $|A| > 1$*. If* $t \precsim u$*, and* x *is a summand of* t*, then* x *is also a summand of* u*.*
2. *If* $t \precsim u$*, then* $depth(t) \leq depth(u)$*.*
3. *If* $t \precsim u$*, then* $var(t) \subseteq var(u)$*.*

Proof. 1. Let $m > depth(u)$, $a \neq b$, and ρ the closed substitution with $\rho(x) = a^m b\mathbf{0}$ and $\rho(y) = \mathbf{0}$ for any variable $y \neq x$. By assumption, x is a summand of t, so $\rho(t) \stackrel{a^m b}{\rightarrow} \mathbf{0}$. Since $t \precsim u$, $\rho(t) \precsim \rho(u)$. It follows that $\rho(u) \stackrel{a^m b}{\rightarrow} p$ with $\mathbf{0} \precsim p$. Since $m > depth(u)$, clearly $u \stackrel{a^\ell}{\rightarrow} y + u'$ and $\rho(y) \stackrel{a^{m-\ell} b}{\rightarrow} p$, for some $\ell \leq depth(u)$, variable y and term u'. Since $\ell \leq depth(u) < m$, we have $\rho(y) \neq \mathbf{0}$, and hence $y = x$. Since $\rho(y) \stackrel{a^{m-\ell} b}{\rightarrow} p$ and $a \neq b$, it follows that $\ell = 0$. Concluding, x is also a summand of u.

2. Let ρ be the closed substitution with $\rho(x) = \mathbf{0}$ for all variables x. Since $t \preccurlyeq u$, $\rho(t) \precsim \rho(u)$. From the definition of $\precsim$, it follows that $depth(\rho(t)) \leq depth(\rho(u))$. Hence $depth(t) = depth(\rho(t)) \leq depth(\rho(u)) = depth(u)$.
3. Suppose, towards a contradiction, that there exists some $x \in var(t) \backslash var(u)$. Let $m > depth(u)$ and ρ the closed substitution with $\rho(x) = a^m \mathbf{0}$ and $\rho(y) = \mathbf{0}$ for any variable $y \neq x$. Since $t \precsim u$, $\rho(t) \precsim \rho(u)$. Clearly, $depth(\rho(t)) \geq m > depth(\rho(u))$, which contradicts (2). □

We note that Lemma 1(1) would not hold if $|A| = 1$. For instance, in that case, we have $ax + x \simeq ax$.

3 $1 < |A| < \infty$

In this section we present a proof that the (in)equational theory of BCCSP(A) modulo simulation semantics does not have a finite basis, provided that $1 < |A| < \infty$.

3.1 Simulation Preorder

We start with proving that the inequational theory of BCCSP(A) modulo $\precsim$ does not have a finite basis. The corner stone for this negative result is the infinite family of inequations

$$a(x + \Psi_n) \preccurlyeq \sum_{\theta \in A^n} a(x + \Psi_n^\theta) + a\Phi_n$$

for $n \geq 0$. Here, the Φ_n are defined inductively as follows:

$$\begin{cases} \Phi_0 & = \mathbf{0} \\ \Phi_{n+1} & = \sum_{b \in A} b\,\Phi_n \end{cases}$$

Moreover, the Ψ_n and Ψ_n^θ are defined by:

$$\Psi_n = \sum_{b_1 \cdots b_n \in A^n} b_1 \cdots b_n \mathbf{0}$$

$$\Psi_n^\theta = \sum_{b_1 \cdots b_n \in A^n \backslash \{\theta\}} b_1 \cdots b_n \mathbf{0} \qquad \text{for } \theta \in A^n$$

For any p with $depth(p) \leq n$, clearly $p \precsim \Phi_n$. So in particular, $\Psi_n \precsim \Phi_n$.

It is not hard to see that the inequations above are sound modulo $\precsim$. The idea is that, given a closed substitution ρ, either $depth(\rho(x)) < n$, in which case $a(\rho(x) + \Psi_n)$ is simulated by $a\Phi_n$. Or $\rho(x) \stackrel{b_1 \cdots b_n}{\rightarrow}$, in which case $a(\rho(x) + \Psi_n)$ is simulated by $a(\rho(x) + \Psi_n^{b_1 \cdots b_n})$.

Proposition 1. *Let E be a finite axiomatization over* BCCSP(A) *that is sound modulo $\precsim$. Let $n > 1$ be greater than or equal to the depth of any term in E. Then from E we cannot derive the inequation*

$$a(x + \Psi_n) \preccurlyeq \sum_{\theta \in A^n} a(x + \Psi_n^\theta) + a\Phi_n$$

The main part of this section is devoted to proving Proposition 1. We start with two key lemmas.

Lemma 2. *If $a(x + \Psi_n) \precsim at \precsim \sum_{\theta \in A^n} a(x + \Psi_n^\theta) + a\Phi_n$, then $at \simeq a(x + \Psi_n)$.*

Proof. Since $x + \Psi_n \precsim t$, by Lemma 1(1), x is a summand of t. Then (modulo A3) $t = x + t'$ where x is not a summand of t'. We prove that $t' \precsim \Psi_n$.

Since $at \precsim \sum_{\theta \in A^n} a(x + \Psi_n^\theta) + a\Phi_n$, by Lemma 1(3), $var(t') \subseteq var(t) \subseteq \{x\}$. Assume, towards a contradiction, that x occurs in t'. Consider a substitution σ with $\sigma(x) = a^n\mathbf{0}$. Clearly $depth(\sigma(t')) > depth(\sigma(x))$. By assumption, $a\sigma(t) \precsim \sum_{\theta \in A^n} a(\sigma(x) + \Psi_n^\theta) + a\Phi_n$. However, $depth(a\sigma(t)) = depth(\sigma(t)) + 1 \geq depth(\sigma(t')) + 1 > depth(\sigma(x)) + 1 = n + 1$, while $depth(a(\sigma(x) + \Psi_n^\theta) + a\Phi_n) = n + 1$. This is a contradiction according to Lemma 1(2). In summary, t' is a closed term.

Consider a substitution ρ with $\rho(x) = a^{n+1}\mathbf{0}$. By assumption, $a(\rho(x) + t') \precsim \sum_{\theta \in A^n} a(\rho(x) + \Psi_n^\theta) + a\Phi_n$. Clearly, $\rho(x) + t' \not\precsim \Phi_n$, so $\rho(x) + t' \precsim \rho(x) + \Psi_n^\theta$ for some $\theta \in A^n$. Hence $t' \precsim a^{n+1}\mathbf{0} + \Psi_n^\theta$. Since $at \precsim \sum_{\theta \in A^n} a(x + \Psi_n^\theta) + a\Phi_n$, by Lemma 1(2), $depth(t') \leq depth(t) \leq n$. So it follows that $t' \precsim a^n\mathbf{0} + \Psi_n^\theta \precsim \Psi_n$.

Then $at = a(x + t') \precsim a(x + \Psi_n)$. By assumption, $a(x + \Psi_n) \precsim at$. Hence $at \simeq a(x + \Psi_n)$. □

Lemma 3. *Assume that:*

- *$t \precsim u$;*
- *$n \geq depth(u)$ and $n > 1$;*
- *$\sigma(t)$ has a summand similar to $a(x + \Psi_n)$; and*
- *$\sigma(u) \precsim \sum_{\theta \in A^n} a(x + \Psi_n^\theta) + a\Phi_n$.*

Then $\sigma(u)$ has a summand similar to $a(x + \Psi_n)$.

Proof. We can write $t = \sum_{i \in I} t_i$ and $u = \sum_{j \in J} u_j$ for some finite index sets I and J, where each term t_i and u_j is either a variable or of the form av. According to the third proviso of this lemma, for some $i_0 \in I$, $\sigma(t_{i_0})$ has a summand similar to $a(x + \Psi_n)$. We proceed by a case analysis on the form of t_{i_0}.

1. Let $t_{i_0} \in V$. Since $t \precsim u$ and $t_{i_0} \in V$, by Lemma 1(1), u also has t_{i_0} as a summand. Since $\sigma(t_{i_0})$ has a summand similar to $a(x + \Psi_n)$, the same holds for $\sigma(u)$.

2. Let $t_{i_0} = at'$ for some term t'. Then $a\sigma(t') \simeq a(x+\Psi_n)$. Let $\{y_k \mid k \in K\}$ be the collection of variable summands of t', for some finite index set K. Since $\sigma(t') \simeq x+\Psi_n$, by Lemma 1(1), x is a summand of $\sigma(t')$. So x is a summand of $\sigma(y_{k_0})$ for some $k_0 \in K$. In particular, $K \neq \emptyset$.

   Since V is countable, there exists an injective function $\ulcorner\cdot\urcorner : V \to \mathbb{N}$. Let the closed substitution ρ be defined by

$$\rho(z) = a^{\ulcorner z \urcorner \cdot n} b\mathbf{0} \qquad \text{for all } z \in V.$$

   $t \precsim u$ implies $\rho(t) \precsim \rho(u)$. Since $\rho(t) \xrightarrow{a} \rho(t')$, there is a $j_0 \in J$ such that $\rho(u_{j_0}) \xrightarrow{a} p$ with $\rho(t') \precsim p$.

   The term u_{j_0} cannot be a variable. Namely, in that case we would have $p = a^{\ulcorner u_{j_0} \urcorner \cdot n-1} b\mathbf{0}$. On the other hand, $K \neq \emptyset$ implies that $\rho(t') \xrightarrow{a^{\ulcorner y_k \urcorner \cdot n} b} \mathbf{0}$ for some $k \in K$. Since $a \neq b$ and $n > 1$, this would clearly contradict $\rho(t') \precsim p$. So it follows that $u_{j_0} = au'$ for some term u' with $p = \rho(u')$.

   Consider a trace $t' \xrightarrow{b_1 \cdots b_m} z + t''$ for some $0 \leq m < n$, variable z and term t''. We will now prove that there exists a trace $u' \xrightarrow{b_1 \cdots b_m} z + u''$. Since $\rho(t') \precsim \rho(u')$, there is a trace $\rho(u') \xrightarrow{b_1 \cdots b_m} p'$ with $\rho(z+t'') \precsim p'$. Assume, towards a contradiction, that $u' \xrightarrow{b_1 \cdots b_\ell} y + u_1$ and $\rho(y) \xrightarrow{b_{\ell+1} \cdots b_m} p'$ for some $0 \leq \ell < m$, variable y and term u_1. Since $\rho(y) = a^{\ulcorner y \urcorner \cdot n} b\mathbf{0}$, $0 < m - \ell < n$, and $a \neq b$, it follows that p' cannot simulate the trace $\rho(z+t'') \xrightarrow{a^{\ulcorner z \urcorner \cdot n} b} \mathbf{0}$. This contradicts $\rho(z+t'') \precsim p'$. Hence, since $\rho(u') \xrightarrow{b_1 \cdots b_m} p'$, we have $u' \xrightarrow{b_1 \cdots b_m} u_2$ for some term u_2 with $\rho(u_2) = p'$. By the second proviso of this lemma, $depth(u_2) < n$. Since moreover $\rho(u_2)$ can simulate $\rho(z+t'') \xrightarrow{a^{\ulcorner z \urcorner \cdot n} b} \mathbf{0}$, it follows from the definition of ρ that $u_2 = z + u''$ for some term u''. Concluding, $t' \xrightarrow{b_1 \cdots b_m} z + t''$ implies $u' \xrightarrow{b_1 \cdots b_m} z + u''$.

   Now consider any $b_1 \cdots b_n \in A^n$. Since $\Psi_n \precsim \sigma(t')$ and (by the second proviso of this lemma together with Lemma 1(2)) $depth(t') < n$, we have $t' \xrightarrow{b_1 \cdots b_m} z + t''$ and $\sigma(z) \xrightarrow{b_{m+1} \cdots b_n}$ for some $0 \leq m < n$, variable z and term t''. We proved above that $t' \xrightarrow{b_1 \cdots b_m} z + t''$ implies $u' \xrightarrow{b_1 \cdots b_m} z + u''$ for some term u''. Since $\sigma(z) \xrightarrow{b_{m+1} \cdots b_n}$, this yields $\sigma(u') \xrightarrow{b_1 \cdots b_n}$. This holds for all $b_1 \cdots b_n \in A^n$, so $\Psi_n \precsim \sigma(u')$.

   Furthermore, recall that y_{k_0} is a summand of t', and that x is a summand of $\sigma(y_{k_0})$. Since $t' \xrightarrow{\lambda} t'$ (where λ denotes the empty trace), we proved above that $u' \xrightarrow{\lambda} y_{k_0} + u''$ for some term u''. So y_{k_0} is a summand of u'. Hence x is a summand of $\sigma(u')$.

   Concluding, $x+\Psi_n \precsim \sigma(u')$, so $a(x+\Psi_n) \precsim a\sigma(u')$. By the fourth proviso of this lemma, $a\sigma(u') \precsim \sigma(u) \precsim \sum_{\theta \in A^n} a(x + \Psi_n^\theta) + a\Phi_n$. So by Lemma 2, $a\sigma(u') \simeq a(x+\Psi_n)$. □

The following lemma paves the way for the proof of Proposition 1.

Lemma 4. *Let E be a finite axiomatization that is sound modulo $\precsim$. Assume that:*

- *$E \vdash v \preccurlyeq w$;*
- *$n > 1$ is greater than or equal to the depth of any term in E;*
- *v has a summand similar to $a(x + \Psi_n)$; and*
- *$w \precsim \sum_{\theta \in A^n} a(x + \Psi_n^\theta) + a\Phi_n$;*

Then w has a summand similar to $a(x + \Psi_n)$.

Proof. By induction on the depth of the proof of the inequation $v \preccurlyeq w$ from E. We proceed by a case analysis on the last rule used in the derivation of $v \preccurlyeq w$ from E. The case of reflexivity is trivial. Below we consider the other possibilities.

- Case $E \vdash v \preccurlyeq w$ because $\sigma(t) = v$ and $\sigma(u) = w$ for some $t \preccurlyeq u \in E$ and substitution σ. The claim follows by Lemma 3.
- Case $E \vdash v \preccurlyeq w$ because $E \vdash v \preccurlyeq t$ and $E \vdash t \preccurlyeq w$ for some term t. By the soundness of E, $t \precsim w \precsim \sum_{\theta \in A^n} a(x + \Psi_n^\theta) + a\Phi_n$, so by induction, t has a summand similar to $a(x+\Psi_n)$. Hence, again by induction, w has a summand similar to $a(x + \Psi_n)$.
- Case $E \vdash v \preccurlyeq w$ because $v = v' + v''$ and $w = w' + w''$ with $E \vdash v' \preccurlyeq w'$ and $E \vdash v'' \preccurlyeq w''$. Since v has a summand similar to $a(x + \Psi_n)$, so does either v' or v''. Assume, without loss of generality, that v' has a summand similar to $a(x + \Psi_n)$. Since $w' \precsim w \precsim \sum_{\theta \in A^n} a(x + \Psi_n^\theta) + a\Phi_n$, by induction, w' has a summand similar to $a(x + \Psi_n)$.
- Case $E \vdash v \preccurlyeq w$ because $v = av'$ and $w = aw'$ with $E \vdash v' \preccurlyeq w'$. Then $av' \simeq a(x + \Psi_n)$. Since $aw' \precsim \sum_{\theta \in A^n} a(x + \Psi_n^\theta) + a\Phi_n$, by Lemma 2, $aw' \simeq a(x + \Psi_n)$. □

Now we are in a position to prove **Proposition 1**.

Proof. Let E be a finite axiomatization over BCCSP(A) that is sound modulo $\precsim$. Let $n > 1$ be greater than or equal to the depth of any term in E.

$\sum_{\theta \in A^n} a(x + \Psi_n^\theta) + a\Phi_n$ does not contain a summand similar to $a(x + \Psi_n)$. So according to Lemma 4, the inequation $a(x + \Psi_n) \preccurlyeq \sum_{\theta \in A^n} a(x + \Psi_n^\theta) + a\Phi_n$, which is sound modulo $\precsim$, cannot be derived from E. □

Theorem 1. *The inequational theory of* BCCSP(A) *modulo $\precsim$ is not finitely based.*

Proof. By Proposition 1, no finite axiomatization over BCCSP(A) that is sound modulo $\precsim$ proves all inequations that are sound modulo $\precsim$. □

3.2 Simulation Equivalence

Following the same line as in Section 3.1, we can prove that the equational theory of BCCSP(A) modulo $\simeq$ does not have a finite basis. The following lemma is the counterpart of Lemma 4 for simulation equivalence.

Lemma 5. *Let E be a finite axiomatization that is sound modulo $\simeq$. Assume that:*

- $E \vdash v \approx w$;
- $n > 1$ *is greater than or equal to the depth of any term in* E;
- v *has a summand similar to* $a(x + \Psi_n)$; *and*
- $w \simeq \sum_{\theta \in A^n} a(x + \Psi_n^\theta) + a\Phi_n$;

Then w *has a summand similar to* $a(x + \Psi_n)$.

Proof. Note that Lemma 3 remains true if all occurrences of $\precsim$ are replaced with $\simeq$, owing to the fact that the relation $\simeq$ is included in $\precsim$.

By postulating that for each axiom $t \approx u$ in E also its symmetric counterpart $t \approx u$ is present, one may assume, without loss of generality, that applications of symmetry happen first in equational derivations.

Now the proof proceeds by a case analysis on the last rule used in the derivation of $v \approx w$ from E, similar to the proof of Lemma 4. This case analysis is omitted here. □

Proposition 2. *Let* E *be a finite axiomatization over* BCCSP(A) *that is sound modulo* $\simeq$. *Let* $n > 1$ *be greater than or equal to the depth of any term in* E. *Then from* E *we cannot derive the equation*

$$a(x + \Psi_n) + \sum_{\theta \in A^n} a(x + \Psi_n^\theta) + a\Phi_n \approx \sum_{\theta \in A^n} a(x + \Psi_n^\theta) + a\Phi_n$$

Proof. $\sum_{\theta \in A^n} a(x+\Psi_n^\theta)+a\Phi_n$ does not contain a summand similar to $a(x+\Psi_n)$. So according to Lemma 5, the equation $a(x + \Psi_n) + \sum_{\theta \in A^n} a(x + \Psi_n^\theta) + a\Phi_n \approx \sum_{\theta \in A^n} a(x+\Psi_n^\theta)+a\Phi_n$, which is sound modulo $\simeq$, cannot be derived from E. □

Theorem 2. *The equational theory of* BCCSP(A) *modulo* $\simeq$ *is not finitely based.*

Proof. By Proposition 2, no finite axiomatization over BCCSP(A) that is sound modulo $\simeq$ proves all equations that are sound modulo $\simeq$. □

4 Simulation Equivalence with $|A| = \infty$

In [9], van Glabbeek gave a finite axiomatization that is sound and ground-complete for BCCSP(A) modulo $\simeq$. It consists of axioms A1-4 (see Section 2) together with

$$\text{S} \qquad a(x + y) \approx a(x + y) + ax$$

Likewise, a finite sound and ground-complete axiomatization for BCCSP(A) modulo $\precsim$ is obtained by adding $x \preccurlyeq x + y$ to A1-4.

It was stated in [9, p78] and in [2, p355] that if A is infinite, then the axiomatization A1-4 + S is ω-complete. In both articles it was claimed that this could be proved using the technique of inverted substitutions from Groote [10], but the proof itself was never given.

For the sake of completeness, here we present a proof that A1-4 + S is ω-complete, using inverted substitutions. This technique works as follows. Consider an axiomatization E. For each equation $t \approx u$ of which all closed instances can be derived from E, one must define a closed substitution ρ and a mapping $R : \mathrm{T}(\mathrm{BCCSP}) \to \mathbb{T}(\mathrm{BCCSP})$ such that:

(1) $E \vdash R(\rho(t)) \approx t$ and $E \vdash R(\rho(u)) \approx u$;

(2) for each function symbol f (with arity n), $E \cup \{p_i \approx q_i,\ R(p_i) \approx R(q_i) \mid i = 1, \ldots, n\} \vdash R(f(p_1, \ldots, p_n)) \approx R(f(q_1, \ldots, q_n))$ for all closed terms $p_1, \ldots, p_n, q_1, \ldots, q_n$; and

(3) $E \vdash R(\sigma(v)) \approx R(\sigma(w))$ for each $v \approx w \in E$ and closed substitution σ.

Then, as proved in [10], E is ω-complete.

Theorem 3. *If $|A| = \infty$, then A1-4+S is ω-complete.*

Proof. Consider terms t and u. Define $\rho : V \to \mathrm{T}(\mathrm{BCCSP})$ by $\rho(x) = a_x\mathbf{0}$, where a_x is a unique action for $x \in V$ that occurs in neither t nor u. Such actions exist because A is infinite. We define $R : \mathrm{T}(\mathrm{BCCSP}) \to \mathbb{T}(\mathrm{BCCSP})$ as follows:

$$\begin{cases} R(\mathbf{0}) & = \mathbf{0} \\ R(ap) & = aR(p) \text{ if } a \neq a_x \text{ for all } x \in V \\ R(a_x p) & = x \\ R(p_1 + p_2) & = R(p_1) + R(p_2) \end{cases}$$

We now check the three properties from [10]:

(1) Since t and u do not contain actions of the form a_x, clearly $R(\rho(t)) = t$ and $R(\rho(u)) = u$.

(2) Consider the operator $\_ + \_$. From $R(p_1) \approx R(q_1)$ and $R(p_2) \approx R(q_2)$ we derive $R(p_1 + p_2) = R(p_1) + R(p_2) \approx R(q_1) + R(q_2) = R(q_1 + q_2)$.
Consider the prefix operator $a\_$. We distinguish two cases.
   - $a \neq a_y$ for all $y \in V$. Then from $R(p_1) \approx R(q_1)$ we derive $R(ap_1) = aR(p_1) \approx aR(q_1) = R(aq_1)$.
   - $a = a_y$ for some $y \in V$. Then $R(a_y p_1) = y = R(a_y q_1)$.

(3) For A1-4, the proof is trivial. We check the remaining case S. Let σ be a closed substitution. We consider two cases.
   - $a = a_z$ for some $z \in V$. Then

$$\begin{aligned} R(a(\sigma(x) + \sigma(y))) &= z \\ &\approx z + z \\ &= R(a_z(\sigma(x) + \sigma(y))) + R(a_z\sigma(x)) \end{aligned}$$

   - $a \neq a_z$ for all $z \in V$. Then

$$\begin{aligned} R(a(\sigma(x) + \sigma(y))) &= a(R(\sigma(x)) + R(\sigma(y))) \\ &\approx a(R(\sigma(x)) + R(\sigma(y))) + aR(\sigma(x)) \\ &= R(a(\sigma(x) + \sigma(y)) + a\sigma(x)) \end{aligned}$$

This completes the proof. □

Acknowledgement. We thank Bas Luttik for his constructive comments.

References

1. L. Aceto, W. Fokkink, R. van Glabbeek, and A. Ingolfsdottir. Nested semantics over finite trees are equationally hard. *Information and Computation*, 191(2):203–232, 2004.
2. L. Aceto, W. Fokkink, A. Ingolfsdottir and B. Luttik. Finite equational bases in process algebra: Results and open questions. In *Processes, Terms and Cycles: Steps on the Road to Infinity, Essays Dedicated to Jan Willem Klop, on the Occasion of his 60th Birthday*, Amsterdam, LNCS 3838, pp. 338–367. Springer 2005.
3. L. Aceto, W. Fokkink, A. Ingolfsdottir and B. Luttik. A finite equational base for CCS with left merge and communication merge. In *Proceedings 33rd Colloquium on Automata, Languages and Programming (ICALP'06)*, Venice, LNCS. Springer, 2006. To appear.
4. S. Blom, W. Fokkink, and S. Nain. On the axiomatizability of ready traces, ready simulation and failure traces. In *Proceedings 30th Colloquium on Automata, Languages and Programming (ICALP'03)*, Eindhoven, LNCS 2719, pp. 109–118. Springer, 2003.
5. T. Chen, W. Fokkink, and S. Nain. On finite alphabets and infinite bases II: Completed and ready simulation. In *Proceedings 9th Conference on Foundations of Software Science and Computation Structures (FOSSACS'06)*, Vienna, LNCS 3921, pp. 1–15. Springer, 2006.
6. W. Fokkink and B. Luttik. An ω-complete equational specification of interleaving. In *Proceedings 27th Colloquium on Automata, Languages and Programming (ICALP'00)*, Geneva, LNCS 1853, pp. 729–743. Springer, 2000.
7. W. Fokkink and S. Nain. On finite alphabets and infinite bases: From ready pairs to possible worlds. In *Proceedings 7th Conference on Foundations of Software Science and Computation Structures (FOSSACS'04)*, Barcelona, LNCS 2987, pp. 182–194. Springer, 2004.
8. W. Fokkink and S. Nain. A finite basis for failure semantics. In *Proceedings 32nd Colloquium on Automata, Languages and Programming (ICALP'05)*, Lisbon, LNCS 3580, pp. 755–765. Springer, 2005.
9. R. van Glabbeek. The linear time – branching time spectrum I. The semantics of concrete, sequential processes. In J.A. Bergstra, A. Ponse, and S.A. Smolka, eds, *Handbook of Process Algebra*, pp. 3–99. Elsevier, 2001.
10. J.F. Groote. A new strategy for proving ω-completeness with applications in process algebra. In *Proceedings 1st Conference on Concurrency Theory (CONCUR'90)*, Amsterdam, LNCS 458, pp. 314–331. Springer, 1990.
11. R. Gurevič. Equational theory of positive natural numbers with exponentiation is not finitely axiomatizable. *Annals of Pure and Applied Logic*, 49:1–30, 1990.
12. J. Heering. Partial evaluation and ω-completeness of algebraic specifications. *Theoretical Computer Science*, 43:149–167, 1986.
13. L. Henkin. The logic of equality. *American Mathematical Monthly*, 84(8):597–612, 1977.
14. P. Jancar, A. Kucera, and F. Moller. Simulation and bisimulation over one-counter processes. In *Proceedings 17th Symposium on Theoretical Aspects of Computer Science (STACS'2000)*, Lille, LNCS 1770, pp. 334–345. Springer, 2000.
15. H. Lin. PAM: A process algebra manipulator. *Formal Methods in System Design*, 7(3):243–259, 1995.
16. A. Lazrek, P. Lescanne, and J.-J. Thiel. Tools for proving inductive equalities, relative completeness, and ω-completeness. *Information and Computation*, 84(1):47–70, 1990.

17. N. Lynch and M. Tuttle. An introduction to input/output automata. *CWI Quarterly*, 2(3):219–246, 1989.
18. R. Lyndon. Identities in two-valued calculi. *Transactions of the American Mathematical Society*, 71:457–465, 1951.
19. R. McKenzie. Tarski's finite basis problem is undecidable. *Journal of Algebra and Computation*, 6(1):49–104, 1996.
20. R. McKenzie, G. McNulty, and W. Taylor. *Algebras, Varieties, Lattices.* Wadsworth & Brooks/Cole, 1987.
21. R. Milner. *A Calculus of Communicating Systems.* LNCS 92. Springer, 1980.
22. R. Milner. *Communication and Concurrency.* Prentice Hall, 1989.
23. F. Moller. *Axioms for Concurrency.* PhD thesis, University of Edinburgh, 1989.
24. F. Moller. The importance of the left merge operator in process algebras. In *Proceedings 17th Colloquium on Automata, Languages and Programming (ICALP'90)*, Warwick, LNCS 443, pp. 752–764. Springer, 1990.
25. V.L. Murskiĭ. The existence in the three-valued logic of a closed class with a finite basis having no finite complete system of identities. *Doklady Akademii Nauk SSSR*, 163:815–818, 1965. In Russian.
26. V.L. Murskiĭ. The existence of a finite basis of identities, and other properties of "almost all" finite algebras. *Problemy Kibernetiki*, 30:43–56, 1975. In Russian.
27. D.M.R. Park. Concurrency and automata on infinite sequences. In *Proceedings 5th GI Conference*, Karlsruhe, LNCS 104, pp. 167–183. Springer, 1981.
28. G.D. Plotkin. The λ-calculus is ω-incomplete. *Journal of Symbolic Logic*, 39(2):313–317, 1974.

Inference of Event-Recording Automata Using Timed Decision Trees*
(Extended Abstract)

Olga Grinchtein, Bengt Jonsson, and Paul Pettersson

Department of Computer Systems, Uppsala University, Sweden
{olgag, bengt, paupet}@it.uu.se

Abstract. We present an algorithm for inferring a timed-automaton model of a system from information obtained by observing its external behavior. Since timed automata can not in general be determinized, we restrict our attention to systems that can be described by deterministic *event-recording automata*. In previous work we have presented algorithms for event-recording automata that satisfy the restriction that there is at most one transition per alphabet symbol from each state. This restriction was lifted in subsequent work by an algorithm based on the region graph.

In this paper, we extend previous work by considering the full class of event-recording automata, while still avoiding to base it on the (usually prohibitively large) region graph. Our construction deviates from previous work on inference of automata in that it first constructs a so called timed decision tree from observations of system behavior, which is thereafter folded into an automaton.

1 Introduction

Research during the last decades has developed powerful techniques for using models of reactive systems in specification, automated verification (e.g., [7]), test case generation (e.g., [9,23]), implementation (e.g., [15]), and validation of reactive systems in telecommunication, embedded control, and related application areas. Typically, such models are assumed to be developed *a priori* during the specification and design phases of system development. In practice, however, often no formal specification is available, or becomes outdated as the system evolves over time. One must then construct a model that describes the behavior of an existing system or implementation. In software verification, techniques are being developed for generating abstract models of software modules by static analysis of source code (e.g., [8,18]). However, peripheral hardware components, library modules, or third-party software systems do not allow static analysis. In practice, such systems must be analyzed by observing their external behavior.

* This work was supported in part by the Swedish Research Council, by the European Network of Excellence ARTIST2, and by the European Research Training Network Games.

C. Baier and H. Hermanns (Eds.): CONCUR 2006, LNCS 4137, pp. 435–449, 2006.

Techniques for constructing finite-state models by analysis of externally observable behavior (black-box techniques) have been used, e.g., in regression testing [14,19]), and in model checking [13] of finite-state systems for which no model or source code is available.

The construction of models from observations of system behavior can be seen as a learning problem. For finite-state reactive systems, this can be formulated as the problem of *regular inference:* to infer a (deterministic) finite automaton by posing a finite set of *membership queries*, each of which asks whether a certain word is accepted by the automaton or not. There are several slightly different algorithms for regular inference (e.g., [3,10,20,22,4]), which guarantee that a correct automaton will be constructed if "sufficiently many" membership queries have been posed. In some settings, the inference algorithm may also pose *equivalence queries* that ask whether a hypothesized automaton is equivalent to the one that is being investigated: such a query is answered either by *yes* or by a counterexample on which the hypothesis and the correct automata disagree.

In this paper, we extend the inference algorithm of Angluin and others to the setting of timed systems, more precisely systems that can be described by a timed automaton [1], i.e., a finite automaton equipped with clocks that constrain the times of occurrences of actions. One motivation is to develop techniques for creating abstract timed models of hardware components, device drivers, etc. for analysis of timed reactive systems. Since timed automata can not in general be determinized [1], we restrict consideration to the class of *event-recording automata* [2]. These are timed automata that, for every action a, use a clock that records the time of the last occurrence of a. Event-recording automata can be determinized, and are sufficiently expressive to model many interesting timed systems; for instance, they are as powerful as timed transition systems [16,2], another popular model for timed systems. We assume that an inference algorithm observes a system by checking whether certain actions can be performed at certain moments in time, and that it is able to control and record precisely the timing of the occurrence of each action.

In previous work, authors of this paper [11] have presented algorithms for the restricted class of event-recording automata that have most one outgoing transition per action; under this restriction, the time of an action occurrence depends only on the (untimed) past sequence of actions, and not on their timing. In this paper, we consider the full class of event-recording automata. This is much more challenging, since it must be inferred how the timing of an action occurrence may depend on timing of previous actions. One way to address this problem is to infer an explicit representation of the region graph, as in [12]; this can be done using techniques for untimed regular inference, but at the cost of a high blow-up. In this paper, we avoid the region graph, but must then develop techniques for inferring guards on transitions of a timed automaton.

A novel feature of our algorithm (in comparison with other regular inference algorithms) is that it contains two constructions: the first construction generates a so-called *timed decision tree* from the answers to the membership queries that have been performed so far. The conditions (or guards) that distinguish between branches in this tree should correspond to guard in the inferred automaton. A guard is therefore introduced only if there is a pair of observations with different outcomes, where this guard is the only means to distinguish between them. The algorithm includes a systematic search for such pairs of observations. The second construction consist in folding the timed decision tree into an event-recording automaton by appropriate merging of nodes, in an analogous manner as in algorithms for (untimed) regular inference.

Previous work on inference of timed systems include work of authors of this paper [11,12]. Several papers are concerned with finding a definition of timed languages which is suitable as a basis for inference algorithms. There are several works that define determinizable classes of timed automata (e.g., [2,24]) and right-congruences of timed languages (e.g., [21,17,25]), motivated by testing and verification.

The paper is structured as follows. After preliminaries and a definition of event-recording automata in the next section, the construction of timed decision trees is described in Section 3 and 4, followed by a technique for folding them into automata in Section 5. An illustrating example is given in Section 6, and finally Section 7 concludes the paper. The proofs are omitted due to lack of space but will appear in the full version of this paper.

2 Preliminaries

We write $\mathbb{R}^{\geq 0}$ for the set of nonnegative real numbers, and $\mathbb{N}$ for the set of natural numbers. Let Σ be a finite alphabet of size $|\Sigma|$. A *timed word* over Σ is a finite sequence $(a_1, t_1)(a_2, t_2) \ldots (a_n, t_n)$ of symbols $a_i \in \Sigma$ paired with nonnegative real numbers $t_i \in \mathbb{R}^{\geq 0}$ such that the sequence $t_1 t_2 \ldots t_n$ of time-stamps is nondecreasing. We use λ to denote the empty word.

An event-recording automaton contains for every symbol $a \in \Sigma$ a clock x_a, called the *event-recording clock* of a. Intuitively, x_a records the time elapsed since the last occurrence of the symbol a. We write C_Σ for the set $\{x_a \mid a \in \Sigma\}$ of event-recording clocks. A *clock valuation* γ is a mapping from C_Σ to $\mathbb{R}^{\geq 0}$.

Throughout the paper, we will use an alternative, equivalent, representation of timed words, namely clocked words. A *clocked word* over Σ is a sequence $w_c = (a_1, \gamma_1)(a_2, \gamma_2) \ldots (a_n, \gamma_n)$ of symbols $a_i \in \Sigma$ that are paired with clock valuations which satisfies

- $\gamma_1(x_a) = \gamma_1(x_b)$ for all $a, b \in \Sigma$, and
- $\gamma_i(x_a) = \gamma_i(x_{a_{i-1}}) + \gamma_{i-1}(x_a)$ whenever $1 < i \leq n$ and $a \neq a_{i-1}$.

Each timed word $(a_1, t_1)(a_2, t_2) \ldots (a_n, t_n)$ can be naturally transformed into the clocked word $(a_1, \gamma_1)(a_2, \gamma_2) \ldots (a_n, \gamma_n)$ where for each i with $1 \leq i \leq n$,

- $\gamma_i(x_a) = t_i$ if $a_j \neq a$ for $1 \leq j < i$,
- $\gamma_i(x_a) = t_i - t_j$ if there is a j with $1 \leq j < i$ and $a_j = a$, such that $a_k \neq a$ for $j < k < i$.

A *timed language* over Σ is a set of clocked words over Σ.

A *clock constraint* is a conjunction of atomic constraints of the form $x \sim n$ or $x - y \sim n$ for $x, y \in C_\Sigma$, $\sim \in \{<, \leq, >, \geq\}$, and $n \in \mathbb{N}$. We use $\gamma \models \varphi$ to denote that the clock valuation γ satisfies the clock constraint φ. A clock constraint is K-*bounded* if it contains no constant larger than K. A *clock guard* is a clock constraint whose conjuncts are only of the form $x \sim n$ (for $x \in C_\Sigma$, $\sim \in \{<, \leq, >, \geq\}$), i.e., comparison between clocks is not permitted. The set of clock guards is denoted by G_Σ.

A *constrained word* is a sequence $w_\varphi = (a_1, \varphi_1)(a_2, \varphi_2) \ldots (a_n, \varphi_n)$ of symbols $a_i \in \Sigma$ that are paired with clock constraints. A *guarded word* is a sequence $w_g = (a_1, g_1)(a_2, g_2) \ldots (a_n, g_n)$ of symbols $a_i \in \Sigma$ that are paired with clock guards. For a clocked word $w_c = (a_1, \gamma_1)(a_2, \gamma_2) \ldots (a_n, \gamma_n)$ we use $w_c \models w_g$ to denote that $\gamma_i \models g_i$ for $1 \leq i \leq n$.

For a guarded word w_g, we introduce the *strongest postcondition* of w_g, denoted by $sp(w_g)$, as the constraint on clock values that are induced by w_g on any following occurrence of a symbol. Postcondition computation is central in tools for symbolic verification of timed automata [6,5], and can be done inductively as follows:

- $sp(\lambda) = \bigwedge_{a,b \in \Sigma} x_a = x_b$,
- $sp(w_g(a, g)) = ((sp(w_g) \wedge g)[x_a \mapsto 0]) \uparrow$,

where for clock constraint φ and clock x,

- $\varphi[x \mapsto 0]$ is the condition $x = 0 \wedge \exists x.\varphi$,
- $\varphi \uparrow$ is the condition $\exists d.\varphi'$, where d ranges over $\mathbb{R}^{\geq 0}$ and where φ' is obtained from φ by replacing each clock y by $y - d$.

Both operations can be expressed as corresponding operations on clock constraints.

Definition 1. *An* event-recording automaton *(ERA) over Σ is a tuple $\mathcal{A} = \langle L, L_0, L^f, E \rangle$ consisting of a finite set L of* locations, *a set $L_0 \subseteq L$ of* start locations, *a set L^f of accepting locations, and a finite set E of edges. Each edge is a quadruple (l, l', a, g) with a source location $l \in L$, a target location $l' \in L$, an input symbol $a \in \Sigma$, and a clock guard $g \in G_\Sigma$.*

A *run* of the event-recording automaton $\mathcal{A}$ over the clocked word $w_c = (a_1, \gamma_1) \ \ldots \ (a_n, \gamma_n)$ is a finite sequence

$$l_0 \stackrel{e_1}{\rightarrow} l_1 \stackrel{e_2}{\rightarrow} l_2 \cdots \stackrel{e_{n-1}}{\rightarrow} l_{n-1} \stackrel{e_n}{\rightarrow} l_n$$

of locations $l_i \in L$ and edges $e_i = (l_{i-1}, l_i, a_i, g_i) \in E$ such that $l_0 \in L_0$ and $\gamma_i \models g_i$ for all $1 \leq i \leq n$. The run is *accepting* if $l_n \in L_f$. The clocked word w_c is *accepted* by $\mathcal{A}$ if there is an accepting run of $\mathcal{A}$ over w_c, otherwise w_c is *rejected.* The timed language $\mathcal{L}(\mathcal{A})$ defined by $\mathcal{A}$ consists of all clocked words accepted by $\mathcal{A}$.

We call an ERA *time-deterministic* (TDERA) iff it has a single start location and for each location l and input symbol a, the guards $g_1, \ldots, g_n$ of edges from l labeled a are total and mutually exclusive, i.e., $g_1 \vee \ldots \vee g_n \equiv$ *true* and $g_i \wedge g_j \equiv$ *false* whenever $1 \leq i < j \leq n$.

3 Overview of Our Inference Algorithm

In this section, we define timed decision trees and give an overview of our inference algorithm. Our algorithm is designed to infer a TDERA which defines the same timed language as a given TDERA $\mathcal{A}$. In this algorithm a so called *Learner*, who initially knows nothing about $\mathcal{A}$, is trying to learn $\mathcal{L}(\mathcal{A})$ by asking queries to a *Teacher*, who knows $\mathcal{A}$. There are two kinds of queries:

- A *membership query* consists in asking whether a clocked word w_c over Σ is in $\mathcal{L}(\mathcal{A})$.
- An *equivalence query* consists in asking whether a hypothesized TDERA $\mathcal{H}$ is correct, i.e., whether $\mathcal{L}(\mathcal{H}) = \mathcal{L}(\mathcal{A})$. The *Teacher* will answer *yes* if $\mathcal{H}$ is correct, or else supply a counterexample, i.e, a clocked word w_c which is either in $\mathcal{L}(\mathcal{A}) \setminus \mathcal{L}(\mathcal{H})$ or in $\mathcal{L}(\mathcal{H}) \setminus \mathcal{L}(\mathcal{A})$.

The typical behavior of a *Learner* is to start by asking a sequence of membership queries, and gradually build a hypothesized TDERA $\mathcal{H}$ using the obtained answers. When the *Learner* feels that she has built a hypothesis $\mathcal{H}$, she makes an equivalence query to find out whether $\mathcal{H}$ is correct. If the answer is *yes*, the *Learner* has succeeded, otherwise she uses the returned counterexample to revise $\mathcal{H}$ and perform subsequent membership queries until arriving at a new hypothesized TDERA, etc.

We assume that the upper bound K on the constants occurring in the guards of event-recording automaton is known a priori.

Let us represent the information gained by the *Learner* at any point during the learning process as a partial mapping *Obs* from clocked words to $\{+, -\}$, where $+$ stands for *accepted* and $-$ for *rejected.* The domain *Dom*(*Obs*) of *Obs* is the set of clocked words for which membership queries have been performed, or which have been given as counterexamples in equivalence queries. An inference algorithm should prescribe how to pose additional membership queries and thereafter transform *Obs* into a TDERA $\mathcal{H} = \langle L, L_0, L^f, E\rangle$, which is *conformant* with *Obs*, in the sense that any string $w_c \in Dom(Obs)$ is accepted by $\mathcal{H}$ if $Obs(w_c) = +$, and rejected by $\mathcal{H}$ if $Obs(w_c) = -$.

Timed Decision Trees. Our algorithm first organizes *Obs* into a timed decision tree.

Definition 2. *A* timed decision tree *(TDT) is a prefix-closed set N of guarded words, such that for any node $w_g \in N$ and symbol a, the set of nodes $w_g(a, g_1), \ldots, w_g(a, g_n)$ in N that extend w_g by the symbol a is either empty, or have the properties that $g_1 \vee \cdots \vee g_n = true$ and $g_i \wedge g_j = false$ whenever $i \neq j$.*

To transfer the information in *Obs* to a timed decision tree, we extend the definition of *Obs* to guarded words, as follows.

$Obs(\lambda) = +$
$Obs((b,0)) = +$
$Obs((a,0)) = -$
$Obs((a,0)(a,0)) = +$
$Obs((a,0)(b,0)) = +$
$Obs((a,0)(b,0.5)) = -$
$Obs((a,1.5)(b,1.5)) = -$

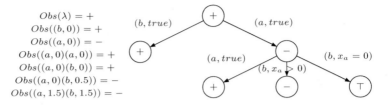

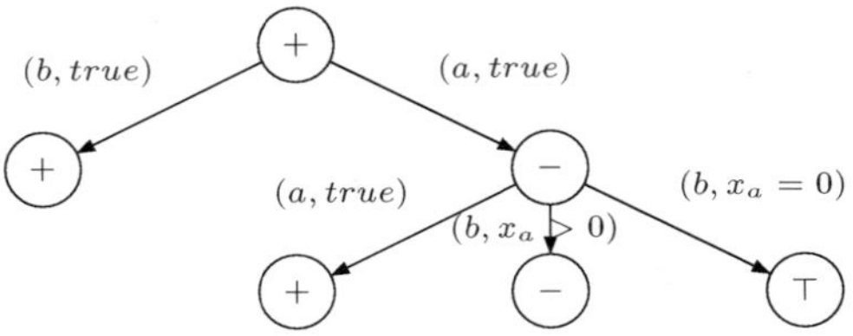

Fig. 1. A timed decision tree N

$$Obs(w_g) = \begin{cases} \top & \text{if there are } w_c, w'_c \in Dom(Obs) \text{ with } w_c \models w_g \text{ and } w'_c \models w_g \text{ such that } Obs(w_c) \neq Obs(w'_c) \\ Obs(w_c) & \text{if there is } w_c \in Dom(Obs) \text{ with } w_c \models w_g \text{ such that } Obs(w'_c) = Obs(w_c) \text{ for all } w'_c \in Dom(Obs) \text{ with } w'_c \models w_g \\ \bot & \text{if there is no } w_c \in Dom(Obs) \text{ with } w_c \models w_g \end{cases}$$

By this definition, the function *Obs* is overloaded so that it can also be regarded as a labeling of nodes in a timed decision tree. A node is labeled by $+$ (or $-$) if every observation that "leads to" the node is accepted (or rejected). A node is labeled by $\top$, and called *inconsistent*, if there are both accepted and rejected observations that lead to the node. If there are no observations that lead to the node, the node is labeled by $\bot$. A timed decision tree N is *consistent* w.r.t. *Obs* if it has no inconsistent nodes.

Definition 3. *A timed decision tree N* reflects *the partial mapping Obs if*

- *for any $w_c \in Dom(Obs)$ there is a $w_g \in N$ such that $w_c \models w_g$,*
- *N has no leaf w_g with $Obs(w_g) = \bot$.*

Example 1. Figure 1 shows an example of a set of observations[1] and a timed decision tree that reflects it[2]. □

Overview of Algorithm. From *Obs*, our algorithm constructs a timed decision tree which reflects *Obs*. Since each run of a TDERA corresponds to a guarded word, our ambition is that the tree will be a prefix of the unfolding of the learned TDERA. A main problem when constructing the tree is to find suitable guards that occur in edges of the TDERA. The *Learner* does not know *a priori* which guards to use in the final TDERA. Therefore, guards will be introduced "by need", when the information in *Obs* shows that they are necessary. Initially, the guarded words in the tree will use only *true* in guards. Whenever there is an inconsistent node w_g in the tree, it will be split into (at least) two guarded

[1] To simplify the presentation we use timed words as a short representation of clocked words.

[2] In the figures we label the edges of a timed decision tree with pairs of the form (a, g) where $a \in \Sigma$ and $g \in G$. The guarded word of a node is the sequence of all labels on the path reaching the node.

words, by splitting some guarded action in w_g according to whether a particular atomic clock guard is true or false. The appropriate clock guard is generated by posing additional membership queries in order to find a pair of observations with different outcomes (i.e., one accepted and one rejected), such that this guard is the only means to distinguish between them.

In order to fold the tree into an automaton, the inference algorithm also maintains a prefixed closed set U of nodes in the tree, which will be used to represent states in the TDERA. We let $succ(U)$ be the set of children of nodes in U which are not themselves in U. These nodes are used to construct transitions between nodes in U. The construction of U is based on a relation $\preceq_{un}$ between nodes of the tree which states which tree nodes may be merged when constructing an automaton. Intuitively $v_g \preceq_{un} u_g$ if the information about future behavior from the node v_g is contained in the information about future behavior from the node u_g, so that the node v_g can be merged with the node u_g when constructing an automaton.

When the tree satisfies certain properties the *Learner* constructs a hypothesized TDERA by merging each node in V with the corresponding node in U, and asks the *Teacher* an equivalence query. If a counterexample is returned, the *Learner* adds the counterexample to the timed decision tree, and the algorithm iterates. The algorithm terminates when a TDERA is found, for which the *Teacher* returns no counterexample.

In the next section we describe how to split inconsistent nodes in a timed decision tree, and in Section 5 we describe how to fold a timed decision tree into a TDERA by merging nodes.

4 Splitting Inconsistent Nodes

In this section, we describe our procedure for splitting inconsistent nodes in a timed decision tree. If $Obs(w_g) = \top$, then there are two clocked words $w_c, w'_c \in Dom(Obs)$ with $w_c \models w_g$ and $w'_c \models w_g$, such that $Obs(w_c) \neq Obs(w'_c)$. That is, w_c and w'_c both correspond to the same node, but one is accepted and one is rejected. In this section, we present our procedure for splitting some parent of w_g into two nodes using a suitable atomic clock guard that separates w_c and w'_c. More precisely, if $w_g = (a_1, g_1) \dots (a_n, g_n)$, then we must find an atomic guard g and a position i in w_g, and then split node $(a_1, g_1) \dots (a_i, g_i)$ into $(a_1, g_1) \dots (a_i, (g_i \wedge g))$ and $(a_1, g_1) \dots (a_i, (g_i \wedge \neg g))$.

4.1 Finding Critical Pairs

For two nonnegative real numbers p, p', define $p \approx p'$ if either

- $p > K$ and $p' > K$, or
- both p and p' are integers with $p = p'$, or
- both p and p' are non-integer with $\lfloor p \rfloor = \lfloor p' \rfloor$ (i.e., they have the same integer parts).

For two clock valuations γ and γ', define $\gamma \approx \gamma'$ if $\gamma(x_a) \approx \gamma'(x_a)$ for all event-recording clocks x_a. For two clocked words $w_c = (a_1, \gamma_1) \ldots (a_n, \gamma_n)$ and $w'_c = (a'_1, \gamma'_1) \ldots (a'_n, \gamma'_n)$, define $w_c \approx w'_c$ if $a_i = a'_i$ and $\gamma_i \approx \gamma'_i$ for all $1 \leq i \leq n$.

Definition 4. *The clocked word $w'_c = (a_1, \gamma'_1) \ldots (a_n, \gamma'_n)$ is* adjacent *to the clocked word $w_c = (a_1, \gamma_1) \ldots (a_n, \gamma_n)$ if $w_c \not\approx w'_c$ and for all i with $1 \leq i \leq n$ and symbols $a \in \Sigma$,*

- *whenever $\gamma'_i(x_a)$ is an integer, then $\gamma_i(x_a) = \gamma'_i(x_a)$,*
- *whenever $\gamma_i(x_a)$ is an integer, and $\gamma'_i(x_a)$ is not, then $|\gamma_i(x_a) - \gamma'_i(x_a)| < 1$,*
- *whenever $\gamma_i(x_a)$ is not an integer, then $\gamma_i(x_a) \approx \gamma'_i(x_a)$,*

Definition 5. *Let w_g be a guarded word. A* critical pair *in w_g is a pair of clocked words w_c, w'_c such that*

- *$Obs(w_c) \neq Obs(w'_c)$,*
- *$w_c \models w_g$ and $w'_c \models w_g$,*
- *w'_c is adjacent to w_c,*
- *there is no $w''_c \models w_g$ such that w'_c is adjacent to w''_c, and w''_c is adjacent to w_c.*

Intuitively, one clocked word in a critical pair is accepted and one is rejected, both correspond to the same inconsistent node, and they are "as adjacent as possible". The point of critical pairs is that they allow a natural construction of guards that split some parents of inconsistent nodes.

Theorem 1. *If there is a node w_g in the timed decision tree N such that $Obs(w_g) = \top$, then a critical pair in w_g can be found by $O(m|\Sigma| \log K)$ membership queries, where m is the length of w_g.*

Proof. We use binary search to find two adjacent clocked words and then solve a constraint satisfaction problem to find a critical pair. □

4.2 Splitting the Tree

In order to resolve inconsistency in a timed decision tree, we use a separating guard that can be inferred from a critical pair. A node is split according to the separating guard and subtree of the node is reconstructed. In general we maintain the property that every guard in a timed decision tree is inferred from a critical pair.

Definition 6. *Let w_c, w'_c be a critical pair in w_g, where $w_c = (a_1, \gamma_1) \ldots (a_n, \gamma_n)$ and $w'_c = (a_1, \gamma'_1) \ldots (a_n, \gamma'_n)$. The* separating guard *$x_a \leq k$ at position i is* inferred from *w_c, w'_c if*

- *$k \leq K$,*
- *$\gamma_i(x_a) = k$ and $\gamma'_i(x_a) > k$,*
- *$\gamma_j \approx \gamma'_j$ for all $j < i$.*

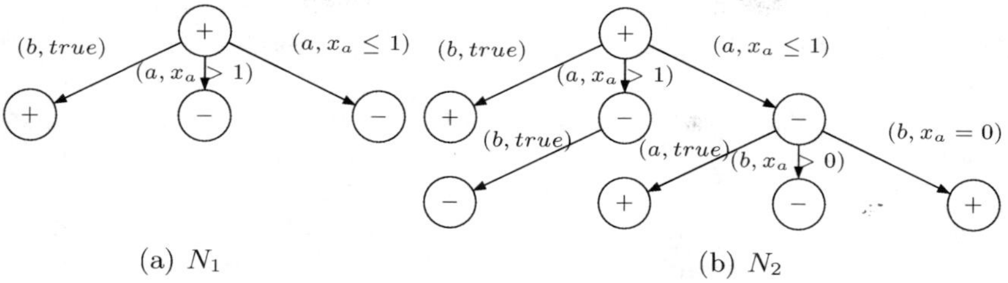

Fig. 2. Introducing a split into the tree N

Similarly, from the dual case the separating guard $x_a \geq k$ can be inferred.

Example 2. Suppose that we have observations $u_c = (a, \gamma_1(x_a){=}0.8, \gamma_1(x_b){=}0.8)(b, \gamma_2(x_a){=}0.2, \gamma_2(x_b){=}1.0)$ and $w_c = (a, \gamma_1'(x_a){=}0.8, \gamma_1'(x_b){=}0.8)(b, \gamma_2'(x_a){=}0.3, \gamma_2'(x_b){=}1.1)$ such that $Obs(u_c) \neq Obs(w_c)$. The clocked word w_c is adjacent to u_c. We see that u_c, w_c is a critical pair and that the only guard that can be inferred is $x_b \leq 1$, which separates γ_2 and γ_2'. □

We show an example how a split is introduced to the tree. Recall the tree N shown in Figure 1. The node $(a, true)(b, x_a = 0)$ is inconsistent. In order to resolve inconsistency we need to find a critical pair. Suppose that the critical pair is $(a, \gamma(x_a) = 1, \gamma(x_b) = 1)(b, \gamma(x_a) = 0, \gamma(x_b) = 1)$, $(a, \gamma(x_a) = 1.5, \gamma(x_b) = 1.5)(b, \gamma(x_a) = 0, \gamma(x_b) = 1.5)$. We infer guard $x_a \leq 1$ from it. Then we construct tree N_1 shown in Figure 2(a) by splitting node $(a, true)$ into nodes $(a, x_a \leq 1)$ and $(a, x_a > 1)$, we also remove successors of node $(a, true)$ from the tree N. Then we copy subtree of node $(a, true)$ of N to the subtree of node $(a, x_a \leq 1)$ of N_1 and construct tree N_2 shown in Figure 2(b). The node $(a, x_a > 1)(a, true)$ is missing since there is no corresponding observation.

5 Constructing Automata from Timed Decision Trees

In this section, we consider how to fold a timed decision tree into an event recording automaton by merging nodes.

Let N be a timed decision tree. In order to fold it into a TDERA, we maintain a prefix-closed subset U of N, which will be used as states of the automaton. Given a set U, the set $succ(U)$ is defined as the children of nodes in U which are not themselves in U. An automaton is formed by merging each node in $succ(U)$ with some node in U. This is done on the basis of a relation between nodes in N which say how nodes may be merged.

Definition 7. *Let N be a timed decision tree. A node $v_g \in N$ is* unifiable *with a node $u_g \in N$, denoted $v_g \leq_{un} u_g$, if for every descendant of v_g of form $v_g w_g$ with $Obs(v_g w_g) \in \{+, -\}$ and clocked word w_c with $w_c \models w_g$, there is a descendant of u_g of form $u_g w_g'$ with $w_c \models w_g'$ and $Obs(u_g w_g') = Obs(v_g w_g)$.*

That is, the node v_g is unifiable with node u_g if v_g can use the subtree of u_g to handle suffixes of clocked words. This means that the subtree at u_g must agree with the subtree at v_g on all descendants of v_g that are accepted or rejected.

The relation $v_g \preceq_{un} u_g$ on nodes in N can be checked symbolically in the following way. Say that two guarded words w_g and w'_g *overlap* if there is a clocked word w_c such that both $w_c \models w_g$ and $w_c \models w'_g$. This can be checked by propagating the constraints imposed by prefixes of w_g and w'_g on later clock constraints. For a clock constraint φ and a guarded word w_g we define (recursively) the constrained word $\varphi \,;w_g$ to be

$$\begin{aligned}\varphi \,;\lambda &= \lambda \\ \varphi \,;(a,g)\ w_g &= (a,\varphi\wedge g)\big(\ ((\varphi\wedge g)[x_a\mapsto 0])\uparrow \,;\ w_g\ \big)\end{aligned}$$

If φ is a postcondition of v_g, then $\varphi \,;w_g$ exactly characterizes the set of clocked words w_c that may appear as suffixes of clocked words $u_c w_c$ with $v_c w_c \models v_g w_g$. It follows that w_g and w'_g overlap if for $true; w_g = (a_1,g_1)\ldots(a_n,g_n)$ and $true; w'_g = (a_1,g'_1)\ldots(a_n,g'_n)$, we have $g_i \wedge g'_i \neq false$ for all $i = 1,\ldots,n$. Now $v_g \preceq_{un} u_g$ if for any descendant $v_g w_g$ of v_g with $Obs(v_g w_g) = \{+,-\}$,

– there is at least one descendant $u_g w'_g$ of u_g such that w_g and w'_g overlap, and
– for any descendant $u_g w'_g$ of u_g such that w_g and w'_g overlap, we have $Obs(v_g w_g) = Obs(u_g w'_g)$.

In the case that $v_g \not\preceq_{un} u_g$, there is one situation in which it is certain that v_g and u_g cannot be unified:

Definition 8. *The nodes u_g and v_g are* incompatible, *if they are distinguished by equivalent suffixes, i.e., if $Dom(Obs)$ contains clocked words $u_c w_c$ and $v_c w'_c$ such that*

– $u_c \models u_g$ *and* $v_c \models v_g$,
– $w_c \approx w'_c$, *and*
– $Obs(u_c w_c) \neq Obs(v_c w'_c)$.

The remaining case is when $v_g \not\preceq_{un} u_g$, and u_g and v_g are not incompatible. In this case there are descendants $v_g w_g$ of v_g and $u_g w'_g$ of u_g such that w_g and w'_g overlap, but $Obs(v_g w_g) \neq Obs(u_g w'_g)$. Then we perform the following *unification* procedure. If $sp(v_g); w_g$ and $sp(u_g); w'_g$ overlap, we pose one or two more membership queries to check if v_g and u_g are incompatible. If $sp(v_g); w_g$ and $sp(u_g); w'_g$ do not overlap and $sp(v_g) = sp(u_g)$ we can make v_g unifiable with u_g by the following procedure. We remove all descendants nodes of v_g. If there is a clocked word $v_c(a_1,\gamma_1)\ldots(a_n,\gamma_n) \in Dom(Obs)$, where $v_c \models v_g$ and there is a node $w_g(a_1,g_1)\ldots(a_n,g_n)$ in the tree, then we add a node $v_g(a_1,g_1)\ldots(a_n,g_n)$ to the tree and ask a query if the node is labeled by $\perp$.

In order to fold a TDT N into a TDERA, two natural requirements should be fulfilled.

Definition 9. *Let N be a TDT, and let U be a prefix-closed subset of N. Then N is*

- U-complete *if for all $u_g \in U$ and $a \in \Sigma$ there is some $u_g(a, g) \in N$,*
- U-closed *if for all $v_g \in succ(U)$ there is $u_g \in U$ with $v_g \leq_{un} u_g$.*

We can now describe our algorithm. Initially U contains the root $\{\lambda\}$. The *Learner* then asks membership queries, updates the tree, and maintains the set U, with the goal to make the tree consistent, U-complete, and U-closed. This is done by Algorithm 1.

Algorithm 1. Pseudo code for the construction consistent, U-closed and U-complete tree

---

Function construction(N,U)
  repeat
    while tree N is not consistent **do**
      Find inconsistent node $w_g \in N$.
      Perform splitting procedure which splits some prefix v_g of w_g into nodes v'_g and v''_g with new subtrees.
      if $v_g \in U \cup succ(U)$ **then** Add v'_g and v''_g to $succ(U)$.

    while tree N is not U−complete **do**
      Find $u_g \in U$ such that for some $a \in \Sigma$ there is no $g \in G_\Sigma$ with $u_g(a, g) \in N$.
      Add node $u_g(a, true)$ to N and to $succ(U)$.

    while tree N is not U−closed **do**
      Find $v_g \in succ(U)$ such that $v_g \not\leq_{un} u_g$ for all $u_g \in U$.
      for each $u_g \in U$
        Perform unification procedure for v_g and u_g.
        if $v_g \leq_{un} u_g$ **then continue_while**.
      Add v_g to U and all its successors to $succ(U)$.

  until tree N is consistent, U−closed and U−complete

From a consistent, U-complete, and U-closed timed decision tree we construct an event-recording automaton, called *merged automaton*, that agrees with the current set of observations *Obs*.

Definition 10. *Let the TDT N with set $U \subseteq N$ be a consistent, U-complete, and U-closed timed decision tree. The* merged automaton *of N, denoted $N_{\leq_{un}}$ is the TDERA $\langle U, \{\lambda\}, L^f, E\rangle$, where*

- $L^f = \{ u_g \in U \ : \ Obs(u_g) = + \}$,
- $(u_g, u_g(a, g), a, g) \in E$ *if* $u_g(a, g) \in U$, *otherwise* $(u_g, u'_g, a, g) \in E$ *with* $u_g(a, g) \in succ(U)$, *where* u'_g *for each* $u_g(a, g)$ *is chosen as a unique node with* $u_g(a, g) \leq_{un} u'_g$.

The locations of the merged automaton are nodes from U. For each $u_g(a, g)$ with $u_g \in U$, there is an edge from location u_g to location u'_g labeled with $a \in \Sigma$ and $g \in G_\Sigma$ if $u'_g = u_g(a, g)$ and $u_g(a, g) \in U$, or u'_g is a selected node in $succ(U)$ which is unifiable with $u_g(a, g)$.

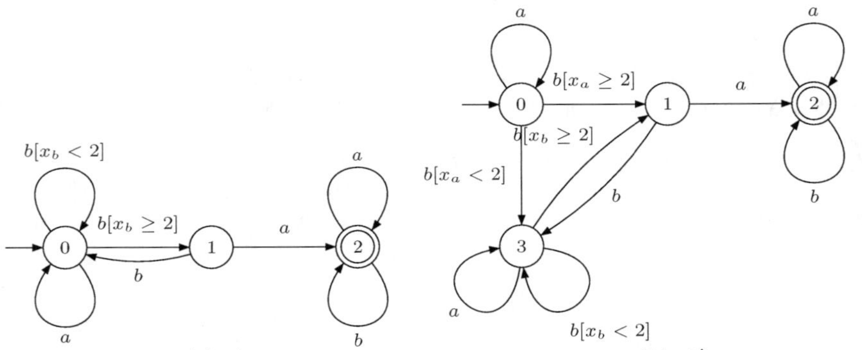

(a) A (b) A'

Fig. 3. Automata A and A'

Theorem 2. *Let A be some TDERA which is equivalent to the one we are learning. Then the inference algorithm for learning a TDERA equivalent to A terminates after $O(|S|^l)$ equivalence queries, and $O(K^{4|\Sigma|(l+|A||S|^{|A|})}+|S|^{l+|A||S|^{|A|}}(l+|A||S|^{|A|})|\Sigma|\log K)$ membership queries, where $|S|$ is the maximal number of splits used in the transitions from a node in A, $|A|$ is the number of locations in A and l is the length of the longest counterexample.*

Let A' be a minimum size TDERA of Theorem 2. The output of our inference algorithm is an event-recording automaton A representing the timed language to be learned. The number of locations in A is less than $m2^n$, where n is the size of A' and m is the number of K-bounded clock constraints, which is $O(4^{|\Sigma|^2}K^{|\Sigma|^2})$. For comparison, in [12] authors of this paper present an algorithm that infers the region graph of some automaton representing the language to be learned. The number of equivalence queries is at most R and the number of membership queries is $O(|\Sigma|^2R^2lK)$, where R is the size of the region graph which is bounded by $2^n|\Sigma|!2^{|\Sigma|}K^{|\Sigma|}$ states, and l is the length of longest counterexample.

6 Example

Suppose the system to learn is the event-recording automaton A in Figure 3(a). We start by asking the queries λ, $(a,0)$, and $(b,0)$, and then construct the timed decision tree N_1, shown in Figure 4(a), with $U = \{\lambda\}$. The tree N_1 is U-complete, consistent and U-closed. The Learner construct hypothesized automaton A_1 which has one location and submits A_1 as equivalence query.

Assume that the counterexample $(b,2)(a,2.4)$ is returned. It is accepted by A but rejected by A_1. Then the counterexample is added to the tree N_1 and the tree N_2, shown in Figure 4(b), is constructed. The tree is not U-closed as $(b, true) \not\leq_{un} \lambda$. Since $sp(\lambda); (a, true)$ and $sp((b, true)); (a, true)$ overlap, we ask query $(b,0)(a,0)$ that is not accepted by A. The node $(b, true)(a, true)$ is now

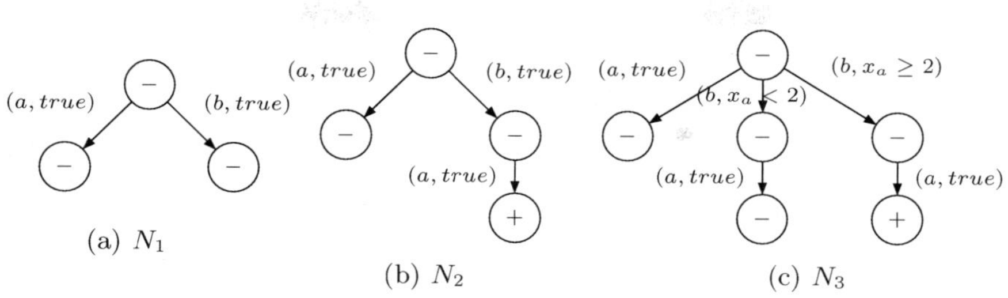

Fig. 4. Trees N_1, N_2 and N_3

labeled $\top$, and thus N_2 is inconsistent. By binary search we find the critical pair $(b, \gamma_1(x_a) = 2, \gamma_1(x_b) = 2)(a, \gamma_2(x_a) = 2.4, \gamma_2(x_b) = 0.4)$, $(b, \gamma'_1(x_a) = 1.75, \gamma'_1(x_b) = 1.75)(a, \gamma'_2(x_a) = 2.1, \gamma'_2(x_b) = 0.35)$ from which we infer the inequalities $x_a \geq 2$ and $x_b \geq 2$.

At this point we (arbitrarily) choose inequality $x_a \geq 2$ and construct timed decision tree N_3, shown in Figure 4(c), by splitting node $(b, true)$. The tree N_3 is not U-closed as $(b, x_a \geq 2) \not\leq_{un} \lambda$. Since $sp(\lambda); (a, true)$ and $sp((b, x_a \geq 2)); (a, true)$ overlap, we ask the queries $(a, 2.4)$ and $(b, 2)(a, 4.4)$ that are rejected and accepted by A respectively. Then λ and $(b, x_a \geq 2)$ are incompatible. We add $(b, x_a \geq 2)$ and $(b, x_a \geq 2)(a, true)$ to U. In order to make the tree U-complete we ask queries $(b, 2)(b, 2)$, $(b, 2)(a, 2)(a, 2)$, and $(b, 2)(a, 2)(b, 2)$. The resulting timed decision tree N_4 is shown in Figure 5(a).

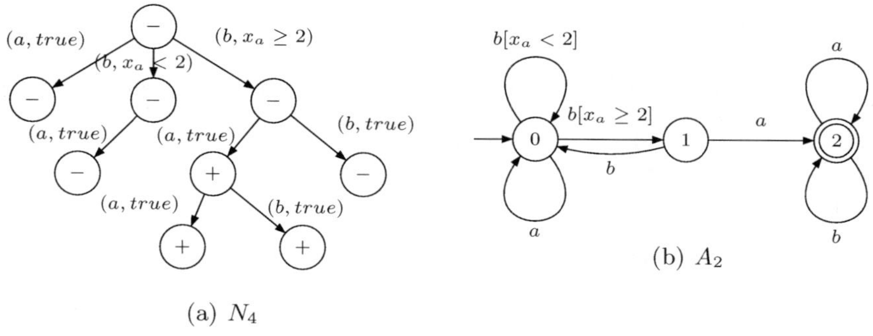

Fig. 5. Tree N_4 and automaton A_2

The tree N_4 is U-complete, consistent, and U-closed. The Learner construct the hypothesized automaton A_2, shown in Figure 5(b).

The procedure continues and the Learner will construct three more automata before automaton A', shown in Figure 3(b), is finally created (due to space limitations these steps are omitted). Note that the automaton A' contains only one state more than the automaton A.

7 Conclusion

We have presented a technique for inference of timed systems that can be represented as event-recording automata. We introduced timed decision tree as a data structure for organizing the results of the membership and equivalence queries. The timed decision tree is folded into an event-recording automaton by a merging procedure that is based on a notion of unifiable nodes. This is the first inference algorithm for the full class of event-recording automata which avoids explicit use of the region graph. We believe that the algorithm can be extended to deterministic timed automata.

References

1. R. Alur and D. Dill. A theory of timed automata. *Theoretical Computer Science*, 126:183–235, 1994.
2. R. Alur, L. Fix, and T. Henzinger. Event-clock automata: A determinizable class of timed automata. *Theoretical Computer Science*, 211:253–273, 1999.
3. D. Angluin. Learning regular sets from queries and counterexamples. *Information and Computation*, 75:87–106, 1987.
4. J. L. Balcázar, J. Díaz, and R. Gavaldá. Algorithms for learning finite automata from queries: A unified view. In *Advances in Algorithms, Languages, and Complexity*, pages 53–72. Kluwer, 1997.
5. J. Bengtsson, K. G. Larsen, F. Larsson, P. Pettersson, and W. Yi. UPPAAL: a tool suite for the automatic verification of real-time systems. In R. Alur, T. A. Henzinger, and E. D. Sontag, editors, *Hybrid Systems III*, volume 1066 of *LNCS*, pages 232–243. Springer-Verlag, 1996.
6. M. Bozga, C. Daws, O. Maler, A. Olivero, S. Tripakis, and S. Yovine. Kronos: A model-checking tool for real-time systems. In A. J. Hu and M. Y. Vardi, editors, *Proc. CAV'98*, volume 1427 of *LNCS*, pages 546–550. Springer-Verlag, 1998.
7. E. Clarke, O. Grumberg, and D. Peled. *Model Checking.* MIT Press, Dec. 1999.
8. J. Corbett, M. Dwyer, J. Hatcliff, S. Laubach, C. Pasareanu, Robby, and H. Zheng. Bandera : Extracting finite-state models from java source code. In *Proc. 22nd Int. Conf. on Software Engineering*, June 2000.
9. J.-C. Fernandez, C. Jard, T. Jéron, and C. Viho. An experiment in automatic generation of test suites for protocols with verification technology. *Science of Computer Programming*, 29, 1997.
10. E. M. Gold. Language identification in the limit. *Information and Control*, 10:447–474, 1967.
11. O. Grinchtein, B. Jonsson, and M. Leucker. Learning of event-recording automata. In *Proceedings of the Joint Conferences FORMATS and FTRTFT*, volume 3253 of *LNCS*, Sept. 2004.
12. O. Grinchtein, B. Jonsson, and M. Leucker. Inference of timed transition systems. *ENCS*, 138(3):87–99, 2005.
13. A. Groce, D. Peled, and M. Yannakakis. Adaptive model checking. In *Proc. TACAS'02*, LNCS, 2002.
14. A. Hagerer, H. Hungar, O. Niese, and B. Steffen. Model generation by moderated regular extrapolation. In R.-D. Kutsche and H. Weber, editors, *Proc. FASE02*, volume 2306 of *LNCS*, pages 80–95. Springer Verlag, 2002.

15. D. Harel, H. Lachover, A. Naamad, A. Pnueli, M. Politi, R. Sherman, A. Shtull-Trauring, and M. Trakhtenbrot. STATEMATE: A working environment for the development of complex reactive systems. *IEEE Trans. on Software Engineering*, 16(4):403–414, April 1990.
16. T. Henzinger, Z. Manna, and A. Pnueli. Temporal proof methodologies for timed transition systems. *Information and Computation*, 112:173–337, 1994.
17. T. Henzinger, J.-F. Raskin, and P.-Y. Schobbens. The regular real-time languages. In K. Larsen, S. Skuym, and G. Winskel, editors, *ICALP98*, volume 1443 of *LNCS*, pages 580–591. Springer Verlag, 1998.
18. G. Holzmann. Logic verification of ANSI-C code with SPIN. In K. Havelund, J. Penix, and W. Visser, editors, *SPIN Model Checking and Software Verification: Proc. 7th Int. SPIN Workshop*, volume 1885 of *LNCS*, pages 131–147, Stanford, CA, 2000. Springer Verlag.
19. H. Hungar, O. Niese, and B. Steffen. Domain-specific optimization in automata learning. In *Proc. CAV'03*, 2003.
20. M. Kearns and U. Vazirani. *An Introduction to Computational Learning Theory*. MIT Press, 1994.
21. O. Maler and A. Pnueli. On recognizable timed languages. In *Proc. FOSSACS04*, LNCS. Springer-Verlag, 2004.
22. R. Rivest and R. Schapire. Inference of finite automata using homing sequences. *Information and Computation*, 103:299–347, 1993.
23. M. Schmitt, M. Ebner, and J. Grabowski. Test generation with autolink and testcomposer. In *Proc. 2nd Workshop of the SDL Forum Society on SDL and MSC - SAM'2000*, June 2000.
24. J. Springintveld and F. Vaandrager. Minimizable timed automata. In B. Jonsson and J. Parrow, editors, *Proc. FTRTFT'96*, volume 1135 of *LNCS*, pages 130–147. Springer Verlag, 1996.
25. T. Wilke. Specifying timed state sequences in powerful decidable logics and timed automata. In H. Langmaack, W. P. de Roever, and J. Vytopil, editors, *Proc. FTRTFT'94*, volume 863 of *LNCS*, pages 694–715. Springer Verlag, 1994.

Controller Synthesis for MTL Specifications*

Patricia Bouyer, Laura Bozzelli, and Fabrice Chevalier

LSV, CNRS & ENS Cachan, France
{bouyer, bozzelli, chevalie}@lsv.ens-cachan.fr

Abstract. We consider the control problem for timed automata against specifications given as MTL formulas. The logic MTL is a linear-time timed temporal logic which extends LTL with timing constraints on modalities, and recently, its model-checking has been proved decidable in several cases. We investigate these decidable fragments of MTL (full MTL when interpreted over finite timed words, and Safety-MTL when interpreted over infinite timed words), and prove two kinds of results. *(1)* We first prove that, contrary to model-checking, the control problem is undecidable. Roughly, the computation of a lossy channel system could be encoded as a model-checking problem, and we prove here that a perfect channel system can be encoded as a control problem. *(2)* We then prove that if we fix the resources of the controller (by resources we mean clocks and constants that the controller can use), the control problem becomes decidable. This decidability result relies on properties of well (and better) quasi-orderings.

1 Introduction

Control of Timed Systems. Timed automata are a well-established and widely used model for representing real-time systems. Since their definition in the 90's [5], many works have investigated this model, and several tools have been developed for model-checking timed automata and have been used for verifying real industrial case studies.

To deal with *open* systems, *i.e.* systems interacting with an environment (which is the case of most embedded systems), model-checking may be not sufficient, and we need to *control* (or guide) the system so that it satisfies the specification, whatever the environment does. More formally, the *control problem* asks, given a system $\mathcal{S}$ and a specification φ, whether there exists a controller $\mathcal{C}$ such that $\mathcal{S}$ guided by $\mathcal{C}$ satisfies φ. Since the mid-90's, the control of real-time systems has developed a lot [8,17,13,16,15,11,4], and several kinds of properties have been investigated, for instance properties based on states of the system [8,17,4], or expressed in LTL [15], or in the branching-time timed temporal logic TCTL [16], or even expressed by timed automata [13]. However, to our knowledge no work has investigated the control problem against properties expressed in a linear-time timed temporal logic.

The Logic MTL. The logic MTL [18] is a linear-time timed temporal logic which extends LTL with timing constraints on Until modalities. For instance, we can write a formula $\psi = \Box\,(p \rightarrow \Diamond_{=1} q)$, which expresses that a request p is always followed one time unit later by a response q. The interest in this logic has encountered a great soar in the last year, since Ouaknine and Worrell proved that the model-checking and the

* Work supported by the ACI Cortos, a program of the French ministry of research.

C. Baier and H. Hermanns (Eds.): CONCUR 2006, LNCS 4137, pp. 450–464, 2006.

satisfiability problems for this logic are decidable [22], as soon as they are interpreted using a *pointwise semantics* over finite timed words. It is worth noticing that MTL, like most real-time logics, can be interpreted either using a pointwise semantics (the system is observed through events), or using a continuous semantics (the system is observed at any point in time). These two points of view lead to pretty different decidability properties: for instance, while the first semantics makes model-checking decidable, the second semantics leads to undecidability [6]. Since this new insight into decidability of linear-time timed temporal logics, works on MTL are flourishing [10,14,23,24]. Let us for instance point out the result of [24], stating that the fragment of MTL called Safety-MTL (which roughly imposes upper bounds on Until modalities) is decidable for the pointwise semantics when interpreted over infinite timed words, while model-checking full MTL is undecidable in this case [23].

Our Contributions. In this paper, we consider the control problem for properties given as MTL or Safety-MTL formulas. We prove the following results:

- The control problem for MTL is undecidable for the pointwise semantics, even when considering finite timed words. In addition, if restricting to Safety-MTL, the control problem is also undecidable when interpreted over infinite timed words. These undecidability results rely on an elegant construction which (roughly) uses (un)controllable actions to check that every p action is preceded one time unit earlier by a q action: this property cannot be expressed in MTL, but is somehow sufficient to lead to undecidability [14].
- When bounding resources of the controller (its set of clocks, and constants it can use in its constraints), the control problem becomes decidable for MTL specifications interpreted over finite timed words, and for Safety-MTL specifications interpreted over infinite timed words. Note that such a restriction to bounded resources is quite common in the framework of synthesis of timed systems [19,13,11]. However, the construction proposed here is much more involved than those done in previous papers, and requires well (and better) quasi-ordering arguments for proving correctness and termination of the construction.

All proofs can be found in the research report [9].

2 Preliminaries

Time, Granularity, and Symbolic Alphabet. Let $\mathbb{R}_{\geq 0}$ be the set of non-negative reals and $\mathbb{Q}_{\geq 0}$ be the set of non-negative rational numbers. Let Σ be an alphabet. A *timed word* over Σ is a word $\sigma = (a_1, \tau_1)(a_2, \tau_2)\ldots$ over $\Sigma \times \mathbb{R}_{\geq 0}$ such that $\tau_1 = 0$ and $\tau_i \leq \tau_{i+1}$ for every $1 \leq i < |\sigma|$ (where $|\sigma|$ denotes the (possibly infinite) length of σ).[1] If σ is infinite, it is *non-Zeno* if the sequence $\{\tau_i\}_{i\in\mathbb{N}}$ is unbounded. Let $T\Sigma^*$ (resp. $T\Sigma^\omega$) be the set of finite (resp. infinite non-Zeno) timed words over Σ.

Let X be a finite set of variables (called *clocks* in our context). The set $\mathcal{G}(X)$ of *clock constraints* g over X is defined by the grammar: $g ::= g \wedge g \mid x \bowtie c$, where

[1] We force timed words to satisfy $\tau_1 = 0$ in order to have a natural way to define initial satisfiability in the semantics of MTL.

$\bowtie \in \{<, \leq, =, \geq, >\}$, $x \in X$, and $c \in \mathbb{Q}_{\geq 0}$. A *valuation* over X is a mapping $\nu : X \rightarrow \mathbb{R}_{\geq 0}$. Whether a valuation ν satisfies a constraint g (written $\nu \models g$) is defined naturally, and we set $[\![g]\!] = \{\nu \mid \nu \models g\}$. For $t \in \mathbb{R}_{\geq 0}$, the valuation $\nu + t$ is defined as $(\nu + t)(x) = \nu(x) + t$ for all $x \in X$. For $Y \subseteq X$, the valuation $\nu[Y \leftarrow 0]$ is defined as $\nu[Y \leftarrow 0](x) = 0$ if $x \in Y$ and $\nu[Y \leftarrow 0](x) = \nu(x)$ otherwise. Also, we use $\overrightarrow{0}$ to denote the valuation which maps every $x \in X$ to 0.

We define a measure of the clocks and constants used in a set of constraints, called its *granularity*. A granularity is specified by a triple $\mu = (X, m, K)$ where X is a finite set of clocks, $m \in \mathbb{N}_{>0}$, and $K \in \mathbb{N}$. A constraint g is *μ-granular* if the clocks it uses belong to X and each constant occurring in g is $\frac{\alpha}{m}$ with $\alpha \leq K$ and $\alpha \in \mathbb{N}$. A granularity μ is *finer* than μ' if all μ'-granular constraints are also μ-granular. Also, we say that $\mu = (X, m, K)$ is the *granularity* of a *finite* set of constraints if X (resp. m, resp. $\frac{K}{m}$) is the exact set of clocks (resp. the lcm of all denominators of constants, resp. the largest constant) mentioned in the constraints. A μ-granular constraint g is *μ-atomic* if for every μ-granular constraint g', either $[\![g]\!] \subseteq [\![g']\!]$, or $[\![g]\!] \cap [\![g']\!] = \emptyset$.

For an alphabet Σ and a set of clocks X, a *symbolic alphabet Γ based on* (Σ, X) is a finite subset of $\Sigma \times \mathcal{G}(X) \times 2^X$. A (symbolic) word $\gamma = (a_1, g_1, Y_1)(a_2, g_2, Y_2)\ldots$ over Γ gives rise to a set of timed words over Σ, denoted $tw(\gamma)$. We interpret the symbolic action (a, g, Y) to mean that action a can happen if the constraint g is satisfied, with the clocks in Y being reset after the action. Formally, $\sigma \in tw(\gamma)$ iff $|\sigma| = |\gamma|$, $\sigma = (a_1, \tau_1)(a_2, \tau_2)\ldots$, and there is a sequence of valuations $\nu_0, \nu_1, \nu_2, \ldots$ over X such that $\nu_0 = \overrightarrow{0}$ and for all $0 \leq i < |\gamma|$, $\nu_i + \tau_{i+1} - \tau_i \in [\![g_{i+1}]\!]$ and $\nu_{i+1} = (\nu_i + \tau_{i+1} - \tau_i)[Y_{i+1} \leftarrow 0]$ (assuming $\tau_0 = 0$).

Symbolic Transition Systems and Timed Automata. A *symbolic transition system* (*STS*) over a symbolic alphabet Γ based on (Σ, X) is a tuple $\mathcal{T} = \langle S, s_0, \rightarrow, F\rangle$ where S is a (possibly infinite) set of states, $s_0 \in S$ is the initial state, $\rightarrow \subseteq S \times \Gamma \times S$ is the transition relation, and $F \subseteq S$ is a set of accepting states.[2] A *timed automaton* (TA, for short) [5] is an *STS* with finitely many states. In the sequel, if $\mathcal{A}$ is a TA, then we will write $\mathcal{T}(\mathcal{A})$ for the *STS* corresponding to $\mathcal{A}$ where all states are considered accepting.

For a finite or infinite path $\pi = s_1 \xrightarrow{b_1} s_2 \xrightarrow{b_2} \ldots$ of $\mathcal{T}$, the *trace* of π is the word over Γ given by $b_1 b_2 \ldots$. Such a finite (resp. infinite) path is accepting if it ends in (resp. visits infinitely often) an accepting state. We denote by $\mathcal{L}^*_{symb}(\mathcal{T})$ (resp. $\mathcal{L}^\omega_{symb}(\mathcal{T})$) the set of finite (resp. infinite) symbolic words over Γ that are traces of finite (resp. infinite) accepting paths starting from the initial state s_0. We set $\mathcal{L}_{symb}(\mathcal{T}) = \mathcal{L}^*_{symb}(\mathcal{T}) \cup \mathcal{L}^\omega_{symb}(\mathcal{T})$. The *STS* $\mathcal{T}$ is *symb-deterministic* whenever $s \xrightarrow{b} s_1$ and $s \xrightarrow{b} s_2$ implies $s_1 = s_2$. For each state $s \in S$, we denote by *enabled*$_{\mathcal{T}}(s)$ the set of symbolic actions $b \in \Gamma$ such that $s \xrightarrow{b} s'$ for some $s' \in S$. If $\mathcal{T}$ is symb-deterministic, then for each word $\gamma \in \mathcal{L}_{symb}(\mathcal{T})$, there is at most one path starting from s_0 whose trace is γ. In this case and assuming that γ is finite, we denote by *state*$_{\mathcal{T}}(\gamma)$, the last state of such a path. Let $\mathcal{T} = \langle S, s_0, \rightarrow\rangle$ be an *STS*. The *deterministic version* of $\mathcal{T}$ is the symb-deterministic *STS* *Det*$(\mathcal{T}) = \langle 2^S, \{s_0\}, \rightarrow_D\rangle$, where $S_1 \xrightarrow{b}_D S_2$ iff $S_2 = \{s_2 \in S \mid \exists s_1 \in S_1.\ s_1 \xrightarrow{b} s_2\}$ and $S_2 \neq \emptyset$. Note that $\mathcal{L}^*_{symb}(Det(\mathcal{T})) = \mathcal{L}^*_{symb}(\mathcal{T})$.

[2] We may omit F in the tuple if all states are accepting.

Let $\mathcal{T}$ be an *STS*. It also recognizes timed words.The *timed language* over finite words accepted by $\mathcal{T}$, denoted $\mathcal{L}^*(\mathcal{T})$, is defined by $\mathcal{L}^*(\mathcal{T}) = tw(\mathcal{L}^*_{symb}(\mathcal{T}))$, while the timed language over infinite words accepted by $\mathcal{T}$, denoted $\mathcal{L}^\omega(\mathcal{T})$, is defined by $\mathcal{L}^\omega(\mathcal{T}) = tw(\mathcal{L}^\omega_{symb}(\mathcal{T})) \cap T\Sigma^\omega$. The *STS* $\mathcal{T}$ is said *deterministic* if there are no distinct transitions $q \xrightarrow{a,g_1,Y_1} q_1$ and $q \xrightarrow{a,g_2,Y_2} q_2$ with $[\![g_1]\!] \cap [\![g_2]\!] \neq \emptyset$. This notion is stronger than symb-determinism.

Let $\mathcal{T}_1 = \langle Q_1, q_0^1, \rightarrow_1, F_1\rangle$ and $\mathcal{T}_2 = \langle Q_2, q_0^2, \rightarrow_2\rangle$ be two *STS* over an alphabet Γ based on (Σ, X). The *parallel composition* of $\mathcal{T}_1$ and $\mathcal{T}_2$, denoted $\mathcal{T}_1 \parallel \mathcal{T}_2$, is the *STS* $\langle Q, q_0, \rightarrow, F\rangle$ where $Q = Q_1 \times Q_2$, $q_0 = (q_0^1, q_0^2)$, $F = F_1 \times Q_2$, and $(p_1, p_2) \xrightarrow{a,g,Y} (q_1, q_2)$ iff $p_1 \xrightarrow{a,g_1,Y_1}_1 q_1$ and $p_2 \xrightarrow{a,g_2,Y_2}_2 q_2$ with $g = g_1 \wedge g_2$ and $Y = Y_1 \cup Y_2$.

2.1 Metric Temporal Logic (MTL)

The logic MTL [18] is a linear-time timed temporal logic which extends LTL with time constraints on Until modalities. The set of MTL formulae over a set Σ of atomic actions is defined inductively as follows:

$$\varphi ::= \top \mid a \mid \neg\varphi \mid \varphi \wedge \varphi \mid \varphi\, \mathcal{U}_I\, \varphi$$

where $\top$ denotes "true", $a \in \Sigma$, and $I \subseteq \mathbb{R}_{\geq 0}$ is an interval with bounds in $\mathbb{Q}_{\geq 0} \cup \{\infty\}$. We will use some classical shortcuts: $\Diamond_I \varphi$ stands for $\top\, \mathcal{U}_I\, \varphi$ (the *constrained eventually* operator), $\Box_I \varphi$ stands for $\neg\Diamond_I\neg\varphi$ (the *constrained always* operator), and $\varphi_1\, \widetilde{\mathcal{U}}_I\, \varphi_2$ stands for $\neg((\neg\varphi_1)\, \mathcal{U}_I\, (\neg\varphi_2))$ (the *dual-until* operator). We also use pseudo-arithmetic expressions (like '≥ 1' or '$= 1$') to denote intervals. We may omit the subscript I when it is equal to $\mathbb{R}_{\geq 0}$.

In this paper we consider the so-called *pointwise semantics*, and thus interpret MTL over timed words [22]. Given a (finite or infinite) timed word $\sigma = (a_1, \tau_1)(a_2, \tau_2)\ldots$ and an MTL formula φ, for each $1 \leq i \leq |\sigma|$, the satisfaction relation $(\sigma, i) \models \varphi$ (which reads as "σ satisfies φ at position i") is defined by induction. The rules for atoms, negation, and conjunction are standard. For the until modality, following [22], we give a *strict-future* interpretation as follows:

$$(\sigma, i) \models \varphi_1\, \mathcal{U}_I\, \varphi_2 \text{ iff there is } j > i \text{ such that } (\sigma, j) \models \varphi_2,\ \tau_j - \tau_i \in I, \text{ and }$$
$$(\sigma, k) \models \varphi_1 \text{ for all } k \text{ with } i < k < j$$

We say that σ satisfies φ, denoted $\sigma \models \varphi$, if $(\sigma, 1) \models \varphi$. The set of finite models of φ is given by $\mathcal{L}^*(\varphi) = \{\sigma \in T\Sigma^* \mid \sigma \models \varphi\}$. The set of infinite models of φ is given by $\mathcal{L}^\omega(\varphi) = \{\sigma \in T\Sigma^\omega \mid \sigma \models \varphi\}$.

Using the dual-until operator and the disjunction we can rewrite every MTL formula into an equivalent formula in *positive normal form, i.e.* where negation is only applied to actions $a \in \Sigma$. We then define the fragment of MTL, called Safety-MTL [22], consisting of those MTL formulas in positive normal form that only include instances of the constrained until operator $\mathcal{U}_I$ in which interval I has bounded length. Note that no restriction is placed on the dual-until operator.

Example 1. Let $\Sigma = \{a, b\}$ and $\varphi_1 := \Box(a \rightarrow \Diamond_{=1} b)$ be the MTL formula requiring that every a-event is followed one time unit later by a b-event. Also, let $\mathcal{L}$ be the language consisting of finite timed words σ such that the untimed of σ is in a^*b^* and two different events do not happen at the same time. It is clear that $\mathcal{L}$ can be specified by some MTL formula φ_2. Now, we note that $\mathit{Untimed}(\mathcal{L}^*(\varphi_1 \wedge \varphi_2)) = \{a^n b^m \mid m \geq n\}$ (where $\mathit{Untimed}(\cdot)$ is the projection over Σ), which is a non-regular language [7].

2.2 Control Problem for MTL Specifications

Let $\Sigma = \Sigma_C \cup \Sigma_E$ be an alphabet partitioned into a set of *controllable* actions Σ_C and a set of *environment* actions Σ_E. A *plant* $\mathcal{P}$ over Σ is a deterministic *TA*. Let the clocks used in $\mathcal{P}$ be $X_\mathcal{P}$, and $\mu = (X_\mathcal{P} \cup X_\mathcal{C}, m, K)$ be a granularity finer than that of the plant. Then, a *μ-controller* for $\mathcal{P}$ is a deterministic *STS* $\mathcal{C}$ over a symbolic alphabet based on $(\Sigma, X_\mathcal{P} \cup X_\mathcal{C})$ having granularity μ and satisfying:

(C1) $\mathcal{C}$ does not reset the clocks of the plant: $q_\mathcal{C} \xrightarrow{a,g,Y} q'_\mathcal{C}$ in $\mathcal{C}$ implies $Y \subseteq X_\mathcal{C}$.
(C2) $\mathcal{C}$ does not restrict environment actions (*non-restricting*): if $\sigma \in \mathcal{L}^*(\mathcal{T}(\mathcal{P}\|\mathcal{C}))$ and $\sigma \cdot (e,t) \in \mathcal{L}^*(\mathcal{T}(\mathcal{P}))$ with $e \in \Sigma_E$, then $\sigma \cdot (e,t) \in \mathcal{L}^*(\mathcal{T}(\mathcal{P}\|\mathcal{C}))$.
(C3) $\mathcal{C}$ is *non-blocking*: if $\sigma \in \mathcal{L}^*(\mathcal{T}(\mathcal{P}\|\mathcal{C}))$ and $\sigma\cdot(a,t) \in \mathcal{L}^*(\mathcal{T}(\mathcal{P}))$, then $\sigma\cdot(b,t') \in \mathcal{L}^*(\mathcal{T}(\mathcal{P}\|\mathcal{C}))$ for some $b \in \Sigma$ and $t' \in \mathbb{R}_{\geq 0}$.
(C4) all states of $\mathcal{C}$ are accepting (*fairness*).

For a timed language $\mathcal{L} \subseteq T\Sigma^*$, we say that a μ-controller $\mathcal{C}$ *controls* $\mathcal{P}$ against the specification of desired (resp. undesired) behaviours $\mathcal{L}$ iff $\mathcal{L}^*(\mathcal{P}\|\mathcal{C}) \subseteq \mathcal{L}$ (resp. $\mathcal{L}^*(\mathcal{P}\|\mathcal{C}) \cap \mathcal{L} = \emptyset$). A similar notion is defined for timed languages over infinite words.

Problem 1. The **control problem with fixed resources against desired (resp. undesired) behaviours** is to decide, given a plant $\mathcal{P}$, a specification $\mathcal{L}$, and a granularity μ finer than that of $\mathcal{P}$, whether there exists a μ-controller $\mathcal{C}$ which controls $\mathcal{P}$ against the specification of desired (resp. undesired) behaviours $\mathcal{L}$.

Problem 2. The **control problem with non-fixed resources** is analogous to the previous one with the important difference that the granularity of the controller is not specified *a priori*.

In this paper we study the decidability of these problems for specifications given as MTL formulas (*i.e.* $\mathcal{L} = \mathcal{L}^\omega(\varphi)$ or $\mathcal{L} = \mathcal{L}^*(\varphi)$ for a given MTL formula φ). However, for MTL specifications over infinite words, it is easy to show that the control problem is undecidable (also for fixed resources) by a trivial reduction from the MTL satisfiability problem over infinite words that is known to be undecidable [23]. Thus, in the following we consider the cases in which either $\mathcal{L}$ is the set of *finite* models of an MTL formula or the set of infinite models of a Safety-MTL formula.

3 Undecidability Results

In this section we show that for non-fixed resources, the control problems for both MTL over finite words and Safety-MTL over infinite words against *desired* behaviours are undecidable. We obtain these undecidability results by a reduction from the reachability problem of channel machines, which is known to be undecidable [12].

A *deterministic channel machine* (*DCM*, for short) $\mathcal{S} = \langle S, s_0, s_{\text{halt}}, M, \Delta \rangle$ is a finite-state automaton acting on an unbounded fifo channel, where S is a finite set of (control) states, $s_0 \in S$ is the initial state, $s_{\text{halt}} \in S$ is the halting state, M is a finite set of messages, and $\Delta \subseteq S \times \{m!, m? \mid m \in M\} \times S$ is the transition relation satisfying the following *determinism* hypothesis: (1) $(s, a, s_1) \in \Delta$ and $(s, a, s_2) \in \Delta$ implies $s_1 = s_2$; and (2) $(s, m!, s_1) \in \Delta$ and $(s, a, s_2) \in \Delta$ implies $a = m!$ and $s_1 = s_2$.

The semantics is described by a labelled graph $G(\mathcal{S})$, whose set of vertices (global states) is the set of pairs (s, x) with $s \in S$ and $x \in M^*$ (representing the channel content), and whose edge relation is defined as follows: $(s, x) \xrightarrow{a} (s', y)$ iff $(s, a, s') \in \Delta$ and either $a = m!$ and $y = x \cdot m$, or $a = m?$ and $x = m \cdot y$. We say that s_{halt} is *reachable* in $\mathcal{S}$ iff there is path in $G(\mathcal{S})$ from (s_0, ε) to (s_{halt}, x) for some $x \in M^*$. The *reachability problem* for *DCM*s then asks whether, given a *DCM* $\mathcal{S}$, s_{halt} is reachable in $\mathcal{S}$.

Proposition 1 ([12]). *The reachability problem for* DCM*s is undecidable.*

Theorem 1. *The control problem with non-fixed resources for* MTL *specifications over* finite *words representing desired or undesired behaviours is undecidable.*

Proof. We reduce the halting problem for *DCM*s to the control problem for MTL specifications against *desired* behaviours (note that since MTL is closed under negation, the undecidability result holds also for specifications of *undesired* behaviours). We first ensure that the *DCM* has additional properties which will be useful in our construction, and then we describe the reduction and give a sketch of proof.

Adding properties to channel machines. Given a *DCM* $\mathcal{S}' = (S', s'_0, s'_{\text{halt}}, M', \Delta')$, we can construct w.l.o.g. (for details see [9]) an equivalent one $\mathcal{S} = (S, s_0, s_{\text{halt}}, M, \Delta)$ (w.r.t. reachability of the halting state) such that:

- s_{halt} is the single state with no outgoing transition,
- there is no cycle in (S, Δ) in which every edge is labelled by a write action,
- if the unique (maximal) path in $G(\mathcal{S})$ from (s_0, ε) is infinite, then the size of the channel content is unbounded (*unbounded channel property*).

Encoding computations with timed words. We encode the executions of $\mathcal{S}$ (*i.e.* the paths of $G(\mathcal{S})$ from (s_0, ε)) [22] by the set $L_{correct}$ of timed words $(a_1, t_1)(a_2, t_2)\cdots$ over $\{m?, m! \mid m \in M\}$ such that:

(R1) there exist $s_1, s_2, \cdots$ such that $s_1 = s_0$ and $(s_i, a_i, s_{i+1}) \in \Delta$ for each $i \geq 1$,
(R2) there is no two actions at the same time: $\forall i, j,\ i \neq j \Rightarrow t_i \neq t_j$,
(R3) every $m!$ action is matched by an $m?$ action one time unit later:
$$\forall i,\ (a_i = m! \text{ and } \exists j\ t_j \geq t_i + 1) \Rightarrow \exists k\ (a_k = m? \text{ and } t_k = t_i + 1),$$
(R4) every $m?$ action is matched by an $m!$ action one time unit earlier:
$$\forall i,\ (a_i = m?) \Rightarrow \exists k\ (a_k = m! \text{ and } t_k = t_i - 1),$$

Reduction to the control problem. Let $\mathcal{S} = (S, s_0, s_{\text{halt}}, M, \Delta)$ be a *DCM* satisfying the above-mentioned properties. The idea of the reduction is the following: the plant will roughly be the channel machine $\mathcal{S}$ with all actions $m!$ and $m?$ being controllable. We add two new uncontrollable actions *Nil* and *Check*. A play will consist of an alternance of controllable and uncontrollable actions. When it is his turn the environment can either play a *Nil* action to continue the simulation or a *Check* action to stop the game (the use of the *Check* action is explained below). The goal of the controller will be to simulate a correct execution of the channel machine reaching state s_{halt} (of course this is possible iff s_{halt} is reachable in $\mathcal{S}$). If s_{halt} is reached at some point, the controller can stop performing actions and wins the game (if the execution played so far is correct).

We now have to ensure that the timed words σ played by the controller simulate a valid execution of the channel machine (that is $\sigma \in L_{correct}$):

- **(R1)** is satisfied because the plant we consider has the same structure as $\mathcal{S}$,
- **(R2)** and **(R3)** can be encoded by an MTL formula in the specification,
- **(R4)** will be checked by the environment. We add a new sink state q_{End} to the plant; at any time the environment can decide to stop the game by playing a *Check* action and going to this new state. In this case, if the *Check* action is played at the same time as an $m?$ action and there is no matching $m!$ action one time unit before, the controller will be declared losing (in the MTL formula). *Otherwise*, (that is when there is no $m?$ action or if there is a matching $m!$ one time unit before), the controller will be declared winning.
  Thus the controller will be forced to simulate a correct execution of $\mathcal{S}$ because if it tries to insert an $m?$ which is not matched by a $m!$, then it may lose if the environment plays *Check* immediately after.

Here is the formal definition of the plant $\mathcal{P}_\mathcal{S}$ and the MTL specification ϕ. $\mathcal{P}_\mathcal{S} = \langle Q, q_0, \rightarrow, F\rangle$ is defined over a symbolic alphabet based on $(\Sigma_C \cup \Sigma_E, X)$, where

- $\Sigma_C = \{m!, m? \mid m \in M\}$, $\Sigma_E = \{\mathit{Nil}, \mathit{Check}\}$, and $X = \{x\}$;
- $Q = S \cup \{q_\delta \mid \delta \in \Delta\} \cup \{q_{End}\}$, $q_0 = s_0$, and $F = Q$;
- $q \xrightarrow{true, a, \{x\}} q_\delta$ iff $\delta = (q, a, q') \in \Delta$,
- $q_\delta \xrightarrow{x=0, Nil} q'$ iff $\delta = (q, a, q')$ for some q and a.
- $q_\delta \xrightarrow{x=0, Check} q_{End}$

The MTL formula ϕ is given by $\phi = \phi_{Sim} \wedge \phi_{Match} \wedge \phi_{Check}$, where $\phi_{C\text{-}action}$ stands for $\bigvee_{a \in \Sigma_C} a$, and:

- $\phi_{Sim} = \overline{\Box}\neg(\phi_{C\text{-}action} \wedge \Diamond_{=0}\, \phi_{C\text{-}action})$ [3] [expresses **(R2)**]
- $\phi_{Match} = \overline{\Box}((m! \wedge \Diamond_{\geq 1}\phi_{C\text{-}action}) \Rightarrow \Diamond_{=1} m?)$ [expresses **(R3)**]
- $\phi_{Check} = \bigwedge_{m \in M} \Big(\big(\overline{\Diamond}(m? \wedge \Diamond_{=0} Check)\big) \Rightarrow \overline{\Diamond}(m! \wedge \Diamond_{=1} Check) \Big)$
  [ensures that if *Check* is played at the same time than (but right after) an $m?$ action, then this $m?$ action must be matched by an $m!$ one time unit earlier]

Sketch of proof. In our control game, the controller can only win if it simulates the maximal execution of $\mathcal{S}$. Now, we show that s_{halt} is reachable in $\mathcal{S}$ if and only if there exists a controller for the plant $\mathcal{P}_\mathcal{S}$ against the specification ϕ of desired behaviours.

If s_{halt} is reachable in $\mathcal{S}$, we consider a controller with one clock (reset after every transition) which simply plays a correct encoding (with timestamps in $\mathbb{Q}_{\geq 0}$) of the execution of $\mathcal{S}$, reaching s_{halt} and staying idle from here.

[3] We use the non-strict version of $\Diamond$ and $\Box$: $\overline{\Diamond}_I\varphi$ stands for $\varphi \vee \Diamond_I\varphi$ and $\overline{\Box}_I\varphi$ stands for $\neg\overline{\Diamond}_I\neg\varphi$.

Assume now that s_{halt} is not reachable in $\mathcal{S}$. Two cases may occur: either (1) $\mathcal{S}$ may be blocking at some point; a controller playing a valid execution will then be stuck in a state different from s_{halt}, however as it is non-blocking, it will have to play an incorrect action and so violate ϕ; or (2) there is an infinite computation in $\mathcal{S}$ not reaching s_{halt}. In this case, since $\mathcal{S}$ has the unbounded channel property, the channel will be unbounded on this execution, and a controller will not be able to simulate such a computation (it would intuitively need an infinite number of clocks). □

The proof for finite words can be adapted to Safety-MTL over finite or infinite words specifying *desired* behaviours (ϕ_{Sim} and ϕ_{Match} can be rewritten in Safety-MTL by just expanding implications; For ϕ_{Check} we need to consider a more involved formula, see [9]). Safety-MTL is not closed under negation and the technique cannot be applied to *undesired* behaviours, thus the problem remains open in this case.

Theorem 2. *The control problem with non-fixed resources for* Safety-MTL *specifications over infinite words representing* desired *behaviours is undecidable.*

4 Decidability Results

In this section, we show that for fixed resources, the control problems for both MTL over finite words and Safety-MTL over infinite words (with respect to both desired and undesired behaviours) are decidable.

In order to solve these problems, we first recall a notion of "timed game" introduced in [13]. Given an alphabet Σ, a *validity function* over Σ is a function $val : 2^{\Sigma} \to 2^{(2^{\Sigma})}$ such that every set of actions $U \in 2^{\Sigma}$ is mapped to a nonempty family of subsets of U. Let $\mathcal{T} = \langle S, s_0, \to \rangle$ be a symb-deterministic *STS* over a symbolic alphabet Γ and *val* be a validity function over Γ. A *strategy* in $\mathcal{T}$ respecting *val* is a mapping $f : D \subseteq \mathcal{L}^*_{symb}(\mathcal{T}) \to 2^{\Gamma}$ such that $\varepsilon \in D$ and for all $\gamma \in D$ and $b \in f(\gamma)$, $f(\gamma) \in val(enabled_{\mathcal{T}}(state_{\mathcal{T}}(\gamma)))$ and $\gamma \cdot b \in D$.

The set of plays of f, denoted by *plays*(f), is the set of words in $\mathcal{L}_{symb}(\mathcal{T})$ that are consistent with the strategy f. Formally, $\gamma \in plays(f)$ iff for every prefix $\gamma' \cdot b$ of γ, $b \in f(\gamma')$. We say that f is a *finite-state* strategy if there is a symb-deterministic finite-state *STS* $\mathcal{T}_{fin}$ such that $\mathcal{L}_{symb}(\mathcal{T}_{fin}) = plays(f)$ and for every finite play γ of f, $f(\gamma)$ is given by the set of symbolic actions enabled at $state_{\mathcal{T}_{fin}}(\gamma)$.

A *timed game over finite (resp. infinite) words* is a pair $\mathbb{G} = (\mathcal{A}, \mathcal{L})$ where $\mathcal{A}$ is a symb-deterministic *TA* over a symbolic alphabet Γ based on (Σ, X), and $\mathcal{L} \subseteq T\Sigma^*$ (resp. $\mathcal{L} \subseteq T\Sigma^{\omega}$) is a timed language over finite (resp. infinite) words. Moreover, we require that $\mathcal{A}$ is *atomic* (each clock constraint of $\mathcal{A}$ is atomic w.r.t. the granularity of $\mathcal{A}$) and is *consistent* ($tw(\mathcal{L}^{\omega}_{symb}(\mathcal{A})) \subseteq T\Sigma^{\omega}$ and for every $\gamma \in \mathcal{L}_{symb}(\mathcal{T}(\mathcal{A}))$, $tw(\gamma) \neq \emptyset$).

Let *val* be a validity function over Γ. A strategy respecting *val* in the timed game $\mathbb{G} = (\mathcal{A}, \mathcal{L})$ is a strategy in $\mathcal{T}(\mathcal{A})$ respecting *val*. A strategy f is *winning with respect to desired behaviours* (resp. *winning with respect to undesired behaviours*) iff for every accepting play $\gamma \in plays(f) \cap \mathcal{L}_{symb}(\mathcal{A})$ (γ is finite if $\mathcal{L} \subseteq T\Sigma^*$ and γ is infinite otherwise), the condition $tw(\gamma) \subseteq \mathcal{L}$ holds (resp. condition $tw(\gamma) \cap \mathcal{L} = \emptyset$ holds).

An MTL *timed game* (resp. a Safety-MTL *timed game*) is a timed game $\mathbb{G} = (\mathcal{A}, \mathcal{L})$ in which $\mathcal{L}$ is the set of finite or infinite models of an MTL (resp. Safety-MTL) formula.

Let us return to the control problem. Slightly extending a result in [13], we easily obtain the following result.

Proposition 2. *Given a plant $\mathcal{P}$ over a symbolic alphabet Γ, a granularity μ finer than that of the plant, and a timed language $\mathcal{L}$ over finite or infinite words, one can construct a timed game $\mathbb{G} = (\mathcal{A}, \mathcal{L})$ and a validity function* val *over Γ s.t. $\mathcal{A}$ has granularity μ and there is a (finite-state) μ-controller $\mathcal{C}$ which controls $\mathcal{P}$ for the specification of desired (resp. undesired) behaviours $\mathcal{L}$ iff there is a (finite-state) winning strategy respecting* val *in $\mathbb{G}$ with respect to desired (resp. undesired) behaviours.*

By Proposition 2, it follows that for fixed resources, the control problem for MTL over finite words (resp. Safety-MTL over infinite words) can be reduced to deciding the existence of a winning strategy in an MTL timed game over finite words (resp. Safety-MTL timed game over infinite words). In the remainder of this section we prove that these problems are decidable. The correctness of our approach relies on a well (and even better) quasi-ordering defined over a suitable symb-deterministic countable infinite-state *STS*. Therefore, we start by recalling some basic results from the theories of well quasi-orderings and better quasi-orderings.

In the following, we assume w.l.o.g. that constants occurring in constraints of *TA* are integers. For granularity $\mu = (X, 1, K)$, we simply write $\mu = (X, K)$.

4.1 Well Quasi-Orderings and Better Quasi-Orderings

A *quasi-ordering* (qo, for short) is a pair $(S, \preceq)$ where $\preceq$ is a reflexive and transitive (binary) relation on a set S. A *well quasi-ordering* (wqo, for short) is a qo $(S, \preceq)$ such that for every infinite sequence $x_0, x_1, x_2, \ldots$ of elements of S there exist indices $i < j$ such that $x_i \preceq x_j$.

Given a qo $(S, \preceq)$, we are interested in the following qo induced by $(S, \preceq)$:

- the *monotone domination order* is the qo $(S^*, \preceq^*)$, where S^* is the set of finite words over S and $x_1, \ldots, x_m \preceq^* y_1, \ldots, y_n$ iff there is a strictly monotone injection $h : \{1, \ldots, m\} \rightarrow \{1, \ldots, n\}$ such that $x_i \preceq y_{h(i)}$ for all $1 \leq i \leq m$;
- the *powerset order* is the qo $(2^S, \sqsubseteq)$, where for all $S_1, S_2 \subseteq S$, $S_1 \sqsubseteq S_2$ if and only if $\forall x_2 \in S_2. \exists x_1 \in S_1. x_1 \preceq x_2$.

A *better quasi-ordering* (bqo, for short) is a stronger relation than wqo. We do not recall the (rather technical) definition of bqo (*e.g.* see [2]). Instead we recall some properties of bqo (see [2,3]), which will be used in the following.

Proposition 3.
1. Each bqo is a wqo.
2. If S is finite, $(2^S, \subseteq)$ is a bqo.
3. If $(S, \preceq)$ is bqo, $(S^*, \preceq^*)$ is a bqo.
4. If $(S, \preceq)$ is bqo, $(2^S, \sqsubseteq)$ is a bqo.

4.2 Alternating Timed Automata

In this subsection we recall the framework of *alternating timed automata* with a single clock (*ATA*, for short) [22,20]. We use x to denote this single clock. For a finite set Q, $\Phi(Q)$ denotes the set of formulas: $\psi ::= \psi \wedge \psi \mid \psi \vee \psi \mid q \mid x \bowtie k \mid x.\psi$, where

$q \in Q$, $k \in \mathbb{N}$, and $\bowtie \in \{<, \leq, =, \geq, >\}$. The expression $x.\psi$ is a binding construct corresponding to the operation of resetting the clock x to 0.

An *ATA* over an alphabet Σ is a tuple $\mathcal{A} = \langle Q, q_0, \delta, F\rangle$ where Q, q_0, and F are defined as for *TA*, and $\delta : Q \times \Sigma \to \Phi(Q)$ is the transition function.

A *configuration* of $\mathcal{A}$ is a finite set of pairs (q, u) where $q \in Q$ is a state and $u \in \mathbb{R}_{\geq 0}$ is a clock value. The *initial configuration* is $\{(q_0, 0)\}$. A configuration C is accepting if for all $(q, u) \in C$, $q \in F$ (note that the empty configuration is accepting).

Given a clock value u, we define a satisfaction relation $\models_u$ between configurations and formulas in $\Phi(Q)$ according to the intuition that when the automaton is in state q with clock value u, then it can make an instantaneous a-transition to configuration C if[4] $C \models_u \delta(q, a)$. Formally, $\models_u$ is defined inductively as follows: $C \models_u q$ if $(q, u) \in C$, $C \models_u x \bowtie k$ if $u \bowtie k$, $C \models_u x.\psi$ if $C \models_0 \psi$, and the boolean connectives are handled in the obvious way. We say that $\mathcal{A}$ is *complete* if for all $q \in Q$, $a \in \Sigma$, and $u \in \mathbb{R}_{\geq 0}$, there is a configuration C such that $C \models_u \delta(q, a)$.

We say that a configuration M is a *minimal model* of $\psi \in \Phi(Q)$ with respect to $u \in \mathbb{R}_{\geq 0}$ if $M \models_u \psi$ and there is no proper subset $C \subset M$ with $C \models_u \psi$.

A *single-step run* is a triple of the form $C \xrightarrow{a,t} C'$ where $a \in \Sigma$, $t \in \mathbb{R}_{\geq 0}$, $C = \{(q_i, u_i)\}_{i \in I}$ and C' are configurations, and $C' = \bigcup_{i \in I}\{M_i \mid M_i$ is a minimal model of $\delta(q_i, a)$ with respect to $u_i + t\}$. A *run* over a (finite or infinite) timed word $\sigma = (a_0, \tau_0)(a_1, \tau_1)\ldots$ is a sequence of the form $C_0 \xrightarrow{a_0,d_0} C_1 \xrightarrow{a_1,d_1} C_2 \ldots$ such that each triple $C_i \xrightarrow{a_i,d_i} C_{i+1}$ is a single-step run and $d_i = \tau_i - \tau_{i-1}$ (assuming $\tau_{-1} = 0$).

We say that a finite timed word σ is *accepted* by $\mathcal{A}$ iff there is a finite run of $\mathcal{A}$ over σ starting from the initial configuration and leading to an accepting configuration. We denote by $\mathcal{L}^*(\mathcal{A})$ the set of finite timed words accepted by $\mathcal{A}$.

4.3 Preliminary Results

In this subsection we recall some results from [22] and state some properties useful in our approach to solve MTL and Safety-MTL timed games. We fix a symb-deterministic, atomic *TA* $\mathcal{A} = \langle Q, q_0, \to, F^{\mathcal{A}}\rangle$ over a symbolic alphabet Γ based on (Σ, X) and with granularity (X, K), and a complete *ATA* $\mathcal{B} = \langle P, p_0, \delta, F^{\mathcal{B}}\rangle$ over Σ whose unique clock is x. We assume that K is greater than all constants appearing in the clock constraints of $\mathcal{B}$.

An $\mathcal{A}/\mathcal{B}$-configuration is a pair $((q, \nu), G)$, where (q, ν) is configuration of $\mathcal{A}$ (*i.e.* $q \in Q$ and ν is a valuation over the set of clocks X) and G is configuration of $\mathcal{B}$. For an $\mathcal{A}/\mathcal{B}$-configuration $((q, \nu), G)$, $t \in \mathbb{R}_{\geq 0}$, and $(a, g, Y) \in \Gamma$, we define

$$\begin{cases} Succ^{\mathcal{A}}((q,\nu), t, (a,g,Y)) = \{(q',\nu') \mid (q,\nu) \xrightarrow[t]{a,g,Y} (q',\nu') \text{ is a single-step of } \mathcal{A}\}^5 \\ Succ^{\mathcal{B}}(G, t, a) = \{G' \mid G \xrightarrow{a,t} G' \text{ is a single-step of } \mathcal{B}\} \end{cases}$$

The *synchronous product* of $\mathcal{A}$ and $\mathcal{B}$ is an uncountable infinite-state *STS* over Γ, denoted by $\mathcal{T}_{\mathcal{A}/\mathcal{B}}$, representing intuitively $\mathcal{A}$ and $\mathcal{B}$ executing in parallel. Formally,

---

4 *I.e.* a simultaneous transition to multiple-copies of $\mathcal{A}$ described by configuration C.

5 *I.e.* $q \xrightarrow{a,g,Y} q'$ is a transition of $\mathcal{A}$, $\nu + t \in [\![g]\!]$, and $\nu' = (\nu + t)[Y \leftarrow 0]$.

$\mathcal{T}_{\mathcal{A}/\mathcal{B}} = \langle S, s_0, \twoheadrightarrow \rangle$, where S is the set of $\mathcal{A}/\mathcal{B}$-configurations, $s_0 = ((q_0, \vec{0}), \{p_0, 0\})$ corresponds to the initial $\mathcal{A}/\mathcal{B}$-configuration, and

$$((q_1, \nu_1), G_1) \xrightarrow{a,g,Y}\!\!\!\!\!\twoheadrightarrow ((q_2, \nu_2), G_2) \text{ iff } \exists t \in \mathbb{R}_{\geq 0} \text{ s.t. } G_2 \in \mathit{Succ}^{\mathcal{B}}(G_1, t, a) \text{ and } (q_2, \nu_2) \in \mathit{Succ}^{\mathcal{A}}((q_1, \nu_1), t, (a, g, Y))$$

Now, we recall the extended region construction presented in [21] to abstract away precise clock values in $\mathcal{A}/\mathcal{B}$-configurations, recording only their values to the nearest integer and the relative order of their fractional part.

Let REG_K be the finite set of one-dimensional regions $\{r_0, r_1, \ldots, r_{2K+1}\}$ defined as follows: for $0 \leq i \leq K$, $r_{2i} = \{i\}$ and $r_{2i+1} = (i, i+1)$, and $r_{2K+1} = (K, \infty)$. For $u \in \mathbb{R}_{\geq 0}$, $\mathit{reg}(u)$ denotes the region in REG_K containing u.

Define the finite alphabet $\Lambda = 2^{(Q \times X \times \mathit{REG}_K) \cup (P \times \mathit{REG}_K)}$: its letters are finite sets of pairs (p, r) and triples (q, y, r), where q and p are states of $\mathcal{A}$ and $\mathcal{B}$ respectively, $y \in X$ is a clock of $\mathcal{A}$, and r is a one-dimensional region in REG_K. Moreover, we denote by $(\Lambda^*, \preceq)$ the monotone domination order induced by the bqo $(\Lambda, \subseteq)$, and by $(2^{\Lambda^*}, \sqsubseteq)$ the powerset order induced by $(\Lambda^*, \preceq)$. Applying Proposition 3, $(\Lambda^*, \preceq)$ and $(2^{\Lambda^*}, \sqsubseteq)$ are bqo (hence, also wqo).

Now, we associate to every $\mathcal{A}/\mathcal{B}$-configuration $s = ((q, \nu), G)$ a canonical word $H(s) \in \Lambda^*$ as follows. First note that s can be equivalently represented as the set G' given by $G \cup \{(q, y, \nu(y)) \mid y \in X\}$. We partition G' into a sequence of subsets $G_1, \ldots, G_n$, such that for all $1 \leq i \leq j \leq n$, for every pair (p, u) or triple (q, y, u) in G_i, and for every pair (p', v) or triple (q', y', v) in G_j, the following holds: $i \leq j$ iff $\mathsf{fract}(u) \leq \mathsf{fract}(v)$.[6] Define $H(s)$ as the word in Λ^* given by $\mathit{Abs}(G_1) \ldots \mathit{Abs}(G_n)$, where for any $1 \leq i \leq n$, $\mathit{Abs}(G_i) = \{(p, \mathit{reg}(u)) \mid (p, u) \in G_i\} \cup \{(q, y, \mathit{reg}(u)) \mid (q, y, u) \in G_i\}$. We say that two $\mathcal{A}/\mathcal{B}$-configurations s and s' are equivalent, written $s \sim s'$, if $H(s) = H(s')$.

Proposition 4 ([22]). *The relation $\sim$ is a bisimulation over $\mathcal{T}_{\mathcal{A}/\mathcal{B}}$, i.e. $s_1 \sim s_1'$ and $s_1 \xrightarrow{a,g,Y}\!\!\!\!\!\twoheadrightarrow s_2$ implies $s_1' \xrightarrow{a,g,Y}\!\!\!\!\!\twoheadrightarrow s_2'$ and $s_2 \sim s_2'$ for some s_2'.*

The *discrete quotient* induced by the bisimulation $\sim$ over $\mathcal{T}_{\mathcal{A}/\mathcal{B}}$ is the *STS* $\mathcal{T}_{\sim} = \langle W, w_0, \hookrightarrow \rangle$, defined as follows:

- $W = \{H(s) \mid s \text{ is an } \mathcal{A}/\mathcal{B}\text{-configuration}\}$;
- $w_0 = H(s_0)$ (*i.e.* the image under H of the initial $\mathcal{A}/\mathcal{B}$-configuration).
- $w_1 \xhookrightarrow{a,g,Y} w_2$ iff there exists $s_1 \in H^{-1}(w_1)$ and $s_2 \in H^{-1}(w_2)$ s.t. $s_1 \xrightarrow{a,g,Y}\!\!\!\!\!\twoheadrightarrow s_2$.

Proposition 5 ([22]). *The following properties hold:*

1. *The set of successors of any word w in $\mathcal{T}_{\sim}$ is finite and effectively computable.*
2. *The transition relation $\hookrightarrow$ of $\mathcal{T}_{\sim}$ is* downward-compatible *with respect to $\preceq$, i.e. $w_1' \preceq w_1$ and $w_1 \xhookrightarrow{a,g,Y} w_2$ implies $w_1' \xhookrightarrow{a,g,Y} w_2'$ for some $w_2' \preceq w_2$.*

---

[6] $\mathsf{fract}(u)$ denotes the fractional part of u.

We conclude this subsection by stating some simple results on the deterministic version of $\mathcal{T}_{\sim}$. For $w \in W$, we note $reg_{\mathcal{A}}(w)$ the maximal subword $u \preceq w$ s.t. u does not contain occurrences of states of $\mathcal{B}$. Since $\mathcal{B}$ is complete and $\mathcal{A}$ is atomic and symb-deterministic, by classical properties of regions in timed automata, it easily follows that for all $w_1, w_2 \in W$ with $reg_{\mathcal{A}}(w_1) = reg_{\mathcal{A}}(w_2)$, $w_1 \xhookrightarrow{a,g,Y} w_1'$ and $w_2 \xhookrightarrow{a,g,Y} w_2'$ imply that $reg_{\mathcal{A}}(w_1') = reg_{\mathcal{A}}(w_2')$. Moreover, $enabled_{\mathcal{T}_{\sim}}(w_1) = enabled_{\mathcal{T}_{\sim}}(w_2)$. Motivated by these observations, we denote by SW the set of nonempty finite sets $\mathcal{C} \subseteq W$ such that for all words $w, w' \in \mathcal{C}$, $reg_{\mathcal{A}}(w) = reg_{\mathcal{A}}(w')$. Moreover, we denote by $\mathcal{DT}_{\sim} = \langle SW, \{w_0\}, \hookrightarrow_{\mathcal{D}} \rangle$ the restriction of $Det(\mathcal{T}_{\sim})$ to the set of states SW. Note that by the observations above, $\mathcal{L}^*_{symb}(\mathcal{DT}_{\sim}) = \mathcal{L}^*_{symb}(Det(\mathcal{T}_{\sim}))$.

Proposition 6. *1. If $\mathcal{C}_1 \sqsubseteq \mathcal{C}_2$, then $enabled_{\mathcal{DT}_{\sim}}(\mathcal{C}_1) = enabled_{\mathcal{DT}_{\sim}}(\mathcal{C}_2)$.*
2. The transition relation $\hookrightarrow_{\mathcal{D}}$ of $\mathcal{DT}_{\sim}$ is downward-compatible *with respect to $\sqsubseteq$, i.e. $\mathcal{C}_1' \sqsubseteq \mathcal{C}_1$ and $\mathcal{C}_1 \xhookrightarrow{a,g,Y}_{\mathcal{D}} \mathcal{C}_2$* implies *$\mathcal{C}_1' \xhookrightarrow{a,g,Y}_{\mathcal{D}} \mathcal{C}_2'$ for some $\mathcal{C}_2' \sqsubseteq \mathcal{C}_2$.*

4.4 Decidability of MTL Timed Games over Finite Timed Words

The logic MTL is closed under negation, thus we only consider MTL timed games against specifications of *undesired* behaviours. We fix an MTL timed game over finite words $\mathbb{G} = (\mathcal{A}, \mathcal{L}^*(\varphi))$ and a validity function *val* over the symbolic alphabet Γ associated with $\mathcal{A}$. Assume $\mathcal{A} = \langle Q, q_0, \rightarrow, F^{\mathcal{A}} \rangle$ has granularity (X, K). Applying [22], one can construct a complete *ATA* $\mathcal{B}_{\varphi} = \langle P, p_0, \delta, F^{\varphi} \rangle$ s.t. $\mathcal{L}^*(\mathcal{B}_{\varphi}) = \mathcal{L}^*(\varphi)$.

Let $\mathcal{T}_{\mathcal{A}/\varphi}$ be the synchronous product of $\mathcal{A}$ and $\mathcal{B}_{\varphi}$, $\mathcal{T}_{\sim} = \langle W, w_0, \hookrightarrow \rangle$ and $\mathcal{DT}_{\sim} = \langle SW, \{w_0\}, \hookrightarrow_{\mathcal{D}} \rangle$ be the *STS* induced by $\mathcal{T}_{\mathcal{A}/\varphi}$ defined in Subsection 4.3.

An $\mathcal{A}/\mathcal{B}_{\varphi}$ configuration $((q, \nu), G)$ is *bad* if both q is accepting (*i.e.* $q \in F^{\mathcal{A}}$) and G is accepting (*i.e.* for all $(p, u) \in G$, $p \in F^{\varphi}$). A word $w \in W$ is said *bad* if there is $s \in H^{-1}(w)$ such that s is bad. Moreover, a word set $\mathcal{C} \in SW$ is *bad* if $\mathcal{C}$ contains some bad word. Finally, a strategy f in $\mathcal{DT}_{\sim}$[7] is *safe* iff for every finite play γ of f, $state_{\mathcal{DT}_{\sim}}(\gamma)$ is *not* bad.

Lemma 1. *There is a (finite-state) winning strategy in the timed game $\mathbb{G}$ with respect to* undesired behaviours *iff there is a (finite-state) safe strategy in $\mathcal{DT}_{\sim}$.*

Proof. Since $\mathcal{B}_{\varphi}$ is complete and $\mathcal{A}$ is consistent, we easily obtain that $\mathcal{L}^*_{symb}(\mathcal{T}(\mathcal{A})) = \mathcal{L}^*_{symb}(\mathcal{T}_{\mathcal{A}/\varphi})$ $(= \mathcal{L}^*_{symb}(Det(\mathcal{T}_{\mathcal{A}/\varphi}) = \mathcal{L}^*_{symb}(\mathcal{DT}_{\sim}))$. This means that for every $f : D \subseteq \Gamma^* \rightarrow 2^{\Gamma}$, f is a strategy in $\mathbb{G}$ iff f is a strategy in $\mathcal{DT}_{\sim}$. If f is a winning strategy in $\mathbb{G}$ w.r.t. undesired behaviours, then we claim that f is safe for $\mathcal{DT}_{\sim}$. Indeed if for some finite play γ, $state_{\mathcal{DT}_{\sim}}(\gamma)$ was bad, then by definition of $\mathcal{DT}_{\sim}$ and Proposition 4 there would be a path in $\mathcal{T}_{\mathcal{A}/\varphi}$ from the initial $\mathcal{A}/\mathcal{B}_{\varphi}$ configuration to a bad $\mathcal{A}/\mathcal{B}_{\varphi}$ configuration whose trace is γ. By construction, this implies $\gamma \in \mathcal{L}^*_{symb}(\mathcal{A})$ and $tw(\gamma) \cap \mathcal{L}^*(\varphi) \neq \emptyset$, which is a contradiction. Thus, the claim holds. In a similar way, if f is safe for $\mathcal{DT}_{\sim}$, then f is a winning strategy in $\mathbb{G}$ w.r.t. undesired behaviours. $\square$

By Lemma 1, deciding the existence of a winning strategy in the timed game $\mathbb{G}$ w.r.t. undesired behaviours can be reduced to checking the existence of a safe strategy f in

[7] In the following we omit the reference to *val*.

$\mathcal{DT}_{\sim}$. Now, we show that this last problem is decidable, by extending the approach proposed in [1] for A-downward closed games. The correctness and termination of our procedure relies on the well quasi-ordering of $(SW, \sqsubseteq)$.

We build a finite portion T of the tree given by the unfolding of $\mathcal{DT}_{\sim}$ from the initial state $\{w_0\}$ as follows. We start from the root, labelled with $\{w_0\}$, and at each step, we pick a leaf x with label $\mathcal{C} \in SW$ and perform one of the following operations:

- if $\mathcal{C}$ *is not bad* and there is an ancestor of x in the portion of the tree built so far with label $\mathcal{C}'$ where $\mathcal{C}' \sqsubseteq \mathcal{C}$, then we declare the node *successful* and close the node (*i.e.* we will not expand the tree further from the node);
- if $\mathcal{C}$ *is bad*, then we declare the node *unsuccessful* and close the node;
- otherwise, for any transition in $\mathcal{DT}_{\sim}$ of the form $\mathcal{C} \xhookrightarrow{a,g,Y}_{\mathcal{D}} \mathcal{C}'$ we add a new node y with label $\mathcal{C}'$ and an edge from the current node x to y labelled by (a, g, Y). If $\mathcal{C}$ has no successor, then we declare the current node x as *dead*.

Note that the procedure is effective. Moreover, termination is guaranteed by König's Lemma and by well quasi-ordering of $(SW, \sqsubseteq)$. The resulting finite tree T is re-labelled in a bottom-up way by elements in $\{\top, \bot\}$ as follows:

- *successful* and *dead* leaves are labelled $\top$ and *unsuccessful* leaves are labelled $\bot$;
- for any internal node x labelled by $\mathcal{C}$, the $\{\top, \bot\}$-labelling is defined as follows: if there is a set of symbolic actions $U \in val(enabled_{\mathcal{DT}_{\sim}}(\mathcal{C}))$ such that for each $(a, g, Y) \in U$, the edge in T from x and with label (a, g, Y) leads to a node labelled by $\top$, then we label x by $\top$; *otherwise*, we label x by $\bot$.

The algorithm answers "yes" if the root is labelled by $\top$. Otherwise, it answers "no".

Correctness of the algorithm is stated by Lemma 2. The first point is simple, and the second point follows from Proposition 6 (a detailed proof is given in [9]).

Lemma 2. *If the algorithm answers "no", then there is* no *safe strategy in $\mathcal{DT}_{\sim}$.*
If the algorithm answers "yes", then there is a finite-state *safe strategy in $\mathcal{DT}_{\sim}$ and we can build it effectively.*

Finally, by Lemmata 1 and 2, the fact that MTL is closed under negation, and Proposition 2, we obtain the main result of this subsection.

Theorem 3. *The control problem for fixed resources against* MTL *specifications over finite words representing desired or undesired behaviours is decidable. Moreover, if there exists a controller, then one can effectively construct a finite-state one.*

Remark 1. As the satisfiability problem for MTL can be reduced to an MTL control problem, the control problem for fixed resources against MTL specifications over finite words has non-primitive recursive complexity [22].

Remark 2. Since our algorithm is based on the translation of MTL over finite words to *ATA*, the result above can be extended to specifications given as languages of finite timed words recognized by *ATA* (note that *ATA* are closed under complementation [22]).

4.5 Decidability of Safety-MTL Timed Games over Infinite Timed Words

First note that Safety-MTL is not closed under negation. Thus, we need to distinguish between specifications representing desired and undesired behaviours. For *desired* behaviours, the construction is not that far from the one for finite timed words, even though it requires some refinement. On the other hand, for *undesired* behaviours, the algorithm is much more involved and require techniques inspired by [24]. The whole construction is reported in [9]. The main result can be summarized as follows.

Theorem 4. *The control problem for fixed resources against* Safety-MTL *specifications over infinite words representing desired or undesired behaviours is decidable. Moreover, for* desired *behaviours, if there exists a controller, then one can effectively construct a finite-state one.*

5 Conclusion

In this paper, we have studied the control problem for MTL and Safety-MTL specifications. Our results are summarized in the following table.

	fixed resources	**non-fixed resources**
MTL over finite words (***desired or undesired behaviours***)	decidable	undecidable
Safety-MTL over infinite words (***desired behaviours***)	decidable	undecidable
Safety-MTL over infinite words (***undesired behaviours***)	decidable	?

There are still open problems, for instance the precise complexity of the control problem for Safety-MTL specifications with fixed resources, and also the decidability of the control problem for Safety-MTL specifications representing undesired behaviours with non-fixed resources. Finally, for Safety-MTL representing undesired behaviours with fixed resources, actually we do not know if the existence of a strategy in a timed game implies the existence of a finite-state one. This means that the question to construct a finite-state controller in this case remains open.

References

1. P. A. Abdulla, A. Bouajjani, and J. d'Orso. Deciding monotonic games. In *Proc. 17th Int. Work. Computer Science Logic (CSL'03)*, volume 2803 of *LNCS*, pages 1–14. Springer, 2003.
2. P. A. Abdulla and A. Nylén. Better is better than well: On efficient verification of infinite-state systems. In *Proc. 15th Ann. Symp. Logic in Computer Science (LICS'00)*, pages 132–140. IEEE Comp. Soc. Press, 2000.
3. P. A. Abdulla and A. Nylén. Timed Petri nets and bqos. In *Proc. 22nd Int. Conf. Application and Theory of Petri Nets (ICATPN'01)*, volume 2075 of *LNCS*, pages 53–70. Springer, 2001.
4. L. d. Alfaro, M. Faella, Th. A. Henzinger, R. Majumdar, and M. Stoelinga. The element of surprise in timed games. In *Proc. 14th Int. Conf. Concurrency Theory (CONCUR'03)*, volume 2761 of *LNCS*, pages 142–156. Springer, 2003.

5. R. Alur and D. Dill. A theory of timed automata. *Theoretical Computer Science*, 126(2):183–235, 1994.
6. R. Alur and Th. A. Henzinger. Real-time logics: Complexity and expressiveness. *Information and Computation*, 104(1):35–77, 1993.
7. R. Alur and P. Madhusudan. Decision problems for timed automata: A survey. In *Proc. 4th Int. School Formal Methods Design of Computer, Communication and Software Systems: Real Time (SFM-04:RT)*, volume 3185 of *LNCS*, pages 122–133. Springer, 2004.
8. E. Asarin, O. Maler, A. Pnueli, and J. Sifakis. Controller synthesis for timed automata. In *Proc. IFAC Symp. System Structure and Control*, pages 469–474. Elsevier Science, 1998.
9. P. Bouyer, L. Bozzelli, and F. Chevalier. Controller synthesis for MTL specifications. Research report, Laboratoire Spécification & Vérification, ENS de Cachan, France, 2006.
10. P. Bouyer, F. Chevalier, and N. Markey. On the expressiveness of TPTL and MTL. In *Proc. 25th Conf. Foundations of Software Technology and Theoretical Computer Science (FST&TCS'05)*, volume 3821 of *LNCS*, pages 432–443. Springer, 2005.
11. P. Bouyer, D. D'Souza, P. Madhusudan, and A. Petit. Timed control with partial observability. In *Proc. 15th Int. Conf. Computer Aided Verification (CAV'03)*, volume 2725 of *LNCS*, pages 180–192. Springer, 2003.
12. D. Brand and P. Zafiropulo. On communicating finite-state machines. *Journal of the ACM*, 30(2):323–342, 1983.
13. D. D'Souza and P. Madhusudan. Timed control synthesis for external specifications. In *Proc. 19th Int. Symp. Theoretical Aspects of Computer Science (STACS'02)*, volume 2285 of *LNCS*, pages 571–582. Springer, 2002.
14. D. D'Souza and P. Prabhakar. On the expressiveness of MTL in the pointwise and continuous semantics. *Formal Methods Letters*, 2006. To appear.
15. M. Faella, S. La Torre, and A. Murano. Automata-theoretic decision of timed games. In *Proc. 3rd Int. Work. Verification, Model Checking, and Abstract Interpretation (VMCAI'02)*, volume 2294 of *LNCS*, pages 94–108. Springer, 2002.
16. M. Faella, S. La Torre, and A. Murano. Dense real-time games. In *Proc. 17th Ann. Symp. Logic in Computer Science (LICS'02)*, pages 167–176. IEEE Comp. Soc. Press, 2002.
17. Th. A. Henzinger and P. W. Kopke. Discrete-time control for rectangular hybrid automata. *Theoretical Computer Science*, 221:369–392, 1999.
18. R. Koymans. Specifying real-time properties with metric temporal logic. *Real-Time Systems*, 2(4):255–299, 1990.
19. F. Laroussinie, K. G. Larsen, and C. Weise. From timed automata to logic – and back. In *Proc. 20th Int. Symp. Mathematical Foundations of Computer Science (MFCS'95)*, volume 969 of *LNCS*, pages 529–539. Springer, 1995.
20. S. Lasota and I. Walukiewicz. Alternating timed automata. In *Proc. 8th Int. Conf. Foundations of Software Science and Computation Structures (FoSSaCS'05)*, volume 3441 of *LNCS*, pages 250–265. Springer, 2005.
21. J. Ouaknine and J. B. Worrell. On the language inclusion problem for timed automata: Closing a decidability gap. In *Proc. 19th Ann. Symp. Logic in Computer Science (LICS'04)*, pages 54–63. IEEE Comp. Soc. Press, 2004.
22. J. Ouaknine and J. B. Worrell. On the decidability of metric temporal logic. In *Proc. 19th Ann. Symp. Logic in Computer Science (LICS'05)*, pages 188–197. IEEE Comp. Soc. Press, 2005.
23. J. Ouaknine and J. B. Worrell. On metric temporal logic and faulty Turing machines. In *Proc. 9th Int. Conf. Foundations of Software Science and Computation Structures (FoSSaCS'06)*, volume 3921 of *LNCS*, pages 217–230. Springer, 2006.
24. J. Ouaknine and J. B. Worrell. Safety metric temporal logic is fully decidable. In *Proc. 12th Int. Conf. Tools and Algorithms for the Construction and Analysis of Systems (TACAS'06)*, volume 3920 of *LNCS*, pages 411–425. Springer, 2006.

On Interleaving in Timed Automata

Ramzi Ben Salah, Marius Bozga, and Oded Maler

VERIMAG, 2, av. de Vignate, 38610 Gieres, France
Ramzi.Salah@imag.fr, Marius.Bozga@imag.fr, Oded.Maler@imag.fr

Abstract. We propose a remedy to that part of the state-explosion problem for timed automata which is due to interleaving of actions. We prove the following quite surprising result: the union of all zones reached by different interleavings of the same set of transitions is *convex*. Consequently we can improve the standard reachability computation for timed automata by merging such zones whenever they are encountered. Since passage of time distributes over union, we can continue the successor computation from the new zone and eliminate completely the explosion due to interleaving.

1 Introduction

Exploring the state space of timed automata [AD94] is a fundamental activity with numerous potential applications in circuit timing analysis, scheduling, verification of real-time software, performance analysis, etc. It is, however, a very difficult problem still waiting for a performance breakthrough despite efforts invested during the last 15 years. We hope that the results of this paper will advance us in this respect.

Partial-order methods have been widely reported in the discrete verification literature. They focus on that part of the state-explosion problem posed by the interleaving semantics, as illustrated by the example of Figure 1 where we see two automata and their asynchronous composition. Actions a and b are mutually independent and hence, in the product automaton, state 11 can be reached via two paths[1] that commute in a "diamond". For certain simple reachability properties that do not mention paths and intermediate states, it is sufficient to explore only one of those paths. However, if additional non-commuting transitions are possible from the intermediate states, or if the properties are more sequential and less invariant under path permutations, the situation is more involved and has been a subject of numerous publications. This is not the topic of the present paper.

In the analysis of timed automata, diamonds pose additional problems. Due to the clock variables, paths that seem to commute on the transition diagram do not necessarily converge to the same extended state which includes also the clock values. Consider the timed automata appearing in Figure 2 together with their composition. In each automaton the transition from 0 to 1 resets the respective clock. The standard reachability computation algorithm for timed automata computes a discrete directed graph, the nodes of which are "symbolic states" of the form (q, Z) where q is a discrete state and Z is a *zone*, a convex set of clock valuations satisfying some conjunction of inequalities.

[1] In general, $n!$ paths when there are n transitions.

C. Baier and H. Hermanns (Eds.): CONCUR 2006, LNCS 4137, pp. 465–476, 2006.

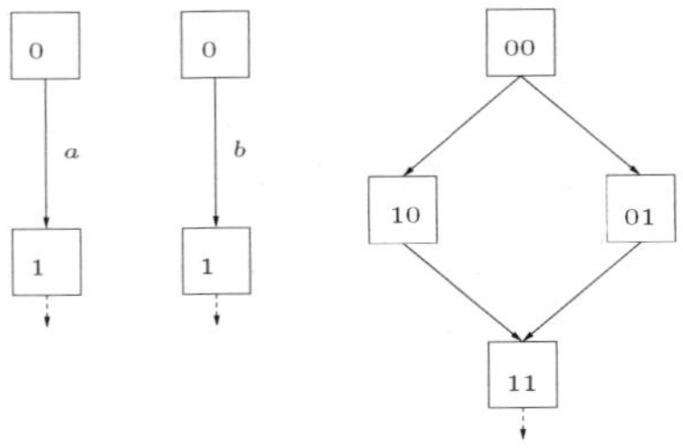

Fig. 1. Two automata with independent action a and b, and their composition

Apply this algorithm to the automaton we obtain two zones associated with state 11, one in which $x \leq y$ (because in all runs along this path x is reset after y) and the other with $y \leq x$. So here, in a situation where untimed reachability will converge to single state, timed reachability will generate several symbolic states from which the computation can be continued, leading very quickly to explosion. Roughly speaking, while the ordinary explosion associated with a product of n automata, each with m states will lead in the worst case to $O(m^n)$ states, the additional splitting due to interleaving may result in $O(n^{mn})$ states, a fact that prevents verification of systems of modest size.[2]

In this paper we propose a solution to this problem, which is based on a new surprising[3] result which shows that the set of all points in the clock space reached by runs consisting of interleaving of the same set of actions is *convex*. Since evolution distributes over union, zones that have been reached through different paths in the transition graph can be merged during reachability computation, thus eliminating the interleaving explosion. The rest of the paper is organized as follows. In Section 2 we give the definition of timed automata and their interaction. In Section 3 we prove our main result which is used in Section 4 to define a modified reachability algorithm whose superiority is experimentally confirmed. In Section 5 we discuss the applicability of the results to various forms of interaction, and conclude in Section 6 with a discussion of related work, in particular the idea of local time scales.

2 Timed Automata

We consider a composition $\mathcal{A}^1||\mathcal{A}^2|| \cdots ||\mathcal{A}^n$ of timed automata. Interaction can be defined using two types of mechanisms, the first one is by synchronized transitions and the other one, which is more expressive and useful, is by shared variables. To simplify the presentation we will use the former to present our result and discuss later its extension to state-based synchronization. For the same pedagogical reasons, we make additional simplifying assumptions concerning the form of invariants and guards, but the results

[2] Note that if we can push the size limit of timed verification toward non-trivial systems, the rest of the battle against explosion can continue from there using abstraction-based methods like the ones we have recently proposed [BBM03, BBM06].

[3] What is surprising is the fact that it has not been discovered before by all those working in the domain, the authors included.

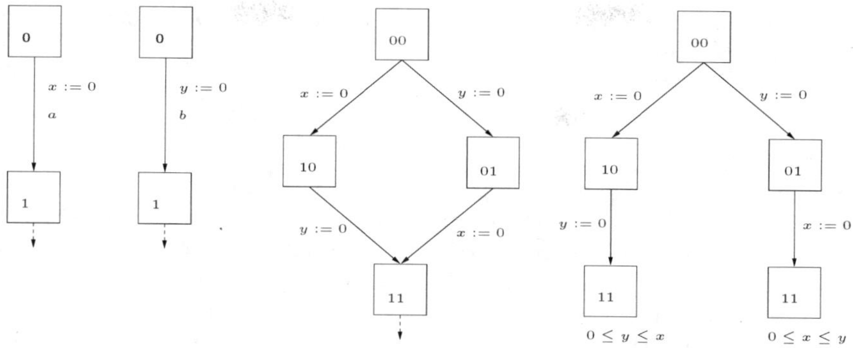

Fig. 2. Two timed automata, their composition and an example of reachability computation

extend naturally to any conjunction of timed inequalities. As for non-convex (disjunctive) conditions allowed by the original definition of timed automata, we have found no use of them in more than 10 years experience in the domain.[4] We also do not pay much attention to the distinction between strict and non strict inequalities which are irrelevant to convexity.

Definition 1 (Timed Automaton). *A timed automaton is $\mathcal{A} = (\Sigma, Q, C, I, \Delta)$ where Σ is a finite set of transition labels, Q is a finite set of states, C is a finite set of clocks, I is the staying condition (invariant), assigning to every $q \in Q$ a conjunction I_q of inequalities of the form $c \leq u$, for some clock c and integer u, and Δ is a transition relation consisting of elements of the form (q, g, a, r, q') where q and q' are states, $a \in \Sigma$ is a transition label, g (the transition guard) is a conjunction of formulae of the form $(c \geq l)$ for some clock c and integer l and $r \subseteq C$ is a set of clocks to be reset by the transition.*

We assume one transition labelled a for every $a \in \Sigma$. A *clock valuation* is a function $v : C \rightarrow \mathbb{R}_{\geq 0}$ and a *configuration* of the automaton is a pair (q, v) consisting of a discrete state (location) and a clock valuation. We use r also to denote the reset function on clock valuation that sets the clock in r to zero and leaves the other intact. We use $v + d$ to denote the clock valuation obtained from v by adding d to all clock values. A *step* of the automaton is one of the following:

- A *discrete step*: $(q, v) \xrightarrow{a} (q', v')$, for some transition $(q, g, a, r, q') \in \Delta$ such that v satisfies g and $v' = r(v)$.
- A *time step*: $(q, v) \xrightarrow{d} (q, v + d)$ for some $d \in \mathbb{R}_{\geq 0}$ such that $v + d$ satisfies I_q.

A *compound step* is a time step (possibly of a zero duration) followed by a discrete step:

$$(q, v) \xrightarrow{d,a} (q', v') \equiv (q, v) \xrightarrow{d} (q, v + d) \xrightarrow{a} (q', v').$$

[4] The tendency to look for results proved for the "most general" definition, inherited uncritically from mathematics, can be sometimes very counter-productive in domains which are still evolving. Perhaps this could be one of the reasons for the sterility of certain branches of theoretical computer science.

A *run* of the automaton starting from a configuration (q_0, v_0) is a finite sequence of compound steps ending in a time step.

$$\xi: \quad (q_0, v_0) \stackrel{d_1,a_1}{\longrightarrow} (q_1, v_1) \stackrel{d_2,a_2}{\longrightarrow} \cdots \stackrel{d_k,a_k}{\longrightarrow} (q_k, v_k) \stackrel{d_*}{\longrightarrow} (q_k, v_k + d_*).$$

We use also the notation $(q, v) \stackrel{\xi}{\longrightarrow} (q', v')$ for runs.

We will define the interaction between the automata via a "distributed alphabet" Σ in the sense of the theory of traces [DR95]. For each automaton $\mathcal{A}^i$, let Σ^i be its local alphabet, that is the set of transition labels it uses. Our composition semantics requires that all $\mathcal{A}_i$ such that $a \in \Sigma^i$ should participate in an a-labelled global transition. Hence in any run of the global automaton an a-transition will be taken the same number of times in all $\mathcal{A}^i$ such that $a \in \Sigma^i$.

Definition 2 (Composition of Timed Automata). *A composition of timed automata is* $\mathcal{A} = \mathcal{A}^1 || \mathcal{A}^2 || \cdots || \mathcal{A}^n$ *where each automaton is of the form* $\mathcal{A}^i = (\Sigma^i, Q^i, C^i, I^i, \Delta^i)$. *The sets of states and clocks of the automata are mutually disjoint.*

The global automaton obtained from the composition is $\mathcal{A} = (\Sigma, Q, C, I, \Delta)$ where $Q = \Pi_{i=1}^n Q^i$, $C = \bigcup_{i=1}^n C^i$ and $\Sigma = \bigcup_{i=1}^n \Sigma^i$. We write global states as $\mathbf{q} = (q^1, \ldots, q^n) \in Q$ and global clock valuations over C as $\mathbf{v} = (v^1, \ldots, v^n)$. The semantics of the composition is given in terms of global steps as follows:

- A discrete step: $(\mathbf{q}, \mathbf{v}) \stackrel{a}{\longrightarrow} (\mathbf{q}', \mathbf{v}')$, such that for every i either $a \in \Sigma^i$ and $(q^i, v^i) \stackrel{a}{\longrightarrow} (q'^i, v'^i)$ is a step of $\mathcal{A}^i$, or $a \notin \Sigma^i$ and $(q'^i, v'^i) = (q^i, v^i)$.
- A time step: $(\mathbf{q}, \mathbf{v}) \stackrel{d}{\longrightarrow} (\mathbf{q}, \mathbf{v} + d)$ for some $d \in \mathbb{R}_+$ such that $v + d$ satisfies $\bigwedge_{i=1}^n I_{q^i}$.

Global compound steps and runs are defined similarly to their local counterparts. It is sometimes (and this time in particular) useful to speak of the projection of a global run on each automaton. The projection ξ^i of a global run ξ is obtained from ξ in two stages. First we "hide" transitions in which $\mathcal{A}^i$ does not participate and collapse the time passages, that is apply successively the following transformation:

$$(\mathbf{q}, \mathbf{v}) \stackrel{d,a}{\longrightarrow} (\mathbf{q}', \mathbf{v}') \stackrel{d',a'}{\longrightarrow} (\mathbf{q}'', \mathbf{v}'') \quad \longmapsto \quad (\mathbf{q}, \mathbf{v}) \stackrel{a,d+d'}{\longrightarrow} (\mathbf{q}'', \mathbf{v}'')$$

whenever $a' \notin \Sigma^i$. After all such external transitions have been eliminated we project the run on the states and clocks of $\mathcal{A}_i$.

Finally let us define two additional notions. Two runs ξ, ξ' of $\mathcal{A}$ are *qualitatively equivalent* if they go through the same sequence of discrete transitions and differ only in timing. We denote this fact by $\xi \approx \xi'$ and write equivalence classes of $\approx$ by $[\xi]$. We say that ξ and ξ' are *locally equivalent*, denoted by $\xi \sim \xi'$, if all their local projections are equivalent, that is, $\xi^i \approx \xi'^i$ for every i. We denote equivalence classes of $\sim$ as $\langle\xi\rangle$. Clearly, $\approx$ is stronger than $\sim$, and perhaps too strong. When $\xi \sim \xi'$, both runs agree on the order of local transitions while $\xi \approx \xi'$ means that they agree also on their interleaving.

3 Main Result

We can now formulate our main result.

Theorem 1 (Convexity). *Let Z be a convex timed polyhedron and let $\mathbf{q}$ and $\mathbf{q}'$ be two global states of $\mathcal{A}$. Let ξ be a run starting at $\mathbf{q}$ and ending in $\mathbf{q}'$. Then the set*

$$R_{Z,\langle\xi\rangle} \equiv \bigcup_{\xi' \in \langle\xi\rangle} \{\mathbf{v}' : \exists \mathbf{v} \in Z \ (\mathbf{q}, \mathbf{v}) \xrightarrow{\xi'} (\mathbf{q}', \mathbf{v}')\}$$

is convex.

The proof is given via a characterization of the reachable clock valuations by a quantified formula consisting of conjunctions of inequalities over clock values and auxiliary variables. Since convex sets are closed under projection the result follows. For economy of notation we assume that ξ is such that each automaton $\mathcal{A}^i$ makes exactly k steps. The restriction of $\mathcal{A}^i$ to the states and transitions involved in the run is of the form depicted in Figure 3.

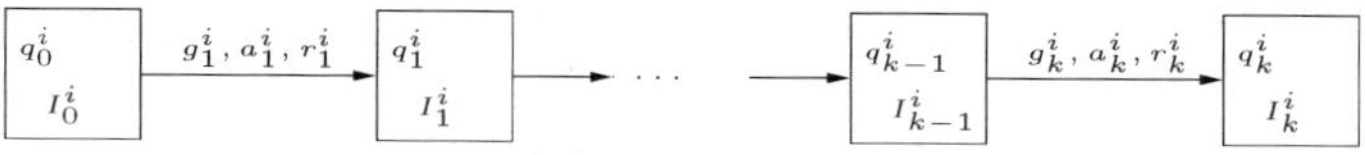

Fig. 3. The part of $\mathcal{A}^i$ which participates in ξ^i

As a first step we extend the description of local runs to include the *time stamps* of the transitions:

$$\xi^i : \ (q_0^i, v_0^i, t_0^i) \to (q_1^i, v_1^i, t_1^i) \to \cdots \to (q_k^i, v_k^i, t_k^i) \to (q_k^i, v_{k+1}^i, t_{k+1}^i).$$

Each t_j^i variable denotes the *absolute time* in which the corresponding transition has been taken. Every global run in $\langle\xi\rangle$ is completely characterized by the values t_j^i and v_j^i for $i = 1..n$ and $j = 0..k+1$. All those runs satisfy the natural local ordering among time stamps, i.e. $t_j^i \leq t_{j+1}^i$, while those that are also $\approx$-equivalent agree also on the ordering of time stamps of different automata, which characterize the particular interleaving (shuffle) of the local runs.

We can now proceed to the logical characterization. We will use the following auxiliary notations and abbreviations: $\mathbf{q}_j = (q_j^1, \ldots q_j^n)$ for global states, $\mathbf{v}_j = (v_j^1, \ldots v_j^n)$, for global clock valuations, $\mathbf{v}^i = \{v_0^i, \ldots, v_k^i\}$, for the set of valuations appearing in a local run ξ^i and $\mathbf{t}^i = \{t_0^i, \ldots, t_k^i\}$ for the set of local time stamps. The set of all values that characterize a run are $\mathbf{v} = \bigcup_i \mathbf{v}_i$, and $\mathbf{t} = \bigcup_i \mathbf{t}^i$. The predicates $\{\Phi_j^i\}$ characterize the clock values and time stamps in a valid step j of $\mathcal{A}^i$.

$$\Phi_j^i(v_{j-1}^i, t_{j-1}^i, v_j^i, t_j^i) \equiv \begin{cases} \exists d \ d = t_j^i - t_{j-1}^i \ \wedge \\ I_{j-1}^i(v_{j-1}^i + d) \ \wedge \\ g_j^i(v_{j-1}^i + d) \ \wedge \\ v_j^i = r_j^i(v_{j-1}^i + d) \end{cases}$$

This is nothing but a recapitulation of the definition of a compound step, namely that time passage does not violate the staying condition, the transition guard is satisfied and that a reset takes place. Note that this definition is invariant under a shift of global time, that is, $\Phi^i_j(v,t,v',t')$ is equivalent to $\Phi^i_j(v,t+d,v',t'+d)$ for every d. We can now define what constitutes a valid run of $\mathcal{A}^i$ *in isolation*, without taking into account synchronization constraints. We keep this definition shift-invariant as well and do not yet insist on the initial zone which is defined globally.

$$\Phi^i(\mathbf{t}^i,\mathbf{v}^i) = \bigwedge_{j=1}^{k} \Phi^i_j(v^i_{j-1},t^i_{j-1},v^i_j,t^i_j)$$

The predicate which defines what constitutes a valid global run is a conjunction of the conditions for local runs with additional conditions that take care of all the synchronization aspects, including the fact that all runs start and terminate simultaneously. For every $a \in \Sigma$ let $S_a = \{(i,j) : a^i_j = a\}$ be the set of steps that synchronize on a. To force all a-transitions to take place at the same time we define the predicate

$$\Psi_a(\mathbf{t}) \equiv \bigwedge_{(i,j),(i',j')\in S_a} t^i_j = t^{i'}_{j'}.$$

The conditions for a valid global run starting at Z_0 are then:

$$\Phi(\mathbf{t},\mathbf{v}) = \begin{cases} t^1_0 = t^2_0 = \cdots = t^n_0 \wedge \\ \mathbf{v}_0 \in Z_0 \wedge \\ \bigwedge_{i=1}^n \Phi^i(\mathbf{v}^i,\mathbf{t}^i) \wedge \\ \bigwedge_{a\in\Sigma} \Psi_a(\mathbf{t}) \wedge \\ t^1_{k+1} = t^2_{k+1} = \cdots = t^n_{k+1} \end{cases}$$

Note that the first and last conditions can be viewed as synchronization conditions for two additional fictitious transitions "start" and "end" in which all automata participate. This set is a convex subset of the space consisting of all valuations and time stamps in the run, and so is its projection on the last n dimensions which is the reachable set:

$$R_{Z,\langle\xi\rangle}(\mathbf{v}_{k+1}) \equiv \exists \mathbf{t} \exists \mathbf{v}_1,\ldots,\mathbf{v}_k\ \Phi(\mathbf{t},\mathbf{v}_1,\ldots\mathbf{v}_k,\mathbf{v}_{k+1}).$$ □

Let us mention that the result extends naturally to arbitrary "linear" hybrid automata with convex guards and invariants.

4 Application to Reachability Computation

4.1 A Modified Algorithm

We will now modify the standard reachability computation algorithm for timed automata to take advantage of this result. The idea is to generate symbolic states in a *breadth-first* manner and at each level merge those reached by the same set of compound steps. To identify those we need to decorate symbolic states with (partially ordered) path information. A *shuffle expression* over Σ is $\alpha = \alpha^1||\ldots||\alpha^n$ with $\alpha^i \in (\Sigma^i)^*$. Concatenation of a shuffle expression and a symbol a is defined as $(\alpha^1||\ldots||\alpha^n) \cdot a = (\beta^1||\ldots||\beta^n)$ where $\beta^i = \alpha^i$ if $a \notin \Sigma^i$ and $\beta^i = \alpha^i \cdot a$ otherwise.

Reachability computation for timed automata [HNSY94] is based on zones (timed polyhedra) which are expressed as conjunctions of rectangular inequalities of the form $c \leq d$ or $c \geq d$ and diagonal inequalities of the form $c - c' \leq d$ for clocks c, c' and integer d. A symbolic state is a pair (q, Z) where Z is a zone. The a-successor of a symbolic state (q, Z) such that q admits an a transition is defined as

$$Suc^a(q, Z) = \{(q', v') : \exists v \in Z\ \exists d \geq 0\ \ (q, v) \xrightarrow{d,a} (q', v').$$

The computation $(q', Z') = Suc^a(q, Z)$ is done by first applying "time passage" to Z, intersecting the result with I_q and with the transition guard and then applying the corresponding reset. This computation costs $O(n^3)$ time for n clocks.

Algorithm 1 performs this computation. At each iteration *Waiting* is a list of extended zones to be explored, all reached by the same number of transitions. We compute the successors of all those symbolic states and put them in a list *New*. The *Merge* procedure scans *New* and replaces every subset of symbolic states of the form

$$\{(q, Z_1, \alpha), \ldots, (q, Z_m, \alpha)\}$$

by a single state (q, Z, α) where Z is the convex hull of all these zones. From our result it follows that Z is exactly the union of the zones. Note that the path labels of a zone need not be kept after its successors have been computed. This also guarantees termination due to the finite number of zones.

Algorithm 1 (New Reachability Algorithm)

Explored:= *New*:=$\emptyset$
Waiting:=$\{(\mathbf{q}_0, Z_0, \varepsilon||..||\varepsilon)\}$
while *Waiting*$\neq \emptyset$ **do**
  for each $(q, Z, \alpha) \in$ *Waiting such that* $(q, Z) \notin$ *Explored* **do**
    for each $a \in \Sigma$ **do**
      New :=*New*$\cup\{(Suc^a(q, Z), \alpha \cdot a)\}$
    Explored := *Explored* $\cup\{(q, Z)\}$
  Waiting := *Merge(New)*
return(*Explored*)

4.2 Experimental Results

To confirm the complexity reduction empirically we have first tested a preliminary implementation of Algorithm 1 restricted to products of chain-like automata. Such automata are notorious for generating state explosion due to interleaving. We have considered two simple families of synthetic benchmarks shown in Figure 4. The first consists of parallel compositions of n independent *reset sequences* of length m each. The second class consists of parallel compositions of k independent synchronization chains, each being a parallel composition of n *synchronized sequences* of length m. A synchronized

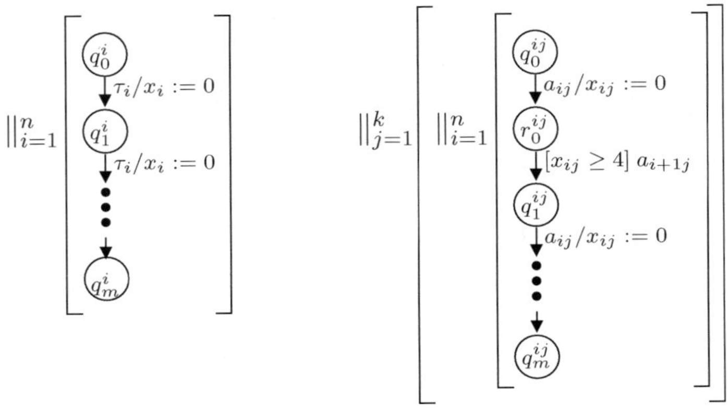

Fig. 4. The structure of the synthetic benchmarks

Table 1. Experimental results on the synthetic acyclic benchmarks

	n=2	n=4	n=6	n=8	n=10
Independent reset sequences					
m=1	5 / 4	65 / 16	1957 / 64	109601 / 256	⊥ / 1024
m=2	13 / 9	633 / 81	75973 / 729	⊥ / 6561	⊥ / 59049
m=3	25 / 16	2713 / 256	732529 / 4096	⊥ / 65536	⊥ / ⊥
Synchronization chains $k = 1$					
m=1	4 / 4	6 / 6	8 / 8	10 / 10	12 / 12
m=2	8 / 8	37 / 17	236 / 30	1600 / 47	10949 / 68
m=3	12 / 12	86 / 32	1441 / 72	30841 / 140	660615 / 244
Synchronization chains $k = 3$					
m=1	2012 / 64	812375 / 216	⊥ / 512	⊥ / 1000	⊥ / 1728
m=2	97142 / 512	⊥ / 4913	⊥ / 27000	⊥ / 103823	⊥ / 314432
m=3	745197 / 1728	⊥ / 32768	⊥ / 373248	⊥ / ⊥	⊥ / ⊥

sequence ($\mathcal{A}^{ij}$) alternates between actions that synchronize with the left ($a_{i,j}$) and the right ($a_{i+1,j}$) neighbor while separating them by at least 4 time units.

The experimental results obtained for the two benchmarks for different values of n, m and k are summarized in Table 1. Each entry in the table is of the form B/C where B is the number of symbolic states encountered in an ordinary breadth-first exploration, while C is the number of states explored by Algorithm 1. We limit ourselves to instances with less than 10^6 symbolic states, and use the $\perp$ symbol to denote the fact that this limit has been reached. Let us note that we achieve an exponential reduction both for the interleaving of *independent* actions (reset sequences) and for strongly-synchronized actions (a single synchronization chain with $k = 1$). The reduction is clearly much

Table 2. Results on the Fisher protocol benchmark. The Uppaal-A column corresponds to results obtained using the convex-hull approximation, while the IF-U column represents our new algorithm. Table entries represent the number of symbolic states and computation time. The symbol "-" means " not reported" (or "irrelevant" for the case of computation time on older computers) and $\perp$ means "too big".

Size	Kronos	Uppaal	Uppaal-A	IF	IF-U
2	-/-	-/0.01s	-/0.00s	29/0.003s	18/0.002s
3	-/-	-/0.03s	-/0.01s	165/0.01s	53/0.01s
4	752/-	-/0.23s	-/0.06s	1099/0.07s	164/0.03s
5	3552/-	-/5.09s	-/0.29s	8453/1.07s	527/0.04s
6	16320/-	-/310.97s	-/1.34s	74939/21.06s	1726/0.20s
7	73620/-	-/51598.17s	-/5.89s	762429/595.75s	5693/1.75s
8	$\perp/\perp$	$\perp/\perp$	-/25.83s	$\perp/\perp$	18792/5.73s
9	$\perp/\perp$	$\perp/\perp$	-/113.53s	$\perp/\perp$	61883/28.42s
10	$\perp/\perp$	$\perp/\perp$	-/498.88s	$\perp/\perp$	202994/367.76s
11	$\perp/\perp$	$\perp/\perp$	-/2525.31s	$\perp/\perp$	662873/4489.23s

more impressive in the synchronized case, where reductions based on partial order or symmetry [HBL+03] are not directly applicable.

We have then implemented Algorithm 1 into the IF toolset [BGM02] and tested its performance on several publicly-available benchmarks. Table 2 compares the performance of the new algorithm on the Fisher mutual-exclusion protocol benchmark with other reported results. We compare with old Kronos results reported in [T98], Uppaal results reported in [U] and results obtained with IF without using the new algorithm. It is interesting to note that although our new algorithm performs much better than the standard Uppaal machinery, their performances are similar when the convex-hull approximation option of the latter is employed. Our result shows that this "approximation" can be easily made exact.

5 Generalizations and Limitations

Let us discuss briefly the applicability of our result to more general modes of interaction between timed automata. A crucial condition for expressing synchronization constraints in a conjunctive form is that in every abstract run, every transition admits a unique set of transitions with which it is has to synchronize. This condition is fulfilled by requiring that whenever an a-transition takes place, all automata having a in their alphabet must participate. If a transition could choose some subset of the other transitions to synchronize with, Φ may contain disjunctions that cannot be eliminated and the result no longer holds.

State-based synchronization in which the state of one or more automata may appear in the invariants and transition guards of other automata is more general and has a more

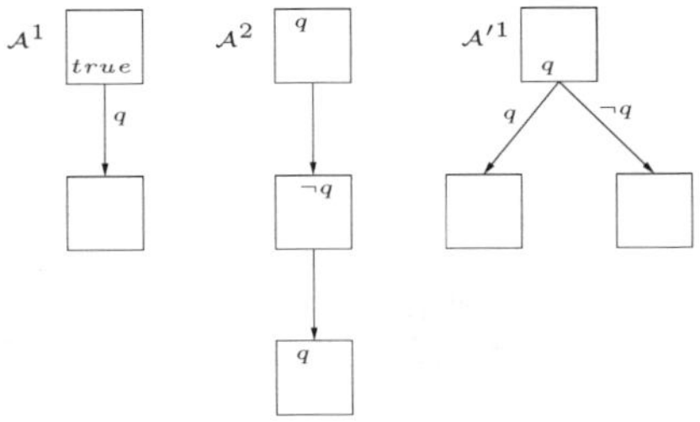

Fig. 5. Automata $\mathcal{A}^1||\mathcal{A}^2$ do not satisfy Theorem 1 while $\mathcal{A}'^1||\mathcal{A}^2$ do

asymmetric flavor as one automaton may enable a transition in the other without being obliged to take a transition by itself. Suppose $\mathcal{A}^1$ can take a transition when $\mathcal{A}^2$ is in state q and consider an abstract run in which $\mathcal{A}^1$ takes this transition and $\mathcal{A}^2$ passes through q twice (see Figure 5). Let t be the time stamp of the $\mathcal{A}^1$ transition, and let $[t_1, t_2]$ and $[t_3, t_4]$ be the time intervals in which $\mathcal{A}^2$ stays in q. The synchronization condition in this case will be disjunctive: $t \in [t_1, t_2] \vee t \in [t_3, t_4]$. If, however, the *disabling* of the $\mathcal{A}^1$ transition is always accompanied by an explicit transition in $\mathcal{A}^1$ the run that synchronizes with the first sojourn in q and the one synchronizing with the second one, are not qualitatively equivalent and the result is preserved. This property holds, for example, in the automata we use to model bi-bounded inertial delays [MP95] as well as in models derived from free-choice Petri nets.

Another illuminating example which is particularly important for our motivating application domain (circuits) is the following: let $\mathcal{A}^x$, $\mathcal{A}^y$ and $\mathcal{A}^z$ be three Boolean automata modeling an AND gate $z = x \wedge y$ and consider runs in which both x and y rise from 0 to 1 and consequently z rises as well. Denoting the respective time stamps by t_x, t_y and t_z, the synchronization condition is of the form

$$(t_x \leq t_y = t_z) \vee (t_y \leq t_x = t_z)$$

or equivalently $t_z = \max\{t_x, t_y\}$, which does not define a convex set. In order to apply Algorithm 1 correctly to systems admitting this type of synchronization we need to split every such transition to several copies, each with a unique synchronization context.

Let us remark that when the local automata are acyclic and reverse-deterministic (no state is entered via two different sequences of transitions), all global symbolic states that agree on the discrete state are reached via the same set of transitions. Hence our result can be exploited without decorating the states with path information.

6 Related Work and Discussion

The application of partial-order techniques to timed systems has been subject to several publications [R94, YS97, DGKK98, BJJY98, M99, LNZ05, ZYN03] but nothing that resembles our simple and easily-usable result has been explicitly stated. Neither has any solution that works in practice been reported so far.

The closest work, at least in spirit, to ours is that of Niebert et al. [ZYN03, LNZ05] who are more ambitious with respect to full-fledged partial-order reductions and use "event zones" rather than the standard "clock zones" used in the present paper. Event zones contain sufficient additional dimensions to represent dependency such that all representatives of a trace lead to the same event zone. It might be the case that the union that we compute here could be extracted (and proved to be convex) using their results. It would be interesting to compare the reductions provided by the two approaches in terms of scope and performance.

An interesting idea which was first proposed in [BJJY98], inspired by distributed simulation, is to use *local time scales*, that is to compute successors for each automaton separately on its own clock subspace, and somehow combine these local zones upon synchronization. Although the idea is aesthetically pleasing, it suffers from several problems including the implicit global synchronization that takes place at time zero, and the fact that you need to augment each automaton with an additional clock that measures its corresponding total elapsed time. This idea, however, inspired our proof of convexity.

We prove, nevertheless, a small result which indicates the circumstances under which local time scales can be effectively exploited. We present the result informally. Consider two automata $\mathcal{A}^1$ and $\mathcal{A}^2$ and a prefix of a global run that reaches a global state (q^1, q^2), and in which each of the two has passed through a local state in which all its clocks were inactive.[5] If no synchronized action has taken place since then, one can see that if $q^1 \rightarrow q'^1$ and $q^2 \rightarrow q'^2$ via synchronization-free local runs, then $(q^1, q^2) \rightarrow (q'^1, q'^2)$ in the product automaton. The reason is that because of the clock inactivity, each of the local runs can be "delayed" and every local state that can be reached at time t can be reached as well at any $t' \geq t$ and hence any pair of local states can be made to be reached simultaneously. This implies that after such a "desynchronization" point, reachable sets can be computed separately for each automaton and be merged via intersection before the next synchronization. This observation can be useful for verifying products of automata that repeatedly go through such inactive states.

As a final remark, let us note that reducing the number of zones by taking their convex hull has been considered in the past [DT98] but always as an *over-approximation*. We speculate that the reason for not discovering the result of the present paper is due to the fact that the systems studied were cyclic, in which the same discrete state could be reached by different paths, not all of which being permutations of the same set of transitions. That is why the possibility of exact convex hull escaped the attention. In general we think that looking at the structure of *individual runs* can give insights that are sometimes masked by focusing exclusively on the reachability graph representation.

Acknowledgment. This paper has benefitted from discussions with P. Niebert.

References

[AD94] R. Alur and D.L. Dill, A Theory of Timed Automata, *Theoretical Computer Science* **126**, 183-235, 1994.

[BJJY98] J. Bengtsson, B. Jonsson, J. Lilius and W. Yi, Partial Order Reductions for Timed Systems, *CONCUR'98*, 485-500, 1998.

[5] A clock is inactive in a state if along any path starting in that state it will be reset before being tested. This fact has been used to reduce the dimension of reachability computation [DY96].

[BBM03] R. Ben Salah, M. Bozga and O. Maler, On Timing Analysis of Combinational Circuits, *FORMATS'03*, 204-219, 2003.

[BBM06] R. Ben Salah, M. Bozga and O. Maler, Automatic Abstraction of Timed Components, submitted, 2006.

[BGM02] M. Bozga, S. Graf and L. Mounier, IF-2.0: A Validation Environment for Component-Based Real-Time Systems, *CAV'02*, 343-348, 2002.

[DGKK98] D. Dams, R. Gerth, B. Knaack and R. Kuiper, Partial-order Reduction Techniques for Real-time Model Checking, *Formal Aspects of Computing* **10**, 469-482, 1998.

[DT98] C. Daws and S. Tripakis, Model Checking of Real-Time Reachability Properties Using Abstractions, *TACAS'98*, 313-329, 1998.

[DY96] C. Daws and S. Yovine, Reducing the Number of Clock Variables of Timed Automata, *RTSS'96*, 73-81, 1996.

[DR95] V. Diekert and G. Rozenberg (Eds.), *The Book of Traces*, World Scientific, 1995.

[HBL$^+$03] M. Hendriks, G. Behrmann, K. Larsen, P. Niebert and F. Vaandrager, Adding Symmetry Reduction to Uppaal, FORMATS'03, 46-59, 2003.

[HNSY94] T. Henzinger, X. Nicollin, J. Sifakis, and S. Yovine, Symbolic Model-checking for Real-time Systems, *Information and Computation* **111**, 193-244, 1994.

[LNZ05] D. Lugiez, P. Niebert and S. Zennou, A Partial Order Semantics Approach to the Clock Explosion Problem of Timed Automata, *Theoretical Computer Science* **345**, 27-59, 2005.

[MP95] O. Maler and A. Pnueli, Timing Analysis of Asynchronous Circuits using Timed Automata, *CHARME'95*, 189-205, 1995.

[M99] M. Minea, Partial Order Reduction for Model Checking of Timed Automata, *CONCUR'99*, 431-446, 1999.

[R94] T.G. Rokicki, *Representing and Modeling Digital Circuits*, PhD Thesis, Stanford University, 1994.

[T98] S. Tripakis, The Analysis of Timed Systems in Practice, PhD Thesis, Université Joseph Fourier, Grenoble, 1998.

[U] Uppaal benchmarks:
`www.it.uu.se/research/group/darts/uppaal/benchmarks`

[YS97] T. Yoneda and B.-H. Schlingloff, Efficient Verification of Parallel Real-Time Systems, *Formal Methods in System Design* **11**, 187-215, 1997.

[ZYN03] S. Zennou, M. Yguel and P. Niebert, ELSE: A New Symbolic State Generator for Timed Automata, *FORMATS'03*, 273-280, 2003.

A Language for Task Orchestration and Its Semantic Properties

David Kitchin, William R. Cook, and Jayadev Misra*

The University of Texas at Austin
{dkitchin, wcook, misra}@cs.utexas.edu

Abstract. Orc is a new language for task orchestration, a form of concurrent programming with applications in workflow, business process management, and web service orchestration. Orc provides constructs to orchestrate the concurrent invocation of services – while managing time-outs, priorities, and failure of services or communication. In this paper, we show a trace-based semantic model for Orc, which induces a congruence on Orc programs and facilitates reasoning about them. Despite the simplicity of the language and its semantic model, Orc is able to express a variety of useful orchestration tasks.

1 Introduction

We describe the semantic properties of *Orc*, a new language for *task orchestration*. Task orchestration is a form of concurrent programming in which multiple services are invoked to achieve a goal – while managing time-outs, priorities, and failures of services and communication. Unlike traditional concurrency models, orchestration introduces an *asymmetric* relationship between a program and the services that constitute its environment. An orchestration invokes and receives responses from the external services, which do not initiate communication.

Many practical problems can be understood as orchestrations – for example, business workflows are naturally expressed as orchestrations [1]. We illustrate the use of Orc in implementing some traditional concurrent computation patterns; larger examples have also been developed [2,3]. Orc has also been used to study service-level agreements for composite web services [4].

The goal of this work is to develop a language based on a simple trace semantics that can still express, and support reasoning about, useful task orchestrations. The key metric for a trace semantics is whether trace equivalence corresponds to observational equivalence of programs. Depending on the language, traces must be extended to include failures, refusals, ready states, etc., in order to adequately model observational equivalence. The trace semantics of Orc is a simple set of traces; the traces include communication events and substitution events, which model synchronization. We prove that the equality of trace sets defines a congruence on programs, in that programs with equivalent trace sets

* Work of the second author is partially supported by National Science Foundation grant CCF-0448128.

C. Baier and H. Hermanns (Eds.): CONCUR 2006, LNCS 4137, pp. 477–491, 2006.

are interchangeable. We show a number of laws about Orc programs, similar to those in Kleene algebra [5]; the laws are based on strong bisimulation. We then introduce a more general congruence based on trace set equivalence which can establish laws not provable by strong bisimulation.

2 Overview of Orc

An Orc program consists of a set of definitions and a *goal* expression which is to be evaluated. Orc assumes that basic services, like sequential computation and data manipulation, are implemented by primitive *sites*. Orc provides constructs to orchestrate the concurrent invocation of sites.

The syntax of Orc is given in Figure 1. A site call $M(\bar{p})$ invokes a site named M with a list of actual parameters $\bar{p}$. If there are no parameters, the site call is written as just 'M'. An actual parameter p may be a variable x or a value v. Calls to defined expressions $E(\bar{p})$ are similar, given a definition with name E and formal parameters $\bar{p}$. There are only three combinators: $>x>$ for sequential composition, $|$ for parallel composition, and **where** for asymmetric parallel composition. The combinators are listed in decreasing order of precedence, so $f >x> g \mid h$ means $(f >x> g) \mid h$, and f **where** $x :\in g \mid h$ means f **where** $x :\in (g \mid h)$. In the remainder of this section, we give an informal overview of the Orc programming model with examples. The formal semantics is given in Section 3.

2.1 Site Calls

The simplest Orc expression is a *site call* $M(\bar{p})$, where M is a site name and $\bar{p}$ is a list of actual parameters. A site is a separately defined procedure, like a web service. The site may be implemented on the client's machine or a remote machine. A site call elicits at most one response; it is possible that a site never responds to a call. For example, a site call $CNN(d)$, where CNN is a news service and d is a date, might download the newspage for the specified date. Site calls are *strict*, i.e., a site is called only if all its parameters have values.

Table 1 defines a few sites that are fundamental to effective programming in Orc (a *signal* is a value which has no additional information). Additionally, **0** represents a site which never responds.

2.2 Combinators

There are three combinators in Orc to compose expressions. Symmetric composition of f and g, written as $f \mid g$, evaluates f and g independently. The sites called

$$\begin{array}{rcll} f,g,h & \in & \textit{Expression} & ::= M(\bar{p}) \mid E(\bar{p}) \mid f \mid g \mid f >x> g \mid f \textbf{ where } x :\in g \\ p & \in & \textit{Actual} & ::= x \mid v \\ & & \textit{Definition} & ::= E(\bar{x}) \;\underline{\Delta}\; f \end{array}$$

Fig. 1. Syntax of Orc

Table 1. Fundamental Sites

$let(x, y, \cdots)$	Returns argument values as a tuple.
$if(b)$	Returns a signal if b is true, and does not respond if b is false.
$Rtimer(t)$	Returns a signal after exactly t time units.

by f and g are the ones called by $f \mid g$ and any value published by either f or g is published by $f \mid g$. There is no direct communication or interaction between these two computations. For example, evaluation of $CNN(d) \mid BBC(d)$ initiates two independent computations; up to two values will be published depending on the number of sites that respond.

In $f >x> g$, expression f is evaluated, each value published by it initiates a fresh instance of g as a separate computation, and the value published by f is called x in g's computation. Evaluation of f continues while (possibly several) instances of g are run. This is the only mechanism in Orc similar to spawning threads. If f publishes no value, g is never instantiated. The values published by the executions of different instances of g are the values published by $f >x> g$. As an example, the following expression calls sites *CNN* and *BBC* in parallel to get the news for date d. Responses from either of these calls are bound to x and then site *email* is called to send the information to address a. Thus, *email* may be called 0, 1 or 2 times.

$$(CNN(d) \mid BBC(d)) >x> email(a, x)$$

Expression $f \gg g$ is a short-hand for $f >x> g$ when x is not used in g.

To evaluate (f **where** $x :\in g$), start by evaluating both f and g in parallel. Evaluation of parts of f which do not depend on x can proceed, but site calls in which x is a parameter are suspended until x has a value. In (($M \mid N(x)$) **where** $x :\in R$), for example, M can be called even before x has a value. If g publishes a value, then x is assigned this value, g's evaluation is terminated and the suspended parts of f can proceed. This is the only mechanism in Orc to block or terminate parts of a computation. Unlike in the previous example, the following expression calls *email* at most once.

$$email(a, x) \textbf{ where } x :\in (CNN(d) \mid BBC(d))$$

2.3 Definitions

Declaration $E(\bar{x}) \;\underline{\Delta}\; f$ defines expression E whose formal parameter list is $\bar{x}$ and body is expression f. A call $E(\bar{p})$ is evaluated by replacing the formal parameters $\bar{x}$ by the actual parameters $\bar{p}$ in the body of the definition f. Sites are called by value, while definitions are called by name.

2.4 Examples

Time-Out. Expression $let(z)$ **where** $z :\in (f \mid Rtimer(t) \gg let(3))$ either publishes the first publication of f, or times out after t units and publishes 3. A typical programming paradigm is to call site M and publish a pair (x, b) as the value, where b is true if M publishes x before the time-out, and false if there is a time-out. In the latter case, x is irrelevant. Below, z is the pair (x, b).

$$let(z) \;\; \textbf{where}\; z :\in (\; M > x > let(x, true) \;\mid\; Rtimer(t) > x > let(x, false)\;)$$

Fork-Join Parallelism. In concurrent programming, one often needs to spawn two independent threads at a point in the computation, and resume the computation after both threads complete. Such an execution style is called *fork-join* parallelism. There is no special construct for fork-join in Orc, but it is easy to code such computations. The following code fragment calls sites M and N in parallel and publishes their values as a tuple after they both complete their executions.

$$(let(u, v) \; \textbf{where}\; u :\in M) \; \textbf{where}\; v :\in N$$

Synchronization. There is no special machinery for synchronization in Orc; a **where** expression provides the necessary ingredients for programming synchronizations. Consider $M \gg f$ and $N \gg g$; we wish to execute them independently, but synchronize f and g by starting them only after *both* M and N have completed.

$$((let(u, v) \; \textbf{where}\; u :\in M) \; \textbf{where}\; v :\in N) \gg (f \mid g)$$

Priority. Call the sites M and N, but give priority to M by publishing its response if it arrives within the first time unit, even if N's response precedes it.

$$let(x) \;\; \textbf{where}\; x :\in (M \mid ((Rtimer(1) \gg let(u)) \; \textbf{where}\; u :\in N))$$

Arbitration. A fundamental problem in concurrent computing is *arbitration*: to choose between two computations and let only one proceed. Arbitration is the essence of mutual exclusion. Consider a process which behaves as process P if event *Alpha* happens and as Q if *Beta* happens. In Orc, events *Alpha* and *Beta* are represented as sites, and P and Q are expressions. Below, *flag* records which of *Alpha* and *Beta* responds first.

$$\begin{array}{l} if(flag) \gg P \mid if(\neg flag) \gg Q \\ \quad \textbf{where}\;\; flag :\in (Alpha \gg let(true) \mid Beta \gg let(false)) \end{array}$$

The Orc model permits more complex arbitration protocols, such as: execute one of P, Q and R, depending how many sites out of *Alpha*, *Beta* and *Gamma* respond within 10 time units.

Recursive Definitions of Expressions. The recursive expression *Metronome*, defined below, publishes a signal every time unit, starting immediately. It is used in the subsequent expression to call site *Poll* each time unit and publish its values.

$Metronome \;\underline{\Delta}\; Signal \mid Rtimer(1) \gg Metronome$
$Metronome \gg Poll$

Non-strict Evaluation; Parallel-or. *Parallel-or* is a classic problem in non-strict evaluation: computation of $x \vee y$ over booleans x and y publishes *true* if either variable value is *true*; therefore, the evaluation may terminate even when one of the variable values is unknown. Here, we state the problem in Orc terms, and give a simple solution.

Suppose sites M and N publish booleans. Compute the *parallel-or* of the two booleans, i.e., (in a non-strict fashion) publish *true* as soon as either site returns *true* and *false* only if both sites return *false*. In the following solution, site $or(x, y)$ returns $x \vee y$. Site $ift(b)$ returns *true* if b is true; it does not respond otherwise: $ift(b) = if(b) \gg let(true)$.

$$\begin{array}{l}(\;(let(z)\ \textbf{where}\ z :\in ift(x) \mid ift(y) \mid or(x, y)\,)\\ \qquad\qquad\textbf{where}\ x :\in M\ \;)\\ \qquad\qquad\qquad\textbf{where}\ y :\in N\end{array}$$

3 Asynchronous Semantics

We develop a formal semantics of Orc in this section. The semantics is operational, asynchronous, and based on labeled transition systems. A synchronous semantics has also been defined [2], while a complete temporal semantics is future work.

As is common in small-step operational semantics, the syntax of Orc must be extended to represent intermediate states. We introduce $?k$ to denote an instance of a site call that has not yet returned a value, where k is a unique handle that identifies the call instance. We also restrict the language to sites and definitions with a single argument; multiple arguments are easily handled by adding tuples to the language.

The transition relation $f \stackrel{a}{\rightarrow} f'$, defined in Figure 2, states that expression f may transition with event a to expression f'. There are four kinds of events, which we call *base events*:

$$a, b \in BaseEvent ::= !v \;\big|\; \tau \;\big|\; M_k(v) \;\big|\; k?v$$

A *publication* event, $!v$, publishes a value v from an expression. As is traditional, τ denotes an *internal* event. The remaining two events, the *site call* event $M_k(v)$ and the *response* event $k?v$, are discussed below.

3.1 Site Calls

A site call involves three steps: invocation of the site, response from the site, and publication of the result. These steps can be arbitrarily interleaved with other site calls, or delayed indefinitely.

$$\frac{k \text{ fresh}}{M(v) \overset{M_k(v)}{\rightarrow} ?k} \quad (\textsc{SiteCall})$$

$$?k \overset{k?v}{\rightarrow} let(v) \quad (\textsc{SiteRet})$$

$$let(v) \overset{!v}{\rightarrow} \mathbf{0} \quad (\textsc{Let})$$

$$\frac{f \overset{a}{\rightarrow} f'}{f \mid g \overset{a}{\rightarrow} f' \mid g} \quad (\textsc{Sym1})$$

$$\frac{g \overset{a}{\rightarrow} g'}{f \mid g \overset{a}{\rightarrow} f \mid g'} \quad (\textsc{Sym2})$$

$$\frac{(E(x) \;\underline{\Delta}\; f) \in D}{E(p) \overset{\tau}{\rightarrow} [p/x].f} \quad (\textsc{Def})$$

$$\frac{f \overset{a}{\rightarrow} f' \qquad a \neq !v}{f > x > g \overset{a}{\rightarrow} f' > x > g} \quad (\textsc{Seq1N})$$

$$\frac{f \overset{!v}{\rightarrow} f'}{f > x > g \overset{\tau}{\rightarrow} (f' > x > g) \mid [v/x].g} \quad (\textsc{Seq1V})$$

$$\frac{f \overset{a}{\rightarrow} f'}{f \textbf{ where } x :\in g \overset{a}{\rightarrow} f' \textbf{ where } x :\in g} \quad (\textsc{Asym1N})$$

$$\frac{g \overset{!v}{\rightarrow} g'}{f \textbf{ where } x :\in g \overset{\tau}{\rightarrow} [v/x].f} \quad (\textsc{Asym1V})$$

$$\frac{g \overset{a}{\rightarrow} g' \qquad a \neq !v}{f \textbf{ where } x :\in g \overset{a}{\rightarrow} f \textbf{ where } x :\in g'} \quad (\textsc{Asym2})$$

Fig. 2. Asynchronous Operational Semantics of Orc

Rule SiteCall specifies that a site call $M(v)$, where v is a value, transitions to $?k$ with event $M_k(v)$. The handle k connects a site call to a site return – a fresh handle is created for each call to identify that call instance. The resulting expression, $?k$, represents a process that is blocked waiting for the response from the call. A site call occurs only when its parameters are values; in $M(x)$, where x is a variable, the call is blocked until x is defined.

In SiteRet a pending site call $?k$ receives a result v from the environment and transitions to the expression $let(v)$. There is no assumption that all site calls eventually respond. If there is no response, then the call blocks indefinitely.

The Let rule generates a publication event $!v$ from its argument value v.

3.2 Composition Rules

The composition rules are straightforward, except in some cases where subexpressions publish values. When f publishes a value ($f \overset{!v}{\rightarrow} f'$), rule Seq1V creates a new instance of the right side, $[v/x].g$, the expression in which all free occurrences of x in g are replaced by v. The publication $!v$ is hidden, and the entire expression performs a τ action. Note that f and all instances of g are executed in parallel. Because the semantics is asynchronous, there is no guarantee that the values published by the first instance will precede the values of later instances. Instead, the values produced by all instances of g are interleaved arbitrarily.

Asymmetric parallel composition is similar to parallel composition, except when g publishes a value v. In this case, rule Asym1V terminates g and x is bound to v in f. One subtlety of these rules is that f may contain both active and blocked subprocesses – any site call that uses x is blocked until g publishes.

Expressions are evaluated using call-by-name in the DEF rule. We assume a single global set of definitions D.

4 Executions and Traces

Define the relation $\Rightarrow$ as the transitive closure of the transition relation $\rightarrow$, together with the empty transition ϵ. If $f \overset{s}{\Rightarrow} f'$, we say that s is an *execution* of f.

$$f \overset{\epsilon}{\Rightarrow} f \qquad \frac{f \overset{a}{\rightarrow} f'',\ f'' \overset{s}{\Rightarrow} f'}{f \overset{as}{\Rightarrow} f'}$$

We write as to denote the concatenation of event a onto execution s. Similarly, st is the concatenation of two executions s and t. We have included $f \overset{\epsilon}{\Rightarrow} f$ to guarantee that the set of executions of an expression is prefix-closed.

A *trace* is obtained by removing all internal events, τ, from an execution. Note that every execution (and trace) is finite in length. However, we can represent an infinite sequence of transitions by the set of all of its finite prefixes.

Example. An execution of $((M(x) \mid let(x)) >y> R(y))$ **where** $x :\in (N \mid S)$ is shown below. In the following, N returns value 5 and $R(5)$ returns 7.

$$S_k \quad N_l \quad l?5 \quad M_m(5) \quad \tau \quad R_n(5) \quad n?7 \quad !7$$

The response from S, if any, is ignored after N responds. The event τ is due to $let(5) \overset{!5}{\rightarrow} \mathbf{0}$. This event causes the event $R_n(5)$. Site call $M_m(5)$ has not yet responded in this execution. The final expression is $(?m >y> R(y))$.

4.1 Laws Proved Using Strong Bisimulation

A *closed* expression is one which has no free variables; an *open* expression has free variables. In this section, we list certain identities over closed expressions, some of them similar to the laws of Kleene algebra [5]. We write $f \sim g$ to denote that f and g are strongly bisimilar [6]. In a later section, we develop a notion of congruence over both closed and open expressions. That notion can be used to show, for example, that $f >x> let(x)$ is congruent to f.

Below, "f is x-free" means that x is not a free variable of f.

1. $f \mid \mathbf{0} \sim f$
2. $f \mid g \sim g \mid f$
3. $f \mid (g \mid h) \sim (f \mid g) \mid h$
4. $f >x> (g >y> h) \sim (f >x> g) >y> h$, if h is x-free.
5. $\mathbf{0} >x> f \sim \mathbf{0}$

6. $(f \mid g) >x> h \sim f >x> h \mid g >x> h$
7. $(f \mid g)$ **where** $x :\in h \sim (f$ **where** $x :\in h) \mid g$, if g is x-free.
8. $(f >y> g)$ **where** $x :\in h \sim (f$ **where** $x :\in h) >y> g$, if g is x-free.
9. $(f$ **where** $x :\in g)$ **where** $y :\in h \sim (f$ **where** $y :\in h)$ **where** $x :\in g$, if g is y-free and h is x-free.
10. $\mathbf{0}$ **where** $x :\in ?k \sim ?k \gg \mathbf{0}$
11. $\mathbf{0}$ **where** $x :\in M \sim M \gg \mathbf{0}$, for any site M.

4.2 Substitution Events

Strong bisimulation is applicable only if each side of an identity is a closed expression. If we relax this restriction, we can use bisimulation to prove, for example, that $\mathbf{0} = let(x)$, because neither has a non-trivial transition. Yet, these two expressions display different behaviors in the same context. For example, $let(1) >x> \mathbf{0}$ never publishes whereas $let(1) >x> let(x)$ always publishes.

To obtain a more general theory we introduce a new kind of event, a *substitution event* of the form $[v/x]$, and the transition rule:

$$f \overset{[v/x]}{\rightarrow} [v/x].f \qquad \text{(SUBST)}$$

A substitution event differs from the base events described in Section 3 in a crucial way: the rules in Figure 2 are defined only over base events. Therefore, given that $f \overset{[v/x]}{\rightarrow} [v/x].f$, (SYM1) can *not* be applied to deduce

$$f \mid g \overset{[v/x]}{\rightarrow} [v/x].f \mid g,$$

Allowing substitution events expands the set of executions (and traces) of expressions. For example, the traces of $let(x)$ are of the form $[v/x]\ !v$, for all possible v, and their prefixes. Introducing substitution events allows us to distinguish between $\mathbf{0}$ and $let(x)$, for instance, because a possible trace of $let(x)$ is $[1/x]\ !1$.

We observe that proofs by strong bisimulation of the laws of Section 4.1 remain valid after allowing for substitution events. This is because both sides of an identity $f \sim g$ are closed. Hence, given $f \overset{a}{\rightarrow} f'$, either a is not a substitution event, or it is of the form $[v/x]$ where x is not free in f. In the latter case, $f' = f$, and this transition corresponds in g to $g \overset{a}{\rightarrow} g$.

Furthermore, we can now show that all the laws of Section 4.1 hold for arbitrary expressions f, g, and h, open or closed. So, we can prove, for instance, that $let(x) \mid let(y) \sim let(y) \mid let(x)$. Each side of an identity has the same set of free variables (except $\mathbf{0} >x> f \sim \mathbf{0}$, which is easily handled). Therefore, a proof by strong bisimulation applies to each identity.

Variable Naming. Free and bound variables of an expression have different names. Hence, in $(f >x> g)$, f does not have a free variable x, and in $(f$ **where** $x :\in g)$, x is not free in g.

5 Characterizations of Traces

Notation. We write $\langle f \rangle$ for the set of traces of f.

In this section, we show that the traces of an expression can be determined from the traces of its constituent subexpressions. In particular, we overload the Orc combinators to apply over trace sets and prove that

$$\langle f \mid g \rangle = \langle f \rangle \mid \langle g \rangle$$
$$\langle f > x > g \rangle = \langle f \rangle > x > \langle g \rangle$$
$$\langle f \textbf{ where } x :\in g \rangle = \langle f \rangle \textbf{ where } x :\in \langle g \rangle$$

5.1 Trace Characterization of Base Expressions

Notation. We use the following notation for quantified expressions: $(\cup r : r \in R : e)$ denotes $\cup_{r \in R}(e)$, where variable r can be free in e. Range R of r may be omitted if it is clear from context, e.g., $(\cup i :: S_i)$.

We show the trace sets of base expressions, i.e, those without constituent subexpressions. We only list the compact versions of traces in which there are no substitutions to irrelevant variables (which have no effect on the rest of the trace). Also, we only list the maximal traces below, whose prefixes constitute the entire trace set. Below, *Values* denotes the set of all possible responses from sites.

$$\langle let(v) \rangle = \{ !v \}$$
$$\langle M(v) \rangle = (\cup w : w \in Values : \{ M_k(v)\ k?w\ !w \})$$
$$\langle M(x) \rangle = (\cup v : v \in Values : (\cup t : t \in \langle M(v) \rangle : \{[v/x]t\}))$$

The trace set for $let(v)$ is easy to see. For $M(v)$, any maximal trace is of the form $M_k(v)\ k?w\ \ !w$, where w is a response from M. Note that k is a bound parameter of the trace (with $M_k(v)$ as its binder) and it can be renamed consistently. The trace set of $M(x)$ starts with a substitution $[v/x]$, for any v, followed by any trace of $M(v)$.

5.2 Trace Characterization for (f | g)

Separation and Merge. Let s, t and p be sequences of events. We call p a *merge* of s and t if (1) s and t are both subsequences of p and every event of p belongs to at least one of s and t, (2) every common event of p (i.e., an event that belongs to both s and t) is a substitution, and (3) for any variable which has a substitution in both s and t, its first substitution in both s and t is a common event of p. We call the pair $(s,\ t)$ a *separation* of p.

Example. Let

$$s = a \quad b \quad [3/x] \quad [4/x] \quad [5/x]$$
$$t = c \quad [2/y] \quad [3/x] \quad [5/x] \quad [4/x]$$
$$u = [3/x] \quad [2/y]$$

Below, we use subscripts on events to identify the sequences to which they belong, when there is ambiguity.

$$\begin{array}{llllllll} a & c & b & [2/y] & [3/x]_{s,t} & [4/x]_s & [5/x]_{s,t} & [4/x]_t \in (s \mid t) \\ a & b & [3/x]_{s,u} & [4/x] & [5/x] & [2/y] & & \in (s \mid u) \end{array}$$

There is no merge for t and u because the orders of first substitutions to x and y are different. Also, if two sequences have $[v/x]$ and $[w/x]$ as their first substitutions for x, and $v \neq w$, then they have no merge, from condition (3). Note that in the merge of s and t, $[5/x]$ appears once, whereas $[4/x]$ appears twice. Condition (3) imposes a constraint only on the first substitution to a variable; subsequent substitutions may or may not be common events in a merge.

Definition. For traces s and t, define $s \mid t$ to be the set of their merges.

$$s \mid t = \{p \mid p \text{ is a merge of } s \text{ and } t\}$$

We lift the definition to trace sets $S \mid T$:

$$S \mid T = \{p \mid p \in s \mid t,\ s \in S,\ t \in T\}$$

Note that $s \mid \epsilon = \{s\}$, $S \mid \{\epsilon\} = S$, and $\mid$ over traces is commutative.

Theorem 1. $\langle f \mid g \rangle = \langle f \rangle \mid \langle g \rangle$

Proof Sketch: The complete proof is in [7]. The proof is in two parts showing that one side is a subset of the other. For $\langle f \mid g \rangle \subseteq \langle f \rangle \mid \langle g \rangle$, we show a separation (s,t) of any trace p of $\langle f \mid g \rangle$ such that $s \in \langle f \rangle$ and $t \in \langle g \rangle$. The proof is by induction on the length of p. In the other direction, to show $\langle f \rangle \mid \langle g \rangle \subseteq \langle f \mid g \rangle$, let p be a trace with separation (s,t) where $s \in \langle f \rangle$ and $t \in \langle g \rangle$. We prove that $p \in \langle f \mid g \rangle$ by induction on the length of p.

5.3 Trace Characterization for $(f >x> g)$

Define operator $\backslash$ as follows: $T\backslash[v/x] = \{t \mid [v/x]t \in T\}$. That is, $T\backslash[v/x]$ discards all traces in T that do not begin with $[v/x]$, and removes the leading $[v/x]$ event from the remaining traces.

We extend this notation to sequences of substitutions:

$$T\backslash\epsilon = T$$
$$T\backslash(cD) = (T\backslash c)\backslash D,$$
where c is a substitution and D a sequence of substitutions.

Definition. For trace s and trace set T define a set of traces $(s >x> T)$ by

$$\begin{cases} \{s\} & \text{if } s \text{ has no publication,} \\ r(t >x> T' \mid (T'\backslash[v/x])) & \text{if } s = r\ !v\ t \text{ and } r \text{ has no publication,} \\ \quad \text{where } D \text{ is the sequence of substitutions in } r, & \\ \quad \text{and } T' = T\backslash D & \end{cases}$$

We lift the definition to $S >x> T$, where S and T are sets of traces.

$$S >x> T = \{p \mid p \in s >x> T,\ s \in S\}$$

Theorem 2. $\langle f >x> g\rangle = \langle f\rangle >x> \langle g\rangle$

Proof Sketch: The complete proof is in [7]. The proof is in two parts showing that one side is a subset of the other. To prove that $\langle f\rangle >x> \langle g\rangle \subseteq \langle f >x> g\rangle$, take any p which is in $\langle f\rangle >x> \langle g\rangle$, i.e., $p \in (s >x> \langle g\rangle)$, where $s \in \langle f\rangle$. Then show, by induction on the number of publications in s, that $p \in \langle f >x> g\rangle$. In the other direction, to show $\langle f >x> g\rangle \subseteq \langle f\rangle >x> \langle g\rangle$, we take a trace p of $\langle f >x> g\rangle$, and construct a sequence s which corresponds to the subsequence of events from f in p. We prove, by induction on the number of publications in s, that $p \in (s >x> \langle g\rangle)$.
Note: Any substitution event $[v/x]$ in s is unrelated to x in $(s >x> T)$.

5.4 Trace Characterization for (f where $x :\in g$)

Definition. For traces s and t define a set of traces (s **where** $x :\in t$) by

$$\begin{cases} (s \mid t) & \text{if } t \text{ has no publication,} \\ (s' \mid t')s'' & \text{if } s = s'\ [v/x]\ s'',\ t = t'\ !v\ t'', \\ & t' \text{ has no publication and } s' \text{ has no substitution for } x \\ \{\} & \text{otherwise .} \end{cases}$$

We lift the definition to (S **where** $x :\in T$), where S and T are sets of traces.

$$(S \textbf{ where } x :\in T) = \{p \mid p \in (s \textbf{ where } x :\in t),\ s \in S,\ t \in T\}$$

Theorem 3. $\langle f \textbf{ where } x :\in g\rangle = \langle f\rangle \textbf{ where } x :\in \langle g\rangle$

Proof Sketch: The complete proof is in [7]. The proof is in two parts showing that one side is a subset of the other. If g never publishes, rule (ASYM1V) is never used; therefore, the operational behavior of (f **where** $x :\in g$) is analogous that of $f \mid g$ because (ASYM1N) and (ASYM2) are the counterparts of (SYM1) and (SYM2), respectively. Then, any trace of (f **where** $x :\in g$) is from $(s \mid t)$, where s and t are traces of f and g. If g has a trace $t'\ !v\ t''$ and f a trace $s'\ [v/x]\ s''$, then $(s' \mid t')s''$ is a trace of (f **where** $x :\in g$), using the above argument and the meaning of substitution.
Note: Any substitution event $[v/x]$ in t is unrelated to x in (s **where** $x :\in t$).

6 Monotonicity and Continuity of Combinators

The results of the last section show that the set of traces of any expression can be obtained from the traces of its constituent subexpressions. This motivates the following definition of *congruence* among expressions: two expressions are congruent, $\cong$, if their trace sets are equal. Similarly, define a partial order, $\sqsubseteq$, over expressions.

$$f \cong g \text{ if } \langle f\rangle = \langle g\rangle, \text{ and } f \sqsubseteq g \text{ if } \langle f\rangle \subseteq \langle g\rangle$$

Each combinator preserves substitution of congruent subexpressions. That is, given $f \cong g$, we claim

1. $f \mid h \cong g \mid h$, and $h \mid f \cong h \mid g$
2. $f >x> h \cong g >x> h$, and $h >x> f \cong h >x> g$
3. f **where** $x :\in h \cong g$ **where** $x :\in h$, and
   h **where** $x :\in f \cong h$ **where** $x :\in g$

We prove the results by showing that each combinator is monotonic in both its arguments. That is, given $f \sqsubseteq g$, we prove the claims (1, 2, 3) with $\sqsubseteq$ replacing $\cong$. Then switching the roles of f and g, we get the congruences. We also prove continuity of the combinators. Underlying most of the proofs is the following lemma.

Lemma 4. Let each of $S_0, S_1, \cdots$ and T be a set of traces. Then,

1. $(\cup i :: S_i * T) = (\cup i :: S_i) * T$, where $*$ is any Orc combinator.
2. $(\cup i :: T * S_i) = T * (\cup i :: S_i)$, where $*$ is any combinator other than $>x>$.

Proof: From the definition of $*$ over trace sets, for arbitrary R and T,

$$R * T = (\cup r : r \in R : r * T), \text{ where } * \text{ is any Orc combinator}$$
$$R * T = (\cup t : t \in T : R * t), \text{ where } * \text{ is any combinator other than } >x> .$$

These follow from the lifting in the definition of the combinators over sets.

6.1 Monotonicity of Orc Combinators

Each Orc combinator is monotonic in its left argument, e.g. $f \sqsubseteq g$ implies $f \mid h \sqsubseteq g \mid h$. This follows from Lemma 4, part(1); see [7] for details.

Monotonicity in the right argument for combinators other than $>x>$, (e.g. $f \sqsubseteq g$ implies (h **where** $x :\in f) \sqsubseteq (h$ **where** $x :\in g$)), follows from Lemma 4, part(2). We give a proof that $f \sqsubseteq g$ implies $(h >x> f) \sqsubseteq (h >x> g)$ in [7].

6.2 Continuity of Orc Combinators

Characterization of Least Upper Bound. Let f denote a sequence of expressions $f_0, f_1, \cdots$, where $f_i \sqsubseteq f_{i+1}$, for all i. Expression F is an upper bound of f if for all i, $f_i \sqsubseteq F$, and F is the least upper bound of f if for any upper bound G of f, $F \sqsubseteq G$. Henceforth, we write $(\sqcup f)$ for the least upper bound of f. The proof of the following theorem is standard, and is given in [7].

Theorem 5. $\langle \sqcup f \rangle = (\cup i :: \langle f_i \rangle)$.

Continuity over Left Argument. Let f be a sequence of expressions, and $h_i = f_i * g$, for all i, where $*$ is any Orc combinator. Then

$$\sqcup h \cong (\sqcup f) * g, \text{ i.e., } \langle \sqcup h \rangle = \langle (\sqcup f) * g \rangle.$$

The proof follows directly from Lemma 4, part(1).

Continuity over Right Argument. Given a sequence g, and $h_i = f * g_i$, for all i, where $*$ is any Orc combinator, we show $\sqcup h \cong f * (\sqcup g)$. The proof follows directly from Lemma 4, part(2), where $*$ is any combinator other than $>x>$. For $>x>$, we prove the result in [7].

6.3 Least Fixed Point for Recursive Definitions

We have shown that $\sqsubseteq$ is a complete partial order over expressions. Next, we show that $\mathbf{0}$ is the bottom element. Any substitution $[v/x]$ is applicable to any expression because $f \overset{[v/x]}{\to} [v/x].f$. Hence, any sequence of substitutions D is a trace of any f (by applying induction on the length of D). Since $\mathbf{0}$ has no other transition,

$$\langle \mathbf{0} \rangle = \{D |\ D \text{ is a finite sequence of substitutions}\}$$

Therefore, for any f, $\langle \mathbf{0} \rangle \subseteq \langle f \rangle$, i.e., $\mathbf{0} \sqsubseteq f$.

Monotonicity and continuity of Orc combinators allow us to treat a recursively defined expression as the least upper bound of a chain of approximations. As an example, consider *Metronome* (described in Section 2.4) which we repeat below in an abbreviated form.

$$M \triangleq S \mid R \gg M$$

Then M is the least upper bound of the chain $M_0 \sqsubseteq M_1 \sqsubseteq \cdots$, where

$$M_0 = \mathbf{0}$$
$$M_{i+1} = S \mid R \gg M_i, \text{ for all } i, \text{ where } i \geq 0$$

6.4 A Proof Using Congruence

Theorem 6. $f >x> let(x) \cong f$

Proof Sketch: The complete proof is in [7]. The proof is by structural induction on f. For the base cases (i.e. when f is any of $let(p)$, $?k$, $M(p)$, or $M(x)$), the result is proved by enumerating the traces (all maximal traces of f are of the form $r\ !v$, where r has no publications). For the inductive case, we consider three possible forms of f which are: $g \mid h$, $g >y> h$ and g **where** $y :\in h$. We apply certain laws from Section 4.1. From law (6), $(g \mid h) >x> let(x)$ is $g >x> let(x) \mid h >x> let(x)$, and inductively, this is $g \mid h$. From law (4), $(g >y> h) >x> let(x)$ is $g >y> (h >x> let(x))$, which is $g >y> h$, using induction on $h >x> let(x)$. From law (8), $(g$ **where** $y :\in h) >x> let(x)$ is $(g >x> let(x))$ **where** $y :\in h$, which is g **where** $y :\in h$, using induction on $g >x> let(x)$.

7 Related Work

There are two primary bodies of work on developing models for task orchestration. On the one hand, commercial workflow and orchestration languages have been the subject of formal study. On the other hand, traditional process algebra theory is being adapted to fit orchestration problems.

Petri nets have been proposed as a semantic model for workflow [8]. To compare commercial systems, Van der Aalst has proposed a set of workflow patterns [1]. These workflow patterns have been also been implemented in Orc [3] and the π-calculus [9]. Others have identified difficult patterns, like time-out [10], which have solutions in Orc.

A new Petri net language, YAWL, has been defined to express the patterns more directly [11]. YAWL's mechanism for multiple instantiation is analogous to Orc's sequential composition, but provides built-in synchronization. The node grouping and cancellation constructs are similar to Orc's **where** operator. Rather than build specific workflow patterns into the language, Orc provides just a few fundamental primitives with a mechanism to define new operators for user-defined composition patterns.

Process calculi, including CSP [12], CCS [6] and π-calculus [13], provide fundamental models of concurrency, with a focus on symmetric communication between threads. Orc has a structured approach to concurrency, and has an asymmetric relationship with its environment. Orc also supports a general sequential composition of expressions, $f \gg g$, and an explicit construct for process termination, which is synchronized with communication. Some variants of the π-calculus include a termination construct [14].

Simon Peyton-Jones suggested a relationship between Orc and the List monad as used in functional programming languages, including Haskell . The sequential composition operator, $>x>$, is analogous to the list bind $>>=$. The **where** operator resembles taking the first item from a lazy list. The standard list monad always produces values in a specific order, whereas the publication order in Orc is non-deterministic.

8 Conclusion

Task orchestration is a form of concurrent programming in which an agent invokes and coordinates the execution of passive, but potentially unreliable, services. Orchestration is well-suited to solving a range of concurrency problems, most notably workflow. Our practical experience in using Orc for orchestration has been very encouraging; we are able to code most concurrent programming paradigms succinctly. This paper shows that Orc has a simple trace semantics, and Orc combinators have many desirable properties such as monotonicity and continuity. The simplicity of the semantics may be a factor in simplicity of programming. We have addressed only the asynchronous aspects of Orc in this paper. We are now developing the full semantics which will combine asynchrony with time-based computations.

References

1. Aalst, W.M.P.V.D., Hofstede, A.H.M.T., Kiepuszewski, B., Barros, A.P.: Workflow patterns. Distrib. Parallel Databases **14**(1) (2003) 5–51
2. Misra, J., Cook, W.R.: Computation orchestration: A basis for wide-area computing. Journal of Software and Systems Modeling **May** (2006) Available for download at `http://dx.doi.org/10.1007/s10270-006-0012-1`.

3. Cook, W.R., Patwardhan, S., Misra, J.: Workflow patterns in Orc. In: Proc. of the International Conference on Coordination Models and Languages (COORDINATION). (2006) to appear.
4. Rosario, S., Benveniste, A., Haar, S., Jard, C.: SLA for web services orchestrations. Unpublished manuscript (2006)
5. Kozen, D.: On Kleene algebras and closed semirings. In: Proceedings, Math. Found. of Comput. Sci. Volume 452 of LNCS., Springer-Verlag (1990) 26–47
6. Milner, R.: Communication and Concurrency. International Series in Computer Science, C.A.R. Hoare, series editor. Prentice-Hall (1989)
7. Kitchin, D., Cook, W.R., Misra, J.: Semantic properties of asynchronous Orc. Technical Report TR-06-32, University of Texas at Austin, Department of Computer Sciences (2006)
8. Eshuis, R., Dehnert, J.: Reactive Petri Nets for workflow modeling. In: International Conference on Applications and Theory of Petri Nets (ICATPN 2003). Volume 2679 of LNCS., Springer-Verlag (2003) 296–315
9. Puhlmann, F., Weske, M.: Using the π-calculus for formalizing workflow patterns. In: Proceedings of the 3rd International Conference on Business Process Management. Volume 3649 of LNCS. (2005)
10. van Glabbeek, R.: On specifying timeouts. In: Workshop on Algebraic Process Calculi: The First Twenty Five Years and Beyond, Electronic Notes in Theoretical Computer Science (2005) to appear.
11. van der Aalst, W.M.P., Aldred, L., Dumas, M., ter Hofstede, A.H.M.: Design and implementation of the YAWL system. In Persson, A., Stirna, J., eds.: CAiSE. Volume 3084 of LNCS., Springer (2004) 142–159
12. Hoare, C.: Communicating Sequential Processes. Prentice Hall International (1984)
13. Milner, R.: Communicating and Mobile Systems: the π-Calculus. Cambridge University Press (1999)
14. Riely, J., Hennessy, M.: Distributed processes and location failures. Theoretical Computer Science **266**(1–2) (2001) 693–735

Finding Shortest Witnesses to the Nonemptiness of Automata on Infinite Words

Orna Kupferman and Sarai Sheinvald-Faragy

Hebrew University, School of Engineering and Computer Science, Jerusalem 91904, Israel
{orna, surke}@cs.huji.ac.il

Abstract. In the automata-theoretic approach to formal verification, the satisfiability and the model-checking problems for linear temporal logics are reduced to the nonemptiness problem of automata on infinite words. Modifying the nonemptiness algorithm to return a shortest witness to the nonemptiness (that is, a word of the form uv^ω that is accepted by the automaton and for which $|uv|$ is minimal) has applications in synthesis and counterexample analysis. Unlike shortest accepting runs, which have been studied in the literature, the definition of shortest witnesses is semantic and is independent on the specification formalism of the property or the system. In particular, its robustness makes it appropriate for analyzing counterexamples of concurrent systems.

We study the problem of finding shortest witnesses in automata with various types of concurrency. We show that while finding shortest witnesses is more complex than just checking nonemptiness in the nondeterministic and in the concurrent models of computation, it is not more complex in the alternating model. It follows that when the system is the composition of concurrent components, finding a shortest counterexample to its correctness is not harder than finding some counterexample. Our results give a computational motivation to translating temporal logic formulas to alternating automata, rather than going all the way to nondeterministic automata.

1 Introduction

The automata-theoretic approach to formal verification uses the theory of automata as a unifying paradigm for system specification, verification, and synthesis. Two fundamental problems in formal verification are reduced to the nonemptiness problem of automata on infinite words: the *satisfiability* problem for a linear temporal logic (LTL) formula ψ is reduced to the nonemptiness problem of an automaton $\mathcal{A}_\psi$ that accepts exactly all the computations that satisfy ψ [5,35], and the *model-checking* problem of a system $\mathcal{S}$ with respect to ψ is reduced to checking the emptiness of the product of $\mathcal{S}$ with an automaton $\mathcal{A}_{\neg\psi}$ that accepts exactly all the computations that violate ψ [35]. Verification methods based on these reductions have been implemented in both academic and industrial automated-verification tools.

Modifying the nonemptiness algorithm to return a *witness* to the nonemptiness of the automaton does not involve an additional computational price and is beneficial in both applications: in the case of satisfiability, the witness is a computation that satisfies the formula. In particular, when the formula describes the desired behavior of a closed

C. Baier and H. Hermanns (Eds.): CONCUR 2006, LNCS 4137, pp. 492–508, 2006.

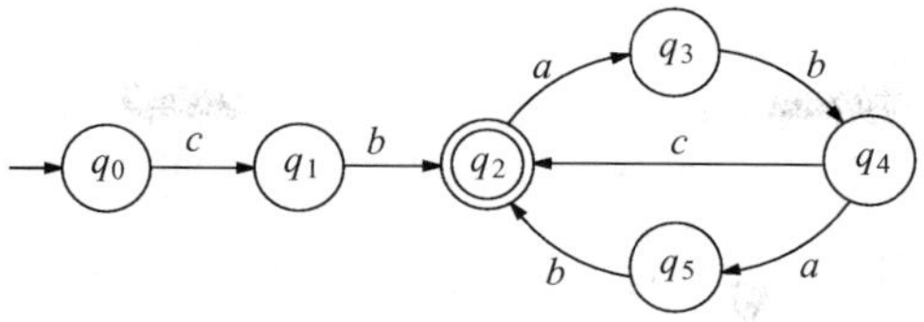

Fig. 1. While the shortest accepting run in $\mathcal{A}$ is $q_0, q_1, (q_2, q_3, q_4)^\omega$, the shortest witness to its nonemptiness is $c(ba)^\omega$

system, finding a witness amounts to *synthesis* [6]. In the case of model checking, a witness points to a computation of the system that violates the specification, and it helps the user to detect errors in the system. Further applications of witnesses exist in *abstraction*, where refinement is directed by an analysis of counterexamples [7], and *vacuity*, where a positive answer from the model checker is accompanied by a trace in which the specification is satisfied non-vacuously [24].

A witness to the nonemptiness of an automaton on infinite words is a word of the form uv^ω, for finite words u and v. The length of the witness is $|u| + |v|$. Modifying the emptiness algorithm further to return a shortest witness (that is, one with a minimal length) has useful applications. One of the weaknesses of automated synthesis is that it may produce systems that are needlessly complicated [2]. Returning a minimal witness amounts to returning the most optimal system that satisfies the specification. In the context of model checking, short witnesses enable the user to find errors in the system as soon as they appear, and they give a compact explanation to the incorrectness of system. Using counterexamples for refinement of an abstract system, shorter counterexamples point better to elements that have to be refined. Finally, using witnesses in the context of vacuity, short witnesses explain better how formulas have been satisfied in a non-vacuous way.

Finding a shortest witness to the nonemptiness of an automaton has the flavor of finding shortest paths in graphs. Indeed, previous work on short witnesses studies the problem of finding minimal fair cycles in graphs [8,14,32]. Nevertheless, the fact that an automaton corresponds to a *labeled* graph, makes things more complicated. To see this, consider for example the deterministic Büchi automaton $\mathcal{A}$ in Figure 1. In the Büchi acceptance condition, a run is accepting if it visits the set of accepting states infinitely often. The shortest accepting run that witnesses the nonemptiness of $\mathcal{A}$ is $q_0, q_1, (q_2, q_3, q_4)^\omega$, which witnesses the membership of the word $cb(abc)^\omega$, of length 5, in the language of $\mathcal{A}$. The automaton $\mathcal{A}$, however, has an even shorter witness to its nonemptiness. Indeed, while the accepting run $q_0, q_1, (q_2, q_3, q_4, q_5)^\omega$ is of length 6, it witnesses the membership of the word $c(ba)^\omega$, which is of length 3.

For the applications mentioned above, it is the shortest witness, rather than the shortest accepting run, that we want to return to the user[1]. Indeed, in the case of synthesis, the shortest witness points to the most optimal system that satisfies the specification, and in the case of model checking, the shortest witness is the shortest computation that

[1] One can consider an even shorter description, where, for example, a subword $aaa \overset{n}{\ldots} a$ is represented by a^n, with n encoded in binary. Then, the description of the word may be logarithmically shorter. We will refer also to such *compressed* descriptions.

violates the property. In particular, in the case of model checking, the automaton is the product of the specification automaton with the system, and considering shortest accepting runs rather than shortest witnesses is sensitive to the structure of the specification automaton.

The length of a shortest witness is a robust measure, as it is independent of the specification formalism: every language $L \subseteq \Sigma^\omega$ has a shortest member, and this member is independent of whether L is specified by an LTL formula, or by a particular type of an automaton. In [32], the authors point to the fact that a shortest witness may not coincide with a shortest accepting run, and studied automata for which the two measures coincide (that is, the shortest witness is read along a shortest run). Here, we take a different approach, and refer to the length of the witness directly, for various specification formalisms. Note that the shortest-witness measure is especially appropriate when we consider the intersection of several automata, as in the case of model checking a system that is given by means of its underlying components. There, the shortest accepting run is defined with respect to the product of the components of the system. A shortest witness, on the other hand, is independent of the presentation of the system, and can be defined with respect to the underlying components.

Classical models of computations, such as Turing machines and automata, have been enriched with features to capture concurrency. *Nondeterminism*, for example, amounts to letting several processes run over the input word, each following different nondeterministic choices. In the case of nondeterminism, no cooperation between the spawned processes takes place, except when time comes to decide whether the input should be accepted. Then, the input is accepted if some process accepts it. A dual type of cooperation is allowed in *universal* automata. There, the input word is accepted if all the processes accept it. It turned out that such limited cooperation is sufficient to make nondeterministic and universal automata exponentially more succinct than deterministic automata, and to make their combination, namely alternating automata, doubly exponentially more succinct than deterministic automata [9]. As studied in [10], enriching automata with real concurrency, where the spawned processes can cooperate all along the computation (technically, a *concurrent* automaton consists of several components that run concurrently, and the transitions of a component depend on the states of the other components), results in even more succinct automata.

The automata-theoretic approach to formal verification was originally developed with nondeterministic automata, and is based on an exponential translation of LTL formulas to nondeterministic Büchi automata [35]. In recent years, however, more and more algorithms and tools are based on *alternating* automata. A significant advantage of alternating automata is the straightforward (and linear) translation of LTL formulas to alternating Büchi automata [26,34]. Solving the nonemptiness problem for alternating Büchi automata is done by translating them to nondeterministic Büchi automata [27]. The translation involves an exponential blow-up. Thus, alternating automata do not lead to an improved complexity, but they do suggest cleaner algorithms with practical advantages: an ability to minimize both the intermediate alternating automaton and the nondeterministic one [12], an ability to use the structure of the alternating automaton in order to generate minimal nondeterministic automata [15], and more.

We study the problem of finding shortest witnesses to Büchi automata with various types of concurrency. The input to the *shortest-witness problem* is an automaton and an integer k, given in binary. The problem is to determine whether a witness uv^ω such that $|uv| \leq k$ exists[2]. We start with nondeterministic automata, and show that the witness problem for them is NP-complete — more complex than the NLOGSPACE-complete nonemptiness problem[3]. We describe a heuristic that does better than checking all candidates, and is based on the observation it is possible to transfer letters from the prefix u of the witness to its cycle v, and vice versa. A similar idea is used in [14] in the context of shortest accepting runs, but is more significant in the context of shortest witnesses. We then show that the increased complexity with respect to the nonemptiness problem is carried over also to concurrent automata, where the witness problem is NEXPTIME-complete — more complex than the PSPACE-complete nonemptiness problem for them [10,21]. It follows that our heuristic can be applied to the nondeterministic automaton obtained by removal of concurrency, but we cannot hope to do much better.

Our main result is that for alternating automata, one can do better, and the shortest-witness problem is not more complex than the nonemptiness problem. The technical point is that while alternating automata are sufficiently strong to count to k with $O(\log k)$ states [3], they are sufficiently weak to let us analyze the run on a word of the form uv^ω by carefully analyzing the run of each of the processes in isolation. This leads to a PSPACE algorithm to the shortest-witness problem for alternating automata. From a practical point of view, our results give another good reason to translate LTL formulas to alternating automata, rather than going all the way to nondeterministic ones. Indeed, not only the algorithm for alternating automata is cleaner, but also it improves the complexity from NEXPTIME to PSPACE. Also, in the context of model checking, our algorithm shows that when the system is given by a set of components (that is, when the language of the system is the intersection of the languages of its underlying components, in which case it can be efficiently translated to an alternating automaton), it is better to avoid the generation of the product system and reason about the components in isolation. ¿From a theoretical point of view, our results extend previous study on the computational price of different types of concurrency. We will go back to this point in Section 6.

2 Preliminaries

Given an alphabet Σ, an *infinite word over* Σ is an infinite sequence $w = \sigma_0 \cdot \sigma_1 \cdot \sigma_2 \cdots$ of letters in Σ. We denote by w^l the suffix $\sigma_l \cdot \sigma_{l+1} \cdot \sigma_{l+2} \cdots$ of w. An *automaton on infinite words* is $\mathcal{A} = \langle \Sigma, Q, Q_0, \rho, \alpha \rangle$, where Σ is the input alphabet, Q is a finite set

[2] We specify the shortest witness problem as a decision problem rather than an optimization problem in order to analyze its complexity in terms of the classical complexity classes. By bounding the length of the shortest witness and performing a binary search for it, our results imply also tight bounds in complexity classes like $\text{FP}^{\text{NP}[\log]}$, which refer to the problem of computing the length of the shortest witness.

[3] This result is different from the NP-completeness result in [8] for the shortest accepting run problem for a nondeterministic generalized Büchi automaton. We refer to this point lengthily in Section 3.

of states, $\rho : Q \times \Sigma \to 2^Q$ is a transition function, $Q_0 \subseteq Q$ is a set of initial states, and α is an acceptance condition (a condition that defines a subset of Q^ω). If $|Q_0| = 1$ and ρ is such that for every $q \in Q$ and $\sigma \in \Sigma$, we have that $|\rho(q, \sigma)| \leq 1$, then $\mathcal{A}$ is *deterministic*.

A *run* of $\mathcal{A}$ on w is a function $r : \mathbb{N} \to Q$ where $r(0) \in Q_0$ and for every $l \geq 0$, we have $r(l+1) \in \rho(r(l), \sigma_l)$. Acceptance is defined according to the set $Inf(r)$ of states that r visits *infinitely often*, i.e., $Inf(r) = \{q \in Q$: for infinitely many $l \in \mathbb{N}$, we have $r(l) = q\}$. The way we refer to $Inf(r)$ depends on the acceptance condition of $\mathcal{A}$. Several acceptance conditions are studied in the literature. We consider here *Büchi* automata, where $\alpha \subseteq Q$, and r is accepting if it visits α infinitely often. Formally, $Inf(r) \cap \alpha \neq \emptyset$.

Since $\mathcal{A}$ is not deterministic, it may have many runs on w. In contrast, a deterministic automaton has a single run on w. There are two dual ways in which we can refer to the many runs. When $\mathcal{A}$ is an *existential* automaton (or simply a *nondeterministic* automaton, as we shall call it in the sequel), it accepts an input word w iff there exists an accepting run of $\mathcal{A}$ on w. When $\mathcal{A}$ is a *universal* automaton, it accepts an input word w iff all the runs of $\mathcal{A}$ on w are accepting. *Alternation* was studied in [9] in the context of Turing machines and in [4,9,27] for finite automata. In particular, [27] studied alternating automata on infinite words. Alternation enables us to have both existential and universal branching choices.

For a given set X, let $\mathcal{B}^+(X)$ be the set of positive Boolean formulas over X (i.e., Boolean formulas built from elements in X using $\wedge$ and $\vee$). For technical convenience, we do not allow the formulas in $\mathcal{B}^+(Q)$ to use the constant **true**. For $Y \subseteq X$, we say that Y *satisfies* a formula $\theta \in \mathcal{B}^+(X)$ iff the truth assignment that assigns *true* to the members of Y and assigns *false* to the members of $X \setminus Y$ satisfies θ. For example, the sets $\{q_1, q_3\}$ and $\{q_2, q_3\}$ both satisfy the formula $(q_1 \vee q_2) \wedge q_3$, while the set $\{q_1, q_2\}$ does not.

An *alternating automaton on infinite words* is a tuple $\mathcal{A} = \langle \Sigma, Q, q_0, \delta, \alpha \rangle$, where Σ, Q, q_0, and α are as in automata, and $\delta : Q \times \Sigma \to \mathcal{B}^+(Q)$ is a transition function. When $\mathcal{A}$ runs on an input word, it generates (an unbounded number of) processes that read the input word. The joint behavior of these processes can be described in a tree; thus a run of an alternating automaton is a tree in which each node is labeled by a state of $\mathcal{A}$. A node in level l that is labeled q, corresponds to a process of $\mathcal{A}$ that visits the state q and has to accept the suffix w^l of w. As proven in [11], runs of alternating Büchi automata are *memoryless* in the sense that if $\mathcal{A}$ accepts a word w, then it also accepts w in a memoryless run — one in which two processes that are in the same state and have to accept the same suffix proceed in the same way[4]. Accordingly, we restrict attention to memoryless runs and define a run of an alternating Büchi automaton to be a DAG (directed acyclic graph).

Formally, a *run*-DAG of $\mathcal{A}$ on an input word $w = \sigma_0 \cdot \sigma_1 \cdots$, is $G_r = \langle V, E \rangle$, where $V \subseteq Q \times \mathbb{N}$ and $E \subseteq \bigcup_{l \geq 0} (Q \times \{l\}) \times (Q \times \{l+1\})$ are such that $\langle q_0, 0 \rangle \in V$, and

[4] [11] proves a stronger result, namely the existence of memoryless accepting runs for parity alternating automata. Since the Büchi acceptance condition is a special case of the parity acceptance condition, the result cited above follows.

for every vertex $\langle q, l\rangle \in V$, there is a set $S = \{q_1, \ldots, q_k\}$ such that S satisfies $\delta(q, \sigma_l)$ and for all $1 \leq c \leq k$, we have $\langle q_c, l+1\rangle \in V$ and $E(\langle q, l\rangle, \langle q_c, l+1\rangle)$.

A run-DAG is *accepting* iff all its paths[5], which are labeled by words in Q^ω, satisfy the acceptance condition. A word w is accepted iff there exists an accepting run-DAG on it. Note that while conjunctions in the transition function of $\mathcal{A}$ are reflected in branches of G_r, disjunctions are reflected in the fact we can have many run-DAGs on the same word.

Recall that when an alternating automaton runs on an input word, it spawns to several processes. All these processes take part in the task of deciding whether the word belongs to the language. No cooperation, however, between the processes takes place, except when time comes to decide whether the input should be accepted. A different type of concurrency is one in which the processes cooperate all along the run. This type of concurrency exists in *nondeterministic Büchi automata with bounded concurrency* (concurrent Büchi automata, for short), introduced in [10][6]. A CBW is a tuple $\mathcal{A} = \langle \Sigma, \mathcal{A}_1, \ldots, \mathcal{A}_n\rangle$ consisting of an alphabet Σ and n *components* $\mathcal{A}_1, \ldots, \mathcal{A}_n$, for some $n \geq 1$. Each component $\mathcal{A}_i$ is a tuple $\langle Q_i, Q_i^0, \delta_i, \alpha_i\rangle$, where Q_i is a finite set of states, and we require the state sets of the different components to be pairwise disjoint. Let $Q = \bigcup_{j=1}^n Q_j$. The set $Q_i^0 \subseteq Q_i$ is the set of initial states, $\delta_i : Q_i \times \Sigma \times \mathcal{B}(Q) \to 2^{Q_i}$ is a transition relation, where $\mathcal{B}(Q)$ denotes the set of all Boolean propositional formulas over Q, and $\alpha \in \mathcal{B}(Q)$ is a Büchi acceptance condition. Note that while each component of Q has its own states and transitions, its transitions depend not only on the component's current state but also on the current states of the other components. Also, the Büchi acceptance condition refers to the states of all components.

A *configuration* of $\mathcal{A}$ is a tuple $c = \langle q_1, q_2, \ldots, q_n\rangle \in Q_1 \times Q_2 \times \cdots \times Q_n$, describing the current state of each of the components. A configuration is *initial* if for all $1 \leq i \leq n$, we have $q_i \in Q_i^0$. We use C to denote the set of all configurations of $\mathcal{A}$, and C_0 to denote the set of all its initial configurations. For a propositional formula θ in $\mathcal{B}(Q)$ and a configuration $c = \langle q_1, q_2, \ldots, q_n\rangle$, we say that c *satisfies* θ if assigning **true** to states in c and **false** to states not in c makes θ true. Given two configurations $c = \langle q_1, q_2, \ldots, q_n\rangle$ and $c' = \langle q'_1, q'_2, \ldots, q'_n\rangle$, and a letter $\sigma \in \Sigma$, we say that c' is a *σ-successor of* c, if for all $1 \leq i \leq n$ there is $\theta_i \in \mathcal{B}(Q)$ such that c satisfies θ_i and $q'_i \in \delta_i(q_i, \sigma, \theta_i)$. In other words, a σ-successor configuration is obtained by simultaneously reading σ in all the components. A run of $\mathcal{A}$ on an input word $w = \sigma_0, \sigma_1, \ldots$ is a function $r : \mathbb{N} \to C$ where $r(0) \in C_0$ and for every $l \geq 0$, we have $r(l+1)$ is a σ_l successor of $r(l)$. Acceptance is defined according to the set $Inf(r)$ of configurations that r visits *infinitely often*. A run is accepting if at least one configuration in this set satisfies α.

We use NBW, ABW, and CBW to denote nondeterministic, alternating, and concurrent Büchi automata, respectively. For all types of automata, the language of $\mathcal{A}$, denoted $L(\mathcal{A})$, is the set of infinite words that $\mathcal{A}$ accepts. Thus, each word automaton defines a

---

5 Recall that we do not allow the formulas in $\mathcal{B}^+(Q)$ to use the constant **true**, thus all the paths of G_r are infinite.

6 The basic motivation for this model comes from the *statecharts* of [17], which can be viewed as nondeterministic automata with both concurrency and hierarchy. Our goal here is to study the role of concurrency, and we eliminate the hierarchy.

subset of Σ^ω. For all types, we refer also to automata on finite words (denoted NFW, AFW, and CFW). There, acceptance is defined according to the last state visited by the run (or a process of the run, in case of the alternating and concurrent models).

A *witness* to the nonemptiness of an automaton $\mathcal{A}$ is a word $w \in L(\mathcal{A})$. For an automaton $\mathcal{A}$ on infinite words, we define a *shortest witness* for $\mathcal{A}$ to be a word $uv^\omega \in L(\mathcal{A})$ such that $|uv|$ is minimal; that is, for all words $u'(v')^\omega \in L(\mathcal{A})$, we have $|uv| \leq |u'v'|$. We refer to $|uv|$ as the length of the witness. For example, as discussed in Section 1, the shortest witness for the automaton of Figure 1 is $c(ba)^\omega$, which is of length 3. The *shortest-witness* problem is to decide, given an automaton $\mathcal{A}$ and an integer $k \geq 0$, given in binary, whether $\mathcal{A}$ has a witness of length at most k.

It is easy to see that for an NBW with n states, the length of a shortest witness is bounded by $2n$. In the case of ABW and CBW, a shortest witness may be exponentially longer than the size of the automaton. Intuitively, the above follows from the fact that intersection of automata can be modeled with no blow-up by both alternating and concurrent automata. For a concrete example, consider, given $k \geq 1$, the intersection of k automata $\mathcal{A}_1, \ldots, \mathcal{A}_k$ defined as follows. For $i \geq 1$, let p_i be the i-th prime number. Let $\mathcal{A}_i$, for $1 \leq i \leq k$, be an NBW that accepts exactly all words of the form $(a^{d_i} b)^\omega$, for $d_i = 0 \bmod p_i$. For example, $\mathcal{A}_1$ accepts $((aa)^* b)^\omega$, $\mathcal{A}_2$ accepts $((aaa)^* b)^\omega$, $\mathcal{A}_3$ accepts $((aaaaa)^* b)^\omega$, and so on. It is easy to see that $\mathcal{A}_i$ needs $O(p_i)$ states. Since $p_i = O(i \log i)$ [20], the size of all components together is polynomial in k. On the other hand, the shortest witness to the nonemptiness of their intersection is $(a^{2 \cdot 3 \cdot 5 \cdots p_k} b)^\omega$. Since $2 \cdot 3 \cdot 5 \cdots p_k$ is exponential in k, we get that the shortest witness is exponential in the size of the components.

Remark 1. Recall that the shortest-witness problem gets as input both an automaton $\mathcal{A}$ and an integer k. Since k is given in binary, an algorithm that is based on checking the membership in $\mathcal{A}$ of all words uv^ω with $|uv| \leq k$, is exponential in the input. By the above discussion, the length of a shortest witness is at most exponential in the size of $\mathcal{A}$. Thus, with k given in binary, $\mathcal{A}$ is always the dominant part of the input (otherwise, we can reduce the shortest-witness problem to the nonemptiness problem, which is independent of k). Consequently, the complexities we get to our decision problem correspond to the complexities of the optimization problem in which only $\mathcal{A}$ is given, and a shortest witness has to be found. □

A naive approach for finding a shortest witness first checks the nonemptiness of the automaton and then tries witnesses of increasing lengths. Our main results in this paper are that for nondeterministic and concurrent automata, one can proceed with algorithms that are likely to perform in average better than the naive algorithm, yet it is impossible to go below the NP and NEXPTIME complexities of the naive approach. On the other hand, for alternating automata, where the naive approach also yields an NEXPTIME algorithm, we are able to suggest a PSPACE algorithm.

3 The Shortest-Witness Problem for Nondeterministic Automata

We start with NBW and prove that the shortest-witness problem for them is NP-complete. The result is technically easy, but is of interest, as it highlights the difference between the shortest-accepting-run and the shortest-witness problems. The shortest-accepting-run problem for NBW can be reduced to the problem of finding shortest paths in a graph and can therefore be solved in polynomial time. On the other hand, it is proven in [8] that the shortest-accepting-run problem for nondeterministic *generalized* Büchi automata (NGBW) is NP-complete. In an NGBW, the acceptance condition is a set of sets of states, and a run is accepting if it visits all sets infinitely often. By the above, hardness of the shortest-accepting-run problem in NP crucially depends on the use of the generalized Büchi condition. An NGBW $\mathcal{A}$ can be translated to an NBW $\mathcal{A}'$ with only a polynomial blow up. How come, then, that the problem is in PTIME for NBW and is NP-hard for NGBW? Well, while $\mathcal{A}'$ accepts the same language as $\mathcal{A}$, it has a different structure, and a shortest accepting run for it says nothing about a shortest accepting run for $\mathcal{A}$. This is a drawback of the shortest-accepting-run measure, which depends on the specification formalism. The shortest-witness measure, on the other hand, is independent of the specification formalism, and the solution of the shortest-witness problem can (and indeed does) involve translations between different specification formalisms.

Theorem 2. *The shortest-witness problem for NBW is NP-complete.*

Proof: We first prove membership in NP. Consider an NBW $\mathcal{A} = \langle \Sigma, Q, \delta, q_0, \alpha \rangle$. When $\mathcal{A}$ is not empty, a witness uv^ω is induced by a simple path (labeled u) from Q_0 to a state in α that is reachable from itself (by a simple cycle labeled v). Thus, the length $|uv|$ of a shortest witness is bounded by $2|Q|$. Since the membership-problem for NBW can be solved in polynomial time, membership in NP follows.

For the lower bound, we do a reduction from the Hamiltonian-cycle problem. There, we are given a graph $G = \langle V, E \rangle$ and we have to decide whether there exists a simple cycle traversing all vertices in V. Given G, let $V = \{1, \ldots, n\}$. We define an NBW $\mathcal{A} = \langle E, V \times V, \{\langle 1, 1 \rangle\}, \delta, \{\langle n, n \rangle\} \rangle$, where $\delta(\langle i, j \rangle, (i, h))$ is $\langle h, (j \bmod n) + 1 \rangle$ if $i = j$, and is $\langle h, j \rangle$ if $i \neq j$. Intuitively, a state $\langle i, j \rangle$ indicates that $\mathcal{A}$ traverses a path that now visits vertex i, and is waiting for a visit in vertex j. Accordingly, from state $\langle i, j \rangle$, the NBW $\mathcal{A}$ can read only edges with source i, and it updates the first element of the successor state to be the target of the edge. In addition, if $i = j$, then the path visits the vertex for which $\mathcal{A}$ waits, and it updates the second element of the successor state to be the next vertex. Consequently, $\mathcal{A}$ visits the state $\langle n, n \rangle$ infinitely many times iff the traversed path has visited all vertices infinitely often.

It is easy to see that $\mathcal{A}$ has a witness of length (at most) n iff G has a Hamiltonian cycle. Indeed, if G has a Hamiltonian cycle C, then for a word w read along C from vertex 1, we have $w^\omega \in L(A)$. For the other direction, assume that $\mathcal{A}$ has a witness uv^ω of length n. An accepting run r on uv^ω visits $\langle n, n \rangle$ infinitely often. By the definition of δ, the run r also visits the states $\langle i, i \rangle$ infinitely often, for all $1 \leq i \leq n$. The transitions to each of these states are labeled by different letters. Therefore, v must include at least n different letters, and can include only n letters only if G has a Hamiltonian cycle. □

Remark 3. Membership in NP holds also for nondeterministic generalized Büchi automata. There, the length of a shortest witness can be bounded by $2k|Q|$, where k is the index of the automaton. Note that the automaton $\mathcal{A}$ used in the hardness proof is deterministic. Moreover, with some more technicality (going to an accepting loop from the state $\langle n, n\rangle$), it is possible to modify $\mathcal{A}$ to be a Büchi automaton with $\alpha = Q$ (also known as a *looping* automaton). Thus, NP-hardness holds already for deterministic looping automata. □

Remark 4. As mentioned in Section 1, a compressed description of a witness is such that subwords consisting of a block of m repetitions of the same subword x are represented by x^m, with m given in binary. For example, if the witness is $aabaab(cccb)^\omega$, a compressed description for it is $(a^2b)^2(c^3b)^\omega$. In the *shortest compressed witness* problem, we are given an automaton $\mathcal{A}$ and an integer k, given in binary, and we have to decide whether a witness of compressed length k exists.

Since the length of a witness is bounded by $2|Q|$, so is the length of a compressed witness, which implies that the shortest compressed-witness problem is in NP. In addition, since our NP-hardness proof for the shortest-witness problem imposes a witness with no repeated letters, NP-hardness holds also for the shortest compressed-witness problem. □

The NP-completeness of the shortest-witness problem for NBW implies that a polynomial algorithm for finding a shortest witness is unlikely to exist. A naive algorithm for finding a shortest witness for a given NBW $\mathcal{A}$ goes over all words of the form uv^ω such that $|uv|$ is bounded by $2|Q|$, and returns the shortest such word that is accepted by $\mathcal{A}$. In the full version, we tighten the $2|Q|$ bound to $|Q|$ and describe an exponential time and polynomial space algorithm that has a better running time than the naive algorithm. Essentially, the improved algorithm is based on the observation that the we can choose the location where the loop starts in such a way that the paths traversed along u and v are disjoint. This observation is also used in [14] in the context of shortest accepting runs, but its applications are more significant in our setting. Formally, we have the following.

Proposition 1. *Consider an NBW $\mathcal{A} = \langle \sigma, Q, \delta, Q_0, \alpha\rangle$. For a state $q \in Q$, let u_q be a word labeling a shortest path from Q_0 to q, and let v_q be a shortest word such that v_q^ω is accepted by $\mathcal{A}$ with initial state q. Then, a shortest witness for $\mathcal{A}$ is $u_q v_q^\omega$, for some $q \in Q$.*

4 The Shortest-Witness Problem for Concurrent Automata

We now turn to study the shortest-witness problem for concurrent automata. Note that for concurrent automata, shortest accepting runs are not defined[7]. On the other hand, the definition of shortest witnesses is semantic, and we can refer to the shortest witnesses of concurrent automata.

Theorem 5. *The shortest-witness problem for CBW is NEXPTIME-complete.*

Proof: A CBW $\mathcal{A}$ can be translated to an NBW with an exponential blow up [10]. Thus, membership in NEXPTIME follows from Theorem 2. For the lower bound, we

[7] One can define shortest accepting runs for CBW by referring to the product of the components, but this gives up the exponential succinctness of the concurrent model.

do a reduction from the *succinct Hamiltonian cycle* problem. A succinct representation of a graph with 2^n nodes is a Boolean circuit C with $2n$ input gates. The graph represented by C is $G_C = \langle \{0, \ldots, 2^n - 1\}, E \rangle$, where $E(i,j)$ iff C has value 1 on the input (of length $2n$) that has the n-bit binary encoding of the integers i and j. The *succinct Hamiltonian circle* problem is to determine, given a circuit C, whether the graph G_C has a Hamiltonian cycle. Like many other problems on succinct graphs whose "non-succinct version" (that is, over graphs given enumeratively) is NP-complete, the succinct Hamiltonian cycle problem is NEXPTIME-complete [16].

Given C with $2n$ input gates, we construct a CBW $\mathcal{A}$ with $|C| + n$ components, each with two states, such that $\mathcal{A}$ has a witness of length at most $n2^n$ iff G_C has a Hamiltonian cycle. We partition the components of $\mathcal{A}$ to $2n$ input components, $|C| - 2n$ internal-gate components, and n counting components. Recall that each component has two states, thus we refer to the *value* of a component, which is either 0 or 1, according to the state it visits.

The alphabet of $\mathcal{A}$ is $\{0, 1\}$, and an input word $w = w_0, w_1, \ldots$ describes an attempt to encode a path $v_0, v_1, \ldots$ in G_C, where the vertex v_i is encoded in the subword $w_{in}, \ldots, w_{(i+1)n-1}$. The word w encodes a path if its partition to blocks of length n indeed describes a path. Thus, there is an edge between v_i and v_{i+1} for all $i \geq 0$. Equivalently, the value of C on $w_{in}, \ldots, w_{(i+2)n-1}$ is 1, for all $i \geq 0$.

Accordingly, $\mathcal{A}$ proceeds as follows. The $2n$ input components maintain the last edge that was taken, and the internal-gate components maintain the value of the internal gates of C with respect to this edge. The automaton $\mathcal{A}$ updates its guess for the next edge whenever a block in the input word starts (that is, once every n letters). The update consists of the following steps: a check that the component of the output gate (the one that maintains the value of C) is 1, a transfer of the values of the input components $n+1, \ldots 2n$ to the input components $1, \ldots, n$, a guess for the new values of the input components $n+1, \ldots, 2n$, and a guess for the value of the internal-gate components. Once the update has been performed, the input and internal-gate components do not change their value until $\mathcal{A}$ finishes reading the current block. They may, however, get stuck (and do so in case of a bad guess), during the reading of the current block. Technically, when the current block is read, the input components $n+1, \ldots, 2n$ check that the guess for the next vertex is correct (that is, in the i-th letter of the block, the input component $n+i+1$ expects to read the letter that agrees with its value. If this is not the case, the component gets stuck, and the run is rejected. In addition, each internal-gate components checks that its guessed value corresponds to the semantics of the gate with which it is associated. For example, an internal-gate component associated with an and gate, stays in its state if its value is the conjunction of the values of the components associated with its operands. If this is not the case, the component gets stuck, and the run is rejecting. For the initial configuration, $\mathcal{A}$ guesses values for all input components. Note that the components of $\mathcal{A}$ make use of its concurrency: the transitions of one component depends on the values of other components.

By the above, $\mathcal{A}$ accepts a word only if it encodes a path in C_G. It is left to describe how $\mathcal{A}$ takes care of the path being a Hamiltonian cycle. This is where the counter components enter the picture. The job of these components is similar to the job of the second element in the pair in the state space of the NBW described in the proof of Theorem 2. While there blowing up the state space of the NBW by the number of vertices is not a problem, here we cannot blow-up the state space by a factor of 2^n, and instead we use the ability of concurrent automata to count to 2^n with n components. Formally, whenever a block is read and the vertex in this block agrees with the value of the counter (that is, the value of the input components $n+1, \ldots, 2n$ agree with the value of the counter components), $\mathcal{A}$ increases the value of the counter by 1. □

Remark 6. Note that our reduction involves a generation of a CBW that accepts a word iff it is a path in a graph represented succinctly. Thus, the technique we developed for the shortest-witness problem is useful for proving NEXPTIME-hardness of a family of problems for which the corresponding problem on NBW is NP-hard [30]. □

5 The Shortest-Witness Problem for Alternating Automata

In the concurrent case, our results indicate that one cannot do better than translating the CBW to an NBW and solving the shortest-witness problem with respect to the NBW. ABW can also be translated to NBW with an exponential blow up [27]. Solving the shortest-witness problem by translating the ABW to an NBW would then result in an NEXPTIME algorithm. In this section we show that the translation to NBW can be avoided, and that a direct algorithm on the ABW requires only polynomial space.

Consider an ABW $\mathcal{A} = \langle \Sigma, Q, \delta, q_0, \alpha \rangle$. For two sets $S, S' \subseteq Q$, let $\mathcal{A}[S, S'] = \langle \Sigma, Q, S, \delta, S' \rangle$ be the alternating automaton on finite words obtained from $\mathcal{A}$ by defining S to be the set of *conjunctively related* initial states and S' to be its set of final states[8]. For simplicity, when $S = \{q\}$ is a singleton, we denote the automaton by $\mathcal{A}[q, S']$. Note that for every sets S, S', and S'', with $S' \subseteq S''$, we have that $L(\mathcal{A}[S, S']) \subseteq L(\mathcal{A}[S, S''])$, and $L(\mathcal{A}[S'', S]) \subseteq L(\mathcal{A}[S', S])$.

For $m \geq 1$, we say that a function $f : Q \rightarrow 2^Q \setminus \{\emptyset\}$ is *m-cyclic on $\mathcal{A}$* if there exists a set $Q' \subseteq Q$ such that

1. $q_0 \in Q'$,
2. $\bigcup_{q \in Q'} f(q) \subseteq Q'$, and
3. there exists a word w such that $|w| = m$ and $w \in \bigcap_{q \in Q'} L(\mathcal{A}[q, f(q)])$.

We say that Q' is a *core* of f. Thus, f is m-cyclic on $\mathcal{A}$ if there is a set Q' of states that contains q_0, the application of f on a state in Q' results in states in Q', and there is a word w of length m such that for all states in Q', the word w is accepted by the AFW with initial states q and accepting set $f(q)$. Intuitively, m-cyclic functions reduce the existence of a witness to the nonemptiness of the alternating automaton to the existence of the same witness to the nonemptiness of several automata.

In order to describe how we use m-cyclic cycles in order to solve the shortest-witness problem for ABW, let us first consider a special case of the Büchi condition, where $\alpha = Q$. In such automata (also known as *looping* automata), every infinite run is accepting. Also, let us first handle the case where the witness is of the form v^ω.

[8] An alternating automaton with a set of conjunctively related initial states has to accept the input word from all the initial states. Automata with a set of conjunctively related initial states can be easily translated to an automaton with a single initial state: the transition from the new initial state is a conjunction of the transitions from the states in the set of initial states.

Lemma 1. *Consider an alternating looping automaton $\mathcal{A}$. For all $m \geq 1$, there exists a witness $w^\omega \in L(A)$ such that $|w| = m$ iff there exists an m-cyclic function on $\mathcal{A}$.*

Proof: Let $\mathcal{A} = \langle \Sigma, Q, \delta, q_0, Q \rangle$. For the first direction, let $w^\omega \in L(A)$ be such that $|w| = m$. Consider an accepting memoryless run r of $\mathcal{A}$ on w^ω. Let $G_r = \langle V, E \rangle$ be the run DAG of r. For each $i \geq 0$, let Q_i denote the set of states in the (im)-th level of G_r; thus, $Q_i = \{q : \langle q, im \rangle \in V\}$. Since the run is accepting, $Q_i \neq \emptyset$ for all $i \geq 0$. Note that for all $i \geq 0$, the set Q_i is the set of states that r visits after reading the prefix w^i of w^ω. For a state $q \in Q_i$, let $S_{q,i}$ denote the subset of Q_{i+1} that contains all states reachable from q. Formally, $q' \in S_{q,i}$ iff $\langle q', (i+1)m \rangle$ is reachable from $\langle q, im \rangle$. Since r is memoryless, then for all $i, j \geq 0$ and $q \in Q_i \cap Q_j$, we have that $S_{q,i} = S_{q,j}$. Indeed, both sets contain the set of states that q "generates" when it reads the prefix w of w^ω. For a state q for which $q \in Q_i$ for some $i \geq 0$, let $S_q = S_{q,i}$. As argued, the definition of S_q is independent of i.

We construct an m-cyclic function f as follows. Let $Q' = \bigcup_{i \geq 0} Q_i$. Thus, the core of f is the set of states that r visits in levels $0, m, 2m, 3m, \ldots$. For $q \in Q'$, we define $f(q) = S_q$. For $q \notin Q'$, we define $f(q)$ arbitrarily. We claim that the three conditions for f being m-cyclic hold. First, since $Q_0 = \{q_0\}$, we have that $q_0 \in Q'$. Second, if $q' \in f(q)$ then $q' \in Q'$, and hence $\bigcup_{q \in Q'} f(q) \subseteq Q'$. Finally, for each $q \in Q_i$, we have that $w \in \mathcal{A}[q, S_q]$, so, by the definition of f, we also have that $w \in L(\mathcal{A}[q, f(q)])$. Hence, as $|w| = m$, there exists a word of length m in $\bigcap_{q \in Q'} L(\mathcal{A}[q, f(q)])$.

For the other direction, let f be an m-cyclic function on $\mathcal{A}$, and let Q' be a core for f. Since f is m-cyclic, there exists a word w of length m in $\bigcap_{q \in Q'} L(\mathcal{A}[q, f(q)])$. We claim that $\mathcal{A}$ accepts w^ω. We define a run r of $\mathcal{A}$ on w^ω as follows. Let r_0 be an accepting run of $\mathcal{A}[q_0, f(q_0)]$ on w. Such a run exists, as by the definition of f, we have that $w \in L(\mathcal{A}[q_0, f(q_0)])$. Let S_1 be the set of states that r_0 visits after reading w. Let r_1 be an accepting run of $\mathcal{A}[S_1, \bigcup_{q \in S_1} f(q)]$ on w. Again, such a run exists, as $S_1 \subseteq Q'$, and hence $w \in \mathcal{L}(\mathcal{A}[q, f(q)])$ for all $q \in S_1$. We continue in the same manner to obtain, for each $i \geq 0$, a set $S_i \subseteq Q'$ and an accepting run r_i of $\mathcal{A}[S_i, \bigcup_{q \in S_i} f(q)]$ on w. Since there are 2^n subsets of Q, it is guaranteed that there are $j' < j \leq 2^n$ such that $S_j = S_{j'}$. The run obtained by concatenating $r_0, r_1, \ldots, r_{j'-1}$ and then repeatedly concatenating $r_{j'}, \ldots, r_{j-1}$ is an infinite accepting run of $\mathcal{A}$ on w^ω. □

We can now extend m-cyclic function to ABW. In [29], Muller et al. introduce *weak alternating automata* (AWW). In an AWW, the acceptance condition is $\alpha \subseteq Q$, and there exists a partition of Q into disjoint sets, Q_i, such that for each set Q_i, either $Q_i \subseteq \alpha$, in which case Q_i is an *accepting set*, or $Q_i \cap \alpha = \emptyset$, in which case Q_i is a *rejecting set*. In addition, there exists a partial order $\leq$ on the collection of the Q_i's such that for every $q \in Q_i$ and $q' \in Q_j$ for which q' occurs in $\delta(q, \sigma)$, for some $\sigma \in \Sigma$, we have $Q_j \leq Q_i$. Thus, transitions from a state in Q_i lead to states in either the same Q_i or a lower one. It follows that every infinite path of a run of a AWW ultimately gets "trapped" within some Q_i. The path then satisfies the acceptance condition if and only if Q_i is an accepting set. Thus, we can view a AWW with an acceptance condition α as both a Büchi automaton with an acceptance condition α, and a co-Büchi automaton with an acceptance condition $Q \setminus \alpha$. Indeed, a run gets trapped in an accepting set iff it visits infinitely many states in α, which is true iff it visits only finitely many states in $Q \setminus \alpha$.

The translation of LTL formulas to alternating automata results in weak automata [26]. Also, ABW can be translated to an AWW with a quadratic blow up [23]. Accordingly, we are going to use m-cyclic functions of AWW in our algorithm for the shortest-witness problem for ABW.

We say that an m-cyclic function f has a *rejecting cycle* if for every core Q' for it, there exists a sequence $q_1, q_2, \ldots, q_k$, with $k \leq |Q|$, of states in $Q' \setminus \alpha$ such that $q_{(i \bmod k)+1} \in f(q_i)$ for all $1 \leq i \leq k$. Note that a rejecting cycle refers only to states in Q' and requires some path in the run induced by f to visit $Q \setminus \alpha$ infinitely often. As we argue in Lemma 2 below, the weakness of the automaton guarantees that the fact a rejecting cycle refers only to states "sampled" by f does not prevent it from characterizing acceptance.

Lemma 2. *Consider an AWW $\mathcal{A}$. For every $m \geq 1$, there exists a word $w^\omega \in L(A)$ such that $|w| = m$ iff there exists an m-cyclic function f on $\mathcal{A}$ that does not have a rejecting cycle.*

Proof: Let $\mathcal{A} = \langle \Sigma, Q, \delta, q_0, \alpha \rangle$. For the first direction, let $w^\omega \in L(\mathcal{A})$ be such that $|w| = m$. Let r be a memoryless accepting run of $\mathcal{A}$ on w and let $G_r = \langle V, E \rangle$ be its run DAG. We claim that the m-cyclic function f defined in the proof of Lemma 1 does not have a rejecting cycle. Assume by way of contradiction that f has a rejecting cycle $q_1, \ldots, q_k$. Since for each $1 \leq i < k$ we have that $q_{(i \bmod k)+1} \in f(q_i)$, then, by the way we have defined f, there exists an index $j \geq 0$ and a vertex $\langle q_1, j \cdot m \rangle$, reachable from $\langle q_0, 0 \rangle$, from which there is a path π_1 to the vertex $\langle q_2, (j+1) \cdot m \rangle$. Again, by the definition of f, there exists a path π_2 from $\langle q_2, (j+1) \cdot m \rangle$ to $\langle q_3, (j+2) \cdot m \rangle$. We can continue in a similar way and generates an infinite path in G_r that visits infinitely many states in $Q \setminus \alpha$, contradicting the fact that G_r is accepting.

For the other direction, let f be an m-cyclic function on $\mathcal{A}$ that does not have a rejecting cycle, and let Q' be the core of f. We claim that the run r constructed in the proof of Lemma 1 is accepting. Assume by way of contradiction that r is rejecting. Then, the DAG G_r has a path $\pi = \langle q_0, 0 \rangle, \langle q_1, 1 \rangle, \ldots$ such that there is an index $l \geq 0$ such that $q_j \notin \alpha$ for all $j \geq l$. By the definition of r, we have that $Q_i \subseteq Q'$ for all $i \geq 0$. Let j be such that $j \cdot m > l$. The sequence $q_{jm}, q_{(j+1)m}, q_{(j+2)m}, \ldots$ is such that for all $i \geq 1$, we have that $q_{(j+i)m} \in Q' \setminus \alpha$, and $q_{(j+i+1)m} \in f(q_{(j+i)m})$. By the pigeonhole principle, there exist i' and i with $i' < i < n$ such that $q_{(j+i')m} = q_{(j+i)m}$. Therefore, the sequence $q_{(j+i')m}, q_{(j+i'+1)m}, \ldots, q_{(j+i-1)m}$ is a rejecting cycle in f, and we reach a contradiction. □

Theorem 7. *The shortest witness problem for ABW is PSPACE-complete.*

Proof: An ABW with n states can be translated to an NBW with 3^n states [27]. Therefore, since by Proposition 1 length of a shortest witness for an NBW is bounded the number of its states, an ABW with n states is empty iff it has no witness of length at most 3^n. Hence, hardness in PSPACE follows from the PSPACE hardness of the non-emptiness problem for ABW. [27].

Let $\mathcal{A}$ be an ABW with n states, and let k be an integer given in binary. We describe an algorithm in NPSPACE for deciding whether $\mathcal{A}$ has a witness of length at most k. Since NPSPACE=PSPACE [31], we are done. First, the algorithm answers "no" if $\mathcal{A}$

is empty and answers "yes" if $\mathcal{A}$ is not empty and $k > 3^n$. Since the nonemptiness problem is in PSPACE, this can be done in PSPACE.

Otherwise, let $\mathcal{A}' = \langle \Sigma, Q, q_0, \delta, \alpha \rangle$ be an AWW equivalent to $\mathcal{A}$. By [23], such an AWW with at most $2n^2$ states exists. The algorithm guesses an integer $0 < m \leq k$, a function $f : Q \to 2^Q \setminus \{\emptyset\}$ and a set $Q' \in Q$. The function f consists of $|Q|$ sets of elements in Q, each of size at most $|Q|$. Hence f can be encoded in space of size $O(n^4 \log n)$. The algorithm then checks that f is m-cyclic as follows. It first checks that $q_0 \subseteq Q'$, and that $\bigcup_{q \in Q'} f(q) \subseteq Q'$. These checks are both performed in polynomial space. It then constructs an AFW $\mathcal{A}_m$ of size $O(\log m)$ that accepts all words $w \in \Sigma^m$ [3]. The algorithm then constructs an AFW $\mathcal{A}[q, f(q)]$ for each $q \in Q'$, and checks that the intersection $L(\bigcap_{q \in Q'} \mathcal{A}[q, f(q)]) \cap L(\mathcal{A}_m)$ is not empty. Since alternation can model intersection, the latter can be checked in PSPACE. Note that the intersection is not empty iff an m-cyclic function on $\mathcal{A}$ exists. It is left to check that f has no rejecting cycle. For that, the algorithm goes over each sequence $q_1, \ldots, q_k$, with $k \leq |Q|$ and checks that it is not a rejecting cycle. If all sequences pass the check successfully, the algorithm returns "yes". By Lemma 2, there exists a witness $v^\omega \in L(A)$ of length $m \leq k$ iff there is an instance of the algorithm that answers "yes".

We now expand the algorithm to account for cases where the witness is of the form uv^ω. The algorithm first guesses the length of u by guessing an integer $t < m$. It then guesses a sequence of t letters and a run of $\mathcal{A}$ on it. Let Q_0' be the set of states the algorithm visits after reading the t letters without getting stuck, and let $\mathcal{A}''$ be the ABW obtained from $\mathcal{A}$ by defining Q_0' to be its set of initial states. The algorithm now proceeds as in the case of witnesses of the form v^ω, with respect to witnesses of length $m - t$. □

Recall that the definition of a shortest witness is semantic and depends on the language of the automaton rather than its structure. Thus, the shortest-witness problem can be defined with respect to any specification formalism that defines ω-regular languages. LTL formulas can be linearly translated to AWW. Hence, together with the PSPACE lower bound for LTL satisfiability, Theorem 7, implies the following.

Theorem 8. *The shortest-witness problem for LTL is PSPACE-complete.*

It follows that finding a shortest witness for the satisfiability of an LTL formula is not harder than just checking its satisfiability.

6 Discussion

We studied the shortest-witness problem in three different models of concurrency. From a theoretical point of view, our results show that the limited concurrency between the processes of an alternating automaton makes reasoning about them simpler than concurrent automata: the shortest-witness problem for ABW is PSPACE-complete, like the nonemptiness problem for it, whereas for concurrent automata, the problem is NEXPTIME-complete. Note that while cooperation between the processes of an alternating automaton is limited, this model does not bound the number of processes that run on the input. Thus, alternation cannot be easily simulated by concurrency. In fact, the translations between the two models involve an exponential blow up in both directions [10].

It is interesting to compare our results with previous results about the computational price of the two models. In Figure 2, we describe such results. The table in the figure refers to six problems that involve automata. Simulation and fair-simulation consider labeled transition systems, which can be viewed as automata with labels at the states rather than on the transitions. In fair simulation, we refer to the definition of [13]; in the case of alternating systems, we refer to the alternating simulation of [1]; the complexity of fair alternating simulation is still open. ELTL satisfiability is the problem of deciding the satisfiability of an LTL formula in which automata are used as temporal modalities.

	nonemptiness	universality	simulation	fair-simulation	ELTL satisfiability	shortest witness
NBW	NLOGSPACE [35]	PSPACE [33]	PTIME [28]	PSPACE [22]	PSPACE [19]	NPTIME Th. 2
CBW	PSPACE [10]	NEXPSPACE [10]	EXPTIME [18]	EXPSPACE [18]	EXPSPACE [19]	NEXPTIME Th. 5
ABW	PSPACE [27]	PSPACE [27]	PTIME [1]	?	EXPSPACE [19]	PSPACE Th. 7

Fig. 2. The computational price of different types of concurrency

As can be seen from the table, all problems become exponentially more complex in the concurrent setting. On the other hand, for some problems, special algorithms for the alternating setting are less complex than an algorithm that first removes alternation, which involves an exponential blow up. The shortest-witness problem falls in this category.

From a practical point of view, our results indicate that alternation can be useful not only thanks to the straightforward translation of temporal logic formulas to alternating automata, but also because of computational considerations. In particular, in case the system is given symbolically by a set of underlying components, and the specification is given by an LTL formula, it is better to translate the formula to an ABW (rather than an NBW) and search for a shortest witness in this setting. Indeed, the intersection of the underlying components can be modeled by an alternating automaton, and the complexity is PSPACE, like the PSPACE complexity for the model-checking problem (note that in the symbolic setting described above, model checking is PSPACE in both the LTL formula and the underlying components).

Another application of the shortest-witness problem is synthesis. In the last years, researches have developed methods for coping with the implementation difficulties of the synthesis problem: its high complexity, and the fact its solution involves determinization of automata on infinite words [25]. With these problems being challenged, there is now room for studying the size of the synthesized system, and developing automated-synthesis algorithms for generating optimal systems. Our study in this paper handles the case of a closed system. In future research, we plan to study the case of open systems, where the problem is to find minimal transducers that generate correct systems.

References

1. R. Alur, T.A. Henzinger, O. Kupferman, and M.Y. Vardi. Alternating refinement relations. In *Proc. 9th CONCUR*, LNCS 1466, pages 163–178, 1998.
2. A. Bouajjani, J.-C. Fernandez, and N. Halbwachs. Minimal model genration. In *Proc. 2nd CAV*, LNCS 531, pages 197–203, 1990.
3. J.C. Birget. State-complexity of finite-state devices, state compressibility and incompressibility. *Mathematical Systems Theory*, 26(3):237–269, 1993.
4. J.A. Brzozowski and E. Leiss. Finite automata and sequential networks. *TCS*, 10:19–35, 1980.
5. J.R. Büchi. On a decision method in restricted second order arithmetic. In *Proc. International Congress on Logic, Method, and Philosophy of Science. 1960*, pages 1–12, Stanford, 1962. Stanford University Press.
6. E.M. Clarke and E.A. Emerson. Design and synthesis of synchronization skeletons using branching time temporal logic. In *Proc. Workshop on LP*, LNCS 131, pages 52–71, 1981.
7. E. M. Clarke, O. Grumberg, S. Jha, Y. Lu, and H. Veith. Counterexample-guided abstraction refinement for symbolic model checking. *J. ACM*, 50(5):752–794, 2003.
8. E.M. Clarke, O. Grumberg, K.L. McMillan, and X. Zhao. Efficient generation of counterexamples and witnesses in symbolic model checking. In *Proc. 32nd DAC*, pages 427–432. IEEE Computer Society, 1995.
9. A.K. Chandra, D.C. Kozen, and L.J. Stockmeyer. Alternation. *J. ACM*, 28(1):114–133, January 1981.
10. D. Drusinsky and D. Harel. On the power of bounded concurrency I: Finite automata. *J. ACM*, 41(3):517–539, 1994.
11. E.A. Emerson and C. Jutla. Tree automata, μ-calculus and determinacy. In *Proc. 32nd FOCS*, pages 368–377, 1991.
12. S. Gurumurthy, O. Kupferman, F. Somenzi, and M.Y. Vardi. On complementing nondeterministic Büchi automata. In *Proc. 12th CHARME*, LNCS 2860, pages 96–110, 2003.
13. O. Grumberg and D.E. Long. Model checking and modular verification. *ACM TOPLAS*, 16(3):843–871, 1994.
14. P. Gastin, P. Moro, and M. Zeitoun. Minimization of counterexamples in spin. In *SPIN Workshop on Model Checking of Software*, pages 92–108, 2004.
15. P. Gastin and D. Oddoux. Fast LTL to büchi automata translation. In *Proc. 13th CAV*, LNCS 2102, pages 53–65, 2001.
16. H. Galperin and A. Wigderson. Succinct representations of graphs. *I& C*, 56(3):183–198, 1983.
17. D. Harel. Statecharts: A visual formalism for complex systems. *Sci. Computer Prog.*, 8:231–274, July 1987.
18. D. Harel, O. Kupferman, and M.Y. Vardi. On the complexity of verifying concurrent transition systems. *I & C*, 173:1–19, 2002.
19. D. Harel, R. Rosner, and M.Y. Vardi. On the power of bounded concurrency iii: Reasoning about programs. In *Proc. 5th LICS*, pages 478-488, 1990.
20. G.A. Jones, J.M. Jones, and J.M. Tyrer-Jones. *Elementary Number Theory*. Springer Undergraduate Mathematics Series, Berlin, 1998.
21. D. Kozen. Lower bounds for natural proof systems. In *Proc. 18th FOCS*, pages 254–266, 1977.
22. O. Kupferman and M.Y. Vardi. Verification of fair transition systems. *CJTCS*, 1998(2), 1998.
23. O. Kupferman and M.Y. Vardi. Weak alternating automata are not that weak. *ACM TOCL*, 2(2):408–429, July 2001.

24. O. Kupferman and M.Y. Vardi. Vacuity detection in temporal model checking. *J. STTT*, 4(2):224–233, February 2003.
25. O. Kupferman and M.Y. Vardi. Safraless decision procedures. In *Proc. 46th FOCS*, pages 531–540, 2005.
26. O. Kupferman, M.Y. Vardi, and P. Wolper. An automata-theoretic approach to branching-time model checking. *J. ACM*, 47(2):312–360, March 2000.
27. S. Miyano and T. Hayashi. Alternating finite automata on ω-words. *TCS*, 32:321–330, 1984.
28. R. Milner. *A Calculus of Communicating Systems*, LNCS 92, 1980.
29. D.E. Muller, A. Saoudi, and P.E. Schupp. Alternating automata, the weak monadic theory of the tree and its complexity. In *Proc. 13th ICALP*, LNCS 226, pages 275 – 283, 1986.
30. C.H. Papadimitriou. *Computational Complexity*. Addison-Wesley, 1994.
31. W.J. Savitch. Relationship between nondeterministic and deterministic tape complexities. *Journal on Computer and System Sciences*, 4:177–192, 1970.
32. V. Schuppan and A. Biere. Shortest counterexamples for symbolic model checking of LTL with past. In *Proc 11th TACAS*, LNCS 3440, pages 493–509, 2005.
33. A.P. Sistla, M.Y. Vardi, and P. Wolper. The complementation problem for Büchi automata with applications to temporal logic. *TCS*, 49:217–237, 1987.
34. M.Y. Vardi. Alternating automata and program verification. In *Computer Science Today – Recent Trends and Developments*, LNCS 1000, pages 471–485, 1995.
35. M.Y. Vardi and P. Wolper. Reasoning about infinite computations. *I& C*, 115(1):1–37, November 1994.

Second-Order Simple Grammars

Colin Stirling

School of Informatics
University of Edinburgh
Edinburgh EH9 3JZ, UK
cps@inf.ed.ac.uk

1 Introduction

Higher-order notations for trees have a venerable history from the 1970s and 1980s when schemes (that is, functional programs without interpretations) and their relationship to formal language theory were first studied. Included are higher-order recursion schemes and pushdown automata. Automata and language theory study finitely presented mechanisms for generating languages. Instead of language generators, one can view them as process calculi, propagators of possibly infinite labelled transition systems. Recently, model-checking techniques have been successfully extended to these higher-order notations in the deterministic case [18,9,8,21].

A long standing open question is: given two nth-order schemes do they generate the same tree? Courcelle [10] showed that for $n = 1$ the problem coincides with the language equivalence problem for deterministic pushdown automata (DPDA) that was subsequently solved positively by Sénizergues [23]. For $n > 1$, equivalence of *safe* nth-order recursion schemes coincides with equivalence between determinisitic nth-order pushdown automata [12,18]. It is not known whether safety is a genuine restriction on expressive power: see [1].

Second-order pushdown automata involve finite-state control over a stack of stacks. They have applications in language theory as they characterize the *indexed* languages introduced by Aho [2]. Also, they generalize the "mildly" context-sensitive languages used in computational linguistics [29]. Aho defined these languages using indexed grammars and also characterized them in terms of nested stack automata [3]. Their characterization in terms of second-order pushdown automata is due to Maslov, who also defined a hierarchy of higher-order indexed languages characterized by higher-order pushdown automata, [20]. A more detailed account is given by Damm and Goerdt [12].

There has been considerable research activity on decision procedures for bisimulation equivalence between first-order systems, initiated with [4] for normed context-free grammars and then extended to classes of pushdown automata [26]. Recent results show that bisimulation equivalence is undecidable [17].

Here, we present a decidability result for equivalence of second-order systems. A configuration of a second-order pushdown automaton is a state and a stack of stacks. The operations pop stacks and push stacks onto it. We examine deterministic second-order pushdown automata which generalize DPDA. A configuration of a DPDA is a state and a stack. Simple grammars are an instance

C. Baier and H. Hermanns (Eds.): CONCUR 2006, LNCS 4137, pp. 509–523, 2006.

of DPDA when there is a single state and no ϵ-transitions. So a configuration of a simple grammar is justa stack. Korenjak and Hopcroft showed that language equivalence is decidable between configurations of simple grammars [19]. Here, we introduce second-order simple grammars as the subset of second-order deterministic pushdown automata when there is a single state and no ϵ-transitions. A configuration of such a grammar is, therefore, a stack of stacks. We show that language equivalence is decidable for a subset of second-order simple grammars. The proof technique is based on bisimulation equivalence and some combinatorics about repetitions of stack extensions (loosely based on ideas from [28]). We view this result as a first step towards understanding the general equivalence problem for higher-order schemes.

In Section 2, we describe 2nd-order (deterministic) pushdown automata and in Section 3 we introduce 2nd-order simple grammars and the subset that we study. Some properties of the grammars are outlined in Section 4. In Sections 5 and 6 we present the equivalence decision procedure, using tableaux.

2 2nd-Order Pushdown Automata

The following four finite sets are ingredients of a 2nd-order pushdown automaton, a 2PDA: states P, stack symbols S, alphabet A and basic transitions T. A basic transition is $pX \xrightarrow{a} q\theta$ where p and q are states in P, X is a stack symbol in S, $a \in \mathsf{A} \cup \{\epsilon\}$ and θ is an operation belonging to $\{\mathrm{swap}_\alpha, \mathrm{push}, \mathrm{pop} : \alpha \in \mathsf{S}^*\}$.

A 2-stack is a sequence of non-empty stacks $\beta_1 : \ldots : \beta_n$, so each $\beta_i \in \mathsf{S}^+$. We use ϵ for the empty stack and capital greek letters Γ, Δ, ... to range over sequences of stacks with Λ for the empty sequence. An operation θ is defined on a 2-stack as follows:

$$\begin{aligned} \mathrm{swap}_\alpha(X\beta : \Gamma) &= \alpha\beta : \Gamma \\ \mathrm{push}(\beta : \Gamma) &= \beta : \beta : \Gamma \\ \mathrm{pop}(\beta : \Gamma) &= \Gamma \end{aligned}$$

A configuration of a 2PDA consists of a state $p \in \mathsf{P}$ and a 2-stack Γ. The transitions of a configuration are defined by the following rule from the basic transitions T.

$$\text{PRE} \quad \text{If } pX \xrightarrow{a} q\theta \in \mathsf{T} \text{ then } pX\beta : \Gamma \xrightarrow{a} q\,\theta(X\beta : \Gamma)$$

A traditional automaton interpretation is that on input a with basic transition $pX \xrightarrow{a} q\theta$ the configuration $pX\beta : \Gamma$ in state p with X at the top of the first stack changes to state q and $\theta(X\beta : \Gamma)$ replaces $X\beta : \Gamma$. Alternatively, with respect to a generational or process calculus perspective the configuration $pX\beta : \Gamma$ generates, or performs, a and becomes $q\theta(X\beta : \Gamma)$. In both accounts ϵ-transitions have a special status. If $a = \epsilon$ then the configuration may change without reading an input or it may become $q\theta(X\beta : \Gamma)$ silently without performing an observable action. In the following we abbreviate a basic transition $pX \xrightarrow{a} q\,\mathrm{swap}_\alpha$ to $pX \xrightarrow{a} q\alpha$.

The *transition graph* $\mathsf{G}(p\Gamma)$ is generated by deriving all possible transitions from $p\Gamma$ and every configuration reachable from it using the rule PRE.

Example 1. Consider the following basic transitions.

$$\begin{array}{llll} pZ \xrightarrow{a} qZ & qZ \xrightarrow{a} qAZ & qA \xrightarrow{a} qAA & qA \xrightarrow{b} r\,\text{push} \\ rA \xrightarrow{b} r\epsilon & rZ \xrightarrow{c} s\,\text{pop} & sA \xrightarrow{c} s\epsilon & sZ \xrightarrow{\epsilon} s\,\text{pop} \end{array}$$

Part of the transition graph $\mathsf{G}(pZ)$ is depicted in Figure 1. □

$$\begin{array}{lllll} pZ \xrightarrow{a} qZ & \xrightarrow{a} qAZ & & \xrightarrow{a} qAAZ & \xrightarrow{a} \dots \\ & & \downarrow b & \downarrow b & \\ & & rAZ : AZ & rAAZ : AAZ & \\ & & \downarrow b & \downarrow b & \\ sZ \xleftarrow{c} & sAZ \xleftarrow{c} & rZ : AZ & rAZ : AAZ & \\ \downarrow \epsilon & \uparrow c & & \downarrow b & \\ s\Lambda & \dots & & \vdots & \end{array}$$

Fig. 1. A 2PDA

A 2PDA is presentable in normal form, up to isomorphism of transition graphs, where each transition of the form $pX \xrightarrow{a} q\alpha \in \mathsf{T}$ obeys the constraint that the length of α, $|\alpha|$, is at most 2. Enforcement of the normal form is easy to achieve, by introducing extra stack symbols.

Definition 1. *The* language *of a configuration* $p\Delta$, $L(p\Delta)$, *is the set of words* $w \in \mathsf{A}^*$ *such that* $p\Delta \xrightarrow{w} q\Lambda$ *for some* q.

When recognising any such word the 2-stack is thereby emptied. For instance, $L(pZ)$ in the case of Example 1 is $\{a^n b^n c^n : n \geq 2\}$ which is a context-sensitive language. This is called *empty stack acceptance.* A word $w \in \mathsf{A}^*$ is in $L(p\Delta)$ if there is a w-path from $p\Delta$ to a terminal state $q\Lambda$ for some q in the graph $\mathsf{G}(p\Delta)$. The languages recognized coincide with those recognized if final states were also included.

Our definition of a 2PDA is based on [18] except that it explicitly extends a standard PDA (because of swap transitions). It is simpler than Maslov's, Damm and Goerdt's definition [20,12]. In their case, a 2-stack is a sequence of pairs (X_i, α_i) where $X_i \in \mathsf{S}$, with operations pop_1, pop_2, $\text{push}_1(\alpha)$, $\text{push}_2(\alpha)$ which work as follows: $\text{pop}_1[(X, \alpha_1) : \Gamma] = \Gamma$, $\text{pop}_2[(X, Y\alpha) : \Gamma] = (X, \alpha) : \Gamma$, $\text{push}_1(Z_1Z_2)[(X, \alpha) : \Gamma] = (Z_1, \alpha) : (Z_2, \alpha) : \Gamma$ and $\text{push}_2(Z_1Z_2)[(X, \alpha) : \Gamma] = (X, Z_1Z_2\alpha) : \Gamma$. There is no loss in expressive power (with respect to language equivalence) as these operations can be simulated by families of 2PDA operations.

The family of languages recognized by 2PDA is the *indexed languages*, introduced by Aho in 1968 [2,3], which permit some context-dependency, as Example 1 illustrates. Aho offers a grammatical method for generating them as well as an automata theoretic method (using nested stack automata) which turns out to be equivalent to the 2PDA, as shown by Maslov [20]. An equivalent, schema-like, formalism is the OI macro-grammars of Fischer [14]. Aho also shows that the indexed languages are context-sensitive which is not obvious because repeated push transitions can increase the size of a configuration non-linearly. They form an AFL and are a proper subset of the context-sensitive languages: $\{(ab^n)^n : n \geq 0\}$ is not an indexed language via a pumping lemma for them [16,5]. The subset of *linear* indexed languages is the mildly context-sensitive languages generated by tree adjoining grammars [29].

A 2PDA is *deterministic* if T obeys the following conditions.

- if $pX \xrightarrow{a} q\theta$ and $pX \xrightarrow{a} r\lambda$ then $q = r$ and $\theta = \lambda$
- if $pX \xrightarrow{\epsilon} q\theta$ and $pX \xrightarrow{a} r\lambda$ then $a = \epsilon$

Example 1 is a determinisitic 2PDA. The equivalence question, whether two configurations of a determinisitic 2PDA recognise the same language, generalizes the DPDA equivalence problem, that was solved positively by Sénizergues [25,23,24,27,28]. A DPDA configuration $p\alpha$ can be coded as a deterministic 2PDA configuration $p\alpha Z$ where Z is a new end of stack marker with the extra transitions $qZ \xrightarrow{\epsilon} q\,\mathrm{pop}$ for each state q.

Due to empty stack acceptance, the language recognized by a deterministic 2PDA has the prefix free property: if $w \in L(p\Delta)$ then no proper prefix v of w can belong to $L(p\Delta)$. However, as with DPDA and empty stack acceptance, for any deterministic indexed language L, when defined in the Maslov style [22] with final state acceptance, there is a deterministic 2PDA that accepts $\{w\$: w \in L\}$ where \$ is a new alphabet symbol: deterministic 2PDA coincide with deterministic Maslov pushdown automata with empty stack acceptance. The deterministic indexed languages are closed under complement (and are therefore a proper subset of the indexed languages) and include inherently ambiguous context-free languages such as $\{a^ib^jc^k : i, j, k > 0 \text{ and } i = j \text{ or } j = k\}$ [22].

3 Second-Order Simple Grammars

In this section we consider second-order simple grammars, 2SGs. These are determinisitic 2PDAs which have just one state and no ϵ-transitions. We can therefore drop the state from transitions and configurations: transitions now have the form $X \xrightarrow{a} \theta$ and a configuration has the form Δ. Reachability properties of their nondeterministic version, at higher-orders, have been examined in [6]. We conjecture that simple grammars defined from Maslov pushdown automata are more expressive than 2SGs.

The DPDA correlate of 2SGs are *simple grammars*. A simple grammar contains basic deterministic transitions $X \xrightarrow{a} \alpha$, $a \in \mathsf{A}$, and the language of a configuration β, $L(\beta)$, is the set $\{w : \beta \xrightarrow{w} \epsilon\}$. Decidability of language equivalence between two configurations of a simple grammar was shown by Korenjak and Hopcroft [19]. However, language containment is undecidable [15].

It is unclear if there are alternative characterizations of 2SGs in terms of subsets of schema or macro-grammars. The restriction to a single state suggests that we should examine their monadic versions. We leave this for further work. The following example illustrates that there are interesting 2SGs.

Example 2. Consider the following 2SG

$$A \overset{a}{\longrightarrow} AA \quad A \overset{b}{\longrightarrow} \text{push} \quad A \overset{c}{\longrightarrow} \epsilon \quad Z \overset{c}{\longrightarrow} \text{pop}$$

Part of the graph $\mathsf{G}(AZ)$ is depicted in Figure 2. $L(AZ) \cap a^*b^*c^*$ is the language

$$\begin{array}{ccccccc}
\Lambda \overset{c}{\longleftarrow} Z & \overset{c}{\longleftarrow} & AZ & \overset{b}{\longrightarrow} & \ldots & & \\
 & & \downarrow a \uparrow c & & \uparrow a & & \\
\ldots & \overset{a}{\longleftarrow} & AAZ & \overset{b}{\longrightarrow} & AAZ : AAZ & \overset{b}{\longrightarrow} & \ldots \\
 & & \uparrow c & & \downarrow c & & \\
 & & Z : AAZ & \overset{c}{\longleftarrow} & AZ : AAZ & \overset{b}{\longrightarrow} & \ldots \\
 & & & & \downarrow a & & \\
 & & & & \ldots & &
\end{array}$$

Fig. 2. A 2SG

$\{a^n b^k c^{(k+1)(n+2)} : n, k \geq 0\}$ which is not context-free by the pumping lemma for context-free languages. Therefore, $L(AZ)$ is also not context-free. Consequently, 2SGs are strictly more expressive than simple grammars. Also, they are not subsumed by pushdown automata. □

Example 3. 2SGs even without push transitions can be complex.

$$\begin{array}{llllll}
X \overset{a}{\longrightarrow} YX & X \overset{b}{\longrightarrow} \epsilon & Y \overset{b}{\longrightarrow} X & Y \overset{c}{\longrightarrow} Z & Z \overset{b}{\longrightarrow} U & U \overset{b}{\longrightarrow} \text{pop} \\
A \overset{a}{\longrightarrow} C & A \overset{b}{\longrightarrow} \epsilon & C \overset{b}{\longrightarrow} AA & C \overset{c}{\longrightarrow} W & W \overset{b}{\longrightarrow} \text{pop} &
\end{array}$$

Here, $L(XZ) = L(AW : W)$. The graph $\mathsf{G}(XZ)$ involves infinite indegree because $UX^nZ \overset{b}{\longrightarrow} \Lambda$ for any n. □

Definition 2. *For each stack symbol X, let $\Lambda(X)$ be the length of a shortest word w, if it exists, such that $X \overset{w}{\longrightarrow} \Lambda$, $\epsilon(X)$ be the length of a shortest word w, if it exists, such that $X \overset{w}{\longrightarrow} \epsilon$ and $P(X)$ be the length of a shortest word wa, if it exists, such that $X \overset{w}{\longrightarrow} Z\alpha$ and $Z \overset{a}{\longrightarrow}$ push $\in \mathsf{T}$.*

It is easy to compute whether $\Lambda(X)$, $\epsilon(X)$ or $P(X)$ are defined, and what their values are when defined. First we start by computing the cases of length 1: there must be basic transitions $X \overset{a}{\longrightarrow}$ pop, $X \overset{a}{\longrightarrow} \epsilon$ or $X \overset{a}{\longrightarrow}$ push. To check for length n, we examine basic transitions $X \overset{a}{\longrightarrow} W$ and $X \overset{a}{\longrightarrow} YZ$: if $\epsilon(X)$ is not yet defined, and $\epsilon(W) = n - 1$ or $\epsilon(Y) + \epsilon(Z) = n - 1$ then $\epsilon(X) = n$; if $\Lambda(X)$ is not yet defined and $\Lambda(W) = n - 1$ or $\Lambda(Y) = n - 1$ or $\epsilon(Y) + \Lambda(Z) = n - 1$ then $\Lambda(X) = n$; and, similarly, for $P(X)$ when it is currently undefined. The iteration stops at the first length $2k + 1$ such that no $\Lambda(X)$, $\epsilon(X)$ or $P(X)$ has length more than k. At this point, any remaining $\Lambda(X)$, $\epsilon(X)$ and $P(X)$ are undefined. Clearly, no $\Lambda(X)$, $\epsilon(X)$, $P(X)$ can exceed $2^{|S|}$. In the case of Example 2, $\Lambda(A)$, $\epsilon(Z)$ and $P(Z)$ are not defined and $\Lambda(Z)$, $\epsilon(A)$ and $P(A)$ are all 1. In Example 3, $\Lambda(X) = 4$, $\Lambda(Y) = 3$ and $\Lambda(A) = 3$.

Definition 3. *A 2SG is* special *if for each X, $\Lambda(X)$ or $P(X)$ is defined.*

The 2SGs in Examples 2 and 3 are special. We now state the main result of the paper.

Theorem 1. *If Γ, Δ are configurations of a special 2SG then it is decidable whether $L(\Gamma) = L(\Delta)$.*

The result strictly generalizes the equivalence problem for simple grammars. Consider a simple grammar with basic transitions of the form $X \xrightarrow{a} \alpha$. We transform it into a special 2SG. First, we extend the alphabet with two new symbols \$, # and add an end of stack marker Z with basic transition $Z \xrightarrow{\$}$ pop. For each stack symbol X we also add the transition $X \xrightarrow{\#}$ push. For any two configurations α and β of the simple grammar, $L(\alpha) = L(\beta)$ iff $L(\alpha Z) = L(\beta Z)$ in the transformed 2SG.

4 Some Properties of Special 2SGs

We quickly consider why language equivalence is decidable for simple grammars. A stack symbol X is *normed* if $\epsilon(X)$ is defined. Clearly, $L(\alpha) = \emptyset$ iff α contains an unnormed stack symbol. So we can put a simple grammar into normal form where all stack symbols are normed. With this assumption language equivalence coincides with bisimulation equivalence because of determinism and normedness. We write $\alpha \sim \beta$ if $L(\alpha) = L(\beta)$.

Proposition 1. *$\alpha\delta \sim \beta\delta$ iff $\alpha \sim \beta$ iff $\delta\alpha \sim \delta\beta$.*

Decidability of equivalence now follows reasonably straightforwardly via decomposition and substitutivity: for instance, if $X\alpha \sim \beta\delta$ and $\alpha \sim \beta'\delta$ then $X\beta' \sim \beta$. Decomposition can be extended to *unique* prime decomposition, see [7] for details.

In the case of 2SGs there are *two* notions of stack composition: one between stacks and the other within a stack. Again, we can easily check if a configuration $L(\Gamma) = \emptyset$ using the definitions of $\Lambda(X)$ and $\epsilon(X)$ from the previous section. Proposition 1 generalizes to composition between stacks for arbitrary 2SGs.

Proposition 2. *Assume $L(\Gamma)$, $L(\Sigma)$ and $L(\Delta)$ are all nonempty. It follows that $L(\Gamma : \Delta) = L(\Sigma : \Delta)$ iff $L(\Gamma) = L(\Sigma)$ iff $L(\Delta : \Gamma) = L(\Delta : \Sigma)$.*

Proof. Assume $L(\Gamma)$, $L(\Sigma)$, $L(\Delta)$ are nonempty and $L(\Gamma : \Delta) = L(\Sigma : \Delta)$. If $w \in L(\Gamma : \Delta)$ then $w = w_1 w_2$ and $w_1 \in L(\Gamma)$ and $w_2 \in L(\Delta)$. Let v be a shortest word in $L(\Delta)$. If $w_1 \notin L(\Sigma)$ then there are two cases. First, a proper prefix w_{11} of w_1 is in $L(\Sigma)$. It follows that $w_{11}v \in L(\Sigma : \Delta)$ and $w_{11}v \notin L(\Gamma : \Delta)$ which is a contradiction. Secondly, $w_1 w_{21} \in L(\Sigma)$ where $w_2 = w_{21} w_{22}$ and $w_{21} \neq \epsilon$. Therefore, $w_1 v \in L(\Gamma : \Delta)$ and $w_1 v \notin L(\Sigma : \Delta)$ which again is a contradiction. Arguments for all the other cases are similar. □

However, there are not the same properties for composition within a stack. It is possible for $L(\alpha) = L(\beta)$ and $L(\alpha\delta) \neq L(\beta\delta)$ and for $L(\alpha\delta) = L(\beta\delta)$ and $L(\alpha) \neq L(\beta)$. A simple case is $X \xrightarrow{a} \epsilon$ and $X \xrightarrow{b}$ pop and $Y \xrightarrow{b}$ pop. Although $L(X) = L(Y)$, $L(XY) \neq L(YY)$ because of the disitinguishing word ab.

We introduce an extra configuration $\emptyset$ with $L(\emptyset) = \emptyset$. In the following we always assume that when we write a configuration $\Gamma \neq \emptyset$ then $L(\Gamma) \neq \emptyset$. We define the operation $\Gamma \cdot a$ as follows for $a \in \mathsf{A}$.

Definition 4. *If $\Gamma \xrightarrow{a} \Gamma'$ and $L(\Gamma') \neq \emptyset$ then $\Gamma \cdot a = \Gamma'$ otherwise $\Gamma \cdot a = \emptyset$.*

Proposition 3. *If $X \xrightarrow{a}$ push $\in \mathsf{T}$ then $((X\alpha : \Gamma) \cdot a) = X\alpha : X\alpha : \Gamma$.*

We extend Definition 4 to words.

Definition 5. *$\Gamma \cdot \epsilon = \Gamma$ and $\Gamma \cdot aw = (\Gamma \cdot a) \cdot w$.*

We now come to a key, perhaps surprizing, property of a special 2SG which is essential to the decidability proof.

Proposition 4. *Assume $L(X\alpha : \Gamma) = L(Y\beta : \Delta)$ for configurations of a special 2SG. If $X \xrightarrow{a}$ push $\in \mathsf{T}$ then $Y \xrightarrow{a}$ push $\in \mathsf{T}$ and $L(X\alpha) = L(Y\beta)$.*

Proof. Suppose $L(X\alpha : \Gamma) = L(Y\beta : \Delta)$ and $X \xrightarrow{a}$ push $\in \mathsf{T}$. By assumption $L(X\alpha : \Gamma) \neq \emptyset$. If $Y \xrightarrow{a}$ push $\notin \mathsf{T}$ then $Y \xrightarrow{a} \theta$ and $\theta =$ pop or swap$_{\gamma_1}$. Consider the case $\theta =$ pop. Therefore, $L(X\alpha : X\alpha : \Gamma) = L(\Delta)$. But then by Proposition 2, $L(X\alpha : X\alpha : \Gamma) = L(X\alpha : Y\beta : \Delta) = L(\Delta)$ which is a contradiction. Consequently, $\theta =$ swap$_{\gamma_1}$ and $L(X\alpha : X\alpha : \Gamma) = L(\beta_1 : \Delta)$ where $\theta(Y\beta) = \beta_1$. Now we repeat the argument for Y_1 which is the head stack symbol of β_1. We show that $Y_1 \xrightarrow{a}$ push $\notin \mathsf{T}$. Assume it is. By Proposition 2, $L(X\alpha : X\alpha : X\alpha : \Gamma) = L(X\alpha : \beta_1 : \Delta) = L(\beta_1 : \beta_1 : \Delta)$ and so $L(X\alpha) = L(\beta_1)$. But $L(X\alpha : X\alpha : \Gamma) = L(\beta_1 : Y\beta : \Delta) = L(\beta_1 : \Delta)$ which is a contradiction. Therefore, $Y_1 \xrightarrow{a} \theta_1$ and $\theta_1 =$ pop or swap$_{\gamma_2}$. The argument above shows that $\theta_1 \neq$ pop. Therefore, $L(X\alpha : X\alpha : X\alpha : \Gamma) = L(\beta_2 : \Delta)$ where $\beta_2 = \theta_1(\beta_1)$. Now, we repeat the argument for Y_2 which is the head of β_2. Again, $X \xrightarrow{a}$ push $\in \mathsf{T}$ and by the arguments above $Y_2 \xrightarrow{a}$ swap$_{\gamma_2}$. After n steps, we have $L((X\alpha)^{n+1} : \Gamma) = L(\beta_n : \Delta)$. As $\Lambda(X\alpha) > 0$, it follows that $\Lambda(\beta_n) = \Lambda(\beta_{n-1}) + \Lambda(X\alpha)$: we now use this property to obtain a contradiction when the 2SG is special. Let $n > 2 \times 2^{|\mathsf{S}|}$. Consider Y_n the head variable of β_n. As the 2SG is special, $\Lambda(Y_n)$ or $P(Y_n)$ is defined. Assume the first, and let w be a shortest word such that $Y_n \xrightarrow{w} \Lambda$. It follows that $L(((X\alpha)^{n+1} : \Gamma) \cdot w) = L(\Lambda)$ which is a contradiction. Similarly, if w is a shortest word that $Y_n \xrightarrow{w}$ push then $\beta_n \cdot w = \beta_{n+1} : \beta_{n+1}$. However, $\Lambda(\beta_{n+1}) > 2^{|\mathsf{S}|}$ which contradicts that $L(((X\alpha)^{n+1} : \Gamma) \cdot w) = L(\beta_{n+1} : \beta_{n+1} : \Delta)$. □

We introduce non-standard bisimulation approximants.

Definition 6. *We define* $\sim_n$, $n \geq 0$, *iteratively as follows.*

1. $\Gamma \sim_0 \Delta$ *iff* $\Gamma = \emptyset = \Delta$ *or* $\Gamma \neq \emptyset$ *and* $\Delta \neq \emptyset$.
2. $\Lambda \sim_{n+1} \Lambda$ *and* $\emptyset \sim_{n+1} \emptyset$
3. $X\alpha : \Gamma \sim_{n+1} Y\beta : \Delta$ *just in case*
   (a) $\Lambda(X\alpha : \Gamma) = \Lambda(Y\beta : \Delta)$
   (b) $X \xrightarrow{a} \text{push}$ *iff* $Y \xrightarrow{a} \text{push}$, *and*
   (c) *for each* $a \in \mathsf{A}$, $(X\alpha : \Gamma) \cdot a \sim_n (Y\beta : \Delta) \cdot a$.

Built into this definition is the idea that an immediate bisimulation error occurs if configurations do not agree on length of their shortest words or if push actions are not matched. These non-standard approximants will be critical to the decidability proof later. We write $\Gamma \sim \Delta$ if for all n, $\Gamma \sim_n \Delta$.

Proposition 5. *1.* $L(\Gamma) = L(\Delta)$ iff $\Gamma \sim \Delta$.
2. If $\Gamma \sim_n \Delta$ and $\Delta \sim_n \Sigma$ then $\Gamma \sim_n \Sigma$.
3. If $\Gamma \not\sim_n \Delta$ and $\Delta \sim_{n+k} \Sigma$ then $\Gamma \not\sim_n \Sigma$.

5 Tableaux

The decision procedure for special 2SGs is a *tableau proof system*, consisting of proof rules which allow goals to be reduced to subgoals. Goals and subgoals are all of the form $\Gamma \doteq \Delta$, "is $\Gamma \sim \Delta$?", where Γ and Δ are configurations of a special 2SG. The tableau proof rules are contained in Figure 3.

The initial tableau proof rule is UNF (unfold). The goal, $\Gamma \doteq \Delta$ reduces to the subgoals $(\Gamma \cdot a) \doteq (\Delta \cdot a)$ for each $a \in \mathsf{A}$. The application of this simple rule is both "complete" and "sound". Completeness is the property that if the goal, $\Gamma \doteq \Delta$, is true then so are all the subgoals, $(\Gamma \cdot a_i) \doteq (\Delta \cdot a_i)$.

Proposition 6. *If* $\Gamma \sim \Delta$, *then for all* $a \in \mathsf{A}$, $(\Gamma \cdot a) \sim (\Delta \cdot a)$.

Soundness is the converse, that if all the subgoals are true then so is the goal which is equivalent to, if the goal is false, $\Gamma \not\sim \Delta$, then so is at least one of the subgoals. However, there is a finer account that uses approximants. We assume that, at least, $\Gamma \sim_1 \Delta$ (so push transitions have to be matched).

Proposition 7. *If* $\Gamma \sim_{n+1} \Delta$ *and* $\Gamma \not\sim_{n+2} \Delta$, *then* $(\Gamma \cdot a) \not\sim_{n+1} (\Delta \cdot a)$ *for some* $a \in \mathsf{A}$.

The second rules are SIMP (simplification) that reduce goals. If $\epsilon(X)$ is not defined then $\alpha X \alpha'$ can be reduced to αX. The following implies soundness and completeness of SIMP.

Proposition 8. *If* $\epsilon(X)$ *is undefined then for all* n *and* Γ $\alpha X \alpha' : \Gamma \sim_n \alpha X : \Gamma$.

The final rules are DEC for decomposition. We only decompose $\alpha : \Gamma = \beta : \Delta$ when Δ is non-empty. The following capture completeness and soundness.

UNF

$$\frac{\Gamma \doteq \Delta}{(\Gamma \cdot a_1) \doteq (\Delta \cdot a_1) \ \ldots \ (\Gamma \cdot a_k) \doteq (\Delta \cdot a_k)} \ \mathsf{A} = \{a_1, \ldots, a_k\}$$

SIMP(L) and SIMP(R)

$$\frac{\alpha X \alpha' : \Gamma \doteq \Delta}{\alpha X : \Gamma \doteq \Delta} \ \epsilon(X) \text{ undefined} \qquad \frac{\Delta \doteq \alpha X \alpha' : \Gamma}{\Delta \doteq \alpha X : \Gamma} \ \epsilon(X) \text{ undefined}$$

DEC(L) and DEC(R)

$$\frac{\alpha : \Gamma \doteq \beta : \Delta}{\alpha : (\beta \cdot w) \doteq \beta \quad \Gamma \doteq (\beta \cdot w) : \Delta} \ C \qquad \frac{\beta : \Delta \doteq \alpha : \Gamma}{\beta \doteq \alpha : (\beta \cdot w) \quad (\beta \cdot w) : \Delta \doteq \Gamma} \ C$$

where C is the condition

1. $\Lambda(\alpha) \leq \Lambda(\beta)$ and $\Delta \neq \Lambda$
2. w is a smallest word such that $\alpha \xrightarrow{w} \Lambda$
3. $(\beta \cdot w) \neq \emptyset$

Fig. 3. Tableau proof rules

Proposition 9. *Assume $\Lambda(\alpha) \leq \Lambda(\beta)$, w is a smallest word such that $\alpha \xrightarrow{w} \Lambda$ and $(\beta \cdot w) \neq \emptyset$.*

1. If $\alpha : \Gamma \sim \beta : \Delta$, then $\alpha : (\beta \cdot w) \sim \beta$ and $\Gamma \sim (\beta \cdot w) : \Delta$.
2. If $\alpha : \Gamma \not\sim_n \beta : \Delta$ then $\alpha : (\beta \cdot w) \not\sim_n \beta$ or $n > |w|$ and $\Gamma \not\sim_{n-|w|} (\beta \cdot w) : \Delta$.

Example 4. The following is an application of DEC(R) to a goal whose 2SG is Example 3.

$$\frac{XXXZ : XZ \doteq AAAW : AW : W}{XXXZ \doteq AAAW : UXXXZ \quad UXXXZ : XZ \doteq AW : W}$$

Here, $AAAW \xrightarrow{acb} \Lambda$ and $UXXXZ = (XXXZ \cdot acb)$. □

6 Successful Tableaux

In the previous section we presented and justified tableau proof rules. We now show that these rules lead to an effective decision procedure for checking equivalence of configurations of special 2SGs. A missing ingredient in the tableau description is when a current goal is final. The tableau procedure starts with an initial goal, $\Gamma \doteq \Delta$, "is $\Gamma \sim \Delta$?", and one then builds a proof tree by applying the tableau rules. Goals are thereby reduced to subgoals. Rules are not applied to final goals.

A 2SG is deterministic, and therefore we would prefer that there is just one tableau proof tree for any starting goal. To achieve uniqueness of tableau, we assume a linear ordering on the alphabet A. This ordering is used in an application of UNF, so the subgoals are ordered relative to this ordering. It is also used in the DEC rules to define a unique smallest word such that $\alpha \xrightarrow{w} \Lambda$: if there is more than one word of the same length with this property, we choose amongst them the word that is lexicographically least with repect to the ordering on A. In the case of the SIMP rules we assume that $\epsilon(\alpha)$ is defined: we always try to find the first stack symbol X in the initial stack such that $\epsilon(X)$ is undefined.

Next, we assume that the tableau proof rules are applied in the following order: DEC(L), DEC(R), SIMP(L), SIMP(R), UNF. Given a goal one tries first to apply DEC(L), and if it is not applicable then one tries DEC(R), and so on. A tableau proof tree is built breadth first starting with leftmost non-final goals.

Example 5. Here is part of the tableau proof tree for the goal $XZ \doteq AW : W$ whose 2SG is Example 3.

$$
\cfrac{XZ \doteq AW : W}{
  \cfrac{YXZ \doteq CW : W}{
    \cfrac{XXZ \doteq AAW : W}{\cfrac{YXXZ \doteq CAW : W}{\ldots}\;\mathrm{UNF} \quad \ldots}\;\mathrm{UNF}
    \qquad
    \cfrac{ZXZ \doteq WW : W}{\cfrac{Z \doteq WW : W}{\ldots}\;\mathrm{SIMP(R)}}\;\mathrm{SIMP(L)}
  }\;\mathrm{UNF}
  \quad \ldots
}\;\mathrm{UNF}
$$

Here we have missed out subgoals of the form $\emptyset \doteq \emptyset$. There is an application of SIMP(L) to $ZXZ \doteq WW : W$ because $\epsilon(Z)$ is not defined. □

To show decidability we intend to show that associated with any starting goal $\Gamma \doteq \Delta$ is a unique boundedly *finite* proof tree. However, in Example 5 there appears to be the following potentially infinite branch of goals.

$$
\cfrac{XZ \doteq AW : W}{\cfrac{YXZ \doteq CW : W}{\cfrac{XXZ \doteq AAW : W}{\cfrac{YXXZ \doteq CAW : W}{\cfrac{XXXZ \doteq AAAW : W}{\ldots}}}}}
$$

This will be dealt with by the definition of *final* goal.

Final goals are either *unsuccessful* or *successful*. There is just one kind of unsuccessful goal: $\Gamma \doteq \Delta$ where $\Gamma \not\sim_1 \Delta$. For successful final goals, first we include the identity, $\Gamma \doteq \Gamma$, which is clearly true. However, there is another kind based on repeating patterns of stack extensions (inspired by the extension theorem in [28] which was generalized to the subwords lemma in [25]).

We are interested in goals $\alpha : \Gamma \doteq \beta$ or $\beta \doteq \alpha : \Gamma$ where one side consists of a single stack only: application of the DEC proof rules yield such subgoals. Given a goal $\alpha\alpha_1 : \Gamma \doteq \beta\beta_1$, where α and β are not ϵ, we say that $\alpha\gamma_1\alpha_1 : \Gamma \doteq \beta\lambda_1\beta_1$ is an (γ_1, λ_1)-*extension* of it and (γ_1, λ_1) is the *extension*. We now come to the key property that will limit the size of a proof tree.

Proposition 10. *If α and β are not ϵ and*

(1) $\alpha\alpha_1 : \Gamma \sim_n \beta\beta_1$	and	(5) $\alpha\alpha_2 : \Gamma \sim_n \beta\beta_2$
(2) $\alpha\gamma_1\alpha_1 : \Gamma \sim_n \beta\lambda_1\beta_1$	and	(6) $\alpha\gamma_1\alpha_2 : \Gamma \sim_n \beta\lambda_1\beta_2$
(3) $\alpha\gamma_2\gamma_1\alpha_1 : \Gamma \sim_n \beta\lambda_2\lambda_1\beta_1$	and	(7) $\alpha\gamma_2\gamma_1\alpha_2 : \Gamma \sim_n \beta\lambda_2\lambda_1\beta_2$
(4) $\alpha\gamma_1\gamma_2\gamma_1\alpha_1 : \Gamma \sim_n \beta\lambda_1\lambda_2\lambda_1\beta_1$		

then (8) $\alpha\gamma_1\gamma_2\gamma_1\alpha_2 : \Gamma \sim_n \beta\lambda_1\lambda_2\lambda_1\beta_2$.

Proof. Assume (1) – (7) but (8) is false. So, $\alpha\gamma_1\gamma_2\gamma_1\alpha_2 : \Gamma \not\sim_n \beta\lambda_1\lambda_2\lambda_1\beta_2$. Because of (1) – (7), the bisimulation error in (8) cannot be caused by the heads α and β. Therefore, by repeated application of Proposition 7 there is a w such that one of the following hold. (An easy argument shows that w cannot involve a push transition.)

A) $\alpha \cdot w = \Lambda$, $\beta \cdot w$ is defined and $\Gamma \not\sim_{n-|w|} (\beta \cdot w)\lambda_1\lambda_2\lambda_1\beta_2$.
B) $\alpha \cdot w = \epsilon$, $\beta \cdot w$ is defined and $\gamma_1\gamma_2\gamma_1\alpha_2 : \Gamma \not\sim_{n-|w|} (\beta \cdot w)\lambda_1\lambda_2\lambda_1\beta_2$.
C) $\beta \cdot w = \epsilon$, $\alpha \cdot w$ is defined and $(\alpha \cdot w)\gamma_1\gamma_2\gamma_1\alpha_2 : \Gamma \not\sim_{n-|w|} \lambda_1\lambda_2\lambda_1\beta_2$.

Consider B): the others are similar. Because of (1) – (7) we know that

(11) $\alpha_1 : \Gamma \sim_{n-|w|} (\beta \cdot w)\beta_1$	(51) $\alpha_2 : \Gamma \sim_{n-|w|} (\beta \cdot w)\beta_2$
(21) $\gamma_1\alpha_1 : \Gamma \sim_{n-|w|} (\beta \cdot w)\lambda_1\beta_1$	(61) $\gamma_1\alpha_2 : \Gamma \sim_{n-|w|} (\beta \cdot w)\lambda_1\beta_2$
(31) $\gamma_2\gamma_1\alpha_1 : \Gamma \sim_{n-|w|} (\beta \cdot w)\lambda_2\lambda_1\beta_1$	(71) $\gamma_2\gamma_1\alpha_2 : \Gamma \sim_{n-|w|} (\beta \cdot w)\lambda_2\lambda_1\beta_2$
(41) $\gamma_1\gamma_2\gamma_1\alpha_1 : \Gamma \sim_{n-|w|} (\beta \cdot w)\lambda_1\lambda_2\lambda_1\beta_1$	

We now consider $\alpha \cdot w = \epsilon$, $\beta \cdot w$ is defined and $\gamma_1\gamma_2\gamma_1\alpha_2 : \Gamma \not\sim_{n-|w|} (\beta \cdot w)\lambda_1\lambda_2\lambda_1\beta_2$ and (21), (41) and (61). There are two cases depending on whether $(\beta \cdot w) = \epsilon$. Assume it is not. The bisimulation error cannot be caused by the heads γ_1 and $(\beta \cdot w)$. Therefore there is a word w_1 such that one of the following hold.

BA) $\gamma_1 \cdot w_1 = \Lambda$, $\beta \cdot ww_1$ is defined and $\Gamma \not\sim_{n-|ww_1|} (\beta \cdot ww_1)\lambda_1\lambda_2\lambda_1\beta_2$.
BB) $\gamma_1 \cdot w_1 = \epsilon$, $\beta \cdot ww_1$ is defined and $\gamma_2\gamma_1\alpha_2 : \Gamma \not\sim_{n-|ww_1|} (\beta \cdot ww_1)\lambda_1\lambda_2\lambda_1\beta_2$.
BC) $\beta \cdot ww_1 = \epsilon$, $\gamma_1 \cdot w_1$ is defined and $(\gamma_1 \cdot w_1)\gamma_2\gamma_1\alpha_2 : \Gamma \not\sim_{n-|ww_1|} \lambda_1\lambda_2\lambda_1\beta_2$.

In the case of BA) we also know

$$(211)\ \Gamma \sim_{n-|ww_1|} (\beta \cdot ww_1)\lambda_1\beta_1$$
$$(411)\ \Gamma \sim_{n-|ww_1|} (\beta \cdot ww_1)\lambda_1\lambda_2\lambda_1\beta_1$$
$$(611)\ \Gamma \sim_{n-|ww_1|} (\beta \cdot ww_1)\lambda_1\beta_2$$

Thus, we now get a contradiction using these because from Proposition 5

$$(\beta \cdot ww_1)\lambda_1\lambda_2\lambda_1\beta_1 \not\sim_{n-|ww_1|} (\beta \cdot ww_1)\lambda_1\lambda_2\lambda_1\beta_2$$
$$(\beta \cdot ww_1)\lambda_1\beta_1 \sim_{n-|ww_1|} (\beta \cdot ww_1)\lambda_1\beta_2$$

In the case of BB) we also know that

$$(212)\ \alpha_1 : \Gamma \sim_{n-|ww_1|} (\beta \cdot ww_1)\lambda_1\beta_1$$
$$(412)\ \gamma_2\gamma_1\alpha_1 : \Gamma \sim_{n-|ww_1|} (\beta \cdot ww_1)\lambda_1\lambda_2\lambda_1\beta_1$$
$$(612)\ \alpha_2 : \Gamma \sim_{n-|ww_1|} (\beta \cdot ww_1)\lambda_1\beta_2$$

Now via Proposition 5, we can use (71), (11), (31) and (51) and derive a contradiction from the following.

$$(\beta \cdot w)\lambda_2\lambda_1\beta_2 \not\sim_{n-|ww_1|} (\beta \cdot ww_1)\lambda_1\lambda_2\lambda_1\beta_2$$
$$(\beta \cdot w)\beta_1 \sim_{n-|ww_1|} (\beta \cdot ww_1)\lambda_1\beta_1$$
$$(\beta \cdot w)\lambda_2\lambda_1\beta_1 \sim_{n-|ww_1|} (\beta \cdot ww_1)\lambda_1\lambda_2\lambda_1\beta_1$$
$$(\beta \cdot w)\beta_2 \sim_{n-|ww_1|} (\beta \cdot ww_1)\lambda_1\beta_2$$

All remaining cases are similar. □

We use Proposition 10 to identify when a goal is final via extensions.

Definition 7. *Assume a family of not necessarily distinct goals*

$g(1)\ \alpha\alpha_1 : \Gamma \doteq \beta\beta_1$	$h(1)\ \alpha\alpha_2 : \Gamma \doteq \beta\beta_2$
$g(2)\ \alpha\gamma_1\alpha_1 : \Gamma \doteq \beta\lambda_1\beta_1$	$h(2)\ \alpha\gamma_1\alpha_2 : \Gamma \doteq \beta\lambda_1\beta_2$
$g(3)\ \alpha\gamma_2\gamma_1\alpha_1 : \Gamma \doteq \beta\lambda_2\lambda_1\beta_1$	$h(3)\ \alpha\gamma_2\gamma_1\alpha_2 : \Gamma \doteq \beta\lambda_2\lambda_1\beta_2$
$g(4)\ \alpha\gamma_1\gamma_2\gamma_1\alpha_1 : \Gamma \doteq \beta\lambda_1\lambda_2\lambda_1\beta_1$	$h(4)\ \alpha\gamma_1\gamma_2\gamma_1\alpha_2 : \Gamma \doteq \beta\lambda_1\lambda_2\lambda_1\beta_2$

(or their symmetric versions) in a branch of a proof tree involving extensions (γ_1, λ_1), (γ_2, λ_2). If $h(4)$ is below all the $g(i)$'s and the other $h(i)$'s, is distinct from $g(4)$ and $h(3)$ and there is an application of UNF between $h(3)$ and $h(4)$ then $h(4)$ is a successful *final goal.*

Example 6. Consider the following goals in the initial part of the potentially infinite branch of Example 5.

$g(1)$	$XZ \doteq AW : W$
$g(2) = h(1)$	$XXZ \doteq AAW : W$
$g(3) = h(2)$	$XXXZ \doteq AAAW : W$
$g(4) = h(3)$	$XXXXZ \doteq AAAAW : W$
$h(4)$	$XXXXXZ \doteq AAAAAW : W$

Here $\beta = X$ and $\alpha = Y$ and the extensions are (X, A). There is at least one application of UNF between $h(3)$ and $h(4)$ in the proof tree. Consequently, the branch stops at the final goal $XXXXXZ \doteq AAAAAW : W$. □

Example 7. If there is a repeat goal in the proof tree

$$\frac{\dfrac{(g)\ \alpha : \Gamma \doteq \beta}{\vdots}}{(h)\ \alpha : \Gamma \doteq \beta}$$

with an application of UNF inbetween, then h is final. Here $g(1) - g(4)$ and $h(1) - h(3)$ is the goal g with extension (ϵ, ϵ) and $\alpha_1 = \alpha_2 = \beta_1 = \epsilon$. □

Definition 8. *A* successful *tableau for $\Gamma \doteq \Delta$ is a finite proof tree with root $\Gamma \doteq \Delta$ and all of whose leaves are successful final goals. Otherwise a tableau is* unsuccessful*: that is, if it is not a finite proof tree or if it contains an unsuccesssful final goal.*

We now come to the main results, which show decidability of language equivalence for special 2SG. The decision procedure is to build the tableau with root $\Gamma \doteq \Delta$ breadth first starting with leftmost non-final goals. If an unsuccessful final goal is met then the procedure terminates with a finite unsuccessful tableau.

Theorem 2. *There is a unique finite tableau for goal $\Gamma \doteq \Delta$.*

Proof. Uniqueness is clear because rules are applied in a particular order. The important part of the proof is to show finiteness. Initially, we have $\Gamma \doteq \Delta$. The DEC rules are applied first in the order DEC(L) then DEC(R). Clearly, in the application of a DEC rule if w is the smallest word such that $\alpha \xrightarrow{w} \Lambda$ then there is no push transition in this sequence of transitions. If $(\beta \cdot w)$ involves a push transition then the tableau construction will terminate with an unsuccesful final goal. Assume the rule is DEC(L), so $\alpha : (\beta \cdot w) \doteq \beta$. Consequently, $w = w_1 a w_2$ and $\alpha \cdot w_1 = \alpha_1$ and $\beta \cdot w_1 = \beta_1$ and $\beta_1 \cdot a = \beta_1 : \beta_1$. The subgoal $\alpha_1 : (\beta \cdot w) \doteq \beta_1$ is, therefore, an unsuccessful final goal. There can not be an infinite sequence of consecutive applications of DEC as each application decreases the the number of stacks in both subgoals. Consequently, non-final subgoals to which DEC and SIMP do not apply have the form $X\alpha : \Gamma \doteq \beta$ or $\beta \doteq X\alpha : \Gamma$. First, consider the case of an application of UNF where $X \xrightarrow{a}$ push. If $\Gamma \neq \Lambda$ then the goal $(X\alpha : \Gamma) \cdot a \doteq (\beta \cdot a)$ is an unsuccessful final goal (and similarly for its symmetric version). If $\Gamma = \Lambda$, then $X\alpha \cdot a \doteq \beta \cdot a$ is $X\alpha : X\alpha \doteq \beta : \beta$ and by DEC(L) this reduces to the two occurrences of successful final goals $X\alpha \doteq \beta$ by Example 7. Consequently, without loss of generality, assume there is an infinite subbranch of goals of the form $\alpha_i : \Gamma \doteq \beta_i$, $i \geq 0$ involving applications of UNF and SIMP only. We show that there is a successful final goal. The size of the goals (that is the sum, $|\alpha_i| + |\beta_i|$) must be eventually increasing, otherwise a repeat goal occurs ensuring a successful final goal. Now we examine the first "low point" with respect to the left stack α_i: $\alpha_i = X\alpha$ is a low point if for all $j \geq i$, $\alpha_j = \alpha'_j\alpha$. With respect to the left side we will find infinitely many repeating patterns of the form $Z\alpha'$, $Z\alpha'_1\alpha'$, $Z\alpha'_2\alpha'_1\alpha'$ and $Z\alpha'_1\alpha'_2\alpha'_1\alpha'$ where α'_1 or α'_2 can be ϵ. Now we consider the right hand stacks with respect to these repeating patterns. Clearly, we will also eventually find repeating patterns too, and consequently a successful final goal. □

Theorem 3. *The tableau for $\Gamma \doteq \Delta$ is successful iff $\Gamma \sim \Delta$.*

Proof. Suppose there is a successful tableau for $\Gamma \doteq \Delta$ but $\Gamma \not\sim \Delta$. By Theorem 2 this tableau is finite. There is a least approximant n such that $\Gamma \not\sim_n \Delta$. We construct an offending path of false goals through the tableau within which the approximant indices decrease whenever UNF is applied (by Proposition 7). The other rules preserve falsity indices. Because the tableau is finite and successful this means that the path of false goals must conclude with a final goal. But this is impossible. Clearly it is not possible to reach a final goal of the form $\Gamma \doteq \Gamma$. Moreover it is not possible to reach a final goal which is a result of extensions because of Proposition 10.

For the other direction, one just builds the tableau for $\Gamma \doteq \Delta$. By Propositions 6, 8 and 9, the applications of rules preserve truth. Therefore it is not possible to reach an unsuccessful final goal, and by Theorem 2 the tableau for $\Gamma \doteq \Delta$ is finite, and therefore successful. □

More work needs to be done to ascertain the exact complexity bound of the decision procedure.

Acknowledgements. Many thanks to Luke Ong for imparting his incisive understanding of higher-order schemes and the safety restriction, to Wong Kariento for a copy of the Maslov paper and to the referees for suggesting improvements.

References

1. Aehlig, K., De Miranda, J., and Ong C.-H. L. (2005) Safety is not a restriction at level 2 for string languages. *Lecture Notes in Computer Science*, **3411**, 490-511.
2. Aho, A. (1968). Indexed grammars–an extension of context-free grammars. *Journal of ACM*, **15**, 647-671.
3. Aho, A. (1969). Nested stack automata. *Journal of ACM*, **16**, 383-406.
4. Baeten, J., Bergstra, J., and Klop, J. (1993). Decidability of bisimulation equivalence for processes generating context-free languages. *Journal of ACM*, **40**, 653-682.
5. Blumensath, A. (2004). A pumping lemma for higher-order pushdown automata. Preprint.
6. Bouajjani, A. and Meyer, A. (2004). Symbolic reachability analysis of higher-order context processes. *Lecture Notes in Computer Science*, **3328**, 135-147.
7. Burkart, O., Caucal, D. Moller, F., and Steffen, B. (2001). Verification on infinite structures. In *Handbook of Process Algebra*, ed. Bergstra, J., Ponse, A., and Smolka, S., 545-623, North-Holland.
8. Cachat, T. (2003). Higher order pushdown automata, the Caucal hierarchy of graphs and parity games. *Lecture Notes in Computer Science*, **2719**, 556-569.
9. Caucal, D. (2002). On infinite terms having a decidable monadic theory. *Lecture Notes in Computer Science*, **2420**, 165-176.

10. Courcelle, B. (1978). A representation of trees by languages I and II. *Theoretical Computer Science*, **6**, 255-279 and **7**, 25-55.
11. Damm, W. (1982). The IO- and OI-hierarchy. *Theoretical Computer Science*, **25**, 95-169.
12. Damm, W., and Goerdt, A. (1986). An automata-theoretical characterization of the OI-hierarchy. *Information and Control*, **71**, 1-32.
13. Engelfriet, J. (1991). Iterated stack automata and complexity classes. *Information and Computation*, **95**, 21-75.
14. Fischer, M. (1968). Grammars with macro-like productions. *Procs. 9th Annual IEEE Symposium on Switching and Automata Theory*, 131-142.
15. Freidman, E. (1976). The inclusion problem for simple languages. *Theoretical Computer Science*, **1**, 297-316.
16. Gilman, R. (1996). A shrinking lemma for indexed languages. *Theoretical Computer Science*, **163**, 277-281.
17. Jančar, P., and Srba, J. (2006). Undecidability results for bisimilarity on prefix rewrite systems. *Lecture Notes in Computer Science*, **3921**, 277-291.
18. Knapik, T., Niwiński, D., and Urzyczyn, P. (2002). Higher-order pushdown trees are easy. *Lecture Notes in Computer Science*, **2303**, 205-222.
19. Korenjak, A and Hopcroft, J. (1966). Simple deterministic languages. *Procs. 7th Annual IEEE Symposium on Switching and Automata Theory*, 36-46.
20. Maslov, A. (1976). Multilevel stack automata. *Problems of Information Transmission*, **12**, 38-43.
21. Ong, C.-H. L. (2006) On model-checking trees generated by higher-order recursion schemes. Preprint.
22. Parchmann, R., Duske, J. and Specht, J. (1980). On deterministic indexed languages. *Information and Control*, **45**, 48-67.
23. Sénizergues, G. (2001). L(A) = L(B)? decidability results from complete formal systems. *Theoretical Computer Science*, **251**, 1-166.
24. Sénizergues, G. (2002). L(A) = L(B)? a simplified decidability proof. *Theoretical Computer Science*, **281**, 555-608.
25. Sénizergues, G. (2003). The equivalence problem for t-turn DPDA is co-NP. *Lecture Notes in Computer Science*, **2719**, 478-489.
26. Sénizergues, G. (2005). The bisimulation problem for equational graphs of finite out-degree. *SIAM Journal of Computing*, **34**, 1025-1106.
27. Stirling, C. (2001). Decidability of DPDA equivalence. *Theoretical Computer Science*, **255**, 1-31.
28. Stirling, C. (2002) Deciding DPDA equivalence is primitive recursive. *Lecture Notes in Computer Science*, **2380**, 821-832.
29. Vijay-Shanker, K. and Weir, D. (1994). The equivalence of four extensions of context-free grammars. *Mathematical Systems Theory*, **27**, 511-546.

Author Index

Lecture Notes in Computer Science

For information about Vols. 1–4024

please contact your bookseller or Springer

Vol. 4144: T. Ball, R.B. Jones (Eds.), Computer Aided Verification. XV, 564 pages. 2006.

Vol. 4139: T. Salakoski, F. Ginter, S. Pyysalo, T. Pahikkala (Eds.), Advances in Natural Language Processing. XIV, 771 pages. 2006. (Sublibrary LNAI).

Vol. 4138: X. Cheng, W. Li, T. Znati (Eds.), Wireless Algorithms, Systems, and Applications. XVI, 709 pages. 2006.

Vol. 4137: C. Baier, H. Hermanns (Eds.), CONCUR 2006 - - Concurrency Theory. XIII, 525 pages. 2006.

Vol. 4130: U. Furbach, N. Shankar (Eds.), Automated Reasoning. XV, 680 pages. 2006. (Sublibrary LNAI).

Vol. 4127: E. Damiani, P. Liu (Eds.), Data and Applications Security XX. X, 319 pages. 2006.

Vol. 4121: A. Biere, C.P. Gomes (Eds.), Theory and Applications of Satisfiability Testing - SAT 2006. XII, 438 pages. 2006.

Vol. 4115: D.-S. Huang, K. Li, G.W. Irwin (Eds.), Computational Intelligence and Bioinformatics, Part III. XXI, 803 pages. 2006. (Sublibrary LNBI).

Vol. 4114: D.-S. Huang, K. Li, G.W. Irwin (Eds.), Computational Intelligence, Part II. XXVII, 1337 pages. 2006. (Sublibrary LNAI).

Vol. 4113: D.-S. Huang, K. Li, G.W. Irwin (Eds.), Intelligent Computing, Part I. XXVII, 1331 pages. 2006.

Vol. 4112: D.Z. Chen, D. T. Lee (Eds.), Computing and Combinatorics. XIV, 528 pages. 2006.

Vol. 4111: F.S. de Boer, M.M. Bonsangue, S. Graf, W.-P. de Roever (Eds.), Formal Methods for Components and Objects. VIII, 447 pages. 2006.

Vol. 4109: D.-Y. Yeung, J.T. Kwok, A. Fred, F. Roli, D. de Ridder (Eds.), Structural, Syntactic, and Statistical Pattern Recognition. XXI, 939 pages. 2006.

Vol. 4108: J.M. Borwein, W.M. Farmer (Eds.), Mathematical Knowledge Management. VIII, 295 pages. 2006. (Sublibrary LNAI).

Vol. 4106: T.R. Roth-Berghofer, M.H. Göker, H. A. Güvenir (Eds.), Advances in Case-Based Reasoning. XIV, 566 pages. 2006. (Sublibrary LNAI).

Vol. 4104: T. Kunz, S.S. Ravi (Eds.), Ad-Hoc, Mobile, and Wireless Networks. XII, 474 pages. 2006.

Vol. 4099: Q. Yang, G. Webb (Eds.), PRICAI 2006: Trends in Artificial Intelligence. XXVIII, 1263 pages. 2006. (Sublibrary LNAI).

Vol. 4098: F. Pfenning (Ed.), Term Rewriting and Applications. XIII, 415 pages. 2006.

Vol. 4097: X. Zhou, O. Sokolsky, L. Yan, E.-S. Jung, Z. Shao, Y. Mu, D.C. Lee, D. Kim, Y.-S. Jeong, C.-Z. Xu (Eds.), Emerging Directions in Embedded and Ubiquitous Computing. XXVII, 1034 pages. 2006.

Vol. 4096: E. Sha, S.-K. Han, C.-Z. Xu, M.H. Kim, L.T. Yang, B. Xiao (Eds.), Embedded and Ubiquitous Computing. XXIV, 1170 pages. 2006.

Vol. 4094: O. H. Ibarra, H.-C. Yen (Eds.), Implementation and Application of Automata. XIII, 291 pages. 2006.

Vol. 4093: X. Li, O.R. Zaïane, Z. Li (Eds.), Advanced Data Mining and Applications. XXI, 1110 pages. 2006. (Sublibrary LNAI).

Vol. 4092: J. Lang, F. Lin, J. Wang (Eds.), Knowledge Science, Engineering and Management. XV, 664 pages. 2006. (Sublibrary LNAI).

Vol. 4091: G.-Z. Yang, T. Jiang, D. Shen, L. Gu, J. Yang (Eds.), Medical Imaging and Augmented Reality. XIII, 399 pages. 2006.

Vol. 4090: S. Spaccapietra, K. Aberer, P. Cudré-Mauroux (Eds.), Journal on Data Semantics VI. XI, 211 pages. 2006.

Vol. 4088: Z.-Z. Shi, R. Sadananda (Eds.), Agent Computing and Multi-Agent Systems. XVII, 827 pages. 2006. (Sublibrary LNAI).

Vol. 4085: J. Misra, T. Nipkow, E. Sekerinski (Eds.), FM 2006: Formal Methods. XV, 620 pages. 2006.

Vol. 4079: S. Etalle, M. Truszczyński (Eds.), Logic Programming. XIV, 474 pages. 2006.

Vol. 4077: M.-S. Kim, K. Shimada (Eds.), Advances in Geometric Modeling and Processing. XVI, 696 pages. 2006.

Vol. 4076: F. Hess, S. Pauli, M. Pohst (Eds.), Algorithmic Number Theory. X, 599 pages. 2006.

Vol. 4075: U. Leser, F. Naumann, B. Eckman (Eds.), Data Integration in the Life Sciences. XI, 298 pages. 2006. (Sublibrary LNBI).

Vol. 4074: M. Burmester, A. Yasinsac (Eds.), Secure Mobile Ad-hoc Networks and Sensors. X, 193 pages. 2006.

Vol. 4073: A. Butz, B. Fisher, A. Krüger, P. Olivier (Eds.), Smart Graphics. XI, 263 pages. 2006.

Vol. 4072: M. Harders, G. Székely (Eds.), Biomedical Simulation. XI, 216 pages. 2006.

Vol. 4071: H. Sundaram, M. Naphade, J.R. Smith, Y. Rui (Eds.), Image and Video Retrieval. XII, 547 pages. 2006.

Vol. 4070: C. Priami, X. Hu, Y. Pan, T.Y. Lin (Eds.), Transactions on Computational Systems Biology V. IX, 129 pages. 2006. (Sublibrary LNBI).

Vol. 4069: F.J. Perales, R.B. Fisher (Eds.), Articulated Motion and Deformable Objects. XV, 526 pages. 2006.

Vol. 4068: H. Schärfe, P. Hitzler, P. Øhrstrøm (Eds.), Conceptual Structures: Inspiration and Application. XI, 455 pages. 2006. (Sublibrary LNAI).

Vol. 4067: D. Thomas (Ed.), ECOOP 2006 – Object-Oriented Programming. XIV, 527 pages. 2006.

Vol. 4066: A. Rensink, J. Warmer (Eds.), Model Driven Architecture – Foundations and Applications. XII, 392 pages. 2006.

Vol. 4065: P. Perner (Ed.), Advances in Data Mining. XI, 592 pages. 2006. (Sublibrary LNAI).

Vol. 4064: R. Büschkes, P. Laskov (Eds.), Detection of Intrusions and Malware & Vulnerability Assessment. X, 195 pages. 2006.

Vol. 4063: I. Gorton, G.T. Heineman, I. Crnkovic, H.W. Schmidt, J.A. Stafford, C.A. Szyperski, K. Wallnau (Eds.), Component-Based Software Engineering. XI, 394 pages. 2006.

Vol. 4062: G. Wang, J.F. Peters, A. Skowron, Y. Yao (Eds.), Rough Sets and Knowledge Technology. XX, 810 pages. 2006. (Sublibrary LNAI).

Vol. 4061: K. Miesenberger, J. Klaus, W. Zagler, A. Karshmer (Eds.), Computers Helping People with Special Needs. XXIX, 1356 pages. 2006.

Vol. 4060: K. Futatsugi, J.-P. Jouannaud, J. Meseguer (Eds.), Algebra, Meaning, and Computation. XXXVIII, 643 pages. 2006.

Vol. 4059: L. Arge, R. Freivalds (Eds.), Algorithm Theory – SWAT 2006. XII, 436 pages. 2006.

Vol. 4058: L.M. Batten, R. Safavi-Naini (Eds.), Information Security and Privacy. XII, 446 pages. 2006.

Vol. 4057: J.P.W. Pluim, B. Likar, F.A. Gerritsen (Eds.), Biomedical Image Registration. XII, 324 pages. 2006.

Vol. 4056: P. Flocchini, L. Gąsieniec (Eds.), Structural Information and Communication Complexity. X, 357 pages. 2006.

Vol. 4055: J. Lee, J. Shim, S.-g. Lee, C. Bussler, S. Shim (Eds.), Data Engineering Issues in E-Commerce and Services. IX, 290 pages. 2006.

Vol. 4054: A. Horváth, M. Telek (Eds.), Formal Methods and Stochastic Models for Performance Evaluation. VIII, 239 pages. 2006.

Vol. 4053: M. Ikeda, K.D. Ashley, T.-W. Chan (Eds.), Intelligent Tutoring Systems. XXVI, 821 pages. 2006.

Vol. 4052: M. Bugliesi, B. Preneel, V. Sassone, I. Wegener (Eds.), Automata, Languages and Programming, Part II. XXIV, 603 pages. 2006.

Vol. 4051: M. Bugliesi, B. Preneel, V. Sassone, I. Wegener (Eds.), Automata, Languages and Programming, Part I. XXIII, 729 pages. 2006.

Vol. 4049: S. Parsons, N. Maudet, P. Moraitis, I. Rahwan (Eds.), Argumentation in Multi-Agent Systems. XIV, 313 pages. 2006. (Sublibrary LNAI).

Vol. 4048: L. Goble, J.-J.C.. Meyer (Eds.), Deontic Logic and Artificial Normative Systems. X, 273 pages. 2006. (Sublibrary LNAI).

Vol. 4047: M. Robshaw (Ed.), Fast Software Encryption. XI, 434 pages. 2006.

Vol. 4046: S.M. Astley, M. Brady, C. Rose, R. Zwiggelaar (Eds.), Digital Mammography. XVI, 654 pages. 2006.

Vol. 4045: D. Barker-Plummer, R. Cox, N. Swoboda (Eds.), Diagrammatic Representation and Inference. XII, 301 pages. 2006. (Sublibrary LNAI).

Vol. 4044: P. Abrahamsson, M. Marchesi, G. Succi (Eds.), Extreme Programming and Agile Processes in Software Engineering. XII, 230 pages. 2006.

Vol. 4043: A.S. Atzeni, A. Lioy (Eds.), Public Key Infrastructure. XI, 261 pages. 2006.

Vol. 4042: D. Bell, J. Hong (Eds.), Flexible and Efficient Information Handling. XVI, 296 pages. 2006.

Vol. 4041: S.-W. Cheng, C.K. Poon (Eds.), Algorithmic Aspects in Information and Management. XI, 395 pages. 2006.

Vol. 4040: R. Reulke, U. Eckardt, B. Flach, U. Knauer, K. Polthier (Eds.), Combinatorial Image Analysis. XII, 482 pages. 2006.

Vol. 4039: M. Morisio (Ed.), Reuse of Off-the-Shelf Components. XIII, 444 pages. 2006.

Vol. 4038: P. Ciancarini, H. Wiklicky (Eds.), Coordination Models and Languages. VIII, 299 pages. 2006.

Vol. 4037: R. Gorrieri, H. Wehrheim (Eds.), Formal Methods for Open Object-Based Distributed Systems. XVII, 474 pages. 2006.

Vol. 4036: O. H. Ibarra, Z. Dang (Eds.), Developments in Language Theory. XII, 456 pages. 2006.

Vol. 4035: T. Nishita, Q. Peng, H.-P. Seidel (Eds.), Advances in Computer Graphics. XX, 771 pages. 2006.

Vol. 4034: J. Münch, M. Vierimaa (Eds.), Product-Focused Software Process Improvement. XVII, 474 pages. 2006.

Vol. 4033: B. Stiller, P. Reichl, B. Tuffin (Eds.), Performability Has its Price. X, 103 pages. 2006.

Vol. 4032: O. Etzion, T. Kuflik, A. Motro (Eds.), Next Generation Information Technologies and Systems. XIII, 365 pages. 2006.

Vol. 4031: M. Ali, R. Dapoigny (Eds.), Advances in Applied Artificial Intelligence. XXIII, 1353 pages. 2006. (Sublibrary LNAI).

Vol. 4029: L. Rutkowski, R. Tadeusiewicz, L.A. Zadeh, J.M. Zurada (Eds.), Artificial Intelligence and Soft Computing – ICAISC 2006. XXI, 1235 pages. 2006. (Sublibrary LNAI).

Vol. 4028: J. Kohlas, B. Meyer, A. Schiper (Eds.), Dependable Systems: Software, Computing, Networks. XII, 295 pages. 2006.

Vol. 4027: H.L. Larsen, G. Pasi, D. Ortiz-Arroyo, T. Andreasen, H. Christiansen (Eds.), Flexible Query Answering Systems. XVIII, 714 pages. 2006. (Sublibrary LNAI).

Vol. 4026: P.B. Gibbons, T. Abdelzaher, J. Aspnes, R. Rao (Eds.), Distributed Computing in Sensor Systems. XIV, 566 pages. 2006.

Vol. 4025: F. Eliassen, A. Montresor (Eds.), Distributed Applications and Interoperable Systems. XI, 355 pages. 2006.